Frommer's

4th Edition

Australia

by Elizabeth Hansen

Assisted by Richard Adams

Macmillan • USA

About the Authors

Elizabeth Hansen has lived in both New Zealand and Australia, where she worked as a barmaid in a pub (and learned *not* to serve "shirts with collars"—beer with a head of foam). Her other illustrious minicareers have included assisting a vet who was pregnancy-testing cattle on a large station in New South Wales. In addition to *Frommer's Australia,* Elizabeth is the author of *Frommer's New Zealand from $45 a Day* and *Frommer's San Diego,* as well as *The Woman's Travel Guide to New Zealand* and *Bed & Breakfast New Zealand.* She is also a contributor to *Frommer's California.* Her articles have appeared in such magazines as *Travel Holiday* and *Travel & Leisure,* and she teaches workshops for Australia- and New Zealand–bound travelers at the University of California at San Diego.

Richard Adams is a photographer (see the front cover of this guide) as well as a co-researcher, luggage schlepper, and good-natured husband. His enthusiasm for classic cars is evidenced by the number of automotive museums included in this book.

When they aren't traveling, Elizabeth and Richard live in La Jolla, California.

MACMILLAN TRAVEL

A Simon & Schuster Macmillan Company
1633 Broadway
New York, NY 10019

Find us online at **http://www.mgr.com/travel**
or on America Online at Keyword: **Frommer's.**

ISBN 0-02-860928-X
ISSN 1040-9408

Editor: Ron Boudreau
Production Editor: Trudy Brown
Design by Michele Laseau
Digital Cartography by Ortelius Design
Maps copyright © by Simon & Schuster, Inc.

Special Sales

Bulk purchases (10+ copies) of Frommer's travel guides are available to corporations at special discounts. The Special Sales Department can produce custom editions to be used as premiums and/or for sales promotion to suit individual needs. Existing editions can be produced with custom cover imprints such as corporate logos. For more information write to: Special Sales, Simon & Schuster, 1633 Broadway, New York, NY 10019.

Manufactured in the United States of America

Contents

3 Planning a Trip to Australia 40

4 Settling into Sydney 84

List of Maps

For Rick, for being there

Acknowledgments

I want to thank Joan Boyd and Robin Byrne of Qantas Airways, Maree George of the New South Wales Tourism Commission, and Linda Zaklikowski of the Queensland Tourist and Travel Corporation for the assistance they provided. I'm also grateful to the various state and regional tourist offices around Australia who provided information and answered my seemingly endless questions.

In addition, I'm indebted to Ron Boudreau, my editor at Macmillan Travel, who did careful and caring work, and special thanks go to Suzanne Osborne, my editorial assistant, who "went to" Australia every day for several months.

Finally, thanks to the numerous readers who've taken the time to share their experiences with me.

An Invitation to the Reader

In researching this book, we discovered many wonderful places—hotels, restaurants, shops, and more. We're sure you'll find others. Please tell us about them, so we can share the information with your fellow travelers in upcoming editions. If you were disappointed with a recommendation, we'd love to know that, too. Please write to:

Elizabeth Hansen
Frommer's Australia, 4th Edition
c/o Macmillan Travel
1633 Broadway
New York, NY 10019

An Additional Note

Please be advised that travel information is subject to change at any time—and this is especially true of prices. We therefore suggest that you write or call ahead for information when making your travel plans. The authors, editors, and publisher cannot be held responsible for the experiences of readers while traveling. Your safety is important to us, however, so we encourage you to stay alert and be aware of your surroundings. Keep a close eye on cameras, purses, and wallets, all favorite targets of thieves and pickpockets.

What the Symbols Mean

✪ Frommer's Favorites

Hotels, restaurants, attractions and entertainment you should not miss.

$ Super-Special Values

Hotels and restaurants that offer great value for your money.

The following abbreviations are used for credit or charge cards:

AE	American Express	EU	Eurocard
CB	Carte Blanche	JCB	Japan Credit Bank
DC	Diners Club	MC	MasterCard
DISC	Discover	V	Visa
ER	enRoute		

1

The Best of Australia

Australia is a land of tremendous diversity: On this expansive island continent you'll find everything from vibrant urban cities to colorful sheep stations, a unique native culture, a landscape that varies from desert to rain forest, native birds whose colors and songs defy imagination, animals that live naturally nowhere else on earth, and a barrier reef of unmatched beauty and size. Australia is the perfect playground, but it can be daunting for those planning their first trip or even for those who've already made an initial visit and would like to expand their experience.

In my role as a self-described Aussiephile, I've talked to many people who are interested in going to Australia but overwhelmed by its size and the number of options it offers. They don't have unlimited time and money (who does?), and because they won't be able to see it all and do it all they either stay home or select a more mundane destination. I liken this to someone who walks into a great restaurant, sees the extensive menu, and then, since she can't eat every dish, just walks out—and maybe ends up dining at a mediocre café that offers fewer choices.

Like that diner, would-be-Australia-bound travelers who cave in to their confusion miss out on extraordinary experiences. And that makes me sad, for I know how wonderful this country is and want to share the wonder with others.

Over a period of 20 years I've made numerous trips to the land of Oz, as Aussies call their homeland. I've snorkeled among colorful tropical fish, walked in the dusty earth of the Red Centre, and marveled at the wonders of the rain forest. I've stroked the head of a joey poking out of his mama's pouch, fed an orphaned wallaby with a baby bottle, ridden a camel through a dry river bed, and—yes—cuddled a koala. On the cerebral side, I've attended world-class theater, studied history in state-of-the-art museums, and been introduced to the remarkable culture of the Aboriginal people.

Because I don't want anyone to miss these and the other memorable experiences Australia has to offer, I often volunteer to help people plan their trips. Recently my next-door neighbor asked for advice on a two-week itinerary she could tack on to the end of a business trip to Sydney. Before that, friends sought help planning their honeymoon. They told me what they wanted to do, and I told them the best places to do it. Then we worked out an itinerary that

Impressions

Australia has a marvellous sky and air and blue clarity and a hoary sort of land beneath it, like a Sleeping Princess on whom the dust of ages has settled. Wonder if she'll ever get up.

—D.H. Lawrence (1922)

focused on their areas of interest and fit geographically within their time constraints. When they wanted to dash from one coast to the other, I reminded them that Australia is the same size as the 48 contiguous United States, and for a two- to three-week trip it made better sense to limit themselves to only a few areas.

And now I get to help you. I've written this book in an effort to simplify your trip planning, but you don't have to read every single page. Just select the most interesting dishes off the varied menu below and peruse the referenced sections. And remember, if you've never been to Oz before you don't have to try to do everything the first time. Australia isn't as far away as many people think, and once you've been here you'll realize that 18 million friendly maître d's are waiting to welcome you back again and again.

1 The Top Three Destinations

- **Sydney, New South Wales:** Why not get tickets for a show at the Opera House and experience this landmark the way the locals do? You can phone the box office prior to arrival in Australia, charge the tickets to your credit card, and pick them up when you get there. I also suggest you take to the water—JetCat to the picturesque seaside suburb of Manly and ferry back, or vice versa. Sydneysiders also love The Rocks Market, where bargains galore await them every weekend in the shadow of the Harbour Bridge. See Chapter 5.
- **The Great Barrier Reef:** While it's possible to day trip to this natural wonder, it's even better to stay on one of the islands on or near it. Green, Heron, and Lizard are my favorites. Here I've seen potato cod, giant clams, and myriad colors of coral. Those who don't want to get wet can do their underwater sightseeing in a semisubmersible boat. See Chapter 10.
- **Ayers Rock, the Red Centre, the Northern Territory:** Burnished red Ayers Rock is Australia's most distinctive landscape symbol, and you'll be amazed by its color changes if you're lucky enough to see it as the sun sets or rises. But just because it's there doesn't mean you have to climb it. Your options include a guided walk with an Aborigine, a self-guided walk around the base, and hiking in the nearby Olgas. See Chapter 11.

2 The Best Off-the-Beaten-Path Experiences

- **Exploring Fraser Island, off the Sunshine and Central Coast, Queensland:** The world's largest sand island and a World Heritage area, Fraser offers dunes, a rain forest, and a magnificent beach. You can hire a four-wheel-drive vehicle or join a bus tour—in either case, travel is on sand tracks. See Chapter 8.
- **Day-Tripping to Daintree & Cape Tribulation National Parks, Northern Queensland:** You'll see rain forests and crocodiles on this excursion. Many companies offer this trip, but my favorite is Australian Wilderness Safari, because

it seems the most sensitive to the environment. The picnic lunch in the bush helps make it memorable. See Chapter 9.

- **Wandering Among Wildflowers in Western Australia:** If fields of flowers tickle your fancy, plan to be in the southwest corner of Australia in September and October. One of the most spectacular flowers, the red-and-green "kangaroo paw" is the state's emblem. See Chapters 12 and 13.
- **Taking a Scenic Drive Along the Great Ocean Road, Victoria:** This section of Victoria is known as the "Shipwreck Coast," and the highlights are the Twelve Apostles and Port Campbell National Park. Here the sea crashes against dramatic cliffs, and it isn't hard to understand why the area has claimed so many vessels. See Chapter 17.
- **Cruising Kangaroo Island with Craig, in South Australia:** Craig Wickham from Adventure Charters of Kangaroo Island provides an in-depth look at the island's native animals. He can also help you find totally private beaches and the best spots for wildlife photography. See Chapter 15.

3 The Best Places for Viewing Wildlife

- **Lamington National Park, Southern Queensland:** Binna Burra Mountain Lodge and O'Reilly's Guest House provide the best bases for watching wildlife. Both organize guided day hikes through splendid rain forest to see native birds and other animals. See Chapter 8.
- **Fogg Dam & Kakadu National Park, the Northern Territory:** If you drive from Darwin to Kakadu be sure to stop at Fogg Dam, which has the greatest concentration of water fowl I've ever seen. But don't stick in your big toe—crocodiles love it here. In Kakadu you'll see more crocs as well as lots of water buffalo. See Chapter 11.
- **Monkey Mia, Western Australia:** This spot is the only place I know where wild dolphins visit daily. There's no guarantee they'll turn up every day, but they almost always do—and then you can stand in waist-deep water and pet them as they frolic and feed. See Chapter 13.
- **Kangaroo Island, South Australia:** Australia's third-largest island is home to its greatest concentration of wildlife in their natural habitats. Here you'll find kangaroos, wallabies, the occasional wombat, lots of koalas, a colony of seals, sea lions, and fairy penguins. This is the best spot in the country to get up close and personal with mammals and marsupials. See Chapter 15.
- **Phillip Island, Victoria:** Most folks go to this area to see the fairy penguins, an experience that's a little too touristy for my taste. However, the island also provides an opportunity to see koalas in their natural surroundings. This is where I first discovered that koalas make a sound that's not in keeping with their cuddly countenance. See Chapter 16.
- **Cradle Mountain National Park, Tasmania:** This area abounds with marsupials and native birds—a treat for unsuspecting hikers. The lodge puts out tidbits that draw all manner of nocturnal creatures to a well-lit viewing area. See Chapter 18.
- **Hervey Bay, Queensland:** The waters here (300km/186 miles north of Brisbane) are a great place to see humpback whales. They migrate north in June and July and south in September and October. Boats leave from the Hervey Bay marina and nearby Fraser Island. See Chapter 8.

4 The Best Places to Experience the Outback

The Australia you've read about and seen in movies really exists. In and around the places below you'll find huge cattle stations, jackeroos in Acubra hats, and red earth as far as your eye can see.

- **Broken Hill, New South Wales:** If you visit this outback town be sure to stop at the Royal Flying Doctor Service base to get a sense of what it's like to live in an isolated area. This is also where the "brushmen of the bush" have their galleries. See Chapter 6.
- **Ayers Rock, the Red Centre, the Northern Territory:** There's a good reason why this is one of the country's top attractions. It provides beautiful scenery as well as an opportunity to learn about the Aboriginal culture firsthand—Aboriginals lead guided tours here. Among other things, you'll learn about "bush tucker," the plants that form the traditional diet of Australia's native people. See Chapter 11.
- **Alice Springs, the Northern Territory:** The consummate outback town, "The Alice" is the heart of the Red Centre and the gateway to the beautiful red rock formations in the Macdonnell Ranges. You'll experience cobalt-blue sky during the day and starlit heavens at night. The Milky Way never looked so good. See Chapter 11.
- **The Kimberley, Western Australia:** This sparsely populated northwest corner of the country is home to huge cattle stations, a prolific diamond mine, and four national parks. The seasons here are known as "the wet" and "the dry" and they live up to their names. See Chapter 13.

5 The Best Ways to Learn About Aboriginal Culture

Australia's native people have a fascinating belief system and an awesome relationship with the land.

- **Watching the Tjapukai Dancers, near Cairns:** This performance is interspersed with information on Aboriginal culture. I doubt you'll ever hear a more haunting didgeridoo. See Chapter 9.
- **Staying at Pajinka Wilderness Lodge, Queensland:** At the top of the Cape York Peninsula, this remote lodge is owned and operated by Aborigines who enjoy sharing their stories. See Chapter 9.
- **Taking a Day Trip to Bathurst & Melville Islands, the Northern Territory:** Here, just a short flight from Darwin, you can visit a mission and have a chance to talk with the locals over morning tea. You'll also see the products they make that help to support their community. See Chapter 11.
- **Doing the Liru Walk at Ayers Rock, the Red Centre, the Northern Territory:** This walk is guided by a local Aborigine who describes how the native people gather food and find water. Would you like to eat a witchetty grub? See Chapter 11.
- **Visiting the Tandanya Aboriginal Cultural Institute, Adelaide, South Australia:** This institute displays the work of Aboriginal artists, and Aboriginal guides are available to answer questions. A great opportunity for cultural exchange. See Chapter 14.

6 The Best Beaches

- **Narrabean, New South Wales:** Only minutes from central Sydney, Narrabean is famous for good surfing waves. In fact, this left-hand break is especially good for "goofy footers." See Chapter 5.
- **Byron Bay, New South Wales:** This excellent surfing spot—one of the longest rides in the world—is on the New South Wales coast, just south of the Queensland border. A scenic lighthouse marks the spot. See Chapter 6.
- **The Gold Coast, Southern Queensland:** Miles and miles of golden-sand beaches await you just south of Brisbane. Surfers Paradise gets hoards of tourists; Burleigh Heads, Kirra, and Coolangatta are less crowded. All offer great waves. See Chapter 8.
- **The Sunshine Coast, Southern Queensland:** The long white beaches in this part of Queensland are never crowded. Near Noosa, surfers enjoy unusually long rides—up to 2 miles long. See Chapter 8.
- **Whitehaven, the Whitsunday Coast, Central Queensland:** This Whitsunday island has beaches of fine white sand—ideal for walking barefoot and lounging. Because it's inside the reef, there's no surf, but the swimming is fantastic. See Chapter 8.
- **Port Douglas, Northern Queensland:** My favorite spot for jogging, Four Mile Beach is a wonderful stretch of golden sand—and it's never crowded. See Chapter 9.
- **Scarborough, Western Australia:** At this beach in a Perth suburb, sun worshipers watch colorful windsurfers bobbing in the waves. The strong wind that blows them around is known as the "Fremantle Doctor." See Chapter 12.
- **Broome, Western Australia:** This beach is a wonderful place for a camel ride at sunset, an early-morning stroll, or some midday windsurfing. See Chapter 13.

7 The Best Diving & Snorkeling Sites

Details and contact information for the experiences below can be found in the referenced chapters. Also be sure to peruse "The Active Vacation Planner" in Chapter 3.

- **Heron Island, the Great Barrier Reef:** This coral island right on the reef provides many and varied dive spots. In just a few minutes you can walk from your lodging to the beach and into the water, where there are beautiful coral formations. Dive boats carry skin and scuba divers to deeper sites 5 to 15 minutes away. See Chapter 10.
- **Orpheus Island, the Great Barrier Reef:** This continental island is encircled by an excellent fringing reef. Snorkelers find plenty of coral right off the beach, and divers can take boat trips to the outer reef. Giant clams abound, and you can visit a marine research facility on the island. See Chapter 10.

Impressions

The most Australian thing you can do is to lie on a clean, wide beautiful beach.

—Ross Terrill

Impressions

There has long been this element in Australia of delighting in life for its vigour and activity, without asking questions about it.

—Donald Horne, *The Lucky Country* (1978)

- **Green Island, the Great Barrier Reef:** This coral cay, accessed from Cairns, is a personal favorite. There's excellent coral right off the beach, plus an underwater observatory. See Chapter 10.
- **Michaelmas Cay, the Great Barrier Reef:** Reached by boat from Cairns, this uninhabited cay is surrounded by marine life. Marine biologists lead guided snorkel tours. See Chapter 9.
- **Lizard Island, the Great Barrier Reef:** The farthest north of the reef islands, Lizard offers coral right off the beach as well as boat trips to the outer reef. I saw a baby octopus here once while snorkeling. See Chapter 10.
- **Cod Hole, the Great Barrier Reef:** Accessed from Lizard Island, the famous Cod Hole is where you'll find potato cod and friendly eels. You can feed them by hand 30 feet down. See Chapter 10.
- **Ningaloo Reef, Western Australia:** The best-known dive spot on the west coast, Ningaloo Reef provides you an opportunity to dive with whale sharks—if you're up to the challenge. See Chapter 13.

8 The Best Places to Hike (Bushwalk)

Walking tracks (trails) lead travelers to the country's best scenery. Details and contact information for the experiences below can be found in the referenced chapters. Also be sure to peruse "The Active Vacation Planner" in Chapter 3.

- **Blue Mountains, New South Wales:** Hiking trails wind throughout the Blue Mountains National Park and carry walkers to the best viewpoints. Proximity to Sydney makes this a good day-trip activity. See Chapter 6.
- **Daintree National Park, Northern Queensland:** North of Cairns and Port Douglas, the Daintree rain forest is a fascinating tangle of trees and other plants. Walking provides the only practical way to see it. See Chapter 9.
- **The Olgas, the Red Centre, the Northern Territory:** The Valley of the Winds at the Olgas isn't for tenderfoots, but if you're energetic you'll be rewarded with beautiful Red Centre scenery. See Chapter 11.
- **Grampians National Park, Victoria:** This area is rich in Aboriginal history, as well as in wildlife and great scenery. The park staff maintain numerous trails that are suitable for all fitness levels. See Chapter 17.
- **Cradle Mountain National Park, Tasmania:** The Overland Track, an 80km (50-mile) route, links Cradle Mountain and Lake St. Clair. This trek takes 5 to 10 days. Other walks in the area can be done as day- or half-day hikes. See Chapter 18.

9 The Best Adventure Activities

Details and contact information for the experiences below can be found in the referenced chapters. Also be sure to peruse "The Active Vacation Planner" in Chapter 3.

- **Abseiling in the Blue Mountains, New South Wales:** While this *sounds* like an activity requiring lots of training, novices can actually try their hand after very little preparation. Several outfitters in Katoomba provide all the gear, instruction, and transportation. See Chapter 6.
- **Sailing in the Whitsundays, Central Queensland:** Many sheltered anchorages and numerous tree-clad islands make this area of Queensland the most popular place in the country for sailing. Local companies offer both skippered and bareboat charters. See Chapter 8.
- **White-Water Rafting on the Tully River, Northern Queensland:** The highest rainfall in Australia supplies the Tully, just south of Cairns, with plenty of white water. Raging Thunder and others organize adventurous rapid experiences. See Chapter 9.
- **Surfing the Sunshine Coast, Southern Queensland:** The long ride at Noosa is one for the record books. Don't be surprised if dolphins surf with you. See Chapter 8.
- **Deep-Sea Fishing at Lizard Island, the Great Barrier Reef:** It's a pricey endeavor, but dedicated anglers flock to Lizard during marlin season. See Chapter 10.
- **Canoeing Katherine Gorge, the Northern Territory:** You couldn't ask for more dramatic scenery than this through which to paddle your canoe. Steep red-rock walls rise up on either side. See Chapter 11.
- **Horse Trekking in the Snowy River Region, Victoria:** Follow in the tracks of the Man from Snowy River. Several operators in this area provide horses and guides. You couldn't ask for better scenery. See Chapter 17.

10 The Best Offbeat Activities

- **Hanging Out at the House, Sydney, New South Wales:** On sunny Sunday afternoons, the patios around the Sydney Opera House are popular gathering spots for locals—and you can join them. Enjoy the mimes, jugglers, people-watching—and the breeze off the harbor. See Chapter 5.
- **Doing a Pub Crawl on Horseback, New South Wales:** In the New England area, Steve Langley conducts six-day trips traversing the countryside and overnighting in historic country pubs. See Chapter 6.
- **Enjoying a Very Private Picnic, the Great Barrier Reef:** On Lizard or Orpheus Island and in the Whitsundays, you and the picnic partner(s) of your choice can have a whole beach to yourselves. See Chapter 10.
- **Stopping for a Drink at a Backcountry Watering Hole, the Northern Territory:** In the remote areas of the Australian countryside, pubs provide the only gathering places. One of the most colorful is the Bark Hut Inn on the road between Darwin and Kakadu National Park. See Chapter 11.
- **Taking a Camel to Dinner, the Northern Territory:** You can also ride a camel to breakfast or lunch. This Alice Springs activity is one of my favorites. See Chapter 11.

Impressions

In Australia alone is to be found the Grotesque, the Weird, the strange scribblings of nature learning how to write . . . the subtle charm of this fantastic land of monstrosities.

—Marcus Clarke, Journalist (1846–81)

- **Eating Dinner in the Bush, the Northern Territory:** There's nothing quite like a barbecue under the southern sky. You'll also boil the billy and learn to make damper bread. Several minibus tour operators in Alice Springs organize these. See Chapter 11.
- **Fossicking for Opals, South Australia or New South Wales:** This is the main occupation and avocation in Coober Pedy, South Australia, and Lightning Ridge, New South Wales. Anyone can try his or her hand. See Chapters 6 and 15.

11 The Best Museums

- **Hyde Park Barracks, Sydney, New South Wales:** Here you can see how the convicts lived and take a good look at Australia's social history. The building was designed by a convict architect. See Chapter 5.
- **Australian National Maritime Museum, Sydney, New South Wales:** This interactive museum, in the Darling Harbour area, traces the country's maritime history. Included is a fascinating social history of those immigrants who arrived by sea. See Chapter 5.
- **Migration Museum, Adelaide, South Australia:** Adelaide is the home of the best place in the country to learn about the various immigrant groups who've arrived on Australia's shores. This is an exciting hands-on kind of place. See Chapter 14.
- **National Wool Museum, near Melbourne, Victoria:** You'll understand the meaning of the expression "Australia was founded on the sheep's back" after you've toured this wonderful place outside Melbourne. See Chapter 16.
- **War Memorial Museum, Canberra, Australian Capital Territory:** This museum provides a chance to learn about another aspect of the country's history. It's informative, not gruesome. See Chapter 19.

12 The Best Luxury Accommodations

- **The Observatory, Sydney, New South Wales** (☎ 02/256 2222; 02/9256 2222 after July 1996): This wonderful—and very special—hotel is my favorite spot to splurge in Sydney. The flotation tank in the health club is a great way to treat jet lag. I also love the clubby feel of the Globe Bar and the fact that the staff quickly learn guests' names. See Chapter 4.
- **Lilianfels, Katoomba, New South Wales** (☎ 047/801 200; 02/4780 1200 after February 1998): This consummate country-house hotel in the Blue Mountains combines five-star amenities and a cozy atmosphere. I particularly like the huge lounge with the two fireplaces where afternoon tea is served. See Chapter 6.
- **Milton Park Country House Hotel, Bowral, New South Wales** (☎ 048/61 1522; 02/4861 1522 after June 1998): One of the few Relais & Châteaux members in Australia, this lovely inn is less than a two-hour drive south of Sydney. The gardens are some of the best in the country, and the meals are outstanding. See Chapter 6.
- **The Convent, Pokolbin, New South Wales** (☎ 049/987 764; 02/4998 7764 after June 1998): In the heart of the Hunter Valley, this relocated structure is the wine country's poshest place to stay. Guests enjoy champagne and canapes in the drawing room before dinner, plus an incredible breakfast buffet. See Chapter 6.
- **Conrad Treasury Casino Hotel, Brisbane, Southern Queensland** (☎ 07/3306 8888): This is Brisbane's best bet for those who want luxurious accommodations in a heritage building with a great central location. It feels more like a grand home than a modern hotel. See Chapter 7.

- **Marriott Surfers Paradise, Surfers Paradise, Southern Queensland** (☎ 07/5592 9800): I expected a cookie-cutter, name-brand hotel and was pleasantly surprised to find a classy high-rise hostelry that successfully incorporates the *feel* of Queensland. The pool area, with its own coral reef and beach, is unique in Australia. See Chapter 8.
- **Hayman Island Resort, Hayman Island, the Great Barrier Reef** (☎ 079/469 1000; 07/4769 1000 after June 1998): In the Whitsunday area of Queensland, this property offers deluxe accommodations, top-notch service, and first-rate facilities. It reminds me of the lovely Mauna Kea on the Big Island of Hawaii—works of art, antiques, and Oriental rugs abound. See Chapter 10.
- **Reef House, Palm Cove, Northern Queensland** (☎ 070/55 3633; 07/4055 3633 after April 1998): I like this place, just north of Cairns, because it offers comfort and luxury without feeling like a hotel. It's steps from the beach and has won awards for its great breakfasts. See Chapter 9.
- **Seven Spirit Bay, Cobourg Peninsula, the Northern Territory** (☎ 08/8979 0277): This unusual secluded place could best be described as a luxurious eco-tourist lodge. I love it—especially the seductive indoor/outdoor bathrooms. See Chapter 11.
- **Cable Beach Club, Broome, Western Australia** (☎ 091/920 4000; 08/9120 4000 after April 1998): On the coast of the Kimberley region, this spot has an ambience that's a cross between Asian and Australian. Proximity to a beautiful beach is a big bonus. See Chapter 13.
- **Windsor Hotel, Melbourne, Victoria** (☎ 03/9653 0653): The oldest deluxe property in Australia, the Windsor offers spacious surroundings and good service. This is a great spot for traditional afternoon tea or a beer in the Cricketers Bar. See Chapter 16.
- **Hyatt Hotel Canberra, Canberra, Australian Capital Territory** (☎ 06/270 1234; 02/6270 1234 after February 1998): Unlike most name-brand hotels, this property reflects the local history and has a gracious, almost genteel, atmosphere. It feels like a country club. See Chapter 19.

13 The Best Moderately Priced Accommodations

- **The Stafford, Sydney, New South Wales** (☎ 02/251 6711; 02/9251 6711 after July 1996): My favorite self-contained Sydney digs provide an ideal location in The Rocks, spacious quarters, and a friendly staff. This is *the* spot for those who want to feel they've found a home away from home. Some quarters even offer an outstanding Opera House view. See Chapter 4.
- **Bahia Beachfront Apartments, Surfers Paradise, Southern Queensland** (☎ 07/5538 3322): This high-rise overlooking the beach at Surfers Paradise is ideal for those who want lots of space and all the comforts of home. See Chapter 8.
- **Townsville Reef International, Townsville, Northern Queensland** (☎ 077/21 1777; 07/4721 1777 after March 1999): A real sleeper, this delightful spot provides pleasant rooms in a good location. There's also a delightful restaurant on the premises and the proprietors are unusually helpful. See Chapter 9.
- **Castaways Beachfront Resort, Mission Beach, Northern Queensland** (☎ 070/68 7444; 07/4068 7444 after April 1998): Right on the beach, this low-rise property provides great value. Most quarters have balconies and water views. See Chapter 9.
- **Coconut Grove Motel, Port Douglas, Northern Queensland** (☎ 070/99 5124; 07/4099 5124 after April 1998): Only a stone's throw from Four Mile Beach, this

friendly little motel finds its way into the hearts of all who stay here. The owner/operator is a former New York stockbroker. See Chapter 9.

- **Novotel Atrium Hotel, Darwin, the Northern Territory** (☎ 08/8941 0755): On the waterfront, the Novotel offers attractive rooms and gives you a choice of several pleasant and reasonably priced eating/drinking options—all adjacent to the plant-filled lobby. See Chapter 11.
- **Apartments on the Park, Adelaide, South Australia** (☎ 08/232 0555; 08/8232 0555 after August 1996): This home away from home is ideal for families. Each unit has two bedrooms, a full kitchen, and a washer/dryer. Great value! See Chapter 14.
- **Magnolia Court Boutique Hotel, Melbourne, Victoria** (☎ 03/9419 4222): I like this property because it's in a residential neighborhood within walking distance of the central business district. Terrace houses give the area an old-world feel, and there's a sunny breakfast room. See Chapter 16.

14 The Best Alternative Accommodations

- **Jemby-Rinjah Lodge, Blackheath, New South Wales** (☎ 047/87 7622; 02/4887 7622 after June 1988): I've received lots of positive feedback from readers who've stayed here. Everyone seems to enjoy these comfortable cabins in the Blue Mountains of New South Wales. See Chapter 6.
- **Runnymede, Upper Hunter Valley, New South Wales** (☎ 063/761 183; 02/6376 1183 after June 1998): This 2,000-acre sheep-and-cattle station between Mudgee and the Hunter Valley gives you an insight into the *real* Australia. The hosts take guests out over the land and into the nearby town (pop. 110). See Chapter 6.
- **Silky Oaks Wilderness Lodge, Mossman River Gorge, Far North Queensland** (☎ 070/98 1666; 07/4098 1666 after March 1999): I have to confess I haven't stayed here since P&O bought out the original owner, but I can still vouch for the ideal location—overlooking the Mossman River Gorge and surrounded by the Daintree National Forest. Young kangaroos can be cuddled in the nursery. See Chapter 9.
- **Daintree Eco Lodge, Daintree, Northern Queensland** (☎ 070/98 6100; 07/4098 6100 after April 1998): At this property, you sleep in well-appointed rooms set atop poles in a patch of rain forest. All accommodations come with screened-in balconies. See Chapter 9.
- **All Seasons Ross River Homestead, Alice Springs, the Northern Territory** (☎ 08/8969 7111): This place provides one-stop shopping for those wishing to sample outback Australia. Horses and camels are available for riding; damper bread is prepared over an open fire for morning tea; and anyone interested will be instructed in the fine art of throwing a boomerang. See Chapter 11.
- **Quamby Homestead, Woolsthorpe, Victoria** (☎ 055/692 395; 03/5569 2395 after March 1997): It's hard to say what I like most about this place—the warm hospitality, the great food, the historic house, or the scenic countryside. All I know is that I keep going back and always have a good time. See Chapter 17.

15 The Best B&Bs & Guesthouses

These bed-and-breakfast inns and guesthouses offer delightful surroundings and helpful hosts.

- **Simpsons of Potts Point, Sydney, New South Wales** (☎ 02/356 2199; 02/9356 2199 after July 1996): This is a good choice for anyone who enjoys historic houses and wants to be within walking distance of the Kings Cross dining and nightlife scene. See Chapter 6.
- **Scotts Guesthouse, Nambucca Heads, New South Wales** (☎ 065/68 6386; 02/6568 6386 after March 1998): This B&B—renowned for its warm hospitality—is a great value. A beautiful beach is nearby. See Chapter 6.
- **Taylor's Guesthouse, Byron Bay, New South Wales** (☎ 066/847 436; 02/6684 7436 after March 1998): The picturesque pool, rain-forest setting, and country decor make this one of my favorite B&Bs. Host Wendy Taylor is a gourmet chef. See Chapter 6.
- **Boomajarril, Brisbane, Southern Queensland** (☎ 07/3268 5764): At this lovely residence in suburban Brisbane you're treated to a three-course silver-service breakfast. See Chapter 7.
- **The Tilba, South Yarra, Victoria** (☎ 03/9347 7811): It's *almost* too gingerbready on the outside, but inside this house is tastefully well appointed. This is a good choice for those who want to be close to central Melbourne but don't enjoy high-rise hostelries. See Chapter 16.
- **Ballarat Terrace, Ballarat, Victoria** (☎ 053/332 216; 03/5333 2216 after February 1997): This National Trust–listed house and the charming hosts who inhabit it mke Ballarat Terrace a great place to stay while visiting the historic attractions of Ballarat. See Chapter 17.
- **Franklin Manor, Strahan, Tasmania** (☎ 004/717 311; 03/6471 7311 after March 1997): The remote West Coast of Tasmania is an unlikely spot for such a wonderful B&B. The rooms are beautiful and furnished with amenities like small refrigerators, tea- and coffee-making facilities, and tub/shower combinations—standard fare in a motel but unusual in a historic inn. See Chapter 18.

16 The Best Restaurants

- **Merrony's, Sydney, New South Wales** (☎ 02/247 9323; 02/9247 9323 after July 1996): I enjoy the imaginative menu and the convenient location of this popular Sydney restaurant. It's at Circular Quay, not far from the Opera House. See Chapter 4.
- **Pasadena Restaurant, Church Point, New South Wales** (☎ 02/979 6633; 02/9979 6633 after July 1996): I chose this spot for its lovely location—right on the water about 45 minutes from Sydney—but I go back because the food is terrific. See Chapter 4.
- **The Rothbury Cafe, Pokolbin, New South Wales** (☎ 049/987 363; 02/4998 7363 after June 1998): Located in the winery of the same name, this Hunter Valley eatery serves lunches that are both creative and delicious. See Chapter 6.
- **Samford Restaurant, Brisbane, Southern Queensland** (☎ 07/3289 1485): Joy Harman makes wonderful desserts! See Chapter 7.
- **Kiplings, Cairns, Northern Queensland** (☎ 070/31 1886; 07/4031 1886 after April 1998): I love ethnic food, so it isn't a wonder that Kiplings is my favorite restaurant in Cairns. Choices include samplings of Indian, Italian, Greek, Filipino, and Austrian fare. See Chapter 9.
- **Jessica's Fine Seafood Restaurant, Perth, Western Australia** (☎ 09/325 2511; 08/9325 2511 after September 1997): Seafood is the specialty at this popular

restaurant. Enjoy it with an oaky chardonnay from the nearby Margaret River winery region. See Chapter 12.

- **The Oxford, North Adelaide, South Australia** (☎ 08/267 2652; 08/8267 2652 after August 1996): The Oxford serves excellent Modern Australian fare in unusually attractive surroundings. Be sure to try the Oxford fries. See Chapter 14.
- **Mure's Upper Deck, Hobart, Tasmania** (☎ 002/312 121; 03/6231 2121 after November 1996): This restaurant serves wonderful fresh seafood in an appealing setting on the dock overlooking Hobart Harbour. See Chapter 18.

17 The Best Shopping

- **Craft Markets:** My favorites are The Rocks Market in Sydney, the Riverside Market in Brisbane, and the Salamanca Market in Hobart. See Chapters 5, 7, and 18, respectively.
- **National Trust Shops:** These are a great place to purchase tasteful memorabilia. Some of the better ones are in Sydney, Brisbane, Melbourne, Hobart, and Launceston. See Chapters 5, 7, 16, and 18, respectively.
- **Produce Markets:** I love browsing through huge stacks of fresh fruit and vegetables and gathering goodies for a picnic or midnight snack. In Australia the best places for such shopping are the Central Markets in Adelaide and Queen Victoria Market in Melbourne. See Chapters 14 and 16, respectively.
- **Factory Stores:** Melbourne is the fashion-design capital of the country, and factory stores abound. There are also some in Sydney. See Chapter 16.

2

Introducing Oz

Australia's wonders attract visitors from all over the world. Some come to see the desolate beauty of the outback; others travel halfway around the globe to witness for themselves the amazing Great Barrier Reef. Most want to cuddle a koala or stroke the head of a joey poking up out of a mother kangaroo's pouch. Birders are fascinated by Australia's colorful winged life, and other people are intrigued by the mysterious Aboriginal culture.

Whatever your reason for heading down under, keep in mind that Australia is about the same size as the 48 contiguous U.S. states and wandering around without a game plan will get you nowhere—literally. Instead, I hope you'll use this guide to help you decide which areas you want to visit and plan your means of getting there. And while I wouldn't for a minute suggest that you skip Sydney, the Great Barrier Reef, and Ayers Rock, I hope you'll let me lead you off the beaten path to at least a couple of the small towns and country areas that aren't promoted as tourist destinations.

Australia is a great, big, wonderful country that I've covered extensively over the years. I want you to enjoy your trip as much as I've enjoyed all of mine, and to that end I look forward to sharing what I've learned with you. My goal is that you'll get not only the best possible value for your time and money but some wonderful memories as well.

1 Australia's Natural World

THE LAY OF THE LAND

The facts belie Australia's youthful appearance: Scientists have determined that the continent dates back 130 million years. Ayers Rock is composed of material deposited in the Precambrian era—over 600 million years ago. The Aborigines have been in residence for at least 40,000 years.

THE OUTBACK When I think of the Australian landscape, I visualize vast expanses of dry reddish brown earth, punctuated by stately ghost gum trees whose branches are host to large colorful birds. The sun is shining and the sky robin's-egg blue. Not all of Australia looks like this, but a lot of it does, and it makes a lasting impression.

Did You Know?

- "Waltzing Matilda" is *not* Australia's national anthem. This honor goes to "Advance Australia Fair," a patriotic song composed by Peter Dodds McCormick in about 1878.
- Australia's legendary rabbit problem started when a nostalgic settler let loose 24 English rabbits for hunting in Victoria in 1859.
- The Northern Territory is the only place in Australia where it's legal to keep a dingo as a pet.
- Australia is the world's largest diamond-producing country.
- Australia has the largest population of free-ranging camels anywhere (about 200,000).
- The secret ballot box was pioneered in Victoria in 1856.
- The world's largest cattle station, Strangeray Springs in South Australia, is almost the same size as Belgium.
- Voting is compulsory in Australia.
- Rupert Murdoch, the newspaper/TV magnate, was born in Australia in 1931. He became a U.S. citizen in 1985.
- Granny Smith apples were originally grown in New South Wales in the 1860s.
- Look carefully when you pull the plug in an Aussie washbasin or bathtub—chances are that the water will drain out counterclockwise rather than clockwise as you're accustomed to in the Northern Hemisphere.
- Before he made it big in the movies, Paul Hogan worked as a bridge rigger and a racetrack bookmaker's assistant.
- The Royal Flying Doctor Service, which provides urgent medical care to outback residents, flies almost 5 million kilometers (3,125,000 miles) annually.
- There are around 24 million head of cattle in Australia, down from over 33.5 million in the mid-1970s. There are about 138 million sheep.

The rust color, which comes from iron in the soil, is the outback's predominant hue. As a result, the middle of the country around Ayers Rock and Alice Springs is commonly called the Red Centre. The clear sky reflects the lack of pollution in the air. These vast arid expanses extend for great distances without so much as a hill to add variety to the horizon. Australia has the distinction of being not only the driest continent but also the flattest. The average elevation is less than 300m (990 ft.)—the world's mean is about 700m (2,310 ft.).

Ghost gums and other varieties of eucalyptus trees manage to survive the harsh conditions in some areas, but they aren't sufficiently drought-resistant for the most barren places, such as the Nullarbor Plain, whose name means "without trees." Passengers on the *Indian Pacific* train, which crosses the Nullarbor on the world's longest stretch of straight track, can look out the windows for hours and not see a living thing, except perhaps a fleeting glimpse of a kangaroo.

Every mainland state except Victoria has its share of this outback wilderness. In addition to the Nullarbor Plain, Western Australia has the Gibson Desert and the Great Sandy Desert. The Simpson Desert covers an area about the size of South Carolina in the adjacent corners of the Northern Territory, Queensland, and South

Australia. And the huge Great Victoria Desert is near the Red Centre and spills into more than one state.

Except for mining towns like Coober Pedy, Mount Isa, Broken Hill, Tennant Creek, and Andamooka, actual settlements don't exist. Instead, families live on large sheep and cattle stations (ranches), where they receive their medical care from the Royal Flying Doctor Service. Children, through two-way radio contact, attend classes via the School of the Air. One of these cattle stations, Strangeray Springs in South Australia, covers 30,028 square km (11,954 square miles) and is almost the same size as Belgium.

THE GREEN RIM In contrast to the inhospitable outback terrain, a fertile band extends inward from the perimeter of the country, providing an agreeable environment for both humans and animals. In fact, 88% of the population lives within 20km (12½ miles) of the coast. Australians like to joke that their founding fathers knew future generations would love the beach, so they built all the state capitals near the coast; but they couldn't put Canberra, the federal capital, there because the politicians wouldn't get any work done.

Australia is about the same size as the 48 contiguous U.S. states, but because it occupies an entire continent, it has much more coastline—36,700km (22,754 miles), as compared with 19,812km (12,283 miles) for the United States. The beaches created by the Indian Ocean on the west and the South Pacific Ocean on the east are some of the most beautiful in the world.

This fertile coastal strip contains not only beaches but also the "bush," what non-Aussies call forest. In most zones the woodland areas are dominated by gum (eucalyptus) trees. Approximately 550 varieties of gum thrive in Australia, and their identification has been the subject of several books. Notable examples are the jarrah in Western Australia, the messmate stringybark in Victoria, and the spotted gum in New South Wales and Queensland.

About 600 species of wattle (acacia) are found in Australia. These colorful shrubs provide vivid yellow flowers that can be seen throughout the country. The golden wattle is the unofficial national floral emblem. Red bottlebrushes and grevilleas, dramatic banksias, and pretty baronias, which are native only to Australia, are other prominent wildflowers. While all the states have endemic flowering plants, Western Australia has by far the greatest number. *National Geographic*'s "Wild Flowers of Western Australia" (January 1995) is a wonderful resource on this topic.

Rain forests, another feature of the coastal strip, are located in damp areas on the eastern side of the mainland as well as on the island of Tasmania; they range from temperate in the south to tropical in the north. Rain forests teem with plant and bird life and are the antithesis of the arid outback. National parks, such as Lamington near the New South Wales–Queensland border, provide an opportunity for visitors to witness the dark, dense, humid splendor of this special kind of forest, with its characteristic strangler figs, bird's-nest ferns, staghorn ferns, and native orchids.

THE GREAT BARRIER REEF The Great Barrier Reef lies off the Queensland coast and extends for some 2,000km (1,240 miles) from Gladstone to the Gulf of Papua near New Guinea. It's the world's largest coral structure and is one of the great wonders. The reef and its unique array of bird, plant, and marine life are covered in Chapter 10.

MOUNTAINS & RIVERS The highest point in the country is New South Wales's Mount Kosciusko, which reaches a height of 2,228m (7,352 ft.) in the Snowy Mountains region of the Great Dividing Range. It's from the southern portion of these mountains that the Murray River, one of the nation's longest, emerges. The other major river, the Darling, has its headwaters in the eastern highlands of New South Wales and southern Queensland. The Murray-Darling system flows for a total of 5,300km (3,286 miles) until it enters the ocean in South Australia.

WILDLIFE FROM KOALAS TO CROCS

The variety and drama of the country's landscape are rivaled only by the animals that inhabit it. Nowhere else but in Australia do kangaroos and emus dash across the highway, and nowhere else is home to as many large, colorful, noisy birds.

Note: Do *not* feed any wildlife you come across while exploring.

NATIVE ANIMALS Most of the unique native animals are marsupials, whose young are born at a very early stage of development and are carried and nursed in an external abdominal pouch while they continue to mature. The two most famous members of this family are kangaroos and their cousins, koalas. Other members are sugar gliders, possums, quokkas, wallabies, bandicoots, Tasmanian devils, and wombats—this last animal being almost as cute as the koala but, lacking a good press agent, not nearly as popular.

Most everyone knows that koalas *aren't* bears, in spite of their cuddly teddy-bear appearance. These marsupials eat only the tender stems, shoots, and leaves of eucalyptus trees. Because of their diet, koalas have a distinctive body odor that isn't as appealing as their countenance. *National Geographic* ran a very interesting article on koalas in April 1995.

Much less is known about kangaroos, and many people are surprised to learn that there are 45 species in Australia. I find it fascinating that mama roos have a continuous reproductive flow—one joey outside the pouch, one inside, and one embryo on hold. In this way the female can produce offspring long after the male has disappeared. She's also capable of limiting reproduction during droughts.

There are two species of crocodiles in Australia—the freshwater type and the saltwater, or estuarine, variety. It's important to know the difference between the two, especially if you're fond of swimming: The freshwater type is generally not a problem, but the saltwater croc can make a quick meal of a horse, cow, or human.

Snakes, too, can make their presence known. Many, like the death adder, taipan, and brown snake, are poisonous. Since most travelers won't have the time or interest to learn the identity of each type of snake, it's a good idea to leave *all* of them alone.

And on the subject of danger, it's important to know that Australian waters are home to about 20 kinds of sharks. While some of these are harmless, white pointers, blue pointers, tiger sharks, and whaler sharks have been involved in attacks on humans. The eastern seaboard, particularly, is heavily infested; most swimming areas are not only carefully patrolled but also protected with shark nets.

Not everything that swims in Australia is ferocious, however. You'll be lucky to catch a glimpse of the shy platypus; fairy penguins come ashore nightly on Victoria's Phillip Island without paying any attention to the human entourage assembled to watch them; the seals on South Australia's Kangaroo Island don't disturb visitors who roam through their colony as long as they keep a respectful distance from any pups;

Impressions

Australia: The world's wildest island.

—Airline advertisement (1980)

Monkey Mia, on the coast of Western Australia, is the only place in the world where you can pet wild dolphins; and most of the marine life on the Great Barrier Reef is perfectly safe.

In addition to aquatic animals, more than 700 species of bird live in Australia. Emus are the largest and, like the strange-looking cassowaries, can't fly. But they aren't as colorful as galahs, sulfur-crested cockatoos, rainbow lorikeets, or king parrots. Other notable birds are the kookaburra, known for its raucous laugh, and the black swan, the symbol of Western Australia.

IMPORTED WILDLIFE Some of the animals associated with Australia aren't indigenous to the continent. They've been introduced, and several have caused unexpected problems. The dingo (wild dog) is thought to have been brought in by the Aborigines 3,000 to 8,000 years ago. In spite of fences thousands of miles long, dingoes continue to prey on sheep and are classified a noxious pest. Rabbits, imported by early British settlers, reproduce at such a rate they still threaten the livestock industry by eating grass intended for cattle and sheep, a serious depredation where rain and water are scarce.

Like rabbits, foxes were brought to Australia in the 1800s by Europeans. Today, the 3 million wild foxes in the state of Victoria are blamed for contributing to the extinction of 18 marsupials.

And water buffalo, introduced in the north during the early 19th century, are currently the target of an eradication program because their presence threatens the natural ecology. Camels were brought in and used by early explorers as a means of traversing the island continent's vast deserts—now large numbers roam wild in the outback.

2 The States & Territories in Brief

Australia consists of six states (New South Wales, Queensland, Western Australia, South Australia, Victoria, and Tasmania) and two internal territories (the Australian Capital Territory and the Northern Territory). The federal capital, Canberra, is in the Australian Capital Territory. Several external territories are also under Australia's control, like Norfolk Island, Christmas Island, Macquarie Island, Cocos Island, Lord Howe Island, and part of Antarctica.

The biggest decision visitors have to make is where to spend their time. Certainly, with very few exceptions, everyone will want to visit Sydney. This is one of the world's great cities, and it wouldn't be outlandish to consider parking yourself here for a week or two. There's lots to do in the city itself, even more a day trip away. I've been to Sydney at least a dozen times and *always* leave wishing I'd had a few more days. The advantage of this approach is that you avoid packing and unpacking many times and would probably be able to negotiate a good long-stay rate at your choice of accommodation.

Outside of Sydney, **New South Wales** provides an opportunity to experience the outback, some really pretty coastal sceenery, and Australia's best mountain terrain.

Queensland is a very popular destination—and deservedly so—because it's the jumping-off point for the Great Barrier Reef. In terms of cities, Brisbane is pleasant, but if your time is really limited you'd be better off basing yourself in Cairns. From here the reef, the rain forest, and the tablelands are all conveniently accessible.

The **Northern Territory**'s main attraction is Ayers Rock, and I think it's a shame that so many people overlook Alice Springs, also in the Red Centre. Frankly the Top End (Darwin and Kakadu National Park) are, by comparison, uninteresting.

Australia

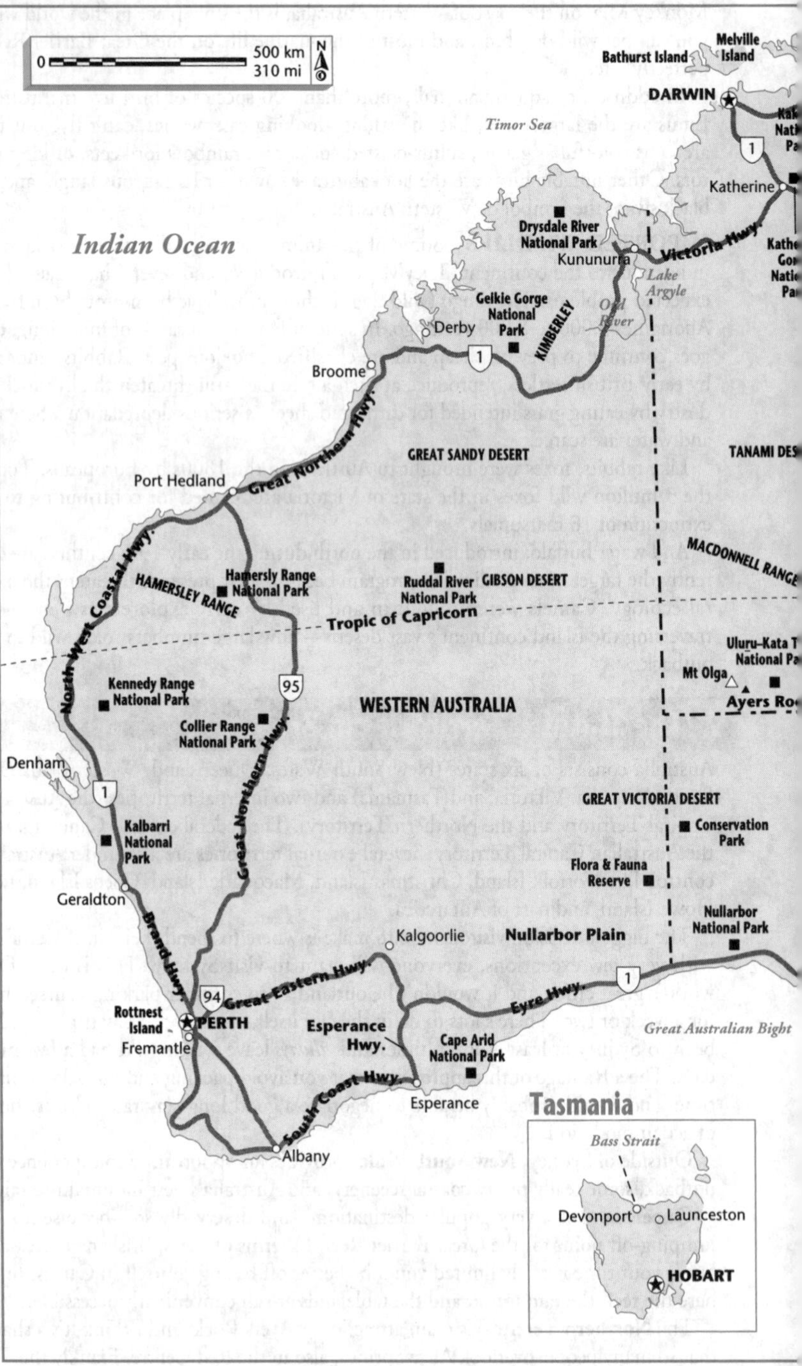
0
500 km
310 mi
N
Bathurst Island
Melville Island
DARWIN
Timor Sea
1
Katherine
Indian Ocean
Drysdale River National Park
Kununurra
Victoria Hwy.
Lake Argyle
Ord River
Geikie Gorge National Park
KIMBERLEY
Derby
1
Broome
Great Northern Hwy.
GREAT SANDY DESERT
TANAMI DES
Port Hedland
MACDONNELL RANGE
North West Coastal Hwy.
HAMERSLEY RANGE
Hamersly Range National Park
Ruddal River National Park
GIBSON DESERT
Tropic of Capricorn
Uluru–Kata T National Pa
Mt Olga
Ayers Ro
95
Kennedy Range National Park
WESTERN AUSTRALIA
Collier Range National Park
Great Northern Hwy.
Denham
1
GREAT VICTORIA DESERT
Kalbarri National Park
Conservation Park
Flora & Fauna Reserve
Geraldton
Brand Hwy.
Nullarbor National Park
Kalgoorlie
Nullarbor Plain
Great Eastern Hwy.
1
94
Eyre Hwy.
Rottnest Island
PERTH
Fremantle
Great Australian Bight
Esperance Hwy.
Cape Arid National Park
South Coast Hwy.
Esperance
Albany
Tasmania
Bass Strait
Devonport
Launceston
HOBART
2317

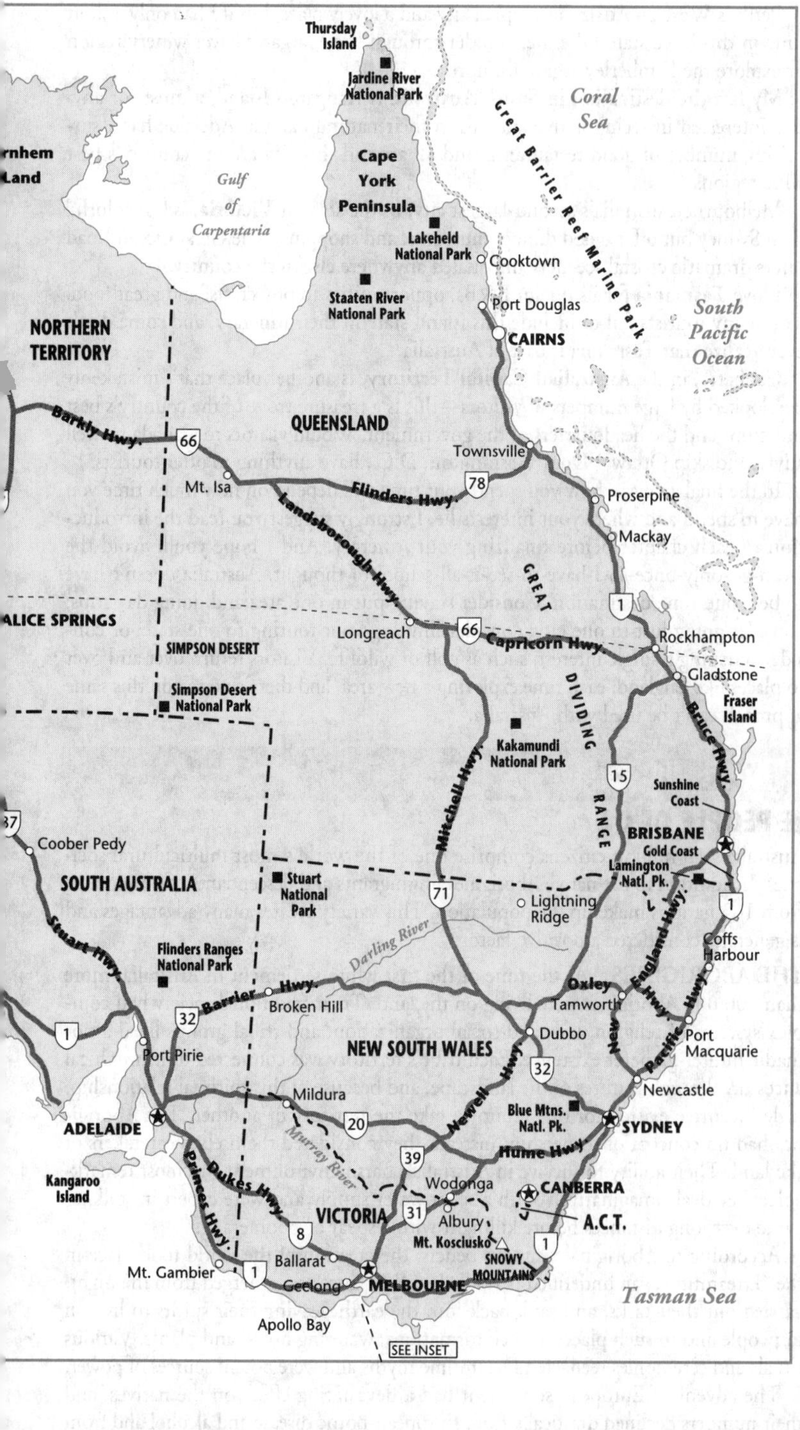
Thursday Island
Jardine River National Park
Coral Sea
Great Barrier Reef Marine Park
rnhem Land
Gulf of Carpentaria
Cape York Peninsula
Lakefield National Park
Cooktown
Staaten River National Park
Port Douglas
CAIRNS
South Pacific Ocean
NORTHERN TERRITORY
QUEENSLAND
Barkly Hwy.
66
Townsville
Mt. Isa
Flinders Hwy.
78
Proserpine
Landsborough Hwy.
Mackay
GREAT
1
ALICE SPRINGS
Longreach
66
Capricorn Hwy.
Rockhampton
SIMPSON DESERT
Gladstone
Simpson Desert National Park
DIVIDING
Fraser Island
Bruce Hwy.
Kakamundi National Park
Mitchell Hwy.
15
RANGE
Sunshine Coast
37
Coober Pedy
BRISBANE
Gold Coast
Lamington Natl. Pk.
SOUTH AUSTRALIA
Stuart National Park
71
Lightning Ridge
1
Stuart Hwy.
Darling River
New England Hwy.
Coffs Harbour
Flinders Ranges National Park
Oxley
Barrier Hwy.
Broken Hill
Tamworth
32
Hwy.
1
Pacific Hwy.
Dubbo
Port Macquarie
Port Pirie
NEW SOUTH WALES
Newell Hwy.
32
Newcastle
Mildura
ADELAIDE
Blue Mtns. Natl. Pk.
SYDNEY
20
Murray River
Hume Hwy.
Princes Hwy.
39
Kangaroo Island
Dukes Hwy.
Wodonga
CANBERRA
VICTORIA
31
Albury
A.C.T.
8
Mt. Kosciusko
1
Ballarat
SNOWY MOUNTAINS
Mt. Gambier
1
Geelong
MELBOURNE
Tasman Sea
Apollo Bay
SEE INSET

Perth is **Western Australia**'s capital city and a lovely place, but if I had only a short time in this huge state I'd either wander through the Margaret River winery region or explore the Kimberley region up north.

My favorite destination in **South Australia** is Kangaroo Island, a must for anyone interested in seeing native animals in their natural habitat. Adelaide has a surprising number of good restaurants, and all around this city are the country's best wine regions.

Melbourne, Australia's second-largest city, in the state of **Victoria,** is less colorful than Sydney but offers good dining, museums, and shopping. The Great Ocean Road offers dramatic coastal sceenery unequaled anywhere else in the country.

I love **Tasmania** for its quaint B&Bs, opportunities to buy crafts, and great food. Too many tourists fail to include this island state in their itinerary, and some don't even realize that Tasmania is part of Australia.

Canberra, in the **Australian Capital Territory,** is another place that's mistakenly overlooked by large numbers of visitors—this is a treasure trove of the country's best museums and the headquarters of the government. Would visitors to Canada be well advised to skip Ottawa? Does Washington, D.C., have anything to offer tourists?

In the final analysis, how you spend your time will depend on how much time you have to spend and where your interests lie. I strongly suggest you read the introduction to each chapter before finalizing your itinerary. And I hope you'll avoid the I-can-go-only-once-so-I-have-to-see-it-all school of thought. Australia doesn't have to be a one-time destination. Consider staying put in one area and doing day trips; consider going just to one city; consider limiting your touring to one state; or consider pursuing a single interest, such as golf or wildlife. Visitors return over and over to places like England, each time exploring a new area, and there's no reason this same approach can't be used with Australia.

3 Australia Today

THE PEOPLE OF OZ

Australia's 18 million citizens comprise one of the world's most multicultural societies. In addition to the native Aborigines, immigrants and descendants of immigrants from 163 nations make up the population. This variety creates many advantages and is generally considered a positive factor.

THE ABORIGINES At the time of the first white settlement in Australia, more than 300,000 Aborigines were living on the land. Their traditional society had complex systems of religion, law, and social organization, and tribal groups lived a nomadic hunter-gatherer existence. Each tribe's territory was connected to its mythical ancestors through features of the landscape, and because of this spiritual relationship, little incentive existed for one group to take the territory of another. The Aborigines had no concept of ownership; instead, they considered themselves caretakers of the land. Their ability to survive in Australia's harsh environment was most remarkable; they dealt imaginatively with a scant water supply and were expert in stalking game over long distances before killing it with a spear or boomerang.

According to Aboriginal religious beliefs, the creation of the world took place in the "Dreamtime," an undefined period when their ancestors emerged from the night, carried out their tasks, and sank back into the earth, leaving their spirits to live on in people and in such places as rock formations, watering holes, and plants. Various rituals and ceremonies reenacted Dreamtime myths and were potent sources of power.

The advent of European settlement had a devastating effect on the natives, and their numbers declined drastically from European-borne disease and alcohol and from the ruthless manner in which they were treated. Conflict arose when the colonists attempted to move tribes off the land to which they had strong spiritual ties. The Aborigines were considered subhuman pests and in some areas, most notably Tasmania, were actually hunted like animals. By 1947 their count had declined to 76,000.

It wasn't until the late 1950s that humane treatment of the Aborigines became an issue in Australia. In 1960 the Aborigines were granted citizenship, and in 1967 a change in the constitution permitted them to be included in the national census. The Aboriginal Land Rights Act of 1978 returned significant tribal territory to its former owners, and in 1983 the government handed back the title to Uluru National Park (Ayers Rock), one of the most sacred Aboriginal sites.

Today, with improved health and welfare programs, the Aborigines account for about 1.5% of the population, approximately 288,000 people. Nearly half of them live in cities and towns, though many still remain in remote areas and prefer a traditional tribal-oriented way of life. In spite of their equal rights and legally improved status, the Aborigines, in general, still have low levels of education, relatively poor health, inadequate housing, and high unemployment rates.

The plight of the Aborigine is an embarrassment for some Australians and a source of resentment for others, who disapprove of the government's aid and assistance efforts. Despite this controversy, the native people are rebuilding their traditional social systems, and their rich culture, with its music, dance, painting, carving, and mythology, is being revitalized.

Aboriginal Beliefs In Aboriginal Dreamtime myths, the mountains, the oceans, the springs, the sky, the sun, the moon, the stars, and all the other natural features were formed by spirits, who afterward returned to the Dreamtime, a sort of Aboriginal heaven. "Dreaming places" are sacred spots associated with a particular mythical ancestor; some can be visited only by initiated males. According to Aboriginal tradition, man can draw on the power of the Dreamtime by reenacting various myths and practicing certain rituals and ceremonies.

One of the most potent of the Aboriginal religious beliefs involved "pointing the bone." In this procedure, an animal or human bone (the forearm of a dead medicine man was preferred) was pointed toward a victim while those doing the pointing sang ritual chants. It was believed the bone would travel invisibly to the victim and pierce his body. So strongly was this belief held that, once someone learned that the bone had been pointed at him, death actually followed.

THE AVERAGE AUSTRALIAN Are Paul Hogan and Bryan Brown typical Aussies? Some Australians might like you to think so, but the facts show that less than 15% of the population live in rural areas. Instead, the average Australian lives in one of the eight capital cities, has never seen native fauna anywhere but in a zoo or wildlife

Impressions

Here I am happy to say we are in full enjoyment of peace and plenty. The colony has improved equal to my most sanguine expectations. My situation is one of considerable fatigue and exertion but this I do not consider any hardship.

—Letter from Lachlan Macquarie,
Governor of the New South Wales Colony (1812)

This is really a wonderful Colony; ancient Rome in her imperial grandeur would not have been ashamed of such an offspring.

—Letter from Charles Darwin (1836)

Modern Aussie Heroes

While spiritual ancestors are held in high esteem by the Aborigines, other Australians have their own heroes.

Robert O'Hara Burke and **William John Wills** were the first Europeans to cross Australia south to north. Their expedition left Melbourne in August 1860 and established a supply camp at Cooper's Creek, nearly the north-south midpoint. From this camp Burke, Wills, and two others set out for the Gulf of Carpentaria on the north coast. After they'd reached their goal, it took them two months to journey back to the supply camp, with one dying en route; when the three arrived at the camp, they discovered that the men who'd been ordered to wait for them had left that morning. Burke, Wills, and John King, desperate for supplies, attempted to reach a distant police outpost at Mount Hopeless. In the meantime, part of the original expedition returned to Cooper's Creek and then, because they didn't find the message left by Burke, set off for Melbourne. In the end, Burke and Wills starved to death at the base camp, while King was saved by Aborigines.

Like the tale of the ill-fated Burke and Wills expedition, the story of **Ned Kelly,** Australia's most famous "bushranger" (outlaw) has been retold in paintings, literature, and film. In April 1878 Ned shot a trooper who was arresting his brother Dan for horse stealing. The two Kellys fled into the bush, where they were joined by Joe Byrne and Stephen Hart. The Kelly Gang, as they were known, proceeded to ambush and kill three police constables, rob banks, hold up stagecoaches, and generally wreak havoc. These men became folk heroes here much the way Jesse James did in America. Ned Kelly was hanged in Melbourne at age 26.

Harry "Breaker" Morant became an Aussie hero for entirely different reasons. Morant, a bush poet and contemporary of "Banjo" ("Waltzing Matilda") Paterson, was sent to South Africa to fight in the Boer War, Britain's conflict with Dutch colonists. During the war, Britain needed a scapegoat to resolve the controversial shooting of several Boer prisoners. Lieutenant Morant was court-martialed for his supposed role in the incident and executed.

A pioneer in the field of aviation, **Kingsford Smith** represents yet another type of hero. In 1928 Smith and Charles Ulm flew from California to Brisbane in 83 hours and 38 minutes. They later made a nonstop flight across Australia and the first trans-Tasman flight to New Zealand. Smith continued to break records, making the first solo flight from England to Australia. He was knighted in 1932 and disappeared while flying in 1935.

Can a horse be a hero? If so, **Phar Lap,** winner of the 1930 Melbourne Cup, certainly qualifies. Though he's Australia's most famous racehorse, Kiwis are quick to point out he was actually born in New Zealand. Phar Lap won 37 of 51 starts in his career, later dying mysteriously in America. A movie, entitled simply *Phar Lap,* was made about his life, and his stuffed body is on display in the Museum of Victoria in Melbourne.

Even though Australians aren't quick to idolize public figures, they make an exception in the area of sports—many of the country's contemporary heroes are, like Phar Lap, outstanding athletes.

park, is much more comfortable in trendy imported clothing than in a Driza-bone coat or Akubra hat, and prefers cappuccino to billy tea. Given the choice, garden-variety Aussies would rather vacation in California than explore the rest of their own country. The "ocker" Aussie (stereotypical uncultured Australian) does exist outside the movies, but not in the numbers you might think. If you're determined to find such a person, head for an isolated sheep or cattle station in the outback.

In cities and towns the people you'll meet may say "G'day, mate," but chances are their pronunciation will have a foreign flavor. About 22% of Australians were born overseas and a further 44% have at least one parent born in another country. These arrivals have more than doubled the population since World War II. The British Isles are the largest source—80%—with Italy, Greece, and the former Yugoslavia close behind. Many Asians have settled in Australia, starting with the Chinese who came out during the gold rush in the mid- and late 19th century and including a significant number of recent Indochinese refugees. Unlike its neighbor, New Zealand, which identifies with Mother England, Australia has a waning interest in things British and tends to see itself as a part of Australasia.

Though the question of who's a true-blue Aussie may plague many Australians in search of a national identity, it doesn't affect visitors. What we notice are personality traits—and these, surprisingly, seem to transcend ethnic origin, tenure in the country, and habitat.

The friendliness of the people—not to mention their sense of humor—is the first thing travelers usually notice. Though Aussies may be descended in good part from English stock, they sure don't exhibit the traditional British reserve. They seem to like just about everyone and don't try to hide it. For example, in a taxi it's quite common for the passenger to sit in front with the driver—so they can talk. Can you imagine that in London or New York?

Love of sports is yet another trait that unites Australians. Whether it's rugby league, Aussie Rules football, cricket, tennis, sailing, surfing, soccer, golf, car racing, or horse racing, the vast majority of people either participate or are avid spectators. Involvement is especially high on weekends, when seemingly every playing field hosts some sort of a competition and the major radio and TV stations devote long hours to coverage.

Gambling, another great passion, goes hand-in-hand with the interest in sports. However, most Aussies don't need a team to bet on; they can get very enthusiastic over the toss of a coin. Anyone who doubts my word should go to one of the country's casinos and watch the crowd play two-up.

Some say that the consuming interest in sports accounts for the sparsely filled pews in Australia's churches, but others suggest that the lack of interest in organized religion stems from the nation's origins as a convict colony, when church representatives doled out some of the harshest punishments.

A strong sense of independence and an innate irreverence and resentment of authority are other characteristics that stem from the country's origins as a convict colony. Aussies love to make fun of their political leaders, law-enforcement officers, and any others who try to set themselves above others. The person who offends the national spirit of egalitarianism is open to a raft of good-hearted verbal ribbing.

If you're getting the idea that the average Australian is dedicated to the enjoyment of life, you're absolutely right. "No worries" is not only a common expression but a prevalent attitude. Aussies dress casually and enjoy a relaxed lifestyle characterized by backyard barbecues and high pub attendance. They even speak casually, adding *y* or *ie* to nearly everything, so that *football* becomes *footy, biscuit* becomes *bickie, mosquito* is *mossie, postie* is the person who delivers the mail, and *barby* is what you slip a shrimp on (except Australians call them prawns). See the Appendix for an Aussie/Yankee lexicon.

Impressions

They're very friendly people, people not prone to, as we say "dip your lid," to others in a sense of recognizing a superiority in one class of people. There is a phrase we have in Australia—the "fair go." The fair go really means that all people are created with the right to develop and express themselves.

—Former Prime Minister Robert Hawke on the Aussie Character

Basic to this way of life is a high regard for the family unit. Parents include their children in most social occasions (and vacations) and only infrequently leave them at home with a sitter. The average Australian couple has 2.2 children, lives in a major urban center, and owns a home.

How is it possible that a population of people from such diverse backgrounds shares so many common attitudes? Why is it that the new arrival from southern Europe who has barely mastered English already loves sports, gambling, barbecues, and going to the pub as much as the descendants of the early settlers? I think it has something to do with pride. Australia has long been known as the "Lucky Country," and those who are able to immigrate consider themselves lucky people. Australia is still the land of opportunity, and the newest of the new Aussies are pleased to embrace its traditions. They happily watch footy on telly, have a barby with their mates, and smile when they say "G'day."

POLITICS

Australia's government is an interesting amalgam of British tradition and American format. While the official head of state is Queen Elizabeth II, the three-tier system of federal, state, and local governments closely resembles that of the United States. There's an active movement toward republicanism, as more and more Australians feel that links with Britain are no longer appropriate. The national flag is an immediate target, with ongoing discussion about replacing the Union Jack presently in its corner. While Australia turns its back on Britain, it seems to focus more and more on what's happening in the United States. A large percentage of TV programming is American, and news items from the United States fill the papers. Even knowing this, I was shocked during a recent visit to see the O.J. verdict two inches high on the front of the country's most prestigious newspaper.

The country's official name is the Commonwealth of Australia, an independent self-governing member of the Commonwealth of Nations. All members of this group were at one time part of the former British Empire. The queen is represented at the federal level by a governor-general and at the state level by governors.

Parliament, the legislative body, consists of the House of Representatives, where the number of members depends on the population of each state, and the Senate, with 12 senators for each state and 2 for each territory.

National elections are held at least every three years, and voting is compulsory. The two major political parties are Labour and Liberal; the minor parties are National and Democrat. The leader of the party or coalition that gets the majority in the House of Representatives becomes the prime minister, or head of government.

Each state has its own parliament, which, with the exception of Queensland's, consists of two chambers. The leader at the state level is called the premier.

Originally there were six separate colonies, but they became a federation of states in 1901. When Australia's founding fathers wrote the constitution and designed the system of government, they were able to pick and choose what they thought best from the examples of other countries. Their Anglo-American blend is unique and seems to be working well.

THE ECONOMY

The financial management of the island continent also represents a combination of styles. Founded "on the sheep's back" and known as a leading producer of wool, beef, lamb, wheat, sugar, and dairy products, Australia has more recently turned its attention to export-oriented mining and energy products. The nation's mineral resources include silver, lead, zinc, oil, gas, bauxite, coal, iron ore, uranium, copper, nickel, and gold. Manufacturing is also a major source of income. Tourism contributes mightily to the economy, with the influx of Asian visitors having a major impact. Happily, growth in the tourist sector is tempered by concern for the environment.

After an all-time low from 1992 to 1993 there has been good economic growth in the past couple of years. This is expected to continue, particularly in the area of tourism, leading up to the year 2000, when Sydney will host the Olympics.

In Australia the free-enterprise system is moderated by protective tariffs and controlled marketing of agricultural products. Considerable taxes are imposed on imported goods. Less than 10% of the federal budget is spent on defense, and more than half goes for social security, health, education, and general public services.

The majority of employed people in Australia belong to trade unions, which are extremely powerful. Nearly everyone works a 38-hour week and receives four weeks' annual vacation. Some Aussies complain that taxes are too high, the unions are too strong, and too much welfare money is doled out. Others rejoice in the opportunity to "have a go," to improve their status in life via the free-enterprise system.

4 A Look at the Past

To begin at the beginning would mean going back 40,000 years to the time when Australia's first inhabitants, the Aborigines, arrived from Asia. However, I'll start with the 17th-century explorations of Dutch, Portuguese, and British navigators. These ambitious sailors confirmed a theory that had been proposed in the 2nd century: that an unknown southern landmass, a *terra australis incognita*, lay to the south of Asia.

EUROPEAN DISCOVERY Willem Jansz, a Dutch explorer, was the first white man to set foot on the mysterious land when he went ashore on the Queensland coast in 1606. Another Dutchman, Abel Tasman, landed on Tasmania in 1642; however, it was the British who actually took possession of the land when Capt. James Cook sailed the *Endeavour* into Botany Bay (near present-day Sydney) in 1770, claimed the east coast of the island continent, and named it New South Wales.

THE FIRST FLEET For George III, Captain Cook's timing couldn't have been better. Britain was having a hard time controlling rebellious colonists in America, and the monarch was looking for

Dateline

- **40,000 B.C.** *Terra australis incognita* is inhabited by Aboriginal people.
- **1606** Dutch explorer Willem Jansz lands on the Queensland coast.
- **1642** Abel Tasman lands on Tasmania.
- **1770** Capt. James Cook sails the *Endeavour* into Botany Bay and takes possession of the land for Britain.
- **1781** America wins the War of Independence.
- **1787** Capt. Arthur Phillip is dispatched from England with the first convicts.
- **1788** Captain Phillip and the First Fleet arrive in Port Jackson.
- **1788–1868** Convicts are transported from England to the colony of Australia.

continues

- 1793 The first free settlers arrive.
- 1797 John Macarthur introduces merino sheep.
- 1807 The first shipment of salable wool is sent from Australia to England.
- 1813 Explorers Blaxland, Wentworth, and Lawson cross the Blue Mountains.
- 1817 The Bank of New South Wales is founded.
- 1828 The first census is taken: 36,000 convicts and free settlers, 2,549 military personnel (no Aborigines counted); explorer Charles Sturt finds and names the Darling River.
- 1850 Sydney University is founded.
- 1851 Gold is discovered in Victoria.
- 1860 The white population of Australia is over one million.
- 1860 The Burke and Wills expedition leaves Melbourne bound for the Gulf of Carpentaria on the north coast.
- 1861–62 John Stuart becomes the first explorer to travel from Adelaide to the coast of the Northern Territory.
- 1863 Gold is discovered in Western Australia.
- 1878 The first telephone is installed in Australia.
- 1883 Silver is discovered in New South Wales.
- 1901 Australia becomes an independent country; the white population is 3,773,801 (no Aborigines counted).
- 1902 Women are granted the right to vote.
- 1908 Canberra is chosen as the site for the federal capital.
- 1911 American Walter Burley Griffin designs Canberra.
- 1914 Australia enters World War I.
- 1920 QANTAS is founded.

continues

a new place to deposit the overflow from English jails; after America won the War of Independence in 1781, the situation became critical. On May 13, 1787, Capt. Arthur Phillip was dispatched from England with 1,030 people, 736 of whom were convicts. He and his fleet of 11 ships arrived in Botany Bay on January 18, 1788. However, they found conditions unsuitable and left after eight days, finally settling nearby at Port Jackson, commonly known now as Sydney Harbour. Today, Australia Day, the anniversary of the arrival of the First Fleet on January 26, is an important holiday celebrated throughout the nation.

RELUCTANT SETTLERS Between 1788 and 1868, 160,000 criminals were transported here from England. Some of these men and women had committed minor acts of thievery or disobedience and were really victims of the social conditions in their home country. The convicts were used to build the new settlement, and without their labor modern-day Sydney would lack some of its most impressive structures. Francis Greenway, who was transported for forgery and arrived in Port Jackson in 1814, was one of the colony's important architects. Since he had trained as an architect, he was given a "ticket of leave" and allowed the freedom to ply his trade. He subsequently designed the lighthouse at the south entrance to Sydney Harbour, St. James Church in Sydney, Hyde Park Barracks in Sydney, the Court House in Windsor, and the building that's now the home of the New South Wales Conservatorium of Music.

Like Greenway, many of the convicts elected to remain in the new colony when they finally attained their freedom. Some of them participated in the exploration of the interior, which, because of the rugged terrain, proceeded slowly. In 1813 Gregory Blaxland, William Charles Wentworth, and William Lawson crossed the Blue Mountains west of Sydney and so provided the colony access to the fertile western plains. In 1860 Robert O'Hara Burke and William John Wills were the first Europeans to cross the continent from south to north; their journey ended tragically when they starved to death during the return trip.

When gold was discovered in Victoria in 1851 and in Western Australia in 1863, the original settlers were joined by droves of pioneers from all over the world. By 1860 the population of Australia was over one million.

FEDERATION & THE GREAT WARS The colony announced its intention to become independent of Britain in 1900, and on January 1, 1901, the Commonwealth of Australia was proclaimed. Nevertheless, in 1914 Australia followed Britain into World War I and, along with New Zealand, sustained devastating casualties on the Gallipoli Peninsula. A large display in the War Memorial in Canberra tells the moving story of this terrible siege.

As part of the ANZAC (Australian and New Zealand Army Corps) forces, Australia again followed Britain into war in 1939. Australia also hosted over a million U.S. servicepeople during their respites from the war in the Pacific. Among these was Gen. Douglas MacArthur, who held some of his important strategy meetings in Melbourne's Australia Hotel.

The Japanese bombing of Darwin in February 1942 brought the war close to home, and the help of the American forces in the decisive Battle of the Coral Sea in May 1942 solidified the already warm relationship between the United States and Australia. To date, in this century Australia and New Zealand are the only allies that've fought alongside America in every major war.

Australia entered the Vietnam conflict in 1965 and was a popular R&R destination for thousands of American service personnel during those years.

RECENT HISTORY In 1972 the White Australia Policy, which had prevented Asians and other nonwhites from immigrating to Australia, formally ended. In 1986, during a visit to Canberra, Elizabeth II signed a proclamation severing some of Australia's legal and political ties with Britain. On January 26, 1988, Australia celebrated the 200th anniversary of the landing of the First Fleet at Port Jackson. And in 1992, as part of a general movement away from Britain, Australia's oath of allegiance was changed, omitting reference to Queen Elizabeth. In the same year the High Court handed down the landmark Mabo decision, enabling Aboriginals with unbroken occupancy of land to claim title. The debate over the resulting claims continues.

In 1993 Australia experienced the highest unemployment rate in its history; the Labour government was reelected; and Sydney was chosen to host the Olympic Games in 2000. Bush fires devastated New South Wales the following year.

- 1927 The federal capital is moved from Melbourne to Canberra.
- 1928 The Flying Doctor Service is founded.
- 1932 The Sydney Harbour Bridge opens.
- 1939 Australia enters World War II.
- 1942 Darwin is bombed; Japanese submarines are detected in Sydney Harbour; the Battle of the Coral Sea takes place.
- 1950 Australian troops join U.N. forces in Korea.
- 1950s Humane treatment of the Aborigines becomes an issue.
- 1951 The ANZUS Security Treaty is signed in Washington, D.C., by Australia, New Zealand, and the United States.
- 1956 The Olympic Games are held in Melbourne.
- 1960 Aborigines are granted citizenship.
- 1961 Extensive iron ore deposits are found in Western Australia.
- 1965 Australia enters the Vietnam conflict.
- 1966 Decimal currency is introduced.
- 1967 Aborigines are included in the national census for the first time.
- 1969 An Arbitration Commission grants equal pay to women.
- 1970 Large antiwar demonstrations take place.
- 1971 Australia ends its fighting role in Vietnam.
- 1972 White Australia Policy is formally ended.
- 1973 The Sydney Opera House is completed.
- 1974 Cyclone Tracy devastates Darwin.
- 1978 The Aboriginal Land Rights Act returns some tribal territory to the native people.

continues

- **1983** Ayers Rock is handed back to the Aborigines.
- **1983** *Australia II* wins the America's Cup Race.
- **1986** Queen Elizabeth II signs a proclamation severing some of Australia's ties with Britain.
- **1988** Australia celebrates the 200th anniversary of the landing of the First Fleet at Port Jackson.
- **1991** Australia's population reaches 17 million.
- **1992** Prime Minister Paul Keating wants the Union Jack off the Australian flag.
- **1993** The Labour government is reelected. Sydney is chosen to host the Olympics in 2000.
- **1994** The debate continues on the Australian Supreme Court's Mabo Decision, recognizing Aboriginal land claims.
- **1995** Australians protest France's nuclear testing in the Pacific Ocean.
- **1996** Australia's population reaches 18 million.

The pope visited Oz in 1995 and Mary McKillop became Australia's first saint. That same year, Australia joined New Zealand in vociferous protest of France's nuclear testing in the Pacific and unemployment fell to a four-year low. In 1996 this "lucky country," with a population reaching 18 million, has a future that seems bright.

5 The Arts from Dreamtime to Done

Australia's first artists were the Aborigines, who painted characters from their spiritual Dreamtime on the walls of caves, on rocks and bark, and even on their bodies. Though their art is a ritual part of their beliefs and will never fully be understood by outsiders, it's greatly admired for its haunting beauty. In the late 1980s some Aboriginal artists at the Papunya settlement near Alice Springs started painting their traditional earth-tone designs on canvas, and these have been well received at galleries around the world. The best known of the Aboriginal landscape artists is Albert Namatjira, whose richly toned watercolors gained worldwide attention in the 1930s and 1940s.

The first European-Australian art emerged in the 1880s, when artists Tom Roberts, Frederick McCubbin, Charles Conder, and Arthur Streeton established the Heidelberg School and created dramatic impressionist paintings of Australia's landscape. These differed from works done by the French impressionists since they frequently included a dramatic incident like a cattle stampede or a bush fire.

Other, more recent artists have retold the nation's legends by painting in series. The best known for this method is Sidney Nolan, who, through his work, has shared the stories of the ill-fated Burke and Wills expedition, the tragedy of Gallipoli, and the adventures of the popular folk hero and outlaw Ned Kelly.

Nolan's *The Trial of Ned Kelly* is on display at the Australian National Gallery in Canberra, one of the best places in the country to see Australian art. The National Gallery of Victoria in Melbourne houses another excellent collection. It's not surprising, given its beauty, that many artists, including Nolan, have painted realistic images of the rugged outback.

In the fashion field, contemporary artist Ken Done (rhymes with *phone*) has won international attention. His colorful designs, depicting Australia, particularly Sydney, at its happiest, adorn everything from T-shirts to bed linens. Done started his

Impressions

It does not read like history, but like the most beautiful lies. And all of a fresh new sort, no mouldy old stale ones. It is full of surprises, and adventures, and incongruities, and incredibilities: but they all are true, they all happened.

—Mark Twain, on his visit to Australia in 1895

professional life in advertising after studying at the East Sydney Technical College, where he was told he'd never make it as an artist. Today, at shops all over Australia and in several other countries, people stand in line to buy his designs. They might even push, grab, and bump, as I discovered recently when I attended the half-price sale at the Ken Done Galleries in The Rocks area of Sydney.

6 Australia's Distinctive Architecture

Australia's climate, terrain, and building materials have always lent a distinctive character to the country's architecture. The early pioneers were quick to realize the need to create buildings suitable for their new surroundings. Their efforts consisted of "wattle and daub" huts—logs and saplings covered with mud, pipe clay, and lime. Later they modified the Georgian, Victorian, and Edwardian homes popular in England to suit Australia's climate. Galvanized iron roofs collected precious moisture from the night air—moisture that could be routed and stored in barrels—and verandas provided shade. Wide eaves and bull-nosed iron hoods over windows were other attempts to keep things cool. In hot, humid Queensland, the settlers built houses on raised platforms supported by stilts for protection against the heat as well as floods and snakes.

Many of the early homes boasted cast-iron railings, balustrades, and trim that had come to the colony as ballast on sailing ships. Later, ironwork was done by skilled craftspeople who emerged from the gold rush and other mining endeavors. The majority of colonial buildings in Sydney were constructed of local sandstone; native timbers, such as cedar and jarrah, and marble from New South Wales and Queensland lent character to the emerging Australian architecture.

Though designed by Danish architect Jörn Utzon in 1957, the famous Sydney Opera House is very much an Australian building. The unique series-of-sails construction suits its position on the water and mirrors the boats that continuously cross the harbor. The white tiles covering the roof reflect the warm Australian sun, and the bold character of the building reflects the Aussie spirit.

In Canberra, the nation's capital, you'll find a similar emphasis on the local landscape. Designed by American architect Walter Burley Griffin in 1911, the city is built on a plain and has the expansive, open feel typical of much of the country. Low-rise buildings complement the natural topography; commercial and housing tracts are decentralized, like the minisettlements that dot the outback. Even the new Parliament House, designed by the American firm of Mitchell, Giurgola, and Thorp and opened in 1988 as part of the bicentennial festivities, is built into a hill so it blends with the environment rather than dominates it.

Environmental conditions also loomed large for Philip Cox & Partners, who within the last decade designed the Yulara Tourist Village, between Ayers Rock and the Olgas in central Australia. The self-contained village, catering to 5,000 visitors a day, has its own power, water, communications, and waste-disposal systems. Because of the harsh desert environment, tentlike fabric roofs providing shade from the strong sun were incorporated into the design.

The first tall buildings had appeared in the 1920s, but it wasn't until the arrival of Austrian architect Harry Seidler in 1948 that skyscraper construction blossomed. From 1961 to 1967 Seidler designed the 170m (561-ft.) glass-and-concrete Australia Square tower, which for many years dominated Sydney's skyline. Today it's overshadowed by others that've grown up around it, like Sydney's Centrepoint, which stands at 305m (1,006 ft.).

As Australia's buildings have become taller, shinier, and more sophisticated, architects have found new ways to cater to the prevailing climatic conditions. One way is by providing open spaces at ground level, often with a cooling fountain and shady places for the public to sit. These plazas and courtyards have created an Aussie institution: the open-air lunch. From noon to about 1:30pm, office workers and vendors selling snacks fill these areas to capacity; the addition of free concerts in many cities adds to the carnival atmosphere. At the end of the lunch break everyone disappears and the canyons created by surrounding tall buildings seem somber and citified once again.

7 Australian Cuisine: More than just Shrimp on the Barby

FOOD

Dining down under has become quite a varied and sophisticated affair, which pleasantly surprises most visitors. Likewise, the local wine industry has blossomed and today offers many exciting options. I tend to think of Australia's cuisine as falling into three categories.

COLONIAL FARE The dishes that either came out from Britain with the settlers or were created by them after they'd arrived are sometimes referred to as colonial fare. Certainly, roast-lamb and roast-beef dinners belong in this category, as do fish and chips and the delicious scones served with morning and afternoon tea. On the other hand, damper bread was created early on by men who lived in the bush; it was originally cooked in the coals of a campfire or in a camp oven, not unlike the sourdough bread that was once a staple in the American West. Life on the frontier also produced billy tea and the now-famous Aussie barbecue. Australians invented the carpetbag steak, a thick cut of beef stuffed with oysters.

Lamingtons, tasty cubes of sponge cake covered with chocolate icing and shredded coconut, were invented by colonists and named after one of their governors. Pavlova, another sweet concoction, was first prepared by Perth chef Herbert Sachse in 1935 and named in honor of Anna Pavlova, the Russian ballerina. A large soft-centered baked meringue filled with whipped cream and garnished with fruit, pavlova has become the unofficial national dessert. See the box "Brava Pavlova" in Chapter 12 for my favorite pavlova recipe.

It's easy to understand the Australian passion for pavlova, but not the fondness for Vegemite, a yeast-based spread for toast that most Aussies (and Kiwis, too) seem to crave. If you were a fan of Men at Work, you may remember them mentioning Vegemite in their hit song "Down Under." Be forewarned: Should you decide to try it, it may be several days before your taste buds forgive you.

Because of Australia's varied climate, which ranges from temperate to tropical, the early settlers found that they were able to grow an extensive variety of fruits and vegetables. Canned plums were one of Australia's first exports, and with today's modern transportation it's possible to enjoy a wide range of fresh produce anywhere in the country throughout the year.

INDIGENOUS FOOD Australia's abundant waters provide large and varied quantities of seafood. Sydney is known for its rock oysters; also popular are barramundi, coral trout, mud crab, jewfish, and John Dory. Moreton Bay bugs and Balmain bugs sound awful, but these lobsterlike shellfish are really delicious.

While the above-mentioned "bugs" aren't of the creepy-crawly type, insects do feature in Australia's indigenous food. Witchetty grubs, giant-size larvae, were consumed by the Aborigines in days past. Only a few places in the country still serve them. It's easier to find restaurants that offer kangaroo, crocodile, and water buffalo; some even serve kangaroo-tail soup. Macadamia nuts, also a native food, find their way into many dishes.

ETHNIC FOOD The large numbers of recent immigrants account for Australia's vast array of ethnic food. For example, one block of Sydney's Oxford Street boasts restaurants serving the cuisines of 16 countries. In Carlton, a Melbourne neighborhood, both sides of Lygon Street are lined with Italian restaurants. Both Adelaide and Melbourne have excellent Greek restaurants. Nationally, Chinese (Cantonese to be specific) is the most popular ethnic food. Recent arrivals also run delis throughout the country, and at lunch it's possible to buy wonderful thick sandwiches and treats like gyros in pita.

And what has America contributed to the Aussie dining experience? According to a song written by Australian folk singer Judy Small, "Every 17 hours another McDonald's opens up"—and, by all appearances, what she says is true. For better or worse, the golden arches stand tall throughout the land and have proven incredibly popular. If the lines are any indication, Quarter Pounders with cheese are more popular than the nation's traditional meat pies.

About the only food item I miss when traveling in Australia is a *really* good poppyseed bagel with cream cheese. I've requested this in various locations and received everything from a blank stare to a stone-cold poppyseedless bagel with catsup and mustard. Should you happen upon the breakfast item of my dreams with the appropriate accoutrements, please let me know. I'd even be willing to reward your efforts with a free copy of the next edition of this book.

DRINK

Coca-Cola has been made in Australia since 1938 and is widely available throughout the country, as are a full array of other soft drinks. Aussies also frequently quench their thirst with fruit-juice beverages, and quite a variety of these are on sale. The water is safe to drink in all parts of the nation.

If your idea of the perfect ending to a day of sightseeing is a nice cold beer or a glass of wine, you'll find both quantity and quality readily available in Australia. You'll also find plenty of company, as Aussies are the largest consumers of alcohol in the English-speaking world.

Fosters ("Australian for beer, mate") is the country's most popular beer, but each state also has its favorite. In New South Wales, Tooheys is the most popular; in Western Australia, Swan Lager is tops; according to the locals in Queensland, Fourex (XXXX) "isn't a beer, it's a religion." Other Aussies swear by Carlton Crown Lager or Reschs. My favorite is Cascade from Tasmania.

Beer is served in 20-ounce pints, half pints (also called "middies"), and 15-ounce schooners. Light drinkers might order a "seven," a 7-ounce glass. Regardless of the size of the vessel, Australian beer is always served ice cold.

Australians are justifiably proud of their wine industry, which in recent years has won some impressive awards. The main grape-growing regions are the Hunter Valley in New South Wales, the Yarra Valley in Victoria, the Barossa and Clare Valleys

Impressions

If you find an Australian indoors, it's a fair bet that he will have a glass in his hand.
—Jonathan Aitken, *Land of Fortune* (1971)

Winning Wines from Down Under

In 1873, judges at a wine competition in Vienna refused to assess the Australian entry, stating that "wines of this quality must clearly be French!" Times have changed. Today, Australian wines are receiving the attention and respect connoisseurs once reserved for Californian and French wines.

One such wine, Penfolds Grange, has been named the "wine of the year" by the most widely read U.S. wine magazine, *Wine Spectator.*

The 1990 Penfolds Grange, a rich, spicy extract from the shiraz grape, is No. 1 on the magazine's eighth annual Top 100 Wines list (Dec. 31 issue). That's the first time a product from outside France or California has been selected for the top award by the editors. A record seven other Australian wines made the list.

"Australian wines, and our exposure to them, are getting better and better," said the *Spectator*'s managing editor, Mr. Jim Gordon.

Grange has been building a large cult following in the U.S. in recent years with fans across the nation organizing tastings and celebratory dinners. The wine also received praise . . . from Robert Parker, regarded as the world's most influential wine critic. He described the wine as "a leading candidate for the richest most concentrated dry red table wine on planet Earth."

[*Author note:* If you're interested in trying Australia's premier red wine, contact Leonard Solomon of **Solomon's Wines & Spirits,** 1456 N. Dayton, Chicago, IL 60622 (☎ 312/915-5911; fax 312/915-0466). He has some bottles of 1988 and 1989 Grange in his cellar. These are collector's wines because they still carry the word *Hermitage.*]

and the Coonawarra district in South Australia, and the Swan Valley and Margaret River area in Western Australia. Overall, South Australia is the state with the greatest wine production.

Penfolds and Lindemans rank as two of the biggest wineries, but smaller houses have won many of the most coveted prizes. In 1986 Philip Shaw of the Rosemont Estate in the Upper Hunter Valley won the Robert Mondavi Winemaker of the Year Award at the International Wine and Spirit Competition in London. This highly regarded recognition went to Greg Clayfield of Lindemans in the Coonawarra district in 1988, and to the Penfolds Group in 1990. Peterson's Hunter Valley chardonnay won in its category in the 1987 Qantas Wine Cup and tied for best white of the show. The Australians beat the Americans overall in this internationally judged competition.

Altogether, the 400 producing wineries in Australia sell about five times more white than red. They also make a great many dessert wines, especially port, and sparkling-wine production is on the increase. The famous French champagne company Domaine Chandon started growing grapes in Victoria's Yarra Valley in 1985 and released its first bubbly late in 1988.

Australian vintners have only recently begun to actively market their wines overseas. "Before that," one winemaker told me, "we knew it was good enough, but we didn't make huge quantities; and we were afraid if we exported it, there wouldn't be enough to go around at home."

This philosophy still exists to some degree, and the traveler in Australia is in the enviable position of being able to visit the wineries and sample the country's best wines—the ones the Aussies keep for themselves.

8 The Performing Arts & After-Dark Scene

THE PERFORMING ARTS

OPERA, CONCERTS, THEATER & DANCE Australia is home to some of the most beautiful and technically perfect theater complexes in the world. The Sydney Opera House, with its five stages, is the best known, but Brisbane's Performing Arts Complex, Adelaide's Festival Centre, and Melbourne's Victorian Arts Centre are also quite impressive.

Australia's most famous performing artist was soprano Dame Nellie Melba. She made her European debut in 1887, and before her death in 1931 she sang in virtually every major opera house in the world. (In 1893 French master chef Auguste Escoffier created a dessert in her honor: peach Melba.) Joan Sutherland, another Aussie opera star, became as well known as her illustrious predecessor. During her career she regularly appeared at the Sydney Opera House, in addition to fulfilling the overseas demand for her talent. Dame Joan's final performance was in 1990.

In the area of conducting, Australians Charles Mackerras and Richard Bonynge (the latter married to Joan Sutherland) have both earned excellent international reputations.

Australian theater has come a long way since 1789, when 12 convicts performed a comedy called *The Recruiting Officer* as part of the birthday celebration for George III. The theater was lit by candles stuck into mud walls, and tickets were purchased with rum, tobacco, or even turnips. Today, plays written and performed by Australians are regularly presented around the country. David Williamson is one of the country's most successful playwrights.

Barry Humphries is easily the king of Aussie comedy. A sometimes biting satirist, Humphries comments on local politics, fashions, and follies via the now-famous character he created: Dame Edna Everage, a frumpy, pretentious, outspoken housewife.

Since Anna Pavlova's famous Australian tour, there has been an interest in dance in Australia. Robert Helpmann, who emigrated to Europe, was one of the best-known Australian dancers. Today there's a lively dance scene here, and the Sydney Dance Company has won an international reputation.

MUSIC Australia's popular music, with its fresh, vital, and imaginative sounds, is attracting world attention.

Rock & Pop The Bee Gees were one of the first Australian groups to become popular overseas. The Little River Band, the Seekers, Olivia Newton-John, and Rick Springfield were other successful exports in the 1970s. More recently, Men at Work, INXS, John Farnham, Icehouse, Midnight Oil, Crowded House, Jason Donovan, Kylie Minogue, and the Aboriginal rock band Yothu Yindi have scored big hits, making Australia the third-largest supplier of repertoire to the world's charts, behind the United States and Britain.

Classical, Jazz & Country Sadly, the vitality of the rock and pop industry is lacking in other types of music in Australia. Classical composers, for instance, haven't been nearly as well received in foreign markets. Percy Grainger, a gifted pianist/composer, was one of the few who won international recognition (he became an American citizen and died in New York in 1961). Malcolm Williamson, who has spent much of his professional life in England, is another talented Australian composer. Alfred Hill is yet another. For many years Australian opera companies performed predominantly European works. In recent years, however, local composers have created their own success stories. The first was *Voss*, a grand opera composed by Richard Meale and premiered at the 1986 Adelaide Festival. Brian Howard's *Metamorphosis,* a chamber opera, is another locally written work.

Jazz musicians and composers have received even less acclaim than their classical counterparts. One exception is Don Burrows, the nation's top jazzman, who has been awarded an MBE, has hosted his own TV program, and is a well-known composer/instrumentalist/public figure.

Country music is relatively popular, especially around Tamworth in New South Wales. Every January a music festival is held in this town, 453km (280 miles) north of Sydney, which calls itself the "Nashville of Australia." Slim Dusty, Chad Morgan, and Reg Lindsay are the top performers.

Native Sounds Only one type of music is purely Australian, of course, and that's Aboriginal. These songs tell of Dreamtime legends, tribal rituals, and heroic deeds. The didgeridoo, a wind instrument made from a slender tree trunk hollowed out by termites, lends a haunting sound to these stories. Unfortunately, many Aborigines have lost interest in their traditional music, and opportunities to hear it being performed in public are infrequent. For better or worse, many of Australia's native people seem to prefer rock 'n' roll.

FILMMAKING

What do Errol Flynn and Paul Hogan have in common? Nothing, if you visualize the suave and debonair Flynn standing next to rough-and-ready Hogan. But there's more here than meets the eye: To begin with, both are Australian and both made their fame in film. However, one major difference exists between the two men. The career of Tasmanian-born Flynn started before the movie industry in Australia had a strong national identity. As a result, the actor defected to Hollywood only two years after making his 1933 debut in Charles Chauvel's *In the Wake of the Bounty*. Hogan, on the other hand, entered the scene after stars like Chips Rafferty and, later, Bryan Brown and Jack Thompson had popularized the role of the rugged outback male. As Crocodile Dundee, Paul Hogan took over where the others had left off and has raised being an ocker Aussie to an art form.

EARLY MOVIEMAKING The success of *Crocodile Dundee, Mad Max,* and the "surfie" drama *Puberty Blues* is ironic when you consider that the first feature-length movie in the world was the religious epic *Soldiers of the Cross,* produced by the Australian Salvation Army in 1900. This film was followed in 1906 by *The Story of the Kelly Gang,* but after an auspicious start the movie industry failed to keep up the pace. Australia was used as the setting of *The Overlanders* in 1946, *On the Beach* in 1959, and *The Sundowners* in 1960, but it wasn't until the 1970s that Aussie filmmaking really came into its own. In the meantime, actor Peter Finch had left for London, where he made the now-classic 1956 version of *A Town Like Alice.*

AUSTRALIAN SUCCESS STORIES *Picnic at Hanging Rock,* released in 1975, was the first significant contemporary film to feature both a domestic story line and a home-grown director, in the person of Peter Weir. *The Last Wave,* another Weir success, introduced the world to Aboriginal folklore. *My Brilliant Career, Breaker Morant,* and *Mad Max* further improved the fortunes of the Australian film industry. In 1993, Weir's *Fearless,* which starred Jeff Bridges as the survivor of a plane crash, won great critical acclaim. Judy Davis, the star of *My Brilliant Career,* was named Best Actress and Best Newcomer in a Leading Role at the 1981 British Academy Awards. More recently, she was nominated for an American Best Actress Oscar for her role in Woody Allen's *Husbands and Wives.* Jack Thompson won a Best Supporting Actor Award for *Breaker Morant,* and Bryan Brown received praise for his part in the film. *Breaker* also brought acclaim to Aussie director Bruce Beresford. *Mad Max,* a worldwide smash hit, grossed over $100 million and launched Mel Gibson to international stardom.

Peter Weir followed with *Gallipoli,* the moving story of Australia's World War I tragedy, and the political suspense thriller *The Year of Living Dangerously,* based on the novel by Australian writer Christopher Koch. George Miller's *The Man from Snowy River* was equally successful. Gillian Armstrong, the first woman director in Australia since the 1930s, established her reputation with *My Brilliant Career* and secured it with *Mrs. Soffel,* starring Mel Gibson and Diane Keaton. Her *Careful He Might Hear You* was voted one of the top 10 films of 1984 by American critics.

In 1986 Australia topped its string of critical successes with the commercial blockbuster *Crocodile Dundee,* which irrevocably proved the popularity of the country's national characteristics. *Crocodile Dundee II* and *Evil Angels* (released as *A Cry in the Dark* in the United States and Canada), with Meryl Streep and Sam Neill, attracted more attention. In the early 1990s, Paul Cox directed two successful films: *A Woman's Tale* (1991) and *The Nun & the Bandit* (1992). Neither of these was as popular, however, as *Strictly Ballroom* (1993) directed by Baz Luhrman. *Hammers Over the Anvil* (1993), directed by Ann Turner, was also well received. Successes of 1994 included *The Adventures of Priscilla, Queen of the Desert, Muriel's Wedding,* and the Academy Award–winning *Babe.* As we go to press, I'm eagerly awaiting the arrival of *All Men Are Liars,* which has been heralded down under as a comic triumph. And mid-1995 brought the fact-based *Race the Sun,* about a team of kids from Hawaii racing a solar car across Australia.

It's now clear that in the movie industry, not only is it okay to be Australian, it's practically a requirement for success.

AFTER DARK

If, after a day of sightseeing or sporting activity you still have the energy for nightlife, you'll be able to find something of interest in any of Australia's cities.

PUBS Pubs are discussed under "Tips on Accommodations" in Chapter 3, but their main function is the dispensing of alcoholic beverages, primarily—but not limited to—beer. The word *pub* is shorthand for "public licensed hotel," that is, a place where it's legal to sell "spirituous liquors" to the public. We normally think of pubs as noisy, smoky, jovial places where no one would notice if you used the floor for an ashtray; actually, asking for an ashtray would probably cause more of a stir. However, lots of Hiltons, Sheratons, and the like are also public licensed hotels. Each has a public bar that keeps the legal pub hours, and anyone can drink there; the public bar in one of these top-class hotels has an ambience that's a cross between a traditional pub and a cocktail lounge. Obviously, these hotels also have piano bars and other posher places to drink. These areas are open later than the public bar, and the dress code prohibits jeans, thongs, and singlets (sleeveless undershirts that are part of the "Aussie uniform").

There are also hotels with liquor licenses that limit the dispensing of alcohol to their registered guests and people who are dining in their restaurants. You'll know you've wandered into such a place when you order a drink and the barmaid asks, "Do you intend to dine?" Legally she can't serve you unless you respond in the affirmative. Likewise, restaurants are licensed to serve drinks only to their dining patrons.

Pub hours vary but usually run Monday to Saturday from 10am to 11pm; some places are closed on Sunday, and those that are open don't get started until noon and close by 10pm. The drinking age throughout the country is 18.

Pub etiquette is simple: If you're drinking with a group, each member takes a turn "shouting"—buying a round.

DANCE CLUBS Unlike the pub scene, where "shouting" refers to the opening of one's wallet, shouting in a disco is what's usually required for conversation. If this is your cup of tea, you'll be happy to know that every capital city in Australia has at least a couple of these high-decibel dancing dens. The better ones are located in the big hotels. Dance clubs are often closed on Sunday and Monday and stay open until the wee hours other nights; cover charges range from A$8 to A$15 (U.S. $6.40 to $12).

CASINOS & CLUBS Most major cities have casinos. Craps, roulette, blackjack, minidice, poker, and two-up are the favorite games. Poker machines (slots) are illegal in some states but are found in private clubs.

In addition to being venues for gambling, casinos often have cabarets (nightclubs) with floor shows or a band for dancing.

Private clubs are an important part of the nightlife scene, especially in areas outside the big cities, where there's often a dearth of evening entertainment. Places like RSL (Returned Services League) Clubs provide a legal way around Australia's sometimes parochial drinking and gambling laws. Visitors are welcome at any of these clubs as long as they're properly dressed and sign in at the door.

In addition to RSLs, football-leagues clubs offer the same facilities: poker machines, bars, restaurants, floor shows, and sometimes discos. It's also not unusual for the clubs to have weight rooms, aerobics classes, and other gym facilities. The cost of dining and drinking in these places is normally reasonable, probably because the overhead expenses are subsidized by gambling revenues.

OTHER ENTERTAINMENT Australian cities offer a wide range of cultural performances—everything from grand opera to intimate dramatic works. There are also comedy clubs, venues for listening to particular types of music (such as jazz), and lots of movie theaters. Overseas visitors also often enjoy after-dark harbor cruises and restaurants with Australiana entertainment.

Last, like all the world's major cities, Australian capitals offer pornographic movie houses and miscellaneous sexual sideshows. The area best known for this is Sydney's Kings Cross, where those willing to pay the price can see just about everything—from women-who-used-to-be-men doing the cancan to women-who-still-are-women performing in seedy striptease shows. American servicemen who took their R&R in Sydney during the Vietnam era helped make Kings Cross what it is today; the country's other red-light districts pale by comparison.

9 Recommended Books, Films & Recordings

BOOKS

Veteran travelers agree that reading about a destination adds to the enjoyment of a trip. If "know before you go" is your motto, here are some suggestions:

The Australians by Ross Terrill is a richly anecdotal personal essay of the country written by a distinguished scholar/journalist. Patrick White won the Nobel Prize in Literature for his 1973 *The Eye of the Storm.* His earlier work, *Voss,* formed the basis of an opera of the same name. *The Fatal Shore,* written by *Time* magazine art critic Robert Hughes, provides good background on early life in the colony, complete with gruesome accounts of prisoners' punishments. *A Fortunate Life* by A.B. Facey is a classic Australian story tracing the remarkable course of an 87-year-old man's life.

One of my favorite books is *From Alice to Ocean* by Rick Smolan, telling the inspiring story of a young woman who crossed the vast desert between Alice Springs and the Indian Ocean accompanied by several camels. The book is illustrated with wonderful color photographs and comes with a computer CD-ROM disk. *Kings in Grass Castles* by Mary Durack is another Australian classic, telling the true story of the author's grandfather and his descendants and their struggle to settle the Kimberley district of Western Australia. It was first published in 1959. Also recommendable is its sequel, *Sons in the Saddle.*

My Brilliant Career by Miles Franklin was first published in 1901, and you may have seen the movie of the same name in which a young woman must choose between marriage and a career. *The Road from Coorain* by Jill Ker Conway is an autobiography tracing the life of a girl raised on a remote New South Wales sheep station who becomes the president of Smith College. Her later book *True North* continues her story.

I think practically everybody in the world has read *The Thorn Birds* by Colleen McCullough, but if you missed it, and the incredibly popular miniseries that followed, it does provide a worthwhile glimpse into the outback. *Walkabout* by James V. Marshall is another classic tale of Australia, about two children who are the sole survivors of a plane crash in the outback and their relationship with the Aborigines who save them; the book was made into an excellent movie by Nicholas Roeg in 1970. Another Australian classic, *We of the Never-Never,* was written by Mrs. Aeneas Gunn in 1908. This book tells the story of a young woman who left the comfort of her Melbourne home to live on an isolated cattle station in the Northern Territory. More recently there has been *From Strength to Strength.* Like *We of the Never-Never,* this autobiography by Sara Henderson is the contemporary story of a woman's strugle on an isolated cattle station.

Thomas Keneally (*Schindler's List*) is one of Australia's best-known authors and has written many wonderful books about his homeland. These include *Outback* (about the history, geology, and culture of the Northern Territory) and *A River Town* (based on real events in the life of his grandfather Tim Shea in turn-of-the-century Kempsey in Northern New South Wales). *Publishers Weekly* described *A River Town* as Keneally's "most masterfully crafted, morally searching, and compassionate work."

For the Aboriginal point of view, I recommend *Dreamkeepers: A Spirit-Journey into Aboriginal Australia* by Harvey Arden. The author is a former staff writer and photographer with *National Geographic* who traveled to Australia to write the magazine's cover story on northwest Australia in 1991. The most-discussed-book-of-the-moment is *Mutant Messages Down Under* by Marlo Morgan, which she claims is nonfiction but many in-the-know feel is a work of fiction inspired by her experiences in Australia.

Also well worth a look is the February 1988 issue of *National Geographic.* The entire issue is devoted to Australia and contains good background information as well as travel ideas. Also see the January 1991 issue, with a piece on Northwest Australia; the October 1991 issue, with an article on Lord Howe Island; the December 1991 issue, with a piece on Australia's pearling industry; the April 1992 issue, with an article on the Simpson outback; the January 1995 issue, with a piece on the wildflowers of Western Australia; and the April 1995 issue, with an article on koalas.

FILMS

The following films are available on video. Each provides a very different view of Australia. (Be aware that videos purchased in Australia will need to be converted before they can be shown on U.S. VCRs and TVs. Australia uses the PAL system, while the United States uses the NTSC system.)

Adventure & Comedy

The Adventures of Priscilla, Queen of the Desert (1994). Terence Stamp stars as a soul-searching transsexual who, with two drag queens, goes on the road in the outback aboard a bus named Priscilla. Much merriment ensues. The outageous costumes won an Oscar.

Babe (1994). This charming comedy—nominated for multiple Oscars—is about a young pig who would rather herd sheep than be bacon. Though aimed at children, it's a rare treat adults can also love. Featuring wonderful Oscar-winning animatronic effects from the late Jim Henson's company, this surprisingly good film appeared on many "Top 10" lists for 1995.

Crocodile Dundee (1986). Paul Hogan and Linda Kozlowski star in the story of a free-spirited Aussie who hunts crocodiles with his bare hands until he comes to the attention of an American reporter who brings him to the jungles of New York City.

Crocodile Dundee II (1988). Crocodile Dundee finds himself up against a gang of ruthless Colombian drug dealers in New York.

Mad Max (1980). Mel Gibson stars in this super-action movie about the ultimate gang of motorcycle bandits. Sequel: *The Road Warrior* (1982).

Mad Max Beyond Thunderdome (1985). This time Mel is joined by Tina Turner in another slam-bang, chase-and-crash thriller.

Muriel's Wedding (1994). This is a bittersweet comedy about a plain young woman who wants nothing more than to listen to her ABBA albums and have a wedding. Eventually she escapes her dreary home and is able to have both in this film with a strong cult following in the United States.

Quigley Down Under (1990). Tom Selleck and Laura San Giacomo star in this adventure set in Western Australia in the 1860s. The movie provides some great laughs, but also an all-too-realistic look at the relationship between the Aborigines and the colonial ranchers.

Drama

Breaker Morant (1980). Jack Thompson and Edward Woodward star as two of the Australians court-martialed by the British during the Boer War. Bruce Beresford directed this wrenching, dramatic movie filmed in South Australia.

Burke & Wills (1987). Jack Thompson stars in this docudrama about the first white men to cross central Australia's vast desert. A gripping true story.

A Cry in the Dark (1989). Known as *Evil Angels* outside North America, this heavy drama is based on the true story of a mother accused of murdering her baby. Starring Meryl Streep and Sam Neill and directed by Fred Schepisi, the movie was filmed at Ayers Rock and Darwin in the Northern Territory.

Gallipoli (1981). Australian director Peter Weir (*Picnic at Hanging Rock, Witness*) tells the story of the futile ANZAC campaign against the Turks on the beach of Gallipoli during World War I. Mark Lee and Mel Gibson are two of the stars in this powerful military drama.

The Last Wave (1977). Richard Chamberlain stars in this film about an Australian lawyer given the task of defending Aborigines charged with ritual murder. Directed by Peter Weir.

The Man From Snowy River (1982). Kirk Douglas stars in this turn-of-the-century story about a young man coming of age on the frontier. The movie was filmed at the foot of the Great Diving Range in Victoria and features lots of beautiful bush scenery and amazing horse riding. *Return to Snowy River Part II* is the sequel.

Phar Lap (1984). Based on a true story, this movie tells of a champion racehorse that won an incredible number of races in the 1930s.

RECORDINGS

Because Aussie rock groups are often at the top of the charts, their recordings are readily available around the globe. It's a bit more difficult, however, to find recordings of other types of Australian music. If you have trouble locating what you want, contact the **Australian Catalogue Company,** 7412 Wingfoot Dr., Raleigh, NC 27615 (☎ 800/808-0938; fax 919/878-0553; e-mail auscat@metaplex.com). They also sell Australian foodstuffs, clothing, gifts, and cookbooks.

In Australia, the best source of CDs and cassettes is **Sounds Australian,** upstairs in The Rocks Centre in Sydney (☎ 02/247 4677; fax 02/241 2873). Look for country music by Slim Dusty and John Williamson; jazz by musicans like James Morrison and Vince Jones; traditional Aboriginal music; contemporary Aboriginal groups like Yothu Yindi; Australian contemporary orchestral works; pop stars like Kylie Minogue, Midnight Oil, INXS, and Crowded House; as well as videocassettes of Australian Opera productions.

3 Planning a Trip to Australia

Advance preparation is imperative if you want to get the most possible enjoyment for the time and the money you spend on a trip. Careful planning pays off in successful sojourns without any nasty surprises, and since I want your Australian experience to be a great one, I've compiled this chapter of nuts-and-bolts background information.

1 Visitor Information & Entry Requirements

VISITOR INFORMATION

TRAVEL AGENTS Since the services provided by a travel agent are free, take advantage of them. If you don't already have an agent you especially like, ask well-traveled friends who they use. Then phone two or three of those recommended and ask the same questions about Australia, making note of who seems the best informed. You can also contact the **Australian Tourist Commission** (below) and ask for a **"Certified Aussie Specialist"** travel agent in your area.

Be careful that the agent doesn't talk you into a package tour if you really want to travel independently. This would save the agent a lot of trouble, but in the end you'd be settling for something you didn't want. The same is true when it comes to accommodations: It's easier for an agent to book you into one of the large international chain hotels that have worldwide toll-free numbers than to ferret out the quaint country inn or B&B you've heard about. In addition, keep an eye on the travel section of your local newspaper for information on bargain promotional fares—and be sure your agent knows about them.

AUSTRALIAN TOURIST COMMISSION The Australian Tourist Commission is extremely helpful and maintains the following offices in North America, Britain, and New Zealand:

- 2049 Century Park E., Suite 1920, **Los Angeles,** CA 9006 (☎ 310/229-4870; fax 310/552-1215).
- 100 Park Ave., 25th Floor, **New York,** NY 10017 (☎ 212/687-6300).

- Gemini House, 10–18 Putney Hill, Putney, **London,** England SW15 6AA (☎ 0181/780-2227).
- Level 13, 44–48 Emily Place, **Auckland,** New Zealand 1 (☎ 09/379-9594).

Americans and Canadians can request a complimentary copy of the ATC's 130-page booklet ***Destination Australia*** by calling 800/285-9113 or 800/333-0262. The ATC's **Aussie Help Line** for travel agents—800/433-AUSSIE—is answered Monday to Friday from 9am to 5pm Chicago time. The **consumer's line** at 708/296-4900 is answered Monday to Friday from 8am to 7pm CST.

STATE TOURIST OFFICES If you'd like to request information from individual Australian states, the following addresses may be useful:

- **New South Wales Tourism Commission,** 13737 Fiji Way, Suite C-10, Marina del Rey, CA 90292 (☎ 310/301-1903).
- **Queensland Tourist & Travel Corporation,** 1800 Century Park E., Suite 330, Los Angeles, CA 90067 (☎ 310/788-0997 or 800/333-6050).
- **South Australian Tourism,** 1600 Dove St., Newport Beach, CA 92660 (☎ 714/852-2270 or 800/546-2155).
- **Victoria Tourist Commission,** 2049 Century Park E., 19th Floor, Los Angeles, CA 90067 (☎ 310/229-4892).
- **Australia's Northern Territory,** 5855 Green Valley Circle, Suite 204, Culver City, CA 90230 (☎ 310/645-9875 or 800/4-OUTBAC).

NEWSLETTERS The ***Word From Down Under*** newsletter (P.O. Box 5434, Balboa Island, CA 92662; fax 714/725-0060; e-mail <72056.23@compuserve.com>), published twice a month, is chock full of Australian news and sports. Fax, write, or e-mail for a free sample copy. Subscribers get a 10% discount on airfares and itineraries booked through Qantas Vacations (see later in this chapter). The Australian Embassy puts out two publications: ***Miscellenea*** (from the Cultural Affairs Office) and ***Australia Report*** (political news). To get on the mailing list for *Miscellanea* call 202/797-3176 or fax 202/797-3414; for *Australia Report* call 202/797-3373 or fax 202/797-3414.

INTERNET WEB SITES Web sites providing information on Australia include the following:

- The Australian Embassy has a site at http://www.aust.emb.nw.dc.us.
- Australia Online is at http://australia-online.com/index.html.
- Australian news can be found at http://www.ee.latrobe.edu.au/~khorsel/OZNEWS. (*Note:* OZNEWS must be typed uppercase.)
- The *Sydney Morning Herald* has a site at http://www.smh.com.au/news/index.html.
- Australian Visual Arts and Music at the Institute of the Arts has a site with over 400 contemporary Australian art images at http://ausarts.anu.edu.au/ITA/AusArts/index.html.
- General information about Australia is available at http://www.Australia-online.com or at http://www.oxonline.com.au/netcafe.

There are many **aus.*** newsgroups on the Internet, but here are a few worth singling out: soc.culture.australian; aus.sport for latest Aussie sport info; aus.sport.aussie-rules for the latest Aussie Rules information; and aus.music for the Aussie top 50 each week.

America Online (AOL) users can now access information on travel to Australia through a joint venture of the Australian Tourist Commission and Sain Australia Tours. Listed under AOL's Traveler's Corner, **Virtual Australia** allows you to plan an itinerary, preview vacation packages, and order travel literature.

ENTRY REQUIREMENTS

Everyone visiting Australia must have a **passport** valid for a period longer than the intended length of stay. In addition, everyone except holders of Australian and New Zealand passports needs a **visa,** *which must be obtained prior to arriving in Australia.*

Visas are free of charge for stays of up to three months (valid for one year). A fee of U.S. $27 (£15 in Britain, $30 in Canada) is charged for longer stays and visa validity longer than one year. Don't wait until the last minute to apply, because in peak periods of travel it can take a month or more to process your visa application by mail. It's possible to obtain a visa in less time, but this requires you delivering and picking up the documents in person. A self-addressed stamped envelope is necessary if you're applying by mail. Application forms are available from the consulate, embassy, or high commission nearest you or from a travel agent.

IN THE U.S. Contact the **Australian Embassy,** 1601 Massachusetts Ave. NW, Washington, DC 20036-2273 (☎ 202/797-3000; fax 202/797-3168), or the nearest Australian Consulate-General: One Peachtree Center, Suite 2920, 303 Peachtree St. NE, **Atlanta,** GA 30308 (☎ 404/880-1700; fax 404/880-1701); 1000 Bishop St., Penthouse, **Honolulu,** HI 96813-4299 (☎ 808/524-5050; fax 808/531-5142); 1990 S. Post Oak Blvd., Suite 800, **Houston,** TX 77056-9998 (☎ 713/629-9131; fax 713/622-6924); 2049 Century Park E., 19th Floor, **Los Angeles,** CA 90067 (☎ 310/229-4800 or 229-4840; fax 310/277-2258 for general information or 310/277-5620 for visas); 630 Fifth Ave., **New York,** NY 10111 (☎ 212/245-4000; fax 212/265-4917); 1 Bush St., **San Francisco,** CA 94104 (☎ 415/362-6160; fax 415/986-5440).

In addition, U.S. residents traveling to Australia on Qantas can obtain visas at the airline's ticket offices in Los Angeles and San Francisco.

IN CANADA Contact the Australian High Commission, 50 O'Connor St., Suite 710, **Ottawa,** ON K1P 6L2 (☎ 613/236-0841); the Australian Consulate-General, 175 Bloor St. E., Suite 314, **Toronto,** ON M4W 3R8 (☎ 416/323-1155); or the Australian Consulate, World Trade Centre Office Complex, 999 Canada Place, Suite 602, **Vancouver,** BC V6C 3E1 (☎ 604/684-1177).

IN BRITAIN & IRELAND Contact the Australian Embassy, Fitzwilliam House, Wilton Terrace, **Dublin** 2 (☎ 01/76-1517); the Australian High Commission, Australia House, The Strand, **London** WC2B 4LA (☎ 071/379-4334); or the Australian Consulate, Chatsworth House, Lever Street, **Manchester** M1 2QL (☎ 0161/228-1344).

Upon landing in Australia, you'll be required to produce both your passport with the visa stamped in it and a completed incoming passenger card (distributed on all ships and aircraft prior to arrival). You may also be asked to show your outbound airline ticket. It's not permissible to work or go to school in Australia if you've entered the country on a Visitor Visa. Those who are 18 to 25 from some countries are eligible for Working Holiday Visas.

Vaccination certificates are required only of travelers who have within six days been in areas infected with yellow fever.

Be sure you don't bring fresh or packaged food of any kind or such things as fruit, vegetables, or seeds. These items, as well as the importation of plants and animals, are strictly controlled.

2 Money

CASH & CURRENCY Australians use a decimal currency. The **Australian dollar (A$)** is made up of 100 **cents.** Notes come in $5, $10, $20, $50, and $100 denominations. Coins are minted in 5¢, 10¢, 20¢, 50¢, $1, and $2 units. (Australia was the first country to introduce plastic bank notes.)

TRAVELER'S CHECKS, CREDIT CARDS & ATMS When you look for a bank to cash **traveler's checks,** keep in mind that service charges vary widely. The National Australia Bank charges A$5 (U.S. $4) to cash a foreign-currency traveler's check. The Commonwealth Bank charges A$10 (U.S. $8), ANZ Bank charges A$2 (U.S. $1.60) or more for the same service, and most Westpac Banks charge nothing.

The Australian Dollar, the U.S. Dollar & the British Pound

For U.S. Readers The rate of $1 U.S. = approximately A$1.40 (or A$1.00 = U.S. 80¢) was the rate of exchange used to calculate the dollar values given in this book (rounded up to the nearest nickel).

For British Readers The rate of £1 U.K. = approximately A$1.92 (or A$1 = £.52 U.K.) was the rate of exchange used to calculate the pound values in the accompanying table.

Note: International exchange rates fluctuate from time to time depending on complicated political and economic factors. Thus the rates given in the accompanying table may not be the same when you travel to Australia, and so this table should be used only as a guide.

A$	U.S.$	U.K.£	A$	U.S.$	U.K.£
0.25	0.20	0.13	30.00	24.00	15.60
0.50	0.40	0.26	35.00	28.00	18.20
1.00	0.80	0.52	40.00	32.00	20.80
2.00	1.60	1.04	45.00	36.00	23.40
3.00	2.40	1.56	50.00	40.00	26.00
4.00	3.20	2.08	55.00	44.00	28.60
5.00	4.00	2.60	60.00	48.00	31.20
6.00	4.80	3.12	65.00	52.00	33.80
7.00	5.60	3.64	70.00	56.00	36.40
8.00	6.40	4.16	75.00	60.00	39.00
9.00	7.20	4.68	80.00	64.00	41.60
10.00	8.00	5.20	85.00	68.00	44.20
15.00	12.00	7.80	90.00	72.00	46.80
20.00	16.00	10.40	95.00	76.00	49.40
25.00	20.00	13.00	100.00	80.00	52.00

What Things Cost in Sydney	U.S. $
Taxi from the airport to the city center	14.50
Bus from Central Station to downtown	1.00
Local telephone call from a pay phone	.25
Double at the Park Hyatt Sydney (deluxe)	384.00
Double at the Holiday Inn Park Suites, Sydney (moderate)	152.00
Double at the Wattle Private Hotel (inexpensive)	64.00
Lunch for one at Bobby McGee's (moderate)	13.00
Lunch for one at the Harbour Takeaway (inexpensive)	6.00
Dinner for one, without wine, at Bilson's (deluxe)	40.00
Dinner for one, without wine, at Paragon Bistro (moderate)	19.00
Dinner for one, without wine, at the Craig Brewery Bar & Grill (inexpensive)	8.00
Can of Fosters (beer)	3.00
Coca-Cola (375ml)	1.75
Cup of coffee	1.20
Roll of ASA 100 Kodacolor film, 36 exposures	6.00
Admission to the Sydney Aquarium	11.20
Movie ticket	9.20
One liter unleaded petrol (gas)	.60

If you run out of traveler's checks, you can buy more at any American Express office if you're one of their cardmembers and have remembered to bring a personal check on your home account. The **American Express headquarters** in Australia is 92 Pitt St., Sydney, NSW 2000 (☎ 02/239 0666 or 13 26 39).

It can be awkward to purchase items at a shop or pay for meals with foreign-currency traveler's checks since the personnel involved will probably not know the value of your check in Australian dollars. During banking hours this dilemma is easily solved, but after hours it can be a real problem. *The simplest way to buy things and pay the tab in restaurants and hotels is to use a credit or charge card.*

Another alternative is to buy Aussie-dollar traveler's checks. These are sold, for no fee, at Thomas Cook offices in the United States. Once you're down under, you can get a cash advance against your MasterCard or Visa and use the money to buy traveler's checks in the local currency. Then you'd have the convenience of cash and the security of traveler's checks.

Credit and charge cards that are widely accepted at hotels, restaurants, and stores throughout Australia are American Express, Bankcard, Diners Club, MasterCard, and Visa. Carte Blanche can be used in some places. Since some establishments take one card and not another, I suggest you carry two. You can get a cash advance with a credit or charge card at most banks in Australia.

Another alternative is to use the **automated-teller machines (ATMs)** that access funds directly from your home bank account. ATMs at ANZ Banks accept cards with either the Cirrus or the Plus symbol, while only Cirrus cards work at Commonwealth Banks. If you intend to use ATMs while you're down under, ask your bank for a

What Things Cost in Mudgee, NSW	U.S.$
Taxi from the airport to the city center	4.40
Local telephone call from a pay phone	.32
Double at the Country Comfort Inn (deluxe)	80.00
Double at the Winning Post Motel (moderate)	62.00
Double at the Riverside Caravan Park (inexpensive)	22.40
Lunch for one at the Colonial Eatery (moderate)	6.40
Lunch for one at the Tramp Cafe (inexpensive)	4.00
Dinner for one, without wine, at the Craigmoor Restaurant (deluxe)	28.00
Dinner for one, without wine, at the Augustine Vineyard Restaurant (moderate)	14.00
Dinner for one, without wine, at the Soldiers' Club (inexpensive)	6.40
Can of Fosters (beer)	2.25
Coca-Cola (375ml)	.90
Cup of coffee	.80
Roll of ASA 100 Kodacolor film, 36 exposures	6.00
Admission to the Colonial Inn Museum	2.00
Movie ticket	6.40
One liter unleaded petrol (gas)	.57

directory of locations where you can use your card. The advantage of using an ATM is that you're charged only a minimal fee and get the bank's best exchange rate (not the higher commercial exchange rate given at currency-exchange bureaus).

3 When to Go

THE CLIMATE

The time of year you visit Australia will be determined chiefly by the type of weather you hope to encounter and the activities you'd like to pursue. Keep in mind that the seasons are reversed in the Southern Hemisphere: Winter is June to August; spring is September to November; summer is December to February; and fall is March to May. Also remember that the northern part of the country is the warmest and that the southern states, particularly Tasmania, are where you might encounter some cool weather during their winter.

The skiing in Victoria and southern New South Wales is good between June and September, but snow almost never falls in any of the cities. Wildflower buffs should head to Western Australia when it's spring down under—September to November. The prime time on the Great Barrier Reef for those who like hot weather is September to December; for those who prefer more temperate days, May to August is better.

In general, the northern half of the country is at its best from April to October; during other times it can be *very* hot and *very* wet. The southern states are most pleasant from October to April. The ideal situation would be to arrive in Australia in August and travel through Queensland and the Northern Territory before the

Australia's Average Temperatures (°F) & Rainfall (in.)

		June	July	Aug	Sept	Oct	Nov	Dec	Jan	Feb	Mar	Apr	May
Adelaide	Max. Temp.	61	59	62	66	73	79	83	86	86	81	73	66
	Min. Temp.	47	45	46	48	51	55	59	61	62	59	55	50
	Rainfall	3	3	2	2	2	1	1	1	1	1	2	3
Alice Springs	Max. Temp.	67	67	73	81	88	93	96	97	95	90	81	73
	Min. Temp.	41	39	43	49	58	64	68	70	69	63	54	46
	Rainfall	1	1	1	1	1	1	0	2	1	1	1	1
Brisbane	Max. Temp.	69	68	71	76	80	82	85	85	85	82	79	74
	Min. Temp.	51	49	50	55	60	64	67	69	68	66	61	56
	Rainfall	3	2	2	2	3	4	5	7	6	6	4	3
Cairns	Max. Temp.	79	78	80	83	86	88	90	90	89	87	85	81
	Min. Temp.	64	61	62	64	68	70	73	74	74	73	70	66
	Rainfall	3	2	2	2	2	4	9	17	16	18	11	4
Canberra	Max. Temp.	53	52	55	61	68	75	80	82	82	76	67	60
	Min. Temp.	34	33	35	38	43	48	53	55	55	51	44	37
	Rainfall	2	2	2	2	2	2	2	2	2	2	2	2
Darwin	Max. Temp.	88	87	89	91	93	94	92	90	90	91	92	91
	Min. Temp.	69	67	70	74	77	78	78	77	77	77	76	73
	Rainfall	0	0	0	1	2	5	9	15	12	10	4	1
Hobart	Max. Temp.	53	52	55	59	63	66	69	71	71	68	63	58
	Min. Temp.	41	40	41	43	46	48	51	53	53	51	48	44
	Rainfall	2	2	2	2	2	2	2	2	2	2	2	2
Melbourne	Max. Temp.	57	56	59	63	67	71	75	78	78	75	68	62
	Min. Temp.	44	42	43	46	48	51	54	57	57	55	51	47
	Rainfall	2	2	2	2	3	2	2	2	2	2	3	2
Perth	Max. Temp.	64	63	67	70	76	81	73	85	85	81	76	69
	Min. Temp.	50	48	48	50	53	57	61	63	63	61	57	53
	Rainfall	7	7	6	3	2	1	1	0	0	1	2	5
Sydney	Max. Temp.	61	60	63	67	71	74	77	78	78	76	71	66
	Min. Temp.	48	46	48	51	56	60	63	65	65	63	58	52
	Rainfall	5	5	3	3	3	3	3	4	4	5	5	5

Source: Australian Tourist Commission, *Destination Australia.*

weather gets unbearably hot. Then head to Western Australia in time for the wildflowers and continue on to South Australia, Victoria, and Tasmania in October. Sydney's temperatures are pleasant year-round, but February to June can be rainy. Consult the following table of average temperatures when you do your planning.

HOLIDAYS

NATIONAL HOLIDAYS

New Year's Day	Jan 1
Australia Day	Jan 26 or the Mon following (varies by state)
Labor Day	first Mon in Mar (WA and TAS)
Labor Day	second Mon in Mar (VIC)
Canberra Day	third Mon in Mar (ACT)
Good Friday	varies

Easter Saturday	varies
Easter	varies
Easter Monday	varies
Easter Tuesday	varies (VIC and TAS)
ANZAC Day	Apr 25 or the Mon following (varies by state)
May Day/Labour Day	first Mon in May (NT and QLD)
Queen's Birthday	second Mon in June (except WA)
Queen's Birthday	first Mon in Oct (WA)
Labour Day	first Mon in Oct (NSW, ACT, and SA)
Melbourne Cup Day	first Tues in Nov (VIC)
Christmas Day	Dec 25
Boxing Day	Dec 26
Additional holiday	Dec 27
Additional holiday	Dec 28 (all states except QLD)

It's a good idea to avoid traveling in Australia from mid-December to the end of January, when Aussies take their summer holidays; accommodations become both scarce and expensive, and traffic delays can be a real nuisance. Easter vacation (from the Thursday before Easter through the Tuesday after) is another period it's wise to avoid.

School Holidays

In addition to checking the list of holidays above, consult the following schedules of school vacation periods when planning your trip:

New South Wales

1996	1997
Summer: Dec 16 (1995)–Jan 4 (1996)	Dec 20 (1996)–Jan 26 (1997)
Fall: Mar 30–Apr 14	Mar 30–Apr 23
Winter: June 29–July 14	June 30–July 11
Spring: Sept 28–Oct 6	Sept 29–Oct 10

Queensland

1996	1997
Summer: Dec 14 (1995)–Jan 27 (1996)	Dec 19 (1996)–Jan 28 (1997)
Fall: Apr 5–15	Apr 12–28
Winter: June 22–July 8	June 28–July 13
Spring: Sept 21–Oct 7	Sept 20–Oct 5

Northern Territory

1996	1997
Summer: Dec 14 (1995)–Jan 28 (1996)	Dec 14 (1996)–Jan 26 (1997)
Fall: Apr 5–12	Apr 5–13
Winter: June 24–July 19	June 21–July 20
Spring: Sept 30–Oct 4	Sept 27–Oct 5

Western Australia

1996	1997
Summer: Dec 19 (1995)–Jan 26 (1996)	Dec 19 (1996)–Jan 28 (1997)
Fall: Apr 5–19	Apr 5–21
Winter: July 8–19	July 6–21
Spring: Sept 9–Oct 11	Sept 28–Oct 13

South Australia

1996	1997
Summer: Dec 21 (1995)–Jan 28 (1996)	Dec 19 (1996)–Jan 27 (1997)
Fall: Apr 13–29	Apr 12–27
Winter: July 6–22	July 5–20
Spring: Sept 10–Oct 13	Sept 27–Oct 12

Victoria

1996	1997
Summer: Dec 22 (1995)–Jan 29 (1996)	Dec 21 (1996)–Jan 26 (1997)
Fall: Apr 5–21	Apr 12–27
Winter: July 6–21	June 28–July 14
Spring: Sept 28–Oct 13	Sept 20–Oct 5

Tasmania

1996	1997
Summer: Dec 19 (1996)–Feb 4 (1997)	Dec 18 (1997)–Feb 1 (1998)
Fall: (no holiday)	(no holiday)
Winter: June 1–16	May 30–June 16
Spring: Sept 7–23	Sept 5–22

Australian Capital Territory (ACT)

1996	1997
Summer: Dec 16 (1995)–Jan 4 (1996)	Dec 20 (1996)–Jan 26 (1997)
Fall: Mar 30–Apr 14	Mar 30–Apr 23
Winter: June 29–July 14	July 1–11
Spring: Sept 28–Oct 6	Sept 29–Oct 10

AUSTRALIA CALENDAR OF EVENTS

January

- **Australia Day.** National day of celebration, rather like a down-under Fourth of July. January 26.

March

- **Moomba Festival,** Melbourne. 10-day festival including street theater, films, parades, and exhibitions. Early March.
- **Canberra Festival.** Ten days of performing arts and sporting events culminating in Canberra Day hoopla. Canberra Day is the third Monday.

✪ **Adelaide Festival of Arts.** Australia's major arts festival takes place in Adelaide in even-numbered years. Dance, theater, opera, and music are included, as are the literary and visual arts. More than a million attendances were recorded at the 40-plus venues around the city in 1996.

Where: Adelaide. **When:** March 1 to 17, 1996. **How:** For more information, contact the General Manager, Adelaide Festival Centre, G.P.O. Box 1269, Adelaide, SA 5001 (☎ 08/213 4788 for inquiries, or 08/213 4777 for bookings; fax 08/212 7849).

May

- **Camel Cup,** Alice Springs. Camel races are the highlight of this annual event.

September

- **Warana,** Brisbane. Two-week fête including parades, concerts, and lots of outdoor entertainment.

- **Australian Rules Grand Final,** Melbourne. The Super Bowl of Aussie Rules footy is held annually.
- **Floriade Canberra Spring Festival.** Canberra's annual floral festival includes spectacular floral displays, complemented by music, dance, and theater events. Call 06/257 5092 or 1800/026 166 in Australia. Between mid-September and mid-October.

October

- **Henley-on-Todd Regatta,** Alice Springs. Race in which contestants run up a dry riverbed carrying homemade boats. Late September or early October.

November

- **Australian Formula One Grand Prix,** Melbourne. The country's most exciting car race. It's the last race on the international Formula One racing calendar, often the most crucial one.
- **Melbourne Cup.** "The race that stops the nation" takes place at Flemington Racecourse in Melbourne. First Tuesday.

SYDNEY CALENDAR OF EVENTS

January

- **Festival of Sydney.** Performing arts, sporting events, and fireworks are included in this month-long festival. Many of the free concerts are held in the Domain and at Harbourside in Darling Harbour. Call 02/267 4622 or 02/267 2311.

February

- **Gay and Lesbian Mardi Gras.** This month-long celebration includes theatrical events and the highlight, a parade. Call 02/557 4332.

March–April

- **Royal Easter Agricultural Show.** Home arts, farming equipment, games, contests, and agricultural products share the spotlight at this two-week popular annual event. Call 02/331 9111. Begins 10 days before Easter.

June

- **Manly Food & Wine Festival.** This popular gathering is held in the seaside suburb of Manly, easily accessible by ferry and JetCat. Call 02/9977 1088. Usually the first weekend (June 1–2, 1996).
- **Sydney Film Festival.** For two weeks a full schedule of movies is shown at various venues. Call 02/660 3844.

August

- **City to Surf Run.** During this race 30,000 participants run the 14km (8.7 miles) from Sydney Town Hall to Bondi Beach. Call 02/282 2747 or 1800/63 1349.

December

- **Sydney to Hobart Yacht Race.** Sailors and nonsailors alike turn out to see the participants off on this exciting race. Call 02/363 9731. December 26.

4 Health & Insurance

STAYING HEALTHY There are few health hazards to worry about in Australia. The water is safe to drink, and high standards regulate food handling and preparation. Doctors and dentists are highly trained and hospitals well equipped. Your hotel will locate a doctor for you if necessary.

Visitors are permitted to import reasonable quantities of prescription medication. It's also a good idea to bring along a copy of your written prescription using the generic name for the medication in case a question arises, although local pharmacies (chemists) can fill prescriptions written by Australian doctors only. Pack all medication in your carry-on luggage, so you'll still have it with you even if your checked suitcase is lost.

Ask your doctor for recommendations for headaches, head colds, indigestion, motion sickness, constipation, diarrhea, and difficulty sleeping—all maladies that can affect travelers.

Be sure to pack sunscreen, sunglasses, and a visor or hat. Don't underestimate the strength of the Australian sun: It's no coincidence that Aussies have the highest rate of skin cancer in the world.

Vaccinations aren't required if you're traveling direct from the United States, Canada, Britain, or New Zealand, unless you've come from or visited a yellow fever–infected country or zone within six days prior to arrival. You don't need any other health certificate to enter Australia.

INSURANCE Check your policy to make sure your health/accident insurance covers you while traveling abroad, and if it doesn't buy a short-term policy that will. Likewise, check that your homeowner's or renter's policy covers your possessions while you're away. It's also possible that the credit or charge card to which you charge your airline ticket automatically provides some sort of baggage insurance.

If you'll be driving down under, check to see if your auto insurance will cover you in case of accident or other loss. Also find out if the credit or charge card with which you pay for the rental car provides any coverage. Many do these days.

5 Tips for Special Travelers

FOR TRAVELERS WITH DISABILITIES The Australian tourism industry is very conscientious in providing facilities for the handicapped. Easy access at attractions, appropriate restroom facilities in public areas, and specially designed hotel rooms make it possible for the disabled person to enjoy a holiday down under.

General information and news about special tours is available from **Nautilus Tours,** 17277 Ventura Blvd., Suite 207, Encino, CA 91316 (☎ 818/788-8747). It may also be helpful to contact the **NICAN,** P.O. Box 407, Curtin, ACT 2605 (☎ 06/285 3713; fax 06/285 3714; TTY 06/282 4333).

FOR GAY & LESBIAN TRAVELERS *OutRage* is Australia's leading monthly magazine for gay men. *The Sydney Star Observer* is a free fortnightly (biweekly) newspaper for gays. To reach the **AIDS hotline,** call 02/332 4000. The **Bookshop Darlinghurst,** 207 Oxford St., Darlinghurst (☎ 02/331 1103), near Taylor Square, is a good source of information and offers the most comprehensive supply of gay and lesbian literature in Australia.

Tasmania is the only Australian state where male homosexuality is illegal. The U.N. Human Rights Committee's adverse decision on Tasmania's stance may force the Commonwealth to use its external affairs power to bring Tassie into line with the more progressive mainland. Lesbian sex has never been outlawed in Australia.

Sydney is the host for the 13th World Congress of the International Gay Travel Association (IGTA) in 1996. This is the first time the Congress has been held outside North America. The members of the Australian Gay and Lesbian Travel Association say the "pink dollar is a rapidly growing commodity down under."

Publications *Our World,* 1104 N. Nova Rd., Suite 251, Daytona Beach, FL 32117 (☎ 904/441-5367), is a magazine about gay and lesbian travel worldwide; it costs

$35 for 10 issues. *Out & About*, 8 W. 19th St., Suite 401, New York, NY 10011 (☎ 800/929-2268), has been hailed for its "straight" reporting about gay travel. It profiles the best gay or gay-friendly hotels, gyms, clubs, and other places, with coverage ranging from Key West to Paris. Its cost is $49 per year for 10 information-packed issues. Aimed at the more upscale gay traveler, it's been praised by everybody from *Travel & Leisure* to *The New York Times*.

An Organization The **International Gay Travel Association (IGTA),** P.O. Box 4974, Key West, FL 33041 (☎ 305/292-0217 or voice mail 800/448-8550), is an international network of travel-industry businesses and professionals who encourage gay/lesbian travel worldwide. It offers quarterly newsletters, marketing mailings, and a membership directory that's updated quarterly. Membership often includes gay or lesbian businesses but is open to individuals for $125 yearly, plus a $25 administration fee for new members. Members are kept informed of gay or gay-friendly hoteliers, tour operators, airline/cruise line representatives, plus such ancillary businesses as the contacts at travel guide publishers and gay-related travel clubs.

FOR SENIORS In most cases, senior citizens from other countries aren't eligible for posted "pensioner" prices, reduced admission costs that are just for older Australians. However, if you're a member of an organization such as the American Association of Retired Persons (AARP), bring your card and give it a try.

It should also be noted that members of the AARP, 601 E St. NW, Washington, DC 20049 (☎ 202/434-2277), are eligible for discounts on car rentals and hotels.

FOR FAMILIES Australia is the ideal place for a family vacation. If you have any doubts, ask your offspring if they'd rather tour the churches and museums of Europe or romp with 'roos down under. You can easily focus a trip to Australia on beaches, wildlife, forests, sports, and adventure—all of which appeal to the younger set. Another advantage is the relative safety. If children go "walkabout" at the beach, parents needn't worry that they'll never see them again. In addition, the informal lifestyle is comfortable with kids.

Because family travel is common here, a good selection of suitable accommodations is available. Serviced apartments are very convenient because meals can be prepared "at home," thus saving the expense of a restaurant. Campgrounds provide handy facilities for people traveling in campers or motor homes. Those who prefer to stay in hotels will be happy to note that most hostelries allow children to stay in the same room with their parents at no additional charge. Another important fact: Hotels and motels will help arrange for baby-sitters. Some resorts even have separate supervised children's meals and almost all have cots (cribs) on hand.

Even the airlines make it easy for families to travel together. On the major domestic and international carriers, children 2 to 11 are charged 67% of the adult fare; infants are charged 10%. Australian railways also offer a child's fare.

Half-price child admission is standard at attractions, as are family packages that typically admit two adults and two children; "mother's rooms" for changing babies' nappies (diapers) are found adjacent to public restrooms (disposable diapers are more expensive and most Aussie parents still use cloth); picnic and barbecue areas are plentiful. Most car-rental companies supply baby and child seats at a slight charge.

And what if the kids get homesick? No worries if they're American—just take them to McDonald's.

FOR STUDENTS It's not surprising that Australia is a popular destination for traveling students. While backpackers are shunned in some countries, they're welcomed with open arms in Oz. Youth hostels, campgrounds, and other types of budget accommodations help keep costs down, sports and adventure opportunities abound, and the pubs are lots of fun.

STA Travel (also known as Student Travel Network), with its West Coast headquarters at 7202 Melrose Ave., Los Angeles, CA 90046 (☎ 213/934-8722, 212/627-3111 in New York, or 800/777-0112 in the rest of the U.S.; 071/737-9921 in London; 09/309-9995 in Auckland), offers discounted international airfares on the major carriers for students and youth under 26. These favorable rates sometimes extend to recent graduates or academic staff. Contact STA Travel for other ways they can save you money. They have 45 offices in Australia, too; national headquarters are in Melbourne: 220 Faraday St., Carlton, VIC 3053 (☎ 03/347-6911).

Another good travel agency for the 18 to 35 crowd is **Council Travel,** also known as Council on International Education Exchange, which has offices in most U.S. Cities and on many college campuses. Look in your local phone book or call 800/226-8624. This is the only company authorized to issue Australian student work visas from most universities and it specializes in budget airfares, Hostelling International cards, work abroad and language programs, and dollarwise rail and bus passes.

Contiki Holidays offers special tours for those in the 18-to-35 age group. Trips last from 5 to 19 days and cost U.S. $449 to $1,375. Ask your travel agent to contact Contiki Holidays, 300 Plaza Alicante, Suite 900, Garden Grove, CA 92640 (☎ 714/740-0808, or 800/466-0610 in the U.S.; fax 714/740-0818).

Study Abroad Australian universities and other institutions of higher education accept overseas students—both from within the Commonwealth and from the United States. In 1990, nearly 2,000 U.S. students attended school in Australia. Marine biology majors relish the opportunity to study the proliferation of sea life around the Great Barrier Reef. Australia is also the obvious place to study the Aboriginal culture and related archeology. Other students study the same subjects they would've taken at their home universities.

If you're interested in attending school in Australia, write to the Student Enquires Officer at the nearest Australian consulate (see "Visitor Information & Entry Requirements" earlier in this chapter).

FOR SINGLE TRAVELERS The good news is that Aussies are gregarious, and solo travelers can easily strike up conversations and make new friends; the bad news is that hoteliers price their rooms as if they were renting out the ark. About the only way to avoid paying for a double when traveling alone is to stay at youth hostels, in private homes, or on farms, where charges are per person, not per room. Even though bed-and-breakfast inns don't charge much less for a single than for a double, I usually favor them when I'm on my own because I like the homey environment and a chance to meet fellow travelers.

I also suggest you join a short adventure tour (see "The Active Vacation Planner" later in this chapter) when you feel like hiking, riding a camel, sailing, or doing other activities where having a buddy is a definite advantage.

6 Getting There

Whoever said "getting there is half the fun" wasn't talking about journeying down under. To get to Oz you may not have to travel in a house whisked away by a cyclone like Dorothy did, but the airborne North American or European visitor must cross the Equator and several time zones before reaching Australia.

"Getting there is what will consume half the budget for the trip" would be a more accurate statement. Even with the lowest fares, the cost of an airline ticket is still a major expense, so you should take the time to study all the options carefully.

BY PLANE

More than two dozen airlines fly to Australia from North America, Asia, Britain, and the rest of Europe. **Qantas** (☎ 800/227-4500 in the U.S. and Canada, 1800/062 123 in Australia), the national carrier, has the most convenient schedule, offers the most nonstops and the only no-smoking flights, and allows for the most flexibility.

Other airlines have very good in-flight service, but the advantage of flying Qantas is that passengers are immersed in Aussie ambience as soon as they step on board. They're also treated to in-flight videos of Australian current events and up-to-date "what's on" entertainment and sports information, as well as Aussie newspapers. All this gives the new arrival a valuable leg up.

In addition, Qantas's safety record is unblemished. Remember the scene in *Rain Man* when Raymond refuses to board the flight his hustler brother has booked for them, citing the statistics on air crashes and fatalities? At least 15 major airlines excised the airport scene before showing the movie aboard their planes, and it isn't surprising that Australia's national carrier was the only one to show it with the four-minute sequence intact: "Qantas?" Charlie demanded in exasperation. "Never crashed," Raymond muttered.

Other international carriers flying to Australia include **British Airways** (☎ 800/247-9297 in the U.S., 800/668-1080 in Canada), **Canadian Airlines International** (☎ 800/426-7000 in the U.S., 800/665-9933 in Canada), **Air New Zealand** (☎ 800/262-1234 in the U.S., 800/663-5494 in Canada), and **United Airlines** (☎ 800/241-6522 in the U.S. and Canada).

FINDING THE BEST AIRFARE Airlines change their rates more often than some people change their socks. Your best bet is to query the airlines directly to find out what they're selling *today,* or you should work with a travel agent who stays abreast of current fares. Remember that tickets are considerably less expensive when you fly off-season. The cheapest period is April to August, which I think is an excellent time to travel down under. Shop all the airlines that fly to Australia and watch your newspaper travel section for special promotions. Don't be afraid to ask lots of questions when you phone the airlines or talk to your travel agent. You may qualify for a lower fare by slightly adjusting your travel plans. And buy your ticket as far ahead as possible. Only a certain number of less expensive seats are allocated for each flight. Remember to take advantage of stopovers offered at no additional charge. If you're a member of an airline mileage club, look into the possibility of getting a free ticket or earning bonus miles or using your miles to obtain an upgrade to business- or first-class.

Another possibility is to go through a firm that specializes in down-under fares, such as **Discover Australia Marketing** of Sacramento, Calif. (☎ 800/637-3273). They offer airline tickets at discounted prices.

Remember that each airline has at least half a dozen fare levels, ranging from first class down to various advance-purchase tickets. The lowest fares come with the most restrictions: They have to be purchased ahead (usually 14 days, but sometimes 21), and maximum and minimum stays are stipulated. The time of year you travel also affects the price of your ticket. Presently, Qantas's round-trip Los Angeles–Sydney **Super APEX fare,** which requires a 21-day advance purchase, a minimum stay of 7 days, and allows a maximum stay of one month, costs U.S. $1,048 in the low season (April to August), U.S. $1,148 in the shoulder season (March and September to November), and U.S. $1,348 in the peak season (December to February). To qualify for these bargains, your travel from North America must commence Sunday to Wednesday and departure from Australia must be Monday to Thursday. An extra U.S. $60 is charged for travel on other days. No stopovers are allowed on the Super APEX Fare, but passengers have the choice of flying to Sydney, Cairns, Brisbane, or Melbourne. A 50% cancellation penalty applies.

Passengers wishing to stay longer than one month could use Qantas's **Custom APEX fare,** which allows a three-month stay. The price of a Custom APEX ticket is U.S. $1,148 for the low season, U.S. $1,098 in the shoulder period, and U.S. $1,448 during the high season. The Custom APEX fare allows for one free stopover, which could be Hawaii, New Zealand, Fiji, Tahiti, or an Australian city other than the chosen gateway. Extra stopovers can be purchased for U.S. $100 each. A 14-day advance purchase, a minimum stay of 7 days, and a 35% cancellation penalty apply. Full economy, business, and first class don't require an advance purchase, don't have cancellation penalties, and aren't seasonal. Qantas's regular round-trip **economy fare** (Los Angeles–Sydney) is U.S. $3,454; **business class** costs U.S. $5,572; and **first class** costs U.S. $8,744. A tax of U.S. $21.60 applies to all tickets.

Qantas flies to Australia from these points in North America: Los Angeles, Honolulu, Toronto, and Vancouver. All flights from Canada go via Honolulu, but nonstops operate out of Los Angeles. Australia's national carrier also flies down under from five European cities: London, Amsterdam, Rome, Frankfurt, and Athens. Flights from North America land in Sydney, Melbourne, Brisbane, and Cairns. Flights from Europe and the United Kingdom arrive in Sydney, Melbourne, Perth, Cairns, and Darwin.

Other airlines also offer nonstop flights to Australia and have three fare seasons. Each has its own assorted fares, different restrictions, and varying stopover policies, so it's important to inquire about these before reserving a flight. My favorite flight from Los Angeles departs LAX at 1pm and arrives Sydney at 8:45pm the next night—just in time to get a good night's sleep in preparation for the next day's sightseeing.

Preselect your seat when you book your flight to Australia, if that's an option, or as soon as you arrive at the airport. Otherwise you'll find that the only spots available are in the middle of the center section. If you're a member of an airline mileage club, look into the possibility of using your points to upgrade to a higher class of service. For comfort you can't beat business class, but if that isn't in your budget request bulkhead or exit row seats in the economy section. These provide the most leg room. For the best arrival view of Sydney Harbour and the Opera House, request a window seat on the left side of the plane. Special meal requests must be made ahead of time.

IN-FLIGHT COMFORT The flight to Sydney from Los Angeles is only slightly longer than the flight to Europe—about 13½ hours. If you're coming from New Zealand, Southeast Asia, or the Orient, it's even shorter. However, if you're starting on the east coast of North America or in Europe, it's a long haul, and if I were you I'd seriously consider taking advantage of the free stopovers offered by most airlines.

In any case, I suggest bringing along a good book and a travel-size board game if you know your seat partner. Wear loose clothing and comfortable shoes that'll still fit if your feet swell a bit. Apply moisturizing lotion during the flight to counteract high-altitude dryness. Keep alcohol consumption to a minimum; drink an eight-ounce glass of water for each hour in the air; and get as much exercise and sleep as possible. The airlines will do the rest by feeding you more often than most infants dine and by running movies almost back to back. If you're lucky enough to travel in business class on Qantas, you'll enjoy channel surfing on your individual 10-channel video screen. On my last trip, I watched two movies, took a nap, ate two meals, read the Sunday *New York Times,* and arrived in Sydney before I'd even started the book I brought along to read.

BY SHIP

Long-distance ship voyages are rare these days, but for those with a real fear of flying or a love of cruising, the **Cunard Line,** 555 Fifth Ave., New York, NY 10017 (☎ 800/528-6273), often includes Australia on the world-cruise itineraries of the *QE2* and the *Sagafjord.* **Princess Cruises,** 10100 Santa Monica Blvd., Los Angeles, CA 90067 (☎ 800/421-0522), and the **Royal Viking Line,** 95 Merrick Way, Coral Gables, FL 33134 (☎ 800/422-8000), position vessels in the South Pacific, and passengers who fly down and join the ships visit several Aussie ports.

PACKAGE TOURS

If you don't want to travel independently, you may be interested in the plethora of package tours available. Some are specialized, ranging from general adventure, cycling, nature, and horseback-riding trips to luxury tours in chartered planes—see "The Active Vacation Planner" later in this chapter for a list of companies with such offerings. Some are all-inclusive, with airfare, transfers, accommodations, and some meals for one price, and some are short group experiences that can be incorporated into an independent itinerary.

In addition to specialty trips, your travel agent should be able to show you a selection of brochures about general-interest group tours and fly-drive packages. Some are fully inclusive escorted tours; others are short trips of a few days' duration that can be mixed and matched with periods of independent travel.

The following companies offer comprehensive package tours to Australia: **Austravel,** 360 Post St., Suite 606, San Francisco, CA 94108 (☎ 800/633-3404 in the U.S.; fax 415/781-4358); **Swain Australia Tours,** 2121 Avenue of the Stars, Suite 1265, Los Angeles, CA 90067 (☎ 800/22-SWAIN in the U.S.; fax 310/788-0299); and **Qantas Vacations,** 300 N. Continental Blvd., Suite 610, El Segundo, CA 90245 (☎ 800/641-8772 in the U.S., 800/567-5144 in Ontario and Québec, or 800/268-7525 in the rest of Canada; fax 310/535-1057).

CREATE YOUR OWN TOUR

If what you want is a preplanned itinerary but don't want to go with a group, one alternative would be to book your international air ticket and domestic air sectors from home and have **Premier Tourist Services,** P.O. Box 105, French Forest, NSW 2086 (☎ 02/451 5901; mobile phone 015 270 077; fax 02/9975 1545), organize your accommodations and touring down under. It offers day trips and transfers by coach, minibus, or limo throughout Australia and can obtain dollarwise hotel and motel rates.

7 Getting Around

Transportation is an important element of any vacation, but because of the considerable mileage between Australia's cities, it becomes critical when planning a trip here. Crisscrossing the continent uses up valuable time and money, so practical itineraries and economical modes of travel are a must.

Your mode of interstate transportation will be determined by the amount of time and money you have to spend and whether you're interested more in cities or in the countryside between them. Renting a car and driving from point to point consumes a lot of time and a fair amount of money, but it's the best way to see the scenery. Taking a coach (bus) is less expensive but less flexible. Trains are fun but don't allow for stopovers at places that strike your fancy. Flying from place to place is the fastest way to get around, but it's relatively expensive and excludes the possibility of touring rural environs on the way. Interstate ferry service comes into play only on the Melbourne–Tasmania route.

BY PLANE

In a country as big as Australia, a certain amount of flying is required for those who want to see a good cross section of sights in a limited amount of time. Since you can't see the scenery from 30,000 feet, a well-planned itinerary will use flights for the greatest distances and some sort of ground transportation for the shorter spans.

The two major Aussie domestic carriers, with extensive networks of routes throughout the country, are **Qantas** (☎ 800/227-4500 in the U.S. and Canada, 13 13 13 in Australia) and **Ansett** (☎ 800/366-1300 in the U.S. and Canada, 13 13 00 in Australia). As far as I can tell, the only difference between the two is that the Qantas personnel are consistently friendlier and more helpful. (I think of this airline as the Nordstrom of Australian air travel.) Many smaller lines service particular regions. *Note:* Qantas flights with numbers QF001 to QF399 depart from the international terminals and flights with numbers QF400 to QF999 depart from the domestic terminals.

Because of their country's vastness and sparse population, Aussies use planes as often as Londoners use the Tube. But don't let the casual attitude of a bush pilot in a little plane fool you—Australian aviation standards are high. In-flight services are also very good. Federal regulations prohibit smoking on all domestic flights, and cabin baggage allowance is more restrictive than North American regulations (readers have complained that the hand luggage they use at home wasn't considered a carry-on on Australian domestic flights). I suggest you save yourself a hassle and check with the domestic carrier you plan to use to find out their policy. Always reconfirm onward reservations.

AIR PASSES & SPECIAL FARES Overseas visitors should take advantage of the bargain airfares available to them, some of which require purchase prior to leaving home, rather than buying regular point-to-point air tickets after arriving in Australia.

Qantas offers the **Australia Explorer Pass,** which requires a minimum purchase of four flight coupons for U.S. $132 to $160 each (or $161 to $196 Canadian each). Passengers can purchase up to a total of eight coupons good for passage to 19 Australian cities. This pass is available only to North American residents and must be purchased prior to arrival. Ansett offers the comparably priced **Visit Australia New Zealand Airpass.** As with the Australia Explorer Pass, the minimum purchase is four flight coupons with a maximum of eight coupons. The original four coupons must be purchased prior to arrival in Australia or New Zealand.

Because of the changing nature of air travel, at the time of booking or before heading down under confirm any information I've provided here.

BY TRAIN

Australian rail service falls somewhere between the fast, efficient mode of transportation available in Europe and the almost-nonexistent, mediocre passenger-railroad system found in America. A dozen train routes link cities on the east coast of the continent with Melbourne, Broken Hill, Adelaide, Alice Springs, Kalgoorlie, and Perth. Each state operates its own rail service, and they join under the **Rail Australia** umbrella to provide interstate transportation.

Australia's Main Air Routes

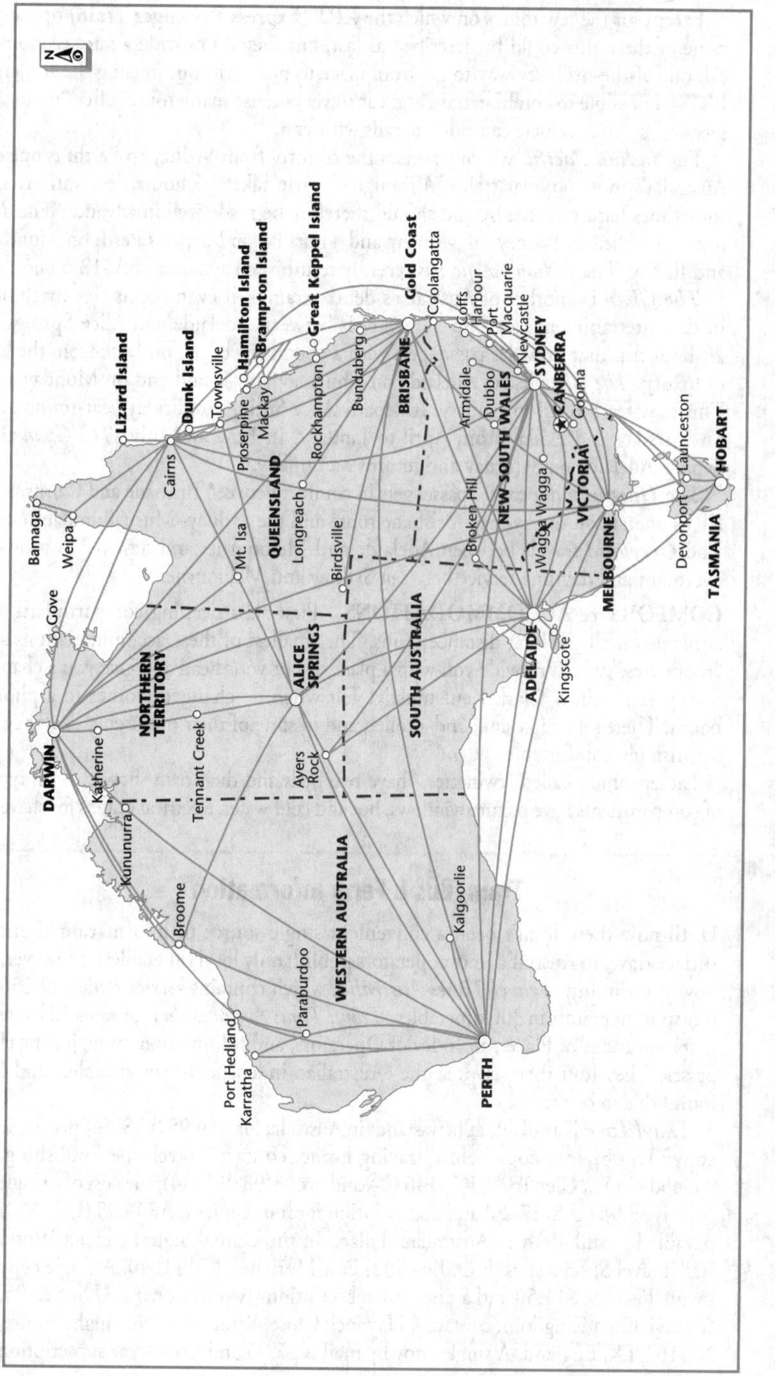

Except for the few routes on which the **XPT (Express Passenger Train)** operates, none of the trains could be described as fast, but they do provide a safe, economical, out-of-the-ordinary way to get from place to place without missing the scenery. It's even possible to combine train and car travel because many routes offer "motorail service," so your vehicle can ride the rails with you.

The ***Indian Pacific,*** which traverses the country from Sydney to Perth, is one of Australia's most popular trains. Although the trip takes 65 hours, reservations are sometimes hard to come by and should therefore be made well in advance. The *Indian Pacific* leaves Sydney on Monday and Thursday and departs Perth on Monday and Friday. The *Indian Pacific* was recently refurbished at a cost of A$12 million.

The Ghan is another of Australia's deluxe trains—it even boasts slot machines in the entertainment car. The train travels between Adelaide and Alice Springs, a 20-hour trip that provides passengers with a good view of the outback from the lap of luxury. *The Ghan* leaves Adelaide on Thursday year-round and on Monday and Thursday from April to January. It departs Alice Springs on Friday year-round and on Tuesday and Friday from April to January. In June and July, *The Ghan* also departs Adelaide on Saturday and returns on Sunday.

The ***Queenslander*** carries passengers in comfort between Brisbane and Cairns, and XPTs operate on the Sydney–Brisbane route and the Sydney–Murwillumbah route. The ***Overland*** travels between Adelaide and Melbourne; and new XPTs provide overnight and daytime service between Sydney and Melbourne.

COMFORT & ACCOMMODATIONS First-class sleeping compartments are available on all the long-distance trains. The smallest of these accommodations are "roomettes," which provide you with a place to put your head and give you a chance to experience how Clark Kent must've felt when he changed clothes in a phone booth. There's a bed, a sink, and a toilet, and in spite of their minuscule size, they're surprisingly comfortable.

Larger cabins, called "twinettes," have two beds and their own shower. Both types of compartments have picture windows, hot and cold water, electrical outlets for shavers,

Train, Bus & Ferry Information

Until now there hasn't been a convenient single source of information about surface travel in Australia (most operators publish only local timetables). However, now you can buy ***Travel Times Australia,*** which contains service details of 250 transport operators in 300 timetables. *Travel Times Australia* also contains 10 route maps, an Index of Places, an Index of Operators, and information on major travel passes. They tout themselves as the "Australian independent travel bible," and I found this to be true.

Travel Times is available at newsstands in Australia for A$4.95 (U.S. $4) per single copy. To obtain a copy before leaving home, contact Traveltime Publishing, 3 Goodwin St., Glen Iris, VIC 3146 (☎ and fax 03/9889 3344); the cost of a single copy is $8.95 (U.S. $7.20) and a subsciption for four copies is A$34.95 (U.S. $28) payable by bank draft in Australian dollars. In the United States, contact World Rail Travel Specialistics, P.O. Box 732, East Moriches, NY 11940. A single copy by mail is U.S. $11.50 and a one-year subscription (two editions) is U.S. $22.95. In the United Kingdom, contact 4 Haydock Close, Kimberley, Nottinghamshire, NG16 2TX, England. A single copy by mail is £7.95 and a one-year subscription is £14.95.

Australia's Main Train Routes

and comfortable beds with crisp linens. "Deluxe compartments" are the most spacious and feature three-quarter beds. Holiday-class (economy) twinettes don't include private toilets and showers. The trains are kept spotless by a staff of ever-present porters. Since there's an extra charge for compartments, cost-conscious travelers might prefer to ride in a chair car, where the seats recline for sleeping. In either case, all interstate rail passengers are allowed up to 80 kg (176 lb.) of luggage, which can be checked, carried in your cabin, or kept by your seat. If you wish to check luggage, keep in mind that the baggage counter closes half an hour before the train leaves.

In addition to sleeping facilities, the majority of long-distance trains in Australia have dining cars with full meal service. The food is good, and the wine list adequate (though not extensive). Dining-car stewards routinely serve and clear four-course dinners in less than an hour—so don't plan to linger at the table.

Another popular feature is the club car, which offers abundant opportunities for socializing. Aussie senior citizens and overseas visitors, the two groups with whom Australian train travel seems the most popular, often play cards and chat their way across the continent.

Smoking is permitted in most club and lounge cars, but not in dining or sleeping cars.

SPECIAL PASSES & DISCOUNTS Visitors who intend to use trains as a major form of transportation may want to consider buying an **Austrailpass,** available in first class or economy for anywhere from two weeks to three months. The pass, which allows unlimited travel, must be purchased prior to arrival down under and doesn't include charges for berths (compartments) and meals. A 14-day Austrailpass costs A$780 (U.S. $624) in first class and A$460 (U.S. $368) in economy. The 21-day pass is A$985 (U.S. $788) in first class and A$595 (U.S. $476) in economy. The price of a one-month pass is A$1,210 (U.S. $968) in first class and A$720 (U.S. $576) in economy. A two-month pass is A$1,540 (U.S. $1,232) in first class and A$945 (U.S. $756) in economy; for three months, the cost is A$1,950 (U.S. $1,560) in first class and A$1,180 (U.S. $944) in economy. Seven-day extensions cost A$410 (U.S. $328) in first class and A$250 (U.S. $200) in economy.

Another possibility is the **Austrail Flexipass.** This offers any 8 days of travel within 6 months (A$650/U.S. $520 in first class or A$550/U.S. $440 in economy) or any 15 days of travel within 6 months (A$915/U.S. $732 in first class or A$550/U.S. $440 in economy). You can also get passes for 22 days (A$1,270/U.S. $1,016 in first class or A$770/U.S. $616 in economy) or for 29 days (A$1,620/U.S. $1,296 in first class or A$995/U.S. $796 in economy). It's ideal for those who wish to make extensive stopovers.

In addition to the above-mentioned passes, Rail Australia sells **Caper Fares,** seven-day advance-purchase fares that provide a discount of 30% off the full fare. These good-value tickets can be purchased after your arrival in Australia.

To make reservations and to buy either of these dollarwise passes, contact ATS Tours (☎ 800/423-2880 in the U.S.). In Canada, phone Goway Travel Ltd. (☎ 416/322-1034 in Toronto, 604/687-4004 in Vancouver, or 800/387-8850 in the rest of Canada). Or contact Rail Australia directly in Australia at 08/217 4321 (fax 08/217 4567).

BY BUS

Interstate bus service in America is often a case of dingy bus stations and questionable traveling companions—but not so in Australia. Clean motorcoaches, equipped with adjustable seats, air conditioning, and bathrooms, provide economical express transportation between cities. They also ply an extensive network of minor roads, carrying passengers to small towns and out-of-the-way places. Smoking isn't allowed on coaches; the terminals are modern, and your seatmates are likely to be companionable Australians or other overseas tourists. In addition, coach captains (drivers) are traditionally very friendly and informative.

Greyhound-Pioneer Australia and **McCafferty**'s are the largest express-coach companies. Greyhound-Pioneer has a slightly more extensive network in some areas, but because McCafferty's coaches don't cover the Perth-Adelaide route, its passes

Sample Travel Times & Fares for Bus Travel

Route	Hours	Fare
Sydney–Adelaide	24	A$95 (U.S. $76)
Sydney–Canberra	4 1/4	A$30 (U.S. $24)
Sydney–Melbourne	14 1/2	A$61 (U.S. $48.80)
Adelaide–Alice Springs	20	A$142 (U.S. $133.60)
Cairns–Brisbane	25	A$137 (U.S. $109.60)
Brisbane–Sydney	17	A$79 (U.S. $63.20)

Greyhound-Pioneer & McCafferty's Adult Bus Pass Fares

No. of Travel Days	Duration of Pass	Greyhound-Pioneer Aussie Pass	McCafferty's Discover Australia Pass
7	1 month	A$475 (U.S. $380)	A$470 (U.S. $376)
10	1 month	A$610 (U.S. $488)	A$605 (U.S. $484)
15	1 month	A$710 (U.S. $568)	A$705 (U.S. $564)
21	2 months	A$935 (U.S. $748)	A$930 (U.S. $744)
30	2 months	A$1,135 (U.S. $908)	A$1,130 (U.S. $904)
60	3 months	A$1,695 (U.S. $1,356)	A$1,690 (U.S. $1,352)
90	6 months	A$2,335 (U.S. $1,868)	A$2,330 (U.S. $1,864)

Lower fares available to children and backpackers.

allow you to take the *Indian Pacific*—one of Australia's great trains—between these two cities. Reservations should be made in advance on main express routes and during school holidays. Two pieces of luggage per person are carried free of charge.

SPECIAL PASSES & DISCOUNTS Greyhound-Pioneer Australia and McCafferty's offer travel passes that represent considerable savings when compared to the cost of purchasing individual tickets. Greyhound-Pioneer's **Aussie Pass** and McCafferty's **Discover Australia Pass** allow travel for a predetermined number of days within a specified period. The 7-, 10-, and 15-day passes are good for one month, 21- and 30-day passes are good for two months, 60-day passes for three months, and 90-day passes for six months.

Greyhound-Pioneer Australia also offers several **Kilometre Passes,** allowing you to travel anywhere from 2,000km to 20,000km for a set price. McCafferty's offers a range of 15 **Travel Australia** passes that allow unlimited travel on preset routes.

Tasmanian Redline Coaches offers a **Tassie Pass** providing unlimited travel around Tasmania. It costs A$98 (U.S. $78.40) for 7 days, A$139 (U.S. $111.20) for 15 days, and A$178 (U.S. $142.40) for 30 days. The Aussie Pass, the Kilometre Pass, the Discover Australia Pass, and the Tassie Pass can be purchased in Australia, but they're less expensive abroad.

To purchase any of the Greyhound-Pioneer Australia, Tasmanian Redline Coaches, or McCafferty's passes, contact Inta-Aussie Tours (☎ 800/531-9222 in the U.S.). In Canada, contact Goway Travel (☎ 800/387-8850).

BY CAR

The availability of good public transportation makes cars superfluous in most Australian cities, but they're wonderful for wandering rural backroads and proceeding from city to city at your own pace. Tourists can drive with valid foreign licenses for up to three months, and the various motoring organizations provide maps and other information to card-carrying members of overseas auto clubs. For stays of longer than three months, you have to obtain an international driving permit.

For help with the rules of the road Aussie style, advice on outback motoring, and other questions, contact one of the following: **NRMA Travel,** 151 Clarence St., Sydney, NSW 2000 (☎ 13 11 22); the **Royal Automobile Club of Victoria (RACV),** 230 Collins St., Melbourne, VIC 3000 (☎ 03/9650 1522, fax 03/9550 1212); the **Royal Automobile Club of Queensland (RACQ),** G.P.O. Building,

261 Queen St., Brisbane, QLD 4000 (☎ 07/3361 2444); the **Royal Automobile Club of Western Australia (RACWA),** 228 Adelaide Terrace, Perth, WA 6000 (☎ 09/421 4444); the **Royal Automobile Association of South Australia (RAA),** 41 Hindmarsh Sq., Adelaide, SA 5000 (☎ 08/202 4500); the **Automobile Association of the Northern Territory (AANT),** 79 Smith St., Darwin, NT 0800 (☎ 089/81 3837); or the **Royal Automobile Club of Tasmania (RACT),** corner of Patrick and Murray streets, Hobart, TAS 7000 (☎ 002/38 2200).

CAR RENTALS The big four—**Avis, Budget, Hertz,** and **Thrifty**—have offices in all the big cities, in many small towns, and at most of the airports. All are reliable and offer a wide range of vehicles, from economy-class cars like a Daihatsu Charade or a Toyota Corolla to eight-seater vans.

After driving many different rental cars in Australia, I've concluded that my favorite is the Holden Commodore by General Motors. I couldn't tell you what's under the hood, but I do know that this five-seater sedan gets very good mileage, that its body is extremely sturdy, that its boot (trunk) is commodious, and that its interior is well designed. Avis has many Commodores; they rent for A$81 to A$100 (U.S. $64.80 to $80) per day, depending on the length of the hire and time of year. A Toyota Camry with air conditioning, power steering, and so forth rents for A$70 to A$89 (U.S. $56 to $71.20) per day. These rates include unlimited kilometers and insurance.

It's sometimes possible to save money on a car rental by getting a fly-drive package. Airline mileage clubs also offer their members bargains with their car-rental partners.

In addition to the major car-rental companies, many local firms rent vehicles, sometimes at lower rates. The disadvantage of the smaller independents is that since they don't have many offices, they generally don't offer one-way rentals and can't provide the backup services of the larger companies.

The minimum age for renting a car in Australia is 21, but many companies impose their own limit of 25 or over. Thrifty's minimum age is 23. Avis's is 21.

For reservations for rental cars in Australia, call **Avis** (☎ 800/331-1084 in the U.S.), **Budget** (☎ 800/472-3325 in the U.S., 800/268-8900 in Canada), **Hertz** (☎ 800/654-3001 in the U.S., 800/268-1311 in Canada), **National** (☎ 800/227-3876 in the U.S. and Canada), or **Thrifty** (☎ 800/367-2277 in the U.S. and Canada).

BUYING A CAR If your stay in Australia will be a long one, you might want to think about buying a car instead of renting one. While recommending used-car dealers is a risky business, there's one in a Sydney suburb I feel I should mention. **Mach I Autos,** 495 New Canterbury Rd., Dulwich Hill, NSW 2203 (☎ 02/569 3374; fax 02/569 2307), is owned by friendly Frank McCorquodale, who has become well known for his guaranteed buy-back price agreement. Here's how it works: You buy a car from Mach I and drive it as much as you want for as long

Readers Recommend

Let's Travel, 165 Victoria St., Kings Cross, Sydney, NSW 2011 (☎ 02/358 2295; fax 02/358 5220). *"Lets Travel really put us onto some real travel deals in Australia. They found us a good price on a rental car and the least expensive internal airfares."* —Capt. Tom Allor, Farmington, Mich.

Author's Note: Let's Travel Australia is a travel agency specializing in making domestic travel arrangements for backpackers and other budget travelers.

as you want. When you're ready to leave the country, he buys the vehicle back at a previously agreed-on price—assuming it's still in driveable condition. The buy-back price is usually about 40% to 50% of what you paid.

GAS The price of gas (petrol) varies from state to state but tends to be cheapest on the east coast and highest in the Northern Territory. Presently it's selling for approximately A70¢ to A80¢ a liter (U.S. $2.20 to $2.50 a gallon).

Petrol stations accept credit and charge cards and are generally open during business hours and the early part of the evening. *Note:* Some stations are closed on weekends, and few stay open around the clock.

ROAD CONDITIONS Australian roads are no great shakes. The main highway between Sydney and Brisbane, for instance, is a two-lane road in some places and a multilane freeway for short stretches. In some places, little shoulder exists and passing can be treacherous. Conditions in Queensland are slightly better; the motorway to Surfers Paradise stands out in my mind as one of the best in the country. The Hume Highway/Freeway between Sydney and Melbourne is another good road. Generally, drivers should expect nondivided one-lane-in-each-direction highways and be pleasantly surprised when they encounter something more spiffy.

"You can't get there from here" is another principle to keep in mind. You can't jump in the car and drive from Cairns to the tip of the Cape York Peninsula, for instance. Not without a four-wheel-drive vehicle and someone who knows the way, because there isn't a road. The same is true in other parts of the country, so consult a recent road map before planning your itinerary.

You should also consider the weather. In the Northern Territory there aren't many roads, and the ones that exist are often closed during "the wet," the monsoon season that descends on the area from December to April.

Another thing to watch for in the Northern Territory: "road trains," up to three truck trailers linked together forming one major hazard. They're nearly impossible to pass on a narrow road, and the drivers have been known to be less than chivalrous.

It really isn't a good idea to drive on Australian highways after dark because you could be unlucky and encounter wandering stock. Dawn and dusk are also hazardous times, for that's when kangaroos hop across the road and drivers who swerve to miss them can end up in considerable strife. Locals who live in rural areas attach "roo bars" to the front of their cars. In some areas wandering camels and water buffalo also pose a problem.

DRIVING RULES Australians drive on the left, give way (yield) to the car on the right, and turn left on red only where signs indicate that it's permissible. It's all very straightforward, and the average competent driver shouldn't be afraid of driving down under. Roundabouts (traffic circles) are one of the few areas that cause concern to North American drivers. Remember to give way to any vehicle already in the traffic circle.

Wearing seat belts is compulsory for drivers *and* passengers. Drinking-and-driving laws are strict ("under .05 or under arrest" —"Drink, Drunk . . . you're sunk. Keep under .05"). Random-stopping breath tests are common, and the police officers involved certainly don't seem to be concerned with public relations. The speed limit in built-up areas is 60km per hour (35 m.p.h.); on the open highway it's 100 to 110km per hour (60 to 66 m.p.h.).

MAPS The best maps are those available at the auto clubs listed earlier in this section. They're free of charge if you present a membership card from your home-country club.

BREAKDOWNS & ASSISTANCE If you experience difficulty while driving a rental car in Australia, phone the company from which you rented the car. The other alternative is to call the nearest auto club. The numbers for their breakdown service are listed in all telephone directories.

BY FERRY

While many vessels provide transfers to and from Great Barrier Reef islands and a boat that carries both passengers and vehicles links Adelaide with Kangaroo Island, the only regularly scheduled interstate ferry service in Australia operates from Victoria to Tasmania. The ***Spirit of Tasmania*** makes regular trips between Melbourne and Devonport (see "Exploring the Island State" in Chapter 18 for details).

HITCHHIKING

Regardless of how much success you've had with thumbing in other parts of the world, don't plan on it in Australia. It's illegal in Queensland and Victoria and frowned on by the police in other states. In addition, given Oz's great distances and sometimes less-than-temperate weather, hitching is highly impractical.

FAST FACTS: Australia

American Express Services available at American Express offices throughout Australia include reconfirmation, rerouting, and reissuing of airline tickets; emergency check cashing; emergency card replacement; traveler's check sales and refunds; sightseeing reservations; and client letter service. The head office is at 92 Pitt St., Sydney (☎ 02/886 0666; fax 02/235 0192). For emergency services or lost or stolen cards, call 1800/230 100; for traveler's checks, call 1800/251 902 (24 hours).

Banks/ATM Networks See "Money" earlier in this chapter.

Business Hours In general, city **banks** are open Monday to Thursday from 9:30am to 4pm and Friday from 9:30am to 5pm. Most **businesses** are open Monday to Friday from 9am to 5pm. **Stores** are generally open Monday to Friday from 9am to 5:30pm and Saturday from 9am to 5pm; in addition, stores are open either Thursday or Friday until 9pm, and some shops are open Saturday from 9am to 4pm and Sunday from 10am to 5pm. In tourist areas it's not uncommon to find stores open seven days a week.

Cameras/Film Most major brands and types of film are available in the larger cities. Prices are reasonable considering that most of them include processing, which can be done anywhere in the world. Prints can be developed quickly, but slides, especially Kodachrome, take much longer.

Car Rentals See "Getting Around" earlier in this chapter.

Cigarettes Smokes in Australia are expensive compared with their Yankee counterparts. I suggest you bring your own. Each traveler over the age of 18 is allowed to bring in 250 cigarettes or 250 grams (8.75 oz.) of cigars or tobacco.

Climate See "When to Go" earlier in this chapter.

Currency See "Money" earlier in this chapter.

Customs Visitors may bring their personal effects into Australia without paying a duty. These include cigarettes (see above) and one liter of liquor. Don't even think about bringing in narcotics and other controlled substances. If you buy wine or spirits in Australia to take home, keep in mind that U.S. residents are allowed

1 liter per person; Canadians are allowed 1.1 liters per person; New Zealanders can take home 1125ml of spirits and 4.5 liters of champagne, port, sherry, or vermouth or 4.5 liters of still table wine; and residents of the United Kingdom can take home 1 liter of spirits or 2 liters of champagne, port, sherry, or vermouth and 2 liters of still table wine.

Dates Aussies, like Europeans, put the day before the month and year; therefore, 8/12/96 in America is equivalent to 12/8/96 down under.

Documents Required See "Visitor Information & Entry Requirements" earlier in this chapter.

Driving Rules See "Getting Around" earlier in this chapter.

Drugstores The down-under equivalent of the North American drugstore is called a "chemist shop."

Electricity The electricity in Australia is 220–240 volts AC, 50 Hertz. North American and Japanese visitors can't use the same 110-voltage appliances they use at home. I recommend dual-voltage hairdryers, curling irons, and other implements. In addition, everyone except New Zealanders will need an adapter plug because the power outlets require a socket with three flat prongs. Universal outlets for 240-volt and 110-volt shavers are found in the better hotels. In order to get power from an electrical outlet, it's necessary to turn the adjacent switch to the on (down) position.

Embassies/Consulates Since Canberra is the capital, that's where you'll find the foreign embassies. In case of an emergency, the following information may be helpful: **Canadian High Commission,** Commonwealth Avenue, Yarralumla, ACT 2600 (☎ 06/273 3844); **Embassy of Ireland,** 20 Arkana St., Yarralumla, ACT 2600 (☎ 06/273 3022); **New Zealand High Commission,** Commonwealth Avenue, Yarralumla, ACT 2600 (☎ 06/270 4211); **Embassy of the United Kingdom,** Commonwealth Avenue, Yarralumla, ACT 2600 (☎ 06/270 6666); **United States Embassy,** Moonah Place, Yarralumla, ACT 2600 (☎ 06/270 5000).

The following countries have consulates in Sydney: **Canada,** Level 5, Quay West 111 Harrington St. (☎ 02/364 3000, general info; or 02/364 3050, immigration 9:30am–12:30pm and 1:30pm–3pm); **New Zealand,** 25th floor, State Bank Bldg., 52 Martin Place (☎ 02/233 8388); **United Kingdom,** Level 16 Gateway, 1 Macquarie Place (☎ 02/247 7521); **United States,** at the corner of Elizabeth and Park streets (☎ 02/261 9200).

Emergencies Dial 000 anywhere in Australia to summon the fire department, police, or ambulance.

Etiquette One of the few vestiges of their British ancestry is the Australians' propensity to queue (line up) for things. Other than that, be polite, keep your voice down (but always return a shout in the pub), and you'll be right, mate.

Holidays See "When to Go" earlier in this chapter.

Information See "Visitor Information & Entry Requirements" earlier in this chapter and individual city chapters for local information offices.

Language Aussie English has to be heard to be believed. For a sampling, see the lexicon in the Appendix of this book.

Laundry Many hotels and motels in Australia have coin-operated washing machines and dryers for guests' use (irons are also widely available). For laundries, see the individual city chapters for details.

Liquor Laws Pub (bar) hours vary but usually run Monday to Saturday from 10am to 11pm; some places are closed on Sunday and those that are open don't get started until noon and close by 10pm. The drinking age throughout the country is 18. And Aussie laws are very strict about drinking and driving, so don't.

Mail Letters can be sent to you in care of General Delivery (poste restante) at any post office in Australia. For example: Ms. H. Traveler, c/o General Delivery, GPO, Sydney, Australia. The GPO is the main post office in each city.

A postcard to the United States costs A95¢ (U.S. 76¢); a letter to the United States costs A$1.05 (U.S. 84¢). A postcard to New Zealand costs A70¢ (U.S. 56¢); a letter to New Zealand costs A75¢ (U.S. 60¢). A postcard to the United Kingdom costs A$1 (U.S. 80¢) and a letter to the United Kingdom costs A$1.20 (U.S. $1).

If you send packages home or buy quantities of stamps, you can use a MasterCard or Visa to pay for purchases (an A$10 minimum is required). If you post any domestic mail, be sure to use the postal code, which is the equivalent of the American ZIP Code. A postcard or letter sent within Australia costs A45¢ (U.S. 36¢).

You can also receive mail in care of the local American Express office if you're a cardmember or carry their brand of traveler's checks.

Maps For information on obtaining the best maps, see "Getting Around" earlier in this chapter.

Newspapers The most widely read daily newspapers are listed in the "Fast Facts" section of every city chapter. I think you'll be surprised at the amount of U.S. news.

Passports See "Visitor Information & Entry Requirements" earlier in this chapter.

Pets Pets from North America must spend four months in quarantine in Hawaii and a further five months in quarantine in Australia before they're allowed to live in or visit Australia.

Police Dial 000 anywhere in Australia to summon the police.

Safety One of Australia's attractions is its relative safety. Crime is not a big worry here, and generally you can feel safe wherever you go. However, whenever you're traveling in an unfamiliar city or country, stay alert. Every society has its criminals: It's your responsibility to be aware of your surroundings in even the most heavily touristed areas.

Taxes As of June 1996, the A$27 (U.S. $21.60) departure tax will be included in the cost of your airline ticket; formerly it was collected at the airport as you were leaving.

Telephone/Mobile Phone/Telex/Fax Austel (Australian Telecommunications Authority) supervises the telephone industry in Australia. The three biggest suppliers of service are Telstra, Optus, and Vodafon.

Austel is in the process of changing all Australian phone numbers from seven digits to eight digits. The planned completion of this changeover is the end of 1998. Under the new numbering system Australia will have four area codes—Queensland will be 07; New South Wales 02; Victoria and Tasmania 03; and the Northern Territory, Western Australia, and South Australia 08. I've done my best to provide the appropriate numbers in this book, but be sure to notice the changeover schedules at the beginning of each chapter or each individual section.

Most hotels in Australia (and in the world, for that matter) place high surcharges on calls made from guest rooms, so you should use pay phones whenever possible, call collect, or use a credit card. If you're making a direct-dial call the International Access code is 0011; the International Fax code is 0015. The easiest way to make an overseas call is dial the appropriate "country direct" number. This will put you in touch with an operator in that country who'll handle your collect or credit-card call. The following are country direct numbers: 1800/55 11 77 (Canada); 1800/55 11 64 (New Zealand); 1800/55 11 55 (U.S. AT&T); 1800/55 11 11 (U.S. MCI); 1800/55 11 10 (U.S. Sprint); 1800/88 14 40 (U.K. British Telecomm); 1800/88 14 41 (U.K. Automated); 1800/55 11 04 (U.K. Mercury).

At one time all toll-free numbers within Australia began with 008; however, as part of the massive changeover of all Australian telephone numbers, toll-free numbers are gradually being changed and will eventually (perhaps by the time you get there) begin with 1800. "One 3" numbers (like Qantas 13 13 13) don't require an area code and are charged as local calls. Mobile phone numbers start with 018 or 015.

When dialing long distance in Australia, be sure to use the right city code: 02 for Sydney, 03 for Melbourne, 07 for Brisbane, and so forth. When dialing these places from overseas, omit the zero. The cheapest time to make long-distance calls within Australia is Monday to Friday from 10pm to 8am or from 6pm Saturday to 8am Monday; try to avoid using the phone from 8am to 6pm Monday to Saturday, which is the most expensive time.

For local directory assistance dial 013; for national, 0175; and for overseas, 0103.

It's possible to use your cellular phone while in Australia. Many countries have reciprocal agreements in place allowing you to use your phone as soon as you get off the plane. Check with your cellular company. For travelers from the United States, the easiest thing to do is to call Telstra at 08/230-2492 (fax 08/231-9305 or in Australia 018 018 468). Upon your completion of a registration form (which requires the Electronic Serial Number of your phone), Telstra will issue you a roaming number to use in Australia. They charge A$3 (U.S. $2.40) per day with a minimum of A$30 (U.S. $24), plus air time.

Telex and fax messages can be sent from post offices or, if you're willing to pay a service charge, from your hotel.

A local call from a pay phone costs A40¢; from a hotel, the charge can be as high as A95¢. You can also use a phone card in a pay phone, available in A$5, A$10, and A$20 denominations from newsstands.

Time There are three time zones in Australia. When it's noon (standard time) on the east coast, it's 11:30am in the center of the country and 10am in Western Australia. Daylight saving time starts the last Sunday in October and ends the first Sunday in March in New South Wales, South Australia, Victoria, and the ACT (it starts October 1 in Tasmania). Queensland, the Northern Territory, and Western Australia don't participate in daylight saving time. (During daylight saving time, Brisbane is 1 hour behind Sydney, Darwin is 1 1/2 hours behind, and Perth is 3 hours behind.)

When it's noon (standard time) on Australia's east coast, it's 2am in London, 3am in Berlin, 4am in Cape Town, 10am in Hong Kong, and 11am in Tokyo; and—all the previous day—4pm in Hawaii, 6pm in Los Angeles, 7pm in Denver, 8pm in Chicago, and 9pm in New York City.

Tipping A 10% tip is customary in the capital cities. Restaurant employees in country areas don't necessarily expect a gratuity; the Aussies who choose to tip leave 10%. In addition, Aussies usually leave a small amount of change for bar service, give taxi drivers 10% of the fare, and give A$1 (U.S. 80¢) per bag to porters. It's not customary to tip hairdressers and barbers.

Tourist Offices See "Visitor Information & Entry Requirements" earlier in this chapter and also the individual city chapters.

Visas See "Visitor Information & Entry Requirements" earlier in this chapter.

Water You can drink Australian water without any worry.

8 Suggested Itineraries

CITY HIGHLIGHTS

The majority of visitors include Sydney on their itinerary, as it should be. The city has one of the most beautiful harbors in the world and provides a plethora of enjoyable activities. However, it would be a mistake to visit Australia's largest city and not any others. Adelaide, Perth, and Hobart are my favorites, and I hope you'll consider stopping in at least one of them. These smaller cities offer something Sydney doesn't have: residents who haven't been inundated with tourists over the past few years and are therefore extremely friendly and helpful.

I'm not saying that Sydneysiders are always rude, but since coastal New South Wales and Queensland are very popular with visitors, the locals have become a little jaded. To experience real Aussie hospitality, venture into South Australia or Western Australia or onto Tasmania. These are also three of the best places for good food and wine at less than sky-high prices.

Alice Springs in the Northern Territory is another spot I heartily recommend. There's nowhere else like it in the country, and the surrounding scenery is breathtaking. And it's a mistake to overlook Canberra, the national capital. This beautiful city is a treasure trove of the country's accomplishments.

PLANNING YOUR ITINERARY

If You Have 1 Week With limited time you'd be wise to confine your touring to one of the capital cities or one state. You could, for instance, spend a few days in Sydney, make an overnight visit to Canberra, and finish with a stay on an outback New South Wales cattle station. Alternatively, you could base yourself in Cairns, Queensland, and do a different day trip every day for a week. This way you'd experience the Great Barrier Reef, the rain forest of Daintree National Park, and the contrasting climate of the Atherton Tablelands.

If You Have 2 Weeks If you have two weeks, try to confine your travels to either a northern route or a southern one. Late autumn, winter, and spring visitors (May to November) can fly into Sydney, spend a few days, and then fly to Ayers Rock. After a day or two at the rock, you can take a bus to Alice Springs and get an eye-level look at the Red Centre. From "the Alice," a flight to Cairns puts you within striking distance of the Great Barrier Reef and in the heart of one of Australia's most exciting tourist areas. Since Cairns has an international airport, you won't have to return to Sydney to get your homebound flight.

If your two weeks happen to come during Australia's late spring to mid-autumn (November to April), why not try a southern circuit, starting at Sydney and including Canberra, Melbourne, Tasmania, and Adelaide? This itinerary works well with train and coach schedules.

If You Have 3 Weeks With more time, combine these shorter plans or add a week in Western Australia to either of them.

HIGHLIGHTS OUTSIDE THE CITIES

EXPLORING THE GREAT BARRIER REEF For some people, witnessing the wonders of the Great Barrier Reef is a life's ambition. If this applies to you, let me suggest a few places on which to focus your attention.

Heron Island, off the coast of Gladstone, 528km (327 miles) north of Brisbane, is one of the few coral cays with its own resort. Whether you want to snorkel, scuba, or walk on the reef at low tide, this is the place. Farther north, **Orpheus Island** (reached via Townsville or Cairns) and **Lizard Island** (out of Cairns) have excellent coral viewing on fringe reefs and launch trips to the outer reef.

While Heron, Orpheus, and Lizard prohibit day-trippers, regular catamaran service shuttles visitors back and forth between Cairns and **Green Island,** one of the other true coral cays. Since accommodations on the islands are relatively pricey, this convenient service makes Green Island the best bet for budget-conscious barrier buffs. The ***Quicksilver*** boat trip from Port Douglas (just north of Cairns) is another way to see the reef without having to pay for a room in a luxury resort.

A Safety Note: Keep in mind when planning your itinerary that northern Queensland's coastal waters are hazardous from October to May, when deadly marine stingers can be present. The beaches are safe, but swimming should be restricted to a pool. This condition also affects the closer Barrier Reef islands, such as Hinchinbrook and Magnetic, but it's okay to swim around the islands that are farther out.

SEEING OUTBACK OZ The most interesting and accessible spots in the outback—**Broken Hill, Coober Pedy, Alice Springs,** and **Ayers Rock**—can easily be linked into a workable itinerary. Those who like train travel can ride the *Indian Pacific* from Sydney to Broken Hill. *The Ghan,* the train from Adelaide to Alice Springs, doesn't go to Coober Pedy, but this odd opal-mining town is on the route of those who choose to drive between the two places.

If your time is limited, taking the train or driving is out of the question. However, **Kendell Airlines** has a flight that goes from Adelaide to Ayers Rock on Saturday, with a brief stop in Coober Pedy. The complete itinerary for those who want to see a lot of the outback would start with this flight and include a coach trip to Alice Springs from Ayers Rock. Coaches from Sydney to Alice Springs travel via Broken Hill and Coober Pedy.

CHECKING OUT WANDERING WILDLIFE If Australia's native fauna are the focus of your trip and you want to see them in their natural habitat, you should probably rent a car. It's not easy, for instance, to get to **Lamington National Park** by public transportation (though day-tour buses do make the trip), and this wonderful spot on the New South Wales/Queensland border is a paradise for birdwatchers and fauna fans. **Cradle Mountain National Park** in Tasmania and **Kakadu** in the Northern Territory are accessible by coach, but you'll want a car for looking around once you get there.

If you don't want to drive or go on an all-inclusive escorted tour, a few parks are still handy. You can easily fly to **Kangaroo Island** from Adelaide, and once on the island you can pick up bus tours that go to **Flinders Chase National Park.** In one memorable afternoon there I saw koalas, emus, Cape Barren geese, and many colorful birds; I also petted kangaroos and wallabies and their joeys and walked through a seal colony. "K.I.," as the locals refer to it, is a not-to-be-missed experience for those who enjoy wildlife.

If time doesn't permit touring the national parks, you can look at native animals in one of the country's many wildlife reserves. **Healesville Sanctuary** outside of Melbourne is one of the best.

9 The Active Vacation Planner

The Aussies' passion for sports is almost legendary. They play cricket, rugby union, rugby league, golf, tennis, squash, Australian Rules football, soccer, and hockey. They sail, cycle, surf, swim, box, balloon, run, row, race horses, snow ski, and waterski—with gusto. And the good news is that you're welcome to join them.

Don't forget, you can call the Aussie Help Line at 708/296-4900 between 8am and 7pm CST, Monday to Friday. You can also get more information on your favorite sports and adventure activities from the state tourist offices listed under "Visitor Information & Entry Requirements" in this chapter.

Serious adventurers might want to pick up a copy of *The Ultimate Australian Adventure Guide*, edited by Chris Darwin and John Amy (Pan Macmillan Australia, Sydney). I bought my copy at Dymocks in Sydney for A$19.95 (U.S. $16) in 1995. The book can pay for itself, because many of the adventure companies listed in it give a discount to those using it.

ACTIVITIES A TO Z

ABSEILING Known also as rappelling, this sport has recently become very popular in Australia. The cliffs of the Blue Mountains in New South Wales (see Chapter 6) are the perfect place to descend on a rope, which is what abseiling is. Anyone who's reasonably fit can "have a go"—no prior experience is necessary. Almost all operators offer instruction.

BUSHWALKING (HIKING) The best way to see Australia's national parks is walking through them. Most have designated trails and track notes are usually available in the visitor centers. Several companies also offer guided walks through the country's beauty spots (see "Outfitters & Operators" at the end of the chapter). In any case, be sure to check the weather information in this chapter (including the temperature and rainfall chart) before planning a hiking holiday and remember to bring comfortable shoes or boots, a day pack, a water bottle, sunglasses, a torch (flashlight), a hat, and—of course—a map. You might like to peruse Tyrone Thomas's *20 Best Walks in Australia* (Hill of Content, Melbourne). For my favorite spots, see "The Best Places to Hike (Bushwalk)" in Chapter 1.

CAMEL TREKKING Many people are surprised to learn that Australia has a large wild camel population, the descendants of the ones imported for exploration of the Outback before cars became a practical alternative. Most visitors are satified with "taking a camel to breakfast, lunch, or dinner," an offer made by the Frontier Camel Farm in Alice Springs. If you'd like a longer expedition, contact Noel Fullerton's Camel Outback Safaris, also in Alice Springs (see Chapter 11). In either case, stick to the cooler winter months. If you're enchanted by camels, you'll want to read Robyn Davidson's *Tracks* or Rick Smolan's *From Alice to Ocean.*

Impressions

Australia is an outdoor country. People only go inside to use the toilet, And that's only a recent development.

—Barry Humphries, quoted by Peter Nichols, *Sunday Times* (Jan. 11, 1981)

CANOEING & KAYAKING Flat water canoeing, sea kayaking, and white-water canoeing are all popular in Australia. Inexperienced visitors who decide to try this sport should do so only if they're good swimmers and have a fair amount of upper-body strength. Katherine Gorge in the Northern Territory (see Chapter 11) and Lake Burley Griffin in Canberra (see Chapter 19) are the best for flat-water canoeing. Kangaroo Island in South Australia (see Chapter 15) and Wilsons Promontory in Victoria (see Chapter 17) are good for sea kayak trips. Several places on Tasmania, including the Huon River west of Hobart, offer excellent white-water canoeing (see Chapter 18).

CANYONING Once you've learned to abseil (above), you can try your hand at canyoning: lowering yourself—sometimes through waterfalls—into a sandstone gorge with a river. You then swim, float on a mat, and scramble over wet rocks to the entrance. This is best done in warm weather and only by capable swimmers. The Blue Mountains in New South Wales is the best place (see Chapter 6).

CAVING Exploring caves is some people's passionate pursuit. If you're one of them, head for the Jenolan Caves in New South Wales (see Chapter 6), the three caves in the Margaret River area of Western Australia (see Chapter 13), and the Naracoorte Caves in South Australia (see Chapter 15).

DIVING & SNORKELING Most, but not all, of the great diving and snorkeling spots in Australia are on the Great Barrier Reef—the largest marine park in the world. Here you can take lessons and get your scuba certification, readily rent equipment (even underwater cameras), arrange for a dive buddy (if you didn't bring your own), and do day trips or longer excursions to coral cays, patches of fringing reef, and various ribbon reefs. The beauty here is amazing, and experienced divers estimate it would take a thousand dives to see just the reef's highlights. August to December are the prime months—true aficionados try to be here during a full moon around November or December when the coral is spawning. No matter when you go, remember that the reef is a fragile environment: Don't stand on coral formations and don't even think about breaking off a piece of anything to take home.

Most internationally recognized certificates are valid, including PADI, NAUI, and BSAC. Bring proof of certification and your dive log. For general information, see Chapter 10, which features a "Great Barrier Reef Resorts at a Glance" chart. You might want to ask the nearest Queensland Tourist and Travel Corporation office for a free copy of the "Dive Queensland" brochure. The office also offers an IBM-compatible computer disk, "The Queensland Scuba Diving Holiday Planner," for a small charge. Information on dive operators, locations, training, and events can be obtained from Dive Queensland, P.O. Box 5120, Cairns, QLD 4870 (☎ 070/511 510, 07/4051 1510 after April 1998; fax 070/511 519, 07/4051 1519). For my list of the best places to go, see "The Best Diving & Snorkeling Sites" in Chapter 1.

FISHING On the Ord River in the Kimberley region of Western Australia and other places in the Far North you can try to hook a barramundi; on Lizard Island, the marlin will give you a run for your money. In Noosa, on Queensland's Sunshine Coast, whiting and flathead can be hooked year round. Trout fishing is popular in Tasmania. Ask the nearest Queensland Tourist and Travel Corporation office for a free copy of the "A Guide to Sport Fishing in Queensland" video.

GOLF Wherever you are in Australia, you'll find there's likely a golf course nearby. This is the country that produced Greg Norman, who has since joined the PGA circuit in the United States. The mates he left behind just *love* to hit the links

Health & Safety in the Great Outdoors

You'll need to keep your wits about you when you're in the bush and on the beach in Oz. While I don't want to alarm you unnecessarily, I couldn't live with myself—and you might not live at all—if I didn't mention the following:

- **Bush fires:** Please be extremely careful with matches and campfires anywhere in Australia.
- **Crocodiles:** While freshwater crocs are rarely a problem, "salties" would just as soon eat you as look at you. *Heed all warning signs!* These will be found in rivers and along the coast in Far North Queensland, the Top End of the Northern Territory, and northern Western Australia. See "Wildlife from Koalas to Crocs" under "Australia's Natural World" in Chapter 2.
- **Dehydration:** Australia is, for the most part, a hot, dry country. Always carry a water bottle when you're outdoors.
- **Emergencies:** Anywhere in Australia, dial 000 to summon police, fire, coastguard, or ambulance.
- **Marine stingers (box jellyfish):** Be sure to read "A Few Precautions" in Chapter 10 and stay out of the water when warnings for marine stingers are posted—they're deadly.
- **Rip currents:** These are hardly exclusive to Australia. The lifesavers (lifeguards) generally know where they are, so ask. If you do get caught in one of these strong water currents, don't panic. Swim across the current diagonally to shore, *not* against it. If you need assistance, raise one hand above your head for help.
- **Sharks:** As with crocs, the people who get hurt generally chose to ignore the posted warning signs. When in doubt, ask the locals. See "Wildlife from Koalas to Crocs" under "Australia's Natural World" in Chapter 2.
- **Snakes:** Australia has lots of poisonous ones. When you're walking in the bush, watch where you put your feet. See "Wildlife from Koalas to Crocs" under "Australia's Natural World" in Chapter 2.
- **Spiders:** The redback is a particularly poisonous one. Shake out your boots before sticking in your feet.
- **Sunburn:** Aussies have the highest rate of skin cancer in the world, and this is one case where "when in Rome" *isn't* a good adage to follow. Wear a hat, sunglasses, and lots of sunscreen.

whenever they can. More than 80 courses can be found within a 40km (25-mile) radius of the Sydney Harbour Bridge, for instance. Most courses rent clubs, so you don't have to drag yours from home. Green fees start at A$20 (U.S. $16) for 18 holes (with clubs).

If you have questions, you can phone the New South Wales Golf Association (☎ 02/264 8433) or Victoria Golf Association (☎ 03/9889 6731). You can also ask the Queensland Tourist and Travel Corporation for a copy of the "Golf Queensland" brochure. Good courses can be found in and around all the capital cities. The Cypress Lakes Golf & Country Club in the Hunter Valley of New South Wales is Australia's newest international-standard course.

HORSE TREKKING If you're a keen horseperson, you might like to read the monthly magazine *Australian Horse News.* If you're an inexperienced rider, expect some stiffness at the end of a long day in the saddle. The trekking season is November to April, and the best places are the Snowy Mountains and the Blue Mountains, both in New South Wales (see Chapter 6), and the Snowy River National Park in Victoria (see Chapter 17). You may also be interested in doing a pub crawl on horseback, which is possible in the New England region of New South Wales (see Chapter 6).

MOUNTAIN BIKING You don't need to BYO if this is your sport. Bikes and helmets can be hired (rented) and tour operators (see "Outfitters & Adventure-Travel Operators" at the end of this section) supply them. Try to avoid hot and extremely wet weather. The Blue Mountains of New South Wales (see Chapter 6) and several places on Tasmania (see Chapter 18) have great mountain-bike terrain and good trails.

MOUNTAINEERING Because Australia is the flattest continent on earth, it's hardly a mecca for mountaineering. However, if climbing to the summit of a snow-covered peak is your heart's desire, head to the Snowy Mountains in New South Wales (see Chapter 6) between July and September.

RAFTING A good activity for a hot summer day, white-water rafting requires no prior experience—just nerve, swimming ability, and a sense of humor. This makes an enjoyable day trip or can be combined with camping in a multiday excursion. Be sure to wear a helmet, a buoyancy vest, and lots of sunscreen. Ask your guide how best to deal with contact lenses. At opposite ends of the country, Tasmania's Franklin River (see Chapter 18) and Queensland's Tully River (see Chapter 9) offer Australia's best rafting.

ROCK CLIMBING Not to be confused with mountaineering (above), this sport involves defying gravity by climbing to the tops of mountains or cliffs by the use of foot and hand holds. Don't try this unless you're extremely physically fit. The Australian Sport Climbing Federation (☎ 02/264 2908) can provide more information. This is a popular activity in the Blue Mountains of New South Wales (see Chapter 6).

SAILING Whether you choose bareboat or skippered, it's hard to beat the sailing conditions in the Whitsundays. The many uninhabited islands in this area of central Queensland provide ideal sheltered anchorages (see Chapter 8).

SKIING I doubt that very many visitors are chomping at the bit to ski in Australia. Those who want to shuss down under during the Northern Hemisphere summer usually head for New Zealand's alps. However, should you get the urge in Oz between June and September, head for the Snowy Mountains—either the New South Wales or the Victoria side. Equipment rental is readily available. Cross-country skiers might like to read *Ski Touring Australia* by John Siseman, Warren Peck, and John Brownlie (Algona Publications, Northcote, VIC). Between June and October, it's possible to cross-country ski in Tasmania's Cradle Mountain/Lake St. Clair National Park (see Chapter 18).

SPECTATOR SPORTS It wouldn't be summer down under without cricket. Coverage of this sport dominates weekend TV programming and extensive reportage appears in every newspaper. The rules confound anyone not born in a Commonwealth country, but you can be clueless and still have a good time at a match. Dennis Lillee, Greg Chappell, and Rodney Marsh were elevated to star status for their performances on the cricket pitch. Mention their names to break the ice with the Aussies sitting nearby.

Likewise, the Aboriginal Ella brothers—Mark, Glen, and Gary—gained great respect for their rugby union prowess. A variation on the sport, rugby league, is very popular in Sydney. Both are played April to September.

Australia competes against other Commonwealth nations in most sports, but since Australian Rules football is played only at home, the competition is between various interstate clubs. Victoria is the hotbed of Aussie Rules, or "footy," as it's called by the locals, but other states share the passion. The Australian Rules Grand Final, the Super Bowl of footy, is held every September—and televised all over the world. Gary Abblett from Geelong (near Melbourne) is presently the nation's top player.

The ultimate spectator events will take place in September 2000, when Sydney plays host to the Olympic Games.

SURFING Great waves surround the island continent, and if you hang 10 at home, why not try it here? Board-rental places aren't plentiful, but I've tried to list at least one in each key location. Be sure to check with local lifeguards about rip currents and the possible presence of sharks and marine stingers. Other questions? Contact the NSW Surfboard Riders' Association (☎ 02/977 4799); the Association of Surfing Professionals, P.O. Box 1015, Coolangatta, QLD 4225 (☎ 07/5536 3411; fax 07/5536 4490); or the Surf Lifesaving Association of Australia, P.O. Box 36, Newstead, QLD 4006 (☎ 07/3852 1496; fax 07/3252 4511). The best surf spots in the country include Narrabeen in suburban Sydney (see Chapter 5), Byron Bay in New South Wales (see Chapter 6), Burleigh Heads on the Queensland Gold Coast (see Chapter 8), Noosa Heads on the Queensland Sunshine Coast (see Chapter 8), Yallingup in Western Australia (see Chapter 13), and Bells Beach in Victoria (see Chapter 17).

TENNIS Do these names sound familiar: Rod Laver, Ken Rosewall, Margaret Smith Court, Roy Emerson, John Newcombe, Evonne Goolagong, and Pat Cash? Australians, it would seem, are born knowing how to wield a racquet. Nearly every community has public courts, and many hotels and resorts offer theirs to their guests. For example, the Hyatt Regency Coolum on Queensland's Sunshine Coast boasts nine courts (see Chapter 8). In central Sydney, both the Novotel on Darling Harbour and The Observatory near The Rocks offer tennis facilities (see Chapter 4).

WILDLIFE WATCHING Australia's native and imported animals are fascinating. Brief background information can be found in "Wildlife from Koalas to Crocs" in

The Race that Stops the Nation

Horse racing captures the country's attention on the first Tuesday in November, when the Melbourne Cup is run. I'd heard the event referred to as "the race that stops the nation," but I didn't believe it until I saw it with my own eyes. I was in Sydney, in the public bar of the Regent Hotel. It was midday and the room was crowded with office workers hovering over the "Cup Day" buffet, talking about the big race, and placing wagers. Half a dozen TVs brought in for the occasion relayed the happenings at the Flemington Racecourse in Melbourne, including lavish parties, women dressed to the nines, and interviews with international jet-setters and others for whom this was the highlight of the social season.

Through the windows of the pub I could watch the activity on Sydney's busiest street. Buses and taxis stopped; not one person remained outside the window. For three minutes Sydney and, I assume, the rest of the nation were transfixed by horses galloping around the track at the Flemington Racecourse in Melbourne. For three minutes the only audible sound was the pounding of horses' hooves and the pounding of punters' hearts.

Chapter 2. For a list of my favorite spots to observe kangaroos, koalas, whales, and more, see "The Best Places for Viewing Wildlife" in Chapter 1.

WINDSURFING Places to practice this sport abound throughout Australia, and it's easy to hire (rent) the equipment. You can even take lessons at the Rose Bay Windsurfer School on Sydney Harbour (see Chapter 5).

OUTFITTERS & ADVENTURE-TRAVEL OPERATORS

Australian Academic Tours Pty Ltd., 27/7 Bungan St., Mona Vale, NSW 2103 (☎ 02/9979 9813 or 1800/810 921 in Australia; fax 02/9979 5540), offers a series of tours ranging from Sydney region day tours to major Australian expeditions. They feel more like field trips than strictly-for-fun holidays. Prices range from A$1,495 to A$2,850 (U.S. $1,196 to $2,280) for extended tours and from A$385 to A$640 (U.S. $308 to $512) for four- to six-day Short Breaks.

Australian Wilderness Tours, Mount Seaview Resort, Tours & Safaris, Oxley Highway, Wauchope, NSW 2446 (☎ 065/87 7144 or 065/87 7155, or 1800/81 8804 in Australia; fax 065/87 7195), offers tours for those who enjoy the outdoors and have a genuine interest in nature. Travel to scenic out-of-the-way places is in six-passenger four-wheel-drive vehicles. Mount Seaview offers City Link Safaris in which passengers are transported in four-wheel-drive vehicles between Australia's major cities via nontraditional routes and various national parks. The four-day/three-night Sydney–Brisbane trip costs A$755 (U.S. $604) and the seven-day/six-night Cairns–Brisbane trip costs A$1,494 (U.S. $1,195)

Auswalk, P.O. Box 13, Northcote, VIC 3070 (☎ and fax 03/9482 1206), offers an interesting compromise between stumbling about in the bush on your own or taking a guided walk. This company provides a minimum of two people with walking notes that describe the route they're to follow. It also organizes lodgings and meals and moves your luggage from one night's accommodation to the next. All you have to carry is a daypack. Now Auswalk offers four itineraries—two in New South Wales and two in Victoria—but, due to popular demand, it's about to add others. The five-day "Melbourne's Playground" costs A$590 (U.S. $472) and the seven-day "Roof of Australia" costs A$930 (U.S. $744).

Backroads, 1516 Fifth St., Berkeley, CA 94710-1740 (☎ 510/527-1555 or 800/245-3874; fax 510/527-1444), offers a nine-day bike trip to Tasmania. The experience includes a stop at the Port Arthur penal colony and overnights at some off-the-beaten-path properties. The cost is U.S. $2,398, plus mountain bike rental of U.S. $159. Airfare is extra. Trips depart in December.

Equitour, P.O. Box 807, Dubois, WY 82513 (☎ 307/455-336 or 800/545-0019; fax 307/455-2354), offers horseback-riding holidays down under. Its week-long riding tour in Queensland, on Arab/thoroughbred crosses, can be done throughout the year for about U.S. $850. This company also offers a five-day Snowy Mountains ride from early November to late April at a cost of about U.S. $900. Special trips are possible.

FITS Equestrian, 685 Lateen Rd., Solvang, CA 93463 (☎ 805/688-9494 or 800/666-FITS; fax 805/688-2943), offers two horseback-riding vacations in Australia. One trip includes a pub crawl in the New England region of New South Wales and overnight lodging in historic bush pubs; this five-day adventure costs A$990 (U.S. $792). There are departures throughout the year. Another trip includes riding and camping in the beautiful Snowy Mountains. The cost is A$540 to A$900 (U.S. $432 to $720), and departures are November to April.

Great Australian Walks, 81 Elliott St., Balmain, NSW 2041 (☎ 02/555 7580), offers guided walking tours around Australia. Most of these are all-inclusive/

sans backpack: the support team prepares camp and has a cuppa ready when you and your trailmates arrive. Trips are rated from "easy" to "adventurous." Prices range from A$299 (U.S. $239.20) for the three-day Katoomba to Jenolan Caves "Six Foot Track" to A$1,495 (U.S. $1,196) for the fully accommodated 14-day "Tasmania Circle." The majority of participants are Australians.

Koala Golf, P.O. Box 93, Sandringham, VIC 3191 (☎ 03/9598 2574; fax 03/9598 8172), offers golf tours in Sydney and Brisbane, on the Gold Coast of Queensland, and in Cairns, Perth, Adelaide, and Melbourne. This company can help you decide which course to play, assist you in renting equipment, obtain permission for you to play at private clubs, and provide transportation.

Morrell Adventure Travel, 1/8 Newcastle St., Rose Bay, NSW 2029 (☎ 02/388 1200 or 1800/066 126 in Australia; fax 02/388 1318), offers guided mountain-biking and hiking trips in Kosciusko National Park and the Southern Highlands areas of New South Wales. It provides all the necessary equipment and meals. Prices range from A$75 (U.S. $60) for one day freewheeling in the Southern Highlands to A$950 (U.S. $760) for the eight-day "Kosciusko Explorer," which includes cycling, bushwalking, rafting, camping, and overnighting in a lodge.

Questers Worldwide Nature Tours, 257 Park Ave. S., New York, NY 10010-7369 (☎ 212/673-3120 or 800/468-8668 in the U.S.), as its name implies, designs excursions for birders, wildlife photographers, and anyone "curious about the world." Prices vary according to the duration of the tour; the 18-day trip costs U.S. $4,279. Questers' 22-day Australia tour costs U.S. $6,247.

Swagman Tours, 16 Gheringhap St., Geelong, VIC 3220 (☎ 052/22 2855; fax 052/23 1047), offers 9- to 37-day camping safaris throughout Australia. Its 10-day trip around Tasmania costs A$775 (U.S. $620) and its 37-day West Coast, Kimberley, and Northern Territory tour costs A$2,595 (U.S. $2,076). Transportation is via luxury coaches and accommodation is in two-person tents. Other amenities include tables, stools, electric camp lights, and clean toilet facilities. Tours include meals, camping equipment, camp fees, and national park entry.

The Tasmanian Outdoor Experience Company, P.O. Box 2053, Launceston, TAS 7250 (☎ 003/344 442; fax 003/342 029) offers soft adventure tours throughout the island state. Some excursions include cycling and bushwalking, others wildlife watching, camping, and sailing. One even offers cable hang gliding, another caving and rafting. Prices start at A$60 (U.S. $48) for the one-day Launceston cable hang gliding/cycle trip. The two-day "Cycle & Sail" costs A$256 (U.S. $204.80), with meals, accommodation, support vehicle, bike, sailing, and guiding.

Travelabout, 88 Guthrie St., Osborne Park, WA 6017 (☎ 09/244 1200; fax 09/445 2284), offers four-wheel-drive tours around Western Australia. Its 16-day trip through the beautiful Kimberley region costs A$1,450 (U.S. $1,160). The four-day Monkey Mia excursion to see the dolphins costs A$320 (U.S. $256). Travelabout also journeys to the Hammersley Ranges, Ayers Rock, and the scenic southwestern portion of the state.

Women's Outdoor Network, P.O. Box 21, Mt. Victoria, NSW 2786 (☎ 047/871 592 or mobile 015/704 582), is an organization run by outdoorswomen from all over the world for the purpose of bringing outdoor adventure to women. It offers abseiling, canoeing, bushwalking, canyoning, and rockclimbing excursions in the Blue Mountains of New South Wales and other areas. This organization is "sensitive to the issues connected to women in the bush and committed to supporting you in fulfilling your needs." Prices range from A$250 (U.S. $200) for a two-day introductory rockclimbing course to A$1,680 (U.S. $1,344) for a 14-day canoeing, camping, bushwalking trip in the Kimberley region of Western Australia.

10 Tips on Accommodations

Australia offers a wide range of accommodations, from deluxe international hotels to modest motels and bed-and-breakfast inns. Some of the terms used down under are unusual, but the following overview should help to clarify things.

HOTELS Australia has its fair share of the big hotels found in the world's major cities. Travelers who enjoy the familiarity, predictability, and high standards offered by these international hostelries will be glad to know that **Sheratons, Hiltons, Regents, Hyatts, Ramadas, Holiday Inns,** and **Inter-Continentals** are available down under.

Many other hotels, of course, are part of regional chains. These are often less expensive, while offering standards similar to those found in the internationals. Look for **Parkroyals, Travelodges, Gazebos,** and **Olims.** By the way, Travelodge Hotels in Australia are owned by a different corporation and offer a much higher standard of accommodation than the motels of the same name in the United States.

In addition to hotels that are part of a chain, numerous independent hostelries are available. These often represent good value but have remained a local secret because they don't advertise overseas. Many have a charming atmosphere that reflects the surrounding environment, as well as personal service that the big hotels may lack. I discovered many such spots while doing the research for this book and was delighted to include them. Since their rates are lower than those of the internationals, you'll find most of these gems listed in the "Moderate" category in the accommodations section of each city chapter.

All rooms in modern Australian hotels have en suite bathrooms (but not necessarily bathtubs, sometimes just showers), heating, air conditioning, phones, TVs, radios, and minibars. In addition, coffee- and tea-making facilities and a small refrigerator are almost always supplied. Meals are served in a dining room or restaurant, with drinks available in at least one bar. Most places also offer room service and provide laundry facilities.

Saving Money City hotels can be very accommodating to tourists on weekends, when the business travelers who occupy most of the rooms during the week have gone home. Discounts of 40% to 50% are not unusual, but *you have to ask for them.* In hotel parlance, a weekend is Friday, Saturday, and Sunday nights. Sometimes you can also get off-season specials and long-stay rates that are much lower than standard room rates. It's also possible to get the "corporate rate" just for asking or an "early-bird discount" when a room is booked and paid for a week in advance. When business is slow, hotels offer special packages that may include breakfast, champagne, or a similar enticement. These can represent very good value, assuming you want whatever the extras are.

Another way to save on accommodations is presenting your auto-club card at one of the **Aussie motoring clubs** (see "By Car" under "Getting Around" above) and ask them to make reservations in the hotels and motels that give their members a discount. Some hostelries will even give discounts to auto-club members on the spot, even if the room wasn't prebooked through one of the clubs.

In addition, your airline mileage club membership might entitle you to hotel discounts.

Hotel Passes Two companies offer prepaid coupons that represent a discount on their regular room rates. Southern Pacific Hotels sells a **Freedom Down Under Hotel Pass** that may be used at any of their more than 75 deluxe and first-class Parkroyal, Centra, THC, or Travelodge hotels in Australia, New Zealand, Asia, Tahiti, and Fiji.

Each coupon costs U.S. $99 ($130 Canadian) and can be redeemed for one room (single, double, or triple) for one night. At some hotels a supplemental payment is required. The hotel pass can be purchased only by U.S. and Canadian residents prior to departure. To order a Freedom Down Under Hotel Pass, contact Southern Pacific Hotels, 1973 Friendship Dr., El Cajon, CA 92020 (☎ 800/441-3847 in the U.S. and Canada; fax 619/596-6236).

Another hotel discount voucher system is offered by Flag International, which has 400 properties in Australia. Flag hotels and motels are graded into six categories, and the **Flag Hotel Pass** costs U.S. $44 to $133 per room, single or double, per night depending on which category you choose. To get a copy of the Flag directory, purchase a pass, or make reservations, call 800/624-3524 in the U.S. and Canada. Reservations can be made before departing or as you travel around Australia via Flag's nationwide toll-free number.

Reservations Many people like the flexibility of making hotel reservations as they need them, instead of reserving ahead. This system works well in most cases, but I recommend prearranging the first couple of nights in the country, regardless of where you arrive. There's nothing worse than trying to find a home away from home while suffering from jet lag.

It's possible to make reservations at many Australian hotels and motels by making toll-free calls in North America. If you want to do this, you can contact the following chains: **Accor** (Novotel, Mercure, and Ibis) (☎ 800/221-4542 in the U.S. and Canada), **Best Western International** (☎ 800/528-1234 in the U.S. and Canada), **Flag International Hotels and Resorts** (☎ 800/624-3524 in the U.S. and Canada), **Hilton International** (☎ 800/445-8667 in the U.S., 800/268-9275 in Canada), **Holiday Inns** (☎ 800/HOLIDAY in the U.S. and Canada), **Hyatt Hotels** (☎ 800/233-1234 in the U.S. and Canada), **Inter-Continental Hotels** (☎ 800/327-0200 in the U.S. and Canada), **Regent International Hotels** (☎ 800/545-4000 in the U.S. and Canada), **Sheraton Corporation** (☎ 800/325-3535 in the U.S. and Canada), and **Southern Pacific Hotels** (Travelodges and Parkroyals) (☎ 800/835-SPHC in the U.S. and Canada).

COUNTRY PUBS Hotels in Australia were originally built as places for dispensing "grog," but to comply with the licensing laws they had to have a certain number of guest rooms as well. Most of the pubs built during the era of these regulations are functioning today as "grog shops" only. However, some of them—primarily in country towns—offer inexpensive, atmospheric accommodations to travelers. Some of the old public licensed hotels in the city also offer overnight stays.

If you're interested in staying in a pub, contact **AUSRES/Australian Reservation Service,** Suite 1, 27–33 Raglan St., South Melbourne, VIC 3205 (☎ 03/9696 0422 or 13 10 66; fax 03/9696 0329). Prices vary from approximately A$38 to A$83 (U.S. $30.40 to $66.40) for a single and A$55 to A$100 (U.S. $44 to $80) for a double, including breakfast.

MOTELS & MOTOR INNS While hotels are licensed to serve alcoholic beverages and usually furnish all meals, most motels limit themselves to lodging and breakfast only. Further, while hotels often provide both shower stalls and bathtubs, motels frequently offer only showers. Because they cater to motorists, motels and motor inns have ample free parking available. The majority of them also provide laundry facilities, phones, TVs, radios, and heating and air conditioning, as well as coffee- and tea-making facilities and a small refrigerator.

SERVICED APARTMENTS Overseas visitors to Australia are usually surprised to find a large number of fully furnished apartments for rent on a daily basis.

Meeting the Aussies

Aussies are known for their friendliness, and you'll have no trouble meeting them while you're down under. In case you'd prefer a formal introduction, you might like to know about the following opportunities:

Friends Overseas-Australia, 68-01 Dartmouth St., Forest Hills, NY 11375 (☎ 718/261-0534), is an organization that operates a meet-the-people program in Australia. It puts visitors in touch with residents who've expressed an interest in meeting Americans with similar interests and backgrounds. This is a great opportunity to experience Australia—off the tourist track. Visitors spend time with local residents, but don't stay in their homes. There's a $25 membership fee (individual or family). Send a self-addressed stamped business-size envelope for more information.

AUSRES (see "Homestays & Farmstays" below) arranges dinners in private homes at a cost of A$50 to A$70 (U.S. $40 to $56) per person.

Meet the People, P.O. Box 370, Randwick, NSW 2031 (☎ 02/314 6987; fax 02/314 6180), operates only in Sydney and specializes in familiarizing overseas visitors with everyday Sydney. Small groups of four to six people might go to a local home for lunch or dinner, stopping enroute to visit a supermarket or other untouristy spot. They specialize in matching local people with visitors who have the same interests. Prices for touring and guiding vary. Meet the People has a site on the Internet at http://www.meetoz.com.au/g_day.

These convenient places have all the kitchen equipment necessary for preparing a meal and often have a lounge (living room) in addition to one or two bedrooms. Sometimes meals are available, but rarely are serviced apartments licensed to serve alcohol. Daily cleaning service is usually included (but they don't wash dishes); all linens are supplied. Rates are generally lower than they would be for the same space at a comparable hotel. A "holiday flat" is basically the same thing as a serviced apartment, but without the daily cleaning service. Aussies are starting to use the term *all-suite hotel* to describe certain serviced apartments, and they are very similar.

HOMESTAYS & FARMSTAYS Staying with an Australian family is a great way to get to know the country. Many families throughout Australia, in big cities and small towns, love to have a visitor stay for a night or a few days. **Bed & Breakfast Australia,** P.O. Box 408, Gordon, NSW 2072 (☎ 02/498 5344; fax 02/498 6438), has been operating successfully for 16 years, matching up guests and hosts. All homes have been personally visited by Clare and Adrian Webster, owners of the company. Rates range from A$50 to A$65 (U.S. $40 to $52) per night for a single and from A$84 to A$98 (U.S. $67.20 to $78.40) per night for a double, including breakfast. Bed & Breakfast Australia offers three categories of rooms; in the top two categories guests normally have their own bath. In economy rooms, hosts and guests share the facilities.

Other firms to contact are **AUSRES/Australian Reservation Service,** 27–33 Raglan St., Suite 1, South Melbourne, VIC 3205 (☎ 03/9696 0422 or 13 10 66; fax 03/9696 0329); **National Bed & Breakfast Reservations,** "Lilybank" 75 Kamerunga Rd., Stratford, QLD 4870 (☎ 070/551 123; fax 070/581 990); **Bed & Breakfast Booking Service,** P.O. Box 298, Edgecliff, NSW 2027 (☎ 02/314 7203; fax 02/314 6803); or **West Coast Homestays,** P.O. Box 854, Hillarys, WA 6923 (☎ 09/401 8149; fax 09/307 2347).

The best way to experience rural life down under is to stay on a farm or station with a family, and there are many places to do this. Guests can try their hand at mustering or shearing or can simply lie back and enjoy the beautiful countryside and the hospitality of their hosts. Several companies specialize in arranging farm stays. If you're interested contact **Bed & Breakfast Australia** (see above); **AUSRES/Australian Reservation Service** (see above); **Australian Farmhost Holidays,** P.O. Box 65, Culcairn, NSW 2660 (☎ 060/29 8621; fax 060/29 8770); or **Host Farms Association,** c/o Intaussie (☎ 800/531-9222 in the U.S.). **Countrylink** provides train-farmstay holiday packages from Sydney (☎ 13 22 32).

If you decide to try a farmstay after arriving, you can contact the offices above or make reservations through any of the tourist offices listed in the city and state chapters.

YOUTH HOSTELS The YHA has 143 hostels spread around Australia. For information on this economical form of lodging open to all ages, contact either **Hostelling International/American Youth Hostels National Office,** P.O. Box 37613, Washington, DC 20013-7613 (☎ 202/783-6161 or 800/444-6111), or **Hostelling International-Canada, National Office,** 400-205 Catherine St., Ottawa, Ontario K2P 1C3 (☎ 613/237-7884 or 800/663-5777). Once in Australia, you should direct all questions to **Hostelling International/Australian Youth Hostel Association,** Level 3, 10 Mallet St., Camperdown, NSW 2050 (☎ 02/565 1699; fax 02/565 1325). Fees are around A$15 (U.S. $12) per night.

BED & BREAKFAST INNS I have to confess a partiality toward these cozy inns where rooms sometimes come without a bath but where you get a wonderful breakfast. Every city in Australia has at least a few, though finding them requires diligent sleuthing: They often don't advertise and aren't promoted by travel agents because some of them don't pay commissions. Not only are B&Bs cozier and less expensive than hotels, they also provide a level of hospitality matched only by that experienced at farm- and homestays.

The Bed & Breakfast Booking Service, P.O. Box 298, Edgecliff, NSW 2027 (☎ 02/314 7203; fax 02/314 6803), can make B&B reservations for you in Queensland, New South Wales, and Victoria. You also might like to order a copy of the 253-page book ***A Guide to Bed & Breakfast Australia & New Zealand*** by Jennie Fairlie, from The Crossing Press, 97 Hangar Way, Watsonville, CA 95076 (☎ 408/722-0711; fax 408/722-2749). This guide, which costs A$12.95 in Australia or U.S. $9.95 in the United States, gives the details for arranging accommodation in farmstays, homestays, and guesthouses throughout Australia and New Zealand, with an emphasis on Queensland.

CAMPING & CARAVAN PARKS If you're one of the many people who choose to rent a campervan or motor home down under and stay at caravan parks and campgrounds, you'll probably be pleasantly surprised by the facilities. Clean restrooms, communal kitchens, barbecues, electricity hookups, and laundry facilities are almost always provided. Many also have children's playgrounds, a small grocery store, and a recreation room. Nonpowered sites (without electrical hookup) are available for tent camping, and on-site caravans (mobile homes) can be rented.

One company that handles such rentals is **Brits: Australia Rentals,** 200 Gipps St., Abbotsford, Australia, VIC 3067 (☎ 03/9417 1888; fax 03/9416 2933). For reservations in North America, call Qantas Vacations in the United States at 800/641-8772 or 310/322-6359 or Goway Travel in Canada at 800/387-8850. You can also try **Maui Australia,** 9–11 Wollongong Rd., Arncliffe, Sydney, NSW 2205 (☎ 02/597 6155; 800/351-2317 within California; 800/351-2323 outside

California), or **Koala Camper Rentals,** 180 Great Eastern Hwy., Belmont, WA 6104, Australia (☎ 09/277 1000; fax 09/478 2565); for reservations in North America, write to 188 MacIntosh Dr., Stoney Creek, Ontario, L8E 4C1, or call 800/461-3226 in the United States and Canada (fax 905/664-4234).

HOME EXCHANGES For an authentic taste of living in Australia, you might like to exchange homes for a period of time. If that's the case, contact **Vacation Exchange Club,** P.O. Box 650, Key West, FL 33041 (☎ and fax 305/294-1448 or 800/638-3841).

11 Tips on Dining

Australian dining spots are almost identical to restaurants in other parts of the world, but a few cultural differences are worth mentioning. To begin with, on most menus everything is à la carte and every desired dish must be specifically ordered. This confuses some Americans, who are accustomed to finding bread and soup or salad included with all meals. Another caution for my compatriots: Don't ask for "doggie bags"; Aussies don't call them that, and they use them less frequently than we do. Don't be surprised when you have to ask for ice water and remember that no-smoking sections aren't as common there as they are in North America.

We Yanks are sometimes accused of being surly over what we consider slow service. Just keep in mind that if you want everything just the way it is at home, then home is where you should stay.

Labor costs are high in Australia, and many restaurants add a surcharge on weekends and holidays, when they must pay overtime wages to their staff. A 10% tip is customary in Sydney and other capital cities; in country areas the locals don't tip or leave a maximum of 10% for exceptionally good service.

Many restaurants, especially ethnic ones, offer take-away (take-out) meals. Because there's less labor involved, these are sometimes considerably less expensive than the sit-down variety.

Another way to save money on meals is to dine in BYO (Bring Your Own) restaurants. In these places, diners bring their own wine or beer, purchased at a bottle shop (liquor store), and avoid paying inflated restaurant prices. It's important to find out ahead of time if an establishment is licensed to sell spirits or if it's BYO. In all the restaurant write-ups in this book I've stated whether each place is BYO, but it's a good idea to confirm my information when you phone to make reservations. BYOs tend to be fairly casual, as are bistros and brasseries.

The "Aussie/Yankee Lexicon" and "Menu Savvy" sections in the Appendix of this book provide most of the dining definitions you'll need, but before you read any further I want to point out a few major vocabulary differences. An *entree* in Australia is a smallish first course, similar to an appetizer in the United States. A *main course* down under is an entree in America. *Tea* is sometimes used as a synonym for dinner. A *salad bar* doesn't consist of ingredients for making a tossed green salad but is a buffet of already mixed salads, such as coleslaw, three bean, potato, pasta, and so forth. And on the subject of salad, if you order a mixed green one it'll be served with your meal, not before it.

A *counter tea* is a casual meal served in a pub from 6 to 7:30 or 8pm. The cost is in the vicinity of A$5 to A$7 (U.S. $4 to $5.60). Pubs are also agreeable places to have lunch, but keep in mind that they serve food for only a limited time, usually from noon to 2:30pm, but sometimes just until 2pm. Pub lunches can be quite economical—curry and rice or roast of the day frequently costs only A$4 (U.S. $3.20). Meat pies and sandwiches can be had for even less. Every traveler should try a pie-and-a-pint pub lunch at least once. It's a significant part of the Australian dining scene—and they don't charge extra for the ambience.

Pub meals are great value, as are lunches and dinners at RSL (Returned Services League) clubs, which are like VFW clubs in the States. Another way to economize is picnicking in one of the country's many parks; most areas have barbecue facilities and clean restrooms.

If you stay in serviced apartments, you can do your own cooking, which is cheaper than dining out. Even if you stay in regular hotels or motels, you can avoid paying for breakfast by buying a box of cereal and a carton of milk. Refrigerators and coffee- and tea-making facilities are standard features of accommodations down under.

12 Tips on Shopping

There was a time when opals were about the only exciting purchase available to visitors in Australia, but that was before Aussie designers caught the attention of the world with their appealing colors and patterns. Nowadays, shoppers have fun buying traditional outback garments, contemporary fashions, and attractive souvenir items, as well as the pretty precious and semiprecious stones.

WHAT TO BUY Australian movies have helped popularize the **work clothes** worn by rugged bushmen and drovers. *The Man from Snowy River* launched Driza-bone riding coats onto the international fashion scene. Akubra hats and moleskin pants gained wide exposure in *A Town Like Alice, Phar Lap,* and *Crocodile Dundee.* These items and a variety of sturdy boots are manufactured and sold throughout Australia by the firms of R.M. Williams and Morrisons.

Sheepskin products are also popular, but I think travelers who are visiting both Australia and New Zealand will find that Kiwi shops offer more variety and better selection. On the other hand, Aussie designers can't be beat when it comes to colorful, creative **wool sweaters.** Ken Done and his contemporaries also turn T-shirts, sweatshirts, tea towels, aprons, and coasters into works of art.

Aboriginal arts and crafts—artifacts and paintings, bark pictures, wood carvings, and watercolors—make good investments as well as attractive mementos. You may have to go to the Northern Territory to buy Aboriginal art directly from the tribe that created it, but it's also sold at galleries throughout the country. Likewise, handcrafts produced in various states are available in craft shops in all the capital cities. **Glass** and **pottery** from Tasmania and South Australia are especially interesting. And don't overlook **Australian books** and **Australian wine** as good souvenir and gift items.

Melbourne is the best place for buying designer clothing. Australia's top fashion designers are Prue Acton, Carla Zampatti, Adele Palmer, Trent Nathan, Perri Cutten, and Anthea Crawford.

While **opals** can be purchased in almost every country, the best values are to be found in Australia, which produces 95% of the world's supply. Stores that sell opal jewelry are in all the major cities and provide the best shopping for the majority of visitors. Those who prefer to travel to the remote areas where the gemstones are mined might get a good buy on unset stones if they're knowledgeable and drive a hard bargain. Lightning Ridge, New South Wales, is the home of the black opal. Coober Pedy, South Australia, is the major center for white or milk opals. Other fields are at Mintabie in South Australia and Quilpie in Western Queensland.

When purchasing opals, you should consider three factors: color, brightness, and pattern. Very expensive stones should have a lot of red showing. Other visible hues, in descending order of value, are orange, green, and blue. A valuable opal should also be bright, and large splashes of strong color are preferable to numerous small ones.

The most expensive opals are solid, but doublets and triplets are usually found in souvenir-quality jewelry. Be sure you know what you're buying. Triplets consist of a thin veneer of opal glued on a plastic backing and topped with a clear quartz dome. A doublet is the same thing without the quartz top.

Most stores will deduct the Australian sales tax levied on opal jewelry when overseas purchasers show their passport and airline ticket. This can result in substantial savings.

WHERE TO BUY IT Nearly every city in Australia has a pedestrian **shopping mall** in the center of the downtown area. These handy precincts are usually dominated by one or two major department stores, like David Jones, which caters to the carriage trade, and Grace Bros., which appeals more to the middle market. Seemingly endless small shops surround the department stores and fill attractive arcades.

In addition to traditional shopping venues, there are large **public markets.** These bargain barns sell everything from fruits and vegetables to clothing, costume jewelry, and household goods. Some markets are similar to American swap meets and others are more reminiscent of European flea markets. Like the markets, **factory outlets** offer savings to the shopper with a good eye.

In all these cases, the Australian sales tax is included in the price of all goods and isn't added at the time of purchase.

Duty-free stores, which sell imported jewelry, perfume, porcelain figurines, handbags, liquor, cameras, and other items, intrigue many travelers because they sound like a great place to save money. However, while these stores are popular with Aussies and Kiwis, who must normally pay high rates of Customs duty on these luxury goods, the average American tourist will not find bargains in these shops. I encourage you to exercise caution when you feel yourself lured by the words *duty free.* The best bet is to call around before you leave home and find out what you'd pay for the items in your local stores. I've yet to find a perfume in a duty-free store at a lower price than I pay for the exact same thing in the States.

4 Settling into Sydney

Sydney is a collage, a patchwork of colors and textures. The sparkling waters of the harbor splash against the seawall surrounding the Royal Botanic Gardens. The lush green park abuts the downtown core, where smooth chrome-and-glass office towers turn the streets into shaded canyons. The neon lights of Kings Cross create a small rainbow at one side of the picture; while in The Rocks area the vivid hues of redevelopment have brightened the somber tones of working warehouses and convict-cut stone cottages.

The city's 3.7 million inhabitants present contrasts no less dramatic than the background against which they live. Women in English woolens take afternoon tea at one of the traditional old hotels and down the street the lines at McDonald's stretch out the door.

The parks are popular with "new" Australians, and on Sunday scores of extended families can be seen strolling and picnicking, with grandma in the same black dress she'd be wearing were she still in Greece or Italy. On the same day, the harbor will be full of top-of-the-line sailboats whose occupants could be models for trendy sportswear.

This chapter will help you familiarize yourself with Sydney and begin to settle in—it covers everything from a general city orientation to specifics on transportation, a quick rundown of facts you might need to know, and listings of accommodations and dining choices.

1 Orientation

ARRIVING

BY PLANE Sydney's **Kingsford Smith Airport** is well equipped to meet the needs of travelers. In the international terminal you'll find bureaux de change (open 6am–9pm), car-rental companies (Avis, Budget, Hertz, Thrifty), elevators, information, mail boxes, a message board, a post office for mail and faxes (open Mon–Fri 9am–5pm), shops (including Australiana, Australian produce, duty-free, and pharmacy), restaurants and bars, showers, strollers, a children's play area, a prayer room, wheelchairs, and trolleys (luggage carts). The airport is totally no-smoking. A shuttle bus transfers passengers between the international and the domestic terminals.

In addition to their counters at the airport, the following airlines have offices in Sydney: **Air France** (formerly UTA French Airlines), 12 Castlereagh St. (☎ 02/321 1030); **Air New Zealand,** 5 Elizabeth St. (☎ 02/223 4666); **Ansett,** at the corner of Oxford and Riley streets (☎ 02/13 13 00); **British Airways,** 64 Castlereagh St. (☎ 02/258 3200); **Canadian Airlines International,** 30 Clarence St. (☎ 02/299 7843); **Qantas,** 70 Hunter St. (☎ 02/691 3636; reservations—international 02/9957 0111, domestic 02/13 13 13), or 70 Hunter St. (☎ 02/693 3333); and **United,** 10 Barrack St. (☎ 02/13 17 77).

Getting into Town You can travel to the city center either on the **Kingsford Smith Airport Coach** for A$6 (U.S. $4.80) or on the **Airport Express** operated by State Transit for A$5 (U.S. $4) one-way or A$8 (U.S. $6.40) return for adults, half price for children under 12. Both leave the airport every 20 minutes for the half an hour trip into town. The buses run from 5am to 11pm and serve both the international and the domestic terminals.

The Kingsford Smith bus drops its passengers at the door of their hotel or motel; the Airport Express delivers people to one of 33 predetermined points, from which they must walk or take a taxi. A **taxi** to Sydney from the airport costs about A$22 (U.S. $17.60).

Departing passengers can arrange for the Kingsford Smith Airport Coach to pick them up at their hotel if they call at least an hour in advance (☎ 02/667 3221).

Premier Limousines (☎ 02/451 5901; mobile phone 015 270 077; fax 02/9975 1545) offers airport transfers for up to four people for A$60 (U.S. $48).

BY TRAIN Should you arrive by train from another Australian state, it's a short taxi ride to the city center from **Central Station** at the end of Pitt Street.

BY BUS The **Greyhound-Pioneer Australia terminal** is on the corner of Oxford and Riley streets, Darlinghurst (☎ 13 20 30 or 02/283 5977). The Sydney Coach Terminal is at Central Station, at the corner of Eddy Avenue and Pitt Street (☎ 02/281 9366).

BY CRUISE SHIP Should you arrive by cruise ship, you'll find that the **Overseas Passenger Terminal** is ideally located near The Rocks and Circular Quay, only a short distance from the Opera House.

BY CAR The **Pacific Highway** brings visitors from the north, the **Great Western Highway** is the main route to Sydney from the west, and the **Hume Highway** and **Princes Highway** enter Sydney from the south.

VISITOR INFORMATION

A plethora of information is available to Sydney's visitors. The **New South Wales Tourism Centre** at the international airport terminal is open daily from 6am until the last flight arrives. Its staff are helpful with hotel reservations and can sometimes arrange *very* favorable rates for those who didn't reserve in advance. They can arrange cruises and coach tours. Their free phone information service operates daily from 5am to 10pm (☎ 02/669 1583 or 669 1584).

Impressions

Sydney: It's part San Francisco. A bit of England. The flavor of New York.

—Airline advertisement (1980)

What's Special About Sydney

Beaches

- Manly Beach, just a short ferry ride from the central business district, where Norfolk pines line the boardwalk.
- Bondi Beach, known for great waves, with many trendy spots to eat nearby.

Museums

- Hyde Park Barracks, designed by convict architect Francis Greenway in 1818.
- The Australian National Maritime Museum, in Darling Harbour, with an exhibit on U.S.–Australian links.

For Kids of All Ages

- Sydney Aquarium, in Darling Harbour, where sharks swim inches away from you.
- Featherdale Wildlife Park, where you can cuddle a koala or kiss a kangaroo.

Activities

- A harbor cruise, which lets you admire the city from the water.
- Surfing—Narrabeen is the top spot.

Top Attractions

- Sydney Harbour, surely one of the world's most beautiful.
- Sydney Opera House, a world-famous landmark offering drama, orchestral concerts, opera, and more.

Shopping

- Queen Victoria Building, a restored Victorian beauty open seven days a week.

Sunday Selections

- Free entertainment around the Opera House, popular with locals and visitors alike.

Wonderful Walks

- From Circular Quay to Mrs. Macquarie's Chair, along the waterfront and around the Opera House.
- Through The Rocks, admiring cottages of convict-cut stone—lots of good shops and atmospheric pubs.

In the city center, information is available at the **Countrylink/New South Wales Travel Centre,** Transport House, at the corner of Margaret and York streets (☎ 02/231 4444; fax 02/232 6080). The staff at this well-stocked office, open Monday to Friday from 9am to 5pm, is ready and willing to answer questions and make reservations for you. The **Sydney Visitors Information Booth** (shared with Halftix), on Martin Place between Castlereagh and Elizabeth streets (☎ 02/235 2424), is a good place to get information on Monday to Friday from 9am to 5pm.

Daily from 9am to 5pm, the people at **The Rocks Visitor Centre and Exhibition Gallery,** 106 George St. (☎ 02/255 1788), answer questions about their part of town. Here you'll find displays, maps, brochures, an audiovisual presentation on the area's history, and a gift shop. The center is in a restored building from the 1860s, formerly used as the Sydney Sailors' Home.

You can get good tourist information at **NRMA Travel,** 151 Clarence St. (between Barrack and King streets) (☎ 13 11 22), if you're a member of an affiliated club—so be sure to bring your membership card. It's open Monday to Friday from 8am to 5pm and Saturday from 8:30 to 11:30am.

For information about the seaside suburb of Manly, contact **Manly Visitors Information Bureau,** South Steyne Street, Manly (☎ 02/9977 1088). It's open daily from 10am to 4pm; closed Christmas.

Interstate information is available by contacting the following: **Canberra Reservation Centre,** Wingello House, 1–12 Angel Place, 6th floor (☎ 02/233 3666); **Northern Territory Holiday Centre Helpline** (☎ 1800/621 336); **Queensland Government Travel Centre,** 75 Castlereagh St. (☎ 02/232 1788); **South Australian Government Travel Centre,** 247 Pitt St., mezzanine level (☎ 02/264 3375); **Tasmanian Visitor Information Network** (☎ 02/202 2022); **Tourism Victoria,** 403 George St. (☎ 02/299 2288); and **Western Australian Tourist Centre,** 247 Pitt St., mezzanine level (☎ 02/261 2031).

CITY LAYOUT

Sydney is Australia's largest and oldest city. Founded at the harbor, it has gradually spread inland and the metropolitan region now covers 1,730 sq. km (668 sq. miles)—an area considerably greater than that of sprawling Los Angeles. Sydney is about the same distance from the Equator as San Diego and enjoys a similar sunny climate.

Two major bodies of water—the South Pacific Ocean and the harbor, a major inlet of the ocean—have given Sydney its shape. The **harbor** divides the downtown core on the south from the suburbs, which stretch out to the north. The **Sydney Harbour Bridge** and a tunnel connect the two sides. The inland waterway's irregular coastline has determined where the most expensive real estate is and where the most picturesque neighborhoods have developed. The harbor has dozens of bays, separated by arms of land. From the bridge eastward are marinas filled with private yachts. West of the bridge is commercial and industrial activity. Just 11km (7 miles) to the east, large surf rolls up onto some of the most beautiful beaches in the world.

MAIN ARTERIES & STREETS Downtown Sydney has grown from **Circular Quay** (pronounced "key"), the terminal for dozens of ferries and fast catamarans that regularly cross the harbor, to the south along Macquarie, Elizabeth, Castlereagh, Pitt, and George streets. The major east–west thoroughfares are Bridge, Hunter, King, Market, and Park. The twisted maze of streets near the quay evolved from ruts created by bullock carts in colonial days. Now taxis, buses, and cars inch their way through the area. **Martin Place,** a pedestrian mall from Macquarie to George streets, is the city center's heart. While sleek modern buildings predominate here, some beautiful examples of colonial architecture remain on Macquarie Street. **Centrepoint Tower,** on Market Street between Pitt and Castlereagh, is a lofty, easy-to-spot landmark.

STREET MAPS Get maps of Sydney and the surrounding area from the **New South Wales Travel Centre,** 19 Castlereagh St. (☎ 02/231 4444). If you're a member of an affiliated club, get maps from **NRMA Travel,** 151 Clarence St. (☎ 13 11 22).

NEIGHBORHOODS IN BRIEF

Circular Quay Because of the harbor ferries coming and going frequently, the train station, and the bus stop, Circular Quay is a major transport hub. It's also a picturesque spot for strolling and has both indoor and outdoor eateries. The Opera House is only steps away at the end of Bennelong Point. From Circular Quay you get a great view of the Sydney Harbour Bridge, also known as "the coat hanger."

Sydney & Suburbs

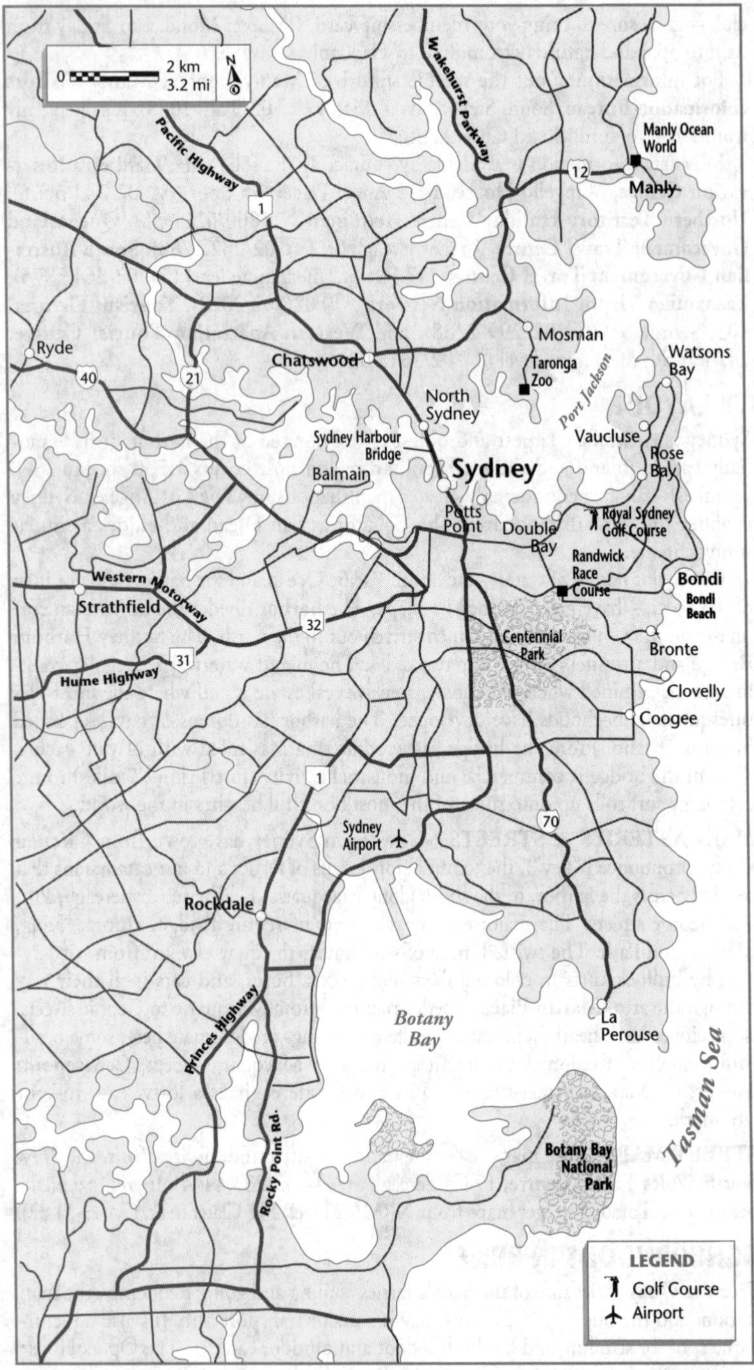

North Sydney Once a repository for the overflow of Sydney's office buildings and now an important business district in its own right, this area is located at the north end of the Harbour Bridge.

Northern Suburbs Beyond North Sydney, Chatswood, Lindfield, Killara, and other suburbs are strung out along Pacific Highway. The easiest way to get here is by train.

North Shore Communities Kirribilli and Neutral Bay are only two of the popular neighborhoods on the north side of the harbor. The Taronga Park Zoo is also here. Ferries provide frequent access.

Manly & the Northern Beaches Easily reached by ferry or fast catamaran, the seaside suburb of Manly is known for its wonderful beach. Other beaches along the coast north of the harbor entrance are Curl Curl, Dee Why, Collaroy, Avalon, and Whale.

The Rocks This is a historic area of colonial stone buildings that now house myriad shops and popular pubs, as well as a string of excellent restaurants. The Rocks is west of Circular Quay.

Millers Point Adjacent to The Rocks, Millers Point is a historic neighborhood where terrace houses and buildings of convict-cut stone line the streets. The waters of Walsh Bay and Darling Harbour form the perimeter on two sides. The city's observatory is the area's focal point.

Darling Harbour At the southwest edge of the main business district is this former industrial area that now hosts many sights of interest. Darling Harbour's convention center, Sydney Aquarium, exhibition center, waterfront promenade, Harbourside Marketplace, and Chinese garden were opened in 1988 as part of the bicentennial celebrations. The Australian National Maritime Museum has opened since then. This area is easily reached by monorail.

Kings Cross & Beyond About a mile from the city center lies the infamous red-light district called Kings Cross. Beyond "the Cross," attractive suburbs—Elizabeth Bay, Double Bay, Rose Bay, and Watsons Bay—hug the waterfront.

Paddington Inland from Double Bay, this Sydney neighborhood is a down-under version of New York's Greenwich Village.

Bondi & Other Southern Beaches Sydney's famous beaches face the South Pacific Ocean on both sides of the harbor entrance: to the south, Bondi, Bronte, Clovelly, and Coogee.

Parramatta This major manufacturing area is within the metropolitan region, about 45 minutes by train or RiverCat from the central business district.

2 Getting Around

BY PUBLIC TRANSPORTATION

State Transit operates an excellent network of buses and ferries in Sydney, coordinated with the urban and suburban trains run by CityRail. For **timetable information** on all State Transit lines, call the InfoLine (☎ 13 15 00 daily 6am–10pm). In addition, a monorail connects the city center to Darling Harbour. Be sure to pick up a copy of the **Sydney Transport Map** (a guide to train, bus, and ferry service) at the New South Wales Travel Centre or at any rail, bus, or ferry information office.

MONEY-SAVING PASSES Visitors who'll be using public transport frequently would be wise to purchase the **SydneyPass,** which includes three, five, or seven days'

Sydney Transportation Systems

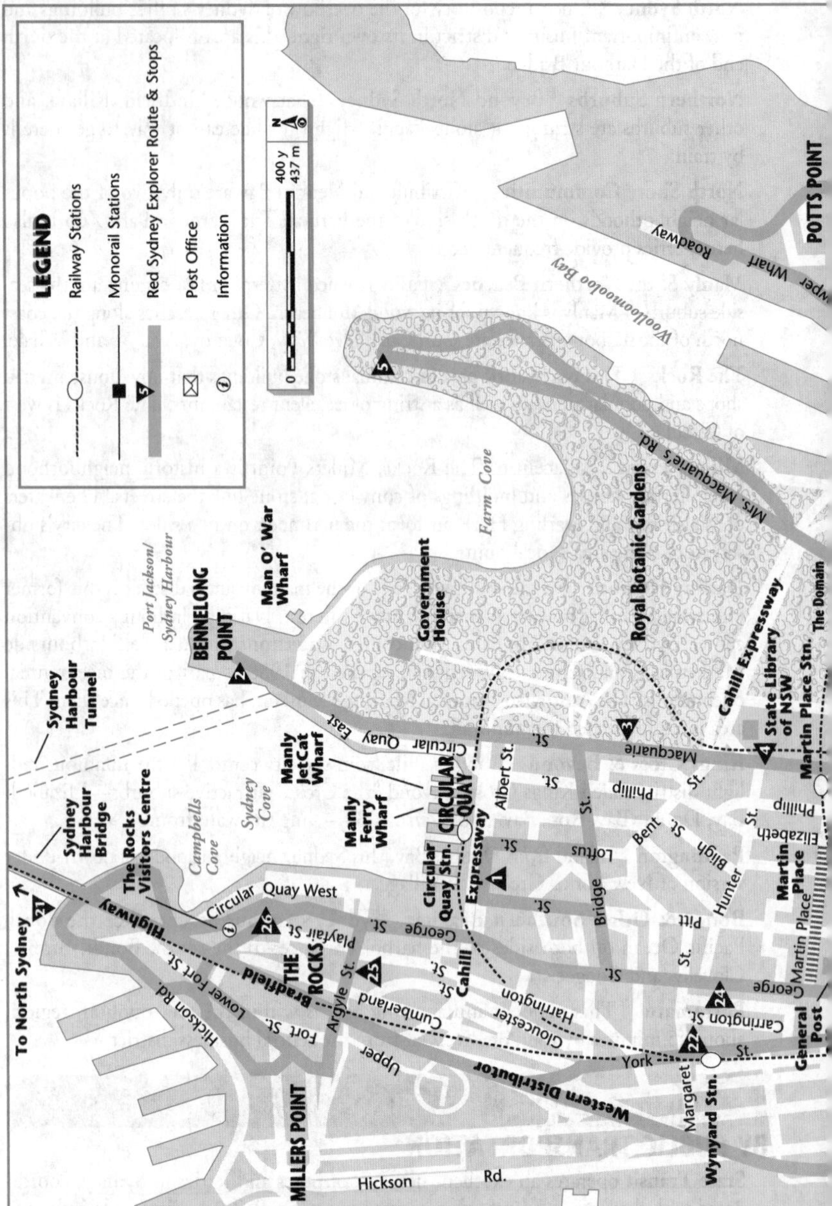

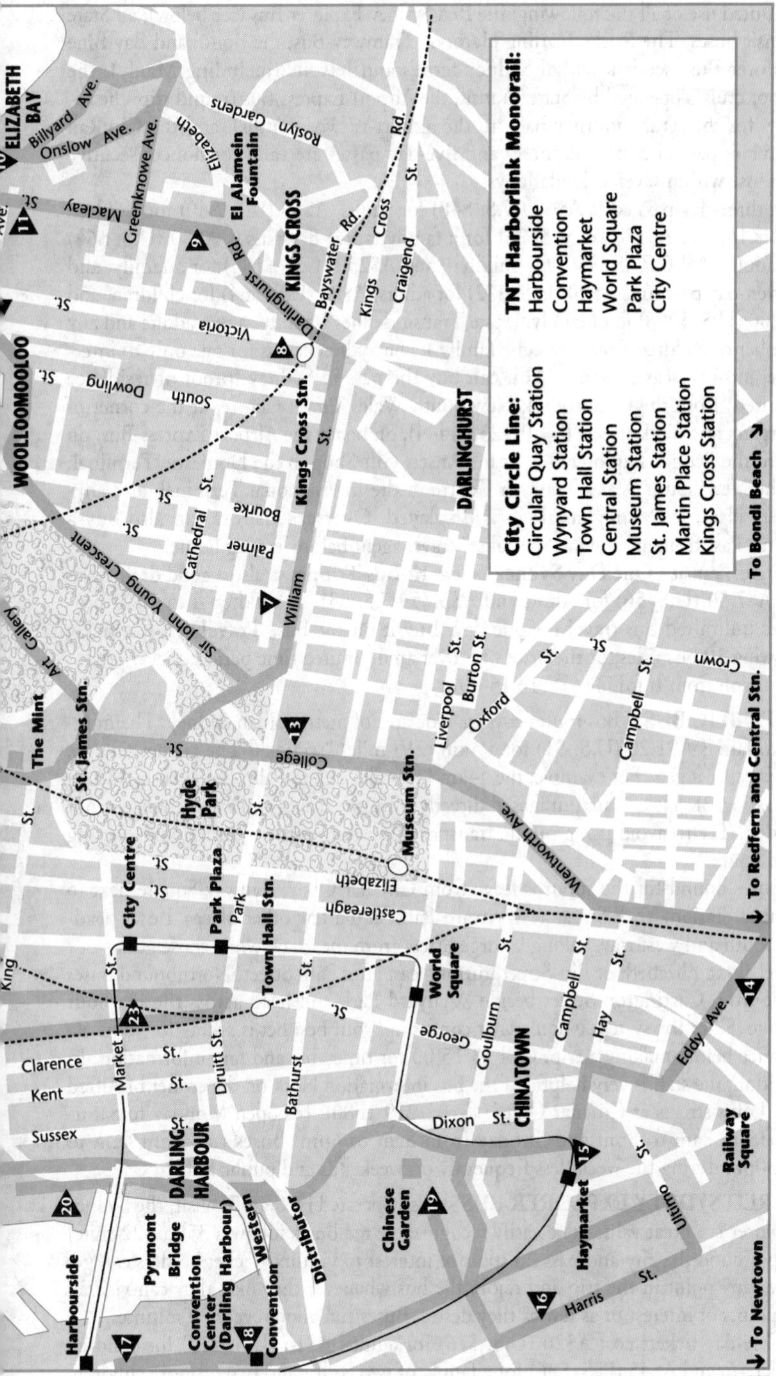

City Circle Line:
Circular Quay Station
Wynyard Station
Town Hall Station
Central Station
Museum Station
St. James Station
Martin Place Station
Kings Cross Station
TNT Harborlink Monorail:
Harbourside
Convention
Haymarket
World Square
Park Plaza
City Centre
ELIZABETH BAY
WOOLLOOMOOLOO
KINGS CROSS
DARLINGHURST
DARLING HARBOUR
CHINATOWN
El Alamein Fountain
The Mint
Hyde Park
Chinese Garden
Railway Square
Pyrmont Bridge
Convention Center (Darling Harbour)
Kings Cross Stn.
St. James Stn.
Museum Stn.
Town Hall Stn.
Billyard Ave.
Onslow Ave.
Greenknowe Ave.
Macleay St.
Roslyn Gardens
Darlinghurst Rd.
Bayswater Rd.
Kings Cross Rd.
Craigend St.
Victoria St.
Dowling St.
South
Cathedral St.
Palmer St.
Bourke St.
William St.
Sir John Young Crescent
Art Gallery
College St.
Liverpool St.
Burton St.
Oxford St.
Campbell St.
Crown St.
Wentworth Ave.
Elizabeth St.
Castlereagh St.
Park St.
King St.
Market St.
Clarence St.
Kent St.
Sussex St.
Druitt St.
Bathurst St.
George St.
Goulburn St.
Dixon St.
Hay St.
Eddy Ave.
Harris St.
Ultimo
Western Distributor
To Bondi Beach
To Redfern and Central Stn.
To Newtown

unlimited use of all the following: the Red Sydney Explorer Bus (see below), all State Transit buses, The Rocks-Darling Harbour Tramway Bus, the Bondi and Bay Blue Explorer Bus (see below), all Sydney ferries and JetCats (including Manly), the harbor cruises operated by State Transit, the Airport Express Bus (round trip; the validity for the return journey back to the airport is two months), and the CityRail "CityHopper" circuit. The three- and five-day passes are valid for nonconsecutive days' use within seven calendar days.

A three-day pass costs A$60 (U.S. $48) for adults, A$50 (U.S. $40) for children under 16, and A$170 (U.S. $136) for a family; a five-day pass is A$80 (U.S. $64) for adults, A$70 (U.S. $56) for children, and A$230 (U.S. $184) for a family; and a seven-day pass runs A$90 (U.S. $72) for adults, A$80 (U.S. $64) for children, and A$260 (U.S. $208) for a family. (State Transit defines a family as two adults and any number of children from the same family.) The SydneyPass is for sale only to interstate and overseas residents. You can buy the pass in Sydney (proof of residence required) from the Countrylink/New South Wales Travel Centre, at the corner of Margaret and York streets (☎ 02/231 4444), on board the Airport Express Bus, on board the Sydney Explorer Bus, at the Ansett Gift Shop in the Domestic Terminal, at the New South Wales Tourism Centre in the International Terminal, and anywhere else the SydneyPass logo is displayed. Overseas visitors can also buy a SydneyPass from an "Aussie Specialist" travel agent before leaving home.

State Transit's **One Day Sydney Network Bus Tripper** is also a good deal. Costing A$7.50 (U.S. $6) for adults and A$3.75 (U.S. $3) for children 4 to 16, it provides unlimited bus travel for one day. Buy it on the bus. **TravelTen** is a ticket allowing 10 bus rides for the price of 8 over an unlimited time period. Get more information from InfoLine (☎ 13 15 00).

BY PUBLIC BUS Bus routes cover a wide area of metropolitan Sydney. The minimum fare is A$1.20 (U.S. $1) for a 4km (2½-mile) "section." The farther you go, the cheaper it gets. For example, the 44km (27-mile) trek to Palm Beach costs A$4.40 (U.S. $3.52). Tickets are purchased directly from the driver and exact change is not needed. Try to avoid using public transportation during the morning and evening rush hours.

Buses bound for the suburbs leave from Circular Quay, Railway Square next to Central Station, York Street at Wynyard Park, and a few other places. Buses heading south and west travel along George Street from the quay, while those going east travel along Elizabeth or Pitt Street, turning east after Park Street. Northbound buses leave from Carrington Street beside Wynyard Park and head across the Harbour Bridge. Since the system is somewhat confusing, your best bet is asking for some assistance before making a trip. Call 13 15 00 for timetable and fare information. In addition, the staff is very helpful at the bus information kiosk on the corner of Alfred and Lofus streets at Circular Quay (☎ 02/219 1680). It's open Monday to Saturday from 8am to 8pm and Sunday from 8am to 6pm. Buses run from 4am to 11:30pm during the week, less frequently on weekends and public holidays.

BY RED SYDNEY EXPLORER BUS Also operated by State Transit, the Sydney Explorer is a great value. The easily recognizable red buses follow a 35km (22-mile) loop around the city and pass 26 spots of interest to visitors. Ticket holders can get off at any point in the trip and rejoin the bus whenever they like; they can visit all 26 points of interest or as few as they desire. Buses run about every 20 minutes.

One-day tickets cost A$20 (U.S. $16) for adults, A$15 (U.S. $12) for children under 16, and A$45 (U.S. $36) for a family of two adults and two or more children. Two-day Explorer tickets costs A$35 (U.S. $28) for adults, A$25 (U.S. $20) for children, and A$70 (U.S. $56) for a family. Tickets are valid on the day of purchase only, so it makes sense to start riding the Explorer Bus early in the day. The buses operate daily from 9:15am to 7pm and tickets are sold on board. Bus stops are marked with distinctive red-and-green Sydney Explorer signs. A Sydney Explorer ticket also entitles you to free travel on any State Transit bus within the Explorer route until midnight on the day of purchase.

BY BLUE BONDI & BAY EXPLORER BUS Cousin to the Red Sydney Explorer Bus, the Blue Bondi & Bay Explorer sets out every 30 minutes from Circular Quay on a path that passes through the harborside suburbs of Double Bay and Rose Bay en route to Watsons Bay. It also travels down the coast to Bondi Beach and the oceanfront suburbs of Bronte and Clovelly. On the way back to the city center, the Blue Bus passes the Royal Randwick Racecourse and Sydney Cricket Ground and Football Stadium. As with the Red Explorer Bus, ticket holders can get off at any point during the trip and rejoin the bus whenever they like.

A one-day pass costs A$20 (U.S. $16) for adults, A$15 (U.S. $12) for children, and A$45 (U.S. $36) for a family. Two-day Explorer tickets cost A$35 (U.S. $28) for adults, A$25 (U.S. $20) for children, and A$70 (U.S. $56) for a family.

BY BOOMERANG BEACH BUS Operated by a private company, the Boomerang Beach Bus (☎ 02/9913 8402) provides daily service and informative commentary from the suburb of Manly to Palm Beach. The continuous round trip follows the coastline and takes three hours. Fifteen stops are made along the 70km (43-mile) route; passengers can disembark and rejoin the tour wherever they like. Buses depart Manly hourly from 9:15am with a last departure at 2:15pm. Complimentary pick-ups are available from central points within Sydney. Advance reservations are advisable. The fare is A$20 (U.S. $16) for adults, A$15 (U.S. $12) for children and seniors, and A$60 (U.S. $48.00) for families.

BY FERRIES & JETCATS The most scenic way to get around Sydney is on one of the picturesque ferries or JetCats that regularly cross the harbor.

If you'd like to go to Manly and see the seaside suburb's ocean beach, take the ferry from no. 3 jetty at Circular Quay. The trip takes 35 minutes and costs A$3.60 (U.S. $2.90) for adults and A$1.80 (U.S. $1.45) for children one way. If you opt for the high-speed JetCat you'll leave from no. 2 jetty. The cost is A$4.80 (U.S. $3.85) for adults or children one way.

You can also take the ferry from no. 2 jetty to the Taronga Zoo, just across the harbor. At the wharf the ferry connects with a bus that carries passengers uphill to the entrance gates. A combined ferry, bus, aerial safari, and zoo admission ticket costs A$17 (U.S. $13.60) return (round trip). Children pay A$8.70 (U.S. $6.95).

Ferries operate daily from 5:30am to 12:30am. Other places that can be reached by ferry are Darling Harbour, Neutral Bay, Kirribilli, Cremorne, Balmain, Greenwich, Cockatoo Island, Hunters Hill, Meadowbank, and Parramatta. A one-way trip on the inner harbor costs A$2.60 (U.S. $2.10) for adults and A$1.30 (U.S. $1.05) for children. Frequency of service varies. For ferry information, call 13 15 00 or stop in the ferry information office opposite Wharf 4 at Circular Quay. It's open Monday to Saturday from 7:30am to 6:30pm and Sunday from 8:30am to 5:30pm.

BY HARBOUR EXPRESS Matilda Cruises (☎ 02/264 7377) operates **The Rocket Harbour Express,** which circumnavigates Sydney Harbour and cruises up the Parramatta River to the Homebush Bay Olympic Site. One ticket, costing A$20 (U.S. $16) for adults and A$12 (U.S. $9.60) for children, is valid for the whole day. Stops include Darling Harbour, the Sydney Aquarium, the Olympic Site,

Sydney Ferries

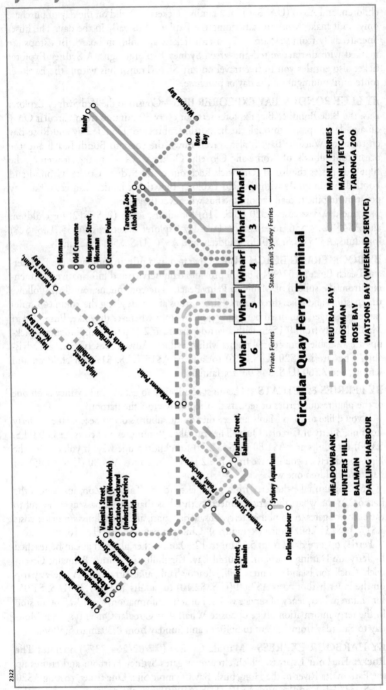

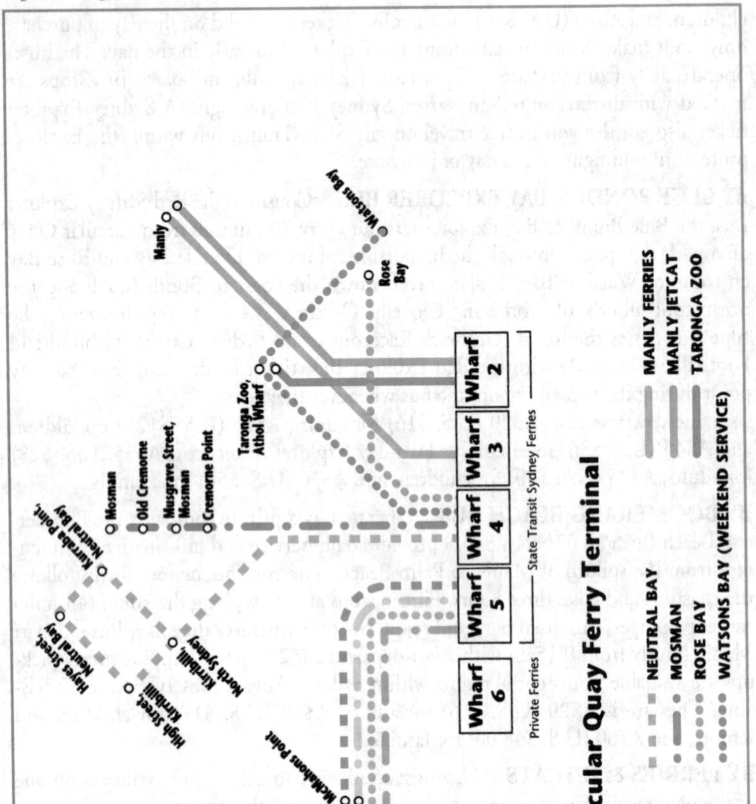

Circular Quay Ferry Terminal
Wharf 2
Wharf 3
Wharf 4
Wharf 5
Wharf 6
State Transit Sydney Ferries
Private Ferries
Watsons Bay
Manly
Rose Bay
Taronga Zoo, Athol Wharf
Mosman
Old Cremorne
Musgrave Street, Mosman
Cremorne Point
Neutral Bay
Kurraba Point
Hayes Street, Neutral Bay
Kirribilli
North Sydney
High Street, Kirribilli
McMahons Point
Darling Street, Balmain
Longnose Point, Birchgrove
Thames Street, Balmain
Sydney Aquarium
Darling Harbour
Elliott Street, Balmain
Valentia Street, Hunters Hill (Woolwich)
Cockatoo Dockyard (Industrial Service)
Greenwich
Wolseley Street, Drummoyne
Gladesville
Abbotsford
Meadowbank
John Street, Rydalmere
MANLY FERRIES
MANLY JETCAT
TARONGA ZOO
NEUTRAL BAY
MOSMAN
ROSE BAY
WATSONS BAY (WEEKEND SERVICE)
MEADOWBANK
HUNTERS HILL
BALMAIN
DARLING HARBOUR
2322

the Taronga Zoo, and Circular Quay. You can get on and off whenever you like between 9am and 5pm.

BY TRAIN Because of traffic congestion, it's usually quicker to get to your destination in Sydney and its suburbs by train rather than bus. In the central region, the **City Circle** train line runs underground. Stations on this route are Central, Town Hall, Wynyard, Circular Quay, St. James, and Museum. Off-peak return (round-trip) fares, which must be purchased after 9am, are the least expensive. The minimum one-way ticket is A$1.20 (U.S. 95¢).

CityRail's **CityHopper pass** costs A$2.20 (U.S. $1.75) and provides unlimited off-peak train travel for one day. Tickets are half price for children under 16 and can be used after 9am on weekdays and all day on weekends around the City Circle, including Milson's Point, North Sydney, Martin Place, and Kings Cross. The **Train Weekly** allows unlimited train usage for seven days between two stations you nominate. Information is available from InfoLine (☎ 13 15 00) and at the CityRail Host Centres opposite Wharf 4 at Circular Quay (☎ 02/224 2649; open daily 9am–5pm) and at Central Station (☎ 02/219 1977; open daily 6am–10pm).

State Rail operates CityRail service and Countrylink trains carrying passengers farther afield. For Countrylink reservations call 13 22 32 between 6:30am and 10pm; or you can stop in at the Countrylink Travel Centre, 11–31 York St. (☎ 02/224 4744; open Mon–Fri 8:30am–5pm), or the Countrylink Travel Centre at Circular Quay (open Mon–Fri 9am–5:30pm and Sat 8am–3pm).

BY MONORAIL Like the underground train, the speedy monorail connecting the central business district to Darling Harbour doesn't compete with vehicular traffic. Instead, Sydney's sleek state-of-the-art system glides over the heads of pedestrians and above congested streets. The system usually operates Monday to Saturday from 7am to midnight and Sunday from 8am to 9pm, but do check the hours on signs posted in the stations. The city center/Darling Harbour round trip takes approximately 12 minutes. Tickets cost A$2.50 (U.S. $2); children under 5 are free; an all-day monorail pass is A$6 (U.S. $4.80). The monorail connects with trains at Town Hall Station. For more information, call TNT Harbourlink at 02/552 2288.

BY TAXI

Sydney and its suburbs are well serviced by taxis. Fares are set by the Department of Motor Transport and all cabs are metered. Extra charges apply for a taxi request by phone, waiting time, luggage weighing over 25kg (55 lb.), and crossing the Harbour Bridge.

The main cab companies are **Taxis Combined Services** (☎ 02/332 8888), **RSL Cabs** (☎ 02/581 1111), and **Legion Cabs** (☎ 02/289 9000). All three accept American Express or Diners Club cards. Fares start at A$2 (U.S. $1.60) and go up about A97¢ (U.S. 78¢) per kilometer.

Taxis line up at ranks throughout the city, but I find it easiest to catch them in front of the big hotels. A light on the roof of the car indicates whether it's "vacant" or "engaged." To order modified vehicles for people with disabilities, call 02/339 0200.

A word of warning: The shift change of drivers takes place between 2:30 and 3pm, and during this time cabs will pick you up only if you're going in the direction of their company's base. Taxis also become scarce as soon as it starts to rain.

If you think you've been treated unfairly by a Sydney taxi driver, call the **Taxi Complaint Hotline** (☎ 02/9916 5244) or **Roads and Traffic Authority NSW** (☎ 02/218 6888) to file a complaint.

Networks & Resources

- **Students:** For travel information, contact the Student Travel Association (☎ 02/519 9866). The general information number at the University of Sydney is 02/692 2222. The YHA NSW Membership and Travel Centre is at 422 Kent St. (☎ 02/261 1111) and can help with membership, hostel bookings, and travel arrangements.
- **Gays & Lesbians:** To reach the gay and lesbian hotline, call 02/360 2211 between 4pm and midnight. For the Gay and Lesbian "What's On" line, call 02/319 6320 or 02/361 0655 (for 24-hour recorded information). *OutRage* is Australia's leading monthly magazine for gay men. *The Sydney Star Observer* is a free fortnightly (biweekly) newspaper. To reach the AIDS hotline, call 02/332 4000. The Bookshop Darlinghurst, 207 Oxford St., Darlinghurst (☎ 02/331 1103), near Taylor Square, is a good source of information and offers the most comprehensive supply of gay and lesbian literature in Australia.
- **Women:** See "Safety" in "Fast Facts: Sydney." The number of the Rape Crisis Hotline is 02/819 6565. You might also want to contact the Women's Refuge and Resource Centre, 61 Palace St., Petersham (☎ 02/560 1605). The YWCA, 5–11 Wentworth Ave. (☎ 02/264 2451), offers women and couples centrally located low-cost accommodations as well as counseling and community support services.

WATER TAXIS Should you wish to rent your own harbor transportation, try **Taxis Afloat** (☎ 02/9955 3222). The trip from Watsons Bay to Circular Quay costs about A$40 (U.S. $32) for two.

BY CAR

I suggest you take advantage of Sydney's good public transport and not rent a car. Traffic congestion is a problem and parking very limited (and expensive when you can find it). However, if you do decide to drive you'll be impressed with the quality of sign posting.

CAR RENTALS The big four (Avis, Budget, Hertz, and Thrifty) have desks at the airport. Car-rental agencies in Sydney include **Avis,** 214 William St. (☎ 02/357 2000); **Budget,** 93 William St. (☎ 02/339 8888); **Dollar,** Sir John Young Crescent (☎ 02/223 1444); **Hertz,** at the corner of William and Riley streets (☎ 02/360 6621 or 13 30 39); and **Thrifty,** 75 William St. (☎ 02/360 4055).

LIMOUSINES If you want your own chauffeur and limo, call **Premier Limousines** (☎ 02/451 5901; mobile phone 015 270 077).

FAST FACTS: Sydney

American Express Traveler's checks can be cashed at 92 Pitt St. (☎ 02/239 0666 or 886 1111) on Monday to Friday from 8:30am to 5:30pm and Saturday from 9am to noon.

Area Code Sydney telephone numbers are in the 02 area code.

Baby-Sitters The All Sydney Baby Sitting Service (☎ 02/521 3333) comes to your hotel and charges about A$8 (U.S. $6.40) per hour, with a four-hour minimum, plus traveling charges of A$8 (U.S. $6.40).

Business Hours Sydney **banks** are open Monday to Thursday from 9:30am to 4pm and Friday from 9:30am to 5pm. **Stores** are generally open Monday to Wednesday and Friday from 9am to 5pm, Thursday from 9am to 9pm, and Saturday from 9am to 5pm; many are also open Sunday from 10am to 4pm. Some shops stay open later on Friday (David Jones is open until 7pm, for instance) and some are open only until noon on Saturday.

Car Rentals See "Getting Around" earlier in this chapter.

Currency See "Money" in Chapter 3.

Currency Exchange In addition to the American Express office, you can cash traveler's checks at Thomas Cook, Kingsgate Shopping Centre, Kings Cross (☎ 02/356 2211), Monday to Friday from 8:45am to 5:15pm and Saturday from 9am to 1pm. The Thomas Cook office on the lower ground floor of the Queen Victoria Building, George Street, Sydney (☎ 02/264 1133), is open Monday to Wednesday from 9am to 6pm, Thursday from 9am to 9pm, Friday and Saturday from 9am to 6pm, and Sunday and public holidays from 11am to 5pm. The Interforex Money Exchanges, at no. 6 jetty, Circular Quay (☎ 02/247 2082), and 140 George St. (☎ 02/247 5555), are open daily from 8am to 9:30pm. Other Interforex Money Exchanges are at Darling Harbour and in the Pitt Street Mall.

While there are many Westpac banks in Sydney, one of the most convenient for tourists is at 47 George St., The Rocks (☎ 02/226 2388); it's open during regular bank hours (see "Business Hours" above).

Dentist For dental problems, contact the Dental Emergency Information Service, an official service of the Australian Dental Association (☎ 02/9962 6557).

Doctor Look under "Medical Practitioners" in the yellow pages of the Sydney directory.

Drugstores Most pharmacies (chemist shops) keep regular shopping hours, but Wu's Pharmacy, 629 George St. (☎ 02/211 1805), is open Monday to Saturday from 9am to 9pm and Sunday from 9am to 7pm.

Embassies/Consulates All embassies are in Canberra, the capital. Sydney is home to the following consulates: **Canada,** 5/111 Harrington St. (☎ 02/364 3000 or 364 3050); **New Zealand,** 14/1 Alford St. (☎ 02/247 1999); **United Kingdom,** 1 Macquarie Place (☎ 02/247 7512 or 1900/20273); and **United States,** 59 MLC Centre, 19–29 Martin Place (☎ 02/373 9200).

Emergencies In an emergency, dial 000 to summon an ambulance, the fire department, or the police.

Eyeglasses Replace lost or broken prescription glasses at OPSM Express, 383 George St., opposite the Strand Arcade (☎ 02/299 3061). It's open Monday to Wednesday and Friday from 8:30am to 5:15pm, Thursday from 8:30am to 7:15pm, and Saturday from 8:30am to 2:30pm. One-hour service is available.

Holidays See "When to Go" in Chapter 3. In addition, New South Wales observes Labour Day the first Monday in October.

Hospitals You'll find Sydney Hospital on Macquarie Street (☎ 02/228 2111).

Hotlines The following numbers may be useful in an emergency: Crisis Centre, 02/358 6577; Poison Information, 02/692 6111; and the Rape Crisis Centre, 02/819 6565.

Library The State Library of New South Wales is on Macquarie Street (☎ 02/230 1414).

Lost Property If you lost something at the airport, go to the Federal Airport Corporation's administration office on the top floor of the International Terminal (☎ 02/667 9583). If you left something in a taxi, phone the office of the taxi company. If you lost something on trains in New South Wales, go to 490 Pitt St., near the Central Railway Station, on Monday to Friday from 8:30am to 4:30pm (☎ 02/211 4535 or 02/211 1176). There's no general lost-property bureau in Sydney. Other than the above suggestions, go to the police station closest to where you lost the item.

Luggage Storage There's luggage storage at the Travellers' Information Service at Kingsford Smith Airport.

Newspapers The *Sydney Morning Herald* is the major metropolitan newspaper. *The Australian,* distributed across the country, is also widely read. *The International Herald Tribune* and *USA Today* are also available. The Sydney Library, 3rd level, Town Hall, receives most major overseas newspapers.

Photographic Needs Paxton's Photographics, 285 George St. (☎ 02/299 2999), is open Monday to Wednesday and Friday from 8:45am to 5:30pm, Thursday from 8:45am to 8pm, and Saturday from 9am to 4pm. Whilton Camera Service, 251 Elizabeth St. (☎ 02/267 8429), is open Monday to Friday from 8am to 6pm and Saturday from 8am to 2pm. Clock Tower 1 Hour Photo, at the corner of Harrington and Argyle streets, The Rocks (☎ 02/247 8396), offers fast photo processing.

Police In an emergency, dial 000 to reach the police.

Postal Code Central Sydney addresses have a 2000 postal code.

Post Office The General Post Office (GPO), 159–171 Pitt St., at Martin Place (☎ 02/13 13 17), is open Monday to Friday from 8:15am to 5:30pm and Saturday from 8am to noon. Letters can be sent to you c/o General Delivery, GPO, Sydney, Australia.

Restrooms In the central business district, you can avail yourself of the facilities in the Queen Victoria Building, any department store, or (outside of business hours) any hotel. In Darling Harbour, there are nice restrooms in the Harbourside Marketplace.

Safety Avoid The Rocks on Friday and Saturday around 11pm when the pubs close and Kings Cross in the wee hours. And, of course, stay out of parks and gardens after dark.

Taxes Sales tax is not added to purchases anywhere in Australia, and there's no GST. Sydney doesn't have a hotel tax.

Taxis See "Getting Around" earlier in this chapter.

Telegrams/Telex/Fax The least expensive way to send these is from a post office. Hotels will do it but will probably add a service charge.

Telephone Numbers As part of the telephone changeover, **in July 1996 all seven-digit phone numbers within the 02 area code will be changing to 02/9xxx xxxx and all six-digit numbers within the 02 area code will be changing to 02/91xx xxxx.** Note that the numbers listed as 02/99xx xxxx will remain unchanged.

Telephones The Telstra Pay Phone Centre, 130 Pitt St., has more than 48 pay phones for local or overseas calls.

Television Sydney has five TV stations: three commercial networks and two government-owned. Channel 1, SBS TV, offers multicultural programming; Channel 2, ABC (Australian Broadcasting Corporation), is the equivalent of PBS in the

United States; Channel 7, ATN, runs a variety of programs, including the NBC *Today* show with Katie Couric and Bryant Gumbel at 12:30am; Channel 9, TCN, shows excerpts from CBS and ABC news from the States, as well as *Murphy Brown, The Late Show with David Letterman,* and *Matlock;* this channel also airs an Australian version of *60 Minutes.* Channel 10, TEN TV, has varied programming, including *Seinfeld, Mad About You,* and *Melrose Place,* and CNN International runs day and night. The stations are required to run at least 40% Australian programming but manage to include a large number of U.S. shows.

Transit Information Call the InfoLine at 13 15 00 (daily 6am–10pm).

Useful Telephone Numbers News, 1199; phone directory assistance/information, 013; time, 1194; Traveller's Aid Society, 02/211 2469.

Weather For the local weather forecast, dial 1196.

3 Accommodations

An ultramodern room with a view? A traditional room in a cozy B&B? A room in an atmospheric pub? No worries—Sydney and its suburbs have them all, in all price ranges. Whether you want to be completely pampered, cook your own meals, or stay in a more homey environment, Sydney can accommodate you well.

General information can be found in "Tips on Accommodations" in Chapter 3. Note that most hotel rates are the same for a single or double occupancy, and where there's a single rate it's usually only slightly less than the double rate. Unless otherwise specified, the rates given below are for a double or twin room shared by two people and all rooms have a private bath. Hotel rates have remained fairly steady the last few years but are likely to climb as the city comes closer to hosting the Olympic Games in 2000. Happily, more and more B&Bs are opening, and these homey alternatives offer good value as well as warm hospitality.

***Note:* As part of the telephone changeover, in July 1996 all seven-digit phone numbers in the 02 area code will change to 02/9xxx xxxx and all six-digit numbers will change to 02/91xx xxxx. Phone numbers listed as 02/99xx xxxx will remain unchanged.**

The following rate categories apply for accommodations: **Very Expensive,** more than A$225 (U.S. $180); **Expensive,** A$131 to A$225 (U.S. $104.80 to $180); **Moderate,** A$81 to A$130 (U.S. $65 to $104); and **Inexpensive,** less than A$80 (U.S. $64).

INSIDER TIPS I recommend prebooking accommodations in Sydney, but if you're willing to take a chance on the city being "full up" when you arrive you may be able to get a great standby deal through the New South Wales Tourism Centre at the airport.

To save money, ask about weekend discounts, corporate rates, long-stay rates, off-season (May to August) rates, and lower rates available through Australian auto clubs, such as the NRMA. Special packages, like ones that include breakfast and a bottle of champagne for the normal rate, are also a good value, as are serviced apartments, which help save on dining costs. Hotel passes are discussed in "Tips on Accommodations" in Chapter 3. It never hurts to ask about a lower rate—when a property isn't full, they'd rather sell a room to you at a discount than have it be empty.

I also advise you to avoid minibars, where every item costs about 50% more than it would elsewhere, and hotel laundry service (you could buy new underwear for what some of them charge to wash it). It's also a good idea to avoid making phone calls

Central Sydney Accommodations

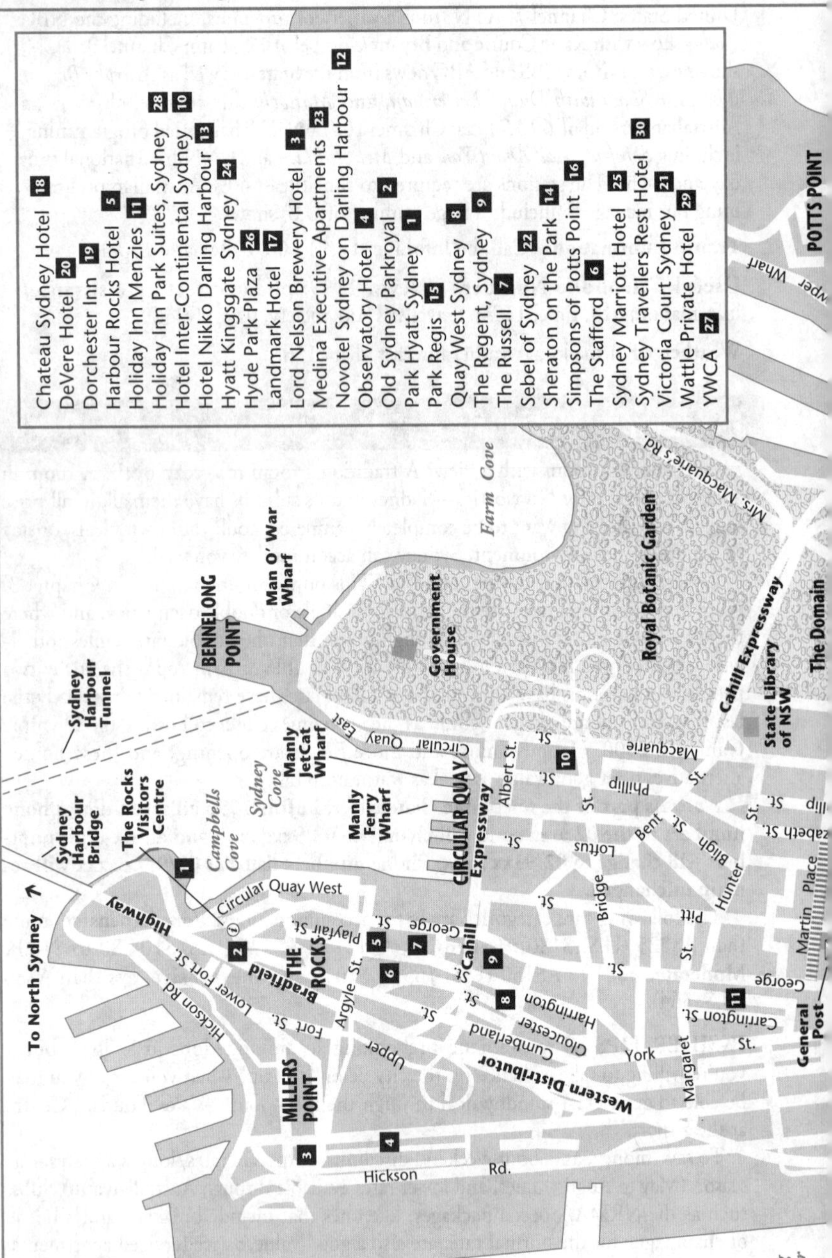

Chateau Sydney Hotel 18
DeVere Hotel 20
Dorchester Inn 19
Harbour Rocks Hotel 5
Holiday Inn Menzies 11
Holiday Inn Park Suites, Sydney 28
Hotel Inter-Continental Sydney 10
Hotel Nikko Darling Harbour 13
Hyatt Kingsgate Sydney 24
Hyde Park Plaza 26
Landmark Hotel 17
Lord Nelson Brewery Hotel 3
Medina Executive Apartments 23
Novotel Sydney on Darling Harbour 12
Observatory Hotel 4
Old Sydney Parkroyal 2
Park Hyatt Sydney 1
Park Regis 15
Quay West Sydney 8
The Regent, Sydney 9
The Russell 7
Sebel of Sydney 22
Sheraton on the Park 14
Simpsons of Potts Point 16
The Stafford 6
Sydney Marriott Hotel 25
Sydney Travellers Rest Hotel 30
Victoria Court Sydney 21
Wattle Private Hotel 29
YWCA 27
To North Sydney
Sydney Harbour Bridge
The Rocks Visitors Centre
Sydney Harbour Tunnel
Campbells Cove
Sydney Cove
BENNELONG POINT
Man O' War Wharf
Farm Cove
Manly JetCat Wharf
Manly Ferry Wharf
CIRCULAR QUAY
Circular Quay West
Circular Quay East
Government House
Royal Botanic Garden
Mrs. Macquarie's Rd.
Cahill Expressway
State Library of NSW
The Domain
POTTS POINT
Bradfield Highway
THE ROCKS
MILLERS POINT
Hickson Rd.
Lower Fort St.
Fort St.
Argyle St.
Playfair St.
George St.
Cahill Expressway
Upper Fort St.
Cumberland St.
Gloucester St.
Harrington St.
Western Distributor
York St.
Margaret St.
Carrington St.
George St.
General Post
Martin Place
Pitt St.
Hunter St.
Bligh St.
Bent St.
Loftus St.
Bridge St.
Phillip St.
Albert St.
Macquarie St.
Darling Harbour

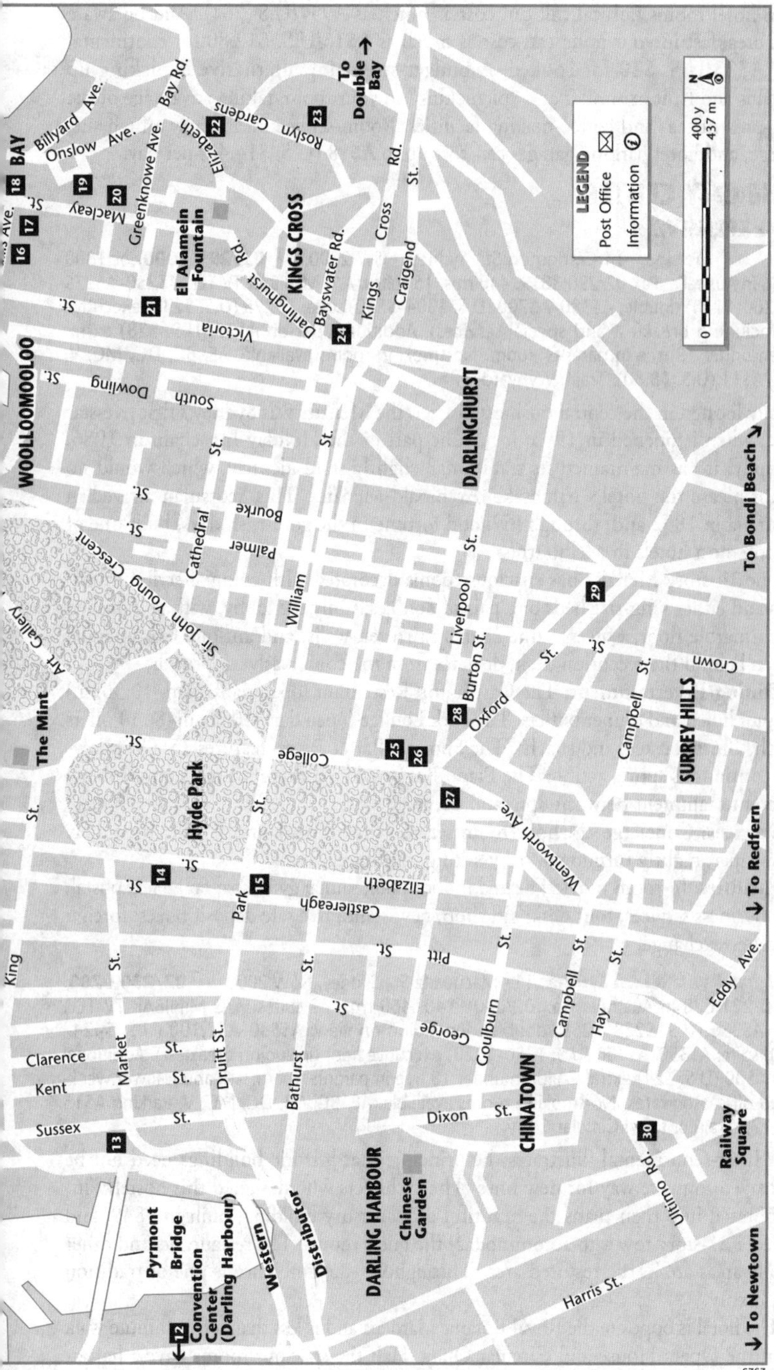
WOOLLOOMOOLOO
BAY
KINGS CROSS
DARLINGHURST
SURREY HILLS
CHINATOWN
DARLING HARBOUR
Hyde Park
The Mint
El Alamein Fountain
Chinese Garden
Railway Square
Pyrmont Bridge
Convention Center (Darling Harbour)
Western Distributor
To Double Bay →
To Bondi Beach
To Redfern
To Newtown
LEGEND
Post Office
Information
400 y
437 m
Billyard Ave.
Onslow Ave.
Bay Rd.
Greenknowe Ave.
Elizabeth
Roslyn Gardens
Macleay St.
Victoria St.
Darlinghurst Rd.
Bayswater Rd.
Kings Cross Rd.
Craigend St.
South Dowling St.
Cathedral St.
Bourke St.
Palmer St.
William St.
Sir John Young Crescent
Art Gallery
Liverpool St.
Burton St.
Oxford St.
Crown St.
Campbell St.
College St.
Wentworth Ave.
Elizabeth St.
Castlereagh St.
Park St.
Pitt St.
George St.
King St.
Market St.
Clarence St.
Kent St.
Sussex St.
Druitt St.
Bathurst St.
Goulburn St.
Dixon St.
Hay St.
Eddy Ave.
Ultimo Rd.
Harris St.
2323

from hotel rooms (a local call can cost as much as A95¢/U.S. 76¢). And be aware that breakfast in your hotel can cost as much as A$16/U.S. $12.80 for continental and A$25/U.S. $20 for cooked. A budget-stretching alternative is picking up muffins and fruit or similar and "picnicking" in your room, taking advantage of the ever-present tea- and coffee-making facilities. Room-service meals carry a high surcharge, and hotel parking garages can cost up to A$18 (U.S. $14.40) per day.

IN THE CITY CENTER

VERY EXPENSIVE

Holiday Inn Menzies. 14 Carrington St., Sydney, NSW 2000. ☎ **02/299 1000,** or 1800 221 066 in Australia. Fax 02/290 3819. 440 rms, 15 suites. A/C MINIBAR TV TEL. A$250–A$275 (U.S. $200–$220) double; A$380–A$700 (U.S. $304–$560) suite; A$295 (U.S. $236) executive floor (including breakfast and special services). Additional person A$35 (U.S. $28) extra. Children under 18 free in parents' room. No-smoking rooms available. AE, BC, DC, MC, V. Parking A$11 (U.S. $8.80). Train: Wynyard.

Ideally located in the central business district, the Menzies was Sydney's first five-star hotel when it opened in 1963; it became part of the Holiday Inn chain in 1986. Happily, it has maintained its traditional, slightly staid identity, which would no doubt please the hotel's namesake, Archibald Menzies. This Scotsman arrived in Australia in 1852 and, through his good fortune in the gold-rush days, built one of the foremost hotels in Melbourne.

The 14-story Menzies has spacious rooms decorated with colonial-style furnishings and either king-size beds or a pair of doubles. Only the lobby, with its polished black marble floor, Queen Anne chairs, mirrored walls, and antique Coromandel screen behind the reception desk, deviates from the conservative approach.

Dining/Entertainment: The Carrington Restaurant (open daily 6am–10:30pm) features lunch and dinner buffets. The Park Lounge (open daily 10:30am–8pm) offers lunch, afternoon tea, and snacks. The Sporters Bar & Bistro features 15 TVs showing continuous sports action. The Piano Bar provides a more intimate atmosphere, with entertainment between 8pm and 11pm.

Services: Concierge, 24-hour room service, shoeshine, laundry, valet, free daily newspaper, nightly turndown, baby-sitting, massage.

Facilities: In-room movies; heated indoor pool; sauna; gym; spa; fax, telex, postal, and business services; tour desk; gift shop; newsstand; free safe deposit boxes; foreign currency exchange.

Hotel Inter-Continental Sydney. 117 Macquarie St., Sydney, NSW 2000. ☎ **02/230 0200,** or 1800/221 828 in Australia. Fax 02/240 1240. 460 rms, 42 suites. A/C MINIBAR TV TEL. A$285–A$335 (U.S. $228–$268) double, depending on view; A$530–A$2,100 (U.S. $424–$1,680) suite; A$350–A$400 (U.S. $280–$320) executive floor (including breakfast). Additional person A$30 (U.S. $24) extra. Children under 18 free in parents' room. Ask about lower weekend and off-season rates. No-smoking rooms available. AE, BC, CB, DC, MC, V. Parking A$15 (U.S. $12). Train or ferry: Circular Quay.

The Inter-Continental illustrates the principle that historic buildings need not be destroyed to make way for new ones. The architects who designed this hostelry incorporated into their plans the beautiful old Treasury building, built in 1849, and added a 31-story tower to accommodate the guest rooms. The restaurants and other public areas are in the restored area. Throughout, the ambience is one of tradition and luxury.

The hotel is opposite the Royal Botanic Gardens and is less than a five-minute walk from the Opera House and Circular Quay. Half the spacious rooms have a harbor view. Regular rooms have queen-size or twin beds, while king-size beds are found only in the suites. In addition to the standard refrigerator and coffee- and tea-making facilities, the rooms come equipped with toasters. All baths have phones and hairdryers, and two rooms are designed to accommodate handicapped guests.

Dining/Entertainment: Tea, light lunches, and cocktails are served in the skylit central Cortile, a lobby bar surrounded by the sandstone arcades and arches of the Treasury's old-world facade. Lunch is served in this area from noon to 3pm and tea is available from 3 to 5:30pm; snacks may be ordered from 5:30 to 11pm. The Treasury is the hotel's fine-dining venue. The 30 Something Lounge on the 31st floor is a good spot for a drink with a panoramic view. Café Opera offers informal dining daily from 6:30am to midnight. Sketches Pasta Bar & Bistro serves freshly made pasta (for more details, see "Dining" below).

Services: Concierge, 24-hour room service, shoeshine, laundry, valet, free daily newspapers, nightly turndown, massage, baby-sitting.

Facilities: One of the best hotel fitness clubs in the city: the Clark Hatch Fitness Centre, with indoor pool, sauna, spa, gym with exercise equipment, power-walking classes, and massage therapists; business center, hair/beauty salon, gift shop, newsstand, early-arrivals/late-departures lounge.

✪ **The Regent, Sydney.** 199 George St., Sydney, NSW 2000. ☎ **02/238 0000,** or 1800/222 200 in Australia. Fax 02/251 2851. 594 rms, 64 suites. A/C MINIBAR TV TEL. A$270–A$375 (U.S. $216–$300) double depending on view; A$500–A$2,000 (U.S. $40–$1,600) suite. Children under 16 free in parents' room. Weekend packages and no-smoking floors available. AE, BE, CB, MC, V. Parking A$12 (U.S. $9.60). Train or ferry: Circular Quay.

The Regent established a benchmark for hotel luxury and service when it opened in 1982, and it subsequently won the Australian government's National Tourism Award for Excellence in Accommodation several years in a row. Each room features an Italian marble bath, blackout curtains for those who wish to sleep during the day, a choice of king-size or twin beds, three dual-line phones, modern Tasmanian oak furnishings, fresh flowers, a remote-control TV and videos, a fax machine, lights on dimmers, and towels that are weighed regularly to ensure adequate thickness for the pampered guests. Each suite has its own telescope.

A three-story atrium rises from a lobby floor of gleaming South Australian granite, and each level is rimmed with brass balustrades and a profusion of greenery. The 36-story hotel has a great location near Circular Quay and The Rocks and expansive views from most of its rooms.

Dining/Entertainment: Kable's, the Regent's fine-dining restaurant, is one of the best spots in the city. The cuisine and service here are truly outstanding. The Club Bar has an elegant country-club ambience. The Mezzanine Lounge is a delightful place for light lunches, afternoon tea, or after-theater snacks. The Lobby Restaurant is open from 6:30am to 1am. The George Street Bar is an upmarket pub. For more details on these venues, see "Dining" below.

Services: Concierge, 24-hour room service, laundry, valet, nightly turndown, shoeshine, baby-sitting, massage, free daily newspapers, complimentary in-room movies; floor stewards to greet guests, pack/unpack, reconfirm airline reservations, and provide myriad other services; a Mercedes-Benz limousine ready for airport transfers.

Facilities: Outdoor pool, health club, business center, hair salon, gift shop, newsstand.

Sheraton on the Park. 161 Elizabeth St., Sydney, NSW 2000. ☎ **02/286 6000,** or 1800/80 2782 in Australia. Fax 02/286 6686. 510 rms, 49 suites. A/C MINIBAR TV TEL. A$315–A$450 (U.S. $252–$360) double; A$750–A$3,000 (U.S. $600–$2,400) suite. Children under 12 free in parents' room. Ask about lower weekend rates and packages. No-smoking floors available. AE, BC, DC, MC, V. Parking A$12 (U.S. $9.60). Train: St. James. Monorail: City Centre.

The Sheraton on the Park's impressive lobby, where marble columns rise three stories from the highly polished floor, sets the tone for this rather formal, sophisticated property. Muted colors are used throughout, and the long upstairs halls are accented by original art commissioned for the hotel—each with its own portrait light.

The hotel is across from Hyde Park, and 70% of its rooms have a park or a city view. Each offers contemporary furnishings, a marble bath with the shower separate from the tub, three phones, a remote-control TV, and an in-room safe. Some rooms and all suites also have CD players. Guests can choose between twin beds or a king-size.

Dining/Entertainment: The Botanica Brasserie offers all-day dining. The Conservatory is an elegant area where a cascading fountain, lily pads, and lots of window area give you the sense of sitting in a conservatory. Traditional high tea is served from 2pm, and light lunches and cocktails are also offered. Modern Australian cuisine is served in Gekko, where there's a walk-through wine cellar and an indoor garden of native plants.

Services: Concierge, 24-hour room service, laundry, valet, shoeshine, free daily newspapers, nightly turndown, baby-sitting, massage, valet parking, limo service.

Facilities: Rooftop pool, large health club, spa, sauna, steamroom, foreign currency exchange.

Serviced Apartments

Quay West Sydney. 98 Gloucester St., Sydney, NSW 2000. ☎ **02/240 6000.** Fax 02/240 6060. 129 apts. A/C MINIBAR TV TEL. A$270–A$360 (U.S. $216–$288) one-bedroom apt; A$485 (U.S. $388) two-bedroom apt; A$1,000–A$1,300 (U.S. $800–$1,040) penthouse for one to six. Additional person A$30 (U.S. $24) extra. Ask about lower long-stay rates and weekend packages. AE, BC, DC, JCB, MC, V. Parking A$14 (U.S. $11.20).

Well located between The Rocks and the central business district, Quay West is a good choice if you'll be staying longer than a few days, if you'll be entertaining, or if you prefer cooking for yourself. The apartment hotel occupies the top 31 floors of a tower; the first 7 floors contain offices. Each apartment has a fully equipped kitchen, laundry facilities, a CD player, two remote-control TVs, and a VCR. The outdoor sundeck on the 24th floor offers a fantastic view, as do the huge windows in many of the apartments. Kitchens feature marble counters, dishwashers, ovens, stoves, and refrigerators. A grocery shopping service will deliver supplies from the food hall at David Jones department store. Two-bedroom apartments have king-size beds and two baths, and all have very modern furnishings. Every penthouse has two bedrooms, two baths (one with a Jacuzzi), and a choice of a city or harbor view. Request a "north view" if you want to see the Opera House.

Dining/Entertainment: Harringtons Restaurant and Bar is open daily for breakfast and Monday to Saturday for dinner.

Services: 24-hour room service, complimentary daily newspaper.

Facilities: Pool, sauna, spa, gym, recreation deck, business center, safe deposit boxes.

EXPENSIVE

Ⓢ **Sydney Marriott Hotel.** 36 College St., Sydney, NSW 2010. ☎ **02/361 8400,** or 1800/02 5419 in Australia. Fax 02/361 8599. 241 rms and suites. A/C MINIBAR TV TEL. A$180 (U.S. $144) standard double; A$300 (U.S. $240) junior suite; A$450–A$600 (U.S. $360–$480) premier suite. Additional person A$20 (U.S. $16) extra. Children under 12 free in parents' room. Ask about lower weekend rates and dollarwise honeymoon packages. No-smoking floors available. AE, BC, DC, MC, V. Free parking. Train: Museum.

I learned of the Marriott from thoughtful readers who wrote to me about their enjoyable stay. Having now visited this "new-ish" property, I can see why they were so impressed. In addition to the amenities you might expect (like a hairdryer, bathrobes, a small refrigerator, tea- and coffee-making facilities, three phones), the Marriott outfits all quarters with plates, cutlery, a toaster, a wetbar, and a microwave. One-third of the rooms also have hotplates and cooking utensils, and each has its own iron and ironing board. These conveniences contribute to the overall user-friendly atmosphere. The oversize triangular bathtubs in every room provide a luxurious touch.

Dining/Entertainment: The Park Bench Coffee Shop, adjacent to the informal welcoming lobby, is open daily. Windows on the Park Restaurant overlooks Hyde Park and offers à la carte meals. Drinks and live entertainment are available in Archibald's Cocktail Bar.

Facilities: Heated rooftop pool and sundeck with great view, health club, small gym, steam room, sauna, spa.

Serviced Apartments

$ Holiday Inn Park Suites, Sydney. 16–32 Oxford St., Sydney, NSW 2010. ☎ **02/331 7728,** or 1800/22 1813 in Australia. Fax 02/360 2583. Reservations can be made through Holiday Inn Worldwide at 800/HOLIDAY in the U.S. and Canada. 135 apts. A/C MINIBAR TV TEL. A$190 (U.S. $152) one-bedroom apt for one or two; A$215 (U.S. $172) two-bedroom apt for one or two. Additional person A$15 (U.S. $12) extra. Children under 12 free in parents' apt. Ask about lower rates on weekends and June–July; lower weekly rates; lower rates through Aussie auto clubs. AE, BC, DC, MC, V. Free parking. Train: Museum.

Holiday Inn Park Suites is the most luxurious of the centrally located apartment hotels I've listed. Each of the one- or two-bedroom units has a spacious kitchen with a dishwasher, an oven, and a full-size refrigerator. In addition, every apartment has its own washing machine, dryer, iron, ironing board, and balcony with table and chairs. "Harbourside" apartments are on the 7th to 15th floors and overlook the water.

Dining/Entertainment: The licensed Park Brasserie is open daily and Clancy's supermarket is conveniently across the street.

Services: Room service (7am–9pm), laundry, baby-sitting.

Facilities: Heated outdoor pool, spa, sauna.

Hyde Park Plaza. 38 College St., Sydney, NSW 2000. ☎ **02/331 6933,** or 1800/22 2442 in Australia. Fax 02/331 6022. 182 suites. A/C MINIBAR TV TEL. A$185 (U.S. $148) double; A$195 (U.S. $156) suite; A$210 (U.S. $168) executive floor. Additional person A$15 (U.S. $12) extra. Ask about lower weekend and seasonal rates and lower rates through Aussie auto clubs. AE, BC, DC, MC, V. Free parking. Train: Museum.

The rooms at the Hyde Park Plaza range in size from studios to "executive flexi-suites" that accommodate up to eight. All the spacious quarters have full kitchens, either a dining table or a breakfast bar, attractive contemporary furnishings, tub/shower combinations, VCRs, irons, ironing boards, and windows that open. The two-bedroom apartments also have walk-in closets and full-size refrigerators. Rooms on the Oxford Street side have balconies.

Dining/Entertainment: Hyde Park Plaza has a licensed restaurant open daily.

Services: Concierge, laundry, free daily newspaper.

Facilities: Rooftop sundeck, spa, sauna, heated pool, gym.

MODERATE

Park Regis. 27 Park St. (at Castlereagh St.), Sydney, NSW 2000. ☎ **02/267 6511,** or 1800/221138 in Australia. Fax 02/264 2252. 112 rms, 8 suites. A/C TV TEL. A$130 (U.S. $104) double; A$160 (U.S. $128) suite. Additional person A$15 (U.S. $12) extra. Children under 14 free in parents' room. Ask about lower rates available through Aussie auto clubs. No-smoking floor available. AE, BC, DC, MC, V. Free parking. Monorail: Park Plaza. Train: Town Hall.

The hotel occupies the first 15 floors of a 45-story building near Hyde Park, the Queen Victoria Building, and Sydney Tower. Condominiums fill the other floors, and a licensed restaurant is adjacent. The recently refurbished average-size rooms are light, attractive, and modern. All have the standard coffee- and tea-making facilities and a refrigerator; the baths have shower only. Front rooms have park and city views, but even without a view the room rate is a good value.

Dining/Entertainment: The hotel's restaurant offers a continental breakfast at a reasonable price.

Services: Concierge, room service (7am–10pm), laundry.

Facilities: Outdoor pool.

INEXPENSIVE

YWCA. 5–11 Wentworth Ave., Sydney, NSW 2010. ☎ **02/264 2451.** Fax 02/283 2485. 124 rms (16 with bath); 14 suites. A$60 (U.S. $48) double without bath, A$85 (U.S. $68) double with bath; A$15 (U.S. $12) per person in dormitory (four people sharing; maximum stay three nights). Additional person A$10 (U.S. $8) extra, including children under 12. Children under 4 free in parents' room. No-smoking. BC, MC, V. Parking moderate charge. Train: Museum.

Central Sydney's YWCA (Young Women's Christian Association) has convenient, inexpensive accommodations. The rooms are a bit spartan, but those familiar with college dormitories should feel at home. The rooms with a bath have tub/shower combinations and coffee- and tea-making facilities; all beds are twins, and one room and three baths are equipped for handicapped travelers. TV lounges and laundry facilities are available. Aerobics and yoga classes are held on the premises. A cafeteria adjacent to the lobby is open daily.

A Bed-&-Breakfast Inn

$ **Wattle Private Hotel.** 108 Oxford St. (at Palmer St.), Darlinghurst (Sydney), NSW 2010. ☎ **02/332 4118.** Fax 02/331 2074. 12 rms. MINIBAR TV TEL. A$80 (U.S. $64) double. Additional person A$10 (U.S. $8) extra. Rates include continental breakfast. BC, MC, V. Parking not available. Bus: Taylor Square.

I visited this place on Melbourne Cup Day and found a merry group of guests gathered around a TV in the breakfast room. Michael Wu, the congenial host, was enjoying the prerace program as much as the others, and I had the feeling I was in a big family home.

The Wattle's attractive exterior is best described as "remodeled Edwardian." The house, built between 1900 and 1910, has been altered more than once. Luckily, the Federation-period stained-glass windows remain in the breakfast room. Upstairs (four stories, no elevator or "lift"), each guest room has large windows that make it bright. The decor is a hodgepodge of French provincial headboards, Chinese vases, tropical fans, Victorian high ceilings, and contemporary bedspreads, but all quarters are clean and comfortable, and the mattresses are firm. Each room has coffee- and tea-making facilities and a small refrigerator. Laundry facilities are on the premises.

IN KINGS CROSS & VICINITY

VERY EXPENSIVE

Sebel of Sydney. 23 Elizabeth Bay Rd., Elizabeth Bay, NSW 2011. ☎ **02/358 3244,** or 1800/222 266 (reservations only) in Australia. Fax 02/357 1926. 166 rms, 23 suites. A/C MINIBAR TV TEL. A$265 (U.S. $212) double; from A$450 (U.S. $360) suite; A$1,300 (U.S. $1,040) Presidential Suite. Additional person A$25 (U.S. $20) extra. Children under 12 free in parents' room. Ask about much lower weekend and off-season rates. No-smoking rooms available. AE, BC, DC, MC, V. Free parking. Train: Kings Cross.

In the inner suburb of Elizabeth Bay, about a block from the bright lights of Kings Cross, the Sebel has long been the choice of the theatrical set. It has hosted such

Family-Friendly Accommodations

Holiday Inn Park Suites, Sydney *(see p. 105)* No other central-city hostelry feels more like a home away from home. Each roomy unit has a full kitchen and its own washing machine and dryer. The heated pool is popular with kids, and the management can organize baby-sitters.

Manly Paradise Motel and Beach Plaza Apartments *(see p. 114)* What kid wouldn't want to be right across the street from the beach? The apartments are spacious and have full kitchens, balconies, and laundry facilities—and there's a pool on the roof. Another fun bonus is going back and forth to Sydney on a ferry or JetCat.

Novotel Sydney on Darling Harbour *(see p. 115)* A pool and tennis courts add to the "kid appeal" of this place, but the biggest factor is location. The adjacent Darling Harbour development boasts dozens of quick and casual places to dine, a playground for small fry, the National Maritime Museum, the Powerhouse Museum (with lots of hands-on exhibits for the younger set), and the Sydney Aquarium. The Novotel likes families so much that children under 16 get a free breakfast daily and a children's menu is available in the restaurant. Another plus: Access is by monorail or ferry.

luminaries as Elton John, Bob Hope, Rex Harrison, Lauren Bacall, Rod Stewart, Glenda Jackson, and Bette Davis, to name a few.

The stars are attracted by the hotel's reputation for excellent personal service. For Richard Harris, a certain type of rolled oats was imported from Britain; Elton John's wedding reception was held in the ballroom, and cases of his favorite champagne are always kept on hand when he's in residence. Rex Harrison lived in the Sebel for three months while he performed locally. Happily, it isn't just recognizable guests who receive this mollycoddling. Everyone is called by name; the restaurant and bar hours can be adjusted to suit individual needs; and shoes left outside the door are shined overnight. More important, the security is very tight. The Beatles wanted to stay at the Sebel but were asked to go elsewhere because it was feared that their fans would disturb the other guests.

The spacious rooms have traditional furnishings, including built-in mahogany cabinets, windows that open, and terry robes. In the junior suites, luxury suites, and magnificent penthouse, the decor is "theatrical" and facilities include minikitchens, VCRs, and audiocassette systems. Guests have a choice of queen- or king-size beds, and about half of the accommodations offer a view of the marina at Rushcutters Bay. A nearby park is ideal for jogging.

Dining/Entertainment: An à la carte restaurant and cozy bar are on the premises.

Services: Concierge, 24-hour room service, laundry, valet, nightly turndown, free daily newspaper, shoeshine, baby-sitting.

Facilities: Rooftop outdoor pool, gym, sauna, business center, gift shop.

EXPENSIVE

Chateau Sydney Hotel. 14 Macleay St., Potts Point, NSW 2011. ☎ **02/358 2500,** or 1800/22 1412 (reservations only) in Australia. Fax 02/358 1959. Reservations can be made through Flag International at 800/624-3524 in the U.S. and Canada. 94 rms, 2 suites. MINIBAR TV TEL. A$120–A$180 (U.S. $96–$144) double, depending on view; A$195 (U.S. $156) executive floor; A$350 (U.S. $280) suite. Additional person A$15 (U.S. $12) extra. Children under 12 free in parents' room. Ask about lower weekend rates that include continental breakfast and about lower winter rates. AE, BC, DC, MC, V. Free parking. Train: Kings Cross, about 1km (1/2 mile) away. Bus: 311 from Circular Quay.

Many rooms here offer expansive views of the peaceful sailboats on Elizabeth Bay, and all have been recently renovated and redecorated in light neutral colors. Each has a tub/shower combination. Queen- and king-size beds are available. In-room movies, hairdryers, clock radios, bathroom scales, and tea- and coffee-making facilities are provided. I've received many letters from readers reporting superb service.

Dining/Entertainment: The licensed Poolside Brasserie offers a view and provides casual dining day and night.

Services: Concierge, 24-hour room service, free daily newspapers, shoeshine, laundry, valet, baby-sitting.

Facilities: Outdoor heated pool.

Hyatt Kingsgate Sydney. William Street, Kings Cross, NSW 2011. ☎ **02/356 1234.** Fax 02/356 4150. 389 rms, 6 suites. A/C MINIBAR TV TEL. A$175–A$190 (U.S. $140–$152) double; A$215–A$230 (U.S. $172–$184) executive floor (including continental breakfast); A$750 (U.S. $600) suite. Additional person A$30 (U.S. $24) extra. Children under 12 free in parents' room. No-smoking rooms available. AE, BC, DC, MC, V. Parking A$15 (U.S. $12). Train: Kings Cross.

The surrounding colorful nightlife makes this 33-story hotel a great option for late-night revelers. It's also an ideal place for those who wish handy access to the good dining spots in the area. The city center is about 2km (1 mile) to the west, and the train provides frequent inexpensive transportation. Those who opt for a taxi will pay about A$4 (U.S. $3.20).

The Hyatt is a three-tower complex whose rooms are connected by a maze of corridors and elevators. The recently renovated rooms are spacious, each with a tub/shower combination, a king-size bed or twin beds, and windows that open.

Dining/Entertainment: Yoshino is a Japanese restaurant; Red is an all-day restaurant and bar open daily.

Services: 24-hour room service, nightly turndown, laundry, valet, concierge, baby-sitting.

Facilities: Outdoor pool, business center, hair salon, gift shop, newsstand.

Landmark Hotel. 81 Macleay St., Potts Point, NSW 2011. ☎ **02/368 3000,** or 1800/02 3665 in Australia. Fax 02/358 6631. 450 rms, 13 suites. A/C MINIBAR TV TEL. A$160–A$180 (U.S. $128–$144) double; A$160–A$180 (U.S. $128–$144) Parkroyal Floor (including cocktails and business amenities); A$985 (U.S. $788) Presidential Suite, Parkroyal Floor. Extra bed A$25 (U.S. $20). Children under 19 free in parents' room. Ask about weekend packages. No-smoking rooms available. AE, BC, DC, MC, V. Parking A$9 (U.S. $7.20). Train: Kings Cross, about 1km (1/2 mile) away. Bus: 311 from Circular Quay.

The Landmark Hotel, in the pleasant suburb of Potts Point about 3km (almost 2 miles) east of central Sydney, offers excellent views of the city and Sydney Harbour. Those using the Explorer Bus will find that stop no. 10 is in front of the hotel. The bright and airy rooms feature modern Tasmanian oak furnishings and pastel decors; both king- and queen-size beds are available. As in all Sydney's five-star hostelries, the rooms at the Landmark include clock radios, hairdryers, tea- and coffee-making facilities, small refrigerators, and in-room movies; terry robes are provided free if requested. All suites feature walk-in closets, a shower stall separate from the tub, and double sinks. Facilities for the handicapped have been provided throughout.

Dining/Entertainment: All the hotel's several food and beverage outlets are on the ground floor. Cafe Maclacy (open daily until midnight) is a popular spot for Sunday brunch. Genoi serves authentic Japanese cuisine. The Point, boasting a tile floor, mahogany doors with stained-glass transoms, and dark wooden chairs, has the feel of a San Francisco bistro; it serves breakfast.

Services: Concierge, 24-hour room service, nightly turndown, free daily newspaper, shoeshine, laundry, valet, baby-sitting.

Facilities: Outdoor pool, gift shop.

A Bed-&-Breakfast Inn

✪ **Simpsons of Potts Point.** 8 Challis Ave., Potts Point, NSW 2011. ☎ **02/356 2199.** Fax 02/356 4476. 14 rms. A/C MINIBAR TV TEL. A$140 (U.S. $112) double; A$155 (U.S. $124) queen room; A$245 (U.S. $196) Cloud Suite (including private spa). Children under 12 not allowed. BC, MC, V. Free parking. Train: Kings Cross, about 1km (1/2 mile) away. Bus: 311 from Circular Quay.

Simpsons was designed in 1892 by John Bede Barlow, one of Sydney's best-known colonial architects. This elegant mansion was built to be the family residence of John Lane-Mullins, MLC, a member of the New South Wales Colonial Parliament. Carefully restored in 1988, it won the New South Wales State Tourism Award the following year for excellence in accommodation.

The house is imbued with the genteel ambience usually associated with bygone eras. Beautiful stained-glass windows grace the lounge and halls and some of the guest rooms. Imported English fabrics have been used on upholstered pieces as well as for bedspreads and draperies. Most of the furniture is antique. A French Pleyel piano is in the lounge, and every room has framed reproductions of Ellis Rowan's Australian wildflower paintings (copied from the originals in Sydney's Powerhouse Museum). Classical music is played in the lounge and dining area.

The guest rooms are furnished with clock radios, hairdryers, ceiling fans, and small refrigerators; some have queen-size beds. Four rooms have tub/shower combinations; the others have showers only. Terry robes are available on request, and tea- and coffee-making facilities are provided all day in a picturesque courtyard conservatory.

Dining/Entertainment: Breakfast in the conservatory is complimentary with a stay of three or more nights and with Cloud Suite accommodation or is available for A$10 (U.S. $8).

Services: Laundry, free daily newspaper.

MODERATE

A Bed-&-Breakfast Inn

Victoria Court Sydney. 122 Victoria St., Potts Point, NSW 2011. ☎ **02/357 3200** or 1800/63 0505 in Australia. Fax 02/357 7606. 22 rms. A/C TV TEL. A$99–A$115 (U.S. $79.20–$92) double; A$165 (U.S. $132) deluxe double with sundeck or honeymoon suite with balcony. Additional person A$15 (U.S. $12) extra. Rates include buffet breakfast. AE, BC, DC, MC, V. Parking free in a security area. Train or bus: Kings Cross.

Two elegant Victorian terrace homes have been joined and restored to create this B&B on the edge of Kings Cross. The property is named after Australian poet Henry Kendall (1830–82), an ancestor of the owner. All rooms have ceiling fans, showers (no tubs), and clock radios; four have small refrigerators. Queen- and king-size beds are standard. The honeymoon suite has a four-poster queen-size bed and a balcony. Tea- and coffee-making facilities are located in a pretty plant-filled conservatory and an adjacent cozy sitting room. Comments in the visitors' book reflect guests' appreciation of the old-world character and friendly service.

Dining/Entertainment: Breakfast is served in the glass-ceilinged conservatory with a bubbling fountain.

Services: Laundry, baby-sitting.

Serviced Apartments

Dorchester Inn. 38 Macleay St., Potts Point, NSW 2011. ☎ **02/358 2400.** Fax 02/357 7579. 14 apts. A/C TV TEL. A$95 (U.S. $76) studio double; A$160 (U.S. $128) executive studio or

Readers Recommend

De Vere Hotel, 44 Macleay St., Potts Point, NSW 2011 (☎ 02/358 1211; fax 02/358 4685). *"The De Vere Hotel, in the Potts Point area of Sydney, charges A$45 for two people. Buses for everything are out the front door and the hotel staff—all shifts—were wonderful. We made our arrangements through the information desk at the airport."*
—Capt. Tom Allor, Farmington, Mich., U.S.A.

Author's Note: The regular rate at the De Vere is A$65 to A$75 (U.S. $52 to $60) but, as mentioned in "Visitor Information" earlier in this chapter, the airport information office often offers dollarwise deals.

---

one-bedroom apt; A$140 (U.S. $112) two-bedroom apt. Additional person A$15 (U.S. $12) extra. AE, BC, DC, MC, V. Parking A$8 (U.S. $6.40). Train: Kings Cross. Bus: 311.

In this hundred-plus-year-old mansion on the same block as the Chateau Sydney, the tiny reception desk consumes most of the space in the tiny lobby. The inn's decor is colonial, its charm clearly old world. Each of the apartments is spacious, bright, and cheerful. Ten studio, two one-bedroom, and two two-bedroom units are available. Some have tub/shower combinations, but most have showers only. All have full kitchens and some have queen-size beds. The management can arrange baby-sitting.

$ **Medina Executive Apartments.** 70 Roslyn Gardens, Elizabeth Bay, NSW 2011. ☎ **02/356 7400** or 1800/808 453 in Australia. Fax 02/357 2505. 58 studio apts. A/C TV TEL. A$100 (U.S. $80) double (special rate for Frommer's readers). Additional person A$12 (U.S. $9.60) extra. No-smoking rooms available. AE, BC, DC, MC, V. Parking free in a security area. Train: Kings Cross.

The Medina Apartments are in residential Elizabeth Bay, between Kings Cross and scenic Rushcutters Bay, about 3km (2 miles) from central Sydney. The studio apartments are bright, airy, and immaculate. Rooms open onto a six-story atrium with cascading green plants. Each unit has a kitchenette, a small dining table and two chairs, and double, queen-size, or twin beds. Twelve apartments have tub/shower combinations, but the rest have showers only.

Dining/Entertainment: Medina lacks a restaurant or bar, but the Cuisine Courier service, which delivers meals from more than 40 local restaurants, is available, and a grocery shop is nearby. Guests may use the rooftop barbecue, from which there's a great view.

Services: Concierge, valet, baby-sitting.

Facilities: Guest laundry.

IN THE ROCKS & MILLERS POINT

VERY EXPENSIVE

✪ **Observatory Hotel.** 89–113 Kent St., Sydney, NSW 2000. ☎ **02/256 2222** or 1800/806 245 in Australia. Fax 02/256 2233. 100 rms and suites. A/C MINIBAR TV TEL. A$335–A$405 (U.S. $268-324) double; A$500–A$1,250 (U.S. $400–$1,000) suite. Additional person A$30 (U.S. $24) extra. Children under 14 free in parents' room. AE, BC, DC, JCB, MC, V. Parking A$15 (U.S. $12). Bus: 339, 431, or 433 to Millers Point.

The area's first choice in luxury accommodation, the Observatory offers a turn-of-the-century Australian ambience and traditional furnishings—including cloisonné objets d'art, Irish-Georgian furniture, and the finest draperies, upholstery, and carpeting. The fireplace in the elegant Drawing Room was removed from Elizabeth Bay House when this historic home was being remodeled. Because of the relatively small number of rooms, guests enjoy attentive personal service. Each room features a safe, an umbrella, terry robes, slippers, a hairdryer, a remote-control TV, a CD player, a VCR, four two-line phones, and a fax line; the suites have fax machines. A free video library is available from the concierge. The rooms boast the most responsive heating/cooling system I've ever experienced in a hotel. Second-floor rooms are reserved for nonsmokers and have doonas. The spacious marble baths include heated towel racks and two-headed shower stalls separate from large tubs. Executive suites have a separate living room, and junior suites have a large sitting area. (Room 313 is my favorite junior suite.) The state-of-the-art health club includes a flotation tank, and arriving overseas guests are offered a free float to help them recover from jet lag. Location is the only drawback to this outstanding hotel—it's a 10-minute walk to George Street. The Observatory is an Orient Express Hotel, and if it's in your budget I highly recommend making this boutique hotel your home away from home.

Dining/Entertainment: The Orient Café serves breakfast and lunch daily and dinner on weekends. The candlelit Galileo Restaurant, an elegant fine-dining option, features handmade silk wall coverings (see "Dining" later in this chapter). The Globe Bar has a wonderful clubby feel (see "Sydney After Dark" in Chapter 5).

Services: Concierge, 24-hour room service, newspaper delivery, dry cleaning/laundry, nightly turndown, twice-daily maid service, valet parking.

Facilities: Gorgeous 20-meter chemical-free indoor pool (fiber optics in the ceiling over the pool are in the pattern of Southern Hemisphere constellations); sauna, steam room, flotation tank, state-of-the-art health club; tennis courts, business center.

Park Hyatt Sydney. 7 Hickson Rd., The Rocks, Sydney, NSW 2000. ☎ **02/241 1234,** or 1800/222 188 in Australia. Fax 02/256 1555. 158 rms and suites. A/C MINIBAR TV TEL. A$480–A$620 (U.S. $384–$496) double; A$700–A$750 (U.S. $560–$600) executive studio; A$850 (U.S. $680) premier suite; A$3,000 (U.S. $2,400) Governor Suite. Extra bed A$30 (U.S. $24). Children under 18 free in parents' room. Ask about lower weekend rates and packages. No-smoking rooms available. AE, BC, DC, MC, V. Parking A$15 (U.S. $12). Train or ferry: Circular Quay.

The Park Hyatt occupies an enviable position in the Campbell's Cove area of Sydney Harbour. This location affords spectacular views of the Opera House, the harbor, and the city and has attracted such guests as Billy Joel and Frank Sinatra. Seemingly every possible luxury has been incorporated into the rooms. Guests have a choice of either king-size or twin beds; all rooms have remote-control curtains (sheer and blackout), double-glazed windows for total quiet, three two-line phones, stereo systems including CD players, VCRs, walk-in closets, dressing rooms, safes, and a shower shall separate from the tub in a marble bath. The loan of videos and CDs is complimentary, and fax machines are available (they come in all suites). Each of the 33 executive studios has two balconies and a telescope.

Dining/Entertainment: Verandah at the Park, the hotel's casual dining area, is open daily from 6:30am till late. No. 7 at the Park is for formal dining with a spectacular waterfront view. The Bar, which has a fireplace, resembles an English club. In the health club is a juice bar.

Readers Recommend

Old Sydney Parkroyal, 55 George St., The Rocks, NSW 2000 (☎ 02/252 0524, fax 02/251 2093). *"In Sydney, we found the Old Sydney Parkroyal in The Rocks to be terrific. The staff was wonderful and couldn't do enough to meet our needs."*

—Chad and Colleen Seymour, Scottsdale, Ariz., U.S.A.

Services: Concierge, butler (several on each floor), 24-hour room service, nightly turndown, free newspaper, laundry, shoeshine, valet, baby-sitting, massage.

Facilities: Outdoor pool, health club, gym, steam room, sauna, spa, business center, lobby shop.

EXPENSIVE

Harbour Rocks Hotel. 34–52 Harrington St., The Rocks, Sydney, NSW 2000. ☎ **02/251 8944,** or 1800/251 210 in Australia. Fax 02/251 8900. 55 rms. MINIBAR TV TEL. A$165 (U.S. $132) double. Additional person A$20 (U.S. $16) extra. Children under 16 free in parents' room. AE, BC, DC, MC, V. Parking A$15 (U.S. $12), across the road. Train or ferry: Circular Quay.

Location is the biggest advantage of this four-story hotel, for many of Sydney's premier attractions are within a short walk. The building is over 100 years old, and some of the rooms were once workmen's cottages. All rooms are clean and tidy and have ceiling fans, small refrigerators, free in-house videos, tea- and coffee-making facilities, clock radios, and either twin or double beds. There's a luggage lift (elevator), but guests must climb the stairs. One ground-floor room is equipped for the handicapped.

Dining/Entertainment: The Harbour Rocks Cafe overlooks a leafy balcony and provides indoor and outdoor dining. All meals are served daily in this casual café. A continental breakfast costs A$8 (U.S. $6.40) and a full buffet breakfast runs A$12 (U.S. $9.60). The Harbour Rocks Bar is open until 10pm daily.

Services: Limited room service, laundry, baby-sitting.

Facilities: Coin-operated laundry.

Serviced Apartments

✪ **The Stafford.** 75 Harrington St., The Rocks, Sydney, NSW 2000. ☎ **02/251 6711.** Fax 02/251 3458. 61 apts. A/C TV TEL. A$170 (U.S. $136) studio double; A$185 (U.S. $148) executive studio; A$195 (U.S. $156) one-bedroom apt; A$210 (U.S. $168) executive one-bedroom; A$195 (U.S. $156) terrace house; A$235 (U.S. $188) penthouse. Additional person A$15 (U.S. $12) extra. Children under 16 free in parents' room. Ask about lower weekly and weekend rates and lower rates through Aussie auto clubs. AE, BC, DC, MC, V. Parking A$15 (U.S. $12). Train or ferry: Circular Quay.

Ideally located in the historic Rocks area, where atmospheric pubs, shops, and dining spots abound, the six-story Stafford offers harbor and Opera House views from the top three floors. The property consists of seven two-story terrace houses dating from 1870 to 1895 and 54 modern apartments. All units have modern furnishings, tub/shower combinations, and full kitchens (the 49 studio apartments lack dishwashers). Some queen-size beds are available. Everyone receives a free daily newspaper. Half the lodgings have balconies. The Stafford's personable staff and spacious quarters make this a highly recommended hostelry.

Dining/Entertainment: The nearby Clocktower Cafe provides room-service breakfasts and light meals.

Facilities: Complimentary self-service laundry, outdoor pool, gym, sauna, spa.

MODERATE

A Bed-&-Breakfast Inn

The Russell. 143A George St., The Rocks, Sydney, NSW 2000. ☎ **02/241 3543.** Fax 02/252 1652. 29 rms and suites, 19 with bath. TV TEL. A$105–A$200 (U.S. $84–$160) double; A$220 (U.S. $176) suite. Additional person A$15 (U.S. $12) extra. No-smoking rooms available. Rates include continental breakfast. AE, BC, DC, MC, V. Parking not available. Train or ferry: Circular Quay.

The Russell offers Victorian-style accommodations in the heart of the historic Rocks area. All rooms have recently been refurbished and are decorated with wicker and cane furniture, ceiling fans, and antique iron beds. An open fire warms the reception area, and a rooftop garden provides views of Circular Quay and the harbor. With a cozy atmosphere, the Russell is popular with honeymooners and romantic overseas visitors, but the narrow stairs make this 100-year-old inn a poor choice for the elderly or handicapped. The Russell is licensed. All guests are provided bathrobes, tea- and coffee-making facilities, and free daily newspapers. The 11 rooms without en suite facilities share five baths.

Dining/Entertainment: Breakfast is served in a picturesque café or in bed. Those who are not guests may enjoy breakfast in the Dining Room between 7 and 9am (A$8.50/U.S. $6.80).

Services: Nightly turndown, laundry, baby-sitting, massage.

INEXPENSIVE

Pub Lodging

The Lord Nelson Brewery Hotel. At the corner of Kent and Argyle streets, The Rocks, Sydney, NSW 2000. ☎ **02/251 4044.** Fax 02/251 1532. 6 rms, none with bath. TEL. A$80–A$100 (U.S. $64–$80) double, depending on room size. Additional person A$10 (U.S. $8) extra. Rates include continental breakfast. AE, BC, DC, MC, V. Parking not available. Train or ferry: Circular Quay.

The Lord Nelson is a wonderful old atmospheric pub in The Rocks. Downstairs, crowds of happy folks eat and drink surrounded by sandstone block walls and brewery bric-a-brac. Upstairs, the six guest rooms are decorated in Laura Ashley–type prints and antique furniture. Tea- and coffee-making facilities are provided and shared by guests. The overall atmosphere is one of colonial charm. Since the Lord Nelson is Sydney's oldest licensed hotel, you couldn't sleep in a more historic setting.

IN MANLY

EXPENSIVE

Manly Pacific Parkroyal. 55 N. Steyne, Manly, NSW 2095. ☎ **02/9977 7666.** Fax 02/9977 7822. Reservations can be made through Southern Pacific Hotels at 800/835-7742 in the U.S. and Canada. 145 rms, 24 suites. A/C MINIBAR TV TEL. A$165 (U.S. $132) double; A$405–A$455 (U.S. $324–$364) suite. Additional person A$20 (U.S. $16) extra. AE, BC, DC, MC, V. Free parking. Ferry: Manly (30 minutes). JetCat: Manly (15 minutes).

The only top-class hotel on the Sydney beachfront, the Manly Pacific Parkroyal has an atmosphere entirely different from that of the city hotels I've described. Everything in this seven-story building is spacious and bright, which is one of the reasons it feels more like a resort than a metropolitan-area hotel. Wide hallways lead to rooms that have two double beds or one queen, generous closet space, free in-house movies, and balconies. On the ocean side, lower floors have a better view because the pines lining the boardwalk aren't in the way; upper floors are quieter. All ocean-view rooms have tub/shower combinations, and the king-size studios have king-size beds and an ocean view. Facilities for the handicapped are available.

Taxi fare to the hotel from the Manly Wharf is about A$3 (U.S. $2.40), but most people without much luggage prefer the 8- to 10-minute walk.

Dining/Entertainment: Gilbert's Restaurant, the fine-dining venue, is one level above the street, overlooking Manly Beach and the Pacific Ocean; breakfast, lunch, and dinner are served daily. Nells Brasserie & Cocktail Bar serves a buffet breakfast and dinner daily, with a menu ranging from light snacks to complete meals. The Charlton Bar and Grill and Dallys Night Club are also in the hotel.

Services: 24-hour room service, concierge, laundry.

Facilities: Rooftop spa, pool, gym, sauna.

Inexpensive

A Motel

$ Manly Paradise Motel and Beach Plaza Apartments. 54 N. Steyne, Manly, NSW 2095. ☎ **02/9977 5799.** Fax 02/9977-6848. 20 rms, 16 apts. A/C TV TEL. A$75–A$95 (U.S. $60–$76) double motel unit; A$180 (U.S. $144) two-bedroom apt. Additional person A$10 (U.S. $8) extra. Ask about lower long-stay rates. AE, BC, DC, MC, V. Parking free, with undercover security. Ferry: Manly.

For midprice accommodations just steps from the beach, the Manly Paradise is the best choice. The motel units are air-conditioned and have showers, tea- and coffee-making facilities, small refrigerators, toasters, hairdryers, and clock radios; some have ocean views. Each spacious apartment has two bedrooms, two baths, a full kitchen with dishwasher, laundry facilities, a tub/shower combination, and a large balcony overlooking the beach. The motel units receive daily chamber service; the apartments are cleaned weekly (or daily for a small additional charge). The phones in all rooms are direct dial.

Manly Paradise lacks a restaurant and bar, but these abound in the surrounding commercial area and next door at the four-star Manly Pacific Parkroyal. Breakfast can be served to the units. A rooftop pool and sundeck are available to guests. Ferries and JetCats provide frequent service to central Sydney.

A Guesthouse

Periwinkle-Manly Cove Guesthouse. 19 East Esplanade, Manly, NSW 2095. ☎ **02/9977 4668.** Fax 02/9977 6308. 18 rms, some with bath. TV. A$80 (U.S. $64) double without bath, A$90 (U.S. $72) double with bath. Additional person A$15 (U.S. $12) extra. View room A$5 (U.S. $4) extra. Ask about lower weekly rates. No-smoking rooms available. Rates include continental breakfast. BC, MC, V. Free parking. Ferry: Manly.

The Periwinkle is a homey guesthouse where visitors prepare their own meals in a communal kitchen, often barbecue together in the central courtyard, and gather around the fireplace in the cozy lounge (living room) during cool spells. The inn occupies an 1895 harborside house in the suburb of Manly. The previous owner added a wisteria-covered pergola on the front to hide an unflattering 1920s addition and chose a name for the guesthouse that "sounded friendly." Each spacious room has a refrigerator and ceiling fan; some have sinks. Accommodations at the front of the two-story house have a harbor view. A self-serve laundry is available. The Periwinkle is 20 minutes from the city by high-speed catamaran.

At Darling Harbour

Very Expensive

Hotel Nikko Darling Harbour. 161 Sussex St. (at Market St.), Sydney, NSW 2000. ☎ **02/299 1231,** or 1800/222 700 in Australia; 800/NIKKOUS in the U.S. and Canada. Fax 02/299 3340. 645 rms and suites. A/C MINIBAR TV TEL. A$260–A$320 (U.S. $208–$256) double, depending on view; A$400–A$550 (U.S. $320–$440) suite; A$1,000 (U.S. $800) deluxe suite; A$1,600 (U.S. $1,280) Presidential Suite. Add a A$25 per-person supplement for Nikko floor rooms. Extra bed A$25 (U.S. $20). Ask about special dollarwise packages. No-smoking and handicapped-accessible rooms available. AE, BC, DC, MC, V. Parking available. Train: Town Hall. Ferry: Darling Harbour/Aquarium.

On the city side of Darling Harbour, the Nikko is, at least for now, Australia's largest tourist hotel. It incorporates the Corn Exchange building built by Sydney's City Council in 1887, the Dundee Arms Hotel, and two sandstone maritime warehouses from the 1850s. The interior has been done in nautical art deco. To reach the National Maritime Museum, the Harbourside Marketplace, and the Convention Centre, guests take the short walk across the Pyrmont Bridge; the Sydney Aquarium and ferries to Circular Quay are even closer. Most rooms in the 15-story hotel have harbor views, some have balconies, and all offer polished granite baths, in-room movies, and music and radio systems. Guests on the Nikko Floor rate special services.

Dining/Entertainment: The Corn Exchange Brasserie, Lobby Bar, Kamogawa Japanese Restaurant, Dundee Arms Tavern, and a disco are located on the ground floor.

Services: Concierge, 24-hour room service, laundry, valet.

Facilities: Business center, early-arrival lounge, roof garden, tour desk, duty-free shops.

Expensive

Novotel Sydney on Darling Harbour. 100 Murray St., Pyrmont, NSW 2009. ☎ **02/9934 0000,** or 1800/642 2444 in Australia, 800/221-4542 in the U.S. Fax 02/9934 0099. 527 rms and suites. A/C MINIBAR TV TEL. A$200–A$240 (U.S. $160–$192) double; A$290 (U.S. $232) junior suite; A$405–A$475 (U.S. $324–$380) two-story penthouse. Extra bed A$20 (U.S. $16). Children under 16 free in parents' room and receive free breakfast. Ask about the good-value weekend packages. AE, BC, DC, MC, V. Parking free in a secure area. Monorail: Harbourside or Convention.

Adjacent to Sydney's Convention and Exhibition Centre and close to Darling Harbour's Festival Marketplace, the Novotel Sydney is linked to the central business district by the city's sleek monorail. Each of the hotel's guest rooms features a remote-control TV, a radio, tea- and coffee-making facilities, a small refrigerator, in-house movies, and tub/shower combinations. Many have harbor and city-skyline views. Fax machines are available.

Dining/Entertainment: Food and beverage outlets include the Pool Bar, Baudin's (all-day dining with a great view), and La Terrasse Lounge Bar.

Services: 24-hour room service, laundry.

Facilities: Outdoor pool, gym, sauna, nightlit tennis courts, business center, sundries shop.

In Chinatown

Inexpensive

Sydney Travellers Rest Hotel. 37 Ultimo Rd., Sydney, NSW 2000. ☎ **02/281 5555** or 1800/023 071 in Australia. Fax 02/281 2666. 104 rooms, 95 with bath. TV TEL. A$69 (U.S. $55.20) double without bath, A$89–A$104 (U.S. $71.20–$83.20) double with bath. Additional person A$10 (U.S. $8) extra. Children under 18 free when sharing with two adults. Ask about lower rates for auto club members. AE, BC, DC, MC, V. Limited parking. Monorail: Haymarket. Train: Central Station.

This property was on the verge of a major renovation when I last visited. With any luck, the refit will be complete by the time you get there. Across the street from Paddy's Market and within walking distance of Darling Harbour, the Travellers Rest was clean and tidy but in need of modernization. The management was planning to add a new lobby and restaurant, but heating and air cooling will still not be available. Ceiling fans help in summer, and there were plans to add electric blankets by winter. Every room has a small refrigerator, a clock radio, and tea- and coffee-making facilities. Family rooms sleep four to six. The age of the hotel (1908) accounts for the odd-shaped rooms. A coin-operated laundry is on the premises.

In Suburban Sydney

Expensive

Centra Hotel North Sydney. 17 Blue St., North Sydney, NSW 2060. ☎ **02/9955 0499** or 1800/22 466 in Australia. Fax 02/9922 3689. 220 rms, 2 suites. A/C MINIBAR TV TEL. A$195

(U.S. $156) double; A$350 (U.S. $280) suite. Additional person A$15 (U.S. $12) extra. Ask about lower weekend rates. No-smoking rooms available. AE, BC, CB, DC, MC, V. Free parking. Train: North Sydney. Ferry: Lavendar Bay.

The Centra Hotel North Sydney is your best bet if you want to be across the Harbour Bridge. Because of the hotel's semicircular design, almost all rooms have breathtaking harbor views—back across the water to the Opera House and the impressive skyline. The hotel is especially popular with business travelers. All rooms have clock radios, tea- and coffee-making facilities, and small refrigerators; queen-size beds and in-room movies are available. The train ride to central Sydney takes 10 minutes; the bus takes about 5 minutes longer. Adventurous folks, of course, could walk across the bridge (not recommended for the faint-hearted).

Dining/Entertainment: Meals are available in the Blues Bar and Restaurant.

Services: Concierge, 24-hour room service, free daily newspaper, shoeshine, laundry, valet, baby-sitting.

Facilities: Outdoor pool, business center.

Ritz-Carlton Double Bay. 33 Cross St., Double Bay, NSW 2028. ☎ **02/362 4455** or 1800/252 888 in Australia. Fax 02/362 4744. 140 rms and suites. A/C MINIBAR TV TEL. A$199–A$249 (U.S. $159.20–$199.20) double; A$425–A$2,000 (U.S. $340–$1,600) suite; A$239–A$249 (U.S. $191.20–$199.20) Club floor. AE, BC, DC, MC, V. Parking A$15 (U.S. $12).

The Ritz-Carlton offers the first five-star accommodations in Sydney's poshest suburb. "Double Bay, double pay" has often been said about the area's chic boutiques and shops. Designed in the French provincial style, the six-story property is situated in the heart of the community, 4km (2½ miles) east of central Sydney. Each spacious room offers a marble bath with a separate shower stall, three phones, a safe, a remote-control TV, a radio, a small refrigerator, and fluffy robes. All rooms have French doors leading to balconies; most have water views. Quarters on the Ritz-Carlton Club floor offer additional comfort and privacy.

Dining/Entertainment: Try The Grill for continental cuisine in an intimate, elegant environment; The Bar for cocktails; or The Lobby Lounge for breakfast, buffet lunch, or afternoon tea.

Services: Concierge, 24-hour room service, valet, twice-daily maid service, nightly turndown, baby-sitting.

Facilities: Heated rooftop pool, fitness center, business center, meeting facilities, sundry/gift shop, currency exchange.

Serviced Apartments

Medina Paddington Executive Apartments. 400 Glenmore Rd., Paddington, NSW 2021. ☎ **02/361 9000** or 1800/80 8453 in Australia. Fax 02/332 3484. 48 apts. A/C TV TEL. A$230 (U.S. $184) two-bedroom apt for four; A$280 (U.S. $224) three-bedroom apt for six. Rates include continental breakfast on first day. Children under 15 free in parents' room. Ask about discounts for weekly and monthly stays. AE, BC, DC, MC, V. Free parking. Train: Edgecliff.

On the edge of the White City Tennis Complex, Sydney's answer to Wimbledon, these sleek, spacious low-rise apartments are a tennis buff's delight. They're also well located for travelers who wish easy access to the posh shops in Double Bay or the bohemian cafés and markets in Paddington. Central Sydney is a little more than 3km (2 miles) away. The recently refurbished two- and three-bedroom apartments are appointed attractively, with decorative prints, large sprays of fresh flowers, leather couches, and lacquer tables. Some units have expansive city-skyline views, and all have patios or balconies, large kitchens with dishwashers, and laundry facilities. The Cuisine Courier service brings meals from a variety of restaurants, and the management provides a grocery- and liquor-shopping service. Laundry and baby-sitting can be arranged. The facilities include an outdoor pool, a business center, and a barbecue. Tennis courts, some of the best in the country, are steps away.

INEXPENSIVE

Homestays

$ **Filla's Cottage.** 213 Ryde Rd., West Pymble, NSW 2073. ☎ **02/498 7184.** One self-contained cottage. TV TEL. U.S. $35 per day; U.S. $200 per week. No credit cards. Minimum three-day stay. Free parking. Train: Gordon Station, then bus.

I *had* to add this property to the book, as I've been deluged by readers recommending it and chastising me for its omission from earlier editions. Herb and Renate Filla have a lovely studio cottage in the garden behind their house, with a pool beside it. Its tiny kitchenette contains a refrigerator, a microwave, a hot plate, a toaster, a sink, and dishes. There's a shower in the bath, and fresh towels are supplied every other day. The Fillas are warm, gracious, and gregarious, going out of their way to make visitors feel welcome. If you phone them, let it ring at least 10 times; they're often in the garden. Central Sydney is 40 minutes away by public transport. Herb and Renate enjoy traveling America and prefer payment be made in "good old greenbacks."

Syl's Sydney Homestay. 75 Beresford Rd., Rose Bay, NSW 2029. ☎ **02/327 7079.** Mobile phone 018/464682. Fax 02/327 8419. 3 rms, 2 with bath; 1 apt. TV. A$85–A$90 (U.S. $68–$72) double. Additional person A$15–A$20 (U.S. $12–$16) extra. Children under 5 free in parents' room. Ask about lower weekly and long-term rates. Rates include breakfast. BC, MC, V. Free parking. Ferry: Rose Bay. Bus: 323, 324, or 325.

Sylvia and Paul Ure welcome guests from all over the world into their home and provide them with all the necessary sightseeing and transportation details. Energetic Syl even conducts day tours (A$55/U.S. $44 per person) and offers dinner (A$13/U.S. $10.40). The house is close to Bondi Beach, where Paul bodysurfs every morning; it's also only 20 minutes by ferry or 30 minutes by bus from central Sydney. The Ures have three school-age children and welcome families. The apartment sleeps up to five; guests are welcome to gather in the family room or kitchen to watch a movie, make coffee, or chat. The fax, phone, and laundry facilities can be used for a nominal charge. Smoking isn't permitted in the rooms.

INEXPENSIVE

For those on a tight budget, **YHA Hostels** are dotted around the Sydney suburbs. **Glebe Point,** 262 Glebe Point Rd., Glebe, NSW 2037 (☎ 02/692 8418; fax 02/660 0431), is near the water in a cosmopolitan inner suberb. Nearby is **Hereford Lodge,** 51 Hereford St., Glebe, NSW 2037 (☎ 02/660 5577; fax 02/552 1771), the YHA's Australian flagship. All rooms are en suite; this facility also has a pool and sauna. Charges at Glebe Point and Hereford Lodge are A$16 to A$24 (U.S. $12.80 to $19.20). Children are charged half price.

Readers Recommend

Gemini Hotel Sydney, 65–71 Belmore Rd., Randwick, Sydney, NSW 2031 (☎ 02/399 9011, or 1800/222 300 in Australia; fax 02/398 9708). *"In Sydney, we recommend Gemini as a reasonable, recently refurbished hotel, with easy access by bus to downtown. There were many restaurants and shopping malls nearby, but we especially liked Sophie's Place, 124 Belmore Rd. It seemed like a place where all the locals went. They had a very diverse and inexpensive menu."*

—Jacques E. Linder, Sarasota, Fla., U.S.A.

Readers Recommend

Australian Sunrise Lodge, 485 King St., Newtown, NSW 2042 (☎ 02/550 4999). *"We stayed several nights at this property, which is between the airport and downtown Sydney. The rooms are small but sunny and very clean. The owner is especially attentive to his guests and supplies information on transportation, tours, and restaurants in the area. I believe this is a 'gem' and deserves consideration."*

—Dick Schoenman, Bellevue, Wash., U.S.A.

Author's Note: The rate at the Australian Sunrise Lodge is A$55 to A$65 (U.S. $44 to $52) for two. All rooms have TVs, coffee- and tea-making facilities, toasters, and small refrigerators. Of the 18 rooms, 14 have baths. Guests can prepare meals in a communal kitchen.

NEAR THE AIRPORT

Sydney Airport Parkroyal. Bourke Road (at O'Riordan St.), Mascot, NSW 2020. ☎ **02/330 0600.** Fax 02/667 4517. 246 rms, 2 suites. A/C MINIBAR TV TEL. A$225 (U.S. $180) double. Additional person A$20 (U.S. $16) extra. Ask about special discounts, including a A$135 (U.S. $111.20) "international stopover" rate. Flexistay A$40 (U.S. $32) first hour, A$10 (U.S. $8) each additional hour. No-smoking floors available. AE, BC, DC, MC, V. Free parking. Round-the-clock complimentary shuttle to/from Sydney Airport.

If what you want is a bed close to the airport the night before an early-morning flight or a convenient spot for a meeting near the airport, the Parkroyal is your best bet. This is also the ideal place if you want a shower and a nap between flights, as rooms can be rented on an hourly "flexistay" basis. All quarters have clock radios, bathrobes, hairdryers, tea- and coffee-making facilities, in-room movies, fax connections, and small refrigerators. King- and queen-size beds are available, and all guests receive a complimentary daily newspaper. Flight details can be accessed on each room's TV screen. Guests may leave their car at the hotel while they travel.

Dining/Entertainment: Biggles Tavern Bar is a lively spot for a pub lunch, and Amelia's Brasserie & Bar serves both buffet and à la carte meals.

4 Dining

Boasting more than 2,000 dining spots offering dozens of ethnic cuisines (with Thai the current favorite) as well as indigenous Australian specialties, Sydney's restaurant scene presents a challenge for visitors. The greatest concentration of spots is in The Rocks—this area once known only for its "rough pubs" is now the location of the best chefs. All over the city you can find all kinds of food at all price levels. And it'd be a mistake for you to leave this harborside metropolis without sampling the local seafood, such as Sydney rock oysters, Balmain bugs (rock lobster), and John Dory.

In the following listings you'll find restaurants that float and others that are perched on top of a tower. A handful are outdoors and several are in pubs. Some have harbor views, a few offer entertainment, many have excellent wine lists, and some are BYOs. Almost all the very expensive and most of the moderately priced places accept major credit cards; weekend and public-holiday surcharges are de rigueur; and reservations are recommended in all but the most casual eateries. A few other delightful eateries are included in Chapter 5 under "Side Trips from Sydney."

Regarding tipping, it used to be rare for Aussies to leave a gratuity in restaurants, but nowadays in Sydney they tend to leave about 10%. If your service is satisfactory, I suggest you follow suit.

My price categories are as follows: Restaurants in which a three-course dinner for one costs A$50 (U.S. $40) or more are **Very Expensive;** places where the same number of courses cost A$38 to A$49 (U.S. $30.40 to $39.20) are **Expensive;** those where three courses cost A$25 to A$37 (U.S. $20 to $29.60) are **Moderate;** and those where three courses cost less than A$24 (U.S. $19.20) are **Inexpensive.**

***Note:* As part of the telephone changeover, in July 1996 all seven-digit phone numbers within the 02 area code will change to 02/9xxx xxxx and all six-digit numbers will change to 02/91xx xxxx. Numbers listed as 02/99xx xxxx will remain unchanged.**

IN THE CITY CENTER

VERY EXPENSIVE

Kable's. In The Regent, Sydney, 199 George St. ☎ **02/238 0000.** Reservations recommended. Main courses A$19.50–A$29.50 (U.S. $15.60–$23.60); fixed-price three-course lunch A$39.50 (U.S. $31.60). AE, BC, DC, MC, V. Mon noon–2:30pm, Tues–Fri noon–10:30pm, Sat 6:30–10:30pm. Train or ferry: Circular Quay. AUSTRALIAN.

Kable's is Sydney's finest hotel dining venue and one of Australia's best restaurants. It has won numerous awards, including the New South Wales Tourism Award for Best Restaurant several years in a row. Ironically named after the first convict to step ashore in the new colony (he carried Governor Phillip to land on his shoulders), Kable's is extravagant and elegant in every detail. Expensive tableware and crystal complement the stylish black, white, and gray art deco space, and the service is flawless.

Executive chef Serge Dansereau oversees the preparation of the superb dishes on a menu that changes daily to take advantage of the best available produce. You might order wild barramundi filets, pan-fried breast of Guinea fowl with scorched witlof, or roasted Balmain bug tails with lime butter. The restaurant also has an extensive wine list. You won't be disappointed.

Level One—Sydney Tower Restaurant. In Centrepoint Tower, Market Street (between Pitts and Castlereagh sts.). ☎ **02/233 3722.** Reservations recommended. Main courses A$24.50–A$29.50 (U.S. $19.60–$23.60); fixed-price lunch or early dinner A$32–A$36 (U.S. $25.60–$28.80); fixed-price dinner A$36–A$52 (U.S. $28.80–$41.60). Minimum A$20 (U.S. $16) per person; Sat surcharge 10%. AE, BC, DC, MC, V. Mon–Fri 11:30am–11:45pm, Sat 5–11:45pm. Closed public holidays. Train: St. James. Monorail: City Centre. INTERNATIONAL.

Rotating 85 stories above the city, this restaurant provides a spectacular view as well as excellent food and service. The Tower is the tallest public building in the Southern Hemisphere, and diners are treated to a 360-degree view of the city, harbor, and suburbs. Restaurant patrons don't pay the A$6 (U.S. $4.80) normally charged for the 40-second ride to the observation level; instead, they enter via Market Street, take the elevator to the Gallery Level, and proceed to the reception lounge, where they're given tokens for the "lift up" to the restaurant.

Level One's international à la carte menu, served in an intimate candlelit environment, includes local seafood as well as a variety of carefully prepared meat dishes. A special menu for children 3 to 12 is available for lunch and early dinner, which finishes at 7:30pm. A less expensive self-service dining spot is on Level Two (see "Moderate" below).

EXPENSIVE

Bennelong Restaurant. In the Sydney Opera House, Bennelong Point. ☎ **02/250 7548** or 250 7578. Reservations recommended. Main courses A$25–A$33 (U.S. $20–$26.40). AE, BC, DC, MC, V. Mon–Fri 7–10:30pm. Train or ferry: Circular Quay. MODERN AUSTRALIAN.

When in Sydney, I wouldn't miss dining in the Bennelong any more than I'd visit Paris without having a meal aloft in one of the restaurants in the Eiffel Tower. This

Central Sydney Dining

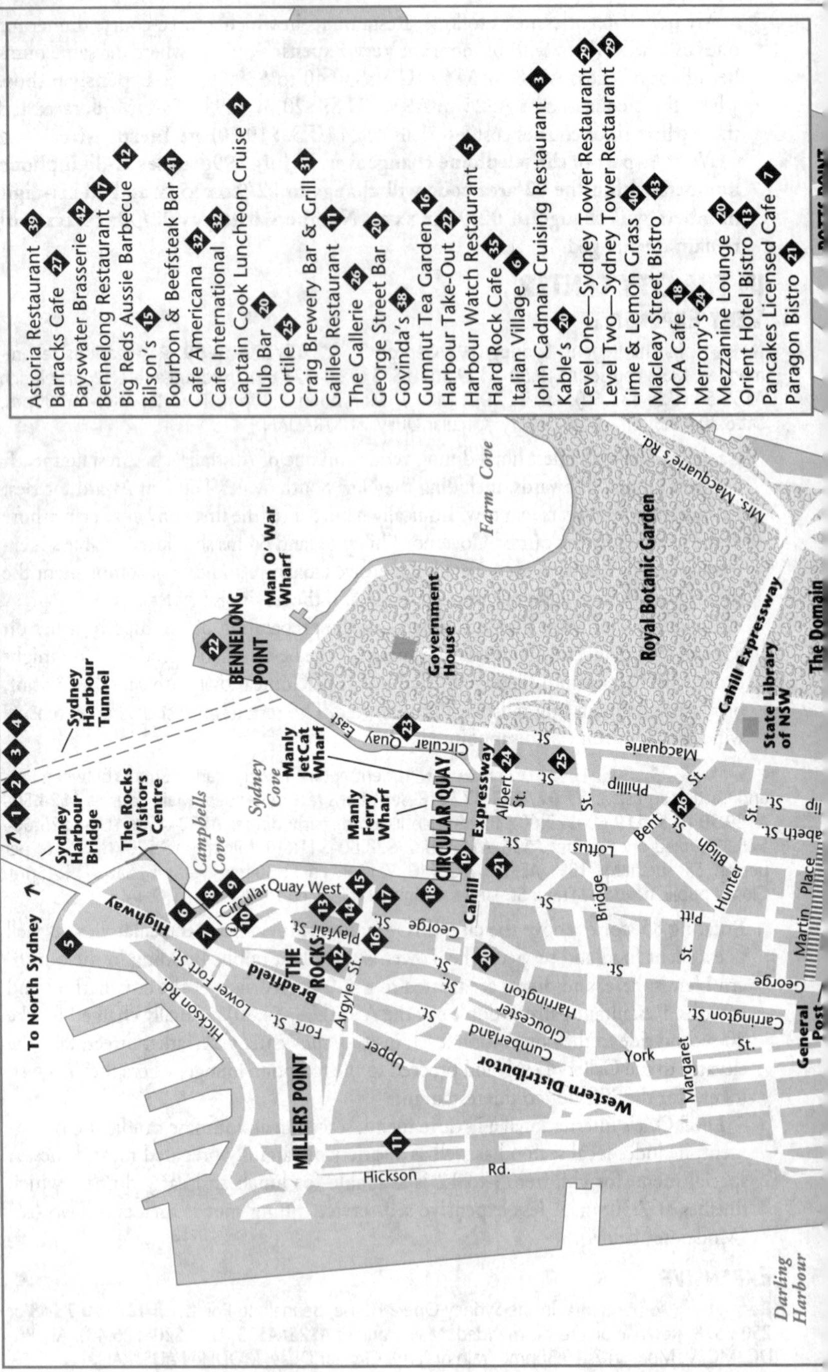
Astoria Restaurant 39
Barracks Cafe 27
Bayswater Brasserie 42
Bennelong Restaurant 17
Big Reds Aussie Barbecue 12
Bilson's 15
Bourbon & Beefsteak Bar 41
Cafe Americana 32
Cafe International 32
Captain Cook Luncheon Cruise 2
Club Bar 20
Cortile 25
Craig Brewery Bar & Grill 31
Galileo Restaurant 11
The Gallerie 26
George Street Bar 20
Govinda's 38
Gumnut Tea Garden 16
Harbour Take-Out 22
Harbour Watch Restaurant 5
Hard Rock Cafe 35
Italian Village 6
John Cadman Cruising Restaurant 3
Kable's 20
Level One—Sydney Tower Restaurant 29
Level Two—Sydney Tower Restaurant 29
Lime & Lemon Grass 40
Macleay Street Bistro 43
MCA Cafe 18
Merrony's 24
Mezzanine Lounge 20
Orient Hotel Bistro 13
Pancakes Licensed Cafe 7
Paragon Bistro 21
To North Sydney
Sydney Harbour Bridge
Sydney Harbour Tunnel
The Rocks Visitors Centre
Campbells Cove
Sydney Cove
Manly JetCat Wharf
Manly Ferry Wharf
CIRCULAR QUAY
Circular Quay West
Circular Quay East
BENNELONG POINT
Man O' War Wharf
Farm Cove
Government House
Royal Botanic Garden
Mrs. Macquarie's Rd.
Cahill Expressway
State Library of NSW
The Domain
THE ROCKS
MILLERS POINT
Bradfield Highway
Western Distributor
Hickson Rd.
Darling Harbour
General Post
Martin Place

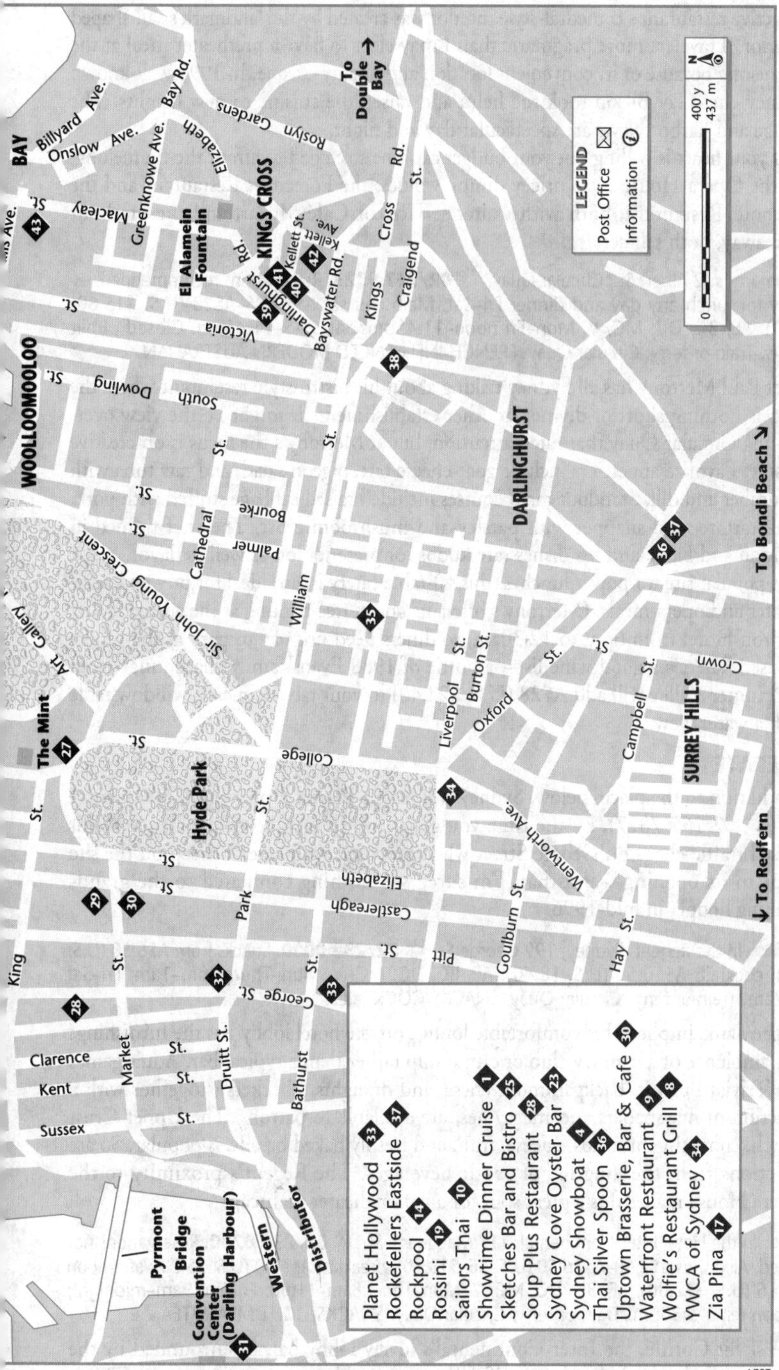
WOOLLOOMOOLOO
BAY
KINGS CROSS
DARLINGHURST
SURREY HILLS
Hyde Park
The Mint
El Alamein Fountain
Pymont Bridge
Convention Center (Darling Harbour)
Western Distributor
To Double Bay →
To Bondi Beach ↘
↓ To Redfern
Billyard Ave.
Onslow Ave.
Greenknowe Ave.
Bay Rd.
Elizabeth
Roslyn Gardens
Macleay St.
Kellett St.
Kellett Ave.
Darlinghurst Rd.
Bayswater Rd.
Victoria St.
Kings Cross Rd.
Craigend St.
South Dowling St.
Cathedral St.
Bourke St.
Palmer St.
William St.
Sir John Young Crescent
Art Gallery
College St.
Park St.
Elizabeth
Castlereagh St.
Pitt St.
George St.
Liverpool St.
Burton St.
Oxford St.
Campbell St.
Crown St.
Wentworth Ave.
Goulburn St.
Hay St.
Bathurst St.
Druitt St.
Market St.
King St.
Clarence St.
Kent St.
Sussex St.
LEGEND
Post Office
Information
0
400 y
437 m
N
Planet Hollywood 33
Rockefellers Eastside 37
Rockpool 14
Rossini 19
Sailors Thai 10
Showtime Dinner Cruise 1
Sketches Bar and Bistro 25
Soup Plus Restaurant 28
Sydney Cove Oyster Bar 23
Sydney Showboat 4
Thai Silver Spoon 36
Uptown Brasserie, Bar & Cafe 30
Waterfront Restaurant 9
Wolfie's Restaurant Grill 8
YWCA of Sydney 34
Zia Pina 17
2324

attractive restaurant's cathedral-style interior was created by the landmark's sail-shaped exterior. Travelers more pragmatic than I may elect to have a pretheater meal at the Bennelong because of its convenient location and quality cuisine. In 1995 well-known Sydney chef Gay Bilson took the helm and raised the cuisine to new heights. The bridge and harbor views are spectacular day and night.

If your heart is willing but your budget can't be stretched to afford the Bennelong, try the Opera House's less pricey dining venues: the Forecourt Restaurant and the Harbour Restaurant, both with waiter service; or Café Mozart and the Harbour Takeaway, both self-service.

✪ **Merrony's.** 2 Albert St., Circular Quay. ☎ **02/247 9323.** Reservations recommended, especially for lunch any day and dinner Fri–Sat. Main courses A$19.75–A$23 (U.S. $15.80–$18.40). AE, BC, DC, MC, V. Mon–Fri noon–11:45pm, Sat 5:45–11:45pm. Closed public holidays. Train or ferry: Circular Quay. FRENCH-INFLUENCED MODERN AUSTRALIAN.

Chef Paul Merrony has all Sydney talking about his bistro-style restaurant where the food is nothing short of divine. In other establishments it might be the view overlooking Circular Quay that rated attention, but at Merrony's the focus is on creative cuisine. Favorite appetizers include goat-cheese tart, pigeon salad, and raw tuna with cucumber and dill. Standout main courses include braised cabbage stuffed with pork, steak tartare, and snapper with parsley-and-mushroom crust. The chef trained in London and Paris, and his dishes rate kudos for presentation as well as flavor.

A popular site for power lunches, this 40-table eatery is also ideal for pre- and post-theater and opera meals. (Merrony's offers its guests free parking at the adjacent Ritz Carlton Hotel from 6pm to 12:30am, so diners need not pay to park at the Opera House.) There's a good wine list—a bottle of 1988 Evans family chardonnay from the Hunter Valley will add A$28 (U.S. $22.40) to your tab. Request a window table with a water view.

MODERATE

In addition to the places below, Sydney will have a **Planet Hollywood,** 600 George St. (☎ 02/267 7827), by the time you get there. In fact, co-owner Bruce Willis caused traffic chaos on George Street when he posed with several sheep on the site prior to its opening—and that, I'm sure, was nothing compared to the grand-opening hoopla in mid-1996.

Club Bar. In the Regent, Sydney, 199 George St. ☎ **02/238 0000.** Snacks from A$6.50 (U.S. $5.20); cocktails A$10.50 (U.S. $8.40). AE, BC, DC, MC, V. Mon–Thurs 4pm–1am, Fri–Sat 4pm–2am. Train or ferry: Circular Quay. SNACKS/COCKTAILS.

As the name implies, this comfortable lounge off the hotel lobby has the furnishings and ambience of a country club or cruise ship rather than a typical bar. Adult games like Trivial Pursuit, backgammon, chess, and draughts (checkers), together with a selection of newspapers and magazines, are available to patrons. The Upper Crust Lunch, consisting of salads, cheese, fruit, and freshly baked breads, is popular. So are selections from the long list of exotic beverages. The Regent's proximity to the Opera House makes this a great spot for an after-theater nightcap.

Cortile. In the Hotel Inter-Continental, 117 Macquarie St. ☎ **02/230 0200.** Reservations not accepted. All dishes A$7.50–A$16.50 (U.S. $6–$13.20); breakfast A$6.50 (U.S. $5.20); afternoon tea A$16 (U.S. $12.80). AE, BC, DC, MC, V. Mon–Thurs 8am–11pm, Fri–Sun 9am–midnight; afternoon tea 3–5:30pm. Train or ferry: Circular Quay. SNACKS/LIGHT MEALS/TEA.

The skylit Cortile, the Inter-Continental's lovely lobby bar, is surrounded by the sandstone arches of Sydney's beautiful Treasury Building, dating from 1849. This is a delightful site for light meals, teas, and cocktails. The traditional English afternoon tea includes a selection of finger sandwiches, freshly baked scones with King Island cream and strawberry preserves, or a gateau slice of your choice. You could also have English fruitcake or French pastries. A string quartet accompanies.

On the "All Day" menu is a wide selection of sandwiches prepared with assorted breads or a baguette and a choice of fillings, as well as other light dishes, like smoked ocean trout with rockette lettuce, homemade soups, or spicy Malaysian laksa.

Level Two—Sydney Tower Restaurant. In Centrepoint Tower, Market Street (between Pitt and Castlereagh sts.). ☎ **02/233 3722.** Reservations recommended. Early dinner A$27.50–A$35 (U.S. $22–$28); dinner A$30–A$33 (U.S. $24–$26.40). A$12 (U.S. $9.60) for children 3–12 at lunch and early dinner. Weekend and public holiday surcharge of 10%-15% on drinks only. AE, BC, DC, MC, V. Tues–Sat 11:30am–11:45pm, Sun 5–6:15pm. Train: St. James. Monorail: City Centre. BUFFET (GRILLS/ROASTS/SEAFOOD/ASIAN).

Level Two is one floor up from Level One, the tower's more expensive dining spot (see "Very Expensive" above). The view from these places is obviously the same—spectacular. Both complete an entire rotation in about an hour, providing diners with the best bird's-eye view in town. The main difference is that Level Two is self-service, sans tablecloths. The extensive buffet consists of five appetizers, at least a dozen main courses, and six desserts. Should you choose this Sydney Tower restaurant, you can heap your plate with just-carved roast, steak, Chinese dishes, and specialties like pork knuckle, chicken Maryland, and lasagne. Trust me, you won't go away hungry. Restaurant patrons purchase a voucher at the gallery-level reception area and receive a complimentary "lift up" instead of paying the regular charge for the fast elevator ride up the tower.

Note: If budget or time constraints make this aerial carvery out of the question, light refreshments and drinks are available before 5pm at a snack bar, the Sydney Tower Sky Lounge, on Level Three.

✪ **MCA Cafe.** In the Museum of Contemporary Art, Circular Quay West. ☎ **02/252 1888.** Reservations accepted. Main courses A$11–A$13.50 (U.S. $8.80–$10.80). Minimum charge A$8.50 (U.S. $6.80) per person noon–2:30pm. Weekend and public holiday surcharge 10%. AE, BC, MC, V. Daily 11am–5:30pm. Train or ferry: Circular Quay. MODERN AUSTRALIAN.

If you sit at one of this café's 16 outside tables, you'll be treated to a wonderful view of the Opera House and Circular Quay. The café consists of a wooden deck at the front of the museum and an adjacent inside dining area. Regardless of the location of your table, the fare is excellent. Neil Perry, the chef/owner of the pricey Rockpool restaurant across the street, designed the menu here and oversees the food preparation. I recommend the focaccia of grilled lamb and sun-dried tomatoes, but you might also like the grilled minute steak with salsa verde or the lamb shank–and–lentil soup. And be sure to save room for some heavenly chocolate cake.

The MCA is housed in the old Maritime Services Board building, designed in the 1930s—hence the art deco ambience. I suggest you book early.

✪ **Mezzanine Lounge.** In The Regent, Sydney, 199 George St. ☎ **02/238 0000.** Reservations not required. Breakfast A$20–A$26.50 (U.S. $16–$21.20); light lunch A$9–A$17 (U.S. $7.20–$13.60); afternoon tea A$16 (U.S. $12.80). AE, BC, DC, MC, V. Mon–Thurs 7am–midnight, Fri 7am–1am, Sat 7:30am–1am, Sun 7:30am–midnight. Train or ferry: Circular Quay. LIGHT MEALS/AFTERNOON TEA.

A three-story atrium rises from the polished marble floor of The Regent's lobby, each level trimmed with brass railings and cascading green plants. The second-floor Mezzanine Lounge provides a bird's-eye view of the hotel's front doors and the activity

Family-Friendly Restaurants

Big Reds Aussie Barbecue Restaurant *(see p. 130)* Paul Hogan promised to slip a shrimp on the barby for you and this is where it happens. The kids enjoy the Aussie blokes and sheilas who comprise the wait staff.

Hard Rock Cafe *(see p. 127)* The teen and preteen set thrive on these rock 'n' roll eateries. The music is loud, and that's how they like it.

Planet Hollywood *(see p. 122)* As is the case with the other Planet Hollywoods around the world, this place appeals to movie buffs of all ages.

in the elegant foyer. Surely there isn't a better perch in all of Sydney for a quick breakfast, a light lunch, afternoon tea, an after-work cocktail, or an after-theater snack. The price for afternoon tea includes sandwiches, scones, French pastries, an assortment of cakes, sorbet, ice cream, and a selection of Twinings teas. A classical ensemble provides accompaniment.

The Paragon Bistro. In the Paragon Hotel, Loftus Street, Circular Quay. ☎ **02/241 3888.** Reservations recommended. Main courses A$9–A$14 (U.S. $7.20–$11.20); two-course lunch and pretheater specials A$11.50 (U.S. $9.20). AE, BC, MC, V. Mon–Fri noon–2:30pm and 6–10pm, Sat 6–10pm. Train or ferry: Circular Quay. MODERN AUSTRALIAN.

The Paragon Bistro occupies the second floor of the Paragon Hotel, dating from 1865. The restaurant's art deco atmosphere reflects a 1930s refurbishment and provides a pleasant dining space. Chef Michael Bengtsson's menu changes continuously, based on his ingredients' seasonal availability. Typical appetizers include half a dozen Sydney rock oysters with salmon caviar, chives, and champagne as well as grilled mushrooms and pancetta, spinach-and-garlic croutons, and smoked salmon with ginger, lime, cherry tomatoes, and fried leek. The main courses might feature tagliatelle with crabmeat, smoked salmon, and vodka-dill cream sauce; barbecued honey lamb and rosemary sausages with kumera; or Nasi goreng (Indonesian fried rice) with bacon, prawns, chiles, eggs, and sprouts. The light evening menu makes this an ideal spot for pretheater dining.

Uptown Brasserie, Bar & Cafe. In the Skygarden shopping arcade, Level 3, 77 Castlereagh St. ☎ **02/223 4211.** Reservations recommended. Main courses A$8–A$14 (U.S. $6.40–$11.20). AE, BC, MC, V. Mon–Fri 11:30am–8:30pm, Sat 5:30–8:30pm. Train: St. James. Monorail: City Centre. MULTICULTURAL.

The menu and the decor of this trendy spot are best described as eclectic. The designer created "a metaphorical cityscape," a place where diners can view "images of urban life through the ages." The walls boast assorted facades of buildings from various parts of the world and from different periods in history. The result is very colorful and avant-garde. Like the decor, the menu comes from various corners of the globe. Items may include angel-hair pasta with smoked salmon, goat cheese, and rocket; mole of charcoal-grilled chicken breast on pinto-bean purée with sweet-potato fritters; or roast loin of lamb with vegetable paysanne on a bed of fragrant rosemary and tomato consommé.

Uptown is a restaurant/café/bar, so even if you aren't hungry you can have a drink and ogle the "cityscape." A draft beer costs A$2.30 (U.S. $1.84).

INEXPENSIVE

The Barracks Cafe. On Queen's Square, Macquarie Street. ☎ **02/223 1155.** Reservations not accepted. Main courses A$7.50–A$12.50 (U.S. $6–$10); sandwiches A$3.75 (U.S. $3). AE, BC, MC, V. Mon–Fri 10am–4pm, Sat–Sun 11am–3pm. Train: Martin Place. CAFÉ.

I revisited this place recently and was disappointed that they no longer serve the wonderful open-face sandwiches I remember, but they do offer shell pasta with pork sausages, tomatoes, and fresh peas; avocado salad with Israeli salsa; and caramelized onion tart served with rocket and parmesan salad—all really tasty. The menu changes monthly, so you may not see anything I've listed. Seating is both inside and outside and there are separate smoking and no-smoking areas. This appealing spot, on the grounds of Hyde Park Barracks, is very popular with locals.

The Gallerie. In the Wentworth Rydges Hotel, 61–101 Phillip St. ☎ **02/230 0700.** Reservations not accepted. Lunch A$8–A$12 (U.S. $6.40–$9.60); coffee A$3.25 (U.S. $2.60). AE, BC, DC, MC, V. Mon–Fri 8am–6:30pm, Sat 10am–4pm. Train: Martin Place. LIGHT MEALS/COFFEE.

Coffee is the specialty of the house in this casual café. Java fans can sample Kona style, Blue Mountain style, royal blend, Colombian, mocha and Kenya blend, or European style. Teas, juices, soft drinks, and milkshakes are also offered. These can be accompanied by pastries, muffins, or scones. The lunch menu consists of salads, open focaccia sandwiches, a cheese-and-fruit plate, and soup.

George Street Bar. In The Regent, Sydney, 199 George St. ☎ **02/256 5171.** Reservations not required. Lunch and light meals from A$8.50 (U.S. $6.80). AE, BC, DC, MC, V. Mon–Thurs noon–10pm, Fri noon–11:30pm. Train or ferry: Circular Quay. PUB FARE.

The Regent's George Street Bar has a lively atmosphere and classic pub decor including brass railings, a brick floor, lots of wood, and pool tables. The bar has two entrances directly on the main thoroughfare from which it gets its name. Large windows allow a view of the city's hustle and bustle. The handsome interior, together with the relative brightness of the place, puts the George Street Bar a cut above the majority of public bars. A full range of drinks, wines, and draft beers is offered, in addition to hearty pub lunches like meat pies and roasts from a chalkboard menu.

The Harbour Take-Out. On the north side of the Sydney Opera House, Bennelong Point. ☎ **02/250 7557.** Reservations not accepted. Fish and chips A$5.50 (U.S. $4.40); seafood box A$9.50 (U.S. $7.60); tea or coffee A$1.50 (U.S. $1.20); cake A$2.50 (U.S. $2); glass of house wine or champagne A$3 (U.S. $2.40); beer A$3.50 (U.S. $2.80). No credit cards. Daily 10am–5pm (to 6pm in summer). Train or ferry: Circular Quay. SEAFOOD.

Walk around the back of the Opera House, past the entrance to the Drama Theatre and the Playhouse, and you'll find two dining spots with million-dollar views. The Harbour Restaurant (☎ 02/250-7191) is a moderately priced seafood place with waiter service. However, for a quick bite I heartily recommend its budget-priced self-service neighbor, the Harbour Take-out. Seating is indoors or out, and the parade of ferries and other vessels on the harbor is almost constant.

$ **Rossini.** Opposite wharf no. 6, Circular Quay. ☎ **02/247 8026.** Reservations not accepted. All dishes A$5–A$12 (U.S. $4–$9.60). No credit cards. Daily 7am–10:30pm. Train or ferry: Circular Quay. ITALIAN.

If you like pasta, this is the place to go. Rossini offers dishes such as cannelloni, maccheroni Rossini bolognese, and penne with chicken, mushrooms, and peppercorn—all for A$7 (U.S. $5.60) each, including bread. Pizzettes are even less expensive and veal dishes only slightly more. You make your choice and pay at the register before choosing a seat either inside or outside adjacent to the hustle and bustle of Circular Quay. Rossini is open for breakfast with your choice of light or full breakfast fare from $A2 to $A7 (U.S. $1.60 to $5.60). All pasta, pizza crust, gelato, and other desserts are made in-house, and they're all very good. Certainly this is one of Sydney's best values.

Sketches Bar and Bistro. In the Hotel Inter-Continental, 117 Macquarie St. ☎ **02/230 0200.** Reservations recommended. Pasta and salad buffet A$14.50 (U.S. $11.60); large dish of pasta A$14.90 (U.S. $11.90). AE, BC, DC, MC, V. Mon–Fri noon–9pm, Sat 5:30–10pm (bar open Mon–Fri 11am–11pm, Sat 5–11pm). Train or ferry: Circular Quay. PASTA.

Large chalkboard menus proclaim the daily choices in this lively create-your-own-plate venue. You pay at the bar, then wander to the pasta bar, where you can choose from about a dozen types of freshly made pasta and a variety of sauces. While waiting for your fettuccine, tortellini, or agnolotti to be cooked, you can start on the salad bar. A jug (pitcher) of draft beer costs A$8.50 (U.S. $6.80). This eatery is so named because the work of the Australian Black & White Artists Club decorates its walls. The cartoons and caricatures of the country's politicians, sports figures, and other celebrities are for sale.

Soup Plus Restaurant. 383 George St. ☎ **02/299 7728.** Reservations recommended. Main courses A$7–A$12 (U.S. $5.60–$9.60). AE, BC, MC, V. Mon–Thurs noon–midnight, Fri–Sat noon–1:30am. Closed New Year's Day, Good Friday, and Christmas. Train: Town Hall. INTERNATIONAL.

Opposite the Strand Arcade between King and Market streets, Soup Plus offers live jazz between 8 and 11:30pm during the week and until 1:30am Friday and Saturday. The quality of the performances is quite high, as is the volume, so don't plan on an intimate conversation during your meal. As the name implies, at least four soups are offered daily, some hot, some chilled. The chalkboard menu also usually lists several kinds of pasta, salads, steak, chicken, and vegetarian dishes. The food is good, and the plain pine furniture, basement location, and self-service setup create a simple yet pleasant atmosphere. This place is a great value and it's not surprising that it's been voted one of the best "cheap eats" in Sydney.

Be aware, however, that a cover charge of A$3 to A$5 (U.S. $2.40 to $4) applies after 8pm, that the minimum purchase if you want to pay by credit card is A$20, and that when I last dined here they were charging A50¢ (U.S. 40¢) for a glass of water.

Sydney Cove Oyster Bar. 1 E. Circular Quay. ☎ **02/247 2937.** Reservations not required. Snacks A$6.50–A$10 (U.S. $5.20–$8); glass of wine A$4.50 (U.S. $3.60); 10-oz. midi of beer A$3.30 (U.S. $2.64); 15-oz. schooner of beer A$4.50 (U.S. $3.60). AE, BC, DC, MC, V. Mon–Thurs noon–11pm, Fri noon–midnight, Sat noon–midnight, Sun noon–9pm. Shorter hours in winter. Train or ferry: Circular Quay. MODERN AUSTRALIAN.

You couldn't ask for a better setting for enjoying a drink and a light meal. The Sydney Cove Oyster Bar is *right* on the water, a stone's throw from the Opera House, in a building that dates from 1906. Ferries and JetCats pass back and forth while patrons seated at umbrella-shaded tables enjoy the view. Those who get hungry can munch on smoked trout pâté, oysters, selections from a cheese platter, or other dishes chosen from a chalkboard menu. This is one of the few places you can drink Hahn beer, a local specialty; the other tap brew is Coopers Ale from South Australia.

The YWCA of Sydney. 5–11 Wentworth Ave. ☎ **02/264 2451.** Reservations not accepted. Main courses A$6.25–A$7.50 (U.S. $5–$6). No credit cards. Mon–Fri 7:30am–7pm, Sat–Sun 7–9am and 5:30–7pm. Train: Museum. HOMESTYLE.

The setting might not be exciting, but you can't beat the Y for economical meals. Remember, it isn't licensed to serve alcoholic beverages and you can't bring your own, and there's no smoking. High chairs are provided for children, and Hyde Park is right across the street.

IN KINGS CROSS & VICINITY

MODERATE

$ Bayswater Brasserie. 32 Bayswater Rd., Kings Cross. ☎ **02/357 2177.** Reservations not accepted. Main courses A$12.50–A$19.50 (U.S. $10–$15.20). AE, BC, DC, MC, V. Mon–Sat noon–midnight, Sun 10 am–10 pm. Train: Kings Cross. MODERN MULTICULTURAL.

The popularity of this brasserie isn't hard to understand: good food, reasonable prices, friendly service, and convenient hours. In addition, the drop-in-and-eat-what-you-like policy and casual ambience are very appealing to locals and visitors alike. You might want to try the spicy seafood fritters, duck-liver mousse and brioche, or linguine with field mushrooms, cream, and parsley. It'd also be perfectly okay to sit in the garden area and nurse a Bloody Mary over the course of an afternoon or drop in for nothing more substantial than pastry and coffee. A disc jockey holds forth in the bar on Friday nights. Highly recommended.

Bourbon & Beefsteak Bar. 24 Darlinghurst Rd., Kings Cross. ☎ **02/358 1144.** Reservations recommended Fri–Sun. Main courses A$9.50–A$21.50 (U.S. $7.60–$17.20). Weekend and public holiday surcharge A$2 (U.S. $1.60). AE, BC, DC, MC, V. Daily 24 hours (happy hour daily 4–7pm). Train: Kings Cross. INTERNATIONAL.

The Bourbon & Beefsteak came into its own during the late 1960s when U.S. servicemen took their R&R in Sydney and frequented the Cross. It still specializes in American breakfasts of Denver omelets, hash browns, pancakes, or eggs Benedict. There's even a chili con carne omelet, which must've brought tears to the eyes of homesick GIs from Texas. Dinners range from a variety of huge steaks to such gourmet dishes as "son-of-a-bitch cowpoke beef stew" and "gawdammit J.R.'s chili." Mexican, Italian, Chinese, and vegetarian dishes are also offered.

Food may be served around the clock at the B&B, but drinks and dancing are just as important to its clientele of tourists, locals, and the colorful transients who work in the "lively half mile" of Darlinghurst Road, where the bar is located. Vying for tables by the picture window near the street, some watch the seedy side of life without having to be part of it, while others crowd onto the dance floor and gyrate to the band playing daily from 9pm to 4am or disco the night away downstairs from 11pm to 5am. The piano bar may be more to your liking from 5 to 9pm.

Hard Rock Cafe. 121–129 Crown St., Darlinghurst. ☎ **02/331 1116.** Reservations not accepted. Main courses A$9.75–A$17.95 (U.S. $7.80–$14.35). Weekend and public holiday surcharge 10%. AE, BC, MC, V. Sun–Thurs noon–midnight, Fri–Sat noon–2am. Closed Christmas. Train: Museum. AMERICAN.

In 1989, almost 20 years after the first Hard Rock Cafe opened in London, Sydney finally got its long-awaited rock 'n' roll burger eatery. The memorabilia adorning the

Readers Recommend

The Cafe Americana and **Cafe International,** on the Lower Level of the Queen Victoria Building, George Street (between Market and Druitt streets.). *"We found both the Cafe Americana and Cafe International quick, tasty, and inexpensive."*

—Jacques E. Linder, Sarasota, Fla., U.S.A.

walls and ceiling includes costumes worn by Elvis, Elton John, and John Lennon, as well as items from Australian groups like INXS and Icehouse. As per the other locations, a Cadillac rides overhead and the menu features bulging burgers with a variety of toppings, salads, chicken, ribs, and so on.

Lime & Lemon Grass. 42 Kellett St., Kings Cross. ☎ **02/358 5577.** Reservations accepted. Main courses A$9.50–A$16.50 (U.S. $7.60–$13.20). A$2 (U.S. $1.60) surcharge on Sundays and public holidays. AE, BC, DC, MC, V. Daily 6:30–10:30pm. Train: Kings Cross. THAI.

If you love Thai food, Lime & Lemon Grass may provide your favorite Sydney dining experience. The specials chalkboard changes monthly, but you can expect to find delicacies like green curry of fish filet with wild ginger, roast duck salad with herbs and coconut, and steamed fish curry with vegetables. The octopus is especially popular. All meals are served in dishes made from hollowed-out coconuts. This is a good spot for vegetarians, as the management provides meatless alternatives on request. There's also a good selection of local wines. Be sure to let your waiter know ahead how hot you can take your Thai. Ask for a table on the back terrace if you'd like a quieter setting.

INEXPENSIVE

Astoria Restaurant. 7 Darlinghurst Rd., Kings Cross. ☎ **02/358 6327.** Reservations not required. Main courses A$4.70–A$7.80 (U.S. $3.80–$6.25); desserts A$1¢–A$1.60 (U.S. 80¢–$1.28). Public holiday surcharge A50¢ (U.S. 40¢) per person. No credit cards. Mon–Sat 11–2:30pm and 4–8:30pm. Train: Kings Cross. TRADITIONAL AUSTRALIAN.

Across from the Bourbon & Beefsteak Bar (see "Moderate" above), the Astoria is a welcome sight for those whose budgets have worn thin. Roast dinners with vegetables cost less than A$5 (U.S. $4), as do other homestyle dishes, such as pork chops and applesauce and American fried chicken. Jelly (Jell-O), ice cream, tinned (canned) fruit salad, and trifle are offered for dessert. The decor is dated, but at these prices, who cares? The Astoria is BYO.

$ **Govinda's.** 112 Darlinghurst Rd., Darlinghurst. ☎ **02/380 5162.** Reservations accepted. Dinner A$12.50 (U.S. $10), including free movies. BC, MC, V. Daily 5:30–11pm. Train: Kings Cross. VEGETARIAN.

Govinda's is on the second floor in the Hare Krishna Centre, but diners are not exposed to doctrine. Instead, they're treated to a delicious all-you-can-eat buffet of vegetarian dishes, some of which have an Indian flavor. The decor, including a tile floor and black lacquer tables, is simple and pleasant. There are nine tables inside and four on a balcony. No smoking is allowed on the premises. BYO.

Rockerfellers Eastside. 225 Oxford St., Darlinghurst. ☎ **02/361 6968.** Reservations recommended. Main courses A$9.90–A$15.90 (U.S. $7.95–$12.75). Sun surcharge A50¢ (U.S. 40¢)

Readers Recommend

Macleay Street Bistro, 73-A Macleay St., Potts Point (☎ 02/358 4891). *"This wonderful restaurant is owned by an expatriate Frenchman named Daniel. The food is typical of a French bistro but uses very fresh Australian ingredients. The attitude is warm and friendly, and there's a sidewalk café with moderate prices."*

—Joel P. Smith, San Benito, Tex., U.S.A.

Author's Note: The Macleay Street Bistro is open for lunch and dinner Tuesday to Sunday; no reservations; BYO.

per person. AE, BC, MC, V. Mon–Sat 6pm–midnight, Sun 6–11pm. Bus: Taylor Square, then walk one block east. AMERICAN.

Seemingly every symbol of the United States has been incorporated into this restaurant's decor, including Mickey and Minnie Mouse, "grid-iron" (football) players suspended from the ceiling, and jelly beans on the counter. The food is also stereotypical Yank: burgers, ribs, barbecued chicken, and so forth. This eatery is licensed, but you may bring your own alcohol if you wish.

Thai Silver Spoon. 203 Oxford St., Darlinghurst. ☎ **02/360 4669.** Reservations recommended on weekends. Main courses A$9.90–A$12.90 (U.S. $6.35–$10.32). Public holiday surcharge A$1 (U.S. 80¢). AE, BC, MC, V. Daily 11:30 am–3 pm and 6–11 pm. Bus: 380 to the Darlinghurst Court House; the restaurant is across the street. THAI.

This is the place if you like green-curry chicken, pork chili dip, garlic squid, or whole chili fish. Two soups are offered: tom khar kai (chicken with coconut milk) and tom yum (prawn or chicken soup with lemon grass and galanga). Like many of the ethnic eateries on Oxford Street, the Thai Silver Spoon is BYO.

IN THE ROCKS & MILLERS POINT

VERY EXPENSIVE

✪ **Bilson's.** On the Upper Level of the Overseas Passenger Terminal, Circular Quay West, The Rocks. ☎ **02/251 5600.** Reservations recommended well in advance. Main courses A$26–A$32 (U.S. $20.80–$25.60). AE, BC, DC, MC, V. Daily noon–9:30pm. Train or ferry: Circular Quay. MODERN AUSTRALIAN.

Bilson's occupies two glass-walled levels at the northern end of the cruise-ship terminal and offers the finest view in Sydney. By day, diners can take in the sparkling water of the sun-drenched harbor, the Opera House, the north-shore suburbs, the ferries bustling to and from Circular Quay, and the Harbour Bridge. At night, the scene becomes a fairyland of reflected lights. It's no surprise that Bilson's is "a must" for many visitors. The members of INXS dined here when they were in town, as did Mick Jagger and King Juan Carlos and Queen Sofia of Spain.

The creative cuisine prepared by chef Jimmy Tsimikas is as spectacular as the view, and the menu changes daily in order to take advantage of seasonal specialties. The extensive wine list includes fine Australian wines. In deference to North American visitors who expect such things, Bilson's provides a no-smoking section and will organize quick service for guests who are in a hurry. However, I can't imagine wanting to leave this beautiful spot in less than two or three hours.

✪ **Galileo Restaurant.** In the Observatory Hotel, 89–113 Kent St., Sydney, NSW 2000. ☎ **02/256 2222.** Reservations accepted. Main courses A$17–A$36 (U.S. $13.60–$28.80). AE, BC, DC, JCB, MC, V. Mon–Fri noon–2:30pm, Mon–Sat 6:30–10:30pm. ITALIAN-INFLUENCED MODERN AUSTRALIAN.

The Observatory's premier restaurant has an elegant candlelit atmosphere. The wallcovering is Fortuny silk, and there are fine tapestries and polished walnut furniture, as well as original Venetian etchings and Australian impressionist works of art. The focal point is a magnificent central antique crystal chandelier. Main courses include potato gnocchi with roasted capsicum and marscapone fondue; deep sea ocean perch filet, spinach, pinenuts, and raisins with crab dressing; and roasted squab with oyster mushrooms, pumpkin, and rosemary-risotto cake. Desserts include tiramisú, marsala chocolate cake, and my favorite—apple torte with cinnamon ice cream. The wine list and service are excellent. Take a taxi—this isn't a neighborhood for walking around after dark.

Rockpool. 109 George St., The Rocks. ☎ **02/252 1888.** Reservations required. Main courses A$28 (U.S. $22.40). AE, BC, DC, MC, V. Mon–Fri noon–10pm, Sat 6:30–10pm. Train or ferry: Circular Quay. MODERN AUSTRALIAN.

This two-story restaurant across from the Museum of Contemporary Art has a 1950s-modern decor, with crisp white tablecloths. Chef Neil Perry prepares Australian seafood like no one else. His innovative menu includes such dishes as crayfish ravioli with burnt butter and yogurt, red curry of blue-eye cod, and herb- and spice-crusted tuna with braised eggplant. Some nonfish dishes are roasted Illabo milk-fed lamb with fried artichoke and aïoli, and veal with potato-and-fennel gratin and pea purée. A bottle of 1989 Paulette Polish River chardonnay from South Australia, which I highly recommend, will add A$25 (U.S. $20) to your tab. The oyster bar section is less expensive.

EXPENSIVE

Big Reds Aussie Barbecue Restaurant. In the Argyle Centre, 12 Argyle St., The Rocks. ☎ **02/247 1011.** Reservations recommended. Main courses A$12–A$37 (U.S. $9.60–$29.60), half price for children under 14. AE, BC, DC, MC, V. Daily noon–3pm and 5:30–10:30pm. Train or ferry: Circular Quay. AUSSIE BARBECUE.

The Argyle Centre, where Big Reds is located, was built in 1828 as a bond store and warehouse. It served this purpose until 1966, when it was converted to its present use. The original walls have been retained, making an ideal setting for this lively eatery. They claim to serve "Australia's finest, juiciest steaks," as well as seafood dishes, like barbecued jumbo ocean prawns wrapped in paper bark with potato wedges and Queensland mango chutney.

The Harbour Watch Restaurant. On the top level, Pier One, Hickson Road and Lower Fort Street, The Rocks. ☎ **02/241 2217** or 241 1717. Reservations recommended. Main courses A$18.50–A$39 (U.S. $14.80–$31.20); children's menu A$8 (U.S. $6.40). Weekend and public holiday surcharge A$2.50–A$3.50 (U.S. $2–$2.80). AE, BC, DC, MC, V. Daily noon–10pm. Train or ferry: Circular Quay, then free bus to Pier One. SEAFOOD.

The Harbour Watch is provided with an ever-changing and panoramic backdrop for an enjoyable meal. Ferries, large container ships, and various private craft continuously ply the waters in front of the restaurant. The 300-seat room is divided into three levels, so nearly every table shares the remarkable vista.

The very good menu consists almost entirely of fish and shellfish, though steak and veal are offered as a concession to those who prefer meals from the turf. Popular dishes include the barbecued green prawns, Queensland Mud crab, live lobsters, and seafood platter (a small banquet in itself). The seafood is always fresh, with most of it caught locally and brought from the markets or flown in fresh daily.

Waterfront Restaurant. In Campbell's Storehouse, 27 Circular Quay West, The Rocks. ☎ **02/247 3666.** Reservations recommended. Main courses A$19.95–A$42.50 (U.S. $15.96–$34). Weekend surcharge A$2.50 (U.S. $2); public holiday surcharge A$5 (U.S. $4). AE, BC, DC, MC, V. Daily 11:30am–10:30pm. Train or ferry: Circular Quay. SEAFOOD.

Readers Recommend

Pancakes Licensed Cafe, 10 Hickson Rd., The Rocks (☎ 02/247 6371), open 24 hours. *"This is a great place for breakfast. It's not the cheapest place in the world, but the pancakes were, well, perfect."*

—John Rosenthal, New York, N.Y., U.S.A.

The Waterfront is in the historic Campbell's Storehouse, Sydney's first commercial building, on the harbor's edge. Adjacent to the restaurant stands a monument to Robert Campbell, who constructed the building in the colonial period. The large inside and outside seating areas are decorated in a 19th-century nautical motif, and the open-air plaza is shaded by sails suspended from a ship's mast; indoors, three levels of tables are surrounded by brass lanterns, fish nets, tea chests, barrels, and halyards.

Of course, fresh seafood is the specialty of the house. John Dory, barramundi, whole snapper, and filet of Tasmanian salmon are served either grilled or pan-fried. In addition, Sydney rock oysters, fresh ocean prawns, blue swimmer crabs, and Moreton Bay bugs (rock lobster) are regularly available. Though most of the fish is caught locally, some, like the barramundi, is flown in from Queensland. Live lobsters also arrive daily from Tasmania. The food is very good, as is the service.

Wolfie's Restaurant Grill. In Campbell's Storehouse, 17–21 Circular Quay West, The Rocks. ☎ **02/241 5577.** Reservations recommended. Main courses A$19.95–A$25.95 (U.S. $15.95–$20.75). Weekend surcharge A$2.50 (U.S. $2) per person; public holiday surcharge A$5 (U.S. $4) per person. AE, BC, DC, MC, V. Daily 11:30am–10:30pm. Train or ferry: Circular Quay. SEAFOOD/STEAK.

Rounding out the good dining spots in the Storehouse—and named after the man who owns them—Wolfie's opened in 1992. It shares the same priceless harborside location as the Italian Village and the Waterfront Restaurant, but this time Wolfie Pizem decided to specialize in Australia's prime grain-fed beef and local seafood. The menu includes appetizers like Wallis Lake oysters, Chinese barbecued ribs, and salad niçoise with miso dressing. The main courses include prawns "Outback," kangaroo filet, prime sirloin (300 grams), and filet of buffalo. These can be accompanied by excellent herb bread and your choice from a wine list that's both interesting and affordable.

Wolfie's decor includes sandstone walls, earthy terra cotta tones and natural leather, and several colorful murals depicting Sydney Harbour and the Opera House. The result is a warm, relaxed atmosphere. For a view of the Opera House, request a window table or dine out on the large patio. The last time I ate here, Brooke Shields and her mother were at the next table. I can't guarantee you'll dine with celebrities, but I *am* sure you'll have a good meal.

Moderate

✪ **Italian Village.** In Campbell's Storehouse, 7 Circular Quay West, The Rocks. ☎ **02/247 6111.** Reservations recommended. Main courses A$19.95–A$42.50 (U.S. $16–$34). Weekend surcharge A$2.50 (U.S. $2) per person; public holiday surcharge A$5 (U.S. $4) per person. AE, BC, DC, MC, V. Daily 11:30am–10:30pm. Train or ferry: Circular Quay. ITALIAN.

Like the Waterfront Restaurant (above), the Italian Village is in the historic Campbell's Storehouse, on the harbor. Three levels featuring Italian decor and artifacts, a quarry-tile floor, and rustic bric-a-brac combine to create a pleasant country-taverna ambience. The waiters' uniforms are not unlike those of Venetian gondoliers. Seating is both indoors and outside overlooking the water. The appetizers include calamari, penne Matriciana, and lasagne. Sample main courses are pan-fried chicken breast, veal Boscaiola, and Zuppa Di Pesce (lobster, prawns, calamari, Balmain bugs, fish, and scallops, served with garlic croutons and a tomato, onion, shallot, and white-wine sauce). Everything served here is very tasty.

Inexpensive

✪ **The Gumnut Tea Garden.** 28 Harrington St., The Rocks. ☎ **02/247 9591.** Reservations recommended for lunch Mon–Fri. Breakfast from A$5.50 (U.S. $4.40); light lunch from A$8

Quick Bites & 24-Hour Eateries

Sydney's **food courts** provide welcome relief to visitors who'd prefer that their credit-card statement not resemble the national debt. These clusters of minikitchens can be found at several places around town. Inexpensive, mostly ethnic, food is sold take-out style and consumed at tables provided in a central area.

One of the best of these food courts is on the bottom level of the **Queen Victoria Building,** on George Street between Market and Druitt; another good one is on the Pitt Street level at **Centrepoint,** on Market Street between Pitt and Castlereagh. Similar spots are on the waterfront in the **Pier One** complex, at Darling Harbour in the **Harbourside Festival Marketplace,** on the **Manly Wharf,** in **Australia Square** on George Street, and in the **Skygarden** shopping arcade on Level 3.

For better or for worse, American fast food is available in Sydney. If you're pining for a really good chocolate-chip cookie, you'll be glad to know there's a **Mrs. Fields** on the lower level of Martin Place (☎ 02/221 5596). A **Kentucky Fried Chicken** graces the corner of Bathhurst and George streets in the central business district. And there are **McDonald's** golden arches at 375, 505, 600, and 863 George St., as well as on the corner of Pitt and Park, on the Wynyard Station concourse, and across from Circular Quay.

The **Bourbon & Beefsteak Bar** and **Pancakes Licensed Cafe,** 10 Hickson Rd., The Rocks (☎ 02/247 6371), are open 24 hours daily.

(U.S. $6.40); pot of Twinings tea A$2.50 (U.S. $2); order of scones ("enough to share," includes tea or coffee for one) A$6 (U.S. $4.80). BC, MC, V. Daily 8am–5pm. Closed New Year's Day, Good Friday, and three days at Christmas. Train or ferry: Circular Quay. BREAKFAST/LIGHT MEALS/COFFEE/TEA.

This wonderful little cottage, with its crooked windows, sloping floor, and uneven plaster walls, was built in 1835 by blacksmith convict William Reynolds, who'd been sent to Australia as punishment for stealing a horse in Dublin. The original fireplace is still used during cool winter months. You have a choice of sitting in one of several tiny rooms inside or at an umbrella-shaded table on a leafy brick patio. The Gumnut's scones, made only on weekends, are legendary, and their recipe for lemon-hazelnut meringue was requested by the editors of *Gourmet* and printed in the magazine. You might also like to try their fresh fruit juices. BYO.

The Orient Hotel Bistro. 89 George St., The Rocks. ☎ **02/251 1255.** Reservations not required. Main courses A$9.50–A$14.50 (U.S. $7.60–$11.60). AE, BC, CB, DC, MC, V. Daily noon–10pm. Train or ferry: Circular Quay. AUSTRALIAN BARBECUE.

This is a historic Aussie pub with simple good-value meals. The Orient Grill serves charcoal-grilled steaks or a range of dishes from charcoal-grilled fish, pork, chicken, seafood, lamb shish kebab, and even tofu and vegetable skewers for vegetarians. All main courses are served with salad.

Sailors Thai. 106 George St., The Rocks. ☎ **02/251 2466.** Reservations accepted well in advance in restaurant, not accepted in canteen. Main courses A$14–A$20 (U.S. $11.20–$16) in restaurant, A$12–$13 (U.S. $9.60–$10.40) in canteen. AE, BC, DC, MC, V. Restaurant, Mon–Fri noon–3pm, Mon–Sat 6pm–closing; canteen, daily noon–8pm. Ferry, train, or bus: Circular Quay. THAI.

Sailors Thai has quickly become one of Sydney's most popular Thai restaurants. A long line wends out the door of the street-level canteen every day at lunch. Indoor and outdoor seating is offered here. If indoors, expect to be seated at the only table—a very unusual stainless steel item with 21 bentwood chairs on each side. Four tables on the wooden balcony overlook the cruise-ship terminal and the quay. Downstairs in the restaurant the decor is equally modern. The food is *very* good and *very* spicy. In the cantina you might like to try grilled octopus with sweet chili sauce; Kao man gai—poached chicken, rice, soup, and black-bean and ginger sauce; or Parlow—pork, eggs, and bean curd braised with star anise and served with Chinese broccoli. Popular dishes in the restaurant include red curry of bean curd, baby corn, and sugar snap peas as well as beef ribs with chiles.

Zia Pina. 93 George St., The Rocks. ☎ **02/247 2255.** Reservations recommended well in advance. All dishes A$7.20–A$17.60 (U.S. $5.76–$14.08). AE, BC, DC, MC, V. Daily noon–3pm; Sun–Mon 5–9pm, Tues–Thurs 5–10pm, Fri–Sat 5–11:30pm. Train or ferry: Circular Quay. PIZZA/PASTA.

This must be the most popular dining spot in The Rocks. The tiny room with its wooden floor and red-and-white-checked tablecloths always seems to be packed. Pizza comes in two sizes and with a large variety of toppings.

IN MANLY

INEXPENSIVE

Cafe Steyne. 14 S. Steyne. ☎ **02/9977 0116.** Reservations not required. Breakfast (cooked) A$6.80–A$9.60 (U.S. $5.45–$7.70); burgers A$7.90–A$10.90 (U.S. $6.32–$8.75); children's menu A$4.80 (U.S. $3.85). AE, BC, MC, V. Mon–Fri 11am–late evening; weekends and public holidays 8am–late evening. Ferry or JetCat: Manly. BREAKFAST/SANDWICHES/BURGERS/PASTA.

The beachfront location makes this eatery ideal for a casual meal or a cold beer. The menu is much like an American coffee shop's, offering everything from cooked and continental breakfasts to steaks and seafood. A Cobb salad or a Creole chicken salad might appeal if you're watching your waistline; otherwise try one of the big juicy burgers. The home-baked pies are a specialty. Children under 12 can have junior-size burgers, breakfasts, or fish and chips.

AT DARLING HARBOUR

INEXPENSIVE

$ **The Craig Brewery Bar & Grill.** In the Harbourside Festival Marketplace, North Pavilion, Darling Harbour. ☎ **02/281 3922.** Reservations recommended Thurs–Sat night. Lunch or dinner Mon–Sat A$9.90 (U.S. $7.90); lunch Sun A$9.90 (U.S. $7.90). AE, BC, MC, V. Mon–Sat 10am–midnight or later, Sun 10am–midnight. Closed Good Friday and Christmas. Monorail: Harbourside. AUSTRALIAN BARBECUE.

Though it can accommodate up to 1,500 people, the Craig is often jammed. You won't be surprised on seeing the menu, the three bars, the waterfront location, the poker machines, and the live bands on Friday, Saturday, and Sunday nights. You have a choice of rump steak, sirloin steak, pepper steak, Scotch filet steak, and Cajun chicken breast, and can make unlimited trips to the salad bar. Jacket (baked) potatoes, bread rolls, and onions are also included. There's also an extensive chalkboard menu ranging from $A5.50 to A$12 (U.S. $4.4 to $9.60). Nine beers are on tap and a selection of cocktails and Australian wines are available. A schooner (15 oz.) will set you back A$3.10 (U.S. $2.48).

IN SUBURBAN SYDNEY

EXPENSIVE

The Coachmen Restaurant. 763 Bourke St., Redfern. ☎ **02/319 7705.** Reservations recommended. Main courses A$17–A$23 (U.S. $13.60–18.40). AE, BC, DC, MC, V. Mon–Fri noon–3:30pm; Tues–Sat 6pm–midnight. Taxi from city center costs about A$10 (U.S. $8). INTERNATIONAL.

The Coachmen is in an 1826 building constructed by convicts. The home first belonged to Thomas Campbell and was a Sydney landmark, and the nine rooms used for dining reflect its colonial heritage. The exposed brick and stone walls are complemented by subdued lighting. Ronnie Fabri provides soft music for dancing six nights a week. The menu includes such seafood and meat dishes as grilled barramundi, rack of lamb, veal Oscar, and grain-fed beef. Herb-and-garlic bread, baked on the premises, makes a delicious accompaniment. The Coachmen has an excellent wine list and displays vintage wine in the impressive "wine room."

DINING ON THE WATER

Captain Cook Luncheon Cruise. Departing no. 6 Jetty, Circular Quay. ☎ **02/206 1111.** Reservations recommended. Buffet lunch and cruise A$40 (U.S. $32) adults, A$30 (U.S. $24) children 5–14. AE, BC, DC, MC, V. Lunch cruise only, daily 12:30–2pm. Train or ferry: Circular Quay. INTERNATIONAL.

In addition to the Showtime Dinner Cruise (below), Captain Cook Cruises offers a $1^1/_2$-hour luncheon cruise with a commentary on passing sights, allowing busy tourists to do some sightseeing while they enjoy a very good buffet. The meal includes oysters, trout, ham, roast beef, chicken, a variety of salads, lots of fresh fruit, and a cheese platter. Beer and wine can be purchased separately.

John Cadman Cruising Restaurant. Departing no. 6 Jetty, Circular Quay. ☎ **02/206 6666.** Reservations required. $3\ ^1/_2$-hour cruise, three-course dinner, and entertainment A$79 (U.S. $63.20) adults, A$44 (U.S. $35.20) children 5–14. AE, BC, DC, MC, V. Daily 7:30–11pm. Train or ferry: Circular Quay. INTERNATIONAL.

"Sydney's cruising restaurant" departs from Circular Quay every evening at 7:30pm and meanders around Sydney Harbour for $3^1/_2$ hours while passengers enjoy drinks, dinner, and dancing to live music. Visitors staying on the north shore can join the boat at the Jeffrey Street wharf, Kirribilli. A $2^3/_4$-hour Sunset Dinner Cruise is offered for A$56 (U.S. $44.80) for adults and A$40 (U.S. $32) for children 5 to 14. The Sunset Cruise offers champagne and canapes on boarding, a two-course dinner, and wine. Passengers have the option of disembarking at the Opera House at 6:45pm to attend evening performances.

Showtime Dinner Cruise. Departing no. 6 Jetty, Circular Quay. ☎ **02/206 1111.** Reservations required. Three-course dinner, show, and $2^1/_2$- or 4-hour cruise A$75 (U.S. $60) adults, A$42 (U.S. $33.60) children. AE, BC, DC, MC, V. Sun–Thurs 7–9:30pm, Fri–Sat 7–11pm. Train or ferry: Circular Quay. INTERNATIONAL.

Like the John Cadman, the Showtime Dinner Cruise is operated by Captain Cook Cruises. This company, the granddaddy of waterborne sightseeing and dining, operates nine vessels on Sydney Harbour. The Showtime Cruise includes *Under the Southern Cross,* an original production tracing the history of Sydney in song, dance, and comedy.

Sydney Showboat. Departing Campbell's Cove, Circular Quay West, The Rocks. ☎ **02/ 552 2722.** Reservations required. $1^1/_2$-hour luncheon cruise A$40 (U.S. $32) adults, A$32 (U.S. $25.60) children; $3^1/_2$-hour dinner cruise, three-course meal, and entertainment A$95 (U.S. $76). AE, BC, MC, V. Mon–Sat 12:30–2pm, Sun 12:30–3:45pm; daily 7:30–11pm. Train or ferry: Circular Quay. INTERNATIONAL.

It has been more than 100 years since paddlewheelers were working vessels in Australia, but the Sydney Showboat can be seen making daily rounds of Sydney Harbour. In addition to 10:30am and 2:30pm coffee cruises, the Showboat does daily Dixieland jazz buffet luncheon trips (with sightseeing commentary) and nightly dinner cruises featuring a one-hour Showboat Follies Cabaret.

5 What to See & Do in Sydney

Kangaroos don't hop through the central business district, but that's about the only disappointment visitors to Sydney are likely to experience. If your ideas about Australia's largest city are even just *slightly* more down to earth, you'll be pleased with what you encounter.

Public transportation here is inexpensive and easy to use. The sightseeing attractions are truly interesting and rarely evoke the "We really should visit this church because it's famous" syndrome. (Most museums, for instance, are designed to be hands-on experiences.) Shopping in Sydney can be great fun, and you'll find many opportunities to enjoy spectator sports and recreational activities. And the city's after-dark options range from high-brow to red-light.

***Note:* As part of the telephone changeover, in July 1996 all seven-digit phone numbers within the 02 area code will change to 02/9xxx xxxx and all six-digit numbers will change to 02/91xx xxxx. Numbers listed as 02/99xx xxxx will remain the same.**

SIGHTSEEING SUGGESTIONS FOR THE FIRST-TIME VISITOR

If You Have 1 Day Confine your sightseeing to a limited area, such as The Rocks, Circular Quay, and the Opera House. Start with the film at The Rocks Visitors Centre and Exhibition Gallery, 106 George St., The Rocks, which provides a good background on the city's history. Then pick up an area map at the center and browse around the surrounding lanes with their cottages of convict-cut stone. Wander along Circular Quay and then go over to the Opera House for a guided tour. If there's time, take a ferry or JetCat to Manly and back. Another option is to take a lunch cruise, so you can dine and savor the sights simultaneously. For information on cruising, see "Dining on the Water" at the end of Chapter 4.

If You Have 2 Days Spend your first day at The Rocks, Circular Quay, and the Opera House, as suggested above. Your second day could take in the attractions in the Darling Harbour area, formerly a main shipping area of Sydney's port known as Cockle Bay. These include the Sydney Aquarium, the National Maritime Museum, the Powerhouse Museum, and the Chinese Garden. The myriad eateries in the Harbourside Festival Marketplace provide a logical lunch stop. Use the monorail to get here.

✪ Frommer's Favorite Sydney Experiences

Enjoying Sunday Around the House. Each Sunday there's free entertainment on the patios around the Opera House, but it's not just the mimes and musicians that make the scene special. Sydneysiders of all ages gather for this happening, and it's fun to see how people from another nation play. The breeze off the harbor and the continuous parade of sailboats and ferries add to the experience. Perhaps my favorite Sydney experience is taking a walk around the Opera House (see Walking Tour 3 in "Strolling Around Sydney" later in this chapter).

Spending an Evening at the House. There's something magical about attending a performance at the Opera House—maybe it's the wonderful view of lights sparkling on the harbor that you have from the bar and lounge areas during the interval (intermission).

Checking Out The Rocks Market. I always time my trips to Sydney so I'm here over a weekend and can browse through the stalls of The Rocks Market. Over the years I've acquired everything from a lithograph of the Opera House that now hangs in my bedroom to a favorite silver bracelet. Take a tip and take cash—you'll get slightly better prices than those paying with credit cards.

Taking Afternoon Tea at The Regent Hotel. Tea in the Mezzanine Lounge of The Regent, Sydney is a memorable experience. The scones are fluffy, the service is impeccable, and it's fun to watch the comings and going in the lobby one level below. You're sure to see a few tycoons, some famous faces, and maybe even a head of state.

Riding the Ferry to Manly. The JetCats are faster, but there's something wonderfully atmospheric about the old ferries that ply the harbor between Circular Quay and the seaside suburb of Manly. Upon arrival I decide whether I want to visit Oceanworld or take the scenic walk to Shelly Beach.

If You Have 3 Days Follow my suggestions above for Days 1 and 2, then add the Sydney Tower, the Hyde Park Barracks, the Australian Museum, the Queen Victoria Building, and a walk in the Royal Botanic Gardens.

If You Have 4 Days or More After following the above suggestions, the visitor with more time could spend a day at Manly or Bondi exploring the area and experiencing an Australian beach and then another day at one of the wildlife parks, like Featherdale or Koala Park.

1 The Top Attractions

✪ **Sydney Opera House.** Bennelong Point. ☎ **02/250 7111** (general inquiries), 02/250 7250 (tours), 02/250 7870 or fax 02/250 7321 (Tourism Services Department), or 02/250 7777 or fax 02/251 3943 (box office). Parking available in the Sydney Opera House Car Park. Take a train or ferry to Circular Quay or take the Red Explorer Bus or State Transit bus: 438.

Whether you think the Opera House looks like a cleverly folded dinner napkin or, as some say, like a pair of armadillos in heat, you'll be impressed by the size and the drama of Sydney's—and Australia's—top attraction. Most visitors are surprised to learn that this famous landmark isn't really an opera house per se—it's a performing arts complex with four main auditoriums, a reception hall, four restaurants, six theater bars, a library, an archives, and extensive foyer and lounge areas. And don't let its avant-garde appearance make you think the Opera House was built just recently—it celebrates its 23rd birthday in 1996.

Central Sydney Attractions

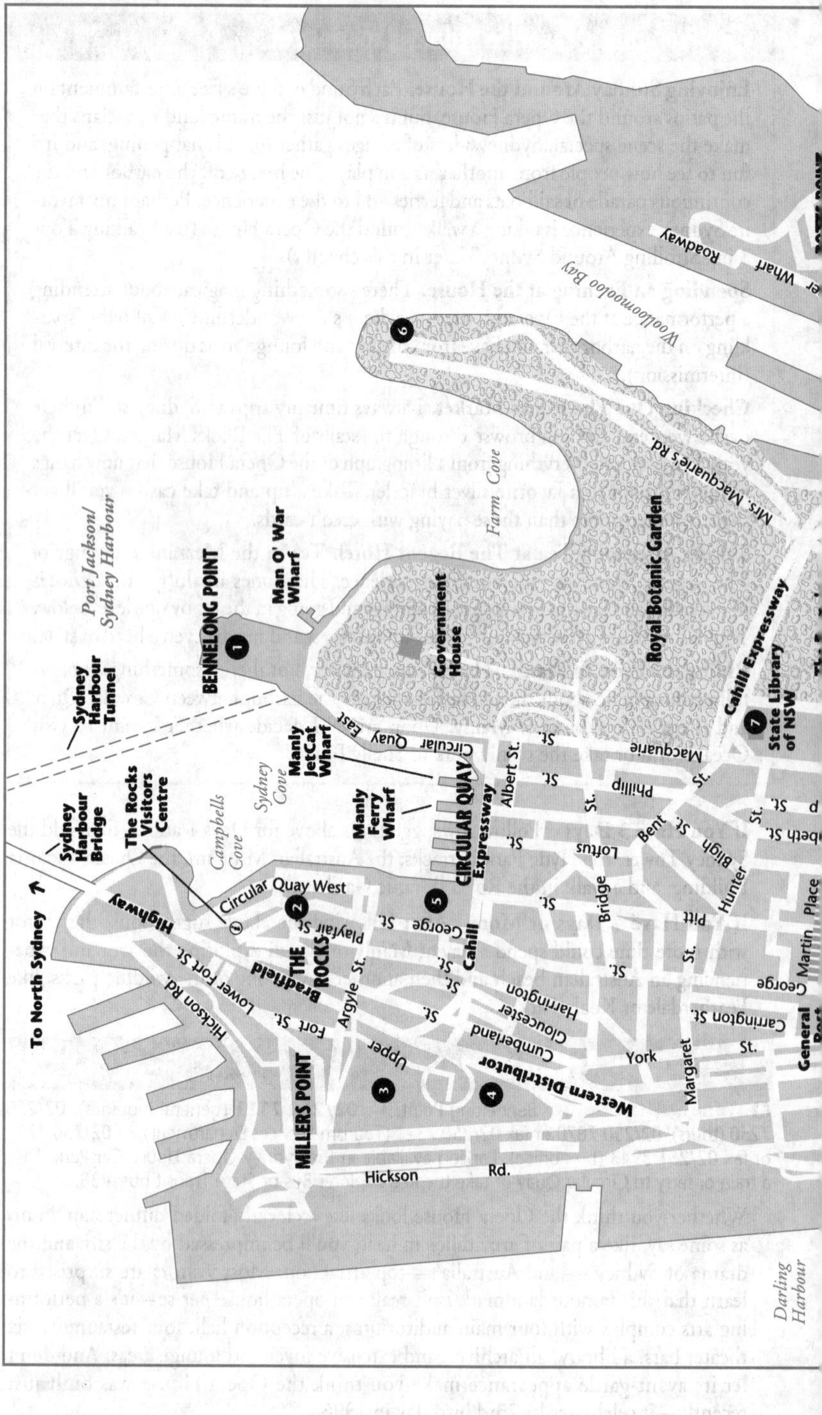

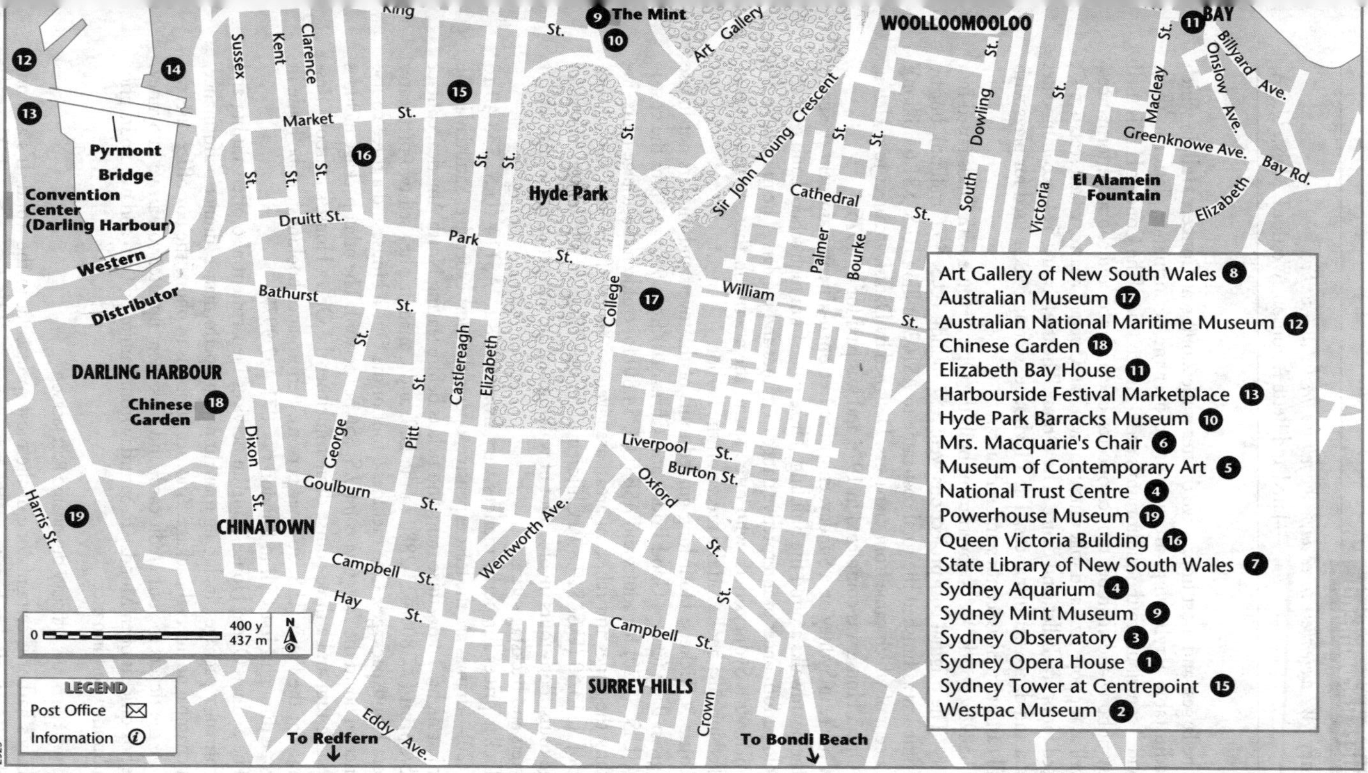

The Mint
WOOLLOOMOOLOO
BAY
Billyard Ave.
Onslow Ave.
Greenknowe Ave.
Bay Rd.
Elizabeth
Macleay St.
El Alamein Fountain
Victoria St.
South Dowling St.
Cathedral St.
Palmer St.
Bourke St.
William St.
Sir John Young Crescent
Art Gallery
Hyde Park
College St.
Liverpool St.
Burton St.
Oxford St.
Wentworth Ave.
Campbell St.
Crown St.
SURREY HILLS
To Bondi Beach
To Redfern
Eddy Ave.
Hay St.
Campbell St.
Goulburn St.
CHINATOWN
Dixon St.
George St.
Pitt St.
Castlereagh St.
Elizabeth St.
Park St.
Bathurst St.
Druitt St.
Market St.
King St.
Sussex St.
Kent St.
Clarence St.
Pyrmont Bridge
Convention Center (Darling Harbour)
Western Distributor
DARLING HARBOUR
Chinese Garden
Harris St.
0
400 y
437 m
N
LEGEND
Post Office
Information
Art Gallery of New South Wales 8
Australian Museum 17
Australian National Maritime Museum 12
Chinese Garden 18
Elizabeth Bay House 11
Harbourside Festival Marketplace 13
Hyde Park Barracks Museum 10
Mrs. Macquarie's Chair 6
Museum of Contemporary Art 5
National Trust Centre 4
Powerhouse Museum 19
Queen Victoria Building 16
State Library of New South Wales 7
Sydney Aquarium 4
Sydney Mint Museum 9
Sydney Observatory 3
Sydney Opera House 1
Sydney Tower at Centrepoint 15
Westpac Museum 2
2325

Readers Recommend

Sydney *"We were there three days. We felt we needed at least five."*

—Jared and Bette Aaronson, Westford, Mass., U.S.A.

The largest and most impressive theater is the 2,690-seat **Concert Hall,** in which 18 adjustable acrylic rings are suspended over the performance platform; these "clouds" contribute to the auditorium's excellent acoustics. The Concert Hall is used for symphony and chamber music concerts, opera, dance, and choral performances, as well as for pop, jazz, and folk music shows. The **Opera Theatre,** which seats 1,547, is used for opera, ballet, and dance. The **Drama Theatre,** seating 544, accommodates drama and dance performances. The **Playhouse,** seating 398, is used for plays with small casts, as well as lectures and seminars.

The New South Wales government built the Opera House with funds raised in a lottery. The original cost projections were A$7 million (U.S. $5.6 million), but by the time it was finished the total cost came to A$102 million (U.S. $81.6 million), not a cent of which came from taxpayers. Designed by Danish architect Jørn Utzon, the Opera House was completed in 1973 and was paid for by 1975.

If you're in Sydney on a Sunday, enjoy the **free open-air entertainment** presented on the boardwalks around the building. These range from high school band concerts to solo performances of interpretive dance to mimes and jugglers. The minishows are popular with Sydneysiders, who often spend the afternoon there with friends, a packed lunch, a book, and the breeze off the harbor.

Tours & Tickets: Hour-long guided tours of the foyers and theaters not in use are given daily (except Good Friday and Christmas) from 9am to 4pm; the cost is A$9 (U.S. $7.20) for adults and A$6 (U.S. $4.80) for children. Backstage tours, including the stages and rehearsal areas, are given on Sunday from 9am to 4pm at a cost of A$13.50 (U.S. $10.80). Children under age 12 aren't allowed on the backstage tours. Both tours involve a lot of walking and are subject to the availability of theaters and backstage areas.

Ticket prices for performances vary from A$48 to A$114 (U.S. $38.40 to $91.20)—dramas are the least expensive, operas the most expensive; Saturday is the costliest night. To organize tours and tickets before leaving North America, contact **ATS/Sprint** (☎ 800/423-2880 in the U.S. and Canada). They sell two pretheater Opera House packages: One includes a tour of the Opera House and a three-course dinner on board the *John Cadman* (U.S. $56 per person). The other package includes the same tour and a three-course dinner in either the Opera House's Harbour Restaurant or the Foyer (U.S. $67 per person). Performance bookings can be made in Europe through **First Call** in London (☎ 071/497 9977).

The Sydney Opera House Tourism Services Department also offers dining and performance packages, including tour/dinner and performance, dinner/performance, or a champagne interval package. Another option is to phone the box office directly, charge the tickets to your credit card, and pick them up after you arrive in Sydney. The box office is open Monday to Saturday from 9am to 8:30pm and two hours prior to a Sunday performance.

✪ **Sydney Harbour.** Officially designated Port Jackson.

Sydney's harbor is certainly one of the most spectacular in the world. It's also one of the busiest, playing host to an almost constant parade of container ships, cruise ships, ferries, JetCats, water taxis, and private yachts. The extensive waterway, with

A House like no Other in the World

When I first met her she was a sweet young thing—all gleaming white and nearly brand new. The year was 1975. I was a schoolteacher on summer vacation. She—the Sydney Opera House—was an architectural wonder on her way to becoming the most famous landmark in the Southern Hemisphere.

When I think of this occasion, of walking down Macquarie Street—actually dashing down Macquarie because I was late and afraid I'd miss the tour I'd booked—and looking up and seeing the House for the first time, I hear Roberta Flack's voice. I hear "The first time ever I saw your face."

I know it sounds corny, but I really was "knocked off my pins" as they say in Australia. The building itself, all gleaming white and looking like nothing I'd ever seen before, would've been impressive on its own, but in combination with its site, it took my breath away.

The Opera House occupies a finger of land extending into Sydney Harbour. This extrusion, called Bennelong Point, is surrounded by water on three sides. A wonderful breeze blows here, refreshing all who stop to admire the passing parade of massive container ships, peripatetic ferries, and dutiful tug boats. I was blown away by the beauty of it all, so much so that my legs trembled as I climbed the stairs spreading across the front of the building.

That night I attended *Simon Boccanegra,* and the next night I managed to get tickets for an orchestral performance in the Concert Hall. The sights during the "interval" were every bit as impressive as the show on stage: I stood in an unoccupied spot next to one of the expansive windows in the northern foyer and looked out into the dark winter night. The Harbour Bridge was outlined in lights and their reflection sparkled on the water; a soft glow emanated from the ferries trudging back and forth on their way to and from Circular Quay; brightly lit party boats cha-chad to and fro. I drank in the view, not champagne, but I still felt giddy when I returned to my seat for the second act.

In recent years when I've returned to Sydney, I've tried to analyze what makes this building so special. What gives it the charisma, the magical quality that no other has. I'm sure it has something to do with the way sunlight and moonlight reflect off the roof tiles, making it seem almost alive. I've also noticed that its appearance seems to be constantly changing, and I find myself studying each view like I do an especially beautiful pattern in a kaleidoscope, knowing I'll never see it exactly the same again.

When I first met her she was all gleaming white and nearly brand new. She has mellowed now but is more beautiful than ever.

a shoreline of 240km (149 miles), is the focal point of the city. Major streets lead to it, the Opera House is perched above it, the Royal Botanic Gardens abut it, and homes, hotels, and office buildings are designed to face it. Container ships berth in the Darling Harbour area of the port and private yachts fill myriad marinas along the waterfront, but ferries and JetCats come and go day and night from busy **Circular Quay.** This colorful hub, described by reader Karen Amster as "what you'd get if you crossed the Reading Terminal with the Atlantic City boardwalk," is well worth a wander. A small island in the middle of the harbor was once used to confine convicts and got the nickname Pinchgut from prisoners who were kept there on short rations. **Fort Denison,** as it's properly known, provides superb water and city views.

Captain Cook Tours conducts excursions to the isle (see "Organized Tours" later in this chapter).

Until about 65 years ago, the only way to cross the harbor was by boat—a scenic, but not always convenient, mode of transport. However, in 1932 construction of the **Harbour Bridge,** known locally as the "coat hanger," was completed. The 1,150-meter (3,795-ft.) bridge spans the 503-meter (1,660-ft.) distance between Dawes Point on the south and Milson's Point on the north. Accommodated on the bridge are an eight-lane road, two train tracks, a bicycle path, and a pedestrian walkway. The **Pylon Lookout** (☎ 02/247 3408), where you can view displays relating to the bridge's history, can be visited daily from 10am to 5pm. Admission is A$2 (U.S. $1.60). *Note:* Touring the Pylon involves climbing 200 steps. You can also use your feet to explore **The Rocks,** the historic area at the south end of the Harbour Bridge. Walking Tour 2, later in this chapter, gives you a detailed view of this area.

You shouldn't leave Sydney without taking a cruise on the harbor. I've detailed several in "Organized Tours" later in this chapter.

Here's a bit of Harbour Bridge humor you might enjoy:

An American and an Australian are sitting in a bar overlooking Sydney Harbour. "Do you know why America is the greatest country in the world?" asks the American. "It's because we build big and we build fast. We put up the Empire State Building in six weeks. And you," he continues, turning to the Australian, "what has Australia done to match that?"

"Nuthin', mate. Not that *I* know of."

The American points at the Harbour Bridge. "What about that?"

The Australian looks over his shoulder. "Dunno, mate. Wasn't there yesterday."

Sydney Tower at Centrepoint. Market Street, between Pitt and Castlereagh sts. ☎ **02/229 7444.** Admission A$9 (U.S. $7.20) adults, A$7 (U.S. $5.60) students, A$4 (U.S. $3.20) children, A$20 (U.S. $16) family (2 adults, 2 children). Sun–Fri 9:30am–9:30pm, Sat 9:30am–11:30pm. Train: St. James. Monorail: City Centre.

Rising 304 meters (988 ft.) above the Centrepoint Shopping Complex, Sydney Tower is the Southern Hemisphere's tallest and one of Australia's most spectacular buildings. You ride one of the three double-decker elevators for the 41 seconds it takes to get to the top, and there you're treated to a spectacular 360-degree view. The tower houses two revolving restaurants and an observation area. This is Sydney's version of the Eiffel Tower.

✪ **Hyde Park Barracks Museum.** Queen's Square, at the top of Macquarie St. ☎ **02/223 8922.** Admission A$5 (U.S. $4) adults, A$3 (U.S. 2.40) children, A$12 (U.S. $ 9.60) family. Daily 10am–5pm. Closed Good Friday and Christmas. Train: St. James. Sydney Explorer Bus: Stop 4, then short walk.

This adapted Georgian-style building was designed by convict architect Francis Greenway in 1818. Over the years it has served as convict barracks, a female immigration depot, courts and legal offices, and a museum. In 1990 it was taken over by the Historic Houses Trust of New South Wales, and now the building is being

Impressions

We got into Port Jackson in the afternoon and had the satisfaction of finding the finest harbour in the world, in which a thousand sail of the line may ride in the most perfect security.

—Capt. Arthur Phillip, Recounting His Arrival with the First Fleet in 1788 allowed to speak for itself. Various periods of social history are demonstrated by the structure and the alterations that've been made to it. Actual Victorian color schemes have been restored on the second floor; the original whitewashed brick walls can be seen on the third floor, a reconstruction of the convict dormitories that originally occupied the entire building. This top floor also provides rare insight into the daily lives of the convicts, and you can lie in reconstructed jute hammocks and listen to the dreams and nightmares of the first occupants. Throughout this significant historic building exhibits address the various contrasting groups of people who've lived and worked within its walls.

The relationship between the barracks and the colonial buildings and parks around it is also addressed. These neighbors include St. James Church, the Mint, the Supreme Court, Hyde Park, and the Domain.

The Barracks Cafe, in the courtyard, is open Monday to Friday from 10am to 4pm and Saturday and Sunday from 11am to 3pm.

Museum of Contemporary Art (MCA). Circular Quay West. ☎ **02/241 5876** or 241 5892. Admission A$8 (U.S. $6.40) adults, A$3 (U.S. $2.40) children, A$15 (U.S. $12) family. Daily 11am–6pm. Closed Good Friday and Christmas. Train or ferry: Circular Quay.

This museum dedicated to contemporary visual arts houses the J. W. Power Collection of more than 4,000 pieces, including works by Marcel Duchamp, Christo, Robert Rauschenberg, and Andy Warhol, plus a special representation of Aboriginal art. The MCA also offers changing art shows and related films and lectures. Free guided tours are given daily at noon and 2pm.

The MCA Store is a good place to shop for innovative merchandise, and the MCA Cafe is a popular Sydney eating and meeting spot (see "Dining" at the end of Chapter 4).

Oceanworld. West Esplanade, Manly. ☎ **02/9949 2644.** Admission A$13.50 (U.S. $10.80) adults, A$7 (U.S. $5.60) children 4–14; under 4 free. Daily 10am–5:30pm. Closed Christmas. Ferry or JetCat: Manly.

This aquarium displays a wide range of marine animals, including many colorful living corals, and several unusual species, such as the giant cuttlefish and leafy sea dragon. Tropical fish from the Great Barrier Reef can be seen, as well as sea life from Sydney Harbour. Sharks are the main research emphasis at Oceanworld, and feedings take place twice a day. An after-hours dive in the shark tank can even be arranged for the more adventurous. Seal shows take place four times a day.

Oceanworld is only a short walk from the Manly Wharf, where ferries and JetCats arrive from Sydney. Meals and snacks are served in the Coral Cafe.

Sydney Aquarium. Darling Harbour—East Side. ☎ **02/262 2300.** Admission A$14.90 (U.S. $11.90) adults, A$7 (U.S. $5.60) children under 16. Daily 9:30am–9pm. Ferry: Darling Harbour/ Aquarium. Monorail: Darling Park. Sydney Explorer Bus: Stop 20.

Shaped like a great breaking wave, the aquarium stands 15 meters (50 ft.) high and 140 meters (462 ft.) long and until recently was listed in the *Guinness Book of World Records* as the largest aquarium in the world. Inside are extensive exhibits of purely Australian aquatic species. A major feature is the "Open Ocean" oceanarium where many species of sharks and rays can be observed at very close range from underwater transparent tunnels. There's also a marine mammal sanctuary for seals. The Great Barrier Reef display, live crocodiles, and exhibits relating to Australian fish are other good reasons to come here.

The Aquarium Coffee Shop serves all meals, and a gift shop is in the main lobby.

Did You Know?

- It takes 30,000 liters (7,800 gal.) of paint to cover the Sydney Harbour Bridge with one coat.
- When it first opened in 1932, the toll on the Sydney Harbour Bridge was 6 pence for a car and 3 pence for a horse and rider.
- The first road from Sydney to Liverpool was paid for with 400 gallons of rum.
- Sydney Harbour, also known as Port Jackson, covers an area of 55 square kilometers (22 sq. miles).
- From 1897 to 1905, Sydney's Kings Cross was called Queen's Cross.
- The *Sydney Morning Herald* is the oldest daily newspaper in the Southern Hemisphere, founded in 1831.
- San Francisco and Sydney are sister cities.
- Sydney got its name from Viscount Sydney, British home secretary at the time the city was founded.
- Sydney will host the Olympic Games in the year 2000.

✪ **Australian National Maritime Museum.** Darling Harbour. ☎ **02/552 7777.** Fax 02/552 2318. Admission A$7 (U.S. $5.60) adults, A$4.50 (U.S. $3.60) children 5–15, A$18.50 (U.S. $14.80) family; under 5 free. Daily 9:30am–5pm. Monorail: Harbourside. Sydney Explorer Bus: Stop 17.

This museum houses historic vessels, artifacts, and displays depicting Australia's relationship with the sea, from the Aboriginal seafarers to America's Cup contenders. Visitors can climb aboard a navy destroyer and see the fastest boat in the world. The USA Gallery, America's Bicentennial gift, reflects Australia's close maritime relationship with the United States over the last 200 years. This is a wonderful interactive museum that provides meaningful social history. Allow several hours for your visit; on our first visit my husband and I almost had to be forcibly removed at closing time. Highly recommended.

Powerhouse Museum. 500 Harris St., Ultimo. ☎ **02/217 0100.** Admission A$5 (U.S. $4) adults, A$2 (U.S. $1.80) children 5–15 (under 5 free); A$12 (U.S. $9.60) family. Free highlight tour daily at 1:30pm. Daily 10am–5pm. Closed Christmas. Monorail: Haymarket. Sydney Explorer Bus: Stop 16.

One of the Southern Hemisphere's largest museums, the Powerhouse (formerly the Ultimo Power Station) near Darling Harbour is notable for the innovation of its displays. Its attractive architectural space is filled with information about science, transportation, human achievement, technology, decorative arts, and social history. Participation is encouraged here. Interactive computers and experiments capture the attention of people who think they don't like museums. This place is a treasure house of Australia's past and present. The Kids Interactive Discovery Spaces (KIDS) are designed to appeal to those under 8.

The Powerhouse Garden Restaurant, painted by colorful contemporary artist Ken Done, is on Level 5, and the kiosk in the Grace Bros. Courtyard on Level 2 serves light lunches and snacks.

Chinese Garden. Darling Harbour. ☎ **02/281 6863.** Admission A$2 (U.S. $1.60) adults, A50 (U.S. 40) children under 15. Daily 9:30am–sunset. Sydney Explorer Bus: Stop 19.

This is the largest traditional Chinese garden of its type outside China. It embodies principles dating back to the 5th century and is a refreshing hideaway in the heart of Sydney. The garden was designed by Guangdong Landscape Bureau in Guangzhou, China—Sydney's sister city.

Taronga Zoo. Bradleys Head Road, Mosman. ☎ **02/9969 2777.** Fax 02/9969 7515. Admission A$14 (U.S. $11.20) adults, A$7 (U.S. $5.60) children 4–15; there are a variety of family packages. Combination ferry, bus, aerial safari, and zoo admission tickets (Zoopass) are sold at Circular Quay (see "Getting Around" in Chapter 4). Daily 9am–5pm. Ferry: Taronga Zoo; then bus or aerial safari uphill to the entrance gate. Bus: 247 from Wynard station.

In a suburb on the north side of the harbor, this zoo has the world's finest collection of Australian fauna and wonderful harbor and city views. Animals are displayed in 30 hectares (74 acres) of gardens that slope down to the water's edge.

The highlights include the koala exhibit, where a spiral staircase permits good viewing from ground to treetop; the nocturnal house; the rain-forest aviary with over 30 species of birds; and the only platypus display area in Sydney. Phone ahead to find out the koalas' feeding time or you're likely to see just their little furry bodies asleep in the forks of trees. And for the best look at the platypus, try to be there between 11am and noon or between 2 and 3pm. Travelers with young children won't want to miss the Discovery Park, where the zoo displays its baby animals, or the seal shows.

Aerial safari rides and guided walking tours are available at a small charge, and large souvenir shops sell Australian products and publications. "Koala Encounters" provides an opportunity for visitors to have their picture taken standing next to koalas. This area is open twice daily; phone for times.

Featherdale Wildlife Park. 217 Kildare Rd., Doonside. ☎ **02/622 1644** or 671 4981 for 24-hour information. Admission A$8.50 (U.S. $6.80) adults, A$4.25 (U.S. $3.40) children 4–14; under 4 free. Daily 9am–5pm. Closed Christmas. Featherdale is also included on Great Sights Day Tours (☎ 02/241 2294). Train: Blacktown; then bus 725.

If you've got the time, it's well worth the effort to make your way to the Featherdale Wildlife Park, 41km (25 miles) west of Sydney. The park is the home of Syd, the Qantas koala, and dozens of his adorable furry friends. If you want to cuddle, be there between 10am and 4:30pm. (Phone to confirm these hours if it's really important to you; also note that this cuddling may change in 1997 if a proposed New South Wales law goes into effect.) Kangaroos and wallabies can be petted all day. Allow time for admiring the colorful native birds and wincing at the ferocious Tasmanian devil. There are also lots of wonderful wombats—animals that would be as popular as koalas if they had a better press agent.

Snacks are sold from a kiosk on the premises, and there's a good souvenir shop.

✪ **Koala Park.** 84 Castle Hill Rd., West Pennant Hills. ☎ **02/484 3141** or 875 2777. Admission A$8.50 (U.S. $6.80) adults, A$4.50 (U.S. $3.60) children 4–14; under 4 free. Sydney Day Tours offers a Koala Park package including bus to park, park admission, guided tour, billy tea, and damper for A$40 (U.S. $32), or A$38 (U.S. $30.40) in the afternoon when the stockman's camp has closed. Daily 9am–5pm. Closed Christmas. Take train to Pennant Hills Station via North Strathfield (45 min.), transfer to bus 651-655 Koala Park.

This pretty park is spread across 4.1 hectares (10 acres) where 55 koalas come and go from one tree to another. The rain forest was planted here in 1922, and the park opened in 1930. Koala feeding/informative chat times are 10:20 and 11:45am and 2 and 3pm, and visitors can pet and be photographed with one of the little animals at this time. For animal-welfare reasons, Koala Park has never allowed guests to hold koalas, but you can put your arm around one and take pictures with your own camera. Featherdale Wildlife Park allows guests to hold koalas, but that may change in 1997 (see above). At Koala Park, there are also wombats, dingos, kangaroos, wallabies, emus, and native birds. Be sure to say hello to Matilda the wombat and a charming dingo named Marinda. Of the four wildlife parks in the greater Sydney area, I like Koala Park the best because of their concern for the animals' wellbeing. Their new koala hospital will open in 1996.

Gledswood Homestead. Camden Valley Way, Catherine Field. ☎ **02/606 5111.** Fax 02/606 5897. Admission A$60 (U.S. $48) adults; 10% discount to Frommer's readers who show this book. Daily 10am–4pm. Tours: Sydney Day Tours and Premier Tourist Services offer tours. By Car: Take the M5 to Camden Valley Way (Exit 89)—an hour from Sydney. By Train: CityRail train to Campbelltown and transfer to local Busways service from outside station.

Gledswood is a 61.5-hectare (150-acre) farm and winery affording you a realistic look at the agricultural lifestyle. Here you can see an authentic sheep shearing (not an abhorrent staged one like the Australian Wildlife Park offers) at noon and 2pm, try boomerang throwing, milk a cow, have billy tea and damper bread in the stockmans' camp, watch sheep dogs working, take a tour of the colonial homestead dating from 1810, taste wine, and meander through the pretty gardens. The admission includes all of the above, plus a hearty lunch served by staff in period costumes. Horse riding is available at an extra cost. An adjacent golf course is the only reminder that this is no longer a working property; otherwise, it feels like a completely rural experience, and it's more authentic than any similar option you'll find within an hour's drive of any capital city in Australia. Plan to spend the day.

2 More Attractions

HISTORIC HOUSES

Elizabeth Bay House. 7 Onslow Ave., Elizabeth Bay. ☎ **02/358 2344** or 356 3022. Admission A$5 (U.S. $4) adults, A$3 (U.S. $2.40) children, A$12 (U.S. $9.60) family. Tues–Sun 10am–4:30pm. Closed Good Friday and Christmas. Bus: 311. Sydney Explorer Bus: Stop 10.

An elegant mansion built in 1835, Elizabeth Bay House was described at the time as the "finest house in the colony." A domed ceiling covers a central oval foyer, and an impressive winding staircase leads to rooms on the second floor. Close to the harbor, Elizabeth Bay House commands some of the best views in Sydney.

Vaucluse House. Wentworth Road, Vaucluse. ☎ **02/388 7922.** Admission A$5 (U.S. $4) adults, A$3 (U.S. $2.40) children, A$12 (U.S. $9.60) family. Tues–Sun 10am–4:30pm. Closed Good Friday and Christmas. Bus: 325 from Circular Quay.

Vaucluse House is a 15-room mansion built in the Gothic style and splendidly sited on Sydney Harbour. From 1827 to 1853 it was the home of William Charles Wentworth, father of the Australian constitution. Vaucluse House Tearooms is a licensed restaurant serving à la carte lunch and morning and afternoon tea.

MUSEUMS, GALLERIES & MORE

Art Gallery of New South Wales. Art Gallery Road, The Domain. ☎ **02/225 1744.** Free admission. Daily 10am–5pm. Train: Martin Place. Sydney Explorer Bus: Stop 6.

The gallery houses a comprehensive collection, including various Australian schools. There are continuous temporary exhibitions.

Sydney Mint Museum. Macquarie Street, opposite Queen's Square. ☎ **02/217 0311.** Admission A$5 (U.S. $4) adults, A$2 (U.S. $1.60) children. Daily 10am–5pm. Closed Christmas. Train: St. James. Sydney Explorer Bus: Stop 4, then short walk.

In addition to stamp, coin, and gold exhibits, various Australian decorative arts are displayed in the museum, housed in Sydney's oldest public building. It's next to the Hyde Park Barracks.

Australian Museum. 6 College St. ☎ **02/320 6000.** Admission A$5 (U.S. $4) adults, A$2 (U.S. $1.60) children, A$10 (U.S. $8) family. Daily 9:30am–5pm. Closed Christmas. Train: Museum or Town Hall. Sydney Explorer Bus: Stop 13.

The Australian Museum holds the country's largest natural-history and anthropology collection, including many Aboriginal artifacts. Take advantage of the free guided tours. Children will enjoy the hands-on activities in the Discovery Space. A restaurant with low-cost meals is open daily from 9:30am to 5pm.

The State Library of New South Wales. Macquarie Street. ☎ **02/230 1414.** Free admission. Mon–Fri 9am–9pm, Sat, Sun and selected holidays 9am–5pm, Sun 11am–5pm. Closed New Year's Day, Good Friday, Christmas, and Boxing Day. Train: Martin Place. Sydney Explorer Bus: Stop 4.

In addition to containing a huge amount of reference material, the library is a venue for exhibits and films. Be sure to notice the marble mosaic Tasman Map on the floor in the vestibule—it depicts the discoveries made by Abel Tasman on his voyages to terra australis in 1642–43 and 1644.

Light lunch and tea are available in the Glasshouse Cafe. The Library Shop offers a good selection of books on Australia.

Westpac Museum. 6–8 Playfair St., The Rocks. ☎ **02/251 1419.** Free admission. Mon 1–4pm, Tues–Fri 10:30am–4pm, Sat 1–4pm, Sun noon–4pm. Closed Good Friday and Christmas. Train or ferry: Circular Quay. Sydney Explorer Bus: Stop 26.

The Westpac Museum details the history of Australia's oldest bank, the Bank of New South Wales, and the economic growth of the country. A dateline around the main gallery traces major events in the financial history. A computer answers banking-related questions like "Why is a cashier called a teller?" You can even cash a traveler's check in an 1890s-style bank.

Sydney Observatory. Watson Road, Observatory Hill, The Rocks. ☎ **02/217 0485.** Admission daytime, free; night visits, A$5 (U.S. $4) adults, A$2 (U.S. $1.60) children, A$12 (U.S. $9.60) family. Mon–Fri 2–5pm, Sat–Sun 10am–5pm; Thurs–Tues evenings (times vary). Bookings made well in advance are essential for evening session. Closed Good Friday and Christmas. Bus: Millers Point. Sydney Explorer Bus: Stop 25, then walk up hill.

The observatory was built in 1858 and included a dome for an equatorial telescope, a room with slits in the roof for a transit telescope, an office, a time-ball tower, and a residence for the astronomer. In those days the time ball would drop at exactly 1pm daily to signal the correct time to the city and harbor below. Today, you can use the observatory's telescopes to discover the wonders of the southern sky. The evening program includes a short talk and tour of the building, films or videos, and telescope viewing of the night sky.

National Trust Centre. Watson Road, Observatory Hill, The Rocks. ☎ **02/258 0123.** Admission: Centre, free; gallery, A$4 (U.S. $3.20) adults, A$2 (U.S. $1.60) children. Tues–Fri 11am–5pm, Sat–Sun noon–5pm. Train or ferry: Circular Quay. Sydney Explorer Bus: Stop 25.

The headquarters of the National Trust was built in 1815 as the colony's military hospital. From 1850 to 1974 it was the Fort Street High School. The centre includes the S. H. Ervin Gallery, a pleasant café (BYO), and a book/gift shop.

PARKS & GARDENS

Looking at a map of Sydney, you'll quickly recognize the major role that parks and gardens play in the city's profile. **Hyde Park,** bordered by Elizabeth, College, and Liverpool streets and St. James Road, is the most central. Named after London's well-known park, it has at various times served as a military training reserve, a cricket ground, and a racecourse. Today it provides a shady spot for office workers'

Full of Fun & Free of Charge

CONCERTS In The Rocks Square, **The Rocks Stage** offers free concerts on Saturday and Sunday from 11am to 4pm. **Darling Harbour** regularly has free entertainment on weekends.

On Sunday you can find **open-air entertainment** on the broadwalks surrounding the Opera House. These range from high school band concerts to solo performances of interpretive dance to mimes and jugglers. The minishows are popular with Sydneysiders, who often spend the afternoon there with friends, a packed lunch, a book, and the breeze off the harbor.

Lunch performances are held in the Martin Place Amphitheatre, Martin Place, on Monday to Friday from 12:15 to 2pm. You can phone the Sydney City Council at 02/265-9110 to find out what's planned.

FILMS The **State Library**, Macquarie Street (☎ 02/230 1414), has free films every Friday and every second Sunday. The **Hare Krishna Centre,** 112 Darlinghurst Rd., Darlinghurst (☎ 02/380 5162), offers free recent-release films to those who dine in Govinda's, their restaurant.

MUSEUMS & GALLERIES All the following offer free admission: the **Art Gallery of New South Wales,** Art Gallery Rd., The Domain (☎ 02/225 1744); the **National Trust Centre,** Watson Rd., Observatory Hill, The Rocks (☎ 02/258 0123); the **Sydney Observatory,** Watson Road, Observatory Hill, The Rocks (☎ 02/217 0485), this is free during the daytime; and the **Westpac Museum,** 6–8 Playfair St., The Rocks (☎ 02/251 1419).

PARKS, GARDENS & BEACHES You can't beat a free stroll through the Royal Botanic Gardens or the Domain. Likewise, Manly, Bondi, and the other great beaches in the area are free. And remember, you've already paid for this book, which means you can take the walking tours in this chapter without spending a penny.

lunchtime retreats and is popular for chess games. During the Sydney Festival in January, Hyde Park is the site of frivolity and free entertainment. At the northern end is the **Archibald Fountain,** designed by artist François Sicard to commemorate the Australian-French alliance of 1914–18.

The **Domain,** adjacent to the Royal Botanic Gardens, is the home of the Art Gallery of New South Wales and the Boy Charlton Pool (public), but the area most visited by Sydneysiders and overseas travelers is **Mrs. Macquarie's Point,** a shady expanse of lawn with sweeping harbor views that gets its name from a seat carved into a rock face near the water's edge—said to have been used by Governor Macquarie's wife during her daily walks in the area. On Sunday the Domain is frequented by soapbox orators.

Early settlers once tried to grow vegetables on the land where the ✪ **Royal Botanic Gardens Sydney** (☎ 02/231 8125) now bloom. Today they'd surely be surprised to see the array of exotic and native trees, shrubs, and flowers thriving near the shores of Sydney Harbour. The herbarium and pyramid glasshouse (greenhouse) are of special interest, as is the Sydney Tropical Centre. The gardens are open daily from 6:30am to sunset. Entry is free of charge, and free guided walks leave from the Visitor Centre on Wednesday and Friday at 10am and Sunday at 1pm. The Sydney Tropical Centre is open daily from 10am to 4pm. Admission is A$5 (U.S. $4) for adults, A$2 (U.S. $1.60) for children, and A$12 (U.S. $9.60) for a family. Very good meals are available at the Botanic Gardens Restaurant.

SURF & SAND

Even if you have no intention of going in the water, try not to leave Sydney until you've seen one of its famous ocean beaches.

Located 8km (5 miles) southeast of the city, **Bondi** is one of Australia's best-known beaches. Access is via train to Bondi Junction and then a no. 380 bus to the beach or the blue Bondi & Bay Explorer Bus (see "Getting Around" in Chapter 4). Bondi's popularity is due to its good surf and fine sand, as well as the lively pubs and trendy bistros nearby. Should you decide to take a dip, there are showers and changing rooms. If you like walking, follow the scenic seaside footpath that starts near the baths (pool) at the south end of the beach and winds along the water to **Bronte Beach.**

✪ **Manly** is 15km (9 miles) from Sydney and has the only surf beach on the north side of the harbor that's patrolled year-round, but safety isn't the only drawing card at this well-patronized beach. Its beauty is in part due to the row of stately Norfolk pines lining the boardwalk. Take the ferry or JetCat from Circular Quay and walk through the Corso to the ocean. As with Bondi, a lovely waterfront walkway starts at the baths and ends at picturesque **Shelly Beach.**

In addition to a nice beach, Manly's attractions include **Oceanworld** (☎ 02/9949 2644), a state-of-the art aquarium that exhibits living coral gardens, tropical fish, and a host of exotic creatures (see "The Top Attractions" at the beginning of this chapter).

You may also want to visit the **New Manly Wharf,** which has restaurants, shops, and amusement facilities. If you plan to be in Sydney in June, you may want to check out the two-day **Manly Food & Wine Festival.** The **Manly Visitors Information Bureau,** South Steyne Street (☎ 02/9977 1088), can tell you more.

ESPECIALLY FOR KIDS

Almost all of Sydney's attractions are fun for families, but the following places are especially appealing for youngsters (the attractions are discussed in full above).

At the **Sydney Aquarium** *(see p. 143)* and Manly's **Oceanworld** *(see p. 143)* sharks and rays swim overhead as you walk through an acrylic tunnel. Kids of all ages are sure to enjoy going aboard the ships that are part of the **Australian National Maritime Museum** *(see p. 144).*

Kids Interactive Discovery Spaces (KIDS) at the **Powerhouse Museum** *(see p. 144)* are designed to appeal to children under 8. Those who are older can use the computers, videos, and other hands-on aspects of this museum to learn about science, technology, and more. At the **Australian Museum** *(see p. 147)* kids enjoy hands-on activities in the Discovery Space.

At **Taronga Zoo** *(see p. 145),* first it's the ferry ride from Circular Quay, then a lift in an aerial tram to the entrance gates. Your offspring haven't even seen the animals yet and they're already having a good time. The whole family can be photographed holding a koala, and the kids can pet kangaroos and other native animals at **Featherdale Wildlife Park** *(see p. 145).* They can also get up close and personal with native animals at **Koala Park** *(see p. 145).*

I've yet to meet a child who doesn't think a day spent at the beach is a day well spent. **Bondi Beach** *(see above)* and **Manly Beach** *(see above)* are both good ones.

SPECIAL-INTEREST SIGHTSEEING

FOR THE LITERARY ENTHUSIAST Of interest to both readers and writers is the ✪ **Writers Walk,** starting just south of the Overseas Passenger Terminal, continuing along Circular Quay, and proceeding toward the Opera House. A project of the New South Wales Ministry for the Arts, round bronze plaques set in the brick footpath recognize Australian authors or authors from other countries who wrote about Australia.

One disk commemorates the completion of the project: "What we are and how we see ourselves evolves fundamentally from the written and spoken word. The Writers Walk demonstrates that this evolutionary process continues to channel the thoughts and perceptions, the hopes and the fears of writers who have known this great city and its people. Dedicated 13 February 1991."

Some of the authors included on the walk are Miles Franklin, Eleanor Dark, Charles Darwin, David Williamson, A. B. "Banjo" Paterson, C.J. Dennis, Christopher Brennan, Oodgeroo Noonuccal, Kenneth Slessor, D.H. Lawrence, Jack London, and Henry Lawson.

Miles Franklin's circle contains a quote from *My Brilliant Career,* and Eleanor Dark's has a passage from *The Timeless Land.* David Williamson, who is still living, is Australia's best-known 20th-century dramatist. Oodgeroo Noonuccal is the Aboriginal name of poet Kath Walker. She adopted the name of her tribe in 1988 to honor the Aboriginal peoples' cause.

FOR THE ARCHITECTURE ENTHUSIAST Sydney's architecture is a case of majestic colonial buildings successfully juxtaposed with contemporary high-rises. These structures are of particular interest:

The **Mint** and **Hyde Park Barracks** stand next to each other on Macquarie Street, a testimonial to the colonial period. The Mint was originally the south wing of the 1816 Rum Hospital, which was converted into the Royal Mint in 1856. It has been restored to its 1870 appearance. Convict architect Francis Greenway designed the Hyde Park Barracks in 1818 for Governor Macquarie and it has been restored to its original appearance. The **Strand Arcade,** 412 George St., was first opened in 1892, then was destroyed by fire in the 1970s and subsequently restored. The **Queen Victoria Building,** 455 George St., was built in 1883 and is probably Sydney's best example of adaptive reuse. More than 150 specialty shops and dining venues have been sensitively fitted into the grand old structure.

Other good examples of successful reuse include the **Powerhouse Museum,** once the Ultimo Power Station where the electricity to run the city's tram system was generated, and the **Hotel Nikko Darling Harbour,** which incorporates the Corn Exchange building built by Sydney's City Council in 1887. Architecture enthusiasts will also want to visit the **Hotel Inter-Continental,** 117 Macquarie St., and admire the way the facade of the old Treasury Building was incorporated into the present use.

On the modern side of things, of course the **Sydney Opera House,** designed by Danish architect Jørn Utzon, is of great interest. Likewise, **Sydney Tower**—the tallest building in the Southern Hemisphere—is notable. The **MLC Centre,** surrounded by Martin Place, Castlereagh and King streets, was designed in 1977 by Harry Seidler, the Austrian-born architect who introduced the high-rise to Australia in the 1960s when he designed the **Australia Square** tower, between George, Bond, and Pitt streets. The MLC Centre is one of the tallest reinforced-concrete towers in the world.

More recently, the **Sydney Aquarium** and the **Australian National Maritime Museum** in Darling Harbour were both designed by Phillip Cox Richardson

Readers Recommend

Manly *"Wish I'd planned more time to stay here."*

—Beverly Carr, Toronto, Ontario, Canada.

Taylor and Partners. **Chifley Tower,** 92–122 Phillip St., a 49-story office building, was completed in 1992. The **World Square Development,** surrounded by Liverpool, Pitt, Goulburn, and George streets, is the largest consolidated development to date in Sydney.

FOR GETTING TO KNOW SYDNEYSIDERS

Meet the People, P.O. Box 370, Randwick, NSW 2031 (☎ 02/314 6987; fax 02/314 6180), specializes in familiarizing visitors with everyday Sydney. Small groups of four to six might go to a local home for lunch or dinner, stopping en route to visit a supermarket or other untouristy spot. They specialize in matching local people with visitors who have the same interests. Prices for touring and guiding vary. Meet the People has a site on the Internet at http://www.meetoz.com.au/g_day.

3 Strolling Around Sydney

Sydney is a great city for walking. The lack of hills, super water views, and handsome architecture are all pluses. Following are three detailed strolls: Walking Tour 1 incorporates some significant shopping venues along George Street. Walking Tour 2, of The Rocks area, is best for history buffs. And Walking Tour 3 covers the Opera House area—it's my favorite and is perfect for photographers seeking waterfront vantage points.

WALKING TOUR 1
George Street

Start: Bathurst and George streets.
Finish: Alfred and George streets.
Time: Allow at least half an hour, not including shopping stops and viewing time at Sydney Tower.
Best Times: Weekdays, but not during business rush hours, when the sidewalks are packed with office workers.
Worst Times: Sunday, when services are held in St. Andrew's Cathedral and shops in the Strand Arcade are closed.

Sydney's main street starts near Central Station and ends in The Rocks. A walk from one end to the other, a distance of about $2^1/_2$km ($1^1/_2$ miles), takes you past a good selection of historic buildings and four McDonald's eateries. The most interesting section, the $1^1/_2$km (1 mile) from Bathurst to Alfred Streets, is detailed here. George Street was named by Governor Macquarie in 1810 in honor of George III of England. Australia's oldest thoroughfare, it was originally called Sergeant Major's Row, Spring Row, and High Street.

Begin your walk at:

1. **St. Andrew's Cathedral,** at Sydney Square on the northwest corner of Bathurst and George streets. The cathedral dates from 1868 and is the oldest Anglican cathedral in Australia. It was constructed from Hawkesbury sandstone and built in the Gothic style. Adjacent to St. Andrew's is the:
2. **Town Hall,** which opened in 1889 and is still an impressive site for welcoming visiting dignitaries. The Lord Mayor holds official receptions in this grand building, which is also used for exhibitions and public meetings. After crossing Druitt Street, you'll see the:

Walking Tour 1—George Street

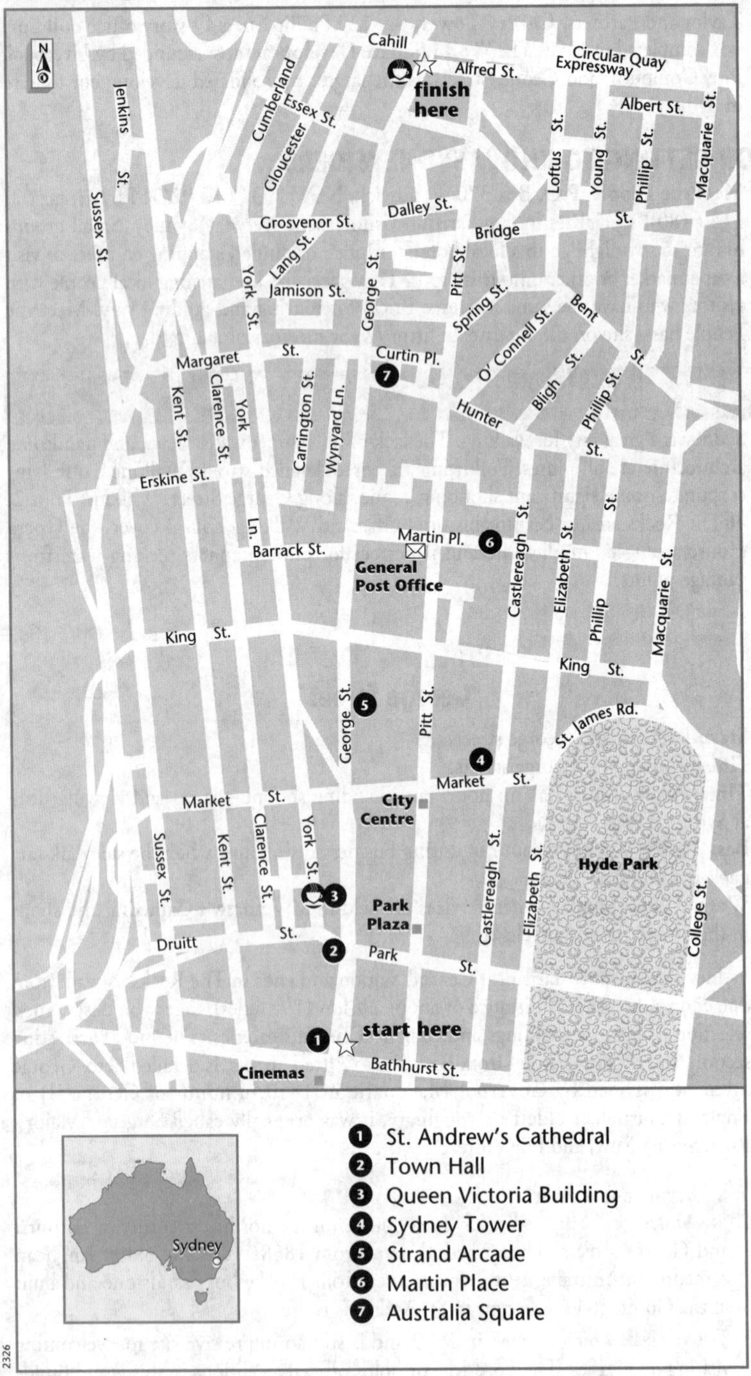

1. St. Andrew's Cathedral
2. Town Hall
3. Queen Victoria Building
4. Sydney Tower
5. Strand Arcade
6. Martin Place
7. Australia Square

3. **Queen Victoria Building,** known locally as the QVB. This huge Romanesque edifice, covering an entire city block, housed the city's main produce markets when it opened in 1898. Allowed to deteriorate from the 1930s on, it reopened in 1986 with all its Byzantine splendor restored and containing nearly 200 shops, cafés, and restaurants. Pierre Cardin is supposed to have called the QVB "the most beautiful shopping center in the world," and I can understand why. The spacious interior is characterized by tall arches, intricate tile patterns, and magnificent stained-glass windows. A curved glass roof allows natural light to illuminate ornate plasterwork, grand columns, and a unique clock that displays scenes of English history on the hour. The building is open for shopping daily. The statue of Queen Victoria in the plaza at the south end was donated by the government and people of Ireland. Until 1947 it stood in front of Leinster House in Dublin—the seat of the Irish Parliament. The sculptor was John Huges, RHA, Dublin (1865–1941).

TAKE A BREAK **Eat Street,** the food court on the lower level of the QVB, offers an array of dining options. You can purchase light meals takeout style and eat in a central area where tables and chairs are provided. A dozen moderately priced cafés also sell meals and snacks.

As you leave the Queen Victoria Building, head east on Market Street to:

4. **Sydney Tower,** where you can zoom 304 meters (988 ft.) to the top in one of three double-decker lifts (elevators). The cost is A$6 (U.S. $4.80) for adults and A$2.50 (U.S. $2) for children, and the view is fantastic.

   Leaving Sydney Tower, walk north through the Pitt Street Mall and turn left into the:

5. **Strand Arcade,** running from Pitt to George streets. When this shopping area opened in 1892, it was described in the *Daily Telegraph* as "the finest public thoroughfare in the Australasian Colonies." Today it boasts three levels with 80 shops and a charming 19th-century atmosphere.

   Continue walking north on George Street to:

6. **Martin Place.** The original General Post Office (GPO) occupies the corner (Australia Post has moved to an adjacent building). As you pass it, note the large clock tower. Martin Place is a popular midday spot for office workers, who share their brown-bag lunches with the pigeons and enjoy free concerts presented Monday to Friday at 12:15pm in the amphitheater.

   In contrast to the historic buildings found along the upper reaches of George Street, the:

7. **Australia Square** high-rise between Hunter and Bond streets is a young whippersnapper. Constructed in 1968, the tower is 170 meters (561 ft.) high.

WINDING DOWN If you've walked all this way, you must be thirsty. Go just a bit farther and you can wander into **The Regent, Sydney** hotel and have a drink or meal. See "Dining" at the end of Chapter 4 for information on the Regent's Club Bar, George Street Bar, and Mezzanine Lounge.

WALKING TOUR 2
Around The Rocks

Start: The Rocks Visitor Centre and Exhibition Gallery, 106 George St.
Finish: Museum of Contemporary Art, Circular Quay West.

Time: Allow a minimum of an hour, much more if you stop to shop or visit any of the attractions.
Best Time: Any day.
The site of the first European settlement in Australia, The Rocks was once a neglected area of convict-built stone buildings. Today it's Sydney's most historic and lively neighborhood. Because the streets are narrow, exploring is best done on foot.

Start your walk at:

1. **The Rocks Visitor Centre and Exhibition Gallery,** 106 George St. (☎ 02/ 255 1788), open daily from 9am to 5pm. Here you'll find a permanent exhibit highlighting the social, archeological, and architectural heritage of the area, brochures, and an audiovisual presentation on the area's history. The center is in the former Sydney Sailors' Home, dating from the 1860s.

   After you've looked around, walk out the door, turn right, and walk a couple of doors down to the:
2. **Australasian Steam Navigation Co. Building** (1884), 1 Hickson Road. This significant Sydney landmark has distinctive Flemish gables and tower. The tower was once used for sighting ships.

   Cross the road and descend the Customs Officers Stairs to reach:
3. **Campbell's Storehouse** (1839–90), Sydney's first commercial building, which once housed tea, sugar, cloth, and liquor imported from the Far East. A monument to Robert Campbell is near the stairs. These colonial warehouses have been restored and are now a row of wonderful waterfront restaurants. See "Dining" at the end of Chapter 4 for complete information on Wolfie's, the Waterfront Restaurant, and the Italian Village.

   Walk in front of the restaurants and around the Park Hyatt Sydney to:
4. **Dawes Point Park,** from which there's a superb harbor view. This is a good place to rest if you plan to climb the 200 stairs in the:
5. **Harbour Bridge's Pylon Lookout.** See "The Top Attractions" at the beginning of this chapter for complete information.

   Return to Hickson Road and proceed to:
6. **No. 18,** contructed in 1902 to be an electric light station but never used for this purpose.

   Continue up George Street past historic terrace houses and the Westpac Banking Museum (see "More Attractions" earlier in this chapter) and turn right onto Playfair Street. You'll soon come to:
7. ***First Impressions,*** a sandstone sculpture by Bud Dumas. It shows a soldier, a settler, and a convict and tells the story of the hardship they experienced.

   Continue a few steps farther to the:
8. **Argyle Terraces,** a row of terrace houses that contain shops. They date from 1875 to 1877 and were once workmen's cottages.

   Continue walking along Playfair Street, with The Rocks Square on your left. Turn right on Argyle Street. The entrance to the:
9. **Argyle Stores** is on your right. Built in 1828 as a bond store and warehouse, it served this purpose until 1966, when it was converted. It's now the home of Big Reds Aussie Barbecue Restaurant (see "Dining" at the end of Chapter 4).

   Continue up Argyle Street and through the:
10. **Argyle Cut,** excavated from 1843 to 1845 by chain gangs of convicts and completed with the aid of explosives in 1859. The Bradfield Highway and Cumberland Street are overhead.

    Continue walking to the:

Walking Tour 2—Around The Rocks

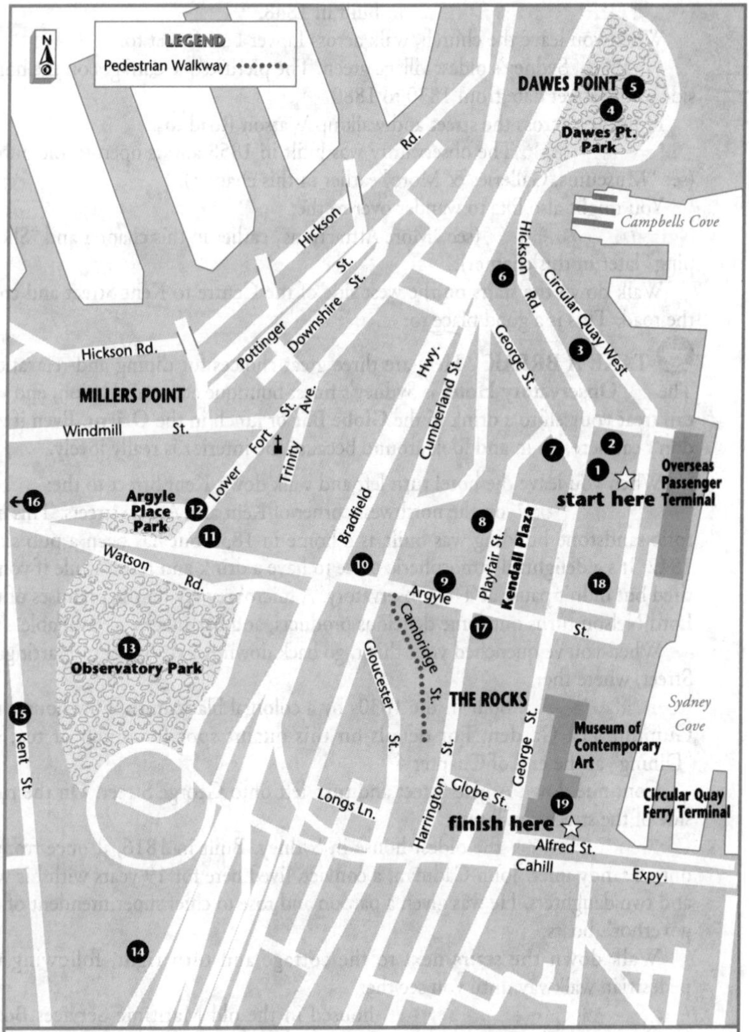

1. The Rocks Visitors Center and Exhibition Gallery
2. Australasian Steam Navigation Co. Building
3. Campbell's Storehouse
4. Dawes Point Park
5. Harbour Bridge's Pylon Lookout
6. No. 18 Hickson Rd.
7. *First Impressions*
8. Argyle Terraces
9. Argyle Stores
10. Argyle Cut
11. Holy Trinity (Garrison) Church
12. Argyle Place
13. Observatory Park
14. National Trust Centre
15. Observatory Hotel
16. Lord Nelson Hotel
17. Reynold's Cottage
18. Cadman's Cottage
19. Museum of Contemporary Art

11. Holy Trinity (Garrison) Church, built in 1848.

When you leave the church, walk across Lower Fort Street to:

12. Argyle Place, Sydney's oldest village green. The picturesque cottages on the north side of the street date from 1830 to 1880.

From here, cross the street and walk up Watson Road to:

13. Observatory Park. The observatory was built in 1858 and is open to the public (see "Museums, Galleries & More" earlier in this chapter).

You might also like to wander over to the:

14. National Trust Centre (see "More Attractions" earlier in this chapter and "Shopping" later in this chapter).

Walk down the stairs on the west side of the Centre to Kent Street and cross the road. This is a good place to:

TAKE A BREAK Here are three great choices for dining and relaxation. The 15. **Observatory Hotel** is Sydney's finest boutique accommodation, and you can treat yourself to a drink in the **Globe Bar** or lunch in the **Orient.** Even if you don't eat here, go in and look around because the interior is really lovely.

When you leave the hotel turn left and walk down Kent Street to the:

16. Lord Nelson Hotel, on the northwest corner of Kent and Argyle streets. This historic sandstone building was built as a home in 1834 but has been a pub since 1842. It's a delightful atmospheric place to have a drink and rest a while if you're tired but didn't pause at The Observatory. A microbrewery on the premises of the Lord Nelson turns out some delicious products, and bar snacks are available.

When you've quenched your thirst, go back down Argyle Street to Harrington Street, where the:

17. Reynolds Cottage, built in the 1830s by a colonial blacksmith, now houses the Gumnut Tea Garden. For details on this quaint spot for lunch or tea, see "Dining" at the end of Chapter 4.

Continue down Argyle Street and turn left onto George Street. On the right side of the street you'll see:

18. Cadman's Cottage, the oldest house in Sydney. Built in 1816, it once fronted onto a sandy inlet. John Cadman, a convict, lived here for 19 years with his wife and two daughters. He was given a pardon and rose to chief superintendent of the governor's boats.

Walk down the stairs next to the cottage and turn right, following the pedestrian walkway until you see the:

19. Museum of Contemporary Art, housed in the old Maritime Services Board building (see "The Top Attractions" at the beginning of this chapter).

WALKING TOUR 3
Around the House

Start: On the pedestrian walkway just south of the Overseas Passenger Terminal and east of John Cadman's Cottage.
Finish: Mrs. Macquarie's Chair, the Domain.
Time: One to two hours, depending on your pace.
Best Times: Weekends, when the harbor is dotted with sailboats.
Worst Time: There isn't a bad time to do this walk.

Walking Tour 3—Around the House

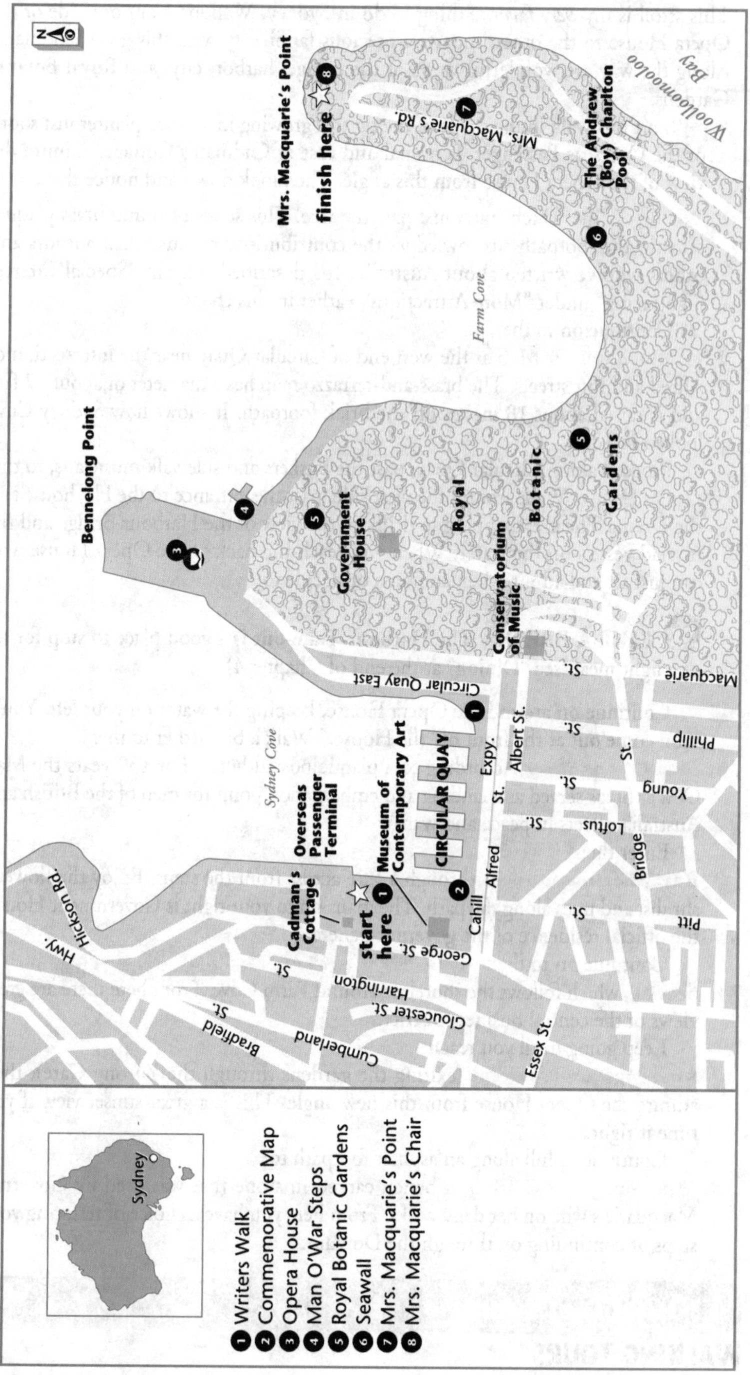
1 Writers Walk
2 Commemorative Map
3 Opera House
4 Man O'War Steps
5 Royal Botanic Gardens
6 Seawall
7 Mrs. Macquarie's Point
8 Mrs. Macquarie's Chair
Sydney
2328
Bennelong Point
Government House
Royal Botanic Gardens
Conservatorium of Music
Farm Cove
Mrs. Macquarie's Point
finish here
Mrs. Macquarie's Rd.
The Andrew (Boy) Charlton Pool
Woolloomooloo Bay
Sydney Cove
Overseas Passenger Terminal
Museum of Contemporary Art
CIRCULAR QUAY
Cadman's Cottage
start here
Circular Quay East
Macquarie St.
Phillip St.
Young St.
Loftus St.
Bridge St.
Pitt St.
Albert St.
Alfred St.
Cahill Expy.
George St.
Harrington St.
Gloucester St.
Cumberland St.
Bradfield Hwy.
Hickson Rd.
Essex St.

This stroll is my *very favorite* thing to do in Sydney. Walking from one side of the Opera House to the other imparts a precious familiarity with this great landmark. Along the way are wonderful views of the bridge, harbor, city, and Royal Botanic Gardens.

Start this walk in the shade of the fig tree growing in a raised planter just south of the Overseas Passenger Terminal and east of Cadman's Cottage. Admire the view of the Opera House from this angle. Then look down and notice the:

1. Writers Walk, which starts just past the tree. This series of round brass plaques set into the footpath acknowledges the contributions of Australian authors and others who've written about Australia. It's described fully in "Special-Interest Sightseeing" under "More Attractions" earlier in this chapter.

   Continue on to the:

2. Commemorative Map at the west end of Circular Quay near the intersection of Alfred and Pitt streets. The brass-and-terrazzo map has a diameter of about 12 feet and is raised about 18 inches off the brick footpath. It shows how Sydney Cove looked in 1808.

   Proceed along Circular Quay, past the buskers and sidewalk musicians, to the:

3. Opera House. Walk around the west side, past the entrance to the Playhouse and the Drama Theatre, stopping to drink in the view of the Harbour Bridge and the myriad vessels on the water. When you reach the back of the Opera House, you can just sit and admire the panorama or decide to:

TAKE A BREAK The **Harbour Take-out** is a good place to stop for tea or a light meal (see "Dining" at the end of Chapter 4).

Continue on around the Opera House, keeping the water on your left. You'll soon come out at the front of "the House." Walk a bit farther to the:

4. Man O'War Steps. According to a plaque posted here, "For 150 years the Man O'War Steps served as a landing and embarkation point for men of the British and Australian fleets in peace and war."

   Enter the:

5. Royal Botanic Gardens through a gate across from the steps. Enjoy the flowers, shrubs, and trees along the path. The mansion to your right is Government House, the official residence of the governor-general.

   Continue on to the:

6. Seawall, which follows the shoreline around Farm Cove. From here there are great views of the central business district.

   Keep going until you reach:

7. Mrs. Macquarie's Point (exiting the gardens through the Yurong Gate), then admire the Opera House from this new angle. This is a great sunset view if you time it right.

   Continue uphill along an asphalt footpath to:

8. Mrs. Macquarie's Chair, a bench carved in stone that was used by Governor Macquarie's wife on her daily walks. From here you have a choice of retracing your steps or continuing on through the Domain.

4 Organized Tours

WALKING TOURS

Because Sydney is compact, it's an ideal place for those who like exploring on foot. If you enjoy guided excursions, try **The Rocks Walking Tour** (☎ 02/247 6678) given Monday to Friday at 10:30am and 12:30 and 2:30pm and Saturday and Sunday at 11:30am and 2pm. The 1½-hour tours depart The Rocks Visitors Centre, 106 George St.. The cost is A$10 (U.S. $8) for adults and A$6.50 (U.S. $5.20) for children. Accompanied children under 10 are free.

For other escorted walks, contact **Maureen Fry Guided Tours** (☎ 02/660 7157). Her two-hour tours operate daily, cover various parts of the city, and cost A$15 (U.S. $12).

If you prefer to go exploring on your own, follow the tours I've laid out above. However, there are also a few other areas worth a wander. For instance, you'll find restored terrace houses trimmed with cast-iron "lace" along tree-lined residential streets in **Paddington.** The New Edition Bookshop, 328 Oxford St., Paddington (☎ 02/360 6913), distributes a booklet on "Paddo," as the locals call it, for A$2.95 (U.S. $2.36). Bus no. 378, 380, or 389 will get you there, but the no. 389 (from Circular Quay) is best for an overview of the restored houses. Paddington is only 4½km (less than 3 miles) from the city center. There's a café conveniently located in the bookstore if you want a snack before you set off on your adventure.

Sydney doesn't have a huge Chinatown, but **Dixon and Sussex streets** near Darling Harbour have lots of Chinese restaurants and some Asian shops.

If **Kings Cross** is too seedy for you after dark, you can get the general idea by strolling through there during the day.

In addition, walkers may want to pick up State Transit's **"Go Walkabout with Sydney Ferries"** brochure. This guide describes a dozen scenic harborside walks accessed by ferry.

BUS & CAR TOURS

If you don't want to use public transportation and do want to see the sights, organized bus tours are available. Some of these are operated by **Sydney Day Tours** (☎ 02/251 6101), **Great Sights South Pacific** (☎ 02/252 4380), **AAT King's** (☎ 02/252 2788), and **Australian Pacific Tours** (☎ 02/313 3312 or 252 2988).

You can book sightseeing excursions over the phone, but if you'd rather do it in person the **Day Tour Booking Office** is at the south end of the Overseas Passenger Terminal. Most coaches depart just steps from the office on Circular Quay West. Sydney Day Tours depart from Clocktower Square, at the corner of Harrington and Argyle streets.

You might also like to travel about the city and environs in a sedan, a stretch limo, or a minibus. While this sounds like a big splurge, it's really good value for a family or two couples traveling together because the cost is *per vehicle.* For instance, **Premier Tourist Services** (☎ 02/451 5901; mobile phone 015 270 077; fax 02/9975 1545) charges up to four people A$130 (U.S. $104) for three hours of touring. That's A$32.50 (U.S. $26) per person. The average three-hour bus tour costs A$35 (U.S. $28) per person.

CRUISES

You shouldn't leave Sydney without taking a cruise on the harbor. In addition to the ones I've listed below, a variety of cruises are operated by **State Transit** (☎ 13 15 00 or 02/256 4670). You can also cruise Sydney Harbour on a paddle-wheeler: **Sydney Showboat** (☎ 02/552 2722) departs from Campbells Cove in The Rocks. Buy tickets at No. 2 Jetty, Circular Quay. You can also sail the harbor in a replica of Captain Bligh's **Bounty** (☎ 02/247 1789). **Sail Venture Cruises** (☎ 02/262 3595) offers cruises on their large sailing catamarans.

Tickets and information on harbor cruises are available at the Quayside Booking Centre, Jettys 2 and 6, Circular Quay; Darling Harbour; and Manly Wharf (☎ 02/247 5151).

Captain Cook Cruises. Departing no. 6 Jetty, Circular Quay. ☎ **02/206 1111.**

The granddaddy of operators on Sydney Harbour, Captain Cook Cruises offers a variety of cruise possibilities. All excursions include a full commentary.

The 2 1/3-hour **Coffee Cruise** departs daily at 10am and 2:15pm. Including cake and coffee or tea, it costs A$28 (U.S. $22.40) for adults and A$17 (U.S. $13.60) for children 5 to 14.

The 1 1/4-hour **Highlights Cruise**, departing daily at 9:30 and 11am and 2:30 and 4pm, costs A$16 (U.S. $12.80) for adults and A$11 (U.S. $8.80) for children 5 to 14. When combined with a visit to the Sydney Aquarium, this excursion becomes the **Aquarium Cruise,** and the cost (including aquarium admission) rises to A$24 (U.S. $19.20) for adults and A$15 (U.S. $12) for children 5 to 14.

The **Luncheon Cruise** and the **Showtime Dinner Cruise** are both described in detail in "Dining on the Water" at the end of Chapter 4. The **Sundowner Cruise** departs Darling Harbour at 5pm and Circular Quay at 5:30pm daily and costs A$16 (U.S. $12.80) for adults and A$11 (U.S. $8.80) for children 5 to 14.

The **Fort Denison Tour** departs Tuesday to Sunday at 10am, noon, and 2pm and costs A$8.50 (U.S. $6.80) for adults and A$6 (U.S. $4.80) for children 5 to 14.

Matilda Cruises. Departing Aquarium Wharf, Darling Harbour. ☎ **02/264 7377.** Fax 02/261 8483.

The Matilda fleet of 12 vessels, based at Darling Harbour, offers several cruise options. All trips include a full commentary. Two-hour morning, lunch, and afternoon **Discovery Cruises** are offered daily on catamarans, sailing at 11:30am and 1:30pm. Discovery Cruises cost A$25 (U.S. $20) for adults and A$12.50 (U.S. $10) for children under 12.

The 125-foot gaff-rigged topsail schooner ***Solway Lass*** is the flagship of the fleet. This classic tall ship, with 10 working sails, was built in 1902 and accommodates up to 60 passengers. It sails on lunch cruises daily at noon, afternoon cruises daily at 2pm, and dinner cruises on Friday and Saturday at 7pm. The lunch cruise costs A$38 (U.S. $30.40) for adults and A$25 (U.S. $20.40) for children under 12; the afternoon cruise (including tea or coffee) costs A$25 (U.S. $20) for adults and A$12.50 (U.S. $10) for children under 12; and the dinner cruise costs A$60 (U.S. $48) for adults and A$45 (U.S. $36) for children under 12.

In addition, Matilda Cruises is included in a good-value package: The **Darling Harbour Superticket,** valid for one month, includes a Rocket Express, a ride on the monorail, entrance to the Sydney Aquarium, entrance to the Chinese Garden, lunch or dinner at the Aquarium, and 10% off at participating stores in the Harbourside Festival Marketplace. The Superticket costs A$29.90 (U.S. $23.90) for adults and A$19.50 (U.S. $15.60) for children under 12.

5 Outdoor Activities & Spectator Sports

Playing games and keeping up your fitness routine while traveling not only means that you stand a chance of returning home in good shape but also can be a pleasant way to meet local people. This is certainly true in Australia, where sport is king.

OUTDOOR ACTIVITIES

BALLOONING You can float over Sydney's rural environs with **Balloon Aloft** (☎ 1800/028 568 in Australia). The cost is about A$175 (U.S. $140), with city hotel pickup available.

BOOMERANG THROWING What could be more Australian? Boomerangs and information on lessons are available from the **Australian Boomerang Association (ABA Inc.)** at 02/419 3537.

CYCLING Rent bikes from **Centennial Park Cycles,** 50 Clovelly Rd., Randwick (☎ 02/398 5027), 200 meters from Centennial Park, the best place to ride. The cost is A$6 (U.S. $4.80) for the first hour, A$10 (U.S. $8) for two hours, and A$14 (U.S. $11.20) for three hours; the fourth hour is free. There are no cycle pathways around the city. The **Bicycle Institute of New South Wales** (☎ 02/212 5628) organizes rides through Sydney and beyond.

FOUR-WHEEL-DRIVE TOURING **Australian Wild Escapes** (☎ 02/482 2881; fax 02/477 3114) conducts eco-tours in the greater Sydney area, including the Blue Mountains, the Hunter Valley, the South Coast, and Southern Highlands. These include bushwalking and sometimes abseiling and mountain biking.

GOLF There are dozens of courses to choose from because this is one of Sydney's favorite sports. You might like the **Lakes Golf Club,** near the airport (☎ 02/669 1311), costing A$90 (U.S. $72) for 18 holes. The **Royal Sydney Golf Club** at Rose Bay (☎ 02/371 4333) and the **Australian Golf Club** (☎ 02/663 2273) are prestigious private clubs, but they sometimes allow members of "recognized" overseas golf clubs to play, provided arrangements are made in advance. No matter where you play, reservations must be made ahead of time. Club rental costs about A$25 (U.S. $20). If you want to improve your stroke but don't have time for a game, try **City Golf Driving Range,** 123 Pitt St. (☎ 02/223 2600). **The New South Wales Golf Association** (☎ 02/264 8433) can answer any other questions.

GRASS SKIING Long hot summers and short warm winters are responsible for the popularity of this somewhat strange sport (literally skiing on grass with special skis). You can try it any weekend in **Moore Park,** at the corner of South Dowling and Cleveland streets (☎ 02/663 2070). The cost is about A$20 (U.S. $16) for two hours. Tobogganning is also available for A$5 (U.S. $4) per half an hour.

GYM WORKOUTS The **Clark Hatch Fitness Centre** in the Hotel Inter-Continental, 117 Macquarie St. (☎ 02/251 3486), is one of the best in the city.

HORSEBACK RIDING Centennial Park is the best place to ride near the city center. Rent your steed from **Centennial Park Horse Hire,** at the Sydney Showgrounds in Paddington (☎ 02/361 4513). The cost is about A$18 (U.S. $14.40) per hour.

JOGGING The Domain, Hyde Park, and the Royal Botanic Gardens are scenic spots for stretching your legs.

SURFING Bondi, Cronulla, Long Reef, Avalon, Narrabeen, and Manly are just a few of Sydney's best surfing spots. Unfortunately, Bondi and Manly have a pollution problem. Narrabeen has a left-hand break good for "goofy footers." The **NSW Surfboard Riders' Association** (☎ 02/9977 4799) can tell you about other places and has the scoop on the various surfing competitions. You can rent a board at the **Bondi Surf Beat,** 72 Campbell Parade, Bondi (☎ 02/365 0870). The rate of about A$25 (U.S. $20) per day includes a wetsuit.

SWIMMING Both **harbor and ocean beaches** abound, and between October and March seemingly every Sydneysider takes to his or her favorite sandy spot and stays there. Lady Jane Beach at Watsons Bay is popular with nude bathers.

The **Andrew (Boy) Charlton Pool** (☎ 02/358 6686) in the Domain is open daily from 6:30am to 7:15pm from September to June. For winter workouts, the **North Sydney Olympic Pool** (☎ 02/9955 2309) is preferable.

TENNIS National and international tournaments, including the Davis Cup, are held on the White City courts (☎ 02/331 4144), 3km (1.8 miles) from the city, and you can play there, subject to availability. You might also try Rushcutters Bay Tennis Centre, Waratah Street, Rushcutters Bay (☎ 02/357 1675), or Moore Park Tennis Courts (☎ 02/313 8000). Darling Harbour Sports (☎ 02/212 1666) offers facilities for tennis, basketball, volleyball, and netball. The NSW Tennis Association at 02/331 4144 can advise you on the location of other courts.

WINDSURFING Rent your gear from **Balmoral Marine,** Balmoral Beach (☎ 02/9969 6006), or **Longreef Sailboard & Surf** (☎ 02/9982 4829) and head for Long Reef Beach, the premier spot for wave jumping. It costs about A$15 (U.S. $12) per hour to rent a windsurfer. You can take lessons at the **Rose Bay Windsurfing School** (☎ 02/371 7036).

YACHTING If you'd like to be on one of the beautiful white boats in the harbor rather than admiring them from the shore, contact the **Cruising Yacht Club of Australia** (☎ 02/363 9731) about the possibility of crewing for one of their members. You can rent a sailboat, powerboat, rowboat, canoe, or dinghy from **Balmoral Marine** at Balmoral Beach (☎ 02/9969 6006). Catamaran rental costs about A$20 (U.S. $16) per hour. Serious sailors should contact **Harbour Days Sailing Experience** at 02/9968 1578; it offers two-day/one-night skippered cruises in Sydney Harbour. Stops are made for sightseeing, swimming, and fishing, and accommodations, cocktails, and meals are included in the price of A$275 (U.S. $220) per person, based on double occupancy. Harbour Days also offers a less expensive "One Day Interlude." The **Yachting Association of New South Wales** at 02/660 1266 may also be helpful.

SPECTATOR SPORTS

CRICKET Cricket is played from October to March. The Sydney Cricket Ground (SCG) is the city's best-known site. Phone the **New South Wales Cricket Association** at 02/261 5155 for more information.

FOOTBALL This sport (rugby, rugby league, soccer, and Aussie Rules) draws large crowds from May to September. Each club has its own playing field. The Sydney Football Stadium is the best-known football ground in Sydney. Tours are available.

HORSE RACING Races take place on Saturday throughout the year. Sydney's four tracks are Randwick, Canterbury, Rosehill, and Warwick Farm. Admission is about A$6 (U.S. $4.80) per person. Call the **Australian Jockey Club** at 02/663 8400 with questions.

SURFING CARNIVALS These are a uniquely Australian phenomenon where volunteer life savers (lifeguards) demonstrate their talents at ocean beaches; these events take place from September to March. Call the **Surf Life Saving Association** at 02/663 4298 for times and locations.

YACHT RACING The start of the **Sydney-to-Hobart Yacht Race** is a not-to-be-missed sight if you're in town on Boxing Day (the day after Christmas).

6 Shopping

Sydney is a shopper's delight. Whether you're interested in Australian fashions, opals, local wines, quality souvenirs, or gifts, you'll find a wide selection in hundreds of stores. (This would be a good time to reread "Tips on Shopping" in Chapter 3.)

THE SHOPPING SCENE

GREAT HUNTING GROUNDS A good place to start is the **Queen Victoria Building,** occupying an entire block in the city center. The QVB, bounded by George, Market, York, and Druitt streets, is open seven days a week. The beautifully restored Victorian center has nearly 200 shops, including many fashion specialty stores, with Pierre Cardin and lots of other high-fashion moguls. The **Strand Arcade,** which dates from 1892, runs from the Pitt Street Mall through to George Street between King and Market and shares the QVB's Victorian grace and elegance. Like the majority of Sydney's stores, the three levels of shops in the Strand Arcade are open Monday to Saturday from 9am to 5:30pm and Thursday from 9am to 9pm. Some places close at noon or 4pm on Saturday, and a few stay open a bit later on Friday. Some Sydney stores are also open on Sunday.

Centrepoint, on Market Street between Pitt and Castlereagh, has a colorful array of places to spend money, as do the nearby **Imperial Arcade** and **Mid City Centre.** The **Royal Arcade** under the Hilton Hotel, **Sydney Square** between the Town Hall and St. Andrews Cathedral on George Street, and the **Pitt Street Mall** between King and Market streets offer hundreds more opportunities to browse boutiques, search for souvenirs, and generally shop till you drop. The **Skygarden** arcade, running from the Pitt Street Mall through to Castlereagh Street, is one of Sydney's newest, most-talked-about shopping venues.

A short distance from the city center, some of Sydney's most interesting shops are dotted around **The Rocks,** and most are open daily. This is where ✪ **The Rocks Market** is held every Saturday and Sunday under the Harbour Bridge on George Street (☎ 02/255 1717). Items you can purchase here include jewelry, posters, prints, curios, crafts, and books.

More purchases await at Darling Harbour's **Harbourside Festival Marketplace** and at the shops on the **Manly Wharf.**

Truly dedicated bargain hunters will want to head for **Surry Hills,** the area just east of the Central Railway Station, where factory shops (factory outlets) abound. Three companies offer shopping tours in this area—mostly to groups—but they might let you join them if they have a spare seat on the bus. Try **Fashion Frolic** (☎ 02/798 6755), **Bargain Buyers** (☎ 02/310 1088), or **Legend Shopping Tours** (☎ 02/524 2876). If you decide to go it alone, wander down Foveaux Street between Elizabeth and Waterloo streets.

Most suburbs have their own shopping meccas, but probably the only one worth trekking out to is **Double Bay,** about a mile east of the city center, also known as "double pay" because of the posh designer boutiques that line Knox Street, Cross Street, and Transvaal Avenue.

BEST BUYS There was a time when opals were about the only exciting purchase available in Australia. Nowadays, shoppers have fun buying traditional outback garments, contemporary Australian fashions, Aboriginal artwork and crafts, and attractive souvenir items, as well as the pretty precious and semiprecious stones.

SHOPPING A TO Z

ABORIGINAL ARTIFACTS & CRAFTS

Coo-ee Aboriginal Art and Australian Emporium. 98 Oxford St., Paddington. ☎ **02/332 1544.**

The proprietors collect artifacts and fine art from more than 30 Aboriginal communities and dozens of individual artists throughout Australia. The gallery stocks a large collection of limited-edition prints and paintings by desert, Arnhem Land, and urban Aboriginal artists. In the emporium you'll find hand-printed fabrics, didgeridoos, books, and jewelry. Open Monday to Saturday from 10am to 6pm and Sunday from 11am to 5pm.

Art Prints & Originals

✪ **Affordable Art Company.** 513 Alfred St. (near Pitt St.), Circular Quay. ☎ **02/251 2813.** Fax 02/386 1848.

I stumbled on this delightful spot when I sought shelter from a downpour, and I now consider it a must for anyone—like me—who considers lithographs, silkscreens, and the like to be the ideal trip souvenir. Here you'll find original images and prints of Sydney scenes by Maggie Finn, Bruce Munro, Dorota Mears, Joe Spellman, and others. (I bought my Maggie Finn lithograph at The Rocks Market, but I'm glad to know they carry her work here, because the market is held only on weekends.) The store offers worldwide mailing service and free hotel delivery. Open Monday to Friday from 9:30am to 9pm and Saturday and Sunday from 9:30am to 7pm.

The Done Art and Design Centre. 1 Hickson Rd. (at George St.). ☎ **02/247 2740.** Fax 02/251 4884.

Silkscreens and huge colorful acrylic paintings by artist/designer Ken Done are sold here. Done's colorful and exuberant work captures the essence of Sydney and reflects the city's high energy level. Open daily from 10am to 6pm.

Ken Duncan Gallery. 73 George St., The Rocks (opposite The Rocks Visitors Centre). ☎ **02/241 3460.** Fax 02/241 3462.

This gallery exhibits the large colorful landscape photos of Ken Duncan. His subject is Australia—and he successfully captures the country's vivid colors and moods. The gallery also sells a limited range of books and some gift items. Open daily from 9am to 6pm.

The Quay Gallery. Nurses Walk, The Rocks. ☎ **02/247 3199.**

The Quay Gallery sells charming original artworks by well-known Australian artists. Nurses Walk is a quaint little lane one block west of George Street. Open daily from 10am to 5pm.

Books

In addition to the following emporia, the various museum gift shops also sell a good selection of books; try the ones listed below under "Gifts & Souvenirs."

Angus & Robertson Bookstore. In the Imperial Arcade, 168 Pitt St. ☎ **02/235 1188.**

One of the granddaddies of Australian bookselling, this bookstore in the Pitt Street Mall is open Monday to Wednesday and Friday from 8:30am to 6pm, Thursday from 8:30am to 9pm, Saturday from 9am to 5:30pm, and Sunday from 10:30am to 5pm.

Readers Recommend

Shopping Spree Tours, P.O. Box 361, Darlinghurst, NSW 2010 (☎ 02/360 6220 or 1800/625 969 in Australia; fax 02/332 2641). *"This company offers fully escorted tours of Sydney's best factories and warehouses. Tours run Monday to Saturday, visiting approximately eight to ten outlets and enjoying a two-course lunch at a well-known restaurant. The price is A$43 (U.S. $34.40) per person."*

—Nancy L. Mirata, Rohnert Park, Calif., U.S.A.

Bookshop Darlinghurst. 207 Oxford St. (near Taylor Square), Darlinghurst. ☎ **02/331 1103).**

This shop is a good source of information and offers the most comprehensive supply of gay and lesbian literature in Australia. Open Monday to Wednesday from 10am to 10pm, Thursday to Saturday from 10am to midnight, and Sunday from noon to 10pm.

Dymocks Book Arcade. 426 George St. (just north of Market St.). ☎ **02/235 0155.**

Like Angus & Robertson, Dymocks (pronounced *Dim*-icks) sells a complete range of books, and the sales staff is very helpful. Open Monday to Wednesday and Friday from 9am to 6pm, Thursday from 9am to 9pm, Saturday from 9am to 5pm, and Sunday from 10am to 5pm.

The MCA Store. In the Museum of Contemporary Art, 140 George St. ☎ **02/241 5865.**

Looking for a book on contemporary art? This store claims to have the best selection in Australia, including some on Aboriginal art and culture. Also sold here are jewelry, glassware, and pottery by contemporary Australian designers.

The Travel Bookshop. 20 Bridge St. ☎ **02/241 3554.**

As the name implies, this store specializes in travel books of all kinds. Open Monday to Friday from 9am to 6pm, Saturday from 9am to 5pm, and Sunday from 11am ro 4pm.

Crafts

Australian Craftworks. 127 George St., The Rocks. ☎ **02/247 7156.**

Here you'll find the products of more than 300 Aussie craftspeople who work in glass, leather, textiles, clothing, wood, ceramics, and jewelry. The building that houses the shop was once a police station and dates from 1882. It's interesting to see even if you aren't shopping for crafts. Some of the old gaol (jail) cells are used as exhibit spaces. Open Monday to Saturday from 9am to 7pm and Sunday from 10am to 7pm.

The Craft Centre. 88 George St., The Rocks. ☎ **02/247 7984.**

In this store the work of members of the Crafts Council of New South Wales is sold. Look for blown-glass pieces, wood turnings, pottery, textiles, silkscreens, and jewelry. Open Monday to Friday from 10am to 5:30pm and Saturday and Sunday from 10am to 5pm.

Telopea Gallery. Shop 2 in the Metcalfe Arcade, 80–84 George St., The Rocks. ☎ **02/241 1673.**

Telopea is the botanical name of the waratah, New South Wales's state flower. This shop is run by the Society of Arts and Crafts of New South Wales, an organization that has been in existence since 1906, and only the work of members is exhibited. Each individually crafted piece was made in New South Wales. The shop, staffed by members, is open Monday to Friday from 9:30am to 5:30pm and Saturday and Sunday from 10am to 6pm.

Department Stores

Sydney's major department stores are **David Jones** (☎ 02/266 5544), between Castlereagh and Elizabeth streets, at Market Street, and **Grace Bros.** (☎ 02/238 9111), on the corner of George and Market streets. David Jones is open Monday to Wednesday and Friday from 9am to 6pm, Thursday from 9am to 9pm, Saturday from 9am to 5pm, and Sunday from 11am to 5pm. Grace Bros. is open

Monday to Wednesday from 9am to 6pm, Thursday from 9am to 9pm, Saturday from 9am to 6pm, and Sunday from 11am to 5pm.

DUTY-FREE SHOPS

Downtown Duty Free. 84 Pitt St. ☎ **02/221 4444.**

This duty-free shop has additional branches on the second floor of the Queen Victoria Building (☎ 02/267 7944) and in the Strand Arcade (☎ 02/233 3166). Photographic, sound, and video equipment are sold, as well as souvenirs, leather goods, and the like. Prices are about 30% lower than they'd be in regular stores but may or may not be less than those at home. You must present your plane ticket and passport to buy duty free.

FASHIONS

Australian Outback Clothing

Outback Style. Shop 131 in the Harbourside Marketplace, Darling Harbour. ☎ **02/212 3143.**

This store specializes in outback clothing for women and men, including Driza-bone coats. All Australian-made. Open Monday to Saturday from 9:30am to 9pm and Sunday from 9:30am to 7pm.

R.M. Williams. 389 George St. ☎ **02/262 2228.**

After Thomas Cook (below), this is the other good place to look for Man from Snowy River clothes; they're original bushmen's outfitters. They also sell jeans, jodhpurs, shirts, and their legendary books. Open Monday to Wednesday and Friday from 9am to 5:30pm, Thursday from 9am to 9pm, Saturday from 9am to 4pm, and Sunday from 11am to 4pm.

Thomas Cook Boot & Clothing Company. 790 George St., Haymarket. ☎ **02/212 6616.**

Outback clothes are the specialty here, including Driza-bone coats and Akubra hats. Open Monday to Friday from 9am to 5:30pm and Saturday from 9am to 4pm.

Casual Clothing

Done Art and Design. 123–125 George St., The Rocks. ☎ **02/251 6099.**

Artist Ken Done and his designer wife, Judy, offer a wide range of products based on Ken's colorful original art. Here you'll find swimwear, children's clothes, T-shirts and sweatshirts, manchester (household linen), clever clothes and accessories, and glassware. This shop is the original Ken Done retail outlet. Open Monday to Friday from 9am to 6:45pm, Saturday from 9am to 5:45pm, and Sunday from 10am to 5:45pm.

Other Done Art and Design stores are in the Harbourside Festival Marketplace in Darling Harbour (☎ 02/281 3818), in the Queen Victoria Building (☎ 02/283 1167), and at the Sydney international airport (☎ 02/667 0996). There's a seconds shop at Skygarden (☎ 02/232 6625). Other Australia locations are in Melbourne, Perth, Surfers Paradise, and Cairns.

✪ **Treasures of Australia.** Level 2 in the Queen Victoria Building, George Street. ☎ **02/261 3574.**

The charming Viva La Wombat items can be found in many stores throughout Australia, but this place has one of the best selections. You're bound to fall in love with the wonderful prints that adorn kids' clothes, sweaters, housewares, boxer shorts, socks, and even shoes. Other designers are also represented. Open Thursday from 10am to 9pm and Friday to Wednesday from 10am to 6pm.

Men's Fashions

Country Road. 142–146 Pitt St. ☎ **02/394 1818.**

There are Country Road stores all over Australia and in quite a few U.S. cities. Their casual fashions are popular with both men and women. Additional Sydney locations include the Queen Victoria Building, Skygarden, Bondi Junction, Darling Harbour, Double Bay, Manly, Mosman, and Chatswood.

David Jones. Market and Elizabeth streets. ☎ **02/266 5544.**

Established in 1838, David Jones (called DJs by locals) is Australia's premier department store. Designers such as Armani, Valentino, Ungaro, and Dior are featured.

Women's Fashions

Also see the Country Road listing under "Men's Fashions" above.

Bec Pierce. Nurses Walk, The Rocks. ☎ **02/241 1209.**

This is a good spot to look for colorful clothing, accessories, and gifts for adults and children. Open daily from 10am to 5:30pm.

Carla Zampatti. 435 Kent St. ☎ **02/264 8244.**

This is the place for "stylish, understated high fashion." There are 29 Carla Zampatti stores throughout Australia, and her designs are sold in David Jones (above).

Dorian Scott. 105 George St., The Rocks. ☎ **02/221 8145.** Fax 02/251 8553.

Hand-knit sweaters—known as jumpers in Australia—are one of the specialties at Dorian Scott. Look for the clever, colorful ones designed by Click Go the Shears. My favorites sport cuddly flag-waving or formally attired koalas (and A$350/U.S. $280 price tags). Don't overlook the Coogi sweaters made by an Italian family in Melbourne. They're featured on the ground floor of this two-story emporium. The sweaters are sold at Bloomingdale's and Saks, too, at much higher prices. Ms. Scott displays the work of over 200 leading Australian designers and artists, including Maggie Shepherd, Moreen Clark, Amy Hamilton, Robyn Malcolm, and Ruth Fitzpatrick. Clothing and accessories for men and children, as well as women, are also sold here. Look for Jungle Party gymwear, Hot Tuna surfwear, and Thomas Cook adventure clothing. A mail-order service is available. Open Monday to Friday from 9:30am to 7pm, Saturday from 9:30am to 6pm, and Sunday from 10am to 6pm.

There's also a Dorian Scott store at the Sydney International Airport (first floor, departures level), and one at the Inter-Continental Hotel, 117 Macquarie St.

Perri Cutten. 770 Military Rd., Mosman. ☎ **02/9969 9614.**

Cutten is one of Australia's top fashion designers. If you fall in love with her fashions, you may be interested in visiting her seconds store in Melbourne.

Sydneyscope. Shop 24, first floor in the Queen Victoria Building. ☎ **02/264 8240.** Fax 02/2111 081.

This store specializes in the popular computer-knitted Coogi sweaters from Melbourne and claims to offer Australia's largest selection. Other Sydneyscope shops are located in Darling Harbour and the Wentworth Hotel in Chifley Square. Open daily from 10am to 6pm.

FOOD

David Jones. Castlereagh and Market streets. ☎ **02/266 5544.**

The food hall here has everything you could ever want for a picnic in the park or a midnight snack in your hotel room. This place is a real feast for the senses—all of them.

The Old Sydney Coffee Shop. On the concourse level in the Strand Arcade. ☎ **02/231 3002.**

You won't want to miss this emporium. Believe it or not, this shop is one of the originals in the arcade, which means that it has been around since 1892.

Gifts & Souvenirs

In addition to the following stores, there are excellent shops for quality souvenirs and gifts, including books, at the Opera House, the Taronga Zoo, the Australian Museum, and the Hyde Park Barracks Museum.

Bluegum Designs. Shop 32 on Level 2 in the Queen Victoria Building. ☎ **02/264 8070.**

This shop sells a wide range of quality Australian crafts and souvenirs, including T-shirts, soft toys, and scarves and ties in Aboriginal designs. It also sells Aboriginal items, especially didgeridoos. Be sure to notice the Australian floral fragrances and the hand-painted koalas and kangaroos. Most items are made in Australia. Open Monday to Wednesday, Friday, and Saturday from 9:30am to 6pm; Thursday from 9:30am to 9pm; and Sunday from 10am to 6pm.

Koala Bear. Shop 35, top level of the Queen Victoria Building. ☎ **02/267 3187.**

All types of souvenirs are sold here, including toys, T-shirts, sheepskin products, Aboriginal items, crystal, and opal jewelry. The Koala Bear Shop also stocks Driza-bone coats and Thomas Cook clothing. Open Friday to Wednesday from 9am to 6:30pm and Thursday from 9am to 9pm.

National Trust Gift and Bookshop. Observatory Hill, The Rocks. ☎ **02/258 0173.**

This shop in a historic building is a good place for souvenirs, placemats, stuffed animals, T-shirts, and so forth. Many items are specifically designed for the National Trust. Open daily.

Markets

Paddington Bazaar. At the corner of Newcombe and Oxford streets, Paddington. ☎ **02/331 2646.**

This popular bargain mart is also known as the Paddington Village Church Bazaar because it's held on the grounds of the Village Church in Paddington. The specialties are crafts, costume jewelry, funky clothing (new and used), curios, and other items of interest to devotees of alternative lifestyles. This is a great place for people-watching—bizarre dress is standard. The 250 or so stalls of the Paddington Bazaar set up shop on Saturday from 10am to 4pm.

Paddy's Market. At the corner of Thomas and Hay streets, in Chinatown, Haymarket. ☎ **02/325 6200.**

If you like big public markets, you'll love Paddy's. This swap meet–like place sells an assortment of farm produce, plants, food, clothing, crafts, household goods, and general merchandise. Open Saturday and Sunday from 9am to 4:30pm. There's easy access by train—the closest stations are Town Hall and Central. Another Paddy's Market is held in Flemington on Friday and Sunday.

✪ **The Rocks Market.** At the end of George Street under the Harbour Bridge, The Rocks. ☎ **02/255 1717.**

If you like browsing through colorful craft and gift markets, it's worth planning your trip so you'll be in Sydney over a weekend when this lovely event takes place. Over 100 stalls are arranged under a sail-like canopy, and others spill onto adjacent sidewalks. Expect to find homewares, antiques, posters and prints, jewelry, books, curios, and more. Shopping tip: You get better deals when paying cash. Open Saturday and Sunday from 9am to 5pm (until 6pm in summer).

Music

✪ **Sounds Australian.** Shop 33, upstairs in The Rocks Centre, 10–26 Playfair St. (near Argyle St.), The Rocks. ☎ **02/247 7290.** Fax 02/241 2873.

Music buffs love this place. The commercial arm of the Australian Music Centre, Sounds Australian sells CDs and some cassettes of music performed by Australian artists. Styles include contemporary Aboriginal (Yothu Yindi), jazz (James Morrison, Vince Jones), pop (INXS, Kylie Minogue, Crowded House), country (Slim Dusty, John Williamson), traditional Aboriginal, folk, environmental, soundtracks from Australian films, and more. Their listening facility allows you to try before you buy. Open Monday to Friday from 9:30am to 5:30pm and Saturday and Sunday from 10:30am to 5:30pm.

Opals

This is a good time to reread the information about opals in "Tips on Shopping" in Chapter 3. And remember, we overseas visitors are entitled to a 32% reduction in price when presenting our passport and plane tickets because we don't have to pay the luxury tax. Further discounts aren't unusual.

Costello's of Australia. 280 George St. ☎ **02/232 1011.**

Formerly known as the Opal Skymine, Costello's is next door to its old Australia Square location, where it was in business for over 20 years. Ask to view a video and an educational gem display. In addition to opals, Costello's offers a good selection of South Seas pearls and Argyle diamonds. Both loose stones and designer jewelry are sold with a worldwide money-back guarantee. Open Monday to Friday from 9:30am to 6pm, Saturday from 9:30am to 5:30pm, and Sunday from 1 to 5pm. Mention that you're a Frommer's reader and receive a free gift with your purchase.

✪ **Flame Opals.** 119 George St., The Rocks (opposite the Museum of Contemporary Art). ☎ **02/247 3446.**

Only solid opals from the major mining fields are sold here. These include boulder opal, black opal, and white (or "milk") opal. A wide range of handcrafted opal jewelry in 18-carat gold and sterling silver is available, too. Flame Opals is known for its straight talk and fair prices, and numerous readers have commented on the knowledgeable and helpful service they received. Open Monday to Friday 9am to 7pm, Saturday from 10am to 5pm, and Sunday from 11:30am to 5pm.

House of Giulians. At the corner of George and Bridge streets. ☎ **02/252 2051.** Fax 02/252 4495.

Established in 1966 by brothers Ivan and Eric Vortuni, Giulians offers beautiful custom-designed pieces. Whether you want to plan your own and have them make it or buy one of their creations, I don't think you'll be disappointed. They also offer a range of loose opals, as well as pearls and diamonds. Open Monday to Saturday from 9:30am to 6:30pm and Sunday from noon to 6:30pm.

Sheepskin Products

Ausfurs. Shop 4 in Clocktower Square, Argyle Street (at the corner of Harrington St.), The Rocks. ☎ **02/247 3160.**

This shop sells the products they manufacture at their factory in suburban Sydney, so they have real quality control. Sheepskin coats and rugs are the most popular items, but you'll also find footwear, car-seat covers, and little sheepskins for babies. Open daily from 9am to 7pm.

There's a second Ausfurs in the Queen Victoria Building (☎ 02/264 6072) and a third at the airport. You can sometimes buy bargain-priced seconds at the factory: 414 Bourke St., Surry Hills (☎ 02/361 3075).

Lambswool Trader. 80–84 George St., The Rocks. ☎ **02/247 9174.**

The Lambswool Trader sells sheepskin boots and rugs, as well as Driza bones, wildlife sculptures, and general souvenirs. Open daily from 9:30am to 5:30pm.

WINE

✪ **Australian Wine Centre.** 1 Alfred St., Shop 3 in Goldfields House, Circular Quay. ☎ **02/247 2755.** Fax 02/247 2756.

This is probably the best place in the country to buy cases of wine to send home. The proprietors stock an extensive selection of fine Australian wines, and the staff are completely clued in to each state's and counttry's liquor laws and shipping procedures. Their packing is almost breakage free, and they provide competent, personal service. Premium wine from all the major growing areas in the country are sold, including vintages from some boutique wineries that don't export overseas. One of New South Wales's largest stocks of Penfolds Grange Hermitage and other rare wines are on hand. Informal tastings are held Friday and Saturday throughout the day. See "Customs" in "Fast Facts: Australia" in Chapter 3 for duty-free allowances. Open Monday to Saturday from 9:30am to 6:30pm and Sunday from 11am to 5pm.

7 Sydney After Dark

Whether your idea of after-dark entertainment is an atmospheric pub, some hot jazz spot, or a lively dance club, you'll find something that pleases you in Sydney. For a review of licensing restrictions and pub hours, see "The Performing Arts & After-Dark Scene" in Chapter 2. For up-to-date information on current shows and appearances, check the *Sydney Morning Herald* (especially the "Metro" section on Friday) or look for a complimentary copy of *Where* magazine in your hotel.

If you'd like company on your evening excursion, several operators offer "Sydney by Night" tours (see "Organized Tours" in "More Attractions" earlier in this chapter).

For any of the theaters mentioned here and many more, you can get half-price day-of-performance tickets at the $ **Halftix** booth in Martin Place, between Elizabeth and Castlereagh streets. You can call them at 005526655 from 11am Monday to Saturday and listen to a recorded message with list of available shows, but this costs about A75¢ (U.S. 60¢) per minute. Tickets must be purchased in person, and sales are made by cash or credit card only. No refunds or exchanges are allowed. Halftix is open Monday to Friday from noon to 5:30pm and Saturday from noon to 5pm. The booth sells full-price tickets to all events in Sydney Monday to Friday from 9am. Halftix also sells half-price admissions to museums, exhibitions, bus tours, harbor cruises, and other tourist activities.

THE PERFORMING ARTS

The **Australian Chamber Orchestra,** the **Sydney Philharmonia Choir,** the **Sydney Symphony Orchestra,** the **Australian Ballet,** and the **Australian Opera** are all based at the Sydney Opera House. The **Sydney Theatre Company** and the **Sydney Dance Company** are associated with the Wharf Theatre but sometimes perform in the Opera House. **One Extra Dance Company** is usually at the Belvoir Street Theatre.

Major Performing Arts Complexes

Sydney Opera House. Bennelong Point. ☎ **02/250 7111.**

Performances are held in four theaters—opera, ballet, dance, symphony and chamber concerts, drama, experimental theater, and pop, jazz, and folk-music shows. Consult the *Sydney Morning Herald* to find out what's on or stop by the Opera House and pick up a copy of the bimonthly *Diary,* which lists all events. Buy your tickets at the box office or phone (☎ 02/250-7777 or fax 02/251-3943) and charge them to a credit card and have them held for you.

For information about ordering tickets before arrival in Australia, see the Opera House listing in "The Top Attractions" at the beginning of this chapter. It's important to arrive on time for performances at the Opera House because the ushers are very sticky about seating latecomers. And don't bother too much about dressing up—Australians are fairly casual. The box office is open Monday to Saturday from 9am to 8:30pm and for two hours prior to a Sunday performance. Prices vary. Opera is the most expensive, followed by major ballet performances; plays and concerts are less costly.

Seymour Centre. At the corner of Cleveland Street and City Road, Chippendale. ☎ **02/364 9400.**

Across from Sydney University, this center is another notable complex, and it contains the York, Everett, and Downstairs Theaters. Music, dance, musicals, and dramas are performed. Many productions are held during the Festival of Sydney in January.

Theaters

Belvoir Street Theatre. 25 Belvoir St., Surry Hills. ☎ **02/699 3444.**

The Belvoir is owned by a syndicate of entertainment and media professionals, including Nicole Kidman, Sam Neill, Mel Gibson, Patrick White, Judy Davis, and Dame Joan Sutherland. The company arranges for Australia's most prominent and promising directors, actors, and designers to present razor-sharp programs. The productions range from classics to cutting-edge Australian, Aboriginal, and foreign works, plus productions that are part of the Gay and Lesbian Mardi Gras (February). Ticket prices range from A$18 to A$30 (U.S. $14.40 to $24).

Capital Theatre. 3 Campbells St., Haymarket. ☎ **02/320 5000** (information); 02/320 9122 (First Call ticket agency); 1900/957 313 (toll call in Australia; 24-hour recorded information).

Miss Saigon, a modern retelling of Puccini's *Madame Butterfly* set in 1975 Saigon, opened here in July 1995 and is expected to run until at least the end of 1996. The Capital Theatre was rebuilt at a cost of A$35 million for the event. The stalls (orchestra section) seat 1,031, and the dress circle capacity is 1,033. Ticket prices are A$25 (U.S. $20), A$50 (U.S. $40), and A$75 (U.S. $60).

Footbridge Theatre. Sydney University, Parramatta Road, Broadway. ☎ **02/692 9955** or 320 9000.

The Footbridge is used by professional theater companies, except once a year when the various departments of Sydney University put on revues. The theater seats about 600.

Her Majesty's Theatre. 107 Quay St. ☎ **02/212 3411.**

42nd Street was performed here during the 1990 season. Before that Her Majesty's hosted *Evita, Sweeney Todd, 9,* and other musicals. At press time, *Me and My Girl* was on stage. Average ticket prices are A$40 to A$60 (U.S. $32 to $48).

New Theatre. 542 King St., Newtown. ☎ **02/519 3403.**

This comfortable fringe theater, which opened in 1932, seats 160 in a raked auditorium. The New Theatre was started in the Great Depression and continues to do plays that reflect the "problems confronting mankind." Dramas, comedies, musicals, and classics performed by the resident company tend to have a left-wing point of view. Ticket prices vary from A$15 to A$20 (U.S. $12 to $16).

Theatre Royal In the MLC Centre. King Street (neat Pitt Street). ☎ **02/224 8444** (general inquiries) or 320 9111 (box office). Fax 02/223 3994.

Phantom of the Opera opened here in July 1993 and is expected to run until at least mid-1996. The lead is played by talented New Zealander Rob Guest. Tickets cost around A$75 (U.S. $60) and can be purchased in the United States and Canada through ATS Tours' Sprint Department (☎ 800/423-2880).

The theater has a history of hosting major musicals. *Cats* and *Les Misérables* were performed here. The theater accommodates 1,133 in continental seating: 731 in the stalls (orchestra section) and 402 in the dress circle (mezzanine). Since it opened in 1976, Peter O'Toole, Deborah Kerr, Peter Ustinov, and Vincent Price have graced its stage.

Wharf Theatre. Pier 4, Hickson Road, The Rocks. ☎ **02/250 1700.**

Home of the Sydney Theatre Company, the Wharf Theatre is located on a refurbished wharf on the edge of Sydney Harbour.

A CASINO

Sydney Harbour Casino. Wharves 12 and 13, Pyrmont Bay. ☎ **1300/300 711.**

Sydney's first casino, albeit a temporary one, opened in September 1995. Located on Darling Harbour north of the Maritime Museum, it offers all the usual gaming, dining, and drinking facilities. It's open 24 hours a day, and entry is prohibited to those under 18. Jeans, T-shirts, beachwear, sport shoes, and the like aren't permitted. The permanent casino is under construction nearby and expected to open in 1998. If you take the monorail, get off at Harbourside. You could also take bus no. 21 from the Queen Victoria Building. The Darling Harbour Rocket Ferry is also a good transportation option.

THE CLUB & MUSIC SCENE

FOLK & ROCK

See "Dance Clubs" below for more nightspots featuring rock.

The Craig Brewery Bar & Grill. In the Harbourside Festival Marketplace, Darling Harbour. ☎ **02/281 3922.**

Live rock bands make this a popular place Sundays from 5:30pm. The scenic waterfront location is great, too. For more details, see "Dining" at the end of Chapter 4.

Hard Rock Cafe. 121–129 Crown St., Darlinghurst. ☎ **02/331 1116.**

This is a great spot to listen to *loud* rock while you dine and/or drink, with rock memorabilia hanging from the ceilings and walls. For more details, see "Dining" at the end of Chapter 4.

Rose, Shamrock and Thistle. 193 Evans St., Rozelle. ☎ **02/555 7755.** Cover varies in performance area, about A$5 (U.S. $4).

Known locally as the "Three Weeds," this popular place features blues as well as folk music. The Rose Cafe, specializing in Australian cuisine, is open Tuesday to Sunday from 6:30pm. The performance area opens about 7:30pm. There's Irish entertainment most nights. Call for recorded "what's on" info.

Jazz & Blues

Sydney is the jazz capital of Australia.

The Basement. 29 Reiby Place, Circular Quay. ☎ **02/251 2797.** Cover A$7–A$25 (U.S. $5.60–$19.20), depending on who's performing.

Sydney's beloved Basement was closed for a couple of years, and the loss was mourned by the city's jazz fans. Open again it offers live jazz nightly; lunch Monday to Friday from noon to 2:30pm; and dinner Monday to Sunday from 7pm till late.

Soup Plus. 383 George St. ☎ **02/299 7728.** Cover A$4–A$5 (U.S. $3.20–$4).

Not all Sydney's settings for jazz are elegant and sophisticated. Soup Plus is a casual self-service eatery where hot jazz is performed between 7:30pm and midnight Sunday to Thursday and until the wee hours on Friday and Saturday. For details on the restaurant, see "Dining" at the end of Chapter 4.

Dance Clubs

Bourbon & Beefsteak Bar. 24 Darlinghurst Rd., Kings Cross. ☎ **02/358 1144.** Cover Fri–Sat A$2–A$5 (U.S. $1.60–$4).

This is a hot spot for dancing—its ad reads: "Band on the main level 9pm to 5am and disco downstairs nightly 11pm to 5am." There's also a piano bar from 5pm to 9pm, and the restaurant serves food and drinks 24 hours a day. If you need a breather, snag a window table and watch the human parade on Darlinghurst Road. The Bourbon & Beefsteak is in the heart of the red-light district. For details on the restaurant, see "Dining" at the end of Chapter 4.

Juliana's Nightclub. In the Sydney Hilton, 259 Pitt St. ☎ **02/266 0610.** Cover: Hotel guests, free; nonguests, A$7 (U.S. $5.60) Wed, A$5 (U.S. $4) Thurs, A$10 (U.S. $8) Fri, A$10–A$15 (U.S. $8–$12) Sat after 10pm.

If you prefer dance clubs, glittery Juliana's is a good choice. The club is open on Wednesday, Thursday, and Saturday from 9pm to 4am, and Friday from 5pm to 4am. If you don't feel like dancing, go to watch the flashy people or have supper. Popular with the over-25 crowd.

Studebaker's. 33 Bayswater Rd., Kings Cross. ☎ **02/358 5656.** Cover: Tues A$6 (U.S. $4.80) for men, A$10 (U.S. $8) for women (who drink free all night); Fri and Sat A$5 (U.S. $4) before 9pm, A$10 (U.S. $8) after 9pm.

This lively spot, with its red diner motif, caters to the 21- to 40-year-old crowd with an interest in 1950s and 1960s rock. It's show time once every half an hour and entertainers lip-sync songs and do dance routines. No live music here, but good DJs. Open Tuesday, Friday, and Saturday from 7pm until 3am. A buffet supper is included in the cover charge up until 9pm on Friday. This place promises "nonstop bop"—anddelivers. Look for the 1951 red bullet-nose Studebaker in the entrance.

Gay & Lesbian Clubs

Most of Sydney's gay and lesbian nightspots are on Oxford Street between Whitlam Square in Darlinghurst and Centennial Park in Paddington—known as "the Golden Mile." For more information, pick up a copy of the city's free gay newspaper, the *Sydney Star Observer*.

DCM ("Don't Cry Mamas"). 33 Oxford St. ☎ **02/267 7036.** Cover varies.

This mixed nightclub is popular with gays and lesbians of all ages. There's a large dance floor and two bars. Open Thursday to Sunday 11pm to late.

Midnight Shift. 85 Oxford St. ☎ **02/360 4319.** Cover A$5 (U.S. $4) Wed–Fri, A$10 (U.S. $8) Sat.

This nightspot is popular with gays and lesbians in the 25- to 45-year-old crowd. There's a disco upstairs and a bar downstairs. Open Monday to Saturday from midnight till very late and Sunday from 4pm to midnight. The upstairs is open Wednesday to Saturday.

Oxford Hotel. 134 Oxford St., Darlinghurst. ☎ **02/331 3467.** No cover.

This popular community pub attracts a mainly male crowd—hip and of the moment—similar to that at Midnight Shift (above). There are two DJs: one downstairs and one upstairs in Gilligan's Bar. Open daily 5pm to 2am.

The Bar Scene

For a quiet drink with a beautiful view, head to **The Lounge,** on top of the Boulevard Hotel, 90 William St. (☎ 02/356 2222). Soft piano music adds to the sophisticated surroundings. The **Club Bar,** in the Regent, Sydney, 199 George St. (☎ 02/238 0000), is a great spot for people-watching. See also the listing for the Globe Bar in The Observatory Hotel below. And the George Street Bar is described in "Dining" at the end of Chapter 4.

America's Cup Bar. In the Sydney Hilton, 259 Pitt St. ☎ **02/266 0610.**

With its nautical decor featuring mementos of the famous yacht race, the America's Cup Bar is a must for sailing buffs and sports fans who want to watch cricket, rugby, and so forth on the pub's wide-screen TV. Open Sunday to Thursday from noon to midnight and Friday and Saturday from noon to 1am. Draft beer costs A$3 (U.S. $2.40); bottled beer, A$4.10 (U.S. $3.30).

The Globe Bar. In the Observatory Hotel, 89–113 Kent St., Millers Point. ☎ **02/256 2222.**

I can't think of a lovelier place in Sydney to enjoy a quiet drink with friends. The walls are lined with shelves of old books, seating is in handsome leather wing chairs, original oil paintings hang on cedar-paneled walls—in short this feels like a traditional gentlemen's club. You can also enjoy a light meal here: Between 5 and 11pm the choices include caesar salad, curry of the day, pizza Margarita, and chili potato chinks with a yogurt mint dip (from A$8 to 15/U.S. $6.40 to 12). The Globe Bar is open Monday to Saturday from 3pm to midnight and Sunday from 2 to 10pm. Afternoon tea is offered daily from 3 to 5pm.

Hero of Waterloo Hotel. 81 Lower Fort St., The Rocks. ☎ **02/252 4553.**

Built from 1843 to 1844 and granted a license in 1845, the Hero of Waterloo is an atmospheric colonial pub. A tunnel running from the cellar of the hotel to the harbor was used for smuggling rum and the "involuntary recruitment" of sailors. This sandstone landmark is classified by the National Trust. Live music adds to the ambience on the weekends. A schooner of draft beer costs A$2.80 (U.S. $2.24), and a can of beer is A$3 (U.S. $2.40). Open Monday to Saturday from 10am to 11pm and Sunday from 10am to 10pm. Don't walk around this neighborhood on your own after dark.

Lord Dudley Hotel. 236 Jersey Rd., Woollahra. ☎ **02/327 5399.**

Outside the city center on a tree-lined street near Paddington, this pub has an Olde English atmosphere and a trendy following. An open fire makes this an especially congenial place on cool days. A schooner of draft beer runs A$2.60 (U.S. $2.08); a can of beer, A$3.10 (U.S. $2.48). Open Monday to Wednesday from 11am to 11pm, Thursday to Saturday from 11am to midnight, and Sunday from noon to 10pm. A restaurant on the premises serves modern-Australian lunches and dinners daily.

Lord Nelson. At Kent and Argyle streets, The Rocks. ☎ **02/251 4044.**

The Lord Nelson was granted a license in 1842, which makes it the city's oldest hotel. The thing that's particularly interesting is that the proprietor, Blair Hayden, makes his own beer, and patrons can sample this as well as established brands. Blair's award-winning brews include Old Admiral, Victory Bitter, Trafalger Pale Ale, Three Sheets, and Quayle Ale. Substantial bar snacks are available daily, and there's a brasserie upstairs, so there's no risk of going hungry while you soak up the historic ambience and some suds. Beer goes for A$2.30 to A$4.90 (U.S. $1.85 to $3.90). The "pub that restored Nelson's eyesight" is a gathering point for yuppies and similar friendly, fun-loving types. I highly recommend it. There's more information on the Lord Nelson in Walking Tour 2 under "Strolling Around Sydney" earlier in this chapter and in "Accommodations" in Chapter 4.

Marble Bar. In the Sydney Hilton, 259 Pitt St. ☎ **02/266 0610.**

The bar was built in 1893 at a cost of £32,000 sterling and was at that time part of Adams' Hotel, which stood on the site where the Hilton is now. The decoration of the bar was carried out in the style of the 15th-century Italian Renaissance. (The capitals of the Corinthian columns are solid bronze.) Artist Julian Ashton was commissioned to paint 18 rural scenes with nudes, for which the bar became famous.

In 1968 the decision was made to sell and demolish the Adams' Hotel while preserving as much as possible of the Marble Bar. The bar was then closed, the paintings were removed, the marble was tagged and photographed, casts were taken of the plasterwork, and the stained-glass windows were carefully packed away. On July 19, 1973, the rebuilt Marble Bar was opened as part of the Hilton International. The main difference between the original and the present bar is that it now boasts a carpeted floor. Some 14 of the big paintings remain, and it's still a significant watering hole for Sydneysiders—as it has been for more than 100 years. It's open Monday to Wednesday from noon to 11pm, Thursday from noon to midnight, Friday from noon to 2am, and Saturday from 3pm to 2am. There's live entertainment—everything from jazz to rhythm and blues—Wednesday to Saturday (no cover charge) and happy hour from 7 to 9pm on Monday to Saturday. A schooner of draft beer costs A$2.60 (U.S. $2.08), while a bottle of beer goes for A$4.20 (U.S. $3.36).

Oaks Hotel. 118 Military Rd., Neutral Bay. ☎ **02/9953 5515.**

Over in Neutral Bay on the north shore of the harbor, the Oaks Hotel is a place where upscale singles mingle while downing a few beers and cooking their own steaks. There are six drinking areas, including a beer garden and the Tramway Bar, which contains the front half of a real tram. A schooner of beer goes for A$2.90 (U.S. $2.30) and a can of beer is A$3.75 (U.S. $3). To get there, take a ferry from no. 4 jetty, Circular Quay, a bus from Wynyard, or a taxi. The bar is open Monday to Saturday from 10am to midnight and Sunday from 11:30am to 10pm.

Pumphouse Brewery Tavern. 17 Little Pier St., Darling Harbour. ☎ **02/281 3967.**

Conveniently located only steps from the Convention Centre in Darling Harbour, the Pumphouse Brewery Tavern offers indoor and outdoor seating, lunches and dinners from a chalkboard menu, and six house-brewed beers on tap: Brewer's Draught, Golden Wheat Beer, Thunderbolt Ale, Bull's Head Best Bitter, Federation

Ale, and Pumphouse Extra. Brewery tours are conducted on request. A half pint of Brewer's Draught will set you back A$2.30 (U.S. $1.85); a pint costs A$4.50 (U.S. $3.60). This atmospheric pub is open Sunday to Thursday from 11am to midnight and Friday and Saturday from 11am to 2am. Live music is provided upstairs on Friday and Saturday nights.

MORE ENTERTAINMENT

DINNER CRUISES The **John Cadman Cruising Restaurant,** the **Showtime Dinner Cruise,** and the **Sydney Showboat** (described in "Dining on the Water" in Chapter 4), and Matilda Cruises' ***Solway Lass* Dinner Cruise** (described in "Organized Tours" earlier in this chapter) are all pleasant options for an evening in Sydney.

MOVIES Three multiscreen cinemas are cheek-to-jowl on George Street between Liverpool and Bathurst streets. The **Village Cinema 6 Plex** is next to the **Greater Union** multiscreen, which is next to the **Hoyts Centre,** which has seven screens. The cost is about A$11.50 (U.S. $9.20) for adults and A$6 (U.S. $4.80) for children.

In addition, recent-release films are shown nightly in a small theater in the **$ Hare Krishna Centre** in Darlinghurst. Govinda's, the wonderful dining spot in the same place, is described in "Dining" at the end of Chapter 4. The movies are free of charge to diners.

ADULT ENTERTAINMENT The "dirty half mile" of Darlinghurst Road in Kings Cross offers a plethora of sex shows, porn movies, adult bookshops, and prostitutes. Places like the **Pink Panther Club,** 41 Darlinghurst Rd. (☎ 02/358 5070), advertise nude dancers, strippers, and "live sex on stage," and they mean what they say. Admission is officially A$20 (U.S. $16), but if they aren't busy it's negotiable.

Speaking of negotiable, brothels will soon be legal in New South Wales.

8 Side Trips from Sydney

In addition to seeing the destinations described here, you can make day trips to the **Blue Mountains** and the **Hunter Valley** (see Chapter 6).

THE HAWKESBURY RIVER & PITTWATER AREA

43km (27 miles) N of Sydney

In 1788 Governor Phillip discovered the Hawkesbury River and was grateful for its fertile soil, which was needed to grow food for the struggling colony to the south. The river enters the ocean at Broken Bay, about 43km (27 miles) north of Sydney, and was named for Baron Hawkesbury, president of the Board of Trade and Plantations in England at the time. As a result of Phillip's discovery, the earliest farming settlements in Australia were along the Hawkesbury River. To this day, the riverlands have remained rural and provide the background for a peaceful, picturesque respite from the rigors of urban existence.

ESSENTIALS

GETTING THERE To **Palm Beach:** Drive or take State Transit (☎ 13 15 00) bus 190 (A$3.80/U.S. $3.05 one way). The end of the line is steps from the sand. You could also take the Boomerang Bus (☎ 02/9913 8402; see Chapter 4). To **Brooklyn:** Drive up the Sydney-Newcastle Freeway or Pacific Highway or take a train from Central Station to the Hawkesbury River Railway Station. To **Church Point:** Take bus 155 from the Manly Wharf or, if you're driving, allow about 45 minutes.

Sydney & Environs

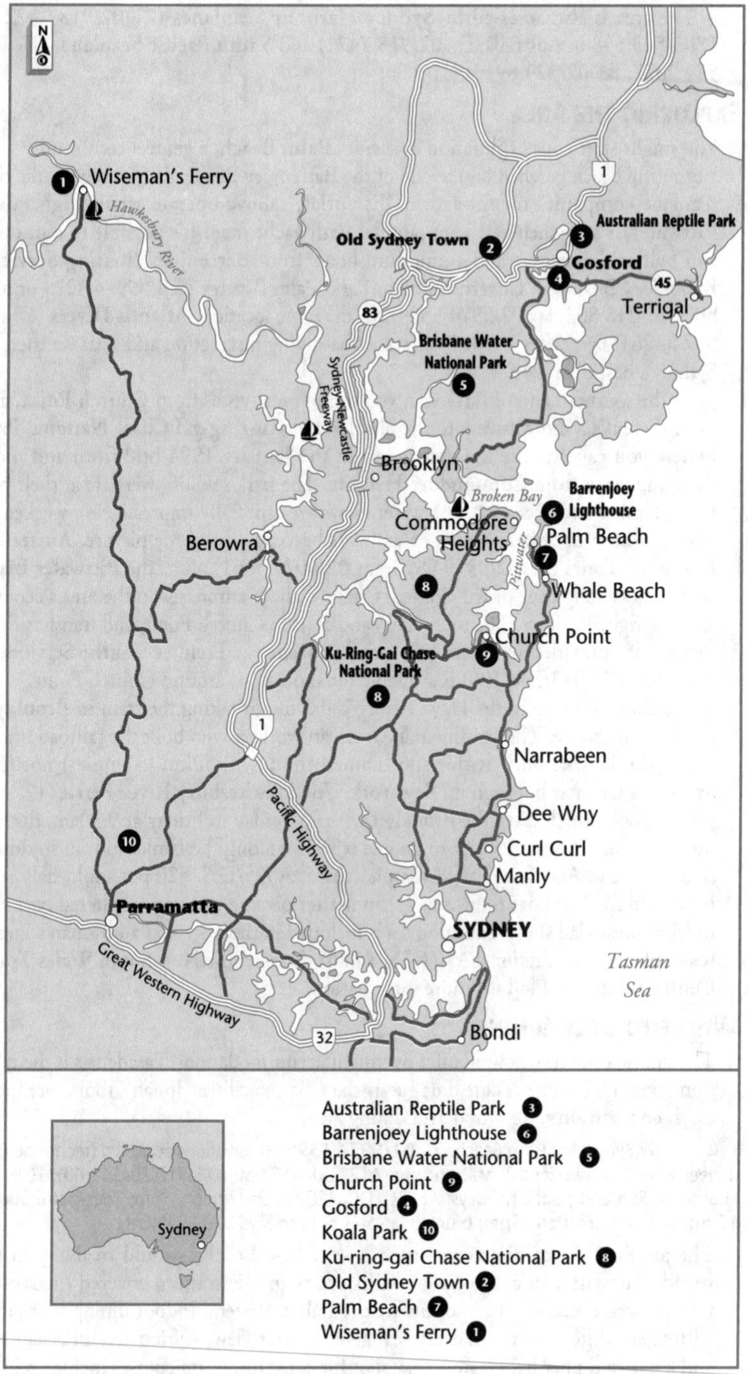

The area is also accessed by **Sydney Harbour Seaplanes** (☎ 02/918 7472 or 1800/803 558 in Australia; fax 02/918 7471) and **South Pacific Seaplanes** (☎ 02/544 0077; fax 02/523 6919).

Exploring the Area

You might start your exploration in scenic **Palm Beach,** a genteel community with a beautiful beach perched on the end of the Barrenjoey Peninsula. From here, the two seaplane companies mentioned in "Essentials" above operate scenic flights over **Pittwater,** a long sheltered inlet popular with yachtsmen. It's possible to rent open and half-cabin cruisers and aluminium boats from **Barrenjoey Boating Services,** Barrenjoey Boatshed, Governor Phillip Park, Palm Beach (☎ 02/9974 4229 or mobile 015/218 868; fax 02/9974 5534). In the same location, **Atlantis Divers** (☎ 02/9974 4261; fax 02/9974 5009) offers scuba-diving instruction and boat transfers to Sydney's best dive spots.

At the southern end of Pittwater, you'll find great vistas from **Church Point,** and from there it's a short drive into the bushland of **Ku-ring-gai Chase National Park** (where you can still see the damage from the January 1994 bushfires) and more sweeping views from **Commodore Heights.** The park's wildflowers are at their best in September and October. The water views are especially impressive on weekends, when millions of dollars' worth of sailboats become part of the picture. **Australian Academic Tours** (☎ 02/9979 9813; fax 02/9979 5561) offers the **Pittwater Experience,** a walking tour of Ku-ring-gai Chase with an emphasis on the area's ecology and Aboriginal culture. The tours starts and ends in Church Point, and transfers from Sydney are provided by Australian Pacific coaches or Premier Tourist Services. A water taxi (☎ 018/238 190) is available for short hops around Church Point.

Another approach to the Hawkesbury is driving or taking the train to **Brooklyn,** on the south shore. The sentimental American workers who built the railroad bridge across the Hawkesbury at this spot named the town, 50km (31 miles) north of Sydney, after their borough in New York. The **Hawkesbury River Ferries** (☎ 02/9985 7566), which leave the Brooklyn wharf Monday to Friday at 9:30am, distribute mail and other necessities to people who live along the banks and, in so doing, share a slice of Australiana with visitors (cost is A$25/U.S. $20 per adult, half price for children). The boat returns at 1:15pm after passing countless sheltered bays and miles of bush-clad shore. Morning tea is included in the price and a Postman's Lunch is available for an additional A$6 (U.S. $4.80). Contact the **New South Wales Travel Centre** at 02/231 4444 for more information.

Where to Stay & Dine

The dining options below all offer overnight accommodations. Pasadena's is the most upmarket. La Palma's is cute, but guests share bath facilities. Jonah's rooms are modest in comparison to its wonderful dining area.

Jonah's. 69 Bynya Rd., Palm Beach. ☎ **02/9974 5599.** Reservations accepted (recommended a week ahead for weekends). Main courses A$21.50–A$24.50 (U.S.$17.20–$19.60). 10% surcharge on Sun and public holidays. AE, BC, DC, MC, V. Daily noon–3pm; Tues–Sat 6:30pm–10pm, Sun–Mon 6:30pm–9pm; brunch Sat–Sun 8–10am. MEDITERRANEAN.

The absolutely exquisite view—high over Whale Beach—would rival any in the world. The vista, in combination with pretty gardens and a covered quarry-tile terrace, create an ambience not unlike the Italian Riviera. Indoor dining is at tables with crisp white cloths, and every seat gives a water view. A fireplace, a Persian rug, and a native timber bar create a cozy spot for cocktails. Main courses include roasted squab breast, spicy duck pie, and honey-glazed turnips; seared wild barramundi with creamed fennel, grilled zucchini, and brown-butter calabraise; and scallops in their shells with warm oysters, compote of leeks and wild rice, and lemon-thyme beurre blanc. There's a good wine list, and the staff provides transfers for guests who arrive by seaplane. The eight motel-like guest rooms cost A$140 to A$170 (U.S. $112 to $136) double.

La Palma Restaurant. 1108 Barrenjoey Rd., Palm Beach. ☎ **02/9974 4001.** Reservations recommended. Main courses A$17–A$26.50 (U.S. $13.60–$21.20), AE, BC, MC, V. Daily noon–10pm. MODERN ITALIAN.

A perfect spot for a summer lunch, La Palma's canvas-covered outdoor dining space has a conservatorylike feel, but airy indoor seating is available, too. The well-prepared cuisine puts its emphasis on fresh ingredients. Main courses might include roasted veal loin with forest mushrooms and rosemary or degustazione of seafood with herb puff pastry. Desserts include tiramisú, spumone, and homemade gelato. The guest rooms cost A$80 to A$130 (U.S. $64 to $104) double with light breakfast; one room has a bath.

Pasadena Restaurant. 1858 Pittwater Rd., Church Point. ☎ **02/9979 6633.** Reservations accepted. Main courses A$17–A$23 (U.S. $13.60–$18.40). Sun surcharge A$1.50 (U.S. $1.20) per person, public holiday surcharge A$2 (U.S. $1.60) per person. AE, BC, DC, MC, V. Daily 7am–10pm. SEAFOOD.

I was first attracted to this spot by its wonderful waterfront setting and open, leafy ambience, but I soon realized the food was every bit as impressive. My baked pesto ricotta served on olive bread was wonderful. The menu also offers grilled John Dory filets, scallop-and-prawn brochette with eggplant, roast capsicum and pesto, barbecued Tasmanian ocean trout filets on a bed of olive oil mashed potato and capsicum coulis and herb cream. When I was there, three sides of the restaurant consisted of plastic curtains that can be rolled up or down, depending on the weather (I understand that the owner plans to put in French doors). The quarry-tile floor, abundance of potted ficus trees, and sailcloth roof help to make this a very special place. The attractive guest rooms cost A$100 to A$120 (U.S. $80 to $96) double.

GOSFORD

84km (52 miles) N of Sydney

Gosford (pop. 129,000) is a picturesque town on the edge of **Brisbane Water National Park,** an area renowned for its beaches and waterways. Area activities include boating, fishing, golf, scenic drives, and bowls (lawn bowling).

ESSENTIALS

GETTING THERE Drive up the Pacific Highway and the Sydney-Newcastle Freeway, take the train, or catch the Central Coast Airbus (☎ 043/32 8655). Several Sydney sightseeing companies, like Australian Pacific Tours, run excursions to Old Sydney Town (see below).

VISITOR INFORMATION The **telephone area code** for Gosford is 043. As part of the telephone changeover, all phone numbers with an 043 area code will be changing to 02/43xx xxxx in May 1998. The **Gosford City Visitors Information Centre** is at 200 Mann St. (☎ 043/25 2835); it's open daily.

SEEING THE TOP ATTRACTIONS

Australian Reptile Park. Pacific Highway, Gosford. ☎ **043/28 4311.** Admission A$9.50 (U.S. $7.60) adults, A$4 (U.S. $3.20) children. Daily 9am–5pm. Closed Christmas.

Besides a plethora of snakes, lizards, and other reptiles, this fauna park has koalas, birds, and two platypuses (named Eb and Flo). There are also turtles, iguanas, and funnel web spiders. Visitors who are game can hold a python.

Old Sydney Town. Pacific Highway, Somersby, 9km (5 1/2 miles) south of Gosford. ☎ **043/40 1104.** Admission A$15 (U.S. $12) adults, A$8.50 (U.S. $6.80) children 5–16; A$40 (U.S. $32) family pass; under 5 free. Wed–Sun 10am–4pm; daily during NSW school and public holidays. Closed Christmas.

This attraction is a must if you're traveling with children (and maybe even if you aren't). Old Sydney Town is where Australia is re-created as it was 200 years ago. Costumed characters live out colonists' lives against a backdrop of historic buildings. Kids particularly enjoy the reenactment of activities that took place in 1806 and 1807. These include floggings and hangings, as well as wagon rides. Allow an hour to drive to Old Sydney Town from Sydney. There's a connecting bus from the Gosford train station. Meals are available at Rosetta's Eating Establishment, the King's Head Tavern, and a snack bar.

Where to Stay & Dine

Holiday Inn Crowne Plaza. Pine Tree Lane, Terrigal, NSW 2260. ☎ **043/84 9111,** or 1800/02 4966 in Australia. Fax 043/84 5798. 196 rms and suites. A/C MINIBAR TV TEL. A$175–A$250 (U.S. $140–$200) single or double; A$315–A$430 (U.S. $252–$344) suite; A$210–A$430 (U.S. $168–$344) 7th floor. Additional person A$35 (U.S. $28) extra. Children under 20 free in parents' room. AE, BC, DC, MC, V. Parking A$5 (U.S. $4). Take bus or taxi from Gosford or the Central Coast Airbus from Sydney.

Terrigal is a beach community about 1 1/2 hours north of Sydney and 15 to 20 minutes east of Gosford. This attractive resort, built at a cost of A$60 million (U.S. $48 million), provides a getaway for harried Sydneysiders who flock to it on weekends. The eight-story property looks a bit like a Mediterranean villa. All but six rooms face the ocean and have bougainvillea-trimmed balconies. They have either two double beds or a queen-size bed. In-room movies, bathrobes, tea- and coffee-making facilities, small refrigerators, and radios are provided. Children aren't permitted on the 7th floor.

Dining/Entertainment: The hotel offers a wide range of dining venues—from casual to the formal. The thing they have in common is great-tasting food, attractively presented. La Mer is the formal à la carte restaurant for gourmet dining. Fresh seafood and French cuisine are featured, and the wine list is extensive. La Mer is open for dinner Wednesday to Saturday. The Norfolk Brasserie is a casual dining spot where the hardwood floor, bouquets of garden flowers, ceiling fans, and blue-and-white tablecloths create a chic country decor. This eatery is open for dinner daily. The Conservatory overlooks the ocean and is also open daily.

Services: Concierge, 24-hour room service, laundry, valet, nightly turndown, complimentary daily newspaper, baby-sitting, massage.

Facilities: Outdoor pool, extensive health club, gym, sauna, spa, the Adventure Club for children's activities, children's center, hair salon, gift shop, newsstand.

Kims Beachside Retreat. Toowoon Bay, NSW 2261. ☎ **043/32 1566.** Fax 043/33 1544. 34 bungalows. TV TEL. From A$189 (U.S. $151.20) per person. Rates include three buffet meals daily. Seasonal discounts available. AE, BC, DC, MC. Free off-street parking.

For more than 100 years this beachfront site, a 20-minute drive from Gosford (just over an hour north of Sydney), has been a stopping place for vacationers, but until recently, when Kim's bungalows were built, accommodation here was limited to camping. Now guests relax in comfortable, but not self-consciously posh, surroundings. This is very much an adult retreat—families are not encouraged. Instead, the privacy and natural beauty of the area appeal to honeymooners and others with a need to get away. The lush tropical foliage (all imported) makes this place look more like Queensland than New South Wales. About a third of the quarters are right on the beach; others are just a short stroll away. Many rooms have fireplaces, all have balconies, most have outdoor spa pools or indoor spa baths, and four have private pools. All have tea- and coffee-making facilities and small refrigerators; the majority also have video players. Some beds are king-size, the rest queen-size.

Dining/Entertainment: A bell rings to call guests to meals, which are served buffet style. Extensive deck areas allow for alfresco dining. The menu changes daily, with an emphasis on fresh local ingredients. A pianist plays popular and classical music in the cocktail bar most evenings.

Services: Limited room service.

Facilities: Complimentary video library, beauty and massage therapist.

YERRANDERIE

96km (60 miles) NW of Sydney

During the silver-mining boom from 1907 to 1914, Yeranderie had a population of 2,000. The richest silver in Australia came from these mines bordered by the Blue Mountains National Park. However, the mines closed in 1928 and the place became a ghost town. It was further isolated when the Sydney Water Board flooded the nearby Burragorang Valley in 1957, cutting the direct-access road from Sydney.

At this point Yerranderie was officially removed from most maps of the area and would've disappeared completely had it not been for the interest of one of the former stockholders of Tonalli Mining & Engineering Pty. Ltd., Miss Val Lhuede. This stalwart lady bought the ghost town and the 462 hectares (1,141 acres) of bushland surrounding it and is gradually restoring the original buildings. The town now has a permanent population of one, its caretaker. Kangaroos, wallabies, and other native animals thrive in the peaceful environment, making it an ideal location for nature study. Conducted tours of the town cost A$8 (U.S. $6.40).

ESSENTIALS

GETTING THERE You can drive to Yerranderie from Sydney in about six hours, from Katoomba in four hours, or from the Jenolan Caves in just under three hours. Another option is going with Australian Academic Tours (☎ 02/9979 9813; fax 02/9979 5561), who include it on their "Yerranderie, Blue Mountains Ghost Town" tour. Curtis Aviation (☎ 046/556 789) provides round-trip air transport from Camden at A$122 (U.S. $97.60) per person.

VISITOR INFORMATION If you have questions or want to book accommodations, get in touch with **Val Lhuede,** Yerranderie Village Project, 8½ Parkes St., Kirribilli, NSW 2061 (☎ 046/59 6165 [this number will change to 02/4659 6165 in April 1998] or 02/9955 8083 in Sydney).

WHERE TO STAY

Guests can sleep in a rustic lodge that formerly housed the post office at a cost of A$32 (U.S. $25.60) per adult; camping costs A$8 (U.S. $6.40). Children under 12 are half price. You must bring your own linen and provisions, as there are no food shops or petrol (gas) stations. No credit cards are accepted.

6 New South Wales

"It's more than a bridge and an Opera House," residents of New South Wales continually remind visitors. And they're right: Their state boasts more than its share of wonders. Beyond Sydney's borders lie beaches, mountains, bushland, vineyards, rivers, mining country, and outback wilderness.

Because New South Wales is relatively small (occupying only 10% of the continent), you can sample its assorted features with relative ease without putting an inordinate strain on your time and dollar budgets. For example, within a week you can fossick for opals in Lightning Ridge, overnight on an outback cattle station, tour some Hunter Valley wineries, pick bananas in Coffs Harbour, and then bushwalk through a forest of eucalyptus. And, depending on the time of year, you could add sunbathing or skiing to the itinerary.

New South Wales's four main geographical regions are the fertile coastal strip, the high tablelands and peaks of the Great Dividing Range, the pastoral farmland on the western slopes of the range, and the sparsely populated western plains covering two-thirds of the state. The climate varies from subtropical to alpine. This state is the home of Sydney, the country's largest city; Mount Kosciusko, the highest peak; and the first Australian island to be registered on the World Heritage List (Lord Howe). The Australian Capital Territory (Canberra) is contained within its borders.

Along with this wealth of diversity, New South Wales is economically the richest of Australia's six states because it's the country's main wheat, coal, and sheep producer. In addition, the Newcastle/Sydney/Wollongong region is the nation's industrial heart. New South Wales is the oldest state and the most populous. Approximately 35% of all Australians live here.

EXPLORING THE STATE

Good highways link the major cities and towns in New South Wales. The **Pacific Highway** heads north over Sydney's Harbour Bridge and follows the coast north. The **Sydney-Newcastle Freeway** connects the two commercial industrial centers. The Princes Highway meanders along the south coast. The New England Highway, passing through Tamworth and Armidale, is parallel to and inland from the Pacific Highway. The **Great Western Highway** and

What's Special About New South Wales

Beaches

- Byron Bay, the most easterly point in Australia, with some of the country's best beaches and great surfing.
- Coffs Harbour, just one of the places on the coast north of Sydney where the beaches stretch for miles.

Events & Festivals

- Each October, the "Toohey's 1000 Touring Car Championship" auto race, Bathurst, in the Golden West.
- Each spring (September/October), the Tulip Festival, Bowral, in the Southern Highlands. Call 048/613 133.
- Each January, the Australasian Country Music Awards and a music festival, Tamworth, in the New England region. Call 067/684 462 or 684 467.

Natural Spectacles

- Mount Kosciusko, in the Snowy Mountains, the highest point in the country, with good skiing June to September.
- The Blue Mountains—superbly scenic, with good hiking trails and lodging in cozy guesthouses.

Ace Attractions

- The Hunter Valley, the oldest commercial wine-producing area in Australia, with dozens of wineries open for tours and tasting.
- The Jenolan Caves, slightly southwest of the Blue Mountains; guided tours take place daily.

Offbeat Places

- Lord Howe Island, due east of Port Macquarie, one of only a handful of islands on the World Heritage List—rare plants, birds, and marine life abound.

Unusual Activities

- Taking a pub crawl on horseback through the New England region—a great way to meet the locals.
- Fossicking for opals in Lightning Ridge.

Galleries

- Broken Hill's "Brushmen of the Bush" exhibit their work at several galleries in this outback town.

Western Motorway head west from Sydney and through the Blue Mountains. The **Hume Highway** and **South Western Freeway** connect Sydney and Melbourne. Travelers should consult **NRMA Travel**, 151 Clarence St., Sydney (☎ 02/260 9222 or 13 11 22), before setting out by car across the state.

If you aren't driving, **Ansett, Qantas, Hazelton Airlines,** and **Eastern Australia Airlines** provide intercity air service. If you'd rather get into training, **CityRail** and **Countrylink** can get you to most areas of the state.

VISITOR INFORMATION The **New South Wales Travel Centre,** 19 Castlereagh St., Sydney, NSW 2000 (☎ 02/231 4444), is the best information source.

1 The Southern Highlands & the South Coast

Two main roads lead south from Sydney: the Hume Highway (and South Western Freeway) and the Princes Highway. Both connect Australia's two biggest cities, but the Hume is the faster and therefore popular with truck drivers and others who must get to their destinations quickly. Using this road, you can get to Melbourne in 12 hours. If taking the Princes Highway, following the coast and passing small towns and beachfront resorts, you'll need at least two days.

Many travelers, taking the most scenic route, start out on the Hume, which goes through the picturesque Southern Highlands, and then cross over to the Princes via the Illawarra Highway, which connects the two roads about 140km (87 miles) south of Sydney. By following this path, you can enjoy the gardens and forests of the highlands; the route reaches the ocean just in time for the most beautiful beach vistas. Berrima, Bowral, Mittagong, Moss Vale, and other quaint towns in the highlands make pleasant overnight stops for those who lack the time or desire for the full trip along the coast. If you wish to follow the Hume all the way to Melbourne, see "Victoria to New South Wales: Along the Hume Freeway & Highway" in Chapter 17.

BERRIMA

122km (98 miles) SW of Sydney

The historic village of Berrima was founded in 1829 by settlers attracted to the fertile farmlands surrounding it. A courthouse, a jail, a public school, an inn, and other buildings were constructed of local sandstone, and the town was expected to become a major center in this part of the state. However, the railroad bypassed Berrima in the 1860s and the town failed to thrive. Today it retains its 19th-century appearance and has a population of 850.

The colonial sandstone buildings that give Berrima its charm are open to the public. Of special note are the **Surveyor General Inn,** the **Court House,** the **Gaol** (jail), the **Church of Holy Trinity,** and **St. Francis Xavier Roman Catholic Church.** Also of interest are the many antiques and craft shops and the scenic countryside around the village.

ESSENTIALS

GETTING THERE You'll need your own vehicle if you want to go to Berrima; you'll find the village on the Hume Highway. The closest train station and bus depot are in Mittagong, 18km (11 miles) northeast. The bus ride from Sydney to Mittagong takes $2^1/_2$ hours.

VISITOR INFORMATION The **Southern Highlands Visitor Information Centre** (☎ 048/712 888), in Winifred West Park on the Old Hume Highway in Mittagong, is open daily from 9am to 4:30pm. Ask for the "Two Foot Tour" booklet if you'd like to do a self-guided walk past Berrima's historic buildings. The **telephone area code** is 048. As part of the telephone changeover, all numbers with a 048 area code will be changing to 02/48xx xxxx in June 1998.

WHERE TO STAY

Berrima Bakehouse Motel. At the corner of the Old Hume Highway and Wingecarribee Street, Berrima, NSW 2577. ☎ **048/77 1381.** Fax 048/77 1047. 18 units. TV TEL. A$60–A$90 (U.S. $48–$72) double. Additional person A$15 (U.S. $12) extra. AE, BC, DC, MC, V.

Each unit has a shower and coffee- and tea-making facilities. The two-story property, set in several acres of gardens, also offers laundry facilities, a playground, and a pool.

New South Wales

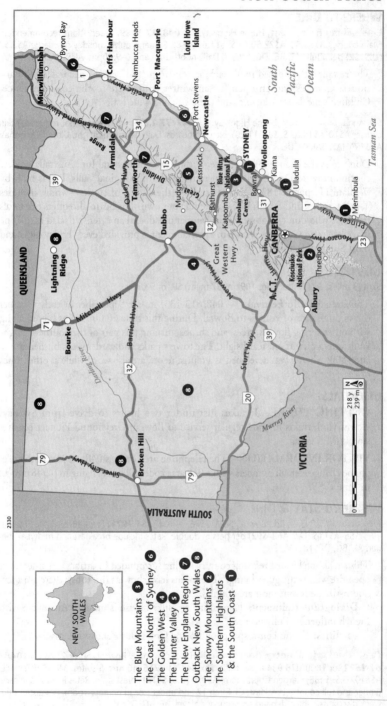

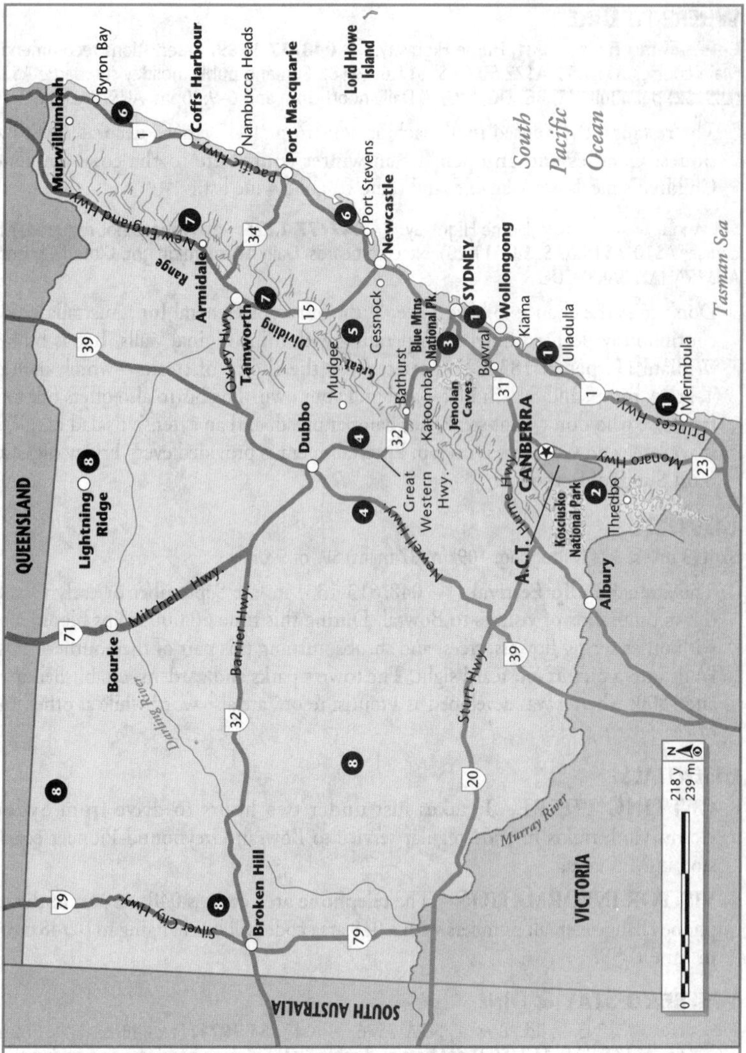

Where to Dine

Colonial Inn Restaurant. Hume Highway. ☎ **048/77 1389.** Reservations recommended. Main courses A$14.50–A$22.50 (U.S. $11.60–$18). Sun and public holiday surcharge A$2.50 (U.S. $2) per adult. AE, BC, DC, MC, V. Daily noon–3pm and 6–9:30pm. AUSTRALIAN.

The restaurant is housed in a coaching inn (from 1842) that's decorated with antiques. Candles and an open fire in winter contribute to the cozy ambience. Children's meals are available, and there's a good wine list.

Surveyor General Inn. Hume Highway. ☎ **047/77 1226.** Reservations not required. Main courses A$10–A$14 (U.S. $8–$11.20). No credit cards. Daily 10am–midnight. Closed Christmas. AUSTRALIAN BARBECUE.

Don't miss the chance to have a beer at the Surveyor General Inn, Australia's oldest continuously licensed hotel still operating within its original walls. It was built by William Harper in 1834. You select from the choice of steaks—which includes T-bone, rump, and Scotch filet—and grill your own. The bistro also offers full meals for those who don't want steak, hot damper bread, and an extensive salad bar. Wine is available and Guinness is on tap. Entertainment is provided every Friday night and most Sunday afternoons.

BOWRAL

5km (3 miles) S of Mittagong, 109km (87 miles) SW of Sydney

The annual **Tulip Festival** (☎ 048/613 133) in late September or early October draws thousands of visitors to Bowral. During this time 60,000 tulips bloom along with other spring flowers, trees, and shrubs, turning this part of the Southern Highlands into a picture-postcard sight. The town's parks and gardens, established in the late 1800s when it was developed as a tourist resort, are also worthwhile at other times of year.

Essentials

GETTING THERE It takes just under two hours to drive from Sydney. Countrylink trains provide regular service to Bowral; Greyhound-Pioneer coaches stop in Mittagong.

VISITOR INFORMATION The **telephone area code** is 048. As part of the telephone changeover, all numbers with a 048 area code will be changing to 02/48xx xxxx in June 1998.

Where to Stay & Dine

Links House. 17 Links Rd., Bowral, NSW 2576. ☎ **048/61 1977.** Fax 048/62-1706. 16 rms. TV. A$85–A$115 (U.S. $68–$92) per person double. Rates include breakfast and midweek dinner. AE, BC, DC, MC, V.

This small hotel is in a relaxing country setting surrounded by attractive gardens. An open fire warms the guest lounge. The rooms have showers (no tubs); there are a few queen-size beds, but most are doubles.

Dining/Entertainment: The cuisine at Links House is modern Australian with French influence. Fully licensed.

Facilities: Tennis court, spa, pool; Bowral Golf Course across the road.

✪ **Milton Park Country House Hotel.** Horderns Road, Bowral, NSW 2576. ☎ **048/61 1522,** or 1800/028 954 in Australia. Fax 048/61 4716. 46 rms, 5 suites. MINIBAR TV TEL. A$610 (U.S. $488) Garden Court room; A$770 (U.S. $616) Forest suite. Rates include à la carte dinner and full country breakfast. Children 12 and under free in parents' room. Ask about midweek discounts, which depend on occupancy level. AE, BC, DC, V.

This Relais & Châteaux member is the grandest lodging in the Southern Highlands. Its artistically landscaped gardens are Australia's finest and were once rated in the world's top 10. In spring, lilacs, dogwoods, rhododendrons, azaleas, and daffodils are at their peak; in fall (March to May), the leaves of the ash, elm, and maple trees turn various shades of red, gold, and ocher. When the estate was the home of the Anthony Hordern family, it hosted such notables as Princess Margaret and Lyndon B. Johnson. Today the Edwardian manor house has been remodeled and expanded. The most frequent guests are affluent Sydneysiders soaking up the ambience of peace and luxury. All the accommodations are attractive, offering king-size beds, plenty of space, heated towel racks, and plush terry robes. The suites have fireplaces, spa baths, and coffee- and tea-making facilities.

Dining/Entertainment: Milton Park's contemporary country cuisine is another popular feature. Roast lamb with fig tapenade, house-smoked duck, chowder of salmon and wild rice, and fresh pastas with local wild mushrooms are a few items on the extensive menu. Lunch and dinner are served daily and nonguests are welcome; a three-course lunch is A$26 (U.S. $20.80), a three-course dinner is A$48 (U.S. $38.40), and reservations are necessary.

Services: Limited room service.

Facilities: Tennis, croquet, pool, bicycles, horseback riding, spectacular gardens (open to the public only during Tulip Time).

KIAMA

119km (74 miles) S of Sydney

Kiama (pop. 7,716) is on the **Illawarra Coastline,** stretching 295km (183 miles) from Sydney to Bateman's Bay. The town is known for its **blowhole,** spurting up through a rock fissure water jets that *can* reach heights of 60 meters (198 ft.); however, its performance is anything but consistent. The blowhole is floodlit until 1am.

A **Heritage Walk** is available, taking you around the historic precinct of this pretty harborside village, including the timber terraces built in 1896 as workers' cottages. They're now classified by the National Trust and house craft and gift shops (most open daily from 10am to 5pm). Kiama's **beaches** are good for surfing, swimming, and fishing.

ESSENTIALS

GETTING THERE If you take the Illawarra Highway from Moss Vale in the Southern Highlands down to the coast, you'll come out just north of Kiama (ki—rhymes with *sky*—ama). The other alternative, if you're driving, is heading straight south from Sydney through Wollongong on the Princes Highway.

There's regular train and coach service from Sydney. The bus trip with Greyhound-Pioneer takes about two hours (A$16/U.S. $12.80).

VISITOR INFORMATION The **Kiama Visitors Centre,** Blowhole Point (☎ 042/323 322), can answer your questions. The **telephone area code** is 042. As part of the telephone changeover, all numbers with a 042 area code will be changing to 02/42xx xxxx in March 1998.

WHERE TO STAY & DINE

Kiama Terrace Motor Lodge. 51 Collins St., Kiama, NSW 2533. ☎ **042/33 1100.** Fax 042/33 1235. 50 rms. A/C TV TEL. A$98 (U.S. $78.40) double. Additional person A$10 (U.S. $8) extra. Reservations can be made through Best Western. Ask about lower rates through Aussie auto clubs and about weekend packages. AE, BC, DC, MC, V.

Readers Recommend

*"We feel **Torreys Restaurant** in Ulladulla is worth recommending. The seafood was good and the service satisfactory."*

—Jack and Eileen Esterkin, Paoli, Penn., U.S.A.

Kiama's newest motor inn is three stories and has a restaurant on the premises. All rooms have bathtubs as well as showers, and 22 have roomy spa tubs. Videos, clock radios, queen-size beds, coffee- and tea-making facilities, and small refrigerators are standard throughout. Meals can be brought to your room or eaten in the restaurant. Facilities include a self-service laundry, a barbecue, and a saltwater pool.

ULLADULLA

233km (140 miles) S of Sydney

Farther along the Illawarra Coast, Ulladulla (pop. 9,962) is a picturesque fishing port whose catch more often than not ends up on a menu in Sydney. If you're in the area at Easter, don't miss the colorful **Blessing of the Fleet Carnival and ceremony** (☎ 044/54 1778). Surfing, swimming, golf, and fishing are popular local activities, and bushwalkers can make the trek to **Pigeon House Mountain,** a rocky outcrop at the south end of Morton National Park. It's easy to net prawns in season, and the rock and offshore fishing is good.

ESSENTIALS

GETTING THERE A daily bus transports passengers from the railhead at Nowra. The trip from Sydney on Greyhound-Pioneer takes about five hours.

VISITOR INFORMATION The **telephone area code** is 044. As part of the telephone changeover, all numbers with a 044 area code will be changing to 02/44xx xxxx in June 1998.

WHERE TO STAY

Pigeon House Motor Inn. 156 Princes Hwy., Ulladulla, NSW 2539. ☎ **044/55 1811.** Fax 044/55 5256. 16 rms. TV TEL. A$65 (U.S. $52) double. Additional person A$15 (U.S. $12) extra. Holiday surcharges in Jan and at Easter and Christmas. Reservations can be made through Flag Inns. AE, BC, DC, MC, V.

This motor inn is half a kilometer (a few blocks) south of the center of town. All rooms have the standard coffee- and tea-making facilities and refrigerators, plus toasters and clock radios. There's also an outdoor pool.

MERIMBULA

480km (384 miles) S of Sydney, 580km (464 miles) NE of Melbourne

The focal point for the coastal country between Bega and Eden, Merimbula (pop. 4,251) has developed into a successful seaside resort. It's also the last point of interest before the Princes Highway crosses the state border into Victoria.

ESSENTIALS

GETTING THERE Driving from Sydney takes about 7 hours, from Melbourne about 7½ hours, and from Canberra 3 hours. Kendell Airlines and Hazelton Airlines operate flights to Merimbula. The Greyhound-Pioneer bus trip from Sydney takes 8 hours and 40 minutes.

VISITOR INFORMATION The **Tourist Information Centre,** Beach Street, Merimbula, NSW 2548 (☎ 064/95 1129), is open daily from 9am to 5pm. The

telephone area code is 064. As part of the telephone changeover, all numbers with a 064 area code will be changing to 02/64xx xxxx in March 1998.

SEEING THE AREA

Eden, near Merimbula, was once a major whaling port, and the town's **Killer Whale Museum,** on Imlay Street (☎ 064/96 2094), displays an array of maritime relics relating to the whaling, fishing, and timber industries. It's open Monday to Friday from 10am to 4pm and Saturday and Sunday from 11am to 4pm. The admission is A$4 (U.S. $3.20) for adults and A$1 (U.S. 80¢) for children.

You may be interested in seeing the **Brogo Valley Rotolactor,** 16km (10 miles) north of Bega, where cows are milked on a rotary turnstile at 3pm daily. There are also tours at the **Bega cheese factory** Monday to Friday.

Golf is the main game in Merimbula, and the area's most popular venue is the **Pambula-Merimbula Golf Club** (☎ 064/95 6154), where kangaroos regularly graze on the fairways of the 27-hole course. Another favorite is the **Tura Beach Country Club** (☎ 064/95 9002), at **Tura Beach,** 4km (2½ miles) north of town. This course is known for its excellent coastline views. (Greens fees are about A$15/U.S. $12.) Besides golf, Merimbula has good **beaches** for surfing and windsurfing. Fishing, oystering, and prawning are also popular.

If jazz is a passion, the **Merimbula Jazz Festival** is held in June. For information, contact Stan Delle Vergin at 064/95 1399 or Ken Gordon at 064/92 1723.

WHERE TO STAY

Ocean View Motor Inn. At Princes Highway and View Street, Merimbula, NSW 2548. ☎ **064/95 2300,** or 1800/02 8293 in Australia. Fax 064/95 3443. 19 rms. A/C TEL TV. A$45–A$95 (U.S. $36–$76) double. Additional person A$10 (U.S. $8) extra. BC, MC, V.

All rooms in this two-story motor inn have showers (no tubs), clock radios, coffee- and tea-making facilities, and small refrigerators. Ten have queen-size beds, and 13 have kitchenettes. A saltwater pool, recreation room, barbecue, and self-service laundry are provided for guests' use.

2 The Snowy Mountains

In a country like Australia, best known for its beaches and outback barrenness, the Snowys are a rarity. While snow falls in other places, these mountains have the only ski facilities. Aussies love the Snowys and flock to the area for both winter and summer sports.

The loftiest point is Mount Kosciusko, reaching a height of 2,228 meters (7,352 ft.) and dominating **Kosciusko National Park.** The major ski areas—Thredbo, Perisher Blue (which includes Perisher Valley, Smiggens, Guthega, and Blue Cow Mountain), Charlotte Pass, and Mount Selwyn—are in the park. In addition to their fame as a winter-sports venue, the Snowys are known for high-country horseback riding, an activity that got great exposure in *The Man from Snowy River* movies. The ballad on which the film was based was written by bush poet Banjo Paterson in 1895 and set in the area around Kiandra in the northern part of the park.

Some of the action in the movie takes place in the neighboring state of Victoria, which borders Kosciusko National Park on the south and is separated from New South Wales by the Murray River.

THREDBO

519km (322 miles) SW of Sydney, 208km (129 miles) SW of Canberra, 534km (331 miles) NE of Melbourne

Easily the area's most popular ski resort, this alpine village has facilities on a par with those of similar resorts around the world. Thredbo is the site of international skiing events and offers a wide range of accommodations and dining options.

ESSENTIALS

GETTING THERE Motorists can follow the Hume Highway through Goulburn, connecting with the Federal Highway to Canberra. From there the Monaro Highway leads to Cooma. The Alpine Way then takes you through Jindabyne and into Thredbo Village. Chains must be carried during winter if you plan on traveling past Thredbo.

Those coming from Sydney can fly to Cooma, 95km (59 miles) to the northeast, on Impulse through Ansett (☎ 13 13 00) or Eastern Australia through Qantas (☎ 13 13 13). The connecting bus trip to Thredbo takes 1½ hours and is available only from June to October.

From June to October, Greyhound-Pioneer offer two trips a day from Sydney to Thredbo (duration: 8 hr.). The cost is A$52 (U.S. $41.60). You could also take a Countrylink train from Sydney to Canberra and catch a Greyhound-Pioneer coach from there to Thredbo.

The Sydney-Canberra train ride takes four hours; the connecting Countrylink coach goes only as far as Cooma.

VISITOR INFORMATION Information is available (☎ 064/57 6275) and lodging arrangements can be made through the **Thredbo Resort Centre** (☎ 064/57 6360), open daily from 9am to 6pm. **Snow reports** are as close as the phone (☎ 1900/63 253 from anywhere in New South Wales).

The village, which feels more like it's in Switzerland than in Australia, is a compact cluster of lodges, restaurants, and a hotel; a **free shuttle bus** operates to the valley terminal, even though the lifts are within easy walking distance. An underground **Skitube** is midway between Thredbo and Jindabyne on the Alpine Way and travels through the mountain to Perisher Valley and then on to Blue Cow Mountain.

Perisher Blue is the largest ski resort in Australia, covering 1,250 hectares (3,088 acres) and offering a wide variety of lodging and dining options. For information, call 1800/654 681 or the Perisher Blue Reservation Centre at 1800/020 808.

Blue Cow Mountain is the newest ski area. It's a day resort only, and access is via the Skitube or road. For information, call 1800/654 681, 064/57 5444, or 02/580 6555.

The **telephone area code** is 064. As part of the telephone changeover, all numbers with a 064 area code will be changing to 02/64xx xxxx in March 1998.

WHAT TO SEE & DO

In spite of efforts to promote summer activities in the village, **skiing** is still the sport that brings most people to Thredbo and other resorts in the Snowy Mountains. The season runs from June to September. Equipment rental (skis, poles, boots, and clothing) is available in the valley terminal. Lift tickets cost A$56 (U.S. $44.80) per day, lessons are available, and there are over 100km (62 miles) of trails.

Summer attractions include bushwalking, canoeing, fishing, playing golf or tennis, and swimming. The chair lift runs year round, and at the top you can have a beer and a bite in the cafeteria or head for the top of Mount Kosciusko, a 13km (8-mile) trek round trip. Brochures available from the Resort Centre describe other alpine hikes of varying degrees of difficulty.

Tennis courts can be rented in the village, as can fishing rods. You can also play golf.

Horseback riding is available in the village, but for that real *Man from Snowy River* experience, you should contact Roslyn and John Rudd at **Reynella Horseback Adventures,** Adaminaby, NSW 2630 (☎ 064/54 2386 or 54 2469). They lead alpine horseback trips into Kosciusko National Park and host guests at their Reynella Country Lodge, nestled in the foothills of the Snowy Mountains. The trekking season is November to April. The rest of the year you can join one of their Riverina Cattle Drives (à la *City Slickers*).

Where to Stay

Bernti's Mountain Inn. Mowamba Place, Thredbo, NSW 2627. ☎ **064/57 6332** or 1800/ 500 105. 27 rms, 4 apts. TV TEL. Summer, A$70 (U.S. $56) double. Winter, A$80–A$170 (U.S. $64–$136) per person. Rates include breakfast. BC, MC, V.

This inn is a cozy stone-and-timber alpine lodge operated by Tricia and Bernd Hecher. It features a pleasant lounge with an open fire, a popular bar and licensed restaurant, an open-air café, a sauna, a spa, and attractive rooms. The apartments have cooking facilities, and the whole place has rustic charm.

$ **Kara's Apartments.** Bobuck Lane, Thredbo, NSW 2627. ☎ **064/57 6385.** Fax 064/57 6060. 9 apts. TV. High season (July to mid-Sept), A$1,355 (U.S. $1,084) per week for two in a bed-sitter (studio); A$2,415 (U.S. $1,932) per week for four in a one-bedroom apt; A$2,520 (U.S. $2,016) for six in a two-bedroom apt. Off-season, rates are lower and daily tariffs are available. No credit cards. Closed Oct–May.

Kara's is a good choice for those who want self-contained living with daily chamber service. Each studio, one-bedroom, or two-bedroom unit has a fully equipped kitchen and all the necessary bed and bath linens. All have balconies from which there's a view of Crackenback Mountain; a sauna is shared by guests.

Thredbo Alpine Hotel. Thredbo, NSW 2627. ☎ **064/59 4200.** 64 rms, 2 suites. MINIBAR TV TEL. Summer, A$125 (U.S. $100) double. Winter, A$280–A$340 (U.S. $224–$272) double. Ask about weekly rates and lower rates through Aussie auto clubs. Rates include breakfast. AE, BC, DC, MC, V.

The three-story Thredbo Alpine has comfortable rooms, a heated pool, a sauna, a spa, a licensed restaurant and bistro, and several bars. The hotel is the social center of the community since it's the village's only licensed hotel, and it's the ideal place for people who like being in the thick of things.

3 The Blue Mountains

They were an unwelcome obstacle for the explorers who tried to cross them in the early 1800s, but for the past century the Blue Mountains have provided a scenic retreat for harried Sydneysiders in search of peace and relaxation. Waterfalls now run down the sandstone plateaus that thwarted colonists' westward movement, and some of the eroded cliffs have taken on fanciful shapes. The area is heavily timbered with eucalyptus, and it's the oil vapor from these trees that makes the mountains look blue. While superb scenery is the major draw, the hospitality and good food at the region's cozy guesthouses also contribute to its popularity.

The mountains are most popular in winter (June to August), when the thermometer registers an average daytime maximum of 10°C (50°F) and guesthouse proprietors, celebrating Yulefest, serve traditional English-style Christmas dinners, accompanied by caroling. Summer temperatures average 22°C (72°F). For more about Yulefest, call 047/396 266.

Katoomba is the largest of the 26 townships in the Blue Mountains area. Other resort communities along the Great Western Highway include Wentworth Falls,

Leura, Medlow Bath, Blackheath, and Mount Victoria. The combined Katoomba–Wentworth Falls area has a population of 16,901.

KATOOMBA

100km (62 miles) W of Sydney

In the late 1870s the first vacationers made the lengthy trip in Cobb & Co. stagecoaches, but today you can hop on a train or bus or rent a car and be in the mountains in only two hours. One-day tours are available too, but to appreciate the area fully, you'll need more time.

ESSENTIALS

GETTING THERE Those who opt to drive can make it in slightly less than two hours from Sydney via the Western Motorway (M4) and the Great Western Highway (Hwy. 32). There's frequent train service between Sydney and Katoomba; the trip takes about two hours and costs A$18 (U.S. $14.40) round trip for adults. In addition, CityRail (☎ 13 15 00) offers a Blue Mountains Special Tour that includes round-trip transportation to Katoomba and a bus tour of the area. The Monday to Friday fare is A$40 (U.S. $32) for adults and A$20 (U.S. $16) for children; the Saturday and Sunday fare is A$27 (U.S. $21.60).

One-day coach tours are operated by AAT King's, Australian Pacific Tours, Sydney Day Tours, and others. Greyhound-Pioneer provides regular bus service (duration: 2¾ hr.).

VISITOR INFORMATION Information is dispensed at centers staffed by the **Blue Mountains Tourism Authority,** centrally located at Echo Point, Katoomba, NSW 2780, and on the Great Western Highway at Glenbrook (☎ 047/39 6266); both places are open daily from 9am to 5pm. The **telephone area code** is 047. As part of the telephone changeover, all numbers with a 047 area code will be changing to 02/47xx xxxx in February 1998.

SEEING THE TOWN

Mountain scenery is the main attraction in Katoomba, and **The Three Sisters** is the best-known and most popular sight. The trio of pinnacles is best viewed from Echo Point off Cliff Drive, near the Visitor Information Centre. Other good viewpoints include **Evans Lookout, Govetts Leap,** and **Hargreaves Lookout.** Serious scenery buffs with their own cars should pick up a touring map outlining the main scenic drives in the Blue Mountains, available at the area's Information Centres for A$4.50 (U.S. $3.60).

The **Skyway,** a cable car that glides 300 meters (990 ft.) above the floor of the Jamison Valley and provides a breathtaking view of **Orphan Rock** and **Katoomba Falls,** and the **Scenic Railway,** the world's steepest, are two popular rides. Each costs A$4 (U.S. $3.20) round trip. Both the Skyway and railway (☎ 047/82 2699) operate daily from 9am to 5pm (last trip at 4:50pm). The Skyway Revolving Restaurant (☎ 047/82 2577) is open daily from 9:30am to 4:30pm.

If you take the train to Katoomba, you can connect with the **Explorer Bus,** which operates on weekends and goes to the major attractions (A$16/U.S. $12.80 for adults, A$8/U.S. $6.40 for children), or take the three-hour Blue Mountains Highlights Tour offered Monday to Friday (A$29/U.S. $23.20 for adults, A$18/U.S. $12 for children). Both are operated by **Fantastic Aussie Tours** (☎ 047/82 1866).

Another alternative for getting around is provided by **Cliff Edge Cruisers** (☎ 047/824 462 or 015/073 216). Graham and Paul Geddes, father and son, invite you to jump on the back of their Harleys and tool around scenic byways with them. They provide leather jackets, helmets, and gloves. A half-hour spin costs A$40 (U.S. $32); a full hour is A$50 (U.S. $40); and an all-day ride to the Jenolan Caves or Bathurst is A$250 (U.S. $200), including teas and lunch. This isn't just for daredevils—they've had 80-year-olds on board.

Besides the various viewpoints, the **Norman Lindsay Gallery,** 14 Norman Lindsay Crescent (via Chapman Parade), Faulconbridge, east of Katoomba (☎ 047/51 1067), is a worthwhile stop. Lindsay was an imaginative Australian artist/writer (1879-1969). The gallery, his former home, is a National Trust property and open Wednesday to Sunday from 11am to 5pm; admission is A$5 (U.S. $4) for adults and A$1 (U.S. 80¢) for children. Lindsay's best-known work is *The Magic Pudding,* a children's classic, and his drawings of the book's characters are displayed in one room. The landscaped gardens around the gallery are dotted with 15 of his fountains. The **Old Etching Studio Coffee Shop** serves Devonshire teas and boasts "We bake the best scones in town."

By the time you get there, the new **IMAX Theatre** will have opened on the Great Western Highway in Katoomba, about 200 meters (217 yards) from the railway station. The plan is to show the Blue Mountains destination movie *The Edge* every 50 minutes from 10am to 3pm.

Seeking Adventure

If you read "The Active Vacation Planner" in Chapter 3, you know that the Blue Mountains are one of Australia's best areas for adventure activities. Rock climbing, abseiling, mountain biking, horse riding, bushwalking, and canyoning are just a few of the popular pastimes. One of the best local operators is the **Blue Mountains Adventure Company,** P.O. Box 242, Katoomba, NSW 2780 (☎ 047/821 271; fax 047/821 277). Its headquarters are in the Mountain Designs shop, 190 Katoomba St. The other well-known local adventure specialist is the **Australian School of Mountaineering,** located in Rock Craft, 182 Katoomba St, Katoomba, NSW 2780 (☎ 047/822 014; fax 047/825 787). Both can organize your abseiling, canyoning, or rock-climbing experience. Blue Mountain Adventure Company also offers caving and mountain biking. The Australian School of Mountaining also offers mountaineering, bushcraft, trekking, survival, rescue, and outdoor training.

Other adventure companies operating in the Blue Mountains, including the **Womens' Outdoor Network** and **Great Australian Walks,** are listed in "The Active Vacation Planner" in Chapter 3.

Where to Stay

The wise traveler will plan to be in the Blue Mountains on Sunday to Thursday, when rates are much lower than they are on weekends.

Avonleigh Guest House. 174 Lurline St., Katoomba, NSW 2780. ☎ **047/82 1534.** Fax 047/82 5688. 12 rms. Midweek, A$105 (U.S. $84) per person double; weekend, A$125 (U.S. $100) per person double. Rates include breakfast and dinner. AE, BC, DC, MC, V. Closed late Dec to early Jan. Free parking.

This cozy Federation period (1900–1915) mountain home has comfortable guest rooms, a cozy ambience created by open fires and classical music, and cuisine that could compete favorably with that of the best city restaurants. Hosts Belinda and Ivan Harris are responsible for the success of the inn. While Belinda acts as hostess, Ivan, who trained as a chef in Lausanne and London, works his magic in the kitchen.

The home is a mixture of Edwardian and Victorian decor. The guest rooms feature double beds with antique headboards, and tufted velvet chairs, double cameo couches, sprays of dried flowers, and a high ceiling of ornamental white pressed metal create a Victorian air in the living room. You receive a complimentary glass of sherry before dinner, as well as free coffee and tea in the lounge day and night. Avonleigh is only a five-minute walk from Echo Point; the hosts provide transfers to the railway station. Because of the inn's delicate decor and peaceful nature, Belinda and Ivan don't encourage guests to bring children, and the stairs make it inappropriate for handicapped travelers. A heated spa and tennis court are available.

Ivan's gourmet dinners start with an entree (appetizer) like leek, mushroom, and sherry soup or vegetable timbale with tomato coulis. The main course may include turkey with green peppercorns and avocado. The delicious desserts include vanilla bavarois or apple-and-banana brûlée followed by homemade chocolates. Popular Christmas dinners are served on Saturday night throughout July. The dining room is open to nonguests on a space-available basis; dinners cost A$38 (U.S. $30.40) per person. Bring your own wine.

$ Echos Guesthouse. 3 Lilianfels Ave., Echo Point, Katoomba, NSW 2780. ☎ **047/821 966.** Fax 047/823 707. 12 rms. MINIBAR TV TEL. Midweek, A$100 (U.S. $80) per person with breakfast, A$145 (U.S. $116) per person with dinner and breakfast; weekend, A$320–A$330 (U.S. $256–$264) per person with two dinners and two breakfasts. AE, MC, V. Free parking.

Echoes is across from the much pricier Lilianfels (below) and enjoys the same proximity to Echo Point. However, Echoes actually has a better view than Lilianfels because it's *right* on the edge of the Jamison Valley, not separated by a road the way Lilianfels is. Many rooms in this chic guesthouse offer tile balconies overlooking the legendary scenery that draws travelers to the Blue Mountains. The decors could best be described as "smart country"—Ralph Lauren–type fabrics predominate in the simply furnished rooms. All offer underfloor heating; two corner rooms have Jacuzzi tubs. Upstairs, a contemporary open space contains a restaurant, a lounge, an open fire, and a bar (all with huge windows), plus a large tile deck from which there's a panoramic vista. Guests enjoy good French cuisine and relaxing in the sauna. Smoking isn't allowed, and children aren't accepted.

Fairmont Resort. 1 Sublime Point Rd., Leura, NSW 2780. ☎ **047/82 5222.** Fax 047/84 1685. 210 rms, 20 suites. A/C MINIBAR TV TEL. A$242 (U.S. $193.60) double; A$341–A$726 (U.S. $272.80–$580.80) suite. Additional person A$35 (U.S. $28) extra. Ask about lower rates Sun–Thur, with two-night minimum stay on weekends, and lower rates through Aussie auto clubs. AE, BC, DC, MC, V. Free parking.

Compared to the area's cozy guesthouses, the Fairmont Resort is like a gigantic palace. The modern four-story hotel overlooking the beautiful Jamison Valley opened in 1988, giving the Blue Mountains its first deluxe accommodations. Each room has tea- and coffee-making facilities, a small refrigerator, a clock radio, and a fluffy bathrobe. Queen-size beds are the norm, but king-size are available. The resort cost A$52 million (U.S. $42 million), has won numerous awards, and is understandably popular with those seeking extensive recreation facilities.

Dining/Entertainment: Embers is a cozy lounge with a huge stone fireplace and an expansive mountain view; Misty's is the fine-dining room, and Jamison's Restaurant is a casual brasserie.

Services: Concierge, 24-hour room service, laundry, valet, nightly turndown, massage, baby-sitting.

Facilities: Indoor and outdoor pools, health club, gym, spas, sauna, four floodlit tennis courts, two glass-backed squash courts, adjacent Leura Golf Course, children's center and supervised activity program, business center, gift shop.

✪ **Lilianfels Blue Mountains.** Lilianfels Avenue, Echo Point, Katoomba, NSW 2780. ☎ **047/801 200** or 1800/024 452 in Australia. Fax 047/801 300. 86 rms and suites; 1 cottage. A/C MINIBAR TV TEL. A$260–A$310 (U.S. $208–$248) double, A$400–A$490 (U.S. $320–$392) suite; A$700 (U.S. $560) cottage. Ask about dollarwise off-season packages. AE, BC, DC, MC, V. Free parking.

This charming country-house hotel manages to combine the coziness of a guesthouse with the facilities of a top-class resort. The rooms are extremely spacious and well appointed—all offer fluffy doonas, remote-control TVs, VCRs, and large marble baths with separate tub and shower. The focal point of the property is a gracious large lounge overlooking the Jamison Valley. Here two open fires, traditional furnishings, and classical piano music create a stately feel. There are also a billiards room; a reading room with a selection of books, games, and puzzles; and a tennis court and croquet lawn. If you stay here, be sure to request a valley view—these rooms cost a bit more but are worth it.

Dining/Entertainment: Darley's Restaurant (see "Where to Dine" below) offers fine dining in historic surroundings; Lilians is more casual; and the Lobby Lounge is a wonderful spot for light meals and teas.

Services: Room service, dry cleaning/laundry, nightly turndown, secretarial services.

Facilities: A tile deck with wicker chairs surrounding an attractive heated indoor pool; a health club including a flotation tank, an herbal bath, a gym, steam and sauna rooms, and Jacuzzis; massage therapist and beautician; tennis, croquet, and mountain bikes.

The Little Company Guest House. 2 Eastview Ave., Leura, NSW 2781. ☎ **047/82 4023.** Fax 047/82 5361. 35 rms, 6 country houses. TV TEL. Mon–Thurs, A$120 (U.S. $96) per person; Fri–Sun, A$140 (U.S. $112) per person. Rates include breakfast and dinner. Reduced rates for children under 12. AE, BC, DC, MC, V.

A few kilometers east of Katoomba, in the community of Leura, the Little Company Guest House sits on parklike grounds surrounded by tennis courts, gardens, a putting green, a croquet lawn, a barbecue area, and a pool. Hosts Margaret and Alan Hair have converted the original house (built 1906), which for 50 years served as a retreat for nuns from the Little Company of Mary, into a charming inn. Ten homey front rooms have views of Mount Hay and Mount Wilson. There are also six country houses of four rooms each that are suitable for small groups. One room is set up to accommodate handicapped travelers. Soufflés, croissants, homemade yogurt, and eggs cocotte are served for breakfast, and three-course "homestyle gourmet" dinners are served in a delightful dining room with turn-of-the-century decor. Yulefest dinners enliven Saturday nights during June, July, and August. Regular evening meals for nonguests cost A$35 (U.S. $28). BYO.

Where to Dine

Darley's Restaurant. In Lilianfels Blue Mountains, Lilianfels Avenue, Echo Point, Katoomba. ☎ **047/801 200.** Reservations essential. Dinner and Sun lunch: two courses A$48 (U.S. $38.40); three courses A$58 (U.S. $46.40). Wed–Sat lunch: two courses A$32 (U.S. $25.60); three courses A$38.50 (U.S. $30.80). AE, BC, DC, MC, V. Wed–Sun noon–2:30pm, and 6:30–9:30pm. COUNTRY AUSTRALIAN.

In 1889 a fine country house was built for Sir Frederick Darley, Chief Justice and Lieutenant Governor of New South Wales. Today this home is the fine-dining restaurant on the grounds of Lilianfels, the country-house hotel described above. The original drawing room—where there are two fireplaces, stained-glass windows, and a mahogany ceiling and woodwork—is now the main dining area. Smaller rooms are used for cocktails and extra-intimate meals. What was an upstairs guest room is now the history room—be sure to look at the photo of the drawing room taken in the early 1900s. The à la carte menu includes starters like cream of mussel soup and mousseline of trout with salmon, saffron, ginger, coriander, and sugar snap peas. Typical main courses are duck pie with red wine, black olives, mushrooms, and sweet potato mash as well as casserole of braised pork cheeks with stock pot vegetables, bacon, and forest mushrooms. For dessert, try the hot chocolate soufflé with orange marmalade and King Island cream or homemade caramel, ginger, and vanilla bean ice cream. Darley's seats only 36, so book well ahead.

$ **Parakeet Cafe.** 195B Katoomba St., Katoomba. ☎ **047/82 1815.** Main courses A$8–A$12 (U.S. $6.40–$9.60). No credit cards. Mon–Thurs and Sun 7am–9pm, Fri–Sat 7am–10pm. MODERN AUSTRALIAN/CAFE.

Conveniently located on the main drag, only 1/2km (1/3 mile) from the train station, this very casual café serves top-notch food. Don't be put off by the kinda divey, cluttered appearance. Gerard Rio serves great homemade soup, focaccia, and pastas. On a recent visit the chalkboard offerings included fresh ricotta ravioli, beef nachos with avocado and sour cream, and chef's salad. Walk to the back and turn right to find the no-smoking section. BYO.

BLACKHEATH

14km (9 miles) W of Katoomba, 114km (71 miles) W of Sydney

Like neighboring Katoomba, Blackheath is surrounded by scenic rock formations and waterfalls. Four kilometers (2 1/2 miles) farther west, the township of Mount Victoria, perched on the highest peak in the Blue Mountains, is known for its antiques and craft shops and adventurous bushwalks.

ESSENTIALS

GETTING THERE Motorists proceed west from Katoomba on the Great Western Highway. CityRail trains provide frequent service from Sydney to Blackheath.

VISITOR INFORMATION The **telephone area code** is 047. As part of the telephone changeover, all numbers with a 047 area code will be changing to 02/47xx xxxx in February 1998.

EXPLORING THE AREA

You don't have to be an experienced rider to enjoy the "holidays on horseback" offered by ✪ **Mountain River Riders,** P.O. Box 95, Oberon, NSW 2787 (☎ 063/36 1890). All you need are an appreciation of the wilderness and a desire to see part of the real Australia. Warwick and Beryl Armstrong come from families who first bought property in this region when the country was only 70 years old; now they want to share with visitors the beauty of the bush they know so well. Pack trips can be tailored to suit individual needs but typically last three days. They start at River Downs, the Armstrongs' home on the edge of Blue Mountains National Park, 20km (12 miles) south of Blackheath. From there, two experienced guides lead six to eight riders into a remote cattleman's outstation in the bush, making 17 river crossings along the way. Guests spend two nights in huts equipped with a fireplace, and during the day they fish (trout season is October to June), hike, swim, or just enjoy the silence afforded by the location. The three-day/two-night experience costs A$540 (U.S. $432) per person, or more if helicopter transfers from Sydney are required. Alternatively, day rides cost A$120 (U.S. $96) per person and include morning and afternoon tea, lunch in the bush, and five hours of riding.

Readers Recommend

Cleopatra's, Blackheath (☎ 047/878 456). *"Here we found superb food, good ambience, a large grassy lawn with iron tables under majestic shady trees. Co-owners Trish Mullene and Dany Choet grow their own herbs and salad greens. Set-price dinners cost A$65 (U.S. $52) BYO. They also offer well-decorated rooms, some with private baths, and one delightful suite. Lodging costs A$150 to A$200 (U.S. $120 to $160) per person, including dinner and breakfast. They accept American Express, Diners Club, MasterCard, and Visa."*

—David Robinson, Mill Valley, Calif., U.S.A.

Mountain River Riders has recently extended its operation to include four-wheel-drive trips, too. These day excursions are designed for a minimum of 4 people and a maximum of 10; costing A$150 (U.S. $120) per person, they offer lots of beautiful scenery, morning and afternoon tea, and a barbecue lunch. Horseback riding is included in the tour they call River Downs Roamer. Highly recommended.

Where to Stay & Dine

For dining, **Roast and Rolls,** 18 Govetts Leap Rd., Blackheath (☎ 047/876 615), is easy to find—at the traffic light on the highway as it passes through town. Here the specialty is good roast meat sandwiches, to eat in or to go. Nearby, the **Blackheath Patisserie** is almost a legend in the Blue Mountains.

$ Amani Bed and Breakfast. 31 Days Cresent, Blackheath, NSW 2785. ☎ **047/87 8610.** 3 rms (2 with bath). A$80 (U.S. $64) double. Rates include breakfast. No credit cards.

Rosemary and Bill Chapple have a lovely home surrounded by extensive rhododendron and azalea gardens, but the most impressive feature is the view of Grose Valley from their lounge (living room). They serve tea to new arrivals. Upstairs are two guest rooms, with views and walk-in closets and smallish baths with skylights. Though guests are always welcome downstairs, they also have their own lounge upstairs with tea- and coffee-making facilities, a TV, a microwave, a toaster, and a refrigerator. Rosemary even keeps a supply of her homemade biscuits (cookies) in this area. A twin room downstairs shares a bath with the hosts. Children are welcome.

$ Jemby-Rinjah Lodge. 336 Evans Lookout Rd., Blackheath, NSW 2785. ☎ **047/87 7622.** Fax 047/87 6230. 9 cabins, lodge with 15 rms. Mon–Thurs, A$85 (U.S. $68) cabin (occupied by up to two adults and two children); Fri–Sun, A$105 (U.S. $84) cabin; additional adult A$15 (U.S. $12) extra, additional child A$10 (U.S. $8) extra; A$49 (U.S. $39.20) per person bed and breakfast in lodge. BC, MC, V.

Jemby-Rinjah Lodge consists of nine deluxe cabins (two one-bedroom and seven two-bedroom) sleeping up to six people and a lodge bunkhouse in a lovely wooded setting on the edge of the Grose Valley section of Blue Mountains National Park. This is a wonderful place for those who like hiking; the start of the grand canyon and clifftop walk are nearby. The two-bedroom/one-bath cabins are carpeted, have wood stoves in the living rooms, and boast fully equipped kitchens, including microwaves. Feather doonas grace each bed. The main lodge complex consists of three separate eco lodges for accommodation, a dining and lounge area, and conference facilities.

Owners Peter and Margaret Quirk have a high regard for the fragility of the bush and designed the accommodations accordingly. Composting toilets and passive solar heating protect the environment, while the lovely wooden cabins provide guests all the comfort they could possibly expect. The Quirks provide courtesy pickup from Blackheath Rail Station and can arrange baby-sitting. Meals are available in the lodge. The local parrots (Jemby-Rinjah) are fed each day at 8:30am, providing a wonderful photo opportunity. To quote some readers who were recent guests: "It's a splendid place."

JENOLAN CAVES

182km (113 miles) W of Sydney

Underground limestone caves can be found in several places in New South Wales, but the best known are the Jenolan Caves, a short distance from the Kanangra Boyd National Park on a spur of the Great Dividing Range. Several million people have visited the caves since they were opened in 1866, and I doubt many have been disappointed—the stalactites and stalagmites combine with underground rivers to create a magical scene.

ESSENTIALS

GETTING THERE It takes about 1½ hours to drive to the Jenolan Caves from Katoomba (turning left onto Jenolan Caves Road just after the township of Hartley). You can take a CityRail train to Katoomba and link up with daily Jenolan Caves excursions conducted by Fantastic Aussie Tours (☎ 047/82 1866). The CityRail combination train/coach tour ticket costs A$59 (U.S. $47.20) for adults and A$26 (U.S. $20.80) for children. The tour alone costs A$48 (U.S. $38.40) for adults and A$26 (U.S. $20.80) for children. These prices don't include cave tours.

One-day round-trip coach tours that include the Jenolan Caves are operated by AAT King's and Australian Pacific Tours. Greyhound-Pioneer provides regular bus service to Katoomba from Sydney.

VISITOR INFORMATION The **telephone area code** is 063. As part of the telephone changeover, all numbers with a 063 area code will be changing to 02/63xx xxxx in January 1998.

EXPLORING THE CAVES

Nine caverns are open to the public and guided tours are conducted by the staff of the Jenolan Caves Reserve Trust (☎ 063/59 3311). The first cave tour starts at 9:45am weekdays and 9:15am weekends and holidays. The final tour starts at 5pm every day. Each costs A$12 to A$20 (U.S. $9.60 to $16) and lasts 1½ to 2 hours. Children under 16 pay A$6 to A$20 (U.S. $4.80 to $16). Multiple cave packages are also available. A kiosk sells snacks, and meals are available at Jenolan Caves House (below).

WHERE TO STAY & DINE

Jenolan Caves House. Jenolan Caves, NSW 2790. ☎ **063/59 3304** or 1800/02 7927 in Australia. Fax 063/59 3227. 99 rms (some with bath). Midweek, from A$193 (U.S. $154.40) per adult double; higher on weekends. Rates include breakfast and dinner. AE, BC, DC, MC, V.

This three-story hotel was built between 1888 and 1906 and is a classic example of late Victorian architecture. Constructed of limestone blocks, it boasts grandness that's strictly old world. Residents of New South Wales feel "100 years of affection" for this property, and the present owners have undertaken extensive refurbishment to restore this grand guesthouse to its former glory. The integrity of the building has been preserved while adding modern conveniences. The wildlife reserve surrounding the hotel is ideal for walking and scenic drives. Wildflowers make it especially pretty in the spring.

In addition to the grand dining room, with its 16-foot ceiling and huge antique sideboards, a café lounge on the ground floor serves light lunches and Devonshire teas.

4 The Golden West

West of the Blue Mountains and the Great Dividing Range is a region of New South Wales called the Golden West, so named because Australia's first assayable gold was found here in 1851.

The discovery of the precious metal brought diggers and Chinese workers into an area that was previously not heavily populated. Towns grew overnight, and many fine homes were constructed with goldfield money. Some 13 tons of gold were found around Gulgong within five years; today Gulgong is known as "the town on the 10-dollar note" (even though it no longer is).

While for all practical purposes mining has come to a halt, this part of the state continues to thrive as an important agricultural area. The city of Orange is known as "Australia's Big Apple," not because it in any way resembles its U.S. namesake, but because two-thirds of all the apples in New South Wales are grown there. Mudgee has emerged in the last few years as an important grape-growing district; sheep and cattle thrive in the region's fertile pastures.

The main points of interest are relics of the gold-mining days—and a chance to understand this important part of Australia's history a bit better.

BATHURST

211km (131 miles) W of Sydney

It's ironic that the two main attractions in this sedate old city (pop. 27,500) are its historic connections to the past and its very modern racing circuit.

ESSENTIALS

GETTING THERE Motorists follow the Great Western Highway through the Blue Mountains. Hazelton Airlines has flights to Bathurst from Sydney. Countrylink offers direct XPT rail service from Sydney's Central Station (A$26/U.S. $20.80). Greyhound-Pioneer offers daily service (A$21/U.S. $16.80), as does CityRail (A$25/U.S. $20); travel time is about four hours.

VISITOR INFORMATION Information is available at the **Bathurst Visitors' Centre,** 28 William St., Bathurst, NSW 2795 (☎ 063/32 1444; fax 063/32 2333), open daily from 9am to 5pm. The **telephone area code** is 063. As part of the telephone changeover, all numbers with a 063 area code will be changing to 02/63xx xxxx in January 1998.

SEEING THE TOWN

The modern **Mount Panorama Motor Racing Circuit** hosts the internationally renowned **Toohey's 1000 Touring Car Championship** held annually in late September or October (☎ 063/32 1444). This race and the Touring Car Championships in March lure drivers and spectators from all over the world. Visitors who aren't here at these times can drive the circuit (no charge) and visit the **Bathurst Motor Racing Hall of Fame** (☎ 063/32 1872) in the pit area. It's open daily from 9am to 4:30pm (A$4/U.S. $3.20 for adults, A$1/U.S. 80¢ for children).

At the **Bathurst Sheep and Cattle Drome** (☎ 063/37 3634), you can learn about milking and shearing and watch sheepdog demonstrations. Shows are daily at 11:30am.

Bathurst has more than its fair share of attractive historical buildings. Of particular interest are **Abercrombie House,** a huge mansion built in the late 1870s (tours are welcome by appointment (☎ 063/31 4929); the **Court House** (which contains the Bathurst Historical Society and Museum); and **Miss Traill's House,** a colonial Georgian cottage built in 1845 (open Monday to Saturday from 1 to 4:30pm).

Bathurst Gold Diggings, located at Karingal Village, Mount Panorama (☎ 063/32 2022), is an authentic reconstruction of an 1860s gold mine, complete with restored machines in action and a film on gold discoveries. You can try your luck at panning, and while I can't promise you results, it sometimes still happens in the Golden West: At Ophir, near Orange, a nugget worth more than A$100,000 (U.S. $80,000) was found in 1979.

Where to Stay & Dine

Governor Macquarie Motor Inn. 19 Charlotte St., Bathurst, NSW 2795. ☎ **063/31 2211.** Fax 063/31 4754. 37 rms, 2 suites. A/C MINIBAR TV TEL. A$99 (U.S. $79.20) double. Additional person A$10 (U.S. $9.60) extra. AE, BC, DC, MC, V.

The Governor Macquarie is a centrally located two-story motel. All units have showers, coffee- and tea-making facilities, and small refrigerators; 19 have bathtubs. Other features include a guest laundry and a pool. A la carte meals are served in the Governors and drinks are available in the Ribbon Gang Bar.

MUDGEE

264km (164 miles) NW of Sydney

Once known for its "Mudgee mud," beer with sediment in the bottom of the bottle, this attractively laid-out town (pop. 7,500) has become known for its vineyards and their fine wines. Besides grapes, the area produces stud cattle and sheep, fine wool, and honey.

Essentials

GETTING THERE Take the Great Western Highway and connect with Highway 86 if you're driving; allow about four hours. Hazelton Airlines flies between Sydney and Mudgee. A Countrylink coach—not train—ticket costs about A$36 (U.S. $28.80).

VISITOR INFORMATION Take your questions to the **Tourist Information Centre,** 84 Market St., Mudgee, NSW 2850 (☎ 063/72 5875 or 72 5874), open Monday to Friday from 9am to 5pm, Saturday from 9am to 3:30pm, and Sunday from 9:30am to 2pm; pick up a free visitors' guide. The **telephone area code** is 063. As part of the telephone changeover, all numbers with a 063 area code will be changing to 02/63xx xxxx in January 1998.

SPECIAL EVENTS The **Mudgee Wine Festival** (☎ 063/73 5875), which includes eating, drinking, listening to good music, and enjoying spring weather, takes place in September (the 7th to 29th in 1996). The **Small Farm Field Days** are held each July (☎ 063/72 3615).

Seeing the Town

Mudgee's meadery and 18 wineries are open daily and welcome visitors. For the most part, they're small operations, and often it's the proprietor who conducts the tastings in the cellar. **Craigmoor Winery,** Craigmoor Lane (☎ 063/722 208), is open Monday to Saturday from 10am to 4:30pm and Sunday from 11am to 4pm. **Montrose Winery,** Henry Lawson Drive (☎ 063/733 853), is open Monday to Friday from 9am to 4pm and Saturday and Sunday from 10am to 4pm. **Miramar,** Henry Lawson Drive (☎ 063/733 874), is open daily from 9am to 5pm. The wineries are clustered only a short way out of town; they're easy to find using the map in the visitors' guide supplied free at the Tourist Information Centre.

After you've learned about the local vino, you may want to investigate the two major honey factories. At the **Mudgee Honey Company,** 28 Robertson St. (☎ 063/722 359), you can see bees working under glass and taste various types of the pure natural product; it's open weekdays from 9am to 5pm and weekends from 9am to 4pm. And **Honey Haven,** Gulgong Road (☎ 063/724 478), sells 70 flavors of honey, conducts tours, and offers tastings.

After looking around Mudgee, you may want to take a trip to **Gulgong,** an atmospheric town 27km (17 miles) to the north. The quaint place has been described as "a Walt Disney set." The **Pioneers Museum,** 73 Herbert St. (☎ 063/74 1513), is worth a peek.

WHERE TO STAY

In addition to the places below, accommodation is available at Runnymede Station, an hour from Mudgee in the Upper Hunter Valley (see "Hunter Valley" below).

Country Comfort Inn, Mudgee. Cassilis Road, Mudgee, NSW 2850. ☎ **063/72 4500,** or 1800/005 064 in Australia. Fax 063/72 4525. 66 rms, 4 suites. A/C TV TEL. A$88–A$108 (U.S. $70.40–$86.40) double; A$139–A$159 (U.S. $111.20–$127.20) suite. Additional person A$10 (U.S. $8) extra. AE, BC, DC, MC, V.

This two-story property is the newest lodging in Mudgee. Each guest room has a clock radio, coffee- and tea-making facilities, a toaster oven, and a small refrigerator. A la carte meals are served in the Paradise Restaurant, and limited room service is available. The cocktail lounge, Holtermans, is named after Bernardt Holterman, who found the largest gold specimen in the world. Guests can use the heated indoor pool, spa, and sauna.

Winning Post Motor Inn. 101 Church St., Mudgee, NSW 2850. ☎ **063/72 3333,** or 1800/02 7915 in Australia. Fax 063/72 1208. Reservations can be made through Flag Inns. 43 rms, 2 suites. A/C MINIBAR TV TEL. A$78–A$99 (U.S. $62.40–$79.20) double; A$88–A$160 (U.S. $70.40–$128) suite. Additional person A$8 (U.S. $6.40) extra. Surcharge Sat night and public holidays. No-smoking rooms available. AE, BC, DC, MC, V.

This motor inn has all the usual modern amenities, plus a licensed restaurant, a laundry, an outdoor pool, a spa, half-court tennis, and a playground. In-room videos, clock radios, coffee- and tea-making facilities, and small refrigerators are in all quarters. Limited room service is available.

WHERE TO DINE

$ **Augustine Vineyard Restaurant.** George Campbell Drive. ☎ **063/72 6816.** Reservations required for dinner. Main courses A$12–A$13 (U.S. $9.60–$10.40); Devonshire tea A$5 (U.S. $4); cheese-and-fruit plate A$5 (U.S. $4) per person. AE, BC, MC, V. Wed–Sun 10am–noon (morning tea), noon–2pm, and 2–4pm (afternoon tea); Fri–Sat dinner by advance reservation only; wine tasting daily 10am–4pm. AUSTRALIAN.

Light lunch or Devonshire teas can be enjoyed here at picnic tables in a patio shaded by grape vines, giving credence to their slogan: "Dine beneath the vines at Augustine Wines." The view of the vineyard on two sides is delightful. In addition to the alfresco dining, meals are served inside in a large room with a colonial ambience. Main courses include charcoal-grilled Mudgee sirloin of beef, roast rack of lamb, and baked rainbow trout. The tasting room is nearby, and there's a children's play area.

$ **Tramp Cafe.** 61 Market St. ☎ **063/726 665.** A$3–A$3.50 (U.S. $2.40–$2.80) sandwiches, A$5 (U.S. $4) pasta of the day. No credit cards. Mon–Fri 8am–5pm, Sat–Sun 8am–3pm. CAFE.

Look for this cute little spot a few steps off the main drag at the back of a courtyard. The sign on the door says "Cafe Open," and the first time I came here the South Australian friend I was traveling with tried to convince me that was the name of eatery. Luckily, I recognized the great Australian leg pull. In fact, the café is named after the character made famous by Charlie Chaplin. Breakfast is served all day, and there are lots of good sandwiches and tempting tea tidbits. During winter the homemade soup is so popular that latecomers often miss out.

DUBBO

420km (260 miles) NW of Sydney

Sited on the Macquarie River, Dubbo (pop. 35,000) is the regional capital for this part of the state. The city is best known as the home of the Western Plains Zoo.

ESSENTIALS

GETTING THERE If you're driving, Dubbo lies at the intersection of the Newell and Mitchell Highways. Eastern Australia Airlines and Hazelton Airlines provide air service between Sydney and Dubbo. The flight lasts 55 minutes.

Countrylink trains take $6^1/_2$ hours. Dubbo is a popular stopover point for many coach companies, including Greyhound-Pioneer, on the routes between Melbourne and Brisbane, Adelaide and Brisbane, and Sydney and Adelaide. A Sydney-Dubbo coach ticket costs A$51 (U.S. $40.80).

VISITOR INFORMATION Information is available at the **Dubbo Visitors Centre,** at the corner of Macquarie and Erskine streets, Dubbo, NSW 2830 (☎ 068/84 1422; fax 068/84 1445); it's open daily from 9am to 5pm, except Christmas. Another information center is at the **Dubbo Museum and Historical Society,** 232–234 Macquarie St. (☎ 068/82 5359). The **telephone area code** is 068. As part of the telephone changeover, all numbers with a 068 area code will be changing to 02/68xx xxxx in January 1998.

SEEING THE TOP ATTRACTIONS

Old Dubbo Gaol (Jail). Macquarie Street. ☎ **068/82 8122** or 84 2859. Admission A$3 (U.S. $2.40) adults, A$1 (U.S. 80¢) children. Daily 9am–5pm (no admission after 4:30pm). Closed Good Friday and Christmas.

In the center of the city between the State and Commonwealth banks, the old gaol has been restored. It was actually in use until 1966, and a tour of the gallows, padded cells, and hangman's kit gives some insight into Australia's slightly gruesome past. Animated models of prisoners reveal their lives of crime to visitors.

Western Plains Zoo. Obley Road, 5km (3 miles) south of town. ☎ **068/82 5888.** Admission A$14 (U.S. $11.20) adults, A$7 (U.S. $5.60) children 4–16, A$33 (U.S. $26.40) family of two adults and two children (extra children A$5 (U.S. $4) each); under 4 free. Daily 9am–4pm. Take Newell Highway south and turn left on Obley Road.

This is by far the largest open-range zoo in the country. Animals from six continents, including giraffes, elephants, rhinoceroses, tigers, zebras, and monkeys, are displayed in natural settings throughout the wildlife park's 300 landscaped hectares (741 acres). Since the animals are contained by moats and other subtle means, they give the illusion of roaming free; the absence of cages and bars is much appreciated by visitors. Native Australian fauna, like koalas, kangaroos, dingoes, and emus, are included in the collection. Because of the zoo's size, you have a choice of walking, renting a bike or Jeep, or driving your car past the exhibits. Children can pet young animals in the Friendship Farm. A bistro and fast-food kiosk overlook a lake. Bike rental is A$8 (U.S. $6.40) for four hours; mopeds cost A$30 (U.S. $24) for three hours.

Where to Stay

Ashwood Country Club Motel. Whylandra Street (Newell Hwy.), Dubbo, NSW 2830. ☎ **068/81 8700** or 1800/33 5005 in Australia. Fax 068/81 8930. Reservations can be made through Flag Inns. 39 rms and suites. A/C MINIBAR TV TEL. A$89 (U.S. $71.20) double; A$95 (U.S. $76) suite. Additional person A$10 (U.S. $8) extra. AE, BC, DC, MC, V.

This motel is a cut above the average. Each room has a queen-size bed, a toaster, and an ironing board, in addition to the usual coffee- and tea-making facilities and small refrigerator. For an extra A$10 (U.S. $8) you can rent a VCR and as many videos as you like. The facilities include a guests' laundry, an outdoor pool, a spa, a tennis court, and a playground. Meals are served in a licensed restaurant or delivered to the units. Some quarters have water beds; eight have bathtubs. Handicapped facilities are available. This lodging is conveniently located 1km (0.6 mile) from the zoo.

Cascades Motor Inn. 147 Cobra St., Dubbo, NSW 2830. ☎ **068/82 3888,** or 1800/02 7256 in Australia. Fax 068/82 0906. Reservations can be made through Flag Inns. 36 rms. A/C MINIBAR TV TEL. A$70–A$80 (U.S. $56–$64) double. Additional person A$10 (U.S. $8) extra. AE, BC, DC, MC, V.

This two-story property has all the normal amenities, plus bathtubs in 14 units and a spa bath in one. There's a licensed restaurant on the premises and limited room service. Guests can use the laundry facilities and pool.

Where to Dine

$ Matilda's Family Steakhouses. At the corner of Mitchell and Newell Highways. ☎ **068/84 3333.** Reservations recommended for dinner Thurs–Sun. Main courses A$8.95–A$14.45 (U.S. $7.20–$11.60); children's meals A$4.49–A$4.99 (U.S. $3.60–$4). Public holiday surcharge 10%. BC, MC, V. Daily noon–2:30pm and 6–9:30pm. CONTEMPORARY AUSTRALIAN.

If you've ever eaten at a Sizzler in the States, you might have a spell of déjà vu at Matilda's. Both offer wholesome, inexpensive meals and both welcome families. Dubbo's Matilda's (another is in Orange) has an attractive Australiana decor, with bentwood chairs, wooden tables, exposed-brick walls painted mushroom, and forest-green woodwork. All is very smart and clean.

Sample main courses include lemon and tandoori chicken, rump steak, and a seafood platter. All main-course prices include a trip to the extensive salad bar. Matilda's is licensed to serve alcohol, but you can bring your own. The slogan here is "Good times, good tucker."

5 The Hunter Valley

The Hunter Valley is Australia's oldest commercial wine-producing area. The first vines were planted more than 150 years ago after attempts at establishing vineyards around Sydney Cove literally proved fruitless. South Australia produces more wine, but with its rich, fertile soil and its pleasant, often sunny climate, the Hunter Valley is the second most important region and has the advantage, from the traveler's point of view, of being relatively close to Sydney. Since this is the Southern Hemisphere, the harvest months are February and March.

The Hunter Valley boasts beautiful rolling countryside, with sections of farmland interspersed between the vineyards. There's an unreal feeling here, like this section of the state somehow isn't part of the real world. No banks, fast-food restaurants, or stores selling anything of a practical nature interfere with the pursuit of good food and wine. Stressed-out Sydneysiders escape to Pokolbin on weekends, and the area's guesthouses try to outdo one another in providing a retreat atmosphere.

If you have transportation, it's easy to get around during the day; however, at night signposts on the rural roads aren't lit, so you have to go slowly and take care as you make your way back to your accommodations after dinner.

In addition to wine-related activities, the Hunter presents opportunities for gallery browsing, craft shopping, golfing, and even hot-air ballooning.

CESSNOCK & POKOLBIN

190km (118 miles) N of Sydney

A few wineries are in the Upper Hunter Valley, but if you have only a day or two for tasting and touring, I suggest you confine yourself to the 35 places found in the lower part. Cessnock is the only town of any size (pop. 16,916) and provides commercial support for the wineries that dot the rolling countryside of the Lower Hunter Valley. Most of the wineries are nearby in an area that spreads out from the village of Pokolbin. Cessnock and Pokolbin are so close it's hard to tell where one ends and the other begins.

ESSENTIALS

GETTING THERE If you drive from Sydney, the trip will take about two hours via the Pacific Highway and the Sydney-Newcastle Freeway. Dakota Air flies DC3's between Sydney and Cessnock two days a week; planes are met by coach for vineyard tour and lunch.

Countrylink trains go to Maitland, about 30km (19 miles) away. The train costs A$24 (U.S. $19.20). A taxi from Maitland to Cessnock will set you back about A$20 (U.S. $16). Keans Travel Express (☎ 02/281 9366) coach travels directly between Sydney and Cessnock and Pokolbin. The coach costs A$20 (U.S. $16). Several Sydney sightseeing companies, such as AAT King's and Australian Pacific Tours, operate one- and two-day excursions to the Hunter Valley.

VISITOR INFORMATION The **Cessnock Tourist Information Centre,** Aberdare Road, Cessnock, NSW 2325 (☎ 049/90 4477), is open Monday to Friday from 9am to 5pm, Saturday from 9:30am to 5pm, and Sunday from 9:30am to 3:30pm. Its staff can answer your questions and make accommodations bookings. The **telephone area code** is 049. As part of the telephone changeover, all numbers with a 049 area code will be changing to 02/49xx xxxx in June 1998.

WHAT TO SEE & DO

SEEING THE AREA The best place to start your exploration is at the **Hunter Valley Wine Society,** at the corner of Broke and Branxton roads in Pokolbin, next door to the Gateway Kitchen and in front of Petersons Champagne House (☎ 049/98 7397), where every vineyard in the area is represented under one roof. This is a good place to get an overview before you start out on your own because the staff consists of locals who know each company's products. It's open daily from 10am to 4:30pm for tastings and bottle sales.

Almost all the more than 50 valley wineries welcome visitors to their cellars, where generous tasting policies prevail. Some operations, like Petersons (below), are family businesses producing small quantities of exceptionally good wine. At the other extreme, **McGuigan Bros Wines** has created an entire "wine village," including a children's playground, the Cellar Restaurant, a picnic area, and a couple of casual eateries.

Tyrrell's, established in 1858, is the oldest family-owned Hunter Valley winery; it's open Monday to Saturday from 8am to 5pm. The **Rothbury Estate,** open daily, is another good example of a successful operation.

There's always a member of the family or a longtime employee in the tasting room at **Petersons,** whose chardonnays have won some impressive awards. Ironically, Shirley and Ian Peterson never dreamed of growing grapes when they bought their Hunter Valley property in 1964. They intended to run cattle, but by 1971 the pharmacist and his wife were planting their first crop. In 1974 they crushed some grapes and squeezed them through pantyhose to make wine for themselves. Their 1986 chardonnay won the 1987 Qantas Cup, a prestigious America vs. Australia competition. They've since won many other awards, including several prizes for their 1991 and 1995 chardonnays.

In addition to tasting, **Lindeman's Winery** provides picnic tables, barbecues, a children's play area, and a small museum of wine-making equipment. Other well-known companies include **Wyndham Estate, Tulloch's, McWilliams,** and **Draytons.**

If you don't have a car, you can explore the area with the **Hunter Vineyard Tours** (☎ 049/911 659 or 018/497 451). These last all day and cost A$45 (U.S. $36) with lunch and A$29 (U.S. $23.20) without a meal. Even if you do have a car, this might be a good option because Australia's driving-under-the-influence laws are very strict. The most romantic means of travel are the elegant horse-drawn carriages operated by **Somerset Carriages** (☎ 049/98 7591) and several others in the valley. Somerset offers an all-day excursion that includes a gourmet picnic, with wine served by a lake, and transportation to four wineries for tasting. **Pokolbin Horse Coaches** (☎ 049/747 258) takes you from one restaurant to another, and you have one course in each place.

Hot-air ballooning takes place daily at sunrise year round. If you'd like to glide over the Hunter Valley, call **Balloon Aloft** in Cessnock (☎ 049/38 1955, or 1800/02 8568 in Australia). The cost is about A$200 (U.S. $160) weekends and public holidays and A$185 (U.S. $148) weekdays for adults and A$120 (U.S. $96) for children 8 to 12 and includes a champagne breakfast.

PLAYING GOLF The **Cypress Lakes Golf & Country Club,** at the corner of Thompsons and McDonalds roads, Pokolbin (☎ 049/987 371, or 1800/061 818 in Australia), is the newest international-standard course in the country. The 18-hole course is a par 72 and features Australia's longest par 5—the 8th hole at 573 meters (621 yards). It was designed by American golf architect Steve Smyers and Australian Bob Stanton. Golf clubs, shoes, carts, and buggies can be hired, and a driving range provides an opportunity to practice. Green fees for 9 holes are A$27 (U.S. $21.60) Monday to Thursday and A$34 (U.S. $27.20) Friday to Sunday; 18 holes are A$39 (U.S. $31.20) Monday to Thursday and A$52 (U.S. $41.60) Friday to Sunday. The course is open daily from 7:30am to dusk. A restaurant serves breakfast and lunch daily.

SHOPPING Don't miss **Butterflies Gallery,** Broke Road, Pokolbin (☎ 049/98 7724), where Robert Kay and Jane Brabon display the paintings and crafts of some of Australia's most talented artists. Much of the artwork, pottery, glass, wood, and hand-painted silk is made by New South Wales craftspeople. Look for Alan Williams's wood work, Pat Cahill's pottery, and John Trier's cattle-horn objects and pewter ware. All work is by Australians. Robert and Jane will ship your purchases if necessary. The gallery, set in a pretty country garden, is open daily from 10am to 5pm. Butterflies Tea Room is adjacent (see "Where to Dine" below).

Peppers Creek Antiques, at the corner of Broke and Ekerts roads, Pokolbin, near Peppers Guest House (☎ 049/98 7532), sells antique jewelry, Georgian and Victorian furniture, and old-world bric-a-brac on Wednesday to Sunday from 10am to 5pm. Cafe Enzo (see "Where to Dine" below) shares the premises.

Where to Stay

Value-conscious travelers should plan to be in the Hunter Valley during the week, when the rates for lodging are *significantly lower* than they are on weekends.

$ **Carriages Guest House.** Halls Road, Pokolbin, NSW 2321. ☎ **049/987 591.** Fax 049/987 839. 8 rms. A/C TV TEL. A$110–A$170 (U.S. $88–$136) double per night (minimum two-night stay on weekends). Ask about lower midweek and standby rates. AE, BC, DC, MC, V.

The ideal spot for a honeymoon retreat, Carriages offers charming rooms in a two-story wooden building with a distinctive double-gable roof. Since the house is located on the edge of a patch of bushland, the feel here is distinctly secluded. Downstairs rooms have ceiling fans and hardwood floors and open onto a big wooden veranda. Upstairs, the two gable suites have skylights, stained-glass windows, lofty open-beam ceilings, a sitting area in front of a brick fireplace, bathtubs, and balconies overlooking the pretty garden and bush beyond. The country decor in all quarters includes doonas and fresh flowers. The Carriages doesn't have a restaurant, but breakfast can be delivered to the room. Guests enjoy the tennis court and pool and, perhaps most of all, the quiet.

The Convent. In the Pepper Tree complex, Halls Road, Pokolbin, NSW 2320. ☎ **049/987 764.** Fax 049/987 323. 17 rms. A/C MINIBAR TEL. Midweek, A$245–A$270 (U.S. $196–$216) double; weekend, A$645–A$695 (U.S. $516–$556) two-night package with one dinner. All rates include country breakfast buffet and predinner wine and canapés. Children under 12 free with an adult. AE, BC, DC, MC, V.

My stay at the Convent provided me with a new benchmark for a great breakfast buffet. I can still taste the out-of-this-world rice pudding, the equally delicious bread-and-butter pudding, and the fresh mushrooms served on wholemeal toast. And I remember how light and bright the breakfast room is and the obvious attention paid to detail throughout the building and grounds. It's almost hard to believe that the structure started life in 1909 as a real convent for the Brigidine nuns, was dismantled and carted 600km (372 miles), and was reconstructed to its original condition here in 1991. I guess it isn't surprising that cherub prints and figurines are found throughout—including in the elegant sitting area where predinner wine is served. The guest rooms are gorgeous: Each has a high ceiling with a delicate plaster frieze, wicker furniture, padded headboards, and miles of drapery fabric covering large windows and French doors. Unfortunately, the rooms are *not* soundproof. Recreational facilities include a tennis court, a pool, an enclosed spa, and complimentary use of bikes. Breakfast is the only meal served here; the restaurant, Robert's, is nearby. This special place has won numerous awards.

Hunter Resort. Hermitage Road, Pokolbin, Hunter Valley, NSW 2320. ☎ **049/98 7777.** Fax 049/98 7787. 30 rms, 4 spa suites, 1 cottage. A/C TV TEL. A$130 (U.S. $104) double. Additional person A$15 (U.S. $12) extra. Ask about lower midweek rates and lower rates through Aussie auto clubs. AE, BC, DC, MC, V.

All units here have a view of vineyards in the foreground and the Brokenback Mountain Range in the distance. The place has a natural-log look on the outside, but features modern amenities inside. These include clock radios, coffee- and tea-making setup, small refrigerators, and queen-size beds. Additional facilities are a self-service laundry, an outdoor pool, a spa, a children's playground, tennis courts, and a barbecue area with benches and a covered pergola. The friendly management can arrange baby-sitting and will deliver breakfast to the rooms. The Hermitage Restaurant is adjacent.

Pokolbin Village Resort. 188 Broke Rd., Pokolbin, NSW 2320. ☎ **049/98 7670.** Fax 049/98 7670. 17 two-bedroom units. A/C MINIBAR TV TEL. A$190 (U.S. $152) double; A$280–A$320 (U.S. $224–$256) for four. Ask about lower midweek rates and lower rates through Aussie auto clubs. BC, MC, V.

This motel is part of a village-style commercial area that includes a general store, a deli, a café, and two licensed restaurants. All units have two bedrooms and a bath with a shower, except one has a tub and one a spa bath. I really like the skylights in the bathroom. Three units have full kitchens, and all quarters have tea- and coffee-making facilities, small refrigerators, toasters, microwaves, and balconies. On the premises are a saltwater pool, a playground, a volleyball court, a tennis court, and a picnic area.

Thalgara Estate. Debeyers Road, Pokolbin, NSW 2320. ☎ **049/98 7717.** 3 studios, 3 one-bedroom units. A/C TV TEL. A$120 (U.S. $96) studio for two; A$180 (U.S. $144) one-bedroom for two to four. Ask about much lower midweek rates and lower rates for stays of more than two nights. BC, MC, V.

Steve and Sue Lamb have built six units near their home in a countryside setting surrounded by many acres of vineyards. The studios and one-bedroom units can sleep from two to four; each has a bath, a fully equipped kitchen, open-beam ceilings, contemporary furnishings, and a patio with table and chairs. The hosts can arrange baby-sitting and enjoy showing guests around their winery, but they don't provide breakfast. This is a great spot if you're prepared to prepare your own morning meal.

$ **Vineyard Hill Country Motel.** Lovedale Road, Pokolbin, NSW 2321. ☎ **049/904 166.** Fax 049/914 431. 8 units. A/C MINIBAR TV TEL. A$118 (U.S. $94.40) one-bedroom unit; A$198 (U.S. $158.40) two-bedroom unit. Additional person A$15 (U.S. $12) extra. Ask about lower midweek rates. AE, BC, MC, V.

This is a good spot for those wanting self-contained accommodations. Each of Alan and Pattie Wattman's neat and tidy units has cooking facilities as well as balconies overlooking a pretty view. The spacious A-frames also offer oversize showers, ceiling fans, and covered parking. The two-bedroom units have an especially large lounge/kitchen area. A pool is on the premises, and the hosts sell premade casseroles, pies, cheese-and-pâté plates, desserts, and so forth, so you can eat in without going out for groceries. They also supply breakfast. Vineyard Hill is about 5km (3 miles) outside the main winery district.

A Cattle Station in the Upper Hunter

$ **Runnymede.** Runnymede, Cassilis, NSW 2329. ☎ **063/761 183.** Fax 063/761 187. (These numbers will change to 02/6376 1183 and fax 02/6376 1187 in January 1998.) 2 rooms (1 with bath). A$80 (U.S. $64) double. A$20 (U.S. $16) per person dinner (BYO). Rates include breakfast. No credit cards. Located on Hwy. 84, an hour from Mudgee; 2 1/2 hours from Cessnock; 4 hours from Sydney.

If you want to understand the agricultural side of Australia, you couldn't find a better place than Runnnymede, a 2,000-acre sheep-and-cattle station where Libby and David Morrow are the wonderful hosts. David's grandfather designed the brick California bungalow built in 1930. The homestead provides beautiful views over farmland to the Liverpool Range, an open fire in the living room, and homey farmstyle lodgings. Native birds thrive in the garden, where the lighted tennis court and pool are located. One room with an antique double bed has an en suite bath; occupants of the twin room share the hosts' bath down the hall or the en suite. If you're here in May, you might get to see shearing; August is best for lambing and calving. The Morrows offer full- and half-day tours in their area (for an extra charge) and enjoy classical music, theater, and traveling. Ask David to tell you about whitewater rafting on the Zambezi River.

Where to Dine

The top three places to eat in the Hunter are **Chez Pok** in Peppers Guesthouse; **Robert's,** which like The Convent is part of the Pepper Tree complex; and **Casuarina** (below). Because these spots are expensive, I've included information on a few casual places.

✪ **Blaxland's Restaurant.** Broke Road, Pokolbin. ☎ **049/98 7550.** Reservations recommended. Main courses A$19–A$22 (U.S. $15.20–$17.60). Weekend and public holiday surcharge A$2 (U.S. $1.60) per person. AE, BC, DC, MC, V. Daily noon–7pm. INTERNATIONAL.

The restaurant was constructed from the remains of the Blaxland homestead built in the nearby town of Broke in 1827. Proprietor Chris Barnes had the idea of recycling the convict-made sandstone blocks and bricks when the colonial house was razed. Despite the unusual architecture and historic atmosphere, Blaxland's most outstanding feature is its extensive wine list. Chris bottles his own wine, manages to keep more than 100 wines available, and has a license to sell wine by the bottle or case. On a recent visit, I very much enjoyed the Blaxland's chardonnay.

On a typical evening the menu may list such main courses as barbecued loin of lamb, seafood tempura, and roast duckling. Typical desserts are raspberry crumble (terrific), marinated figs, pavlova, strawberry millefeuille, and a selection of fine Australian cheeses and Hunter pecans. I suggest you make a point of meeting the hosts, who are very knowledgeable about the area and its wines.

Butterflies Gallery and Garden Cafe. Broke Road, Pokolbin. ☎ **049/98 7724.** Reservations recommended at lunch. Devonshire tea A$6 (U.S. $4.80); light lunch about A$9 (U.S. $7.20). BC, DC, MC, V. Daily 10am–5pm. HOMESTYLE AUSTRALIAN.

Everything Jane Brabon and Robert Kaye serve is made in their kitchen. My mother's meatloaf is wonderful, but it doesn't compare with Butterflies', served with damper bread and salad. Their version of a ploughman's lunch contains cheese, salami, and roast beef. This is also a great place for tea: The sideboard holds tins of Twinings and cakestands bearing mouth-watering delights. Part of the pleasure of this pretty place, with its light-blue walls, open fire, and view of the countryside, is meeting the congenial hosts. BYO.

Casuarina Restaurant. Hermitage Road, Pokolbin. ☎ **049/98 7888.** Reservations recommended. Main courses A$22–A$25 (U.S. $17.60–$20). Children's meals 50% discount. Public holiday and weekend surcharge A$3 (U.S. $2.40) per person. AE, DC, MC, V. Sat–Sun from noon; daily from 7pm. INTERNATIONAL WITH ASIAN OVERTONES.

Casuarina is a very special dining venue, housed in a building owner/chef Peter Meier bought and enlarged in 1982. He named it after a native Australian tree because "when the wind blows through casuarinas, it makes a beautiful sound." A cozy bar with sofas and easy chairs is adjacent to the dining room, where a dozen huge white paper lanterns hang from the cathedral ceilings. The sandstone-block walls have been painted rose and large flower arrangements rest on antique mahogany sideboards.

Peter believes that "the greatness of food lies in its simplicity," so he prepares fare that's light and healthful. This surprises many people who know Peter is German and learned his trade in hotels in Salzburg and Paris. "I also believe in custom-made food and food that's cooked very quickly," he says, so many dishes are flambéed at the table. Typical entrees are stir-fried prawns, pan-fried duck livers, and sugar-cured Atlantic salmon. Three popular main courses are roast veal filet, rolled chicken breast, and rack of lamb. Flambés include chili lobster and prawns and seafood Thai style. Because Casuarina is popular with local vintners, the wine list often includes vintages unobtainable at other dining spots.

Adjacent to the restaurant, the Casuarina Country Inn, with eight themed minisuites and three cottages, is owned/supervised by Peter Meier. Guests have the use of a pool, a tennis court, a sauna, and a really pretty lounge with an open fire.

Cafe Enzo. At the corner of Broke and Ekerts roads, Pokolbin, adjacent to Peppers Creek Antiques, near Peppers Guest House. ☎ **049/987 599.** Lunch A$8–A$12 (U.S. $6.40–$9.60); afternoon tea about A$5 (U.S.$4). BC, MC, V. Wed–Sun 10am–5pm. TUSCAN.

Owner Peter Island likes Ferraris and named this cute little café after the famous carmaker. Both the menu and the ambience feel Tuscan. Diners are seated at 6 tables inside and 12 out. Offered are a handful of simple dishes like pizzetta of the day, seafood salad, and grilled focaccia of the day. This is a great place for lunch or afternoon tea. BYO.

✪ **The Rothbury Cafe.** Upstairs at The Rothbury Estate, Broke Road, Pokolbin. ☎ **049/987 363.** Main courses A$9.50–A$14.50 (U.S. $7.60–$11.60). Weekend surcharge 10%. Corkage charge A$3 (U.S. $2.40). AE, BC, DC, MC, V. Daily noon–3pm. MODERN AUSTRALIAN.

The view of the vineyards and countryside from here is terrific, but I bet it's the food you'll remember. I recently enjoyed a divine salad of chicken and wild rice with a Thai peanut sauce. Chef Brian Means's menu changes frequently, so it's hard to say what your choices will be. However, look for spinach-and-ricotta terrine, penne pasta with double cheese and grilled red-wine-and-garlic salami, and a selection of avant-garde pizzas. Desserts include sticky banana pudding with hot buttered rum sauce and rich chocolate-chestnut torte with berries. This place is a good choice on a really hot day: The 12 tables are inside, and the premises are air-conditioned. BYO or buy a bottle of their Rothbury wine.

Sangas on the Hill. In the McGuigan Hunter Wine Village, Broke Road, Pokolbin. ☎ **049/98 7518.** Reservations not required. Meals about A$5–A$7 (U.S. $4–$5.60) per person. No credit cards. Mon–Fri 10am–"4ish"pm, Sat–Sun 10am–5pm. LIGHT LUNCHES.

Sangas on the Hill sells unusual sandwiches like smoked salmon, caper, onion, sprouts, and lettuce. More traditional fare such as pumpkin soup with hot crusty damper bread is also available. You might like to try Australian ANZAC biscuits or homemade carrot and banana cake. Seating is outside at picnic tables. BYO.

If you can't find what you want at Sangas, try the adjacent **Vineyard Kitchen,** which offers indoor seating and hot meals.

6 The Coast North of Sydney

The **Pacific Highway** leads over Sydney's Harbour Bridge, through the white-collar northern suburbs, and to the bushland at the metropolitan region's edge where it merges for a while with the Sydney-Newcastle Freeway. Farther on it passes the Hawkesbury River and the resort district around Gosford. The highway skirts the recreation areas of Tuggerah Lake and Lake Macquarie and the city of Newcastle, and then it hugs the coast, while the other major north-south road, the **New England Highway,** heads inland. Many people elect to follow the Pacific Highway all the way to Brisbane, a distance of 1,000km (620 miles), which is best covered in at least two days and could easily occupy a week at a leisurely pace.

The popularity of this route can be attributed both to the varied scenery and to the good lodging and dining facilities found along the way. The beach vistas are excellent, and when the highway leaves the coast at places like Taree and Kempsey, you encounter heavily timbered terrain, as well as inland lakes, rivers, and green mountain slopes. Most of the ocean viewpoints require a detour of at least a few kilometers, which can add to the time the journey takes. Even if time is limited, don't miss the views from **Crescent Head, Nambucca Head, Yamba,** and—best of all—**Byron Bay,** where a picturesque lighthouse marks the most easterly point in Australia.

The biggest coastal resort centers are Coffs Harbour and Byron Bay. Murwillumbah, near the Queensland border, is the gateway to the beautiful Tweed Valley and Mount Warning National Park. In between these places are great surf, several outstanding fishing spots, award-winning resorts, a down-under dude ranch, and a banana 10 meters (33 ft.) long. How's that for a trip?

PORT MACQUARIE

423km (262 miles) N of Sydney

Roughly midway between Sydney and the border with neighboring Queensland, "Port," as the locals call it (pop. 28,000), is at the mouth of the Hastings River, an ideal spot for boating. There are also wonderful ocean beaches, including Flynn's, which is exceptionally good for surfing. Horton Street is the main shopping area.

ESSENTIALS

GETTING THERE Motorists follow the Pacific Highway and Sydney-Newcastle Freeway north from Sydney. Eastern Australia Airlines flies between Sydney and Port Macquarie. The one-way fare ranges from A$108 to A$174 (U.S. $86.40 to $139.20). The airport is close to town and a taxi costs about A$5 (U.S. $4).

The coach fare from Sydney is A$49 (U.S. $39.20), and the trip takes about seven hours. The trip from Brisbane takes almost 11 hours and costs A$51 (U.S. $40.80).

VISITOR INFORMATION The **Visitor Information Centre,** at the corner of Clarence and Hay streets, under the Civic Centre (☎ 065/83 1293, or 1800/02 5935 in Australia), is open Monday to Friday from 8:30am to 5pm and Saturday and Sunday from 9 to 4pm. The **telephone area code** is 065. As part of the telephone changeover, all numbers with a 065 area code will be changing to 02/65xx xxxx in January 1998.

EXPLORING THE AREA

Timbertown, 23km (14 miles) west of Port Macquarie on the Oxley Highway (☎ 065/85 2322), is a re-creation of a turn-of-the-century timber-cutting and logging settlement, and you walk through and watch timber workers splitting logs, blacksmiths at work, and a steam train that still runs. Timbertown is open Sunday to Friday from 9am to 5pm. The entrance fee is A$13 (U.S. $10.40) for adults, half price for children, and A$35 (U.S. $28) for a family.

River cruises are another popular Port Macquarie activity. The 257-passenger vessel *Port Venture* (☎ 065/83 3058) departs from the foot of Clarence Street daily at 10am and 2pm. Tickets for the two-hour cruise on the scenic Hastings River are A$15 (U.S. $12) for adults, A$5.50 (U.S. $4.40) for children, and A$35 (U.S. $28) for a family. Reservations are essential.

WHERE TO STAY

El Paso Motor Inn. 29 Clarence St., Port Macquarie, NSW 2444. ☎ **065/83 1944,** or 1800/02 7965 in Australia. Fax 065/84 1021. 55 rms, 2 suites. A/C MINIBAR TV TEL. A$75–A$87 (U.S. $60–$69.60) double; A$104–A$124 (U.S. $83.20–$99.20) suite. Additional person A$10 (U.S. $8) extra. A$15 (U.S. $12) surcharge Easter, Christmas, and some long weekends. BC, DC, MC, V.

Readers Recommend

Billabong Koala and Aussie Wildlife Park, 61 Billabong Drive, Port Macquarie (☎ 065/85 1060). *"This is a family-owned park where koalas have been hand-raised. Three times a day Bob takes out two of the koalas and allows visitors to pat and photo them. There are also kangaroos and many types of birds, as well as wombats, emus, and peacocks. I like Billabong more than other zoos I've visited because I was able to have contact with the animals, not just look at them from a distance. The admission is A$6 (U.S. $4.80) for adults and A$4 (U.S. $3.20) for children."*

—Laura B. Roemmele, Temecula, Calif., U.S.A.

El Paso is on the waterfront in the heart of town. Many of the rooms in the three-story building have kitchenettes, and they all have the standard Aussie motel amenities. There are also a heated pool, a sauna, a spa, a recreation room, a licensed restaurant, and a cocktail bar. Facilities for the handicapped are offered.

Sails Resort. Park Street, Port Macquarie, NSW 2444. ☎ **065/83 3999,** or 1800/02 5271 in Australia. Fax 065/84 0397. 83 rms. A/C MINIBAR TV TEL. A$150–A$180 (U.S. $120–$144) double; A$200–A$240 (U.S. $160–$192) family room; A$300–A$450 (U.S. $240–$360) executive room. Additional person A$20 (U.S. $16) extra. Children under 14 free in parents' room using existing bedding. BC, DC, MC, V.

Sails Resort offers the most luxurious accommodations in town. As its name implies, the resort is located on the waterfront, and sea birds, as well as boats of all sizes and shapes, pass back and forth in front of the two-story property. Each room has a queen-size bed or two twins, coffee- and tea-making facilities, a small refrigerator, a toaster, and various other amenities. The family rooms have kitchenettes and queen-size beds, with twin beds in screened-off areas; the executive rooms offer king-size beds, expansive water views, kitchenettes, and spa baths. All have private balconies, ceiling fans, free in-house movies, and tub/shower combinations. Two rooms have been specially equipped for the disabled.

Dining/Entertainment: Spinnakers Restaurant and bar overlook the water.

Services: 24-hour room service, laundry, nightly turndown, baby-sitting, massage.

Facilities: Indoor and outdoor spas, heated seawater pool, children's pool, steamroom, tennis courts, volleyball court, children's playroom and playground, bicycle rental, mini-golf, complimentary kids club during holiday periods; boats and canoes can be rented next door at the marina.

A Nearby Place to Stay

$ **Mount Seaview Resort.** Near Yarras, NSW 2446. ☎ **065/87 7144.** Fax 065/87 7195. 26 motel rms, 24 lodge rms. A/C TEL. A$42 (U.S. $33.60) double in lodge; A$66 (U.S. $52.80) double motel unit; A$90 (U.S. $72) suite. Additional person A$10 (U.S. $8) extra. Three-day/two-night package (including accommodations, meals, four-wheel-drive safari, and transfer from Port Macquarie) A$145 (U.S. $116) per person double. Children under 12 half price. AE, BC, MC, V. You can be picked up at the train station in Wauchope or at the Port Macquarie coach depot or airport.

Mount Seaview is 80km (50 miles) west of Port on the Oxley Highway (and 55km/34 miles west of Wauchope, which the locals inexplicably pronounce "war hope"). Here you can ride horses, swim in the Hastings River, hike, ride mountain bikes, or take four-wheel-drive safaris. The resort is on a beautiful 1,200-hectare (2,964-acre) cattle-breeding ranch with majestic hills, pockets of rain forest, a crystal-clear river, and "fair dinkum" Aussie bush. Strangler figs, staghorn ferns, wild orchids, and flame trees give the rain forest a wondrous storybook appearance. Native animals thrive throughout the area.

The accommodations here are comfortable motel-type rooms, a bunkhouse, a rustic lodge, and a camping/caravan area. Hearty home-cooked meals are available in the lodge (licensed or BYO), or you can prepare your own food in the communal kitchen. Host Ralph Clissold and his staff join guests around the big log fire at night and create a welcoming, friendly atmosphere.

The facilities include a pool table, table tennis, a putting green and driving range, a tennis court, indoor bowling, and a playground. Horseback riding is an additional A$15 (U.S. $12) an hour and full-day safaris cost about A$35 (U.S. $28). The cost of four-wheel-drive trips varies from A$12 to A$50 (U.S. $9.60 to $40) per person.

After Dark

Visitors are welcome at the **Port Macquarie RSL Club,** Park Street (☎ 065/83 1999), the focal point of nightlife. In addition to one fancy restaurant and four casual eateries, it has five bars, floor shows, and a disco. Dining and drinking in RSLs are generally very good values because costs are subsidized by poker (slot)-machine revenues. This particular club also has an indoor pool, a gym, and aerobics classes.

LORD HOWE ISLAND

702km (435 miles) NE of Sydney, due E of Port Macquarie

Little known even to Australians, this tiny island is 11km (less than 7 miles) long and no more than 2km (about 1¼ miles) wide. Lord Howe has the southernmost coral reef in the world and boasts some of the rarest flora, birds, and marine life anywhere. The Howea palm (also known as Kentia palm), indigenous to the island, provides the only income, apart from tourism. Seeds from these palms have been collected and sold throughout the world for more than 100 years. Lord Howe is one of only a few islands on the World Heritage List.

Lord Howe is a good destination for those wishing to truly get away from it all and experience a casual island where you'll find yourself on a first-name basis with other visitors and with the locals after a short time. There are refreshingly few cars and not very many phones. And where else in the world is it still safe to leave the key in your car or front door? Anyone interested in this destination should read the feature on Lord Howe Island in the October 1991 *National Geographic*.

Essentials

GETTING THERE Year-round access to Lord Howe is via Eastern Australia Airlines from Sydney. September to May, you can take Sunstate Airline from Brisbane.

For the adventurous, the freighter *Island Trader* takes up to six passengers. It departs from Yamba on the North Coast of New South Wales every fortnight (two weeks).

VISITOR INFORMATION The **New South Wales Travel Centre,** 19 Castlereagh St., Sydney, NSW 2000 (☎ 02/231-4444), is the best source. The **telephone area code** is 065. As part of the telephone changeover, all numbers with a 065 area code will be changing to 02/65xx xxxx in January 1998.

Enjoying the Island

Lord Howe's subtropical climate, varying from 16°C (61°F) in winter to 26°C (79°F) in summer, and its unspoiled water and land make it a virtual playground. You can swim, surf, snorkel, scuba dive, play tennis, golf, fish, hike, and bird watch. And you can even hand-feed the fish at Ned's Beach. The most common form of transport on the island is bicycle. Glass-bottom boats make it possible for nonswimmers to view the sea life and two-hour cruises circle the island, providing a good look at its mountains, rising straight from the ocean. Golf sticks (clubs), tennis rackets, bicycles, masks and flippers for snorkeling, and all scuba gear can be rented.

WHERE TO STAY & DINE

Island lodging is mainly at guesthouses like the one below, but self-contained apartments are also available. Lord Howe doesn't have a pub, but bars are in the various accommodations houses and in several restaurants. Hosts provide transport to and from the airport.

Pinetrees Lodge. Lord Howe Island, NSW 2898. ☎ **065/63 2177,** or 1800/22 6142 in Australia. Fax 065/63 2156. Sydney booking office: 72 Erskine St. (☎ 02/262 6585). 27 rms, 7 cottages. From A$160 (U.S. $128) per person double; from A$340 (U.S. $272) per person garden cottage. Higher rates in summer (Dec–Jan). Ask about four-night package holidays. Rates include all meals. No credit cards.

Opened in 1900, Pinetrees is the island's largest and oldest guesthouse resort. It's run by descendants of the first hosts, and the family homestead, built in 1884, still stands as part of the lounge/bar/dining room complex. Accommodation is in motel-style units, one-bedroom garden cottages, a four-bedroom/three-bath cottage, and a 2½-bedroom cottage. You'll also find a Supergrasse tennis court, a small library, and a billiard table. The lagoon beach is just across the road. Guests ride bicycles to the golf course and surf beach.

COFFS HARBOUR

150km (93 miles) N of Port Macquarie, 572km (355 miles) N of Sydney, 427km (265 miles) S of Brisbane.

As you drive north in Australia, the pace at which people move slows down and their lifestyle relaxes. Melburnians have little in common with residents of far-north Queensland, and were you to travel between those two by road, you'd see a gradual loosening of dress standards and general reduction of formalities.

My husband and I drove up the coast from Sydney to Cairns while doing the research for this book, and I remember thinking when we got to Coffs Harbour (pop. 55,700) that it was our first contact with an area that felt tropical. It certainly isn't steamy and lush like Cairns or Port Douglas, but banana plantations are a common sight, the beaches stretch for miles, the weather is warmer, and it's the first place I remember seeing houses built up on poles the way they are in Queensland.

High Street is the main drag in Coffs Harbour. Most stores are east of Pacific Highway, the main north-south street.

ESSENTIALS

GETTING THERE Travel time by car up the Pacific Highway from Sydney is at least seven hours without stops; the trip from Brisbane takes five hours. Qantas, Eastern Australia Airlines, and Ansett Airlines fly nonstop to Coffs Harbour from Sydney.

A Countrylink train from Sydney costs A$67 (U.S. $53.60). Several coach companies, including Greyhound-Pioneer and McCafferty, make the trip from Sydney in about nine hours. A ticket costs about A$56 (U.S. $44.80). A bus from Brisbane takes about seven hours and costs A$42 (U.S. $33.60).

VISITOR INFORMATION The **Visitors and Convention Bureau** (☎ 066/52 1522) is just off Pacific Highway at the corner of Rose Avenue and Marcia Street, two blocks north of the city center. It's open daily from 9am to 5pm. The **telephone area code** is 066. As part of the telephone changeover, all numbers with a 066 area code will be changing to 02/66xx xxxx in March 1998.

EXPLORING THE AREA

The sight you won't be able to miss is the 10-meter (33-ft.) banana I mentioned earlier. You'll find it alongside the highway at the **Big Banana** theme park (☎ 066/52 4355), 3km (2 miles) north of town. This pièce de résistance is made of reinforced Ferro concrete.

At the Big Banana you can take a ride in an air-conditioned plantation train around the 45-acre banana plantation on which a variety of exhibits have been built. The theme park is open daily from 9am to 4pm. Admission is free; the train tour costs A$9.50 (U.S. $7.60) for adults, A$5.50 (U.S. $4.40) for children, and A$22 (U.S. $17.60) for a family of up to two adults and two children. A coffee shop and restaurant serve banana bread, banana cake, banana splits, banana shakes—you get the idea. The local favorite seems to be chocolate-covered bananas from the Snowy Mountains Ice Creamery. Other shops sell souveniers, crafts, clothing, and handmade candy. This is high-tack Australia at its finest.

In contrast, **Green Pastures Studio,** Sharp Close (☎ 066/561 005), 12km (7.3 miles) north of the Big Banana, was one of the favorite finds of my last trip to Oz. Here you can buy **Australian Wildflower Jewelry**—gold- or silver-plated necklaces, bracelets, earrings, and more—all designed by Wolfgang Schulze, who finds inspiration in the nation's native plants. These aren't plated plant parts, but metal shaped to look like eucalyptus leaves, orchid flowers, wattle buds, and more. The artist works with lead-free pewter and an old-fashioned dentist's drill. The prices are extremely reasonable. The studio is open Monday to Saturday 9am to 5pm. To get here, head north on the Pacific Highway; turn left into Sharp Close and watch for the sign.

You might also be interested in **George's Gold Mine,** 38km (23 miles) inland from Pacific Highway on Bushman's Range Road (☎ 066/54 5355). It's open Wednesday to Sunday from 10am to 4pm; admission is A$8.50 (U.S. $6.80) for adults and A$4 (U.S. $3.20) for children. At the **Clog Barn** (also known as Holland Downunder), 1.6km (1.3 miles) north of the Coffs post office on the highway (☎ 066/52 4633), you can watch traditional Dutch wooden shoes being made daily at 11am and 4pm. The attraction is open from 8am to 5pm; admission to the model village display is A$3 (U.S. $2.40) for adults and A$2 (U.S. $1.60) for children.

If you don't have your own car, **Coffs Harbour Coach and Travel,** 42 Moonee St. (☎ 066/52 2686), operates full- and half-day tours of the surrounding area.

If you drive north of Coffs during the last week in October or the first week in November, allow time for enjoying the **Jacaranda Festival** in Grafton (☎ 066/42 3959). Past Grafton at Yamba, the **Surf Carnival** takes place in January and the **Family Fishing Festival** in July.

Wildwater Adventures, 26 Butlers Rd., Bonville, via Coffs Harbour, NSW 2441 (☎ 066/53 4469), will take you white-water rafting on the Nymboida River or the Gwydir River for a charge beginning at A$109 (U.S. $87.20) per person. These adventurous one-day expeditions operate most days, year round, depending on water levels. Extended two-, three-, and four-day tours begin at A$265 (U.S. $212) per person. These prices include all meals; participants camp out by the river on overnight trips. Rafting is especially exciting from November to June, the "wet season." The minimum age for participants is 12. Bonville is 14km (9 miles) south of Coffs Harbour (halfway between Sydney and Brisbane), and the operators provide transfers.

Where to Stay

$ Nautilus on-the-Beach. Pacific Highway, Coffs Harbour, NSW 2450. ☎ **066/53 6699,** or 1800/02 9966 in Australia. Fax 066/53 7039. Reservations can be made through Flag Inns. 18 rms, 50 apartments. MINIBAR TV TEL. A$110 (U.S. $88) double; A$130 (U.S. $104) deluxe double; A$150 (U.S. $120) one-bedroom apt for up to four; A$195 (U.S. $156) two-bedroom apt for up to seven; A$215 (U.S. $172) three-bedroom apt for up to eight. Children under 12 free in parents' room. Rates 25% higher during NSW school holidays. AE, BC, DC, MC, V.

Nautilus on-the-Beach enjoys a "beaut pozzie" on a long stretch of white sand 7km (4.2 miles) north of Coffs Harbour. Nautilus's beach is a continuation of the one belonging to its next-door neighbor, Pelican Beach. In spite of the resorts' proximity to each other, their personalities are quite different. At Nautilus the emphasis is on do-it-yourself living and family activities. Only the standard rooms lack a full kitchen. The deluxe rooms and the one-, two-, and three-bedroom apartments all have completely equipped kitchens and laundry facilities. All units are modern, spacious, and bright with high-quality furnishing; all baths have tub/shower combinations. Queen- and king-size beds are available. Covered parking is adjacent to each low-rise duplex. The apartments are set on 9 acres of landscaped grounds.

During school holidays, the rates are significantly higher, the minimum stay is one week, and the resort is fully booked a year in advance.

Dining/Entertainment: The Deck Chairs Bar and Grill (à la carte dining) is open daily.

Services: Massage, baby-sitting, complimentary newspaper.

Facilities: Three heated pools, sauna, spa, small gym, two full-size "mod grass" tennis courts, barbecue area, children's games room and playground.

Pelican Beach Travelodge Resort. Pacific Highway, Coffs Harbour, NSW 2450. ☎ **066/53 7000,** or 1800/02 8882 in Australia. Fax 066/53 7066. 112 rms. A/C MINIBAR TV TEL. A$120–A$140 (U.S. $96–$112) standard for one or two; A$175–A$265 (U.S. $140–$212) family room for up to four; A$260–A$420 (U.S. $208–$336) suite for one or two. Additional person A$20 (U.S. $16) extra. The higher rates are for holiday periods. AE, BC, DC, MC, V.

Located 7km (4.2 miles) north of Coffs Harbour, Pelican Beach has an ideal location. The 7½ acres of landscaped grounds around the resort are adjacent to a lovely stretch of white-sand beach. The outdoors is brought into interior halls with the effective use of large container gardens, streams diverted from the pool, and natural light streaming through the glass ceiling of a multistory atrium. The accommodations are arranged on six levels that have been terraced into a hillside so many rooms have a view over the lagoonlike pool to the beach. Each room has a balcony and spacious modern decor, with a tub/shower combination. Family rooms have kitchenettes, and two rooms are equipped for the handicapped.

Dining/Entertainment: Your dining options here include The Shores, overlooking the pool area and offering an extensive à la carte menu and wine list (about A$85/U.S. $68 for a three-course dinner for two, plus wine). Lunch is served at the Beach Grill by the pool.

Services: 24-hour room service, laundry/dry cleaning, baby-sitting, courtesy airport transfers.

Facilities: A 48-meter (50-yd.) free-form heated seawater pool, glass-enclosed spa, children's pool, nine holes of mini-golf, three full-size floodlit tennis courts, volleyball court, cricket pitch; gym, sauna, spa, children's games room.

Sanctuary Resort. Pacific Highway, Coffs Harbour, NSW 2450. ☎ **066/52 2111.** 37 rms. TV TEL. A$85 (U.S. $68) double. Additional person A$10 (U.S. $8) extra. Holiday surcharges. Ask about lower rates through Aussie auto clubs. AE, BC, MC, V.

The Sanctuary is a 37-unit low-rise motel about 2km ($1^1/_4$ miles) south of town, in an animal sanctuary where kangaroos, peacocks, and native birds roam. The resort has all the "mod cons" (modern conveniences), including a pool, a spa, a sauna, a rec room, a playground, tennis and squash courts, and a gym. The Treehouse Restaurant is a lofty retreat overlooking the gardens and sanctuary.

Nearby in Nambucca Heads

Smaller than Coffs Harbour and much less touristy, Nambucca (pronounced nam-*buck*-a) Heads—44km/27 miles south—presents another coastal option. Here you'll find the 18-hole **Nambucca Heads Golf Club** in an unusual island location (☎ 065/686 073 or 688 172). The **Visitor Information Centre**, next to the post office on Ridge Street (☎ 065/686 954), is very helpful.

$ Scotts Guesthouse. 4 Wellington Dr., Nambucca Heads, NSW 2448. ☎ **065/68 6386.** Fax 065/69 4169. 7 rms. TV. A$60–A$80 (U.S. $48–$64) double. Rates include continental breakfast. BC, MC, V.

I have reader E. Hope Stewart of Nanaimo, B.C., Canada, to thank for introducing me to this good-value guesthouse and its charming pair of proprietors. "The Irish couple who own and run it are delightful and made us feel at home immediately," she wrote. And right she was. Joan and Robert Scott have modernized a house from 1887. Be sure to peek in their kitchen and look at their antique wood-burning stove. The rooms are quite spacious, modern, and comfortable. Each offers a shower, a TV, a refrigerator, a balcony, a ceiling fan, coffee- and tea-making facilities, and an electric blanket in winter. I think Room 1 has the best view, and Room 2 the prettiest furnishings. Breakfast is served downstairs, where pretty china sits atop an antique sideboard.

Where to Dine

The jetty end of High Street is Coffs Harbour's restaurant row, with a dozen or so little ethnic restaurants in one block. Since they post their menus in the window, you can easily peruse the scene and make your decision on the spot. You might also like to grab a snack at the **Fishermens Co-op,** at the Boat Harbour, which offers take-away meals Monday to Thursday from 10:30am to 7pm and Friday to Sunday 10:30am to 7:30pm. This is a scenic area with plenty of good spots to enjoy your meal. If you're staying in a place with cooking facilities, the Fishermans Co-op has a seafood market open daily from 8:30am to 5:30pm. In the same area, the **Tide & Pilot Brasserie** (☎ 066/51 6046) is a licensed seafood restaurant with a great view from the upstairs deck. Another fast-food option is the 530-seat **McDonald's** on the Pacific Highway at North Boambee Road (☎ 066/52 7200).

In addition to these places and the dining spots above in "Where to Stay," I want you to know about a special place:

✪ Seafood Mama's. Pacific Highway. ☎ **066/53 6733.** Reservations recommended. Main courses A$11.50–A$25 (U.S. $9.20–$20). AE, BC, DC, MC, V. Wed–Fri noon–2pm; daily 6–10pm. ITALIAN/SEAFOOD.

This restaurant overlooking the Pacific Ocean near the Pelican Beach and Nautilus resorts, 7km (4.2 miles) north of Coffs Harbour, was named by the jazz-fan proprietors and Fats Waller's song "Hold Tight." The present mama-in-residence is Diane Strachan, who looks nothing like the plump fishwife on the menu. As you might guess from the restaurant's name, the specialty here is local—and so very fresh—seafood done in a tasty southern Italian style, as well as pasta and veal dishes. Favorite items include scaloppine del mare, spaghetti chili octopus, and fettuccine marinara. The atmosphere is cheerful, friendly, and informal, and the food is great, so it's not surprising that Seafood Mama's has recently won several awards. The restaurant also delivers and does take-out.

After Dark

Coffs Harbour Ex-Services Club. At Pacific Highway and Vernon Street. ☎ **066/52 3888.** No cover, but neat dress is required.

This is one of the popular local nightlife spots. Live bands often perform in Crystal's Disco and other bars and lounges. This place also has poker (slot) machines, if you're feeling lucky, as well as six bars, a bistro, and an à la carte dining room.

BYRON BAY

78 km (48 miles) SE of Murwillumbah

Australia's most easterly point is a majestic sheer-sided buttress topped with a picturesque lighthouse. From here you get spectacular views across the South Pacific Ocean. Byron Bay's white-sand beaches are renowned for their excellent surfing.

The **Byron Bay Lighthouse** on Cape Byron is one of Australia's most powerful—its beacon is visible more than 40km (25 miles) out to sea. The sparkling white tower is not open for inspection, but the point on which it's located affords a spectacular ocean view daily, weather permitting.

Watego's Beach, under Cape Byron, is one of the best surfing beaches on the east coast. **Julian Rocks,** a marine reserve in the same vicinity, is a good area for skin- and scuba diving.

For many years, Byron Bay was the almost-exclusive haunt of surfers and travelers who thrived on getting off the beaten path. However, the town and its environs have now become *the* place to go. The affluent (Paul Hogan has a house here) mingle with long-haired alternative-lifestyle types—and everyone agrees that the beaches (which face both east and north), rain forest, and climate here are the best. You might like to visit for the blues festival at Easter or the first Sunday of the month, when the public market is held.

Essentials

GETTING THERE Byron Bay is on the coast, 6km (almost 4 miles) east of the Pacific Highway. If you're driving from the south, leave the highway at Ballina and take the scenic coast road via Lennox Head. Ansett Express Airlines flies from Sydney to Ballina, 20km (12.4 miles) northwest of Byron Bay. The Coolangatta airport is just north of the Queensland border, 112km (69.4 miles) away. A Qantas Sydney-Coolangatta ticket costs A$131 to A$166 (U.S. $104.80 to $132.80). Coolangatta is also serviced by most major airlines.

A Sydney–Byron Bay coach ticket costs A$70 (U.S. $56). A Brisbane–Byron Bay ticket costs A$22 (U.S. $17.60).

VISITOR INFORMATION If you have questions, stop at the **Tourist Information Office,** 69 Jonson St., Byron Bay, NSW 2481 (☎ 066/85 8050). The **telephone area code** is 066. As part of the telephone changeover, all numbers with a 066 area code will be changing to 02/66xx xxxx in March 1998.

Where to Stay

In addition to the options below, you might be interested in **The Wheel Resort,** 39–51 Broken Head Rd., Byron Bay, NSW 2481 (☎ 066/85 6139; fax 066/85 8754), comprised of comfortable self-contained cabins with screened verandas (wheelchair-accessible).

Cape Byron Resort Motel. 16 Lawson St., Byron Bay, NSW 2481. ☎ **066/85 7663,** or 1800/02 8909 in Australia. Fax 066/85 7439. 30 rms. TV TEL. A$105–A$200 (U.S. $84–$160) double (depending on time of year). Additional person A$15 (U.S. $12) extra. AE, BC, DC, MC, V.

One block from Byron's main beach, this two-story red-brick motel has a garden of native trees and shrubs. All rooms have clock radios, ceiling fans, heaters, and kitchenettes, and two have spa baths. There's a solar-heated pool and a hot spa, as well as a playground and laundry facilities. The management can arrange baby-sitting. The Rocks Restaurant is open daily.

✪ **Taylor's Guesthouse.** McGettigan's Lane, Ewingsdale, Byron Bay, NSW 2481. ☎ **066/847 436.** Fax 066/847 526. 5 rms, 1 cottage. TV. A$160–A$180 (U.S. $128–$144) double;. A$210–A$250 (U.S. $172–$200) self-contained cottage. Rates include breakfast, afternoon tea, and predinner sherry or port. Surcharge Christmas and Easter. A$40–A$45 (U.S. $36) three-course dinner. BYO. AE, BC, DC, MC, V. Not suitable for children.

A perfect place for a honeymoon—whether it be first, second, or trial—Taylor's positively exudes romance. The guest rooms are perfect: Each has a great country decor with crisp linen, fluffy bathrobes, ceiling fans, and fresh flowers and opens onto a private veranda. The secluded rain-forest setting and beautiful 18-meter (19½ yards) pool help to create a relaxing atmosphere.

Hosts Wendy and Ross Taylor are experts at helping folks feel at home, and Wendy is an amazing cook. A recent meal started with emu, chicken, sliced pear, and rocket (arugula) salad, followed by Atlantic salmon from Tasmania and then a fine apple tart with palm sugar sauce for dessert. The atmosphere at their table is not unlike that of a dinner party. Naturally, they offer locally grown coffee and herb tea. Breakfast is served at tables for two out on a tile deck overlooking the pool. "No one should have to be sociable before they've had coffee," explains Wendy. I couldn't agree more.

Where to Dine

The Pavilion, a beach kiosk near the swimming baths (pool), is open daily from 10am to 7pm (shorter hours in winter). You can get great fish and chips for about A$5 (U.S. $4).

The Pass Cafe. At the end of Brooke Drive, on the Cape Byron Walking Track, Palm Valley. ☎ **066/85 6074.** Reservations accepted. Main courses A$7–A$12 (U.S. $5.60–$9.60) at lunch, A$14–A$17.50 (U.S. $11.20–$13.80) at dinner. BC, MC, V. Sun–Thur 8am–3pm, Fri–Sat 8am–9:30pm (Tues–Sat in summer). MEDITERRANEAN.

Whether you walk, drive, or bike here, you won't be disappointed with the setting, steps from the beach between the town center and the lighthouse. Hosts John and Josy Bassett have made it easy for you to have what you want. They offer breakfast, teas, lunch, and dinner—and if you're in a hurry they even sell pies and sandwiches from a kiosk. Dinner main courses include veal steak with field mushrooms, rosemary, Chianti sauce, and risotto fritters; Atlantic salmon with saffron mash and braised leeks; or Moroccan-style blue-eye cod filet with grilled vegetable salsa. For lunch you could have a salad, a burger, or pasta. BYO.

Rae's Restaurant and Bar. Watego's Beach, Byron Bay. ☎ **066/85 8246.** Reservations recommended. Dinner main courses A$17–A$20 (U.S. $13.60–$16); light lunch A$6–A$16 (U.S.$7.80–$12.80). AE, BC, DC, MC, V. Mon–Fri noon–10pm, Sat–Sun 9am–10pm. MODERN AUSTRALIAN/SEAFOOD.

The setting overlooking Watego's Beach is clearly Australian, but the very plain architecture is purely Mediterranean—white walls with blue woodwork are more reminiscent of Greece than Oz. Even if the food weren't good (which it is) the view alone would be sufficient reason to dine here. Entrees (appetizers) include Peking pancakes with blue swimmer crab and broccoli with oyster sauce or tea-smoked sea scallops tossed with rag pasta and lemon crème fraîche. Sample main courses are risotto of four pumpkins with red-basil pesto and oven-roasted snapper filet in green-chile broth.

MURWILLUMBAH

321km (200 miles) N of Coffs Harbour, 893km (554 miles) N of Sydney, 30km (19 miles) S of Queensland border

The forested slopes of **Mount Warning,** picturesque country towns, and the razzmatazz of licensed clubs near the Queensland border are all within a short drive of Murwillumbah (pop. 8,000), the focal point of the scenic **Tweed Valley.** In addition to being a good base for touring, Murwillumbah is an important commercial center. Throughout the area you'll see evidence of the sugarcane, banana, timber, dairy, and beef cattle industries.

ESSENTIALS

GETTING THERE Murwillumbah is inland from the coast on the Pacific Highway, which connects Sydney and Brisbane. The Coolangatta airport is just north of the Queensland border, 34km (21 miles) away. A Qantas Sydney-Coolangatta ticket costs A$131 to A$166 (U.S. $104.80 to $132.80) one-way.

Direct Countrylink XPT trains link Murwillumbah to Sydney. A first-class ticket costs A$112 (U.S. $89.60) one way; economy class costs A$80.80 (U.S. $64.60). The trip takes 12 hours and 40 minutes. By coach, the trip takes 14 hours and costs A$73 (U.S. $58.40) one way.

VISITOR INFORMATION Check in at the **Visitors Centre,** at the corner of the Pacific Highway and Alma Street, Murwillumbah, NSW 2484 (☎ 066/72 1340), before heading out through more of the Tweed Valley or east to the beaches. You can also stop by the **Tweed Heads Visitors Centre,** at the corner of Bay and Wharf streets, Tweed Heads, NSW 2485 (☎ 07/5536 4244). The **telephone area code** for Murwillumbah is 066. As part of the telephone changeover, all numbers with a 066 area code will be changing to 02/66xx xxxx in March 1998.

SEEING THE AREA

Tropical Fruit World (formerly Avocado Adventureland), on the Pacific Highway (☎ 066/77 7222), 15km (9 miles) north of Murwillumbah and 15km south of Coolangatta, is the home of the Big Avocado, as well as the Garden of the Lost Inca Crops. Tractor-train safaris across the 200-acre tropical fruit plantation, four-wheel-drive rain-forest adventure rides, and riverboat rides are offered. A plantation restaurant, kiosk, fruit market, and gift shop are also available. Tropical Fruit World grows 400 varieties of tropical fruit and is open daily from 10am to 5pm (10am to 6pm during daylight savings time). Admission to food and shopping areas is free. Guided tours cost A$12 (U.S. $9.60) for adults and A$6 (U.S. $4.80) for children. This is the Tweed Valley's top attraction.

Many good bushwalks circle and lead to the top of 1,156-meter (3,815-ft.) ✪ **Mount Warning,** from where there's a good view of the caldera formed from volcanic action 20 to 23 million years ago. Mount Warning National Park is one of four World Heritage Parks in the area.

WHERE TO STAY & DINE

Those on a tight budget will appreciate the **Mt. Warning/Murwillumbah Backpackers YHA,** 1 Tumbulgum Rd., Murwillumbah, NSW 2484 (☎ 066/72 3763), with two eight-bed dorms and four double/twin rooms. The hostel is right on the

Pub Problems: A Self-Diagnosis

The following is a handwritten sign on the wall of the pub in the Tyalgum Hotel, Tyalgum:

Symptoms	Fault	Action to be Taken
Drinking fails to give satisfaction and taste, shirt front wet.	Mouth not open while drinking or glass applied to wrong part of face.	Buy another schooner and practice in front of mirror. Continue with as many schooners as is necessary until drinking technique is perfect.
Drinking fails to give satisfaction and taste. Beer unusually pale and clear.	Glass empty.	Look for someone who will buy you another schooner.
Feet cold and wet.	Glass being held at incorrect angle.	Turn the other way so that open end is pointing toward the ceiling.
Feet warm and wet.	Incorrect bladder control.	Go and stand next to the nearest dog—after a while complain to its owner about its lack of house training—then demand a schooner for compensation.
Bar blurred.	You are looking through the bottom of your glass.	Look for someone who will buy you another schooner.
Bar sways.	Air turbulence unusually high—may be due to a darts match in progress.	Insert broom handle down the back of your jacket.
Bar moving.	You are being carried out.	Find out if you are being taken to another pub—if not, complain loudly that you are being hijacked by the Salvation Army.
You notice that the wall opposite is covered with ceiling tiles and has a fluorescent light strip across it.	You have fallen over.	If glass is still full and no one is standing on your drinking arm, stay put. If not, get someone to help you up and lash yourself to the bar.
Everything has gone dim, you have a mouthful of dog-ends and broken teeth.	You have fallen over, forward.	See above.
Everything has gone dark. You have woken up and found your bed hard, cold, and wet, and you cannot see your bedroom wall or ceiling.	The pub is closed. You have spent the night in the gutter	PANIC! Check your watch to see if it's opening time—if not, treat yourself to a sleep-in.

banks of the Tweed River, and a canoe and rowboat are available. Charges are A$13 to A$15 (U.S. $10.40 to $12) per person.

Those who visit this area on a weekend might like to know about **Pullman's Retreat,** Coolman Street, Tyalgum (☎ 066/793 415). Dinner is served here on Friday and Saturday and lunch is often offered on Sunday. Tyalgum is a tiny village 22km (13 miles) west of Murwillumbah. The restaurant is housed in a former bank building dating from 1911. The town's hotel, nearby, is an authentic Aussie country pub and a good spot for a cold beer. The veranda sports a most amazing collection of staghorn ferns.

$ Crystal Creek Rainforest Retreat. Brookers Road, Upper Crystal Creek, Murwillumbah, NSW 2484. ☎ **066/791 591.** Fax 066/791 596. 5 cabins. TV. A$130 (U.S. $104) double without spa; A$170 (U.S. $136) double with spa. Ask about lower midweek rates and weekly specials. Breakfast A$10 (U.S. $8); lunch A$18 (U.S. $14.40); dinner A$35 (U.S. $28). BC, MC, V. Not suitable for children and no smoking is permitted.

This eco-retreat is only 25 minutes off the Pacific Highway, but it feels a world away. The self-contained cabins are set in a rain forest on the edge of the World Heritage–listed Border Ranges National Park. Walking tracks crisscross the region, and guests have a good chance of seeing a wide variety of native birds. Area animals include bandicoots, wallabies, echidnas, and possums. Hosts Judy Rimmer and Ralph Kraemer hang hammocks *over* the river, where everyone swims in the natural pools in December and January. Guests can cook for themselves, have meals delivered to them, or join Ralph and Judy in the dining room. Three cabins have two bedrooms (one of these has two baths). Each cabin offers a balcony, a barbecue, a TV, a VCR, a full sound system including a CD player, and lots of privacy. Massage can be arranged.

Midginbil Hill Holiday Farm. Uki, NSW 2484, via Murwillumbah. ☎ **066/79 7158.** Fax 066/79 7120. 8 lodge rms, 30 tent sites. Lodge rooms (including all meals), A$90 (U.S. $72) adults, A$35 (U.S. $28) children 4-15; under 4 free. Tent sites, A$6 (U.S. $4.80) adults, A$3 (U.S. $2.40) children. BC, MC, V.

Midginbil Hill is a holiday farm designed for relaxed family fun. Located 30km (19 miles) west of Murwillumbah and surrounded by beautiful views of the Tweed Valley, the 160-hectare (395-acre) cattle property (ranch) is great for folks who want to ride horses, go on four-wheel-drive safaris, try canoeing, or, depending on the time of year, help out with mustering livestock. (Horseback riding is A$18/U.S. $14.40; a wildlife canoeing safari costs A$24/U.S. $19.20.) Proprietors Annette and John Flower create a welcoming atmosphere and encourage kids to help feed the farm animals. Archery, swimming, tennis, pool, and table tennis keep even the most active youngsters happy. "Mountain morning tea" provides a real Aussie-style experience: One group rides out into the bush on horseback and another goes on a four-wheel-drive safari. They meet, boil the billy for morning tea, and switch conveyances to return to the farm.

Healthful home-cooked meals are enjoyed in the original colonial homestead, sometimes also used for bush dances. Accommodations are in rustic lodges with bunk beds and private baths or in tents.

After Dark

Several clubs thrive on the New South Wales/Queensland border at Tweed Heads.

Seagulls Rugby League Football Club. Gollan Drive, Tweed Heads. ☎ **07/5536 3433.** No cover.

This is a popular spot for dining, entertainment, drinking, and gambling. Top-name stars often perform in the club's Stardust Room, which seats up to 1,600. In the past few years Seagulls has hosted such performers as Tom Jones, Joe Cocker, and Bob Hope. Local award-winning performers include Julie Anthony, Tina Arena, and Kate Cebrano. There are also five eateries, three lounges, nine bars, and a casino with 522 poker machines. Open daily 24 hours.

Twin Towns Services Club. Wharf Street, Tweed Heads. ☎ **07/5536 2277.** No cover.

As with most clubs like this in Australia, food and beverages at Twin Towns are a great value. Dining options range from a coffee shop to an à la carte restaurant. In the Bistro/Carvery a roast dinner with four vegetables costs about A$7.50 (U.S. $6). Entertainment and dancing go every afternoon and evening. On Monday nights they show free movies in the auditorium. Casual dress is acceptable during the day at this poker-machine and entertainment complex, but after 7:30pm shorts and thongs are prohibited. Children under 18 aren't allowed in the gambling area but may be left in the children's lounge on level three. Open Monday to Thursday from 9am to 12:30am, Friday from 9am to 1am, Saturday from 9am to 1:30am, and Sunday from 9am to midnight.

7 The New England Region

If you've ever wanted to sample autumn in New England, you might like to visit Tamworth, Armidale, Tenterfield, or Glen Innes between April and June, when trees in the area turn lovely shades of gold, red, and orange. Unlike the north-coast region on the other side of the Great Divide, New England is about 1,000 meters (3,300 ft.) above sea level and has four distinct seasons—fall is one of the nicest.

The area spreads out on either side of the New England Highway from the Hunter Valley to the Queensland border. This highway roughly parallels the coastal Pacific Highway from Sydney to Brisbane and, instead of beaches, offers rugged gorges, lofty waterfalls, dense forests, wide green paddocks, and bracing highland air. If you want to sample a real variety of scenery, start out on one highway and cross the Great Dividing Range to the other road partway up. Three highways—the Oxley, Gwydir, and Bruxner—make it possible to do this. And wherever you are in New England, keep your eyes on the ground. The area is rich in gemstones, and it's possible to stumble across jasper, crystal, serpentine, quartz, and chalcedony. If you're very lucky, you might even find sapphires, diamonds, and gold.

TAMWORTH

453km (281 miles) NW of Sydney

Except during the music festival in January, Tamworth (pop. 35,000) is an attractive quiet city in the center of a rich pastoral and agricultural area. Before its musical identity was established by a radio program called "Hoedown," popular in the 1960s, Tamworth was known as the "city of lights" because it was the first place in Australia to have electric streetlights. It's situated at the junction of the New England and Oxley Highways, so it makes a good stopover on the route from Sydney or Melbourne to Brisbane.

ESSENTIALS

GETTING THERE Tamworth is about a 5½-hour drive from Sydney, north on the Pacific Highway/Sydney-Newcastle Freeway and then west and north on the New England Highway. Motorists traveling from Brisbane should allow 6½ hours.

The fare for flights from Sydney on Eastern Australia Airlines is A$157 to A$164 (U.S. $125.60 to $131.20). On Tamair it's A$144 to A$162 (U.S. $115.20 to $129.60).

A Countrylink XPT train ticket from Sydney to Tamworth costs A$52.80 (U.S. $42.24) in economy class and A$74.60 (U.S. $59.68) in first class. Countrylink also offers three- and six-day packages to Tamworth. Several coach companies, including Greyhound-Pioneer and McCafferty's, travel the New England Highway. A one-way ticket from Sydney to Tamworth costs about A$53 (U.S. $42.40). The trip takes 8¼ hours or more.

VISITOR INFORMATION Tourist information is dispensed at the **Visitors Centre,** at the corner of Peel and Murray streets, Tamworth, NSW 2340 (☎ 067/66 9422), open Monday to Friday from 8:30am to 4:45pm, Saturday from 9am to 3:30pm, and Sunday from 9am to 3pm. The **telephone area code** is 067. As part of the telephone changeover, all numbers with a 067 area code will be changing to 02/67xx xxxx in January 1998.

SPECIAL EVENTS Known as the "country music capital of the nation," Tamworth hosts the **Australasian Country Music Awards,** a 10-day festival every January. More than 700 shows, concerts, and talent quests are staged during this time, and the city is packed with musicians and their fans.

Seeing the Town

If you're feeling lucky, drive the **Fossicker's Way** from Tamworth to Glen Innes. The route was so named after numerous gemstones were found in its vicinity.

If you like country music, you won't want to miss **Hands of Fame Park,** at the New England Highway and Kable Avenue, where country music musicians have their handprints recorded in concrete à la Mann's Chinese Theater in Hollywood. At the **Country Collection,** models of Chad Morgan, Frank Ifield, Buddy Williams, and Slim Dusty, to name just a few, tell their stories via tape. The clothes on the wax figures are the real thing, donated by the performers or their families.

The **Powerstation Museum,** 216 Peel St., Tamworth, NSW 2340 (☎ 067/66 1999), is the first working steam-powered electricity-generating museum in Australia. It commemorates the fact that Tamworth had the first electric streetlights in the nation. Open Tuesday to Friday from 9am to 1pm. Free admission.

Oxley Park, at the top of Brisbane Street (☎ 067/66 3641), is a sanctuary for kangaroos and other native wildlife. It's open daily from 8am to 5pm. Nice picnic area. Free admission.

Where to Stay & Dine

Powerhouse Motor Inn. New England Highway, Tamworth, NSW 2340. ☎ **067/66 7000.** Fax 067/66 7748. Reservations can be made through Flag Inns. 60 rms, 10 suites. A/C MINIBAR TV TEL. A$105 (U.S. $84) double; A$150–A$170 (U.S. $120–$136) suite. Additional person A$10 (U.S. $8) extra. AE, BC, DC, MC, V.

Besides the standard amenities, the two-story Powerhouse offers queen-size beds, waterbeds, ironing boards, hairdryers, spa baths, a gym, and 24-hour room service. A licensed restaurant, a large pool, a sauna, a hot spa, a children's playground, and a self-service laundry are available. Two rooms have cooking facilities, and there are specially equipped quarters for the disabled. Baby-sitting can be arranged.

Staying on a Farm

$ **Lalla Rookh Country House.** Duri, NSW 2344. ☎ **067/68 0216.** Fax 067/68 0330. Mobile 015/29 3938. 4 rms (2 with bath). A$84 (U.S. $67.20) double. BC, MC, V. Rates include breakfast. Closed Christmas week.

Bob and Sue Moore welcome guests to Lalla Rookh and treat them like members of the family. Their 160-hectare (395-acre) grazing property is 20km (12 miles) south of Tamworth, and visitors are accommodated in the guest wing of the Moores' modern home. This is a great spot for gaining insight into Australian agricultural production and enjoying warm country hospitality. Both hosts have traveled widely; Sue is a potter. Two twin rooms have their own baths, while the other twin and a double share another (guests-only) bath. Breakfast is included, and other meals are available at an extra charge. Only children over the age of 15 are welcome. Hosts will pick up guests in Tamworth. I recommend that you treat yourself to Lalla Rookh and the Moores' hospitality.

ARMIDALE

110km (68 miles) N of Tamworth, 563km (349 miles) NW of Sydney, 464km (288 miles) S of Brisbane

Being both a major commercial center and a university city, Armidale (pop. 22,000) is the focal point of the New England region. Its university, cathedral, parks, and gardens are reminiscent of old England, an impression reinforced by the cool weather often experienced at the city's 1,035-meter (3,416-ft.) elevation. Several other educational institutions are here, giving Armidale the bookish appearance of Cambridge—either Massachusetts or England. The surrounding area is known for its merino wool, cattle, apples, stone fruit, and vegetables. Spring and fall are the best times to visit.

ESSENTIALS

GETTING THERE From Tamworth it's about a 1½-hour drive on the New England Highway; it's about a 7½-hour drive from Sydney. The Sydney-Armidale flight on Eastern Australia Airlines or Hazelton Airlines ranges from A$120 to A$193 (U.S. $96 to $154.40).

A Countrylink train ticket from Sydney costs A$60 (U.S. $48). A Greyhound-Pioneer or McCafferty's coach ticket from Sydney costs A$52 (U.S. $41.60). The coach fare from Brisbane is A$47 to A$52 (U.S. $37.60 to $41.60).

VISITOR INFORMATION Your questions will be answered at the **Visitors Centre and Coach Station,** 82 Marsh St., Armidale, NSW 2350 (☎ 067/73 8527 or 1800/62 7736 in Australia). It's open Monday to Friday from 9am to 5pm, Saturday from 9am to 4pm, and Sunday from 10am to 4pm. The **telephone area code** is 067. As part of the telephone changeover, all numbers with a 067 area code will be changing to 02/67xx xxxx in January 1998.

EXPLORING THE TOWN

You can tour the 260-hectare (642-acre) campus of the **University of New England** (☎ 067/73 3333) daily from 9am to 4:30pm. The "Uni" is off Queen Elizabeth Drive, 5km (3 miles) northwest of the city. Be sure to stop at the entrance to Booloominbah, built between 1883 and 1888 as a homestead for Frederick White, and sign the visitors' book. This impressive building, with its gables, stained-glass windows, and great cedar staircase, was purchased and donated to the University of Sydney in 1937; it eventually resulted in the founding of the University of New England in Armidale. Today "Bool" is an administrative center, and the campus with its many historic buildings has a strong traditional feel. Fallow deer, kangaroos, and wallabies wander nearby in **Deer Park,** adding to the peaceful atmosphere.

Some 39km (24 miles) east of Armidale on the road to Ebor, the 220-meter (726-ft.) **Wollomombi Falls** plunge into a rugged gorge. These falls are one of the highest in Australia and well worth a look. Good picnic facilities are nearby.

Armidale and District Folk Museum. At Rusden and Faulkner streets. ☎ **067/72 8666,** ext. 536. Free admission. Daily 1–4pm.

Set in a National Trust building, this folk museum contains a display of pioneer relics and room settings from a 19th-century parlor, bedroom, and kitchen.

Armidale Art Museum. Kentucky Street. ☎ **067/72 5255.** Admission A$5 (U.S. $4) adults; school-age children free. Storeroom tour additional A$2 (U.S. $1.60). Mon–Sat 10am–5pm, Sun 1–5pm.

This museum houses the famous Hinton Art Collection, the Armidale City Art Collection, and the Coventry Collection. The Howard Hinton Collection, which contains over 1,100 pictures, bronzes, medallions, and craft works, is the most valuable provincial collection in the country.

WHERE TO STAY & DINE

Both farm stay and bed-and-breakfast accommodations are popular in the Armidale area. If you're interested in savoring the local hospitality, contact the **Armidale Visitors Centre,** 82 Marsh St., Armidale, NSW 2350 (☎ 067/73 8527; fax 067/71 4486).

Cattleman's Motor Inn. 31 Marsh St. (New England Hwy.), Armidale, NSW 2350. ☎ **067/72 7788,** or 1800/02 8910 in Australia. 54 units. A/C TV TEL. A$95–A$120 (U.S. $76–$96) double; A$130–A$170 (U.S. $104–$136) suite. Additional person A$10 (U.S. $8) extra. AE, BC, DC, MC, V.

Set in a modern two-story building, the guest rooms have toasters in addition to the standard coffee- and tea-making facilities; 14 have tubs as well as showers. A licensed restaurant, a laundry, a barbecue, a pool, a spa, a sauna, and facilities for the disabled are also available.

Cotswold Gardens Motor Inn. 34 Marsh St. (New England Hwy.), Armidale, NSW 2350. ☎ **067/72 8222.** Fax 067/72 5139. Reservations can be made through Flag Inns. 25 rms. MINIBAR TV TEL. A$80 (U.S. $64) double. Additional person A$6 (U.S. $4.80) extra. AE, BC, CB, DC, MC, V.

What could be more appropriate in this town with its English feel than this single-story hostelry with a gabled roof and colonial appearance? The rooms have modern amenities, and a licensed restaurant, cocktail bar, and games room are on the premises. Baby-sitting can be arranged.

8 Outback New South Wales

The western two-thirds of New South Wales consists of arid rust-colored plains periodically broken by low, rocky ranges and dry, or nearly dry, riverbeds. Only rugged souls can live in this inhospitable terrain. Heat, distance, and low rainfall are a constant threat, even to visitors if they stray off the main roads. If it weren't for the discovery of valuable minerals and gemstones, the outback would probably have remained unsettled.

As it is, large deposits of silver, lead, and zinc have put Broken Hill on the map, and black opals draw residents to Lightning Ridge. Other towns, like Bourke, serve as commercial centers for the surrounding sheep or cattle country, where vast stations (ranches) go on for miles.

To many visitors, the outback is the real Australia, a land of great expanses, kangaroos, Aborigines, miners, sheep and cattle stations, and the Flying Doctor Service. While this is true, I encourage you to be realistic and careful about traveling in this region, especially from November to March, when temperatures often reach 38°C (100°F) and flies and dust can be thick and annoying. Running out of petrol (gas), food, or water can be a very serious matter. On the other hand, substantial improvements have been made to roads and amenities in recent years, and, if you're cautious, your experience could be one of watching Aussie folklore come to life, meeting some unusual outback characters, and having a fair dinkum good time.

BROKEN HILL

1,157km (717 miles) W of Sydney, 508km (315 miles) NE of Adelaide

More than 100 years ago, Charles Rasp, a German boundary rider, found what he thought was tin ore on a broken hill in the vicinity of the Mount Gipps Station. Rasp's samples turned out to be silver and lead, and by 1885 the Broken Hill Proprietary Company had been launched. The ore deposits turned out to be the largest and richest of their kind in the world, and through the years the BHP has played a major role in transforming Australia from a pastoral nation to an important industrial force. The mines continue to operate and produce two million tons of ore annually, though the BHP, Australia's largest company, pulled out of the community in 1940.

Broken Hill (pop. 24,450) is very close to the South Australian border. The fact that it operates on South Australian time (central standard time, half an hour behind eastern standard time), though located in New South Wales, is symbolic of its proximity to Adelaide and distance from Sydney. Access to this outback oasis is surprisingly easy.

ESSENTIALS

GETTING THERE If you're driving from Sydney, take the Great Western Highway to Dubbo, then the Mitchell Highway to the Barrier Highway and the Barrier Highway on to Broken Hill. There are regular flights on Kendell Airlines to and from Adelaide. Hazelton Airlines goes back and forth from Sydney. Southern Australia Airlines connects Broken Hill to Melbourne, Adelaide, and Mildura.

The *Indian Pacific* train stops on its way to Perth. An Australian National rail ticket from Sydney to Broken Hill costs A$97 (U.S. $77.60) in economy class and A$119 (U.S. $95.20) in first class. A Countrylink ticket costs A$70 (U.S. $56).

Greyhound-Pioneer provides coach service. A Sydney-Broken Hill bus ticket costs A$95 (U.S. $76), and the journey lasts nearly 16 hours.

GETTING AROUND **Broken Hill's Outback Tours,** 166–170 Crystal St. (P.O. Box 199), Broken Hill, NSW 2880 (☎ 080/877 800 or 874 064, or 1800/670 120 in Australia; fax 080/883 813), conduct three- to six-day tours in the area. You can also contact them on the Internet at brkhill@outbtour.com.au.

VISITOR INFORMATION Information is available at the **Broken Hill Tourist and Travellers Centre,** at Blende and Bromide streets, Broken Hill, NSW 2880 (☎ 080/87 6077), open daily from 8:30am to 5pm. In the same location are a car-rental desk, a souvenir shop, a bus terminal, and a cafeteria. The **telephone area code** is 080. As part of the telephone changeover, all numbers with a 080 area code will be changing to 08/80xx xxxx in March 1997.

EXPLORING THE TOWN

If you arrive in Broken Hill without a car, **Silver City Tours,** 328 Argent St. (☎ 080/87 6956), conducts coach and minicoach tours to most of the places below.

Interesting galleries around town include the **Hugh Schulz Gallery,** 51 Morgan St. (☎ 080/87 6624), and the **Pro Hart Gallery,** 108 Wyman St. (☎ 080/87 2441). Both are open daily.

A Pub Crawl on Horseback

Here's something you can't do at home: Congenial host Steve Langley, P.O. Box 379, Glen Innes, NSW 2370 (☎ 067/32 1599), conducts six-day trips that start at his Bullock Mountain Homestead, 113km (70 miles) north of Armidale near Glen Innes. Riders traverse the beautiful New England countryside and stay overnight in historic country pubs. Along the way they meet local stockmen, farmhands, miners, prospectors, horse breakers, and other colorful people. Steve welcomes children as well as adults, as long as they have "a smattering of horsemanship"—six hours a day is spent in the saddle for six days. The trip covers 150km (93 miles). One night is spent in the town of Emmaville (pop. 500; two hotels), two nights in Torrington (pop. 80; one hotel), and yet another in Deepwater (pop. 350), where the original Cobb & Co. stagecoaches stopped. Groups are kept to a maximum of 20 participants; horses range from docile to spirited. The tariff of A$999 (U.S. $799) includes horses, accommodations, and all meals. If you like horses, beautiful scenery, getting off the beaten path, and cold beer, this could really be fun. Don't forget to pack your broad-brimmed hat and riding boots. If you don't have one, stockman's coats can be rented (A$20/U.S. $16). Steve picks guests up upon arrival in Glen Innes. Shorter rides are also available.

This trip can also be arranged through **FITS Equestrian** (see "Outfitters & Adventure-Travel Operators" under "The Active Vacation Planner" in Chapter 3).

Major Attractions

Broken Hill City Art Gallery. Chloride Street, between Blende and Beryl streets. ☎ **080/88 9252.** Fax 080/87 1411. Admission A$2 (U.S. $1.60) adults, A$1 (U.S. 80¢) children. Mon–Fri 10am–5pm, Sat–Sun 1pm–5pm. Closed Good Friday and Christmas.

This gallery, in the modern Entertainment Centre, is the state's oldest gallery outside Sydney (est. 1904) and houses an extensive collection of Australian colonial and Australian impressionist works. Of particular interest is the *Silver Tree,* wrought from pure silver from the Broken Hill mines for Charles Rasp, discoverer of the rich mineral deposits. This is a good place to see the work of the **Brushmen of the Bush,** a well-known group of artists who live in the outback and attempt to capture its unique scenery on canvas. Look for paintings by Pro Hart, Jack Absalom, Eric Minchin, and Hugh Schulz. Their pictures of the local landscape have been exhibited worldwide.

Railway and Historical Museum. At Blende and Bromide streets. ☎ **080/88 4660.** Admission A$2 (U.S. $1.60) adults, A$1.50 (U.S. $1.20) children, A$5 (U.S. $4) family. Daily 10am–3pm.

This technical museum, opposite the Tourist Information Centre, has displays that explain how the railway lines from Sydney and Melbourne, together with the wealth of the mining industry, transformed Broken Hill into a relatively modern oasis in the middle of the otherwise desolate outback. On display in the stone railway station, built in 1905, are old photos and books relating to the Silverton Tramway Company.

White's Mineral Art and Mining Museum. 1 Allendale St. ☎ **080/87 2878.** Admission A$4 (U.S. $3.20) adults, A$2 (U.S. $1.60) children under 12. Daily 9am–6pm.

Here you can visit a replica of a mine and see a mining video and models.

Broken Hill's Mosque. At the corner of Williams and Buck streets. Admission A$.20 (U.S. 15¢). Sun 2:30–4:30pm.

The mosque was built around 1891 by Afghan and Indian camel drivers on the site of the camp where they loaded and unloaded their camel teams.

More Attractions

TOURING MINES Underground mine tours are conducted at **Delprat's Mine** (☎ 080/88 1604 or 87 4905) Monday to Friday at 10:30am and Saturday at 2pm. Visitors go 120 meters (396 ft.) below the surface and gain an understanding of what it's like to work in one of Broken Hill's mines. Children under 6 aren't permitted. Cameras are okay. The two-hour tours cost A$18 (U.S. $14.40).

✪ **VISITING THE SCHOOL OF THE AIR & THE RFDS** You might also like to visit the School of the Air and the Royal Flying Doctor Service base. Both of these places provide real insight into the "tyranny of distance" that historian Geoffrey Blainey speaks of when describing Australia's remote regions. The School of the Air, which conducts lessons via two-way radio for children on isolated stations, requires that visits be booked by the Tourist Information Centre. The Royal Flying Doctor Service base is at the Broken Hill Airport (☎ 080/88 0777). The RFDS maintains communication with over 400 outback stations, providing long-range diagnosis of problems and, if necessary, dispatching a physician by air. The Broken Hill base covers 25% of New South Wales as well as parts of Queensland and South Australia. Explanatory sessions lasting 45 minutes are held at the base Monday to Friday at 10:30am and 3:30pm and Saturday and Sunday at 10:30am. Admission is A$2 (U.S. $1.60) for adults; under 12 free.

CHECKING OUT A GHOST TOWN **Silverton** (pop. 50), 23km (14 miles) northwest of Broken Hill, is a popular location for moviemakers. *A Town Like Alice, Mad Max II (The Road Warrior),* and many other films have been shot there. Silverton was home to a population of 3,000 after silver chlorides were discovered there in 1882, but the field closed in 1889 and nearly everyone left. Its restored buildings include a hotel and a jail.

TAKING AN OUTBACK ADVENTURE If you really want to get a feel for the outback, join an airborne postman as he flies the Saturday bush mail run to a string of about 16 isolated sheep stations along a 560km (347-mile) loop outside Broken Hill. The tour departs at 6:30am and can carry four sightseers in addition to the pilot. Along the way you'll see lots of kangaroos and other native animals, land at strips on remote stations, and meet some quite out-of-the-ordinary people. The experience costs A$210 (U.S. $168), including lunch and a tour of White Cliffs, an opal-mining town. To book your seat, contact **Crittenden Aviation,** P.O. Box 346, Broken Hill, NSW 2880 (☎ 080/88 5702).

Where to Stay

Broken Hill Overlander Motor Inn. 142 Iodide St., Broken Hill, NSW 2880. ☎ **080/88 2566.** Fax 080/88 4377. Reservations can be made through Best Western. 15 rms. A/C TV TEL. A$64–A$82 (U.S. $51.20–$65.60) double. Additional person A$10 (U.S. $8) extra. AE, BC, DC, MC, V.

Barry and Kerry Josephs offer 15 modern units, as well as an outdoor pool, a sauna, and a spa. Each room has a clock radio, tea- and coffee-making facilities, and a small refrigerator. Facilities for the handicapped are available, as are in-house movies and a guest laundry. Baby-sitting can be arranged.

Tourist Lodge. 100 Argent St., Broken Hill, NSW 2880. ☎ **080/88 2086.** 33 rms (none with bath). A$24–A$32 (U.S. $19.20–$25.60) double. AE, BC, MC, V.

The centrally located Tourist Lodge has both private rooms and dormitory facilities, all at budget prices. Shared kitchen facilities are provided, as are laundry facilities, a communal TV lounge, a solar-heated pool, and barbecue facilities.

DINING & AFTER-DARK ENTERTAINMENT

Broken Hill Musicians Club. 276 Crystal St. ☎ **080/881 777.**

This spot, open daily for lunch and dinner, is licensed to serve alcohol. Live entertainment is provided.

RSL Club. 2 Chloride St. ☎ **080/872 653.**

This club provides meals, drinks, and a chance to play one-arm bandits.

LIGHTNING RIDGE

765km (474 miles) NW of Sydney, 572km (355 miles) SW of Brisbane

While most people move to Lightning Ridge with the hopes of finding a large vein of black opal, it's the frontier atmosphere and relaxed lifestyle that keep them here. The township is home to 7,000 people who've chosen an unorthodox way of life over urban conformity. In the town pub, the Digger's Rest Hotel, locals tantalize visiting fossickers with tales of great strikes and legendary riches, but their wealth isn't as apparent as their love of the "great Aussie leg pull." Consider yourself lucky if you find even one or two dirt-encrusted opal pebbles. Lightning Ridge is one of three main opal fields in Australia and the only source of black opals in the world. The other two important fields are Quilpie, Queensland, and Coober Pedy, South Australia.

ESSENTIALS

GETTING THERE Lightning Ridge is most easily accessible via Hazelton Airlines. A Countrylink coach/rail ticket costs A$73 (U.S. $58.40); travel is via Dubbo.

VISITOR INFORMATION Information is available from the **Lightning Ridge Tourist Information Centre,** P.O. Box 1779, Lightning Ridge, NSW 2834 (☎ 068/29 1466 or 29 1462; fax/recorded message 068/29 0565). The **telephone area code** is 068. As part of the telephone changeover, all numbers with a 068 area code will be changing to 02/68xx xxxx in January 1998.

SEEING THE TOWN

The **Artesian Bore Baths,** 2km (1 mile) from the post office on Pandora Street (☎ 068/291 466), are free of charge and open 24 hours a day. The artesian hot water is believed to be of therapeutic value.

At the **Opal Bazaar,** on Three Mile Road (☎ 068/290 247), you can watch cutting demonstrations, go on a guided mine tour, and fossick in the mine tailings. Also known as the Big Opal, this place sells loose stones and jewelry. You can also visit **Spectrum Opal Mines,** 1km (0.6 mile) north of the post office on Bald Hill Road (☎ 068/29 0581), where admission is free and films are shown daily. Also on display here are black opals from their mines. Jewelry, loose stones, and souvenirs are for sale. There's a nice picnic area, too.

If you're in Lightning Ridge in April you can attend the **Great Goat Race** (☎ 068/290 429), and in early October visitors are welcome to participate in the two-day **Opal Festival** (☎ 068/290 565).

Where to Stay

Black Opal Motel. Opal Street, Lightning Ridge, NSW 2834. ☎ **068/29 0518.** Fax 068/29 0884. 12 rms. A/C TV TEL. A$59–A$63 (U.S. $47.20–$50.40) double. Additional person A$10 (U.S. $8) extra. AE, BC, MC, V.

The rooms in the Black Opal have showers and are equipped with coffee- and tea-making facilities, small refrigerators, clock radios, and safes (in case you need a place to stash your opals).

Brisbane 7

"Send the worst convicts somewhere else" was a demand often voiced by the free settlers in New South Wales in the 1820s. As a result, Gov. Sir Thomas Macdougall Brisbane (pronounced *"Briz*-bun" by Aussies) sent explorers north to find a suitable spot for a new penal colony. They searched the coast for a site on a river, for in those days all long-distance transport was by sea, and Lt. John Oxley in the cutter *Mermaid* discovered the waterway extending inland from Moreton Bay, 1,031km (639 miles) north of Sydney. The location was ideal: Fresh water was plentiful, grazing land was lush, and it was a long way from the free settlers. Within a year a colony had been established on the Brisbane River, named after the governor who had precipitated its discovery.

The Australian colony continued to expand, and in 1837 free settlers joined the convicts at Brisbane Town. In 1842 the original penal settlement was closed. The fledgling community remained under the control of New South Wales until 1859, when the state of Queensland was declared. By 1891 more than 104,000 people, attracted by gold, rich farmland, and local industries like shipbuilding, had chosen to live in Brisbane.

During World War II, Gen. Douglas MacArthur set up his South Pacific headquarters here, and thousands of American troops were housed in the area. By the early 1960s Brisbane had amassed a city-size population but still had a reputation in Australia of being "just an overgrown country town." This bothered forward-thinking civic leaders, who set about to use the wealth of the state's newly developed mineral resources to change their community's image.

When Brisbane hosted the Commonwealth Games in 1982, Australians and others became aware that the Queensland capital was no longer a Sleepy Hollow down under. Even more people were attracted to the area, the population figures rising nearly as fast as the height of the office towers that appeared on the skyline. In the mid-1980s Brisbane's voters took their modern ideas to the ballot box and elected a woman, popular Sallyanne Atkinson, as Lord Mayor. In 1991 Atkinson was succeeded by Alderman Jim Soorley, who earned his M.A. in Organizational Development at Loyola University in Chicago.

Today Brisbane has a population of 1.2 million; only Sydney and Melbourne are larger. It has a slower pace and doesn't take itself as seriously as the southern capitals. Like the Sunbelt cities in North

What's Special About Brisbane

Top Attraction

- The Australian Woolshed, a chance to learn about sheep, milk a cow, and generally become conversant in the agricultural side of life in Australia. Highly recommended.

Architectural Highlights

- The Queensland Cultural Centre, a low-rise complex of buildings surrounded by imaginative pools and fountains—a visual treat.

Regional Food

- Excellent opportunities for savoring seafood at the city's dining spots. Don't miss the Moreton Bay bugs.

For Kids of All Ages

- Lone Pine Koala Sanctuary, containing the world's largest population of the cuddly creatures.

Shopping

- Wonderful markets at the South Bank Parklands and at the Riverside Centre.

After Dark

- Eating dinner at one of the restaurants in the South Bank Parklands and walking along the waterfront promenade with a view back to the city lights.

America, Brisbane attracts young people who enjoy and perpetuate the area's relaxed lifestyle. Sports clothes are commonplace in the city center and a do-your-own-thing atmosphere prevails.

1 Orientation

ARRIVING

BY PLANE **Qantas, Air New Zealand, United Airlines,** and **British Airways** operate direct flights to Brisbane from Europe, New Zealand, and North America; passengers on other international carriers may have to change to a domestic airline in another gateway city.

If you're traveling to the Queensland capital from within Australia, you'll find frequent air, rail, and bus services. **Ansett** and **Qantas** fly in and out several times a day. Qantas's Sydney-Brisbane fare is about A$159 (U.S. $127.20) one way.

Brisbane's new **international airport,** about 13km (8 miles) from the city center, opened in late 1995 and provides all the "mod cons" (modern conveniences), including the requisite food, beverage, and retail outlets. Passengers take a shuttle bus from here to the nearby domestic terminal.

Coachtrans (☎ 07/3236 1000 or 5573 3777; 6:30am–8:30pm) operates a half-hourly shuttle bus service from each terminal to the city center (A$6.50/U.S. $5.20) and between terminals; taxis are also available at about A$16 (U.S. $12.80). The major car-rental companies have desks in both buildings. The large Shell petrol (gas) station opposite the International Terminal is handy for the final fill of a rental car.

BY TRAIN The ***Spirit of Capricorn*** brings visitors from Rockhampton; the trip takes almost 10 hours and costs A$67 (U.S. $53.60) one way in economy class; the ***Spirit of the Outback*** carries passengers from Longreach. The ***Sunlander*** and ***Queenslander*** carry passengers from Cairns on a journey that lasts about 32 hours.

Greater Brisbane

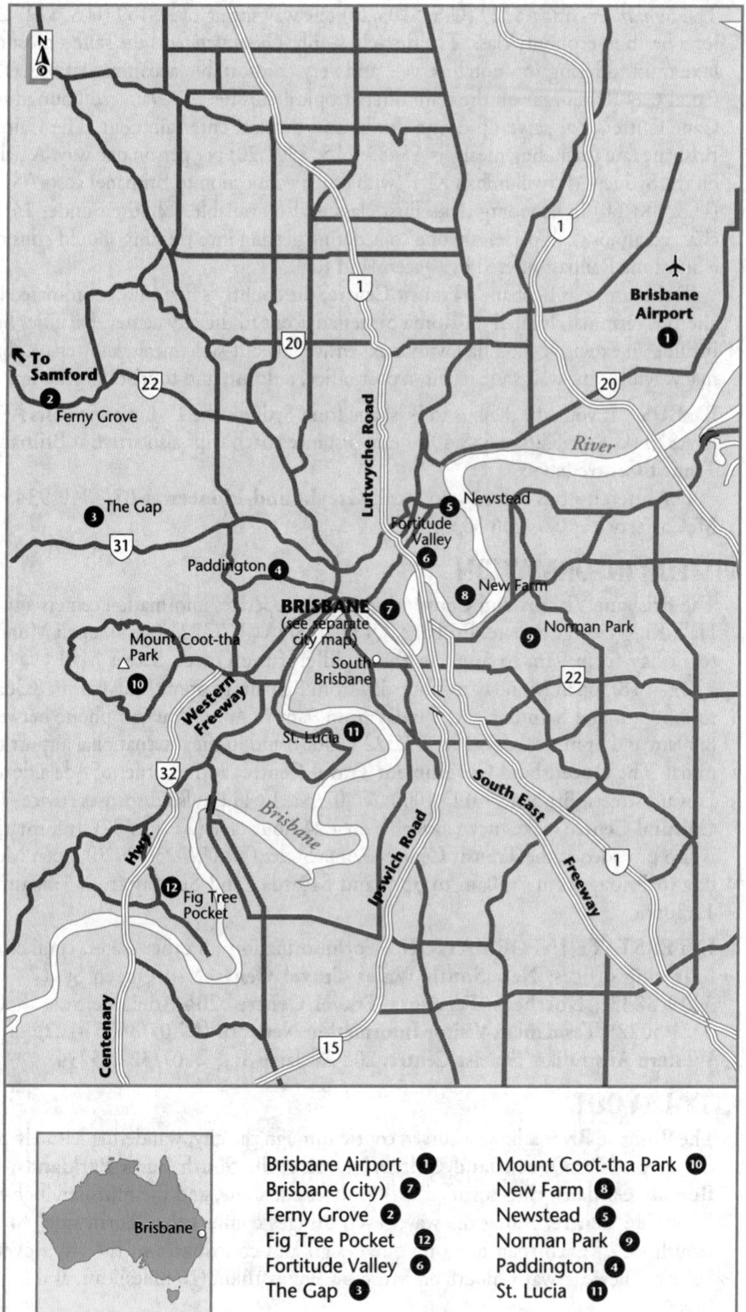

The *Sunlander* costs A$129 (U.S. $103.20) one way sitting or A$159 (U.S. $127.20) for a berth in economy class. The first-class-only *Queenslander* is the state's most deluxe train, offering top-notch service and very comfortable accommodations. The Coral Cay Restaurant on the train offers tropical cuisine; the Daintree Lounge and Cane Cutters Bar serve up exotic drinks and musical entertainment. The Cairns-Brisbane fare (including meals) is A$489 (U.S. $391.20) per person one way. A ticket on the Sydney-Murwillumbah XPT (with coach connection to Brisbane) costs A$102 (U.S. $81.60) in economy class. First class is also available. Children under 14 are charged almost half price. Anyone considering getting into training should consider a Sunshine Railpass offered by Queensland Rail.

Trains arrive at Brisbane's **Transit Centre,** the country's first fully coordinated rail and bus terminal, located on **Roma Street** adjacent to the city center. Facilities here include an extensive food hall with inexpensive takeout-style meals, showers, a pharmacy, while-you-wait shoe repair, a post office, a florist, and tourist information.

BY BUS If you take the bus to Brisbane from Sydney, the 17-hour trip costs A$69 to A$73 (U.S. $55.20 to $58.40). Long-distance coach trips also arrive at Brisbane's **Transit Centre** (above).

For intercity bus information, call **Greyhound-Pioneer** at 07/3840 9343 or **McCafferty's** at 07/3236 3033.

VISITOR INFORMATION

The **Brisbane Visitors and Convention Bureau** operates information centers at City Hall, King George Square, Brisbane, QLD 4000 (☎ 07/3221 8411), open Monday to Friday from 9am to 5pm; in the middle of the Queen Street Mall (☎ 07/3229 5918), open Monday to Thursday from 8:30am to 5pm, Friday from 8:30am to 8:30pm, and Saturday and Sunday from 9am to 4pm. You can phone between 8:30am and 5pm weekdays (☎ 07/3225 4360); and in the international airport terminal. The **Queensland Government Travel Centre,** at the corner of Adelaide and Edward streets, Brisbane, QLD 4000 (☎ 07/3221 6111), also dispenses advice. The **Cultural Centre** makes news available on a 24-hour tape (☎ 11 632). Information is also provided at the **Transit Centre,** Roma Street (☎ 07/3236 2020), open Monday to Friday from 7:30am to 5pm and Saturday and Sunday from 7:30am to 12:30pm.

INTERSTATE INFORMATION For information on other states, contact the following offices: **New South Wales Travel Centre,** 40 Queen St. (☎ 07/3229 8833); **Northern Territory Travel Centre,** 204 Adelaide St. (☎ 07/3221 5022); **Tasmanian Visitor Information Network** (☎ 07/3405 4122); or the **Western Australian Tourist Centre,** 204 Adelaide St. (☎ 07/3229 5794).

CITY LAYOUT

The Brisbane River follows a curved course through the city, wandering leisurely past the spectacular **Queensland Cultural Centre,** the **South Bank Parklands,** the **Botanic Gardens,** cliffs fortified with convict-cut stone, and the mirrored high-rise **Riverside Centre.** Along the way, seven bridges connect the "north side" to the "south side." Each span has a unique design and contributes to the city's overall beauty. The waterway's mouth on **Moreton Bay** is 16km (10 miles) east, as the crow flies.

The city sprawls over a wide area and is encircled by suburbs and parks that rise from low hills. One of the best views of Brisbane is from **Mt. Coot-tha Park**, perched on a summit 7km (4.2 miles) to the west. From this point you can see the central business district is triangular, with the river on two sides.

In the residential neighborhoods, Queenslanders—houses built on stilts to avoid flood danger, termite destruction, and heat—can still be seen. Downtown, the standard-setting A$480-million (U.S. $384-million) **Myer Shopping Centre** dominates the **Queen Street Pedestrian Mall,** and traditional landmarks like the French Renaissance–style **Parliament House** and the Queensland sandstone **City Hall** are cheek by jowl with ultramodern high-rises. Some historic buildings have been converted: The elegant **Treasury Building** now contains a casino, and the former Lands Administration Building houses the Conrad Treasury Casino hotel. **Queen Street** is the main thoroughfare, and parallel streets are named after royal women: **Ann, Adelaide, Elizabeth, Charlotte,** and **Mary.** Cross streets are named after royal men: **George, Albert,** and **Edward.**

South Brisbane, across the **Victoria Bridge** from the city, was extensively developed as the site of World Expo 88 and now boasts the **South Bank Parklands** and **Queensland Cultural Centre** with its wonderful **Performing Arts Complex,** art gallery, and museum. **Spring Hill** is an inner suburb on a rise just north of the city center. **Chinatown** is in **Fortitude Valley,** another close-in area. **Paddington,** a popular suburb northwest of the central business district, is known for historic buildings that house boutiques, craft shops, and restaurants. Park Road, in the inner suburb of **Milton,** has some cute cafés and shops.

2 Getting Around

BY PUBLIC TRANSPORTATION Brisbane is well served by public buses, suburban trains, and cross-river ferries. In addition, a **City Sights** specialty bus makes the rounds of the major attractions. This handy transport operates Sunday to Friday from 9am to 4pm and costs A$12 (U.S. $9.60) for adults and A$8 (U.S. $6.40) for children. See also "Organized Tours" in "Attractions" later in this chapter.

By Bus The Brisbane City Council operates a service throughout the city and suburban areas. Buses operate Monday to Friday from 5:30am to 11pm, with reduced frequency on weekends. Timetables and information are available from the **Public Transport Information Centre,** Brisbane Administration Centre, at the corner of George and Ann streets (☎ 13 12 30 or 07/3225 4444), or the information kiosk in the Queen Street Mall. A single-zone ticket costs A$1.20 (U.S. 96¢) for adults and A60¢ (U.S. 48¢) for children. A special reduced-price **City Heart fare** of A60¢ (U.S. 48¢) is available in the central business district; bus stops in this zone display a sign with a red heart in a black triangle. **Off Peak Saver** tickets cost A$3 (U.S. $2.40) and provide unlimited bus and ferry travel for one day Monday to Friday between 9am and 3:30pm and after 7pm and all day weekends and holidays. **Day Rover** tickets (A$5.50/U.S. $4.40) can be used at any time.

By Train Brisbane's suburban trains service a wide area and operate daily from 4:30am to 1:30am. Maps and timetables are available from the information desk at the **Central Railway Station,** Ann Street (☎ 07/3235 2222). **Day Rover** tickets are available.

By Ferry Cross-river ferries operate from several places, including South Bank, Edward Street, Eagle Street, and the Riverside Centre, at approximately 15-minute intervals. Individual tickets cost A$1.20 (U.S. 96¢) and a book of 10 adult tickets, the **Ferry Fare Saver,** is A$9 (U.S. $7.20). For information, call the **Brisbane City Council Ferries** (☎ 13 12 30 or 07/3399 4768).

BY TAXI The five major cab companies, all operating 24 hours a day, are **Ascot Taxi Service** (☎ 07/3213 1222), **Black and White Cab Company**

Brisbane

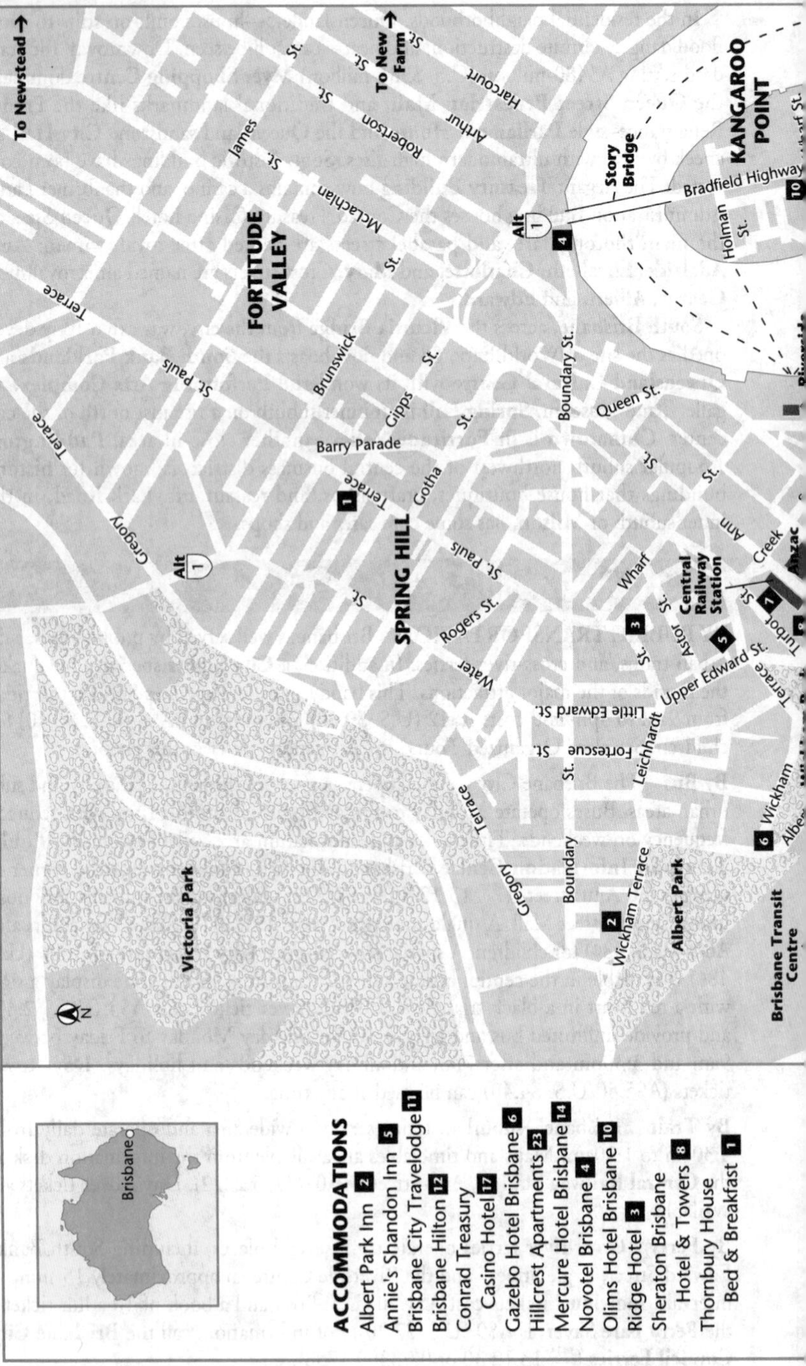
ACCOMMODATIONS
Albert Park Inn 2
Annie's Shandon Inn 5
Brisbane City Travelodge 11
Brisbane Hilton 12
Conrad Treasury Casino Hotel 17
Gazebo Hotel Brisbane 6
Hillcrest Apartments 23
Mercure Hotel Brisbane 14
Novotel Brisbane 4
Olims Hotel Brisbane 10
Ridge Hotel 3
Sheraton Brisbane Hotel & Towers 8
Thornbury House Bed & Breakfast 1
Brisbane
To Newstead →
To New Farm →
FORTITUDE VALLEY
SPRING HILL
KANGAROO POINT
Story Bridge
Bradfield Highway
Victoria Park
Albert Park
Brisbane Transit Centre
Central Railway Station
Boundary St.
Wickham Terrace
Gregory Terrace
St. Pauls Terrace
Brunswick St.
Gipps St.
Barry Parade
Gotha St.
Water St.
Rogers St.
Queen St.
Ann St.
Wharf St.
Astor St.
Upper Edward St.
Little Edward St.
Fortescue St.
Leichhardt St.
Turbot St.
Creek St.
James St.
McLachlan St.
Robertson St.
Arthur St.
Harcourt St.
Holman St.
Alt 1

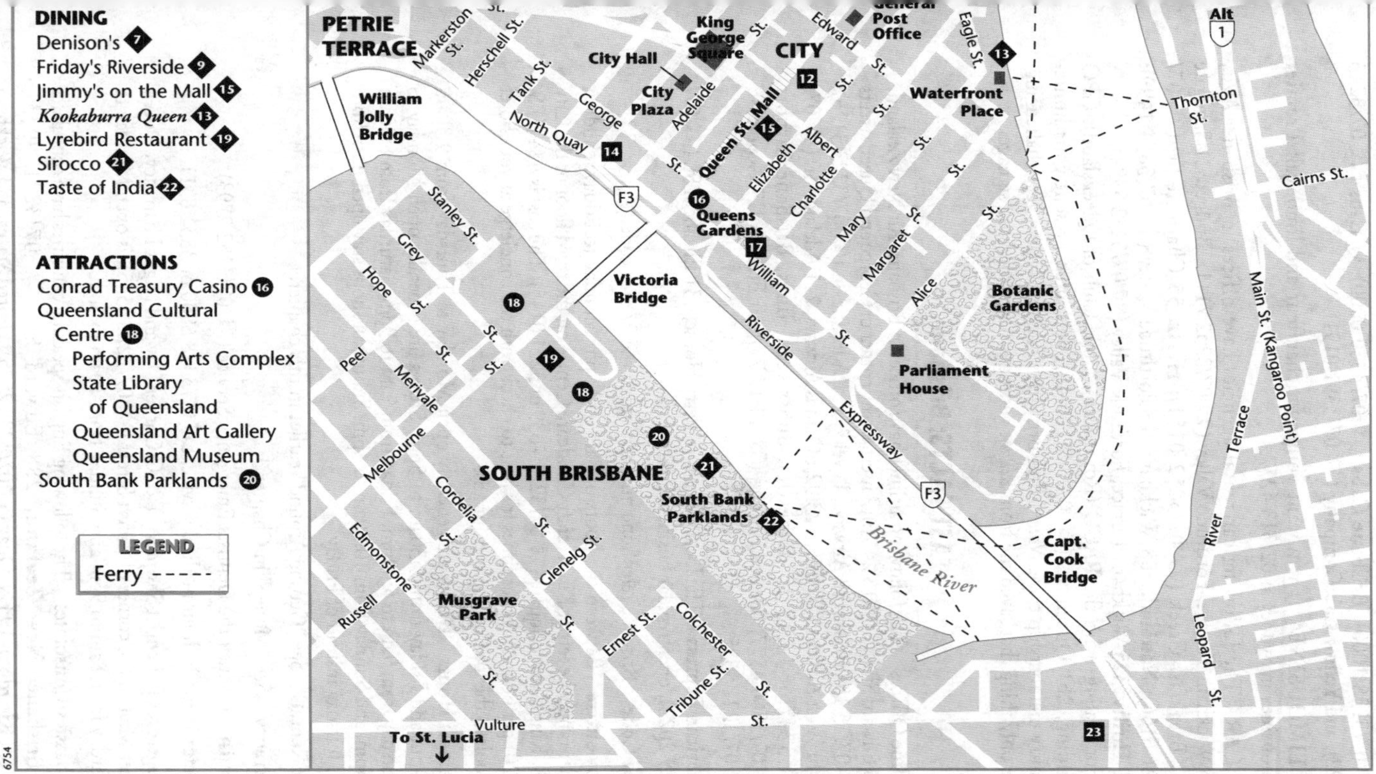

DINING
Denison's 7
Friday's Riverside 9
Jimmy's on the Mall 15
Kookaburra Queen 13
Lyrebird Restaurant 19
Sirocco 21
Taste of India 22
ATTRACTIONS
Conrad Treasury Casino 16
Queensland Cultural Centre 18
Performing Arts Complex
State Library of Queensland
Queensland Art Gallery
Queensland Museum
South Bank Parklands 20
LEGEND
Ferry
PETRIE TERRACE
William Jolly Bridge
Markerston St.
Herschell St.
Tank St.
George
North Quay
City Hall
City Plaza
King George Square
Adelaide
CITY
Edward
Post Office
Eagle St.
Waterfront Place
Queen St. Mall
Elizabeth
Albert
Charlotte
Mary
Margaret
Alice
Queens Gardens
William
Riverside
Expressway
F3
Victoria Bridge
Botanic Gardens
Parliament House
Capt. Cook Bridge
Brisbane River
Thornton St.
Alt 1
Cairns St.
Main St. (Kangaroo Point)
River Terrace
Leopard St.
Stanley St.
Grey
Hope
Peel
Merivale
Melbourne
Cordelia
Glenelg St.
Edmonstone
Russell
Musgrave Park
Ernest St.
Colchester
Tribune St.
Vulture St.
To St. Lucia
SOUTH BRISBANE
South Bank Parklands
6754

(☎ 07/3238 1000), **Brisbane Cabs** (☎ 07/3360 0000), **Q Cabs** (☎ 07/3213 1222), and **Yellow Cab Company** (☎ 07/3391 0191).

BY LIMOUSINE If you want your own chauffeur and limo, call **Premier Limousines** in Sydney at 02/313 4277.

BY CAR The following car-rental agencies have offices in Brisbane: **Avis,** 275 Wickham Terrace, Fortitude Valley (☎ 07/3252 7111); **Budget,** 21 Sandgate Rd., Breakfast Creek (☎ 07/3252 0151); **Hertz,** 55 Charlotte St. (☎ 07/3221 6166); **National,** 388 Wickham St., Fortitude Valley (☎ 07/3854 1499); and **Thrifty,** 325 Wickham Terrace, Fortitude Valley (☎ 07/3252 5994).

For dealings with the **RACQ** (Royal Automobile Club of Queensland), GPO Building, 261 Queen St. (☎ 07/3361 2444), you must present your home-country membership card. *Note:* I find Brisbane's one-way system very challenging. The only thing that saved me from *always* getting lost was the good signage.

FAST FACTS: Brisbane

Airline Offices The following airlines have offices in Brisbane: Air New Zealand, 288 Edward St. (☎ 07/13 24 76); Ansett, at the corner of George and Queen streets (☎ 07/13 13 00); British Airways, Level 7, 241 Adelaide St. (☎ 07/3223 3123); Flight West Airlines (☎ 07/13 23 92); Qantas Airways, 241 Adelaide St. (☎ 07/234 3747 or 13 13 13 domestic); Sunstate Airlines, Brisbane Airport (☎ 07/3860 4577); United Airlines (☎ 13 17 77); Air France, 217 George St. (☎ 07/3221 5655).

American Express The local office is in Perry House, 131 Elizabeth St. (☎ 07/3229 2022), open regular business hours.

Area Code Brisbane telephone numbers are in the 07 area code.

Baby-sitters Between the hours of 8am and 5pm Monday to Friday, children under 6 may be left at Kindercraft Childcare Centre on the third floor of the City Hall, King George Square (☎ 07/3221 7639 or 3221 0145). The cost is A$4 (U.S. $3.20) per hour. At other times it's best to check with the concierge at your hotel or look in the local newspaper for ads.

Business Hours **Banks** are generally open Monday to Thursday from 9:30am to 4pm and Friday from 9:30am to 5pm. **Stores** are generally open Monday to Thursday from 9am to 5:30pm, Friday from 9am to 9pm, Saturday from 8:30am to 4pm, and Sunday from 10:30am to 4pm. Suburban shops stay open until 9pm on Thursday instead of Friday.

Car Rentals See "Getting Around" earlier in this chapter.

Currency See "Money" in Chapter 3.

Dentist Contact the Dentists Emergency Service (☎ 07/3252 2793).

Doctor For 24-hour medical service, call 07/3378 6900 or 3831 8311.

Drugstores (Chemist Shops) T & G Corner Day and Night Pharmacy, Queen Street Mall, at the corner of Albert Street (☎ 07/3221 4585), is open Monday to Saturday from 8am to 9pm and Sunday from 10am to 5pm.

Embassies/Consulates The following English-speaking countries have consulates in Brisbane: **New Zealand,** 288 Edward St. (☎ 07/3221 9933); **United Kingdom,** 193 N. Quay (☎ 07/3236 2575); **United States,** 383 Wickham Terrace (☎ 07/3839 8955).

Emergencies Dial **000** to summon an ambulance, the fire department, or the police in an emergency.

Eyeglasses Eyewear Now, Shop 17 in the Myer Centre (☎ 07/3221 4055), is open Monday to Thursday from 8:30am to 5:30pm, Friday from 8:30am to 9pm, and Saturday from 8:30am to 4pm. It can make new prescription lenses in an hour.

Holidays See "When to Go" in Chapter 3.

Hospitals Royal Brisbane Hospital, Herston Road, Herston (☎ 07/3253 8111), is about 10 minutes from the city center.

Hotlines If you're in need, call the Brisbane Crisis Line (☎ 07/3252 1111) or the Rape Crisis Line (☎ 07/3844 4008).

Information See "Visitor Information" earlier in this chapter.

Laundry/Dry Cleaning Alex's Laundromat, at the corner of Gympie Road and Boothby Street, Kedron (☎ 07/3359 3059), is open daily from 5:30am to 10pm. Same-day service is available from the dry cleaner in the Myer Centre, Shop 18 (☎ 07/3221 5742).

Libraries The State Library of Queensland, in the Cultural Centre (☎ 07/3840 7666), is open Sunday to Friday from 10am to 5pm.

Luggage Storage/Lockers There are lockers on the third floor of the Transit Centre, Roma Street (☎ 07/3236 1400).

Newspapers/Magazines The *Courier-Mail* is the major metropolitan daily. *The Australian* is a nationwide daily. A wide range of overseas and domestic newspapers and magazines is available at Currans Corner Souvenirs, at the corner of Adelaide and Edward streets (☎ 07/3229 3690). Currans is open daily from 8am to 9pm.

Photographic Needs Camera Tech, 270 Adelaide St. (☎ 07/3229 5406), does repairs on the premises and gives free estimates.

Postal Code Central Brisbane addresses have a 4000 postal code.

Post Office The General Post Office (GPO), 261 Queen St. (☎ 07/3405 1202), is open Monday to Friday from 7am to 7pm. Other post offices in the city, such as the one in the Transit Centre, are open Monday to Friday from 9am to 5pm. Use the GPO for general delivery (poste restante).

Radio Classical, 106.1 FM or 103.7 FM; country western, 101.1 FM; news and weather, 612 AM; rock, 105.3 FM, 104.5 FM, or 1008 AM.

Taxes No sales tax or Goods and Services Tax (GST) is added to purchases. Neither is there a hotel tax.

Taxis See "Getting Around" earlier in this chapter.

Telegrams/Telex These can be sent from the GPO (see "Post Office" above).

Television Brisbane receives Channels 2, 7, 9, 10, and SBS. For more information, see "Fast Facts: Sydney" in Chapter 4.

Transit Information If you have bus or ferry questions, call TransInfo at 13 12 30. Address queries about suburban train service to 07/3235 2222.

Useful Telephone Numbers Weather information, 1196; time, 1194; Tourist Infoline, 11 654; B105 FM News Service, 1197; Brisbane Entertainment Centre, 11 611; Women's Community Health Centre, 07/3844 1935; Women's Information Service, 07/3229 1580; Gay and Lesbian Counselling and Information Service, 07/3844 2967.

3 Accommodations

Those on a tight budget who are coming to Brisbane from Sydney will be pleasantly surprised—the hotels and motels in Brisbane generally cost less than those in Sydney. And the quality standards are quite good, with a wide range available—from top class to inexpensive.

If you'd like to stay with a local family in their home, contact **National Bed & Breakfast Reservations**, 75 Kamerunga Rd., Stratford, QLD 4870 (☎ 070/55 1123; fax 070/58 1990). Bed-and-breakfast in city, town, and country homes in and around Brisbane, as well as in other parts of Queensland, can be arranged. You might also like to order a copy of the 253-page ***A Guide to Bed & Breakfast Australia & New Zealand*** from from The Crossing Press, 97 Hangar Way, Watsonville, CA 95076 (☎ 408/722-0711; fax 408/722-2749). This guide, which costs A$12.95 in Australia or U.S. $9.95 in the United States, gives details for arranging farmstays, homestays, and guesthouse stays all around Australia and New Zealand, with an emphasis on Queensland.

IN THE CITY CENTER

VERY EXPENSIVE

✪ **Conrad Treasury Casino Hotel.** William Street, Brisbane, QLD 4001. ☎ **07/3306 8888.** Fax 07/3306 8880. 97 rms and suites. A/C MINIBAR TV TEL. A$280–A$400 (U.S. $224–$320) double; A$675–A$975 (U.S. $540–$780) suite. Children free in parents' room. Ask about weekend packages. AE, BC, DC, MC, V. Parking A$12 (U.S. $9.60).

If you think all casino hotels are chrome-and-glass neon nightmares, think again. Brisbane's Conrad Treasury Casino occupies two of the city's most beloved historic buildings. The hotel is in the former Lands Administration Building, a prime example of Edwardian Baroque architecture. It was constructed in 1905, housed the premier and cabinet until 1971, and was the first permanent home of the Queensland National Art Gallery. The hotel feels like a beautiful home, especially in the carpeted lobby, where the traditional furnishings are in conversation areas. My room had a 15-foot-plus ceiling, a view over Queens Park, terry robes, a hairdryer, an iron and ironing board, a safe, a good-size desk, and a large marble bath with an excellent lighted makeup/shaving mirror. My only complaint was that the spacious quarters made it a challenge to work the remote-control TV from the bed. The central location is another big plus.

Dining/Entertainment: Ryans on the Park serves contemporary Australian cuisine. The Gallery Bar is a great spot for a drink (see "Brisbane After Dark" later in this chapter). In addition to the dining and drinking options in the hotel, three restaurants and several bars can be found steps away in the casino.

Services: 24-hour room service, daily newspaper delivery, twice-daily maid service, laundry/dry cleaning, concierge, valet parking, baby-sitting, business and secretarial services.

Sheraton Brisbane Hotel & Towers. 249 Turbot St., Brisbane, QLD 4000. ☎ **07/3835 3535.** Fax 07/3835 4960. 386 rms, 25 suites. A/C MINIBAR TV TEL. A$300–A$375 (U.S. $240–$300) double; A$450–A$530 (U.S. $360–$424) suite. Additional person A$55 (U.S. $44) extra. Children free in parents' room. Ask about lower weekend rates. No-smoking floors available. AE, BC, CB, DC, MC, V. Free parking.

The hotel is built over the Central Railway Station in the heart of the city and, as with the Travelodge above the Transit Centre, the train noise cannot be heard. I assumed a hotel over a train station would have a mundane atmosphere, but I was wrong. The lobby is glamorous, with Oriental-pattern carpets, potted palms in brass planters, and overstuffed chairs. A doorman in top hat and tails welcomes guests at the porte cochère.

The Sheraton is really two hotels in one, for aside from the regular rooms, Tower accommodations constitute a kind of hotel within a hotel. These premium quarters are ideal for those who wish special treatment and are happy to pay for it. Personalized stationery, terry robes, upgraded amenities, daily newspaper, and nightly turndown are all provided. In addition, Tower residents can use a special lounge where a butler is on duty from 6am to 1am, hors d'oeuvres and cocktails are served for an hour each evening, local calls are free, and a complimentary breakfast buffet is offered every morning. Rooms in the main part of the Sheraton are also luxurious. Sixteen are outfitted for the handicapped.

Dining/Entertainment: All meals are served daily in the Sidewalk Cafe, where large windows overlook the city and Post Office Square. Denison's, the fine-dining venue, is open for dinner Tuesday to Saturday (see "Dining" later in this chapter). There are six bars, including Someplace Else—which has to be seen to be believed.

Services: Concierge, 24-hour room service, shoeshine, laundry, valet, nightly turndown, massage, baby-sitting.

Facilities: Outdoor pool, health club, sauna, spa (the club is free to Tower guests), squash courts; business center, hair salon, gift shop.

EXPENSIVE

$ Brisbane City Travelodge. Roma Street, Brisbane, QLD 4000. ☎ **07/3238 2222.** Fax 07/3238 2288. 169 rms, 22 king suites. A/C MINIBAR TV TEL. A$160 (U.S. $128) standard double; A$180 (U.S. $144) king suite. Additional person A$20 (U.S. $16) extra. Children under 16 free in parents' room. Ask about weekend discounts and lower rates through Aussie auto clubs. No-smoking floors available. AE, BC, DC, MC, V. Free parking.

Though the hotel is on top of the Transit Centre, where coaches and trains come and go, its rooms are well insulated against noise. The center's dry cleaner, tourist information desk, and food hall are just steps from the hotel. State-of-the-art elevators give time and weather information via an electronic readout, announce other messages with the aid of a computer-operated voice, and whisk guests between floors in a matter of seconds.

The Travelodge is one of Brisbane's best values. This 18-story hotel offers spacious rooms with large windows that frame lofty city views. All quarters feature contemporary blond wood built-in desks and dressers, his-and-hers closets, and pleasing decors of teal and light brown. The staff is unusually helpful and friendly.

Dining/Entertainment: The Jazz-n-Blues Bar is just off the lobby foyer, and the Queenslander public bar is accessed from the Transit Centre; the Eight Plates, a Mediterranean restaurant and bar, is on the fifth floor, and the casual Morton Jacks Bar & Grill is on the second floor.

Services: 24-hour room service, laundry, nightly turndown, baby-sitting.

Facilities: Two hot spas, gym, sauna, self-service laundry.

Brisbane Hilton. 190 Elizabeth St., Brisbane, QLD 4000. ☎ **07/3231 3131,** or 1800/22 2255 in Australia. Fax 07/3231 3199. 321 rms and suites. A/C MINIBAR TV TEL. A$195–A$305 (U.S. $156–$244) double; A$680–A$925 (U.S. $544–$740) suite; A$305 (U.S. $244) executive floor. Additional person A$40 (U.S. $32) extra. Children free in parents' room. Ask about lower weekend rates. No-smoking rooms available. AE, BC, CB, DC, MC, V. Parking A$10 (U.S. $8).

The Hilton is on the Queen Street pedestrian shopping mall. Inside, glass elevators run from the 5th to the 25th floor under Australia's largest glass-domed atrium. All the attractively furnished guest rooms have hairdryers, videos, clock radios, and coffee- and tea-making facilities. Accommodations on the north side have a city view;

south-side rooms have river vistas. Like the Sheraton, the Hilton offers extra pampering and facilities for guests who pay a premium rate: Executive Floor residents are provided with terry robes, free local calls, and complimentary breakfast and evening cocktails, plus a butler on call.

Dining/Entertainment: The Atrium Lounge, with cane chairs and potted palms, is popular with locals as well as visitors. Just off the lobby, it's a convenient and agreeable spot for a drink. The Hilton also offers a piano bar, the open-air Tropicana Restaurant, the America's Cup Bar, the Prince Edward Pub, and Her Majesty's Bar. Dining options range from the casual Atrium Cafe to Victoria's Fine Dining Room.

Service: Concierge, 24-hour room service, laundry, valet, nightly turndown, massage, baby-sitting.

Facilities: Eighth-floor outdoor pool (free), the World Executive Club one level down (free for Executive Floor guests, A$15/U.S. $12 for others), tennis court (free for Executive Floor guests, A$16/U.S. $12.80 for others).

$ Novotel Brisbane. 200 Creek St., Brisbane, QLD 4001. ☎ **07/3309 3309,** or 1800/642 244 in Australia, 800/221-4542 in the U.S. Fax 07/3309 3308. 296 rms and suites. A/C MINIBAR TV TEL. A$170–A$185 (U.S. $136–$148) double; A$250 (U.S. $200) suite. Additional person A$20 (U.S. $16) extra. Children under 16 free in parents' room and get free breakfast. AE, BC, DC, MC, V. Free parking.

No fuss, no muss. Just good-value dining and lodging—that's what this new Novotel offers. The room decors are plain, but all quarters come with modern amenities like hairdryers, irons and ironing boards, remote-control TVs, and in-house movies. All have either king beds or two doubles; each suite has a spa bath, a separate lounge, and a microwave. This is a great spot for families: Kids get a free turn at the extensive breakfast buffet. Fill them up here and they won't want lunch. The only drawback is slightly awkward pedestrian access from the central business district.

Dining/Entertainment: Henri's Brasserie is open daily from 6am to midnight and offers indoor and outdoor dining. The Loose Goose Bar & Cafe is a casual spot for a drink, a light lunch, or coffee and tea. It's open Monday to Saturday. Entertainment is provided in the lobby bar Monday to Saturday.

Services: 24-hour room service, baby-sitting, laundry/dry cleaning, concierge.

Facilities: Business center, outdoor pool, gym, sauna.

MODERATE

Gazebo Hotel Brisbane. 345 Wickham Terrace, Brisbane, QLD 4000. ☎ **07/3831 6177** or 1800/77 7789 in Australia. Fax 07/3832 5919. Reservations can be made through Flag Inns. 167 rms, 13 suites. A/C TV TEL. A$95–A$126 (U.S. $76–$100.80) double; A$160–A$200 (U.S. $128–$160) suite. Additional person A$15 (U.S. $12) extra. Children under 12 free in parents' room. Ask about lower weekend rates and packages and lower rates through Aussie auto clubs. No-smoking rooms available. AE, BC, DC, MC, V. Free parking.

Between the city and the inner suburb of Spring Hill, this hotel is out of the hustle and bustle but within walking distance of shops and sights. Because of the building's contemporary terraced architecture, every room at the 11-story Gazebo has a balcony. These provide lots of fresh air and good views of either the city or the surrounding hills. Only ground-floor quarters lack views. Rooms on two floors lack minibars; 90 rooms have bathtubs; and 13 offer cooking facilities. The hotel has 24-hour room service, but if you'd rather dine out, the Terrace Brasserie is a pleasant coffee shop with indoor and outdoor seating. The Gazebo's other dining option, Wickham's Restaurant on the 10th floor, has a wonderful city-lights view at night. Laundry facilities and a pool are also provided.

Mercure Hotel Brisbane. 85 North Quay, Brisbane, QLD 4000. ☎ **07/3236 3300** or 1800/ 64 2244 in Australia. Fax 07/3236 1035. 175 rms, 15 suites. A/C MINIBAR TV TEL. A$120 (U.S. $96) double; A$150–A$250 (U.S. $120–$200) suite. Additional person A$20 (U.S. $16) extra. No-smoking floors available. AE, BC, DC, MC, V. Free parking.

On the Brisbane River with views across to the beautiful Queensland Cultural Centre and the South Bank Parklands, this 13-story hotel is close to the Conrad Treasury Casino. All rooms feature AM/FM clock radios, coffee- and tea-making facilities, toasters, small refrigerators, and tub/shower combinations. The hotel was completely remodeled in 1988. Floors 9 and 10 are reserved for nonsmokers, and rooms on Floors 4 and 5 lack minibars. The hotel provides in-house movies, 24-hour room service, a pool, a sauna, and a spa.

Gillies Restaurant, an à la carte seafood eatery with an old-world atmosphere created by crystal chandeliers and Louis XVI chairs, is open daily for all meals. The garden terrace area of the piano bar is a great spot for a drink with a river view.

IN SPRING HILL

MODERATE

Albert Park Inn. 551 Wickham Terrace, Spring Hill, QLD 4000. ☎ **07/3831 3111** or 1800/ 77 7702 in Australia. Fax 07/3832 1290. Reservations can be made through Flag Inns. 95 rms. A/C TV TEL. A$88 (U.S. $70.40) double; A$110 (U.S. $88) executive floor. Additional person A$10 (U.S. $8) extra. Children under 18 free in parents' room. Ask about lower weekend rates. No-smoking rooms available. AE, BC, DC, MC, V. Free parking. Bus: 23 or 61.

This hotel's pleasant guest rooms overlook Albert Park, about a 10-minute walk from the city center. It's in the inner suburb of Spring Hill, an interesting older area with many restored terrace houses. The Transit Centre is a kilometer (about half a mile) to the south. The rooms have showers (no tubs), clock radios, coffee- and tea-making facilities, small refrigerators, and queen-size or double beds. Room service is available 24 hours a day. Guests also have use of the pool and business center. Albert Park's restaurant serves all meals Monday to Saturday.

Ridge Hotel. 189 Leichhardt St. (at the corner of Henry St.), Spring Hill, QLD 4000. ☎ **07/ 3831 5000,** 07/3832 2589, or 1800/07 7777 in Australia. Fax 07/3832 2589. 63 rms, 21 suites. A/C MINIBAR TV TEL. A$110 (U.S. $88) double; A$125 (U.S. $100) suite. Additional person A$10 (U.S. $8) extra. Ask about weekend discounts and lower rates through Aussie auto clubs. AE, BC, DC, MC, V. Free parking. Bus: City precinct express bus.

On the edge of the city center near the inner suburb of Spring Hill, this 10-story hotel has large family suites that are ideal if four or five of you are traveling together. Each large unit has a kitchenette that's well stocked with dishes and cutlery; a table and chairs; and a generous amount of closet space. There are also regular rooms without cooking facilities. All quarters have showers only, and beds are either queen-size or twin. Every room has a clock radio, coffee- and tea-making facilities, and a small refrigerator. Guests are also provided with 24-hour room service and use of the hotel's laundry room and pool.

The Rooftop Restaurant, with a great city view, is one of the few dining spots in Brisbane with live dance music: On Friday and Saturday nights a band and vocalist present traditional music. Breakfast is served daily in this room, and Italian fare is offered at lunch Monday to Friday and dinner nightly.

$ **Thornbury House Bed & Breakfast.** 1 Thornbury Street, Spring Hill, Brisbane, QLD 4000. ☎ **07/3832 5985.** Fax 07/3832 5985. 9 rms (1 with bath). TV. A$80 (U.S. $64) double without bath, A$85 (U.S. $68) double with bath. Rates include breakfast. AE, BC, MC, V. No smoking allowed. Bus: 108. Parking free off street.

Stairs makes this a poor choice for the handicapped, but it's a good place for thrifty folks who don't mind sharing the three baths and using the hall's pay phone. Hostess Michelle Mullens provides bathrobes, serves a good breakfast, and lets guests use her laundry facilities, microwave, and refrigerator. The atmosphere is cheerful, light, and bright. The rooms are simply furnished, but each has a TV and is more than adequate. The bed and bath linens, including doonas, are very good quality. The one double room with a bath is especially good value; I'd avoid the upstairs quarters because you have to walk downstairs to the bath.

INEXPENSIVE

Annie's Shandon Inn. 405 Upper Edward St., Brisbane, QLD 4000. ☎ **07/3831 8684.** Fax 07/3831 3073. 19 rms (4 with bath). A$48–A$58 (U.S. $38.40–$46.40) double. Additional adult A$10 (U.S. $8) extra; additional child A$5 (U.S. $4) extra. Rates include continental breakfast. AE, BC, MC, V. Free parking.

On the edge of the city center, Annie's Shandon Inn is owned by Carmel Nicholson, whose grandmother came from Ireland in 1888. "She worked as a maid in this hotel, which was called Shandon then," the proprietor told me. "Later she borrowed money from Irish bank managers and bought the place." The property, built in 1854, is one of the oldest in Brisbane and has an eye-catching blue stucco exterior with pink shutters. Carmel has decorated the B&B's rooms with coordinated country-print curtains, bedspreads, and sheets. The rooms are charming but not large; eight have sinks and four have a shower, sink, and toilet. There's no smoking in the communal breakfast and TV rooms. The downstairs hall is lined with old family photos, and the proprietress, who is exceptionally friendly and cheerful, never seems to tire of telling guests about them.

IN SOUTH BRISBANE

Hillcrest Apartments. 311 Vulture St., South Brisbane, QLD 4101. ☎ **07/3846 3000,** or 1800/07 7777 in Australia. Fax 07/3846 3578. 80 units. A/C TV TEL. A$79–A$109 (U.S. $63.20–$87.20) double. Ask about weekly and monthly discounts and lower rates through Aussie auto clubs. AE, BC, DC, MC, V. Free parking. Bus: 160, 170, or 180.

These spacious, modern apartments are very good value for folks who wish all the comforts of home when they travel. All but 16 units have full kitchens, and the two-bedroom apartments have washing machines and dryers. Some quarters have tub/showers, some just showers, and a choice of either one queen-size bed or two singles is offered. The contemporary decors of pale gray and aqua include stylish furnishings imported from Italy. All two-bedroom apartments have balconies, and all but a few units have wonderful city/river outlooks. All guests have access to the pool, tennis court, sauna, spa, games room, and playground. One apartment in the nine-story building is equipped for the handicapped.

A bistro in the lobby is open for breakfast and casual dinners. Some guests take their meals up to their apartments, while others carry them out to the pool area.

IN KANGAROO POINT

Olims Hotel Brisbane. 355 Main St., Kangaroo Point, QLD 4169. ☎ **07/3217 3366.** Fax 07/3217 4122. 91 rms. A/C MINIBAR TV TEL. A$79 (U.S. $63.20) double. Additional person A$12 (U.S. $9.60) extra. No-smoking rooms available. AE, BC, DC, MC, V. Free parking. Bus: 30, 31, or 367. Ferry: From the foot of Edward Street to Thornton Street.

This eight-story motor inn is on the south bank of the Brisbane River, and many of the rooms have excellent views across to the city and Botanic Gardens. Accommodations are divided between the riverside block, with the best views, and a tall building behind it. The rooms are spacious, with contemporary decors. Ladies' quarters, with special accessories, are available. Guests have the use of a pool and laundry room.

The Restaurant, above the riverside section, affords a breathtaking view and is open for breakfast daily, lunch during the week, and dinner nightly. Limited room service is offered.

IN SUBURBAN BRISBANE

Boomajarril. 58 Derby St., Hendra, Brisbane, QLD 4011. ☎ **07/3268 5764.** Fax 07/ 3268 2064. 3 rms. A$220 (U.S. $176) double. Rates include breakfast. A$50 per person for three-course dinner (BYO). BC, DC, MC, V.

This elegant turn-of-the-century home provides an unusual lodging option. Dianna and Jack Smart welcome guests; serve a three-course, silver-service breakfast; offer afternoon tea; lead neighborhood walks to see interesting Queensland mansions; and can arrange golf at private courses. The decor of their house includes traditional furnishings, antiques, Oriental rugs, original art, crystal, fine china, and fresh flowers. More silver serving pieces and flatware grace their breakfast table—where Jack's porridge (oatmeal) and Dianna's omelets compete for attention—than I use for big Thanksgiving dinners. One double guest room opens onto a terrace overlooking the pool; the middle room has a half-tester bed; the front room is the largest but gets some traffic noise. Each comes with decanters of filtered water and sherry and a slate-floored bath. It's 15 minutes from here to central Brisbane by car. The airport is nearby, as are several nice dining spots.

4 Dining

I must confess that I expected Australia's best restaurants to be in Sydney and Melbourne, an idea reinforced by residents of those southern cities, so I was pleasantly surprised to stumble onto some incredibly good dining spots in Brisbane. For the most part, they're unpretentious, but dish for dish they more than hold their own. The seafood places are especially wonderful and offer you an opportunity to sample local specialties like Moreton Bay bugs (a delectable shellfish with a flavor similar to that of lobster), Queensland mud crabs, and fresh fish from the Great Barrier Reef. The Sunshine State's tropical products—pawpaws (papayas), mangoes, pineapples, and avocados—also come as an unexpected treat, as does the excellent beef.

I particularly enjoy dining in the **South Bank Parklands,** where all the restaurants have a good view across the river to the city. Besides those below, look for **Ned Kelly's Bush Tucker** in the Boardwalk area and **Wang Dynasty** and **Cafe San Marco** in the Riverside area.

Another good area for restaurants is **Park Road,** in the inner suburb of Milton, where chic bistros line both sides of the street for a couple of blocks.

IN THE CITY CENTER

EXPENSIVE

Denison's. In the Sheraton Brisbane Hotel & Towers, 249 Turbot St. ☎ **07/3835 3535.** Reservations recommended at all times, required on weekends. Main courses A$19–A$30 (U.S. $15.20–$24). AE, BC, DC, MC, V. Tues–Sat 6:30–10pm. Train: Central Station. MODERN INTERNATIONAL.

On the 30th floor of the Sheraton and approached via glass-walled elevators, this eatery provides mountain views from the dining area and city vistas from the cocktail lounge. The decor is formal and yet warm; imported linen and silver and fine crystal appear on every table. Tropical Queensland foliage is the subject of an etched-glass panel that forms one wall of the restaurant.

The menu includes dishes like lemongrass-flavored barramundi filets baked in parchment and king prawns braised in young cabbage leaves. Beluga caviar served in ice with Russian vodka, roast wild duck with green-apple Rosti and cassis sauce, and venison medallions with morel cream sauce and candied chestnuts are also available. The restaurant's extensive wine list includes a large number of domestic and imported vintages.

MODERATE

Friday's Riverside. 123 Eagle St. ☎ **07/3832 2122.** Reservations recommended, especially for lunchtime window table in Friday's East. Main courses A$5.95–A$19.50 (U.S. $4.75–$15.60); luncheon buffet A$24 (U.S. $19.20). AE, BC, DC, MC, V. Sun–Fri 11:30am–10pm, Sat 5–10pm. Ferry: Riverside Centre. Bus: City Circle. CONTEMPORARY INTERNATIONAL.

Friday's Riverside is really three contemporary-style restaurants in one. The complex enjoys a delightful location on the north bank of the Brisbane River adjacent to the 40-story ultramodern Riverside Centre office tower. From the second-floor site, diners can watch the movement of boats of all sizes and types.

Club Friday's is an outside charcoal grill where the lunch and dinner menus include hamburgers, pastas, fish and chips, salads, seafood, and grain-fed Queensland beef. This is also a popular spot for Sunday brunch. An extensive smorgasbord lunch of international cuisines is offered in Friday's East, and the restaurant is transformed into a nightclub after dark. Friday's West, specializing in steaks and grills, is popular with those wanting a light meal or a quick snack and is open only Monday to Friday at lunch. Friday's East has the most extensive wine list.

Jimmy's on the Mall. Queen Street Mall. ☎ **07/3229 9999.** Reservations not required. Main courses A$8.90–A$18.90 (U.S. $7.10–$15.10); kids' meals A$4.50–A$7.90 (U.S. $3.60–$6.35); snacks A$4–A$5 (U.S. $3.20–$4). Weekend and public holiday surcharge 20%. BC, MC, V. Daily 24 hours. Bus: Any bus to Queen Street Station. CONTEMPORARY INTERNATIONAL.

There are three Jimmy's, one at either end of the plaza and one in the middle. Their location in the city center and reasonable prices contribute to their popularity. All are casual, with friendly staff. The menu has breakfast dishes as well as lunch, dinner, and supper items. Fancy cocktails with Queensland's good fresh fruit are a specialty, as is seafood, which the proprietor buys direct at the market each morning. Bagels, baguettes, and croissants can be filled with pàté, smoked salmon, prawns, or several other choices (sadly, on a recent occassion my bagel arrived cold, but I've come to think of this as an occupational hazard). You can also choose from nachos with melted cheese, chili sauce, and sour cream; spicy Singapore noodles; or a Weight Watcher's salad. Main courses include sea perch, pasta, and sirloin steak.

IN NEWSTEAD & ALBION

EXPENSIVE

Roseville Restaurant. 56 Chester St., Newstead. ☎ **07/3358 1377.** Reservations recommended. Main courses A$16.50–A$22 (U.S. $13.20–$17.60); fixed-price three-course meal A$25 (U.S. $20) at lunch, A$29.50 (U.S. $23.60) at dinner. AE, BC, DC, MC, V. Mon–Fri 10:30am–noon (tea) and 11:30am–2:30pm (lunch); Mon–Sat 6pm–closing (dinner). INTERNATIONAL.

It's hard to know where to start describing this charming restaurant. The Victorian colonial house, restored by previous owners, has high ceilings, crystal chandeliers, stained-glass windows, and other earmarks of homes constructed in the early 1880s. Diners are seated in six rooms of the house and on the veranda. Outside tables have floral cloths; inside, lace cloths and bouquets of fresh flowers complement English and Australian antiques and an impressive collection of 16th- and 17th-century oil portraits in heavy gilded frames.

While the house is impressive, it's the one-acre gardens that continue to win awards—300 rosebushes, 100 azaleas, and assorted flowers and shrubs. September to March are the best months for a visit. Most things are in bloom then, including the century-old magnolia in front of the house.

The cuisine and service are equal to the gracious setting and have won their share of awards. Tuxedoed waiters with red bow ties deliver superb gourmet dishes. You might choose something exotic, like Windsor royale—lamb brains in a light beer batter with a sauce of bourbon and pink peppercorns—or a more basic dish like roast beef and Yorkshire pudding. I can attest to the delectability of reef Sotheby, fresh filets of reef fish pocketed with sea scallops and served with a sauce of dill and white wine.

Moderate

Breakfast Creek Wharf Seafood Restaurant. 192 Breakfast Creek Rd., Newstead. ☎ **07/3252 2451.** Reservations not accepted. Main courses A$14.50–A$19.75 (U.S. $11.60–$15.80); kids' meals A$7.95 (U.S. $6.35). Public holiday surcharge A$2.50 (U.S. $2) per adult. AE, BC, DC, MC, V. Mon–Sat noon–2:30pm and 6–10pm, Sun 8am–9pm. SEAFOOD.

Breakfast Creek Wharf is located in the suburb of Newstead on the banks of Breakfast Creek, a stream that feeds into the Brisbane River. The waterfront setting is appropriate for a restaurant that specializes in fresh Australian seafood and has a 19th-century nautical motif. Seating is both inside and out, and a ship's wheel, portholes, and wooden floors help create a briny atmosphere. The focal point of the restaurant is a full-scale reproduction of the vessel used by early explorer John Oxley.

The house specialty is the Flagship Platter, a tray for two or more people containing a combination of cold and hot seafood, including whole Moreton Bay bugs, Queensland sand crabs, calamari, oysters, scallops, filets of fish, and large prawns. Other popular items on the tabloid-style menu are coral trout, sea perch, barramundi, crayfish, and whole lemon sole. There's a good wine list.

Inexpensive

$ **Breakfast Creek Hotel.** 2 Kingsford Smith Dr., Albion. ☎ **07/3262 5988.** Reservations not accepted. Main courses A$11.90–A$14.80 (U.S. $9.50–$11.80). AE, BC, DC, MC, V. Meals, Mon–Fri noon–2:30pm and 5:30–9:30pm, Sat 5–9:30pm, Sun 5–8:30pm. Pub, Mon–Thurs 10am–10pm, Fri–Sat 10am–11pm, Sun 11am–6pm. AUSTRALIAN BARBECUE.

"Everyone goes to the Breckie Creek for a steak after a footie match," an Australian friend informed me. Well, *I* don't eat steak but figured I'd better go anyway and see why this place has been a Brisbane favorite for decades. What I found are huge portions and a jolly crowd having a great time. To describe this place as casual would be an understatement. Diners sit on plastic chairs at oilcloth-covered umbrella-shaded tables on a concrete floor. The stated minimum dress is "shorts, T-shirt, and thongs." My non-steak position turned out not to be a problem: sea perch, barbecued chicken, and grilled ham steak are served in addition to rump, T-bone, Scotch filet, and eye filet steaks. No matter what you order, it'll arrive with a jacket (baked) potato, salad, bread, and coffee if you want it. The procedure is to order and pay at the counter.

Readers Recommend

Sirocco, part of the Waterways Cafes-North in South Bank Parklands (☎ 07/3846 1803). *"Next time you're in Brisbane visit Sirocco, a Mediterranean café. I guarantee their quality."*

—Bruce Faecher, San Luis Obispo, Calif., U.S.A.

Food Courts

At the Riverside Centre on Eagle Street, **On the Deck** (☎ 07/3833 2333) is an economical eatery where a dozen or so outlets sell a variety of food; seating is in a central area. **Designer Sandwiches** cost about A$4 (U.S. $3.20) and **Dr. Wok's** combination plate is less than A$8 (U.S. $6.40). **Cappucines** sells wonderful cappuccino, and **Mediterrani** offers pastas, moussaka, pizzas, and other southern European treats. On the Deck is open Monday to Friday from 7am to 4pm and Sunday from 10am to 3pm. You can dine indoors or out, and most tables have a river view. Get there on a City Circle bus or a ferry.

Other economical places to eat are the **City Plaza food court** on Adelaide near George Street, where there's also a **Starbucks; Eatz on Broadway** on the Mall; and **Level E,** in the Meyer Centre, where the food court includes a **Mrs. Fields.**

The wait staff deliver meals and take drink orders. Have a Fourex (XXXX)—you're in Queensland.

IN MT. COOT-THA PARK

EXPENSIVE

Mt. Coot-tha Summit Restaurant. Sir Samuel Griffith Drive, Mt. Coot-tha "At the Lookout." ☎ **07/3369 9922**, ext. 23. Reservations recommended. Main courses A$17.90–A$24.90 (U.S. $14.30–$19.90); fixed-price three-course lunch A$24.50 (U.S. $19.60). Public holiday surcharge 10%. AE, BC, DC, MC, V. Daily 10am–10pm. INTERNATIONAL.

Located 8km (5 miles) from the city, this restaurant offers both a splendid view of Brisbane's skyline and delicious meals served in a charming old-world atmosphere. It's housed in a renovated summer home and caretaker's cottage constructed by the Brisbane City Council in the 1920s. The wife of one of the park's first caretakers began serving teas to visitors more than 100 years ago, a tradition continued to the present day.

Entrees (appetizers) include barbecued prawns, oysters, fresh pasta, and mountain mushrooms. Main courses range from chicken-and-prawn roulade to steak and crayfish, pork Normandy, and Moreton Bay bugs in seafood mousse (sweet lobsterlike shellfish with a heavenly flavor). All main courses are served with vegetables or a generous tossed green salad; wonderful whole-grain rolls, baked on the premises, are accompanied by a variety of spreads. The setting is charming, the service good, and the food delicious. A taxi to Mt. Coot-tha costs about A$10 (U.S. $8). Adjacent to the restaurant is the Kuta Cafe and a very nice craft shop (below).

INEXPENSIVE

$ **Kuta Cafe.** Sir Samuel Griffith Drive, Mt. Coot-tha "At the Lookout." ☎ **07/3369 9922.** Reservations not accepted. Lunch and dinner A$5.50–A$9.90 (U.S. $4.40–$7.90); sandwiches A$3–A$5 (U.S. $2.40–$4). AE, BC, DC, MC, V. Daily 8am–11pm, noon–2pm, and 6–9pm. CAFE.

Nestled between the more expensive Mt. Coot-tha Summit Restaurant (above) and the lookout platform, this cute little café is a dollarwise diner's dream. Here you can overlook a million-dollar view while enjoying a deli-style sandwich or an inexpensive hot meal. Unlike many eateries in this price category, Kute Cafe is fully licensed, so you can enjoy a drink while savoring the vista. Seating is inside, with ceiling fans in summer and heaters in winter, or outside. Be sure to notice the Aboriginal mosaic design inlaid on the floor. The lunch and dinner buffet includes such dishes as macaroni and cheese, lemon chicken breast, lamb chops, and shepherd's pie.

IN ST. LUCIA

MODERATE

Pasta Pasta Etc. Etc.. 242 Hawken Dr. ☎ **07/3371 1403.** Reservations recommended. Full meal under A$12 (U.S. $9.60). AE, BC, DC, MC, V. Sun–Thurs 11am–9:30pm, Fri–Sat 11am–10pm. Bus: Cityxpress 11/12 or 512. PASTA/DESSERTS.

Pasta Pasta is a colorful lively spot for moderately priced pasta meals, wonderful ice cream, and fun. Everything is made on the premises: the ice cream from an egg-custard base and also the sorbets. Very fresh eggs, herbs, and produce contribute to the ultimate success of dishes. Salads and garlic bread are also available. Luscious cakes go with the ice cream, which comes in a creative assortment of flavors. You can eat in or take out. BYO (there's a bottle shop across the road).

IN SOUTH BRISBANE

MODERATE

Lyrebird Restaurant. In the Performing Arts Complex on the south bank of the Brisbane River. ☎ **07/3846 2434,** ext. 23. Reservations recommended. Main courses A$10.90–A$19 (U.S. $8.70–$15.20); two-course pretheater meal A$27.50 (U.S. $22). Public holiday surcharge 15%. AE, BC, DC, MC, V. Mon–Sat noon–2pm; 5:30–midnight on performance nights. Bus: Cityxpress 502 or others. INTERNATIONAL.

The Lyrebird is an ideal spot for pretheater and posttheater dining. The casual bistro overlooks one of the plazas in the complex where a fountain sends up a cooling spray. The Lyrebird offers the convenient option of a meal immediately before a performance, followed by dessert after the show. It's also handy because it sells a dozen or so very good wines by the glass, so a concertgoing duo doesn't feel compelled to split a bottle of wine with dinner. If you dine here, you can choose barramundi filet, prime eye filet, prune-stuffed chicken breast, or an onion tart with stuffed mushrooms.

The nearby **Promenade Cafe** (☎ 07/840 7575) offers a less expensive, even more casual option for those who want light meals or snacks. Most seating is out by a fountain. This inexpensive eatery is open Monday to Saturday from 10am to 4pm and until curtain time on performance nights.

Tastes of India. The Boardwalk, South Bank Parklands. ☎ **07/3846 1866** or 3846 7033. Reservations accepted. Main courses A$11.80–A$18.80 (U.S. $9.44–$15). BC, DC, MC, V. Daily 11am–11pm (11am–3pm lunch buffet). Ferry: South Bank. INDIAN.

I love Indian food, and I've had better than what they serve here, but not with this great view of the river and the city beyond. You might like to try chicken sagwala (boneless chicken, spinach, and mild curry), prawns masala, or a vegetarian dish like dhaal (yellow lentils cooked with herbs, onion, garlic, and cumin). Palak paneer—cottage cheese, spinach, onion, and curry—is another good chice. The menu also includes three non-Indian dishes and some kids' meals. It's licensed. Try to go at sunset.

IN SAMFORD

✪ **Samford Restaurant.** Main Street, Samford Village. ☎ **07/3289 1485.** Reservations recommended. Main courses A$16–A$21.50 (U.S. $12.80–$17.20); "Young diners" meals A$6 (U.S. $4.80). AE, BC, DC, MC, V. Sat–Sun 10am–midnight, Mon–Fri 6:30pm–midnight. Train: Ferny Grove; then five-minute taxi. INNOVATIVE INTERNATIONAL.

The quality of the cuisine here is such that diners willingly make the half-hour drive to the township of Samford, 21km (13 miles) northwest of the city. Housed in a cottage, the restaurant offers seating indoors or in a covered courtyard. Ceiling fans, fringed shades on hanging lights, an open fireplace, a fireside bar, and a profusion of greenery contribute to the old-world atmosphere.

Proprietress Joy Harman has designed an adventurous menu that focuses on two things: fresh seasonal produce and wonderful desserts. Most main courses are available in two sizes, so you can match your order to your appetite. For an appetizer you might like "oysters de joie" in a smoked cheese Mornay or thick and hearty pea-and-ham soup flavored with pita crisps. Main courses include fettuccine with smoked salmon, rack of pork with sherry-soaked raisins and onion-ginger sauce, Snowy Mountains rainbow trout deboned and filled with Moreton Bay bugs and prawns, and aged rib filet with a rich demiglaze.

Of all the delicious homemade desserts, Black Forest cake has evolved as the specialty of the house. Joy's version includes Bavarian cream, cherries soaked in brandy and cinnamon, and "extremely rich" chocolate cake. The result is a delight that avoids the sickly sweet trap that can be the downfall of this particular dish. Other treats worth leaving room for are treacle pudding and Bombé Vacherin, a warm meringue filled with macadamia nut–and–mango ice cream and served with Malibu sauce. The restaurant is both BYO and licensed; a bottle shop, open daily, is two doors away.

IN SUBURBAN BRISBANE

✪ **Baguette.** 150 Racecourse Rd., Ascot. ☎ **07/3268 6168.** Fax 07/3268 2607. Reservations accepted in restaurant; accepted only for five or more in brasserie section. Main courses in restaurant A$16–A$29 (U.S. $12.80–$23.20); dishes in brasserie section A$9.50–A$16.90 (U.S. $7.60–$13.50). AE, BC, DC, MC, V. Restaurant, Mon–Fri noon–10pm, Sat 6pm–10pm; brasserie section, daily 11am–11pm. MODERN FRENCH.

It's no wonder this attractive eatery has won numerous awards: The food, atmosphere, and service are all wonderful. Baguette also has the distinction of being Brisbane's oldest licensed restaurant (opened 1976) operated by the original owner, Francis Domenech. The brasserie section occupies the area at the front and a sidewalk patio; the restaurant is through the brasserie. Be sure to try the caesar salad with seared scallops and shaved parmesan—excellent. Be aware that if you order the tasty milk-fed lamb with timbale of ratatouille, honey, and thyme jus, the meat will arrive pink in the middle. Popular brasserie dishes include Thai beef salad with roasted peanuts, green pawpaw, and Asian greens as well as veal cutlet with roasted pumpkin, smoked bacon, and wilted rocket (arugula) leaves. The decor is modern Queensland: The exposed-brick walls are painted the color of mellow sunshine; the high cathedral ceiling has exposed beams. The children's menu is priced at A$1 (U.S. 80¢) per year of age. There's a good wine list or you can BYO. Be here Sunday between 3 and 5pm if you like jazz. The trip from the city will take about 15 minutes and cost about A$9 (U.S. $7.20) in a taxi.

DINING ON THE WATER

Kookaburra Queen. Departing from the Pier at Waterfront Place, 1 Eagle St. ☎ **07/3221 1300**, ext. 23. Reservations recommended. Cruise with morning Devonshire tea A$18 (U.S. $14.40); lunch cruise A$25–A$40 (U.S. $20–$32); dinner cruise A$35–A$50 (U.S. $28–$40). Children 4–14 half price. AE, BC, DC, MC, V. Morning tea cruise, daily 10–11:30am; lunch cruise, daily 12:45–2:15pm; dinner cruise, Mon–Thurs 7:30–10pm, Fri–Sat 7:30–10:30pm, Sun 6:30–9:30pm. These are departure times—board earlier. Bus: City Circle. INTERNATIONAL.

This elegant paddlewheeler, built in 1986 of fine Australian timber, cruises the Brisbane River while patrons enjoy fine food, live entertainment, and sightseeing. The handcrafted curved decks and sweeping staircases create a classic ambience, while the modern galleys allow chefs to prepare meals.

The price you pay depends on your choice of meal. At lunch this varies from the buffet to a seafood platter. Evening meals offer a choice of a buffet or a three-course meal. Morning tea and lunch cruises include descriptive commentary. There's a pianist and music for dancing in the evening. Note that you can also enjoy this cruise without taking a meal—see "Attractions" below.

5 Attractions

SIGHTSEEING SUGGESTIONS FOR THE FIRST-TIME VISITOR

If You Have 1 Day Visit the Australian Woolshed, arriving in time for the 10 or 11am or the 2pm show. Plan to have billy tea and damper and/or lunch while there. Allow time for browsing in the excellent craft shop. At night, attend a play, an opera, or a concert at the Performing Arts Complex in the Queensland Cultural Centre or take a *Kookaburra Queen* dinner cruise.

If You Have 2 Days Follow my suggestions for the first day and go to Lone Pine Koala Sanctuary on the second. Take my walking tour as outlined later in this section or wander over to the South Bank Parklands.

If You Have 3 Days Follow the itinerary for Days 1 and 2, then choose between Mt. Coot-tha Park or the Art Gallery and Museum in the Queensland Cultural Centre for Day 3.

THE TOP ATTRACTIONS

Lone Pine Koala Sanctuary. Jesmond Road, Fig Tree Pocket. ☎ **07/3378 1366,** or 07/3241 4419 for information. Admission A$11 (U.S. $8.80) adults, A$6 (U.S. $4.80) children 3–13, A$25 (U.S. $20) family. Daily 8am–4:45pm. Closed ANZAC Day morning.

Today wildlife parks dot Australia, but when Lone Pine opened in 1927 it was the only place in the country where visitors could cuddle a koala. While the park is no longer unique, it's still a good place to see, hold, and be photographed with one of the balls of fur that've brought recognition to Qantas Airways and become the unofficial symbol of the nation. Who can resist the adorable faces on the front cover of this book?

For koala addicts, Lone Pine is nirvana because this is the world's largest collection. More than 130 of the creatures are housed at the park, and in order to feed them all Lone Pine maintains a plantation of 40,000 eucalyptus leaves. This bit of trivia and other koala facts are explained during a short show presented three times a day. Many colorful Australian birds and other indigenous animals are also on display. If you've never seen a dingo, a kookaburra, an echidna, or a pink-and-gray galah, this is a good opportunity. A Polaroid photo of you holding a koala costs about A$7 (U.S. $5.60). You can cuddle a koala at any time during the day, but the best time is around 2:30pm, because that's when the animals are fed and they're most active. Slide talks take place at 11:30am and 1:15 and 2:45pm; call to confirm these times if this is really important to you.

Getting There: The sanctuary, 12km (7.4 miles) from city, can be reached by car or by the boats operated by Mirimar Cruises (☎ 07/3221 0300). A round-trip river cruise costs A$15 (U.S. $12) for adults and A$8 (U.S. $6.40) for children 3 to 15. It departs North Quay at 10am. Passengers have 1½ hours at Lone Pine before the boat returns to the city. Courtesy transfers are provided from inner-city hotels. Many sightseeing excursions stop at the park, or you can take public bus no. 581 from the koala platform at the Myer Centre.

Full of Fun & Free of Charge

The city's favorite festival, **Warana** (meaning "blue skies" in Aborigine) is a two-week fete that includes parades, concerts, picnics, and lots of outdoor entertainment. It's held every September, when Brisbane's weather is at its best. The Warana hotline is 07/3852 2468.

FREEPS (Free Recreation and Entertainment for Everyone in Parks) concerts, sponsored by the Brisbane City Council, are held every Sunday afternoon—often in the Botanic Gardens but sometimes in the Albert Park Amphitheatre or a suburban park. FREEPS caters to all ages with bands, dance exhibitions, jazz, country music, and holiday programs. For details, call 07/3225 6766 or check the local newspaper.

The Australian Woolshed. 148 Samford Rd., Ferny Hills. ☎ **07/3351 5366.** Admission A$11 (U.S. $8.80) adults, A$5 (U.S. $4) children 3–14. Daily 9:30am–5pm.

You probably never thought that learning about sheep could be fun, but after you've been to the Australian Woolshed, you'll know it can be. Sheep are integral to Australia's agricultural economy, and more than 155 million of them grow the wool that's one of the country's most important exports. At the Woolshed, proprietor Ken Mander-Jones explains about the different breeds, shears a sheep to the tune of "Click Go the Shears," and shows the important role sheepdogs play in farm life. Spinning is also demonstrated, and a lucky volunteer gets a try at milking a cow.

During the impressive Ram Show, various breeds of sheep walk up the aisle and take an assigned place onstage. This behavior plays havoc with the widely held belief that sheep are incredibly dumb and can never be taught anything. After the performance you can pet a kangaroo, feed a goat kid with a bottle, and learn about koalas. The Woolshed doesn't have nearly as many of the cuddly creatures as Lone Pine (above), but Ken feeds his specimens while he talks about them, so they're quite active. A photo of you holding a koala costs A$7.50 (U.S. $6).

Lest you think my enthusiastic endorsement of this place is exaggerated, I quote from a reader letter I received recently: "Re: the Woolshed. Keep raving about it because it was great."

In addition to animal-oriented enjoyment, the "Supply Store" offers quality Australian-made products. In 1985 this shop was voted the best of its kind in the country, and Ken and his wife, Margaret, work hard to maintain the quality and variety of goods.

The one-hour Ram Show takes place daily at 10 and 11am and 2pm, and I suggest you go early and have billy tea and delicious damper bread with butter and golden syrup before the performance. If you stay for lunch, you can try a hearty shearer's sandwich (lamb on damper with gravy) or have steak and salad. If you want to experience another aspect of outback Oz, stay for a woolshed (barn) dance held on Friday and Saturday evenings.

Getting There: The Woolshed is 14km (9 miles) from the city center. You can drive or take a train to Ferny Grove. The station is 800 meters (half a mile) from the Woolshed. The other option is to join a day tour (see "Organized Tours" below).

Queensland Cultural Centre. Across the Victoria Bridge on the south side of the Brisbane River. ☎ **07/3840 7100.** Bus: 165, 169, 175, 185, 189, or others. Train: South Brisbane. Ferry: South Bank.

The Queensland Cultural Centre is a beautiful complex of low-rise modern buildings surrounded by imaginative pools and fountains. You may choose to wander through the area, admiring the creative use of water and the way it complements the terraced architecture of the structures, or you may wish to explore the interiors of the various theaters and museums.

The A$67-million (U.S. $53.6-million) **Performing Arts Complex** was officially opened by the duke of Kent in 1985. It contains three auditoriums for music and stage productions. The overall effect of spacious carpeted lobbies and foyers with aggregate concrete walls, glass, and stainless-steel railings is most impressive. Free tours of the three theaters leave the tour desk in the ticket sales foyer Monday to Friday at noon. For performance information, call 07/3846 4444.

The **State Library of Queensland** (☎ 07/3840 7666), the last building in the complex to be completed, was officially opened in 1988 and houses the state's reference collection—the John Oxley Library of Queensland History and Special Collections.

The **Queensland Art Gallery** is the permanent home of the state's extensive collection and is often the site of touring exhibitions. The Gallery is open daily from 10am to 5pm and admission is free except for special exhibitions. Guided tours are conducted by volunteers Monday to Friday at 11am and 1 and 2pm and Saturday and Sunday at 2 and 3pm. The Gallery Bistro, serving light meals and snacks, is open daily. Call 07/3840 7350 or 3840 7303 for more information.

The **Queensland Museum,** with more than two million items that relate to the natural, human, and technological history of the Sunshine State, is open Thursday to Tuesday from 9am to 5pm and Wednesday from 9am to 8pm. Admission to regular exhibits is free, and prices for visiting displays vary. The Museum Cafe is open daily. For further information, call 07/3840 7555.

The museums and theaters of the Queensland Cultural Centre are fully accessible to the handicapped. To make arrangements, call 07/3840 7100.

If you plan to dine in this area, see the description of the Lyrebird Restaurant and Cafe in "Dining" earlier in this chapter.

✪ **South Bank Parklands.** On the south side of the Brisbane River just east of the Victoria Bridge. ☎ **07/3846 2051** (07/3867 2020 after-hours recorded message). Free admission to general area; Gondwana, A$9 (U.S. $7.20) adults, A$6 (U.S. $4.80) children; Our World, A$6 (U.S. $4.80) adults, A$5 (U.S. $4) children; Butterfly and Insect House, A$6.50 (U.S. $5.20) adults, A$3.50 (U.S. $2.80) children; boat ride, A$5 (U.S. $4) adults, A$2 (U.S. $1.60) children. Dollarwise Parklands Discovery Tickets (A$18/U.S. $14.40 adult; A$10/U.S. $8 children; A$50/U.S. $40 family) are also available. Daily 6am–midnight. Take a ferry, bus, or train from the city center.

Brisbane's newest attraction is a 16-hectare (39-acre) recreation area featuring a large swimming lagoon complete with palm trees and a beach, lots of dining options, picnic places, and impromptu appearances by street entertainers. The Gondwana Rainforest Sanctuary features about 100 species of wildlife; Our World Environment provides an opportunity to learn about our planet; the Butterfly and Insect House boasts the world's largest collection of Australian butterfly species; and the Southship ferries carry passengers along the waterways meandering around the parklands. There are also pathways to stroll and cycle and shops and markets in which to browse. The South Bank Market is held here Friday from 5 to 10pm, Saturday from 10am to 10:30pm, and Sunday from 9am to 5pm (hours change seasonally).

MORE ATTRACTIONS

The following sights are mentioned for the benefit of those who can spend more than a day or two in Brisbane.

Brisbane Forest Park. 60 Mt. Nebo Rd., The Gap. ☎ **07/3300 4855,** ext. 23. Walk-about Creek Centre, A$3.50 (U.S. $2.80) adults, A$2 (U.S. $1.60) children. Walk-about Creek Centre, Mon–Fri 9am–4:30pm, Sat–Sun 10am–4:30pm.

This 28,500-hectare (7,395-acre) bushland park is a 20-minute drive from the center of Brisbane. Bush Ranger Tours are offered and those interested in native fauna won't want to miss Walk-about Creek Freshwater Study Centre (see "Hiking & Nature Study" in "Outdoor Activities" later in this chapter).

The Walk-about Creek Restaurant offers superb treetop views as well as tea, lunch, and dinner.

Earlystreet Historical Village. 75 McIlwraith Ave., Norman Park. ☎ **07/3398 6866,** ext. 23. Admission A$6 (U.S. $4.80) adults, A$4 (U.S. $3.20) children. Mon–Sat 10am–4:30pm, Sun 11am–4:30pm. Closed Good Friday and Christmas. Bus: 8A, 8B, 8C, or 8D. Train: Norman Park Station; then a 1km (half-mile) walk.

For a glimpse into Queensland's early history, walk through the gardens and colonial buildings at Earlystreet, where real pioneer-period structures have been moved onto the grounds of a stately suburban residence 6km (4 miles) from downtown Brisbane. The general store was relocated from Rocky Water Holes, the slab hut is equally authentic, and the pub was constructed from parts saved from many celebrated hotels before they were destroyed. Typical of old-time watering holes, this building features a collection of old bottles, a traditional brass footrail, and a black-and-white tile floor. "Stromness" is a typical early Queensland home, ca. 1870. The half dozen or so structures are surrounded by beautiful mature trees, some of which were growing in their present locations before John Oxley discovered Brisbane.

Kookaburra Queen. Departing from the Pier at Waterfront Place, 1 Eagle St. ☎ **07/3221 1300.** Midday cruise (without lunch) A$18 (U.S. $14.40). Board at 12:15pm, depart at 12:45pm, return at 2:15pm.

I described this atmospheric paddlewheeler in "Dining" earlier in this chapter because of the meals and tea served on board, but it's worth mentioning again purely as a sightseeing attraction. Full commentary about the vessel and the places it passes is supplied over a loudspeaker on all but the evening cruises. Only this midday cruise offers you an option of not having a meal or tea.

Mt. Coot-tha Park. Mt. Coot-tha Road, Toowong. ☎ **07/3377 8893.** Botanic Gardens, free; Planetarium, A$7.50 (U.S. $6) adults, A$3.50 (U.S. $2.80) children under 15. Gardens, daily 8am–5:30pm (closing 5pm Apr–Aug). Planetarium "Sky Theatre" shows, Wed–Fri 3:30 and 7:30pm; Sat 1:30, 3:30, and 7:30pm; Sun 1:30 and 3:30pm. Closed Late Jan–Feb 15. Bus: 37A from Ann Street in the city.

A scenic wooded area only 6km (4 miles) from downtown, Mt. Coot-tha Park is the home of the **Brisbane Botanic Gardens** and the **Sir Thomas Brisbane Planetarium.** In addition, the lofty open forest region affords excellent views of the city. The 52 hectares (128 acres) of gardens include a dome-shaped glasshouse (greenhouse) with over 2,000 tropical shrubs and trees, a Japanese Garden, and an extensive collection of Australian native plants. Experienced volunteer guides conduct informative tours Monday to Saturday at 11am and 1pm. For information call 07/3377 8896. If you want to dine at Mt. Coot-tha, read about the Summit Restaurant and Kuta Cafe in "Dining" earlier in this chapter.

ORGANIZED TOURS

Sunstate Tours (☎ 07/3236 3355) and **Boomerang Tours** (☎ 07/3236 3614) operate half-day city-sights tours (A$34/U.S. $27.20 for adults, A$18/U.S. $14.40 for children) and full-day trips north to the Sunshine Coast (A$63/U.S. $50.40 for adults, A$34/U.S. $27.20 for children) or south to the Gold Coast (A$49/U.S. $39.20 for adults, A$28/U.S. $22.40 for children).

G'Day Australia Bush Tours (☎ 07/3891 5544) operates four-wheel-drive day tours. And don't overlook the possibility of doing a self-guided tour using the **City Sights** bus (see "Getting Around" earlier in this chapter). It stops at 20 places and you can get on and off as often as you like. The fare is A$12 (U.S. $9.60) for adults and A$8 (U.S. $6.40) for children. Call 07/3225 4444 for more information.

I also recommend the **Bush Ranger Tours** offered at Brisbane Forest Park (see "Hiking & Nature Study" in "Outdoor Activities" later in this chapter).

WALKING TOUR
Brisbane's Heritage Trail

Start: King George Square, between Adelaide and Ann streets.
Finish: Treasury Building, between Queen and Elizabeth streets at George Street.
Time: One to two hours.
Best Times: Anytime except Monday to Friday during rush hours, when the sidewalks are crowded.

The best way to see Brisbane's impressive historic buildings is on foot. I suggest you begin at King George Square, from which there's an excellent view of:

1. Brisbane City Hall, erected of Queensland sandstone between 1920 and 1930. The nicely detailed main entrance is topped by a 91-meter (300-ft.) clock tower that affords excellent views of the city and the surrounding area. Even if you don't go up in the tower, poke your head in the door and notice the marble staircase and ornate ceiling. Before leaving the square, look at *The Petrie Tableau,* a statue honoring Brisbane's early families. A plaque explains the story depicted by the figures. The large bronze kangaroos in front is a favorite place for visitors to have their picture taken. Note the joey sticking his head and legs out of his mother's pouch.

From the Ann Street side of King George Square you can see the:

2. Albert Street Uniting Church, built of Oamaru (New Zealand) limestone and dark brick in the Victorian Gothic Revival style. Services are held here Sunday at 10am and 7pm and Tuesday at 1:15pm. In the same block and on the same side of the street is the:

3. Brisbane School of Arts, wedged in among modern high-rises. The original building was constructed about 1865, when it served as the servants home—a clearing house and hostel for new domestic servants who'd been attracted to work in the colony. A sign on the fence, on the right side near the entrance, explains the building's history in detail. Note the verandas, typical of Queensland colonial architecture. Colonial architects borrowed the idea from India, where verandas were used for their cooling effect. (Across from the School of Arts, 157 Ann St., is where you have to go to dispute a parking ticket. Ask me how I know.)

Cross Edward Street to the:

4. Central Railway Station, a fine example of Victorian railway stations, erected in 1901. The building is predominantly brick with white and pink sandstone trim. Be sure to notice the central clock tower and the iron gates to the entrance hall.

Opposite the train station you'll see the:

5. Shrine of Remembrance, erected in honor of the Australian soldiers who died in World War I. Down the stairs below it, ANZAC Square is a pretty park with seating.

Walk back to Edward Street and, on the corner, you'll notice the:

6. **Salvation Army Headquarters,** designed by a Salvation Army architect and built as low-cost accommodation, known at the time as the People's Palace. It opened in 1911 and the elaborate cast-iron balustrades and deep verandas are typical of that time.

Walk down Edward Street, cross Adelaide Street, and notice on your left the:

7. **Rowes Arcade,** which appears to be one building but is really two. The building to the left features the words *Rothwell's* and *Established 1897.* The structure on the right is labeled *Rowes.* Be sure to notice the pretty ceiling with its ornamental plaster octagons in the arcade.

TAKE A BREAK There are several lunch and tea spots in Rowes Arcade. My personal favorite is **Dougall's Gourmet Foods** (☎ 07/3229 5991), open Monday to Thursday from 6am to 5pm and Friday from 6am to 6pm. Sandwiches cost A$2 to A$3 (U.S. $1.60 to $2.40). You can sit at the umbrella-shaded tables next to the fountain.

After some refreshments, duck down Queen Street for a look at the:

8. **General Post Office,** built on the site of the convict settlement's Female Factory Prison. The northern wing was built by John Petrie from 1871 to 1872 and the central tower and southern wing were added from 1877 to 1879. Notice the crest within the balustrade at the first-floor level. (Remember that in Australia the first floor is one above ground.)

Proceed through the GPO Arcade and across Elizabeth Street to:

9. **St. Stephen's Cathedral,** designed by well-known architect Benjamin Backhouse in the early English Gothic style. It was begun in 1863 and completed in 1874. Adjacent to the cathedral is:
10. **Old St. Stephen's Church,** the oldest church in Brisbane, built in 1850.

Walk through to Charlotte Street, turn right, and then turn left into Edward Street. Now walk down Edward, past the Heritage Hotel, and take a short detour down to the ferry landing on the river to admire the view. Return to Edward Street and enter the:

11. **Botanic Gardens.** The present gardens occupy the site of the former Government Garden established in 1824 on instructions of Sir Thomas Brisbane. Of particular interest are an avenue of Bunya pines planted in the 1850s by Walter Hill, the first colonial botanist, and rows of weeping figs planted in the 1870s.

At the George Street end of the gardens you have a good view of:

12. **Parliament House.** The design for this building, conceived by colonial architect Charles Tiffin, was chosen in an Australia-wide competition. The French Renaissance–style building was opened in 1868.

Nearby on George Street is:

13. **The Mansions,** constructed in 1889 as a row of six terrace houses. The architects designed the houses to suit local climatic conditions. Note the recessing of the main wall behind a wide veranda that provides a cooling effect to internal rooms.

Continue to the corner of Queen and George streets, where you have a good view of the:

14. **Treasury Building,** designed primarily in the Italian Renaissance style and built between 1885 and 1928. For nearly 100 years the Treasury was the hub of government administration. Today it's the home of the Conrad Treasury Casino. Across the street, the Conrad Treasury Casino Hotel is housed in the former Land

Walking Tour—Brisbane's Heritage Trail

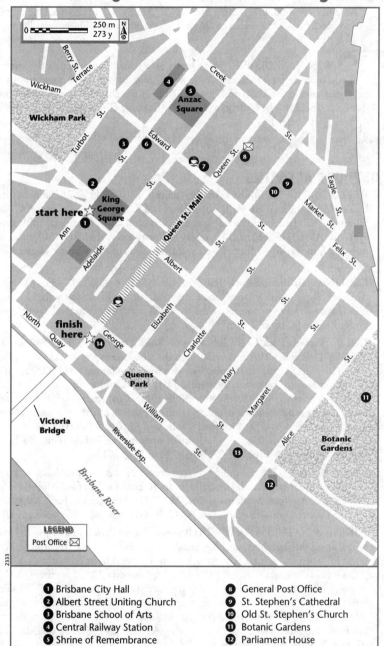

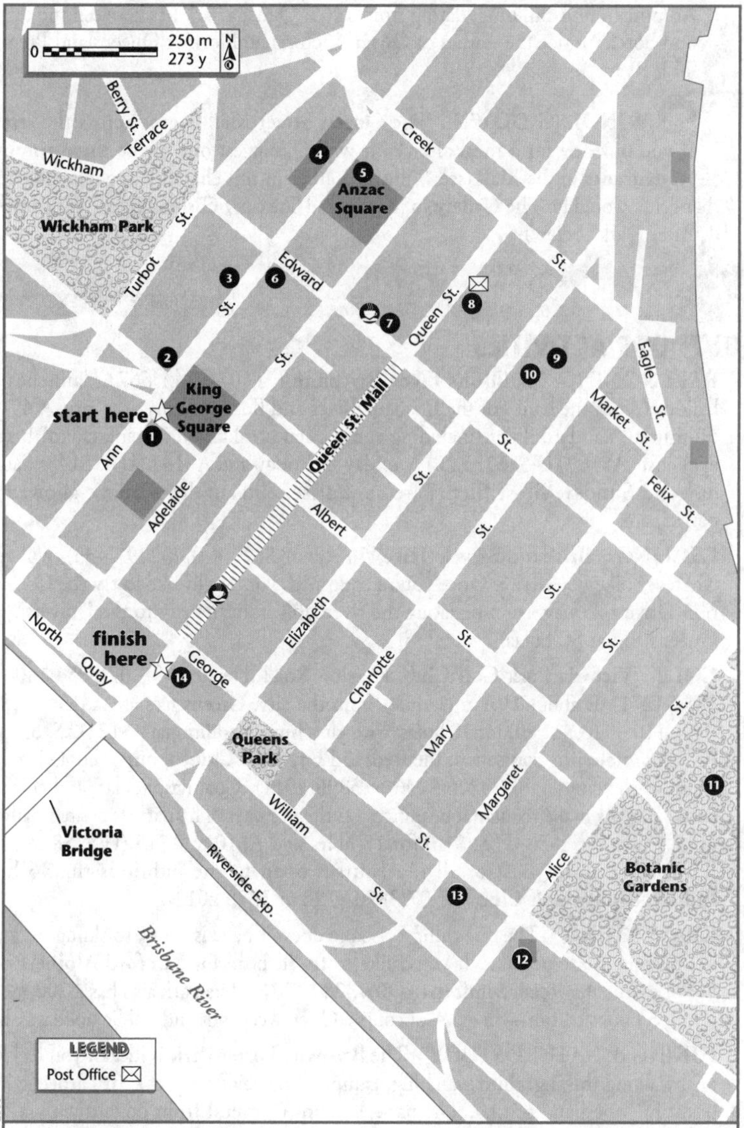

1 Brisbane City Hall
2 Albert Street Uniting Church
3 Brisbane School of Arts
4 Central Railway Station
5 Shrine of Remembrance
6 Salvation Army Headquarters
7 Rowes Arcade
8 General Post Office
9 St. Stephen's Cathedral
10 Old St. Stephen's Church
11 Botanic Gardens
12 Parliament House
13 The Mansions
14 Treasury Building

Administration Building, dating from 1905. Queens Park lies between the casino and hotel. Notice the statues of Queen Victoria and former Queensland Premier T. J. Ryan.

WINDING DOWN The Queen Street Mall begins across the street. If you're ready for a meal after your walk, I suggest one of the three **Jimmy's Restaurants** in the Mall (see "Dining" earlier in this chapter). A good choice for a drink would be **The Gallery** in the Conrad Treasury Casino Hotel (see "Brisbane After Dark" below).

6 Outdoor Activities & Spectator Sports

OUTDOOR ACTIVITIES

BALLOONING **Balloons Over Brisbane** (☎ 07/3844 6671) launches its balloons from the banks of the Brisbane River and floats you over the city. A 45- to 60-minute standard flight (including continental breakfast and "pink cloud" beverage) costs A$169 (U.S. $135.20) Monday to Friday and A$185 (U.S. $148) Saturday and Sunday. Most flights are at sunrise. Kids under 8 aren't allowed to participate.

CYCLING **Brisbane Bicycle Hire,** 50 Albert St. (☎ 07/3229 2433), will rent whatever bike you desire. Once you're equipped, you might like to try the Coronation Drive Bikeway, running along the riverbank from the city to the University of Queensland at St. Lucia.

GOLF **Victoria Park Golf Club,** Herston Road, Herston (☎ 07/3854 1406 or 3852 1271), is about 1½km (1 mile) from the city. Greens fees are A$13 to A$16 (U.S. $10.40 to $12.80) for 18 holes, with club hire an additional A$12 (U.S. $9.60). Another interesting course is at the **Redland Bay Golf Club,** about 35km (21 miles) south of the city (☎ 07/3206 7236 or 3206 7011). Goannas, koalas, and colorful native parrots make regular appearances on the fairways. The parrots are fed daily at 4pm. Costs are A$20 (U.S. $16) for 18 holes and A$10 to A$15 (U.S. $8 to $12) for renting clubs. Best of all the courses open to the public is the 36-hole **Indooroorpilly Golf Club** (☎ 07/3870 3728 or 3870 2012).

GRASS SKIING The one thing Brisbane doesn't have is snow, so skiing on grass has become quite popular. If you'd like to try it, head for **Samford Alpine Park,** Eaton's Crossing Road, Samford (☎ 07/3289 1581). The park also has a 700-meter (763-yd.) bobsled run—on grass, of course. Open weekends and public holidays only.

HIKING & NATURE STUDY The **Brisbane Forest Park** is ideal if you feel like bushwalking (hiking), bird watching, camping, or having a picnic or barbecue in a beautiful woodland setting. The park is 12km (7 miles) from downtown via Mt. Nebo Road, The Gap (☎ 07/300 4855). BFP spreads over 28,500 hectares (70,395 acres) of mountainous bushland containing eucalyptus forest and subtropical rain forest and offers good views of surrounding terrain and the distant city skyline. The scenic Northbrook Parkway travels right through the park, offering great sights. **Go Bush Programs** offers bush tours costing A$5 to A$40 (U.S. $4 to $32). Call 07/3300 5381 for more information.

Also located here is the popular **Walk-about Creek Freshwater Study Centre.** Admission to this center is A$3.50 (U.S. $2.80) for adults and A$2 (U.S. $1.60) for children. Brisbane Forest Park is open daily. A tearoom, restaurant, and bush crafts shop are at the headquarters.

JOGGING The **Botanic Gardens** in the city are a picturesque venue for your workout.

SQUASH Courts are available at the **Royal Queensland Lawn Tennis Association,** Milton Road, Milton (☎ 07/3368 2433), open daily from 6:30am to 10pm. Courts cost A$9 (U.S. $7.20) per hour before 5pm, A$14 (U.S. $11.20) after 5pm. You can also play at the **Brisbane Squash Centre,** Waterloo Street, Newstead (☎ 07/3252 3400).

SWIMMING The **Valley Heated Olympic Pool,** 432 Wickham St., Fortitude Valley (☎ 07/3852 1231), is open Monday to Saturday from 5:30am and Sunday from 7:30am; closing times vary. Admission is A$1.70 (U.S. $1.36) for an unlimited stay.

TENNIS The **Royal Queensland Lawn Tennis Association,** Milton Road, Milton (☎ 07/3368 2433), has both grass courts and hard ones. Charges are the same as for squash (see above). The inner suburb of Milton, about 2km (a mile) from downtown, is easily reached by train.

SPECTATOR SPORTS

HORSE & GREYHOUND RACING The **Queensland Winter Racing Carnival** is the highlight of Queensland's horse-racing season, combining racing, sports, art, and entertainment. These events are held at the **Eagle Farm, Doomben,** and **Bundamba** tracks during May and June.

Trotting (harness racing) takes place at the **Albion Park Raceway,** Amy Street, Albion Park (☎ 07/3262 2577), every Saturday and Wednesday evening. Greyhounds race at the **Brisbane Greyhound Racing Club** (Albion) each Thursday (☎ 07/3862 1744).

7 Shopping

Brisbane has good shopping facilities, including one of the largest central-business-district shopping centers in Australia: the A$480-million (U.S. $384-million) **Myer Centre,** completely filling the block bounded by Queen, Elizabeth, Albert, and George streets. Within the center's five levels are a huge department store, 250 specialty shops, 8 cinemas, taverns, a food fair, and a 1,500-space parking lot.

If you want to continue your spree after the Myer Centre, I suggest you wander along the **Queen Street Pedestrian Mall,** which extends from Edward to George streets. Of particular interest is the **Wintergarden** complex under the Hilton Hotel.

Park Road, in the inner suburb of Milton, is another good area for browsing. Galleries and antiques stores are interspersed with coffeehouses. **Paddington Circle** is an area of boutiques, antiques stores, galleries, craft shops, and restaurants in one of Brisbane's oldest suburbs. Information is available from **Paddington Pharmacy,** 212 Given Terrace (☎ 07/3369 9561). Most places are open Monday to Friday from

Readers Recommend

Decorators Gallery, 57 Elizabeth St. (☎ 07/3229 5946). *"During my last day in Brisbane I found some wonderful things—including a beautiful ikat, indigo, a Japanese kimono, and two brass water containers used in Hindu ceremonies—at Ian Thomson's Decorators Gallery. I was surprised at the range of prices that, unlike at many commercial galleries, included many very affordable items."*

—Jennifer Fisher, Montréal, Québec, Canada.

9am to 5pm and Saturday from 9am to noon; some close at 9pm Thursday and a few are open daily.

Stores in the downtown area are generally open Monday to Thursday from 9am to 5:30pm, Friday from 9am to 9pm, Saturday from 9am to 4pm, and Sunday from 10:30am to 4pm.

SHOPPING A TO Z

ABORIGINAL & ETHNIC ARTIFACTS & CRAFTS

Queensland Aboriginal Creations. 135 George St. ☎ **07/3224 5730.**

This shop sells original handcrafts and artifacts, including leather products, bark paintings, weapons, jewelry, shells, and artwork. Of particular interest is the handmade Aboriginal pottery. Sales directly benefit the Aboriginal community. Open Monday to Friday from 9am to 4:30pm and Saturday from 9am to 4pm.

ANTIQUES

Paddington Antique Centre. 167 Latrobe Terrace, Paddington. ☎ **07/3369 8088.**

This center, in a 1930s cinema building, is the combined effort of 60 individual antiques dealers. Items range from furniture and bric-a-brac to Australiana and jewelry. Open daily from 10am to 5pm.

BOOKS

Dymocks. 239 Albert St. ☎ **07/3229 4266.**

Easily the biggest bookstore in Brisbane, Dymocks has a huge selection of every kind of book. It touts that only the State Library has more volumes, and Dymocks is probably right. It also stocks stationery. Open Monday to Friday from 8:30am to 7pm, Saturday from 8:30am to 5:30pm, and Sunday from 8:30am to 4pm.

Pulp Fiction. Shop 9 in the Anzac Square Arcade, 265–269 Edward St. (between Ann and Adelaide streets). ☎ **07/3236 2750.** Fax 07/3236 2752.

As the name implies, this is the place to look for science fiction, fantasy, crime, and mystery. Open Monday to Thursday from 8:30am to 5:30pm, Friday from 8:30am to 8pm, and Saturday from 8:30am to 12:30am.

CRAFTS

Australian Woolshed. 148 Samford Rd., Ferny Hills. ☎ **07/3351 5366.**

Quality handcrafts are sold at this shop, part of one of the city's top sights (see "Attractions" earlier in this chapter). The award-winning "supply store" stocks only Australian-made crafts and souvenirs. There are ten themed areas in the shop, including one for Aboriginal goods, another where skin and fur items are displayed, and another for men's gifts. Open daily from 8:30am to 4:30pm.

The Needlewoman. 2 Latrobe Terrace, Paddington. ☎ **07/3369 7959.**

This shop sells everything imaginable for needleworkers, including a full range of kits, canvases, books, threads—and even heirloom sewing materials. This is Queensland's only specialized needlework shop and school. Open Monday to Friday from 9:30am to 5pm and Saturday from 9:30am to 1pm.

DEPARTMENT STORE

David Jones Department Store. 194 Queen St. ☎ **07/3227 1111.**

This is the granddaddy and senior partner of Australian department stores—and the oldest in the world still trading under its original name. While David Jones sells a full range of goods, the emphasis is definitely on the top end. This store is open Monday to Thursday from 8:30am to 5:30pm, Friday from 8:30am to 9pm, Saturday from 9am to 4pm, and Sunday from 10:30am to 4pm.

Duty-Free Shops

Allders Duty Free. 78 Queen Street Mall. ☎ **07/3229 2922.**

Like most duty-free shops, Allders has the usual range of items: liquor, cigarettes, perfume, cameras, and small electrical appliances. Open Monday to Thursday from 9am to 5:30pm, Friday from 9am to 9pm, Saturday from 8:30am to 4pm, and Sunday from 10:30am to 4pm.

Fashions

R.M. Williams. In the Wintergarden Complex on the Queen Street Mall, next to McDonald's. ☎ **07/3229 7724.**

Look for country clothes here—Drizabone coats, Acubra hats, that sort of thing. Open Monday to Thursday from 9am to 5pm, Friday from 9am to 9pm, Saturday from 9am to 4pm, and Sunday from 10:30am to 4pm.

Gifts & Souvenirs

Break of Day Gift Shop. Shop 50 at 283 Given Terrace, Paddington. ☎ **07/3368 2921.**

Break of Day Gift Shop has a nice selection of handmade gifts, including teddy bears, baby items, pressed-flower designs, and patchwork quilts. It also sells a variety of miniatures, like dollhouse furniture and accessories, cottages, and animals. The Joanna Sheen pressed-flower designs and David Winter cottages are especially popular. The toiletries in Australian floral fragrances make nice gifts for friends at home. Open Monday to Wednesday and Friday from 9am to 5pm, Thursday from 9am to 8pm, and Saturday from 9am to 4pm.

National Trust Gift Shop. In The Mansions, 40 George St. ☎ **07/3221 1887.**

Everything on sale here is Australian made, like manchester (household linens), stationery, prints, novelties, and souvenirs. Many designs are exclusive to the National Trust. The volunteers who staff the shop are helpful and friendly. Open Monday to Friday from 10am to 4pm.

Post Australia Shop, GPO. Queen Street. ☎ **07/3405 1380.**

In Brisbane's main post office, the Post Australia Shop offers the convenience of selling gift items with purpose-designed packaging for mailing. A variety of quality Australian-made products is available. Open Monday to Friday from 8am to 5:30pm.

Jewelry

Quilpie Opals. In the Lennons Plaza Building, 66–68 Queen Street Mall. ☎ **07/3221 7369.**

Named after Quilpie, a small town in Western Queensland that's the center of the boulder-opal industry, this store sells an extensive range of black, white, and boulder opals as well as a large selection of Australian handmade souvenirs. Open Monday to Friday from 9am to 7pm, Saturday from 9am to 4pm, and Sunday from 10am to 2pm.

Markets

Paddy's Markets. Florence and Macquarie streets, New Farm. ☎ **07/3252 4151.**

Here you'll find 5 acres of undercover merchandise and hundreds of individual stallholders selling everything from native Australian birds to luggage. This is the ideal place to look for army surplus, bric-a-brac, old-fashioned shoes and clothing, hard-to-find tools, books, and out-of-the-ordinary gifts. It also offers a huge selection of fabric. Open Monday to Friday from 9am to 4pm and Saturday and Sunday from 8:30am to 4pm.

Riverside Crafts Market. In the Riverside Complex, Eagle Street. ☎ **07/3371 1452** or 3371 1789.

Hundreds of arts and crafts stalls crowd the plazas and boardwalks of the Riverside Complex and surrounding area every Sunday from 8:15am to 3pm. Besides original wares, look for street performers and food stalls. This is one of the country's best markets. If you're a shopper, it's worth arranging your itinerary to be here.

South Bank Parklands Market. On the south side of the Brisbane River just east of the Victoria Bridge. ☎ **07/3846 2051** (07/3867 2020 after-hours recorded message).

This market sells much the same merchandise as is offered at the Riverside Markets: arts and crafts, toys, jewelry, handmade clothing, pottery, and so forth. The setting, surrounded by the eating spots and attractions of South Bank, is really pleasant. Open Friday from 5 to 10pm, Saturday from 10am to 10:30pm, and Sunday from 9am to 5pm (hours change seasonally).

SPORTS EQUIPMENT

Robinson's Sports Store. 300 Queen St., adjacent to Post Office Square. ☎ **07/3221 5011.**

When my husband and I were last in Brisbane, my husband realized he'd forgotten his swim goggles, and this is where he found a replacement pair. They also sell tennis, squash, golf, fishing, and cricket gear, as well as diving equipment, sports clothes, and so forth. Open Monday to Friday from 8am to 5pm.

SWEATERS

Australian Woolshed. 148 Samford Rd., Ferny Hills. ☎ **07/3351 5366.**

The Australian Woolshed sells beautiful hand-spun, hand-knitted wool garments that Aussies call "jumpers" and Americans refer to as "sweaters." For more information, see "Attractions" earlier in this chapter. Open daily from 8:30am to 4:30pm.

Baa Baa Black Sheep. Shop 17 on the Balcony Level in the Brisbane Arcade, Queen Street. ☎ **07/3221 0484.**

As its name implies, this shop specializes in hand-knitted Australian woolen products. Owner Debra Kolkka makes many of the items herself. Sweaters are the most popular. Open Monday to Thursday from 11am to 4pm, Friday from 11am to 6pm, and Saturday from 10am to 1pm.

8 Brisbane After Dark

The daily *Courier-Mail* newspaper lists entertainment information. I also suggest you pick up a copy of *Time Off*, a free weekly that's primarily a gig guide but does list cultural events and movies besides the performance schedules of myriad rock groups.

THE PERFORMING ARTS

THE MAJOR MULTIPURPOSE PERFORMANCE HALL

Performing Arts Complex. In the Queensland Cultural Centre. ☎ **07/3846 4444.**

This is the principal venue for Brisbane's stage productions. Within the complex, the 2,000-seat **Lyric Theatre** is designed for opera, dance, and musical comedy; the 2,000-seat **Concert Hall** handily accommodates a full symphony orchestra; and the 300-seat **Cremorne** is an experimental studio theater. If you wish to purchase tickets for events at the Performing Arts Complex, call 07/3846-4646 between 9am and 8:30pm Monday to Saturday. All major credit cards are accepted. The PAC has a nationwide toll-free number (☎ 1800/77 7699), and tickets can be purchased through any **Bass** ticket agency in Australia or through **ATS Tours' Sprint Department** in the United States and Canada (☎ 800/423-2880); ask for Showbiz Bookings. The box office is open Monday to Saturday from 9am to 9pm.

THEATERS

Brisbane Arts Theatre. 210 Petrie Terrace. ☎ **07/3369 2344.**

Brisbane's leading little-theater company has been playing for the city for over 50 years. Classics, musicals, comedies, Australian works, and mainstream plays are all presented. This includes the work of Shaw, Pinter, Coward, Ayckbourn, Simon, and so forth. The theater has 157 seats; Masks Bar is open for all performances. Ticket prices are usually about A$15 (U.S. $12).

La Boîte Theatre. 57 Hale St. ☎ **07/3369 1622.**

This theater in the round has been around for nearly 70 years. Recently it has presented such varied productions as *Angry Housewives, A Midsummer Night's Dream, On the Verge,* and *The Three Sisters.* Ticket prices are around A$22.50 (U.S. $18).

Princess Theatre. 8 Annerley Rd., Woolloongabba. ☎ **07/3891 6022.**

This theater, the home of the TN Theatre Company, was founded in 1888 and is the third-oldest working theater in Australia and the oldest in Brisbane. Both classical productions and new Australian works are presented. The 276 seats sell for A$12 to A$24 (U.S. $9.60 to $19.20).

THE CLUB & MUSIC SCENE

Brisbane is a young person's city, and the after-dark options are aimed mainly at under-30s. The gig guide in the free weekly *Time Off* lists pages of rock-club engagements. In addition, dance clubs abound. Happily, hotel cocktail lounges and friendly pubs offer an alternative for those of us looking back at 30.

No matter where you choose to have fun, be sure to try a Fourex (XXXX) or a Power's, Queensland's two most popular beers. The legal age for alcohol consumption here is 18.

NIGHTCLUBS

Friday's on the Water. 123 Eagle St. ☎ **07/3832 2122.** Cover Sun, Tues, and Wed A$4 (U.S. $3.20), Thurs A$5 (U.S. $4), Fri–Sat A$6 (U.S. $4.80).

Friday's is a popular bar/restaurant/nightclub complex adjacent to the lofty Riverside Centre. It opens Sunday to Thursday from 8pm until 3am, Friday and Saturday until 5am. This is the place to be—especially on a Friday night—and it's customary to wait in line to get in. Young professionals and "uni" (university) students make up the usual crowd. The action is both indoors and out, overlooking the Brisbane River with bands and dance music.

Ridge Restaurant. In the Ridge Hotel, 189 Leichhardt St. (at the corner of Henry Street). ☎ **07/3831 5000.**

The Ridge Restaurant is the only restaurant in Brisbane with a live dance band. Traditional tunes are played on Friday and Saturday from 8pm to midnight, and a lovely city-lights view from the ninth-floor "pozzie" (position) provides another good reason to dine here. The menu features Italian and seafood dishes.

Jazz

Caxton Hotel. 38 Caxton St., Petrie Terrace. ☎ **07/3369 5544.** No cover.

The historic Caxton Hotel, built in 1884, offers multiple entertainment choices. On Friday and Saturday nights the resident Piano Man plays singalong favorites in the bar; the DJ spins all the latest hits in the nightclub; and karaoke is the focus in the side bar. The mostly single crowd is 25 to 40 and knows how to party. This venerable spot claims to serve Brisbane's best charcoal-grilled steaks, set below a canopy of trees and palms. The Caxton Hotel is open Monday to Thursday from 10am to 10pm, Friday from 10am to 3am, and Saturday from 10am to 5am. The Australian National Marble Championships is held at the Caxton in June or July. No kidding.

Dance Clubs

Brisbane Underground. 61 Petrie Terrace. ☎ **07/3236 1511.** Cover A$4 (U.S. $3.20) Wed, A$7 (U.S. $5.60) Fri–Sat.

The Brisbane Underground is a popular dance club where queuing up is de rigueur. Open Friday and Saturday from 8pm to 5am and Wednesday from 8pm to 1am or later.

Margaux's. On level five in the Brisbane Hilton, 190 Elizabeth St. ☎ **07/3231 3131.** Free Weds–Thurs, A$5 (U.S. $4) Fri–Sat (free for hotel guests).

This club has an elegant yet relaxed atmosphere, open Wednesday to Saturday to 3am. The crowd is mature, professional, and for the most part over 25. A complete range of beverages and a supper menu are offered. For the sophisticated night owl.

THE BAR SCENE

America's Cup Bar. In the Brisbane Hilton, 190 Elizabeth St. ☎ **07/3231 3131.** No cover.

A pianist plays nightly in this pleasant pub where large yachting pictures line the walls and sailcloth banners extend overhead. The bar, on the lobby level, serves up good cheer Monday to Thursday from 5 to 10pm and Friday and Saturday from 5pm to 1am. Happy hour is 5 to 6:30pm. The America's Cup Bar caters to the yuppie/professonal crowd.

Breakfast Creek Hotel. 2 Kingsford Smith Dr., Albion. ☎ **07/3262 5988.** No cover.

This hotel, built in 1889, has won many awards for its popular beergarden and reasonably priced barbecue meals. Patrons pick their own cut and size of steak. This is the only pub in Brisbane to which beer is delivered in a wooden barrel. Dinner (see "Dining" above) costs about A$14 (U.S. $11.20).

✪ **The Gallery.** In the Conrad Treasury Casino Hotel, William Street. ☎ **07/3306 8888.** No cover.

What a delightful spot for a drink. The historic ambience is created by a high ceiling, a beautiful old bar that was at one time in the Brisbane Polo Club, a polished jarrah floor, and the fact that the pay phones are in a vault—this was formerly the Land Administration Building and the vault held the maps. Caricatures of well-known Aussies line the walls. The Gallery is open daily from 10am to 10pm, with light meals and snacks served from 11am to 8pm. A wide range of domestic and imported beers is served.

Pavillion Bar. In the Heritage Hotel, Edward Street. ☎ **07/3221 1999.** No cover.

A huge TV screen makes this the perfect place to watch sporting events and music videos. In addition, there's outdoor seating overlooking the lily pond. The Heritage is one of Bribane's best hotels, and this bar is classy—in contrast to the Port Office Hotel across the street (see below). The Pavillion draws a crowd of over-25s—professional types. The barbecue lunch served Monday to Friday from noon to 2pm is very popular (A$6/U.S. $4.80). The bar is open Monday to Thursday from 11:30am to 10pm and Friday and Saturday from noon to midnight. Happy hour is Friday from 5 to 7pm. A stubbie of Fourex (XXXX) is A$3.30 (U.S. $2.65).

Port Office Hotel. 38 Edward St., at the corner of Margaret Street. ☎ **07/3221 0072.** No cover.

This is a popular pub housed in a lovely old colonial building; the Port Office Hotel has both indoor and outdoor seating. The historic building, which once held the original port offices for Brisbane, is now a favorite blue-collar hangout. A stubbie of XXXX is A$3.30 (U.S. $2.60). Meals are served in PM's Bar & Palmers Bistro. Open Monday to Thursday from noon to 10pm and Friday and Saturday from noon to 1am.

A CASINO

Conrad Treasury Casino. At the top of Queen Street at George Street. ☎ **07/3306 8888.**

Brisbane's first casino opened in 1995 and occupies the former Treasury Building, a historic gem from 1886. Even if you don't gamble, walk past and admire the exterior. If you do like gaming, this place has roulette, blackjack, baccarat, craps, big six, sic-bo, and that Australian favorite, two-up. A total of 104 gaming tables and 1,200 machines await your money.

There are also several dining and drinking options: The most upmarket is the second-floor Marco Polo East West Cuisine, which serves Asian food; the 24 Hour Restaurant is on the first floor; and the ground-floor Blackjacks Casino Cafe offers inexpensive buffets (A$9.80/U.S. $7.80 lunch; A$11.80/U.S. $9.40 dinner). You must be 18 to enter the casino, and dress standards prohibit singlets, thongs, and workboots.

8 Southern & Central Queensland

Sun, sand, and surf typify southern and central Queensland. The major part of the state lies inland, but it's the coastal area that attracts travelers. The famed beaches of the Gold Coast and the Sunshine Coast make them one of Australia's most popular holiday destinations. Proserpine, Gladstone, and other cities of the central and Whitsunday regions serve as jumping-off points for the fascinating Great Barrier Reef, which lies offshore. Only the hinterland areas lack the three *S*'s; instead, they lure visitors with bird-watching, bushwalking, and beautiful scenery.

The southern half of the Sunshine State constitutes an area about the size of the U.S. state of Texas and is separated into two distinct climatic zones by the Great Dividing Range. East of the mountains is a rich coastal strip; to the west, vast dry plains stretch over great distances. Sugarcane, timber, and tourism, along with pineapples, bananas, and citrus, form the basis of the coastal economy. Inland, hardy farmers grow grain and raise cattle and sheep. Opals are found near the tiny township of Quilpie in the south and coal is mined in the central region.

Queensland's population tends to be more decentralized than that of other parts of the country. Only half of the state's 2.4 million residents live in Brisbane, and a string of middle-size cities are found along the ocean. Queenslanders also tend to be more ethnically homogeneous than residents of other states. Most migrants come from within Australia, not from Asia and southern Europe; therefore, little international influence is apparent.

Winter (June to August) is the best time to visit. Spring and fall are pleasant, but you should probably avoid "the wet" season, from December to March. Central Queensland straddles the Tropic of Capricorn, and temperatures to the north can get quite hot, while the southern portion has a temperate subtropical climate. For details, see "When to Go" in Chapter 3.

EXPLORING THE STATE'S COASTAL AREA

If you're traveling by public transportation, Queensland Railways carries passengers up and down the coast: The *Spirit of Capricorn* provides daily service between Rockhampton and Brisbane. The *Sunlander* and luxurious *Queenslander* travel between Cairns and Brisbane, stopping at Nambour on the Sunshine Coast, Proserpine on the Whitsunday Coast, and Bundaberg, Gladstone,

What's Special About Southern & Central Queensland

Beaches
- Gold Coast beaches, stretching for 42km (26 miles).
- Sunshine Coast beaches—long and uncrowded.

Top Attraction
- Dreamworld, near the Gold Coast, an enchanting down-under Disneyland.

Events & Festivals
- Burleigh Heads, on the Gold Coast, the site of numerous surfing championships and contests.
- The Gold Coast Indy Car Grand Prix every March.

National Parks
- Lamington National Park, one of the best places in the country to observe native fauna in its natural habitat.

Activities
- Surfing—what draws young people to the Sunshine Coast and, to a lesser extent, to the Gold Coast.
- Sailing, the big attraction in the Whitsundays.

Rockhampton, and Mackay on the Central Coast. The *Spirit of the Outback* provides service between Brisbane and Longreach in the outback.

Queensland Rail offers a six-day **Sunshine Rail Tour** with train travel from Brisbane to Cairns or vice versa. Passengers stay overnight in resorts and hotels along the way. This fully escorted experience includes tours of local areas and meals. Trips depart Brisbane on Monday and Cairns on Sunday. The per-person cost (based on two people sharing) ranges from U.S. $910 to $999. For details, contact the **Queensland Tourist and Travel Corporation** in Los Angeles (☎ 310/788-0997).

Queensland Rail also offers a **Sunshine Railpass** that provides travel on Queensland Rail and Brisbane CityTrain services. An additional fee is payable on the *Queenslander* for meals and sleeping berths. The 14-day pass costs A$388 (U.S. $310.40) in first class and A$267 (U.S. 213.60) in economy; 21 days cost A$477 (U.S. $381.60) in first class and A$309 (U.S. $247.20) in economy; and 30 days cost A$582 (U.S. $465.60) in first class and A$388 (U.S. $310.40) in economy. For further information, contact QTTC in Los Angeles at 310/788-0997 or Queensland Rail in Brisbane at 07/3235 2222.

Several regional airlines supplement the routes of the major carriers, so all places of interest in the Sunshine State are accessible by air. McCafferty's and Greyhound-Pioneer provide frequent coach service up and down the coast from Brisbane.

If you're going to drive, contact the **RACQ** (Royal Automobile Club of Queensland), GPO Building, 261 Queen St., Brisbane, QLD 4000 (☎ 07/3361 2444). The trek from Brisbane to Cairns is equal to motoring from Paris to Lisbon (1,717km/1,065 miles).

For information on accommodations in private homes around Brisbane and along the coast, see "Accommodations" in Chapter 7.

VISITOR INFORMATION The best source of information is the **Queensland Government Travel Centre** located in each state capital and many major cities overseas.

1 The Gold Coast

The Gold Coast is the most developed, commercialized, advertised, and controversial vacation destination in Australia. Its fans point to the 300 or more days of sunshine each year, the 42km (26 miles) of golden-sand beaches, the 70km (43 miles) of coastline, the 60 golf courses, and the nonstop entertainment options. Its critics point to the rows of high-rise hotels and apartments, the general overcrowding and traffic congestion, and the constant Mardi Gras atmosphere. About 4 million people vacation on the Gold Coast yearly—some come especially in March for the annual Indy car race that takes place on the streets of Surfer Paradise. Of course the area is popular with Australians, but you'll also find many Japanese and New Zealanders.

Both admirers and critics agree that the area strongly resembles Waikiki and Miami Beach. In fact, one stretch of sand known for its rows of hotels is named after the Florida city. The Gold Coast starts about an hour's drive south of Brisbane and stretches past the New South Wales border. The major centers are Surfers Paradise, Broadbeach, Southport, and the twin towns of Tweed Heads and Coolangatta, where many of the accommodations and entertainment venues are found. Southport is the commercial center and Burleigh Heads and Coolangatta are less congested resort areas. The whole region has a population of about 400,000.

SURFERS PARADISE

70km (44 miles) S of Brisbane

Happily crowded onto a strip of land between the South Pacific Ocean and the Nerang River, Surfers is ideal for both sun worshipers and action seekers. Tourists fill the sidewalks at all hours. So casual is the atmosphere that brief beachwear worn in shopping centers barely draws a stare. As on Waikiki, the hotels, souvenir shops, and entertainment centers here create a carnival atmosphere. The **Paradise Centre,** with its 117 shops and 20 fast-food outlets, is one focal point. **Cavill Avenue** is the main drag; it runs east-west and ends in the Cavill Mall, steps from golden sand and surf. The main north-south thoroughfare is the **Gold Coast Highway,** which becomes one-way south in the heart of town while **Ferny Avenue** carries the traffic one-way north.

ESSENTIALS

GETTING THERE It takes about an hour to drive to Surfers Paradise from Brisbane. International flights arrive in Brisbane, and Coachtrans operates a shuttle every 45 minutes to Surfers Paradise. The one-way fare is A$26 (U.S. $20.80). To contact Coachtrans on the Gold Coast, call 07/5592 3488; in Brisbane, call 07/3236 1000. Domestic flights come into the Gold Coast/Coolangatta Airport, adjacent to the New South Wales–Queensland border, and transfers to Surfers Paradise cost A$8 (U.S. $6.40). If you arrive on Qantas, call Gold Coast Airport Transit at 07/5536 6841 to arrange a coach transfer; if you come in on Ansett, call Silverbrae Coaches at 07/5576 4000. Qantas's fares between Sydney and Gold Coast/Coolangatta range from A$131 to A$166 (U.S. $104.80 to $132.80).

Citytrain offers service from Brisbane to Beenleigh and Helensvale at the northern end of the Gold Coast. Train service is scheduled to expand to Central Gold Coast by 1997. Travelers coming from the north can also take a train to Brisbane and then catch a coach to the Gold Coast; those arriving from the south can go as far as Murwillumbah, New South Wales, by train and then transfer to a coach.

Greyhound-Pioneer and McCafferty's offer coach service between Sydney and Surfers Paradise, the 14-hour trip costing A$80.80 (U.S. $64.60) one way.
The 80-minute trip from Brisbane costs A$15 (U.S. $12).

The Gold Coast

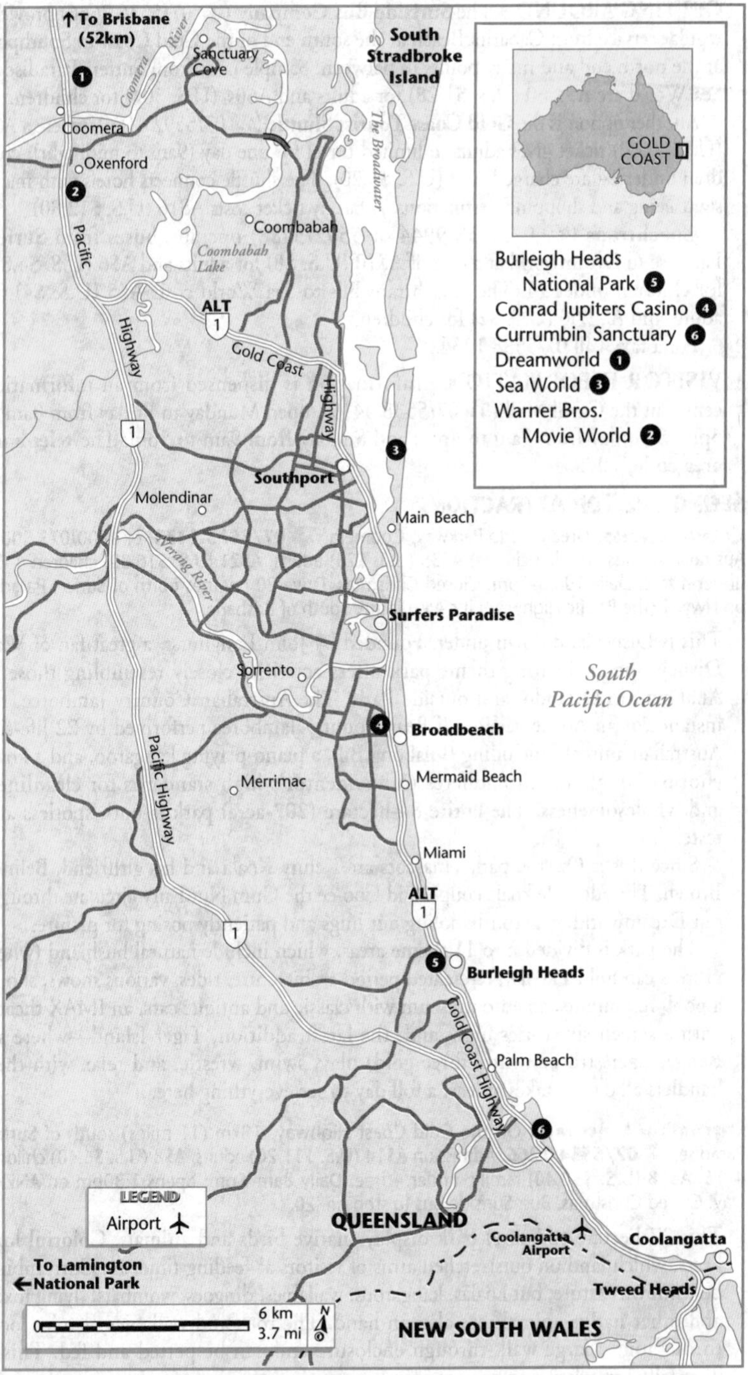

To Brisbane (52km)
Sanctuary Cove
Coomera River
South Stradbroke Island
The Broadwater
Coomera
Oxenford
Coombabah
Coombabah Lake
Pacific Highway
ALT 1
Gold Coast Highway
1
Southport
Molendinar
Main Beach
Nerang River
Surfers Paradise
Sorrento
South Pacific Ocean
Broadbeach
Merrimac
Mermaid Beach
Miami
Burleigh Heads
Palm Beach
QUEENSLAND
Coolangatta Airport
Coolangatta
Tweed Heads
NEW SOUTH WALES
To Lamington National Park
LEGEND
Airport
6 km
3.7 mi
N
GOLD COAST
Burleigh Heads National Park 5
Conrad Jupiters Casino 4
Currumbin Sanctuary 6
Dreamworld 1
Sea World 3
Warner Bros. Movie World 2
2334

GETTING AROUND The **Surfside Bus Company** (☎ 07/5536 7666) provides regular service from Cabarita Beach at the south end of the Gold Coast to Southport at the north end and many points in between. Sample fares from Surfers Paradise to Sea World are A$1.60 (U.S. $1.28) for adults and A60¢ (U.S. 50¢) for children.

Another option is the **Gold Coast Tourist Shuttle** (☎ 07/5592 4166), where a A$7 (U.S. $5.60) ticket gives adults unlimited travel for one day (9am to midnight); children under 14 are charged A$4 (U.S. $3.20). The shuttle connects hotels with major sightseeing and shopping destinations. A family ticket costs A$16 (U.S. $12.80).

Coachtrans (☎ 07/5538 9944 or 5592 3488) operates buses from Surfers Paradise to Dreamworld at a cost of A$10 (U.S. $8) for adults and A$6 (U.S. $4.80) for children under 14. The Coachtrans bus to Sea World costs A$5 (U.S. $4) for adults and A$2.50 (U.S. $2) for children.

For a taxi, call 07/5588 1234.

VISITOR INFORMATION Information is dispensed from an information center in the Cavill Mall (☎ 07/5538 4419), open Monday to Friday from 8am to 5pm, Saturday from 9am to 4pm, and Sunday from 9am to 5pm. The **telephone area code** is 07.

SEEING THE TOP ATTRACTIONS

✪ **Dreamworld.** Dreamworld Parkway, Coomera. ☎ **07/5573 1133,** or 1800/073 300 in Australia. Admission (all inclusive) A$35 (U.S. $28) adults, A$21 (U.S. $16.80) children 4–13; under 4 free. Daily 10am–5pm. Closed Christmas. Drive 20 minutes north of Surfers Paradise on Hwy. 1 (the Pacific Highway); it's 45 minutes south of Brisbane.

This is Disneyland down under. Founded by John Longhurst, a great fan of Walt Disney, the enchanting theme park offers activities closely resembling those in Anaheim, in Orlando, and outside Paris. The Australian Country Jamboree, for instance, is an Aussie version of Bear Country Jamboree performed by 22 life-size Australian animals, including Billabong Bill, a piano-playing kangaroo, and a koala chorus. Longhurst also adheres to his mentor's high standards for cleanliness and wholesomeness. The entire 84-hectare (207-acre) park is both spotless and tasteful.

Since this is Oz, the park's mascots are Kenny Koala and his girlfriend, Belinda Brown. The adorable koala couple and Coo-ee the Gum Nut Fairy circulate throughout Dreamworld, generously doling out hugs and patiently posing for pictures.

The park is divided into 11 theme areas, which include natural bushland (where visitors can hold a koala), re-created period architecture, rides, various shows, shops, a pool, restaurants, an auto museum with classic and antique cars, an IMAX theater with a screen six stories high, and, the latest addition, Tiger Island—where six Bengal tigers (three white, three gold) play, swim, wrestle, and relax with their handlers all day. It takes at least a full day to see everything here.

Currumbin Sanctuary. On the Gold Coast Highway, 18km (11 miles) south of Surfers Paradise. ☎ **07/5534 1266.** Admission A$14 (U.S. $11.20) adults, A$8 (U.S. $6.40) children 4–15, A$38 (U.S. $30.40) family; under 4 free. Daily 8am–5pm; opens 1:30pm on ANZAC Day. Closed Christmas. Bus: Surfside bus to stop no. 20.

This 27-hectare (67-acre) park displays native birds and animals. Colorful lorikeets, which land on outstretched arms of visitors at feeding time, are Currumbin's best-known feature, but koalas, kangaroos, wallabies, dingoes, wombats, flying foxes, and other native animals are also on hand. The roos and wallabies wander loose throughout a large walk-through enclosure and can be petted and fed. This is especially fun when one has a joey in her pouch. A miniature train circles the park, but walking provides the best access to animals.

Be sure to allow time for browsing through the several shops, which sell rocks, shells, jewelry, and gemstones in addition to souvenirs. It's also a good idea to phone ahead and find out the activity times of your favorite animals. The lorikeets usually dine between 8 and 9am and 4 and 5pm.

You can also dine here. Enjoy "Breakfast with the Birds," "Lunch with Nature," or a "Wild Snack" in the Terrace Cafe, Reserve Kiosk, or Main Station ice-cream parlor.

Sea World. On the Spit at Main Beach, 3km (2 miles) north of Surfers Paradise. ☎ **07/5588 2222.** Admission (all inclusive, except helicopter rides and dolphin tours) A$34 (U.S. $27.20) adults, A$22 (U.S. $17.60) children 4–13; under 4 free. Daily 10am–5pm. Bus: Surfside bus.

Except for the name, there's little resemblance between this park and those in America. Queensland's Sea World is basically an elaborate amusement park with a marine theme, and very few of the shows include animals. Action-packed rides like Bermuda Triangle, the Corkscrew, and the Flume Ride get much more attention. At this Sea World you can also ride Australia's first monorail and be taken on helicopter joy flights. If you go, allow four hours to see everything.

Warner Bros. Movie World. Pacific Highway, Oxenford. ☎ **07/5573 3999** or 5573 3891 (for recorded information). Admission A$34 (U.S. $27.20) adults, A$22 (U.S. $17.60) children 4–13; under 4 free. Daily 10am–5pm. Closed Christmas.

Just south of Dreamworld, this attraction is based on the famous Hollywood movie studio and has working sets. A first in the Southern Hemisphere, Movie World offers the Police Academy Stunt Show, the Great Gremlins Adventure, Outback Action, the Looney Tunes Studio (featuring the Warner Bros. cartoon favorites), and Batman Adventure—The Ride. The most recent additions are The Riddler's Lair, Lethal Weapon—The Ride, and Maverick Grand Illusion Show.

Themed restaurants, including Yosemite Sam's Place, Blazing Saddles Café, and Rick's Café Americain, offer meals and snacks.

Sir Bruce Cruises. At the river end of Cavill Avenue. ☎ **07/5531 3236.** Admission A$24 (U.S. $19.20) adults, A$18 (U.S. $14.40) children. Departs daily at 10:30am and 2pm.

This company offers a variety of calm-water cruises on the inland waterways adjacent to Surfers Paradise. The two-hour Canal and Harbour Cruise glides past palatial waterfront residences and provides a good look at an array of yachts. This waterborne sightseeing tour also takes you past hotels, shopping centers, and restaurants. Complimentary fresh scones with jam and cream are served, as are tea, coffee, and soft drinks.

Gold Coast Arts Centre. 135 Bundall Rd. ☎ **07/5581 6500.** Admission free to art gallery (☎ 07/5581 6517 or 5581 6521). Art gallery, Tues–Fri 10am–5pm, Sat–Sun 1–5pm.

The arts center provides a cultural retreat from the bright lights and commercial attractions of the Gold Coast. About five minutes' drive from Surfers Paradise on the banks of the Nerang River, the A$16-million (U.S. $12.8-million) complex includes two theaters and is the home of the **Gold Coast City Art Gallery**. Classical music concerts, plays, and ballet are staged regularly. Call 07/5581 6900 for tickets. The Harlequin Restaurant (☎ 07/5581 6584 or 5581 6568) in the complex serves lunch Monday to Friday and pretheater dinners.

SHOPPING

This is a major activity in the Surfers Paradise area. **Pacific Fair,** across from the Conrad Jupiters Hotel and Casino in Broadbeach, is Australia's only theme shopping complex and features cobbled streets and architecture designed to resemble the world's famous trading areas. Nearby, **The Oasis** is connected to the casino complex by monorail. Other places to spend your money include the **Australia Fair shopping center** in Southport, the **Paradise Centre** and **Cavill Avenue Mall** in Surfers Paradise, and **Marina Mirage**, at The Spit, Main Beach, Surfers Paradise. The centers are open Monday to Saturday from about 8:30am to 5:30pm. Most stores stay open until 9pm on Thursday and stores that cater to tourists and some centers are open on Sunday from 10:30am to 4pm. And don't forget—Dreamworld, Sea World, and Currumbin all have their own shops.

Outdoor Activities

Many of the Gold Coast's fun and games are, not surprisingly, waterborne activities. **Aussie Bob's Water Sports** (☎ 07/5591 7577) can organize water sleigh rides, seaplane joy flights, waterskiing, fishing charters, windsurfing boards, and speedboat fun rides. **Budds Beach Water Sportz** (☎ 07/5592 0644) rents catamarans, windsurfing boards, paddleboats, surf skis, canoes, aqua bikes, and more. Boogie boards and surfboards can be rented at **Brothers Neilsen** (☎ 07/5570 1186) at several locations in the area.

If you're traveling with kids, you may want to visit the **Wet n' Wild Water Park**, 15 minutes north of Surfers Paradise (☎ 07/5573 2277, or 5573 2255 for info). Besides wet rides, this spot offers new release films at their "Dive-In Movies" outdoor cinema. Seating is in-pool or on the deck.

Parasailing is possible at several beaches in and around Surfers Paradise. Call **Aussie Bob's Watersports** (above) if you're ready for this thrilling experience. The cost is A$50 (U.S. $40) per person.

Golf is also very popular on the Gold Coast, where there are 60 courses. **Hooked on Golf** (☎ 07/5598 2788 or 018/755693; fax 07/5598 2786) will take you to a different 18-hole course every day. **Play-A-Round Golf Tours**, Royal Pines Resort, Ashmore (☎ 07/5571 1800; fax 07/5571 1900) arranges four- to seven-day fully escorted golf tours along the Gold Coast and elsewhere in Queensland.

Where to Stay

Very Expensive

Hyatt Regency Sanctuary Cove. Manor Circle, Sanctuary Cove, via Hope Island, QLD 4212. ☎ **07/5530 1234,** or 1800/659 994 in Australia. Fax 07/5577 8234. 247 rms and suites. A/C MINIBAR TV TEL. A$225 (U.S. $180) standard double; A$285 (U.S. $228) Regency Club double; A$390–A$775 (U.S. $312–$620) one- or two-bedroom junior suite; A$1,100–A$1,345 (U.S. $880–$1,076) premier suite; A$1,400–A$1,645 (U.S. $1,120–$1,316) Presidential Suite. Additional bed A$35 (U.S. $28) extra. Children under 18 free in parents' room. Ask about lower midweek rates. AE, BC, DC, MC, V. Free parking. Coach service from Surfers Paradise, Coolangatta Airport, and Brisbane Airport.

Calling itself "Australia's first world-class resort," the Hyatt Regency Sanctuary Cove offers a dramatic contrast from the bright lights of Surfers Paradise. The resort is in a peaceful setting on the banks of the Coomera River, 25 minutes from Surfers, 40 minutes from Brisbane, and 40 minutes from the Coolangatta Airport. A planned residential community and village is adjacent.

Five low-rise lodges are spread across the property; one contains Regency Club rooms offering complimentary drinks and continental breakfast. All architecture and interiors are in the 1920s Australian homestead theme. Period furniture is used throughout the public spaces and guest rooms. One of the three-story buildings has an elevator (for the disabled). Each room has either a king-size bed or two doubles; all have clock radios, robes, tea- and coffee-making facilities, small refrigerators, and in-room movies. Suites have their own safes.

Dining/Entertainment: The Grange is a specialty restaurant featuring traditional cuisine. The Cove Cafe overlooks the terrace pool, tea and cocktails are served in the Verandah Bar, and Coomeras is a poolside bar and grill restaurant.

Services: Concierge, 24-hour room service, shoeshine, free daily newspaper, laundry, valet, nightly turndown, baby-sitting.

Facilities: Two outdoor pools (one freshwater, one salt—the saltwater pool has a sand bottom and sand "beach" around it), health club, gym, sauna, spa, tennis courts, squash court, two 18-hole golf courses.

Sheraton Mirage Gold Coast. Sea World Drive, Broadwater Spit, Main Beach, QLD 4217. ☎ **07/5591 1488.** Fax 07/5591 2299. 318 rms and suites. A/C MINIBAR TV TEL. A$420–A$500 (U.S. $336–$400) standard double; A$590 (U.S. $472) premium double; A$810–A$1080 (U.S. $648–$864) ocean or executive suite. Rates for Presidential and Royal Suite on request. Additional person A$60 (U.S. $48) extra. Children under 14 free in parents' room. AE, BC, DC, MC, V. Free parking.

The only Gold Coast area resort hotel right on the beach, the Sheraton Mirage offers an extensive sports/health complex, Sports Mirage, and shopping facilities across at Marina Mirage. The Sea World theme park is steps away. I don't recommend a short stay: By the time you find your way around the 30-hectare (75-acre) resort it'll be time to check out. The three-story accommodations blocks are surrounded by 2.5 hectares (6 acres) of shallow lagoons, and there's lots of lush landscaping. While the guest rooms don't have balconies, the 25 Mirage Rooms have their own terrace on a lagoon and are understandably popular.

The tropical decor is stylish, impressive, and (except for the deafening sound of the large fountain in the lobby) pleasant. All rooms have king-size beds or two doubles, tea- and coffee-making facilities, small refrigerators, clock radios, robes, safes, and in-room movies. All have cane furnishings and quarry-tile floors; 40% have ocean views.

Dining/Entertainment: Horizons is the resort's signature restaurant; there's also a coffee shop, Terraces, where large buffet-style meals are offered. Rolls is the nightclub.

Services: Concierge, 24-hour room service, shoeshine, free daily newspaper, laundry, valet, nightly turndown, massage.

Facilities: Two outdoor pools (including a lap pool in the health club and a huge sprawling lagoon-style pool with a swim-up bar and underwater bar stools), health club, gym, sauna, tennis courts, spa, hair salon.

Expensive

Conrad Jupiters Hotel and Casino. Gold Coast Highway, Broadbeach Island, Broadbeach, QLD 4218. ☎ **07/5592 1133** or 5592 8130, or 1800/07 4344 in Australia. Fax 07/5592 8219. 600 rms, 22 suites. A/C MINIBAR TV TEL. A$210–A$260 (U.S. $168–$208) double; A$595–A$1,650 (U.S. $476–$1,320) suite. Additional person A$20 (U.S. $16) extra. Children free in parents' room. No-smoking floor available. AE, BC, CB, DC, JCB, MC, V. Free parking.

Conrad's is a deluxe hotel with a very unique atmosphere. Buses collect patrons from all over Surfers Paradise and bring them to play at the gaming tables and video-gaming machines—thus it has the ambience of a large Las Vegas hostelry. The hotel is south of the center of Surfers Paradise, on its own island in the Nerang River; the beach is a block away, with monorail access. Conrad's is the largest in Australia, with more than 6 acres of landscaped grounds surrounding the property. Included on the 2,500-member staff are 4 full-time Japanese interpreters and 2 full-time people to look after the coach tours. All guest rooms have clock radios, tea- and coffee-making facilities, and in-room movies.

Dining/Entertainment: The hotel has six restaurants, myriad bars, a 950-seat show room, and 24-hour gaming, dining, and imbibing facilities.

Services: Concierge, 24-hour room service, free daily newspaper, laundry, valet, nightly turndown, baby-sitting, massage.

Facilities: Large heated pool complex (with Roman-style pavilion and food and drink service), spas, sauna, health club, four tennis courts, jogging track.

$ Gold Coast International Hotel. Gold Coast Highway and Staghorn Avenue, Surfers Paradise, QLD 4217. ☎ **07/5592 1200,** or 1800/07 4020 in Australia. Fax 07/5592 1180. 296 rms and suites. A/C MINIBAR TV TEL. A$185–A$205 (U.S. $148–$164) double; A$350 (U.S. $280) suite. Additional person A$20 (U.S. $16) extra. Children under 18 free in parents' room. Ask about lower weekend rates. No-smoking floors available. AE, BC, DC, MC, V. Free parking.

The Gold Coast International is both luxurious and centrally located. Arriving guests enter the impressive spacious lobby, where silk ficus trees are inset into a polished marble floor; more marble forms the staircase suspended over the Piano Lounge cocktail bar. Tiny white lights twinkle in the trees and soft music comes from a white-lacquered baby grand. Travertine marble also adorns the entryways and baths of the sleeping quarters. The king rooms are on the 22nd floor, and only these lack tile balconies. Half the rooms have ocean views, and all baths have tub/shower combinations, phones, and hairdryers. Clock radios, in-room movies, robes, tea- and coffee-making facilities, and small refrigerators are standard throughout.

Dining/Entertainment: The hotel has four restaurants and a half-dozen bars.

Services: Concierge, 24-hour room service, free daily newspaper, laundry, valet, nightly turndown, shoeshine, baby-sitting, massage.

Facilities: Outdoor pool with cocktail bar, health club, gym, sauna, massage, spa, squash and tennis courts, business center, hair salon, gift shops.

✪ Marriott Surfers Paradise. 158 Ferny Ave., Surfers Paradise, QLD 4217. ☎ **07/5592 9800,** or 1800/251 259 in Australia. Fax 07/5592 9888. 330 rms and suites. A/C MINIBAR TV TEL. A$320–A$340 (U.S. $256–$272) double; A$475–A$900 (U.S. $380–$720) suite. Free Parking (valet or self).

I was prepared not to like this place, as 28-story "name-brand" hotels are rarely my favorites. However, I came away positively impressed. For one thing, the designers remembered where they were, so instead of that cookie-cutter, could-be-anywhere decor, this Marriott actually reflects its surroundings. The Queensland ambience in the lobby is created by a flagstone floor, wooden shutters, the large constantly waving punkahs hanging from the high ceiling, and the Moreton Bay fig leaf motif used throughout. Outside, guests gather around a manmade beach and a heated saltwater lagoon in which there's an artificial coral reef (with tropical fish) and a waterfall. Scuba lessons are given here. Nearby, a heated pool and spas offer freshwater alternatives. "North-facing" rooms overlook these facilities, and the ocean beyond; I think it's worth the extra money to have this view. Every room has a balcony and either a king bed or two doubles. The resort is on the Nerang River; a walkway leads to Surfers Paradise Beach—about five minutes away. Room amenities include in-room safes and VCRs, but the closet is small and has those nasty nonremovable hangers.

Dining/Entertainment: Cafe on the Lagoon Restaurant serves California cuisine, including wood-fired pizza; drinks are served in the Lagoon Terrace Bar. There's also a Benihana Japanese Steakhouse.

Services: Twice-daily maid service, 24-hour room service, concierge, laundry/valet, shuttle bus to nearby attractions, business services, complimentary child care two hours a day, baby-sitting.

Facilities: Marina, Kid's Klub, heated freshwater pool and spas, saltwater lagoon, artificial coral reef, two tennis courts, jogging track, scuba lessons, coin-op laundry, beauty salon.

✪ **Pan Pacific Hotel Gold Coast.** 81 Surf Parade, Broadbeach, QLD 4218. ☎ **07/5592 2250,** or 1800/07 4465 in Australia. Fax 07/5592 3747. 298 rms and suites. A/C MINIBAR TV TEL. A$220 (U.S. $176) standard double; A$295 (U.S. $236) corner king suite; A$600 (U.S. $480) ocean-view suite; A$1,200 (U.S. $960) Pacific Suite. Additional person A$20 (U.S. $16) extra. Higher in peak season, lower in midweek. Ask about special packages. Children under 15 free in parents' room. No-smoking rooms available. AE, BC, DC, MC, V. Free parking.

The Pan Pacific is the epitome of Gold Coast accommodation. The 23-story hotel is 50 yards from the beach, 5km (3 miles) south of central Surfers Paradise, and is connected to Jupiters Casino by a monorail. Adjacent to it is the Oasis shopping complex, which has a carousel, lots of places to spend money, and many eating options—including a McDonald's (yes, the golden arches).

The marble lobby has a very modern fountain and a pair of three-story-high palm trees. Two-thirds of the guest rooms have ocean views, and all have at least one balcony and a pleasant color scheme. Each bath has a tub separate from the shower stall, and corner "king rooms" and all suites have spa baths. Actually, if your budget allows, I highly recommend the corner king rooms. The view from your spa is great, and each has a king-size bed and a lovely green marble bath. All quarters have safes.

Dining/Entertainment: Meals are served in Cafe Pelicans and Mavericks Restaurant.

Services: 24-hour room service, concierge, laundry/valet, baby-sitting.

Facilities: Two outdoor pools, health club, gym, sauna, spa, running track, two night-lit tennis courts; hair salon, gift shop, and newsstand in adjacent Oasis shopping complex.

Ramada Hotel. Hanlan Street and the Gold Coast Highway, Surfers Paradise, QLD 4217. ☎ **07/5579 3499,** or 1800/07 4317 in Australia. Fax 07/5592 0026. 405 rms and family suites. A/C MINIBAR TV TEL. A$215 (U.S. $172) double; A$250 (U.S. $200) family suite. Additional person A$30 (U.S. $24) extra. Children under 15 free in parents' room. Ask about weekend packages and lower standby rates (same-day bookings for midweek accommodations). No-smoking floors available. AE, BC, DC, MC, V. Free parking.

Smack in the middle of Surfers Paradise, the 36-story Ramada is ideal for those who like to be where the action is. The shops and food outlets of the Paradise Centre are adjacent and the beach is just steps away. The Ramada's spacious rooms have tub/shower combinations and hairdryers and offer either two double beds or a queen-size bed with a twin. The balconies provide a view of the ocean to the north or the hinterland to the west.

Dining/Entertainment: Summerfield's Restaurant is open daily (A$18/U.S. $14.40 for the breakfast buffet). Bamboo Palace serves Asian cuisine.

Services: 24-hour room service, laundry, valet, baby-sitting.

Facilities: Outdoor pool, tennis court, spa pool, Health Club (two steam rooms, gym equipment, massage), badminton, children's playground.

Moderate

Trickett Gardens Holiday Inn. 24–30 Trickett St., Surfers Paradise, QLD 4217. ☎ **07/5539 0988,** or 1800/07 4290 in Australia. Fax 07/5592 0791. 32 apts. TV TEL. A$84 (U.S. $67.20) one-bedroom apt for one or two; A$92 (U.S. $73.60) two-bedroom/one-bath apt for two; A$116 (U.S. $92.80) two-bedroom/two-bath apt for four. Additional person A$12 (U.S. $9.60) extra. "Holiday Season" rates are 35% higher. AE, BC, DC, MC, V. Free parking.

Trickett Gardens is a nice serviced-apartment complex for folks who want to do their own cooking. While a little more modest than the Bahia's (below), the apartments are more than adequate. In the heart of Surfers Paradise and close to the beach, the low-rise units, serviced daily, all have washers and dryers. Cooked or continental breakfast and other meals can be delivered to the units. A pool and spa are in front of the building.

Inexpensive

$ Bahia Beachfront Apartments. 154 Esplanade, Surfers Paradise, QLD 4217. ☎ **07/5538 3322.** Fax 07/5592 0318. 30 apts. TV TEL. A$78 (U.S. $62.40) one-bedroom apt for one or two; A$90 (U.S. $72) two-bedroom apt for one or two. Additional person A$10 (U.S. $8) extra. Higher holiday rates. Ask about weekly discounts. AE, BC, MC, V. Free underground security parking.

The Bahia is ideal for those who wish self-contained lodgings that are serviced daily. The 14-story building is on the beach, 900 meters (half a mile) from the heart of Surfers Paradise. Each unit has a washing machine and dryer, fully equipped kitchen, dishwasher, and private balcony. One-bedroom apartments measure 700 square feet, and the two-bedroom units, with two baths, are 1,300 square feet. Above the third floor, guests look out over the ocean.

The Bahia is a great dollarwise value for folks who want to do their own cooking and don't mind the lack of flashy hotel amenities. Continental breakfast and other meals can be delivered to the apartments. Friendly resident managers Karen and Richard Stephens and Lynne and Kim Adamson staff the reception desk from 8:30am to 6:30pm. Guests can use the heated pool, sauna, and spa at no charge. Mr. and Mrs. John Morris, readers from Richmond, Va., U.S.A., describe the 11th-floor view as "unbelieveable" and the whole place as "very clean, good value."

WHERE TO DINE

Charters Towers. In Conrad Jupiters Hotel and Casino, Gold Coast Highway, Broadbeach. ☎ **07/5592 1133.** Reservations required. Main courses A$19.50–A$34.50 (U.S. $15.60–$27.60). AE, BC, DC, MC, V. Daily from 6pm. STEAK/SEAFOOD.

Named for the township at the heart of Queensland's gold rush in the 1800s, this restaurant boasts walls lined with paintings by one of Australia's leading artists. Its gourmet à la carte menu features top-quality Australian cuisine complemented by attentive service. The specialties include crabmeat- and asparagus-topped oysters, ragout of reef fish and crustaceans, and charcoal-grilled steak. The elegant surroundings overlook the hotel's atrium and across to the casino.

$ Food Fantasy. In Conrad Jupiters Hotel and Casino, Gold Coast Highway, Broadbeach. ☎ **07/5592 1133.** Reservations not accepted. Breakfast buffet A$8.25–A$16.50 (U.S. $6.60–$13.20); lunch buffet A$8.75–A$17.50 (U.S. $7–$14); dinner buffet A$11.25–A$22.50 (U.S. $9–$18). AE, BC, DC, MC, V. Daily 6:30–10am, 11:30am–2:30pm, and 5:30–10:30pm; brunch Sun 6:30am–3pm. Bus: Conrad Jupiters Casino. BUFFET.

Food Fantasy is an appropriate dining spot for those who've yet to hit the jackpot. Themed as a tropical island paradise, the restaurant overlooks the pool and gardens. Quality and quantity make Food Fantasy very popular, and you'll probably have to wait in line.

Grumpy's Wharf. 60–70 Seaworld Dr., Mariner's Cove, The Spit (just north of central Surfers Paradise). ☎ **07/5532 2900.** Fax 07/5532 9165. Reservations accepted. Main courses A$15.90–A$30 (U.S. $12.70–$24). AE, BC, DC, MC, V. Daily noon–10:30pm. SEAFOOD/STEAK.

The decor of this pleasant restaurant overlooking the marina includes both nautical bric-a-brac and memorabilia from the Indy race held annually on the Gold Coast. Grumpy's was named after the original owner, whose stride reminded his friends of one of the Seven Dwarfs. The best dishes are the daily specials of very fresh fish—

Surfers Paradise Food Courts

Fisherman's Wharf is a waterfront complex of shops and eateries 4km (2 1/2 miles) north of Surfers Paradise near the Sea World amusement park. The sprawling collection of low-rise buildings has an early Australian maritime theme and enjoys wonderful views over the picturesque inland waterway, wharves, and jetties. Live entertainment is provided daily.

At one of the Fisherman's Wharf restaurants, the **Hungry Pelican** (☎ 07/5532 7933 or 5532 7944), good seafood meals, as well as steaks, salads, and sandwiches, are available self-service style. Dining is outdoors at umbrella-shaded tables, and the cost averages A$11 (U.S. $8.80) per person. The cocktail bar upstairs, the **Blue Water Bar,** has a wonderful water view and comfy wicker chairs—a delightful place for a drink or snack. Access to Fisherman's Wharf from Surfers Paradise is by boat or via the Surfside bus service.

One of the most economical places to eat in Surfers is **The Picnic Place,** in the Paradise Centre (☎ 07/5592 0155), where 14 great eateries and a licensed bar are located. The Funtasia Amusement Centre is adjacent.

depending on the time of year, these might be coral trout, snapper, or Atlantic salmon. Regular menu items include barbecued "bugs," seafood risotto, barramundi filet, and steak. If you like prawns, you can have them pan-fried with a spicy red Thai curry and coconut sauce and tossed with rice noodles, or crispy, or skewered with crocodile. Take my advice and leave room for dessert—Grumpy's chocolate cake is luscious.

✪ **Oskar's Garden Restaurant.** 2931 Gold Coast Hwy. ☎ **07/5538 5244.** Reservations recommended. Main courses A$19.90–A$23.50 (U.S. $15.92–$18.80). Public holiday surcharge A$3 (U.S. $2.40) per person. AE, BC, DC, MC, V. Daily noon–midnight. Bus: Surfside bus. MODERN MULTICULTURAL/SEAFOOD.

This eatery, 2km (a mile) south of the heart of Surfers Paradise, serves delicious creative cuisine. The à la carte menu features fresh local seafood, like salmon, king prawns, lobster, and mud crab. More unusual dishes like crocodile, emu, and quail are also offered. "Our cuisine has exotic Cajun, Italian, Asian, and Thai influences," the chef explains. All breads, pastas, and ice cream are made on the premises. You might like to try the seafood salad: local seafood tossed with buckwheat noodles, chili, and sesame dressing. Or perhaps try the Moreton Bay bugs baked in the stone oven and drizzled with a chili plum sauce.

This Surfers Paradise eatery has both inside and outside dining. Bright kelly-green fans hanging from wooden-beam ceilings complement the charcoal-gray polished granite tabletops, colorful Native American–style upholstery, and polished wooden floor. The attractive decor, good service, and wonderful food make this spot understandably popular.

Yamagen. In the Gold Coast International Hotel, Gold Coast Highway and Staghorn Avenue. ☎ **07/5592 0088.** Reservations recommended. Average meal A$45 (U.S. $36). AE, BC, DC, MC, V. Mon–Sat noon–2pm and 5:30–10pm. Closed public holidays. JAPANESE.

Authentic decor and architecture complement the cuisine. Yamagen is divided into three areas: the sushi bar, the teppanyaki room, and an à la carte section. The menu, written in Japanese with English subtitles, includes sunomono (marinated vegetables and seasonal seafood), yakitori (bamboo-skewered chicken with teriyaki sauce), sumibiyaki (marinated beef and vegetables charcoal-grilled at the table), and tempura moriawase (a variety of fine seafood and vegetables deep-fried in soybean oil). For dessert, you can choose between tempura ice cream, green-tea ice cream, orange sorbet, assorted fruit, or the pineapple boat special.

After Dark

In spite of everything that's available on the Gold Coast, some folks prefer to go over the border to clubs in New South Wales. Free bus transportation from Surfers Paradise to Tweed Heads is provided by the **Twin Towns Services Club** (☎ 07/5536 2277) and the **Seagulls Rugby League Football Club** (☎ 07/5536 3433). These nightspots are discussed under "Murwillumbah" in Chapter 6.

Those who elect to stay in and around Surfers Paradise can choose from a dozen or so hot dance clubs and nightclubs, including **Fortunes Nightclub** in the Conrad Jupiters Casino, Gold Coast Highway, Broadbeach (☎ 07/5592 1133), open daily from 9am to 3am. The sophisticated nightspot, reached by glass elevators from the gaming levels, features the latest in video, sound, and light effects. Cover charge for those not staying at the hotel is A$5 (U.S. $4) midweek and A$5 to A$10 (U.S. $4 to $8) weekends.

Melba's on the Park, 46 Cavill Ave. (☎ 07/5538 7411), and the **Penthouse Niteclub,** Orchard Avenue (☎ 07/5538 1388), are two other popular nightspots, both with A$7 (U.S. $5.60) cover charges. The Penthouse offers four floors of entertainment: There's a popular piano bar on the fourth floor, with dancing on the first, second, and third floors—until 5am Monday to Saturday, until 3am Sunday.

The best-known dinner theater is **Dracula's Cabaret Restaurant,** 1 Hooker Blvd., Broadbeach Waters (☎ 07/5575 1000)—just a "blood squirt from the casino." Here a three-course dinner and show, offered Tuesday to Friday at 7pm, cost A$35 (U.S. $28) per person. The same thing costs A$45 (U.S. $36) on Saturday. This is a great spot for those who enjoy horror.

The 940-seat **International Showroom,** on the lower level of the Conrad Jupiters Casino, provides spectacular floor shows Las Vegas style. Performances are at 8pm Tuesday to Friday, 7:30 and 10:15pm Saturday, and 6:30pm Sunday, with a Wednesday matinee at 12:30pm. For reservations, call 07/5576 2411 (or 1800/07 4144 in Australia). Tickets cost A$35 (U.S. $28). Children's tickets to the matinee are A$20 (U.S. $16).

Gambling at the **Conrad Jupiters Casino,** with its 114 gaming tables, 1,000 video machines, and numerous "pokies," is another popular activity. Be sure to watch the crowd play two-up, an Australian game where the toss of a coin generates the kind of cheering and yelling usually associated with football contests. The casino is open 24 hours a day; the minimum age is 18.

Also, don't overlook the performances at the **Gold Coast Arts Centre** (see "What to See & Do" above).

BURLEIGH HEADS

91km (56 miles) S of Brisbane, 16km (10 miles) S of Surfers Paradise

Halfway between Surfers Paradise and the New South Wales border, the community of Burleigh Heads has a relaxed, relatively quiet family atmosphere.

Essentials

GETTING THERE Convenient bus service makes the run to and from Surfers Paradise frequently. Motorists simply follow the Gold Coast Highway.

VISITOR INFORMATION The **telephone area code** is 07.

Seeing the Town

Burleigh Heads is best known as the site of various surf championships. The natural headland at Burleigh forms an ideal amphitheater from which you can watch skilled surfers from all over the world who come here to test their mettle against the great waves. Along with **Currumbin Alley, Kirra, Greenmount,** and **Duranbah**, Burleigh Heads is one of the best point breaks on the Gold Coast.

Burleigh Heads National Park is another big draw. A 3km (2-mile) graded track leads around the headland, giving sweeping views of the coast.

Where to Stay

$ **Burleigh Beach Tower.** 52 Goodwin Terrace, Burleigh Heads, QLD 4220. ☎ **07/5535 9222.** Fax 07/5576 1095. 101 apts. TV TEL. A$92 (U.S. $73.60) one-bedroom apt for one or two; A$112 (U.S. $89.60) two-bedroom apt for two. Additional person A$20 (U.S. $16) extra. Three-night minimum stay. Much higher holiday rates. No-smoking rooms available. AE, BC, DC, MC, V. Free parking. Bus: Stop 42.

The Burleigh Beach Tower is just steps from a beautiful white-sand beach. It has a modest lobby, a small pool, an adequate spa, and a tennis court. The apartments are furnished in a traditional decor with good-quality pieces, and each has a balcony and ocean view. Each kitchen is fully equipped (with a dishwasher), while each bath has a washing machine and dryer. Heating and air conditioning aren't provided, but with the Gold Coast's subtropical climate that really isn't a problem. Many dining spots are nearby and several eateries deliver. Weekly chamber service is included, and daily cleaning is available on request at an extra charge.

COOLANGATTA

100km (62 miles) S of Brisbane

The most southerly community on the Gold Coast, Coolangatta, like Burleigh Heads, offers beautiful beaches, relatively inexpensive accommodations, and a peaceful holiday atmosphere. Known with Tweed Heads in New South Wales as one of the "twin towns," Coolangatta is ideal for those who want to be close to the gambling and nightlife that thrive across the border. And access is easy to the Gold Coast's other attractions, nightlife, and shopping. Coolangatta and nearby Kirra are popular with board surfers.

Essentials

GETTING THERE There's frequent bus service along the Gold Coast Highway to and from Coolangatta. The Gold Coast/Coolangatta Airport is nearby.

VISITOR INFORMATION Information is available at the **Gold Coast Tourism Bureau Information Centre,** Beach House Plaza, Marine Parade, Coolangatta, QLD 4225 (☎ 07/5536 7765; fax 07/5536 7841), open Monday to Friday from 8am to 2pm and 3pm to 4pm, Saturday from 8am to 3pm, and public holidays from 8am to 1pm. The **telephone area code** is 07.

Where to Stay

Beach House Seaside Resort. 52 Marine Parade, Coolangatta, QLD 4225. ☎ **07/5536 5566.** Fax 07/5536 5466. 132 apts. TV TEL. A$115 (U.S. $92) double per night for stays of three or more nights; A$125 (U.S. $100) double per night for shorter visits. Additional person A$10 (U.S. $8) extra. Rates about 20% higher during school holidays. AE, BC, DC, MC, V. Free parking. Frequent public bus service.

This is a delightful spot for a self-contained holiday. Each unit has its own dishwasher, microwave, washer, and dryer. Ceramic-tile balconies have wonderful water views. The two-bedroom/two-bath units easily sleep six. The 17-story building is across from a beautiful stretch of golden sand and several eateries and shops are in a ground-level arcade. A supermarket, open daily, is nearby. There are an open-air squash court, a half court for tennis, a nice gym, two barbecues, a pool, a spa, and two saunas.

Activities for children are provided at the Kids Club Monday to Friday. Babysitting can be arranged.

2 The Gold Coast Hinterland

"The green behind the gold," as it's known, is a wonderful forested area just west of the bright lights and beaches that attract most visitors. Here savvy Australians retreat from the heat, hectic pace, and crowds found along the coast.

LAMINGTON NATIONAL PARK

45km (28 miles) W of the Gold Coast, 120km (74 miles) S of Brisbane

One of the few Queensland attractions not on the coast or an offshore island, Lamington National Park is a haven for those who like learning about native animals, hiking, eating hearty meals in a wholesome family environment, and generally admiring the wonders of nature. While the park is geographically fairly close to Surfers Paradise, no two places could be experientially farther apart.

Most of the 20,000-hectare (49,400-acre) park is covered with a dense rain forest—the largest of its type in Australia. Three-thousand-year-old antarctic beech trees are found in the temperate areas of the higher altitudes, and subtropical forest thrives in the warmer valleys. The remaining 30% or so is open forest. Both types of woodland attract native birds and animals, and it's common to see colorful crimson rosellas, king parrots, satin bowerbirds, black-and-gold regent bowerbirds, bandicoots, sugar gliders, pademelons (a species of small wallaby), brush turkeys, and possums while walking on the 160km (99 miles) of trails that wind throughout the park. You might even happen upon a rare Albert's lyrebird, found only in this region. Because of its lofty situation on a plateau of narrow ridges, Lamington is also blessed with some 500 waterfalls.

ESSENTIALS

GETTING THERE The easiest way to get to Lamington is by car. If you're traveling from Brisbane, allow two hours. Take the Pacific Highway south to the Beenleigh turnoff and follow the road that has the TAMBORINE/BEAUDESERT sign. After 20 minutes you'll come to the small village of Tamborine. Follow the signs to Canungra. Once there, follow the signs to either O'Reilly's or Binna Burra, depending on where you're staying. Because of the winding mountain road, the trip from Canungra to O'Reilly's takes an hour; allow similar time to reach Binna Burra.

From Surfers Paradise, head west to Nerang, then to Canungra. The New South Wales–Queensland border forms the southern boundary of the park.

The other arrival alternative is hitching a ride on one of the day-tour buses that visit the park. **All State Scenic Tours** (☎ 07/3285 1777) makes the trip from Brisbane to O'Reilly's Sunday to Friday (A$35/U.S. $28 round trip). The **Mountain Coach Company** (☎ 07/5592 1066) provides daily transportation to O'Reilly's from Surfers Paradise. The cost is A$32 (U.S. $25.60) round trip; half price for children 5 to 14. Binna Burra Lodge offers a coach service leaving the Surfers Paradise Coach Centre daily at 1:15pm (A$32/U.S. $25.60 round trip; half price for children).

VISITOR INFORMATION The **Canungra Visitor Information Centre,** Lamington National Park Road, Canungra, QLD 4275 (☎ 07/5543 5156), 30km

(18 miles) west of Nerang, is open Sunday to Friday from 10am to 4pm and Saturday from 10am to 12:30pm. The **telephone area code** is 07.

Where to Stay & Dine

Camping is permitted in certain areas. For more information, contact **Binna Burra Mountain Lodge** (☎ 07/5533 3622). Sites with power cost A$3 (U.S. $2.40), plus A$7 (U.S. $5.60) per person per night. Safari tents, accommodating two to four, cost A$36 (U.S. $28.80) for two and A$52 (U.S. $41.60) for four (including beds and lighting).

When you're deciding where to stay in Lamington, keep in mind that the food is better at O'Reilly's and the rooms are nicer at Binna Burra. Decide what's important to you and go from there.

Binna Burra Mountain Lodge and Campsite. Beechmont, via Nerang, QLD 4211. ☎ **07/5533 3622,** or 1800/07 4260 in Australia. Fax 07/5533 3658. (North American sales office: ☎ 408/685-8901, or 800/225-9849 in the U.S. and Canada; fax 408/685-8903). 41 cabins (22 with bath), 25 tent sites. A$105–A$160 (U.S. $84–$128) in cabin; A$7 (U.S. $5.60) tent site. Rates are per person based on two people sharing. Cabin price includes all meals and activities. Children under 5 free; those 5–14 half price. Ask about lower weekly rates and midweek specials. MC, V. Free parking. See "Getting There" above for transportation.

This holiday retreat, open since 1933, enjoys a scenic rain-forest site. The rustic timber, stone, and shingle accommodations offer good views of the surrounding terrain. The 22 Acacia cabins have private toilets and showers, plus tea- and coffee-making facilities, small refrigerators, and verandas. The 12 Banksia cabins have sinks, but guests use communal baths. The 7 Casuarina cabins are the most basic. All three lodging types offer heaters and electric blankets.

Homestyle meals are served in the dining room with a view of the Coomera Valley. Breakfast, morning tea, lunch, afternoon tea, dinner, and supper are included in the rates. You can play pool or table tennis in the games room, where there's a cozy fire in the winter. A craft shop and tearoom are also on the premises.

✪ **O'Reilly's Guest House.** Lamington National Park, via Canungra, QLD 4275. ☎ **07/5544 0644.** Fax 07/5544 0638. 51 rms (44 with bath). A$105 (U.S. $84) per person in room without bath, A$150 (U.S. $120) per person in room with bath. Children under 6 stay free; those 6–14 are charged half price. Rates include all meals, activities, and entertainment. AE, BC, DC, MC, V. Free parking. See "Getting There" above for transportation.

In a pocket of lofty serenity, the O'Reillys introduce guests to their woodland wilderness as generations of their family have done since 1926. Their comfortable rustic guesthouse, at an elevation of 900 meters (2,970 ft.), is approached by a road that winds up through the mountains from Canungra. Though only a 2-hour drive from Brisbane and 1½ hours from the Gold Coast, O'Reilly's feels like an entirely different world. You're most often met by a member of the family—usually Shane or Tim these days—and escorted to your accommodations. At the first meal you're seated at a table for six or eight and introduced to the folks you'll be dining with for the rest of the stay (unless you request a change in order to sit with newfound hiking buddies). The rates include early-morning tea, breakfast, morning tea, lunch, afternoon tea, dinner, and supper. Everything is made on the premises; the delicious fare is served family or buffet style. Drinks at the bar or with dinner are extra.

It's not unusual for small marsupials to dine along with guests—on the other side of a floodlit picture window where fruit and other bits have been left for them.

A member of the family stops by each table during meals to explain the day's or evening's activities and ascertain guests' interests. Bird-watching expeditions are conducted by a resident naturalist; four-wheel-drive trips and short guided walks are intended for those whose legs aren't as nimble as they used to be. One track has been surfaced to accommodate wheelchairs. A cleverly constructed canopy walk, suspended above the rain forest, allows a unique perspective. At night, artful slide shows and educational programs highlight native animals and birds of the area, and evening walks are held to search out shy nocturnal creatures or visit glowworm grottoes. All guided walks, bus trips, and evening presentations are included in the rates.

Three categories of rooms are available here. The most comfortable are the 37 motel-style quarters, each with a bath, a queen-size bed, tea- and coffee-making facilities, a small refrigerator, and a view of the surrounding spectacular scenery. Eight single rooms also have toilets and showers. Another eight rooms rely entirely on communal baths. Two rooms are suitable for the handicapped. Nights at this elevation can be pretty nippy, but all accommodations have electric blankets and heaters; the large rustic lounge has a lovely open fire.

There's a tennis court and a nice gift shop on the premises, and baby-sitting can be arranged.

TAMBORINE MOUNTAIN

70km (43.3 miles) S of Brisbane, 40km (24.8 miles) NW of Surfers Paradise

Tambourine Mountain is an off-the-beaten-path retreat—"tourists" may not like it, "travelers" will.

ESSENTIALS

GETTING THERE Driving time from Brisbane is 1 hour; from the Gold Coast, 40 minutes. Logan Coach & Bus Service (☎ 07/5546 3077) brings visitors from Brisbane. Tambourine Mountain Coach Service (☎ 07/5545 1298) provides transportation from the Gold Coast.

VISITOR INFORMATION Information is available from **The Ranger,** QNPWS, Tamborine Mountain, Knoll Road, North Tamborine, QLD 4272 (☎ 07/5545 1171). The **telephone area code** is 07.

SEEING THE AREA

Due west of Sanctuary Cove, Tamborine Mountain isn't a mountain at all, but an undulating plateau some 550 meters (1,788 feet) above sea level. The area is about 4km (2.5 miles) wide and 8km (5 miles) long, and though there's no mountain peak to climb, you'll find subtropical rain forest, beautiful gardens, native birds, galleries, and tea rooms. A country market is held on the second Sunday of each month at the Show Ground in Mount Tamborine. Extensive walking tracks (trails) wind throughout the nine national parks in the area.

WHERE TO STAY

$ Tamborine Mountain Bed and Breakfast. WYUKA 19–23 Witherby Cresent, Eagle Heights, Tamborine Mountain, QLD 4271. ☎ **07/5545 3595.** 4 rms. A/C TV. A$110 (U.S. $88) double weekend. Mon–Thurs 10% discount. A$30 (U.S. $24) three-course dinner. BYO. BC, MC, V. No children under 12.

On a clear day you can see all the way to the coast where Surfers Paradise high-rises look like something from another world. In this natural timber house, native birds and homemade bread are the focus. Carolyn Rose and Michael Perrin have created a most unusual abode: The exposed timber in the lounge walls is from an old New South Wales bridge that was being pulled down. The rocks for the fireplace were collected by the couple from various places on the mountain. The guest rooms have showers, mosquito netting over the beds, doonas, and wood floors and ceilings. One has a four-poster bed. The guest quarters are connected to the main house by a covered walkway. At breakfast everyone enjoys homemade bread and jam, freshly squeezed juice, and homemade muesli. Complimentary tea and coffee are available throughout the day. The bird feeders on the extensive wood decks around the house attract magpies, king parrots, lorikeets, kookaburras, and rosellas. The birds, like the flightless guests, are attracted to this cozy B&B by the great food.

3 The Sunshine Coast

Like the Gold Coast, the Sunshine Coast is blessed with a benign climate and miles of beautiful ocean beaches. The Sunshine Coast starts at Caloundra, 83km (51 miles) north of Brisbane, and extends to Rainbow Beach, taking in the seaside communities of Kawana, Mooloolaba, Maroochydore, Coolum, and Noosa. Unlike the popular resort area south of Brisbane, the Sunshine Coast is low-rise and laid-back. In this part of Queensland, the majority of tourists are Australians who want to enjoy the beaches and go surfing, and R&R means "rest and relaxation," not "rock 'n' roll." Most attractions are designed for families, and much less evidence of commercialization exists. Visitors are more likely to admire the beautiful coastline of Noosa National Park than to dance the night away in a club, and rides at the Big Pineapple are the region's tame answer to the Gold Coast's amusement parks.

NOOSA

150km (93 miles) N of Brisbane

Noosa, the principal township on the Sunshine Coast, is comprised of **Noosa Heads** (restaurants and accommodations), **Noosa Junction** (business area), and **Noosaville** (riverside region and popular fishing spot). **Hastings Street** is the center of activity and main thoroughfare in this seaside resort of 17,000. The oceanfront in town hasn't weathered well, but the coast from the Heads to **Sunshine Beach** is a long sandy paradise. Marked hiking trails and spectacular scenery are adjacent to town in Noosa National Park. The surfing here is excellent.

ESSENTIALS

GETTING THERE If you're driving, allow two hours from Brisbane. Go north on the Bruce Highway and turn east at Eumundi. Travelers bound for Noosa fly Sunstate Airlines, Qantas, Ansett, or Flight West Airlines into the Sunshine Coast Airport near Maroochydore, 25 minutes to the south. A Henry's bus transfer from there costs A$8 (U.S. $6.40); the major resorts offer free shuttle service. A ticket from Sydney costs A$217 to A$269 (U.S. $173.60 to $215.20).

You can't take a train to Noosa. The closest rail station is Cooroy, about 20 minutes west. The main rail depot for the Sunshine Coast is Nambour.

Suncoast Pacific Coaches operates between the Brisbane Airports and Noosa. The fare is A$18 (U.S. $14.40). From downtown Brisbane it's a 2¾-hour ride (A$18/ U.S. $14.40) (☎ 07/3236 1901). Sunair Bus Service (☎ 074/43 7320) also transports passengers from the Brisbane Airport to Noosa; theirs is door-to-door service.

GETTING AROUND Noosa's public transport system runs frequently throughout the township. **Tewamtim Bus Service** (☎ 074/49 7422) operates between Nambour and Noosa.

If you'd like your own car and chauffeur, call **Budget Chauffeur Drive** (☎ 074/ 43 6688).

Suncoast Cabs (☎ 074/13 11 34) is the only taxi company operating on the Sunshine Coast. The rate is A$2.40 (U.S. $1.92) call charge and then A81¢ (U.S. 65¢) per kilometer.

VISITOR INFORMATION Information is available at **Hastings Street Information Centre,** Hastings Street, Noosa Heads, QLD 4567 (☎ 074/47 4988), or down the coast at the **Maroochy Information Centre,** at the corner of Aerodrome Road and Sixth Avenue, Maroochydore, QLD 4558 (☎ 074/79 1566). This latter spot is open Monday to Saturday from 9am to 4:30pm. The **telephone area code** is 074. As part of the telephone changeover, all numbers with a 074 area code will be changing to 07/54xx xxxx in February 1997.

Exploring the Area

The **Big Pineapple,** 6km (3 1/2 miles) south of Nambour on the Bruce Highway (☎ 074/42 1333), is the area's biggest commercial attraction, and there's little chance you'll miss it as you drive up the highway, inland from the Sunshine Coast. Its Big Pineapple landmark, about the size of a water tower, can be seen from quite a distance. These big things are uniquely Australian phenomena. In most cases, the big thing (banana, pineapple, trout, cow, rocking horse, and so forth) represents a local product, and a tourist center with a souvenir shop and an eatery or two has grown up around it.

In the case of the Big Pineapple, you can visit a working fruit plantation, ride the sugarcane train through the orchards, take the Nutmobile to the Macadamia Nut Factory, or take Tomorrow's Harvest Tour, a flume ride through a hydroponic garden. The price of the all-tour ticket is A$10.50 (U.S. $8.40) for adults and A$8 (U.S. $6.40) for children.

The Sunshine Restaurant, with indoor and veranda seating, is open daily from 9am to 5pm. Plantations Licensed Restaurant has an all-you-can-eat smorgasbord for lunch daily. Rap's Restaurant (☎ 074/42 1333) is open Friday to Sunday 6pm–closing. The upper-level tropical market sells everything from resort wear to local fruit, preserves, nuts, and bakery items. On the lower level are a souvenir shop and a plant nursery. The Big Pineapple is open daily from 9am to 5pm.

Farther north, the **Ginger Factory,** also known as **Gingertown,** on Pioneer Road in Yandina (☎ 074/46 7100), is the world's largest such establishment. You can watch Queensland ginger being processed into a variety of products or catch the ginger train that tours through the landscaped gardens while you listen to an informative commentary. The shops of Gingertown sell Australian souvenirs and gifts. The Ginger Shoppe offers the largest selection of ginger-based goods in Australia. Admission to the Ginger Factory is free.

While at Gingertown you may want to visit **Bunya Park** (☎ 074/46 8222 or 46 8555). Within the factory grounds, this wildlife sanctuary is home to koalas, crocodiles, lizards, tortoises, wallabies, wombats, kangaroos, fruit bats, and lots of colorful, noisy native birds. Koala education and handling sessions are conducted four times daily. Admission is A$5 (U.S. $4) for adults and A$2.50 (U.S. $2) for children 4 to 15. Bunya Park is open daily from 9am to 5pm. There's a charge of A$3 to A$6 (U.S. $2.40 to $4.80) per person if you want your picture taken while holding a koala.

Another big attraction, the **Eumundi Markets** are held every Saturday from 6am to noon. I haven't seen it myself, but I'm told that hundreds of cars converge on the tiny village about 18km (11 miles) west of Noosa.

South of Eumundi, on the west side of the Bruce Highway, the **Ettamogah Pub** is the focal point of the Aussie World tourist area. The Ettamogah was built in 1989 but resembles a country pub—complete with a TAB for betting. See the box "Magic Sunshine Coast Brew" for the benefits of the Ettamogah's brew.

Among the area's natural attractions, its beaches are definitely number one. **Sunshine Beach,** starting 2km (1 1/4 miles) south of Noosa Heads, is a marvelous

Magic Sunshine Coast Brew

Aussies love their beer, and those at the Ettamogah Pub on the Bruce Highway are so smitten with the local brew they've listed its positive properties on the outside of the building:

"ETTAMOGAH BEER"
AUSSIE'S BEST BEER.
ERADICATES CANE TOADS.
DESTROYS GROUNDSEL & CHOLESTEROL.
TURNS CROCS INTO TADPOLES.
CLEANS OUT YA CARBI.
TANTALISES YA TASTE BUDS.
IT'S FAIRDINKUM BRAIN FOOD.
KICKS OVER THE STARTER MOTOR.
SETTLES THE DUST.
TAKES THE PUFF OUT OF CYCLONES.
& TASTES FLAMIN' GREAT TOO, MATE!

uncrowded stretch of sand. Before I visited this area, I'd visualized being able to drive along the coast and admire the ocean from the car. However, this wasn't the case. The road parallels the coast but is set back from it 100 to 500 meters (109 to 545 yd.), and water and beach are often obscured by trees and dunes. While they block the view from the road, they protect the beach from erosion. The sand grass grows close to the maximum high-tide line and holds the sand that isn't packed by tidal and wave wash. The grasses cause a protective dune to form, and eventually hearty shrubbery starts to grow inland of the berm. If it weren't for the dunes and the grasses, the relentless pounding of the waves would eventually sweep the beach away. This means that outside the populated areas you'll have to walk through a bit of native bush or over a dune to get a good view of the ocean.

Some of the most dramatic coastal vistas are from **Noosa National Park,** a not-to-be-missed spot for anyone who appreciates natural beauty. Within the 442-hectare (1,105-acre) reserve, walking tracks (trails) provide views of rugged headlands, beautiful stretches of golden-sand beaches, and pockets of rain forest with characteristically gnarled strangler fig trees. The trails, well marked and easy to follow, range from the 600-meter (654-yd.) Palm Grove walk to the 4.2km (2$^1/_2$-mile) Tanglewood Track to Hells Gates, where there's a spectacular view of the rugged coast. The south end of Alexandria Bay is popular with sunbathers (some of whom forgo swimsuits), and surfers find the best waves from Boiling Pot to Granite Bay.

The entrance to the park is about 1km (0.6 mile) east of the post office in Noosa Heads—an easy 10- to 15-minute walk. A ranger is on duty to answer questions daily from 9am to noon and 1 to 4pm. You can also call 074/47 3243. Camping isn't permitted in the park, but barbecues and picnic tables are provided.

Another popular attraction, **Underwater World** (☎ 074/44 8488) is adjacent to the Wharf complex, in Mooloolaba about a half-hour drive south of Noosa. Here visitors are transported, via a moving walkway, through an 80-meter (87-yard) clear-acrylic tunnel and view 12-foot sharks, stingrays, coral, and reef fish all around. The crocodile lagoons and seal habitat can be viewed from above and below the water.

There's also an audiovisual theater and a touch-and-feel lagoon. Underwater World is open daily from 9am to 5pm (closed Christmas). Admission is A$15.50 (U.S. $12.40) for adults and A$8 (U.S. $6.40) for children 5 to 15. Numerous eating options are available at the Wharf.

Outdoor Activities

Some of the most popular surfing spots in Australia are along the Sunshine Coast. Don't be surprised if dolphins surf with you at Sunshine Beach or along the coast of Noosa National Park. For current local information, stop in at or call **Noosa Surf World** in Noosa Junction (☎ 074/47 3538), open daily from 9am to 5:30pm.

Four-wheel-drive day trips to **Fraser Island** are available through several operators in Noosa, including Suncoast Safaris (☎ 074/47 0800). Fraser, the world's largest sand island, is 120km (74 miles) long and an average of 15km (9 miles) wide. Two-thirds of the island is state forest, the balance a national park. Camping is permitted. Suncoast's day trip costs A$110 (U.S. $88) for adults and A$75 (U.S. $60) for children 4 to 14; under 4 free. Included are pickup at any accommodation between Caloundra and Noosa, barbecue lunch, morning and afternoon teas, and ferry fees. Travel is by four-wheel-drive. For more information on Fraser Island, see "The Central Coast" later in this chapter.

The **Noosa River** is one of the popular local fishing spots where whiting and flathead can be caught year round. Bream is bountiful in May, June, and July; the best bass fishing is October to April. During summer (December to February), the ocean provides mackerel, tuna, black marlin, and sailfish. You can buy bait and equipment at **Davo's Bait & Tackle Shop,** 271 Gympie Terrace, Noosaville (☎ 074/49 8099), open daily from 7am to 6pm. Fishing tackle and bicycles can be rented at **Noosa Sea Sports & Hire,** 4 Hastings St. (☎ 074/47 3426). Jetskiing, sailing, diving, yacht charters, and snorkeling can be arranged through **Seawind Charters,** Main Beach, Noosa (☎ 074/47 3042; mobile phone 018/73 5624).

Where to Stay

Besides the properties below, **Accom Noosa Holiday Accommodation,** Hastings Street, Noosa Heads, QLD 4567 (☎ 074/47 3444 or 1800/07 2078; fax 074/47 2224), can arrange your own fully furnished beachfront or riverside house or condominium. Rates range from A$60 (U.S. $48) for a comfortable studio to A$350 (U.S. $280) for positively palatial digs.

Netanya Noosa Resort. 75 Hastings St., Noosa Heads, QLD 4567. ☎ **074/47 4722,** or 1800/07 2072 in Australia. Fax 074/47 3914. 47 suites. A/C MINIBAR TV TEL. A$160 (U.S. $128) one-bedroom garden suite; A$230 (U.S. $184) one-bedroom beachfront suite; A$310 (U.S. $248) two-bedroom beachfront suite; A$400 (U.S. $320) two-bedroom/two-bath penthouse. Children under 18 free in parents' room. Ask about special packages. Higher rates in peak season (school holidays, Easter, and Christmas). AE, BC, DC, MC, V. Free parking.

The four-story Netanya Noosa hotel is right on the beach, just a short walk from the center of town. All quarters have balconies, kitchenettes (some with microwaves), and bedrooms separate from lounge (living) rooms. While not overly spacious, the suites are well designed and have attractive modern decors. Instead of ordinary tub/shower combinations, showers are above two-person spa baths. Hairdryers in the baths and TVs and videos in all lounges and bedrooms are additional nice touches. Some suites have private roof gardens with barbecues and hot tubs, and many have ocean views. One has been designed for the handicapped; only this room lacks a spa bath.

Dining/Entertainment: Pavillions is a delightful à la carte restaurant with seating at umbrella-shaded tables on the terrace or indoors. Sails Beach Cafe is open daily for breakfast and lunch.

Services: Limited room service, laundry, baby-sitting, free daily newspaper, massage, courtesy vehicle.

Facilities: Pool, spa, sauna, gym; sporting goods, like boogie boards, surf skis, and fishing rods, are available.

Noosa International Resort. Edgar Bennett Avenue, Noosa Heads, QLD 4567. ☎ **074/47 4822.** Fax 074/47 2025. 65 apts. A/C TV TEL. A$100–A$160 (U.S. $80–$128) apt for up to four. Higher holiday rates. AE, BC, DC, MC, V. Free parking.

The Noosa International apartment-hotel is 1.5km (1 mile) from the town center. Since the complex is away from the water, the views are of the surrounding foliage, not the ocean. Taking advantage of this, the owners have created a Polynesian atmosphere with the thatched roof over the pool bar and with lush tropical plantings. The units have the advantage of being very spacious and offering full kitchens, washers, dryers, attractive furnishings, video recorders/players, and balconies. Baths have showers only. Each apartment has a master bedroom, and the second bedroom sleeps two adults or four children. Traffic noise is the only drawback to the well-landscaped recreation area.

Dining/Entertainment: The restaurant offers a choice of open-air or indoor dining, and there's live music in the piano bar several nights a week.

Facilities: Two pools, three spas, two saunas, courtesy bus to transfer guests to the beach and shops.

Sheraton Noosa Resort. Hastings Street, Noosa Heads, QLD 4567. ☎ **074/49 4888,** or 1800/07 3535 in Australia. Fax 074/49 2230. 140 rms, 29 suites. A/C MINIBAR TV TEL. A$310–A$390 (U.S. $248–$312) double; A$370–A$650 (U.S. $296–$520) suite. Additional person A$50 (U.S. $40) extra. Higher rates in peak season. Children under 17 free in parents' room using existing bedding. Rates include complimentary child care. Ask about special packages. No-smoking rooms available. AE, BC, DC, MC, V. Free parking.

In the heart of Noosa, with beachfront access, the six-story Sheraton provides the community's most luxurious accommodations. All rooms have kitchenettes, including microwaves and utensils, tea- and coffee-making facilities, small refrigerators, ceiling fans, balconies, spa baths, video players, and a choice of a king-size bed or two doubles. The grounds are nicely landscaped. Facilities for the handicapped are available.

Dining/Entertainment: The Sheraton offers three restaurants: the Charthouse Seafood & Grill, the Tea Tree Cafe, and, on the beach, the Laguna Bay Beach Club. There are also four bars.

Services: Concierge, room service, laundry, complimentary daily child care for children up to 9.

Facilities: Pool, gym, sauna, spa, games room, self-service laundry.

Where to Dine

Besides the restaurants below, you may want to check out Hastings Street, Noosa's restaurant row. **La Monde** and **Lindoni's** are both popular. Also keep in mind that Montville in the Sunshine Coast Hinterland (later in this chapter) offers good dining options.

✪ **Coco's Licensed Restaurant.** In Noosa National Park. ☎ **074/472 440.** Reservations advisable on weekends. Main course A$13.50–A$22 (U.S. $10.80–$17.60). AE, BC, MC, V. Daily 8:30am–10pm. MEDITERRANEAN.

What a delightful spot! Tucked away on the edge of the bush and steps from the ocean, this eatery provides a respite from the touristy atmosphere of Hastings Street. The plant-filled patio and veranda are separated by a white lattice railing; you sit on directors' chairs or white wicker chairs at polished granite tables. Candlelight makes dinners especially nice. If you come then, you'll choose between such dishes as warm roast chicken salad with carmelized carrots, mushrooms, and potato crisps (chips); yellowfin tuna with avocado salsa and crème fraîche; or lamb sweetbreads, minted peas, and balsamic mashed potatoes. Lunch choices include toasted focaccia with mozzarella, tomato, and sweet Piemontese peppers; avocado-and-bacon salad; and oysters with scrambled eggs. Children's meals are available.

La Plage Restaurant. Hastings Street. ☎ **074/47 3308.** Reservations recommended. Main courses A$16.50–A$22.50 (U.S. $13.20–$18). AE, BC, MC, V. Daily 6–9:30pm. FRENCH.

This sidewalk café/brasserie has an appearance and ambience to match its Gallic menu. The tile floor, bright paintings on the walls, bentwood chairs, and hanging plants help to create a casual Mediterranean atmosphere. Local seafood is artfully used in both traditional and contemporary French dishes. You might like to try the fresh tuna steak crusted with pepper and lemon-thyme or pan-fried cuttlefish served on a chiffonade of spinach with gribiche sauce. Meat dishes include eye filet with either béarnaise sauce or Dijon mustard glaze. In keeping with the French fare, the lamb is served pink with a mustard, whiskey, and fresh herb demiglaze. This BYO restaurant offers a messenger pickup from the Sheraton's bottle shop (liquor store).

Pavillions. In the Netanya Noosa Resort, 75 Hastings St. ☎ **074/47 4722.** Reservations recommended. Main courses A$18–A$24 (U.S. $14.40–$19.20). AE, BC, DC, MC, V. Daily 5pm–midnight. MODERN AUSTRALIAN.

On the ground floor of the resort, Pavillions offers dishes like stir-fried lamb with garlic, chiles, and mint in lettuce leaves or fresh king prawns and oysters with peaches and chile-mint dressing. Other choices include peppered duck breast with piquant raspberry sauce, and medallions of beef, lobster, and veal with a trio of sauces. Profiteroles are the most popular dessert. An extensive wine list is offered.

Nearby in a Nursery

✪ **Picnics at Fairhill.** At the Fairhill Nursery, Fairhill Road, Yandina. ☎ **074/46 8191.** Reservations recommended. Lunch A$10–A$13.50 (U.S. $8–$10.80). BC, MC, V. Daily 9am–4pm. INVENTIVE AUSTRALIAN. Turn east off the Bruce Hwy. just north of Yandina. Follow signs for 2.7 km to Fairhill.

It makes perfect sense, and I'm only surprised it isn't done more often: a restaurant opened on the grounds of a plant nursery. You enjoy great food and are surrounded by shrubs and flowers—all for sale. Seating is in a bright brick-floored hexagonal room or outdoors. Sample lunches are chicken breast with avocado salsa; duck and haricots vert cassoulet; and almond-coated lambs brains, fried and served on a caesar-style salad. Morning and afternoon teas include muffins, homemade biscuits (cookies), and a variety of tasty tarts and cakes. Also on the grounds is a very good shop where handcrafts, garden books, and gift items are for sale. BYO.

COOLUM & BEYOND

15km (9 miles) S of Noosa

While international visitors have tended to stay in popular Noosa hotels, Aussies who regularly come to the Sunshine Coast have found more privacy and better values in the less promoted coastal communities. One of these is Coolum (pop. 3,000). The focal point of the area is beautiful Coolum Beach, a long white-sand stretch with good rolling surf. The friendly township offers a variety of shopping, dining, and accommodations options and is convenient to all Sunshine Coast sightseeing attractions.

Essentials

GETTING THERE Travelers bound for Coolum fly into the Sunshine Coast Airport near Maroochydore, 15 minutes to the south (see "Getting to Noosa" above). You can't take a train to Coolum. The main rail depot for the Sunshine Coast is Nambour. For info on buses, see "Getting to Noosa" above. If you're driving, allow 1¾ hours from Brisbane.

VISITOR INFORMATION Information is available at the **Maroochy Tourist Information Centre,** at the corner of Sixth Avenue and Aerodrome Road, Maroochydore, QLD 4558 (☎ 074/79 1566; fax 074/79 1761). This office is open Monday to Saturday from 9am to 5pm. The **telephone area code** is 074. As part of the telephone changeover, all numbers with a 074 area code will be changing to 07/54xx xxxx in February 1997.

Where to Stay

Coolum Caprice. 123–133 The Esplanade, Coolum Beach, QLD 4573. ☎ **074/46 2177.** Fax 074/46 3559. 65 apts. TV TEL. A$105 (U.S. $84) one-bedroom unit for two; A$115 (U.S. $92) two-bedroom/two-bath unit for up to four; A$130 (U.S. $104) three-bedroom unit for up to six. Ask about weekly discounts. Higher holiday rates. BC, MC, V. Free parking.

Coolum Caprice is a good example of the kind of lodgings the locals like. Each of the spacious one-, two-, and three-bedroom units is tastefully furnished and has a balcony, and all but the ground-floor apartments have a wonderful ocean view. Kitchens are fully equipped, and washing machines and dryers are provided. All but the one-bedroom units have walk-in closets. The 14-story complex, across from the beach, lacks a restaurant and bar, but a nearby café will deliver meals. In addition, the management sells a starter pack of breakfast items for new arrivals. Two saunas, a spa, a pool, a gym, and a games room are provided. Baby-sitting can be arranged.

Coolum Dreams Bed & Breakfast. 28 Warran Rd., Yaroomba, Coolum, QLD 4573 (3km/1.9 miles south of Coolum P.O.). ☎ and fax **074/463 868.** 4 rms (1 with bath). A$90 (U.S. $72) double without bath, A$110 (U.S. $88) double with bath; A$130 (U.S. $104) three people with bath. A$10–A$20 (U.S. $8–$16) dinner. BYO. BC, MC, V. No children allowed.

Wendy and Ken Budd welcome guests to their home, across from the *much* more expensive Hyatt (below). If you fly into Maroochydore or take the train to Nambour or Yandina, Wendy will even pick you up. Buses from Brisbane stop nearby. By the time you get there, I think all the rooms will have en suite baths, but what's really memorable about this spot is the lovely open porch where everyone gathers for breakfast and during the day. Wendy bakes homemade bagels, muffins, croissants, and a variety of breads and also serves frittatas, crumpets, and barbecued bacon and eggs. The guest rooms are small, but the bed and bath linens are of good quality and color-coordinated with the decor. If you're lucky, you'll be here when Ken is making his home-brew beer. In any case, ask them to tell you where to get the best fish and chips on the Sunshine Coast.

Hyatt Regency Coolum. Warran Road, Coolum Beach, QLD 4573. ☎ **074/46 1234,** or 1800/22 2188 in Australia. Fax 074/46 2957. 324 suites and villas. A/C MINIBAR TV TEL. A$285 (U.S. $228) Deluxe suite; A$396 (U.S. $316.80) two-bedroom/two-bath President's Villa; A$825 (U.S. $660) two-bedroom/two-bath Ambassador's Club Villa; A$1,320 (U.S. $1,056) three-bedroom/three-bath Ambassador's Club residence. Ambassador accommodation includes continental breakfast and predinner wine in the Ambassador Club Lounge. Children under 18 free in parents' room. Ask about special packages. AE, BC, DC, MC, V. Free parking.

This is one of Australia's most outstanding international-standard spa resorts. The facilities are designed for people who want to relax and unwind on the Sunshine

Coast. The low-rise buildings, set in 149 hectares (373 acres) of subtropical gardens and forests 7km ($4^1/_2$ miles) from the Sunshine Coast Airport and 20 minutes south of Noosa, stretch to the beach. However, what makes this an unusual resort is the Spa, featuring a gymnasium, an aerobics room, Jacuzzis, a sauna, herbal wraps, massage, a sun court, a lap pool, and a health wing with consultation rooms.

Modeled on La Costa Resort and Spa in Southern California, the luxurious Hyatt offers myriad beauty and cosmetic services to both men and women. A wide range of sports facilities, including a challenging 18-hole golf course designed by Ralph Trent Jones, Jr., nine pools, a jogging track, squash courts, and nine tennis courts, are provided. Bicycles and shuttle vehicles get guests around the resort. There are four restaurants and a nightclub. Child care is provided for offspring from six weeks of age.

Novotel Twin Waters Resort. Ocean Drive, Mudjimba Beach, Sunshine Coast, QLD 4564. ☎ **074/48 8000,** or 1800/642 2444 in Australia, 800/221-4542 in the U.S. Fax 074/48 8001. A/C TV TEL. 368 rms and suites. A$170–A$195 (U.S. $136–$156) double; A$260–A$365 (U.S. $208–$292) suite; A$310–A$355 (U.S. $248–$284) two-bedroom suite. Children 16 and under free in superior rooms. Ask about dollarwise packages. AE, BC, MC, V. Free parking. About 15 minutes south of Coolum.

The focal point here is a large artificial lagoon where guests swim and boat. The ocean beach is about five minutes' walk away, but the manmade beach at the lagoon actually seems more popular. There's also a pool. I particularly like the over-water Lagoon Suites that have large porches, king beds, full kitchens, and big spa tubs. Deluxe suites have kitchenettes, and superior rooms have no cooking facilities. All quarters offer contemporary furnishings and a balcony or patio. The variety of complimentary recreational facilities makes this a great spot for families.

Dining/Entertainment: The resort offers three restaurants and four bars.

Services: Concierge, room service, free shuttle from Maroochy Airport, laundry/dry cleaning, secretarial service, baby-sitting.

Facilities: Free laundry; free use of catamarans, paddleboats, canoes, and windurfers; free use of bicycles and gym; six tennis courts (no charge); 18-hole championship golf course; Kid's Club for ages 6-12 during holidays and on weekends (no charge); day care for children; hair and beauty salon; golf pro shop.

4 The Sunshine Coast Hinterland

The Sunshine Coast Hinterland is a scenic area inland from, and parallel to, the Sunshine Coast. The townships of Maleny and Montville are perched atop the Blackall Range escarpment, affording great views of the Glasshouse Mountains and the Pacific Ocean. The area is known for its craft shops, galleries, eating places, and cozy accommodations.

MALENY

80km (49.6 miles) NW of Brisbane

In Maleny you'll find crafts shops and cute B&Bs juxtaposed with rural and commercial enterprises. Maple Street is the main drag. This little town feels "real," as opposed to Montville, which, while *very* appealing, has pretty much been taken over by tourism.

ESSENTIALS

GETTING THERE If you're driving, head north from Brisbane on the Bruce Highway and take the Glasshouse Mountains Scenic Route exit. The climb to Maleny from Landsborough offers great views. I particularly like the lookout point at Mary Cairncross Scenic Reserve, 6km (about 4 miles) before Maleny. The reserve is only

½km (⅓ mile) off the main road and would be a great place for a picnic. There's also bus and train service from Brisbane to Landsborough and connecting bus service from there to Maleny.

VISITOR INFORMATION Contact the **Maleny Tourism Association** (☎ 074/943 916) if you have questions. The **telephone area code** is 074. As part of the telephone changeover, all numbers with a 074 area code will be changing to 07/54xx xxxx in February 1997.

Seeing the Town

I'd picnic in **Mary Cairncross Park**, as mentioned above, and poke around the craft shops. **Rather Bizr**, 38 Maple St. (☎ 074/944 596), sells clothing, jewelry, leatherwork, and gift items. Next door, **Peace of Green Gallery**, 37 Maple St. (☎ 074/999 311), is a collective of artists and craftspeople. Both are open daily 9am to 5pm.

Where to Stay

Maleny Lodge. 58 Maple St., Maleny, QLD 4552. ☎ **074/94 2370.** Fax 074/94 3407. 7 rms (2 with bath). A$100 (U.S. $80) double without bath; A$165 (U.S. $132) double with dinner and without bath; A$125–A$145 (U.S. $100–$116) double with bath; A$190–A$210 (U.S. $152–$168) double with dinner and bath. Rates include breakfast. BYO. Free parking. No children allowed.

This is pretty much the consummate B&B: The house was built in 1894, and guests share a charming parlor where an open fire warms in winter. There are also a plant-filled veranda, a dining room with a beautiful mahagony table and Queen Anne chairs, a pool, and nice gardens. All the guest rooms are appointed with handsome colonial furniture, doonas, electric blankets, and heaters. The five nonfacilitied rooms share two baths. The only possible drawback is that I didn't find hostess Lorraine Duffy as warm and friendly as she might've been. Smoking is allowed in the gazebo but not in the house.

MONTVILLE

95km (59 miles) NW of Brisbane

A shoppers delight, Main Street, Montville, is lined with craft shops, galleries, gift shops, and antiques stores. Several good places to eat are in this area. If you have to choose between Montville or Maleny, pick Montville—it's cuter and has lots more shops.

Essentials

GETTING THERE The most scenic way to get to Montville is taking the escarpment drive from Maleny, stopping at Balmoral Park about 10km (6 miles) north of Maleny. Here there are picnic tables and a vista that includes the ocean to the east and the ranges to the west. You can also access Montville from the Bruce Highway via Nambour and Mapleton. There's bus service if you aren't driving.

VISITOR INFORMATION Montville is small enough that you can get information from any of the shopkeepers. However, if you want to write ahead, address your queries to the **Blackall Range Tourism Association,** c/o Post Office, Montville, QLD 4560. The **telephone area code** is 074. As part of the telephone changeover, all numbers with a 074 area code will be changing to 07/54xx xxxx in February 1997.

Where to Stay

$ **Clouds of Montville.** 166 Balmoral Rd., Montville, QLD 4560. ☎ **074/429 174.** Fax 074/429 485. 10 units. A/C TV TEL. A$85–A$100 (U.S. $68–$80) double. Additional adult A$20 (U.S. $16) extra, additional child 2–12 A$15 (U.S. $12) extra. Ask about lower off-season and weekly rates. AE, BC, DC, MC, V. Free parking.

About 2km (1.2 miles) outside Montville, this attractive motel has a nice pool surrounded by palms and a tennis court, with racquets available for use. Each of the spacious units in the two-story building has exposed-brick walls, pretty floral-print bedspreads, a microwave, an electric frying pan, a toaster, a refrigerator, a sink, and dishes. Continental breakfast can also be provided at a charge of A$7 (U.S. $5.60). Upstairs units sleep four. Guests are welcome to use the laundry and a barbecue. I was surprised to learn that Clouds was built in 1991, because it feels brand new. The owner said that one way they keep things spotless is by prohibiting smoking.

WHERE TO DINE

Besides the places below, the **Montville Patisserie & Bakery** (next door to Nonie's) is a good place to buy desserts, bread, scones, and meat pies as well as coffee.

Nonie's. Main Street. ☎ **074/429 488.** Reservations accepted. Meals A$10 (U.S. $8). No credit cards. Daily 10am–8pm. MODERN AUSTRALIAN.

This casual spot makes a good lunch stop. The menu changes seasonally and includes dishes like vol au vent, fettuccine with eggplant sauce, and Greek salad. The most popular desserts are "orgasmic" chocolate cake and deep-dish apple pie. There's indoor and outdoor seating. BYO.

✪ **Restaurant One Two Eight.** 128 Main St., Montville. ☎ **074/42 9407.** Reservations advisable, essential Sat–Sun. Main courses A$19.50–A$25 (U.S. $15.60–$20). Light meals A$10.50–A$15.50 (U.S. $8.40–$12.40). Sunday surcharge A$2.50 (U.S. $2). AE, BC, MC, V. Sun–Fri 11:30am–4pm, Sat 11:30am–10pm. THAI-INFLUENCED MODERN AUSTRALIAN.

The menu changes daily and includes tasty dishes like warm salad of smoked kangaroo and sugar-cured tuna on a bed of lettuce, wok-fried pearl perch served whole with honey-and-ginger glaze, and Thai peppered chicken, grilled crisp and then served on basmati rice with coriander pawpaw, mint marsala, and snowpeas. The casual decor includes wooden tables—about half on the porch and half inside, where cedar timbers line the walls. The wood-burning fireplace is welcome on cool days. BYO.

5 The Central Coast

Heading north from the Sunshine Coast, you enter an area that's of interest primarily because of the access it provides to offshore islands. Travelers don't flock to the central coast the way they do to other Queensland regions. Instead, the local economies are based on important agricultural and mineral production.

Maryborough (pop. 22,600) is the commercial center for a region that produces sugar, timber, dairy products, grain, fruit, and vegetables. Bundaberg (pop. 32,780) is known as "Queensland's rum city," but sugar is the town's most significant product. Rum, like the manufacturing of sugar-harvesting equipment, is a sideline. Just north of Maryborough, Hervey (pronounced "Harvey") Bay is the jumping-off point for Fraser Island and a popular place from which to do whale-watching excursions from August to October.

If you travel through this central coast region during the cane-harvesting season, July to December, you'll notice the practice of burning off the fields. After dark, huge sections along the highway and in the distance are engulfed in red-orange flames; during the day, smoke from the burnt cane drifts across the highway. In either case, slow down and proceed carefully because your visibility could be impaired. And I don't suggest you inspect the fields on foot—the purpose of the burning is to remove the thick cane's leaves and drive out venomous snakes before the harvesters start cutting. You may also see cane trains chugging alongside the highway or bringing their loads through town.

Farther north, Gladstone and Rockhampton are in the Capricorn region, named for the fact that it straddles the Tropic of Capricorn. Gladstone is a major industrial center and the home of the world's largest aluminum plant. Rockhampton is the beef capital of Australia. While these cities aren't totally without charm, their main interest for tourists is as a jumping-off point to islands on or near the Great Barrier Reef. Delightful Heron Island is a mere 80km (50 miles) by launch or helicopter from Gladstone. Great Keppel Island lies offshore of Rockhampton.

One-third of Australia's sugar comes from the area around Mackay, and seven mills operate in conjunction with the world's largest bulk-sugar-loading terminal. You can tour Pleystowe Sugar Mill from June to December. Mackay is 1,061km (658 miles) north of Brisbane, approximately halfway between the Queensland capital and Cooktown in the Far North region of the state. While Mackay has some nice beaches of its own, they aren't quite as special as the ones found on Brampton Island, 32km (20 miles) off the coast.

FRASER ISLAND

260km (161 miles) N of Brisbane

The world's largest sand island, 124km (77 miles) long and covering an area of 163,000 hectares (402,610 acres), has been World Heritage listed since 1992. Here you'll find pristine lakes, an ocean beach stretching 120km (74.4 miles), dense rain forests, freshwater lakes perched in sand dunes, winding streams, and desertlike sandblows. Fraser is also a bird-watchers nirvana—290 species have been sighted to date. There are also eight kinds of bat, lots of dingos, four types of poisonous snake, and a few small marsupials. Dolphins and whales can be observed off the coast at various times of year. In short, Fraser Island is a naturalist's dream. While a few yahoos choose to roar up and down the beach in four-wheel-drive vehicles, the majority of visitors are—thankfully—sensitive to the island's ecology. This is Australia's finest large-scale example of eco-tourism.

ESSENTIALS

GETTING THERE The drive from Brisbane to Hervey Bay takes three to four hours. Sunstate Airlines and Flight West Airlines provide service from Brisbane to Hervey Bay. Sunstate's one-way fare is A$67 (U.S. $53.60); Flight West's is A$80 (U.S. $65). You can also take a train to Maryborough and bus (Greyhound-Pioneer or McCafferty's) from there to Hervey Bay or bus all the way from Brisbane to Hervey Bay. From Hervey Bay it takes 35 to 45 minutes by catamaran (A$28/U.S. $22.40 per adult return/round trip; half price for kids 4 to 14) to get to Fraser Island. The vehicular barge takes 45 to 90 minutes (A$55/U.S. $44 per vehicle, including driver return/round trip; A$3/U.S. $2.40 per additional person). You can also fly to the east side of the island on Air Fraser Island (A$40/U.S. $32 return/round trip). It's also possible to do a day trip to Fraser Island from Noosa (see "The Sunshine Coast" earlier in this chapter).

VISITOR INFORMATION Information on Fraser Island can be obtained from the **Hervey Bay City Council Tourist Office,** Shop 4, 46 Main St., Pialba (P.O. Box 45, Torquay, Hervey Bay, QLD 4655; ☎ 071/242 448, or 1800/811 728 in Australia; fax 071/242 918). There are also several information offices on the island. The **telephone area code** is 071. As part of the telephone changeover, all numbers with a 071 area code will be changing to 07/41xx xxxx in February 1999.

ENJOYING THE ISLAND

There are no roads, as such, on the island—only sand tracks requiring four-wheel-drive vehicles. You have the choice of going out on a bus excursion, hiring your own vehicle once on the island, or touring in a vehicle brought over from the mainland. If you plan to hire a four-wheel-drive vehicle on the island *be sure to reserve it well in advance* because there aren't many of them. (I found the bus excursion frustrating because I didn't get to go where I wanted and couldn't determine how long I stayed at each place, but when I saw a family dealing with their "bogged" vehicle I felt a little better.) Walking trails provide another alternative. Fishing is a popular activity, as is lake swimming. Sharks make ocean swimming an *extremely* bad idea. Whale-watching excursions are available August to October. The best time to be here is from April to September.

WHERE TO STAY & DINE

Besides the resort below, accommodation and meals are available at **Happy Valley Resort** (☎ 071/279 144; fax 071/ 279 131) on the east side of the island.

Kingfisher Bay Resort. On the west side of Fraser Island. ☎ **071/203 333,** or 1800/072 555 in Australia. Fax 071/279 333. 152 rms, 52 two- or three-bedroom villas. Three-night minimum stay in villas. A/C TV TEL. A$200–A$210 (U.S. $160–$168) hotel room double, A$690–A$1,260 (U.S. $552–$1,008) *three* nights for four to eight adults in two- or three-bedroom villa. Ask about dollarwise packages and off-season specials. Children free in parents' room. AE, BC, MC, V.

Before arriving, I knew this was an eco-tourist resort, so I was prepared for a barebones facility—a place where only truly dedicated evironmentalists could be happy. Boy, was I wrong. There's nothing painful or primitive about this place: It's a full-fledged resort that meets the criterion of eco-tourism. You won't see grim-faced birders here—85% of guests are Australian families having a great time. All the rooms have refrigerators, coffee- and tea-making facilities, hairdryers, irons and ironing boards, and private decks or balconies. The villas have full kitchens. It's no wonder Kingfisher Bay has won so many awards, since it mananges to provide all these creature comforts without damaging the environment. The buildings are below the treeline and painted natural colors; the landscaping is done with native species from the site; the waste is carefully managed; everything that can be recycled is; and the impact to the dunal system is minimized through the use of boardwalks. The goal was to build a resort without disturbing the flora and fauna. I'd say they've accomplished their mission: A dingo patrolling his territory walked right past the table where I was having dinner one night.

Dining/Entertainment: The Maheno Restaurant and Lounge Bar provides casual dining overlooking Great Sandy Strait. Seabelle Restaurant and Cocktail Bar is more elegant. The Sand Bar, overlooking the beach, serves great pizzas in a publike atmosphere.

Services: Free guided walks, Junior Eco Ranger program for kids, baby-sitting, laundry/dry cleaning.

Facilities: Four pools and a spa, four-wheel-drive vehicle hire, shopping village, fishing school, four-wheel-drive guided bus excursions, whale-watching excursions, tennis courts, children's playground.

GLADSTONE

600km (372 miles) N of Brisbane, 126km (78 miles) S of Rockhampton

A boomtown since the 1960s, when the potential for its harbor was realized, Gladstone (pop. 23,800) is one of Australia's most prosperous seaside cities. Handling Queensland's vast supplies of coal, as well as other minerals, wheat, and meat, Gladstone exceeds even Sydney in annual shipping tonnage.

Essentials

GETTING THERE & DEPARTING If you're driving, head up the Bruce Highway. Sunstate Airlines and Flight West Airlines fly to Gladstone. Helicopter flights for Heron Island leave from the Gladstone airport. Launches depart from O'Connell Wharf.

Greyhound-Pioneer makes the trip from Brisbane in eight hours; a ticket costs A$60 (U.S. $48). Gladstone is on the main north-south train route. The *Queenslander, Sunlander, Spirit of Capricorn, Spirit of the Tropics,* and *Spirit of the Outback* all stop there.

VISITOR INFORMATION The **Visitor Information Centre,** 56 Goondoon St., Gladstone, QLD 4680 (☎ 079/72 9922), is open daily. The **telephone area code** is 079. As part of the telephone changeover, all numbers with a 079 area code will be changing to 07/47xx xxxx in June 1998.

Where to Stay

Chances are you'll arrive by air from Brisbane and connect immediately with transportation to Heron Island, but if you're driving, you may need lodging.

Country Plaza International. 100 Goondoon St., Gladstone, QLD 4680. ☎ **079/72 4499.** Fax 079/72 4921. Reservations can be made through Flag Inns. 72 rms. A/C MINIBAR TV TEL. A$97 (U.S. $77.60) double. Additional person A$10 (U.S. $8) extra. AE, BC, DC, MC, V. Free parking.

Conveniently located near the Visitor Information Centre in the heart of town, the Country Plaza's units have all the standard amenities, including coffee- and tea-making facilities, minibars, videos, and clock radios. All rooms have their own balconies, some with an ocean view. The Brass Palm serves all meals, and there's a pool.

Highpoint International. 22 Roseberry St., Gladstone, QLD 4680. ☎ **079/72 4711.** Fax 079/72 4940. 54 suites. A/C TV TEL. A$105 (U.S. $84) suite for one; A$120 (U.S. $96) suite for two. Additional person A$16 (U.S. $12.80) extra. AE, BC, DC, MC, V. Free parking. Transfers to and from airport and launch to Heron Island are provided.

The Highpoint International is the city's poshest hostelry. Each guest room in the eight-story motel has a separate lounge, a fully equipped kitchen, a balcony, and laundry facilities. Videos, clock radios, and tub/shower combinations are standard. The Highpoint has a restaurant, a bar, a pool, and 24-hour room service.

Where to Dine

Swaggy's Australian Restaurant. 56 Goondoon St. ☎ **079/72 1653.** Reservations not required. Main courses A$14.80–A$42.80 (U.S. $11.85–$34.25). AE, BC, DC, MC, V. Mon–Fri noon–closing, Sat 6pm–closing. AUSTRALIAN.

If you find yourself in Gladstone at lunch- or dinnertime, don't fail to sample the fare at Swaggy's. I thoroughly enjoyed my main course, "jolly jumbuck"—a juicy rack of lamb baked with honey and almonds. Other dishes are "Ned Kelly's combination," "chicken Matilda," "billabong filet," and "swagman's surprise." Don't be put off by the folksy names—their careful preparation and presentation belie their frontier appellations. And if you're game, try the barbecued crocodile, kangaroo, emu, and witchetty grub soup. Children's meals are available.

ROCKHAMPTON

726km (450 miles) N of Brisbane

Rockhampton (pop. 55,700) is the beef capital of Australia, but what lures most visitors here is Great Keppel Island (see Chapter 10). **Keppel Tourist Services** (☎ 079/33 6744) offers transfers and day trips.

ESSENTIALS

GETTING THERE & DEPARTING If you're driving, you'll find Rockhampton on the Bruce Highway. Sunstate Airlines, Qantas, Ansett, and Flight West Airlines fly to Rockhampton. The Air Pass fare from Brisbane to Rockhampton ranges from A$140 to A$176 (U.S. $112 to $140.80). Sunstate flights to Great Keppel Island leave from the Rockhampton Airport.

The *Spirit of Capricorn* and several other Queensland Railways trains take nearly 10 hours to reach Rockhampton from Brisbane. An economy-class "sitting" ticket costs A$67 (U.S. $53.60).

The Greyhound-Pioneer bus from Brisbane takes either 9 or 10 hours, depending on whether you're on an express. The fare is A$59 (U.S. $47.20).

VISITOR INFORMATION The 14-meter (46-ft.) **Capricorn Spire** at Curtis Park on the Bruce Highway at the south end of town marks the exact line of the Tropic of Capricorn and is the site of the **Tourist Information Office** (☎ 079/27 2055), open daily. The **telephone area code** is 079. As part of the telephone changeover, all numbers with a 079 area code will be changing to 07/47xx xxxx in June 1998.

WHERE TO STAY

Albert Court. Albert and Alma streets, Rockhampton, QLD 4700. ☎ **079/27 7433.** Fax 079/27 3815. Reservations can be made through Best Western. 44 rms. A/C TV TEL. A$60–A$85 (U.S. $48–$68) double. Additional person A$10 (U.S. $8) extra. AE, BC, DC, MC, V. Free parking.

The Albert Court is a low-rise motel close to the center of town. Three rooms have water beds, and the baths have showers but no tubs. Coffee- and tea-making facilities and small refrigerators are standard throughout. A restaurant and bar are open to the public Monday to Saturday and guests only on Sunday. Guests can use the pool and self-service laundry facilities. There's limited room service.

Country Comfort Inn. 86 Victoria Parade, Rockhampton, QLD 4700. ☎ **079/27 9933.** Fax 079/27 1615. 66 rms, 6 suites. A/C MINIBAR TV TEL. A$108 (U.S. $86.40) double. Additional person A$12 (U.S. $9.60) extra. Ask about lower rates through Aussie auto clubs. AE, BC, DC, MC, V. Free parking.

The Country Comfort Inn is a nine-story hostelry where all the rooms and suites have balconies, clock radios, videos, coffee- and tea-making facilities, and small refrigerators. The restaurant is open for lunch and dinner; there are also a coffee shop, a bar, a self-service laundry, and a pool. Room service is available 24 hours.

MACKAY

1061km (658 miles) N of Brisbane, 335km (208 miles) N of Rockhampton.

Pronounced "mu" (as in *mud*) "ki" (rhymes with *sky*), Mackay (pop. 60,000) is the sugar capital of the country and the departure point for lovely Brampton Island.

ESSENTIALS

GETTING THERE & DEPARTING Motorists follow the Bruce Highway. Qantas, Sunstate Airlines, Flight West, and Ansett fly into Mackay. An Air Pass ticket from Brisbane costs A$206 to A$274 (U.S. $164.80 to $219.20). Qantas and a daily launch provide transportation to Brampton Island. A launch service is also available to Lindeman Island (Club Med).

Two Queensland Railways' trains, the *Sunlander* and the *Queenslander*, stop in Mackay. A Greyhound-Pioneer or McCafferty's ticket from Brisbane costs about A$90 (U.S. $72) and the trip takes about 14½ hours.

VISITOR INFORMATION **Tourism Mackay,** Nebo Road, Mackay, QLD 4740 (☎ 079/52 2677), can answer your questions. The **telephone area code** is 079.

Readers Recommend

Planet Downs, P.O. Box 415, Virginia, QLD 4014 (☎ 07/3265 5022; fax 07/3265 3978). *"Planet Downs is a working cattle station [ranch] with first-class accommodations. It's a family-owned and -operated property consisting of 250,000 acres—about 100 miles long and 15 miles wide. There are 10,000 head of cattle and 50 horses, and wild koalas live on the property. We had a choice of watching or joining in with the daily ranch activities or playing tennis, riding horses, swimming in the pool or creek, or visiting 3,000-year-old Aboriginal cave paintings. The accommodations are extremely nice. Our room had a king-size bed, a modern bath, a pot-belly stove, and tea- and coffee-making facilities (complete with homemade cookies). The meals, shared with members of the family, are great. All-in-all, Planet Downs was one of the highlights of our trip to Australia, and we heartily recommend it to your readers."*

—Marj and Bob Julian, Winnetka, Ill., U.S.A.

Author's Note: Planet Downs has 10 suites with air conditioning and minibars. Rates, including all meals and activities, are A$395 (U.S. $316) per person based on double occupancy. American Express, Bankcard, Diners Club, MasterCard, and Visa are accepted. Planet Downs is 650km (403 miles), a nine-hour drive, northwest of Brisbane and a three-hour drive from Rockhampton. There's an airstrip on the property, and direct flights from Brisbane, Rockhampton, and other Queensland cities are available. Transfer by Planet Downs' four-wheel-drive vehicle from Rockhampton or Gladstone costs A$200 (U.S. $160) per person round-trip. Closed December and January.

As part of the telephone changeover, all numbers with a 079 area code will be changing to 07/47xx xxxx in June 1998.

WHERE TO STAY

Four Dice Motel. 166 Nebo Rd., Mackay, QLD 4740. ☎ **079/51 1555.** Fax 079/51 3655. Reservations can be made through Flag Inns. 34 rms, 2 suites. A/C MINIBAR TV TEL. A$80 (U.S. $64) double; A$140 (U.S. $112) suite. Additional person A$10 (U.S. $8) extra. AE, BC, DC, MC, V. Free parking.

Located 3km (2 miles) from the city and 2km (1¹/₄ miles) from the airport, this comfortable motel offers all the standard amenities: videos, clock radios, tea- and coffee-making facilities, and small refrigerators. Two rooms have a spa bath; one has a water bed. Meals are available in Pipers Grill, and there's a pool. Accommodations for the handicapped are available.

6 The Whitsunday Coast

Surfers flock to the Sunshine Coast, night owls love the Gold Coast, and sailors are sure the Whitsundays are their nirvana. Protected from the open sea by the Great Barrier Reef, the 74 islands in the Whitsunday Passage and the tranquil azure water between them create a mariner's playground. For nonsailors, delightful resorts on seven of the islands offer myriad other pleasures and water-oriented activities. The island resorts are discussed in Chapter 10.

On the coast, most vacation-bound travelers land at the Proserpine Airport; Airlie Beach supplies lodging before and after island idylls. Seaplanes, helicopters, launches, and catamarans shuttle in and out of Shute Harbour, providing transportation to and from such getaway havens as Hayman, South Molle, and Daydream Islands.

The area was named by Captain Cook when he discovered it on Whitsunday (the seventh Sunday after Easter) in 1770.

AIRLIE BEACH

297km (184 miles) S of Townsville

Airlie Beach, the gateway to the Whitsundays, is a laid-back beachfront community closely resembling Los Angeles's Venice or San Diego's Mission Beach. The only street is crammed with stores selling resort wear, water-sports equipment, and souvenirs. Interspersed among these shops are agencies that book day trips to the islands and sailing adventures. The town's population of 1,705 consists of hoteliers, restaurateurs, yacht specialists, and merchants meeting the needs of vacationers who base themselves in Airlie Beach and do a series of one-day island excursions or who stay overnight in the community on their way to an offshore vacation.

Those in the tourist industry are joined by young people who work at the marinas or in hotels while looking for a job crewing on someone's luxury yacht. Airlie (pronounced "*a*-lee") Beach has a tropical feel and is on the same latitude as Tahiti. Toad racing two nights a week draws a big crowd at the local pub, where everyone drinks stubbies—short bottles of beer served in Styrofoam holders. Shorts are the local uniform day and night in all but one or two of the better restaurants.

ESSENTIALS

GETTING THERE If you're driving, the trip from Townsville takes 3½ hours on the Bruce Highway. Qantas and Ansett Airlines fly into Proserpine, 24km (15 miles) inland. An Air Pass ticket from Brisbane costs from A$170 to A$185 (U.S. $136 to $148); from Sydney the fare ranges from A$170 to A$250 (U.S. $136 to $200). Sampson's Bus Service (☎ 079/45 2377) transfers passengers from the airport to Airlie Beach hotels (A$11/U.S. $8.80).

Queensland Railways' *Sunlander* and *Queenslander* stop in Proserpine. McCafferty's and Greyhound-Pioneer provide service to Airlie Beach. From Brisbane the trip takes about 15 hours and costs A$103 (U.S. $82.40). From Townsville it takes about 3½ hours and costs A$38 (U.S. $30.40).

VISITOR INFORMATION Information is dispensed at the **Whitsunday Visitors Bureau Information Centre,** Bruce Highway (☎ 079/45 3711), open daily. The **telephone area code** is 079. As part of the telephone changeover, all numbers with a 079 area code will be changing to 07/47xx xxxx in June 1998.

SPECIAL EVENTS The **Great Whitsunday Fun Race,** held on the Sunday in September with the highest midday tide, is the highlight of Airlie's social season. Each boat must have a live topless figurehead, who draws much more attention than rules, protocol, or even who wins. (First prize is a bottle of rum.) The entire weekend is one of heavy-duty frivolity.

EXPLORING THE AREA

Because it's protected by the Great Barrier Reef many miles to the north and east, Airlie Beach has almost no sandy stretch along its waterfront and almost no surf. Even more important, and actually *a matter of life and death,* is the presence of deadly box jellyfish along the coast from October to April. Commonly referred to as "stingers," the jellyfish kill more humans in Australian tropical waters than sharks, crocodiles, stonefish, and all other harmful marine creatures put together. I implore you to heed signs posted on coastal beaches and close-in islands that tell you to stay out of the water during the late spring, summer, and early autumn. Stingers can be present anywhere north of the Tropic of Capricorn but aren't a problem at the Whitsunday islands, which are far offshore.

With the exception of tours through the **Proserpine Sugar Mill** from July to November, the sights in this area are natural rather than commercial. Forget museums and historic buildings and savor some of the most beautiful scenery Australia has to offer. Fly over forest-clad islands and quiet water with **Island Air** (☎ 079/46 9933), whose tours last 2 1/2 to 3 hours and cost A$130 to A$150 (U.S. $104 to $120). Included are courtesy coach pickup, a scenic flight over such beauty spots as **Whitehaven Beach,** the only long sandy stretch in the Whitsundays, a water landing and takeoff on the Great Barrier Reef (60km/37 miles east of Airlie Beach), a walking tour, snorkeling, and glass-bottom-boat coral viewing. Snorkels, masks, and fins are provided.

Day trips to **Daydream** and **South Molle Islands** are also popular. The round-trip water-taxi fare from Shute Harbour is A$22 to A$30 (U.S. $17.60 to $24). Details of the facilities in each place are in Chapter 10. **Whitsunday All Over** (☎ 079/46 6900 or 46 9499) and half a dozen other operators offer day trips to the Great Barrier Reef, Whitehaven Beach, and Hook Island. Prices range from A$40 to A$110 (U.S. $32 to $88).

Outdoor Activities

The Whitsundays are a watery playground where everyone can—and usually does—try his or her hand at yachting (sailing), scuba diving, snorkeling, fishing, or windsurfing. Bareboat (sail-yourself) charters are especially popular, as they allow total freedom. You can anchor in a sheltered inlet and stay as long as you like, explore uninhabited islands to your heart's content, visit the island resorts, or raft up (tie up alongside) with newfound friends. At the same time, you have the security of checking in twice a day by radio with the people from whom you chartered the boat, and they're always on call should any problems arise.

If you're willing to trade a little privacy for less responsibility, you can rent a boat with a crew who'll do all or some of the work, as you prefer. The third option is joining a sailing adventure organized by one of the charter companies. You'll have less say in the itinerary, but the cost is lower and it's a fun way to meet people. No sailing experience is necessary. Another possibility is a Barrier Reef dive trip, where you live aboard a boat on the reef.

Whitsunday Rent A Yacht, Shute Harbour, QLD 4802 (☎ 079/46 9232, or 1800/07 5111 in Australia), is one of the largest charter companies in the area. The standard and deluxe Beneteau fleet consists of yachts from 27 to 46 feet, plus 34- and 36-foot motor cruisers for rent with or without a crew.

If you want a day sail, try the maxiboat ***Apollo*** (☎ 079/46 6922) or the 1962 America's Cup challenger, ***Gretel*** (☎ 079/46 6224 or 46 7529). The cost of A$58 (U.S. $46.40) for adults and A$29 (U.S. $23.20) for children includes morning and afternoon tea, lunch, and equipment for snorkeling and windsurfing.

The ultimate Whitsunday experience for some may be spending the day or longer on an uninhabited island. **Helijet**, **Coral Air**, and many of the other charter companies will drop you off for a private picnic or your very own camping adventure.

Where to Stay

Coral Sea Resort. 25 Ocean Ave., Airlie Beach, QLD 4802. ☎ **079/46 6458,** or 1800/07 5061 in Australia. Fax 079/46 6516. 24 rms. A/C TV TEL. A$125 (U.S. $100) studio; A$165 (U.S. $132) suite. Additional person A$20 (U.S. $16) extra. AE, BC, DC, MC, V. Free parking.

The Coral Sea Resort occupies a scenic waterfront site at the end of a peninsula less than a 10-minute walk from the heart of Airlie Beach. All but four of the rooms have an ocean view, and some quarters overlook the attractive 25-meter (27-yd.) pool and private boat jetty. A boutique, beauty salon, croquet lawn, spa, and sun deck are also on the premises. Most rooms have balconies and all have the usual coffee- and tea-making facilities.

The resort's restaurant is open Wednesday to Monday; room service is available until 9pm. Even though the management allows nonguests to use the pool for a fee, the Coral Sea has a restful atmosphere.

Whitsunday Wanderers Resort. Shute Harbour Road, Airlie Beach, QLD 4802. ☎ **079/46 6446,** or 1800/07 5069 in Australia. Fax 079/46 6761. 128 rms. A/C TV TEL. A$99 (U.S. $79.20) double, A$109 (U.S. $97.20) double in peak season. Additional adult A$18–A$24 (U.S. $14.40–$19.20) extra; additional child A$7 (U.S. $5.60) extra. Peak season is school-holiday periods and Christmas to late Jan. AE, BC, DC, MC, V. Free parking.

Whitsunday Wanderers is a Polynesian-style property where low-rise units are set in 8.5 hectares (21 acres) of lush tropical plantings. Native lorikeets (parrots) add to the atmosphere (and make this an especially good place for those who like to be up early with the birds). Of all the rooms, the Kookaburra units with wood paneling are the coziest. Others have concrete-block walls and chenille bedspreads on a double and a single (trundle) bed. All quarters come with kitchenettes and sleep up to two adults and two children.

The unusually friendly staff offers an orientation talk and welcome cocktail daily at 3pm. They also provide free scuba-diving lessons, use of windsurfers and paddleskis at the beach, and use of the property's other sports facilities: four pools, archery, table tennis, 18-hole mini-golf course, full- and half-court tennis, volleyball, and aerobics. Whitsunday Wanderers is owned by the Proserpine Sugar Mill, where tours are conducted from July to November. All meals at the resort are served in the Wanderer's Restaurant; no room service is offered. One unit is designed to accommodate the handicapped.

WHERE TO DINE

K.C.'s Chargrill. Shute Harbour Road. ☎ **079/46 6320.** Reservations accepted only for large parties. Main courses from A$15 (U.S. $12). AE, BC, DC, MC, V. Sun noon–4pm; daily 6pm–2am. CHARCOAL-GRILLED MEATS.

K.C.'s is not only a fun, casual site for delicious charcoal-broiled meals but also a popular meeting place and nightspot. Whether you've been out sailing all day or lazing by the pool at your hotel, you're bound to develop an appetite when you see steaks, lamb chops, prawns, ribs, and rack of lamb sizzling on the grill; and if you stay and socialize a while you'll undoubtedly meet some of the friendly yachties who call Airlie Beach home. If you want to look as if you belong, order a Fourex (XXXX) or Powers stubbie, which'll be handed to you in a Styrofoam "cooler," and sit back and enjoy the live music that's performed nightly.

K.C.'s has a down-to-earth atmosphere, created by wooden booths, linoleum floors, and ceiling fans. It feels so tropical and funky that you almost expect to see Humphrey Bogart sitting at the bar. Meals are ordered at a desk and collected by diners; seating is both indoors and out. The portions are large and a trip to the salad bar comes with each main course. Hosts Greg Clee and Geoff Glide welcome guests and keep a loose lid on the frivolity.

AFTER DARK

A big crowd gathers at the local pub, the **Airlie Beach Hotel** (☎ 079/466 233), on Tuesday and Thursday at 7:30pm for toad racing. The large cane toads chew on anything that comes close, so they're kept in cloth bags until race time and are handled with gloves. The hotel also has a disco Tuesday to Friday from 9pm until the wee hours, a live band on Saturday night, and entertainment on Sunday afternoon. The cover charge ranges from A$3 to A$5 (U.S. $2.40 to $4).

9

Northern & Northwestern Queensland

If you like white colonial buildings surrounded by stately coconut palms, jungle-green growth punctuated by vivid bougainvilleas, and miles of beaches edged in mangroves, you're going to love northern Queensland. While the Tropic of Capricorn actually passes through Rockhampton many miles to the south and Mackay gives visitors their first taste of trade winds, safari suits, and a decidedly slower pace, Townsville, Cairns, and Port Douglas are what make you want to sip a long cool drink on the veranda and wait for Clark Gable to appear.

Australians tend to divide the top half of the holiday state into two regions: North Queensland and the Far North. Townsville, capital of North Queensland, is the largest city in the combined area and provides a dress rehearsal for those heading to the true tropics of the Far North. Cairns, which has been entertaining travelers since the 1920s, is the gateway to the refreshingly cool Atherton Tableland, the jungles of the Cape York Peninsula, and the wonders of the Great Barrier Reef. The international airport at Cairns also provides access to popular Palm Cove and Port Douglas—thriving tourist destinations to the north. Like Florida in the United States, northern Queensland is a lush, humid region where mangoes, pawpaws (papayas), bananas, palms, and jacarandas thrive. Older homes were built on stilts to provide ventilation and prevent destruction by floods and termites. Modern houses are air-conditioned and close out the sun with wooden shutters.

Four climate zones running parallel to the coast divide this part of the state. To the west, the Great Artesian Basin is a hot flat region best left to hardy folks in search of minerals—for example, silver, lead, copper, and zinc come in great quantities from the mines at Mount Isa. The tablelands, to the east of the outback, are known for their rich volcanic soils, tobacco plantations, and cattle pastures. Staghorn ferns and orchids thrive in the rain forests that grow on the edge of the tablelands near the Great Dividing Range. Seas of sugarcane characterize the coastal plains, which lead to the water's edge and the Great Barrier Reef beyond.

In northern Queensland, more than in any other area of the country, the tourist industry is prospering. Many new hotels and attractions have opened recently and services for visitors are being finely honed.

What's Special About Northern & Northwestern Queensland

Natural Spectacles

- The Great Barrier Reef, a magical underwater garden that has to be seen to be believed.
- Daintree National Park and Cape Tribulation, featuring large areas of untouched rain forest.

Top Attractions

- Great Barrier Reef Wonderland in Townsville, a must for those who want to learn more about the reef.
- The Tjapukai Dance Theatre, comprised of talented Aborigines; they perform daily.

Beaches

- The coastal communities north of Cairns, each with its own lovely stretch of sand.
- Mission Beach, with almost 9 miles of palm-fringed sand.

Adventurous Activities

- Fishing for black marlin on Lizard Island from late September to early December.
- White-water rafting on the Tully River.
- Scuba diving on the Great Barrier Reef.

Most travelers arrive during winter (July to September), when daytime temperatures are in the high 70s and there's the least chance of rain. The wet period, December to March, is best avoided. Deadly marine stingers are a problem at coastal beaches and on the islands nearest the coast from October to April or May.

Unlike the cities along the central coast of Queensland, Townsville and Cairns are both popular destinations *and* jumping-off points to the reef. Townsville is the gateway to Orpheus and Magnetic Islands, and access to Lizard, Green, and Fitzroy is via Cairns. Dunk and Bedarra can be reached from either city.

EXPLORING THE STATE'S NORTHERN AREA

TRANSPORTATION Queensland Railways' *Sunlander* and *Queenslander* trains provide transportation between Brisbane and Cairns, stopping at most coastal cities.

Sunstate Airlines supplements the routes of the major carriers. McCafferty's and Greyhound-Pioneer buses travel up and down the coast and along the major inland routes.

INFORMATION The **Queensland Government Travel Centres** located in Australian state capitals and **Queensland Tourist and Travel Corporation** offices overseas are the best sources of tourist information. For motoring information, contact the **Royal Automobile Club of Queensland (RACQ),** 202 Ross River Rd., Aitkenvale (near Townsville), QLD 4814 (☎ 077/75 3999), or 112 Sheridan St., Cairns, QLD 4870 (☎ 070/51 4788).

1 Townsville

1,439km (892 miles) N of Brisbane, 347km (215 miles) S of Cairns

Townsville (pop. 130,000) is on Cleveland Bay near the mouths of the Ross River and Ross Creek. A long footpath, ideal for jogging or strolling, follows the waterfront

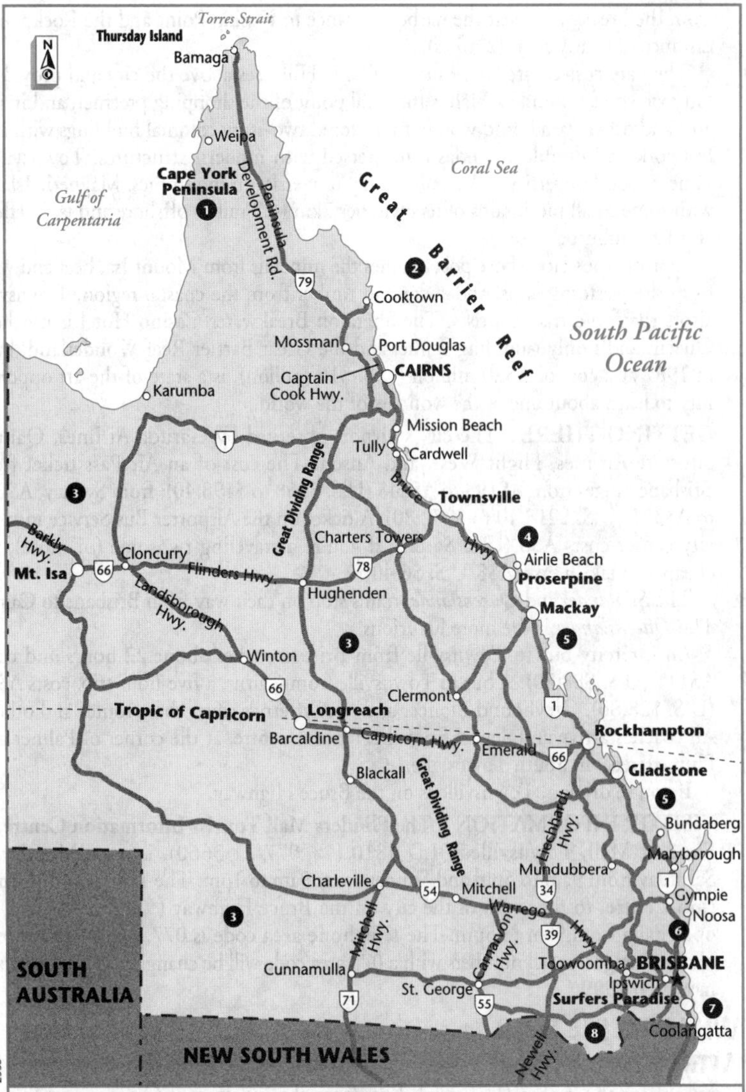
Torres Strait
Thursday Island
Bamaga
Weipa
Cape York Peninsula
Peninsula Development Rd.
Gulf of Carpentaria
Coral Sea
Great Barrier Reef
79
Cooktown
South Pacific Ocean
Mossman
Port Douglas
CAIRNS
Captain Cook Hwy.
Karumba
Mission Beach
1
Tully
Cardwell
Great Dividing Range
Bruce
Townsville
Barkly Hwy.
Charters Towers
Hwy.
Airlie Beach
Cloncurry
Mt. Isa
66
Flinders Hwy.
78
Proserpine
Landsborough Hwy.
Hughenden
Mackay
Winton
66
Clermont
1
Tropic of Capricorn
Longreach
Rockhampton
Barcaldine
Capricorn Hwy.
Emerald
66
Gladstone
Blackall
Great Dividing Range
Leichhardt Hwy.
Bundaberg
Maryborough
Mundubbera
Charleville
54
Mitchell
34
1
Gympie
Noosa
Warrego
Hwy.
39
Mitchell Hwy.
Carnarvon Hwy.
SOUTH AUSTRALIA
Cunnamulla
Toowoomba
BRISBANE
Ipswich
St. George
Surfers Paradise
71
55
Coolangatta
NEW SOUTH WALES
Newell Hwy.
2335
QUEENSLAND
The Cape York Peninsula 1
The Central Coast 5
The Gold Coast 7
The Great Barrier Reef 2
Lamington National Park 8
Outback & Inland Queensland 3
The Sunshine Coast 6
The Whitsunday Coast 4

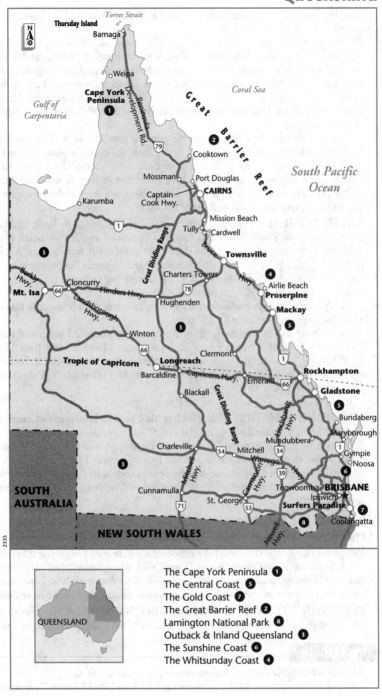

from the breakwater near the harbor entrance to Kissing Point and the Rockpool, a distance of nearly 3km (2 miles).

The bare rust-colored rock face of Castle Hill rises above the city and provides a lofty viewpoint. Flinders Mall is the focal point of the shopping precinct, and in this area and others you'll find wonderful restored two-story colonial buildings with iron fretwork and double verandas interspersed with modern structures. Townsville's James Cook University is Australia's only university in the tropics. Magnetic Island, with some small mountains of its own, lies 7km (4.2 miles) offshore and is, in effect, an island suburb.

A prosperous city whose port handles the minerals from Mount Isa, beef and wool from the western plains, and sugar and timber from the coastal region, Townsville also strives to attract tourists. The Sheraton Breakwater Casino Hotel is northern Queensland's only gambling venue, and the Great Barrier Reef Wonderland, built in 1987 at a cost of A$20 million (U.S. $16 million), is a state-of-the-art opportunity to learn about one of the wonders of the world.

GETTING THERE The city's airport is served by Garuda Airlines, Qantas, Sunstate Airlines, Flight West, and Ansett. The cost of an Air Pass ticket from Brisbane ranges from A$198 to A$248 (U.S. $158 to $198.40); from Sydney, A$273 to A$341 (U.S. $218.40 to $272.80). A ticket on the Airporter Bus Service into the city center costs A$6 (U.S. $4.80); if you're a traveling twosome (or more), it's cheaper to take a taxi (A$8/U.S. $6.40).

The *Sunlander* and *Queenslander* trains stop on their way from Brisbane to Cairns. The *Queenslander* is the more luxurious.

An intercity bus to Townsville from Brisbane takes about 22 hours and costs A$111 (U.S. $88.80). A bus to Townsville from Cairns, a five-hour trip, costs A$36 (U.S. $28.80). Greyhound-Pioneer and McCafferty's cover these routes and others. All coaches arrive and depart from the Transit Centre, at the corner of Palmer and Plume streets in South Townsville.

If you're driving, Townsville is on the Bruce Highway.

VISITOR INFORMATION The **Flinders Mall Tourist Information Centre,** in Flinders Mall, Townsville, QLD 4810 (☎ 077/21 3660), is open Monday to Saturday from 9am to 5pm and Sunday from 9am to 1pm. The **Highway Information Centre,** to the south of the city on the Bruce Highway (☎ 077/78 3555), is open daily from 9am to 5pm. The **telephone area code** is 077. As part of the telephone changeover, all numbers with a 077 area code will be changing to 07/47xx xxxx in March 1999.

WHAT TO SEE & DO

ATTRACTIONS

Except for the 2.5km (1½-mile) drive from the junction of Gregory and Stanley streets to the top of 285-meter (941-ft.) **Castle Hill,** where a panoramic vista awaits, and the **Billabong Sanctuary,** where you can experience Aussie wildlife, Townsville's major attractions involve the water—and, more specifically, the Great Barrier Reef.

✪ ENJOYING THE GREAT BARRIER REEF WONDERLAND For those who want to understand—or at least try to understand—the Great Barrier Reef,

Impressions

When in Australia be prepared to do somewhat as the Australians do.

—Plaque in the Lake Eacham Hotel Lounge, Yungaburra

there's no better place in Australia than Townsville's Great Barrier Reef Wonderland, 2–36 Flinders St. (☎ 077/21 1793 or 21 2411).

The large complex includes three main areas: the largest **live coral reef aquarium** in the world, the first **OMNIMAX** Theater in the Southern Hemisphere, and the **Museum of Tropical Queensland**. These attractions are contained in a covered mall, along with specialty shops, fast-food outlets, dive shops, and the departure area for outer-reef trips and Magnetic Island ferries.

The aquarium is unique to Reef Wonderland. A 20-meter (66-ft.) acrylic tunnel allows you to, in effect, walk through the huge tank where coral, plants, fish, and other animals have been relocated from various parts of the actual Great Barrier Reef. A predator tank, a touch tank, an aquarium theaterette, various educational displays, and a shop with an excellent selection of publications concerning the GBR are in the aquarium area. Upstairs you can see the algae turf filters, which keep the water clean in the tank, and get a bird's-eye view of marine life. The aquarium is operated by the Great Barrier Reef Marine Park Authority, and knowledgeable staff, as well as an army of volunteers, are on hand to answer questions.

The **Museum of Tropical Queensland** contains dinosaur fossils and life-size reconstructions of ancient marine reptiles. This is also a good place to learn about the local bird life as well as tropical insects, snakes, mammals, and shells. If shipwrecks are your thing, this museum houses a model of the *HMS Pandora* (the ship used to retrieve the infamous *Bounty* mutineers—the *Pandora* sank after hitting the Great Barrier Reef in 1791). The museum shop sells books with tropical themes, T-shirts, cards, and gifts.

The Great Barrier Reef Wonderland is between Flinders Street East and Ross Creek, within easy walking distance of the city center. Entry to the aquarium is A$13 (U.S. $10.40) for adults, A$6.50 (U.S. $5.20) for children, and A$32.50 (U.S. $26) for families. The OMNIMAX ticket is A$11 (U.S. $8.80) for adults, A$5.50 (U.S. $4.40) for children, and A$28 (U.S. $22.40) for families. The Museum of Tropical Queensland entrance fee is A$4 (U.S. $3.20) for adults, A$2 (U.S. $1.60) for children, and A$10 (U.S. $8) for families. These attractions are open daily, except Christmas, from 9am to 5pm. Phone the OMNIMAX Theater directly (☎ 077/21 1481) for program information.

GETTING TO THE REEF To fully understand the Great Barrier Reef, you really need to see it from the air. **Island Link Air Charter** (☎ 077/75 3866) will take you on a 1¾-hour flightseeing excursion for A$155 (U.S. $124).

Pure Pleasure Cruises (☎ 077/21 3555) offers trips to the outer reef on a 100-foot, 196-passenger Wave Piercer catamaran. Trips depart Townsville's Great Barrier Reef Wonderland Tuesday to Thursday, Saturday, and Sunday at 8:45am. The fare of A$120 (U.S. $96) for adults, A$60 (U.S. $48) for children 4 to 14, and A$280 (U.S. $224) for a family includes morning and afternoon tea, a buffet lunch, glass-bottom-boat reef viewing, snorkeling equipment, scuba diving, and fishing bait and tackle.

SEEING MAGNETIC ISLAND Eight kilometers (5 miles) offshore from Townsville, Magnetic is somewhat of an island suburb. Many of the permanent population of 2,000 take the 20-minute ferry ride to work daily. **Magnetic Island Ferries** (☎ 077/21 1913) operates frequent services (A$19/U.S. $15.20 round trip), and there are full-day and half-day tours. A lunch cruise costs A$37 (U.S. $29.60) for adults and A$17 (U.S. $13.60) for children, while the price for a cruise and tour is A$26 (U.S. $20.80) for adults and A$11.50 (U.S. $9.20) for children. While good beaches can be found on Magnetic Island, coral is sparse. For more information, see Chapter 10.

Outdoor Activities

If scuba diving is your thing, **Mike Ball Watersports** (☎ 077/72 3022) runs courses and dive trips to the reef. If you'd rather try landing a billfish, sailfish, or black marlin, contact **Challenger Charters** (☎ 077/25 1165). The cost for game fishing is about A$250 (U.S. $200) per day. **Australian Pacific Charters** (☎ 077/71 2534) can also organize your day of angling.

The **Tobruk Olympic Pool,** on the waterfront, is popular from October to April, when marine stingers preclude swimming near the shore or around Magnetic Island. **The Rockpool** at the opposite end of the beachfront at Kissing Point is a rock-walled enclosure that also provides safe swimming year-round as does the enclosure at Pallarenda.

Shopping

Townsville's main shopping area is **Flinders Mall,** where stores are open Monday to Thursday from 9am to 5:30pm, Friday from 9am to 9pm, and Saturday from 9am to 4pm.

The specialty shops at the **Great Barrier Reef Wonderland** are open daily and offer a nice range of souvenirs and sportswear. The work of local artisans is displayed at the **Cotters Market** held in Flinders Mall on Sunday from 8:30am to 12:30pm. The market also features entertainment and food stalls.

WHERE TO STAY

Expensive

Sheraton Breakwater Casino-Hotel. Sir Leslie Thiess Drive, Townsville, QLD 4810. ☎ **077/22 2333,** or 1800/07 9210 in Australia. Fax 077/72 4741. 176 rms, 16 suites. A/C MINIBAR TV TEL. A$200–A$240 (U.S. $160–$192) double; A$300 (U.S. $240) executive suite; A$850 (U.S. $680) Presidential Suite. Additional person A$40 (U.S. $32) extra. Children under 18 free in parents' room. Ask about lower weekend rates and special Oct–Feb packages. No-smoking floors available. AE, BC, DC, MC, V. Free parking. Take courtesy shuttle bus.

The Sheraton is a lovely 11-story building near the entrance to the harbor, about a mile from the city center. Half the rooms have ocean views, while the rest overlook Townsville and the marina. Nine rooms have facilities for the handicapped. Though northern Queensland's only casino is on the premises, the hotel has an exclusive, luxurious ambience. The Lobby Lounge, in restful periwinkle and light blue, complements the marble reception area.

Dining/Entertainment: Melton's, the hotel's elegant fine-dining venue, is open for dinner Tuesday to Saturday. Keno terminals in the Sails Coffee Shop, open daily, allows you to continue gambling while you dine. On Friday and Saturday nights a piano vocalist plays in the Lobby Lounge.

Services: Concierge, 24-hour room service, laundry.

Facilities: Pool, spa, sauna, tennis courts, gym.

Townsville Travelodge. 334 Flinders Mall, Townsville, QLD 4810. ☎ **077/72 2477,** or 1800/079 903 in Australia. Fax 077/21 1263. 186 rms and suites, including 7 Presidential Suites. A/C MINIBAR TV TEL. From A$150 (U.S. $120) standard double; A$230 (U.S. $184) Presidential Suite. Additional person A$20 (U.S. $16) extra. Ask about multinight packages and lower rates through Aussie auto clubs. No-smoking floors available. AE, BC, DC, MC, V. Free parking.

Known as the "sugar shaker" because of its 20-story cylindrical shape, the Travelodge is a local landmark and the tallest in town. It has a convenient midcity location and is within walking distance of tourist attractions and shops. All the standard rooms and suites have traditional furnishings. Some quarters have water views, and all standard rooms have balconies.

Raffles Restaurant is open for breakfast and lunch daily and the intimate Margeaux is open each night. The restaurants, as well as Rogues Piano Bar and Raffles Club Bar, are one floor up from the ground level, which Aussies call the "first floor" and Yanks insist is the "second." A drive-in bottle store—the ubiquitous feature that's part and parcel of life in Oz—is in back of the hotel. There's a great view from the rooftop pool.

MODERATE

✪ **Townsville Reef International.** 63–64 The Strand, Townsville, QLD 4810. ☎ **077/21 1777.** Fax 077/21 1779. 45 rms, 2 suites. A/C MINIBAR TV TEL. A$108 (U.S. $86.40) double; A$120 (U.S. $96) executive double; A$130 (U.S. $104) suite. Additional person A$15 (U.S. $12) extra. Children under 15 free in parents' room. Ask about off-season (Nov–Mar) weekend discounts. No-smoking rooms available. AE, BC, DC, MC, V. Free parking. Take airport courtesy car.

This four-story hotel occupies a picturesque site across from the Cleveland Bay waterfront, approximately 1km (0.6 mile) from the city center. The attractive exterior is pale gray with sky-blue trim; vivid bougainvillea adds a splash of color. Restful grays and beiges characterize the rooms and suites that've been made personal and homey by proprietors Judy and Eric Baker. All quarters have balconies, and 25% have a full water view. (These rooms also get a little traffic noise, so it might be better to request a quieter side room with only a partial bay outlook.)

Large windows give Flutes, the hotel's dining venue, a lovely Cleveland Bay vista and help make the room bright and airy. You also have the option of dining by the pool and spa. The Bakers' willingness to help out with sightseeing arrangements, the property's attractive appearance, and the good-value rates make this place highly recommended.

INEXPENSIVE

Seagulls Resort. 74 The Esplanade, Belgian Gardens, Townsville, QLD 4810. ☎ **077/21 3111.** Fax 077/21 3133. 55 rms. A/C TV TEL. A$72–A$102 (U.S. $57.60–$81.60) double. Additional adult A$12 (U.S. $9.60) extra; additional child A$6 (U.S. $4.80) extra. AE, BC, MC, V. Free parking. Courtesy shuttle available.

Seagulls is a resort set in 1.2 hectares (3 acres) of tropical landscaping on the seafront overlooking Cleveland Bay. Besides adequate rooms, 11 of which have cooking facilities, there are two pools, a restaurant, tennis courts, a playground, a barbecue area, and laundry facilities.

$ **The Summit.** 6 Victoria St., Stanton Hill, Townsville, QLD 4810. ☎ **077/21 2122.** Fax 077/21 3986. 30 rms. A/C TV TEL. A$60–A$65 (U.S. $48–$52) double. Additional person A$10 (U.S. $8) extra. Ask about off-peak discounts. AE, BC, DC, MC, V. Free parking. Take the courtesy coach.

The Summit is nestled in the foothills of Castle Hill, about five blocks from the town center. While the walk downhill to the mall is pleasant, you might prefer to taxi home to the striking two-story hostelry with its cheerful peach exterior. The umbrella-shaded tables on a large sun deck and the white lattice railing seem appropriate in this tropical setting. Horizons Restaurant serves dinner Monday to Saturday and breakfast daily; both meals can be delivered to the rooms. There are laundry facilities and a pool on the premises.

Readers Recommend

Kookabura Holiday Park, 175 Bruce Hwy., Cardwell, QLD 4849 (☎ 070/66 8648; fax 070/66 8910). *"The Kookabura Caravan Park in Cardwell was a wonderful place to stay. We stayed in an on-site caravan [trailer] for A$26 (U.S. $20.80) a night. We played golf at the nearby country club for A$10 (U.S. $8). The caravan park provided us with golf clubs, a bike, and fishing gear. The fishing in the Cardwell area is great."*

—Capt. Tom Allor, Farmington, Mich., U.S.A.

Author's Note: Cardwell is 171km (106 miles) north of Townsville.

WHERE TO DINE

If the restaurants I've listed here fail to tickle your fancy, you could stroll down historic and slightly trendy **Flinders Street East,** where many eateries are located. Most post their menus and will be happy to let you take a peek inside.

EXPENSIVE

Melton's. In the Sheraton Breakwater Casino-Hotel, Sir Leslie Thiess Drive. ☎ **077/22 2333.** Reservations recommended. Main courses A$24–A$27 (U.S. $19.20–$21.60). AE, BC, DC, MC, V. Tues–Sat 6–11pm. Take the courtesy bus. CONTEMPORARY SEAFOOD/MEAT.

Melton's is a sophisticated eatery with an à la carte menu that emphasizes fresh local seafood and prime Queensland beef. To provide light, healthy dishes, the chefs use alternative cooking methods and employ low-sodium and low-fat recipes. You may like to start with seafood salad with an avocado mousse flavored with ginger and chiles, a vegetable pouch on a tomato-and-lemongrass sauce, or king prawns in a Pernod-and-garlic sauce. Main courses include herb-crusted loin of lamb in yogurt sauce, poached beef tenderloin with freshly grated horseradish, or filet of red emperor in zucchini-and-thyme crust and champagne sauce. If you don't have room for dessert, you can linger over espresso, cappuccino, or Jamaican or Irish coffee. Melton's has won several awards, including the American Express Award for the Best Restaurant in Townsville.

MODERATE

✪ **Flutes.** In the Townsville Reef International Hotel, 63–64 The Strand. ☎ **077/21 1777.** Reservations recommended. Main courses A$12.50–A$32 (U.S. $10–$25.60); continental breakfast A$12 (U.S. $9.60); full Australian breakfast A$16.50 (U.S. $13.20). Children's meals offered at 50% discount. AE, BC, CB, DC, MC, V. Daily 7–9:30am and 6–11pm. INTERNATIONAL.

Flutes overlooks Cleveland Bay and has an intimate, exclusive ambience. The soft-gray carpeting, beige rattan chairs, and pink tablecloths are complemented by trellised bougainvillea showing through large windows. Dining is limited to 14 tables. Spicy curry triangles, avocado delight, and fettuccine boscaila are sample entrees (appetizers). Main courses include coconut prawns Palm Island, chicken breast Côte d'Azur, and Cape Cleveland seafood basket.

INEXPENSIVE

Luvit. 205 Flinders St. East. ☎ **077/21 1366.** Reservations not required. All dishes A$3–A$9.50 (U.S. $2.40–$7.60). BC, MC, V. Mon–Fri 6am–2pm and 7–10pm, Sat–Sun 7am–10pm. CONTINENTAL/INDIAN/PANCAKES.

Luvit is a pancake restaurant/coffee shop conveniently located 70 meters (77 yd.) east of the GPO on the shady side of the street. Breakfast is served until 11am. The pancakes—both sweet and savory—are popular. The hosts are Suzanne and Chris Davey. BYO.

AFTER DARK

THE PERFORMING ARTS

Townsville Arts Centre. At the corner of Stanley and Walker streets. ☎ **077/72 2549** or 72 2828.

This historic building is the home of Dance North, one of the nine major ballet/dance companies in Australia, with many performances during the year.

Townsville Civic Theatre. Boundary Street, South Townsville. ☎ **077/71 4188,** or 077/72 2677 for the box office.

With a seating capacity of 1,066, the Civic Theatre hosts a variety of performing arts, including drama, orchestral concerts, comedy, musicals, and dance. The A$4.5-million (U.S. $3.6-million) complex is an important link in the northern touring arts circuit. The box office is open Monday to Friday from 9am to 4:30pm and Saturday from 9am to 1pm. Tickets run A$12 to A$40 (U.S. $9.60 to $32).

CLUBS & CASINOS

The Bank Nightclub. 169 Flinders St. East. ☎ **077/71 6148.** Cover A$5 (U.S. $4) Mon–Thurs, A$6 (U.S. $4.80) Fri–Sun.

This really was a bank at one time. Today it's a popular nightclub, open nightly, which attracts patrons in the 18 to 30 age group. A wide range of beer and spirits (liquor) is offered.

Sheraton Breakwater Casino-Hotel. Sir Leslie Thiess Drive. ☎ **077/22 2333.**

Gambling at this casino is one of Townsville's most popular after-dark activities. Roulette, minidice, baccarat, blackjack, keno, craps, and two-up are played regularly. The casino has seven banks of video gaming machines and plenty of slot machines, plus two bars. It operates daily from 9am to 3am. A courtesy bus brings players from the city center.

2 Mission Beach

1,615km (1,001 miles) N of Brisbane, 25km (16 miles) E of Tully, 140km (87 miles) S of Cairns

Little more than a wide spot in the road, Mission Beach gives you a chance to see how Queensland would look had it been left relatively undeveloped. Between Townsville and Cairns, the resort community (pop. 660) consists of 14km (9 miles) of palm-fringed beach, splendid pockets of rain forest reaching down to the coast, a significant population of rare cassowary birds, and a few tasteful low-rise resorts.

There's really no town to speak of, just a couple of stores, some arts-and-crafts galleries, a Chinese takeout, a handful of casual eateries, and a real estate office. Commercial sightseeing attractions are absent, as are theaters, dance clubs, pollution, and traffic. People come to Mission Beach to get away from those things. Instead, you recline on golden silica sand, walk through rain forests (where vines, creepers, palms, and ferns create a fairy-tale atmosphere), and enjoy local water sports.

Many tourists merely pass through Mission Beach on day tours from Cairns to **Dunk Island** (see Chapter 10). Only the lucky few know they can stay in the tiny community and take a water taxi at their leisure across the 8km (5 miles) to Dunk. There are also trips to the outer reef from Mission Beach.

Named for the Aboriginal mission established here early this century, Mission Beach comprises several small communities that stretch north from Tam O'Shanter Point through South Mission, Wongaling, Mission Beach, and Bingal Bay. At Tam O'Shanter Point a cairn commemorates the ill-fated Cape York expedition of explorer Edmund Kennedy in 1848.

ESSENTIALS

GETTING THERE Motorists on the Bruce Highway should turn east at Tully and follow the signs to Mission Beach. You can get to Mission Beach by flying to Dunk Island on Australian Regional Airlines and catching one of the water taxis that operate a beach-to-beach service. You can also fly into Cairns and catch the Mission Beach Connection shuttle (A$33/U.S. $26.40).

The train station nearest to Mission Beach is in Tully, 25km (16 miles) to the west. Greyhound-Pioneer and McCafferty's buses make the trip from Townsville to Mission Beach in about three hours. Tickets cost A$38 (U.S. $30.40). It's a shorter trip, less than two hours, from Cairns (A$13/U.S. $10.40).

VISITOR INFORMATION The **telephone area code** is 070. As part of the telephone changeover, all numbers with a 070 area code will be changing to 07/40xx xxxx in April 1998.

OUTDOOR ACTIVITIES

Enthusiasts of ✪ **white-water rafting** come from all over Australia to raft the Tully and North Johnstone rivers, both within a short drive of Mission Beach. **Raging Thunder,** whose offices are at 111 Spence St., Cairns (☎ 070/31 1466 or 51 4911), organizes trips lasting from one to seven days. Whether you've never tried rafting or are an old hand, this exciting experience is bound to make an impression on you. There's always plenty of water—Tully boasts Queensland's highest annual rainfall: 4,267 millimeters (171 in.).

The full-day Tully River excursion, Australia's most popular rafting trip, costs A$122 (U.S. $97.60) per person, including transfers, equipment, guides, lunch, and dinner. Departures are daily year round. A two-day experience on the North Johnstone costs A$235 (U.S. $188), including all meals, equipment, transfers by coach, and river guides. Departures are weekly on Tuesday and Saturday from January to October. The minimum age for both trips is 13. Raging Thunder also offers sea kayaking, bicycling, canoeing, diving, ballooning, horse riding, sailing, trekking, and four-wheel-drive adventures. Some even go into the Solomon Islands and Papua, New Guinea.

WHERE TO STAY

EXPENSIVE

The Point. Mitchell Street, South Mission Beach, QLD 4854. ☎ **070/68 8154,** or 1800/07 9090 in Australia. Fax 070/68 8596. 35 suites. A/C TV TEL. A$160 (U.S. $128) double. Additional person A$20 (U.S. $16) extra. AE, BC, DC, MC, V. Free parking. Courtesy round-trip transfers from Cairns Airport are provided for visitors staying more than two nights.

The Point is an attractive resort where the quarters come with balconies that can be enclosed to create additional living space. All rooms have videos, hairdryers, and irons and ironing boards; king-size beds are available. The Point restaurant—where Waterford crystal and Wedgwood china are de rigueur—overlooks the pool, spa, coastline, ocean, and Dunk and Bedarra Islands. A tennis court, a jogging track, and water-sports facilities are provided. Guests enjoy nature walks in the rain forest and take advantage of the "absolute beachfront" location.

MODERATE

$ **Castaways Beachfront Resort.** Seaview Street, Mission Beach, QLD 4854. ☎ **070/68 7444,** or 1800/07 9002 in Australia. Fax 070/68 7429. 54 rms. A/C MINIBAR TV TEL. A$105 (U.S. $84) double; A$140 (U.S. $112) one-bedroom unit; A$160 (U.S. $128) two-bedroom unit;

A$220 (U.S. $176) two-story penthouse. Additional person A$12 (U.S. $9.60) extra. Standby rates (maximum 48-hour advance booking), including meals, A$43 (U.S. $34.40) per person double. Ask about other special packages. No-smoking rooms available. AE, BC, DC, MC, V. Free parking.

Castaways, right on the beach, has a soft-green exterior that blends in nicely with the surrounding palm trees and junglelike landscaping. The hostelry's design, labeled "modern Queensland," consists of three stories topped by gabled roofs and trimmed with crisp white latticework. The rooms have cooling gray-and-beige decors. Spacious motel-style units are available, as are one- and two-bedroom self-contained apartments. Most have balconies and water views. While there's no real surf, guests who leave their windows open can fall asleep to the sound of water lapping up on the beach. One unit is designed for the handicapped.

The bright, airy restaurant overlooks the pool and spa. There are also a tour desk and business center. Some water-sports equipment is free of charge. A 12-meter (40-ft.) game-fishing boat caters to keen anglers, and a high-speed catamaran can whisk you off to the Great Barrier Reef, an hour's cruise away, for an extra charge.

Mission Beach Resort. Wongaling Beach Road, Mission Beach, QLD 4854. ☎ **070/68 8288,** or 1800/07 9024 in Australia. Fax 070/68 8429. 76 rms, 1 suite. A/C MINIBAR TV TEL. A$95 (U.S. $76) double; A$180 (U.S. $144) suite. AE, BC, DC, MC, V. Free parking.

The Mission Beach Resort is a low-rise property blending nicely with its surroundings—in this case, a pocket of majestic rain forest. The resort has a hotel, motel, an à la carte restaurant, a cocktail bar, a bistro, a bottle shop, and a boutique set on 18 hectares (45 acres) of tropical gardens and rain forest. There are also a tennis court, volleyball court, jogging track, games room, children's playground, and sports oval. Accommodations, all on the ground level, are divided into four blocks, each with its own pool, spa, and barbecue area. Some have kitchens. Tourist information is available from reception.

INEXPENSIVE

Treehouse Hostel. Bingil Bay Road, Mission Beach, QLD 4854. ☎ **070/68 7137.** 48 beds in 6 rms, 2 twins, 2 dbl rms, campsites. A$15 (U.S. $12) per person in dorm, A$38 (U.S. $30.40) per person in twin/double, A$10 (U.S. $8) per person in campsite. Discount for YHA members for prepaid accommodation vouchers. BC, MC, V. Free parking. A courtesy bus meets all coaches in Mission Beach.

The Treehouse is a 52-bed pole-framed building set in 34 hectares (84 acres) of lush rain forest. Offering views of the Pacific, it's a quiet, secluded place for relaxing. The recreational facilities include a 12-meter (13-yd.) outdoor pool and table tennis. This hostel is a base from which regular rain-forest excursions are organized. Night walks and full-day walks take place daily; two- and three-day treks are also available. This YHA hostel is open all day, all year.

3 Cairns

347 km (215 miles) N of Townsville, 1,786km (1,107 miles) N of Brisbane

The capital of the Far North is a collage of various appearances and lifestyles. On the one hand, it looks like a colony in the tropics with lots of white buildings, palms, and bougainvillea; on the other, evidence of its thriving tourist industry is everywhere. Since 1984 Cairns (pronounced "cans") has had an international airport, and more recently the area has acquired luxurious Sheraton, Radisson, Ramada, and Hilton hotels. Long a haven for backpackers and the budget-conscious, the community can now welcome travelers at all comfort levels.

In addition to its colonial/tropical feel and obvious success as a tourist destination, Cairns has ethnic influences you won't feel in other Queensland cities. Many Southeast Asians (particularly natives of Indonesia and Papua, New Guinea) have found their way to this part of Australia, and their influence, together with that of neighboring Thursday Islanders, is felt in markets, restaurants, shops, and other places.

Cairns developed first as a port serving an inland gold rush, then later as a railhead from which produce grown on the fertile Atherton Tableland and sugarcane from the coastal plains were transported to other parts of the country. While the warm climate, trade winds, lush tropical foliage, and laid-back lifestyle of the colorful community have been attracting tourists since the 1920s, the industry boomed in the late 1960s, when prolific game-fishing grounds were discovered offshore. Personalities like actor Lee Marvin put Cairns on the must-visit list of dedicated anglers in search of barracuda, shark, marlin, sailfish, and tuna. From September to December, these prize catches continue to attract fishermen from all over the world. In terms of the weather, June to September is the best time to visit. Cairns (pop. 83,000) is 17 degrees south of the Equator, approximately the same distance—and therefore with a similar climate—as the Northern Hemisphere's Hawaii, Acapulco, and Puerto Rico.

Does this collage of many styles result in a pretty picture? The answer is an overwhelming yes. Somehow, upmarket tourists, backpackers, fishermen, Southeast Asian immigrants, Atherton Tableland plantation owners, descendants of colonial settlers, and sugarcane workers coexist copasetically. Even more, they contribute to Cairns's charisma. It isn't surprising that when Queensland's visitors go "troppo," forsaking jobs and extending vacations indefinitely, it's here they often choose to stay. Frankly, I was tempted myself.

ESSENTIALS

GETTING THERE The Bruce Highway, which brings you all the way from Brisbane, ends in the middle of Cairns. Drivers who continue north do so on the Captain Cook Highway, which takes them past the resort communities of Trinity Beach, Clifton Beach, and Palm Cove to Port Douglas. In Cairns, the Captain Cook Highway becomes Sheridan Street.

Carriers presently flying into Cairns include Qantas, Japan Air Lines, Air New Zealand, Garuda, Cathay Pacific, Air Nuigini, Ansett, and several regional carriers. A Sydney-Cairns Air Pass ticket costs A$316 to A$362 (U.S. $252.80 to $289.60). Brisbane-Cairns costs A$240 to A$350 (U.S. $192 to $280). The Airport Shuttle (☎ 070/35 9555) from the airport into town, a distance of 6km (4 miles) will set you back A$4.50 (U.S. $3.60), or you can pay about A$10 (U.S. $5.60) for a taxi. If you're headed to accommodation on the northern beaches or in Port Douglas, Coral Coaches will get you there (☎ 070/98 1611 or 31 7577). The fare to Port Douglas is A$16.80 (U.S. $13.45) for adults and half price for children 3 to 14. To Palm Cove the fare is A$10 (U.S. $8). If you're in a hurry, Helijet (☎ 070/35 9300) can get you to Port Douglas in a matter of minutes.

Facilities in the International Terminal, a five-minute walk or an A$1 (U.S. 80¢) shuttle from the Domestic Terminal, include Avis, Budget, Hertz, and Thrifty car-rental counters, baggage lockers (A$2/U.S. $1.60 for 24 hours), a newsstand, a mailbox, showers, a visitor information counter, a duty-free shop, a coffee shop and bar, a currency exchange open for all arrivals, and free phones to a dozen hostelries. The Domestic Terminal has similar facilities, but no showers or currency exchange. Before you leave the Domestic Terminal, take time to look at the huge ceramic-tile wall map showing the topography of the Far North; it provides a good introduction to this diverse region.

Choosing a Base in the Area

Please consider what day trips you'll be doing before deciding where to stay. **Cairns** is the best base for hopping to the Great Barrier Reef islands, taking the train to Kuranda, going out on *Ocean Spirit,* and rafting on the Tully River. It also offers the best shopping and nightlife.

Base yourself on **the northern beaches** if beaches are really important to you. The only other attractions up that way are a couple of crocodile farms and a great golf course.

Port Douglas and **Mossman** are closer to the northern end of the Atherton Tablelands, the departure point for *Quicksilver* trips to the reef, the Mossman River, and Daintree and Cape Tribulation National Parks. And Port Douglas has a wonderful beach.

Basing yourself in the **Daintree/Cape Tribulation area** gives you immediate access to the World Heritage rain forest, the Daintree River, and Cape Trib's beautiful beach.

This is *not* to say that you can't go out on *Quicksilver* if you're staying in Cairns or can't day trip to Cape Tribulation from the northern beaches. *Day tours pick up from all locations daily.* Basing yourself close to the attractions you're interested in, however, just cuts down on the amount of time you'll spend getting there.

And remember, deadly marine stingers (box jellyfish) make beaches in this area off-limits from October to May. Stinger-resistant enclosures are at Palm Cove, Trinity Beach, Kewarra, Port Douglas, and several other places.

See Chapter 10 for information on the Reef's island resorts.

At the rail station, one block west of Sheridan Street, on McLeod Street at Shields Street, the *Sunlander* and *Queenslander* arrive from Brisbane. The fare from Brisbane to Cairns on the *Queenslander,* the posher of the two, is A$489 (U.S. $391.20) in first class, inclusive of meals and a sleeping berth; children 4 to 15 are charged less. A first-class berth on the *Sunlander* will set you back A$243 (U.S. $194.40); children are charged less. The *Sunlander* sitting-car fare is A$129 (U.S. $103.20) for adults and half price for children.

Greyhound-Pioneer and McCafferty's make the trip to Cairns from Brisbane in 24 to 26 hours. A ticket costs about A$137 (U.S. $109.60).

DEPARTING As of June 1996, the A$27 (U.S. $21.60) departure tax will be included in the price of your airline ticket; formerly it was collected at the airport as you were leaving.

VISITOR INFORMATION If you want to write for information prior to your arrival, contact the **Far North Queensland Promotion Bureau,** P.O. Box 865, Cairns, QLD 4870 (fax 070/51 0127). Once you're in town, information is dispensed at the Visitor Information Centre on The Esplanade (between Shields and Spence streets) Monday to Friday from 9:30am to 5:30pm and Saturday from 9:30am to 1:30pm or you can call 070/51 3588 Monday to Friday from 9am to 5pm and Saturday and public holidays from 9:30am to 1:30pm. The **Cairns Tour Service,** 85 Lake St. (next to Hides), Cairns, QLD 4870 (☎ 070/51 8311), is open daily from 6:30am to 10pm. The **telephone area code** is 070. As part of the telephone changeover, all numbers with a 070 area code will be changing to 07/40xx xxxx in April 1998.

CITY LAYOUT The main thoroughfare is **Sheridan Street,** which becomes the Captain Cook Highway north of the city. The railway station is one block west of Sheridan on McLeod Street at Shields Street. Trinity Wharf and the Marlin Jetty are the main departure points for day trips to the reef. The **Esplanade** runs parallel to Sheridan Street along the waterfront.

GETTING AROUND

BY BUS Local transportation is provided by four privately owned bus companies. Of these, the **Beach Bus** (☎ 070/57 7411), which goes along the northern beaches, is probably of most interest. Fares range from A$3 to A$4 (U.S. $2.40 to $3.20), depending on how far you're going. For example, a city–to–Palm Cove ticket costs A$3.65 (U.S. $2.90). The "10 tripper" and weekly passes make travel cheaper. Seven runs a day stop at Trinity, Clifton, and Palm Cove, but Kewarra service is less frequent.

BY RENTAL CAR As well as the "Big Four" rental-car companies, there are several local ones with competitive rates. Of these, **Leisure Wheels,** 196A Sheridan St. (☎ 070/51 8988; fax 070/51 5656), seems to offer the best deals. It has small cars (VW "bugs"), medium-size cars, vans, and four-wheel-drives.

BY BOAT **Quicksilver** (☎ 070/99 5500 or 31 4299) will take you to Port Douglas on one of its wave-piercing catamarans. The fare is A$20 (U.S. $16) one way or A$30 (U.S. $24) round trip for adults and half price for children. Morning or afternoon tea is included.

BY ORGANIZED TOUR For sightseeing, most people rent a car or take organized day trips rather than using public transport. A plethora of tour companies operates in and around Cairns. **Australian Pacific Tours** (☎ 070/51 9299 or 31 3371), **Tropic Wings** (☎ 070/35 3555), **Cairns Scenic Tours** (☎ 070/32 1381), and **Down Under Tours** (☎ 070/33 1355) are just a few.

BY TAXI Call **Black & White** at 070/51 5333.

EXPLORING THE CITY & ENVIRONS

Cairns is ideally located so that day trips from the city can reach areas as diverse as the Great Barrier Reef, the northern beaches, the Atherton Tableland, Daintree National Park, the Daintree River, Cape Tribulation National Park, Port Douglas, and Mossman. These spots offer some of the most beautiful scenery in Australia, which is one of the important reasons why Cairns has become so popular.

For information on Daintree and Cape Tribulation, see "Port Douglas, Mossman & Beyond" later in this chapter.

AROUND TOWN

In between excursions to places farther afield, take a wander down to the **Marlin Jetty** at the end of Spence Street (September to December) and you might see fishermen weighing in their catch of black marlin or other impressive game fish.

Cairns Museum. In the City Place Mall, at the corner of Lake and Shields streets. ☎ **070/51 5582.** Admission A$2 (U.S. $1.60) adults, A50 (U.S. 40¢) children. Mon–Sat 10am–3pm.

This municipal museum has interesting displays that bring local history to life. These include Aboriginal artifacts, goldfield relics, and a Chinese joss house.

Flecker Botanic Gardens. 94 Collins Ave., Edge Hill. ☎ **070/50 2454.** Free admission. Daily 8:30am–5:30pm.

Cairns

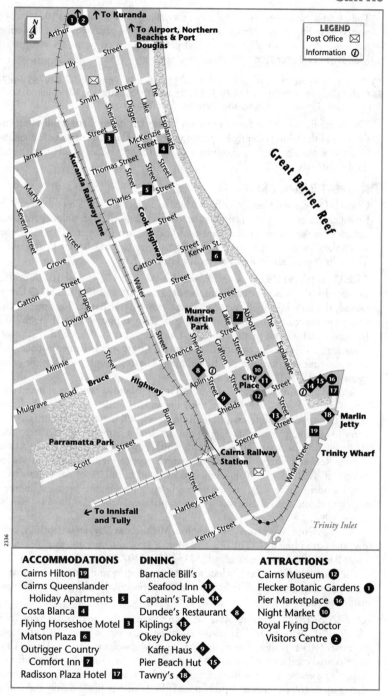

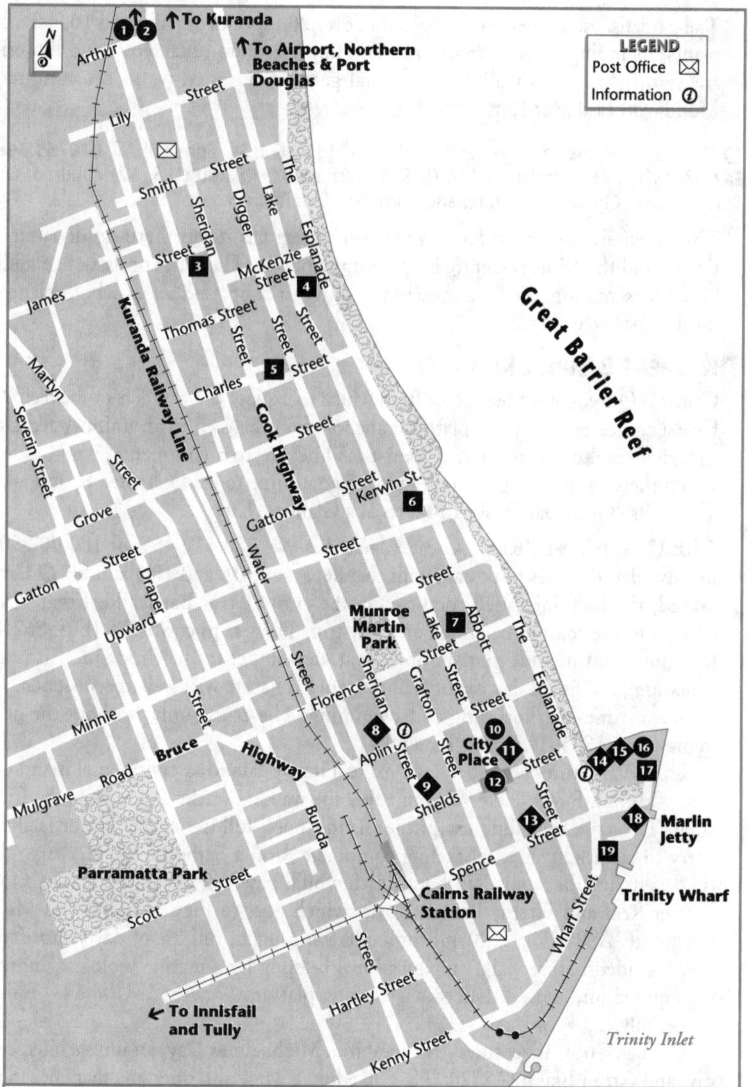

ACCOMMODATIONS

- Cairns Hilton 19
- Cairns Queenslander Holiday Apartments 5
- Costa Blanca 4
- Flying Horseshoe Motel 3
- Matson Plaza 6
- Outrigger Country Comfort Inn 7
- Radisson Plaza Hotel 17

DINING

- Barnacle Bill's Seafood Inn 11
- Captain's Table 14
- Dundee's Restaurant 8
- Kiplings 13
- Okey Dokey Kaffe Haus 9
- Pier Beach Hut 15
- Tawny's 18

ATTRACTIONS

- Cairns Museum 12
- Flecker Botanic Gardens 1
- Pier Marketplace 16
- Night Market 10
- Royal Flying Doctor Visitors Centre 2

The gardens, established in 1886, feature over 200 species of palm and 10,000 other plants, including ferns, orchids, fruit and nut trees, and ornamental and flowering trees and shrubs, as well as Aboriginal gardens. Guided walks are conducted Monday to Friday at 1pm.

✪ **The Royal Flying Doctor Visitors Centre.** 1 Junction St., Edge Hill. ☎ **070/53 5687.** Fax 070/32 1776. Admission A$4 (U.S. $3.20) adults, A$2.50 (U.S. $2) children. Daily 8:30am–5pm. Closed Good Friday and Christmas. Bus: Route 8.

This uniquely Australian famous medical service has its northern headquarters in Cairns and the Visitors Centre is open to the public. The tour consists of an audiovisual presentation, a talk, a museum, a souvenir shop, and an ex-RFDS plane on display for "boarding."

The Great Barrier Reef

Cairns is Queensland's best point from which to explore the wonders of the reef. You have a choice of going to a platform anchored on the reef, to an uninhabited coral cay, to a coral cay with myriad tourist facilities, or to a continental island around which there's some fringing reef. This is a good time to read Chapter 10 and take a look at its "Great Barrier Reef Resorts at a Glance" chart.

GREAT ADVENTURES Great Adventures (☎ 070/51 0455, or 1800/07 9080 in Australia) operates fast catamarans that depart at 8:30 and 10:30am for ✪ **Green Island,** the only inhabited coral cay on the entire Great Barrier Reef that's close enough to the coast to be visited on a day trip. These trips cost A$78 (U.S. $62.40) for adults and include glass-bottom-boat viewing, entry to Crocodile Farm and Aquarium, full use of day visitor facilities, guided nature walk, a barbecue lunch, and plenty of time for snorkeling and swimming. The cruise only, without the other items, costs A$35 (U.S. $28) for adults.

Great Adventures also operates trips to **Fitzroy Island,** a continental island covered with rain forest. Here you can enjoy the walking tracks and explore the fringe coral. This trip, including use of the island's pool, full use of day visitor facilities, entry to clam hatchery, snorkeling equipment, and a barbecue lunch, costs A$58 (U.S. $46.40) for adults. Without lunch, you'll pay A$25 (U.S. $20). The Outer Barrier Reef and Fitzroy Island Cruise, which goes to Fitzroy Island and Moore Reef, costs A$88 (U.S. $70.40) for adults with lunch, full use of day visitor facilities, a guided nature walk, an educational briefing by a marine biologist, snorkeling equipment, and an underwater viewing platform, or A$55 (U.S. $44) for the cruise only.

Another Great Adventures' trip combines **Michaelmas Cay,** an uninhabited coral cay, and Green Island (A$120/U.S. $96 adults). They also offer one that goes to the outer Barrier Reef and Green Island (A$134/U.S. $107.20 adults).

All prices mentioned here include a courtesy pickup at your lodging in Cairns or on the northern beaches. Children under 4 are free, and those 4 to 14 are charged half price.

OCEAN SPIRIT If you'd rather sail than motor to the outer reef, *Ocean Spirit* (☎ 070/31 2920; fax 070/31 4344) might be the vessel for you. This luxurious 32-meter (105-ft.) sailing catamaran goes out to **Michaelmas Cay** and **Upolu Cay,** uninhabited coral cays, where you can snorkel, scuba dive, sun, observe the life of a large bird rookery, and view the reef from a semisubmersible boat. Trips, accommodating up to 160 passengers, depart from Marlin Marina at 8:30am daily and return at 5pm. Snorkeling gear, a delicious buffet lunch, morning and afternoon tea, guided snorkeling with a marine biologist, and pickup from your Cairns or Northern beaches hotel are included in the price of A$125 (U.S. $100) for Michaelmas Cay and A$75 (U.S. $60) for Upolu Cay. For an additional cost you can take an introductory scuba-diving course or, if you're already certified, you can go diving. Coach transfers from Port Douglas are available at an extra charge.

OTHER TOURS Some tour operators offer trips combining bus transport to Mission Beach and a launch to **Dunk Island.** This makes for a long day, in my opinion. If possible, stay overnight in Mission Beach and take the launch or a water taxi from there (see "Mission Beach" earlier in this chapter.)

For information on ***Quicksilver,*** the deluxe 300-passenger high-speed catamaran that makes daily trips to Agincourt Reef, see "Port Douglas, Mossman & Beyond" later in this chapter.

BY HELICOPTER **Helijet** (☎ 070/35 9300) operates trips to the Great Barrier Reef. Its one-hour Reef and Rain Forest Discovery trip costs A$300 (U.S. $240). The Outer Barrier Reef Odyssey takes you to the Agincourt Reef, where you have lunch (on *Quicksilver,* mentioned above) and snorkel for three hours before returning to Cairns (A$375/U.S. $300 per person). Shorter scenic flights range in price from A$75 to A$195 (U.S. $60 to $156).

THE ATHERTON TABLELAND

Cooler weather and wonderful scenery draw visitors to the mountains west of Cairns, where tea plantations, lush rain forests, waterfalls, orchids, lakes, and butterflies await. The Atherton Tableland is only 150km (93 miles) long but contains a wide variety of scenic beauty. Situated west of the Bruce Highway from Innisfail to Cairns, the tableland includes 18 small towns dotted around the lush plateau.

You can drive yourself, of course, but another way to get to the Atherton Tableland is on the **scenic train to Kuranda.** A hostess on the train points out such sights as the Barron River, jungle-covered Freshwater Valley, and waving cane fields. After passing through Redlynch, 11km (7 miles) from Cairns, the train starts a steep winding ascent through dramatic tropical rain forest. You pass through 15 tunnels and stop briefly for photos at Barron Falls Station, 31km (19 miles) from Cairns and 328 meters (1,082 ft.) above sea level. The trip ends at the picturesque Kuranda station, built in 1915 and covered with ferns and other tropical plants. The charge is A$33 (U.S. $26.40) for adults and A$20 (U.S. $16) for children 4 to 14 for a round-trip on Monday, Tuesday, and Saturday; on other days it costs A$39 (U.S. $31.20) for adults and A$20 (U.S. $16) for children round trip. A one-way ticket costs A$23 (U.S. $18.40) for adults and A$10 (U.S. $8) for children. Trains leave from Cairns and Kuranda two to three times daily. To make reservations and to *check the timetable, which varies with seasonal demand,* call Queensland Railways at 070/52 6249 or 55 2222.

Another option is the **Cairns Skyrail** (☎ 070/381 555), the world's longest gondola cableway. Passengers seated in the six-person gondolas travel to or from Kuranda, meters above Far North Queensland's World Heritage Rain Forest. You have an opportunity to get out and explore the rain forest at two stops along the way. At the Red Peak Station you can experience the rain forest with biologists and Aboriginal guides; at Barron Falls Station you can take a short walk to Barron Gorge and Falls and go to the interpretive center to learn more about the rain forest. Stop for as long as you wish and just get on the next available gondola to continue your trip. The cost is A$23 (U.S. $18.40) one way or A$39 (U.S. $31.20) round trip. Many sightseeing coach companies offer packages that allow you to take the train or Skyrail one way and the bus the other. In terms of photography, it's better to go up by train in the morning.

Wednesday, Thursday, Friday, and Sunday are the most popular days to make the Kuranda trip because the **public markets** are open 7am to 1pm. At these popular flea markets you can buy everything from T-shirts and costume jewelry to local craft items, batik clothing, fresh fruit, homemade jam, and baked goods.

Another big draw is the Aboriginal dance program put on by the ✪ **Tjapukai Dance Theatre,** the brainchild of New Yorkers Don and Judy Freeman, who observed during a visit to Australia that there was no place for travelers to see native dances. The show launched the career of David Hudson, who's probably the best didgeridoo player in the world. The unique, exciting, educational one-hour performance takes place in a 300-seat air-conditioned theater at 21 Coondoo St., Kuranda, daily at 11am and 1:30pm. Confirm show times and make bookings by calling 070/93 7544; there's also sometimes a show at 12:15pm on market days. Tickets cost A$16 (U.S. $12.80) for adults and half price for children.

Don't miss an opportunity to see this group—it's the only one of its kind in Australia and has won numerous significant awards, including the PATA Gold Award for Culture and Heritage and the Australian Tourist Commission Award for "Most Significant Local Attraction." A shop and bistro bars are on the premises. Highly recommended.

Note: The Tjapukai Dance Theatre will be moving to the new **Cultural Theme Park** in Smithfield (immediately adjacent to the bottom station of the Skyrail) in mid-1996. Here it'll have three 200-seat indoor theaters, each featuring different shows and the latest in technology. The park, set on 25 acres, is 15 minutes from Cairns, 15 minutes from Kuranda, and 15 minutes from Palm Cove; a shuttle service provides transfers. It'll include a recreation of an Aboriginal village, as well as a restaurant and a gallery. Hours will be daily from 9am to 5pm. Admission will be A$31 (U.S. 24.80) with return transfer or A$21 (U.S. $16.80) without transfer for adults; half price for children 4 to 14. The original shop will remain open in Kuranda.

Other Kuranda attractions include the **Australian Butterfly Sanctuary** (☎ 070/93 7575), open daily from 10am to 3pm, with an admission of A$9.50 (U.S. $7.60) for adults and A$5 (U.S. $4) for children, with free tours every 15 minutes; the **Kuranda Wildlife Noctarium** (☎ 070/93 7334), open daily from 10am to 4pm (be there for the 10:30 and 11:30am and 1:15 and 2:30pm feeding times), with an

Readers Recommend

Kuranda Rainforest Resort, 2 Green Hills Rd. (☎ 070/937 555). *"What a fabulous place. The train trip is nice, but the village is a great base to explore the area. We stayed in a pole cabin that was quite delightful. The pools are the prettiest and most natural I've ever seen. The resort provides frequent complimentary transportation to Kuranda Village, Cairns, and the airport. I found shopping in Kuranda (especially the market) extensive and comparable to or less expensive than elsewhere in Australia."*

—Beverly Carr, Toronto, Ontario, Canada.

A Night in the Rain Forest, Carrowong Fauna Sanctuary, Blackmountain Road, P.O. Box 43, Kuranda, QLD 4872 (☎ 070/937 287). *"An interesting tour is provided by a local mammalogist and his wife. For A$98 (U.S. $78.40) each you get a fabulous steak-and-shrimp dinner in a gazebo in the rain forest, with wallabies wandering around the pool. Then you take a four-wheel-drive tour into restricted (permit required) World Heritage highland rain forest tracks to see nocturnal animals. What an experience. They also offer a cabin for rent."*

—Beverly Carr, Toronto, Ontario, Canada.

admission of A$8 (U.S. $6.40) for adults and A$4 (U.S. $3.20) for children; and river and rain-forest cruises conducted by **Kuranda Rain Forest Tours** (☎ 070/93 7476), at a cost of A$9 (U.S. $7.20) for adults and A$4.50 (U.S. $3.60) for children (note that tours are affected by weather in January and February).

Be sure to allow time for lunch or tea in one of Kuranda's cute cafés and for browsing through the various shops.

ON THE NORTHERN BEACHES

If you don't have time to do a Daintree River cruise and you're dying to see a crocodile, stop at **Wild World,** on the Cook Highway in Palm Cove, 22km (13 miles) north of Cairns (☎ 070/55 3669). It has 150 crocs ranging in size from hatchlings to full-grown specimens some 5 meters (16½ ft.) long.

While the crocodile show is described as "action-packed" in the brochure, I've found the beasts are very sleepy in winter (June to early September). Crocodile shows, cane toad races, a cockatoo show, a snake show, and an Aboriginal cultural show take place throughout the day, so call, get the schedule, and time your visit accordingly. Wild World also has wombats, free-ranging kangaroos, koalas, dingoes, emus, cassowaries, a large range of Australian birds, a walk-through aviary, and a large display of snakes including Australian pythons and the world's most venomous snakes. Admission is A$15 (U.S. $12) for adults and A$8 (U.S. $6.40) for children 4 to 15. Open daily from 8:30am to 5pm. If you aren't driving, the Beach Bus (☎ 070/57 7411) and Coral Coaches (☎ 070/98 2600) stop at Wild World.

You can also see crocodiles at **Hartley's Creek Crocodile Farm** (☎ 070/553 576), 40km (25 miles) north of Cairns. It's open daily from 8:30am to 5pm; show times are 11am and 3pm. Admission is A$10 (U.S. $8) for adults, half price for children. Reader David Klemm of Randwick, NSW, recently wrote: "Although I'm simply an Australian traveling in my own country, I chose your guide to assist me. I had the good fortune to go to Cairns. I highly recommend Hartley's Creek Crocodile Farm, as the guides are pleasant, informed, and helpful. It's strongly advised to go during a show (11am when I went), otherwise the crocs appear 'very sleepy' as you so correctly noted. Thank you for making my trip to Cairns a memorable one."

OUTDOOR ACTIVITIES

Raging Thunder, which offers white-water rafting on the Tully River (see "Mission Beach" earlier in this chapter), also puts together sea-kayaking trips, bicycle tours, adventure holidays, and four-wheel-drive safaris. Its offices are at 111 Spence St., Cairns (☎ 070/51 4911 or 31 1466).

Foaming Fury, 101 The Esplanade (P.O. Box 460), Cairns, QLD 4870 (☎ 070/310 899, or 1800/80 1540 in Australia; fax 070/53 6465), offers half-day, full-day, and two-day white-water rafting and sports-rafting trips. The cost (including transfers) for the half-day trip is A$65 (U.S. $52); the full-day trip is A$99 (U.S. $79.20); the two-day trip is A$240 (U.S. $192). The minimum age for the white-water trips is 13, but family trips—with smaller rapids and where the minimum age is 6—are also available. Tours operate daily from 7:30am to 5:30pm.

Open-cockpit Tiger Moth scenic flights and joy rides are available from **Cairns Tiger Moth Flights** (☎ 070/35 9400). The cost is A$85 to A$350 (U.S. $68 to $280) for flights of 20 minutes to an hour.

Raging Thunder Balloon Adventures, P.O. Box 1109, Cairns 4870 (☎ 070/51 4911; fax 070/51 4010) is another option. The price of A$145 (U.S. $116) includes scenic transfer through the Tablelands, the flight, and breakfast served in the tropical bush.

Several places in Cairns will teach you to scuba dive, but **Pro Dive,** Marlin Parade (☎ 070/31 5255; fax 070/51 9955), is one of the better-known outfits. Its three-day/two-night PADI open-water certification course costs A$420 (U.S. $336) and includes nine dives on the outer reef, free pickup from your accommodation, all dive equipment, live-aboard accommodations (including linen), and all meals on the trip. Courses start on Monday, Tuesday, Thursday, and Friday. Pro Dive also offers a variety of dive trips for those already certified.

Contact **Cairns Reef Charter Services,** Marlin Jetty (☎ 070/31 4742 or 53 4803), if you want to try your luck in marlin, game, and reef fishing. The cost of game fishing begins at A$175 (U.S. $140) per person, reef fishing at A$90 (U.S. $72) per person, and calm-water fishing at A$60 (U.S. $48).

Bicycle rental is available at **Bikeman City,** 105 McLeod St. (☎ 070/51 7135). The price is A$6 (U.S. $4.80) for a half day and A$12 (U.S. $9.60) for 24 hours—plus a A$50 (U.S. $40) refundable deposit. Bikeman City is open Monday to Friday from 8:45am to 5:15pm and Saturday from 8:45am to 12:30pm.

Paradise Palms, Clifton Beach (☎ 070/59 1166), is the most popular golf course in the area. Greens fees are A$80 (U.S. $64) and include motorized buggy (cart) and use of clubhouse. It costs A$20 (U.S. $16) to rent clubs and A$5 (U.S. $4) to rent shoes. There are also tennis courts, a practice (driving) range, a pool, and assorted dining options on the premises.

You may also be interested in knowing that **bungee jumping** has been added to the long list of activities available in Cairns. Organized by A. J. Hackett (☎ 070/31 1119), this thrilling "antigravity" experience costs A$89 (U.S. $71.20) per person.

SHOPPING

Shopping hours in Cairns are generally Monday to Thursday from 8:30am to 5:15pm, Friday from 8:30am to 9pm, and Saturday from 8:30 to 11:30am. In addition, stores in the suburbs are open until 9pm on Thursday; the **Smithfield Shopping Centre,** at the corner of Cook and Kennedy Highways (☎ 070/38 1006), has over 40 specialty stores and is open daily. Shops in the **Pier Marketplace** are open daily, too. If you like local crafts, don't miss the **Mud Markets** held at the marketplace on Saturday and Sunday. There's also a smaller **Night Market** from 5 to 11pm in the alley that runs between The Esplanade and Abbott Street between Aplin and Shields streets.

Bonz on the Reef, at the corner of Lake and Spence streets (☎ 070/31 4165), sells designer hand-knits with Australian themes for men, women, and children, as well as souvenirs and Aussie clothing. Without a doubt, ✪ **Australian Craftworks,** 20 Village Lane—off Lake Street near the Cairns International Hotel—(☎ 070/51 0725), is the best place in town to buy fine Australian handcrafted glass, leather, textiles, clothing, wood, ceramics, and jewelry. This shop is open daily and will ship your purchases. **Done Art & Design,** 4 Spence St. (☎ 070/31 5592), is where the clever T-shirts, sweatshirts, and household items created by Ken and Judy Done are sold. There's even a gallery where you can purchase original pieces of art and posters.

Be sure to take a look in **Presenting Australia** (☎ 070/31 5582), in the Pier Marketplace. Here Australian gifts and the designs of Coogi Knitwear, Bec Pierce, and Viva La Wombat are sold.

If you want to buy Australian art, including Aboriginal and contemporary, try the **Upstairs Gallery,** at 13A Shields St. (☎ 070/51 6150). The **Original Dreamtime Art Gallery,** 22 Orchid Plaza, Abbott Street (☎ 070/21 3222; fax 070/51 3272), specializes in traditional Aboriginal art, crafts, and didgeridoos, and offers free shipping and insurance worldwide. You may also be interested in **City International Duty Free,** 77 Abbott St. (☎ 070/31 1353). Purchases can be picked up within two days of your departure from the country.

WHERE TO STAY

The main decision you have to make before booking your Cairns lodging is whether you want to be in town or on one of the northern beaches. If you want to be near the shops and departure points for Great Barrier Reef cruise boats and Atherton Tableland trains, stay in town. And if being near sand and away from commercialism is a high priority, choose Trinity Beach, Kewarra Beach, or Palm Cove. In either case, day-trip tour buses pick up at all hostelries.

IN TOWN

Very Expensive

Cairns Hilton. Wharf Street, Cairns, QLD 4870. ☎ **070/52 1599,** or 1800/22 2255 in Australia. Fax 070/52 1370. 259 rms, 5 suites. A/C MINIBAR TV TEL. A$240–A$260 (U.S. $192–$208) double; A$750–A$1,050 (U.S. $600–$840) suite; A$50 (U.S. $40) surcharge for executive-floor room. Additional person A$30 (U.S. $24) extra. Children under 18 free in parents' room. No-smoking rooms available. AE, BC, CB, DC, MC, V. Parking A$5 (U.S. $4).

The seven-story hotel's rooms have water views, and many overlook the international cruise terminal and the ferry wharf from which boats leave regularly for Green Island. Each tastefully appointed room has a balcony, either a queen- or a king-size bed, in-room movies, tea- and coffee-making facilities, a small refrigerator, and a hairdryer. As in the Hilton in Sydney, Executive Floor rooms offer extra amenities at premium rates. All guests receive a free daily newspaper.

The main restaurant, Breezes, overlooking the Trinity Inlet marina, provides continuous food service throughout the day. You can get a tasty carvery lunch in the Cane Clipper, the Hilton's public bar. Of all the public spaces, the lobby level, where glass walls permit a 270-degree view, is the most impressive. In addition to a variety of dining choices, you have the use of an attractive pool area, a health club, a sauna, a spa, a gym, and a business center.

✪ **Radisson Plaza Hotel.** Pierpoint Road, Cairns, QLD 4870. ☎ **070/31 1411,** or 1800/25 2553 in Australia. Fax 070/31 3226. 200 rms, 20 suites. A/C MINIBAR TV TEL. A$250–A$290 (U.S. $200–$23.20) double; A$415 (U.S. $332) junior suite; A$505 (U.S. $404) executive suite; A$900–A$1,200 (U.S. $720–$960) Presidential Suite. Additional person A$25 (U.S. $20) extra. Children under 18 free in parents' room. Ask about special packages. No-smoking rooms available. AE, BC, DC, MC, V. Free parking.

The Radisson, with its low-rise colonial Queensland architecture, is in the Pier complex on the Cairns waterfront. In addition to the hotel, there are about 100 shops and numerous food outlets. While most of the property has a distinct nautical theme, you're greeted by a lifelike crocodile in an ersatz rain forest just inside the main entrance. In this area is also a reproduction Aboriginal cave painting.

The nautical decor in the guest rooms includes blue or green color schemes, hardwood cabinets and furniture, and verde marble baths. All quarters have balconies; two-thirds have water views. You have a choice between king-size beds or twins; all rooms have tea- and coffee-making facilities, small refrigerators, ceiling fans, hairdryers, in-room movies, and free daily newspapers.

The Quarterdeck Restaurant serves breakfast, lunch, and dinner daily. The Captain's Table Grill Room has a panoramic view of the harbor. Facilities include an outdoor pool, a fitness center, a sauna, a spa, and a business center.

Moderate

Cairns Colonial Club Resort. 18–26 Cannon St., Cairns, QLD 4870. ☎ **070/53 5111.** Fax 070/53 7072. 267 rms, 79 suites. A/C TV TEL. A$99 (U.S. $79.20) standard double; A$128 (U.S. $102.40) colonial double; A$150 (U.S. $120) one-bedroom suite with cooking facilities; A$250 (U.S. $200) VIP Suite. Additional person A$12 (U.S. $9.60) extra. Children under 3 free in parents' room. No-smoking rooms available. AE, BC, DC, MC, V. Free parking. Airport courtesy van and regular shuttle service to the city center.

The Cairns Colonial Club is in the suburb of Manunda, 6.5km (4 miles) from the city center. The two-story property's rooms are spread over 4 hectares (9³/₄ acres) of tropical landscaped gardens designed to look and feel like an island resort. Of the three free-form saltwater pools, the largest has its own beach made from sand imported onto the property; the medium-size pool is partially shaded by a mango tree that's much appreciated on hot summer days. Two rooms are equipped for the handicapped. The 79 one-bedroom suites offer cooking facilities.

Two large self-service laundry rooms are provided, as are tennis courts, a fitness center, a hair salon, a sauna, a spa, massage, a gift shop, and a tour-booking office. Because of the distances between blocks of lodging, room service isn't offered. Meals are served in three places: the Homestead Restaurant, Jardines, and the Poolside Cafe.

Cairns Queenslander Holiday Apartments. At the corner of Digger and Charles streets, Cairns, QLD 4870. ☎ **070/51 0122.** Fax 070/31 1867. 31 studios, 20 two-bedroom apts. A/C TV TEL. A$115 (U.S. $92) studio apt; A$145 (U.S. $116) two-bedroom apt for up to four. Additional person A$15 (U.S. $12) extra. Lower rates off-season (Oct-Apr). AE, BC, DC, MC, V. Free parking.

This is an ideal place for a family or two couples traveling together. Each apartment has a small kitchen and a balcony or a patio with table and chairs. The colonial Queensland decor includes ceiling fans, lace curtains, and slate floors. You can use the pool, spa, laundry, and barbecue area. Diggers licensed restaurant is open daily for breakfast and dinner. The three-story property is in a quiet area of North Cairns, about a 15-minute walk from the center of town.

$ **Flying Horseshoe Motel.** 281–289 Sheridan St., Cairns, QLD 4870. ☎ **070/51 3022.** Fax 070/31 2761. 51 units sleeping four to six. A/C TV TEL. A$82 (U.S. $65.60) double; A$97 (U.S. $77.60) double with cooking facilities. Additional person A$10 (U.S. $8) extra. AE, BC, DC, MC, V. Free parking. Take the courtesy airport shuttle.

The Flying Horseshoe is in the middle of motel row—an area of economical accommodations about 2km (1 mile) from the center of Cairns. The motel was built in the late 1960s by a former BOAC pilot from Yorkshire whose family coat-of-arms is the horseshoe and wings. The present owners, Margaret and Norton Gill, offer 51 units, some with cooking facilities. All have tea- and coffee-making facilities, small refrigerators, clock radios, and in-room movies. These friendly proprietors also make tour bookings for guests, serve dinner by the pool (A$15/U.S. $12), arrange breakfast delivery to the units, and help organize baby-sitting. You can use the self-service laundry. I'm not surprised, given the reasonable cost and friendly hosts, I've received numerous letters from readers complimenting the Flying Horseshoe.

Outrigger Country Comfort Inn. At the corner of Abbott and Florence streets, Cairns, QLD 4870. ☎ **070/51 6188.** Fax 070/31 1806. 91 rms and suites. A/C MINIBAR TV TEL. A$118–A$138 (U.S. $94.40–$110.40) double; A$185 (U.S. $148) suite. Additional person A$10 (U.S. $8) extra. Ask about lower rates through Aussie auto clubs. No-smoking rooms available. AE, BC, DC, MC, V. Free parking.

This is a most attractive Queensland colonial-style motor inn with white verandas and a multigabled roof. Fifty-five of the rooms are in a two-story section and feature marble baths. While these aren't overly spacious, their decors are very pleasant.

Readers Recommend

Matson Plaza, The Esplanade, Cairns, QLD 4870 (☎ 070/312 211). *"The best hotel we found (and we weren't attempting to stay in top hotels) was Matson Plaza. It may not be in the centre of town, but it's a lot closer than the Cairns Colonial Club and Cairns Queenslander Holiday Apartments."*

—Bruce Alloway, Edmonton, Alberta, Canada.

The 32 rooms in the four-story tower section are also bright, airy, and restful, each with a balcony and a sitting area containing a writing table. The tropical decor of Raffles Restaurant includes cane furniture, potted palms, ceiling fans, shutters, and a cool marble floor. The facilities include a pool and spa.

Inexpensive

$ **Uptop Downunder Holiday Lodge.** 164–170 Spence St., Cairns, QLD 4870. ☎ **070/51 3636.** Fax 070/52 1211. 44 rms (none with bath). A$30 (U.S. $24) double; A$14 (U.S. $11.20) per person in dorm. BC, MC, V. Free parking. Courtesy airport shuttle (free phone at the airport); courtesy pickup from train or bus station; courtesy bus to city center.

Uptop is an inexpensive place to stay, conveniently located only about 1km (0.6 mile) from the town center. You have a choice of single or double rooms or dormitory accommodations. All quarters share baths, a communal kitchen, two TV rooms, a reading/writing area, a pool, and a pool table.

A friendly atmosphere is created by the management and staff, who do day-trip bookings and provide courtesy transfers. A small shop on the premises sells food and everyone eats together at white wooden picnic tables. This is a good spot for budget travelers wanting to meet others who share their style.

On the Northern Beaches

Expensive

The Allamanda. 1 Veivers Rd., Palm Cove, QLD 4879. ☎ **070/55 3000,** or 1800/672 236 in Australia. Fax 070/55 3090. 70 apts. A/C TV TEL. A$235 (U.S. $188) one-bedroom apt; A$285 (U.S. $228) two-bedroom beachfront apt, A$335 (U.S. $268) two-bedroom "absolute beachfront" apt; A$335 (U.S. $268) three-bedroom apt; A$460 (U.S. $368) three-bedroom apt with own pool. No-smoking rooms available. AE, BC, DC, MC, V. Free parking. Take courtesy airport shuttle.

When Australians say "absolute beachfront," they mean right smack on the sand, and this is how they describe The Allamanda. No road or other obstacle stands in the way of your path to the waves. All quarters are luxurious and fully self-contained; the kitchens have dishwashers, microwaves, convection ovens, and everything else you'd expect. Serviced daily, each spacious apartment has a balcony, a white tile floor, ceiling fans, laundry facilities, two baths, and attractive modern furnishings; some have ocean views.

Three saltwater pools and a spa are provided so you can get wet even when marine stingers make the ocean unsafe (October to May). Unfortunately, the three-story building lacks an elevator. Baby-sitting and the amenities already mentioned make this a great place for families. The Far Horizons Restaurant is open daily.

Kewarra Beach Resort. Kewarra Beach (P.O. Box 199, Smithfield, QLD 4878). ☎ **070/57 6666,** or 800/525-4800 in U.S. Fax 070/57 7525. 59 lodge rms and bungalows, 2 suites. A/C MINIBAR TV TEL. A$199 (U.S. $159.20) double *koi moud,* A$272 (U.S. $217.60) double *waraka moud;* A$254 (U.S. $203.20) two adults and two children in *bhutu moud;* A$440 (U.S. $352) two-bedroom Timara Suite. AE, BC, DC, MC, V. Free parking. Complimentary airport shuttle.

The Torres Strait islands are off the tip of the Cape York Peninsula at Australia's most northerly point. Throughout history, the natives of these islands have migrated south for hunting. Many have even settled in the area around Cairns, and it's this South Pacific island culture that provides the theme of the Kewarra Beach Resort. You sip your welcome drinks in the *kudameta,* a spacious open-air entrance foyer with a thatched roof, cane furniture, and a slate floor.

The bungalows and lodges are sited among 30 hectares (78 acres) of lush tropical foliage 20 minutes from central Cairns. The *kois* are lodge-style rooms; the *waraka mouds* are individual bungalows with balconies; the *bhutu mouds* are family bungalows with cooking facilities and bunk beds in one of the two bedrooms. The Timara Suite is an old-world two-bedroom/two-bath cottage built from hand-cut cedar encircled by a large veranda; this is ideal for two couples traveling together.

Excellent meals are served in the Island Kings Restaurant (see "Where to Dine" below). Room service is available from 6:30am to 9:30pm. The resort enjoys a long stretch of private beach frontage, and you can use catamarans, windsurfers, and surf skis free of charge. There are also a very attractive free-form freshwater pool, a tennis court, and a croquet lawn. Free garden and nature tours are conducted daily on the long winding footpaths that crisscross the property. Kewarra Beach is a member of the Relais & Châteaux group and Select Hotels International.

Ramada Great Barrier Reef Resort. At the corner of Williams Esplanade and Veivers Road, Palm Cove, QLD 4879. ☎ **070/55 3999.** Fax 070/55 3902. 175 rms, 4 suites. A/C MINIBAR TV TEL. A$155–A$220 (U.S. $124–$176) double; A$330 (U.S. $264) junior suite; A$429 (U.S. $343.20) executive suite. Additional person A$20 (U.S. $16) extra. No-smoking rooms available. AE, BC, CB, DC, MC, V. Free parking. Airport courtesy coach available.

The Ramada Reef Resort has the largest free-form freshwater pool in the Southern Hemisphere. It sprawls over what seems like a football field–size area on the ocean side of the four-story hotel. Stately melaleucas and palm trees grow through holes cut into the surrounding wooden decking, and a bridge is provided so you won't have to walk all the way around the edge. In addition to the pool and attractive landscaping, the Ramada offers a convenient location just across from Palm Cove Beach, 25km (15 miles) from Cairns.

The rooms are decorated in pleasant blue and green. All have balconies and tub/shower combinations; a few have king-size beds, but most have queen-size beds or twins. Etchings of local scenes by Cairns artist JoAnne Hook add a nice touch. Two rooms for the handicapped are available.

Tropical drinks served in the open-air bar by the pool come in punch bowl–size glasses—and no one ever complains. Meals are served in the Garden Terrace Restaurant and poolside barbecues are popular. Children's activities are planned during Australian school holidays, and free baby-sitting is available then. Besides the huge pool, the resort offers tennis courts, bicycle rental, a spa, and a business center.

Readers Recommend

Costa Blanca, 241 The Esplanade, Cairns, QLD 4870. *"This place should receive special accommodation commendation. My unit was large, airy, and immaculate—the bed was especially comfortable. Julie Forbes, the proprietress, went out of her way to be helpful. All this for A$50 (U.S. $40) a day at the beginning of the winter season. A real bargain."*
—Lois Winsen, San Diego, Calif., U.S.A.

✪ **Reef House.** Williams Esplanade, Palm Cove, QLD 4879. ☎ **070/55 3633,** or 1800/07 9027 in Australia. Fax 070/55 3305. 42 rms and suites. AC MINIBAR TV TEL. A$185 (U.S. $148) Brigadier room double; A$235 (U.S. $188) veranda room double; A$275–A$450 (U.S. $220–$360) suite. Additional person A$32 (U.S. $25.60) extra. AE, BC, DC, MC, V. Free parking. Take courtesy transfer from airport.

The ambience of this very special place is reminiscent of a good private club in a tropical location—say, Palm Beach, Florida. The really caring staff and the tasteful decor contribute to the genteel atmosphere, making Reef House popular with honeymooners and others from around the world.

The Garden Wing was built in the 1970s in classic Queensland colonial architectural style; the northern wing, housing the deluxe rooms, was added in 1987. They're surrounded by magnificent melaleuca trees—one of which is 650 years old—and a plethora of hanging ferns and other tropical plants. All the rooms are spacious and offer kitchenettes, ceiling fans, (decorative) mosquito netting over the beds, terry robes, wicker furniture, cozy comforters, and a choice of a king-size bed or two doubles. Each has either a private patio or terrace.

The property is across from the beach and offers a spa and three pools in a tranquil garden setting. Meals are served in the Corals Restaurant, known for high-quality cuisine. The Poolside Cafe is open for casual daytime dining. It was chosen "one of the world's great places for breakfast" by *Australian Gourmet Traveler* magazine.

Because it feels more like a private club than a hotel and affords a certain amount of privacy, Reef House is a popular retreat for recognizable personalities seeking a respite from the limelight.

Moderate

$ **Paradise Village Resort.** 117 Williams Esplanade, Palm Cove, QLD 4879. ☎ **070/55 3300.** Fax 070/55 3991. 30 rms and suites. A/C TV TEL. A$120 (U.S. $96) double; A$160 (U.S. $128) one-bedroom apt with kitchenette for up to four; A$195 (U.S. $156) suite for up to four; A$275 (U.S. $220) penthouse for up to seven. AE, BC, DC, MC, V. Free parking. Take courtesy airport transfers.

Located 25km (15 miles) from the center of Cairns, Paradise Village really does have the feeling of being an intimate beachside village. Included in the attractive low-rise complex are a small post office, a bistro, an à la carte restaurant, a beauty salon, and 16 shops. The accommodations, on three levels (no elevator), are connected to the bilevel shopping area by a slate-and-ironstone walkway. The pale blue-gray exterior is topped with a traditional Queensland corrugated-iron roof and trimmed with white railings. Parking is under cover.

The lodging is simple but more than adequate, and all quarters have their own balconies. You have a choice of swimming at the beach across the road (June to October, when stingers aren't present) or the pool, where a waterfall flows from the spa. Actually, some people go in the water year-round because a net is used during stinger season. Meals are served in Cafe Paradise and Colonies.

Inexpensive

$ **Tropical Holiday Units.** 63–73 Moore St., Trinity Beach, QLD 4879. ☎ **070/57 6699,** or 1800/07 9022 in Australia. Fax 070/57 6565. 52 apts. A/C TV TEL. A$79 (U.S. $63.20) one-bedroom apt per night, A$485 (U.S. $388) per week; A$99 (U.S. $79.20) two-bedroom apt per night, A$625 (U.S. $500) per week. Additional person A$10 (U.S. $8) extra per night, A$60 (U.S. $48) per week. AE, BC, DC, MC, V. Free parking. Take courtesy transfers from the airport. Bus: Coral Coaches.

Trinity Beach is 15km (9 miles) north of Cairns Airport and south of Palm Cove. Apartments at the three-story Tropical Holiday have one or two bedrooms, full kitchens, ceiling fans, laundry facilities, and balconies. There are three pools with barbecue areas, and the management will help to arrange baby-sitting and day-tour bookings. The beach is a block away.

WHERE TO DINE

IN TOWN

Very Expensive

Tawny's. On the Marlin Wharf, between the Hilton and Radisson Plaza Hotels. ☎ **070/51 1722.** Reservations recommended. Main courses start at A$23.50 (U.S. $18.80). AE, BC, DC, MC, V. Daily 6pm–late. SEAFOOD.

Tawny's is easy to find: Its big turquoise neon sign can be seen from quite a distance, and it's on the waterfront between two of Cairns's best-known hotels. The pleasant atmosphere includes low lights, green plants, and timber paneling, and you're served generous portions of tasty local seafood. Appetizers include Bay Bugs (minilobsters) served hot or cold or succulent roasted quail glazed with tamarind-and-lemongrass sauce. For a main course, you might choose fresh barramundi and avocado or one of the daily chalkboard specials, like fresh reef fish (coral trout or red emperor) or steamed mud crab served cold or hot with a selection of sauces. The printed menu is available in English, French, German, Italian, Mandarin, Korean, and Japanese. Bibs are offered to anyone ordering anything potentially messy.

I suggest you sit on the enclosed veranda on the water side of the restaurant, where one-way windows provide privacy. The glass is mirrored on the outside, and diners get the giggles watching passersby primp.

Expensive

Barnacle Bill's Seafood Inn. 65 The Esplanade. ☎ **070/51 2241.** Reservations recommended. Main courses A$12.90–A$23.90 (U.S. $10.32–$19.12). AE, BC, DC, MC, V. Daily 5pm–late. SEAFOOD.

Barnacle Bill's is on The Esplanade at the south end of the strip of takeaway places that are so popular with backpackers and other budget travelers. A Baskin Robbins is two doors away. The casual decor includes a wooden floor and a blue-and-beige color scheme. As the name implies, seafood is the specialty here. Look for prawns, bugs, scallops, calamari, mud crabs, coral trout, and barramundi as well as pasta and other dishes.

Captain's Table. In the Radisson Plaza Hotel at the Pier, Pierpoint Road. ☎ **070/31 1411.** Reservations recommended. Main courses A$20.50–A$26.50 (U.S. $16.40–$21.20). AE, BC, DC, MC, V. Mon–Sat 6:30pm–late. SEAFOOD/CHARCOAL-GRILLED MEAT.

Commanding a panoramic view of Trinity Bay Inlet and Marlin Marina, this up-market dining spot specializes in grain-fed Queensland beef and fresh seafood. The preparations are modern and multicultural. Appetizers include Southern crayfish tartare on toasted brioche with cabernet-shallot dressing and garden herbs, grilled Nambucca Heads scallops on saffron-flavored soufflé, gnocchi with roasted Roma tomatoes and Chardonnay sauce, and orange-glazed quail with warm red-lentil salad and toasted olive loaf. For a main course you can have salamandre-crusted baby barramundi with lemon myrtle on a spinach fritter and pine-nut dressing, cumin-seared yellowfin tuna with relish of mango and red onions on chili papadums, eye filet of beef with yabbies on a bed of forest mushrooms and garden greens, or herb sabayon and braised venison roulade with fennel on apricot-flavored game sauce. Menus change seasonally.

✪ **Kiplings.** On the Gallery Level of Orchid Plaza, 79–87 Abbott St. ☎ **070/31 1886.** Reservations recommended. Main courses A$18.50–A$26.50 (U.S. $14.40–$21.20). AE, BC, DC, MC, V. Mon–Sat noon–3pm and 6–9:30pm. MODERN AUSTRALIAN.

If I could have only one meal in Cairns, it would be at Kiplings. The attractive restaurant is in the business district, up one flight on an escalator from street level. The decor of sea-foam green and white includes lots of leafy plants. The green iron chairs have pretty padded floral seats and backs. The no-smoking section is in a conservatorylike enclosed balcony overlooking the traffic. Lunch—which might be pasta, curry, a Greek salad, or samosas—is offered from noon to 3pm. Most patrons at this time are local businesspeople needing speedy service.

Chef/owner Herbert Gerzer trained in his native Austria before immigrating to Australia by way of Bermuda. His wife, Jura, hails from the Philippines. The charming couple acquired Kiplings in 1993 and have managed to make a good place even better. Herbert's thoughtful presence projects into the dining room even when he stays in the kitchen. Dinner is served from 6 to 10pm in a much more relaxed atmosphere than lunch. Appetizers include seafood terrine, homemade pasta, fresh oysters, and smoked salmon. Sample main courses are blackened barramundi, roast rack of lamb, and Kipling's curry (Rudyard would be proud).

This is a very special place. Please don't miss it!

Moderate

Dundee's Restaurant. At Sheridan and Aplin streets. ☎ **070/51 0399.** Reservations recommended. Main courses A$13.50–A$35.50 (U.S. $10.80–$28.40). AE, BC, DC, MC, V. Daily 6pm–closing. SEAFOOD/STEAK/PASTA.

Dundee's proved to be a lucky discovery, as the restaurant specializes in grain-fed beef and has a wonderful salad bar. Steak lovers have to make a difficult choice between T-bone, sirloin, rib filet, or rump steak, and Dundee's also offers rack of lamb and beef kebabs. A few unusual dishes include Buffalo Humpty Doo (an eye filet of buffalo with a delicious peanut-and-chili sauce) and Outback Bushman's Pie (beef and veggies covered with creamed potatoes and topped with flaky pastry). You'll also find emu, crocodile, and kangaroo. On the seafood side of things, you might like to try whole baby barramundi, Trinity Bay bugs, or whole crab. Dundee's has a comfortable large bar above the dining area. Children are welcome. The management provides transfers from city hotels.

$ **Homestead Restaurant.** In the Cairns Colonial Club Resort, 18–26 Cannon St., Manunda, Cairns. ☎ **070/53 5111.** Reservations recommended. All-you-can-eat salad bar (including soup, pasta, and bread) A$9.95 (U.S. $8); salad bar with main course A$5.95 (U.S. $4.80); main courses A$8.50–A$17.50 (U.S. $6.80–$14); children's meals A$4.75 (U.S. $3.80). Public holiday surcharge 10%. AE, BC, DC, MC, V. Daily 6:30–10pm. SEAFOOD/CHARCOAL-GRILL.

The Homestead's "Salad Shack"—unlimited trips to a buffet piled high with salad ingredients, a choice of soups, several pastas, and freshly baked bread—is an extremely good value. Main courses include a variety of steaks, local seafood, and a sirloin-and-prawn combination.

The Pier Beach Hut. In the Pier Marketplace, Pierpoint Road. ☎ **070/312 133.** Reservations not required. Main courses A$9.50–A$22 (U.S. $7.60–$17.60); lunchtime Blue Plate special A$11.50 (U.S. $9.20). AE, BC, DC, MC, V. Daily 8am–midnight. STEAK/SEAFOOD.

In the lively Pier Marketplace, one level up, the Pier Beach Hut offers diners an expansive view of Trinity Inlet and the Cairns Yacht Club and Marina (under construction when I last visited). Since the windows surrounding the room are 10 feet high, there's a good view from every table. The lunch and dinner menus include kangaroo-tail soup, barramundi, coral trout, and daily seafood specials. The lunchtime Blue Plate special includes a trip to the dessert bar. Breakfast, served from 8 to 11am, might be blueberry muffins (A$2.50/U.S. $2) or steak and eggs with grilled mushrooms (A$12.50/U.S. $10).

Readers Recommend

Okey Dokey Kaffe Haus, 64 Shields St. (☎ 070/514 744). *"The house specialty, veal schnitzel, was the most tender and delicious we found in four weeks of Australian travel. Enjoying this in the secluded patio in the rear was one of the most delightful dinner experiences of our tour. Gerhard Pfaffelmoser, the owner, is a genial and entertaining host."*
—Bob and Barb Lenz, Cadillac, Mich., U.S.A.

Inexpensive

Cairns has numerous dollarwise food options. The most pleasant are in the Food Court in the **Pier Marketplace,** where a dozen vendors offer everything from pizza to Chinese. The Food Court is open daily from 9am to 9pm. Seating is both indoors and outside with a water view. There are also lots of inexpensive **fast-food places** along The Esplanade from Aplin to Shields streets. And—just for homesick Yanks—Cairns has a Sizzler, Pizza Hut, McDonald's, and KFC.

ON THE NORTHERN BEACHES

Casbah Restaurant. 47 Vasey Esplanade, Trinity Beach. ☎ **070/577 137.** Reservations recommended. Main courses A$12.50–A$18.50 (U.S. $10–$14.80). BC, MC, V. Daily 6pm–late. Take the Beach Bus. TROPICAL/MEDITERRANEAN.

The Casbah is a delightful open-air eatery across from the beach 20km (12 miles) north of Cairns. The menu includes chicken satay, veal Oscar, vegetarian pasta, barramundi, and tiger prawns. BYO.

Colonies. In Paradise Village, Palm Cove. ☎ **070/55 3058.** Reservations recommended. Main courses A$15.80–A$21.50 (U.S. $12.65–$17.20); breakfast A$8.50 (U.S. $6.80); average lunch A$6–A$10 (U.S. $4.80–$8). BC, DC, MC, V. Daily 7:30am–9:30pm. Take the Beach Bus. ITALIAN.

In the whitewashed multilevel Paradise Village, Colonies offers fettuccine, rigatoni, and gnocchi, as well as saltimbocca and scaloppine al la pizzaiola, as well as Southeast Asian dishes and low-fat items for the diet conscious. The homemade Italian gelati and tiramisù are understandably popular. You're seated at nine tables on a pleasant terrace or at a few inside tables one level above ground. Besides full meals, the bistro serves espresso and Devonshire teas. One of the specialties is coffee roasted in the nearby Atherton Tablelands and ground on request. BYO. Takeout is also available.

✪ **Island King's Restaurant.** At the Kewarra Beach Resort, Kewarra Beach. ☎ **070/57 6666.** Reservations recommended. Main courses A$22.50–A$27 (U.S. $18–$21.60). AE, BC, DC, MC, V. Daily 6am–late. Take a taxi (A$22/U.S. $17.60), the Beach Bus, or drive. MODERN AUSTRALIAN.

You couldn't ask for a more delightful setting than the open-air dining at Island King's. Lush foliage surrounds, and you have the sense of being in the wilderness: The restaurant is part of the Kewarra Beach Resort, where most of the 30 hectares (78 acres) is covered in tropical foliage—some native and some from Southeast Asia and Polynesia. Native birds thrive here and little bandicoots have been known to walk through during mealtimes.

Happily, the food is as enjoyable as the ambience. You might start with eggplant, tomato, and feta cheese terrine or green bean, chile, and sour cream soup. Main courses include coral trout with a sauce of black olives and capsicum; escalope of veal with prosciutto, parmesan, and rosemary; and sirloin steak on a bed of mushrooms.

Save room for dessert—I can recommend the steamed ginger pudding in chocolate sauce.

AFTER DARK

Cairns's after-dark scene is nothing to write home about, probably because the area caters more to families than to singles and because everyone is pooped after full-day excursions to the reef, tablelands, and so forth.

However, you'll find some action at the **Playpen Nite Club,** 3 Lake St. (☎ 070/518 211), where there's live music in the main room Wednesday to Sunday nights. The normal cover is A$5 (U.S. $4). The Playpen's Court Jester cocktail bar is open Thursday to Sunday (no cover). Samuels Saloon and Restaurant serves a daily all-you-can-eat buffet (6pm to 2am) popular with backpackers. The A$5 (U.S. $4) cost includes a courtesy coach pickup. A beer at the Playpen will set you back about A$3.80 (U.S. $3.05).

You might also enjoy the **Reno Club International** in the Palm Court Center on Lake Street (☎ 070/521 480 or 518 835). The first (ground) floor is a karaoke club and there's a piano bar upstairs. Reno's is open Monday to Saturday from 8pm to 5am; there's no cover during the week, but it's A$5 (U.S. $4) on weekends.

SIDE TRIPS

Most people are quite happy basing themselves in Cairns or on the northern beaches and doing day trips to area places. However, if you'd like to go farther afield take note of the following.

The **Reef Endeavor** cruiseliner departs from Cairns on three- and four-night trips around the Great Barrier Reef. The ship has accommodations for 168 passengers in 75 cabins. The James Cook Cruise leaves Cairns on Saturday, returns on Wednesday, and visits Port Douglas, Cooktown, Lizard Island, and a Ribbon Reef. The Joseph Banks Cruise departs on Wednesday, returns on Saturday, and goes to Port Douglas, Lizard Island, and a Ribbon Reef. Both itineraries allow ample time for snorkeling and viewing the reef through glass-bottom boats. The ship has a pool, spas, a gym, and a sauna. Prices for the three-night Joseph Banks Cruise range from A$875 to A$1,185 (U.S. $700 to $948) per person based on two people sharing; the cost of the four-night James Cook Cruise is A$1,166 to A$1,576 (U.S. $932.80 to $1,260.80) per person based on two people sharing. The seven-night Combination Cruise is A$1,838 to A$2,485 (U.S. $1,470.40 to $1,988). To get more information or make reservations, contact Captain Cook Cruises, No. 6 Jetty, Circular Quay, Sydney, NSW 2000 (☎ 02/251 5007; fax 02/251 4725).

The **Coral Princess** is a 35-meter (116-ft.) cruising catamaran accommodating up to 54 passengers. You can join the ship in either Cairns or Townsville for a four-day cruise. The itinerary includes Moore Reef, Dunk Island, and Pelorus Island. For more information, contact Coral Princess Cruises, Level 1, Breakwater Marina, Townsville, QLD 4810 (☎ 070/21 1673, or 800/441-6880 in the U.S. and Canada; fax 070/21 1335).

4 Port Douglas, Mossman & Beyond

Port Douglas: 67km (41 miles) N of Cairns. Mossman: 19km (12 miles) N of Port Douglas. Daintree: 116km (72 miles) N of Cairns. Cape Tribulation: 34km (21 miles) N of Daintree

The settlement at Port Douglas got off to a booming start in the late 1870s due to the fervent activity in inland goldfields. In just a few years it amassed a population of 12,000 who supported 27 hotels, 2 newspapers, and a Cobb & Co. coach service. However, the community declined rapidly after 1885, when the government chose to bring the railroad no farther north than Cairns. "Port," as it's known locally, was already a ghost town in 1911, when a cyclone destroyed most of the remaining buildings.

More than 100 years later, the town (pop. 1,500) has been reborn as a trendy tropical resort. Gone are the days when tourists wouldn't consider staying in Port and would drive straight through on their way to the Daintree National Park, Cape Tribulation, Mossman River Gorge, or Cooktown. Now an increasing number are basing themselves in one of the community's new or almost-new resorts. Besides its relaxed lifestyle and tropical ambiance, Port offers a wonderful stretch of golden sand known as **Four Mile Beach.**

Nearby Mossman (pop. 1,600) is Australia's most northerly sugar town, and the gateway to the scenic Mossman River Gorge. North of Port Douglas and Mossman lies the Wet Tropics World Heritage Area, including the Daintree and Cape Tribulation National Parks. Here the oldest continuously surviving rain forest—more than 100 million years old—contains the highest concentration of primitive flowering plants in the world.

Cape Tribulation is the only place on the planet where two World Heritage sites stand side by side: the Wet Tropics and the Great Barrier Reef.

ESSENTIALS

GETTING THERE Take the Captain Cook Highway from Cairns to Port Douglas or Mossman—and be careful, it's a little winding and not too wide. Take the Mossman-Daintree road from Mossman to Daintree township and the Cape Tribulation road from the Daintree River ferry crossing north to Cape Tribulation. A vehicular ferry operates on the Daintree River daily from 6am to midnight. At present only four-wheel-drive rental vehicles are allowed north of the river, but there are plans to pave the road to Cape Tribulation and this restriction may have been lifted by the time you get there.

If you're in a hurry, **Helijet Helicopter Service** (☎ 070/35 9300) can get you from Cairns to Port Douglas or Mossman in a matter of minutes. Bus transport from Cairns to Port Douglas, Mossman, Daintree, and Cape Tribulation is by one of the **Coral Coaches** (☎ 070/98 1611 or 51 9533).

VISITOR INFORMATION The **telephone area code** is 070. As part of the telephone changeover, all numbers with a 070 area code will be changing to 07/40xx xxxx in April 1998.

WHAT TO SEE & DO

EXPLORING THE GREAT BARRIER REEF Of all the large-scale commercial boats that take you to the Great Barrier Reef, ✪ **Quicksilver Connections** is the best organized, most comfortable, and most enjoyable. Jim and Jo Wallace started this highly successful program in 1979; since then, *Quicksilver* has carried more than two million people to where they can experience underwater wonders firsthand.

Quicksilver, a 37-meter (120-ft.) high-speed wave-piercing catamaran, carries up to 300 passengers from Port Douglas to a floating platform anchored in a lagoon at **Agincourt Reef** on the outer Barrier Reef. The platform includes both an underwater observatory and shady seating. Two semisubmersible vessels leave from the platform and cruise through vast coral canyons teeming with marine life. *Quicksilver's* passengers can also snorkel (gear is provided); marine biologists conduct guided snorkel

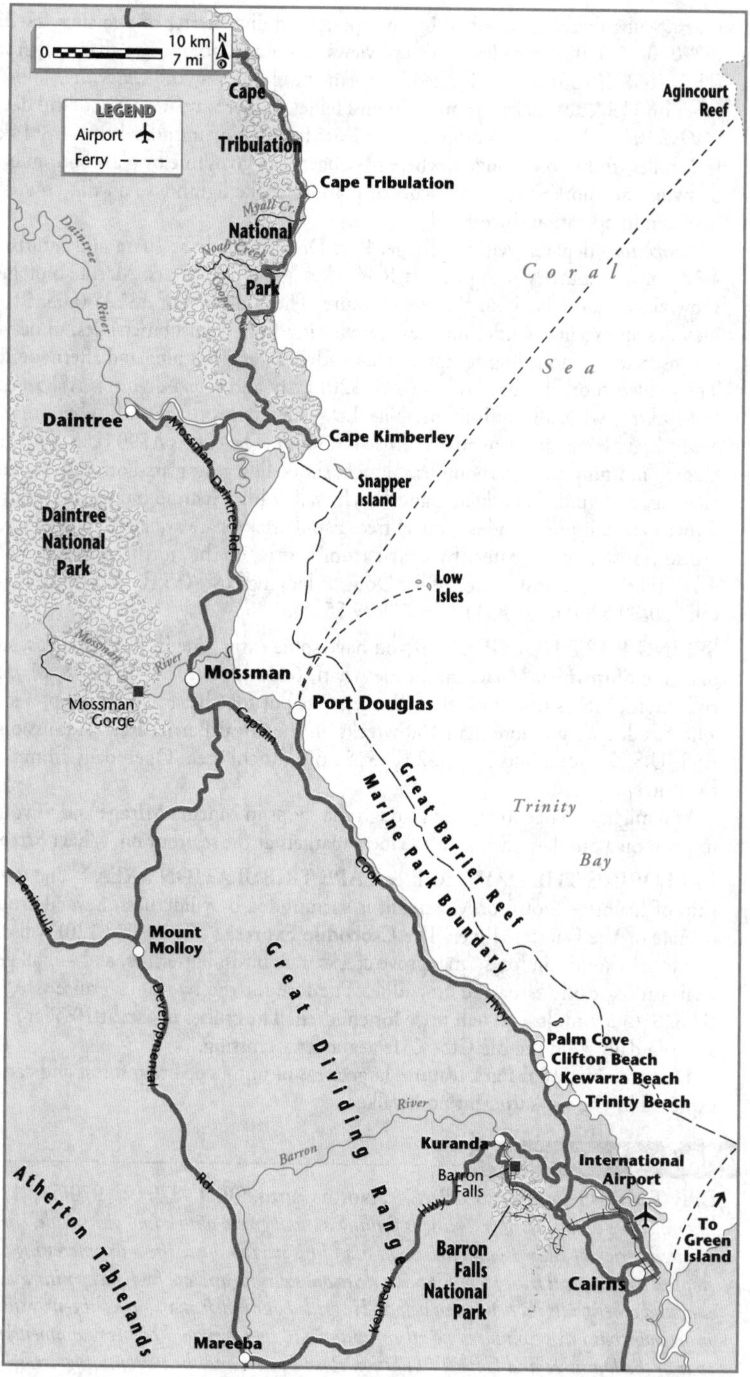
0
10 km
7 mi
N
LEGEND
Airport
Ferry
Cape Tribulation National Park
Cape Tribulation
Myall Cr.
Noah Creek
Cooper Cr.
Daintree River
Daintree
Cape Kimberley
Snapper Island
Daintree National Park
Mossman Daintree Rd.
Low Isles
Coral Sea
Agincourt Reef
Mossman River
Mossman
Mossman Gorge
Port Douglas
Captain Cook Hwy.
Great Barrier Reef Marine Park Boundary
Trinity Bay
Peninsula
Mount Molloy
Developmental Rd
Great Dividing Range
Palm Cove
Clifton Beach
Kewarra Beach
Trinity Beach
Barron River
Kuranda
Barron Falls
International Airport
Kennedy Hwy.
Barron Falls National Park
To Green Island
Cairns
Atherton Tablelands
Mareeba
2337

tours. Scuba divers are escorted by an experienced dive master to two sites. **Helijet** (☎ 070/35 9300) provides bird's-eye views of the reef at an extra charge of A$85 (U.S. $68). If your time is limited, you can travel one way on *Quicksilver* and the other on Helijet or make a round trip on Helijet. Either way, it's a wonderful day.

Quicksilver also operates cruises to the **Low Isles,** a tiny unspoiled coral cay 14km (8½ miles) from Port Douglas, where passengers can go ashore by glass-bottom boat or swim and snorkel from an anchored platform. The lighthouse on the Low Isles has been in operation since 1878.

Quicksilver departs Marina Mirage, Port Douglas, daily at 10am and returns at 4:30pm. The journey to Agincourt Reef takes about 1½ hours. Marine biologists show videos and talk about the reef en route. The adult fare of A$125 (U.S. $100) includes an excellent buffet lunch, coral viewing from semisubmersibles, underwater observatory, snorkeling equipment (and adviser), and morning and afternoon tea. The guided snorkel tour is A$25 (U.S. $20) extra and scuba diving is A$85 (U.S. $68) extra, with all equipment. The Low Isles trip on the sailing catamaran *Wavedancer* leaves at 10am and returns at 4:30pm. The cost is A$90 (U.S. $72), including morning and afternoon teas, lunch, snorkeling gear, glass-bottom-boat coral viewing, and guided snorkeling and beach walk with a marine biologist. Children 4 to 14 are half price; under 4 travel free. Family tickets are available. Wave Piercer cruise transfers or transfers by coach from Cairns or the northern beaches cost A$10 (U.S. $8); transfers from Port Douglas lodging cost A$5 (U.S. $4). To book, call 070/99 5500 or 51 8311 (fax 070/99 5525).

SEEING PORT DOUGLAS If you have some extra time in Port Douglas, stop in at the **Shipwreck Museum,** on the wharf, 6 Dixie St. (☎ 070/99 5858). This collection of relics from historical disasters was put together by Ben Cropp, a local who has discovered more than 100 wrecks on the Great Barrier Reef. Admission is A$5 (U.S. $4) for adults and A$2 (U.S. $1.60) for children. Open daily from 9am to 5pm.

You might also like to browse through the shops in **Marina Mirage** and, if you're in town on a Sunday, check out the local markets at the seafront on **Wharf Street.**

EXPLORING THE DAINTREE & CAPE TRIBULATION AREA The township of Daintree, north of Mossman, is surrounded by wilderness. Several cruises operate on the Daintree River. The **Crocodile Express** (☎ 070/98 6120) will take you to see exotic rain forest, mangrove creeks, rare birds, butterflies, and—if all goes well—at least one estuarine crocodile. The fare for the two-hour cruise is A$20 (U.S. $16) for adults and half price for children. The cruises depart at 10:30am and 1:30pm daily from the Big Croc Cafe at the ferry crossing.

Daintree National Park features large areas of untouched rain forest and can be explored by the self-sufficient bushwalker.

Readers Recommend

Billy Tea Bush Safaris, P.O. Box 77, North Cairns, QLD 4870 (☎ 070/537 115). *"For me, one of the joys of traveling is finding a small group with a knowledgeable, caring guide. Berrick of Billy Tea Safaris went out of his way to make the tour interesting. We stopped at a tropical fruit farm, sipped a delicious soursop, and ate fresh jackfruit, rambutan, and other fruits I'd never seen before. He grilled our lunch at an out-of-the-way swimming hole that I was convinced no other human had ever been to. I highly recommend this tour of the Daintree and Cape Tribulation Rain Forests and the surrounding areas."*

—Deborah Brudno, Washington, D.C., U.S.A.

Cape Tribulation National Park is a wilderness area known for its beautiful coastline, rain forest, and clear creeks. Four-wheel-drive vehicles are required for exploring. And don't miss ✪ **Marrdja Botanical Walk,** north of Noah's Creek, a magical fairyland of strangler figs, palms, and ferns. ✪ **Australian Wilderness Safaris** (☎ 070/981 766; fax 070/981 983) leads environmentally sensitive tours through both Daintree and Cape Tribulation National Parks. The guides are well-informed naturalists. Safari 1—costing A$120 (U.S. $100) for adults and half price for children under 14—includes the transfer by Quicksilver Wave Piercer from Cairns to Port Douglas, the tour in an air-conditioned four-wheel-drive vehicle, a Daintree River cruise, naturalist guides, a guided rain-forest walk, the use of binoculars and reference books, morning tea, a barbecue lunch, and more. If you begin in Port Douglas, this day trip costs A$110 (U.S. $88). Other A.W.S. safaris cost from A$145 to A$160 (U.S. $116 to $128). Highly recommended.

WHERE TO STAY

IN PORT DOUGLAS

Very Expensive

Sheraton Mirage Port Douglas. Port Douglas Road, Port Douglas, QLD 4871. ☎ **070/99 5888,** or 1800/22 2229 in Australia. Fax 070/98 5885. 297 rms, 3 suites. A/C MINIBAR TV TEL. A$470–A$680 (U.S. $376–$544) double; A$1,900 (U.S. $1,520) Presidential Suite; A$2,100 (U.S. $1,680) Royal Suite; A$750–A$950 (U.S. $600–$760) two-, three-, and four-bedroom Reef Mirage Villa. Additional person A$33 (U.S. $26.40) extra. Children under 17 free in parents' room. AE, BC, DC, MC, V. Free parking. Take courtesy shuttle to Marina Mirage.

The Sheraton Mirage is one of the few deluxe hostelries right on the beach in Far North Queensland. The hotel compound, including an 18-hole golf course, 10 tennis courts, and a 2-hectare (5-acre) swimmable saltwater lagoon, occupies an enviable spot on Four Mile Beach. The three-story Sheraton's rooms have king-size beds or two doubles, marble baths with spa tubs and hairdryers, and spacious sitting areas. Hotel facilities include 24-hour room service, a children's activity center, a tour/travel desk, three restaurants, two cocktail lounges, and a health club with gym, steam, sauna, spa, and massage.

Expensive

Radisson Royal Palms Resort. Port Douglas Road, Port Douglas, QLD 4871. ☎ **070/99 5577,** or 1800/02 1211 in Australia, 800/333-3333 in the U.S. and Canada. Fax 070/99 5559. 301 rms, 14 suites. A/C MINIBAR TV TEL. A$155 (U.S. $124) double; A$300 (U.S. $240) garden- or golf-view junior suite; A$430 (U.S. $344) one-bedroom executive suite; A$555 (U.S. $444) two-bedroom executive suite. Additional person A$25 (U.S. $20) extra. Children under 18 free in parents' room or 50% discount in adjacent room. Ask about seven-night packages. No-smoking rooms available. AE, BC, DC, MC, V. Free parking. Take airport courtesy coach from Cairns.

One of the Far North's best values, the colonial Queensland–style Radisson is set on over 3 hectares (8 acres) of landscaped grounds. The rooms in the attractive three-story property (no elevator) aren't overly spacious but have balconies, in-room movies, free daily newspapers, queen-size beds, clock radios, tea- and coffee-making facilities, and small refrigerators. Two rooms are equipped for the handicapped. The hotel charges 23¢ for a local call—the lowest in the country.

Facilities include a large pool with a swim-up bar, a children's center, two tennis courts, a spa, a pool table, bike rental, pitch-and-putt golf, and a self-service laundry. Room service is offered 11am to 11pm; the Guest Activities Office runs a sports-and-crafts program for children. The restaurant serves a three-course buffet dinner for A$28 to A$35 (U.S. $22.40 to $28). There's live entertainment nightly.

Reef Terraces Resort. Port Douglas Road, Port Douglas, QLD 4871. ☎ **070/99 3333.** Fax 070/99 3385. 144 apts. A/C TV TEL. A$160 (U.S. $128) two-bedroom garden-view apt; A$185 (U.S. $148) two-bedroom golf-view apt; A$280 (U.S. $224) three-bedroom St. Crispins Villa. Additional person A$20–A$25 (U.S. $16–$20) extra. Rates 20% higher June–Oct. AE, BC, DC, MC, V. Free parking. Take airport courtesy coach from Cairns.

This property is next to the Radisson Royal Palms (above) and 4km (2½ miles) from the village center. Four Mile Beach is within walking distance, and the Sheraton Mirage is across the road. Here you'll find two-story, two-bedroom apartments with full kitchens, laundry facilities, ceiling fans, two baths, and balconies. They're set on a lushly landscaped 4-hectare (10-acre) site adjacent to the Mirage Country Club Golf Course and include three pools, a tour desk, bike hire, a gym, and the Terracehouse Restaurant and Cocktail Bar.

Inexpensive

✪ **Coconut Grove Motel.** 58 Macrossan St., Port Douglas, QLD 4871. ☎ **070/99 5124.** Fax 070/99 5144. 22 rms. TV. A$55 (U.S. $44) double without air conditioning; A$65 (U.S. $52) double with air conditioning; A$75 (U.S. $60) air-conditioned family room. Additional person A$5 (U.S. $4) extra. AE, BC, DC, MC, V. Free parking.

Surely this is the only motel in Australia owned and managed by an ex–New York stockbroker. Michael Gabour does a great job at maintaining a friendly, welcoming atmosphere. The units are tidy and basic; each has tea- and coffee-making facilities, a small refrigerator, a TV, and a shower. The beach is 100 meters away, and there are two freshwater pools on the premises. It's just a short walk to town and the harborfront. The freshly redecorated Coconut Grove Licensed Restaurant serves reasonably priced meals, such as three-course dinners from A$16 (U.S. $12.80). The bar, where Michael makes "the best margaritas in Queensland," is popular with locals and travelers alike. The bar and restaurant are both closed Wednesday night November to May.

In Mossman

Silky Oaks Wilderness Lodge. 8km (5 miles) west of Mossman on the edge of the Mossman River Gorge (P.O. Box 396, Mossman Gorge, QLD 4873). ☎ **070/98 1666.** Fax 070/98 1983. 60 chalets. A/C MINIBAR. A$350 (U.S. $280) chalet for up to four. Children under 6 not accepted. No-smoking units available. AE, BC, DC, MC, V. Free parking. Transfers from the Cairns Airport (83km/50 miles to the south) are A$110 (U.S. $88) by private car; the Coral Coach costs about A$25 (U.S. $20) per person.

Silky Oaks offers you much more than comfortable accommodations. It provides you a unique opportunity to live amid rain forest and billabongs and be close to native animals, for the lodge is surrounded on three sides by Daintree National Park and overlooks the Mossman River Gorge.

The Lodge is owned by P&O Resort Holidays. Four-wheel-drive Australian Wilderness Safaris conducts excursions into the surrounding wilderness, and when the guides encounter orphaned baby kangaroos or wallabies they bring them back with them. These little ones add a dimension to life at Silky Oaks that's you can't find elsewhere. You can help bottle-feed the babies. The Mossman River Gorge is a haven for native birds, and books in the lodge's nature reference library help to identify them.

Accommodations at Silky Oaks are in 60 comfortable chalets built on poles among the trees near the edge of the river and overlooking the kangaroo nursery. Each has a bath with a shower, a hardwood floor, a ceiling fan, a veranda, and timber furniture; 20 have a kitchenette. There are a boardwalk down to the river and hammocks on the bank. Canoes and kayaks are also available, as are a beautiful pool, a tennis court, bicycles, picnic lunches, and backpacks. Swimming in the river and hiking in adjacent Daintree National Park are popular pastimes.

Guests enjoy meals in an open-air restaurant with a river view; the lodge has a good wine list; no room service.

In the Daintree & Cape Tribulation Area

Coconut Beach Rainforest Resort. Cape Tribulation Road (P.O. Box 6903, Cairns, QLD 4870). ☎ **070/52 1311** or 98 0033. Fax 070/51 6432. 67 rms. A$230 (U.S. $184) double. Additional person A$45 (U.S. $36) extra. Rates include continental breakfast and guided rain-forest walk. AE, BC, DC, MC, V. Free parking. Resort transfers from Cairns cost A$70 (U.S. $56) one-way; you could also arrive on the Coral Coach or hire a four-wheel-drive vehicle (see "Getting There" above).

Located 150km (93 miles) north of Cairns and 2km (1.2 miles) south of Cape Tribulation, the Coconut Beach Resort offers both rain forest and the reef. The accommodations are set among the trees and the sweeping beach lined with palm trees is just steps away. Each unit has simple furnishings, a timber floor, louvered windows for maximum breeze, a balcony, a ceiling fan, coffee- and tea-making facilities, a small refrigerator, and one queen-size or twin beds plus bunk beds. Meals are served in an open-air dining room. There's also a guest lounge, a reference library, and a coin-op laundry.

Guests enjoy two pools, a spa, the beach, adventurous guided four-wheel-drive day tours, excursions to the Great Barrier Reef, and horseback riding on the beach and in the rain forest.

Daintree Eco Lodge. Daintree Road, Daintree (P.O. Box 438, Mossman, QLD 4873). ☎ **070/98 6100,** or 1800/80 8010 in Australia. Fax 070/98 6200. 15 individual lodges. A/C MINIBAR TV TEL. A$360 (U.S. $288) double luxury lodge; additional person A$85 (U.S. $68) extra. A$450 (U.S. $360) double deluxe spa lodge; additional person A$100 (U.S. $80) extra. Rates include cooked breakfast, transfers, and guided rain-forest tour. Ask about three-day packages. Children under 10 not accepted. AE, BC, DC, MC, V. Free parking. The lodge provides complimentary transfer, or take a Coral Coaches bus, or drive (four-wheel-drive not required).

The word *ecotourism* is often misused these days, but in the case of this new property it's completely appropriate. Fifteen lodges are set atop poles in the middle of a patch of rain forest. Each has an uninterrupted up-close view of the trees and wildlife from a screened balcony. Owners Hans and Janice Eymann built the pole structures around the trees, losing only two in the process. They use no chemical pesticide or weed killer and no harmful cleaning products or bleach. The water is recycled, the sanitary system is biocycle, and the habitats of the native animals are never disturbed. Kitchen waste is composted and drinking water comes directly from an underground spring.

The lodge is across from the Daintree River, where you can cruise to see crocodiles and native birds. Walking and fishing are other popular activities. There's also a very nice pool and sun deck.

The Ecotourist Lodge menu features "Daintree cuisine," like fish from the river, rain-forest berries, and organically grown fruit and vegetables. The local Aboriginal people have shown Jan and Hans how to harvest rain-forest food. The proprietors also serve tea made from "environmentally responsive" tea bags in which "oxygen-bleached" paper contains pesticide-free Australian-grown tea. Meals are served in the Baaru House, named for the large three-dimensional crocodile mural on one wall. This handsome animal made of coconut fiber was painted by Garrkarrga Gurruwiwi, an Aboriginal artist from Arnhem Land. (Her brother is the lead singer in the Yotha Yindi rock group.) She painted the crocodile in tribal colors after getting permission from the elders. Holes in the roof and floor of the dining room accommodate a tree and a creek runs under it.

Heritage Lodge. Turpentine Road, Cooper Creek via Mossman, QLD 4873. ☎ **070/98 9138.** Fax 070/98 9004. 20 units. MINIBAR. A$145 (U.S. $11.60) double. Additional person A$15 (U.S. $12) extra. Lower rates off-season. Ask about standby rates. AE, BC, MC, V. Free parking. Access off the Cape Tribulation Road is by four-wheel-drive vehicle; a Coral Coach ticket from Cairns (a 2 1/2-hour trip) costs A$42 (U.S. $33.60) round-trip.

The lodge is 18km (11 miles) north of the Daintree River ferry on the banks of Cooper Creek and adjoins Cape Tribulation National Park. Its units are located in forest clearings. Each has a bath, a minibar, a ceiling fan, and a veranda. The restaurant offers all meals, and there's a bar and pool. This is a great place for bushwalking (a two-hour hike to Alexandra Falls), bird watching, and swimming in nearby Cooper Creek.

WHERE TO DINE

IN PORT DOUGLAS

Besides the two places below, consider the licensed restaurant at the **Coconut Grove Motel.** Several readers have raved about their meals.

Cafe Macrossan. Macrossan Street, Port Douglas. ☎ **070/994 372.** Reservations recommended for dinner. Main courses A$17–A$20 (U.S. $13.60–$16); average lunch A$7 (U.S. $5.60). BC, MC, V. Daily 9am–10pm. MODERN AUSTRALIAN.

This casual BYO is pleasant for an inexpensive meal—especially when the weather's right for dining outdoors. Don't be misled by the Bavarian motif; it's left over from the German restaurant that once occupied this space. Brunch is served from 9am to noon; lunch from noon to 3pm; and dinner from 6:30pm. My midday meal consisted of grilled focaccia with sun-dried tomatoes; my husband enjoyed tortellini. Sample dinner main courses are rack of lamb, coral trout, prawns, and roast duckling.

Nautilus Restaurant. 17 Murphy St., Port Douglas. ☎ **070/99 5330.** Reservations recommended. Main courses A$24–A$29 (U.S. $19.20–$23.20). AE, BC, MC, V. Daily 6:30pm–late. Enter from Macrossan Street. TROPICAL/SEAFOOD.

Nautilus has been luring diners to Port Douglas since 1953 with its creative cuisine and careful cooking. The menu changes daily depending on market availability. Popular modern seafood dishes include fresh tiger prawns dipped in Asian spices and charcoal-grilled, Thai fish curry with steamed rice, and live North Queensland mud crab in chile-and-ginger sauce. Typical meat main courses are grilled lamb cutlets served with beetroot chutney, charcoal-grilled King Island rib of beef with mustard-herb butter, and steamed corned beef with horseradish and creamed potatoes. You might also enjoy deboned baby spatchcock stuffed with mushrooms and parmesan. These gourmet meals are served on a covered veranda or under palm trees on a garden terrace. The tropical foliage is complemented by the candlelight supplied by owner Carmel Forrest. Save room for the house specialty dessert soufflé.

IN MOSSMAN

Silky Oaks Lodge and Restaurant. Mossman Gorge. ☎ **070/98 1666.** Reservations Recommended. Main courses A$19–A$25 (U.S. $15.20–$20). AE, BC, DC, MC, V. Daily noon–2:30pm and 6:30–9:30pm. See Silky Oaks Wilderness Lodge in "Where to Stay" above. INTERNATIONAL.

This is a wonderful open-air setting in which to enjoy lunch or dinner. The restaurant overlooks the Mossman River Gorge and there are lots of native birds and other animals in the area. The menu favors local seafood and international dishes. Coral trout is pan-fried with orange segments; oven-steamed barramundi is wrapped in a banana leaf with vegetables; baked lamb filet is seasoned with mustard and rosemary and wrapped in filo. Lunch guests are welcome to use the resort's recreational facilities. Request one of the seven tables with a view of the river.

5 The Cape York Peninsula

Cooktown: 334km (207 miles) N of Cairns

The northernmost part of the state of Queensland is a triangle-shaped area about $1^1/_2$ times the size of England. It's a land of incredible wilderness inhabited by a few hardy settlers, Torres Strait Islanders, and Aborigines. Camping tours departing from Cairns take at least five days to get to the tip of the Cape York Peninsula, longer if side trips are included. Along the way at least seven rivers are forded.

Cooktown (pop. 1,000) is the last outpost of civilization before heading up the peninsula. Safaris following the **Peninsula Developmental Road,** known locally as the **Telegraph Line,** are first confronted with the up-and-down experience of dealing with high forested ridges and steep river valleys created by water flowing both east and west of the **Great Dividing Range.** Later, detours to the coast reveal spectacular sweeping beaches and evergreen rain forests that possess as many as 50 kinds of orchids and weird insect-eating plants. Farther along, crocodiles thrive in innumerable swamps and creeks. Closer to the top, fascinating termite mounds can be seen, as well as the rich bird life that inhabits the scrubland and open forest. Once at the top, weary adventurers are treated to a breathtaking view of **Endeavour Strait** and the **Torres Strait Islands.**

This is not a trip for inexperienced, albeit enthusiastic, tourists. The lack of sealed roads, bridges, and gas (petrol) stations (the last fuel depot is in Coen)—to say nothing of man-eating crocodiles—makes this a journey to be undertaken only with a jungle-smart Aussie who knows the way and has the proper equipment. In addition to a fully outfitted four-wheel-drive vehicle, your guide will need to obtain written permission for your group to cross Aboriginal land.

ESSENTIALS

GETTING THERE Sunstate Airlines and Flight West Airlines fly from Cairns to Bamaga near the tip of the peninsula. Surface travel is impossible during the wet season, November to May, and even in the optimum period, August to October, only those equipped with a rugged sense of adventure and an equally rugged four-wheel-drive vehicle make it to the top.

VISITOR INFORMATION The **Royal Automobile Club of Queensland (RACQ)** is the best information source for road conditions, and **Queensland Government Travel Centres** can provide you with a list of tour operators who offer camping safaris. The **telephone area code** is 070. As part of the telephone changeover, all numbers with a 070 area code will be changing to 07/40xx xxxx in April 1998.

WHERE TO STAY

Pajinka Wilderness Lodge. 400m (436 yd.) south of Cape York (P.O. Box 7757), Cairns, QLD 4870. ☎ **070/31 3988** or 69 2100, or 1800/80 2968 in Australia. Fax 070/31 3966 or 69 2110. 24 cabins. Three-night packages A$1,290 (U.S. $1,032) per person double; A$1,230 (U.S. $984) per person triple. Ask about lower-priced "green season" packages Nov–Apr. Rates include airfare to/from Cairns, airport transfers, meals, and most sporting activities. AE, BC, DC,

MC, V. Sunstate Airlines and Flight West Airlines fly into Bamaga, 956km (593 miles) north of Cairns and 32km (20 miles) south of Cape York; the lodge provides airport transfers.

The Pajinka Wilderness Lodge (formerly the Cape York Wilderness Lodge) is north of the World War II airstrip at Bamaga and only 400 meters (436 yd.) from the tip of mainland Australia. Each cabin has a modern bath, a ceiling fan, and a balcony with a great view of the surrounding bush. All meals are served buffet style, in an open-sided dining/bar area overlooking the pool. A fully licensed bar is open every day. Guests can sit around the pool, fish, take four-wheel-drive safaris, observe the incredible variety of wildlife in the area, or do day trips to Thursday Island. The staff provides binoculars, flashlights, dinghies with outboard motors, and fishing gear and tackle.

In 1993 Pajinka Wilderness Lodge was purchased by the local Aboriginal community and now provides not only recreational opportunities but also a chance to learn about the Aboriginal culture. The Injinoo people share their heritage with guests and teach them about their traditional food and medicine. They also conduct a variety of field trips to places of special interest.

6 Outback & Inland Queensland

Mount Isa: 900km (558 miles) W of Townsville
Longreach: 682km (423 miles) W of Rockhampton

A long way from the fields of sugarcane and the tropical ambience of the coast, vast stretches of sunburned country cover more than a third of the state. This is where cattle stations, rodeos, and starkly beautiful scenery prevail, and island resorts, rain forests, and beaches seem a world away.

ESSENTIALS

GETTING THERE If you drive to Mount Isa, keep in mind that the Flinders Highway from Townsville passes through 900km (558 miles) of sparsely populated country. Motorists traveling to Longreach from Rockhampton follow the Capricorn Highway. The recently expanded "Matilda Highway" (actually made up of stretches of the Mitchell and Landsborough Highways and the Burke Development Road) goes through several outback towns, including McKinlay—where the Walkabout Creek Hotel of *Crocodile Dundee* fame is located. Always check road conditions with the RACQ before setting out for any outback destination.

Qantas, Ansett, and Flight West fly to Mount Isa. An Air Pass ticket from Townsville to Mount Isa costs A$265 to A$350 (U.S. $212 to $256). Flight West also serves Longreach.

The *Inlander* train leaves Townsville on Wednesday and Sunday at 5pm, arriving in Mount Isa at 1pm the next day. The *Spirit of the Outback* departs Brisbane 7pm Tuesday and Friday and arrives in Longreach at 7pm the next day.

Longreach and Mount Isa can be reached by Greyhound-Pioneer and McCafferty's buses. A Townsville-Mount Isa ticket costs about A$81 (U.S. $64.80). A Longreach-Mount Isa ticket costs about A$56 (U.S. $44.80). Brisbane-Mount Isa will set you back A$135 (U.S. $108).

VISITOR INFORMATION **Queensland Government Travel Centres** in the capital cities throughout Australia and **Queensland Tourist and Travel Corporation** offices in major overseas cities have information on the outback. Another good source is the **Outback Queensland Tourism Authority,** P.O. Box 295, Blackall, QLD 4472 (☎ 076/57 4255; fax 076/57 4437). In addition to providing sightseeing data, these people can make arrangements for you to stay on a working cattle or sheep station. The **telephone area code** is 076 for Longreach and 077 for Mount Isa. As part of the telephone changeover, all numbers with a 076 area code will be changing to 07/46xx xxxx in June 1998, and all numbers with a 077 area code will be changing to 07/47xx xxxx in March 1999.

EXPLORING THE OUTBACK

Longreach (pop. 2,971) is a good place to base yourself if you wish to sample the flavor of the outback. Once there, visit the **Australian Stockman's Hall of Fame and Outback Heritage Centre,** a tribute to the people who pioneered the west. The center was built as part of the 1988 bicentennial celebration and honors explorers, pioneers, stockmen, roughriders, poets, writers, and artists. Longreach was also an early home of **Qantas Airways,** and the original hangar is still at the airport.

In the northwest section of Queensland the terrain is less hostile and dry; instead, outback scenery gives way to rolling plains. Huge stations operate throughout the region, and **Mount Isa** (pop. 23,679) is the site of one of the world's largest copper, silver, lead, and zinc mines. In addition to taking mine tours, visitors to Mount Isa can go to an underground museum and the **Royal Flying Doctor Service/School of the Air** base.

WHERE TO STAY

IN LONGREACH

Jumbuck Motel. Sir Hudson Fysh Drive, Longreach, QLD 4730. ☎ **076/58 1799.** Fax 076/58 1832. 36 rms. A/C TV TEL. A$70 (U.S. $56) double. AE, BC, DC, MC, V. Free parking. Courtesy transfer available.

All quarters here have showers, videos, coffee- and tea-making facilities, and small refrigerators. A restaurant, pool, playground, and barbecue are on the premises.

IN MOUNT ISA

Burke and Wills Mount Isa Motor Inn. At the corner of Grace and Camooweal streets, Mount Isa, QLD 4825. ☎ **077/43 8000.** Fax 077/43 8424. 56 rms. A/C TV TEL. A$85 (U.S. $68) double. AE, BC, DC, MC, V. Free parking. Airport courtesy car on request.

Burke and Wills is a two-story building with all the modern amenities, including water beds, queen-size beds, a pool, hot and cold spas, a restaurant, and facilities for the handicapped. Most rooms have bathtubs as well as showers; all have minibars, tea- and coffee-making facilities, and small refrigerators.

10 The Great Barrier Reef

The world's greatest living structure runs along the Queensland coast from just north of Bundaberg to past the end of the Cape York Peninsula: It's a spectacular coral reef surrounded by tropical fish and other marine life whose shapes and colors put so-called imaginative Hollywood moviemakers to shame. While the coral often appears inert, it's very much alive; anyone who doubts this need only watch it extend its tentacles to feed.

The reef has affected the course of Australia's history since Capt. James Cook encountered it in 1770. Cook's expedition nearly ended in disaster when his ship, the *Endeavour,* was severely damaged when he unknowingly entered through the Whitsunday Passage and tried to find a way out across the outer reef through dense coral shoals. Many northern Queensland place names, including Cooktown, Lizard Island, Magnetic Island, and Cook's Passage, come from this 18th-century voyage. And the labels he bestowed on Cape Tribulation, Weary Bay, Hope Islands, and, finally, Providential Channel indicate the challenge the reef presented.

The Great Barrier Reef continues to amaze, inspire, and challenge the scientists who attempt to understand its fragile, yet enduring, structure and who study the myriad interrelated marine species that thrive in its environs. The reef impacts the nation's economy in the areas of shipping, fishing, and tourism—and, perhaps most important, it's a source of pride for all Australians.

"It is," one Aussie explained to me, "one of the reasons we call ourselves 'the lucky country.'"

REEF FACTS

The Great Barrier Reef extends for 2,000km (1,240 miles) from Lady Elliot Island off Queensland's central coast to the Gulf of Papua near New Guinea. In the south, the reef's outer edge is up to 300km (186 miles) offshore and the closest coral lies about 15km (9 miles) from the coast. In the north, the reef starts about 20km (12 miles) offshore and extends for approximately 30km (18 miles). It covers an area greater than that of Britain and about half the size of the U.S. state of Texas.

NOT REALLY A BARRIER The outer reef isn't a solid wall but a system of coral shoals and individual ribbon and patch reefs upon which waves pound relentlessly. On the far side of the outer reef the Pacific Ocean is hundreds of fathoms deep. The great lagoon

What's Special About the Great Barrier Reef

Activities
- Swimming, snorkeling, scuba diving, reef walking, underwater photography, and viewing the reef from glass-bottom boats or semisubmersibles.

Natural Spectacles
- Coral, in a rainbow of colors and myriad assorted shapes.
- Tropical fish, whose imaginative shapes are rivaled only by their vibrant hues.

Special Pleasures
- Taking private picnics in secluded coves.
- Enjoying candlelit dinners with tropical breezes.
- Reclining under a palm tree and relaxing as only an island idyll allows.

between the outer reef and the mainland is dotted with coral cays, continental islands, and inner patch reefs.

Coral cays are low islands formed from coral rubble and sand, created by the reef on which they stand. Over time, this sedimentary debris is thrown up by wind, waves, and currents onto the sheltered side of the reef top. At first a sandspit forms, and if the cay enlarges with the accumulation of more coral debris it may become a resting site for birds; eventually, plants grow from seeds deposited in bird droppings. Vegetated cays provide ideal places for sea birds and turtles to nest and lay their eggs. Continental islands are drowned mountains rising from the continental shelf. Much larger than coral cays, they're often mountainous and wooded. The Great Barrier Reef is comprised of more than 2,600 separate reefs and over 300 islands, including small bare sand cays, 69 vegetated cays, and many continental islands.

The reef developed because 20 million years ago the waters rose around the ancient continent of Australia, creating a submerged continental shelf and an area of relatively shallow, clear, and warm water. These conditions are ideal for the growth of coral, which began building the first reefs at that time.

ARCHITECTS OF THE REEF During the day, reef-building corals retract their polyps into their limestone skeletons. At night the polyps are extended to feed on microscopic animals drifting in the sea. Over many thousands of years, the limestone skeletons of dead coral polyps have formed reefs. These have a veneer of living coral and provide the perfect environment for many kinds of animals, like fish, worms, sea urchins, sea cucumbers, clams, snails, sponges, crabs, shrimp, and starfish. At least 1,500 species of tropical fish live in the area of the reef, which provides them with both food and protection.

No fewer than 400 kinds of hard and soft coral comprise the Great Barrier Reef. Some of these are shaped like fans, others resemble flowers, tree branches, or mushrooms; brain coral eerily resembles its namesake. Living coral ranges in color from white to pale pink and yellow to vivid purple and red. In spite of the damage done in recent years by the crown of thorns starfish, which actually eats living coral

Impressions

How can you convey the dreamlike fantasy of an undersea forest of seaweed or garden of anemones, the incredible population of tropical fishes, the coral-encrusted clams?

—Elspeth Huxley

polyps, the reef is still incredibly beautiful. Just when you think you've seen all that nature has to offer, a new shade or shape appears.

Coral colonies cluster and form three predominant types of reef. Long narrow ribbon reefs are found along the northern portion of the outer reef, often separated by channels. Patch reefs grow like a platform on the continental shelf, can be up to 20km (12 miles) across, are often oval or round, and frequently have a shallow lagoon in the middle. Fringing reefs form around continental islands, and because most resorts are built on this type of island these reefs are what most tourists see. The coral and marine life of a fringing reef can be just as spectacular as that found at the outer reef or on inner patch reefs.

THE ISLAND RESORTS

CHOOSING A RESORT Nineteen islands near the Great Barrier Reef offer accommodations. Choosing among them is not an easy task, and it's important you give your decision careful consideration. Each resort has its own personality and presents a particular set of options. Some are highly developed and offer a Club Med–ish variety of fun and games. Others are peaceful, secluded, do-your-own-thing places. Several cater to families; a few prohibit children. Please clarify your idea of an island paradise and pick a resort accordingly. I want you to have a wonderful time. For complete guidelines to all 19 islands offering accommodations, see the chart at the end of this chapter.

Keep in mind that three islands with accommodations are actually coral cays: Green, Heron, and Lady Elliot. The first two have resorts, and Lady Elliot offers cabins and tent camping. The advantage of actually being on the reef, as these places are, is the abundance of coral that can be snorkeled over, viewed from a variety of vessels, and walked on at low tide. Coral cays are also rich with bird life and tropical vegetation. Beaches aren't of soft white sand but of tiny bits of coral.

Because a coral cay is actually part of the reef, there's no need to travel to the outer reef for snorkeling, diving, and so forth. In contrast, some continental islands have only very small amounts of fringing coral and a trip in the resort's boat, seaplane, or helicopter to the outer reef or an inner patch reef is required for really good coral viewing. Don't be misled by pictures of coral and tropical fish used in advertisements—the resorts they promote may be a long way from the reef. And beware of pictures of sandy beaches—many near the Great Barrier Reef would be hard to walk on barefoot.

Orpheus and Lizard are examples of continental islands with excellent fringing coral reefs. In contrast, the islands in the Whitsunday group (Hayman, Daydream, South Molle, Long, Lindeman, and Hamilton) offer lots of water sports, but serious reef buffs will want to take an excursion to the outer reef or an inner patch reef to see great coral. Tidal action in the Whitsundays also limits the use of windsurfers and catamarans.

UNDERWATER SIGHTSEEING Nearly every resort has either a **glass-bottom boat** or a **semisubmersible** for coral-viewing excursions. This is a good alternative for nonswimmers. The driver moves the boat slowly over areas of colorful coral and gives descriptive commentary that usually includes the names of fish and other marine life. Another way to view the reef without getting wet is going to an underwater observatory. Good ones are at Hook Island in the Whitsundays, at Middle Island near Great Keppel, and at Green Island.

Reef walking is an additional option for nonswimmers. This is usually done on coral cays, like Heron Island, where trained staff members lead groups to whom they point out and describe the fascinating sea animals.

The Great Barrier Reef

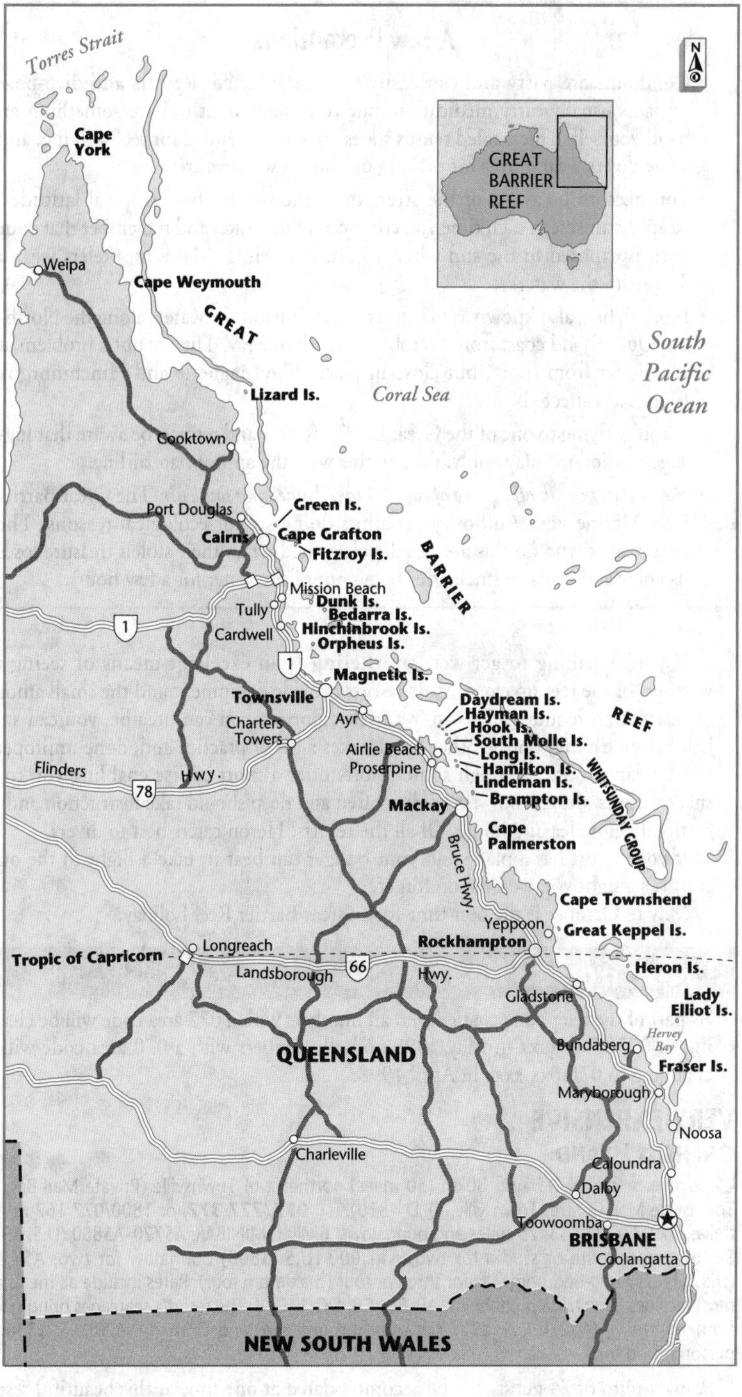

Torres Strait
Cape York
Weipa
Cape Weymouth
GREAT
BARRIER
REEF
GREAT BARRIER REEF
South Pacific Ocean
Lizard Is.
Coral Sea
Cooktown
Port Douglas
Green Is.
Cairns
Cape Grafton
Fitzroy Is.
Mission Beach
Dunk Is.
Tully
Bedarra Is.
Hinchinbrook Is.
Cardwell
Orpheus Is.
1
Magnetic Is.
Townsville
Charters Towers
Ayr
Daydream Is.
Hayman Is.
Hook Is.
South Molle Is.
Long Is.
Airlie Beach
Proserpine
Hamilton Is.
Lindeman Is.
Brampton Is.
Flinders
Hwy.
78
Mackay
Cape Palmerston
WHITSUNDAY GROUP
Bruce Hwy.
Cape Townshend
Yeppoon
Great Keppel Is.
Rockhampton
Longreach
Tropic of Capricorn
Landsborough
66
Hwy.
Heron Is.
Gladstone
Lady Elliot Is.
Hervey Bay
Bundaberg
QUEENSLAND
Fraser Is.
Maryborough
Noosa
Charleville
Caloundra
Dalby
Toowoomba
BRISBANE
Coolangatta
NEW SOUTH WALES

A Few Precautions

- Coral cuts are nasty and can easily become infected. Resorts and dive-boat captains usually carry medication, but you might want to have something on hand yourself. Thick-soled tennis shoes are recommended for reef walking, and some divers wear gloves for picking up thorny sea creatures.
- You need to be aware of the strength of the sun in these tropical latitudes. Reapply sunscreen each time you come out of the water and remember that your back is exposed to the sun when you're snorkeling. Many snorkelers wear a T-shirt in the water.
- Box jellyfish, also known as marine stingers, inhabit the waters along the Northern Queensland coast from October to April or May. They're not a problem at islands far from shore, but close-in places like Magnetic and Hinchinbrook Islands are affected.
- If you're flying to one of the Great Barrier Reef island resorts, be aware that luggage restrictions may apply. Clarify this with the appropriate airline.
- *Please don't break off a piece of coral to take home for a souvenir.* The Great Barrier Reef Marine Park Authority prohibits doing so, for ecological reasons. The selfish sorts who do this are usually chagrined when their stolen treasure loses its color and starts to smell after being out of the water for a few hours.

If you're willing to get wet, **snorkeling** is an excellent means of seeing the wonders of the reef up close. Most resorts provide equipment and the small amount of instruction required. This isn't a tricky sport: If you can breathe, you can snorkel. **Scuba diving,** on the other hand, takes a bit of practice and, done improperly, can be dangerous. Although some resorts offer a short course enabling you to do shallow dives, those who wish to dive often and deep should take instruction and get certified before leaving home. Of all the resorts, Heron caters best to divers.

If your resort has a plane and your budget can bear it, take a flight to the outer reef. It's a sight you won't soon forget.

May to October is the best time for a Great Barrier Reef holiday.

1 The Tropical North

As part of the telephone changeover, all numbers with a 077 area code will be changing to 077/47xx xxxx in May 1999 and all numbers with a 070 area code will be changing to 07/40xx xxxx in April 1998.

VERY EXPENSIVE

ORPHEUS ISLAND

✪ **Orpheus Island Resort.** 80km (50 miles) northeast of Townsville (Private Mail Bag 15, Townsville Mail Centre, Townsville, QLD 4810). ☎ **077/777 377,** or 1800/077 167 in Australia. Fax 077/777 533. 25 suites and bungalows, 6 villas. MINIBAR. A$720–A$850 (U.S. $576–$680) terrace suite or studio for two; A$1,000 (U.S. $800) bungalow for two; A$1,400 (U.S. $1,120) two-bedroom villa for three or four (maximum four). Rates include all meals and most facilities. No children under 15. AE, BC, CB, DC, MC, V. The resort's seaplanes bring guests from Townsville (A$270/U.S. $216 per person round trip) and Cairns (A$420/U.S. $336 per person round trip).

A maximum of 74 guests can be accommodated at one time at this beautiful resort. The absence of TVs, newspapers, day-trippers, and children under 15 contributes to

Orpheus's relaxed, peaceful, private atmosphere, as do graceful palm trees, bougainvilleas, soft breezes, and a good beach. The environment is such that most folks don't bother to lock their doors, and nearly everyone eats breakfast and lunch in swimsuits or other casual attire. In their welcome-to-Orpheus leaflet, the management requests that "swimsuits be the minimum dress."

Once on Orpheus (11km/7 miles long, 1km/half a mile wide), you can choose to lie by the pool, play tennis, bushwalk to lofty lookouts, have a picnic à deux on a secluded beach, snorkel over the excellent fringing reef, go windsurfing, sail a catamaran, waterski, or completely relax and do nothing at all. The open-air, native-style dining room serves all meals, and snorkeling gear, dinghies, windsurfers, paddleskis, catamarans, and one introductory scuba lesson are available free; an extra charge is made for trips to the outer reef, boat charters for deep-sea fishing, additional scuba-diving lessons, or drinks from the bar.

Those who come here usually figure out a way to extend their stay or to make a return visit. I quote from a reader letter I received recently: "There are not enough superlative words to describe the quality of attention and abundance of great food."

Accommodations are in 23 comfortable beachfront units that feature queen-size beds (some draped with mosquito netting), sitting areas, ceramic-tile floors, air conditioning, ceiling fans, high open-beam ceilings, sound systems, and large showers or spa baths. Two bungalows, slightly larger than the others, offer king-size bathtubs and private courtyard gardens. Chamber service is twice daily. The spacious two-bedroom villas, on a rise behind the other structures, lack air conditioning but offer two baths and full kitchens.

Reservations in North America: Contact Utell International at 800/44-UTELL.

LIZARD ISLAND

✪ **Lizard Island Resort.** 241km (149 miles) north of Cairns (Private Mail Bag 40, Cairns, QLD 4870). ☎ **070/60 3999.** Fax 070/60 3991. 40 rms. A/C MINIBAR TEL. A$480–A$567 (U.S. $384–$453.60) per person double; A$235–A$297 (U.S. $188–$237.60) per child 6–14 per night sharing with adult (children under 6 not accepted). Rates include all meals and most activities. Ask about special rates for five-day stays. AE, BC, DC, MC, V. Sunstate Airlines provides transfers; luggage restrictions apply.

The most northerly of Australia's island resorts, Lizard is a real tropical paradise. The surrounding fringing reef is a treasure trove of coral, beautiful fish, and giant clams; the Cod Hole, a well-known dive spot on the outer reef where huge potato cod are so friendly they can be hand-fed and petted, is accessible (but not recommended for the fainthearted). There's a complete dive center and members of the dive team can make videos of your dive (for a fee). In addition to year-round activities like snorkeling, scuba diving, playing tennis, waterskiing, enjoying secluded picnics, walking on the beach, and boating, fishing for black marlin is popular from September to December. The island hosts the annual Black Marlin Classic.

As on Orpheus, no TVs remind guests of the real world. However, there are phones in the rooms, and there's a little less emphasis on privacy and get-away-from-it-all peace and quiet, so children over 6 are permitted. Delicious meals are served in a delightful open-air setting by staff who, like others on the island, are very attentive.

Since the resort is accustomed to catering to Americans, each of the spacious and tastefully decorated units has a king-size bed or two doubles, a tub/shower combination, and double sinks. The eight Sunset Point Villas feature sail-covered decks, timber decor, and an open plan. Other indications that they like Yanks: pancakes on the breakfast menu and ice water on the table at meals.

Day trips to the outer reef, scuba tuition, and fishing excursions cost extra, as do drinks at the bar and wines ordered from an extensive list. A game-fishing boat with a crew who know where to look for black marlin costs A$1,300 (U.S. $1,040) or more per day, which can be divided among four anglers.

Reservations in North America: Contact Australian Resorts at 800/227-4411 or Flag Inn at 800/624-3524.

BEDARRA ISLAND

Bedarra Bay. 125km (78 miles) south of Cairns (Bedarra Bay, Bedarra Island, via Townsville, QLD 4810). ☎ **070/68 8233.** Fax 070/68 8552. 16 villas. A/C TV TEL. A$595 (U.S. $476) per person double. Rates include 24-hour open bar, most sports facilities, and meals. Ask about seven-night packages. Children under 15 not accepted. AE, BC, DC, MC, V. Sunstate Airlines flies to Dunk Island from Cairns and Townsville and transfers to Bedarra are by launch at a cost of A$70 (U.S. $56) per person return/round trip.

Bedarra Bay offers 16 split-level villas with queen-size beds, sunken oval baths, and private balconies. The isle, only 1.5km (1 mile) from end to end, is a pocket of serene beaches and lush rain forest. Because guests are guaranteed privacy, the resort attracts top political leaders, executives, and recognizable folks like the Duchess of York and Princess Caroline of Monaco.

The resort has an indoor/outdoor dining room, a grand piano, a pool, a spa, tennis courts, windsurfers, catamarans, paddleskis, snorkeling and fishing equipment, and dinghies with outboard motors. Guests who wish to participate in motorized water sports use the facilities at Dunk Island, 20 minutes away by launch. The only additional charges are for cruises to the outer reef, game fishing, and other boat charters. Only children over 15 are catered to (but the Duchess of York brought hers).

Like Lizard, Dunk, Brampton, and Great Keppel, Bedarra is owned by Australian Resorts. The resort on Bedarra is the most exclusive and provides the most security and privacy.

Reservations in North America: Contact Australian Resorts at 800/227-4411 or Flag Inn at 800/624-3524.

DUNK ISLAND

Just a short distance offshore of Mission Beach, roughly halfway between Cairns and Townsville, this tropical continental island is 6km (3½ miles) long and approximately 2km (1¼ mile) wide. Launches (45 min.) and water taxis (10 min.) bring you to Dunk from Mission Beach and Clump Point. Dunk is popular with activity-loving day-trippers as well as overnighters. (*Note*: Day-trippers can participate only in water sports and must pay for whatever equipment they use.) There's a national park camping area on the island. The best time to visit, in terms of weather, is May to August (marine stingers sometimes preclude swimming at the beach from September to April).

Dunk Island Resort. Off Mission Beach. ☎ **070/68 8199.** Fax 070/68 8528. 148 rms. A/C MINIBAR TV TEL. A$170–A$247 (U.S. $136–$197.60) per person double; A$20 (U.S. $16) children under 15 in parents' room. Rates include full breakfast and recreational facilities. Ask about much lower standby rates (purchased in three days of arrival) and lower rates for five-night stay. AE, BC, DC, MC, V. Most guests arrive on one of the regularly scheduled flights of Sunstate Airlines; there are also launches and water taxis from Mission Beach (see above).

This resort can accommodate up to 380 people and, when full, is a beehive of activity. Sports and recreation options coordinated by the entertainment team in the Activities Booking Centre include trapshooting, horseback riding, golf (six holes), bird watching, scuba-diving courses, squash, tennis, cricket, volleyball, archery, visiting the island's farm (which supplies the resort with fresh milk and cream), snorkeling, and cruising—the outer reef is the most popular destination. A trip to the outer reef on the **QuickCat** costs extra. You can also lie on the beach, swim in the resort's two lovely pools, or work out in the gym. There's live music nightly in the bar/lounge area and a disco Thursday to Saturday nights.

Special dinner and daytime children's activities for 3- to 12-year-olds are provided free of charge year-round. Baby-sitting is available for a small fee. Accommodations are in three types of room, the nicest of which are the two-level beachfront units. If you opt not to take the breakfast/lunch/dinner package, you can pay separately for meals in the Beachcomber Restaurant or dine in the Rainforest Brasserie, where reasonably priced tasty meals are offered in a pleasant setting.

Reservations in North America: Contact Australian Resorts at 800/227-4411 or Flag Inns at 800/624-3524.

Green Island

Just a stone's throw from Cairns, Green Island probably receives more day-trippers than any other isle around the Great Barrier Reef. However, it isn't just its proximity to a mainland city with an international airport that accounts for the great number of visitors. The island is a coral cay and, as part of the reef, provides several excellent coral-viewing opportunities. The Underwater Observatory has 22 windows from which you can watch the surrounding marine life, and glass-bottom boats make regular sorties. If you're willing to get wet, the snorkeling here is excellent.

The 12-hectare (30-acre) island also offers the Barrier Reef Theatre, guided reef walks, fish feeding, and an outstanding collection of primitive art in Marineland Melanesia. The day-visitor facilities surround a 25-meter (82-ft.) freshwater pool. If you're feeling lazy, stretch out under one of the coconut palms planted a century ago to provide food for shipwrecked sailors.

Great Adventures (☎ 070/51 0455) operates catamarans that make the trip from Cairns in 40 minutes. Besides day trips to Green, Great Adventures offers a two-island excursion including both Green and Fitzroy, a trip going to Green and the outer reef, and a trip combining Green and Michaelmas Cay. For details, see "Exploring the City & Environs" under Cairns in Chapter 9.

Green Island Resort. P.O. Box 898, Cairns, QLD 4870. ☎ **070/313 300,** or 1800/673 366 in Australia. Fax 070/521 511. 36 rms, 10 suites. A/C MINIBAR TV TEL. A$780 (U.S. $624) double room; A$880 (U.S. $704) double suite. Additional adult or child 4–14 A$215–A$240 (U.S. $172–$192) extra. Rates include meals, return boat transfer, use of beach equipment, aqua aerobics, and most nonmotorized activities. AE, BC, DC, JCB, MC, V.

If your budget can bear it, treat yourself to the "new" Green Island Resort, which reopened in 1993 after complete redesign and rebuilding. This five-star property on a small coral cay is surrounded by stunning coral and tropical fish. The resort can accommodate 90 overnight guests in 10 Reef Suites with king-size beds and 36 Island Rooms (9 with king beds and 27 with doubles). All the spacious, well-appointed quarters include safes, robes, complete audiovisual facilities, ceiling fans, and balconies. You can go on guided island and reef walks, lay around the 25-meter freshwater pool, snorkel, scuba dive (instruction provided), go on glass-bottom-boat trips, visit the underwater observatory, or visit the wildlife in Marineland Melanesia. Meals are available in Emerald's Restaurant, The Canopy Grill, and Lite Bites. The advantages of Green Island are its proximity to the mainland (which eliminates expensive and inconvenient transfers) and the fact that it's a coral cay—not an island *near* the reef that necessitates a trip to the outer reef to go snorkeling or diving. And, of course, the place is delightfully posh. The disadvantage is that the resort hosts lots of day guests and so feels less secluded and private than its counterparts.

Reservations in North America: Contact Worldwide Select Hotels and Resorts at 800/525-4800.

MODERATE

MAGNETIC ISLAND

More an island suburb than a resort island, Magnetic is just 8km (5 miles) from Townsville. Ferry service and day tours are provided by **Magnetic Island Ferries** (☎ 077/21 1913). The trip takes 20 minutes and costs A$19 (U.S. $15.60) round trip. Once you're on the island, a regular bus service meets every ferry, as do the courtesy coaches from the two resorts and four major budget accommodations.

Good bushland scenery and white-sand beaches are the biggest draws. Almost 75% of the island is a national park with 22km (13 miles) of walking tracks. Many of these lead to hilltop lookouts and have views of the 40km (25-mile) scenic coastline. Sailing, horse riding, fishing, and parasailing are also popular. Day-trippers can drive themselves around the island on a Mini Moke. The island's four residential areas are Picnic Bay, Nelly Bay, Horseshoe Bay, and Arcadia. From October to April, the presence of marine stingers may preclude swimming, though Picnic Bay has a swimming enclosure with a stinger net in place.

Magnetic International Resort Hotel. Formerly Latitude 19 Resort, Mandalay Avenue, Nelly Bay, QLD 4819. ☎ **077/78 5200**, or 1800/079 902 in Australia. Fax 077/78 5806. Predicted at A$95–A$125 (U.S. $76–$100) per night.

This 25-year-old resort, spread over 4.7 hectares (11.6 acres), closed for refurbishment in 1995 and is expected to reopen in mid-1996. The new resort will contain an entertaining area near the pool with a cocktail bar, a games room with pokies (slot machines), a restaurant, a bistro, and a children's club.

INEXPENSIVE

FITZROY ISLAND

Fitzroy Island Resort. 24km (15 miles) east of Cairns (P.O. Box 2120, Cairns, QLD 4870). ☎ **070/519 588.** Fax 070/521 335. 8 bungalows, 128 bunkhouse beds. A$26 (U.S. $20.80) bunkhouse bed; A$160 (U.S. $128) per person beach cabin for two (including breakfast and dinner); A$75 (U.S. $60) per child 4–14 in beach cabin with parents; A$10 (U.S. $8) camping facilities for two adults (A$2/U.S. $1.60 per additional adult, A$1/U.S. 80¢ per child). AE, BC, DC, MC, V. Daily 45-minute trips from Cairns on Great Adventures (A$27/U.S. $21.60 round trip).

Some of the best inexpensive facilities in the Great Barrier Reef area are on 259-hectare (640-acre) Fitzroy. The continental island with a coarse coral beach and modest fringing reef is known for its wooded mountains, dense rain forest, streams, and waterfalls. Bushwalking (hiking) is a popular pastime.

Accommodations are either in hostel-style bunkhouses, where 32 rooms contain four beds and cooking and bathing facilities are communal, or in a handful of attractive two-bedroom beachfront bungalows with private baths, TVs, and small refrigerators. Each of these also has a ceiling fan, a clock radio, tea- and coffee-making facilities, a hardwood floor, and a porch with patio furniture. There are also campsites; obtain a camping permit from Great Adventures Visitor Centre, Wharf Street, Cairns, QLD 4870 (☎ 070/510 455), before departing. Island facilities include a restaurant, a pool, and dive and snorkel equipment for rent.

Reservations in North America: Contact Antipodes Tours, 9841 Airport Blvd., Suite 820, Los Angeles, CA 90045 (☎ 800/354-7471).

2 The Whitsundays

As part of the telephone changeover, all numbers with a 079 area code will be changing to 077/49xx xxxx in June 1998.

VERY EXPENSIVE

HAYMAN ISLAND

✪ **Hayman Island Resort.** 30km (18 miles) east of the Whitsunday Coast (Hayman, Great Barrier Reef, North Queensland, QLD 4801). ☎ **079/469 100,** or 1800/075 175 in Australia. Fax 079/469 410. 170 rms, 44 suites and penthouses. A/C MINIBAR TV TEL. A$550 (U.S. $440) beachfront double; A$590 (U.S. $472) Ocean View West double; A$650 (U.S. $520) Ocean View East double; A$1,100 (U.S. $880) Ocean View West suite; A$1,300 (U.S. $1,040) Ocean View East suite; A$1,500–A$2,900 (U.S. $1,200–$2,320) penthouse. Rates include extensive breakfast buffet. Children under 14 free in parents' room; second adjoining room occupied by children charged at 50%. Honeymoon and dive packages available. AE, BC, DC, MC, V.

While the emphasis at the other deluxe resorts—Green, Orpheus, Lizard, and Bedarra—is on the natural surroundings, Hayman Island Resort dazzles you with the best man-made luxury. Instead of tropical-style accommodations and relaxed open-air dining, this hostelry offers world-class guest rooms and a choice of sophisticated restaurants. Even the standard accommodations have queen-size beds, video players, wall safes, water views, and 24-hour room service. Forty-four rooms remain from an earlier era, and these have showers only, but other quarters have glamorous marble baths with every modern amenity.

The resort covers a large area with six restaurants, an English club–style bar, an entertainment center, a covey of Rodeo Drive–type boutiques, a billiard room, a beautician, a hair salon, an elaborate health club, a golf target range, racquetball courts, tennis courts, and an absolutely breathtaking saltwater lagoon surrounding a large octagonal freshwater pool. This lagoon covers an area five times the size of an Olympic pool and is surrounded by an expanse of wooden deck, sprinkled with sumptuously comfortable sunbeds. Another oval freshwater pool is nearby. The beach was created by marine engineers and the picturesque date palms were imported from a convent in Victoria.

Works of art, Burmese temple doors, and Persian carpets lend an air of quality and sophistication. In the formal French restaurant, La Fontaine, a pianist plays during dinner while a Louis XVI fountain bubbles away in the middle of the room.

Hayman has a nice beach and some good fringe coral; in addition, you can be transferred to nearby Langford Reef or to the outer reef for snorkeling and diving. Scuba instruction is available through the dive center. When the tide permits, catamaran sailing, parasailing, waterskiing, boardsailing, and other water sports are available. Nonpowered sports are free. A children's activities program operates year-round. September to November is the best time to visit. I can say with some assurance that Hayman is Australia's most luxurious resort.

Getting There: Ansett Airlines flies to Hamilton Island from all major eastern Australian cities. You then transfer to Hayman on the resort's deluxe 35-meter (115-ft.) yacht *Sun Goddess* (A$200/U.S. $160 round trip); champagne is served during the 50-minute trip, and registration is completed so new arrivals can begin enjoying themselves as soon as they set foot on the island. The other access to Hayman Island is via water taxi from Airlie Beach.

Reservations in North America: Contact Ansett Airlines at 800/366-1300 or Leading Hotels of the World at 800/223-6800.

EXPENSIVE

DAYDREAM ISLAND

This 16-hectare (40-acre) Whitsunday isle, surrounded by beautiful turquoise water, is popular with both day-trippers and those wanting a longer holiday. While the beach is hard to walk on barefoot, the island's two large pools are very attractive and a plethora of water sports is offered. The Great Barrier Reef is accessible by boat, seaplane, and helicopter. Day-trippers' transportation to Daydream costs A$18 (U.S. $14.40) for adults and A$12 (U.S. $9.60) for children round trip; once on the island day guests can use the pool at the southern end, rent water-sports equipment, and play tennis. Several dining options are available, plus showers and other amenities. Marine stingers could preclude swimming at the beach from December to April.

Daydream Island Travelodge Resort. 4km (2 1/2 miles) from Shute Harbour (Private Mail Bag 22, Mackay, QLD 4740). ☎ **079/488 488,** or 1800/075 040 in Australia. Fax 079/488 499. 301 rms, 2 suites. A/C TV TEL. A$190–A$265 (U.S. $152–$212) double; A$1,000 (U.S. $800) three-bedroom suite. Rates include meals, use of nonpowered water-sports equipment, tennis courts, and child care for those 12 and under. A$6 (U.S. $4.80) children's meals. Children under 15 free in parents' room. Ask about honeymoon and other packages, much lower standby rates, and lower rates through Aussie auto clubs. AE, BC, DC, MC, V. Fly Qantas or Ansett Airlines to Proserpine, take a coach to Shute Harbour, then catch a Whitsunday Water Taxi to the island; or fly Ansett Airlines to Hamilton Island and get a water taxi from there.

A modern three-story property was built here in 1990 and became a Travelodge Resort in mid-1991. Today guests are accommodated in spacious quarters, many of which have water views. Each has in-house movies, coffee- and tea-making facilities, a radio, an iron and ironing board, and a small refrigerator. The blocks of lodgings are surrounded by extensive picturesque lagoons and landscaping. A four-story atrium-style structure contains the Waterfall Cafe, Langford's Bar, the Entertainment Lounge, and Sunlovers Restaurant. There's live entertainment every night. Only overnight guests can use the large pool with swim-up bar at the north end of the island. The pool at the south end can be used by both day-trippers and house guests. At this end there are also several dining options and a couple of shops. The two sides of the island are connected by a waterfront footpath and a path through the rain forest that covers the center.

Most water sports are at the island's south end. Resort guests may use windsurfers, sailboats, snorkeling equipment, spas, volleyball courts, and tennis courts free of charge. Child-care facilities are available free from 7:45am to 11pm.

The Royal Suite and the Presidential Suite are freestanding houses—about 2,500 square feet each—each comprised of three bedrooms, a full kitchen, 3 1/2 baths, walk-in closets, laundry facilities, and deluxe furnishings. Both have million-dollar views, too.

Reservations in North America: Contact Southern Pacific Hotels at 800/835-SPHC.

MODERATE

LINDEMAN ISLAND

Club Med. Lindeman Island. ☎ **079/469 333,** or 1800/801 823 in Australia. 480 beds. A/C TV TEL. U.S. $1,540 per adult per week, U.S. $770 per child 4–11 per week. Rates are based on double occupancy and include meals, wine and beer with meals, entertainment, and sports. AE, BC, DC, MC, V. Take the launch from Mackay or Shute Harbour or flights from Hamilton Island, Mackay, and Shute Harbour.

Australia's first Club Med village opened on Lindeman in 1992. It's spread over 1,655 acres and offers myriad sports, like golf on an 18-hole course. Accommodation is in bungalows overlooking the sea and bordering the beach and pool; each offers a ceiling fan, a balcony or patio, a small refrigerator, a safe, and a door that locks with a key. The closest airport is on Hamilton Island; transfers by boat from Hamilton, Shute Harbour, and Mackay are available. Children over the age of 4 months are accepted. The Mini Club (ages 4–7) and the Kids Club (ages 8–12) operate year-round. The obvious advantage of this (or any) Club Med is that guests ("GMs") can swim, play tennis or golf, play volleyball, go sailing, and participate in a dozen other sports at a fraction of the cost charged by the luxury resorts. The area around Lindeman isn't good for scuba diving or snorkeling, but the Club offers excursions to the Reef at an extra cost.

Reservations in North America: Contact Club Med at 800/258-2633.

SOUTH MOLLE ISLAND

South Molle Island Resort. 8km (5 miles) from Shute Harbour (Private Mail Bag 21, Mackay, QLD 4817). ☎ **079/469 433,** or 1800/075 080 in Australia. Fax 079/469 580. 202 rms. A/C MINIBAR TV TEL. A$145–A$175 (U.S. $112–$140) twin share; A$180–A$215 (U.S. $144–$172) single. Children 3–14 half price; under 3 free. Rates include all meals and nonpowered sports. Ask about dollarwise packages and lower standby rates. AE, BC, DC, MC, V. Fly Qantas or Ansett Airlines to Proserpine, take a bus to Shute Harbour, then catch a water taxi to the island; or fly Ansett Airlines to Hamilton Island and get a water taxi from there.

Another moderately priced Whitsunday island, South Molle has some modest fringe reef, plus a nice beach, and there are excursions to the outer reef and other islands. In addition to the usual water sports, the island offers two tennis courts, a 25-meter (27-yd.) pool, a gymnasium, a video-games room, and a nine-hole golf course (day-trippers must pay to use these facilities). After-dark activities include theme nights, talent quests, toad races, live bands, and a disco. South Molle hasn't been promoted overseas and caters primarily to Australian families.

All the rooms are more than adequate. The Beachcomber rooms, each a separate bungalow with a balcony and a view, seem the best to me. The 30 Polynesian units, perched on their own hill with a good vista of surrounding clear blue water, are popular with honeymooners.

Reservations in North America: Contact Ansett Airlines at 800/366-1300.

3 The Southern Reef Islands

MODERATE

HERON ISLAND

$ **Heron Island Resort.** 72km (45 miles) northeast of Gladstone (c/o P&O Resorts, GPO Box 5287, Sydney, NSW 2001). ☎ **02/364 8800,** or 13 2469 in Australia; fax 02/299 2477. 109 rms and suites. A$140 (U.S. $112) lodge accommodation; A$198 (U.S. $158.40) Reef Suite; A$215 (U.S. $172) Heron Suite; A$260 (U.S. $208) Beach House or Point Suite. Children 3–14 half price; under 3 free. Single supplement in suites A$60 (U.S. $48). Rates are per person, based on double occupancy, and include all meals. Ask about dollarwise dive packages. AE, BC, DC, MC, V. Lloyd Helicopter (A$364/U.S. $291.20 round trip) for the half-hour flight, or by sea (A$136/U.S. $108.80 round trip) for the two-hour cruise from Gladstone (half price for children; under 3 free).

Heron Island is a true coral cay created by the Great Barrier Reef itself. The island is a mecca for nature lovers who come to see the giant turtles that lay their eggs between late October and March, the humpback whales that skirt the island in August and September, and the thousands of sea birds that make Heron their summer nesting spot. It is, of course, also immensely popular with dedicated divers who want to explore the surrounding coral and the incredible marine life that thrives in the area.

A national park within a marine national park, the waters surrounding the island are renowned for their abundance of protected sea life. It can be seen by reef walkers, snorkelers, or those who choose to explore in the semisubmersible. Heron and its surrounding reefs are generally considered to offer the best scuba diving in Australian waters. A team of helpful guides and instructors is available.

The accommodations for up to 300 guests are comfortable and more than adequate. The Beach House has a separate living room, a tub/shower combination, and tile floors. The Point Suites are spacious and ideally located. Heron Suites and Reef Suites, with private facilities, are near the beach. Lodges, the best for thrifty travelers, can accommodate up to four, and occupants use communal toilets and showers.

Good-quality diving and snorkeling equipment is available for rent or purchase from the well-equipped dive shop on the island. Six-day dive courses, starting on Sunday, are offered (A$350/U.S. $280) for those 15 and over. Two of my favorite activities—sitting by the pool, exquisitely perched on the water's edge, and reef walking at low tide—are free of charge.

If you really want to get away from it all, ask about nearby **Wilson Island,** where eight canvas bungalows provide the only lodging (A$150/U.S. $120 per person per night).

Reservations in North America: Contact P&O Resorts at 408/685-8902 or 800/225-9849.

GREAT KEPPEL ISLAND

Located 56km (35 miles) northeast of Rockhampton (or "Rocky," as the locals refer to it), Great Keppel Island offers a big resort with many activities, plus cabins and camping. Sunstate Airlines makes the 15-minute flight from Rockhampton several times a day, but most campers and some day-trippers come to the island on one of the vessels operated by **Keppel Tourist Services** (☎ 079/336 744), which depart three times a day from Rosslyn Bay, 44km (27 miles) from Rockhampton. It isn't unusual to see the campers, many of whom board the connecting coach at the Rockhampton YHA, off-loading a case of Fourex beer upon arrival at Great Keppel. Day-trippers are free to use the beach and one of the resort's pools.

Great Keppel Island Resort. P.M.B. 8001, North Rockhampton, QLD 4701. ☎ **079/395 044.** Fax 079/391 775. 192 rms. MINIBAR TV TEL. A$270–A$344 (U.S. $216–$275.20) double; A$20 (U.S. $16) children 15 and under in parents' room. Rates include most sports and full breakfast. Ask about special five-night discounts. Meal package A$60 (U.S. $48) adults, A$25 (U.S. $20) children. AE, BC, DC, MC, V. Transportation: See above.

A plethora of activities and facilities is offered: five pools; two spas; 28km (17 miles) of sandy beaches; three tennis courts; two squash courts; a seven-hole golf course; facilities for archery, cricket, volleyball, jumbo tennis, aerobics, catamaran sailing; and sailboards, paddleskis, snorkeling gear, fishing gear, and boom-netting. And there are island cruises. The action continues into the night with live shows, a disco, and live band.

Accommodations are in split-level Ocean View Villas with 250-degree views over the surrounding bays from their hillside location. Sixty of these were added during a recent A$14-million (U.S. $11.2-million) face-lift. Beachfront units also have a water view. Garden Rooms are the least expensive. Each room has its own balcony. The Keppel Kids Klub caters to children 3 to 14. Additional charges are made for drinks, waterskiing, parasailing, scuba diving, cruises to the inner Barrier Reef, tandem skydiving, camel rides, astronomy nights, and guided fishing trips.

Reservations in North America: Contact Australian Resorts at 800/227-4411 or Flag Inns at 800/624-3524.

Keppel Haven. Great Keppel Island, QLD 4700. ☎ **079/391 907.** 12 cabins, 3 "tent villages." A$75 (U.S. $60) cabin; A$12 (U.S. $9.60) per person at "tent village"; A$8 (U.S. $6.40) tent site. Transportation: See above.

For travelers with thinner wallets, Keppel Haven offers a dozen two-bedroom cabins with kitchenettes, as well as three "tent villages" where large tents can be rented, and a BYO tent area for backpacking campers. **Keppel Campout,** another area, is limited to singles 18 to 35.

Great Barrier Reef Resorts at a Glance

	Island	Access	Description	*Rating/ Coral	Beaches	Accommodations	Sports/ Activities	Day Trips	Comments
Far North	Lizard	Cairns	continental island; mountainous	3 fringe	white sand	exclusive deluxe resort; fine dining	all sports with good facilities; marlin fishing; scuba instruction, diving	no	no children under 6; marine research facility near outer reef & "Cod Hole"
	Green	Cairns	coral cay; tropical	3 on reef	fine sand	deluxe resort; great dining	snorkeling and scuba diving; walking track (trail)	yes	good underwater observatory and guided reef walks; glass-bottom boats
	Fitzroy	Cairns	continental island; mountainous; tropical	1 fringe	coarse coral	midprice lodgings; camping; backpacker hostel	fishing; bush walks; scuba-diving instruction	yes	rain forest with streams, waterfalls, wild orchids, butterflies
North	Dunk	Cairns; Townsville; Mission Beach	continental island; tropical	1 fringe	sand	large, relaxed resort	all sports including horseback riding; outer reef trips; bush walks; farm	yes	family resort; national park; rain forest; free child care ages 3–12
	Bedarra	Dunk Island	continental island; tropical	1 fringe	sand	small exclusive resort; tariff includes open bar	some sports; motorized sports at Dunk	no	hideaway for the rich and famous; no kids under 15
	Hinchin-brook	Towns-ville; Cardwell	continental island; large, tropical, rugged	1 fringe	sand	small unsophisticated resort	outer reef trips; bush walks	yes	national park; wildlife; dense rain forest, waterfalls; mangroves; wilderness
	Orpheus	Towns-ville; Cairns	continental island; bush to tropical	3 fringe	white sand	exclusive, informal; good dining	snorkeling, scuba; tennis; bush walks; outer reef trips	no	no kids under 15; ideal honeymoon spot; giant clam research facility

* Ratings: 3 = exellent; 2 = good/fair; 1 = fair/poor. Chart compiled by Richard Adams.

continues

Great Barrier Reef Resorts at a Glance

	Island	Access	Description	*Rating/ Coral	Beaches	Accommodations	Sports/ Activities	Day Trips	Comments
	Magnetic	Towns-ville	continental island; hilly, rocky	1 fringe	white sand	motels	cycling; horseback riding; bush walks; fishing	yes	considered suburb of Townsville; close to mainland
	Whitsun-day	Hayman; Airlie Beach; Hamilton Island	continental island; tropical	2 fringe	soft sand, tidal	five-star luxury; multiple fine-dining options	water sports; outer reef trips; scuba instruction	no	world-class resort; patch reef nearby; easy access
	Daydream	Shute Harbour; Proserpine	continental island; tropical	1 fringe	coarse coral tidal	modern resort built in 1990; hostel	water sports; outer reef trips	yes	free child care, popular with families
South	Molle	Shute Harbour; Proserpine	continental island; tropical	1 fringe	tidal, sand	large resort with various types of lodging	water sports; tennis; golf; outer reef trips; scuba; walking paths	yes	free child care; many activities; good for families with young children
	Long	Shute Harbour; Proserpine	continental island; tropical	1 fringe	tidal sand	midprice	water sports; scuba; bush walks	yes	popular with 18–35 market; rain forest
	Hook	Shute Harbour; Proserpine	continental island; tropical	2 fringe	coarse sand and coral	budget	underwater observatory; snorkeling	yes	dangerous currents preclude swimming at southeast passage; excellent sailboat

	Hamilton	Shute Harbour; Brisbane; Cairns	continental island; dry bush	1 fringe	modest, tidal	large varied; some high-rise; numerous food outlets	water sports; outer reef trips	yes	easy access via island's jet airport
	Lindeman	Shute Harbour; Proserpine; Hamilton	continental island; wooded	2 fringe	tidal	Club Med Village	bush walks; water sports	yes	offers many sports, including golf
Central	Brampton	Mackay	continental island; wooded; mountainous	2 fringe	fine white sand	informal, relaxed	water sports; reef walks at low tide	no	kangaroos on golf course; rain forest
	Great Keppel	Rock-hampton; Yappoon	continental island; large, hilly	1 fringe	fine white sand	resort; camping; cabins	all sports; adjacent underwater observatory	yes	popular with young people; easy access
	Heron	Gladstone	coral cay; tropical	3 on reef	coarse sand and coral	comfortable resort; budget; midprice	water sports including snorkeling, scuba; scuba instruction; birdwatching; guided reef walks	no	outstanding coral reef; marine research facility; turtle-nesting sanctuary; access to Wilson Island
	Lady Elliot	Bunda-berg; Brisbane	coral cay; tropical	3 on reef	coarse sand	camping and cabins	water sports; scuba instruction; guided walks; diving	yes	very little development; southern end of reef

* Ratings: 3 = exellent; 2 = good/fair; 1 = fair/poor. Chart compiled by Richard Adams.

11 The Northern Territory

Vast open spaces characterize the Northern Territory, which occupies one-sixth of the continent but is home to less than 1% of Australia's population. Its climate, rainfall patterns, and soil quality don't encourage permanent settlement. As a result, 171,000 Territorians live in an area six times the size of Great Britain or about the same size as the combined areas of Texas, Oregon, and California in the United States; lack of residents has kept the region from attaining statehood.

However, I'm not saying that the Northern Territory is an unpopular destination. In fact, almost one million tourists flock there every year in search of the outback made famous in *A Town Like Alice* and *Crocodile Dundee I* and *II*. Ayers Rock/Uluṟu, the world's largest monolith, is the most popular attraction, followed closely by Kakadu National Park (where the *Crocodile Dundee* movies were filmed). Many travelers feel this is the real Australia and in a way they're right. The vast openness and harsh terrain found in the Northern Territory are unique to the island continent and are an important part of its projected image. On the other hand, most Aussies live in the green fringe of the country's perimeter.

The Northern Territory is divided into two distinct regions: the Top End and the Red Centre. Fascinating wildlife thrives in the lush tropical environs of the Top End, which stretches from the Gulf of Carpentaria to Darwin and includes Kakadu, Arnhem Land, and Katherine. Most visitors expect to see crocodiles (and they do) but are surprised at the number and variety of water birds. The Red Centre, the area around Alice Springs and Ayers Rock, is characterized by dry reddish brown earth, white-barked ghost gums, and clear azure sky. The best time to visit either place is during "the dry" from May to September. "The wet" brings monsoonal rains to the Top End from November to March, and road closures are common. In this same period, daytime temperatures can reach 36°C (97°F) in the Red Centre. (As strange as this may seem, Darwin's U.S. sister city is Anchorage, Alaska.)

The main industry in the Northern Territory is mining. Gold, bauxite, manganese ore, copper, silver, iron ore, and uranium form the economy's backbone. Tourism is second, with beef cattle third. (The land is so barren that 16 hectares/40 acres are required to support one animal.)

The **Northern Territory Government Tourist Bureaus** found in Australian capital cities are the best sources of information.

What's Special About the Northern Territory

Top Attraction

- Ayers Rock/Uluru, the world's largest monolith.

Cultural Exposure

- The Northern Territory, offering many opportunities for learning about Aboriginal culture.
- The outback way of life, including vast cattle stations, the Royal Flying Doctor Service, the School of the Air, rugged individuals, and long distances between outposts of civilization.

Spectacular Scenery

- The Red Centre, a visual delight with clear blue sky, rust-colored earth, and white-barked ghost gums.
- Katherine Gorge (Nitmiluk)—gorgeous.

Sacred Site

- The Aboriginal cave paintings in Kakadu National Park and around Ayers Rock/Uluru.

Film Locations

- *Crocodile Dundee I* and *II* in Kakadu National Park.
- *Quigley Down Under* near Alice Springs.
- *A Cry in the Dark* in Darwin.
- *The Adventures of Priscilla, Queen of the Desert* in Kings Canyon.

Native & Imported Fauna

- Crocodiles and waterbirds in the Top End.
- Camels roaming the Red Centre.

Activities

- Taking a camel to dinner or spending a night with a camel in Alice Springs.
- Sitting around a campfire and enjoying a bush dinner near Alice Springs.

Shopping

- Aboriginal art and crafts at Alice Springs.

In North America, call 800/4-OUTBAC; in Australia, you can reach the **Northern Territory Holiday Information Helpline** by calling 1800/621 336. While traveling in the Northern Territory, be sure to stop in at the **National Park Information Centres** in Kakadu, Nitmiluk (Katherine Gorge), Simpson's Gap, and Uluru/Kata Tjuta (Ayers Rock/Mount Olga). Rangers are on hand to answer questions and distribute literature on the parks; films and displays enhance understanding of their historical and geological significance, as well as develop an appreciation for the local flora and fauna. The Aboriginal cave paintings at Kakadu and Uluru are the most important in the country, and Katherine has a gorgeous gorge.

Note: The underlined letters in Uluru and Tjuta represent symbols in the Aboriginal language.

EXPLORING THE TERRITORY

The Northern Territory has been self-governing since 1978, and transportation within the region has improved markedly during this time. The Stuart Highway, following the track first blazed by explorer John McDouall Stuart in 1861 and 1862, was finally sealed (paved) in 1987 all the way from Adelaide to Darwin; main

The Northern Territory

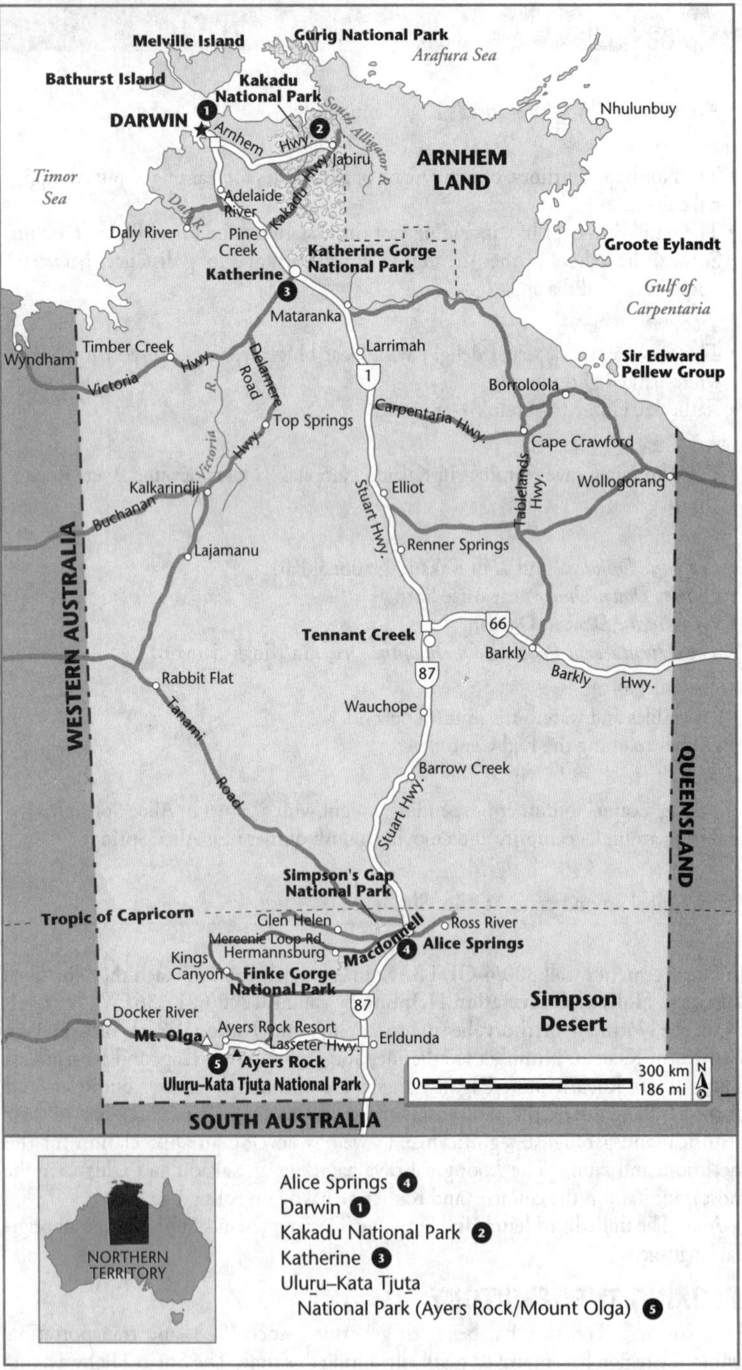

centers of population are along this spine. However, motorists who take this route need to be aware that gas stations are few and far between and wandering animals (cattle, water buffalo, and sometimes camels) make night driving hazardous. Road trains, up to three semitruck trailers linked together, present another driving challenge. *Remember:* Always carry plenty of water and if you have car trouble, stay put; don't attempt to walk to get help.

Alice Springs, in the geographical center of the country, has regular train service. In 1980 the existing railway line, which routinely flooded out during the rainy season, was replaced with all-weather track. Both Alice Springs and Darwin are served by major airlines and coach companies.

Distances in the Northern Territory are significant: The two main centers, Darwin and Alice Springs, are 1,500km (930 miles) apart. Because of this and the distances between towns with tourist facilities, many visitors participate in tours that range from a day or two to a week or more. The tourist offices above have a good selection of brochures describing these excursions, and other operators are listed in Chapter 3. If you decide to go it alone, keep in mind that you'll need permits to enter Aboriginal reserves.

1 Darwin

1,500km (930 miles) N of Alice Springs

The capital of the Northern Territory, named after English naturalist Charles Darwin, has struggled for survival ever since its founding in 1869. At first, development was hampered by the settlement's isolation at the end of a peninsula, surrounded by water on three sides. During World War II, the city was damaged by Japanese bombs. And on Christmas Eve in 1974, Darwin was flattened by Cyclone Tracy. In spite of these difficulties, the community has managed to prevail and today is a busy metropolis with 78,100 residents. Buildings in the city center are modern, having been built after the 1974 disaster. Prosperity is based primarily on the area's mineral wealth.

Darwin is one of Australia's most ethnically mixed places, with inhabitants from 65 or so racial and cultural backgrounds. Chinese have historically constituted part of the population, and today they're joined by numbers of Southeast Asians, Timorese, Greeks, Italians, New Zealanders, and others.

The hot, humid, tropical climate creates a casual lifestyle. The walking shorts and long socks worn by men during summer in southern cities are year-round gear in Darwin, and things tend to move at a relaxed pace. Extensive mangrove swamps, a busy port, and sandy beaches are all nearby. In the downtown area, Smith Street is the main thoroughfare.

While Darwin is an important commercial and governmental hub, its primary interest to tourists is as a jumping-off point to Kakadu National Park and for day trips to Bathurst and Melville Islands.

ESSENTIALS

GETTING THERE Refer to "Exploring the Territory" above for driving information. The **Automobile Association of the Northern Territory (AANT)** provides emergency road service and free maps (☎ 08/8981 3837).

Flights to Darwin cost A$350 to A$439 (U.S. $280 to $351.20) from Sydney, A$259 to A$324 (U.S. $207.20 to $259.20) from Townsville, and A$197 to A$248 (U.S. $157.60 to $198.40) from Alice Springs on the Air Pass fare. Darwin is served by several international carriers, including Qantas, Malaysia Airlines, Singapore Airlines, Garuda, Royal Brunei, and Merparti Airlines. The airport is 7km (4 miles) from the city center. A shuttle bus (☎ 08/8941 1656) meets most flights (A$5/U.S. $4); a taxi to the city costs about A$13 (U.S. $10.40).

There's no train service to Darwin. If you take a bus, your ticket from Alice Springs will cost A$168 (U.S. $134.40) and the trip will take about 17 to 20 hours, depending on whether you get the express. Townsville to Darwin costs A$208 (U.S. $166.40) and takes 33 hours. Greyhound-Pioneer covers these routes.

VISITOR INFORMATION Information is dispensed at the **Darwin Region Tourism Association,** 33 Smith Street Mall, Darwin, NT 0800 (☎ 08/8981 4300), and at the airport. The **telephone area code** is 08.

GETTING AROUND The city bus system operates Monday to Saturday. The main city terminus is on Harry Chan Avenue (near the Bennett Street end of the Smith Street Mall). For information, call 08/8999 6540. The Tour Tub provides another transport option. The bus makes the rounds of various Darwin attractions daily from 9am to 4pm. The cost is A$14.50 (U.S. $11.60) for an all-day ticket.

The main taxi rank is at the end of the Smith Street Mall on Knuckey Street (☎ 08/8981 8777).

EXPLORING THE CITY & ENVIRONS

ATTRACTIONS

Darwin has botanical gardens, the **Musuem and Art Gallery of the Northern Territory,** Conacher Street, Fannie Bay (☎ 08/8989 8211), and **Fannie Bay Gaol** (an incredibly primitive jail in use until 1972 and now a museum), East Point Road, Fannie Bay (☎ 08/8989 8290), but the most interesting thing to do is day-tripping to **Bathurst and Melville Islands.** These two places, 80km (50 miles) offshore, are the home of a group of Aboriginal people known as the Tiwis. Apart from Tasmania, Bathurst and Melville are the largest islands lying off the mainland coast of Australia and together comprise some 8,000 square kilometers (3,089 sq. miles). They're separated by Apsley Strait, less than a kilometer wide in most places.

The day tour starts with a 20-minute flight to Bathurst Island on an Air North Metro or 402. On arrival, you're transferred to the village of **Nguiu,** where about 1,200 Aborigines live. A mission station was established here in 1911 and the Catholic church dates from 1941. When these islands were bombed by the Japanese in 1942, a Tiwi captured the first downed pilot. As the story goes, the Aborigine was a great fan of Western movies and when he took his prisoner he said, "Stick 'em up, pardner, and put your hands on yer head."

After touring the community, you have a chance to shop for Tiwi Pirna wood carvings, Bima Wear clothing, and Tiwi Design screen printing. The Tiwis support themselves with these handcrafts, and prices here are much lower than in Darwin shops. At morning tea, local women demonstrate weaving. The distance between Bathurst and Melville Islands isn't great, but the crossing is made by dinghies with outboard motors because the waters are rife with crocodiles and deadly marine stingers. Since you'll have lunch next to a freshwater spring, it's a good idea to bring your swimsuit. Also handy for the trip: hat, sunglasses, sunscreen, camera. The excursion's price—A$230 (U.S. $184) for adults and A$184 (U.S. $147.20) for children—includes transportation, morning tea, lunch, and Aboriginal land council entry fees.

The full-day tour operates April to November on Monday to Saturday. For information, contact **Tiwi Tours** (☎ 08/8981 5115). In North America, Tiwi Tours is represented by ATS/Sprint (☎ 800/423-2880).

Darwin

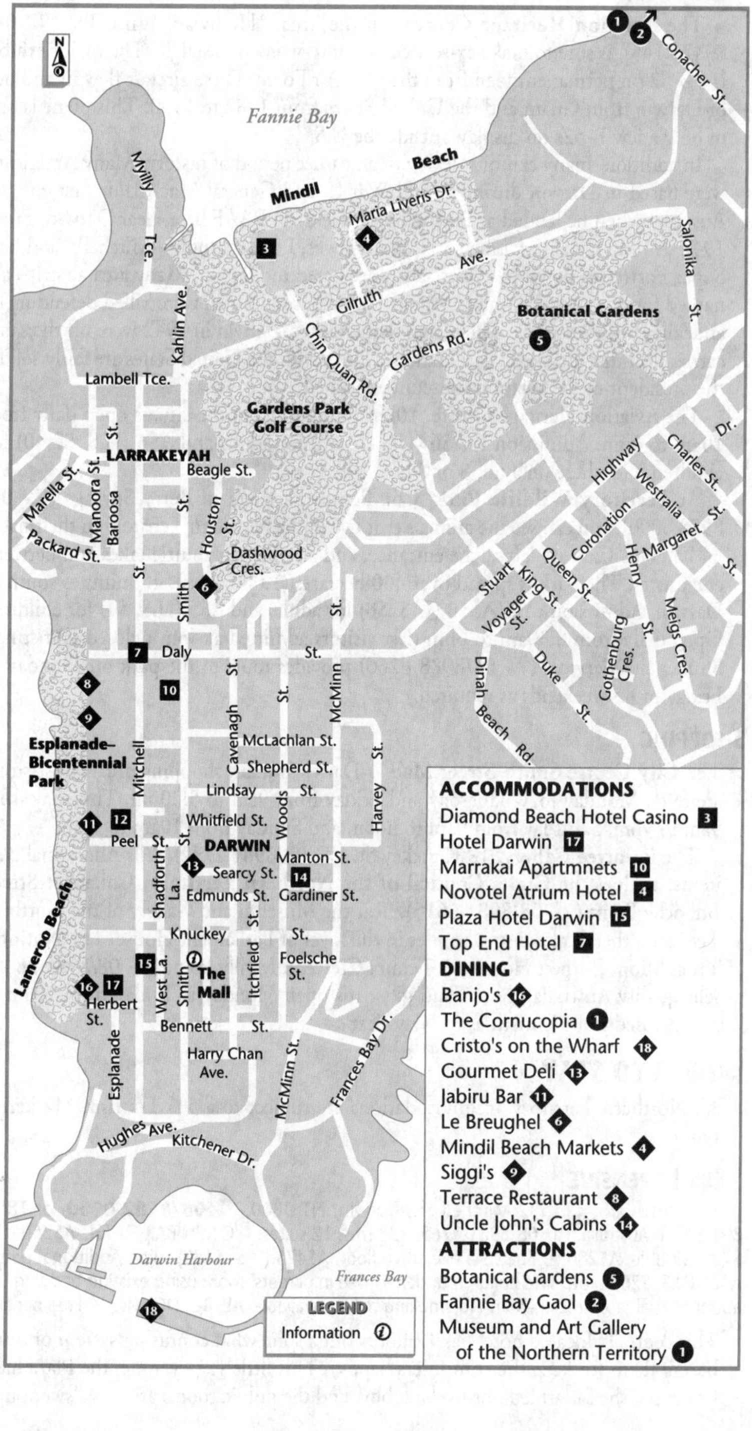
Fannie Bay
Mindil Beach
Conacher St.
Myilly Tce.
Maria Liveris Dr.
Gilruth Ave.
Salonika St.
Botanical Gardens
Kahlin Ave.
Chin Quan Rd.
Gardens Rd.
Lambell Tce.
Gardens Park Golf Course
LARRAKEYAH
Beagle St.
Marella St.
Manoora St.
Barossa St.
Packard St.
Houston St.
Dashwood Cres.
Smith St.
Highway
Charles St.
Dr.
Westralia St.
Coronation
Margaret St.
Henry St.
Queen St.
King St.
Stuart
Voyager St.
Meigs Cres.
Gothenburg Cres.
Duke St.
Dinah Beach Rd.
Daly St.
Cavenagh St.
Woods St.
McMinn St.
Harvey St.
McLachlan St.
Shepherd St.
Lindsay St.
Whitfield St.
Esplanade–Bicentennial Park
Mitchell
Peel St.
DARWIN
Manton St.
Searcy St.
Edmunds St.
Gardiner St.
Shadforth La.
Knuckey St.
Foelsche St.
Itchfield St.
The Mall
West La.
Herbert St.
Bennett St.
Lameroo Beach
Harry Chan Ave.
Esplanade
McMinn St.
Frances Bay Dr.
Hughes Ave.
Kitchener Dr.
Darwin Harbour
Frances Bay
LEGEND
Information
ACCOMMODATIONS
Diamond Beach Hotel Casino 3
Hotel Darwin 17
Marrakai Apartmnets 10
Novotel Atrium Hotel 4
Plaza Hotel Darwin 15
Top End Hotel 7
DINING
Banjo's 16
The Cornucopia 1
Cristo's on the Wharf 18
Gourmet Deli 13
Jabiru Bar 11
Le Breughel 6
Mindil Beach Markets 4
Siggi's 9
Terrace Restaurant 8
Uncle John's Cabins 14
ATTRACTIONS
Botanical Gardens 5
Fannie Bay Gaol 2
Museum and Art Gallery of the Northern Territory 1
2340

The **Aviation Heritage Centre,** on the Stuart Highway, Winnellie (☎ 08/8947 2145), is sure to make ex-servicemen and -women nostalgic. The major exhibit is a B-52 on permanent loan from the U.S. Air Force. These aircraft flew in and out of Darwin from Guam and the United States from 1982 to 1990. This plane is one of only a few B-52s on display outside the U.S.

In addition, many exhibits deal with an earlier period of history. Many Americans were based in Darwin during World War II, and General MacArthur first entered Australia when he landed at Batchelor Air Field, an RAAF base, near Darwin. From 1942 to 1945 Catalinas, Liberators, War Hawks, P38 Lightnings, Mitchells, and B17 Super Fortresses flown by Americans were based in Darwin. Many area airstrips are named for downed U.S. pilots. About 500 U.S. servicemen were killed defending or attacking from Australia. The planes that attacked Darwin in 1942 were off the same carrier fleet that attacked Pearl Harbor. "Links with the United States are fairly solid," the president of the aviation museum explained.

The Aviation Heritage Centre, 10km (6 miles) from the city, is open daily from 10am to 4pm. Admission is A$6 (U.S. $4.80) for adults and A$3 (U.S. $2.40) for children. Get there on a no. 5 or 8 bus.

At **Territory Wildlife Park,** Cox Peninsula Road in Berry Springs (☎ 08/8988 6000), you can see the animals that live in the Northern Territory in their natural habitats. Cars are left at the entrance, and an open-air shuttle takes you between enclosures. The park is spread over 400 hectares (1,000 acres), 40 minutes south of Darwin. Admission costs A$10 (U.S. $8) for adults and A$5 (U.S. $4) for children. Open daily from 8:30am to 6pm (last visitors admitted at 4pm); closed Christmas. Shuker Bus Services (☎ 08/8988 6266) provides tours to the park on Monday to Friday or on weekends as required.

SHOPPING

The **City Centre Smith Street Mall** is Darwin's main shopping area. Most stores are open Monday to Wednesday and Friday from 9am to 5:30pm, Thursday from 9am to 9pm, Saturday from 9am to noon, and Sunday from 10am to 3pm.

The **Raintree Gallery,** 18 Knuckey St. (☎ 08/8981 2732), sells Aboriginal craft items, as does the **Crafts Council of the Northern Territory,** Conacher Street, Bullocky Point (☎ 08/8981 6615), near the Museum and Gallery of the Northern Territory; there's also a small outlet in the foyer of Parliament House. The **National Trust Shop,** Burnett House, 52 Temira Crescent, Myilly Point (☎ 08/8981 2848), sells quality Australian books and gifts. It's open Monday to Friday from 10am to 3pm; closed from Christmas to New Year's.

WHERE TO STAY

All Northern Territory accommodations are subject to a 5% Tourism Marketing Duty.

VERY EXPENSIVE

Plaza Hotel Darwin. 32 Mitchell St., Darwin, NT 0800. ☎ **08/8982 0000,** or 1800/891 107 in Australia. Fax 08/8981 1765. 233 rms, 12 suites. A/C MINIBAR TV TEL. A$250 (U.S. $200) double; A$280 (U.S. $224) executive floor; A$475 (U.S. $380) suite. Additional person A$25 (U.S. $20) extra. Two children under 14 free in parents' room using existing bedding. Ask about special rates in Dec–Mar. No-smoking rooms available. AE, BC, DC, MC, V. Free parking.

This centrally located hotel has 12 floors but a somewhat confusing system of numbering them (to keep the computers happy). This little vagary aside, the Plaza has a lovely polished marble floor in the lobby, and the public rooms are very "swept up," as they say down under (meaning elegant). All quarters have clock radios, bathrobes, hairdryers, tea- and coffee-making facilities, small refrigerators, in-room movies, and king-size or double beds; you also get free daily newspapers. Five rooms are equipped for the handicapped.

Dundee's all-day café is open daily from 6am and the popular Pub Bar is open from 10am to midnight; this latter is a friendly place for a light lunch or a drink or two. The Lobby Bar contains a cocktail bar and relaxing lounge area. The fine-dining venue, Iguana, is closed during the wet season (December to March). Room service is available 24 hours a day. You can use the outdoor pool, gym, spa, business center, and hair salon.

Expensive

Diamond Beach Hotel Casino. Gilruth Avenue, Mindil Beach, Darwin, NT 0800. ☎ **08/8946 2666.** Fax 08/8981 9186. 97 rms and suites. A/C MINIBAR TV TEL. A$150 (U.S. $120) double; A$240 (U.S. $192) suite. AE, BC, DC, MC, V. Free parking. Take a taxi, Tour Tub, or city bus route 6.

This bold, contemporary pyramid-shaped building is on the beach about 2km ($1^1/_4$ mile) outside town. The casino, offering all the standard games from blackjack to baccarat, is popular with groups of high-rolling Asian gamblers. The three-story property's rooms have tub/shower combinations, videos, 24-hour room service, and the other amenities you'd expect in this price range. While the presence of stingers precludes swimming at the beach much of the year, you can use the pool, spa, sauna, gym, and tennis courts year-round.

$ **Novotel Atrium Hotel.** At the corner of Peel Street and The Esplanade, Darwin, NT 0800. ☎ **08/8941 0755,** or 1800/891 102 in Australia. Fax 08/8981 9025. 120 studios, 20 suites. A/C MINIBAR TV TEL. A$155 (U.S. $125) studio for one or two; A$170 (U.S. $136) one-bedroom suite for one or two; A$190 (U.S. $152) two-bedroom suite for one or two; A$215 (U.S. $172) deluxe suite for one or two. Additional person A$20 (U.S. $16) extra. Children under 12 free in parents' room. Ask about lower weekly rates. AE, BC, DC, MC, V. Free parking.

On the waterfront, overlooking Bougainvillea Park and the Timor Sea, this six-story hotel is a five-minute walk from the central business district. The Atrium offers bright, clean accommodations at affordable prices. Each room has its own kitchenette, ceiling fan, queen-size bed, contemporary furnishings, in-house videos, and clock radio. Half have harbor views, and executive and deluxe rooms have spa baths; three are equipped for the handicapped.

There's a nice pool and spa, as well as a children's wading pool, a fitness room, a self-service laundry, and a barbecue area. The Jabiru Cocktail Bar is a popular meeting place; meals are served in Corellas Restaurant and Castaways, which offers alfresco dining. The property's dominant feature is an attractive atrium—with pools, fountains, and tropical foliage—rising from the lobby floor. Room service is available 24 hours a day.

Moderate

Hotel Darwin. 10 Herbert St., Darwin, NT 0800. ☎ **08/8981 9211.** Fax 08/8981 9575. 69 rms, 1 suite. A/C TV TEL. Dry season, A$85 (U.S. $68) double. Additional person A$11 (U.S. $8.80) extra. Wet season, rates are lower. AE, BC, DC, MC, V. Free parking.

I like the centrally located Hotel Darwin because it's over 100 years old and steeped in history and tropical ambience—not unlike that of the Raffles Hotel in Singapore. Opened as the Palmerston Club Hotel in 1883, it survived the 1942 bombing of Darwin but burned down later that year when soldiers rioted over the cutting of their beer ration. Quickly rebuilt, the sturdy two-story building was a command center in

Readers Recommend

Top End Hotel, at the corner of Daly and Mitchell Streets, G.P.O. Box 3795, Darwin, NT 0801 (☎ 08/8981 6511). *"The Top End Hotel is near a park, fish feeding, a casino, and shopping. The large pool in the center of this two-story motel is lovely, and at night you can see the moon through the palms. The rooms have rattan furniture, enclosed fridge (very quiet), and patios with chairs. After check-out they provide luggage storage, use of the pool, and a room to shower and change. They also own the pub next door (Matilda's), so you get a free beer and delicious economical food."*

—Beverly Carr, Toronto, Ontario, Canada.

World War II and again during Cyclone Tracy. Today the Green Room, the large central main bar where trade winds blow in through oversize sliding-glass doors, is often the site of reunions of U.S. service personnel who were there during the war. The management assured me these returnees "don't notice many changes." (The hotel's character has not escaped Hollywood's attention, for part of *Evil Angels*—called *A Cry in the Dark* in the States—was filmed on the premises.)

In addition to the Green Room, the Kakadu Bar is a nice watering hole. Banjo's, the restaurant, is cooled by automatic pankas—oscillating fabric-covered panels hanging from the ceiling. There's a pool on the premises.

Marrakai Apartments. 93 Smith St., Darwin, NT 0800. ☎ **08/8982 3711,** or 1800/891 100 in Australia. Fax 08/8981 9283. 23 apts. A/C TV TEL. A$185–A$215 (U.S. $148–$172) per apt. AE, BC, DC, MC, V. Parking free.

The centrally located Marrakai Apartments are ideal for folks who like to look after themselves. The 16-story property has spacious two-bedroom apartments that sleep up to four—one room has a queen-size bed and the other has twins. The Marrakai offers a pool and spa, as well as a barbecue area and covered parking. All apartments have fully equipped kitchens with dishwashers, laundry facilities, balconies, and two baths with tub/shower combinations. Room-service breakfasts are available.

WHERE TO DINE

EXPENSIVE

The Cornucopia. In the Museum and Art Gallery of the Northern Territory, Fannie Bay. ☎ **08/8981 1002.** Reservations recommended, especially Thurs–Sat night. Main courses A$15–A$21.50 (U.S. $12–$17.20). AE, BC, MC, V. Tues–Sat 9am–10pm; Sun–Mon 9am–5pm. Bus route 4 or taxi. BUSH TUCKER.

This is a great place for lunch with a water view or dinner with a sunset view. The menu features Northern Territory produce—including herbs, fish, fruit, and vegetables. Barramundi encrusted with macadamias is the house specialty. The waterfront setting is lovely.

Siggi's. In the Beaufort Darwin Hotel, Beaufort Centre, The Esplanade. ☎ **08/8982 9911.** Reservations recommended. Main courses A$21.50–A$28 (U.S. $17.20–$22.40). AE, BC, DC, MC, V. Mon–Sat 7–11pm. INNOVATIVE AUSTRALIAN.

Since opening in 1986, this has become one of Darwin's most upmarket eateries. Dining takes place in an intimate atmosphere and waiters use silver service. The à la carte menu is changed monthly according to the season and local availability. The menu and the wine list are extensive and the food is wonderful. Entrees include marinated salmon and capsicums, duck terrine, and oysters gratin. Sample main courses are paupiettes of coral trout and spinach, open ravioli of lobster and bug, and marinated filet of lamb. Next door to the Beaufort Centre is a performing arts complex that includes bars and conference facilities.

Terrace Restaurant. In the Travelodge Hotel, 122 The Esplanade. ☎ **08/8981 5388.** Reservations recommended. Main courses A$17.50–A$27.50 (U.S. $14–$22); breakfast buffet A$15.50 (U.S. $12.40). AE, BC, DC, MC, V. Daily 6:30–10am; Mon–Fri noon–2:30pm; daily 6–10pm. INTERNATIONAL.

The Terrace offers an interesting menu, with appetizers like grilled crocodile kebabs, sliced kangaroo pastrami, and veal satay and main courses like Barramundi filets, New York–cut steak, and buffalo medallions. Some low-cholesterol dishes are offered. The decor, revolving around a Kakadu theme, includes works by local Aboriginal artist Harold Thomas. (Be sure to note the wonderful Harold Thomas mural behind the reception desk in the lobby before you ascend to the Terrace.) Live entertainment is provided two nights a week.

MODERATE

Banjo's. In the Hotel Darwin, 10 Herbert St. ☎ **08/8981 9211.** Reservations not required. Main courses A$12–A$18 (U.S. $9.60–$14.40). AE, BC, DC, MC, V. Daily 7–9pm during "the dry." Closed Sun–Mon during "the wet." LOCAL SPECIALTIES.

Banjo's has a pleasant colonial atmosphere and some unusual menu choices. Camembert Arnhem is a half round of Camembert topped with kiwi fruit and baked in puff pastry served as an entree. Beagle Gulf satay and peanut sambal, skewers of beef marinated in cumin and coriander served with fresh peanut sauce, reflects the ethnic influence so evident in Darwin. Mignon of buffalo Marrakai is Northern Territory buffalo filet served with port-and-mushroom sauce. The restaurant is named after famous bush poet Banjo Paterson (who wrote "Waltzing Mathilda"), and a quote from him appears on the menu: "And the man who goes to the Territory always has a hankering to get back there. Someday it will be civilized and spoilt, but up to the present it has triumphantly overthrown all who have attempted to improve it. It is still 'the Territory.' Long may it wave."

✪ **Le Breughel.** 6 Dashwood Crescent. ☎ **08/8981 2025.** Reservations recommended during "the dry." Main courses A$14.50–A$18.50 (U.S. $11.60–$14.80). AE, BC, MC, V. Tues–Sun 6:30–9:30pm. INTERNATIONAL.

Le Breughel is a casual restaurant on the edge of the central business district. The emphasis is on local seafood, such as scallops, calamari, and gulf bugs. Popular main courses include barramundi Creole, whole baby squid, medallions of buffalo, and Breughel's house curry. The restaurant has a pleasant cocktail lounge for a before-dinner drink. Le Breughel has an additional entrance on Smith Street West (next to the Central Supermarket).

Uncle John's Cabins. 4 Gardiner St. ☎ **08/8981 3358.** Reservations recommended. Main courses A$15.50–A$35 (U.S. $12.40–$28). AE, BC, MC, V. Daily from 7pm during "the dry" (Mar–Sept). SEAFOOD/TERRITORY SPECIALTIES.

At this popular open-air seafood spot the chalkboard menu changes daily to include the catch of the day. Other specialties include kangaroo, crocodile, buffalo, steak, chicken, ribs, and rabbit. This eatery is casual and centrally located. Drinks are served in the Railcar Bar.

INEXPENSIVE

I suggest you plan your trip so you land in Darwin on a Thursday or Sunday between May and October. That way you can head out to the ✪ **Mindil Beach Markets** and enjoy a wide variety of ethnic food at rock-bottom prices. During a recent visit I

Readers Recommend

Cristo's on the Wharf, Stokes Hill Wharf (☎ 08/8981 8658). *"The food was superb and the service was excellent and friendly. I think it's owned by a Greek-Australian."*
—Terence Fu, New York, N.Y., U.S.A.

noted food stalls selling Thai, Philippine, Malaysian, Chinese, Greek, Indonesian, Laotian, Vietnamese, Portuguese, and Italian cuisine. How's that for variety? Everything I tasted was very good, and nothing was over A$4 (U.S. $3.20). This Thursday and Sunday event from 3 to 8pm is popular with locals, some of whom bring their own tables and chairs and set them up near the beach. Entertainment ranges from a Scottish Highland band to folk guitarists. BYO if you want beer or wine with your meal. The Tour Tub provides transportation from 5:30pm or take a public bus, route 6.

The **Gourmet Deli,** at the corner of Smith and Edmunds Streets (☎ 08/8941 2744), is a great place for picnic supplies. Sandwiches cost A$3 to A$4 (U.S. $2.40 to $3.20). This shop is open Monday to Friday from 7am to 5:30pm and Saturday from 8am to 2pm. No credit cards.

Another inexpensive place to eat is the **Jabiru Bar** in the Novotel Atrium Hotel, on The Esplanade (☎ 08/8941 0755), where a carvery lunch is offered Monday to Saturday from noon to 2pm. For about A$4.50 (U.S. $3.60) you'll have a choice of a roast meal with salad or a main course like lasagne or curry with rice.

AFTER DARK

Tickets for performances at the **Darwin Entertainment Centre,** 93 Mitchell St., can be obtained by calling 08/8981 1222. If you're feeling lucky, the **Diamond Beach Casino** (☎ 08/8981 7755) is open daily from noon till the wee hours. Its dress code prohibits the wearing of shorts, thongs, denim, and running shoes.

The ✪ **Hotel Darwin,** Herbert Street (☎ 08/8981 9211), has entertainment in the Green Room lounge bar several nights a week and a disco in the Kakadu Bar on Friday and Saturday nights (no cover). In the Green Room a sign reads THE MINIMUM DRESS FOR THIS ROOM WILL BE SHIRT, SHORTS, SHOES, AND LONG SOCKS. I love the Green Room's tropical atmosphere. It feels as if Humphrey Bogart is right around the corner. The Green Room closes at midnight.

The **Jabiru Bar** in the Novotel Atrium Hotel, on The Esplanade, is another great place for a drink. This popular watering hole is on the ground level of the hotel's six-story atrium, and the picturesque setting includes lots of tropical plants, flowing water, and decorative pools. The crowd includes Darwin's young professionals and overseas visitors. It's open daily from 10am to 1am. A VB draft costs A$2.10 (U.S. $1.68). A can of beer will set you back A$3.50 (U.S. $2.80).

A nightclub, the **Beachcomber Nightspot,** is in the Top End Frontier Hotel, at the corner of Daly and Mitchell Streets (☎ 08/8981 6511). The clientele is 18 to 35—"fun-loving party types." No cover before midnight. Open Wednesday to Sunday from 8pm until very late in "the dry," from 9pm to 2am in "the wet." Draft beer costs A$2.50 (U.S. $2). The **Brewery Bar,** also in the Top End Frontier, is open daily and offers live entertainment and dancing. The crowd here is a little older, maybe 18 to 40. A draft costs A$2.10 (U.S. $1.70).

A SIDE TRIP TO THE COBOURG PENINSULA

The Cobourg Peninsula, 150 nautical miles northeast of Darwin in Arnhem Land, has remained basically unchanged since the last century, when the British established a settlement on the coast. Much of the land is unexplored; Banteng cattle brought here in 1839 roam wild, as do Sambar deer, water buffalo, wild pigs, and Timor ponies. Paperbark swamps, monsoonal vine forests, mangrove swamps, open woodland forests, sandy plains, and flood plains are just some of the kinds of terrain. Saltwater crocodiles, sharks, and marine stingers make the water around the peninsula unsafe for swimming. Because of the peninsula's ecological significance, two national parks have been created: **Gurig National Park** encompasses the land, and **Cobourg Marine Park** consists of the water around it. The land is owned by the Aboriginal people.

WHERE TO STAY

✪ **Seven Spirit Bay.** On the Cobourg Peninsula (P.O. Box 4721, Darwin, NT 0801). ☎ **08/8979 0277**, or 1800/891 189 in Australia. Fax 08/8979 0284. 24 habitats. MINIBAR TEL. May–Oct, A$299 (U.S. $239.20) per adult double occupancy; Nov–Apr, A$249 (U.S. $199.20) per adult double occupancy, A$185.50 (U.S. $148.40) per child 3–6. Children under 3 free in parents' room. Rates include all meals and some activities. AE, BC, DC, MC, V. Executive Air flies you to the Cobourg Peninsula, where you're picked up by a four-wheel-drive vehicle for the transfer to Seven Spirit Bay (A$250/U.S. $200 per person round trip).

This is a wilderness retreat like no other, where a cluster of buildings offers five-star comfort for a handful of people who are keenly interested in wild places and observing an environment yet undisturbed by humans. The Aborigines have leased the land to the owners of Seven Spirit Bay, which opened in 1990, and keep a watchful eye that their property is shown the proper respect.

You sleep in hexagonal "habitats" where two-thirds of the walls are floor-to-ceiling louvers, providing a 240-degree view of the surrounding tropical forest. Each bungalowlike habitat has coffee- and tea-making facilities, a small refrigerator, a minibar, a phone, two ceiling fans, two queen-size beds, lights on rheostats, designer bed linens, comfortable chairs for reading, a highly polished pine floor, an iron and ironing board, a torch (flashlight), a hairdryer, and a pair of cotton kimonos. Each habitat has its own five-star bath steps away, connected by a paving-stone path. Because these facilities are open-air, it's common to see little green frogs in the shower or have a warbler build a nest within view of the loo.

This is true ecotourism, travel for people who share an awareness of the earth's fragility. Guided walks conducted by the resident naturalist explore the microenvironments surrounding this remote property. You can also go fishing for barramundi or giant trevally, go sailing, day-trip to an abandoned British settlement, go birding (285 species live in the area), study the native flora and fauna, or laze by the rock-edged freshwater pool and drink an N.T. Draught.

Meals are served in the Social Hub, a tropical building that includes a restaurant (indoor and outdoor seating), a bar, a reception area, a lounge, and a reading area. Cobourg cuisine is a delightful blend of northern Australian ingredients and modern Australian style.

If you're interested in the environment and like places that are out of the ordinary, I highly recommend Seven Spirit Bay.

Reservations in North America: Contact Adventure Express at 800/443-0799 or ATS Tours at 800/423-2880.

2 Kakadu National Park

220km (136 miles) E of Darwin

If you're driving from Darwin, be sure to stop at **Fogg Dam,** 65km (40 miles) down the Arnhem Highway, where splendid water birds glide from one lily pad to another.

In this and all other areas of the park, *heed warnings to stay out of the water and do not allow children to play near the water's edge*—this is crocodile territory.

Farther along, you'll come to the **Bark Hut Inn,** where food and gas are available. This is also a great spot for witnessing local color, in the form of the burly lads who frequent this watering hole. Most of them are buffalo hunters and look like something out of central casting.

Once inside the park, you'll find that the three centers with any population are **Frontier Kakadu Village, Cooinda,** and **Jabiru.** The first two are motel and camping compounds; the last is a small township where the people who work at the nearby Ranger Uranium Mine live. The **park headquarters** is near Jabiru, as is a small airport served by Kakadu Air Services and Brolga Air. Paved roads connect the main centers, but a dirt road leads to Ubirr (Obiri Rock) and a four-wheel-drive is required to reach Jim Jim Falls.

Kakadu was declared a national park in 1979 and added to the World Heritage List in 1981.

ESSENTIALS

GETTING THERE You can drive to the park from Darwin via the Arnhem Highway. If you aren't keen on driving in these remote parts, several tour operators in Darwin run trips into Kakadu. One of the better known is **Territory Safari Tours** (☎ 08/8948 1877; fax 08/8945 4178). The **Kakadu Air Services** (☎ 08/8979 2411) or **Brolga Air** (☎ 08/8945 3565) tours of Kakadu are good for those with limited time.

VISITOR INFORMATION Information is available at the **park headquarters** (☎ 08/8938 1100), open daily from 8am to 5pm, and in Darwin (☎ 08/8981 5299); or write to the Executive Director, ANCA, G.P.O. Box 1260, Darwin, NT 0801. The **telephone area code** is 08.

EXPLORING THE PARK

Kakadu National Park is famous for its Aboriginal rock art. Over 1,000 sites have been recorded, the best known being those at Ubirr (Obiri Rock) and Nourlangie Rock—both accessible by road during the dry season. Wildlife is another attraction. Boats cruise East Alligator River, South Alligator River, and Yellow Waters, providing a look at fascinating birds and reptiles, including crocodiles. Scenery is yet another draw. The park has saltwater swamps, wetlands, eucalyptus forests, waterfalls, and sandstone escarpments.

While many visitors see Kakadu on a day trip from Darwin, if you have more time and interest you should plan to spend at least one night. The park is about the same size as the U.S. state of Connecticut, and the points of interest are not close together.

Timing is a critical factor concerning a trip to Kakadu. There's no water in Jim Jim or Twin Falls until the wet season from October to March. And while the rain makes Jim Jim Falls and Twin Falls overflow, it also washes out the roads. The best time to visit is between mid-June and mid-August. Otherwise, be prepared for heat, humidity, and flies. The entry fee to Kakadu is A$15 (U.S. $12) per adult; there's no charge for children under 16. Permits are valid for 14 days.

Guests at the Frontier Kakadu Village usually cruise the nearby **South Alligator River** to observe local wildlife (A$27/U.S. $21.60 for two hours, A$60/U.S. $48 for five hours, including a barbecue lunch). Those who stay at the Gagudju Lodge Cooinda take advantage of its proximity to **Yellow Waters,** where a similar experience is possible (A$28/U.S. $22.40 for two hours). The best viewing is in the early morning.

Flightseeing provides another perspective. Kakadu Air operates out of Jabiru Airport and Cooinda (A$50/U.S. $40 for a half hour, A$90/U.S. $72 for an hour).

It's an easy drive to the **park headquarters, Ubirr (Obiri Rock), Nourlangie Rock,** and other points of interest. Sunset at Obiri Rock is spectacular. Besides maintaining the information center, the rangers lead free tours in the park.

WHERE TO STAY & DINE

The number of visitors tends to be higher than the number of available accommodations, so book early. And remember, a Tourism Marketing Duty of 5% is payable on all Northern Territory accommodations.

Frontier Kakadu Village. Arnhem Highway, South Alligator, NT 0886. ☎ **08/8979 0166.** Fax 08/8979 0147. 132 rms, 6 lodges. A/C TV TEL. A$120–A$142 (U.S. $96–$113.60) double. Ask about much lower rates in wet season. AE, BC, DC, MC, V.

The Frontier Kakadu Village is 1km (0.6 mile) from the South Alligator River, a mistakenly labeled stretch of water: There are no alligators in this park. However, the river is inhabited by lots of crocodiles and these are viewed on the motel's boat cruises. This 7-hectare (17-acre) complex includes a motel, a pool, a spa, a tennis court, a walking track, a restaurant, a coffee shop, a general store, a caravan park, and campgrounds.

Gagudju Crocodile Hotel. Flinders Street, Jabiru, NT 0886. ☎ **08/8979 2800,** or 1800/808 123 in Australia. Fax 08/8979 2707. 110 rms. A/C MINIBAR TV TEL. A$190 (U.S. $152) double. Ask about much lower rates in wet season (Nov–Apr). Children under 15 free in parents' room. AE, BC, DC, MC, V.

This hotel is shaped like a 250-meter (825-ft.) crocodile. In Jabiru, the hostelry offers the highest standard of lodging in the park and welcomes new arrivals through a jaw-shaped portico complete with shuttered eyes. The reception area, a marble foyer, a restaurant that serves "bush tucker," bars, a gift shop, and a tour/car hire desk are in the head of the crocodile. Guest rooms are in the reptile's belly, and four stairways represent its legs. A pool (representing the croc's heart), barbecue area, and an Aboriginal art gallery are also on the premises.

Gagudju Lodge Cooinda. Off Kakadu Highway, Cooinda, NT 0886. ☎ **08/8979 0145.** Fax 08/8979 0148. 48 lodge rms, 34 budget rms. A/C. A$120 (U.S. $96) lodge rooms double, A$30 (U.S. $24) plus A$1 (U.S. 80¢) per item of linen budget rooms double. Ask about much lower rates in wet season (Nov–Apr). Children under 15 free in parents' room. AE, BC, DC, MC, V.

The Gagudju Lodge Cooinda has lodge rooms, budget rooms, and a camping/caravan area. The complex also offers a restaurant serving "bush tucker," a casual open-air bistro, a pool, and a beergarden. Since the motel has its own airstrip, it's possible to fly to this part of Kakadu and do day tours, thus eliminating the need for a car.

3 Katherine

350km (217 miles) S of Darwin

The Northern Territory's third-largest town, Katherine (pop. 8,732) is best known for its beautiful river gorge—the focal point of **Nitmiluk (Katherine Gorge) National Park**—32km (20 miles) from town. While a paved road leads out of the city to the north and south, the way to Katherine from Kakadu is partially unsealed. Nevertheless, Darwin, Kakadu, and Katherine make a convenient Top End triangle many visitors follow.

John McDouall Stuart, the first explorer ever to see the Katherine River in 1862, named it for the daughter of a sponsor of his expedition. Katherine has long been the center of a thriving cattle region and has recently had an increase in population due to the reopening of the nearby Tindal Air Force Base.

ESSENTIALS

GETTING THERE It takes just over three hours to drive from Darwin to Katherine. Ansett NT and Skyport provide regular air service from Darwin and Alice Springs. There's no train service to Katherine, but Greyhound-Pioneer provides regular bus service. The four-hour trip from Katherine to Darwin costs A$44 (U.S. $35.20).

VISITOR INFORMATION Information is available at the **Katherine Region Tourism Association,** on the corner of the Stuart Highway and Lindsay Street, Katherine, NT 0850 (☎ 08/8972 2650), open Monday to Friday from 8:45am to 5pm and Saturday from 8:45am to noon. **Travel North,** the company that runs gorge river cruises, has an office in the BP Roadhouse, 6 Katherine Terrace (☎ 08/8972 1044). (The Stuart Highway is called Katherine Terrace within the city limits.)

The **BP Roadhouse** is open 24 hours and sells groceries, light meals, takeout food, and petrol (gasoline). The **telephone area code** is 08.

SEEING THE AREA

Specially designed flat-bottom boats take you through the ✪ **Katherine Gorge.** Birds, fish, and freshwater crocodiles are often seen, and the towering reddish brown rock canyons above the sparkling flowing water are most impressive. Thirteen separate gorges rise from the river, but only a few are passed on the standard sightseeing excursion. These two-hour trips cost A$19 (U.S. $15.20) for adults and A$7.50 (U.S. $6) for children, or A$31 (U.S. $24.80) for adults and A$13.50 (U.S. $10.80) for children if a bus transfer from Katherine is included. Make reservations with **Travel North** (☎ 08/8972 1044). This company also offers a Gorge Adventure Tour lasting four hours and costing A$48 (U.S. $38.40) for adults and A$24 (U.S. $19.20) for children (including transfers); and there's even an eight-hour excursion.

Rental canoes are available for those who wish to see the scenic splendor on their own. Contact **Kookaburra Canoe Hire** (☎ 08/8972 3604). Rates are A$8 (U.S. $6.40) for the first hour; a half-day rental costs A$18 to A$27 (U.S. $14.40 to $21.60) depending on whether it's a one-, two-, or three-person canoe. Full-day rental varies from A$25 to A$45 (U.S. $20 to $36).

Rangers are on hand at the park headquarters to answer your questions about Katherine Gorge, and their displays shed light on area wildlife. I was hesitant when they said the river was safe for swimming because it's inhabited by freshwater, not saltwater, crocs, but I eventually went in and had a refreshing—and uneventful—experience.

No matter how you choose to see the Katherine River Gorge, don't forget to bring sunglasses, insect repellent, sunscreen, and a hat or visor. Sturdy shoes are also required because it's necessary to walk about 500 meters (1,650 ft.) between stretches of the river. If you go upriver in a canoe, you'll need to ford in many places.

The **Edith Falls Nature Reserve,** part of Katherine Gorge National Park, is a picturesque spot for a swim in a large pool at the base of a waterfall. Camping is permitted, too. To reach Edith Falls, drive 42km (26 miles) north of Katherine and turn off at the signpost. Follow this road for another 20km (12 miles) to reach the scenic site. The admission is A$4 (U.S. $3.20) per person (under 5 free).

The **Katherine Low Level Nature Park,** 5km (3 miles) from town via the Victoria Highway, is an ideal riverside picnic location. Swimming is safe here during "the dry," but "the wet" can cause dangerous flooding and strong currents.

WHERE TO STAY

Travelers on a tight budget will be glad to know that Katherine has a **YHA hostel** 2km ($1^1/_4$ miles) south of the Stuart Highway on the Victoria Highway (☎ 08/8972 2942). Charges are A$9 (U.S. $7.20) per person. Bankcard, MasterCard, and Visa are accepted.

The **Gorge Caravan Park** in Katherine Gorge National Park, NT 0850 (☎ 08/8972 1253), offers another inexpensive alternative. Caravan and camping fees are A$13 (U.S. $10.40) for two adults, A$3.50 (U.S. $2.80) for children 5 to 15. Electricity costs an additional A$4 (U.S. $3.20).

All lodging in the Northern Territory except camping is subject to 5% tax.

Knotts Crossing Resort Motel. At the corner of Giles and Cameron Streets, Katherine, NT 0850. ☎ **08/8972 2511.** Fax 08/8972 2628. 65 rms, 18 suites. A/C TV TEL. A$90 (U.S. $72) double; A$94 (U.S. $75.20) executive suite. Additional person A$20 (U.S. $16) extra. Children under 5 free in parents' room. AE, BC, DC, MC, V. Take a taxi; the motel is less than 3km (2 miles) from the town center.

This is the town's poshest place to stay, with an attractive pool area as well as a bistro. The family and executive suites have kitchens. The motel provides covered parking, which is important in this hot climate. Baby-sitting can be arranged.

Pine Tree Motel. 3 Third St., Katherine, NT 0850. ☎ **08/8972 2533.** Fax 08/8972 2920. 50 rms. A/C TV TEL. A$90 (U.S. $72) double. AE, BC, MC, V.

The Pine Tree has standard rooms in a central location. Each has coffee- and tea-making facilities, a refrigerator, and other typical amenities. There are also a pool and a restaurant on the premises.

4 Alice Springs

1,500km (930 miles) S of Darwin

"The Alice," as she's affectionately called by Australians, is at the country's geographical center, surrounded by the Macdonnell ranges and the russet-colored earth and rock formations that give this region its name—the Red Centre. Because of the city's Old West ambience and the area's beautiful scenery, Alice Springs is popular with visitors. Some say the town reminds them of Palm Springs 50 years ago, but I see more of a resemblance to Sedona, Ariz., and other similar beauty spots in the U.S. Southwest.

Nevil Shute immortalized Alice Springs in his best-seller *A Town Like Alice* in 1954; the book, a wonderfully romantic story about the post–World War II reunion of an Englishwoman and a rugged outback Aussie who'd been separated in Malaysia, has subsequently been made into a 1956 British film (with Peter Finch and Virginia McKenna) and a 1981 Australian TV miniseries (with Bryan Brown and Helen Morse).

While Alice Springs (pop. 25,000) is a busy city with modern tourist facilities, it's also the country's consummate outback town. The Royal Flying Doctor Service and School of the Air are based here, and the community is a source of supplies for people who live on far-reaching cattle stations. Many Aborigines work as stockmen on the area's vast stations, and reminders of their rich heritage are everywhere. Wild camels roam throughout the region, and the dry red earth, stately white-barked ghost gums, and deep-blue sky have a sense of otherworldliness to them.

Of all the artists who've tried to capture the area's beauty on canvas, the local Aborigines seem to have done it best. Albert Namatjira, a member of the Arunta tribe who grew up on the Hermannsburg Mission near Alice Springs, is the best known of the landscape watercolorists. Many others have proven their talent, not only with watercolors but also with bark painting and other crafts. Unfortunately, the Aborigines who've found a place in today's Australia constitute only a small minority, and in Alice Springs, where they constitute 25% of the population, you'll see numbers of native people who, dispossessed of their traditional way of life, have found numbing consolation in alcohol.

ESSENTIALS

GETTING THERE Motorists using the Stuart Highway, the only link to other centers of population, refer to "heading up the track" or "down the track." If you decide to do either, be sure to carry plenty of water and watch the fuel gauge. If you experience car trouble, stay with the vehicle; don't attempt to walk to find help.

Ansett and Qantas both have daily flights to Alice Springs. The trip from Sydney costs A$259 to A$325 (U.S. $207.20 to $260); from Adelaide, A$199 to A$250 (U.S. $159.20 to $200). A taxi to town from the airport costs about A$18 (U.S. $14.40), or you can pay A$9 (U.S. $7.20) for the shuttle bus (☎ 08/8953 0310).

The Ghan makes the trip up to Alice Springs from Adelaide once a week year-round (22 hours) and more frequently from April to November. Fares range from A$500 (U.S. $400) for a first-class berth and meals to A$140 (U.S. $112) for economy-class seating. This is one of Australia's nicest trains, a winner of several tourism awards.

A bus to Alice Springs from Adelaide takes 23 hours and costs A$168 (U.S. $134.40). The bus to Alice Springs from Darwin takes 17½ hours and costs A$168 (U.S. $134.40). Greyhound-Pioneer and McCafferty's make the trip.

VISITOR INFORMATION The best time to visit Alice Springs, in terms of **weather,** is from April to late October. Information for new arrivals is dispensed at the airport and train station daily. In town, the **Central Australian Tourism Industry Association,** 37–43 Hartley St., Alice Springs, NT 0870 (☎ 08/8952 5800), is open Monday to Friday from 9am to 6pm and Saturday and Sunday from 10am to 3pm. The **telephone area code** is 08.

SPECIAL EVENTS The **Henley-on-Todd Regatta,** held annually in late September or early October, draws big crowds who laugh and drink beer while watching contestants run up the dry riverbed carrying homemade bottomless boats. Another popular local event, the **Camel Cup,** is held each July.

CITY LAYOUT

The **Todd River,** cutting Alice Springs in two, has water in it only a few months of the year, usually December to February, but it remains a focal point of the community year-round. The **central business district,** where the Todd Mall is the main shopping area, is just west of the river. Many of the new motels are in a separate **tourist district** across the river and about 4km (2½ miles) from town along Barrett Drive. The Royal Flying Doctor Service base is in town, but most of the scenic sights, like Standley Chasm and Simpson's Gap, are 20km (12 miles) or more out of Alice Springs.

GETTING AROUND

BY BUS The **Alice Wanderer** coach (☎ 08/8952 2111) makes the rounds of the sightseeing attractions in town. You get off wherever you like and then board the next bus when you're ready. The fare is A$15 (U.S. $12) for a half day and A$20 (U.S. $16) for a full day. Places on the itinerary include the Royal Flying Doctor base, the School of the Air, the Camel Farm, and the Vintage Auto Museum.

BY TAXI OR LIMOUSINE In addition to its public bus system, Alice Springs has **taxis** readily available (☎ 08/8952 1877). If you want a chauffeured limousine, call **Alice Chauffeur Drive** (☎ 08/8953 1655); it charges approximately A$50 (U.S. $40) per hour for a Ford LTD and A$80 (U.S. $64) per hour for a stretch limo.

BY RENTAL CAR For touring on your own, try **Territory Rent-a-Car,** at the corner of Stott Terrace and Hartley Street (☎08/8952 9999).

BY ORGANIZED TOUR **AAT King's,** 74 Todd St. (☎ 08/8952 1700), operates the most popular half- and full-day tours in the area. Travel is either by air-conditioned coach or a specially designed four-wheel-drive bus called a unimog. **Rod Steinert,** P.O. Box 2058, Alice Springs, NT 0870 (☎ 08/8955 5000), offers group tours that emphasize the traditional Aboriginal lifestyle and expose visitors to real outback cattle stations. Transport is by 10-seater Landcruisers or coaches. Steinert and his vehicles are also available for private charter, and he can arrange a cattle-station stay or a homestay in Alice Springs for you. **Sahara 4-Wheel Drive Tours,** P.O. Box 3891, Alice Springs, NT 0871 (☎ 08/8953 0881), operates overnight camping safaris in the area.

WHAT TO SEE & DO

IN TOWN

✪ **Alice Springs School of the Air.** 80 Head St. ☎ **08/8952 2122.** Admission A$2 (U.S. $1.60) donation requested. Daily 8am–noon and 1pm–4:30pm. Closed Christmas and public holidays.

Like the Royal Flying Doctor Service, the School of the Air was devised to assist people living on isolated cattle stations in the vast, largely unpopulated regions of Australia. A total of 140 pupils, aged 4 to 12, receive their education on the airwaves emanating from this base. These children are spread out over an area two-thirds the size of the U.S. state of Texas. Eleven other schools like this are dotted around the country.

You can visit the school and hear students receiving their lessons on the radio weekdays during the school year, which runs from February to November. Please call ahead and confirm that there's space available for you because sometimes they have as many as 200 guests in one afternoon. Charles and Di even stopped by in 1983. Groups of educators can make special arrangements by writing in advance to the Principal, Alice Springs School of the Air, 80 Head St., Alice Springs, NT 0870.

✪ **The Royal Flying Doctor Service RFDS.** On Stuart Terrace near the end of Hartley Street. ☎ **08/8952 1129.** Admission A$2.50 (U.S. $2) adults, A50¢ (U.S. 40¢) children, for a half-hour tour, which includes a 10-minute video. Mon–Sat 9am–4pm, Sun and public holidays 1–4pm. Closed New Year's Day and Christmas. Walk or take the Alice Wanderer (☎ 08/8952 2111).

The Royal Flying Doctor Service (RFDS) base provides an insight into how Australians have been able to cope with living in the outback. The RFDS was started in 1928 by the Rev. John Flynn and continues to provide medical and communications services to folks who live on isolated cattle stations. Thirteen RFDS bases exist in the country, and this is one of four (Cairns, Mount Isa, and Broken Hill are the others) that welcome tourists.

Nearby

✪ **Frontier Camel Farm.** On the Ross Highway, 8km (5 miles) from central Alice Springs. ☎ **08/8953 0444.** Admission, short camel ride, and guided tour of museum and reptile house, A$10 (U.S. $8) adults, A$5 (U.S. $4) children 5–12; museum and reptile house only, A$5 (U.S. $4) adults, A$2.50 (U.S. $2) children 5–12. For opportunities for longer camel rides, see "Outdoor Activities" and "Where to Dine" below. Daily 9am–5pm. Guided tours and camel rides are given at 10:30am all year, and again at 2pm Apr–Oct. Closed May 8 and Dec 25–Jan 2.

Camels were imported to Australia by the first generations of white settlers, who used them for transport across the country's vast deserts. By 1907 more than 10,000 camels had been brought in. However, the advent of the railroad and motorized transport meant the animals were no longer needed. Some were destroyed, and others were set loose and thrived in the wild. Australia now has the world's largest population of free-ranging camels—about 200,000. The Frontier Camel Farm has tame camels available for riding. It also has a very interesting camel museum and a display of reptiles. A picnic shelter with a gas barbecue is available.

Farther Afield

Simpson's Gap National Park. 23km (14 miles) west of Alice Springs. Free admission. Daily 8am–8pm.

This is a scenic spot in the West Macdonnell ranges. While the parking lot at Standley Chasm (below) boasts a kiosk and souvenir shop, Simpson's Gap is totally uncommercialized. Rangers maintain the Visitor Centre that provides information on the area's flora and fauna. A large colony of rock wallabies lives in the vicinity and can usually be seen. Available brochures describe various bushwalks and tell the way to picturesque picnic places. (Fill your basket at Le Coq en Pâté—see "Where to Dine" below.)

✪ **Standley Chasm.** 50km (31 miles) west of Alice Springs. ☎ **08/8956 7440.** Admission A$2.50 (U.S. $2) adults, A$2 (U.S. $1.60) children. Daily 7:30am–5pm.

Standley Chasm is a steep cleft, 9 meters (30 ft.) wide, in the Macdonnells. The towering red rock walls of the narrow gorge appear to change color when the sun is directly overhead. But while most people rush to the chasm at noon, I find the scenery along the 20-minute walk from the parking lot just as pretty as the midday event. The path follows a streambed and dodges around dusty-green native shrubbery and white-barked ghost gums. The wonderful rust-colored earth and mountains stand out against the cloudless blue sky. Sturdy walking shoes are a must.

Glen Helen Gorge. 135km (84 miles) west of Alice Springs.

This gorge, cut by the Finke River, is a wonderful spot for a swim or a walk. Glen Helen Lodge (see "Where to Stay" and "Where to Dine" below) is at the entrance of the Nature Park.

Readers Recommend

*"In Alice Springs, the **Old Telegraph Station** and the **ANZAC Hill Lookout** were not mentioned in your guide. I felt both were worth visiting."*

—Lee Wadmore, Herts, England.

*"**The Outback Experience,** out of Alice Springs, is on my A+ list. Our guide, Lee Goldman, gave us a day I'll never forget, guiding us skillfully through flood-damaged terrain, pointing out the many nuances of this special territory with unflagging good humor for a full 12 hours."*

—Lois Winsen, San Diego, Calif., U.S.A.

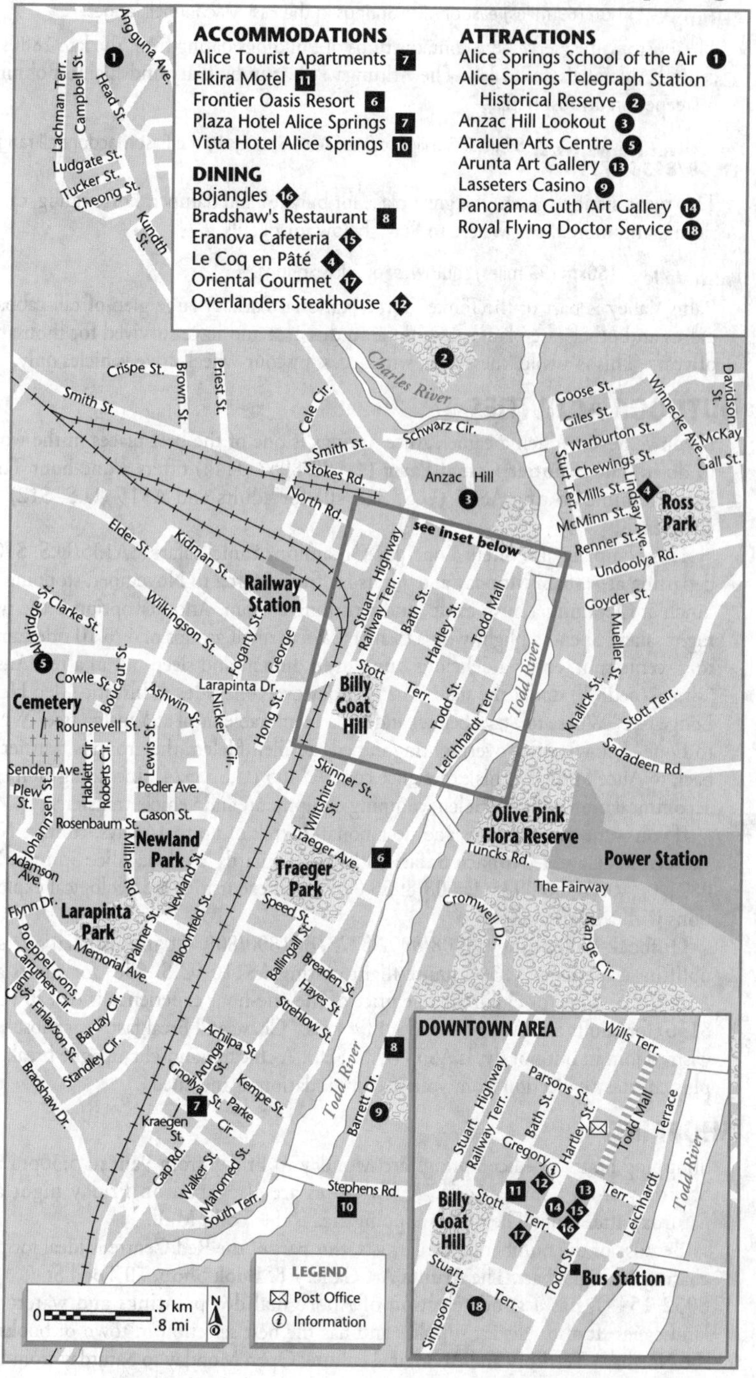
ACCOMMODATIONS
Alice Tourist Apartments 7
Elkira Motel 11
Frontier Oasis Resort 6
Plaza Hotel Alice Springs 7
Vista Hotel Alice Springs 10
DINING
Bojangles 16
Bradshaw's Restaurant 8
Eranova Cafeteria 15
Le Coq en Pâté 4
Oriental Gourmet 17
Overlanders Steakhouse 12
ATTRACTIONS
Alice Springs School of the Air 1
Alice Springs Telegraph Station Historical Reserve 2
Anzac Hill Lookout 3
Araluen Arts Centre 5
Arunta Art Gallery 13
Lasseters Casino 9
Panorama Guth Art Gallery 14
Royal Flying Doctor Service 18
Anguna Ave.
Lachman Terr.
Campbell St.
Head St.
Ludgate St.
Tucker St.
Cheong St.
Kundth St.
Charles River
Crispe St.
Brown St.
Priest St.
Smith St.
Cele Cir.
Schwarz Cir.
Stokes Rd.
North Rd.
Anzac Hill
Goose St.
Giles St.
Warburton St.
Chewings St.
Mills St.
McMinn St.
Renner St.
Undoolya Rd.
Winnecke Ave.
Davidson St.
McKay
Gall St.
Sturt Terr.
Lindsay Ave.
Ross Park
see inset below
Elder St.
Kidman St.
Railway Station
Wilkingson St.
Fogarty St.
George
Stuart Highway
Railway Terr.
Bath St.
Hartley St.
Todd Mall
Todd River
Goyder St.
Mueller St.
Khalick St.
Stott Terr.
Sadadeen Rd.
Aldridge St.
Clarke St.
Cowle St.
Boucaut St.
Larapinta Dr.
Ashwin St.
Nicker Cir.
Hong St.
Billy Goat Hill
Todd St.
Leichhardt Terr.
Cemetery
Rounsevell St.
Senden Ave.
Plew St.
Hablett Cir.
Roberts Cir.
Lewis St.
Pedler Ave.
Johannsen St.
Rosenbaum St.
Gason St.
Newland Park
Milner Rd.
Newland St.
Skinner St.
Wiltshire St.
Olive Pink Flora Reserve
Tuncks Rd.
Power Station
Traeger Ave.
Traeger Park
The Fairway
Adamson Ave.
Flynn Dr.
Larapinta Park
Palmer St.
Bloomfield St.
Speed St.
Cromwell Dr.
Range Cir.
Memorial Ave.
Poeppel Cons.
Carruthers Cir.
Crammond St.
Finlayson St.
Barclay Cir.
Standley Cir.
Ballingall St.
Breaden St.
Hayes St.
Strehlow St.
Achilpa St.
Arunga St.
Kempe St.
Bradshaw Dr.
Gnoilya St.
Parke Cir.
Barrett Dr.
Kraegen St.
Gap Rd.
Walker St.
Mahomed St.
South Terr.
Stephens Rd.
DOWNTOWN AREA
Wills Terr.
Parsons St.
Gregory
Terrace
Stuart Terr.
Simpson St.
Bus Station
LEGEND
Post Office
Information
0
.5 km
.8 mi
N

Arltunga. 111km (69 miles) east of Alice Springs in the East Macdonnell ranges.

The Historical Reserve here contains ruins of buildings dating from the late 1880s—central Australia's gold rush. The Arltunga Pub, run by Gary and Elaine Bohning, is steeped in atmosphere.

Ross River Homestead. 85km (53 miles) east of Alice Springs in the East Macdonnell ranges. ☎ **08/8956 9711.**

This rustic station (ranch) is a great place for billy tea and damper, horse riding, camel riding, and more. See "Where to Stay" below for details.

Palm Valley. 150km (93 miles) southwest of Alice Springs.

Palm Valley is part of the Finke Gorge National Park. A large glen of tall cabbage palms and other rare plants are unique to this area and have survived for thousands of years. This is a wilderness area, with access by four-wheel-drive vehicles only.

OUTDOOR ACTIVITIES

If you've never ridden a camel, Alice Springs is one of the best places in the world to do it. The **Frontier Camel Farm** (☎ 08/8953 0444) offers a one-hour Todd River Ramble costing A$35 (U.S. $28.40) for adults and A$15 (U.S. $12) for children.

This company also offers a one-day Ooraminna camel safari ($A135/U.S. $108) departing at 7:30am Monday and Thursday from March to November, stopping for lunch at Ooraminna bush camp, and returning at 6pm. Another option is the two-night safari "Spend a Night with a Camel," where small groups of 4 to 10 ride camels to a scenic spot, enjoy a delicious camp-oven dinner, and sleep out in a real Aussie "swag" (bedroll) under the stars. The next day everyone rides to historic Glen Helen Lodge (see "Where to Stay" below) and has a memorable meal at Yapalpa (see "Where to Dine" below). After overnighting in beds at Glen Helen, the group is transferred back to Alice Springs. This experience costs A$405 (U.S. $324), including all meals, accommodation at Glen Helen, camping equipment, and vehicle transfers.

If you want to get serious and do a bonafide trek of up to 14 days, contact **Noel Fullerton's Camel Outback Safaris,** PMB 74, Stuart's Well via Alice Springs, NT 0871 (☎ 08/8956 0925; fax 08/8956 0909). All excursions are geological explorations with a safari guide.

Outback Ballooning (☎ 08/8952 8723, or 1800/809 790 in Australia) offers an uplifting experience: a 30-minute flight costing A$110 (U.S. $88) for adults and A$55 (U.S. $44) for children. The price of the one-hour experience is A$170 (U.S. $136) for adults and A$75 (U.S. $60) for kids. "Chase and breakfast," for those who wish to join in but not fly, is A$35 (U.S. $28). A chicken-and-champagne breakfast, plus courtesy collection from your accommodation, is included.

SHOPPING

Shopping hours in Alice Springs are Monday to Friday from 9am to 5:30pm and Saturday from 9am to noon. A few stores are also open on Friday night and Saturday afternoon. The main shopping area is the **Todd Mall.**

Because of the number of local artists, this part of the Red Centre is ideal for purchasing Aboriginal art. The **Arunta Art Gallery & Book Shop,** 70 Todd St. (☎ 08/8952 1544), has a good selection of Aboriginal dot paintings and watercolor landscapes. It also sells art supplies and has the best selection in town of books on the Northern Territory and Aboriginal culture. Open Monday to Saturday from 9am to 5:30pm (sometimes Sunday from March to September).

The **Original Dreamtime Art Gallery,** 63 Todd Mall, opposite Flynn Church (☎ 08/8952 8861), specializes in traditional Aboriginal art, crafts, and didgeridoos and offers free shipping and insurance worldwide. Open Monday to Friday from 9am to 5:30pm and Saturday and Sunday from 9am to 4pm.

The ✪ **Gallery Gondwana,** 43 Todd Mall (☎ 08/8953 1577), sells only top-quality artworks. My favorite is the pottery done by the Hermannsburg craftspeople. Proprietor Roslyn Premont has written a book on Aboriginal art and is knowledgeable on the subject. Full documentation of originality and source is provided with each piece. The Gallery Gondwana is open year-round Monday to Friday from 9:30am to 5:30pm and Saturday from 9:30am to 3pm; also April to October, Sunday from 1 to 5pm. They pack, ship, and insure paintings free of charge.

The **Outcrop Gallery,** at the corner of Todd Mall and Gregory Terrace (☎ 08/8952 3662), sells souvenirs, T-shirts, and some Aboriginal goods like boomerangs and didgeridoos. Open Monday to Friday from 9am to 6pm, Saturday from 9am to 5pm, and Sunday from 2 to 5pm. The **Dreamtime Art Gallery,** opposite Flynn Church, 63 Todd Mall (☎ 08/8952 8861), sells Arnhem Land bark paintings, didgeridoos, batiks from Ernabella, and other local products. Open daily.

WHERE TO STAY

A 5% Tourism Marketing Duty is added to all accommodations in the Northern Territory.

IN OR NEAR TOWN

Expensive

Plaza Hotel Alice Springs. Barrett Drive, Alice Springs, NT 0871. ☎ **08/8952 8000.** Fax 08/8952 3822. 228 rms, 7 suites. A/C MINIBAR TV TEL. A$205 (U.S. $164) double; A$350–A$450 (U.S. $280–$360) suite. Children under 14 free in parents' room. No-smoking rooms available. AE, BC, DC, MC, V. Free parking.

The Plaza Alice Springs is a short distance from the city center in the area known as the tourist district. Lasseter's Casino and the Alice Springs Golf Course are just a stone's throw away. Of the rooms in the three-story hotel, all have balconies—some with a view of the Macdonnell ranges. Most rooms have two queen-size beds and the rest have king-size. All baths have tub/shower combinations. Four rooms have been specially outfitted for the handicapped.

Dining/Entertainment: The hotel has three dining venues: the elegant Bradshaws, the more casual Balloons, and (during summer) an outdoor Mongolian Barbecue. Drinks are available poolside, in the Lobby Bar, or in Simpson's Gap Bar.

Services: Concierge, 24-hour room service, laundry, baby-sitting.

Facilities: Large pool, two tennis courts, gym, sauna, spa, bicycle rental.

Moderate

$ **Frontier Oasis Resort.** 10 Gap Rd., Alice Springs, NT 0870. ☎ **08/8952 1444.** Fax 08/8952 3776. 102 rms. A/C TV TEL. A$95–A$105 (U.S. $76–$84) double. Additional person A$15 (U.S. $12) extra. AE, BC, DC, MC, V. Free parking.

A two-story complex 2km (1¼ miles) from the town center, the Oasis consists of more than 100 units, a large octagonal pool, and an attractive restaurant done in a striking salmon-and-gray decor. There's also a sauna, a spa, a large aviary, a smaller pool, and plenty of garden landscaping. All units have balconies and some have tub/shower combinations. Seven rooms are provided for the handicapped. Barry Partridge is a personable host; he and his staff are sure to make you feel welcome. *Note:* Readers have complained of poor soundproofing and noisy neighbors. Be sure to request a quiet corner.

Vista Hotel Alice Springs. Stephens Road (just off Barrett Drive), Alice Springs, NT 0870. ☎ **08/8952 6100,** or 1800/030 011 in Australia. Fax 08/8952 6234. 140 rms. A/C MINIBAR TV TEL. A$120 (U.S. $96) double. Additional person A$20–A$25 (U.S. $16–$20) extra. Children under 15 free in parents' room. AE, BC, DC, MC, V. Free parking. Complimentary shuttle to town.

This property nestles against the West Macdonnell ranges near Lasseter's Casino. Four large Aboriginal-style carved birds greet new arrivals in the foyer. An atrium rises from the reception level to the second floor, where guests dine in Ainslies Restaurant. Each accommodation has one queen-size bed, one single, and a tub/shower combination, as well as a clock radio, in-room movies, tea- and coffee-making facilities, and a small refrigerator. Room service is provided 16 hours a day. The facilities include a pool, spa, and tennis courts.

Inexpensive

$ **Alice Tourist Apartments.** Gap Road, Alice Springs, NT 0871. ☎ **08/8952 2788.** Fax 08/8953 2950. 24 apts. A/C TV TEL. A$66 (U.S. $52.80) double; A$71 (U.S. $56.80) triple. AE, BC, DC, MC, V. Free parking.

If you want to be completely self-contained, the best value in town is the two-story Alice Tourist Apartments. Owners Phillip and Shirley Webb provide friendly service at their attractive apartments 1.5km (1 mile) south of the city center. All units have a kitchenette and queen-size bed. Of the 24 units, 11 are one-bedroom and sleep four; the others are compact studios that sleep a maximum of three. Continental breakfast is the only meal offered (A$6/U.S. $4.80), but the Piggly Wiggly supermarket across the street is open daily. On the premises are a pool, a barbecue area, and a guest laundry.

Elkira Motel. 65 Bath St., Alice Springs, NT 0870. ☎ **08/8952 1222.** Fax 08/8953 1370. 58 rms. A/C TV TEL. A$75 (U.S. $60) double in older section, A$85 (U.S. $68) double in newer section. Children under 6 free in parents' room. AE, BC, DC, MC, V. Free parking.

The centrally located Elkira offers adequate rooms at reasonable rates. Some 42 units are classified "deluxe," and 7 of those have kitchens. The "moderate" rooms, built in 1958, are small but acceptable. Three rooms are equipped for the handicapped. There's a pool on the premises. The Terrace Restaurant serves à la carte dinners; the Terrace Bistro is open daily for light meals from 6am to 8pm.

Out of Town

All Seasons Glen Helen Homestead. 135km (84 miles) west of Alice Springs in the West Macdonnell ranges (P.O. Box 3020, Alice Springs, NT 0871). ☎ **08/8956 7489.** Fax 08/8956 7495. 25 standard rms, 3 bunkhouses, and camping. A$85 (U.S. $68) double standard room, A$10 (U.S. $8) age 5 and over (under 5 free); A$15 (U.S. $12) per bed in bunkhouse. AE, BC, DC, MC, V. Free parking.

On the bank of the Finke River, the oldest known waterway in the world, the Glen Helen Lodge is renowned for the good food served in its restaurant and its beautiful scenic surroundings. Locals, as well as visitors, drive out, have dinner, and spend the night. The lodge is built on the site of the original Glen Helen station homestead and has a relaxed, homey atmosphere, enhanced by open fires in winter.

The standard rooms are basic but more than adequate. Each has a bath, concrete-block walls, air conditioning, and a pretty patchwork-quilt bedspread.

During the day, you can swim or walk in Glen Helen Gorge, a 5-minute walk from the lodge. A 15-minute flightseeing trip on the helicopter based here costs A$50 (U.S. $40) per person with a minimum of three. Yapalpa Restaurant is open nightly for dinner.

✪ **All Seasons Ross River Homestead.** 88km (55 miles) east of Alice Springs in the East Macdonnell ranges (P.O. Box 3271, Alice Springs, NT 0871). ☎ **08/8956 9711.** Fax 08/ 8956 9823. 30 cabins; also camping area and bunkhouse. A/C. A$80 (U.S. $64) double. Additional person A$15 (U.S. $12) extra. Bunkhouse, A$12 (U.S. $9.60) adults, A$6 (U.S. $4.80) children under 13. Camping, A$4 (U.S. $3.20) adults, A$3 (U.S. $2.40) children. Caravan, A$15 (U.S. $12) powered site. Full-board rates available. BC, MC, V. Ground transfers provided from Alice Springs; light-aircraft transfer also available.

I can't think of a better place to savor the flavor of the Red Centre. The original homestead was built in 1898; it now serves as the dining room on this property covering 62 square kilometers (24 sq. miles) of scenic bushland in the East Macdonnell ranges. The Ross River Homestead provides ample opportunity for guests of all ages to sample the outback activities without experiencing all its discomforts.

Accommodation is in cabins built of red river gum trees; these have stone floors, air conditioning, and electric blankets, as well as baths. During the day, you can ride camels or horses or ride in a wagon pulled by Clydesdales. (Rides cost A$10/U.S. $8 for a half hour, A$18/U.S. $14.40 for an hour, and A$28/U.S. $22.40 for two hours.) This is also a great area for bushwalking (hiking) and bird watching. At night there are sometimes bush dinners; meals are also served in the rustic bar or the historic dining room that features mud-and-stone walls, lace tablecloths, and a colonial decor.

Day visitors and house guests alike are invited to join in for complimentary billy tea and damper every morning. This is usually accompanied by stock-whip-cracking demonstrations and boomerang throwing. If it gets too hot, you can cool off in the pool.

Reservations in North America: Contact Flag Inns at 800/624-3524.

WHERE TO DINE

IN TOWN

Expensive

Bradshaw's Restaurant. In the Plaza Alice Springs Hotel, Barrett Drive. ☎ **08/8952 8000.** Reservations recommended. Main courses A$19.50–A$24.90 (U.S. $15.60–$19.92). 15% surcharge Sun and public holidays. AE, BC, CB, DC, MC, V. Tues–Sat 6:30–11pm. Take a taxi (about A$5/U.S. $4). SEAFOOD.

Bradshaw's is a pleasant spot for a special meal. The room has a colonial atmosphere, which seems appropriate since it was named in honor of Thomas Andrew Bradshaw, an English immigrant who was the post and telegraph stationmaster in Alice Springs from 1899 to 1908. Neville Weston's watercolors, displayed around the room, depict scenes from that period. In one painting, four of the Bradshaw children are shown with their Aboriginal maids at the telegraph station.

The menu primarily features seafood, with a few meat dishes. Prawns, oysters, and scallops are offered as hot appetizers; prawns, baby barramundi, and escallopes of venison are main-course items. You select your wine from an impressive floor-to-ceiling brass wine rack. The Bradshaw won the 1990 Gold Plate Award for Best Silver Service Restaurant in the Northern Territory.

Moderate

✪ **The Overlanders Steakhouse.** 72 Hartley St. ☎ **08/8952 2159.** Reservations recommended. Main courses A$18–A$23.50 (U.S. $14.40–$18.80). AE, BC, DC, MC, V. Daily 6pm–late. OUTBACK AUSTRALIAN.

The Overlander serves generous portions of local fare in a casual Central Australian environment, where the decor includes camel saddles and farm utensils and the "dunnies" (restrooms) are labeled "colts" and "fillies." The kangaroo-tail soup here is excellent. After the soup you can try pan-fried or barbecued barramundi, camel,

Offbeat Red Centre Dining

Where else but Alice Springs could you ✪ **take a camel out to breakfast or dinner?** This opportunity is presented by the Frontier Camel Farm (☎ 08/8953 0444). The Take a Camel to Breakfast experience includes a one-hour ride along the Todd River and a hearty breakfast at the Camel Farm (A$49/U.S. $39.60). The Take a Camel to Dinner evening includes a one-hour ride from the Mecca Date Garden along the Todd River and dinner at the farm (A$75/U.S. $60). Courtesy pickup at your lodging is included. No children under 6. Days vary seasonally, so be sure to make your bookings well in advance of your arrival.

A ✪ **bush dinner** is another Red Centre experience you won't want to miss. Offered by Tailormade Tours (☎ 08/8952 1731) and Camp Oven Kitchen (☎ 08/8953 1411), these include a chance to try your hand at boomerang throwing and stock-whip cracking, as well as a delicious meal served under the stars. Tailormade Tours offers their bush barbecues on Sunday, Tuesday, and Thursday (A$69/U.S. $55.20, including refreshments). Camp Oven Kitchen operates on Monday, Wednesday, Friday, and Saturday (A$59/U.S. $47.20; refreshments available). Transfers included.

kangaroo, buffalo steaks, or a man-size 400-gram (16-oz.) beef rump steak called the Territorian. The damper bread is good, too. Dessert offerings include pavlova, apple-and-cinnamon crêpes, and homemade chocolate eclairs. Host Wayne Kraft helps create a welcoming atmosphere. There's a good wine list (my favorite is the Jim Barry 1989 Clare River Cabernet-Merlot Shiraz), or you can try the local favorite brew: NT Draught.

Inexpensive

Eranova Cafeteria. 72 Todd St. ☎ **08/8952 6094.** Reservations not required. Main courses A$6.50–A$11.50 (U.S. $5.20–$9.20). No credit cards. Mon–Fri 8am–4pm, Sat 8am–late.

This cafeteria's central location and reasonable prices contribute to its popularity. It's a place for filling breakfasts and tasty lunches that won't consume much time or money. BYO.

✪ **Le Coq en Pâté.** Shop 2 in the East Side Shopping Centre, 12 Lindsay Ave. ☎ **08/8952 9759.** Reservations not accepted. Picnic supplies for two A$10 (U.S. $8). No credit cards. Tues–Sun 10am–7pm. FRENCH.

This is the best place in town for buying cheeses, terrines, and pâtés for your picnic basket. Everything is made on the premises, including the baguettes, fruit breads, and croissants. The quiche is my favorite, but they also offer pies, pasties, and assorted savories. Cakes, too, are made fresh daily.

OUT OF TOWN

Yapalpa Restaurant. At the All Seasons Glen Helen Homestead, 135km (84 miles) west of Alice Springs in the heart of the West Macdonnell ranges. ☎ **08/8956 7489.** Reservations required. Main courses A$15–A$25 (U.S. $12–$20). BC, MC, V. Mon–Sat 6:30–9:30pm.

This doesn't look like a place in which you'd find first-class cuisine. The rustic atmosphere and remote location will make you think more of barbecue than exquisitely seasoned sauces. However, if you dine here, chef Shane McCrae's entrees (appetizers) might be warm kangaroo salad with Northern Territory beef jerky with blackberry dressing or a tower of seafood layered between puff pastry. Popular main

Readers Recommend

Bojangles, just past the Todd Mall on Todd Street. *"Their specialty, smoked scotch fillet, is absolutely wonderful. They charge A$20 (U.S. $16) for a main meal."*
—Todd Wagner, New York, N.Y., U.S.A.

Oriental Gourmet, 80 Hartley St. (☎ 08/8953 0888 or 8952 3488). *"A local recommended this Chinese restaurant to us. It's removed a bit from the more touristy places on the Todd Street Mall. All the other patrons seemed to be locals."*
—John Rosenthal, New York, N.Y., U.S.A.

courses are Italian-style whole quail and oven-baked barramundi filets with red-wine beurre blanc.

Up to 46 diners can be seated at Yapalpa's nine tables. The colonial ambience is enhanced by open fires in winter. It's an easy 1½-hour drive to Glen Helen in daylight, but wandering stock and wild animals make the road treacherous after dark. If you dine at Yapalpa, *please stay overnight.*

AFTER DARK

Ted Egan, well-known folksinger and colorful outback character, performs at ✪ **The Winery,** Petrick Road (☎ 08/8955 5133), when he's in town, at 8pm. Because of his popularity, bookings are essential. Egan is the world-champion Fosterphone player. This instrument, in case you haven't heard of it, is an empty Fosters beer carton with some carefully placed strings attached.

If you're determined to do something conventional, try your luck at **Lasseter's Casino,** Barrett Drive. During the casino's "happy hour" (10am–10pm), a 7-ounce glass of wine costs A$1.20 (U.S. $1), a 12-ounce beer costs A$1.60 (U.S. $1.30), and a piña colada costs A$4.60 (U.S. $3.70). Live music is offered in **Aces Cocktail Bar** Wednesday to Sunday from 11pm to 5am. Nearby at the Plaza, there's live entertainment Tuesday to Saturday in the **Simpson's Gap Bar.**

Bojangles Nightclub, 80 Todd St. (☎ 08/8952 2873), is a popular watering hole in the central business district. There's live entertainment Tuesday to Saturday.

The **Araluen Arts Centre** is Alice's venue for the performing and visual arts. Check the local newspaper for schedules or call the box office at 08/8952 5022.

5 Uluṟu–Kata Tjuṯa National Park (Ayers Rock/ Mount Olga)

465km (288 miles) SW of Alice Springs

Overseas visitors and the majority of Australians refer to the world's most famous monolith as Ayers Rock, but its traditional owners, the Aborigines, call it Uluṟu. The site has deep cultural significance for the Aboriginal people, who believe it played an important role in their Dreamtime. The sheltered caves and overhangs around the base of the rock have acted as canvas to hundreds of generations of native artists. There are also many sacred places—four are fenced off and out-of-bounds.

Uluṟu–Kata Tjuṯa (Ayers Rock/Mount Olga) National Park was handed back to the Aborigines in 1985, but they lease it to the Australian government and cooperate in its management with the National Parks and Wildlife Service. Besides Ayers Rock, the park includes the Olgas, beautiful rock formations 56km (34.7 miles) to the west. The Aboriginal people call this range of enormous rock domes, topped by Mount Olga, Kata Tjuṯa, which means "many heads."

Ayers Rock is easily Australia's most distinctive landscape symbol. It has been painted and photographed by millions of visitors and continues to awe all who see it. An indescribable sense of mystery fills those who watch its color change as the sun sets or rises. The rock, standing 348 meters (1,148 ft.) above the surrounding desert, is composed of sandstone with a high iron content—thus its rich red hue. It's 3.1km (2 miles) from east to west and 1.9km (1 mile) from north to south. Aboriginal people still live around the rock, but their community is off-limits to tourists, who are also asked not to photograph these private people.

ESSENTIALS

GETTING THERE The drive to Ayers Rock from Alice Springs is on 465km (288 miles) of paved road—south on the Stuart Highway and west on the Lasseter Highway. Access to Connellan Airport, near the Rock, is by Qantas, Kendall Airlines, Air North, and Ansett. You can also fly to Ayers Rock from Alice Springs on Alice Springs Air Charter. Sydney–Ayers Rock fares range from A$269 to A$339 (U.S. $215.20 to $271.20). Adelaide–Ayers Rock costs A$260 to A$364 (U.S. $208 to $291.20).

Greyhound-Pioneer and McCafferty's run bus service from Alice Springs (A$87/U.S. $69.60; 6½ hr.) and Adelaide (A$142/U.S. $113.60; 19 hr.).

VISITOR INFORMATION The **Visitor Centre,** near the Desert Gardens Hotel, has excellent displays regarding the National Park, its geological basis, flora, and fauna. Staff from the Ayers Rock Resort run the center and provide information from 8am to 9pm daily. The displays in the Visitor Centre will be moved to the new Cultural Centre at the Park Headquarters when it opens about the time this book is published.

In terms of the **weather,** April to October is the best time to come to this area. September and October are best for seeing wildflowers in bloom. The **telephone area code** is 08.

Warning: At any time of year you may encounter annoying black flies in this area. Consider buying an Aussie hat with corks dangling on strings from the brim—and even if the hat doesn't help, it makes an unusual, fun souvenir.

GETTING AROUND **Avis** (☎ 08/8956 2266), **Hertz** (☎ 08/8956 2244), and **Territory Rent-a-Car** (☎ 08/8956 2030) all have an Ayers Rock office at the airport. Despite the proliferation of organized tours, this is a very easy place to rent a car and get around on your own (and probably cheaper, too). There's no traffic out here, and if you can't afford the limo service you don't want to be stuck with a tour bus crowd while you're trying to experience the silence and solitude of Uluṟu.

V.I.P. (☎ 08/8956 2283) has a fleet of Ford LTD Town Cars, stretch limousines, and luxurious four-wheel-drive vehicles in which their driver/guides can squire you around. This is the way to go if you can afford it. The transfer from the airport to the Ayers Rock Resort costs A$52.50 (U.S. $42) per vehicle (one to four passengers).

AAT King's (☎ 08/8956 2171) operates a dozen tours in the area utilizing their large buses (for details on the tours, see "Exploring the Rock & Environs" below). They also do airport transfers. **Uluṟu Experience** offers small-group tours in mid-size vehicles.

EXPLORING THE ROCK & ENVIRONS

Don't be a victim of the "Ayers-Rock-is-just-a-climb-and-a-sunset" myth. There's lots to do here. *Allow several days.*

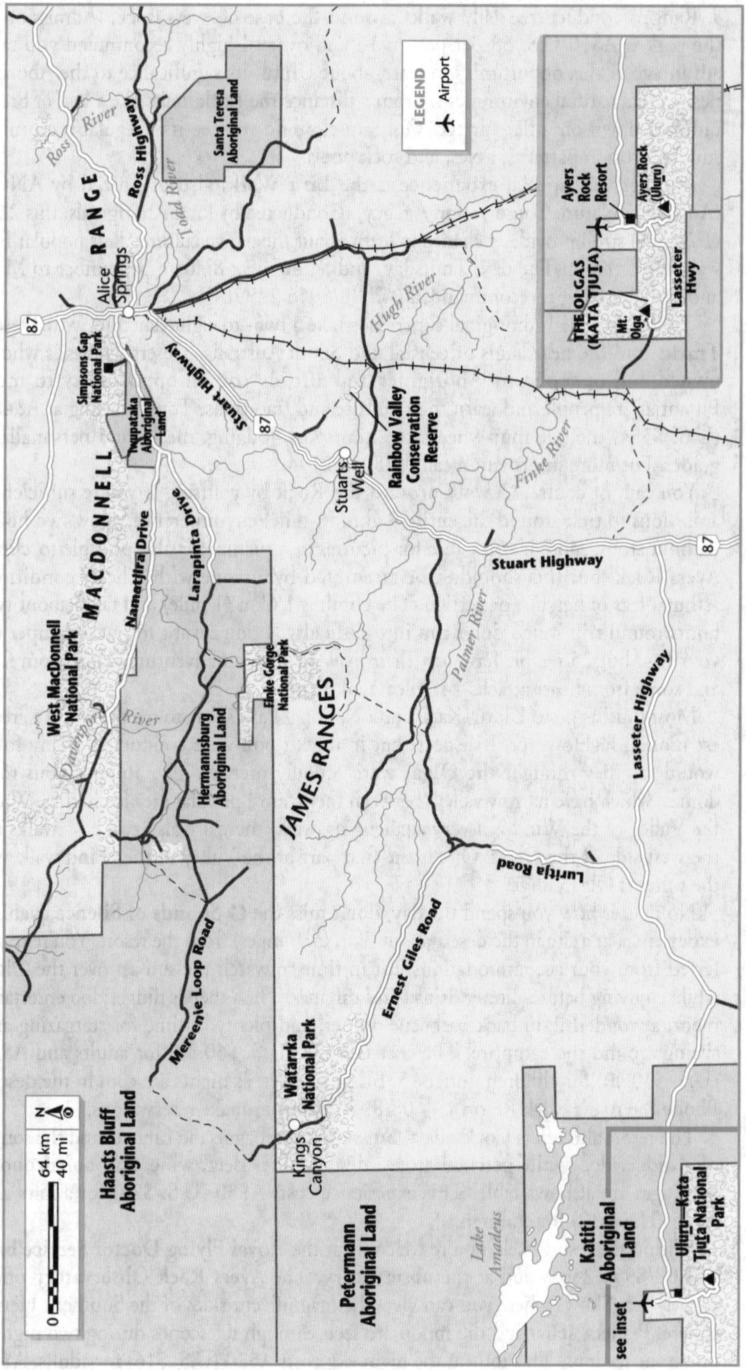
LEGEND
Airport
0
64 km
40 mi
N
Haasts Bluff Aboriginal Land
Petermann Aboriginal Land
Katiti Aboriginal Land
Uluru–Kata Tjuta National Park
see inset
Lake Amadeus
Kings Canyon
Watarrka National Park
Mereenie Loop Road
Ernest Giles Road
Luritja Road
Lasseter Highway
JAMES RANGES
Hermannsburg Aboriginal Land
Finke Gorge National Park
West MacDonnell National Park
Davenport River
Palmer River
Stuart Highway
87
Larapinta Drive
Namatjira Drive
MACDONNELL RANGE
Tnyupataka Aboriginal Land
Simpsons Gap National Park
Alice Springs
Stuarts Well
Rainbow Valley Conservation Reserve
Finke River
Hugh River
Todd River
Ross River
Ross Highway
Santa Teresa Aboriginal Land
THE OLGAS (KATA TJUTA)
Mt. Olga
Ayers Rock Resort
Ayers Rock (Uluru)
Lasseter Hwy

2342

Rangers conduct free daily **walks around the base** of Ayers Rock. (Admission to the park is A$10/U.S. $8 per person 16 and over.) I highly recommend you take advantage of this opportunity to learn about Uluru, its significance to the Aborigines, and its natural environment. From a distance the Rock looks like a loaf of bread plunked down on a flat surface. Only up close do you see its irregular sculptured surface, erosion patterns, caves, and rock pools.

Another very special experience is the **Liru Walk,** also organized by ANCA (Australian Nature Conservation Agency). Conducted by local Aboriginals, this 2km (1¼-mile) stroll provides a chance to learn about the native culture. This popular free walk is offered on Tuesday, Thursday, and Saturday at 8:30am September to May, and early booking is recommended (☎ 08/8956 2299).

For an extended Aboriginal experience take a two- to eight-day tour with **Desert Tracks** into the heartlands of central and South Australia. Desert Tracks is wholly owned and operated by Aborigines and affords you an opportunity to meet Pitjantjatjara people and learn their culture and traditions. Tours starting at A$480 (U.S. $384) include four-wheel-drive transport, lodging, meals, and personalized guides. For more information call 08/8956 2144.

You can, of course, ✪ **walk around the Rock** by yourself. If you're sufficiently ambitious to trek around the entire 9.4km (6-mile) circumference, allow two hours without stops, more if you pause for pictures or a picnic. It's also possible to **climb** Ayers Rock, but this shouldn't be attempted by anyone with a heart condition, asthma, fear of heights, or vertigo. The climb is 1.6km (1 mile) and takes about two hours round trip if you don't run into difficulty. I don't want to put a damper on your fun, but 25 people have lost their lives on such an adventure, some from falls and some from heart attacks—so please take care.

Most tourists go to Uluru–Kata Tjuta National Park solely to see the world's greatest monolith. However, I suspect that if an exit poll were conducted, many folks would say they thought **the Olgas** were actually prettier. The 36 enormous rock domes, which have narrow valleys between them, are a popular area for hiking. While the Valley of the Wind is a very challenging walk, there are also two easy walks on the west side of the Olgas. One is the first part of the Valley of the Wind walk and the other is Olga Gorge.

No matter how you spend the day, don't miss the ✪ **Sounds of Silence evening experience,** at a site in the desert about 7km (4¼ miles) from the resort. You're transferred from your accommodations just in time to watch the sun set over the Olgas while enjoying before-dinner drinks and canapés. Then there's didgeridoo entertainment, a wonderful outback barbecue dinner, and plenty of time for stargazing and sitting around the campfire. The cost is A$76 (U.S. $60.80) for adults and A$38 (U.S. $30.40) for children under 15. Bring a jacket, as nights are cool in the desert. Phone the Ayers Rock Resort (☎ 08/8956 2200) to make reservations.

The resort also offers **Cocktails at Sunset**—champagne and canapés and the sound of a didgeridoo while perched atop a desert dune. Beer, wine, and nonalcoholic beverages are also available. This experience costs A$30 (U.S. $24) for adults and A$15 (U.S. $12) for children.

Within the resort itself, you're welcome at the **Royal Flying Doctor Service base** (☎ 08/8956 2563) and at the **observatory.** The **Ayers Rock Observatory** offers nightly Sky Shows where you can view the magnificent skies of the Southern Hemisphere. Planets, stars, and the moon are seen through telescopes during two nightly one-hour sessions. This tour of the night sky costs A$20 (U.S. $16) for adults, A$11

(U.S. $8.80) for children, and A$53 (U.S. $42.40) for families. For more information call 1800/803 174 in Australia.

Scenic flights over Ayers Rock and the Olgas are another option. These are offered by Rockayer (☎ 08/8956 2345 or 8956 2262) and cost about A$55 (U.S. $44) for 30 minutes. **Air North** (☎ 08/8956 2093) and **Jayrow Helicopters** (☎ 08/8956 2077) also offer arial tours.

The young and the restless might want to jump on the back of a Harley Davidson. **Uluṟu Motor Cycle Tours** (☎ 08/8956 2019 or 8956 2423) run personalized tours of the area with commentary via two-way radios mounted in safety helmets. The cost is A$40 (U.S. $32) for a 30-minute ride, A$70 (U.S. $56) for a one-hour cruise. Self-ride tours are also available.

AAT King's (☎ 08/8956 2171) offers the most tours in and around the Rock. These include the Ayers Rock Climb Tour (A$31/U.S. $24.80), the Ayers Rock Sunrise Tour (A$31/U.S. $24.80), the Ayers Rock Sunset Tour (A$20/U.S. $16), and the Olgas and Sunset Tour (A$54/U.S. $43.20); charges for children are lower. AAT King's also offers a three-day Ayers Rock Pass at A$148 (U.S. $118.40) for adults and A$110 (U.S. $88) for children; it includes several tours and transfers to and from the airport.

Uluṟu Experience (☎ 1800/803 174 in Australia) offers a range of ecotours, including the Spirit of Uluṟu (A$64/U.S. $51.20), Olgas and Dunes (A$49/U.S. $39.20), and Mt. Conner Outback Experience (A$119/U.S. $95.20). Prices for children are lower. Reader Deborah Brudno of Washington, D.C., wrote recently to say how much she had enjoyed their tours.

V.I.P. (☎ 08/8956 2283) offers totally personalized and luxurious tours and experiences in and around Ayers Rock and the Olgas. Its ✪ **Champagne and Sunset Tour** for up to four includes transportation in a chauffeured Ford LTD Town Car and watching the sunset at Ayers Rock while nibbling on canapés and sipping champagne. Despite the rustic surroundings, the glasses are crystal, the champagne bucket is silver, and the tablecloth is lace. This memorable tailgate experience costs A$163.75 (U.S. $131). V.I.P. also offers a Silver Service Dinner in the Desert (price varies according to menu and wines selected) and a Mt. Olga Aussie Barbecue (A$52/U.S. $41.60 per person). Other options are personalized tours to Kings Canyon, Alice Springs, and other Central Australia destinations.

WHERE TO STAY & DINE

All accommodations and dining facilities are within the **Ayers Rock Resort,** an attractive complex 20km (12 miles) from Ayers Rock. Built in 1984, it provides housing for tourists away from the sensitive natural environment of the Rock. The Ayers Rock Resort, 1km (0.6 mile) long and approximately 1km wide, is the only land neighboring the park that's not owned by Aborigines. Because there are no nearby towns, the resort was designed to be completely self-sufficient. The central energy plant cost A$60 million (U.S. $48 million), and the desalinization plant is the largest in the Southern Hemisphere.

Architect Philip Cox appropriately designed the complex to resemble a series of bedouin tents in the desert. The resort is, and looks like, an oasis. In addition to the hotels, there are a post office, bank, variety store, supermarket, café, and child-care center. Each of the contemporary buildings was designed to blend in with the environment and to conserve energy. The "bull-nosed veranda," a curved awning made of corrugated iron, was inspired by colonial Queensland architecture and provides shade over balconies and corridors. The resort, with a permanent staff of 900, can accommodate 5,000 overnight guests, which makes it, when fully occupied, the Northern Territory's fourth-largest population center.

In addition to the three hostelries below, budget travelers might be interested in the **Spinifex Lodge** (☎ 08/8956 2131; fax 08/8956 2163), where 68 rooms share communal baths; and the **Ayers Rock Campground** (☎ 08/8956 2055; fax 08/8956 2260). Families would find the **Emu Walk Apartments** (☎ 08/8956 2100; fax 08/8956 2156) convenient.

Desert Gardens Hotel. 15 Yulara Dr., Yulara, NT 0872. ☎ **08/8956 2100,** or 1800 331 147 in Australia. Fax 08/8956 2156. 100 rms. A/C MINIBAR TV TEL. A$226 (U.S. $180.80) double. Additional person A$20 (U.S. $16) extra. Children under 14 free in parents' room. AE, BC, DC, MC, V.

The Desert Gardens was designed to cater to the domestic market, so its rates are lower. Each modern room has one double and one single bed; the baths have showers (no tubs). There are a pool, facilities for half-court tennis and volleyball, a restaurant, and a cocktail lounge. In addition, because this is an open resort any guest can use the facilities at either hotel. Eight rooms are provided for the handicapped. The White Gums Restaurant is a good place for lunch.

$ **Outback Pioneer Hotel.** Yulara Drive (P.O. Box 10), Yulara, NT 0872. ☎ **08/8956 2170** or 8956 2737. Fax 08/8956 2320. 125 rms, 12 lodge units, 16 lodge cabins, 4 dormitories (none with bath). A/C. A$233 (U.S. $186.40) double; A$99 (U.S. $79.20) lodge unit or cabin; A$20 (U.S. $16) dorm bed. Children under 14 free in parents' room. AE, BC, DC, MC, V.

The Outback Pioneer offers both standard and budget lodging. The rooms have one single and one double bed, TVs, clock radios, coffee- and tea-making facilities, small refrigerators, and baths. The lodge units, cabins, and dormitories share communal baths. A pool, a barbecue, and laundry facilities are on the premises. Meals are served in the Bough House Restaurant.

Sails in the Desert Hotel. Yulara Drive (P.O. Box 21), Yulara, NT 0872. ☎ **08/8956 2200.** Fax 08/8956 2018. 228 rms, 3 suites. A/C MINIBAR TV TEL. A$334–A$372 (U.S. $267.20–$297.60) double; A$600 (U.S. $480) suite. Additional person A$20 (U.S. $16) extra. Children under 14 free in parents' room. No-smoking rooms available. AE, BC, DC, MC, V.

Like the other buildings in the Ayers Rock Resort, the three-story Sails is done in desert tones, with rounded canopies of corrugated iron; large squares of white fabric lend the exterior a tentlike appearance and provide welcome shade. An extensive collection of Aboriginal art and artifacts is displayed throughout the public rooms. All guest rooms have a choice of a king-size bed or two double beds, and 10 have been designed for the handicapped.

Dining/Entertainment: The Desert Rose Brasserie is open daily from 6am to 10pm. The Kunia Room, the fine-dining venue, serves à la carte dinners. Drinks and meals are available around the pool at the Rockpool Restaurant. Cocktails are served in the Piano Bar.

Services: Concierge, 24-hour room service, laundry, baby-sitting.

Facilities: Free-form pool, spa, jogging course, bicycle track, tennis courts, viewing tower.

12

Perth

The most remote capital in the western world, beautiful Perth lies near the coast of the Indian Ocean, isolated from the rest of Australia. The closest urban center, Adelaide, is 2,700km (1,674 miles) to the east. Were it not for Western Australia's mineral wealth, the city might never have gotten off the ground. As it is, the discovery of gold in the state in the 1890s helped Perth become established, and iron ore, diamonds, gold, and other minerals keep it booming today.

I lived in Perth some time ago, and whenever I go back I'm reminded how much it's like my hometown, San Diego, California. They share a delightful Mediterranean climate, a casual outdoorsy lifestyle, large parks adjacent to the city center, beautiful beaches, a love of boating—and an interest in possessing the America's Cup. In addition, both Perth and San Diego have populations of about one million, are in the southwest corners of their respective countries, and are home to people who give meaning to the phrases *laid-back* and *do your own thing.* The two have even been officially designated "sister cities" (Houston, Texas, is Perth's other U.S. sibling).

Unlike other parts of Australia, Perth has dry summers, and what little rain the city does get tends to fall in winter. This is statistically the sunniest capital; temperatures average 29°C (84°F) in summer and 18°C (64°F) in winter. Just when a summer day threatens to get too warm, the Fremantle Doctor, as the stiff breeze off the ocean is known, pays a call and cools things off.

Perth's climate invites visitors throughout the year, but most come in spring, when wildflowers bloom in profusion in the city's parks and environs. September is prime time for wildflower viewing, and if you plan to visit during this popular period I suggest you make reservations well in advance.

1 Orientation

ARRIVING

BY PLANE International air service is provided by Qantas and 13 other carriers, which fly in from Africa, Britain, Europe, Hong Kong, Japan, New Zealand, and Southeast Asia.

Ansett and Qantas provide regular interstate service. The cost of a Sydney-Perth Air Pass ticket ranges from A$386 to A$500 (U.S. $308.80 to $400) for the four-hour trip. Adelaide to Perth (3 hr.)

What's Special About Perth

Beaches

- Scarborough Beach, one of several long sandy stretches within easy reach of Perth.

Natural Spectacles

- Wildflowers blooming in profusion during September and October.

Parks & Gardens

- King's Park, affording great views of the city skyline and Swan River.

Side Trips

- Rottnest Island, a popular resort just offshore.
- Fremantle, a historic seaport downriver.

costs A$310 to A$385 (U.S. $248 to $308). Melbourne to Perth (3½ hr.) costs A$350 to A$483 (U.S. $280 to $386.40).

Perth has separate international and domestic airport terminals northeast of the city. The domestic terminal is 11km (7 miles) from town; the international terminal is 18km (11 miles) away. The shuttle bus to town from the international terminal costs A$7 (U.S. $5.60), or you can take a taxi for about A$18 (U.S. $14.40). The bus from the domestic terminal costs A$6 (U.S. $4.80); the taxi fare is about A$14 (U.S. $11.20). In the unlikely event you need to go directly between the two terminals, that bus trip costs A$6 (U.S. $4.80). If you have questions about the Airport Bus Service, call 09/479 4131.

Duty-free shops, bars, and restaurants are in the airport's international terminal. A bank is open 24 hours. The major car-rental companies have staffed desks, but there isn't a tourist information counter or a post office. Showers are available, as is a baggage-storage facility. The domestic terminal also has car-rental desks, showers, shops, bars, and places to eat. It lacks baggage lockers and a bank, but stamps are available in the newsstand/gift shop and a mailbox is next to the shop. Both terminals have computers that supply tourist information.

When you're leaving Perth, remember to book the **Airport Bus Service** (☎ 09/479 4131) at least an hour ahead. As of June 1996, the A$27 (U.S. $21.60) departure tax will be included in the price of your airline ticket; formerly it was collected at the airport as you were leaving.

BY TRAIN You can also arrive by train. The ***Indian Pacific,*** which makes the 65-hour journey from Sydney three times a week, is Australia's most popular railroad trip even though it crosses the Nullarbor Plain on the world's longest stretch of straight track past scenery that's quite monotonous. If you'd like to sample this experience, make reservations well in advance. First-class berth and meals cost A$1,048 (U.S. $838.40). Economy-class seats are A$320 (U.S. $256). The *Indian Pacific* also travels between Perth and Adelaide (40 hr.) twice a week. First-class berth and meals cost A$672 (U.S. $537.40). Holiday class costs A$438 (U.S. $350.40). Economy sitting is A$200 (U.S. $160). Children's fares are lower. Both trains offer a club/lounge car, as well as dining and sleeping facilities. For information on interstate train service in Perth, call 13 22 32 between 8:30am and 5pm.

If you're departing Perth by train, don't wait until the last minute to get to the station—the baggage check-in counter closes 30 minutes before the train leaves.

ACCOMMODATIONS
Hyatt Regency Perth 23
North Lodge Central City Backpackers 1
Perth Ambassador Hotel 24
Perth Parkroyal 21
Prince's Hotel Perth 13
Sheraton Perth Hotel 20
Wentworth Plaza Hotel 14
YMCA Jewell House 17

DINING
Brass Monkey Pub & Brasserie 8
Cafe Valentino 4
Fast Eddy's Cafe 12
Fishy Affair 6
Horsefeathers 15
Jessica's Fine Seafood Restaurant 22
Ms. Maud's 16
Northbridge Pavillion 5
The Plaka 7
Ted's Cafe 2
Thai House 3

ATTRACTIONS
Art Gallery of Western Australia 11
King's Park 18
Perth Cultural Centre 9
Supreme Court Gardens 19
Western Australia Museum 10

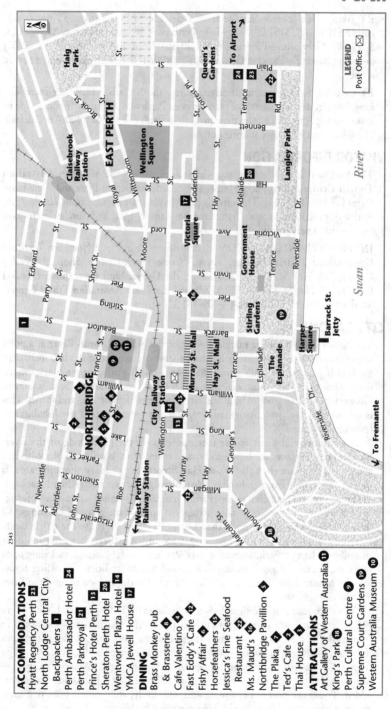

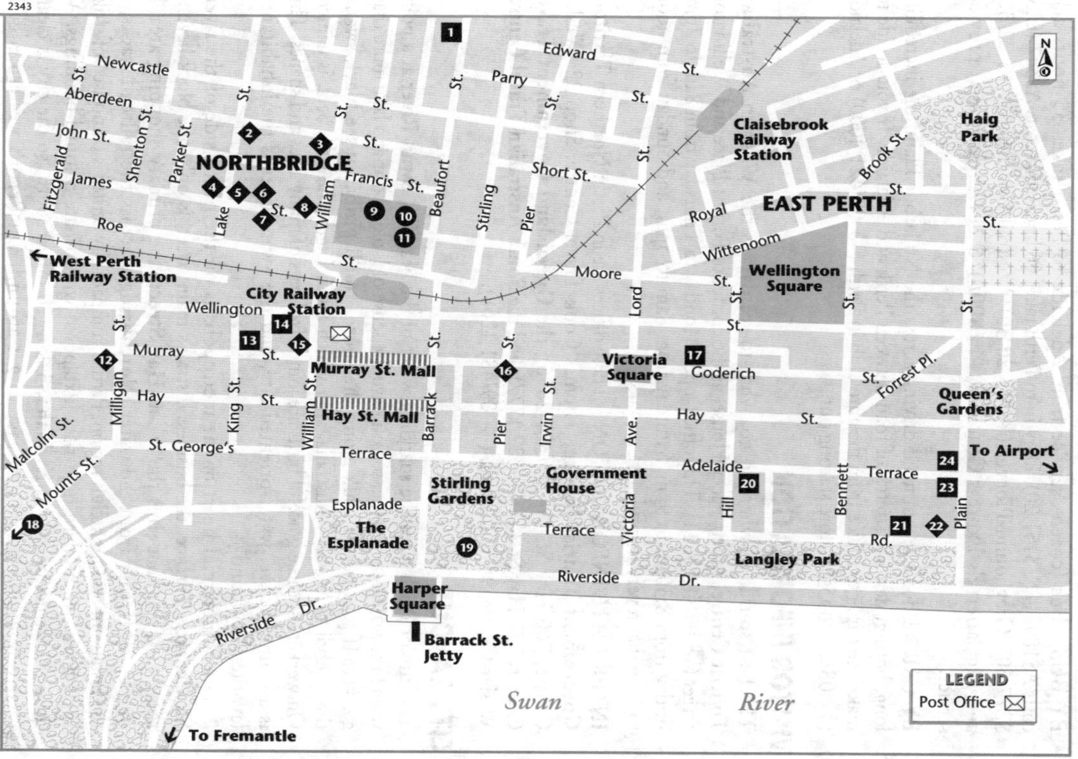

BY BUS Bus (coach) service from Adelaide to Perth takes 35 hours and costs A$189 (U.S. $151.20). Darwin to Perth takes 56 hours and costs A$347 (U.S. $277.60). Greyhound-Pioneer (☎ 13 20 30), Westrail Coaches (☎ 13 22 32) and McCafferty's Express Coaches (☎ 1800/076 211 in Australia) provide service.

BY CAR I don't recommend driving across the Nullarbor Plain, the incredibly long, boring, desolate stretch of road between Perth and Adelaide. If you decide to make the trip, get advice from the auto club in Perth (☎ 09/421 4000) or Adelaide (☎ 08/223 4555) before starting out.

VISITOR INFORMATION

The best source of where-to-go, what-to-see data is the **Western Australian Tourist Centre,** Albert Facey House, at the corner of Forrest Place and Wellington Street (☎ 09/483 1111). This office, open Monday to Thursday from 8am to 7pm, Friday from 8:30am to 9pm, Saturday from 8am to 5pm, and Sunday from noon to 6pm, has a very helpful staff.

INTERSTATE INFORMATION These offices are in Perth: **Northern Territory Government Tourist Bureau,** Thomas Cook Travel Centre, Shop 22, Wesley Centre, 760 Hay St. (☎ 09/321 2896); the **Queensland Government Travel Centre,** 777 Hay St. (☎ 09/322 1777); and the **South Australian Travel Centre,** Wesley Centre, 93 William St. (☎ 09/481 1268).

CITY LAYOUT

The city of Perth faces the sparkling water of the beautiful **Swan River** at a point where the waterway is wide, so you have the sense of looking out at a lake more than a river. If you take a walk along the shore, you'll probably see black swans, the symbol of Western Australia, after which Swan Lager, the state beer, is named. On weekends, these graceful birds are joined by boats of many sizes and shapes. This is a young, active, water-oriented city, and the Swan River is the inhabitants' favorite playground.

The commercial heart of the metropolis is on the north side of the river. **St. George's Terrace,** the business district's main street, is only one block beyond the grassy belt that rims the Swan. **Hay Street,** the primary shopping area, is one block farther from the water. **Northbridge,** across the railroad tracks, is the restaurant and nightclub region. Perth's compact city center is comprised of strikingly attractive modern high-rises juxtaposed with ornate colonial buildings. All industrial structures are at **Kwinana,** 32km (20 miles) south, so the city is clean, relatively uncongested, and easy to get around. On Perth's western edge is magnificent **King's Park,** stretching over 404 hectares (998 acres), including open bushland, botanical gardens, lush lawns, and public facilities. Sprawling across low-rise **Mount Eliza,** the park provides a superb 270-degree view of the Swan River and the city skyline.

On a large-scale map, Perth appears to be right on the Indian Ocean, but it's 19km (12 miles) upstream from the mouth of the Swan, which enters the ocean at **Fremantle.** The location of the port at this distance from the city also contributes to Perth's pleasant appearance. Until 1987, Fremantle wasn't a place where you'd go for a walk, but restoration done in preparation for hosting the America's Cup gave historic buildings a face-lift—parks were relandscaped, new hotels and restaurants added. Today the port is a charming area with lively, atmospheric pubs that draw the after-work crowd from Perth's high-rise office buildings.

North of Fremantle, along the shore of the Indian Ocean, wide beaches invite sunbathers, and the Fremantle Doctor gives windsurfers a thrill. **Cottesloe, Swanbourne,** and **Scarborough** are suburbs named after three of the favorite sandy stretches. Perth is often called "Australia's Dallas" because it's home to many of the country's tycoons. If you'd like to see what a millionaire's row looks like down under, head for the suburb of **Dalkeith. Claremont** is a fashionable shopping district.

2 Getting Around

BY PUBLIC TRANSPORTATION The **Metrobus,** the government-run public transportation system, operates buses, local trains, and cross-river ferries. For timetable brochures, stop in at the Transperth Information Office in the City Arcade (Hay Street Mall level) or the Perth Central Bus Station on Wellington Street near Queen. You can also call 13 22 13 for bus, train, and ferry information between 6am and 9pm daily. The **Sightseers Ticket** is a dollarwise value for visitors. For A$4.80 (U.S. $3.85) you can buy a ticket good for one day on any bus, train, or ferry within the system; a five-day pass is A$19.40 (U.S. $15.55). Children are half price. Tickets can be purchased at any information office or railway station.

Free buses and trains are operated within a city-center **"Free Transit Zone."** This area is bounded by King's Park Road, Thomas Street, Newcastle Street, the Causeway, and the Barrack Street Jetty.

By Train Electric train service started in 1990 and now links the city to the suburbs and towns beyond the metropolitan area. Suburban trains, including the ones to Fremantle, leave from **City Station,** Wellington Street.

By Bus Besides free buses and trains inside the Free Transit Zone, Transperth operates **free City Clipper buses.** Clipper buses are easily distinguished by their blue-and-gold logo on a white background. In addition, each vehicle is color-coded red, yellow, blue, or green according to its designated route. Red and yellow Clippers run Monday to Friday from 7am to 5:30pm and Saturday from 9am to noon; blue and green Clippers operate Monday to Friday. The buses service an area bounded by Outram, Bulwer, and Plain Streets and the Esplanade. A complete map of their routes is printed in the front section of city phone books.

Conducted bus excursions are offered by several companies, including Australian Pacific Tours (☎ 13 13 04), Feature Tours (☎ 09/479 4131), Pinnacle Tours (☎ 09/221 5411), Great Western Tours (☎ 09/421 1411), and Travelabout (☎ 09/244 1200).

By Ferry Ferries across the Swan River to South Perth leave from the **Barrack Street Jetty.** This service operates daily from 7am to 7:15pm. Transperth (☎ 13 22 13) operates river cruises between September and early June.

BY TAXI There are taxi stands throughout the city. Charges are A$2 (U.S. $1.60) at flagfall and A80¢ (U.S. 65¢) per kilometer. The flagfall goes up to A$3 (U.S. $2.40) from 6pm to 6am Monday to Friday and all day Saturday and Sunday. The two companies are **Black & White** (☎ 09/333 3333) and **Swan** (☎ 09/444 9444 in Perth).

BY CAR You can rent cars at these offices: **Avis,** 46 Hill St. (☎ 09/325 7677); **Budget,** 960 Hay St. (☎ 13 27 27); **Capital,** 3/121 Kewdale Rd., Kewdale (☎ 09/350 5799); **Hertz,** 39 Milligan St. (☎ 09/321 7777); **Letz,** 126 Grandstand Rd., Belmont (☎ 09/478 1999); and **Thrifty,** 33 Milligan St. (☎ 09/481 1999).

You'll find an office of the **Royal Automobile Club of Western Australia (RAC)** at 228 Adelaide Terrace (☎ 09/421 4000).

FAST FACTS: Perth

Airlines The following airlines have offices in or near Perth: Air Canada, P.O. Box 76, Whitford City, Hillarys, WA 6025 (☎ 09/421 4000, or 1800/221 015 in Australia); Air New Zealand, 44 St. George's Terrace (☎ 13 24 76); Ansett, 26 St. George's Terrace (☎ 13 13 00 or 13 15 15); British Airways, 80 William St. (☎ 09/483 7711); Garuda Airlines, 111 St. George's Terrace (☎ 09/322 4000); Qantas Airlink, 55 William St. (☎ 09/225 2222, 09/225 8282, or 13 13 13); Rottnest Airbus (☎ 09/478 1322); Skywest, c/o Ansett (see above); and United, 178 St. George's Terrace (☎ 09/321 2719 or 321 8747).

American Express The office is at 78 William St. (☎ 09/426 3777), open regular business hours.

Area Code Perth telephone numbers are in the 09 area code. As part of the telephone changeover, all numbers with a 09 area code will be changing to 08/9xxx xxxx in September 1997.

Baby-Sitters If you're in need of a baby-sitter, call Dial-a-Nanny (☎ 09/321 7485 or after hours 015/42 5096) or Dial an Angel (☎ 09/381 4999).

Business Hours **Banks** are generally open Monday to Thursday from 9:30am to 4pm and Friday from 9:30am to 5pm. **Stores** are generally open Monday to Thursday from 9am to 5:30pm, Friday from 9am to 9pm, Saturday from 9am to 5pm, and Sunday from noon to 4pm (or later).

Car Rental See "Getting Around" earlier in this chapter.

Currency See "Information, Entry Requirements & Money" in Chapter 3.

Currency Exchange Cash traveler's checks at banks or at the larger hotels.

Dentist Look in the yellow pages under "Dentists—Locality Guide."

Doctor Call the Royal Perth Hospital at 09/224 2244.

Drugstore (Chemist Shop) Pharmacity Chemist Supermart, 717 Hay St. Mall (☎ 09/322 6921), is open Monday to Wednesday and Friday from 8am to 6pm, Thursday from 8am to 9pm, and Saturday from 9am to 5pm.

Embassies/Consulates You'll find the following consulates in Perth: **Canada,** 111 St. George's Terrace (☎ 09/322 7930); **United Kingdom,** 77 St. George's Terrace (☎ 09/221 5400); and the **United States,** 16 St. George's Terrace (☎ 09/231 9400).

Emergencies Dial **000** to summon ambulance, fire department, or police in an emergency.

Eyeglass Repair The OPSM Vision Center, 660 Hay St. Mall (☎ 09/221 2882), is open Monday to Thursday from 9am to 5:30pm, Friday from 9am to 9pm, and Saturday from 9am to 5pm.

Hospitals The Royal Perth Hospital is centrally located on Wellington Street (☎ 09/224 2244).

Hotlines Crisis Care Unit, Department of Community Services; call 24 hours a day (☎ 09/325 1111, or 1800/199 008 outside Perth).

Information See "Visitor Information" earlier in this chapter.

Libraries The Alexander Library Building, in the Perth Cultural Centre in Northbridge (☎ 09/427 3111), carries newspapers from around the world as well as a large collection of books, journals, and other library materials.

Lost Property Lost property on trains: call 09/231 1150. On buses: call 09/426 2678.

Luggage Storage/Lockers There are lockers in the East Perth Rail Terminal (A$1/U.S. 80¢ a day).

Newspapers/Magazines The *West Australian* is the major daily.

Photographic Needs KLIKK (camera repair) has 13 locations around Perth. The most central is in Alfred's Photographics, at the corner of Hay and Pier streets (☎ 09/325 5066).

Postal Code Central Perth addresses have a 6000 postal code.

Post Office The General Post Office (GPO), on Forrest Place (☎ 09/326 5211), is open Monday to Friday from 8am to 6pm and Saturday from 9am to 12:30pm. General-delivery mail can be picked up only Monday to Friday from 9am to 5pm, and some other services are also limited to these weekday hours.

Restrooms There are public toilets open 24 hours a day on the mezzanine level of Forrest Place on Wellington Street. The ones on the Esplanade near Barrack Street are open daily from 8am to 7pm. You can also use the facilities in department stores during shopping hours and in hotels at any time.

Safety The area adjacent to Russell Square in Northbridge (Milligan and Aberdeen Streets) is best avoided by women on their own at night.

Taxes Perth has neither a hotel tax nor a GST (Goods and Services Tax). Sales tax is included in the purchase price of merchandise.

Taxis See "Getting Around" earlier in this chapter.

Telegrams/Telex/Fax Send these from the Perth GPO, 3 Forrest Place (☎ 09/326 5211).

Television Channel 2, the Australian Broadcasting Corporation, is the best place to look for news, current affairs, and documentaries. The other channels are 7, 9, and 10, SBS multicultural, and Galaxy pay TV.

Transit Information If you have questions about local public transport, call Metrobus at 13 22 13.

Useful Telephone Numbers Seniors Information Service (☎ 09/328 9155, or 1800 199 087 in Australia), Women's Information Service (☎ 09/264 1900), Gay and Lesbian Counselling Service (☎ 09/328 9044).

3 Accommodations

Several large hotels were built in anticipation of the 1987 America's Cup, and the result is a city with more rooms than it really needs. This oversupply means that lodging rates are quite reasonable, especially on weekends, when reduced rates are often in effect.

For information on available bed-and-breakfasts you can contact **West Coast Homestays,** P.O. Box 854, Hillarys, WA 6923 (☎ 09/401 8149; fax 09/307 2347).

IN THE CITY CENTER

VERY EXPENSIVE

Hyatt Regency Perth. 99 Adelaide Terrace, Perth, WA 6000. ☎ **09/225 1234.** Fax 09/325 8899. 364 rms, 31 suites. A/C MINIBAR TV TEL. A$260–A$280 (U.S. $208–$224) double; A$395–A$950 (U.S. $316–$760) suite. Ask about weekend packages. AE, BC, DC, MC, V. Free parking.

You enter this architectural giant, just minutes from the heart of Perth, one block from Langley Park, and two blocks from the Swan River, under a clear-domed walkway. The Hyatt hosts many conferences, and delegates and their displays frequently spill over into this area. Of the spacious rooms available, half have water views. You have a choice of a king-size bed, twin beds, or a double and a single.

Dining/Entertainment: The hotel is part of the Hyatt Centre, a large modern complex of eating places, shops, and offices. Three restaurants and two bars are in the hotel.

Services: Concierge, 24-hour room service, laundry/dry cleaning.

Facilities: 25-meter heated pool, sauna, fitness center, tennis court, squash courts.

EXPENSIVE

Perth Parkroyal. 54 Terrace Rd., Perth, WA 6004. ☎ **09/325 3811.** Fax 09/221 1564. 99 rms, 2 suites. A/C MINIBAR TV TEL. A$180 (U.S. $144) double; A$320 (U.S. $256) suite. Additional person A$20 (U.S. $16) extra. Children under 16 free in parents' room. Ask about weekend and long-stay discounts. AE, DC, MC, V. Free parking.

The Perth Parkroyal is a 12-story property overlooking Langley Park and the Swan River about four blocks from the city center. An exclusive, private feel prevails in the lobby and public spaces, and the staff gives attentive, personal service.

Pleasant light tones have been used throughout the guest rooms. Each has a balcony or patio and offers a choice of queen-size or twin beds. Some baths have showers only. All quarters come with clock radios, bathrobes, hairdryers, tea- and coffee-making facilities, small refrigerators, in-room movies, and free daily newspapers. Meals and drinks are served in the Royal Palm Restaurant and Lobby Bar. You also have use of the hotel's spa, pool, and gymnasium.

$ Princes Hotel Perth. 334 Murray St. Perth, WA 6000. ☎ **09/322 2844,** or 1800/642 244 in Australia. Fax 09/321 6314. 151 rms, 16 suites. A/C MINIBAR TV TEL. A$144 (U.S. $115.20) double; A$206 (U.S. $164.80) suite. Additional person A$20 (U.S. $16) extra. Ask about weekend packages. AE, BC, DC, MC, V. Free parking.

Princes Hotel is in the heart of town, only a block from the Hay Street Mall and adjacent shopping areas. The hostelry has rooms on nine floors, and these are categorized either "tourist class" or "business class." None of the rooms is spacious; all offer showers only, and a choice between double or twin beds. Tourist-class quarters are on floors one to five and have modest furnishings; business-class rooms occupy loftier levels within the hotel and have upmarket decors. Studio suites have a separate lounge with a sofa sleeper and two baths.

The Prince's Plaza has several pleasant drinking and dining options, including Valentine's Bistro, Valentine's Bar, and the Society Bar and Grill.

Sheraton Perth Hotel. 207 Adelaide Terrace, Perth, WA 6000. ☎ **09/325 0501.** Fax 09/325 4032. 396 rms, 46 suites. A/C MINIBAR TV TEL. A$220–A$335 (U.S. $176–$268) double. Additional person A$40 (U.S. $32) extra. Ask about weekend packages. AE, BC, DC, MC, V. Parking A$10 (U.S. $8).

The doorman in top hat and tails who greets guests here looks a bit out of place in casual Perth. I suspect he's a prop designed to make businesspeople from the eastern states feel at home. Happily, the friendly staff don't reflect his stuffy attire. The hotel is only a block or so from the city center. All rooms have a window that opens; most have king-size beds. All baths have hairdryers. Quarters on the top four floors have the best view.

Dining/Entertainment: The Tuscany Grill is an upmarket casual Mediterranean-style à la carte restaurant and the Wandarrah is a cheerful coffee shop. Two lounge bars, a public bar, and a disco are also on the premises.

Services: Concierge, 24-hour room service, laundry.

Facilities: Pool, sauna, beauty salon.

MODERATE

Perth Ambassador Hotel. 196 Adelaide Terrace, Perth, WA 6000. ☎ **09/325 1455,** or 1800/998 011 in Australia. Fax 09/325 6317. 174 rms, 55 suites. A/C TV TEL. A$110 (U.S. $88) double; A$130 (U.S. $104) suite. Additional person A$20 (U.S. $16) extra. AE, BC, DC, MC, V. Free parking.

This is a pleasant eight-story building a couple of blocks from the heart of the city center. Some of the rooms on upper floors in the front overlook the Swan River. All quarters have large, bright windows and tile baths with separate showers and bathtubs. The Ambassador provides the usual modern amenities. Standard rooms have either a double bed or two twins. Executive studios and Australian suites have either queen- or king-size beds.

The menu at the coffee shop ranges from club sandwiches to three-course meals. You're welcome to use the large sauna and hot spa, but there's no pool.

$ **Wentworth Plaza Hotel.** 300 Murray St., Perth, WA 6000. ☎ **09/481 1000.** Fax 09/321 2443. 93 rms (some without bath), 12 suites. A/C MINIBAR TV TEL. A$55 (U.S. $44) double without bath, A$85 (U.S. $68) double with bath, A$90 (U.S. $72) double with kitchen; A$105 (U.S. $84) apartment. Children under 12 free in parents' room. AE, BC, DC, MC, V. Free parking.

I take my hat off to the architects who designed the midcity Wentworth Plaza. Faced with the task of remodeling and connecting three existing hostelries, they were able to complete the job without destroying the original charm and ambience. Until 1986, the three-story Wentworth Plaza was the Wentworth, the Royal, and the Bohemia—all older hotels, built in 1928, 1882, and 1879, respectively, and all in need of a face-lift.

An attractive gray-and-lavender scheme is used throughout, and the hotel has high ceilings, large wood-framed windows that open, elaborate banisters, and lovely arches in the hallways. In the Royal section, dormer windows and slanted ceilings create an especially cozy feel. Raine Square, a complex of 40 shops, fills the courtyard between the three buildings.

It was the old-world cream exterior that attracted me to the Wentworth Plaza, and when I poked my head inside and saw an aviary I knew I'd found someplace special. The hotel also has four unusual restaurants and bars: Horsefeathers, the Garage, Bobby Dazzlers Eatery & Ale House, and the Moon & Sixpence British Pub.

INEXPENSIVE

The less expensive rooms at the **Wentworth Plaza** qualify as budget digs. Even cheaper is the **YMCA Jewell House,** 180 Goderich St., Perth, WA 6000 (☎ 09/325 8488, or 1800/998 212 in Australia). Doubles cost A$40 (U.S. $32). Jewell House is about a block from the city center, next to the Royal Perth Hospital. They cater to men, women, couples, and families.

Readers Recommend

North Lodge Central City Backpackers, 225 Beaufort St., Perth, WA 6000 (☎ 09/227 7588). *"Friends recommended North Lodge, and I wasn't disappointed. It was close to the city and all public transport, had a clean kitchen, a laundry room, a TV lounge, and most important, large rooms with clean, comfortable beds. It's a real home-away-from-home hostel."*

—Kevin Menham, England.

IN VICTORIA PARK

Burswood Resort Hotel. Great Eastern Highway, Victoria Park, WA 6100. ☎ **09/362 7777.** Fax 09/470 1789. 392 rms, 18 suites. A/C MINIBAR TV TEL. A$260–A$350 (U.S. $208–$280) double; A$600 (U.S. $480) suite. Additional person A$35 (U.S. $28) extra. Ask about special packages. Children under 14 free in parents' room. AE, BC, DC, MC, V. Free parking. Free shuttle from hotel to central business district every hour.

This hotel on the south side of the Swan River is part of a large complex that includes a convention center, a Superdome, an 18-hole golf course, and a casino. The Burswood's lobby is topped by a 12-story cone-shaped atrium where four glass elevators whisk you to your room. Some rooms have king-size beds; in fact, River Suites have two king-size beds. All quarters have clock radios, tea- and coffee-making facilities, small refrigerators, and in-room movies. Each also has a large bath separated from the room by a Japanese sliding screen. Half the rooms have a river view.

Dining/Entertainment: Windows is Burswood's fine-dining venue. The Atrium Bar is in the lobby. There are several other eating options and enough bars to make a Las Vegas veteran feel at home.

Services: Concierge, 24-hour room service, laundry, baby-sitting, massage.

Facilities: Indoor pool, outdoor pool, gym, sauna, hair salon, gift shop, four tennis courts, spa, table tennis, bicycle rental, casino, day-care center, business center.

ON THE BEACH

EXPENSIVE

Radisson Observation City. The Esplanade, Scarborough Beach, WA 6019. ☎ **09/245 1000,** or 800/333-3333 in the U.S. Fax 09/245 1345. 331 rms, 5 suites. A/C MINIBAR TV TEL. A$165–A$230 (U.S. $132–$184) double; A$245 (U.S. $196) Club Room; A$475–A$2,000 (U.S. $380–$1,600) suite. Additional person A$40 (U.S. $32) extra. Ask about lower weekend rates. Children under 18 free in parents' room. AE, BC, CB, DC, MC, V. Free parking. Free shuttle to city center, 18km (11 miles) away; a taxi costs A$17 (U.S. $13.60); Shuttle: 293, A$2 (U.S. $2).

Alan Bond is best known to Americans as the Australian who built the boat that won the America's Cup in 1983. However, in his own country Bond is better known for his entrepreneurial ventures. The 17-story beachfront Observation City Resort is one of these. Opened in 1986, it made a good observation point for the 1987 America's Cup races. The public rooms are done in a potpourri of styles: A waterfall and tropical plants grace one side of the lobby, while plush salmon carpeting and traditional furnishings are across the way. Each guest room has an ocean view and balcony. You have a choice of king-size beds or a queen-size bed with a single. Hairdryers and toasters are standard throughout.

The rates vary according to the location of rooms within the hotel. Deluxe quarters facing the beach have two sliding glass doors that open onto balconies. Superior rooms are in the middle of the hotel and have one slider. Standard rooms are at the back and on the lower floors. The hotel employs a run-of-the-house policy, meaning that you're allotted the best available room at the time of your arrival—so you might book a standard room and be given deluxe lodging. (Obviously, if you reserve deluxe that's what you get.)

Dining/Entertainment: Observation City includes the Spice Market eatery, the Pines Bistro, Crusoe's Seafood Restaurant, and the à la carte Ocean Room. There are six bars, plus the Club Atlantis dance club and Nero's Nightclub.

Services: Concierge, 24-hour room service, shoeshine, laundry, valet, nightly turndown, free child care 9am to 5pm and coordinated children's activities on scheduled days.

Facilities: Lagoon-style pool, health club, gym, spa, sauna, two tennis courts, child-care center, salon with masseuse and beautician.

MODERATE

$ All Seasons West Beach Lagoon Apartments. 251 West Coast Hwy., Scarborough Beach, WA 6019. ☎ **09/341 6122,** or 1800/999 339 in Australia. Fax 09/341 5944. Reservations can be made through Flag Inns. 69 apts. TV TEL. A$97–A$131 (U.S. $77.60–$104.80) two-bedroom apt. for up to four. Rates are 25% higher Dec–Jan. No-smoking rooms available. AE, BC, DC, MC, V. Free parking. Bus: 268 or 269 to Perth, about 12km (7 miles) inland.

All the two-bedroom units in the West Beach have a full kitchen. They're modestly but adequately furnished; all sleep four and most have ocean views. Only an access road (no through traffic) separates this hostelry from the beach, and a nice pool provides another swimming alternative. The Depot, a casual family-oriented eatery, specializes in steaks. West Beach's other dining spot, Somerset's Restaurant, has a tropical feel created by rattan furniture, slate floors, cane lampshades, and lots of green plants. Pictures of Somerset Maugham and his contemporaries line the walls, and the names of menu items are taken from his novels.

If you'd rather cook for yourself, there's a supermarket down the block.

IN FREMANTLE

Tradewinds Hotel. 59 Canning Hwy., East Fremantle, WA 6158. ☎ **09/339 8188,** or 1800/999 274 in Australia. Fax 09/339 2266. 83 suites. A/C TV TEL. A$125 (U.S. $100) one-bedroom suite; A$155 (U.S. $124) two-bedroom suite. Children under 12 free in parents' room. AE, BC, DC, MC, V. Free parking.

The Tradewinds has a bright, airy feel and a tropical/colonial decor. This pleasant hostelry is on the lower reaches of the Swan River, between the Fremantle Bridge and the Stirling Bridge, with the ocean about 2km (1¼ miles) to the west and Perth almost 18km (11 miles) upriver. The original part of the Tradewinds was built in 1910. The hotel offers 83 units dating from 1986 that are one-bedroom and two-bedroom suites. All have queen-size beds, fully equipped kitchenettes or kitchens, and private baths.

Trader Morgans Bistro has a nautical flavor created by barrels, brass, and halyards. The Tradewinds Lounge Bar serves snacks and lunch. Plympton, the pub, is popular with locals who play darts and pool. The Piazza Bar offers outdoor drinking and a view of the river. Guests also enjoy the property's pool and spa.

4 Dining

In Australia, traditionally, the most formal and most expensive dining spots are in the five-star hotels, and Perth has its share of these places. The **River Room** in the Sheraton Perth Hotel, the **Ocean Room Restaurant** in the Radisson Observation City Resort Hotel, and **Windows** in the Burswood Resort are all excellent. Dinner for two costs about A$100 (U.S. $80), plus wine, and the service is impeccable.

IN THE CITY CENTER

EXPENSIVE

✪ **Jessica's Fine Seafood Restaurant.** In the Hyatt Centre, 23 Plain St. ☎ **09/325 2511.** Reservations recommended. Main courses A$19–A$27.50 (U.S. $15.20–$22). AE, BC, DC, MC, V. Sun–Fri noon–late; Sat 6pm–late. Take any bus down St. George's Terrace to Plain Street. SEAFOOD.

Jessica's is easily Perth's finest seafood restaurant. Fish and shellfish are purchased daily at the market, and the menu changes depending on what's available. Because everything is fresh, the chef doesn't need heavy sauces and lets the natural flavor of the ingredients come through. On a typical night you may have a choice of grilled Exmouth red emperor, grilled Albany King George whiting filets, or barbecued Mandurah prawns with onion-and-herb topping. These dishes come in both entree (appetizer) and main-course portions. If you'd prefer not to have two fish courses, you could start with an entree of fresh steamed asparagus, sautéed calves' liver with fried onions, or homemade leek-and-potato soup. Bouillabaisse, served in a heavy black Dutch oven, is a favorite main-course item.

Jessica's is across from Langley Park with a view of the Swan River. The decor has a postmodernist flavor, with a pale-mint scheme, black lacquer chairs, and polished granite tables. The adequate, but not extensive, wine list emphasizes Western Australian whites.

MODERATE

$ **Horsefeathers.** In the Wentworth Plaza Hotel, Raine Square, William Street. ☎ **09/481 1000.** Reservations not required. Main courses A$7.95–A$16.50 (U.S. $6.40–$13.20). AE, BC, DC, MC, V. Daily 11am–11pm. ECLECTIC.

Horsefeathers is enough to wake up anyone's senses. Described by the managers as a "food and fun emporium," it's decorated with a most amazing collection of memorabilia, including props from the TV series based on the Australian classic *A Fortunate Life.* The menu is large and equally colorful. You can choose from a variety of hamburgers, steaks, and sandwiches or something more exotic like Mexican nachos, Nutty Fruity Chook, or asparagus crêpes.

INEXPENSIVE

Fast Eddy's Cafe. 454 Murray St. (at Milligan Street). ☎ **09/321 2552.** Reservations not required. Average meal A$8 (U.S. $6.40). Eftpos cards only. Daily 24 hours. FAST FOOD.

Fast Eddy's is a budget diner's delight. It offers classic fast food like fish and chips and myriad burgers, pancakes, sundaes, and shakes. More substantial fare—grilled chicken dinners, lasagne, steak, pasta, pizza, salads, and American-style spareribs—is also on the menu. The decor is "colonial" crossed with 1930s American: wrought-iron light fixtures, stools that swivel, and lots of pre–World War II posters. The eatery is divided into two parts, and the full menu is available only on the table-service side. Burgers, chips, and shakes served at the quick-service counter cost considerably less. Fast Eddy's has a 24-hour liquor license.

There's another Fast Eddy's Cafe at 13 Essex St., Fremantle (☎ 09/336 1671).

IN FREMANTLE

Inexpensive ethnic food is sold from stalls at the **Fremantle Markets,** Henderson Street (☎ 09/335 2515), open Friday from 9am to 9pm, Saturday from 9am to 5pm, and Sunday from 11am to 5pm.

Readers Recommend

Ms. Mauds, at the corner of Pier and Murray streets (☎ 09/325 3900). *"For a really splendid meal we visited Ms. Mauds. This is a real experience and not to be missed. They serve a smorgasbord that has everything imaginable."*

—Kathleen Button, East Bentleigh, Victoria, Australia.

Author's Note: Ms. Mauds is open daily from 7am to 10pm.

EXPENSIVE

The Oyster Beds Restaurant. 26 Riverside Rd., East Fremantle. ☎ **09/339 1611.** Reservations recommended on weekends. Main courses A$17.50–A$29.95 (U.S. $14–$24); children's menu A$9.50 (U.S. $7.60). AE, BC, DC, MC, V. Daily noon–3pm and 6pm–late. Take a taxi. SEAFOOD.

The Oyster Beds is a seafood eatery built on stilts out over the Swan River, so you have a view of lights shining on the water and the constant parade of small boats. An informal dining area outside has a nautical decor. Inside, things are a bit more formal, and the decor is pink and burgundy. The restaurant, which was formerly owned by a Perth personality who had a cooking show on TV, has been a local institution for over 40 years. The new management prints the menu in both English and Japanese and attracts lots of tourists.

If you dine here, you could start with shellfish au pesto, chili squid, or brain box (crumbed brains in a pastry box "enhanced by a delicate Gorgonzola cheese sauce"). Main courses include filet of John Dory topped with scallops and prawns, crayfish Mornay, and barramundi topped with crab-and-mushroom sauce. A wonderful pianist entertains on Friday and Saturday night. There's a good wine list and also a complete menu of exotic cocktails.

MODERATE

Left Bank Bar & Cafe. 15 Riverside Dr., East Fremantle. ☎ **09/319 1315.** Reservations recommended, especially Fri–Sat dinner and Sun lunch. Main courses A$9–A$16 (U.S. $7.20–$12.80). AE, BC, CB, MC, V. Mon–Fri noon–10pm, Sat 8–11am and noon–10pm; Sun 8–11am and noon–4pm (bar, Mon–Sat until midnight, Sun until 9pm). Ferry: From Perth's Barrack Street Jetty; then walk or taxi less than 1km (0.6 mile). MULTIETHNIC/SEAFOOD.

Until 1970 the building that now houses the Left Bank Bar & Cafe was a private home. The atmospheric two-story was built between 1896 and 1900, and hardwood floors, potted palms, and bentwood chairs reinforce the old-world atmosphere. Wrought-iron lacework forms a railing around the balcony. Tables on the veranda have a view of the Swan River. Sample entrees (appetizers) are charcoal-grilled eggplant with feta cheese and fresh chili-prawn cakes. Main courses include Thai chicken curry, Tex-Mex, and Shanghai Express. This is a popular spot. On Sunday afternoon it's filled to overflowing by trendy young professionals who gather here to drink on the patio.

IN NORTHBRIDGE

This is Perth's dining/nightlife quarter. Your best bet is to wander James, Francis, Lake, Aberdeen, and William Streets until you spot an eatery that appeals to you. You might enjoy **The Fishy Affair,** 132 James St. (☎ 09/328 3939); the **Brass Monkey Pub & Brasserie,** at the corner of James and William streets (☎ 09/227 9596); **Cafe Valentino,** at the corner of Lake and James Streets (☎ 09/328 2105); or **The Thai House,** 63 Aberdeen St. (☎ 09/3286074).

If you're watching your pennies, try **The Plaka,** 87 James St. (☎ 09/328 1636), which serves Greek fast food until 4am.

MODERATE

✪ **Ted's Cafe.** At the corner of Lake and Aberdeen streets, Northbridge. ☎ **09/227 8520.** Reservations not required. Main courses A$8–A$16.50 (U.S. $6.40–$13.20). AE, BC, MC, V. Coffee and snacks daily 9am to "way past your bedtime." Full menu noon–midnight. Bus: The Northbridge dining and nightlife quarter is within the Free Transit Zone. BISTRO.

"Be fed at Ted's" is the motto at this clever, casual dining spot. Everything—from the George Bernard Shaw words of wisdom on the placemat to the "Let them eat cake" comments on the menu—is witty and slightly off-the-wall. If you're in the mood for a salad, Ted's offers the Campagnola chicken with barbecued chicken filets, avocado, sun-dried tomatoes, cashews, and creamy tarragon dressing, or Ted's Caesar salad, or English spinach with bacon, pine nuts, sun-dried tomatoes, Gruyère cheese, and mustard dressing. You could also have Bombay vegetable curry, "Tex-Mex" nachos, pasta carbonara, a Wall Street burger, or Torre's prime beef. There are also a wide range of coffees and teas, plus cakes and pies baked daily. More than a dozen beers are offered, as well as wine, spirits, liqueurs, and teas. Go for a chuckle and a tasty meal.

INEXPENSIVE

The ⓢ **Northbridge Pavillion,** Lake Street, is an Asian food court where most meals cost A$3 to A$8 (U.S. $2.40 to $6.40). Open Wednesday to Saturday from 11am to 2am and Sunday from noon to 10pm. No credit cards.

IN COTTESLOE

✪ **North Cott Cafe.** 149 Marine Parade, at the corner of Eric Street, Cottesloe. ☎ **09/385 1371.** Reservations recommended for table with ocean view. Main courses A$11.50–A$19.50 (U.S. $9.20–$15.60). Public holiday surcharge 10%. BC, MC, V. Daily 7am–9:30pm. Train or bus: 70-73, 100, 101, 103, or 207. INTERNATIONAL.

This eatery, originally an ice-cream/soft-drink kiosk, is only a few feet from the water and has wraparound windows, brick floors, wooden tables, and a canvas roof. You can watch windsurfers and sailors zip by while enjoying your meal. Breakfast includes a choice of bacon, eggs, and sausage or something lighter like toasted muesli (granola), fresh fruit salad, or a bagel or croissant with coffee or tea. Lunch and dinner include dishes like calamari, king prawns, and a variety of fresh local fish, steaks, and pastas. Desserts include a full range of homemade cakes, ice creams, and pies. The cappuccino is excellent. BYO.

DINING ON THE WATER

The ***Mystique*** (☎ 09/221 5844) will carry you up the Swan River to the wine country, where you can enjoy a multicourse meal at Mulberry Farm on the banks of the Upper Swan. Local wines flow freely on the boat and are served with dinner. The trips depart Pier 4, Barrack Street Jetty, at 6pm on Saturday night (Fridays also during peak season). The cost is A$60 (U.S. $48).

Boat Torque Cruises (☎ 09/325 6033) also offers a dinner cruise to Fremantle with a meal served on board. This trip on Saturday at 7:45pm costs A$55 (U.S. $44).

Captain Cook Cruises (☎ 09/325 3341) offers a dinner/dance cruise to Fremantle with a buffet dinner and disc jockey on board. The cruise departs on Wednesday and Friday at 7:30pm for A$30 (U.S. $24).

5 Attractions

SIGHTSEEING SUGGESTIONS FOR THE FIRST-TIME VISITOR

If You Have 1 Day Take my Perth walking tour (later in this section) to familiarize yourself with the city center. If you visit either the Art Gallery of Western Australia or the Western Australian Museum, you'll finish the tour about lunchtime, so continue to Northbridge for a meal. In the afternoon, walk through King's Park, admiring the views of the city and Swan River, then take a train, bus, or boat to Fremantle. If there's time, do the Fremantle walking tour (see "In Fremantle" below). In any case, be sure to visit the Maritime Museum and then treat yourself to a beer at the historic Sail & Anchor pub.

If You Have 2 Days Spend your first day as suggested above. On Day 2, make an excursion to Rottnest Island.

If You Have 3 Days Spend Days 1 and 2 as outlined above. On the third day, take an excursion to either the Pinnacles or the Swan and/or Avon Valleys.

THE TOP ATTRACTIONS

Because of the region's benign climate and scenic appeal, the majority of Perth's sights and activities are outdoors. You'd be wise to bring casual clothes and comfortable, sturdy shoes.

For six weeks during September and October, the southwest portion of Western Australia is covered with colorful carpets of blooming **native flora.** More than 7,000 varieties are unique to the state, and another 830 types have been introduced from other parts of Australia and from other countries. This is said to be one of the richest wildflower areas in the world. It's believed that certain flowers are found only in this corner of the nation because they're isolated by oceans on two sides and harsh desert on a third, making it impossible for seeds to spread naturally.

Of particular botanical interest are the kangaroo paws, Christmas tree, pitcher plant, dryandras, and many of the banksias, featherflowers, triggerplants, and blackboys.

Within Perth itself, King's Park is the best place for wildflower viewing, the Botanic Gardens containing a collection of 1,500 species; free guided tours are offered several days a week. It's also a good idea to venture out, either in a rental car or on a special bus excursion, to the **Darling Range,** 40 minutes east of the city. **Westrail** (☎ 09/326 2222) organizes excursions. The **Western Australian Tourist Centre** (☎ 09/483 1111) is the best source of what's-blooming-where information.

If you're willing to go farther afield, you'll find beautiful wildflowers blooming around **Kalbarri** in the Midwest region of the state and in the vicinity of the **Margaret River** in the Southwest. For information on these places, see Chapter 13. Westrail offers five- and six-day trips to these areas. Keen gardeners and photographers may want to contact the **Wildflower Society of Western Australia,** P.O. Box 64, Nedlands, WA 6009 (☎ 09/383 7979).

IN PERTH

✪ **King's Park.** Fraser Avenue and King's Park Road. ☎ **09/321 4801.**

Originally known as Perth Park, this expansive open space was renamed in 1901 to mark the accession of Edward VII to the British throne. Spreading gently across the slopes of **Mount Eliza,** King's Park affords grand vistas of the city skyline and the Swan River. War memorials, playgrounds, the extensive **Botanic Gardens,** a restaurant, two kiosks, and walking paths are around the park's 404 hectares (998 acres). An information center, between the restaurant and the huge karri log on display, is open daily from 9am to 3pm; closed Good Friday and Christmas. Free guided walking tours are available from April to October (☎ 09/321 4801). Bicycles can be rented from **Koala Bike Hire** (☎ 09/321 3061) in the parking lot behind the restaurant.

You can walk to the park from the city center or take a green Clipper Bus (free) from the Wellington Street Bus Station or anywhere along the route.

Cohunu Wildlife Park. 287A Mills Rd., Kelmscott. ☎ **09/390 6090.** Admission A$9 (U.S. $7.20) adults, A$4.50 (U.S. $3.60) children. Daily 10am–5pm. Train or bus to Gosnells; then a A$5 (U.S. $4) taxi.

Would you like to cuddle a koala? You can at the Cohunu Wildlife Park, 26km (16 miles) southeast of Perth in the Darling Range. The holding and hugging, for which there's a charge, takes place daily between 11am and 3pm. Cohunu also has a variety of other native animals in natural surroundings, a miniature railway, and a very large walk-through aviary.

Perth Zoo. 20 Labouchere Rd., South Perth. ☎ **09/367 7988.** Admission A$8 (U.S. $6.40) adults, A$4 (U.S. $3.20) children. Daily 10am–5pm. Ferry across the Swan River from the Barrack Street Jetty; bus: 110 from St. Georges Terrace.

If you haven't had your fill of native and exotic fauna, head for the Perth Zoo. Highlights are a nocturnal house, an Australian Bush Walk, and a 360-degree koala viewing platform. This is the only place in the world you can see the endangered numbat. The Harmony Farm and the Conservation Discovery Centre are especially popular with kids.

Underwater World. Hillarys Boat Harbour, West Coast Drive. ☎ **09/447 7500.** Fax 09/447 7856. Admission A$13.90 (U.S. $11.12) adults, A$7 (U.S. $5.60) children 3–14. Daily 9am–5pm. Closed Christmas. Take a train from the Perth Central Station toward Joondalup and get off at Warrick station; bus: 423 or the Sunset Coaster.

At Underwater World, 20 minutes northwest of Perth, you can see dolphins in their harbor enclosure and walk beneath the sea in a submerged acrylic tunnel that brings you face to face with divers feeding 3-meter (10-foot) sharks, rays, octopus, and a variety of other sea life. There are also a Touch Pool where turtles, Port Jackson sharks, starfish, and squid can be handled; the Coral Lagoon; Microworld; a theater; a shop; and a restaurant.

WALKING TOUR

Perth's Central Business District

Start: Town Hall, Hay and Barrack Streets.
Finish: In Northbridge.
Time: Approximately an hour, not including shopping and museum stops.
Best Times: Monday to Saturday.
Worst Times: Friday to Sunday morning, when the Western Australian Museum is closed; Sunday, when the stores are closed and the CBD is deserted.

A stroll around Perth's central business district will give you an appreciation for this city, which is both historically significant and progressive.

Walking Tour—Perth's Central Business District

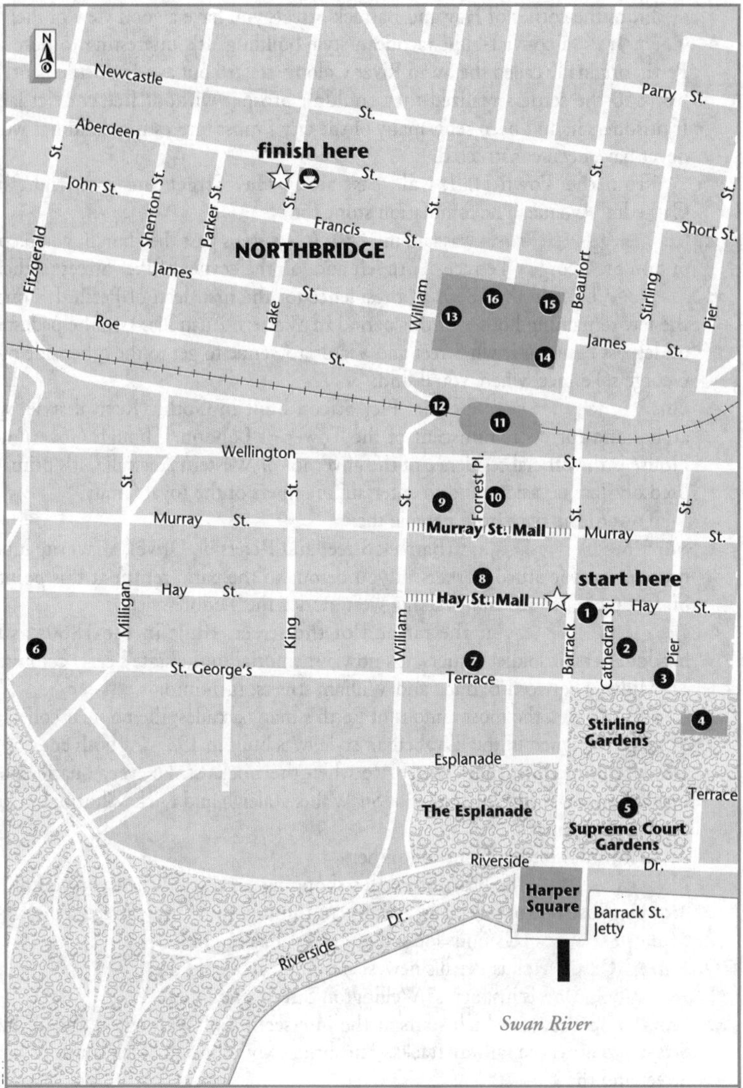

1. Town Hall
2. St. George's Cathedral
3. Deanery
4. Government House
5. Supreme Court Gardens
6. Barracks Archway
7. London Court
8. Hay Street Mall
9. Main post office (GPO)
10. Forest Chase Mall
11. Railway Station
12. Horseshoe Bridge
13. Perth Cultural Centre
14. Art Gallery of Western Australia
15. Western Australian Museum
16. Alexander Library Building

From the corner of Hay and Barrack Streets you have a good view of the:

1. **Town Hall,** a convict-built Jacobean-style building. It's interesting to note that Perth, originally called the Swan River Colony, started out as a free settlement, but by 1850 the settlers realized they couldn't prosper without free convict labor. If prisoners hadn't been sent, many of the city's most interesting buildings would never have been constructed.

From the Town Hall, walk east along Hay Street and turn right into Cathedral Avenue. The foundation stone for:

2. **St. George's Cathedral** was laid in 1880. A few steps past the church, you'll come out on St. George's Terrace. Turn left and, on the corner of Pier Street, is the:
3. **Deanery,** built in the 1850s as a residence for the first dean of Perth. It's one of the few remaining houses of this period in Western Australia. Use the pedestrian underpass between Irwin Street and Victoria Avenue to get to the other side of St. George's Terrace, where you'll find:
4. **Government House,** opposite Pier Street, built in Gothic Revival style, with arches and turrets reminiscent of the Tower of London. Though Government House is the official residence of the governor of Western Australia, it's primarily used on state occasions and to entertain members of the royal family.

Toward the river from here lie the:

5. **Supreme Court Gardens** (Barrack Street and Riverside Drive), a favorite lunch-time retreat for office workers. If you detour to the park, return at this point to St. George's Terrace and, walking west, notice the Tudor-style:
6. **Barracks Archway** at the far end of the street. Built in the 1860s as the headquarters of soldier settlers, it's now a memorial to the state's early colonists.

Midway between Barrack and William streets, turn into:

7. **London Court,** the most famous of Perth's many arcades; the popular collection of shops, designed in the Elizabethan style, was built in 1937. At both ends of the arcade, miniperformances take place when the clocks strike every quarter hour. Inside London Court, likenesses of Sir Walter Raleigh and Dick Whittington keep an eye on shoppers.

Exit from London Court onto the:

8. **Hay Street Mall,** the heart of Perth's shopping precinct. When you've finished browsing, use one of several arcades to cut through to Murray Street. The:
9. **Main post office (GPO)** is located at Forrest Place. The:
10. **Forrest Chase Mall** is Perth's newest shopping area; and the:
11. **Railway Station** is just across Wellington Street. Now use:
12. **Horseshoe Bridge,** which starts at the intersection of Wellington and William Streets, to cross the railway tracks. This brings you out one block south of James Street and the:
13. **Perth Cultural Centre.** You can visit the:
14. **Art Gallery of Western Australia** (☎ 09/328 7233) daily from 10am to 5pm (free), and the:
15. **Western Australian Museum** (☎ 09/328 4411) Monday to Thursday from 10:30am to 5pm and Friday to Sunday from 1 to 5pm (free). The:
16. **Alexander Library Building** (☎ 09/427 3111) is open Monday and Friday from 9am to 5:30pm, Tuesday to Thursday from 9am to 9:30pm, and Saturday and Sunday from 2 to 5:30pm. Admission is free.

WINDING DOWN Finish off your stroll with a cappuccino or a piece of "Awesome Killer Chocolate Cake" at **Ted's,** on the corner of Lake and Aberdeen streets in Northbridge. See "Dining" earlier in this chapter for details.

IN FREMANTLE

"Freo," as the locals call it, was a run-of-the-mill blue-collar port area when I lived in Perth in 1977. I went there to shop at the markets, which were interesting, and felt no urge to linger in the town afterward. Not until the **Royal Perth Yacht Club** hosted the 1987 America's Cup did Fremantle get the sprucing up it needed. Today it's an area of attractive restored historic buildings, atmospheric pubs, unusual shops, and sights worth a visitor's time. While Perth, 19km (12 miles) upriver, has the appearance of a modern city, Fremantle has the hearty character of a 19th-century port.

GETTING THERE & GETTING AROUND The two places are connected by frequent bus and train service, as well as **Captain Cook Ferries** (☎ 09/325 3341). A one-way cruise from Perth to Fremantle is A$10 (U.S. $8) for adults and A$6 (U.S. $4.80) for children.

Narrow one-way streets make driving here frustrating. The best way to tour Fremantle is on foot, but if you leave your Reeboks at home, selected spots from the stroll below can be reached by taxi or rental car. You might also be interested in the 45-minute tram tours that operate daily, stopping at significant sites (☎ 09/339-8719) for A$6 (U.S. $4.80).

STROLLING THROUGH HISTORIC FREMANTLE A walk through Fremantle allows you to appreciate its historic atmosphere. Begin at the **train station,** which opened in 1907. Turn left onto Elder Place, then right onto Edward Place, then left onto Quarry Street.

The third street on the right is James Street, which leads to the **Fremantle Arts Centre and the Fremantle Museum,** 1 Finnerty St. (☎ 09/335 8244). This restored Gothic building was constructed by convicts as a lunatic asylum in 1861. Today it houses the works of many well-known Australian artists, printmakers, and potters and is open daily from 10am to 5pm. There are a craft shop and a bookshop on the premises, as well as a café with seating inside or in a leafy limestone-walled courtyard. Admission is free.

When you're ready to leave, head down Ord Street to High Street and turn right. Walk up High Street to **St. John's Square,** where you'll see St. John's Church (1882) and the Town Hall (1887). Walk down William Street to Henderson and turn right, continuing to South Terrace.

The **Sail & Anchor Pub Brewery,** 64 South Terrace (☎ 09/335 8433), is without a doubt the most atmospheric spot for a drink or a meal in Fremantle (see "After Dark" later in this chapter for more details). Founded as a Freemason's Hotel in 1854, this popular pub has led a colorful life and was refurbished and renamed in 1985. The bar offers a wide selection of beers brewed both on and off the premises and traditional bar food like a ploughman's lunch, fish and chips, and meat pies. Breakfast, lunch, and dinner are served in a charming brasserie upstairs.

Across from the Sail & Anchor is the entrance to the historic **Fremantle Markets.** Built in 1897 for the Fremantle Municipality, these wholesale markets continued in their original function for more than 70 years. The impressive size of the building indicates the vitality of Fremantle at the turn of the century. Today, arts and crafts, herbs and spices, fruits and vegetables, wooden and cane wares, antiques and bric-a-brac, and fresh seafood are sold from 140 stalls. The 19th-century architecture provides an atmospheric background for the popular markets, open Friday from 9am to 9pm, Saturday from 9am to 5pm, and Sunday from 11am to 5pm.

When you leave the markets, walk down Essex Street until you come to the **Esplanade Hotel,** on the corner of Essex and Marine Terrace, overlooking the

Brava Pavlova

The first pavlova—now considered the national dessert of both Australia and New Zealand—was prepared in 1935 by chef Herbert Sachse at the Esplanade Hotel in Perth. He named it after the legendary Russian prima ballerina Anna Pavlova.

The following recipe is for the best pavlova I've ever eaten. I got it from my friend Susan Goode, an expatriate Kiwi living in San Diego. She got the recipe from her "nana"—Esther Ellen Goode of Marshlands, Christchurch, New Zealand. I thank them both.

4 egg whites
1 cup sugar
1 tsp. vanilla
1 tsp. malt vinegar
1 tsp. water
whipped cream
kiwis, strawberries, raspberries, bananas, and/or nuts to garnish
chocolate pudding or lemon honey (optional)

Beat the egg whites until stiff. Fold in the sugar softly and beat until the sugar dissolves and the mixture is shiny. Fold in the vanilla, malt vinegar, and water. Spread into a circle on waxed paper placed on a greased cookie sheet and bake at 300°F (150°C) for approximately an hour. When the circle is cool, cover it with whipped cream and decorate with fruit and/or nuts. (Before spreading on the cream, perhaps try covering the round with a layer of chocolate pudding or lemon honey.) Enjoy!

Esplanade and boat harbor; at this hotel the pavlova was created (see the "Brava Pavlova" box). Walk along the Esplanade, past the **statue of Captain Fremantle,** after whom the colony was named. You'll soon come upon the **Western Australia Maritime Museum,** on Cliff Street (☎ 09/431 8444). The main entrance and gallery were built by convicts in 1851 to house stores from the Commissariat Department. Today, exhibits relating to Western Australia's maritime history, including Australia's earliest shipwrecks, are on display. These include relics from the Dutch ship *Batavia,* wrecked off the coast in 1629. The museum is open daily from 10:30am to 5pm, ANZAC Day and Boxing Day from 1pm to 5pm; closed Good Friday and Christmas. Admission is free.

As you leave the museum, walk up Cliff Street to High Street, from where you'll have a good view of the **Round House,** 10 Arthur Head (☎ 09/430 2326). This structure, which is not round but has 12 sides, is Western Australia's oldest surviving public building. It dates back to 1831 and was Fremantle's first prison. A prime example of colonial Georgian design, the Round House is open daily from 10am to 5pm. The grounds, which include an information center, a craft shop, and a tearoom, afford a good view of the harbor. Admission is free. From here, return to the train station on Philimore Street.

6 Outdoor Activities & Spectator Sports

OUTDOOR ACTIVITIES

BICYCLING The longest stretch of cycleway in Australia extends along the Swan River, through King's Park, and all the way to Fremantle. The **Western Australian Ministry of Sport and Recreation** (☎ 09/421 4666) publishes a series of brochures describing this ride and many others. **Koala Bike Hire,** in King's Park (☎ 09/321 3061), rents bikes. **Bikewest** in Fremantle (☎ 09/430 7550) has information on interesting rides to take around Perth.

GOLF Many private and public courses are within easy reach of Perth. Private clubs welcome overseas and interstate visitors with a letter of introduction from their clubs. Average greens fees for public courses are A$20 to A$35 (U.S. $16 to $28) for 18 holes. Club rental is an additional A$20 (U.S. $16). Some popular public courses are **South Perth City Council,** Como (☎ 09/450 6187); **Joondalup Country Club,** Connolly (☎ 09/300 1538); **Burswood Park,** Burswood Resort Casino Complex, Great Eastern Highway (☎ 09/362 7576); and **The Vines,** Millhouse Road, Upper Swan (☎ 09/297 0222).

PARASAILING Rob Thompson (☎ 09/446 1835) operates from the Narrows, South Perth. A 10- to 12-minute ride costs A$40 (U.S. $32). The season is November to May.

SAILING Rent a Surf Cat, a 14-foot Windrush catamaran, from **Jack Freeman Fun Cats,** Coode Street Jetty, South Perth (☎ (018)926 003). The cost is A$15 (U.S. $12) an hour. Operates September to May.

SWIMMING The metropolitan Perth area has 19 beautiful beaches spread over less than 35km (22 miles) from South Fremantle to Mullaloo in the northern suburbs. All are within easy access of the city.

You might share Prince Charles's preference for North Cottesloe Beach, or maybe you'd like Swanbourne, where sunning and swimming are done in one's birthday suit. City Beach and Scarborough are also popular. Mullaloo is the calmest while Trigg Island Beach is one of the better ones for surfing. Most of the Indian Ocean shoreline is patrolled by surf lifesaving clubs (lifeguards), who keep watch over surfers, sailboarders, swimmers, and boaters.

Beatty Park Aquatic Centre, Vincent Street, North Perth (☎ 09/328 4099), has a heated Olympic-size pool.

TENNIS Many tennis clubs are in and around Perth. The average outdoor rental cost is about A$5 (U.S. $4) per hour. Courts for hire: **Town of Victoria Park** (☎ 09/311 8111); **McCallum Tennis Courts,** Fitzgerald Street, North Perth (☎ 09/361 2273); and **Burswood Park Tennis Courts** (☎ 09/361 2273).

WATERSKIING Contact **Cables Water Park,** 3 Troode St., Spearwood (☎ 09/418 6888 or 418 6111), if you'd like to try your hand at cable waterskiing. The fee of A$12 (U.S. $9.60) per hour includes skis and a life jacket. The park is open daily from 10am to 8pm October to May and noon to 7pm in other months. They also offer mini-golf, water slides, pools, and a children's playground. (Water slides are closed May to October.) Admission is A$1 (U.S. 80¢) in summer and free in winter.

SPECTATOR SPORTS

AUSTRALIAN RULES FOOTBALL Perth's team is called the West Coast Eagles. This sport is played during winter, as are soccer and other football codes. Local matches are played every Saturday during the season. For more information, call the **Western Australian Football League** at 09/381 5599.

CRICKET This is a popular summer sport. A-grade cricket is played on weekends in summer at ovals throughout the metropolitan area. The **Western Australian Cricket Association** and the **Western Australian Women's Cricket Association** (☎ 09/325 9800) can answer your questions.

HORSE & DOG RACING Regular horse races are held at Ascot Track in summer and at Belmont Track in winter. Trotting (harness racing) takes place at Gloucester Park most Friday nights. For more information, call the **Western Australian Greyhound Racing Association** at 09/458 4600, the **Western Australian Trotting Association** at 09/325 8822, or the **Western Australian Turf Club** at 09/227 0777.

7 Shopping

Perth has extensive shopping facilities centered around the **Hay Street** and **Murray Street** pedestrian malls, running between William and Barrack Streets, and the **Forrest Chase** shopping center, running between Murray and Wellington Streets. Several arcades lead off the malls, the best known of these being **London Court,** with its Elizabethan-style facade.

Away from the city center, the suburb of **Claremont** is known for its fashionable boutiques and women's dress shops. **Fremantle,** of course, has its popular markets, open Friday from 9am to 9pm, Saturday from 9am to 5pm, and Sunday from 11am to 5pm. This is the place to purchase funky clothes and handcrafted accessories.

ABORIGINAL ARTIFACTS & CRAFTS

✪ **Creative Native,** 32 King St. (☎ 09/322 3398 or 322 3397), is the best place in Perth to buy contemporary and traditional Aboriginal art. It sells carved emu eggs, boomerangs, and other artifacts—all handmade by Aboriginal artisans. Open Monday to Thursday from 9am to 5:30pm, Friday from 9am to 9pm, Saturday from 9am to 5pm, and Sunday from 11am to 5pm.

There's also a store in Fremantle at 65 High St. (☎ 09/335 6995), open Monday to Wednesday and Friday from 9am to 5:30pm, Thursday from 9am to 9pm, Saturday from 9am to 5pm, and Sunday from 11am to 5pm.

CRAFTS

On the first floor in the Perth City Railway Station, Wellington Street, the ✪ **Crafts Council of Western Australia Craft West Gallery and Shop** (☎ 09/325 2799) is where you'll find the work of Western Australia's leading contemporary craft designers and makers. A wide variety of glass, leather, paper, silver, ceramics, textiles, and wood items is on sale. Open Tuesday to Friday from 10am to 5pm and Sunday from 2 to 5pm.

DEPARTMENT STORES

Perth's major department stores are **Aherns,** 622 Hay St. (☎ 09/323 0101; open Mon–Thurs and Sat 9am–5pm, Fri 9am–9pm, and Sun noon–5pm), and **Myer,** in the Forrest Chase center, 200 Murray St. (☎ 09/221 3444; open Mon–Thurs 9am–5:30pm, Fri 9am–9pm, Sat 9am–5pm, Sun noon–6pm).

FASHIONS

Bates Saddlery, 430 Newcastle St. (☎ 09/328 6988), is known for excellent horse saddles and also sells Akubra hats, Driza-bone oilskin coats, and R. M. Williams moleskin trousers and boots. This is the place to look for Wintec and Caprilli riding saddles and riding/stockmen's clothing. Open Monday to Wednesday and Friday from 8:30am to 5:30pm, Thursday from 8:30am to 8:30pm, and Saturday from 8:30am to 3pm. Similar outback clothing is sold at **R.M. Williams,** in the Carillion Centre (☎ 09/321 7786).

A half dozen **Purely Australian** shops are dotted around Perth, all selling quality T-shirts and sweatshirts emblazoned with Ken Done prints and other Aussie graphics. Most of Purely Australian's merchandise is made in Western Australia and sold nationwide. The shop at 731 Hay Street Mall (☎ 09/321 4697) is open Monday to Saturday from 9am to 9pm and Sunday from 10am to 5pm. Other P.A. stores are in the London Court arcade (☎ 09/325 4328), in the City Arcade (☎ 09/321 4951), in Sorrento Quay (☎ 09/246 1016), in Fremantle (☎ 09/430 4401), and in the domestic terminal at the airport (☎ 09/277 6424).

St. Quentin Avenue, Claremont, is the best area for boutiques and dress shops. The **Mid 70's Boutique,** Raine Square Shopping Plaza, 277 Murray St. (☎ 09/481 3262), stocks top Australian designs for casual, day, and evening wear. Look for shoes at **Pearse & Swan,** 706 Hay St. (☎ 09/321 6141).

FOOD

Claremont Fresh Markets, 333 Stirling Hwy., Claremont (☎ 09/383 3066), is the place to buy the fruits, vegetables, and other goodies for the picnic you'll take to Rottnest Island or the Swan Valley. Open daily from 7am to 7pm.

Going to a BYO? Pick your beverage from the extensive selection at **Liquorland**, 712 Hay St. (☎ 09/322 7487). At **Perth Central Markets**, 100 Roe St., Northbridge (☎ 09/227 5230), you can buy a variety of produce, including fruits, vegetables, fish, and meat; discounts are available for tourists. Open Monday to Saturday from 7am to 6pm.

GIFTS & SOUVENIRS

Walkabout Souvenirs, Shop 11, Forrest Place (☎ 09/325 2190), sells nicely framed dried wildflowers and other items typical of Western Australia. Open Monday to Saturday from 9am to 9pm and Sunday from 10am to 5pm. Walkabout Souvenirs also has a shop in London Court. The **Koala Bear Shop** in London Court (☎ 09/325 2297) sells wildflower seeds. Open Monday to Thursday from 8:30am to 5:30pm, Friday from 8:30am to 9pm, Saturday from 8:30am to 5pm, and Sunday from 10am to 5pm. The **National Trust Information Centre and Gift Shop,** 139 St. George's Terrace (☎ 09/321 2754), is housed in the Old Perth Boys School and offers a nice selection of Australian souvenirs and gifts. This shop is staffed by volunteers and profits are used for the upkeep of historic buildings. Information on heritage sites is available. Open Monday to Friday from 9am to 5pm. The **G.P.O. Shop** on Forrest Place is another place to look for gifts and souvenirs.

JEWELRY

Remember, when you're buying opals and other "luxury" items in Australia, overseas travelers receive a 30% discount on presentation of their airline ticket and passport.

You might like to look at **Charles Edward Jewellers,** at the corner of Piccadilly Arcade, 704 Hay Street Mall (☎ 09/321 5111). This store sells items designed and handcrafted on the premises. These include Argyle diamonds—pinks, champagne, and cognacs—from the northern part of the state. Open Monday to Wednesday and Friday from 9am to 6pm, Thursday from 9am to 9pm, and Saturday from 10am to 2pm. Diamonds from the Argyle Mine are also sold at **Kalli Brinkhaus,** 1/24 St. Quentin Ave., Claremont (☎ 09/383 3600), and at **Swan Diamonds,** Shop 4, London Court (☎ 09/325 8166).

Another spot for this state's products is **Linneys,** 37 Rokeby Rd., Subiaco (☎ 09/382 4077; fax 09/388 2835), where the jewelry is made of Broome pearls, Argyle diamonds, and Kalgoorlie gold. Several of their designers have won major international awards. Open Monday to Wednesday and Friday from 9am to 5pm, Thursday from 9am to 8pm, and Saturday from 9am to 1pm.

If it's opals you're after, try the **Opal Centre/Costello's,** Shop 1–5, St. Martin's Arcade (downstairs) off London Court (☎ 09/325 8588). It sells both loose opals and opal jewelry, and you can tour its authentic replica working opal mine complete with life-size animated miners and full sound effects. Open Monday to Friday 9am to 5:30pm and Saturday from 9am to 4pm.

8 Perth After Dark

THE PERFORMING ARTS

Visitors perusing the entertainment pages of ***The West Australian*** or ***This Week in Perth*** are usually surprised to see the number of concerts, recitals, and shows available in Perth and Fremantle. The annual **Festival of Perth,** held in February or March, provides a busy schedule of music, dance, film, and theater performances and complements the cultural activities that take place in the city throughout the year. *Variety* is the key word in describing Perth's after-dark activities, catering to a wide range of ages and interests.

THE MAJOR PERFORMANCE HALLS & THEATERS

Dolphin Theatre. At the University of Western Australia, Nedlands 6009. ☎ **09/380 2691** or 380 2440. Tickets A$10–A$30 (U.S. $8–$24).

This 198-seat theater is one of several on the University of Western Australia campus. The Dolphin is is an intimate proscenium-arch theater where the productions of the university's Dramatic Society are often staged. Tours are given on request.

His Majesty's Theatre. 825 Hay St. (at the corner of King Street). ☎ **09/322 2929.** Tickets A$20–A$50 (U.S. $16–$40).

A major venue, His Majesty's is the home of the West Australian Ballet and the West Australian Opera. The theater, which has 1,225 seats, was built in 1904 and is one of the city's most beautiful and graciously restored buildings. Displays in the stalls and dress circle foyers illustrate the theater's colorful history. Over the years many legendary figures have been associated with His Majesty's, including Dame Nellie Melba, Anna Pavlova, Percy Grainger, Yehudi Menuhin, and Dame Margot Fonteyn. State-of-the-art technology is tastefully incorporated into the Edwardian environment. Tours are given Monday to Friday from 10am to 4pm.

New Fortune Theatre. On the campus of the University of Western Australia, Nedlands. ☎ **09/380 2441** or 380 2440. Tickets A$10–A$30 (U.S. $8–$24).

The only theater in the world built to the known dimensions of a 17th-century Elizabethan theater is in the Arts Building on the University of WA campus. Named the New Fortune, it's a unique setting for Shakespearean and other theatrical performances. Without an orchestra pit, the theater seats 508. Tours are given on request.

Perth Concert Hall. 5 St. George's Terrace. ☎ **09/325 9944.** Tickets A$15–A$50 (U.S. $12–$40).

This concert hall is one of Australia's most acoustically perfect venues. It stands on a 1.2-hectare (3-acre) site next to Government House Gardens and has a wide view of the Swan River. Among the international orchestras that've graced this stage are the Chicago Symphony, the London Philharmonic, and the Israel Philharmonic. It's also used for other types of concerts.

Playhouse Theatre. 3 Pier St. ☎ **09/325 3500** or 484 1133. Tickets A$16–A$23 (U.S. $12.80–$18.40).

This is the home of the Western Australian Theatre Company, and a wide variety of productions is presented here. This includes classics, comedies, dramas, and musicals.

Regal Theatre. 474 Hay St., Subiaco. ☎ **09/381 5522.** Tickets A$20–A$40 (U.S. $16–$32).

The Regal, where some of Perth's best plays and musicals are staged, is a converted cinema built in the 1930s in art nouveau style. The theater is now listed by the National Estate as a heritage building.

Subiaco Theatre Centre. 180 Hamersley Rd., Subiaco. ☎ **09/381 2633** or 381 2403. Tickets A$17–A$25 (U.S. $13.60–$20).

This intimate 302-seat theater is the home of the State Theatre Company of Western Australia, which has presented everything from Shakespeare to premiers of new Australian plays. Acting Out is also located here.

THE CLUB & MUSIC SCENE

X-Press is a free magazine that lists live music performances. Look for it at bars, pubs, and clubs around Perth.

The majority of Perth's nightclubs are in Northbridge. The **Arcadia,** 268 Newcastle St., at Lake Street (☎ 09/328 6770), is a popular club—or "super pub" as it's sometimes called. It's open Monday to Saturday from 6pm to 4am. No cover.

Havana, 69 Lake St., at Aberdeen Street (☎ 09/328 1065), is popular with "Perth corporate workers and fashion-conscious people between 25 and 40." The admission to this large disco is A$6 (U.S. $4.80) after 9pm. It's open Wednesday to Sunday nights until the wee hours.

Outside Northbridge, you can dance the night away at **Margeaux's** in the Perth Parmelia Hilton, Mill Street (☎ 09/322 3622), open Tuesday to Saturday from 9pm to 2am. An A$6 (U.S. $4.80) admission is charged. A local beer costs about A$4 (U.S. $3.20), and an import is about A$5 (U.S. $4). Cocktails cost A$8.50 to A$10 (U.S. $6.80 to $8).

A special hotline exists for jazz fans. To find out what's on, call **Jazzline** at 09/271 2755.

THE BAR SCENE

✪ **Millstrasse Lounge and Bar.** In the Perth Parmelia Hilton, Mill Street. ☎ **09/322 3622.**

The Millstrasse is an elegant cocktail lounge/piano bar just off the Hilton's lobby. The decor includes antiques, paintings, marble tables, and handcrafted armchairs. This is a favorite watering hole of Perth's movers and shakers. If you're feeling game, try a "Flaming Lambourgini." Millstrasse opens at 6pm Monday to Saturday.

✪ **Sail & Anchor Pub Brewery.** 64 South Terrace, Fremantle. ☎ **09/335 8433.**

You can't leave Perth without sampling the state's own beer, Swan Lager, but here you may be tempted to try something more exotic. Of the 14 draft beers on tap, 4 are brewed on-site at the Sail & Anchor Brewery. Another 45 bottled beers from around the world are also offered. This lively pub, with its old-world atmosphere, is open Monday to Saturday from 11am to midnight and Sunday from noon to 9pm. Food is served in the bar and upstairs in a charming brasserie. A bottle of beer costs A$3 to A$5.50 (U.S. $2.40 to $4.40). A small glass of draft costs A$2.60 to A$3 (U.S. $2.08 to $2.40). A glass of wine will set you back A$3.50 (U.S. $2.80).

Formerly called the Freemason's Hotel, the Sail & Anchor dates from 1854. The restoration of the historic property, which left the hearty seaport atmosphere intact while modernizing the facilities, received an award from the Royal Australian Institute of Architects. Highly recommended. (See also the walking tour under "In Fremantle" in "Attractions" earlier in this chapter.)

Tradewinds Hotel. 59 Canning Hwy., East Fremantle. ☎ **09/339 8188.**

This hotel, on the south side of the Swan River between the Fremantle and Stirling Bridges, offers a large outdoor patio where you can have a drink and watch the passing parade of boats. This courtyard venue is called the Piazza Bar. Drinks are also served in Plympton or Trader Morgans cocktail bars.

MOVIES

Lumière Cinemas, in the Entertainment Centre, Wellington Street (☎ 09/321 1575), presents innovative first-release films, the annual Jump Cut film festival, meet-the-filmmaker sessions, and screenings of national and international short films. Admission is A$10 (U.S. $8).

Perth also has its share of multiscreen venues. These include **Ace Theatres,** 451 Murray St. (☎ 09/322 2711); **Greater Union,** 139 Murray St. (☎ 09/325 2844); and **Cinema City,** 580 Hay St. (☎ 09/325 2377).

A CASINO

Burswood Resort Casino, Great Eastern Highway, Victoria Park (☎ 09/362 7777), is the city's only casino. It's open 24 hours and offers the traditional gambling games in a sumptuous art deco setting. The casino has 124 gaming tables, plus restaurants, cocktail bars, and a theater cabaret. Games include blackjack, roulette, baccarat, craps, minidice, money wheel, keno, minibaccarat, two-up dice, video machines, and—that Aussie favorite—two-up.

9 Side Trips from Perth

ROTTNEST ISLAND

A popular resort island 19km (12 miles) off Fremantle's coast, "Rotto" can be reached by air or sea—only 15 minutes by light aircraft or an hour by high-speed ferry. **Rottnest Airbus** (☎ 09/478 1322) charges A$66.50 (U.S. $53.20) round trip for adults and A$36.50 (U.S. $29.20) for children for their flights, which depart from Perth Airport. The fare on the boat **Star Flyte** (☎ 09/221 5844), which departs from Perth's Barrack Street No. 4 Jetty, is A$50 (U.S. $40) for adults and A$11 (U.S. $8.80) for children. **Boat Torque** (☎ 09/221 5844) offers a package that includes transportation, a two-course lunch at the Rottnest Hotel, and a bus tour of the island for A$75 (U.S. $80) for adults and A$41 (U.S. $32.80) for children 4 to 12.

Once on the island, you can swim, snorkel, dive, cycle, windsurf, fish, or lie on one of the beaches (many of which are secluded). A golf course, tennis courts, boat rentals, and conducted tours over land and water offer more alternatives. Rottnest, 11km (7 miles) long and 5km (3 miles) wide, is almost completely undeveloped. The only vehicles are a few tour buses and some service trucks. Bicycles, which you can rent from **Rottnest Bike Hire** (☎ 09/292 5043 or 372 9722), are the most common form of transportation. Scuba divers should contact **Diving Ventures** in Perth (☎ 09/336 1664 or 430 5130). The lack of population, as well as favorable environmental conditions, makes Rottnest a haven for a variety of sea birds.

The island got its name from the little marsupials found there: Quokkas are not rats, but Dutch navigator Willem de Vlamingh didn't know that when he landed there in 1696, so he named the island Rottnest—Dutch for "rat's nest." In spite of what he perceived to be large rodents, Commodore de Vlamingh still described the low sandy isle as "a terrestrial paradise," a feeling shared by the thousands of day trippers who flock to Rottnest today.

WHERE TO STAY & DINE

The **Rottnest Island Authority** (☎ 09/372 9729) can arrange accommodation for you in over 250 houses and cottages on the island. It also offers camping facilities nestled in an area of mature eucalyptus trees planted by World War I prisoners of war. In addition, Rottnest has one upmarket lodge and a traditional Aussie hotel.

Rottnest Hotel. Rottnest Island, WA 6161. ☎ **09/292 5011.** Fax 09/292 5188. 18 rms. A$150 (U.S. $120) standard double, A$180 (U.S. $144) Bay View double. Additional person A$60 (U.S. $48) extra. Rates include breakfast. AE, BC, MC, V.

The Rottnest Hotel, built in 1864 and commonly known as the Quokka Arms, offers both accommodations and a lively beergarden. Brolly's Restaurant, overlooking Thomson Bay, serves breakfast, lunch, and dinner. The hotel recently underwent a major refurbishing.

Rottnest Lodge. Rottnest Island, WA 6161. ☎ **09/292 5161.** 62 units. A$140 (U.S.$112) deluxe double, A$190 (U.S. $152) "lakeside" double. Ask about low season rates. AE, BC, DC, MC, V.

This is "Rotto's" first first-class resort. Lodge units have a Mediterranean decor, including French windows. Lakeside quarters have a lounge area with a pot-belly stove and view of Garden Lake.

SWAN VALLEY

Some of Western Australia's best wine comes from the Swan Valley, 20km (12 miles) northeast of Perth. Originally known for their fortified wines, Swan vignerons are now producing full-bodied, or "flavorsome" (as the Aussies say), whites. Over 21 wineries in the region are open for tasting and sales, but even if you aren't interested in vineyards, this is still a good day trip because of its appealing scenery and interesting historic sights.

The village of **Guildford,** classified by the National Trust, is at the Perth end of the valley. From there, wineries, craft shops, and picturesque picnic spots fan out to the north, near such places as **Middle Swan, Henley Brook,** and **Herne Hill.** The **Western Australian Tourist Centre** in Perth has maps and information.

Boat Torque (☎ 09/221 5844) operates cruises from the Barrack Street Jetty in Perth. The Swan Valley River and Vineyard Cruise offers a trip upstream into the Swan Valley and includes a visit to historic Woodbridge Manor and premium wine tasting at either Houghton or Sandleford Vineyard. A buffet lunch, served at Mulberry Farm, is included in the cost of A$55 (U.S. $44).

Great Western Tours (☎ 09/328 4542) offers half-day coach tours of the valley on Wednesday and Saturday. If you drive yourself on this trip, bring a picnic lunch and enjoy it under the trees at Houghton Wines. Another alternative would be to visit **Jane Brook Estate Wines,** a small boutique winery that, like other area places, is generous with samples. At **Jane Brook,** Toodyay Road, Middle Swan (☎ 09/274 1432), they offer a lunch platter that serves three people (A$22/ U.S. $17.60). Proprietor David Atkinson is president of the **Swan Valley Vintners Association** and a knowledgeable source of information on this area. The Atkinsons will happily ship their product to the eastern (Australian) states for you.

Another nice spot to visit is **Evans & Tate Winery,** Swan Street, Henley Brook (☎ 09/296 4666). Most of the Swan Valley wineries are open for tasting and bottle sales seven days a week.

Just off the Great Eastern Highway and overlooking the river, the gracious two-story **Woodbridge Manor House,** Ford Street, West Midland (☎ 09/274 2432), dates from 1885 and is a National Trust property. Afternoon teas are available in the restored coach house on the grounds. Beverly Atkinson of Jane Brook Estate Wines also runs the Woodbridge Coach House Tea Room, open from noon to 4pm. The house is open Monday, Tuesday, and Thursday to Saturday from 1 to 4pm and Sunday from 11am to 5pm; closed July. Admission is A$3 (U.S. $2.40) for adults and A$1.25 (U.S. $1) for children.

WHERE TO STAY

The Vines Resort. Verdelho Drive, Ellen Brook, WA 6056. ☎ **09/297 3000,** or 1800/ 999 005 in Australia. Fax 09/297 3333. 46 town houses. A/C TV TEL. A$230 (U.S. $184) town house for two. Additional person A$50 (U.S. $40) extra. Ask about weekend and other packages. AE, BC, DC, MC, V. Free parking. The resort is 30km (19 miles) from central Perth; the management can arrange transfers from the city or airport.

This luxurious resort, amid vineyards and bushland, was designed with the sports enthusiast in mind. Each spacious unit has a full kitchen and laundry facilities. The master bedroom has a queen-size bed; other bedrooms have two single beds each. The two-bedroom units have two baths, and the three-bedrooms have $2^1/_2$ baths. Meals are served in Copley's Bistro. The facilities include pools, a gym, eight tennis courts, squash courts, a 27-hole golf course, a lawn bowling green, and a pro shop.

WHERE TO DINE

Rose and Crown Hotel. 105 Swan St., Guildford. ☎ **09/279 8444,** or 1800/090 600 in Australia. Reservations required. Main courses A$10.50–A$19.50 (U.S. $8.40–$15.60). AE, BC, DC, MC, V. Daily 7–9am and noon–2pm; Mon–Sat 6–8pm. Bus or train to Guildford; then walk two blocks east. MODERN AUSTRALIAN.

The Rose and Crown offers you an opportunity to dine in old-world surroundings. Its menu includes kangaroo, rabbit, steak, and several ethnic dishes.

AVON VALLEY

If you've ever been to the Cotswolds in England, you may have a sense of déjà vu when you travel through the Avon Valley. The lush countryside, historic homes, and B&Bs are very appealing, seemingly more British than Australian. The valley is about 100km (62 miles) outside Perth, a one-hour drive on the Great Eastern Highway. York, Northam, and Toodyay are the principal towns. Try to visit from April to late October, when the area is at its best; wildflowers bloom in September and October.

YORK

The state's oldest inland settlement dates from 1830 and is a treasure trove of interesting turn-of-the-century architecture. Many of the current population of about 800 live in old brick cottages with white wooden verandas, and all cherish the quality of life the village affords. Vegetables come right out of the garden, fresh eggs are always available, and pollution is nonexistent.

As part of the telephone changeover, all numbers with a 096 area code will be changing to 08/96xx xxxx in April 1998.

The lack of commercialization hasn't kept York's popularity from growing. In fact, it's the absence of commercialization that draws people here. Most folks stroll along Avon Terrace, the main street, stopping to browse through arts and crafts shops and have a cup of coffee or tea at one of the many colonial-style tearooms. Bicycling along country lanes is also popular.

Buildings of note in the area include the splendid York Town Hall, completed in 1911; the Railway Station; the Court House and Police Station; and the Residency Museum. A **jazz festival** is held in York every September and the community hosts a large **Music Festival** in odd-numbered years. The **"Flying 50" Speed Classic** for sports and racing cars built before 1960 also draws large crowds each October.

You can experience farming activities as they were in the 1831–35 period at **Historic Balladong Farm,** 5 Parker Rd. (☎ 096/411 279), a working farm/museum. Balladong Farm was built in 1831; the buildings have been faithfully restored. Many animals can be petted and hand-fed. Free rides on the Clydesdale horses are offered on weekend afternoons. Traditional crafts like spinning and smithing are demonstrated. The farm is open Saturday to Thursday from 10am to 5pm (opening times vary from December to February). Admission is A$5 (U.S. $4) for adults and A$3 (U.S. $2.40) for children 3 to 14.

More than 100 antique and classic cars are on display at the **York Motor Museum,** 116 Avon Terrace (☎ 096/411 288), the town's biggest attraction. Established in 1979, the York Motor Museum is now recognized as the finest collection of veteran, vintage, classic, and racing cars in Australia. The collection presents the evolution of motor transport with prime examples of the finest-quality workmanship from each era. These range from an 1894 Peugeot to the racecar driven by 1980 Grand Prix world champion Alan Jones. Hours are daily from 9am to 5pm; closed Christmas. Admission is A$6 (U.S. $4.80) for adults and A$2 (U.S. $1.60) for children. Daily buses to York depart from East Perth Terminal; bookings necessary.

WHERE TO STAY

If you go to York for the day and decide to stay overnight, you won't be the first to make this on-the-spot decision. The community's charm has had a similar effect on others. Bed-and-breakfast is offered in several private homes (about A$30 to A$50/U.S. $24 to $40 per person). Contact the **York Tourist Bureau,** 105 Avon Terrace, York, WA 6302 (☎ 096/411 301), open daily from 9am to 5pm (closed Christmas); they'll endeavor to find you a room in a cozy B&B and also have a list of farms that accept guests.

The Imperial Inn. 83 Avon Terrace, York, WA 6302. ☎ **096/411 010.** 16 rms (4 with bath). A$60 (U.S. $48) double without bath, A$70–A$75 (U.S. $56–$60) double with bath. BC, MC. Free parking.

The Imperial, across from the Town Hall, was built more than 100 years ago and is rich in old-world charm. The accommodations are modest but adequate. The four rooms in the converted stables have their own baths, as well as tea- and coffee-making facilities. The inn's restaurant is BYO. The historic structure's veranda was lost in a 1968 earthquake.

Settler's House. 125 Avon Terrace, York, WA 6302. ☎ **096/411 096.** 20 rms. A/C. A$73–A$104 (U.S. $58.40–$83.20) double. Additional person A$12 (U.S. $9.60) extra. AE, BC, DC, MC, V. Free parking.

If you'd like to spend the night at an inn, I suggest Settler's House, which has the quaint decor you'd expect from a property built in 1840. All the rooms face a brick courtyard where flower carts, old-fashioned streetlamps, and a wisteria-covered trellis create a colonial feel. The quarters are called after original area settlers, and each contains photos and information on the person after which it's named. Four-poster and canopied beds supply atmosphere, while modern baths provide convenience.

Even if you don't spend the night, drop in and have a meal in the restaurant, which was at one time a Cobb & Co. coaching station. If you're hungry and hurried, grab a bite in the country-style tearoom with its pot-bellied stove. Only à la carte dinners are served in the restaurant; the tearoom is open daily from 10am to 4:30pm.

IRISHTOWN & NORTHAM

As long as you're in the Avon Valley, travel north to Irishtown and nearby **Buckland,** "the state's most stately home." Built in 1874 and set in magnificent landscaped gardens, the recently restored Buckland (☎ 096/221 130) contains a priceless collection of antique furniture, silver, and paintings.

Buckland is the home of Tony and Penny Motion, a friendly, down-to-earth couple who offer bed-and-breakfast in their wonderful mansion. Rates, including a full breakfast, are A$140 (U.S. $112) double.

Nearby in Northam, light lunches and dinners are served in another beautifully restored mansion. **Byfield House,** 30 Gordon St. (☎ 096/223 380), is open Wednesday to Friday from noon to 2pm and Wednesday to Saturday from 6:30pm. This late Victorian (1898) is classified by the National Trust of Australia. BYO.

THE PINNACLES

In the **Nambung National Park,** 260km (162 miles) north of Perth, fossilized remains of an ancient forest stretch eerily across the desert landscape. They're best approached by four-wheel-drive with an experienced driver. If this day-trip destination appeals to you, contact **Travelabout,** 88 Guthrie St., Osborne Park, WA 6017 (☎ 09/244-1200; fax 09/445-2284). Their Pinnacles day tour departs daily at 8am, returning about 6:30pm. The cost is about A$85 (U.S. $68) for adults and A$60 (U.S. $48) for kids. A picnic lunch is included. In spite of the Pinnacles being the destination, the highlight of the day for many is the return trip along the beach, where there are incredible sand dunes as far as the eye can see.

13

Western Australia

Rugged landscapes, delicate wildflowers, and vast distances are all part of Western Australia. The nation's biggest state covers about one-third of the continent and includes goldfields, ghost towns, majestic karri forests, a seemingly endless desert, booming mining towns, and dramatic coastal scenery. The distance from the state's northern edge to its southern side is the same as from Oslo to Madrid. Much of this land is sparsely populated: Perth houses a million of Western Australia's 1.4 million population, leaving precious few inhabitants for the remaining area, the equivalent of Texas, Japan, New Zealand, and Great Britain combined. Because of the state's size and areas of harsh terrain, travel here is usually limited to three or four popular regions.

One of the prettiest places is the Southwest, where wildflowers bloom in spring, wineries produce some of the country's best vintages, and apple orchards, small farms, and B&Bs create a picture reminiscent of the English countryside. The south coast is known for rugged cliffs and spectacular beaches on which the Southern Ocean pounds continuously. Albany and Esperance are the best spots for witnessing this awesome action.

Kalgoorlie and Coolgardie are the main centers in the goldfields region, which can be reached from Perth by car in six hours or by train (the *Prospector*) in eight. In the 1890s, Kalgoorlie's Golden Mile was the richest square mile of gold-bearing earth in the world; gold and nickel are still mined there. Coolgardie is an interesting ghost town. Many passengers disembark from the *Indian Pacific* train en route between Perth and Adelaide to take a quick bus tour of Kalgoorlie. East of the region, the train crosses the Nullarbor Plain on the longest stretch of straight track in the world.

Kalbarri National Park and friendly wild dolphins are the main attractions in Western Australia's Midwest region. Farther north, the Pilbara is mining country where company towns like Tom Price, Paraburdoo, and Newman exist solely because of the vast quantities of iron ore found in the Hamersley and Ophthalmia ranges. Dampier and Port Hedland are mining ports from which the iron ore is shipped. Ningaloo Reef, Australia's closest fringing reef, is 1,081km (670 miles) north of Perth between Exmouth and Coral Bay. The Ningaloo Marine Park is popular with snorkelers and scuba divers.

What's Special About Western Australia

Beaches

- Yallingup and Prevelly Park in the southwest corner of the state—beautiful beaches with wild surf.
- The long expanse of sand right in front of Nanga Station in the Midwest region.

Natural Spectacles

- The coastal scenery around Albany.
- The rugged landscape of the Kimberley region.
- Wildflowers in profusion in various areas during September and October.

Top Attraction

- Monkey Mia, in the Midwest, where you can pet wild dolphins.

Great Towns

- Margaret River, the center of an area known for excellent wineries, beautiful beaches, and pretty rural countryside.

Some of the most dramatic scenery in Australia is found in the rugged Kimberley region in the far north of the state. From the pearling port of Broome, 2,230km (1,383 miles) north of Perth, to the Northern Territory border, the area boasts beautiful cliffs, gorges, and plains. Even though the highway to the Kimberley is now paved, this is a remote and rough area in which to travel.

EXPLORING THE STATE

The **Western Australian Tourism Commission** offices overseas and **Western Australian Tourist Centres** within Australia are the best sources of travel information. They offer several helpful booklets, including "Pubstay Holidays," "Farm & Station Holiday Experience," "Country Style," and "Wildflower Discovery." Anyone interested in Western Australia's wildflowers will want to peruse the January 1995 *National Geographic.*

Ansett WA, Skywest Airlines, and intercity coaches provide transport to the major centers in the state. Westrail provides both train and coach service. If you drive, you may find it helpful to know that the green-and-gold route markers indicate the national highways linking capital cities. The black-on-white signs identify Rte. 1, the highway that completely circles the country. The blue-and-white signs indicate the state routes, and the brown signs denote tourist drives. Consult the **Royal Automobile Club of Western Australia** in Perth (☎ 09/421 4444) before setting out across this vast state.

Home-Away of W.A., 40 Union Rd., Carmel, WA 6076 (☎ 09/293 5347), can arrange homestays throughout Western Australia. They provide airport pickup from Perth.

1 Margaret River & the Southwest

280km (174 miles) S of Perth

Often called "Australia's prettiest corner," the area between Busselton and Augusta is renowned for its gentle countryside, cozy accommodations, and outstanding wineries. Margaret River (pop. 3,000) is the focal point, but the craft shops, beaches, vineyards, caves, and picturesque scenery that make the Southwest a favorite

Western Australia

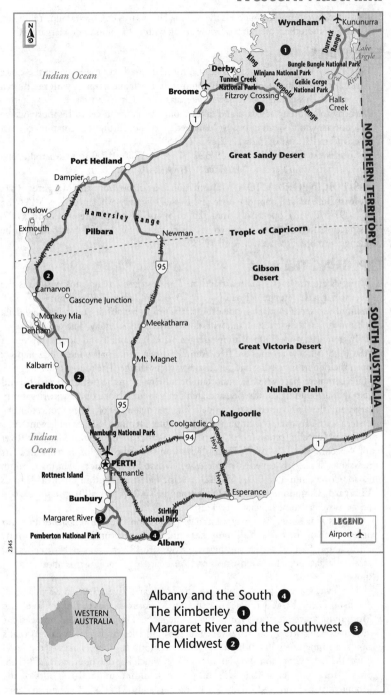

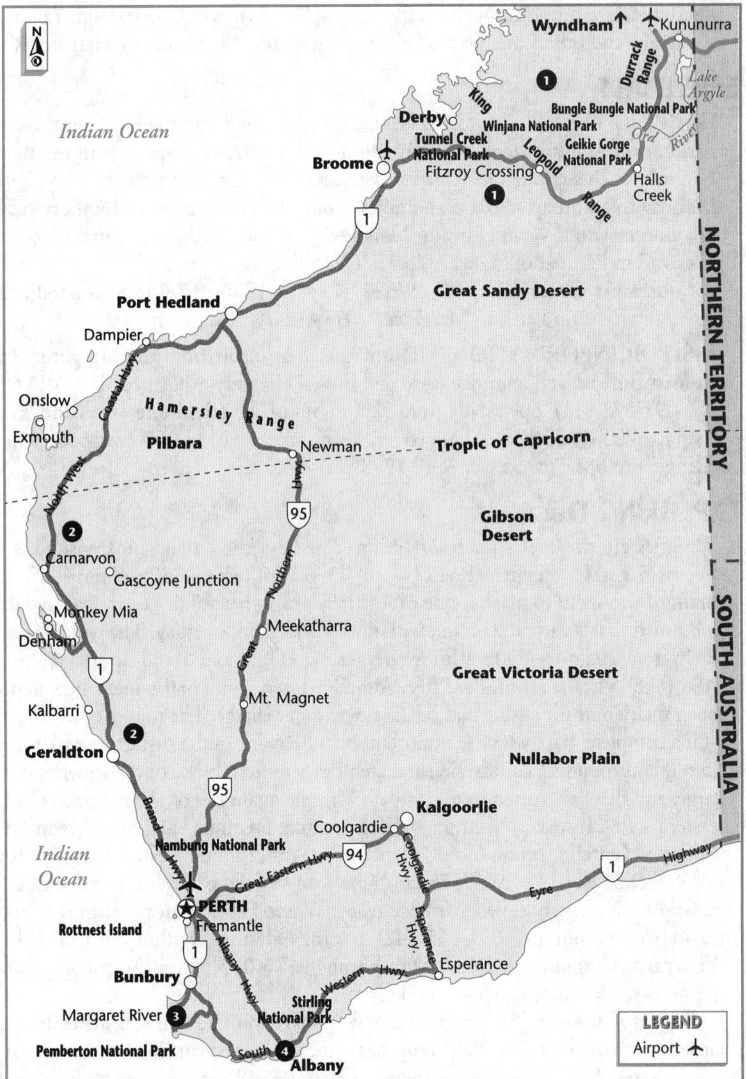

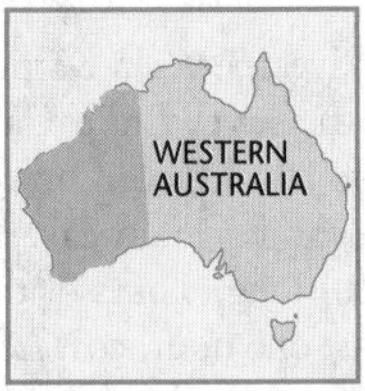

Albany and the South 4
The Kimberley 1
Margaret River and the Southwest 3
The Midwest 2

destination are spread throughout the region. The villages of Cowaramup, Yallingup, Karridale, and others mentioned below are all within 45 minutes of Margaret River.

ESSENTIALS

GETTING THERE Motorists headed for Margaret River follow either the Coast Road or the Southwestern Highway south from Perth and connect with the Bussell Highway at Busselton. The *Australind* departs Perth City (Central) Railway Station Monday to Saturday at 10am and takes about two hours to get to Bunbury, where it connects with a Westrail bus to Margaret River. For further information, contact **Westrail** in Perth at 09/326 2222 or 326 2159.

Southwest Coachlines (☎ 09/322 5173, or 1800/017 033 in Australia) has direct service from Perth to Margaret River (A$24/U.S. $19.20).

VISITOR INFORMATION Information is available from the **Margaret River Tourist Bureau,** at Tunbridge Road and Bussell Highway, Margaret River, WA 6285 (☎ 097/572 911), open daily from 9am to 5pm. The **telephone area code** is 097. As part of the telephone changeover, all numbers with a 097 area code will be changing to 08/97xx xxxx in April 1998.

EXPLORING THE AREA

Wineries are this area's main attraction. The best known and most visited is the **Leeuwin Estate,** Stephens Road (☎ 097/576 253), where A$7 million (U.S. $5.6 million) was spent to make it one of Australia's most beautiful. Lunch is served daily in Leeuwin's à la carte restaurant, with dinner added on Saturday. The winery is open daily from 10am to 4:30pm; tours are given at 11am and 1 and 3pm. The tour is A$6 (U.S. $4.80); tastings are free. Another dozen and a half winemakers happily open their doors for tasting and cellar sales without charge. The tourist office will give you a complete map, which is important because many of the rustic properties blend into the surrounding countryside and aren't easy to find. None of the wineries is very large, and there's no attempt to compete with the quantities of wine produced in the eastern states. Instead, the emphasis is on creating premium-quality table wines.

Cape Mentelle (pronounced "Men-*tell*"), 3km (2 miles) west of Margaret River off Wallcliffe Road (☎ 097/573 266), has won coveted prizes for its red wines. (Its newsletter is cleverly called *Mentelle Notes.*) **Vasse Felix Winery,** Harmans South Road, Cowaramup (☎ 097/555 242), has the oldest vineyard in the area. **Happ's Vineyard,** Commonage Road, Dunsborough (☎ 097/553 300), produces good ports, as well as some delicious dry reds.

Besides wine tasting, you may want to visit the region's **beautiful beaches** and **tour at least one of the caves. Yallingup** has some of the best surf in the state. **Prevelly Park,** about 8km (5 miles) southwest of Margaret River, can get 18-foot waves, creating a challenge for windsurfers and surfboarders. Gracetown is another good spot.

The **Jewel Cave,** 37km (23 miles) south of Margaret River, between Karridale and Augusta, is the best in the area, although **Mammoth Cave, Lake Cave,** and **Moondyne Cave** are also open to the public daily. The Jewel Cave features some unusually long straw stalactites, an underground lake, and a main cavern that's almost 100 meters (330 ft.) high and 91 meters (300 ft.) long. Tours of the Jewel Cave, the Lake Cave, and the Mammoth Cave, which last one hour, cost A$8 (U.S. $6.40) for adults and A$3 (U.S. $2.40) for children under 14. Tours of the Moondyne Cave cost A$25 (U.S. $20) for adults and A$15 (U.S. $12) for students. The minimum age for Moondyne Cave is 12. For information about cave tours, call 097/572 911.

Whatever you do, don't miss the spectacular **Boranup Forest,** starting just south of the Lake Cave. Plan to drive slowly through this patch of wonderland and perhaps even have a picnic under one of the big karri trees. In spring (September and October), the Margaret River region has one of the loveliest wildflower displays in the state.

Two churches deserve your attention: **St. Thomas More Catholic Church,** Mitchell Street, Margaret River, is built of rammed earth and local timbers and has beautiful leadlight and stained-glass windows. The other religious structure is the little whitewashed **Greek Chapel** at Prevelly Park built in honor of the Australian, New Zealand, British, and Greek soldiers who lost their lives in Greece in World War II.

SHOPPING

The Margaret River region abounds in craft shops. The better ones include **Cowaramup Pottery,** Bussell Highway, Cowaramup (☎ 097/555 467), where they do glassblowing as well as stoneware, and **Happ's Pottery,** Commonage Road, Dunsborough (☎ 097/553 300), part of the winery of the same name. At Happ's, potters work with clay dug right there on the property and you're welcome to watch. The complex's mud-brick buildings are also interesting, and the gardens are pretty. Open daily from 10am to 5pm.

Rivendell Gardens, Wildwood Road (at the corner of Commonage Road), Yallingup (☎ 097/552 090), is the place to head if you want to buy homemade jams and preserves, herbs, or flowers or pick your own berries in season. It's open daily from 10am to 5pm, and the staff serve lunches and teas and wine and welcome you to stroll around the gallery and through the cottage and herb garden. Pete and Lu Standish named their farm after Tolkien's haven for weary travelers in *Lord of the Rings*—"a homely house east of the sea in the high pass overlooking the misty mountains . . . merely to be there was a cure."

WHERE TO STAY

IN MARGARET RIVER

Gilgara Homestead. At the corner of Caves and Carter Roads, Margaret River, WA 6285. ☎ **097/572 705.** Fax 097/573 259. 6 rms. A$130–A$150 (U.S. $104–$120) double. Ask about lower midweek rates. Rate includes breakfast. Children under 15 not accepted. BC, MC, V.

Gilgara is a replica 1870s homestead, with a classic tin roof and encircling veranda, which offers cozy guesthouse accommodations for up to 14. The house is set on a 23-acre property that's 6km (4 miles) from Margaret River. Log fires, ceiling fans, and antiques help to establish the old-world ambience. Host Pamela Kimmel creates a welcoming atmosphere.

IN COWARAMUP

Quality Captain Freycinet Inn. Bussell Highway and Tunbridge Street, Margaret River, WA 6285. ☎ **097/572 033,** or 1800/090 600 in Australia. 62 rms. TV TEL. A$98–A$118 (U.S. $78.40–$94.40) double. Additional person A$15 (U.S. $12) extra. AE, BC, DC, MC, V.

All the rooms here have the standard amenities, plus toasters. The baths have showers only. A licensed restaurant, laundry facilities, and a pool are on the premises, as are facilities for the handicapped.

IN YALLINGUP

Caves House Hotel. Caves Road, Yallingup, WA 6282. ☎ **097/552 131.** Fax 097/552 041. 43 rms (21 with bath). TV. A$95 (U.S. $76) double without bath, A$105 (U.S. $84) double with bath; A$150–A$175 (U.S. $120–$140) suite. BC, MC, V. Train to Bunbury, then bus; or bus direct.

This 1901 hotel in Yallingup, 45km (27 miles) north of Margaret River and 300km (186 miles) south of Perth, was almost totally rebuilt after a disastrous fire in 1930. The two-story red-brick property has an appealing old-fashioned decor and is just a kilometer from one of the best beaches in the state. Only a patch of very pretty garden separates Caves House from the water's edge. Many of the rooms have ocean views and all have coffee- and tea-making facilities, ceiling fans, and electric blankets. Most have televisions. Guests are welcome to use the tennis courts or play table tennis, croquet, or pool.

WHERE TO DINE

Above I've mentioned several dining options—the Leeuwin Estate Winery, Rivendell Gardens, and places to stay with lovely on-site restaurants. Here are two more ideas:

Arumvale Siding Teahouse. Caves Road, Karridale. ☎ **097/586 745.** Reservations not required. Light lunches A$2–A$10 (U.S. $1.60–$8). No credit cards. Wed–Sun 10am–5pm (daily during school holidays). TEA/LIGHT LUNCHES.

This is a delightful place for afternoon teas and light lunches. The drive to this picturesque eatery takes you about 30km (19 miles) south of the Margaret River township through a patch of forest that's fairy-tale beautiful. Seating is provided indoors or outside in the shade of karri and peppermint trees. The menu includes Devonshire teas, sandwiches, cakes, soups, quiches, and daily specials like lasagne or vegetarian casseroles.

Margaret River Marron Farm Cafe. Wickham Road, just south of Margaret River. ☎ **097/576 279.** Reservations not required. Main courses A$10–A$22 (U.S. $8–$17.60). No credit cards. Daily 10am–4pm. MARRON & TROUT/SNACKS.

At the Margaret River Marron Farm, 11km (7 miles) south of Margaret River, you can dine on marron, which are freshwater crustaceans. They also serve trout, mussels, and homemade soups. Enjoy the facilities on the property, which include trout fishing, wine and dressing tastings, farm tour, a children's playground, and spring-fed swimming hole.

2 Albany & the South

402km (249 miles) SE of Perth

In 1826 a military post was established on the southwest coast of Australia in order to secure England's position in this part of the world. (There were rumors that the French were thinking of launching a colonizing effort.) From that primitive settlement, inhabited by 45 men, grew Western Australia's first town. Because of its excellent natural harbor, Albany (pop. 26,500) has always been an important port and now, because of its age, it's also an important reservoir of historic buildings.

ESSENTIALS

GETTING THERE Using the most direct route, the Albany Highway, the road trip from Perth takes about 4½ hours. Skywest Airlines has daily flights from Perth for about A$148 (U.S. $118.40). Westrail offers coach service from Perth for A$35.10 (U.S. $28.08).

VISITOR INFORMATION Information is available at the **Albany Tourist Bureau,** Old Railway Station, Proudlove Parade, Albany, WA 6330 (☎ 098/411 088), open Monday to Friday from 8:30am to 5:30pm and Saturday and Sunday from 9am to 5pm. The **telephone area code** is 098. As part of the telephone changeover, all numbers with a 098 area code will be changing to 08/98xx xxxx in April 1998.

GETTING AROUND **Escape Tours** (☎ 098/412 865) operate Wednesday to Sunday year-round. Half-day trips cost A$28 (U.S. $22.40) for adults and A$20 (U.S. $16) for children 3 to 11. Full-day trips cost A$55 (U.S. $44) for adults and A$40 (U.S. $32) for children; the full-day price includes a picnic lunch. Contact the Albany Tourist Bureau at 098/411 088 or 417 000 to make reservations.

Taxis (☎ 098/444 444 or 098/417 000) are also available for sightseeing or other transportation. If you want to rent a car, try **Albany Car Rental** at 098/417 077.

SEEING THE CITY & ENVIRONS

IN OR NEAR ALBANY

The main thoroughfare, **York Street,** slopes down to the sea and is the site of many fine Victorian buildings, like the **Headmaster's House** (1880), **Albany Town Hall** (1886), and **St. John's Anglican Church** (1848).

Not far away, you can follow the steep winding road to the top of **Mount Clarence** for a good view. The **Light Horse Memorial statue** near the top is a replica of the one erected in Suez in 1932 in honor of Australian soldiers. It was badly damaged during the Suez crisis and the granite blocks were shipped back to Australia; bullet marks are still visible on them. **Mount Melville** also has a lookout and a historic military fort has been reconstructed on the slopes of **Mount Adelaide,** another viewpoint.

The most significant historic site is the **Old Farm Strawberry Hill,** 172–174 Middleton Rd. (☎ 098/413 735), the home of Capt. Richard Spencer, Albany's governor-resident in 1833. The homestead, modeled on 18th-century English estates, has period-style furnishings and pretty gardens. The Old Farm is open daily from 10am to 5pm; closed Good Friday, Christmas, and June. Light lunches and Devonshire teas are served in a cottage on the grounds (A$3.50/U.S. $2.80). Admission is A$3 (U.S. $2.40) for adults and A$2 (U.S. $1.60) for children.

Some 20km (12 miles) from town, the rocky cliffs along the ocean create some of the most dramatic coastal scenery in Australia. A few of the best viewing spots are **The Gap, Natural Bridge,** and **The Blowholes.** The holes, you'll discover, are a bit of a walk from the parking lot and blow only in heavy seas, but the area is so pretty you won't be disappointed. However, be careful because the cliffs are slippery and the winds are strong. As you might guess, Natural Bridge is a huge chunk of granite that has been eroded into the shape of a bridge, and the Gap is a steep crevasse between two cliffs.

Nearby, tours are conducted through a former whaling station that has been converted into an impressive museum. The fate of the historic property (whaling was a major industry from the 1840s to 1978) in Frenchman's Bay, 21km (13 miles) from central Albany, hung in limbo till the Jaycees took it over in 1980. They did a great job and put together the **Whaleworld** museum, tracing the history of whaling in Albany and allowing you to examine a boat used for chasing whales. Relics and old lithographs shed light on the development of whaling from the days of "iron men and wooden ships." Guided tours led by former employees (ours was a pilot who looked for whales from the air) take groups over the premises. There's also a souvenir shop and a pleasant eatery, the Whalers Gallery Restaurant. Whaleworld (☎ 098/444 021) is open daily from 9am to 5pm, with guided tours on the hour from 10am to 4pm. Admission is A$5 (U.S. $4) for adults and A$2 (U.S. $1.60) for children.

AROUND THE SOUTHERN REGION

Albany is the focal point of Western Australia's most popular holiday region. The area offers a look at tall trees, magnificent coastal scenery, and beautiful historic buildings. Leaving Perth, most people head down the South Western Highway to **Manjimup** and **Pemberton.** These towns, just over 300km (186 miles) southeast of the capital, are in the heart of tall-timber country. You'll find forests of towering jarrah, karri, tuart, tingle, wandoo, marri, and blackbutt throughout the region. Karri and jarrah, both superb hardwoods, predominate. About 3km (2 miles) from Pemberton, the world's highest fire lookout is built in the **Gloucester Tree,** a giant karri named following a visit by the duke of Gloucester. You're welcome to climb the 153 rungs to the top, where a lookout platform is perched 61 meters (201 ft.) aboveground. You may also want to visit the **local trout hatchery** and drive the **Rainbow Trail,** a scenic route through splendid forest. The **Pemberton Tourist Centre,** Brockman Street, Pemberton, WA 6260 (☎ 097/761 133), is open daily from 9am to 5pm to answer questions and make sure you have good area maps.

Highway 1 is called the South Western Highway until it reaches the coast, where it's, not surprisingly, labeled the South Coast Highway. Along this road, **Walpole** and **Denmark** are a pair of attractive towns offering seaside scenery and good fishing opportunities.

Two national parks north of Albany, **Stirling Range** and **Porongurup,** have fantastic springtime (September and October) displays of wildflowers. March and April are the other optimum months for visiting this southern region of Western Australia.

SHOPPING

The **Nyoongah Art Shop,** on Peel Place (☎ 098/421 330), sells ceramics, paintings, spears, boomerangs, and other artifacts crafted by Aborigines. Ask to see the work of artist Lance Chadd (Tjyllyungoo).

Amity Crafts, Stirling Terrace West (☎ 098/411 766), has an excellent selection of homespun wool sweaters (called "jumpers" in Oz), wooden pieces, pottery, scrimshaw, hand-blown glass, and leatherwork, and they're conveniently open daily from 10am to 5pm. If you're traveling with someone who doesn't like to shop, **Alkoomi Wines** is next door, and they welcome tasters.

WHERE TO STAY

Albany Dog Rock Motel. 303 Middleton Rd., Albany, WA 6330. ☎ **098/414 422,** or 1800/017 024 in Australia. Fax 098/421 027. 81 rms and suites. TV TEL. A$70 (U.S. $56) double; A$82–A$94 (U.S. $65.60–$75.20) suite. AE, BC, DC, MC, V. Walk 300 meters (325 yd.) down Middleton Road from the top end of York Street.

The Dog Rock is Albany's largest and best-appointed motel. The rooms have all the modern amenities you might expect; some have bathtubs and air conditioning. There's a nice dining room on the premises, and room service is available during limited hours. The centrally located motel gets its name from a nearby granite boulder that resembles the head of a bloodhound.

Frederickstown Motor Lodge. 41 Fredericks St., Albany, WA 6330. ☎ **098/411 600.** Fax 098/418 630. 34 rms. A/C TV TEL. A$70–A$82 (U.S. $56–$65.60) double. AE, BC, DC, MC, V.

This motor lodge has units with showers, coffee- and tea-making facilities, and refrigerators. It's situated in the town center, and some rooms have ocean views. The dining room is BYO. Office hours are 7:15am to 9:30pm.

WHERE TO DINE

In addition to the restaurant at Whaleworld and the tearoom the Old Farm Strawberry Hill, you may enjoy this casual city-center eatery:

✪ **Poppies Coffee Shop.** In the Mews Arcade on Lower York Street. ☎ **098/417 595.** Reservations not required. Lunch under A$6 (U.S. $4.80). No credit cards. Mon–Fri 9am–4:30pm, Sat 9am–noon. LUNCH/TEA.

This is my favorite place for a light meal or tea. The decor is light and bright and the service friendly. You might enjoy quiche and salad, a filled croissant, or pâté with salad and toast for lunch. Bob and Dianne Morache also serve cappuccino, a wonderful Black Forest cake, and homemade soup—among other things. It isn't hard to understand why this little place is popular with the locals, who gather here to chat over a "cuppa."

3 The Midwest

While the southwest and the south of Western Australia are established tourist areas, the Midwest region has caught the attention of travelers only in recent years. The region stretches from the shores of the Indian Ocean to the Great Victorian Desert and from Moora, 145km (90 miles) north of Perth, almost to Carnarvon. It's a sunny area, and while winter weather happily allows for tanning, summers can be just plain hot.

Geraldton (pop. 20,895) is the main center in this sparsely populated rural area and serves as a commercial base for surrounding agricultural endeavors, including grain, wool, fat lambs, pigs, and beef cattle. **Kalbarri,** an emerging resort community north of Geraldton, and **Monkey Mia,** where friendly wild dolphins allow humans to pet them, are the most interesting spots for visitors.

If you travel in the Midwest, you may notice the oceanfront strip is referred to as the Batavia Coast, named after the Dutch ship that went aground on the offshore Abrolhos Islands in 1629. Most of the crew survived, but a subsequent mutiny resulted in the slaughter of 125 men, women, and children. Two men whose lives were spared were marooned on the mainland, thus becoming Australia's first European settlers. Their presence accounts for the number of local Aborigines with blond hair and blue eyes.

KALBARRI

661km (410 miles) N of Perth

The tiny seaside community of Kalbarri (pop. 820) has been discovered of late by those seeking sun, sea, scenery, and sports. The town is ideally set at the mouth of the Murchison River, and swimmers, fishers, and boating enthusiasts have a choice of calm water or Indian Ocean rollers. I can think of few coastal sites in the country that are as beautiful as Kalbarri's: The Murchison winds its way slowly to the sea, and right at the river's mouth a long sandbar creates a tranquil estuary while breakers crash only a short distance away. Inland, the colorful gorges of the Murchison and a spectacular springtime display of wildflowers draw visitors to Kalbarri National Park.

ESSENTIALS

GETTING THERE The drive to Kalbarri from Perth takes seven to eight hours. The Western Australian Tourist Centre in Perth is the best source of detailed driving data. **Western Airlines** has flights directly to Kalbarri from Perth by way of Geraldton (A$167/U.S. $133.60 one way). The alternative is to fly Ansett WA, Skywest, or Western to Geraldton (A$109 to A$143/U.S. $87.20 to $114.40) and either take a local bus or rent a car for the final leg. The drive to Kalbarri from Geraldton takes about two hours.

You can also take a Westrail coach to Kalbarri from Perth (8 hr.; A$59.40/U.S. $47.52) or join an organized coach tour from Perth that includes sightseeing and accommodation.

VISITOR INFORMATION Information is provided at the **Kalbarri Visitor Centre,** Kalbarri, WA 6536 (☎ 099/371 474), open daily from 9am to 5pm. The **telephone area code** is 099. As part of the telephone changeover, all numbers with a 099 area code will be changing to 08/99xx xxxx in April 1998.

Exploring the Area

Coastal scenery and the magnificent gorges cut by the Murchison River as it wanders through **Kalbarri National Park** are the area's big attractions. Some of the canyons cut into the reddish sandstone are over 130 meters (429 ft.) deep; some are very narrow and others contain pools and streams. Be sure you don't miss the **Hawkes Head Lookout, Z-bend, the Loop,** and **Meenarra Lookout.** The park totals 1,000 square kilometers (386 sq. miles) of virgin bushland, and kangaroos, emus, and wild pigs are plentiful. The pigs are descended from domestic pigs introduced by a man named Harry Leever. Harry had plans to start a piggery at Lockwood Springs, but he let his animals loose to graze and they never came back. The southern boundary of Kalbarri National Park is a rabbit-proof fence that runs from the coast through all of Western Australia and neighboring South Australia. **Kalbarri Coachline** (☎ 099/371 104) conducts tours in the park or you can drive yourself.

South of Kalbarri, beautiful coastal cliffs have been eroded into fanciful shapes. **Madman's Gorge, Castle Cove, Grandstand Rocks,** and **Shell House** are the special spots to see.

Where to Stay & Dine

Kalbarri Palm Resort. Porter Street, Kalbarri, WA 6536. ☎ **099/372 333.** Fax 099/371 324. 50 rms. A/C TV TEL. A$78 (U.S. $62.40) double. AE, BC, DC, MC, V.

Some units at the Kalbarri Palm Resort have cooking facilities and other modern amenities. A restaurant, tennis court, and pool are on the grounds.

MONKEY MIA

24km (15 miles) E of Denham, 838km (520 miles) N of Perth

The only place I know in the world where you can play with *wild* dolphins is a place on Shark Bay between Carnarvon and Geraldton called Monkey Mia. Monkey Mia is a long way from anywhere, and I hesitate to tell you about it because there's never a guarantee that the dolphins will show up—but they almost always do.

The Shark Bay area can be unpleasantly windy during November and December and extremely hot until the end of March. The best time to visit this region is from late March to mid-October.

Essentials

GETTING THERE One option is flying to Geraldton (see "Kalbarri" above) and then renting a car for the 432km (268-mile) drive to Monkey Mia. Western Airlines operates a service from Perth to Denham; the one-way fare is A$219 (U.S. $175.20). Coach transfers are available to Monkey Mia.

Greyhound-Pioneer provides bus service from Perth to Monkey Mia on Monday, Thursday, and Saturday. The fare is A$120 (U.S. $96). The drive from Perth takes about nine hours.

If you want to join a group, several Perth companies conduct excursions. **Pinnacle Tours** (☎ 09/221 5411, or 1800/999 069 in Australia), **W.A. Coach Service**

(☎ 09/309 1680), **Westrail** (☎ 09/326 2159), and **Travelabout** (☎ 09/244 1200; fax 09/445 2284) are some. One operator, **Peter Wieland's Flightseeing Tours** (☎ 09/314 2224; fax 09/314 1926), makes it possible to visit Monkey Mia on a day trip from Perth. This option costs about A$550 (U.S. $440) and includes a scenic flight over Perth, the Pinnacles Desert, Geraldton, and Kalbarri; a visit to the dolphins; lunch; and time to swim and relax. Peter Wieland also offers air tours to other Western Australia destinations and will custom-tailor a trip to your interests.

VISITOR INFORMATION The **Shark Bay Tourist Centre,** 83 Knight Terrace, Denham, WA 6537 (☎ 099/481 253), is open daily. The **telephone area code** is 099. As part of the telephone changeover, all numbers with a 099 area code will be changing to 08/99xx xxxx in April 1998.

Enjoying the Dolphins

No one is exactly sure why the Indian Ocean bottle-nosed **dolphins** first started coming to Monkey Mia in the 1960s, but six or seven of them usually turn up every day. They swim in water only a few feet deep and enjoy being petted on their sides. They seem to be as curious about humans as we are about them. A few things annoy them, like being petted on their head and having someone touch their dorsal fin or blowhole, and the ranger on duty asks you to refrain from these actions. The dolphins are completely free to leave, and sometimes do for hours at a time, but so far they've always come back. The **Dolphin Welfare Centre** presents films and displays about these fascinating animals. According to directions prepared by the Project Jonah staff, it's bad form to return a fish given to you by a dolphin. Instead, you are to "accept it with gratitude."

Diving with Whale Sharks

The best-known dive spot on the west coast, **Ningaloo Reef** provides you an opportunity to dive with whale sharks. For details, contact the Exmouth Tourist Bureau at 099/491 176, the Exmouth Diving Centre at 099/491 201, or Ningaloo Reef Dive at 099/491 999. Exmouth is about 350km (217 miles) north of Carnarvon.

Where to Stay & Dine

Monkey Mia Dolphin Resort. Monkey Mia (P.O. Box 119, Denham, WA 6537). ☎ **099/481 320,** or 09/368 2100 in Perth. Fax 099/481 034. 36 motel units, 6 on-site vans, 18 "park homes." A$120–A$130 (U.S. $96–$104) double motel; A$25–A$50 (U.S. $20–$40) on-site van for four or six; A$80 (U.S. $64) "park home" for four; A$75 (U.S. $60) "canvas condo." Lower rates off-season (Feb–Mar). AE, BC, MC, V.

This is the place to stay if you want to be near the water and the wild dolphins that have put Monkey Mia on the map. The motel units have private toilets and showers, tea- and coffee-making facilities, and small refrigerators. There are also four- and six-berth on-site vans which have cooking facilities but shared toilets and showers. The "park homes" have the best "possie" (position), right on the beach with a "beaut" water view. These mobile homes are fully furnished and have cooking facilities, but use communal baths. The outdoor restaurant is open from 7:30am to 9pm daily.

Nanga Bay Resort Holiday Village & Caravan Park. Nanga Station, Shark Bay (c/o Post Office, Denham, WA 6537). ☎ **099/483 992.** Fax 099/483 996. 24 motel units, 3 houses, 8 cabins, 15 backpackers twin-share rooms, caravan and tent sites. A$77 (U.S. $61.60) double in motel unit; A$85 (U.S. $68) house for up to four; A$45–A$55 (U.S. $36–$44) cabin; A$18 (U.S. $14.40) per person in a bunkhouse; A$10 (U.S. $8) unpowered caravan site; A$15 (U.S. $12) powered caravan site. Lower weekly rates. BC, MC, V.

Located 50km (31 miles) southeast of Denham on Shark Bay, a 40-minute drive from Monkey Mia, Nanga Station offers the area's widest range of accommodations. The historic homestead on a half-million-acre sheep property is built of shell blocks. The station is owned by Maureen and Ted Sears, who are—and I say this with all kindness—virtual caricatures of outback Aussies. Ted's quick wit, gift of gab, and entrepreneurial talents will remind you of Crocodile Dundee. Starting in business with a chicken farm at age 16, he has worked his way up to Nanga Station, where there are 6,000 sheep. Even more amazing, he has made this remote piece of land attractive to tourists.

At present, Nanga Station offers an 80-seat BYO restaurant (the Nanga Barn), a general store (which sells liquor), a take-out food shop, 24 air-conditioned motel units, 3 large self-contained two-bedroom rental houses, a caravan park, 8 cabins with kitchens (but no baths), 15 bunkhouse rooms with communal baths and kitchens, tennis courts, a large pool, and a spa. Energetic Ted sees that everything is kept clean and tidy. Only the houses and motel rooms are supplied with bed and bath linen. It's very handy to bring a flashlight.

The property is on a beautiful beach, ideal for fishing, swimming, and sunning. During the three weeks of shearing, which start on Boxing Day (December 26), visitors who can stand the heat and flies are welcome to go out on the station and help. March, April, and May are the best months for fishing. The week after Easter, Ted and Maureen host a huge angling competition that concludes with a *hangi* dinner (a New Zealand Maori-style meal where food is cooked in a pit) and a "helluva party."

4 The Kimberley

This is Australia's "last frontier"—an area about the size of the U.S. state of California with a population of less than 15,000. A place where temperatures during "the dry" season can hit 120°F and rain during "the wet" can come at the rate of a foot a month. The Kimberley region covers the top half of Western Australia—stretching from the Northern Territory border to the Indian Ocean and from the Timor Sea to the Great Sandy Desert. The first settlers here tried to raise sheep, but the land was too barren. Today, cattle stations, each averaging over half a million acres, cover much of the land. The hardy folks who live on these outback outposts muster (round up) their livestock with helicopters, rely on the Royal Flying Doctor Service for medical care, and send their children to the School of the Air. Though in Western Australia, residents of the Kimberley identify more with the Top End of the Northern Territory than with Perth many miles to the south, and there's a grass-roots movement to change the region's clocks to Darwin time.

Until recently, the Kimberley lacked tourist facilities, and it was the rare traveler who ventured into this remote and, in some ways, inhospitable corner of the country. However, the completion of a paved road through the region in 1986 opened the door for visitors and made it possible to tour the area in some degree of comfort. The Great Northern Highway connects the two biggest towns: **Kununurra** in the East Kimberley and **Broome** in the West Kimberley. It also provides access to such beauty spots as **Windjana Gorge National Park, Geikie Gorge National Park, Tunnel Creek National Park,** and the **Bungle Bungle Range.** It's these scenic wonders and the chance to experience a real frontier that lure adventurous travelers.

Good background information on the Kimberley is contained in the January 1991 *National Geographic.*

The Kimberley Region

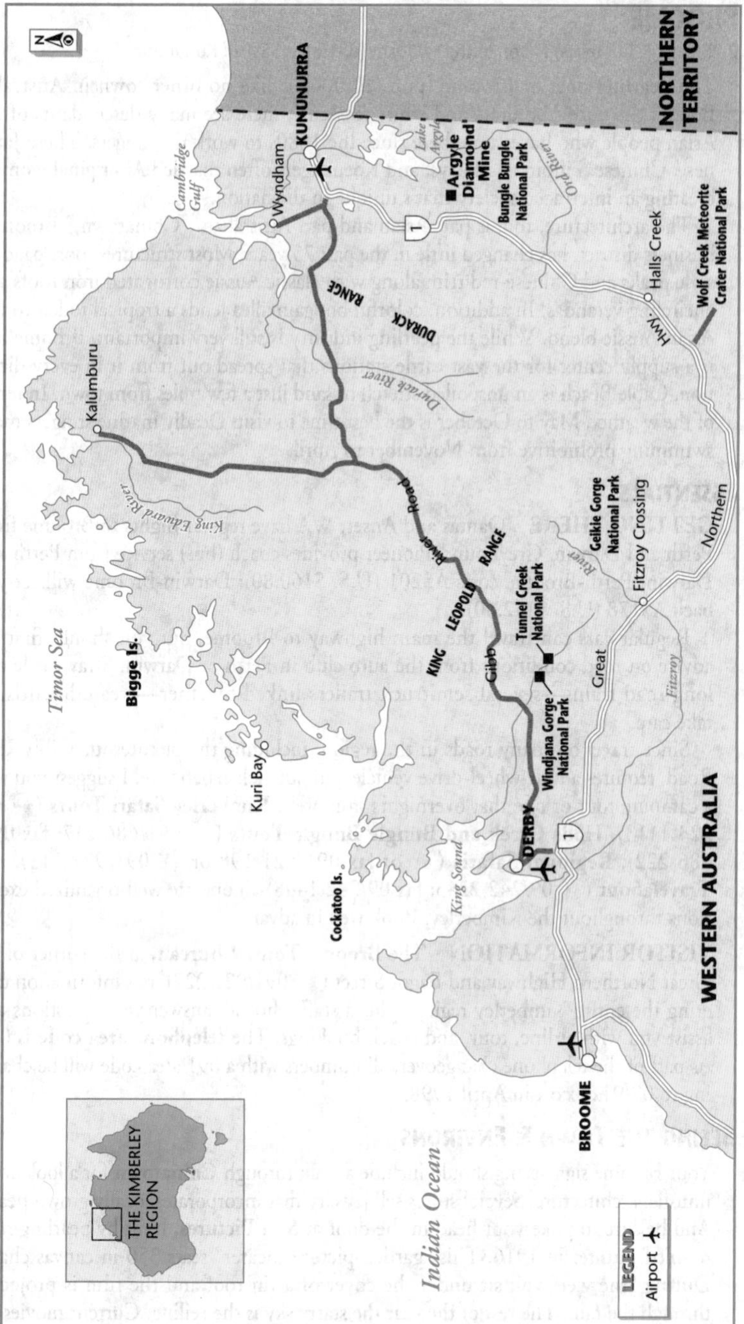

BROOME

2,250km (1,395 miles) NE of Perth, 1,050km (651 miles) SW of Kununurra

The pearling port of Broome (pop. 10,000) is like no other town in Australia. Besides the pure Aborigine and white residents, there are many descendants of the Asian people who have come here since the 1880s to work the luggers. These Japanese, Chinese, Filipinos, Malays, and Koepangers often married Aboriginal women, creating an interracial society that's unique in the nation.

The architecture, too, is part Asian and part Australian. "Chinatown," Broome's business district, has changed little in the past 75 years. Most structures sport pagoda-style peaks and Chinese-red trim along with classic Aussie corrugated iron roofs and encircling verandas. In addition, colorful bougainvillea lends a tropical touch to this Asian/Aussie blend. While the pearling industry is still very important, Broome also is a supply center for the vast cattle stations that spread out from it in every direction. Cable Beach is an unspoiled stretch of sand just a few miles from town. In terms of the weather, May to October is the best time to visit. Deadly marine stingers make swimming prohibitive from November to April.

ESSENTIALS

GETTING THERE Qantas and Ansett WA have regular flights to Broome from Perth and Darwin. Greyhound-Pioneer provides coach (bus) service from Perth and Darwin. Perth-Broome costs A$201 (U.S. $160.80); Darwin-Broome will set you back A$178 (U.S. $142.40).

Regular cars can travel the main highway to Broome, but you should first get advice on road conditions from the auto club in Perth or Darwin. Stray cattle and long road trains—several semitruck trailers linked together—create hazards, so take care.

Since travel on many roads in the region, including the picturesque Gibb River Road, requires a four-wheel-drive vehicle and outback experience, I suggest you join a camping tour or one that overnights in motels. **Kimberley Safari Tours** (☎ 09/323 1113), **Halls Creek and Bungle Bungle Tours** (☎ 091/686 217; fax 091/686 222), **Regional Safaris** (☎ or fax 091/921 198 or ☎ 091/921 113), and **Travelabout** (☎ 09/242 2243; fax 09/242 1448) all operate well-organized excursions throughout the Kimberley. Book well in advance.

VISITOR INFORMATION The **Broome Tourist Bureau,** at the corner of the Great Northern Highway and Bagot Street (☎ 091/922 222), has information covering the entire Kimberley region, plus a staff who can answer your questions and assist you with airline, tour, and coach bookings. The **telephone area code** is 091. As part of the telephone changeover, all numbers with a 091 area code will be changing to 08/91xx xxxx in April 1998.

SEEING THE TOWN & ENVIRONS

Your Broome sightseeing should include a walk through **Chinatown** for a look at the unusual architecture. Several stores sell jewelry that incorporates locally grown pearls. And be sure to poke your head in the door at **Sun Pictures,** built by pearling master Ted Hunter in 1916. This "garden picture theater" seats 350 in canvas chairs. During "the wet" you sit under the cover of a tin roof and the film is projected through the rain. The rest of the year the starry sky is the ceiling. Current movies are shown. Admission is A$9 (U.S. $7.20).

Cable Beach, 24km (15 miles) long, is another "must see," but I wouldn't go out of my way to do the "Ships of the Desert" camel ride offered there, unless they replace the extremely uncomfortable saddles that were in use the last time I tried it. It's better to walk on the beach and take pictures of the experience, which is, admittedly, picturesque with the setting sun behind them. **Surf Cat rental** from a kiosk on the beach March to November (☎ 091/935 551) costs A$16 (U.S. $12.80) per hour; **surfboards** cost A$5 (U.S. $4) per hour. The **Broome Crocodile Park** (☎ 091/921 489) is open daily from April to October. Admission is A$10 (U.S. $8) for adults and A$5 (U.S. $4) for children. You might also like to visit the **Willie Creek Pearl Farm** (☎ 091/924 918).

Local tour operators conduct excursions within the region to such places as **Cape Leveque,** where you can visit the Beagle Bay and Lombadina Aboriginal communities, and to the **Roebuck Plains Cattle Station,** where 10,000 cattle roam 300,000 hectares (750,000 acres) and visitors are exposed to a slice of outback life. There are also Hovercraft tours of **Roebuck Bay** and **fishing excursions.**

WHERE TO STAY & DINE

In or Near Broome

Cable Beach Club. Cable Beach Road, Broome, WA 6725. ☎ **091/920 400,** or 1800/095 508 in Australia. Fax 091/922 249. Reservations can be made through Flag Inns. 260 rms, 3 suites. A/C MINIBAR TV TEL. A$219–A$268 (U.S. $175.20–$214.40) double; A$311 (U.S. $248.80) one-bedroom bungalow for one to four; A$461 (U.S. $368.80) two-bedroom bungalow for one to six; A$922–A$1,383 (U.S. $738–$1,106.40) suite. Lower rates off-season (Oct–Apr). Higher rates in July. AE, BC, DC, MC, V. Free parking. Courtesy airport transfers are provided; or take a taxi (A$10/U.S. $8) from town 6km (4 miles) away.

The only property in the area located adjacent to Cable Beach, this luxurious hotel features Dutch colonial furnishings from Indonesia in the sleeping quarters and antique artifacts from Asia outdoors and in the public spaces. The attractive low-rise structures on the 10 hectares (25 acres) of landscaped grounds are built in typical Broome style, combining both Asian and Australian elements. The Cable Beach Club was built in 1988 by Lord McAlpine from Britain. This gentleman fell in love with the West Kimberley region during a visit there and has contributed significantly to its development as a tourist destination.

All guest rooms are spacious and offer ceiling fans, radios, tea- and coffee-making facilities, small refrigerators, toasters, remote-control TVs, in-house movies, and hairdryers. The bungalows also have kitchenettes and irons and ironing boards. The suites are named after Australian artists (like Sidney Nolan and Elizabeth Durack) and their original works are displayed within.

Dining/Entertainment: Meals are served in Lord Mac's Restaurant, the Club Restaurant, and the Asian Affair. Drinks are served in four bars.

Services: Limited room service, laundry, baby-sitting.

Facilities: Day-tour desk, in-house activities program (including tennis tournaments, water-volleyball games, Surf Cat regattas), free bikes for kids, two free-form pools, spa, 12 tennis courts, Children's Fun Club, diving center.

Continental Hotel. At the corner of Weld and Louis streets, Broome, WA 6725. ☎ **091/921 002,** or 1800/015 519 in Australia. Fax 091/921 715. 66 rms. A/C TV TEL. A$120 (U.S. $96) double; A$140 (U.S. $112) suite. Additional adult A$10 (U.S. $8) extra; children 3–14 A$6 (U.S. $4.80). Lower rates off-season. AE, BC, DC, MC, V. Free parking. Courtesy airport pickup.

The "Conti" is a two-story property across the road from Roebuck Bay and a 10-minute walk from Chinatown. Each modern room has tea- and coffee-making facilities, a small refrigerator, in-house movies, a ceiling fan, and a balcony. The staff is unusually friendly.

Dining/Entertainment: Pearling memorabilia makes the Lugger Bar an atmospheric place for a drink. Three other bars also serve drinks. The Weld Street Bistro is an economical self-serve eatery. There's also an à la carte dining room.

Services: Limited room service.

Facilities: Large pool, tennis court, laundry.

In Fitzroy Crossing

Fitzroy River Lodge. Great Northern Highway, Fitzroy Crossing, WA 6765. ☎ **091/915 141.** Fax 091/915 142. 38 rms, 2 suites. A/C TV TEL. A$100 (U.S. $80) double motel; A$80 (U.S. $64) double safari room. Additional person A$10 (U.S. $8) extra. BC, MC, V.

On the banks of the Fitzroy, 397km (246 miles) east of Broome, this lodge offers accommodation in four buildings, elevated above the flood level of the river, with parking below. These motel units offer coffee- and tea-making facilities, ceiling fans, small refrigerators, and baths. Safari lodges have canvas sides, solid timber floors, baths, small refrigerators, and coffee- and tea-making facilities. There's also a caravan park. On the premises are a restaurant, bar, a pool, and a nine-hole golf course. Geikie Gorge is 18km (11 miles) away, and there are daily tours.

KUNUNURRA

3,192km (1,979 miles) NE of Perth, 1,050km (651 miles) NE of Broome, 525km (326 miles) SW of Katherine (NT)

Barely 30 years old, the town of Kununurra came into being when the decision was made to impound the Ord River and use the water to irrigate the surrounding land. Known as the Ord River Project, this scheme has created hundreds of miles of fertile agricultural land. Man-made Lake Argyle, covering an area nine times as large as Sydney Harbour, is where the Ord's "wet" season flow is stored. Local farmers are still experimenting with various crops. Cotton, rice, and peanuts weren't as successful as it was hoped they would be, but mangoes, bananas, and melons do well.

While many of Kununurra's 4,500 residents came from other Australian states and overseas to try their hand in agriculture, a large number came to work in the area's two highly productive diamond mines. Since these gemstones were first discovered here in 1979, Australia has become the largest diamond-producing country in the world. The Argyle Diamond Mine, open since 1985, yields 34 million carats a year.

ESSENTIALS

GETTING THERE The Victoria Highway brings visitors from the Northern Territory, and the Great Northern Highway connects Kununurra to the West Kimberley region. Ansett WA has regular flights from Darwin and Perth. Greyhound-Pioneer and McCafferty's provide coach (bus) service. A ticket from Darwin costs A$100 (U.S. $80). A ticket from Broome to Kununurra costs A$121 (U.S. $96.80).

VISITOR INFORMATION Contact the **Kununurra Visitors Centre,** Coolibah Drive (☎ 091/681 177). The **telephone area code** is 091. As part of the telephone changeover, all numbers with a 091 area code will be changing to 08/91xx xxxx in April 1998.

EXPLORING THE AREA

Kununurra is the gateway to the beautiful **Bungle Bungle Range,** with intricately sculptured chasms and beehive-shaped sandstone domes. Alligator Airways (☎ 091/681 333) and Sling Air (☎ 091/681 259 or 681 255) offer two-hour flightseeing trips that include the Bungle Bungles, Lake Argyle, and the Argyle Diamond Mine (A$150/U.S. $120 per person). If you drive to the Bungle Bungles, you can take a Sling Air helicopter flight from there.

It's also possible to tour the **Argyle Diamond Mine** with Belray Diamond Tours (☎ 091/681 014). These tours, which include a flight over the Bungle Bungles as well as an on-site tour of the mine, operate Monday to Friday, last five hours, and cost A$265 (U.S. $212) and up per person.

Another really enjoyable experience is offered by ✪ **Triple J Tours Boat Cruises** (☎ 091/682 682). Their boats cruise **Lake Kununurra to Lake Argyle.** Along the way (via the Ord River) you see native birds, crocodiles, and lots of beautiful scenery. The knowledgeable driver/guide provides a running commentary on the flora and fauna, the creation of the lake, how the dam was built, and so forth. Trips vary from 5½ to 7 hours and cost A$70 to A$95 (U.S. $56 to $76). Children 2 to 13 are half price. Highly recommended.

Besides being scenic, the **Ord River** is one of the best places in Australia to **fish for barramundi.** If this interests you, contact the Bush Camp (☎ 091/691 214). Bruce Ellison and Dave Swansson, proprietors of this business, will make sure the wily barra doesn't escape your line. Lodging is at the Bush Camp, described below.

Where to Stay & Dine

In or Near Kununurra

El Questro Station. Gibb River Road (P.O. Box 909, Kununurra, WA 6743). ☎ or fax **091/614 320.** Various lodging options. A$640 (U.S. $512) per person per night in Homestead (including transfers, meals, open bar, and all activities except helicopter flights; minimum stay two nights; A$90 (U.S. $72) double in bush cabin at Emma Gorge; A$120 (U.S. $96) twin, A$150 (U.S. $120) triple, and A$180 (U.S. $144) quad at El Questro Bungalow; A$7.50 (U.S. $6) per person per night for campsite on the banks of the Pentecost River. AE, BC, MC, V. Questro is 120km (74 miles) southwest of Kununurra. The hosts provide transfers.

It's hard to imagine, but this working cattle station actually sprawls over more than 400,000 hectares (one million acres) of rugged outback terrain. Guests can go hiking, boating, fishing, swimming, or flightseeing; soak in a thermal pool; or learn the basics of cattle management. All this amid spectacular gorges, waterholes, and towering cliffs.

El Questro is owned by Englishman Will Burrell, a member of the family that owns Royal Dalton and Penguin Books. He bought the station in 1991 and has subsequently added the various lodging options.

Quality Inn. Duncan Highway, Kununurra, WA 6743. ☎ **091/681 455,** or 1800/090 600 in Australia. Fax 091/854 325. 60 rms. A/C MINIBAR TV TEL. A$117–A$119 (U.S. $93.60–$95.20) double. Additional person A$20 (U.S. $16) extra. AE, BC, DC, MC. Free parking.

Near the center of Kununurra, this motel offers adequate rooms with modern amenities like coffee- and tea-making facilities, small refrigerators, and radios. Other facilities include a restaurant, laundry, and pool.

In Halls Creek

Halls Creek is 359km (223 miles) southwest of Kununurra on the Great Northern Highway.

Halls Creek Kimberley Hotel. Roberta Avenue (P.O. Box 244), Halls Creek, WA 6770. ☎ **091/686 101.** Fax 091/686 071. 44 rms. A/C TV TEL. A$80–A$100 (U.S. $64–$80) double. Additional person A$10 (U.S. $8) extra. Lower rates off-season (Nov–Apr). AE, BC, DC, MC, V. Free parking.

All quarters offer coffee- and tea-making facilities and small fridges. Five bars serve drinks, and meals are available indoors and out. Try to be in Halls Creek on Sunday—barbecue night at this hotel. You can use the nice pool and spa. Scenic flights to the Bungle Bungles and the Wolfe Creek Meteorite Crater operate from Halls Creek.

14 Adelaide

One of the country's best-kept secrets, this capital of South Australia is a beautiful, well-planned city with much to offer. Wide tree-lined streets, sidewalk cafés, colonnaded colonial buildings, and grassy parks with elaborate fountains and statuary create a strong European ambience. The sunny Mediterranean climate, an old-fashioned tram rumbling down its track, and a busy public market further underscore the continental feel.

Adelaide, founded in 1836, was the only colony comprised totally of free settlers. Perhaps it's the absence of convict history that gives this city of 1.1 million its characteristic gentility. Australia's largest arts festival is held here for two weeks in even-numbered years, and the Festival Centre hosts a year-round program of cultural events. Adelaide lacks the hustle and bustle of other capitals, and this might be why it remains undiscovered by most tourists. Wine aficionados, however, have long recognized the city's status as the gateway to the country's most prolific vineyards. German refugees were among the area's first settlers, and they lost no time planting grapes in the ideal climates of the Barossa Valley, Clare Valley, and Southern Vales. Today, two-thirds of Australia's wine comes from this state, much of it within a short drive of Adelaide.

In terms of the weather, September to November and March and April are the best months to visit the Festival City.

1 Orientation

ARRIVING

BY PLANE Adelaide is served by several international and domestic airlines, including British Airways, Qantas, Singapore Airlines, Malaysia Airlines, Ansett, and Kendell Airlines. Fares from Alice Springs are A$225 to A$270 (U.S. $180 to $216); from Melbourne, fares range from A$145 to A$180 (U.S. $116 to $144). The fare from Sydney to Adelaide is A$208 (U.S. $166.40).

The major car-rental companies (Avis, Budget, Hertz, and Thrifty) have desks or contact phones in both the international and domestic terminals. Visitor information is available and several hotels provide phones from which you can call for reservations free of charge. On the domestic side are a post office and a bank; in the international area you can buy stamps from a machine. Both terminals

What's Special About Adelaide

Great Places to Visit

- The Barossa Valley, for wine tasting.
- The Adelaide Hills, for picturesque countryside and interesting villages.

Festivals

- Adelaide Festival of Arts, the country's best, held in late February and early March of even-numbered years.
- Barossa Valley Vintage Festival.

Museums

- The Migration Museum, a must for anyone interested in Australia's immigrant history.
- South Australian Maritime Museum, especially about ships and the sea.

Unusual Transportation

- The historic Glenelg Tram, making frequent trips between Victoria Square and the seaside suburb of Glenelg.
- The Adelaide O-Bahn, a state-of-the-art means of moving.

have showers, currency-exchange desks, shops, and eateries. No baggage lockers are available.

Transit Regency (☎ 08/381 5311) provides service to major Adelaide hotels from the international and domestic terminals at the airport and from the interstate railway station in the suburb of Keswick. The buses run daily approximately every half an hour from 7am to 9pm. The fare into the city from the airport is A$4 (U.S. $3.20); from the train depot, the fare is A$2.50 (U.S. $2). A taxi to town from the airport costs about A$12 (U.S. $9.60).

BY TRAIN The *Indian Pacific* will transport you from Perth or Sydney; the *Ghan* will deliver you from Alice Springs; and the *Overland* provides daily service from Melbourne. Actually, I should say "nightly" because the train departs Melbourne in the evening and takes 12 hours to get to Adelaide. *Overland* fares are A$170 (U.S. $136) for a first-class berth, A$104 (U.S. $83.20) for first-class sitting, and A$50 (U.S. $40) for economy sitting. Call **Australian National Railways** in Adelaide at 08/217 4086 if you have questions about interstate train travel; for reservations, call 08/231 7699.

BY BUS **Greyhound-Pioneer's** (☎ 13 20 30) express bus takes 10 hours to cross the 800km (496 miles) from Melbourne (A$55/U.S. $44). **McCafferty's** also provides service on this route. Sydney is 1,540km (955 miles) and 22 hours away by way of the Hume and Stuart Highways. That ticket costs A$97 (U.S. $77.60). Intercity coaches terminate at the **Adelaide Central Bus Terminal,** 105–111 Franklin St., near Morphett Street in the city center (☎ 08/415 5533).

VISITOR INFORMATION

Take your questions to the friendly folks at the **Tourism South Australia Travel Centre,** in the AMP Building, 1 King William St., Adelaide, SA 5000 (☎ 08/212 1505). This office is open Monday and Wednesday to Friday from 8:45am to 5pm, Tuesday from 9am to 5pm, and Saturday, Sunday, and public holidays from 9am to 2pm (for information only). Its staff supply excellent free maps and guides of Adelaide and environs and can make reservations on your behalf. The **Adelaide City**

Council Information Office, 5 Pirie St. (☎ 08/203 7442), has details on events, venues, and times of Adelaide's annual program of free public concerts and organ recitals. This office is open Monday to Friday from 8:45am to 5pm.

INTERSTATE INFORMATION You'll find the following offices in Adelaide: the **Western Australia Tourist Information Centre,** 41 Currie St. (☎ 08/211 8455); the **Northern Territory Information Centre,** Millers Arcade, 28 Hindley St. (☎ 08/231 3944); the **Queensland Government Travel Centre,** 10 Grenfell St. (☎ 08/212 2399); the **Tasmanian Government Travel Centre,** 32 King William St. (☎ 08/400 5522); **Tourism Victoria,** 16 Grenfell St. (☎ 08/231 4129); and the **New South Wales Travel Centre,** at the corner of King William and Grenfell streets (☎ 08/231 3167).

CITY LAYOUT

Adelaide's orderly community plan was designed in 1836 by the surveyor general, Col. William Light. The central business district is contained in a square mile, and a grid pattern of streets makes it easy for you to find your way around. **Victoria Square** is in the center of the grid; similar, but smaller, plazas are in each quarter. The **River Torrens,** with its wide grassy banks, separates the city center from **North Adelaide,** and a greenbelt of parkland surrounds the combined areas.

King William Street, running north and south, is the main thoroughfare. **Rundle Mall,** perpendicular to the main street, is a pedestrians-only shopping area; more than a dozen arcades adjacent to the mall provide space for more shops. **Rundle Street East,** with avant-garde boutiques and ethnic restaurants, is Adelaide's answer to New York City's Greenwich Village. X-rated nightclubs and ladies of the night can be found on **Hindley Street. Adelaide Plaza,** on the riverbanks just north of the central business district, is the site of the Festival Centre, the city's A$30-million (U.S. $24-million) Casino, and the Convention Centre.

The mouth of the river is 10km (6 miles) to the west on the Gulf of St. Vincent, an inlet of the Southern Ocean. Of the many swimming beaches along the gulf, **Glenelg** is the most popular. Northwest of the city, **Port Adelaide** is both a working port and a picturesque place with an excellent maritime museum and lively pubs. The **Adelaide Hills,** 20 minutes to the west of town, are dotted with delightful day-trip destinations. **Hahndorf** is a charming village settled by Germans fleeing Silesia in 1839. The grateful refugees named their new home after Capt. Dirk Hahn, who commanded their ship, and many original buildings and a Teutonic atmosphere remain. In **Birdwood,** a historic flour mill has been converted to the National Motor Museum and houses an impressive vintage-car collection.

These and other charming villages, nestled among tree-clad hills and valleys, offer craft shops and cozy B&Bs. The Adelaide Hills are part of the **Mount Lofty Range** and encompass **Cleland Wildlife Park,** where koalas and other native animals are on display. The **Barossa Valley,** the best known of South Australia's wine districts, begins 55km (34 miles) northeast of Adelaide.

2 Getting Around

BY PUBLIC TRANSPORTATION

BY BUS Adelaide has a good system of public transportation. **TransAdelaide** (☎ 08/210 1000) operates the free **Beeline Buses** around the inner city, and you can wait for these 99B buses anywhere you see a bumblebee on the bus stop. For timetable information, call TransAdelaide daily from 7am to 8pm. It also has the

TransAdelaide Information Bureau (☎ 08/218 2439), on the corner of King William and Currie Streets and on the platform of the Adelaide Railway Station on North Terrace. Both are open Monday to Thursday from 8am to 6pm, Friday from 8am to 9pm, and Saturday from 8am to 5pm.

The **Adelaide Explorer Bus** (A$20/U.S. $16) takes you to half a dozen sights around town—however, keep in mind that the bus (a replica tram) stops at each destination only every 2½ hours. Depending on how interested you are in the various sights, you might end up wasting valuable sightseeing time waiting for the next bus. Tickets are available through Adelaide Sightseeing (☎ 08/231 4144).

Premier Tours (☎ 08/415 5566), **Adelaide Sightseeing** (☎ 08/231 4144), and **Transit** (☎ 08/381 5311) operate full- and half-day escorted tours.

BY TRAM TransAdelaide also runs the **Glenelg Tram,** which departs from Victoria Square and carries passengers to the seaside suburb of Glenelg. The regular price of tickets, good for two hours, is A$2.70 (U.S. $2.15); between 9:01am and 3pm Monday to Friday, however, the fare is only A$1.60 (U.S. $1.30). The journey takes 29 minutes.

City and suburban buses and suburban trains are also provided by TransAdelaide. You could, for instance, take a train to Port Adelaide in order to visit the Port Dock Railway Museum or the South Australian Maritime Museum. This train runs every 30 minutes and the fare is A$2.70 (U.S. $2.15), except from 9am to 3pm during the week, when it's A$1.60 (U.S. $1.30). The same fares apply to buses, and budget-minded travelers should keep in mind that **Daytrip tickets** are the best value. These cost A$4.40 (U.S. $3.52) if purchased at the Customer Service Centre and are valid all day. Contact TransAdelaide at the above phone numbers or stop in at one of their offices for more details.

BY TAXI & CAR

Taxis operate throughout the city. The major companies are **United Yellow** (☎ 08/223 3111), **Suburban** (☎ 08/211 8888), and **Amalgamated** (☎ 08/223 3333). The flagfall during the day is A$2 (U.S. $1.60); from 7pm to 6am, it's A$2.90 (U.S. $2.30).

The main car-rental companies in the area are **Avis,** 136 North Terrace (☎ 08/410 5727); **Budget,** 274 North Terrace (☎ 08/223 1400); **Hertz,** 233 Morphett St. (☎ 08/231 2856); and **Thrifty,** 100 Franklin St. (☎ 08/211 8788). You might want to try **Action Rent-A-Car** at 08/352 7044.

If you need to get in touch with an auto club, contact the **Royal Automobile Association of South Australia (RAA),** 41 Hindmarsh Square (☎ 08/202 4500).

FAST FACTS: Adelaide

Airline Offices Airlines with offices in Adelaide are Air New Zealand, ANZ House, 13 Grenfell St., 8th floor (☎ 08/212 3544); Air Kangaroo Island, 440 King William St. (☎ 08/410 2466); Ansett, 142 North Terrace (☎ 08/233 3111); British Airways, 33 King William St. (☎ 08/238 2000); Kendell Airlines, 33 King William St. (☎ 08/233 3322); Malaysia Airlines, 144 North Terrace, fifth floor (☎ 08/231 6171); Qantas, 144 North Terrace (☎ 08/237 8541); Singapore Airlines, 50 King William St. (☎ 08/238 2747); and United Airlines, 144 North Terrace, 7th floor (☎ 08/231 2821).

American Express The office, 13 Grenfell St. (☎ 08/212 7099), is open regular business hours.

Area Code Adelaide phone numbers are in the 08 area code. As part of the telephone changeover, all six-digit numbers with a 08 area code will be changing to 08/84x xxxx in August 1996, and all seven-digit numbers with a 08 area code will be changing to 08/8xxx xxxx in August 1996.

Business Hours **Banks** are generally open Monday to Thursday from 9:30am to 4pm and Friday from 9:30am to 5pm. **Stores** are generally open Monday to Thursday from 9am to 5:30pm, Friday from 9am to 9pm, Saturday from 9am to 5pm, and Sunday from 11am to 5pm.

Car Rentals See "Getting Around" earlier in this chapter.

Currency See "Information, Entry Requirements & Money" in Chapter 3.

Currency Exchange In addition to banks and hotels, the Casino and Myer in Rundle Mall will cash traveler's checks.

Dentist Contact the Australian Dental Association emergency information service at 08/272 8111.

Doctor Contact the Royal Adelaide Hospital, on North Terrace (☎ 08/223 0230).

Drugstores They're called "chemist shops" in Australia. Burden Chemists, in the CML Building, at the corner of King William and Hindley streets (☎ 08/231 4701), is open Monday to Friday from 8am to 7pm and Saturday from 9am to 7pm.

Emergencies Dial **000** to summon an ambulance, the fire department, or the police.

Eyeglass Repairs OPSM (Optical Prescription Spectacle Makers), 198 North Terrace (☎ 08/305 1000), or Shop 34, City Cross, Grenfell Street (☎ 08/212 5192), is open Monday to Friday from 9am to 5:30pm and Saturday from 9 to 11:30am. OPSM 29 Rundle Mall (☎ 08/231 8166) is open until 9pm Friday and 5pm Saturday.

Hospitals The Royal Adelaide Hospital, North Terrace (☎ 08/223 0230), is centrally located.

Hotlines Crisis Care Centre, 13 16 11.

Information See "Information, Entry Requirements & Money" in Chapter 3.

Laundry/Dry Cleaning Tip Top Dry Cleaners, 184 Gawler Place (☎ 08/232 0075), offers same-day cleaning service ("90 minutes where possible") and mending.

Libraries The State Library of South Australia is on Kintore Avenue. The newspaper room is in a separate building on North Terrace.

Lost Property The TransAdelaide (public transport) Lost Property Office is on the main concourse of the Adelaide Railway Station on North Terrace (☎ 08/218 2552). It's open Monday to Friday from 9am to 5pm.

Luggage Storage/Lockers There are no lockers at the Adelaide Airport. There are no lockers at Australian National's train station at Keswick (☎ 08/217 4111); however, there's a cloak service costing (A$1/U.S. 80¢) per item per day. At the Central Bus Station on Franklin Street (☎ 08/415 5533) are luggage lockers that cost A$2 (U.S. $1.60) for 24 hours. Premier Roadlines at the bus station will hold luggage at A$2 (U.S. $1.60) per piece if all lockers are in use.

Newspapers/Magazines *The Advertiser* is the morning paper and *The Sunday Mail* is published Sunday only; many people read the national newspaper, *The Australian.*

Photographic Needs Ted's Camera Store is at 212 Rundle St. (☎ 08/223 3449) and Twin Street Camera and Watch Repairs is at 24 Twin St. (☎ 08/223 1050).

Post Office The General Post Office (GPO), 141 King William St., is near Victoria Square (☎ 08/216 2222). The hours are Monday to Friday from 8am to 6pm and Saturday from 8:30am to noon. General delivery mail (poste restante) can be collected only Monday to Friday from 8am to 6pm. A few other services are also limited to these hours. Central Adelaide addresses have a 5000 postal code.

Radio For classical music tune to ABC (103.9 FM).

Restrooms Public restrooms are located at the Central Market Arcade, between Grote and Gouger streets, at Victoria Square, Hindmarsh Square, and James Place (off Rundle Mall).

Safety Avoid walking along the River Torrens at night. Likewise, stay out of the side streets near Hindley Street after dark.

Taxes Sales tax, where levied, is contained in the retail price of goods, not added separately. There is no GST or hotel tax in South Australia.

Taxis See "Getting Around" earlier in this chapter.

Television ABC (Channel 2) is the Australian Broadcasting Corporation (government) station. It offers quality dramas, documentaries, concerts, news, and so forth. SBS offers ethnic programming. Channels 7, 9, and 10 are the commercial stations and offer a variety of movies, soaps, news, and sports.

Telegrams/Telex The better hotels and the GPO offer these services.

Transit Information See "Getting Around" earlier in this chapter.

Useful Telephone Numbers Citizens' Advice Bureau, 08/212 4070; Youth Enquiry Service, 08/211 8466; Rape and Sexual Assault Service, 08/267 8282, or 1800/817 421 in Australia, or 08/267 8292 after hours; Women's Information Switchboard, 08/223 1244; Gay Line, 08/362 3223 (7–10pm); AIDS Hotline, 08/223 3666; Lifeline, 08/212 3444.

3 Accommodations

Adelaide offers lots of lodgings, but be sure to reserve well in advance if you plan to be in town during the Adelaide Festival. You may also be interested in the accommodations I cover in "Side Trips from Adelaide" at the end of this chapter. If you like bed-and-breakfast inns and homestays, request a copy of the "South Australian Bed and Breakfast Town and Country" booklet from any South Australian Government Travel Centre.

IN THE CITY CENTER

VERY EXPENSIVE

Hyatt Regency Adelaide. North Terrace, Adelaide, SA 5000. ☎ **08/231 1234.** Fax 08/231 1120. 367 rms and suites. A/C MINIBAR TV TEL. A$290 (U.S. $232) double; A$320 (U.S. $256) Regency Club (including breakfast); A$600 (U.S. $480) Executive Suite. Additional person A$30 (U.S. $24) extra. Lower weekend rates. Children under 18 free in parents' room. No-smoking rooms available. AE, BC, DC, JCB, MC, V. Parking A$15 (U.S. $12).

At the north end of the city center, the Hyatt Regency is part of the riverside complex that includes the Adelaide Festival Centre, the Casino, and the Convention Centre. It offers rooms on more than 20 floors, including 4 Regency Club floors. All quarters have contemporary decors (each marble bath with a tub and a shower) and include tea- and coffee-making facilities, a small refrigerator, a clock radio, bathrobes, and in-room movies. A plaza on the back of the hotel overlooks the River Torrens.

Dining/Entertainment: Blake's, for fine dining, focuses on South Australia's importance as a wine-growing and culinary center. Shiki, for authentic Japanese, features five teppanyaki bars and one tempura bar. The Riverside Restaurant serves all meals. Waves, the California-style cabaret/nightclub, offers a lively combination of video, disco, and live music. Drinks and afternoon tea are served in the Atrium Lounge.

Services: Concierge, 24-hour room service, shoeshine, free daily newspaper, laundry, valet, nightly turndown, baby-sitting, massage.

Facilities: Hyatt Fitness Centre with sauna, solarium, sports shop, whirlpool, plunge pool, massage room, weight room, and juice bar—all connected to the heated outdoor pool; business center.

EXPENSIVE

Adelaide Hilton. 233 Victoria Square, Adelaide, SA 5000. ☎ **08/217 0711.** Fax 08/231 0158. 380 rms, 15 suites. A/C MINIBAR TV TEL. A$215–A$248 (U.S. $172–$198.40) double; A$300 (U.S. $240) executive floor; A$385–A$990 (U.S. $308–$792) suite. Additional person A$30 (U.S. $24) extra. Children under 18 free in parents' room. No-smoking rooms available. AE, BC, DC, MC, V. Parking A$15 (U.S. $12). The tram stops in front of the hotel; a bus stop is adjacent.

The luxurious 18-story Adelaide Hilton is set on picturesque Victoria Square. A doorman in top hat and tails will greet you as you enter the lobby with its polished marble floor and cascading fountain. Piano music from the adjacent Lobby Lounge will fill the air. Upstairs, the guest rooms offer a choice of king-size, queen-size, or twin beds; all have in-room movies, clock radios, tea- and coffee-making facilities, and small refrigerators. All baths have tub/shower combinations, except those in the 11 rooms specially equipped for the handicapped. The 9th floor is reserved for nonsmokers and the 16th is the Executive Floor.

Dining/Entertainment: The dining and drinking venues include a coffee shop and the Grange, a posh à la carte eatery. The Lobby Lounge is popular, but my favorite spot is Charlie's Bar. I like the English pub decor, which includes pictures of lots of famous Charlies—Bronson, Brown, de Gaulle, King Charles I, and Prince Charles among them.

Services: Concierge, 24-hour room service, free daily newspaper, laundry, valet, baby-sitting.

Facilities: Heated outdoor pool, spa pool, gym, sauna, tennis court (A$20/U.S. $16 per hour), jogging track, business center, unisex hair salon.

Hindley Parkroyal. 65 Hindley St., Adelaide, SA 5000. ☎ **08/231 5552.** Fax 08/237 3800. 177 rms and suites. A/C MINIBAR TV TEL. A$190 (U.S. $152) double; A$240 (U.S. $192) suite; A$500 (U.S. $400) executive suite. Children under 15 free in parents' room. Weekend rates about 50% lower. No-smoking rooms available. AE, BC, DC, MC, V. Free parking.

In the central business district, this property opened under a different name in 1989. The Southern Pacific Hotel Corporation took over in 1990, adding this property to its upmarket Parkroyal Collection. You enter the marble-floored lobby where there's an attractive fountain. Sebastians bar is just inside the front door. All the guest rooms have light wood interiors complemented by muted earth tones and modern furnishings. Standard rooms have either two double beds or one queen, a clock radio, tea- and coffee-making facilities, a small refrigerator, in-room movies, free daily newspapers, and irons and ironing boards. There's 24-hour room service, a heated outdoor pool, a well-equipped gym, a spa, a sauna, and a nice business center. Meals are served in casual Cafe Mo and the fancier Oliphants.

MODERATE

Barron Townhouse. 164 Hindley St., Adelaide, SA 5000. ☎ **08/211 8255**, or 1800/888 241 in Australia. Fax 08/231 1179. Reservations can be made through Flag Inns. 68 rms. A/C MINIBAR TV TEL. A$100 (U.S. $80) double standard, A$134 (U.S. $107.20) double deluxe; A$139 (U.S. $111.20) executive room. Additional person A$12 (U.S. $9.60) extra. Rates include snack-pack breakfast. Children under 12 free in parents' room. Lower rates off-season and weekends. No-smoking rooms available. AE, BC, DC, MC, V. Free parking.

The Barron Townhouse is on the edge of the city center, not far from the nightlife district. Some might find the neighborhood too lively; others might find the small hotel just their cup of tea. This place is ideal for travelers with lots of luggage because the rooms are spacious. Toasters are supplied in addition to the standard coffee-and-tea setup. Everyone has in-room movies and receives a free daily newspaper. Downstairs, Flamingo's Bistro is an informal eatery. Room service is available 24 hours. There's a nice outdoor heated pool on the fifth floor, along with a sauna.

Serviced Apartments

$ **Apartments on the Park.** 274 South Terrace, Adelaide, SA 5000. ☎ **08/232 0555,** or 1800/882 774 in Australia. Fax 08/223 3457. Reservations can be made through Flag Inns. 50 apts. A/C MINIBAR TV TEL. A$110 (U.S. $88) apt for one or two. Additional adult A$15 (U.S. $12) extra, additional child A$5 (U.S. $4) extra. No-smoking rooms available. AE, BC, CB, DC, MC, V. Free parking. Bus: 161.

This apartment complex is on the southern edge of the city center overlooking a scenic greenbelt. Each of the fully furnished units has a full kitchen, two bedrooms, a separate lounge and dining area, and a washing machine and dryer. This modern lodging offers a choice between a beige-and-apricot or beige-on-beige scheme. Baby-sitting can be arranged, and there's a spa on the premises. Valet and breakfast service can be arranged.

$ **The Mansions Apartments.** 21 Pulteney St., Adelaide, SA 5000. ☎ **08/232 0033,** or 1800/888 292 in Australia. Fax 08/223 4559. 51 apts. A/C TV TEL. A$85 (U.S. $68) studio apt for one or two; A$98 (U.S. $78.40) one-bedroom apt for one or two; A$108 (U.S. $86.40) executive one-bedroom apt. Additional person A$10 (U.S. $8) extra. AE, BC, MC, V. Parking A$8 (U.S. $6.40).

This was Australia's first "high-rise" apartment building and is now one of those exceptional values I look forward to sharing with you. All the spacious studio and one-bedroom units have full kitchens and attractive decors. The property was built in 1912, and the high ceilings and traditional furnishings underscore the old-world atmosphere. The apartments are ideally in the city center near North Terrace and within a short walk of museums, the Festival Centre, and the Rundle Mall. Shops and eating places are in the Renaissance Arcade on the street level. A sauna and spa are on the premises.

✪ **North Adelaide Heritage Apartments & Cottages.** Office: 109 Glen Osmond Rd., Eastwood, SA 5063. ☎ and fax **08/272 1355** or 018/832 232 (mobile phone). 6 apts, 6 cottages. TV TEL. A$100–A$160 (U.S. $$80–$128) double. Additional person A$35 (U.S. $28) extra. Two-night minimum. Rates include self-catered breakfast. AE, DC, JCB, MC, V.

The apartments and cottages (11 separate properties in North Adelaide and Eastwood) owned by Rodney and Regina Twiss are all heritage listed. Each building has been restored to its former elegance, and the Twisses have drawn on stock from their antique business to create an authentic yet comfortable

19th-century atmosphere. They decided to create typically Adelaide-style heritage lodgings while honeymooning in the United States. The accommodations vary in size, furnishings, and decoration, but each has a bath, a sitting room, a kitchen, at least one bedroom (many have two or three) and is a short walk from the business, entertainment, and sports districts through Adelaide's parklands. You receive a complimentary country breakfast basket with bacon and eggs on your first morning; children are welcome.

INEXPENSIVE

Moore's Brecknock Hotel. 401 King William St., Adelaide, SA 5000. ☎ **08/231 5467.** Fax 08/410 1968. 10 rms (none with bath). A/C. A$45 (U.S. $36) double; A$60 (U.S. $48) triple. Rates include continental breakfast. AE, BC, DC, MC, V. Free parking. The tram stops in front of the hotel.

Four blocks from Victoria Square, the Brecknock was built in 1851 and has been in the Moore family since 1901. Today it's run by Kyran (Kerry) Moore and his Canadian wife, Tricia, who has refurbished each room with period wallpaper and homey touches. High ceilings and stained-glass windows add to the hotel's charm. Each room has a sink, an electric blanket, and coffee- and tea-making facilities. Guests enjoy breakfasting together and exchanging travel tips. Downstairs, they serve great hamburgers in C J's Bistro and you can get an inexpensive meal in the front bar and outdoor courtyard. There's also a cook-your-own barbecue area.

IN NORTH ADELAIDE

Quality Hotel Adelaide. 62 Brougham Place (at the corner of O'Connell Street), North Adelaide, SA 5006. ☎ **08/267 3444,** or 1800/090 600 in Australia. Fax 08/239 0189. 129 rms, 11 suites. A/C MINIBAR TV TEL. A$120 (U.S. $96) double; A$140 (U.S. $112) suite; A$195 (U.S. $156) executive floor. Additional person A$12 (U.S. $9.60) extra. Children under 14 free in parents' room. Lower weekend rates. AE, BC, DC, MC, V. Free parking. Take bus 181, 182, or 222 1km (0.6 mile) north of the city.

Because it has been renovated, few would guess that the Hotel Adelaide, three blocks north of the River Torrens, is more than 30 years old. The lobby has a contemporary reception counter, the cocktail lounge is off to one side, and a floating staircase leads to the mezzanine. The guest rooms have an unusual French provincial decor, including gray carpeting, rose-and-gray bedspreads, and lavender draperies with sheer white festoons for privacy. Each room has coffee- and tea-making facilities, a small refrigerator, a clock radio, and in-room movies. Closet space is a bit limited, though. Each suite is named and decorated in recognition of one of Adelaide's sister cities: Christchurch, New Zealand; Austin, Texas; Penang, Malaysia; and Himeji, Japan. I think the designer of the Texas suite was inspired by the TV show *Dallas.*

More than half the rooms and suites have an excellent view of the city or surrounding hills. The hotel is within walking distance of the Festival Centre and the central business district. The Brougham Restaurant atop the seven-story hotel has an especially nice vista. Twenty-four-hour room service is available. Facilities include an outdoor pool, a business center, a hair salon, two restaurants, three bars, and a newsstand.

IN GLENELG

Stamford Grand Adelaide. Moseley Square (P.O. Box 600), Glenelg, SA 5045. ☎ **08/376 1222,** or 1800/882 777 in Australia. Fax 08/376 1111. 220 rms and suites. A/C MINIBAR TV TEL. A$165–A$235 (U.S. $132–$188) double, depending on floor; A$240–A$500 (U.S. $192–$400) suite. Ocean-view room A$20 (U.S. $16) extra; additional person A$30 (U.S. $24) extra. Children under 12 free in parents' room. No-smoking rooms available. AE, BC, DC, MC, V. Parking A$6 (U.S. $4.80). The tram from Adelaide takes 29 minutes and stops in front of the hotel.

Adelaide Accommodations & Dining

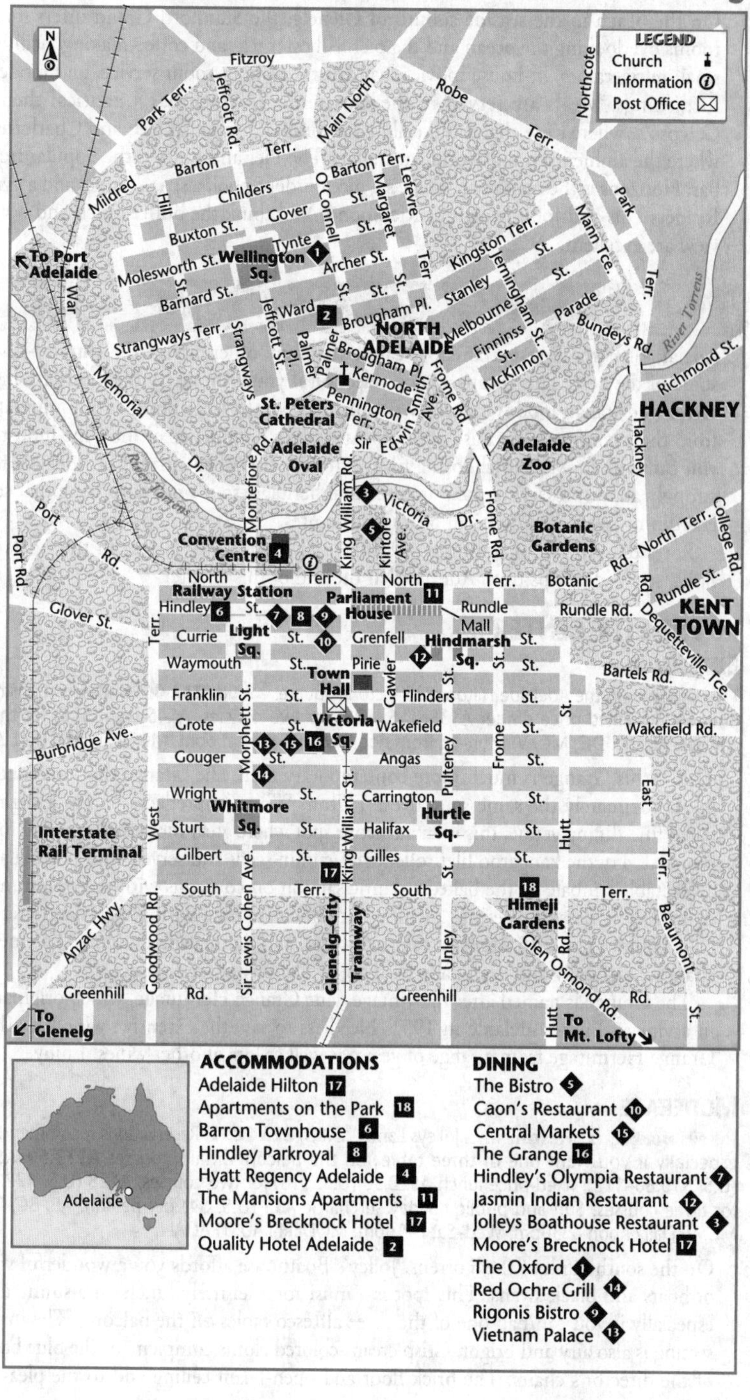

On the beach in the seaside suburb of Glenelg, the Stamford Grand offers many rooms overlooking the ocean and the pier. All offer tea- and coffee-making facilities, small refrigerators, in-house movies, hairdryers, 24-hour room service, and modern furnishings. Meals are served in the Quarterdeck, which has a nautical theme; Calypso's, where cane chairs and ceiling fans impart a tropical feel; and Charlotte's, where the ambience is old-world Australian. The Pier and Pines is the popular front bar; Horizons is the piano bar. There's a nice outdoor pool, a spa, a sauna, and a gym. Readers Lois and John Morris of Richmond, Va., think the buffet lunch and beach view are excellent.

4 Dining

Adelaide has more restaurants per capita than any other city in the country—and some of the best. This means a good selection if you want to try the local offerings. Greek and Italian food is especially popular, due to the large number of immigrants from these countries. Because of South Australia's dominance of the wine industry, you can look forward to choosing from extensive lists. The citizens of Adelaide feel strongly about preserving their architectural heritage, so it's not surprising that several dining spots are housed in historic structures.

For a description of dining possibilities at Mount Lofty House in the Adelaide Hills, see "Side Trips from Adelaide" at the end of this chapter.

IN THE CITY CENTER

EXPENSIVE

The Grange. In the Adelaide Hilton, 233 Victoria Square. ☎ **08/237 0698.** Reservations recommended. Fixed-price dinner A$35 (U.S. $28) for two courses, A$45 (U.S. $36) for three courses. AE, BC, DC, MC, V. Mon–Fri from noon; Mon–Sat from 6pm. MODERN AUSTRALIAN.

This 1990s Grange is much more contemporary than The Grange that preceded it in approximately the same spot at the Hilton. While its predecessor was a slightly dated fine-dining venue, this is an attractive spot where great modern Australian food is served. Try the kangaroo filet rolled with cumin seeds and served with polenta and a vegetable timbale or the baked Atlantic salmon on couscous with red-onion marmalade. The dessert offerings include hot-chocolate cake with King Island cream, baked quince tart with vanilla-cream reduction, and marmalade pudding. The menu changes seasonally and even daily with the availability of fresh items.

The Grange is named after the vintage wine Grange Hermitage, which originated in a vineyard near Adelaide in 1951. Needless to say, the extensive wine list offers Grange Hermitage from a range of years, as well as lots of other wines. Enjoy.

MODERATE

Jolleys Boathouse Restaurant. Jolleys Lane. ☎ **08/223 2891.** Reservations recommended, especially if you want one of three tables on the balcony. Main courses A$13.50–A$15 (U.S. $10.80–$12); fixed-price lunch A$22.50 (U.S. $18) for two courses, A$28 (U.S. $22.40) for three courses. Sun and public holiday surcharge A$5 (U.S. $4) per person. AE, BC, DC, MC, V. Daily noon–2:30pm; Wed–Sat 6–10pm. MODERN AUSTRALIAN.

On the south bank of the Torrens, Jolley's Boathouse affords you a wonderful view of boats and black swans. This spot is a must for a leisurely lunch on a sunny day, especially if you can nab one of the three alfresco tables on the balcony. The inside seating is also airy and bright. Crisp cream-colored cloths complement the blue backs of the director's chairs. The brick floor and open-beam ceiling add to the pleasant ambience.

Food Courts

At the rear of the **City Cross Arcade,** leading off Rundle Mall, there's an extensive **Food Plaza,** where you can purchase many kinds of quick meals (like Chinese, seafood, and Italian) takeout style and eat them at tables provided in a central area. Food is sold during the day Monday to Friday, Friday night, and until 4pm Saturday. You can eat well for A$8.50 (U.S. $6.80). A similar place, this one selling the cuisine of 12 countries, is adjacent to the Central Markets between Gouger and Grote streets. The **International Food Plaza** is open Monday to Thursday from 11am to 4pm and Friday, Saturday, and Sunday from 11am to 9pm. Again, meals cost less than A$10 (U.S. $8). There's also a food court in the **Myer Centre,** where the cuisines include Chinese, Japanese, Mexican, health food, pasta, jacket potatoes, sandwiches, crêpes, and salads—to eat in or take away. My only complaint is that it can be very noisy when busy. The prices are on a par with City Cross's.

Speaking of the **Central Markets,** this is an excellent place to buy cheese, bread, pâté, salami, fresh fruit, and so forth to put in the picnic basket you'll take on day trips to the Barossa Valley or Adelaide Hills. The markets (☎ 08/203 7494 or 203 7345) are open Tuesday from 7am to 5:30pm, Thursday from 11am to 5:30pm, Friday from 7am to 9pm, and Saturday from 7am to 1pm.

You could start with goat cheese, charred capsicum, eggplant, zucchini, and black olives on dried tomato damper or a salad of charcoal-grilled octopus with chili sambal. Main courses include duck leg and lentil curry with jasmine rice and pickles, fresh fish, and seafood stir-fry with coriander, lemongrass, and noodles. Try the passionfruit ice cream or rich chocolate cake with double cream for dessert. This is good for a pretheater meal as the Festival Centre is nearby.

✪ **Red Ochre Grill.** 129 Gouger St. ☎ **08/212 7266.** Fax 08/212 6686. Reservations essential. Main courses A$15–A$24 (U.S. $12–$19.20). AE, BC, DC, MC, V. Daily 11am–late. CREATIVE NATIVE AUSTRALIAN.

The decor of the Red Ochre reflects the colors of Australia, with a subtle Aboriginal/outback influence. The walls are trimmed with an Aboriginal design border and feature Aboriginal art. The restaurant area is more formal, with carpeted floors and white tablecloths, while the café is more casual, with bare floors and tables. Entrees include Ochre antipasto consisting of emu pâté, rare kangaroo, yabby tail, lemon myrtle, cured ocean trout, wild aniseed-pickled octopus, eggplant, and sea parsley; and Point Lincoln scallops baked with bunya nut and wild lime butter. For a main course you could choose kangaroo filet with wild mint polenta and quandong chile glaze or emu steak with braised emu pot sticker dumplings in an aniseed, myrtle, and soya glaze. Desserts range from wattle-seed pavlova to lemon Aspen tart. This restaurant is highly recommended by several readers, as well as by many locals.

Rigonis Bistro. 27 Leigh St. ☎ **08/231 5160.** Reservations recommended. Main courses A$10–A$14 (U.S. $8–$11.20); antipasto bar (lunch only) A$7.90–A$9.90 (U.S. $6.30–$7.90). AE, BC, DC, MC, V. Mon–Fri noon–3pm and 5:30–10pm. ITALIAN.

Tucked away on a narrow lane west of King William Street in the central business district, the restaurant brings the flavors of old-world Italy to present-day Australia. The chalkboard luncheon menu, which changes daily, often includes lasagne della casa, vitello arrosto (baby veal pot-roasted in white wine, herbs, and butter), pesce persico (marinated perch filets lightly pan-fried in butter and sage), and fettuccine carciofi salsicce (fettuccine tossed with artichokes and Italian pork sausage). In addition, there's an extensive salad bar with a variety of antipasto.

The bistro has a casual atmosphere created by Italian travel posters, Michelangelo "sketches," and autographed black-and-white photos of personalities who've dined in this popular spot—like Liza Minnelli and Andy Williams. Wooden tables are set on a rust-colored tiled floor. Licensed and BYO.

Note that this restaurant provides complimentary courtesy car transfers to and from your hotel or the theater at lunch and dinner.

INEXPENSIVE

The Bistro. In the Adelaide Festival Centre, King William Road. ☎ **08/216 8744.** Reservations recommended. Main courses A$9–A$12.50 (U.S. $7.20–$10). AE, BC, DC, MC, V. Mon–Sat 11am until late. MODERN AUSTRALIAN.

The Bistro offers a casual atmosphere for an à la carte meal or a light supper. The location couldn't be better for those attending a performance at the Festival Centre. The terrace area has floor-to-ceiling windows that offer a view of the River Torrens and surrounding parklands.

✪ **Jasmin Indian Restaurant.** 31 Hindmarsh Square. ☎ **08/223 7837.** Reservations recommended. Main courses A$9.50–A$12.50 (U.S. $7.60–$10); lunch buffet A$14.50 (U.S. $11.60); dinner buffet A$20 (U.S. $16). Weekend and public holiday surcharge A$1 (U.S. 80¢) per person. AE, BC, DC, MC, V. Tues–Fri noon–2:30pm; Tues–Sat 5:30–9:30pm. NORTH INDIAN.

Jasmin is a family affair. Amrik Singh is the proprietor and his mother is the chef. A block south of the Rundle Mall in a cozy cellar pozzie, the place has a simple attractive decor, including Indian tapestries and paintings. The low ceiling makes things a little noisy, but that's a small price to pay for the delicious northern Indian food. Beef vindaloo is the house specialty, but those who like chicken tandoori, malabari beef, curry, lamb korma, and prawn sambal won't be disappointed. Traditional breads—chapati, paratha, bhatura, and pappadum—are available. The wine list, a notebook full of labels, is extensive and reasonably priced.

IN KENT TOWN

Chloe's. 36 College Rd., Kent Town. ☎ **08/362 2574** or 363 1001. Reservations recommended. Main courses A$21–A$26 (U.S. $16.80–$20.80); dinner for two about A$80 (U.S. $64). Lunchtime prices much lower. AE, BC, DC, MC, V. Mon–Fri noon–2pm; Mon–Sat from 7pm. CREATIVE FRENCH.

Quick Bites

The front (public) bar and cocktail bar at the **Brecknock Hotel,** 401 King William St. (☎ 08/231 5467), serves very inexpensive counter meals Monday to Saturday from noon to 2pm and 6:30 to 8:30pm. You eat in any of the hotel's three bars or the covered courtyard. Roast beef and vegetables, pasta, burgers, and similar staples cost about A$6 (U.S. $4.80).

Homesick Yanks may want to head for the golden arches—yes, **McDonald's**—in Rundle Mall and at 44 Hindley St. (☎ 08/231 9565). Another familiar sight, **Pizza Hut,** can be found at 9 Hindley St. (☎ 08/231 2281).

Another budget dining spot in Adelaide is **$ Hindley's Olympia Restaurant,** 137–139 Hindley St. (☎ 08/231 9093). Traditional Greek food is served by an exceptionally friendly staff. The gyro wrapped in pita is delicious and the portions are large. Likewise, the horiatiki salata (Greek-style green salad) is big enough to share. Three-course meals cost about A$20 (U.S. $16).

Readers Recommend

Vietnam Palace, 132 Gouger St. (☎ 08/212 1968). *"It doesn't look like much, but the food was spicy and terrific."*

—John Rosenthal, New York, N.Y., U.S.A.

This grand 1880s mansion, in a suburb on the edge of the city center, has been faithfully restored by proprietor Nicolas Papazahariakis, who named his restaurant after his daughter. A meal here is a memorable experience. Diners at Chloe's are seated in one of four rooms, all with 14-foot ceilings and elaborate chandeliers. Museum-quality oil paintings by Australian artists of the late 1800s are on display. Much of the stained glass in and around the doors is original, and the color scheme is true to the period.

The same attention to detail evident in the decor is obvious in the preparation and presentation of the food. The menu changes every three months—sample entrees are smoked mackerel tartare, marinated quail salad, and cassoulet of rabbit filet. For a main course you have a choice of duck with wontons, braised lamb loin, saddle of kangaroo, suprême of chicken with tortellini and light tarragon sauce, or cornets of trout. Desserts include warm pear-and-almond tart, vacherin of rhubarb, and petite creams of mascarpone with poached satsuma plums.

While the house and the cuisine are impressive, the center of attention at Chloe's is the 20-page wine list, which offers a choice of 600 domestic and imported vintages. Nicholas started collecting wine in 1971, when he came to Australia; his cellar is now stocked with more than 22,000 bottles.

IN NORTH ADELAIDE

The Oxford. 101 O'Connell St., North Adelaide. ☎ **08/267 2652.** Reservations recommended, especially for lunch and dinner Fri and dinner Sat. Main courses A$13.50–A$16.50 (U.S. $10.80–$13.20). AE, BC, DC, MC, V. Sun–Fri noon–3pm; Mon–Sat 6–10pm or later. Bus: 182, 222, 224, 226, 228, or 229. MODERN AUSTRALIAN.

If you can eat only one meal in Adelaide, let it be here. The restaurant is housed in an 1870s building that has recently been renovated and now has a modern European appearance. Crisp white cloths cover the tables laid with simple white crockery (pottery) dishes. The single-sheet menu arrives on an aluminum clipboard. The very high ceiling, open kitchen, and service staff comprised of students from the nearby university contribute to the agreeable ambience.

Chef Peter Harris works wonders with the fresh local ingredients. Order the Oxford fries to munch on while you decide what your other courses will be. I highly recommend the pasta al ceppo with capsicum sauce, fresh and sundried tomato salsa, walnuts, rocket, and goat cheese. You might also like to try charcoal-grilled kangaroo filet with bok choy, fried daikon and wasabi butter served with light soy and sesame dressing, or red-roasted spatchcock with mitzuna and mint salad served with pear-and-cardamom chutney. The wine list is extensive. I like the 1988 Hollick Cabernet-Merlot from the Coonawarra wine district, among others.

5 Attractions

SIGHTSEEING SUGGESTIONS FOR THE FIRST-TIME VISITOR

If You Have 1 Day Start out at the Migration Museum, then walk over to the Festival Centre and take a tour of the facility or just admire the view from the plaza. In the afternoon, take a train to Port Adelaide and visit the South Australian Maritime

Readers Recommend

Caon's Restaurant, 19 Leigh St. (☎ 08/231 3011). *"The seafood there was superb, and the waiters so friendly. I would've gone back the next day to eat there again, but unfortunately it was Sunday and it was closed. Reservations are definitely recommended."*

—Terence Fu, New York, N.Y., U.S.A.

Museum. When you get back to town, hop on a Glenelg tram and make the short journey to Adelaide's most popular seaside suburb.

If You Have 2 Days Follow my suggestions for Day 1 and on Day 2 take a tour of the Barossa Valley and its wineries. Several coach companies (see "Getting Around" earlier in this chapter) conduct such excursions. Of course, this can also be done as a self-drive trip, but remember that Australia's drinking-driving laws are strictly enforced.

If You Have 3 Days Spend Days 1 and 2 as above. On the third day, make a trip through the Adelaide Hills. Tour the National Motor Museum in Birdwood, browse through the shops in Hahndorf, visit Cleland Wildlife Park, and stop for a meal or tea at Mount Lofty House.

If You Have 5 Days Spend your first three days as outlined above. On the fourth day, visit the Tandanya Aboriginal Cultural Institute first, then browse through the Central Markets. In the afternoon, choose two of the following activities: the Adelaide O-Bahn to Tea Tree Plaza or Paradise Interchange, a visit to Carrick Hill, or a craft-shopping excursion to the Jam Factory.

On Day 5, tour another nearby wine region, such as the Clare Valley or McLaren Vale.

THE TOP ATTRACTIONS

It's a pleasure to explore Adelaide and its environs. The city is still slightly off the beaten path of the average traveler, so you'll enjoy a sense of being the first to discover certain sights, shops, and scenic vistas. Most of the area's attractions are low-key and noncommercialized, in keeping with its innate gentility. This isn't a place in which to rush from point to point. I suggest you slow down, put on some casual clothes, sample one of the local vintages, wander along the banks of the Torrens, then explore craft shops, wineries, and picturesque villages.

The **Adelaide O-Bahn** is a new transport technology with buses running on concrete tracks. The vehicles travel up to 100kmph (62 m.p.h.) and pass through lots of pretty scenery along the 12km ($7^1/_2$-mile) route from Adelaide to a major shopping center at Tea Tree Plaza. If you'd like to take this ride, board bus 540-546 at the intersection of Grenfell Street and James Place. More information is available from TransAdelaide at 08/210 1000.

✪ **The Migration Museum.** 82 Kintore Ave. ☎ **08/207 7580** or 207 7570. Free admission. Guided tours, A$4.50 (U.S. $3.60) adults, A$2.50 (U.S. $2) children. Mon–Fri 10am–5pm, Sat–Sun and public holidays 1–5pm. Closed Good Friday and Christmas.

It's impossible to separate Australia's history from the dramatic impact made by immigrants. From the first boatload of convicts in 1788 to the present, Australia's is a story of migration. The British who came in the 19th century suffered untold hardships. The ethnic groups who have arrived in great numbers since World War II have had their own trials. At this museum, part of the North Terrace Cultural Precinct, the stories of individual new arrivals are told in a personal way that

Adelaide Attractions

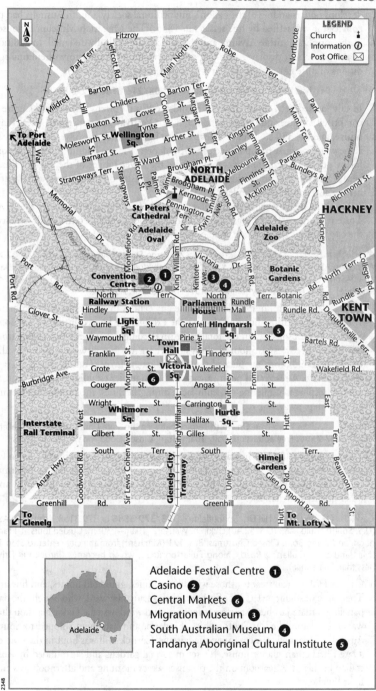

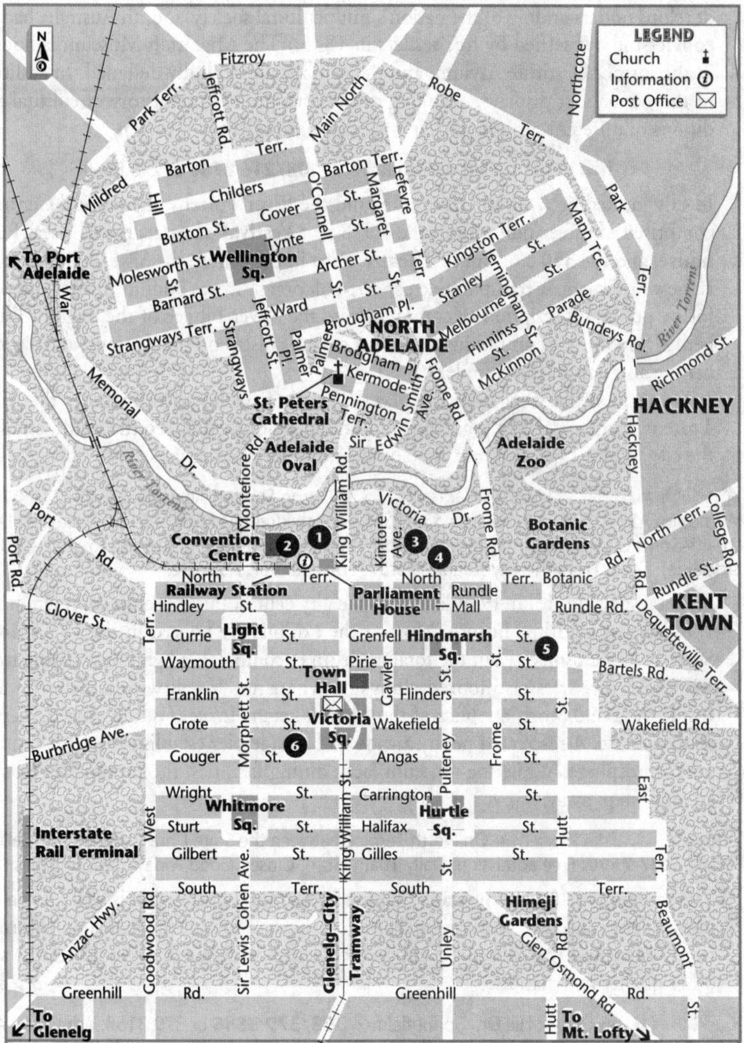

Adelaide Festival Centre 1
Casino 2
Central Markets 6
Migration Museum 3
South Australian Museum 4
Tandanya Aboriginal Cultural Institute 5

develops understanding of the nation's multicultural society. (South Australia had no convicts; it was settled by free settlers in 1836.) The Migration Museum is housed in the former Destitute Asylum, and the exhibits are skillfully designed. In addition to the permanent displays, changing exhibitions present the history of cultural traditions of different groups. This is a hands-on experiential museum.

Adelaide Festival Centre. King William Road. ☎ **08/216 8760** or 216 8600.

Ideally located between the city center and the River Torrens, the Festival Centre is comprised of three auditoriums: the 1,978-seat **Festival Theatre,** the 612-seat **Playhouse,** and the 350-seat **Space Theatre.** Also in the center, the Silver Jubilee Organ is the world's largest transportable concert-hall organ. It was built in Austria and paid for by public subscription to commemorate the Silver Jubilee of the reign of Elizabeth II. An outdoor amphitheater, an art gallery, Bistro on the Torrens, and a piano bar are also part of the complex.

Don't miss the view from the plaza. The vista to the north includes the River Torrens, its grassy banks, a gazebo, and St. Peter's Cathedral. To the south, one sees the city, with its graceful mix of colonial and modern structures.

✪ **South Australian Maritime Museum.** 126 Lipson St., Port Adelaide. ☎ **08/240 0200.** Admission A$7 (U.S. $5.60) adults; A$3 (U.S. $2.40) children; A$17 (U.S. $13.60) families. Daily 10am–5pm. Closed Christmas. Bus: 153-157 from North Terrace in the city to Stop 40 (Port Adelaide). Train: From the city station, North Terrace to Port Adelaide.

In Port Adelaide, 15km (9 miles) from the city center, this museum commemorates 150 years of maritime history. Most of the exhibits are housed in the 1850s Bond Store at 126 Lipson St., but the total museum encompasses a lighthouse dating from 1869 and three vessels moored alongside wharf no. 1—all within a short walk. Inside the Bond Store, a replica of the 54-foot ketch *Active II* is fully rigged, its sails ready to raise. A re-created penny arcade and seaside pier establish the 19th-century port atmosphere. While the museum lacks dining facilities, the Lipton Tea Rooms are only steps away.

South Australian Museum. On North Terrace between the State Library and the Art Gallery. ☎ **08/207 7500.** Free admission. Daily 10am–5pm. Closed Good Friday and Christmas.

The museum focuses on the state's natural and cultural history and is well known for its excellent collection of Aboriginal artifacts. Be sure to visit the hands-on Information Centre and the Museum Shop, which sells a wide range of books, cards, and other quality merchandise.

Carrick Hill. 46 Carrick Hill Dr., Springfield. ☎ **08/379 3886** or 379 3158. Admission A$8 (U.S. $6.40) adults, A$3 (U.S. $2.40) children. Wed–Sun 10am–4:30pm. Guided tours at 11am, noon, and 2 and 3pm. Closed Christmas. Bus: 171 (Mitcham) from the city center to Stop 16 (Maitland Street/Fullarton Road); along Fullarton Road, which becomes Carrick Hill Drive (less than half a mile).

Carrick Hill is a real treat for those who like antiques, grand old homes, and fine art. The house was built in 1939 for Sir Edward and Lady Hayward, who bought the oak paneling, ornate Jacobean staircase, fireplaces, and windows of a Tudor mansion that was to be demolished in Staffordshire, England, and had them shipped to South Australia. Designed to incorporate these items, Carrick Hill was built in the style of a late Elizabethan manor house. It's set in formal gardens and surrounded by Australian bushland. A tearoom on the premises serves morning and afternoon teas and light lunches.

✪ **Tandanya Aboriginal Cultural Institute.** 253 Grenfell St. ☎ **08/223 2467.** Admission A$4 (U.S. $3.20) adults, A$3 (U.S. $2.40) children under 14. Daily 10:30am–5pm.

This is a venue for Aboriginal art, culture, and activities. Changing exhibits provide a glimpse into the past and present life of Australia's indigenous people, and guides are available to answer questions and give informal tours. Films and occasional live performances take place in the theater. The work of Aboriginal artists and books about this mysterious culture are sold in the shop here. The building was originally Adelaide's power-generating station.

IN NEARBY GLENELG

Why not spend a pleasant morning or afternoon making a trip to the seaside suburb of Glenelg? You can start with a 29-minute tram ride from Victoria Square that'll take you through the southern parklands and right out to the coast.

While there you can enjoy a walk along the beach and tour the **HMS *Buffalo*,** Adelphi Terrace, Patawalonga Boat Haven (☎ 08/294 7000), a full-size replica of the original, built from the plans drawn in 1813. This is the ship that brought the first settlers to South Australia in 1836. Today the *Buffalo* contains a small maritime museum and a seafood restaurant. Admission is A$2.50 (U.S. $2) for adults and A90¢ (U.S. 75¢) for children. It's open daily from 10am to 5pm. Take the Glenelg Tram.

The **Old Gum Tree,** under which Governor Hindmarsh read the 1836 proclamation making South Australia a colony, is on MacFarlane Street. The **Glenelg Tourist Information Centre** (☎ 08/294 5833) can answer your questions.

6 Outdoor Activities & Spectator Sports

OUTDOOR ACTIVITIES

BALLOONING **Balloon Adventures,** Bagshaw Road, Kersbrook (☎ 08/389 3195), will take you up, up, and away over Adelaide or the Barossa Valley. The A$195 (U.S. $156) price includes a one-hour flight, a champagne celebration, and ground transfers. Flights are scheduled for very early in the morning.

BICYCLING Adelaide's parklands and recreational areas are popular with cyclists, who turn out in droves on the weekends. Rent your cycle from **Linear Park Bike Hire** (☎ 018/844 588). The charge of A$25 (U.S. $20) includes helmet rental. You can also rent a bike in Glenelg at **Bike & Beach** (☎ 08/294 1477). The **Department of Recreation and Sport** (☎ 08/226 7301) publishes a brochure showing the cycleways through the O-Bahn Park. **The Map Shop,** 16A Peel St. (☎ 08/231 2033), and **Mapland,** 282 Richmond Rd., Netley (☎ 08/226 4946), are also good sources of maps.

CANOEING The Murray River is ideal for paddling a canoe. Contact the **Department of Recreation and Sport** (☎ 08/226 7301) to get the excellent "Canoe Guide," which suggests routes and gives safety tips and other information.

HIKING & JOGGING The banks of the **River Torrens,** just north of the city center, invite you to put on your Nikes and get some exercise. Likewise with the parklands that surround Adelaide. If you wish to go farther afield, contact the **Department of Recreation and Sport** (☎ 08/226 7301) and request a set of their "Jubilee Walks" brochures. You might also ask about the **Heysen Trail,** a 1,600km (992-mile) walking track that starts 80km (50 miles) south of Adelaide and goes to the Flinders Ranges by way of the Adelaide Hills and the Barossa Valley.

HOUSEBOAT CRUISING The Murray River winds along the New South Wales–Victoria border and eventually finds its way to South Australia, where it enters the sea east of Adelaide. The river is a popular place for houseboating. The best place to rent such a vessel is in **Berri,** a riverfront community three hours northeast of Adelaide. Contact Garry and Cheryl Von Bertouch at **Swan Houseboats** (☎ 085/823 077 or 1800/083 183 in Australia; fax 085/823 077). Ski boats, dinghies, and canoes can also be hired and pulled behind the houseboat. Costs vary depending on the time of year and size of vessel, but an average three-night rental for an eight-berth boat is around A$500 (U.S. $400).

SPECTATOR SPORTS

CRICKET The Adelaide Oval is the site of national and international matches during summer.

FOOTBALL Australian Rules Football has a large following. Venues include the Adelaide Oval and Football Park, West Lakes.

HORSE RACING The main tracks are Victoria Park Racecourse and Morphettville Racecourse. The prestigious Adelaide Cup is held at Morphettville in May.

7 Shopping

Adelaide's **Central Markets,** behind the Hilton Hotel between Gouger and Grote streets, are a great place to buy fresh fruits and vegetables, pâté, cheese, and bread to pop into a picnic basket. Even if that isn't your style, the markets are a colorful slice of life you shouldn't miss. Stallholders tout their goods above the din created by bargaining shoppers. The markets, held in a huge warehouselike structure, are open Tuesday from 7am to 5:30pm, Thursday from 11am to 5:30pm, Friday from 7am to 9pm, and Saturday from 7am to 1pm.

In contrast to the chaos of the Central Markets, **Rundle Mall,** the city's main shopping precinct, seems relatively orderly at most times. Friday night, however, is an exception. This is the only evening working people can shop, and the mall becomes a beehive of activity.

ABORIGINAL ARTS & CRAFTS

The **Adelaide Gem Centre/Adella Gallery,** 12 Hindley St. (☎ 08/212 3600), has a comprehensive display of authentic Aboriginal art and crafts, as well as many Aboriginal-designed souvenir items, like a large range of T-shirts and other clothing items. The Gem Centre has a large selection of black, boulder, and white opal from souvenir to investment quality. In addition to finished jewelry, the center offers overnight jewelry manufacturing. Open Monday to Thursday from 9am to 5:30pm, Friday from 9am to 9pm, Saturday from 9am to 5pm, and Sunday from 10am to 5pm.

CRAFTS

L'Unique, Shop 54 in the City Cross Arcade, off the Rundle Mall (☎ 08/231 0030; open Monday to Thursday from 9am to 5:30pm, Friday from 9am to 9pm, and Saturday from 9am to 5pm), or at 33 Main St. in Handorf (☎ 08/388 7934; open daily from 10am to 5pm), sells beautiful South Australian pottery, jewelry, woodcraft, handblown glass, original paintings, and sculpture. The ✪ **Jam Factory Craft and Design Centre,** in the Lion Arts Centre, 19 Morphett St. (☎ 08/410 0727), has an excellent selection of locally made ceramics, glass, furniture, and metal items. This award-winning shop also provides you an opportunity to watch craftspeople at work. Exhibits in the gallery change monthly. Open Monday to Friday from 9am to 5:30pm and Saturday, Sunday, and public holidays from 10am to 5pm. You might also like to browse at the **Jam Factory City Style,** 74 Gawler Place

(☎ 08/223 6809), selling contemporary Australian handcrafted glass, ceramics, wood, leather handbags, silk scarves, and jewelry. Open Monday to Thursday from 9am to 5:30pm, Friday from 9am to 9pm, and Saturday from 10am to 5pm. **Australian Quality Crafts,** Shop 15P on the Promenade Level of the Mayer Centre (☎ 08/212 3340), sells Australian handcrafts like glass, wood, pottery, and Aboriginal art and crafts. Open Monday to Thursday from 9am to 5:30pm, Friday from 9am to 9pm, Saturday from 9:30am to 5pm, and Sunday from 11am to 5pm.

DEPARTMENT STORES

Besides many small and medium-size stores, Adelaide has a **David Jones,** 44 Rundle Mall (☎ 08/305 3000)—Australia's answer to Bloomingdale's and Marshall Field's. **Myer,** 22–38 Rundle Mall (☎ 08/217 0123), and **John Martins,** 100 Rundle Mall (☎ 08/223 0200) are other department stores. All of these are open Monday to Thursday from 9am to 5:30pm, Friday from 9:30am to 9pm, Saturday from 9:30am to 5pm, and Sunday from 11am to 5pm.

FASHIONS

Adelaide is the home of the **R. M. Williams Company,** makers of what locals refer to as "bush gear." If you're looking for kangaroo-leather boots, moleskin pants, Driza-bone coats, or Akubra hats, head to the R. M. Williams shop on Gawler Place (☎ 08/232 3611), open Monday to Thursday from 9:30am to 5:30pm, Friday from 9:30am to 9pm, Saturday from 9am to 5pm, and Sunday from 11am to 4pm.

FOOD

At the corner of King William Street and Rundle Mall, **Haigs** (☎ 08/231 2844) is the favorite chocolate shop of Adelaidians. An exotic confection called "freckles" is especially recommended. **Ditters,** on King William Street (☎ 08/212 5604), is also a local institution; it sells nuts, dried fruit, and the like.

JEWELRY

At least 90% of the world's gem-quality opals come from South Australia, so it's not surprising that Adelaide is a good place to buy these stones. Prices are lower than in other cities and a good selection is available. At **Opal Field Gems,** third floor, 29 King William St. (☎ 08/212 5300), you can view a 10-minute film about opals, watch the cutting, and shop. (Note that this store doesn't stay open on Friday night as do others in the city.) **Opal Gem Mine,** at 5 Rundle Mall and at 142 Melbourne St., North Adelaide (☎ 08/267 5525 or 211 7440), has a simulated opal mine and is another good place to shop.

WINE

Buy your bottle at **Watermans,** King William Street, or at the **Booze Brothers,** 150 Payneham Rd., Evandale.

8 Adelaide After Dark

THE PERFORMING ARTS

Adelaide hosts Australia's largest performing arts festival in March of even-numbered years, one which covers the literary and visual arts as well as dance, theater, opera, and music. More than a million attendees were recorded at 40-plus venues around the city in 1994. The Festival was last held on March 1 to 17, 1996; the dates for 1998 are February 27 to March 15.

The Major Concert Hall

Adelaide Festival Centre. King William Road. ☎ **08/216 8600** or 08/211 8999 for recorded information 24 hours, 08/213 4788 for box office, 08/213 4777 to buy tickets over the phone from the BASS Booking Agency. Tickets A$3.50–A$50 (U.S. $2.80–$40), depending on event.

The **Festival Theatre** accommodates opera, ballet, drama, and orchestral concerts. The Adelaide Symphony Orchestra plays in the Festival Theatre, and the **Playhouse** is the home of the State Theatre Company. Experimental dramas are often done in the **Space Theatre.** For more details, see "Attractions" earlier in this chapter. For information about the Adelaide Festival of Arts, see "Australia Calendar of Events" in Chapter 3. The box office is open Monday to Saturday from 9am to 8:30pm; you can buy tickets over the phone Monday to Saturday from 9am to 6pm.

Theaters

Arts Theatre. 53 Angas St. ☎ **08/212 5777.** Tickets A$14 (U.S. $11.20) for amateur shows, more for professional productions.

This 600-seat venue is the home of the Adelaide Repertory Theatre. The company presents a season of five productions a year, ranging from drama to comedy. A sample of the playwrights whose work is performed is Neil Simon, Alan Ayckbourn, Noël Coward, Agatha Christie, and Terence Rattigan.

The theater is also the home of the Metropolitan Musical Theatre Company, which presents two musical comedy productions a year. A venue for both amateur and professional theater, the Arts Theatre is walking distance from the Hilton and other hotels and restaurants.

Her Majesty's Theatre. 58 Grote St. ☎ **08/216 8600.** Tickets generally A$30–A$55 (U.S. $24–$44).

Opposite Adelaide's famous produce markets in the heart of the city, Her Majesty's is a landmark theater venue with 1,000 seats. Presentations here include drama, comedy, smaller-scale musicals, dance, opera, and recitals. You can purchase tickets through all BASS ticket outlets or on Dial 'n Charge at 13 12 46. All major credit cards are accepted.

The Bar & Club Scene

Adelaide's after-dark options range from slightly sedate to positively X-rated. For strip clubs and raunchy nightspots, head to Hindley Street.

Pubs

Earl of Aberdeen. 316 Pulteney St. (at the corner of Carrington Street). ☎ **08/223 6433.**

This restored 19th-century colonial-style pub is popular with the city's businesspeople. Excellent food is served in the Gazebo Restaurant, renowned for its aged steaks and huge range of beers from Australia and around the world. Locally brewed Coopers beer is a specialty.

Old Botanic Hotel. 309 North Terrace (at the corner of East Terrace). ☎ **08/223 4411.**

This is a favorite watering hole for university students. There's sidewalk dining during summer (December to February).

The Old Lion. 163 Melbourne St., North Adelaide. ☎ **08/267 3766.**

This is a restored brewery hotel built in 1850 with several bars. You can watch as ales and lagers are produced and can sample the Old Lion brew in the Brewery Ale House Bar. The Tavern Bar is also fun. Meals are available at the Grapevine Restaurant and some of the bar areas.

The Port Dock. 10 Todd St., Port Adelaide. ☎ **08/240 0187.**

The Port Dock has three bars: the Upstairs Bar, the P.O.S.H. Bar, and the Long Bar. Four beers are brewed on the premises and pumped to the bars by traditional English beer engines. The Port Dock is a great place to go on Sunday, when it hosts a big crowd from 11am to midnight. The hotel was first licensed in 1865 and has a handsome decor.

PIANO BARS & NIGHTCLUBS

Fezbah Bar. In the Festival Centre, King William Road. ☎ **08/216 8730.**

In the Fezbah Bar you might hear anything from hot jazz to 1950s R&B. You could also happen upon a dance cabaret, South American rhythms, or the big-band sound. Open Saturday from 11pm.

Le Rox. 9 Light Square. ☎ **08/231 3234.** Cover about A$6 (U.S. $4.80).

This nightclub is popular with the 18- to 28-year-old crowd who are "alternative to modern." It's open Friday and Saturday from 9pm to 5am. Live music is offered on Friday. A wide range of drinks is served, but no food.

Lobby Lounge. In the Hilton Hotel, 233 Victoria Square. ☎ **08/217 0711.**

The Lobby Lounge is a good spot for people-watching accompanied by pleasant piano music. Open daily from 4pm to midnight.

A CASINO

Adelaide Casino. North Terrace. ☎ **08/212 2811,** or 1800/888 711 in Australia.

The focal point of the city's nightlife is the Casino with its old-world atmosphere. It's built in the shell of the historic railway station and over the existing train tracks just north of the city center. The Hyatt Regency and Adelaide Convention Centre are nearby. Besides the predictable gaming tables, the Casino has four bars, a café-style food area, a fast-food station, and the Pullman buffet restaurant (serving lunch for A$20.30/U.S. $16.25 Monday to Friday and A$22.30/U.S. $17.85 Saturday and Sunday; and dinner for A$25.30/U.S. $20.25 Monday to Friday and A$27.30/U.S. $21.85 Saturday and Sunday). The casino is open Sunday to Thursday from 10am to 4am and Friday and Saturday from 10am to 6am.

9 Side Trips from Adelaide

BAROSSA VALLEY

South Australia is the country's chief wine-producing state and the Barossa is the state's best-known grape-growing region. The area was settled by Silesian refugees who planted the first vines in 1847. Today over 40 wineries are in operation and the "wine valley" continues to have a German flavor. In addition to visiting wineries, you can poke around in craft shops, admire historic churches, and enjoy the beauty of the valley. **Tanunda** is the focal point of the area, but smaller villages are dotted along the highway from **Lyndoch** to **Nuriootpa.**

Several companies offer conducted tours of the Barossa. If you're driving, this scenic valley is the ideal place for spontaneous travel from one winery to another, stopping for photography, a picnic, or maybe even a nap as the spirit moves. Another alternative is to rent a bike, take the train to Gawler, and cycle through the Barossa. There's no public transportation between wineries.

The wine region starts 45km (28 miles) northeast of Adelaide and extends for about 20km (12 miles). The area is approximately 11km (7 miles) wide. Data on the wineries, detailed maps, and general info are available at the **Barossa Valley Information Centre,** 66 Murray St., Tanunda, SA 5352 (☎ 085/630 600; fax 085/630 616), open Monday to Friday from 9am to 5pm and Saturday, Sunday and public holidays from 10am to 4pm. As part of the telephone changeover, all numbers with a 085 area code will be changing to 08/85xx xxxx in February 1997.

The impressive old buildings that house the wine-making operations in the Barossa set the region apart from Australia's other wine districts. Happily for South Australia, the immigrants who developed this industry built picturesque châteaux to live in and from which to operate their businesses.

Seeing the Wineries

Château Yaldara Winery. Lyndoch. ☎ **085/244 200.** Free admission. Mon–Fri 8:30am–5pm, Sat–Sun 9am–5pm. The Garden Bistro serves lunch noon–2pm; teas and snacks, 10am–4pm. Call to check the times of scheduled tours.

Built of yellow sandstone, this grand house contains valuable period furniture and crystal chandeliers. Extensive collections of porcelain and objets d'art can be viewed on daily house tours. Château Yaldara, the second-largest family-owned winery in the Barossa, was founded in 1947 by emigrant German vintner Hermann Thumm. He bought the ruins of an 1876 flour mill and used the old European-style buildings as the beginning of his estate. Tours of the château and winery, wine tasting, and bottle sales are available. Like most wineries in this area, Château Yaldara has a generous tasting policy.

Charles Cimicky Wines. Lyndoch. ☎ **085/244 025.** Free admission. Daily 10am–4:30pm.

This is another interesting property. A castlelike structure holds the winery and the tasting and sales rooms.

Barossa Settlers Winery. Trial Hill Road, Lyndoch. ☎ **085/244 017.** Fax 085/244 519. Free admission. Mon–Sat 10am–4pm, Sun 1–4pm.

This winery is located in an old stone horse stable built in 1860. The small historic property is owned by Joan and Howard Haese. Wines are sold at cellar door exclusively.

Wolf Blass. Stuart Highway, Nuriootpa. ☎ **085/621 955.** Free admission. Mon–Fri 9:15am–4:30pm, Sat–Sun 10am–4:30pm.

This is an extensive wine-tasting complex with a Germanic style that incorporates an interesting museum on wine making and the history of the Barossa. Wolf Blass consistently produces some of Australia's greatest red wines—the black-label vintages have international reputations. The museum recently won a tourism award.

Penfolds. Nuriootpa. ☎ **085/620 389.** Tasting and sales, Mon–Fri 10am–5pm, Sat 9am–5pm, and Sun 1–5pm.

This is one of the valley's largest wineries, with a storage capacity of 22.5 million liters (5.85 million U.S. gallons). Penfolds got its start in 1844, when Dr. Christopher Rawson Penfold planted a few grapes in the Adelaide foothills so he could make wine for his patients. Penfolds expanded to the Barossa Valley in 1911, and today the winery building covers an area of over 3 hectares (7½ acres) and houses the largest oak barrel maturation cellars in the Southern Hemisphere.

Seppelts. Seppeltsfield. ☎ **085/628 028.** Guided tours, A$3 (U.S. $2.40). Tasting and sales, Mon–Fri 9am–5pm, Sat 10:30am–4:30pm, Sun 11am–4pm.

The business was founded in 1857 by Joseph Seppelt, an immigrant from Silesia who purchased the land to grow tobacco. Today Seppeltsfield is a National Trust site. The winery and storage buildings are built of bluestone and surrounded by attractive gardens. Barbecues are provided in nice picnic areas.

WHERE TO STAY

Barossa Motor Lodge. Murray Street, Tanunda, SA 5352. ☎ **085/632 988.** Reservations can be made through Flag Inns. 40 rms, 2 suites. A/C MINIBAR TV TEL. A$80 (U.S. $64) double; A$87 (U.S. $69.60) suite. Additional person A$10 (U.S. $8) extra. AE, BC, DC, MC, V. Free parking.

It may be that after a day of tasting you'll decide to overnight in the Barossa Valley rather than return to Adelaide. If that's the case, you might consider this motor lodge. All quarters have coffee- and tea-making facilities, small refrigerators, clock radios, and queen-size beds. There are also rooms for the handicapped. A restaurant and a barbecue are on the property. You have the use of a pool, a sauna, half-court tennis, a spa, and a playground. Baby-sitting can be arranged.

Château Yaldara Estate. Barossa Valley Highway, Lyndoch, SA 5351. ☎ **085/244 268.** Reservations can be made through Flag Inns. 34 rms, 1 suite. A/C MINIBAR TV TEL. A$80 (U.S. $64) double. Additional person A$10 (U.S. $8) extra. AE, BC, DC, MC, V. Free parking.

This motel is near the Château Yaldara Winery. All units have single and double beds, showers, and more-than-adequate furnishings. The rates are higher for rooms with the best views of surrounding countryside. A bar, restaurant, playground, and pool are all on the premises.

$ **Lawley Farm.** Krondorf Road (P.O. Box 103), Tanunda, SA 5352. ☎ or fax **085/632 141.** 6 suites. A/C TV TEL. A$110–A$130 (U.S. $88–$104) suite for two. Addition person A$85 (U.S. $68) extra. Rates include breakfast. AE, BC, MC, V. Free parking. Bus to Tanunda; then take a taxi or call Lawley Farm for a ride.

At this cozy property Sancha and Bruce Withers invite you to stay in the "Barn," "Cottage," or "New Cottage" on their 1.2 hectares (3 acres) of native trees and orchard. The Cottage and the Barn date from 1850; all lodging offers old-world charm and scenic surroundings. Each has limited cooking facilities, a bath, a clock radio, and either a king- or queen-size bed; two suites have log-burning stoves. There are laundry facilities, a spa, and a games room with pool table on the property; baby-sitting can be arranged. Breakfast can be served in your room or in the elegant old farm dining room. Hosts can arrange "insider" visits to wineries.

✪ **Tanunda Hotel.** 51 Murray St., Tanunda, SA 5352. ☎ **085/632 030.** Fax 085/632 165. 10 rms (6 with bath). A/C TV. A$49–A$59 (U.S. $39.20–$47.20) double. AE, BC, DC, MC, V. Free parking. Bus: 910 from Adelaide.

The hotel was built of local stone by the early settlers in 1846, and its first liquor license was granted the next year. It was rebuilt after being partially destroyed by fire in 1895, with more renovations following in 1945. Today it's an impressive building with a long veranda supported by wrought-iron columns and lacework that were brought over from England. The Tanunda's popular bars are open daily, and meals are served in several restaurants, ranging from very casual to elegant. All quarters have tea- and coffee-making facilities and small refrigerators. Six have phones, showers, and toilets.

ADELAIDE HILLS

To the east and southeast of Adelaide, tree-clad slopes and valleys and pretty hills dotted with picturesque villages provide a rural getaway. The **Tourism South Australia Travel Centre,** in the AMP Building, 1 King William St., Adelaide, SA 5000 (☎ 08/212 1505), is the best source of information and maps.

BIRDWOOD

Located 46km (28 miles) east and slightly north of Adelaide, Birdwood is best known for its historic flour mill, which has been restored and now contains the ✪ **National Motor Museum**—the best collection of cars (both antique and classic) and motorcycles under one roof anywhere in Australia. Also included in the complex are cottage-style tearooms, a small museum, a gift shop, a playground, and an extensive picnic area alongside the upper reaches of the River Torrens. The museum (☎ 085/685 006) is open daily from 9am to 5pm; closed Christmas. The admission of A$8 (U.S. $6.40) for adults, A$3 (U.S. $2.40) for children, and A$18 (U.S. $14.40) for families includes a ride on a tiny train pulled by a miniature steam engine. There's no public transport to Birdwood: Either drive yourself or join a coach tour that includes this attraction on its itinerary.

HAHNDORF

Hahndorf, 25km (15 miles) from Adelaide, was settled in 1839 by Lutherans fleeing religious persecution in Prussia's eastern provinces. They named their town after Capt. Dirk Hahn, who brought them to Australia in his ship, the *Zebra.* The village, which retains its German appearance and atmosphere, is included on the World Heritage List as a Historical German Settlement. As you walk around town, notice **St. Paul's Lutheran Church,** erected in 1890. In the late 19th century, brides sometimes arrived at this church in a wagon wearing the traditional black wedding gown and a wreath of green and white leaves in their hair. Today, couples married in St. Paul's are often the fourth or fifth generation of their family to do so.

The Wool Factory, Unique, and **Bamfurlong Fine Crafts**—all within walking distance on Main Street—have an extensive range of fine Australian-made gifts and souvenirs. Visitor information and bookings are available through the **Adelaide Hills Tourist Information Centre** (☎ 08/388 1185).

WHERE TO STAY

✪ **Apple Tree Cottage.** P.O. Box 100, Oakbank, SA 5243. ☎ **08/388 4193.** Fax 08/388 4733. 3 cottages. A/C. A$150 (U.S. $120) double. Additional person A$50 (U.S. $40) extra. Lower weekly rates. Rates include breakfast. Two-night minimum stay. No-smoking rooms available. MC, V. Free parking. Drive 35 minutes to Oakbank from Adelaide; it's seven minutes from Hahndorf and less than an hour from the Barossa Valley.

If you're looking for cozy accommodation, here are three self-contained cottages, 1km (0.6 mile) apart, surrounded by 60 hectates (150 acres) of scenic countryside. Owned by Gai and Brenton Adcock, the Apple Tree Cottage, which sleeps up to five and has a spa bath, the Gum Tree Cottage, for up to four, and the Lavender Fields Cottage, which also sleeps up to four, have won several tourism awards. The Apple Tree, circa 1860, overlooks a lake on the Adcock's cattle stud and apple orchard; it's furnished with antiques and has a stone fireplace in the living room. You'll enjoy using kerosene lamps, snuggling under patchwork quilts, and discovering lavender bags beneath your pillows. The Gum Tree Cottage, built of stone and red gum, also has an open log fireplace and superb country views from the windows. The Lavender Fields Cottage has thick stone walls and rustic beams, as well as a log fireplace overlooking a lily-fringed duck pond surrounded with rows of lavender. All three cottages' kitchens are fully equipped, so you can cook your own meals or go out to local restaurants. The Adcocks either fuss over guests or leave them in absolute privacy—as the guests prefer. This is a great place for rowing a boat across the lake, bird watching, fishing, or lazing in a hammock.

Hahndorf Inn Motor Lodge. 35A Main St., Hahndorf, SA 5245. ☎ **08/388 1000,** or 1800/882 682 in Australia. Fax 08/388-1092. Reservations can be made through Best Western. 19 rms. A/C TV TEL. A$75 (U.S. $60) double; A$110 (U.S. $88) deluxe double. Additional person A$10 (U.S. $8) extra. Higher rates during Easter week. AE, BC, DC, MC, V. Free parking. Mount Barker Bus Lines stops in Hahndorf.

If you decide to overnight in this charming community, you'll find this motor lodge to be quite comfortable. All rooms have showers and the standard modern motel amenities, plus toasters. Two rooms have private spas, and a pool, a spa, a sauna, and laundry facilities are provided.

WHERE TO DINE

Several nice places for lunch or tea are on Hahndorf's Main Street. **Stewart's Coffee Shoppe,** near Gumnut Antiques (☎ 08/388 1083), is a tiny spot with only half a dozen tables, but it serves an excellent Devonshire tea. For a tasty German-style meal accompanied by a wide range of German beers, wines, and schnapps, try the restored **German Arms Hotel,** 69 Main St. (☎ 08/388 7013).

MOUNT LOFTY

The summit of Mount Lofty, 20 minutes southeast of Adelaide, provides a panoramic view of the city, suburbs, beaches, valleys, and surrounding hills. It's also the location of one of the area's several bushfire lookout towers. The Adelaide Hills have been badly burned several times and careful watch is kept, especially during the hot, dry summer.

Nearby, off Summit Road in Crafers, native birds and animals are displayed in a natural bush setting at **Cleland Wildlife Park** (☎ 08/339 2444), where you can hold a koala. The park is open daily from 9:30am to 5pm, but koala cuddling is allowed only during the 2 to 4pm photo sessions. A charge of A$8 (U.S. $5) is made for photography. Admission is A$7 (U.S. $5.60) for adults and A$4.50 (U.S. $3.60) for children. Cleland Wildlife Park is included in the itinerary of several coach tours from Adelaide. If you're driving, take Greenhill Road or the South Eastern Freeway and turn onto Summit Road. It's well signposted. Cleland is closed on Christmas and "extreme fire danger days." A kiosk and licensed restaurant are on the premises.

WHERE TO STAY

✪ **Mercure Grand Hotel Mount Lofty House.** 74 Summit Rd., Crafers, SA 5152. ☎ **08/339 6777.** Fax 08/339 5656. 27 rms, 3 suites. A/C TV TEL. A$255–A$300 (U.S. $204–$240) double; A$400–A$470 (U.S. $320–$376) suite. Additional person A$30 (U.S. $24) extra. Rates include continental breakfast. Ask about weekend and other packages. AE, BC, DC, MC, V. Free parking. Chauffeured limousines available for airport transfers and sightseeing. Guests could also take coach to Crafers, then walk 1km (0.6 mile).

Commanding a spectacular view of the Piccadilly Valley and surrounding hills, Mount Lofty House is an elegant English-style country house poised near the summit of the 725-meter (2,393-ft.) peak. Built between 1852 and 1858, it has had many distinguished owners. It was all but destroyed by fire in 1983, and only the efforts of Ross Sands, an Adelaide architect, rescued it from the ashes. Ross and his wife, Janet, bought the remains shortly after the fire and painstakingly restored it. Today it offers tasteful lodging as well as dining in both formal and informal venues.

You'll find that your room is individual in layout and decor, including original works of art and old-world furnishings. Eight rooms have fireplaces. Each has a tub/shower combination, coffee- and tea-making facilities, and queen- and king-size beds or a pair of doubles; some have spa baths. One room has its own conservatory; the Piccadilly Suite affords a wonderful valley view. The grounds of this grand manor house include a heated pool and pleasant gardens. Mount Lofty House is a member of the Accor Asia Pacific Group of Hotels and Resorts and has won several Australian tourism awards.

Dining/Entertainment: For meals, you can choose between casual Piccadilly and formal Hardy's. In addition, before-dinner drinks are available in Tiers Bar and tea is served in the Arthur Waterhouse Lounge (all are described in "Where to Dine" below).

Services: Nightly turndown, laundry, baby-sitting.

Facilities: Pool, tranquil gardens.

Where to Dine

Guests of Mount Lofty House (above) are not the only ones who have access to its beautiful dining venues. Others can enjoy lunch, dinner, and teas daily. Additionally, high tea is served on Sunday. A sample lunch in the casual **Piccadilly** room might start with an entree such as Mount Lofty House antipasto of pickled Octopus, artichokes, vegetable frittata, Italian meatballs, and stuffed mushrooms, followed by a main course of seared kangaroo filet, fig chutney, sautéed snake beans, and marsala glaze and, for dessert, perhaps caramelized quince tart with honeycomb ice cream. This three-course meal would cost about A$25 (U.S. $20).

Hardy's, with its marble fireplace, fine crystal, high ceiling, and fresh flowers, is for fine dining. Its menus change seasonally, but dinner in this elegant environment could include lobster-and-coconut bisque with snapper and lemon quenelles "soup," followed by a main course of loin of venison with beetroot pickle and red-currant peppercorn glaze or pan-seared Atlantic salmon filet with cucumber ribbons and keta caviar and horseradish cream. Dessert could be poached seasonal fruit with henske noble rot jelly and vanilla-seed ice cream or peach crème brûlée with Amaretto ice cream. This dinner would cost about A$42 (U.S. $33.60) per person, plus wine selected from an extensive list.

Before-dinner drinks are enjoyed in **Tiers,** the posh, cozy cocktail bar with its dark woodwork and rust-colored burlap wall covering. The **Arthur Waterhouse Lounge** is a superbly appointed room where traditional furnishings, original oil paintings, high ceilings, and polished-brass fixtures re-create the gracious colonial life. A picture window in this room frames a beautiful view of the Piccadilly Valley.

15

South Australia

Lush and productive vineyards, unspoiled beaches, vast expanses of outback terrain, and incredible wildlife viewing—South Australia is full of contrasts and hidden pleasures.

The Barossa Valley, covered at the end of Chapter 14, is the best known of the winery regions, but vineyards can also be found in other areas. McLaren Vale is the most prolific of the Southern Vales, just south of Adelaide. The Clare Valley, 135km (84 miles) north of the capital, produces excellent red and white table wines. Sevenhill Cellars in Clare was started by two Jesuit priests in 1848 and still operates today. Coonawarra, due north of Mount Gambier near the Victoria border, is another wine-making district.

You'll also find vineyards along the Murray River, where most of the nation's bulk wine is produced. The Riverland is also known for citrus production. The town of Berri, three hours from Adelaide and two hours from Mildura (Victoria), is a popular vacation center.

The Yorke and Eyre Peninsulas, west of Adelaide, produce large quantities of grain and have beautiful unspoiled coasts. These agricultural gulf lands are in sharp contrast to the two-thirds of the state that's desertlike. From Port Augusta northward, very little rain falls and temperatures soar. It isn't surprising that in Coober Pedy, where it can be over 50°C (122°F) in summer, most folks choose to live underground. Were it not for a rich supply of opals, this town would no doubt cease to exist. Likewise with Olympic Dam, the site of huge copper and uranium mines. Though touring these outback areas is fun, 72% of the state's population chooses to live in Adelaide.

The Flinders Ranges, northeast of Port Augusta, are a spectacularly scenic area of peaks and gorges. Wilpena and Arkaroola are tiny rural communities that provide facilities and services to those who explore the area by four-wheel-drive, on horseback, or on foot.

The second "w" in wow stands for wildlife, and if this is your interest head for Kangaroo Island. In addition to friendly kangaroos and wallabies, the occasional wombat, and lots of koalas, Australia's third-largest island has colonies of seals, sea lions, and fairy penguins. If seeing the nation's native fauna is a priority of yours, be sure to allow *at least* three or four days here.

What's Special About South Australia

Oddities
- Coober Pedy, where people live underground to avoid the heat (and the flies).

National Parks
- Flinders Chase National Park, on Kangaroo Island, a treasure trove of native fauna.

Activities
- Houseboating on the Murray River.
- Hiking and camping in the Flinders Ranges.

Beaches
- Seal Bay, on Kangaroo Island, home to a colony of sea lions.

Regional Food & Drink
- The wine regions: the Barossa Valley, the Clare valley, McLaren Vale, and the

EXPLORING THE STATE

South Australia is four times the size of the United Kingdom. Southern Australia Airlines, Kendell Airlines, O'Connor Airways, Augusta Airways, and Sunshine Airlines provide links between cities and towns. The Stuart Highway cuts the state in half diagonally and connects Port Augusta with Alice Springs in the Red Centre. While this road is now paved, the trek between these two places is not without some hazards. Anyone considering this journey should seek advice from the **Royal Automobile Association of South Australia (RAA)** in Adelaide. The **South Australian Government Travel Centres** in major Australian and overseas cities are the best source of visitor information. If you like off-the-beaten-path accommodations, ask for information on farms around the state that welcome visitors.

1 Kangaroo Island

110km (68 miles) S of Adelaide

Of all the places I can think of in Australia to witness native fauna in natural surroundings, none is more impressive than Kangaroo Island, home to dozens of kinds of birds and mammals. The animals are not on display, per se—you can easily see them in the wild if you venture off the beaten track. While koalas, echidnas, and galahs are what I like about K.I., others are equally struck by the rugged coastal scenery, beaches, caves, and good fishing.

The island was named in 1802 by English explorer Capt. Matthew Flinders, who was grateful for the large numbers of kangaroos he discovered and the fresh meat they provided for him and his men. The K.I. kangaroo, not found on the mainland, is a subspecies of the Western Gray variety. In general, K.I. roos are larger and less timid.

The island was officially settled by the South Australia Company in 1836. Since this group's trip was funded by Henry Kingscote, it's not surprising that the main town on the island is named after him. In spite of its early settlement, Kangaroo Island was known to very few people until after World War II, when returned soldiers were set up with farms here. Today there are sheep—more than a million—everywhere you look. The No. 2 industry is tourism and No. 3 is fishing.

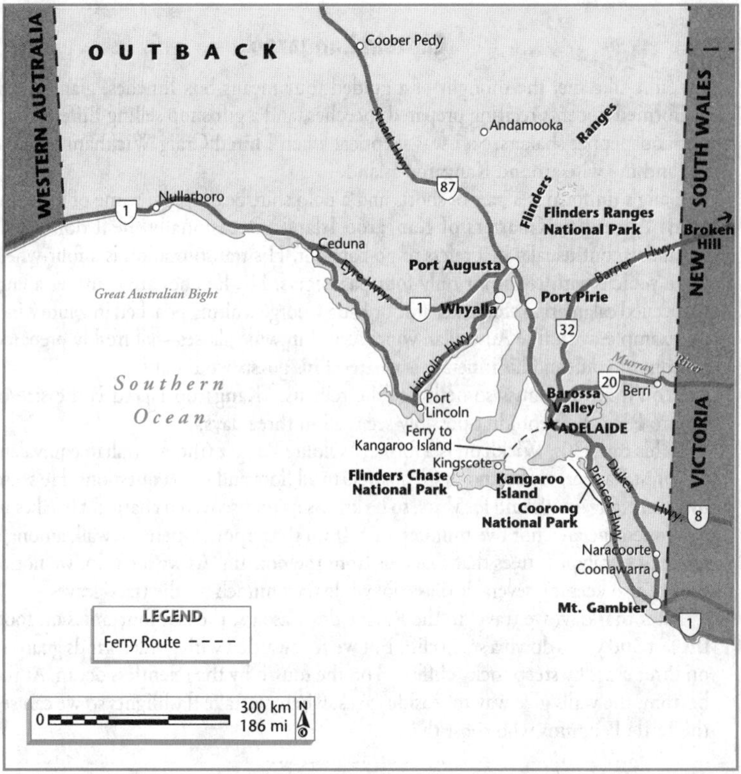

The island is poised at an important crossroads in its development as a tourist destination. It's been "discovered"—particularly by Europeans—and the local authorities are deciding how to manage this growth in tourism while still protecting their environment.

The best time to visit is during November and the first half of December (before the school holidays begin). If you can't get there then, any time between November and March is pleasant, but avoid July and August, which are generally rainy. Midsummer (January and February) guests get the added bonus of being able to watch sheepshearing.

Be sure to allow enough time for Kangaroo Island—at least three days. Don't fall into the trap of flying over for the day and taking a bus tour—you'll be sorry you didn't spend more time here and experience the island without crowds.

ESSENTIALS

GETTING THERE Albatross Airlines, Kendell Airlines, Air Kangaroo Island, and Emu Airways fly to Kingscote from Adelaide, and Air Kangaroo Island also flies into Penneshaw and American River. The round-trip fare is about A$134 (U.S. $107.20).

If you prefer to go by sea, the **Sea Link Ferry,** 440 King William St., Adelaide, SA 5000 (☎ 08/211 8877 or 13 13 01 in Australia), takes an hour to cross the 16km (10 miles) from Cape Jervis on the tip of the mainland to Penneshaw. This journey costs A$60 (U.S. $48) round-trip for people and A$120 (U.S. $96) round-trip for cars. The **Sea Link** operates year-round. Connecting bus service from Adelaide to

Captain Kangaroo

If you're like me, the thought of a guided tour means box lunches, giant buses, uniformed docents reciting prepared speeches, and a gift shop selling Eiffel Tower salt-and-pepper shakers. So I was skeptical when I hired Craig Wickham to show me and my wife around Kangaroo Island.

Craig's uniform is a pair of shorts and a polo shirt bearing the name of his company: Adventure Charters of Kangaroo Island. Occasionally, he'll don a pair of sandals, but usually he prefers to go barefoot. His transportation is a four-wheel drive vehicle with room for only four passengers. His lunches are gourmet affairs barbecued calamari in chili and garlic or King George whiting poached in white wine, for example, with fine Australian wines served in wine glasses—all freshly prepared in front of you. And his itinerary is whatever his guests would like.

"You'll have to miss something," he tells us. "Kangaroo Island is the size of Puerto Rico. You couldn't possibly see it all in three days."

In his early 30s, Wickham is a former Wildlife Ranger (the Australian equivalent of Forest Ranger), so he knows the answers to all flora and fauna questions. He's also lived on Kangaroo Island for years, so he knows its undiscovered charms. He takes us to a lonesome area not five minutes away from the airport, where we walk among a grove of eucalyptus trees that shade us from the hot sun. As we look up, we notice they're also keeping several koalas cool while they munch on the trees' leaves.

Later that day, we travel to the Ravine des Casoars, the last four miles on foot, the last 300 yards down a steep cliff. But we're rewarded with golden sands guarded on three sides by steep rocky cliffs and on the fourth by the relentless ocean. At the bottom, the walls give way to seaside caves, where we take flashlights so we can see the Little Penguins who roost there.

Cape Jervis is provided at an extra A$24 (U.S. $19.20). In addition, the passenger ferry **M.V. *Valarie Jane*** (☎ 0848/31 233, or 1800/018 484 in South Australia) makes the 14km (8³/₄-mile) crossing from Cape Jervis to Penneshaw in 30 minutes and costs A$60 (U.S. $48) for adults and A$30 (U.S. $24) for children round-trip. Combination coach (from Adelaide) and ferry service is available for A$80 (U.S. $64) for adults and A$40(U.S. $32) for children. From September to March **Super Flyte Fast Ferry** (☎ 08/295 2688) transports passengers from Glenelg into Kingscote; this ferry, which doesn't take cars, costs A$65 (U.S. $52) and takes 2 hours and 15 minutes.

VISITOR INFORMATION The **Kangaroo Island Regional Tourist Information Centre** is at the National Parks & Wildlife Service Office, 37 Dauncey St. (P.O. Box 39), Kingscote, SA 5223 (☎ 0848/22 381), open Monday to Friday from 9am to 5pm. In addition, hotel and motel operators on the island are well versed in the area's attractions and will most likely be able to answer your questions.

The **telephone area code** for the communities on Kangaroo Island is 0848. As part of the telephone changeover, all numbers with a 0848 area code will be changing in February 1997 as follows: 0848/22 to 08/8553 2xxx; 0848/23 to 08/8553 3xxx; 0848/28 to 08/8553 8xxx; 0848/29 to 08/8553 9xxx; 0848/31 to 08/8553 1xxx; 0848/33 to 08/8553 7xxx; 0848/35 to 08/8553 5xxx; 0848/36 to 08/8559 2xxx; 0848/37 to 08/8559 7xxx; 0848/93 to 08/8559 3xxx; 0848/94 to 08/8559 4xxx; 0848/96 to 08/8559 6xxx.

Craig's services proved invaluable even at the attractions found in all the brochures. At several stops in Flinders Chase National Park, we seem magically to arrive just as two giant tour buses are departing, leaving the sites empty for us to explore alone. And at Little Sahara, a giant expanse of white-sand dunes towering 10 miles from the nearest shore, we have to scare away only a few kangaroos to have the spot all to ourselves.

Best of all, at Seal Bay, all visitors, whether on a guided tour or exploring by themselves, are limited to a 45-minute stay. But because Craig knows all the rangers, they allow him to stay as long as he (and his guests) like. An hour and a half after we arrive, we're still observing these animals' mating rituals as the bulls grumble and spar over ownership of their harems; only the heat of the sun tells us to move on.

At the end of our tour, Craig takes us not to the gift shop, but to his own home, where his wife is running the business end of things. They grab their swimsuits and take us to the locals' beach. Only the residents of Kangaroo Island know about this beach, and only two people are swimming there. But we have been spoiled by solitude and drive another half mile down the beach to a completely isolated area. As at every other stop on our trip, the beach is ours alone.

—John Rosenthal

John Rosenthal is a freelance writer living in New York City.

Author's Note: John was on a private charter tour and designed his own itinerary (and paid accordingly). Typically, groups run four to six people per guide. Exploring Seal Bay without a guide is no longer permitted.

ISLAND LAYOUT Kangaroo Island is 156km (97 miles) long and 57km (35 miles) wide at the widest point—about the size of Puerto Rico. The distance across at the narrowest point is only 2km ($1^1/_4$ mile). The total population is 4,200, with more than half of these residents in one of three towns: Kingscote (pop. 1,800), Penneshaw (pop. 250), and American River (pop. 200). The others are on scattered farms.

While most people live on the island's north side, closest to the mainland, the most fascinating wildlife is found in Flinders Chase National Park on the west end. Seal Bay and Kelly Hill Caves, two other popular places, are on the south coast.

GETTING AROUND Car rentals are available from Budget (☎ 0848/23 133) and Kangaroo Island Rental Cars (☎ 0848/22 390) at the airport.

The towns on the island are connected by a total of 1,600km (992 miles) of roads, only 300km (186 miles) of which are paved. Since all but the main thoroughfares are reminiscent of a washboard, allow plenty of time and exercise a fair bit of caution when you drive. Keep an eye out for animals crossing the roads—in fact, that's a good reason to avoid driving at night.

EXPLORING THE ISLAND

Kangaroo Island is much larger than you might've imagined and much of it is completely unspoiled. The bush is literally alive with wallabies, kangaroos, and other creatures. I don't have the space to describe all the highlights in detail, but one of the most important places for you to go on Kangaroo Island is ✪ **Flinders Chase National Park,** where you can see koalas perched in the forks of eucalyptus trees. Flinders Chase also has scads of kangaroos and wallabies, so tame and friendly that a fence had to be built around the picnic area so humans could eat lunch without having their sandwiches swiped. This is the first place I ever petted a joey in his mama's pouch, and I remember my surprise when he jumped out and then stuck his head back in for a drink. If you like wildlife, this is one park you shouldn't miss. You'll also see lots of Cape Barren geese, emus, and native birds—like galahs, rainbow lorikeets, and crimson rosellas. If you're very lucky, you could even see a platypus. Entry to Flinders Chase is A$6.50 (U.S. $5.20) per car.

Note: Do not feed any wildlife you come across while exploring.

If I had to choose between Flinders Chase and ✪ **Seal Bay,** I'd be in a real quandary, because I thoroughly enjoyed walking among the magnificent Australian sea lions, watching them snooze and seeing how they care for their young. The rangers who supervise the area charge a small fee (about A$7.50/U.S. $6 per adult and A$5/U.S. $4 per child) to help defray their expenses.

The coastal scenery is also impressive, especially the eerie formations at **Remarkable Rocks** and **Admiral's Arch,** and while caves just aren't my thing, I believe the ones at Kelly Hill are excellent. Tours are conducted at 11am, noon, and 1:30 and 3:30pm. Admission is A$5 (U.S. $4). **Stokes Bay** and **Emu Bay** are good beaches on the north side, but don't swim at Pennington Bay because of dangerous currents. **Sea kayaking** is a popular activity on the north side of Kangaroo Island; contact Adventureland Diving in American Beach (☎ 0848/31 072).

Many of the motels and several independent operators run day tours of the island, and it's a pretty good idea to hook up with one, at least for part of your time here, since the island roads aren't great and you'll want to sightsee with a local. Of these, my favorites are the ones offered by ✪ **Craig Wickham** and his experienced team of guides at **Adventure Charters of Kangaroo Island,** P.O. Box 169, Kingscote, Kangaroo Island, SA 5223 (☎ 0848/29 119). They have extensive knowledge of the island's flora, fauna, and sights and provide you with a very memorable experience. They offer one- to three-day tours of the island, with or without airfare from Adelaide (see the "Captain Kangaroo" box).

Kangaroo Island Wilderness Tours (☎ 0848/35 247) offers similar excursions.

WHERE TO STAY

I've listed a good selection of motels below. If you're a diehard romantic and prefer sleeping in a self-contained farmer's cottage or coastal lodgings, I suggest you contact **Kangaroo Island Remote and Coastal Farm Accommodation** (☎ 0848/31 233). Standards vary and prices range from A$40 to A$100 (U.S. $32 to $80) for each property.

IN & NEAR KINGSCOTE

Graydon Holiday Lodge. 16 Buller St., Kingscote, SA 5223. ☎ **0848/22 713.** Fax 0848/23 289. 7 self-contained units. TV. A$69 (U.S. $55.20) double. Additional adult A$10 (U.S. $8) extra; additional child A$8 (U.S. $6.40) extra. Lower rates during off-season. BC, MC, V.

Graydon Holiday Lodge offers self-catering two-bedroom units that sleep up to six. The all-brick property is a five-minute walk from the shopping area and one minute from the waterfront. Each unit has a clock radio, a kitchen, a ceiling fan, a heater, and electric blankets. All linens and towels are supplied. Barbecue and laundry facilities are on the premises.

Ozone Hotel. The Foreshore (P.O. Box 145), Kingscote, SA 5223. ☎ **0848/22 011,** or 1800/083 133 in Australia. Fax 0848/022 249. 36 rms. TV TEL. A$95 (U.S. $76) double. Additional person A$5 (U.S. $4) extra. Lower rates off-season. No-smoking rooms available. AE, BC, DC, MC, V.

The Ozone is the best known of the K.I. lodging alternatives. The historic hotel has 36 rooms, all with baths, and enjoys a central location on the waterfront. In fact, it gets its name from the aroma of the nearby sea. It's the social center of the island and offers an à la carte restaurant, a casual bistro, and a couple of friendly watering holes. A pool, sauna, and spa are available to guests, and picnic lunches are provided on request.

$ **Wisteria Lodge.** 7 Cygnet Rd., Kingscote, SA 5223. ☎ **0848/22 707.** Fax 0848/22 200. Reservations can be made through Flag Inns. 20 rms. A/C MINIBAR TV TEL. A$110–A$146 (U.S. $88–$116.80) double. Additional adult A$13–A$18 (U.S. $10.40–$14.40) extra; A$11–A$15 (U.S. $8.80–$12) child under 12. Ask about money-saving packages (with transport to the island, transfers, meals, and day tours). AE, BC, DC, MC, V.

The modern Wisteria Lodge is across from Nepean Bay, and each room has a sea view. Recreational facilities include a pool, a spa, a playground, and half-court tennis; meals are served in the Beachcomber Restaurant. Deluxe rooms offer spa baths and queen-size beds.

In American River

Located 37km (23 miles) from Kingscote, American River is popular with fishermen who come looking for whiting from October to March. The area lacks a beach, but the black swans on Pelican Lagoon are a picturesque sight. Wild wallabies abound and have even been known to take a swim in the pool at the American River Resort.

American River Resort. Wattle Avenue, American River, SA 5221. ☎ **0848/33 044.** Fax 0848/33 055. 27 rms. TV TEL. A$90 (U.S. $72) double. Additional person A$10 (U.S. $8) extra. BC, MC, V.

All rooms here offer electric blankets, clock radios, coffee- and tea-making facilities, and small refrigerators. There's also a sauna, spa, pool, restaurant, and bar. Charming hosts Sharon Seabrook and Ron Stewart offer a full complement of escorted island tours and can arrange fishing excursions. Facilities for the handicapped are available.

✪ **Wanderers Rest.** Bayview Road (P.O. Box 34), American River, SA 5221. ☎ **0848/33 140.** Fax 0848/33 282. 8 rms. MINIBAR TV. A$140 (U.S. $112) double. Rates include full breakfast. Children under 12 not accepted. AE, BC, DC, MC, V.

Each room at this pleasant guesthouse has a balcony overlooking the American River, and you wake up to the sound of magpies, egrets, and cockatoos. All rooms have tea- and coffee-making facilities, small refrigerators, and showers (no tubs). A solar-heated pool and spa are available. Congenial hosts Geoff and Pat Wright serve a full breakfast, pack picnic hampers for day trips, and offer memorable evening meals. Their bread is baked fresh daily and fish is caught only after dinner orders are taken in the morning. Local oysters, King George whiting, and Kangaroo Island lobster are the favorites.

In Penneshaw

The most appealing of the three resort communities, Penneshaw is 58km (36 miles) from Kingscote and 32km (20 miles) beyond American River. It has the best beach of the three towns but, while being closest to the mainland, is farthest from island attractions.

Readers Recommend

Muggleton-Mole's Bed & Breakfast, Lots 11–12 Bates Way, Penneshaw, SA 5222 (☎ 0848/31 030; fax 0848/31 290). *"This spectacular house, designed by the Muggleton family, has high beamed ceilings, a terrace with a view of the water, a sunken tub with an ocean view, and a friendly Jack Russell terrier. They offer one room with a double bed and another with a single, sharing a bath. The Muggletons prepare a fabulous dinner for their guests, and Rohan even took us for a drive after dinner so we could spot fairy penguins and wallabies."*

—Lisa Renaud, New York, N.Y., U.S.A.

Author's Note: The rates at Muggleton-Mole's are A$110 (U.S. $88) for a double, breakfast included.

Sorrento Resort. North Terrace (P.O. Box 352), Penneshaw, SA 5222. ☎ **0848/31 028.** Fax 0848/31 204. 27 units. TV. A$92 (U.S. $73.60) double. Additional person A$10 (U.S. $8) extra. Ask about dollarwise packages. AE, BC, DC, MC, V.

Some of the units here have sea views. The Village units, at the back of the property in a garden setting, are separate A-frames with cooking facilities; modern motel rooms face the water, where a colony of fairy penguins resides. A heated pool, a spa, a sauna, half-court tennis, a mini-golf course, a bar, and a restaurant are on the premises. Proprietor Jack Boyd offers packages including transportation to the island and local touring.

2 Outback South Australia

South Australia has the distinction of being the country's driest state. Two-thirds of it gets almost no rainfall and experiences very hot temperatures. The Stuart Highway leads north from Port Augusta and cuts the region in half. Though this is a memorable trip, you shouldn't undertake it if you lack outback driving experience. The town of Woomera, 485km (300 miles) north of Adelaide, supports the Woomera Weapons Testing Range, a restricted area that spreads from the highway across the Great Victoria Desert into Western Australia. The opal towns of Andamooka and Coober Pedy lie to the north.

COOBER PEDY

854km (529 miles) NW of Adelaide, 689km (427 miles) S of Alice Springs

I've been to a lot of strange places in my life and, quite honestly, I think Coober Pedy is one of the strangest. The town, with its population of just over 2,000, is out in the middle of nowhere. Were it not for the fact that most of the world's supply of gem-quality opals are mined here, the town wouldn't even be a wide spot in the road. As it is, Coober Pedy is inhabited by rough-and-ready Aussies and immigrants (some legal and some not) from about 40 nations who live here in the hopes of striking it rich. Aborigines constitute about 10% of the population.

If you approach Coober Pedy by air, which you probably should, you can't help but notice what look like huge gopher holes all around the town. This moonscape is created by miners who continually drill new holes, leaving behind the many dozens that proved to be a disappointment. Once on the ground, you'll find it easy to understand why most residents live in dugout houses to escape the extreme heat, dust, and flies. There are two underground churches and two underground motels. The town itself consists of a few motels, some casual restaurants, shops in which opals are sold, and the necessary service-type businesses. These places are all within walking distance of one another on the main highway, and the only other roads are those leading to the mounds and holes created by those who search for opals.

Unlike other mining areas in Australia, Coober Pedy isn't dominated by one huge company. All mining is done by individuals, and anyone can stake a claim. Even you can "noodle" through the dirt around the top of a shaft looking for a small stone others have failed to see. This free-for-all system of mining attracts colorful characters who add to the town's Wild West atmosphere. Many eccentric old miners, for instance, camp by their staked territory to prevent claim-jumpers from "night mining."

ESSENTIALS

GETTING THERE Kendell Airlines has daily flights to Coober Pedy from Adelaide (A$240/U.S. $192 one way).

If you opt for bus transport (Greyhound-Pioneer or McCafferty's), the trip from Adelaide to Coober Pedy will cost A$87 (U.S. $69.60) and take about 12 hours. The bus from Alice Springs to Coober Pedy costs about A$70 (U.S. $56). Passengers bound for Ayers Rock transfer at Erldunda.

VISITOR INFORMATION The **Coober Pedy Tourist Information Centre,** Hutchison Street, Coober Pedy, SA 5723 (☎ 086/725 298), is open daily. The **telephone area code** is 086. As part of the telephone changeover, all numbers with a 086 area code will be changing to 08/68xx xxxx in February 1997.

SEEING THE TOWN

Excursions are conducted by Tom Compagna, proprietor of **Coober Pedy Tours** (☎ 086/725 333; fax 086/725 352), and Trevor McLeod of **Gem City Opal Tours** (☎ 086/725 408). These provide a look at an underground home and a visit to an underground church. They also take you to visit a working mine and explain a bit of the history and technique involved. Opals were discovered here in 1915, and the miners soon started building dugout houses because they realized their underground workplaces were considerably cooler than the camps they were living in on the surface.

The **Old Timers Mine,** in the Crowders Gully area of Coober Pedy (☎ 086/725 555), provides another opportunity to learn about opals and the people who search for them. It's open for self-guided tours daily from 8:30am to 6pm. Admission is A$3 (U.S. $2.40) for adults and A$1 (U.S. 80¢) for children. You'll see natural opal seams and two underground display homes.

WHERE TO STAY

✪ **Desert Cave.** Hutchison Street, Coober Pedy, SA 5723. ☎ **086/725 688,** or 1800/088 521 in Australia. Fax 086/725 198. 50 rms. A/C MINIBAR TV TEL. A$119 (U.S. $95.20) double. Additional person A$14 (U.S. $11.20) extra. AE, BC, DC, MC, V. Free parking.

The Desert Cave, opposite the bus depot, has the distinction of being the world's only underground hotel "of international standard." Both aboveground and underground lodging is offered. All units have modern motel amenities, including in-room movies and coffee- and tea-making facilities, and a pool, a spa, a sauna, a bar, a

Readers Recommend

Old Miner's Dugout Cafe, Hutchison St., Cooper Pedy (☎ 086/725 541). *"Besides providing lots of local color and ambience, this spot served up some very good food at moderate prices."*

—Phyllis Mayer Brace, Oak Park, Ill., U.S.A.

gaming room, a gift shop, a restaurant, and an underground display are available. They also offer desert cave tours of the town.

Opal Inn Hotel Motel. Hutchison Street (P.O. Box 223), Coober Pedy, SA 5723. ☎ **086/725 054**, or 1800/088 523 in Australia. Fax 086/725 501. 82 rms (70 with bath). Hotel, A$35 (U.S. $28) double. Motel, A$70 (U.S. $56) double. Additional person A$5 (U.S. $4) extra. AE, BC, DC, MC, V. Free parking.

All rooms here are aboveground. In the original hotel the rooms lack baths. The motel rooms come with clock radios, coffee- and tea-making facilities, and small refrigerators. A restaurant and laundry facilities are on the premises.

WHERE TO DINE

It isn't surprising, given the large Greek population, that gyros, salad with feta cheese, and moussaka are all easy to come by in Coober Pedy.

3 The Coonawarra Wine District

381km (236 miles) SE of Adelaide, 424km (263 miles) NW of Melbourne

The Coonawarra is South Australia's, and maybe even Australia's, most elite wine area. The Jimmy Watson Trophy, the country's most important wine award, has been won by Coonawarra wines many times. Wineries like Rouge Homme, Mildara, Lindeman's, Hollick, and Katnook Estate have also won other recognition, including Robert Mondavi's International Winemaker of the Year. There are 16 wineries in an area only 12km (7½ miles) long and 2km (1¼ miles) wide. They produce predominantly red wines, cabernet sauvignon being the most prestigious. All are open to the public for bottle sales and tasting.

There's really no town of Coonawarra—at least not in the sense of stores or gas stations—just a small post office, a motor inn, and half a dozen wineries. There's a bit more at Penola (pop. 1,250), 10km (6 miles) south; Naracoorte (pop. 4,700), 41km (25 miles) north, is a booming metropolis by comparison. Most wineries are between Penola and Coonawarra.

In addition to wineries, the Coonawarra area offers several lovely historic buildings, some unusual caves, a wonderful wool museum, and lots of scenic countryside. Penola, founded in 1838, is the oldest town in southeastern South Australia. Mother Mary MacKillop, Australia's first saint, came to Penola in 1861 to be governess for her uncle's children and later taught school there.

ESSENTIALS

GETTING THERE Kendell Airlines and O'Connor Airways have nonstop flights from Adelaide and Melbourne to Mount Gambier, 61km (38 miles) south of the Coonawarra. Bond's Coach Company stops in Penola in the Coonawarra region.

Motorists following Highway 1 (the Princes Highway) from Victoria turn north at Mount Gambier and follow the signs to Penola. Those coming from Adelaide have a choice between the coastal Highway 1 or Highway 8 (the Dukes Highway).

VISITOR INFORMATION The **Penola Tourist Information Centre and John Riddoch District Interpretation Centre,** Arthur Street, Penola, SA 5277 (☎ 087/372 855), can provide maps and brochures and sells a very informative book, *Your Guide to Penola and Coonawarra,* by Annette Balnaves. The tourist center, housed in the Old Mechanic's Institute built in 1869, is open daily from 10am to 4pm. The **telephone area code** is 087. As part of the telephone changeover, all numbers with a 087 area code will be changing to 08/87xx xxxx in February 1997.

GETTING AROUND This is a destination that requires a rental car, because there are no local public buses or coach tours of the wineries.

SEEING THE WINERIES & ENVIRONS

Wineries are what brings visitors to the Coonawarra. Happily, they're not far apart and all welcome the public to taste their products. Following are just a few of the 16 in the area:

IN COONAWARRA

Rouge Homme Wines. On the main Penola-Naracoorte Road, Coonawarra. ☎ **087/363 205.** Free admission. Daily 10am–4pm.

Be sure to visit this award-winning winery. In 1988 manager Greg Clayfield won the Robert Mondavi International Winemaker award. The winery, established in 1954, specializes in red table wines, specifically shiraz and cabernet.

Mildara Wines. On the main Penola-Naracoorte Road, Coonawarra. ☎ **087/363 380.** Free admission. Mon–Fri 9am–4:30pm, Sat and public holidays 10am–4:30pm.

Mildara specializes in both red and white wine and grows several kinds of grapes, including cabernet sauvignon, shiraz, merlot, cabernet franc, malbec, pinot noir, and chardonnay. You're welcome to use the barbecue and picnic facilities and may taste their award-winning wines.

Penfolds. On the main Penola-Naracoorte Road, Coonawarra. ☎ **087/372 613.** Free admission. Daily 10am–5pm.

Formerly Hungerford Hill Wines, Penfolds is a large winery specializing in premium red and white table wines, as well as champagne and fortified wines. There are a playground and picnic facilities on the premises.

James Haselgrove Wines. On the main Penola-Naracoorte Road, Coonawarra. ☎ **087/372 734.** Free admission. Daily 9am–5pm.

This is one of the newer wineries, established in 1981. Dry and sweet white wines and dry red wines are the specialty.

IN PENOLA

Yallum Park. 8km (5 miles) west of Penola on the Millicent Road. ☎ **087/372 435.** Admission A$3 (U.S. $2.40) adults, A$1 (U.S. 80¢) children under 12. Open by appointment.

This Victorian mansion is a living museum. Owners Glen and Gayee Clifford live here and open the house for tours by appointment. The two-story homestead, built in 1880, is set on an 820-hectare (2,000-acre) working property. If you visit, be sure to notice the original William Morris wallpapers. The acid-etched glass window around the front door came from England by ship and was carried from Port McDonald by bullock cart. Mr. Clifford's father bought the property in 1914. The house is closed when the grandkids are visiting because they play in all the rooms.

IN OR NEAR NARACOORTE

Naracoorte Caves. 12km (7½ miles) southeast of Naracoorte. ☎ **087/622 340.** Guided tours A$4–A$6 (U.S. $3.20–$4.80). Daily—first tour at 9:30am; last tour at 3:30pm.

Guided tours of the Blanche Cave, the Victoria Fossil Cave, and the Alexandra Cave are offered daily at regular intervals, or you can opt for a self-guided tour. You view a bat breeding chamber via a video surveillance system. There are also a campground, walking tracks (trails), a kiosk, and an interpretive center within the Naracoorte Caves Conservation Park. NCCP became a World Heritage Site in 1994.

✪ **The Sheep's Back.** MacDonnell Street, Naracoorte. ☎ **087/621 518.** Admission A$3 (U.S. $2.40) adults, A$1.50 (U.S. 88¢) children, A$7.50 (U.S. $6) family. Daily 10am–4pm.

Exhibits in this wool museum, in a historic 1860 flour mill, illustrate the history of the sheep and wool industry in this part of Australia. A visit here is essential for developing a sense of place and beginning to understand what the lives of the region's early settlers were like. The National Trust, which owns and operates the property, has done an excellent job of creating displays that provide a glimpse into the personal lives of shearers and homesteaders. There's a small craft shop and the local tourist office shares the building.

WHERE TO STAY

IN COONAWARRA

Ⓢ **Chardonnay Lodge.** Penola Road (P.O. Box 15), Coonawarra, SA 5263. ☎ **087/363 309.** Fax 087/363 383. 24 rms. A/C TV TEL. A$88 (U.S. $70.40) double. Additional adult A$12.50 (U.S. $10) extra; A$8.50 (U.S. $6.80) children under 15. Rates include light breakfast. AE, BC, DC, MC, V. Free parking.

With vineyards on one side and extensive lawns on the other, this lodge offers spacious rooms, each offering one queen-size bed and two singles. Each also has coffee- and tea-making facilities, a small refrigerator, a clock radio, a toaster, electric blankets, and windows that open. Two units are for the handicapped.

It's not surprising that the Chardonnay Lodge has won numerous state and regional awards. Its red-brick exterior, stained-glass windows, and gracious grounds set it above other lodging offered in the area. Hosts Anne and James Yates provide a sincere welcome and are well prepared to answer questions about local attractions.

Meals are served in an attractive dining room, where the wine list includes more than 85 Coonawarra wines. An exhibition of paintings by regional artists adds interest to this room. A children's meal is served between 5 and 8:30pm, if parents wish to dine alone later. There are also a pool, playground, self-service laundry, and wine gallery. Room service is available from 7:30am to 8:30pm. Baby-sitting can be arranged.

You may also want to ask Anne and James about staying at **Sarah's Cottage,** their 1870s hideaway.

✪ **Honeysuckle Rise.** Lucindale Road, Coonawarra, SA 5263. ☎ **087/363 311.** 1 cottage, 1 apt. TV. A$130–A$140 (U.S. $104–$112) for two. Rates include breakfast ingredients. BC, DC, MC, V. Free parking.

A stone's throw from the Leconfeld Winery, only 200 yards off the main road, this attractive stone cottage is set among picturesque vineyards. Two queen-size beds, one upstairs and one down, and a full kitchen make this a desirable option. There's also a cozy second-story apartment with a picturesque view of the vines. Each has its own two-person candlelit spa. The charming decor and comfortable appointments are the creation of Americans Dennis and Bonnie Vice, who also own and operate Highbank Winery.

IN PENOLA

Coonawarra Motor Lodge. 114 Church St. (P.O. Box 161), Penola, SA 5277. ☎ **087/372 364.** Fax 087/372 543. Reservations can be made through Flag Inns. 12 rms. A/C MINIBAR TV TEL. A$78 (U.S. $62.40) double. Additional person A$10 (U.S. $8) extra. 10% winter discount June–Aug with minimum two-night stay. AE, BC, DC, MC, V. Free parking.

This modern motel is adjacent to a building that dates from 1868 and today houses a restaurant. All rooms feature tea- and coffee-making facilities, a small refrigerator, electric blankets, in-room movies, queen-size beds, and clock radios; 11 have bathtubs. Meals are served in the atmospheric Bushman's Restaurant. A wine shop, tasting room, pool, and self-service laundry are also on the premises.

WHERE TO DINE

IN COONAWARRA

Chardonnay Lodge. Penola Road. ☎ **087/363 309.** Reservations recommended. Main courses A$14.80–A$19 (U.S. $11.85–$15.20). AE, BC, DC, MC, V. Daily 7:30–9am (breakfast), 8:30am–5pm (snacks and tea), noon–2pm (lunch), 6–8:30pm or later (dinner); children's menu daily 5–8:30pm. INTERNATIONAL.

Local produce is given an international flavor in the dining room of the Chardonnay Lodge motor inn. At dinner you can start with smoked fish in savory cream sauce with crisp potato pikelets, beef satay with spicy soy sauce and a timbale of long grain and wild rice, or a platter of yabbies with coconut dressing. Main courses include turban of trout filet with a ginger-and-cucumber sauce, kangaroo filet pan-fried and served with sherry sauce and pickled walnuts, and beef eye filet filled with oysters and diced bacon, served on Roquefort sauce.

Quiche, filled croissants, other light meals, and Devonshire teas are available throughout the day. The work of local artists, on display in the dining room, is for sale. The extensive wine list includes 85 Coonawarra wines.

IN PENOLA

Bushman's Inn. In the Coonawarra Motor Lodge, 114 Church St. ☎ **087/372 364.** Reservations recommended, especially evenings and weekends. Main courses A$14–A$17.50 (U.S. $11.20–$14). AE, BC, DC, MC, V. Daily 6:30–8:30pm. INTERNATIONAL.

This historic building dating from 1868 has been a hotel, a private home, and a museum. Today it's an atmospheric spot to enjoy dinner. The colonial ambience is enhanced by antiques and lace cloths. Entrees (appetizers) include crumbed lamb brains in lemon-parsley sauce, salad of smoked salmon and avocado, and marinated calamari. The main-course selections include tandori prawns, oven-baked trout, and kangaroo steak with herbed butter. There's a nice selection of wines by the glass as well as a complete wine list.

16 Melbourne

Australia's second-largest city takes itself seriously. Women and men in well-tailored suits march through the central business district on their way to offices where the nation's financial decisions are made. Massive Victorian bluestone buildings and wide tree-lined boulevards create a sense of permanence that dominates the modern appearance of glossy high-rises. Unlike the residents of other Aussie capitals with more relaxed lifestyles, pedestrians here stride purposefully and tend to look slightly somber. In these ways and others, Melbourne (pronounced "*Mel*-bun") is more like London than Sydney, Brisbane, or Perth.

The oft-quoted remark "Sydney is made of plastic, while Melbourne is made of stone" sums up the sentiments of Melburnians toward their archrival. Another old Australian saw claims that in Melbourne you're asked "What school did you go to?" but in Sydney the question is "How much money do you make?"

While these remarks polarize the two cities unrealistically, you can't deny that Melbourne's metropolitan persona is unique. Changeable and sometimes inclement weather has helped to foster a citizenry interested in the arts; sophisticated shopping and dining venues have been developed to meet the requirements of the financially successful; and old-guard Melburnians have fought to retain the Victorian architecture, English-style parks and gardens, and turn-of-the-century tram system that contribute so much to the air of stability, reserve, and tradition. So it seems only natural that Boston is Melbourne's U.S. sister city.

Melbourne's cultural and financial roots were born in the 1850s, when the city boomed with a huge gold rush in the Victorian hills. Following the rush, business and manufacturing continued to thrive as a result of the availability of skilled labor and an excellent natural harbor. By the end of the century, the city was clearly established as the business and cultural capital of the colony. Its British origins were dramatically diversified after World War II by changed immigration policies, which brought in large groups of immigrants from Italy, Greece, Turkey, and elsewhere—adding a vibrant cosmopolitan flavor. These industrious new arrivals further increased the community's prosperity.

This is not to say that the residents of Melbourne don't know how to have a good time. They're the country's most avid supporters of Australian Rules football and follow local teams with

What's Special About Melbourne

Local Transport
- Melbourne's trams, an atmospheric and convenient mode of getting around.

Top Attractions
- The Victorian Arts Centre—to see a production and visit the Performing Arts Museum.

Shopping
- Toorak and South Yarra, offering dozens of fashionable boutiques.
- The Queen Victoria Market, selling almost everything imaginable.

Museums
- The National Gallery of Victoria, one of the country's best.

Parks & Gardens
- The Royal Botanic Gardens and Treasury Gardens, both lovely spots for a walk.
- The Dandenongs—a day trip designed for flower fans.

Monuments
- The Shrine of Remembrance, honoring fallen soldiers and providing a good view of the city.

Zoos & Wildlife Parks
- The Melbourne Zoo—one of the best in the nation.
- Healesville Sanctuary, for native fauna in natural settings.

Events
- Melbourne Grand Prix in early March.
- Melbourne Cup Day, the first Tuesday in November.
- Melbourne International Festival of the Arts, in September.

Side Trips
- The National Wool Museum in Geelong.
- Queenscliff, where time stands still.

something approaching religious zeal. In addition, the entire country stops on the first Tuesday in November to watch horses at Flemington Racecourse compete in the Melbourne Cup and to observe the standard-setting partying that accompanies the race (see the box "The Race That Stops the Nation" in Chapter 3). In early March the city celebrates Moomba, a 10-day carnival whose Aboriginal name translates to "let's get together and have fun."

1 Orientation

ARRIVING

BY PLANE More than 25 international and domestic airlines fly into this capital city's **Tullamarine Airport,** providing overseas access and frequent connections to all Australian states and territories. Some of the carriers are Air China, Air New Zealand, Air Pacific, Alitalia, British Airways, Cathay Pacific, Canadian Airlines International, Garuda, KLM, Lufthansa, Qantas, and United Airlines. Qantas's fare from Sydney to Melbourne is about A$153 (U.S. $122.40); from Brisbane, A$240 (U.S. $192); from Adelaide, A$144 (U.S. $115.20); from Perth, A$347 (U.S. $277.60); from Hobart, A$135 (U.S. $108).

Tullamarine lacks visitor information, but some hotels provide free phones for reservations. A Westpac Bank is open for all arriving and departing flights and baggage lockers are available at A$4 (U.S. $3.20) per day. Duty-free shops are in the international area and there are one restaurant and several snack bars in case you get hungry. Showers are also available. A post office is open daily from 9am to 5pm, with stamps available outside these hours from a vending machine. The big four—Thrifty, Budget, Avis, and Hertz—all maintain car-rental counters.

Melbourne's Tullamarine Airport is 22km (14 miles) northwest of downtown. Transport into the city is provided by the **Skybus Coach Service,** which takes 30 to 35 minutes and costs A$10 (U.S. $8) for adults, half price for children. The service operates daily every half an hour from the airport to the Skybus terminal, Spencer Street Station, Bay 30 (☎ 03/9335 3066). Complimentary transfers are provided to city hotels Monday to Friday from this terminal, and luggage lockers are available. A taxi to the city center from the airport costs about A$22 (U.S. $17.60).

When you're leaving Melbourne, remember to book the Skybus Coach Service (☎ 03/9335 3066 or 9335 2811) ahead of time. As of June 1996, the A$27 (U.S. $21.60) departure tax will be included in the price of your airline ticket; formerly it was collected at the airport as your were leaving.

BY TRAIN Melbourne is well served by interstate trains. The **Sydney-Melbourne XPT** provides daily service between Australia's two largest cities. *The Overland* and Daylink will get you to and from Adelaide, and the Canberra Link provides a combination of rail and coach service to the nation's capital. For train information and reservations, call 03/9619 5000 or 13 22 32 Monday to Saturday from 8am to 8pm and Sunday from 10am to 6pm. Interstate trains come into the Spencer Street Station.

BY BUS Major bus companies connect Melbourne with other Victorian communities and all state capitals. Sample fares: Sydney to Melbourne on the Hume Highway, 14 hours, A$55 (U.S. $44); Sydney to Melbourne along the coastal Princes Highway, 18 hours, A$61 (U.S. $48.80); Canberra to Melbourne, 9 hours, A$61 (U.S. $48.80).

Some interstate buses arrive at the bus terminal on the corner of Franklin and Swanston streets and others come into the bus terminal at the Spencer Street Station. New arrivals can take a tram or taxi from this depot to their final destination.

You can get intercity coach information from **Greyhound-Pioneer** at 03/9600 1687 or 13 12 38. You can reach **McCafferty's** in Melbourne at 03/9670 2533.

BY CAR If you drive to Melbourne from Sydney, the trip will take 12 hours using the **Hume Highway/Freeway** and about two days, with stops, along the more scenic **Princes Highway**.

VISITOR INFORMATION

Start your visit by calling in at the **Melbourne Tourist Information Centre,** Melbourne Town Hall, Swanston Walk (☎ 03/9650 1522; fax 03/9650 1212). The staff can answer your questions, make bookings, and arm you with maps and

Impressions

If Queen Victoria were still alive, not only would she approve of Melbourne, she would probably feel more at home there than in any other city of her former Empire.

—Jonathan Aitken, *Land of Fortune* (1971)

brochures. This office is open Monday to Friday from 9am to 5:15pm and Saturday from 9am to noon.

INTERSTATE INFORMATION For interstate information, contact the following tourist centers: **ACT Tourism Commission** (☎ 1800/026 166 in Australia); **New South Wales Travel Centre,** 388 Bourke St. (☎ 13 20 77 in Australia); **Northern Territory Government Tourist Bureau** (☎ 1800/805 627 in Australia); **Queensland Government Travel Centre,** 257 Collins St. (☎ 03/9654 3866); **Tasmania Visitor Information Network** (☎ 03/9206 7922); or **Western Australian Tourist Centre,** 35 Elizabeth St. (☎ 03/9614 6833).

CITY LAYOUT

Melbourne (pop. 3 million) is on the north side of the **Yarra River,** a few kilometers north of **Port Phillip Bay.** The central business district, where **Swanston Walk** is the main thoroughfare, is bounded by the river on one side and **Spencer, Victoria,** and **Spring Streets** on the others. Finding your way around is simplified by a straightforward grid system and the repeated use of street names. If you walk north from the Yarra, you'll cross—in this order—Flinders Street, Flinders Lane, Collins Street, Little Collins Street, Bourke Street, Little Bourke Street, Lonsdale Street, Little Lonsdale Street, and Latrobe Street.

Parks and gardens lie around the edges of the city center. **Queen Victoria Gardens** and **King's Domain** are across the river on the east side of St. Kilda Road, the southern continuation of Swanston Walk. **Treasury Gardens** and **Fitzroy Gardens** start at Spring Street, the central business district's eastern boundary.

NEIGHBORHOODS IN BRIEF

Greater Melbourne sprawls over 6,110 square kilometers (2,359 sq. miles). For comparison, greater New York covers 3,950 square kilometers (1,525 sq. miles). Within this area are a number of distinct ethnic communities and pockets of historical and scenic interest.

Carlton Italian restaurants line Lygon Street in the inner suburb of Carlton.

Richmond Many Vietnamese live and operate businesses in the vicinity of Bridge Road in Richmond. Swan Street has Greek restaurants. Richmond also has many factory-outlet stores.

Chinatown Sited on Little Bourke Street between Swanston and Exhibition Streets.

Prahran Greek eateries are along Chapel Street in the suburb of Prahran (pronounced "pran"). After Athens, Melbourne is the second-biggest Greek city in the world, but because of the larger population the presence of this ethnic group isn't as evident here as it is in Adelaide.

St. Kilda Road This wide tree-lined boulevard with trams rumbling down the middle is the site of the Victorian Arts Centre, including the Melbourne Concert Hall, the Theatres Building, and the Performing Arts Museum. The National Gallery is adjacent.

St. Kilda At the end of this grand avenue, the waterfront suburb of St. Kilda is known for its red-light district and cake shops—or "tarts and tortes," as Melburnians say.

Toorak Where old money lives.

South Yarra Popular with newly moneyed yuppies.

FARTHER AFIELD

The Yarra River winds down into Melbourne from the heavily forested slopes of the **Dandenong Ranges,** 35km (22 miles) east of the city. The western suburbs are on the edge of a huge volcanic plain extending through western Victoria to the South Australia border.

The **Bellarine Peninsula** and the **Mornington Peninsula** curve around **Port Phillip Bay,** creating a calm waterway for port facilities and pleasure boating. **Phillip Island,** 1½ hours south of Melbourne, is the site of the renowned nightly penguin parade.

2 Getting Around

BY PUBLIC TRANSPORTATION

The **Public Transport Corporation** operates trains, trams, and buses that run throughout the city and suburbs. Generally speaking, trams cover the inner city and trains and buses go farther afield. One ticket is interchangeable among the three modes, so if you want to travel on a tram you can buy a ticket on board or in a train station. If you stay in the inner neighborhoods, the price is A$1.50 (U.S. $1.20) for a short journey, A$2.10 (U.S. $1.70) for a two-hour ticket, or A$4.10 (U.S. $3.28) for an all-day ticket, good from 5:30am to midnight—when all transport stops.

A brochure with detailed route information is available at the **Met office** in the Flinders Street Station or at the **Met Shop,** 103 Elizabeth St. (☎ 13 16 38 or 03/9617 0900).

Discount Passes The **Getabout Travelcard,** which covers two adults and up to four children on weekends only, sells for A$8.50 to A$14.50 (U.S. $6.80 to $11.60), depending on how far you want to go. If you're going to be in Melbourne for an extended period, you might want to get a **Weekly Travelcard,** which costs A$18 (U.S. $14.40) for the inner neighborhoods and A$37.20 (U.S. $29.76) for the entire system.

BY TRAM Melbourne's green-and-yellow trams have become a much-loved symbol of the city. While most communities around the world have phased out this type of transport, the Victorian capital, with over 700 vehicles and 325km (200 miles) of track, is still expanding its system. The old cars have become collector's items. Elton John wants one to use as a summer house in his Berkshire garden; three of the cars run on a tourist line along the Seattle waterfront. The going price for a complete 1920s W-class tram is now about A$10,000 (U.S. $8,000) and it costs over A$20,000 (U.S. $16,000) to transport one of them to North America.

In the mid-1980s, a local artist came up with the idea of turning the trams into canvases in motion. The City Council agreed and six artists were commissioned to create "tramurals." The head-turning designs range from the delights of a Melbourne summer to mythical creatures, and in this conservative city it isn't surprising that the works have met with mixed reviews.

The **City Circle Tram** is a convenient way to get around central Melbourne, and it's *free.* The City Circle Tram travels around the city and links with other tram, train, and light rail routes; it'll take you past shopping malls, arcades, and major attractions. Trams run in both directions every 10 minutes daily between 10am and 6pm except Christmas and Good Friday. To catch the free tram, just wait at any of the specially marked stops on the route.

Note: When standing at a tram stop, hail the tram that you want to get on and pull the left-hand cord once when you wish to disembark. For more information on tram service, contact the **Public Transport Corporation** at 13 16 38 or 03/9617 0900 or visit the **Met Shop** at 103 Elizabeth St. Met tickets can be paid for with a credit card.

BY BUS A compromise between public transport and an escorted tour, the **City Explorer** (☎ 03/9650 1511) allows you to travel around the city on a double-decker bus, stopping at as many sights as you choose. The loop route starts at the Flinders Street Station on the hour from 10am to 4pm. You may get off at the Museum of Victoria, the Old Melbourne Gaol (which we non-British types spell "jail"), Queen Victoria Market, Melbourne Zoo, Lygon Street, and Cook's Cottage in Fitzroy Gardens. You stay as long as you like in each place and reboard the next bus. Tickets cost A$15 (U.S. $12) for adults and A$8 (U.S. $6.40) for children. Ticketholders are entitled to discounted admissions to the zoo, gaol, National Gallery, and Performing Arts Museum.

BY TAXI

Cabs are available throughout the city and cost A$2.60 (U.S. $2.10) at flagfall, plus A68¢ (U.S. 55¢) per kilometer from 6am to midnight. From midnight to 6am the rate jumps to A$3.60 (U.S. $2.90) at flagfall, plus A85¢ (U.S. 70¢) per kilometer. The extra charge for telephone bookings is A60¢ (U.S. 50¢). Three companies are **Silver Top** (☎ 13 10 08), **Taxis Australia** (☎ 13 22 27), and **Embassy** (☎ 03/9320 0320).

BY CAR

Several good reasons for using public transport quickly become evident to the innocent visiting motorist who tries to drive in Melbourne. The most obvious reason is a unique local law about turning right; add to this the generally grumpy attitude of behind-the-wheel Melburnians, the absence of parking lots and spaces, and the double-digit figures hotels charge for parking at their properties, and you'll be turning in your rental car faster than you would've believed. However, if you want a car for a day trip outside the city, here are the rental companies: **Avis,** 400 Elizabeth St. (☎ 03/9663 6366, or 1800/225 533 in Australia); **Budget,** 11 Queens Rd. (☎ 1800/132 727 in Australia); **Hertz,** 97 Franklin St. (☎ 03/9663 6244); **National,** at the corner of Peel and Queensberry streets, North Melbourne (☎ 03/9329 5000); and **Thrifty,** 390 Elizabeth St. (☎ 03/9663 5200).

If you should want to contact the **Royal Automobile Club of Victoria (RACV),** it's at 422 Little Collins St. (☎ 03/9607 2137), open Monday to Friday from 9am to 5pm. Present your home-country auto-club membership card.

BY BICYCLE

Extensive bike paths wind through the city and suburbs. Many bookstores sell "Melbourne Bike Tours," published by Bicycle Victoria (☎ 03/9328 3000), which describes 20 of the most popular routes. You can rent a bike from one of the **Hire a Bicycle** rental shops (☎ 018/534 383) daily from 11am to 5pm. Rates are A$4 (U.S. $3.20) for half an hour, A$6 (U.S. $4.80) for an hour, A$10 (U.S. $8) for two hours, and A$22 (U.S. $17.60) for a full day.

FAST FACTS: Melbourne

Airline Offices The following airlines have offices in Melbourne: Air France, 410 Collins St. (☎ 03/9672 7122); Air New Zealand, 490 Bourke St. (☎ 03/9654 3311 or 9670 3700); Ansett Airlines, 489 Swanston St. (☎ 03/9668 1211);

British Airways, Level 7, 114 William St. (☎ 03/9603 1133); Canadian Airlines International, 174 William St. (☎ 03/9629 6731); Kendall Airlines, c/o Ansett (☎ 03/9668 1211); Qantas, 114 William St. (☎ 03/9602 6026 or 9602 6111); and United Airlines, 233 Collins St. (☎ 03/9602 2544).

American Express The office, at 105 Elizabeth St. (☎ 03/9608 0333), is open during regular business hours.

Area Code Melbourne telephone numbers are in the 03 area code.

Baby-Sitters Call Melbourne Occasional Child Care, 104 A'Beckett St. (☎ 03/9329 9561). It charges A$2.80 (U.S. $2.24) per hour.

Business Hours Stores are generally open Monday to Thursday and Saturday from 9am to 5:30pm, Friday from 9am to 9pm, and Sunday from 10am to 5pm. Two large department stores, David Jones and Myer, both in the Bourke Street Mall, are open Thursday evening. Banks are generally open Monday to Thursday from 9:30am to 4pm and Friday from 9:30am to 5pm.

Car Rentals See "Getting Around" earlier in this chapter.

Currency See "Information, Entry Requirements & Money" in Chapter 3.

Currency Exchange Cash traveler's checks at banks or the larger hotels.

Dentist Call the Dental Emergency Service at 03/9341 0222.

Doctor If you're sick or injured and it's an emergency, go to the "casualty" department of the Royal Melbourne Hospital, Grattan Street, Parkville (☎ 03/9342 7000).

Drugstores They're often called "chemists shops" in Australia. The Galleria Pharmacy, in Galleria Plaza, at the corner of Bourke and Elizabeth Streets (☎ 03/9670 3644), is open Monday to Thursday from 8:30am to 5:30pm, Friday from 8:30am to 6:30pm, and Saturday from 10am to 1pm—and they stock electrical adapters, if you need one. O'Neale's Pharmacy, 300 Lonsdale St. (☎ 03/9663 3339), is open daily from 9am to 9pm.

Embassies/Consulates All embassies are in Canberra, the capital. The following English-speaking countries maintain consulates in Melbourne: **New Zealand,** 60 Albert Rd., South Melbourne (☎ 03/9696 0399); the **United Kingdom,** 90 Collins St. (☎ 03/9650 4155); and the **United States,** 553 St. Kilda Rd. (☎ 03/9526 5900).

Emergencies In an emergency, dial **000** to summon an ambulance, the fire department, or the police.

Eyeglasses O.P.S.M. (Optical Prescriptions Spectacle Makers), 82 Collins St. (☎ 03/9650 3599), can make you new glasses. So can Vision Express, 193–199 Bourke St. (☎ 03/9650 7455).

Hotlines Lifeline, 03/9662 1000; Alcoholics Anonymous, 03/9429 1833.

Laundry/Dry Cleaning Brown Gouge Dry Cleaners is in the Flinders Street Railway Station (☎ 03/9614 3342) and the Myer Department Store (☎ 03/9661 2639). The South Yarra "8 to 8" Laundromat, 326 Toorak Rd., South Yarra (☎ 03/9827 4892), is open daily from 8am to 8pm.

Libraries The State Library of Victoria is at 328 Swanston St., at the corner of Latrobe (☎ 03/9669 9888).

Newspapers/Magazines Melbourne has two major morning newspapers, *The Age* and *The Herald-Sun. The Australian,* distributed throughout the nation, is also widely read.

Photographic Needs Ted's Camera Stores are scattered throughout Melbourne and the suburbs. The best locations for tourists based in the city are 239 Elizabeth St. (☎ 03/9600 0711) and 600 Collins St. (☎ 03/9629 4366).

Post Office The General Post Office (GPO) is on the corner of Bourke and Elizabeth Streets (☎ 03/9660 1344 or 9660 1351). It's open Monday to Friday from 8:15am to 5:30pm and Saturday from 10am to 1pm. There's also a limited service from 9am to noon on public holidays. Many smaller post offices are dotted around the city. Central Melbourne addresses have a 3000 postal code.

Safety Avoid St. Kilda late at night, do your strolling in the city's parks and gardens before it gets dark, and exercise caution when in the area of the King Street nightclubs.

Taxes Taxes on retail items are included in the price. There are no hotel taxes in Melbourne.

Taxis See "Getting Around" earlier in this chapter.

Telephones The Payphone Centre, at 94 Elizabeth St., is open daily from 6am to midnight.

Useful Telephone Numbers Travellers' Aid, 03/9654 2600; Monash University Student Union, 03/9565 3106; Melbourne University Student Union, 03/9344 6966; Latrobe University Student Union, 03/9479 2166; Student Services Australia, 03/9348 1777; Student Counselling and Advice Bureau, 03/9380 5253; the Also Foundation, for gay men and lesbians, 03/9650 8157; Gay Advisory Service, 03/9650 7711; Women Who Want to Be Women, 03/9589 5039; Women's Information and Referral Exchange, 03/9654 6844; Zonta Club of Melbourne, a women's service organization, 03/9809 1084.

Weather For the forecast, call 1196.

3 Accommodations

As you might expect in a city the size of Melbourne, a good selection of lodgings is available. Reservations are fairly easy to come by on weekends, when visiting businesspeople have gone home, but it's a good idea to make weekday room reservations in advance.

The high-powered executives who come to the nation's financial center expect international-class hostelries, and Melbourne gives them a good selection. All are in the central business district—two offer old-world charm, and most charge top rates midweek and offer good value in weekend packages. Moderate lodging is evenly distributed between the city center and the inner suburbs. Additionally, a good choice between hotels and serviced apartments is offered.

I've used the following price categories in this chapter: **Very Expensive,** more than A$275 (U.S. $220) for a double room; **Expensive,** A$185 to A$275 (U.S. $148 to $220); **Moderate,** A$100 to A$184 (U.S. $80 to $147); and **Inexpensive,** less than A$100 (U.S. $80).

Note: In Melbourne there's currently an oversupply of hotels, so the rates I've cited may be negotiable.

IN THE CITY CENTER

VERY EXPENSIVE

Grand Hyatt Melbourne. 123 Collins St., Melbourne, VIC 3000. ☎ **03/9657 1234,** or 1800/339 494 in Australia. Fax 03/9650 3491. 580 rms and suites. A/C MINIBAR TV TEL. A$350 (U.S. $280) superior double; A$385 (U.S. $308) deluxe double; A$420 (U.S. $336)

Regency Club; A$700–A$2,000 (U.S. $560–$1,600) suite. Additional person A$50 (U.S. $40) extra. Children under 18 free in parents' room. Ask about lower weekend rates and weekend packages. Rates 10% higher Nov 1–10. No-smoking rooms available. AE, BC, DC, MC, V. Parking A$18 (U.S. $14.40) per night.

The Grand Hyatt is the largest hotel in Melbourne and the newest in this price category. Throughout, brass, lacquer, and polished marble create a modern, slightly showy atmosphere. In the lobby shop you can buy handy items like a A$210 (U.S. $168) shoehorn and an attaché case for A$1,440 (U.S. $1,152). Each superior and deluxe guest room has the same amenities and decor: camel-and-gray color schemes, modern marble-topped furniture, a king-size bed or twins, and hairdryers. The Regency Club on the top four floors offers upgraded rooms and a complimentary continental breakfast. Prices vary according to the view.

Dining/Entertainment: The Plane Tree Cafe Restaurant is open for breakfast, lunch, dinner, and supper. Max's is a glitzy seafood eatery where the Romanesque decor includes black lacquer and gold chairs. Bar Deco, open nightly, is done in black and white; Monsoon's Entertainment Studio is a nightclub that caters to over-25s. The Hyatt Food Court offers myriad casual options.

Services: Concierge, 24-hour room service, laundry, valet, nightly turndown, shoeshine, baby-sitting, massage.

Facilities: The City Club, with gym, indoor pool, spa, plunge pool, aerobics classes, flotation tanks. Like the tennis court, which costs A$15 (U.S. $12) an hour, there's a charge for the other exercise and fitness facilities. The Business Centre on the ground floor is convenient for traveling executives.

Le Meridien at Rialto Melbourne. 495 Collins St., Melbourne, VIC 3000. ☎ **03/9620 9111,** or 1800/331 330 in Australia. Fax 03/9614 1219. 241 rms, 11 suites. A/C MINIBAR TV TEL. A$370 (U.S. $296) double; A$470–A$560 (U.S. $376–$448) junior or courtyard suite; A$670–A$760 (U.S. $536–$608) deluxe or premier suite. AE, BC, DC, MC, V. Parking A$16 (U.S. $12.80) per night.

This hotel was created by connecting two 19th-century buildings: the Rialto and the Victorian Winfield. In 1984, under the watchful eye of the National Trust, all but the front section of the Winfield was razed and replaced with a brick structure complementing the facade of the Rialto. The space between the buildings was glassed in, turning the bluestone footpath into a covered courtyard. First-class accommodations were fitted into both structures; the preserved front section of the Winfield became a charming drawing room–style lounge, the Edinburgh Bar; the front of the Rialto, from 1891, was turned into tasteful shops; and the courtyard was designated the Portego, Venetian for "meeting place."

The hostelry offers every modern amenity with wonderful old-world ambience. All quarters are spacious and have traditional furnishings as well as hairdryers, terry robes, bath scales, complimentary in-room movies, the normal coffee- and tea-making facilities, and toasters. More than half open onto the atrium between the buildings.

Dining/Entertainment: Dining options vary from the fine-dining Chandelier Room to the Cafe Rialto Brasserie, where breakfast, teas, snacks, and drinks are offered daily.

Services: Concierge, 24-hour room service, laundry, nightly turndown, baby-sitting.

Facilities: Indoor pool, sauna, sun deck, spa, hair salon, chemist shop (drugstore), dentist, doctor, boutiques, business center.

✪ **Windsor Hotel.** 103 Spring St., Melbourne, VIC 3000. ☎ **03/9653 0653,** or 1800/003 100 in Australia. Fax 03/9654 5183. 171 rms, 19 suites. A/C MINIBAR TV TEL. A$280 (U.S.

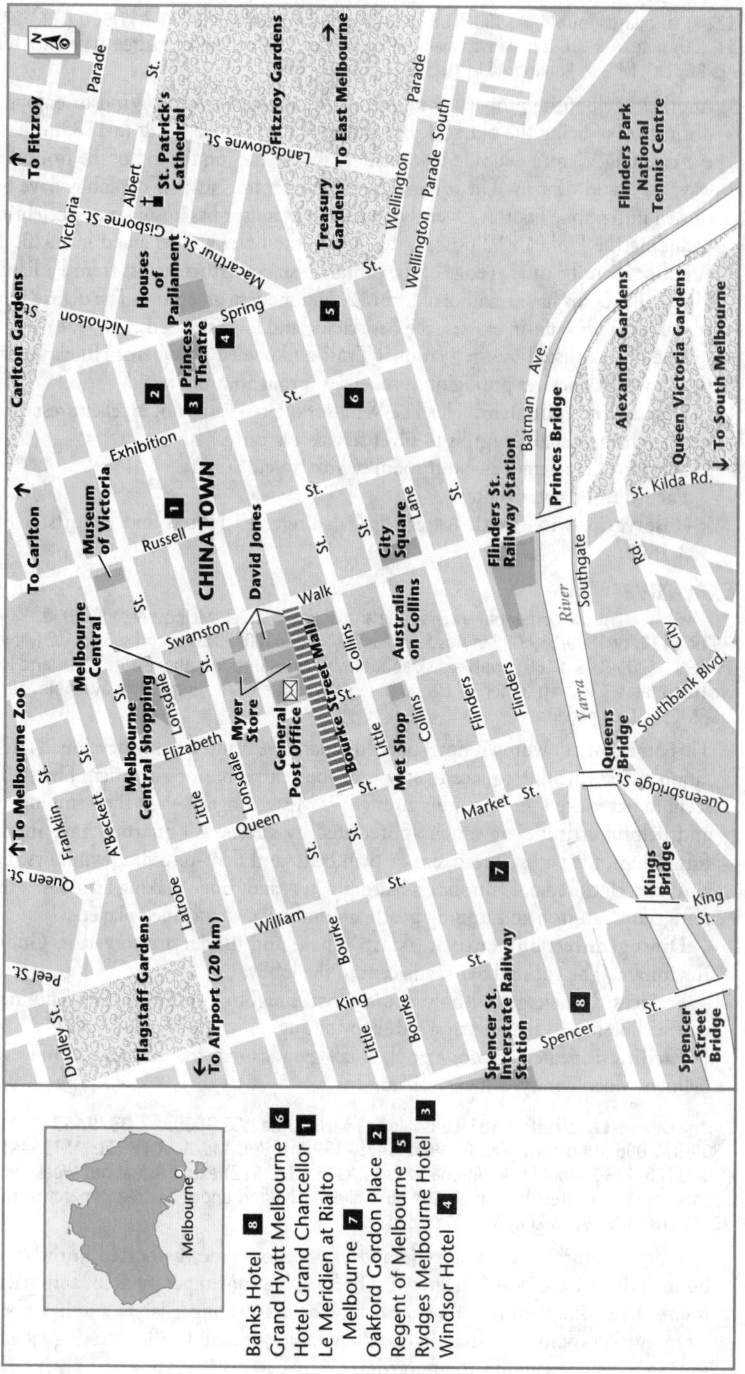
Banks Hotel 8
Grand Hyatt Melbourne 6
Hotel Grand Chancellor 1
Le Meridien at Rialto Melbourne 7
Oakford Gordon Place 2
Regent of Melbourne 5
Rydges Melbourne Hotel 3
Windsor Hotel 4
Melbourne
To Melbourne Zoo
To Carlton
Carlton Gardens
To Fitzroy
Fitzroy Gardens
To East Melbourne
St. Patrick's Cathedral
Houses of Parliament
Princess Theatre
Treasury Gardens
Museum of Victoria
CHINATOWN
Melbourne Central
Melbourne Central Shopping
David Jones
Myer Store
General Post Office
Bourke Street Mall
Met Shop
Australia on Collins
City Square
Flinders St. Railway Station
Princes Bridge
Alexandra Gardens
Queen Victoria Gardens
Flinders Park National Tennis Centre
To South Melbourne
Yarra River
Queens Bridge
Kings Bridge
Spencer Street Bridge
Spencer St. Interstate Railway Station
Flagstaff Gardens
To Airport (20 km)
Southbank Blvd.
St. Kilda Rd.
Batman Ave.
Wellington Parade
Wellington Parade South
Lansdowne St.
Gisborne St.
Macarthur St.
Nicholson St.
Victoria Parade
Albert St.
Spring St.
Exhibition St.
Russell St.
Swanston Walk
Elizabeth St.
Queen St.
William St.
King St.
Spencer St.
Market St.
Collins St.
Little Collins St.
Flinders St.
Flinders Lane
Bourke St.
Little Bourke St.
Lonsdale St.
Little Lonsdale St.
Latrobe St.
A'Beckett St.
Franklin St.
Peel St.
Dudley St.
Queensbridge St.
Southgate
City Rd.
2350

$224) standard double; A$380 (U.S. $304) superior double; A$900–A$1,500 (U.S. $720–$1,200) suite. Ask about dollarwise weekend packages. Children under 12 free in parents' room. AE, BC, DC, MC, V. Parking A$14 (U.S. $11.20) per night.

Another Melbourne property with old-world atmosphere, the Windsor enjoys the distinction of being the oldest deluxe property in Australia. Built in 1883, it has an eye-catching Victorian facade that includes two statues on the top of the front doorway, *Hope* and *Charity.* The original cage-style elevators just off the lobby have been turned into phone booths. Over the years, the Windsor has hosted many celebrities, including the Duke of Windsor, after whom the hotel was renamed in 1920. The Windsor is on the eastern edge of the central business district, across from Parliament House. Its rooms have traditional furniture and modern amenities. The deluxe rooms are larger, with walk-in closets, the best views, and king-size beds.

The hotel is listed by the National Trust and owned by Oberoi Hotels International, which operates prestigious properties throughout the world.

Dining/Entertainment: The The Windsor offers a variety of excellent restaurants catering from casual chargrills to silver service à la carte.

Services: Concierge, 24-hour room service, valet, laundry.

Facilities: Business center.

Reservations in North America: Call Preferred Hotels and Resorts at 800/323-7500.

EXPENSIVE

Banks Hotel. At the corner of Flinders Lane and Spencer Street, Melbourne, VIC 3000. ☎ **03/9629 4111,** or 1800/039 099 in Australia. Fax 03/9629 4300. 204 rms and suites. A/C MINIBAR TV TEL. A$200 (U.S. $160) double. Ask about lower rates through Aussie auto clubs and lower weekend rates. Children under 12 free in parents' room. No-smoking rooms available. AE, BC, DC, MC, V. Free parking.

This nine-story downtown hotel opened in late 1990 and quickly developed a reputation as the friendliest place to stay near the central business district. The staff all seem to have taken their training from TV's Mister Rogers—and their smiling faces and helpful attitude are much appreciated by guests. All quarters have modern furnishings, tile baths, queen-size or twin beds, and floor-to-ceiling windows. Each also has a clock radio, bathrobes, a hairdryer, tea- and coffee-making facilities, a small refrigerator, an iron and ironing board, an umbrella, and a video player.

Dining/Entertainment: Breakfast, lunch, and dinner are served in Gnomes Restaurant. The cocktail bar is adjacent to the lobby.

Services: Concierge, 24-hour room service, nightly turndown, free daily newspaper, shoeshine, valet, courtesy car, baby-sitting.

Facilities: Heated outdoor pool, small gym, sauna, free mountain bikes with helmets, video library, self-service laundry.

Hotel Grand Chancellor. 131 Lonsdale St., Melbourne, VIC 3000. ☎ **03/9663 3161,** or 1800/331 006 in Australia. Fax 03/9662 3479. 159 rms. A/C MINIBAR TV TEL. A$135–A$170 (U.S. $108–$136) double. Additional person A$15 (U.S. $12) extra. Ask about weekend discounts and lower rates through Aussie auto clubs. Children under 15 free in parents' room. AE, BC, DC, MC, V. Parking A$8.50 (U.S. $7).

The newly refurbished 18-story Grand Chancellor is ideally located in the central business district and near Chinatown. The hotel has contemporary decor and spacious rooms. Every standard room has a balcony; deluxe lodging is larger and has a better city view. All rooms have hairdryers, clock radios, tea- and coffee-making facilities, small refrigerators, and in-room movies.

Dining/Entertainment: Dinner and breakfast are served in the Lonsdale Restaurant; there's also a coffee shop.

Services: Concierge, 24-hour room service, valet, free daily newspapers, shoeshine, baby-sitting.

Facilities: Heated rooftop pool, sauna.

✪ **Regent of Melbourne.** 25 Collins St., Melbourne, VIC 3000. ☎ **03/9653 0000,** or 1800/311 123 in Australia. Fax 03/9650 4261. 311 rms, 52 suites. A/C MINIBAR TV TEL. A$240 (U.S. $192) standard double; A$280 (U.S. $224) deluxe double; A$900–A$1,900 (U.S. $720–$1,520) penthouse, premier, or royal suite. Additional person A$30 (U.S. $24) extra. Ask about lower weekend rates and weekend packages. Children under 18 free in parents' room. AE, BC, DC, MC, V. Parking A$10 (U.S. $8) per night.

The Regent offers the town's top accommodations, and you'll find little fault with this superior high-rise. Designed by I. M. Pei, the hotel is entered from a plaza set back from busy Collins Street, so peace and quiet start before you even get in the front door. The lobby, with its reception desk, Green Room Lounge, and Black Swan Bar, is one level above ground. The rest of the hotel is located from the 35th to 50th floors, with the intervening space occupied by offices.

The Regent offers spacious rooms decorated with Italian designer fabrics in muted tones. They boast Portuguese marble baths, "Regent robes," hairdryers, views of the city through floor-to-ceiling windows, and nightly complimentary mineral water. King-size beds are available. All the modern amenities, including toasters, are provided. The hotel's best suites are on the 50th floor. These include the royal and premier suites, which combine elaborate decor with facilities for entertaining in style, and eight theme suites, each with a distinctive atmosphere created by appropriate furnishings and fittings. A well-trained staff provides service reminiscent of fine European hostelries, and the overall ambience is understated elegance and good taste.

Dining/Entertainment: Spectacular views are enjoyed by the dining spots on the 35th floor: Le Restaurant and Café La. The Atrium, encircled by a waterfall almost two stories high, is a casual eatery on the base of the 15-story space around which walkways lead to guest rooms.

Services: Concierge, 24-hour room service, valet, nightly turndown, free daily newspaper, shoeshine, baby-sitting, massage.

Facilities: Health Studio (with gym, spa, sauna, solarium), business center, hair salon, newsstand.

Rydges Melbourne Hotel. 186 Exhibition St., Melbourne, VIC 3000. ☎ **03/9662 0511,** or 1800/333 104 in Australia. Fax 03/9663 6988. 298 rms, 65 suites. A/C MINIBAR TV TEL. A$205 (U.S. $165) superior double; A$230 (U.S. $184) king room; A$260 (U.S. $208) queen suite; A$330 (U.S. $264) king suite; A$440 (U.S. $352) executive suite. Ask about lower weekend rates, lower rates through Aussie auto clubs, and lower long-stay rates. Children under 12 free in parents' room. No-smoking rooms available. AE, BC, DC, MC, V. Free parking.

This 22-story property, in Melbourne's theater district, offers city views from all but the lowest floors. The lobby, with its wood parquet floor and comfortable upholstered chairs, has a welcoming feel. Each guest room is bright (the large windows don't open) and has a homey ambience. The executive suites have remote-control draperies, bidets, spa baths with city views, king-size beds, three phones, two TVs, large living rooms, and double showers. The queen suites have many of the same features and seem to be the best value. The superior rooms offer clock radios, hairdryers, tea- and coffee-making facilities, in-room movies, queen- or king-size beds, and irons and ironing boards.

Dining/Entertainment: Bobby McGee's is open daily from 6:30am to midnight. This dining spot, where the costumed staff do zany stunts, is popular with kids and parents. The entertainment lounge upstairs is open daily from 5pm to 3am. The weekend cover charge is waived for guests.

Services: Concierge, 24-hour room service, laundry, valet, nightly turndown, free daily newspapers, shoeshine, baby-sitting, massage.

Facilities: Outdoor pool, sauna, gift shop.

Serviced Apartments

$ **Oakford Gordon Place.** 24 Little Bourke St., Melbourne, VIC 3000. ☎ **03/9663 2888,** or 1800/331 180 in Australia. Fax 03/9639 1537. 59 apts. A/C MINIBAR TV TEL. A$183 (U.S. $146.40) studio; A$199 (U.S. $159.20) one-bedroom apt; A$265 (U.S. $212) two-bedroom apt; A$386 (U.S. $308.80) split-level three-bedroom apt. Additional person A$15 (U.S. $12) extra. Ask about weekend packages and long-stay rates. AE, BC, DC, MC, V. Parking nearby, A$8 (U.S. $6.40) per night.

These apartments provide a pleasant alternative for those wanting something other than standard hotel accommodations. The property, constructed in 1884, offers studio, one-, two-, and three-bedroom apartments, all with full kitchens including dishwashers. The south block features contemporary furnishings in old-world rooms with high ceilings, built-in wooden bookcases, and marble kitchen counters. Apartments in the north block have a modern appearance, and because it's farther from Little Bourke Street, this might be the quieter of the two sections. An iron and ironing board are provided in all units. Two-bedroom quarters have washing machines and dryers.

Dining/Entertainment: The Terrace Cafe and Bar is a casual eatery between the four-story accommodations blocks. Here tables are set around a huge palm tree, and other green plants create a garden feel; a retractable glass roof makes possible year-round alfresco dining. Breakfast is offered daily; lunch and dinner are served Monday to Friday.

Services: Laundry, nightly turndown.

Facilities: Heated saltwater pool, spa, sauna, small gym, hair salon; supermarket only a block away.

IN CARLTON

$ **Townhouse Hotel.** 701 Swanston St., Carlton, VIC 3053. ☎ **03/9347 7811,** or 1800/333 001 in Australia. Fax 03/9347 8225. 105 rms. A/C TV TEL. A$129 (U.S. $103.20) standard double; A$149 (U.S. $119.20) double on executive floor; A$200 (U.S. $160) suite. Additional person A$15 (U.S. $12) extra. Children under 12 free in parents' room. Ask about lower weekend rates, lower rates through Aussie auto clubs, dollarwise packages, and long-stay rates. AE, BC, DC, MC, V. Free parking. Tram: 1 or 15 from city center (a five-minute ride).

This is one of the best values in this cost category. In the inner suburb of Carlton, the five-story hotel's rooms are quite spacious. A few have tub/shower combinations, but most have just large shower stalls. You have a choice of a rust, light green, or beige color scheme. Some rooms have minibars. This part of Carlton is a mixed neighborhood with both commercial and light industrial activity; a fire station is across from the hotel. Lincoln Park, a grassy patch with a fountain, lies to one side. Lygon Street, with its plethora of dining options and boutique shopping, is a block away.

Dining/Entertainment: Breakfast and dinner are served in Kaynes, where the attractive decor includes cane chairs and exposed-brick walls. Doctor Jazz, as the name implies, is a popular jazz club on the premises.

Services: 24-hour room service, laundry, baby-sitting, secretarial service.

Facilities: Pool, sauna, barbecue area, business center.

IN SOUTH YARRA

The Tilba. 30 W. Toorak Rd. (at Domain Street), South Yarra, VIC 3141. ☎ **03/9867 8844.** Fax 03/9867 6567. 15 rms. TV TEL. A$125–A$170 (U.S. $100–$136) double. Rates include breakfast. Children under 12 not accepted. AE, BC, DC, MC, V. Free parking. Closed last week of Dec, first week of Jan, Easter week. Tram from city center (a 10-minute ride).

An eye-catching Federation-period building trimmed with just the right amount of gingerbread, the Tilba is near St. Kilda Road and across from Fawkner Park. Proprietors Gayle and Bruce McGregor have decorated their guest rooms with antiques, ceiling fans, and period accessories like Victorian shaving mirrors. Each has a shower; two have bathtubs. The rooms have been created from a grand residence and its former loft and stable, dating from 1907. "Pocket parlors" provide breathing space for those whose quarters seem close.

A beautiful stained-glass window over the cedar stairway, the subdued sand-colored decor, and a profusion of potted palms give the Tilba a light, airy feel that's both welcoming and elegant. Housemaids wear black-and-white uniforms; classical music is piped throughout the public rooms at a pleasing volume. The typical clientele includes visiting professors, ballerinas, artists, authors, businesspeople, and travelers—all of whom share an interest in staying somewhere very special.

IN NORTH MELBOURNE

MODERATE

Serviced Apartments

City Gardens Apartments. 335 Abbotsford St., North Melbourne, VIC 3051. ☎ **03/9320 6600,** or 1800/335 730 in Australia. Fax 03/9329 2174. 124 units. TV TEL. A$117 (U.S. $93.60) studio for one or two; A$128 (U.S. $102.40) one-bedroom unit; A$137 (U.S. $109.60) two-bedroom unit; A$195 (U.S. $156) Victorian town house for one to four; A$205 (U.S. $164) three-bedroom unit for one to six. Additional adult A$8 (U.S. $6.40) extra. AE, BC, DC, MC, V. Free parking. Tram from city center (a 12-minute ride).

Spread out over 1.6 hectares (4 acres) of grounds, the two-story Victorian town houses have camel-colored brick exteriors with black wrought-iron lace trim. Each of these spacious two- and three-bedroom dwellings has high-quality furnishings, plus a carport and courtyard with barbecue. City Gardens also offers studio, one-bedroom, and two-bedroom apartments with more modest but still pretty decors. Like the town houses, all have washing machines and dryers and only the studios lack dishwashers. All accommodations are two-story, except the studios. Chamber service is provided weekly and is available more frequently at an extra charge. A grocery store is across the road, and the Melbourne Zoo and North Melbourne City Council pool are in the vicinity.

INEXPENSIVE

Queensberry Hill YHA Hostel. 78 Howard St., North Melbourne, VIC 3051. ☎ **03/9329 8599.** Fax 03/9326 8427. 83 rms, some with bath. A$56 (U.S. $45) double with bath for member; A$62 (U.S. $50) double with bath for nonmember; A$16 (U.S. $12.80) dorm per person for member; A$18 (U.S. $14.40) dorm per person for nonmember. No smoking permitted. MC, V. Free parking. Tram: 55 north along William Street or 19 or 59 north along Elizabeth Street. Airport shuttle bus direct to the hostel.

Forget your previous notions about youth hostels. This state-of-the-art facility offers 24-hour access, a licensed cafeteria, rooms with toilets and showers, wheelchair access, self-service laundry, foreign-currency exchange, free bikes, and full travel-agency services. Each member has his or her own bedside security locker and can use the self-catering kitchen. The hostel is 1.4km (1 mile) from the central business district; the Queen Victoria Market is nearby.

IN EAST MELBOURNE

MODERATE

✪ **Magnolia Court Boutique Hotel.** 101 Powlett St., East Melbourne, VIC 3002. ☎ **03/9419 4222.** Fax 03/9416 0841. Reservations can be made through Flag Inns. 25 rms and suites. A/C TV TEL. A$105 (U.S. $84) double; A$130 (U.S. $104) deluxe double; A$150 (U.S. $120) suite. Additional adult A$15 (U.S. $12) extra; additional child A$7 (U.S. $5.60) extra. AE, BC, DC, MC, V. Free parking. A 10-minute walk or short tram ride from city center.

Magnolia Court is on a quiet residential street in an area known for its charming terrace houses. The oldest part of the property dates from 1858. The three-story building is painted its original Victorian colors—dark and light green—and cast-iron posts with Victorian iron lacework support the second-floor veranda. The sunny breakfast room is popular with residents of the nearby and much-pricier Hilton as well as with the Magnolia Court's own guests.

During the morning meal and at other times of the day, hosts Helen and Taras Maciburko chat with guests and help to plan their sightseeing and dining experiences. This personal attention makes the place feel like a B&B, but the rooms are more reminiscent of a quality motel. All the modern motel amenities—coffee- and tea-making facilities and refrigerators—are provided. There are laundry facilities and a spa on the premises. After 8pm, the front door is locked and you use your own key. No elevator. Breakfast is the only meal offered, and there isn't a bar or a lounge.

Serviced Apartments

$ **Albert Heights Executive Apartments.** 83 Albert St., East Melbourne, VIC 3002. ☎ **03/9419 0955,** or 1800/800 117 in Australia. Fax 03/9419 9517. 36 apts. A/C TV TEL. A$115 (U.S. $92) double. Additional adult A$15 (U.S. $12) extra; additional child A$10 (U.S. $8) extra. Rates include light breakfast on first morning. Ask about lower weekly and weekend rates. AE, BC, DC, MC, V. Free parking. Tram: 42; or a 10-minute walk to central business district.

Albert Heights offers apartments in a neat brick building. Each unit has a full kitchen with a microwave (no conventional oven), cooking utensils, dishes, and cutlery. Irons and ironing boards are also supplied, as are hairdryers. Modern furnishings take their place in a black-and-gray color scheme. Each apartment sleeps four: two in the bedroom and two in the living room. Each offers a VCR, a desk, two phones, and a remote-control color TV.

Albert Heights is everything midprice lodging should be: clean, attractive, and, in this case, an ideal spot for folks who want to do their own cooking. The management is available in the small reception foyer should you have any questions. Chamber service is available Monday to Saturday, and there are a hot spa and a laundry on the premises. Baby-sitting can be arranged.

INEXPENSIVE

A Bed-&-Breakfast

Georgian Court Guest House. 21 George St., East Melbourne, VIC 3002. ☎ **03/9419 6353.** Fax 03/9416 0895. 32 rms (21 with bath). TV. A $65 (U.S. $52) double without bath, A$85 (U.S. $68) double with bath. Additional adult A$20 (U.S. $16) extra; additional child A$10 (U.S. $8) extra. Rates include breakfast. AE, BC, MC, V. Free parking. Tram, train, or bus, and then a one-block walk; Georgian Court is on the street behind the Hilton, a 15-minute walk from city center.

Built in 1910, the Georgian Court retains much of its original appearance. White columns support a porte cochère and a balcony in front. The dining room and guest lounge have high ceilings, period antiques, and an old-world atmosphere. The accommodation section is a modern addition, so the guest rooms, while adequate, are quite plain with cream-colored brick walls and simple pine furniture. Each recently refurbished room has coffee- and tea-making facilities and a clock radio. There are a pay phone and laundry facilities on the premises. Dinner is available at an extra charge. The Georgian Court is gay-friendly.

4 Dining

Melbourne is renowned throughout Australia for the number and variety of its fine dining establishments. These restaurants, bistros, grand hotel dining rooms, delis, and cafés reflect the ethnic origins of the city's residents and its well-heeled heritage. Close to 1,500 options covering 60 national cuisines are listed in the yellow pages. Be sure to book early for all but the budget spots, and remember that BYO means you must bring your own beer or wine if you intend to drink. Be aware that many local restaurants are closed on Sunday.

IN THE CITY CENTER

VERY EXPENSIVE

Flower Drum. 17 Market Lane. ☎ **03/9662 3655.** Reservations recommended. Meal for two about A$120 (U.S. $96), plus drinks. AE, BC, DC, MC, V. Mon–Sat noon–3pm; daily 6–10:30pm. CANTONESE.

The Flower Drum is owned by Gilbert Lau, who serves tasty traditional Cantonese dishes complemented by innovative cuisine. Baked squab with Chinese wine is marinated for a full day and served with a sauce made from its own juice. Specialties of the house are Peking duck, crayfish, and Tasmanian ocean trout. A wide variety of cocktails and a good selection of wines are available.

✪ **Le Restaurant.** In the Regent of Melbourne, 25 Collins St. ☎ **03/9653 0000.** Reservations recommended. Main courses A$31.50–A$40 (U.S. $25.20–$32); six-course *menu dégustation* A$105 (U.S. $84) per person, including wine. AE, BC, DC, MC, V. Tues–Sat 7–10:30pm. MODERN AUSTRALIAN.

Le Restaurant, on the Regent's 35th floor, commands a superb view of Melbourne and the distant Dandenong Ranges. Its cool green contemporary decor creates a sophisticated ambience, complemented by outstanding service and cuisine. You choose from an à la carte menu that changes regularly to include fresh produce and seafood or you can select the multicourse fixed-price menu.

A typical meal might start with smoked duck breast with a marinated mushroom salad or rare peppered tuna medallion on a mudcrab-and-celeriac rémoulade. Main courses may be pot-roasted free-range pheasant with almonds, sultanas, and creamy peppercorn sauce or Tasmanian salmon filet pan-fried in rosemary butter with lemon and sweet capers. A demitasse of consommé can be served between courses to freshen your palate, and fresh spring berries glazed with Cointreau sabayon make a nice light dessert. If you dine here, you'll understand why Le Restaurant has won numerous awards.

Melbourne Oyster Bar Restaurant. 209 King St. ☎ **03/9670 1881.** Reservations recommended. Dinner for two about A$120 (U.S. $96); less for lunch. AE, BC, DC, MC, V. Mon–Fri noon–3pm; daily from 6pm. SEAFOOD.

This restaurant, one floor above street level in the city center, has a nautical decor in keeping with its menu offerings. Its tuxedoed waiters and live organ music create an atmosphere that's a little dated but still elegant. You can dance between courses every night of the week. In addition to regular menu items such as scallops provençal, seafood kebab, and oysters prepared five ways, the "chef's suggestions" are daily fresh offerings that may be barramundi filet, John Dory, trevally, or crayfish—prepared Mornay, thermidor, Newburg, or Mexican style. The specialties of the house are seafood platters, served on a plate big enough to hold a Thanksgiving turkey. A separate dessert menu lists several flambéed dishes, including crêpes Suzette and crêpes Jamaican. Quite a few liqueurs and liqueur coffees are available.

This restaurant is one of several owned by Nick Kadamani, who calls himself "Mr. Seafood." You might also like to know about his casual **Oyster Bar Bistro,** on the ground floor, where the same food is available at lower prices.

EXPENSIVE

Mask of China. 115–117 Little Bourke St. ☎ **03/9662 2116.** Reservations recommended, especially Sat–Sun. Meal for two about A$90 (U.S. $72). AE, BC, DC, MC, V. Daily noon–3pm and 6–11pm. CHINESE.

The Mask of China continues to collect awards for its distinctive Chiu Chow cuisine and consistently high standards. With its trademark of a Chinese opera mask, the decor is more art deco than traditional, though the food is what counts. The cuisine is similar to Cantonese but uses less oil and relies on natural flavors and textures. Fine seafood is a specialty and the game dishes on the menu are well worth trying—the marinated soy goose in particular.

Food Courts & Quick Bites

You wouldn't normally think of a multimillion-dollar hotel as the place to go for a budget bite, but you can at the Grand Hyatt's **Hyatt Food Court,** 123 Collins St. (☎ 03/9657 1234). For a minimum amount of money, you can purchase a variety of items and enjoy them under the vaulted glass dome covering the 400-seat plaza. Perfect Balance serves health food, including beverages from their fresh-juice bar, Hanzleman's will tempt you with Viennese pastries and cakes, and Mr. Tchoo offers quality Asian fare, as does Sushi Q. Can you guess what's served at Fasta Pasta? Bloom's New York Deli has its own seating. The Lone Star Diner serves American Tex-Mex. The Galah Bar provides drinks. The Food Court is open Monday to Thursday from 7am to midnight, Friday from 7am to 2am, and Saturday from 7:30am to 2am.

Southgate, on the south bank of the Yarra River, offers up choices for fast food, ice cream, a glass of wine, and coffee.

Diethnes Coffee Lounge and International Cakes, 185 Lonsdale St. (☎ 03/9663 2092), is a wonderful Greek bakery with seating and incredible pastries, cakes, marzipan, spinach and cheese pastries, and—my favorite—almond horseshoes. It's open daily from 9am to 1am.

Should you get hungry while shopping in South Yarra's fashionable boutiques, I suggest grabbing a bite at the **Divine Cafe,** 311 Toorak Rd. (☎ 03/9827 6046). Good sandwiches made on grainy whole-wheat bread or lovely slices of French loaf will sustain you through the afternoon. Open daily from 7am to 11pm.

Topolinos, 87 Fitzroy St., St. Kilda (☎ 03/9534 4856), is a casual spot for pizza and pasta. It's near the red-light district, but because this is conservative Melbourne you'll hardly notice. Open from Monday to Friday from 5pm to 5am and Saturday and Sunday from 5pm to 6am. Also does takeout and delivers.

Melbourne Dining

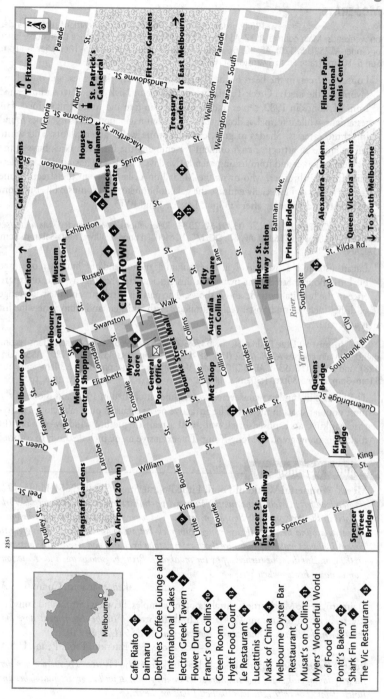

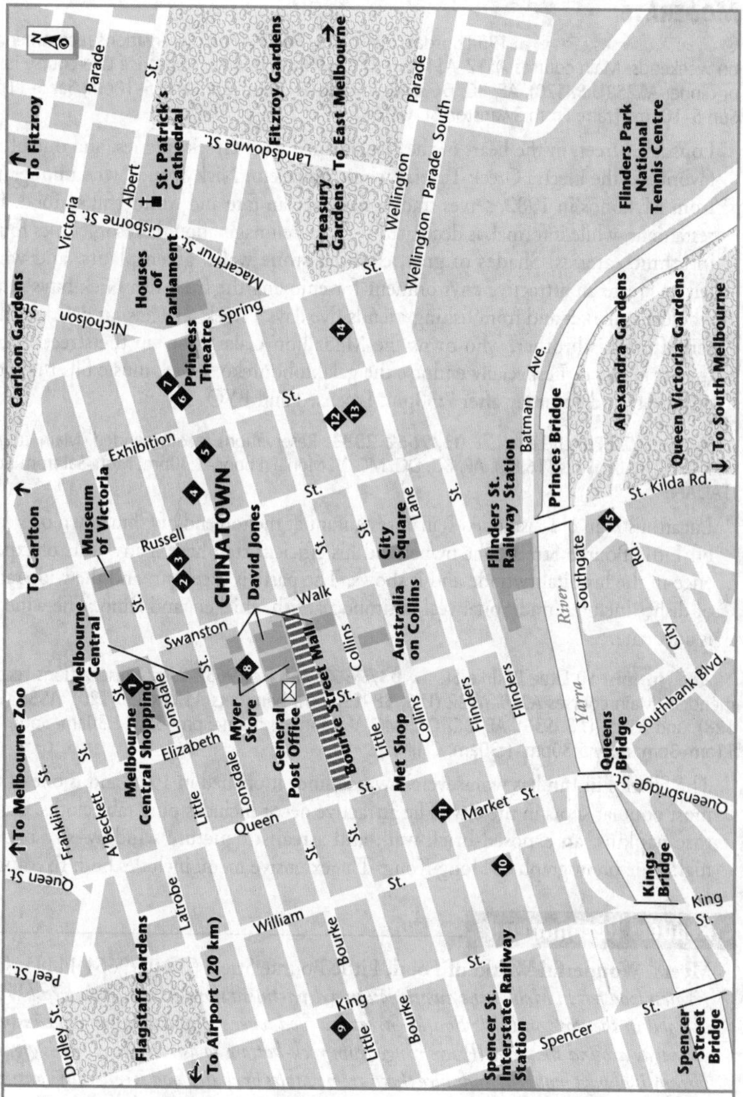

MODERATE

Electra Greek Tavern. 195 Lonsdale St. ☎ **03/9663 4760.** Reservations recommended on weekends. Main courses A$12–A$19.50 (U.S. $9.60–$15.60); fixed-price two-course lunch or dinner A$25 (U.S. $20). AE, BC, DC, MC, V. Mon–Fri noon–3pm and 5–10pm, Sat 5–11pm, Sun 5–10pm. Tram: From Swanston St. GREEK.

Lonsdale Street, in the heart of the city, is lined with Greek eateries, and one of my favorites is the Electra Greek Tavern, where proprietor Nick Spanos, who immigrated from Mykonos in 1982, serves traditional Grecian fare and wonderful seafood. His restaurant, while informal, is decorated with more imagination than sometimes found in ethnic eateries. Shades of gray, exposed stone walls, green plants, and white lattice create an attractive environment for enjoying the fresh fish Nick buys at the wholesale market and from fishing friends five days a week. He gets his delicious desserts from his brother, who owns the Medallion Cake Shop up the street. While they're all good, I especially endorse the galaktoboureko. Greek music fills the room on Friday and Saturday after 7:30pm. Licensed and BYO.

Lucattinis. 22 Punch Lane. ☎ **03/9662 2883.** Reservations recommended. Main courses A$15–A$21 (U.S. $12–$16.80). AE, BC, DC, MC, V. Mon–Fri noon–2:30pm; Mon–Sat from 6pm. ITALIAN.

Lucattinis is an old-fashioned Italian restaurant at the top end of Chinatown on a lane off Little Bourke Street. The owner and his efficient staff have many years of experience in the hospitality trade and it shows. The pasta is excellent, and the wide range of dishes includes traditional veal saltimbocca, fish, chicken, and lamb. The wine list is adequate.

Shark Fin Inn. 50 Little Bourke St. ☎ **03/9662 2681** or 9662 2552. Reservations recommended. Main courses A$10–A$32 (U.S. $8–$25.60); banquets A$25 (U.S. $20), A$35 (U.S. $28), and A$45 (U.S. $36). AE, BC, DC, MC, V. Mon–Fri noon–3pm, Sat 11:30am–3pm, Sun 11am–3pm; daily 5:30pm–1:30am. CHINESE.

The Shark Fin Inn has won several awards since it opened in 1982 and is one of the most popular spots in the city. The attractive decor includes pink tablecloths, dusty-rose napkins, an exposed-brick wall, and a realistic picture window–size backlit nighttime photograph of Hong Kong. The extensive menu includes both fixed-price

Readers Recommend

Myers' Wonderful World of Food, Little Bourke Street (☎ 03/9661 1111). *"The greatest food fest in Melbourne awaits you in a department store. Myers' Wonderful World of Food in the store on Little Bourke Street is a food lover's paradise where you can snack your way around the globe. Prices range from rock-bottom to astronomical. This gigantic bazaar is always mobbed, and since there are no tables or chairs food is generally consumed on the spot. But don't be turned off by the madhouse. Bring bags, load up, and create your own banquet heaven elsewhere."*

—Connie Tonken, Hartford, Conn., U.S.A.

Daimaru, in the Melbourne Central shopping complex, between Latrobe and Lonsdale streets, between Swanston Walk and Elizabeth Street. *"In the department store food court we had a first-rate four-course Indian meal for A$6 (U.S. $4.80)."*

—Jack and Eileen Esterkin, Paoli, Penn., U.S.A.

Ponti's Bakery, on Collins Street, half a block from the Hyatt. *"They had a wonderful selection of croissants, cookies, and other baked goods, as well as great sandwiches and lunch items. The caffe latte was the best I had on the trip."*

—Chad and Colleen Seymour, Scottsdale, Ariz., U.S.A.

"banquets" and à la carte offerings of creative Cantonese cuisine. Give strong consideration to the hot pots (perhaps bone marrow, Chinese mushrooms, and abalone with vegetables) and the daily specials incorporating seasonal produce. Licensed and BYO.

A pricier "sister" restaurant, the **Shark Fin House,** is at 131 Little Bourke St. (☎ 03/9663 1555).

IN SOUTH MELBOURNE

VERY EXPENSIVE

✪ **Rogalsky's.** 440 Clarendon St. ☎ **03/9690 1977.** Reservations recommended. Main courses A$27.50 (U.S. $22). AE, BC, DC, MC, V. Tues–Sat 6:30pm–10pm. MODERN FRENCH.

One of Melbourne's outstanding restaurants, Rogalsky's has amassed a vast collection of awards. For an entree, how about boned quail prepared Peking style, served on small pancakes with scallions and preserved vegetables? Or there's Atlantic salmon marinated in lemon juice and dressed with virgin olive oil and sea salt. Main courses include beef filet marinated in red wine and stuffed with tapenade, roasted and served on tomato pasta; crisp roasted duck breast with the braised leg in a tangy orange glaze served with vegetable stir-fry; and pan-fried filet of deep-sea fish with an herb crust served on an eggplant purée. If you leave room for dessert, try the wild-strawberry soufflé with a pineapple ice-cream sandwich.

The excellent meals are complemented by an attractive dark-green and coral-pink decor. There's no smoking in the dining room.

EXPENSIVE

The Vic Restaurant. In the Theatres Building at the Victorian Arts Centre. ☎ **03/9281 8000.** Reservations recommended. Main courses A$11.80–A$21.50 (U.S. $9.40–$17.20). Public holiday surcharge 15%. AE, BC, DC, MC, V. Mon–Sat 5:30–8pm (pretheater dinner) and 8–11pm (supper). INTERNATIONAL.

The Vic is a convenient place for dining before or after a performance. The modern evening menu features light fare with a slight foreign flavor. Before a show you might have a soufflé of prawns, followed by waterzooi of chicken. The streamlined supper menu is limited to lighter fare like creamy field mushroom soup, English spinach salad, spicy beef noodles, or a selection of cheeses. Framed costume sketches are displayed on the Vic's walls, and an Italianate painted ceiling floats high overhead. An adjacent coffee shop is open Monday to Friday from 11am to 4pm.

IN CARLTON

MODERATE

$ **Il Primo.** 242 Lygon St., Carlton. ☎ **03/9663 6100.** Reservations recommended. Main courses A$12.50–A$22 (U.S. $10–$17.60). AE, BC, DC, MC, V. Sun–Tues 6:30am–1am, Wed–Sat 6:30am–3am. Bus: 203 traveling north on Russell Street. Tram: 1, 15, 21, or 22 traveling north on Swanston Street (Stop 12). SOUTHERN EUROPEAN.

Il Primo is in a pair of historic terrace houses in the Italian sector of Melbourne 1km (0.6 mile) from the central business district. The cozy decor in each of three dining areas is created by used-brick walls, wooden open-beam ceilings, and quarry-tile floors. The eatery feels a little like a wine cellar and the wine list is extensive, including a range of inexpensive, "cleanskin" (unlabeled) local wines.

This is a spot you definitely don't want to miss. Chef Graham Quick offers dishes like charcoal-grilled marinated quail in warm eggplant salad; rack of lamb filled with pinenuts, bacon, and fresh herbs, finished with marsala sauce; and "calabrese" pasta (with hot salami and tomato concassé). All are delicious. BYO and licensed. You can enjoy live jazz on Tuesday to Sunday from 10 or 11pm to closing.

Breakfast, Brunch or Tea

Musat's on Collins, 412 Collins St., between Queen and William streets (☎ 03/ 9670 2280), presents a pleasant alternative to pricey hotel breakfasts. American pancakes cost A$5.90 (U.S. $4.70); eggs Benedict and omelets will set you back about A$9.50 (U.S. $7.60). Musat's is open Monday to Friday from 7am to 4pm. In addition to breakfast, lunch is offered from 11:30am to 3pm, and morning and afternoon tea are available.

The **Green Room,** in the Regent of Melbourne, 25 Collins St. (☎ 03/ 9653 0000), is an elegant spot for afternoon or evening refreshments. Located one level above ground with a view of the hotel's entrance, this is also a good place for people-watching. The Green Room is open from noon to midnight daily. High tea is offered from 2:30 to 5:30pm.

The **Cafe Rialto** and **Franc's on Collins,** in Le Meridien at Rialto Melbourne, 495 Collins St. (☎ 03/9620 9111), and the **Lounge,** in the Windsor Hotel, 103 Spring St. (☎ 03/9653 0653), are other delightful spots in which to have a cuppa. Afternoon tea at the Windsor is served Monday to Saturday from 3:15 to 5:30pm and costs A$22 (U.S. $17.60). High tea with chamber music is offered on Sunday from 2:30 to 5:30pm at a cost of A$28 (U.S. $22.40) per person.

$ La Spaghettata. 238 Lygon St., Carlton. ☎ **03/9663 6102.** Reservations recommended Sat–Sun. Main courses A$11.80–A$19.50 (U.S. $9.44–$15.60). AE, BC, DC, MC, V. Daily noon–3pm and 5–11pm or later. Bus: 203 traveling north on Russell Street. Tram: 1, 15, 21, or 22 traveling north on Swanston Street (Stop 12). ITALIAN.

The proprietors caught my attention with a boast printed on their napkins: "The best spaghetti house in Australia." The casual decor, including red-and-white-checked tablecloths and exposed-brick walls, made a good first impression. Outside seating under red, white, and green umbrellas, as well as the friendly and prompt service, also scored points. Sicilian-born proprietor Tony Cattafi stops at each table to chat with patrons. The eatery is usually filled with the pleasantly noisy hum of happy diners, and it's easy to see that La Spaghettata is popular with locals, especially students from the nearby university.

Chalkboards list specials and homemade desserts that are available in addition to regular menu items. All pasta is made on the premises and, the hosts claim, people come from all over to have the spaghetti marinara. I chose the spaghetti carbonara from the list of nearly two dozen pastas and thoroughly enjoyed it. Happily, I took the waitress's advice and ordered the generous entree size instead of the huge main course. Chicken parmigiana or cacciatore, veal parmigiana or scaloppine, tournedos Rossini, and prime eye filet are also on the menu. The desserts include zabaglione freddo, profiteroles with hot chocolate sauce, and strawberries in a basket. BYO and licensed.

IN FITZROY

Ambrosia. 363 Brunswick St. ☎ **03/9417 7415.** Reservations recommended Thurs–Sat. Main courses A$10.90–A$16 (U.S. $8.75–$12.80). BC, MC, V. Daily 6pm–midnight. Tram: 10 or 11 traveling east on Collins Street. GREEK.

No less than two dozen eateries line Brunswick Street in Fitzroy, Melbourne's newest trendy dining neighborhood. Unlike Lygon Street in Carlton, where most spots serve Italian fare, Brunswick Street's offerings are definitely multiethnic. At Ambrosia, winner of several awards, a clever trompe l'oeil creates the sense of being in a Greek café. Wooden chairs with hemp seats, wooden tables, the tile floor with mosaic border, and ceiling fans enhance the Mediterranean ambience. Patrons at the 15 or so tables can choose such traditional dishes as saganaki ("pan-fried sheep's cheese"), tzatziki (yogurt-and-cucumber dip), barbecued baby octopus, chicken souvlaki, Greek sausage, and baklava. Licensed and BYO.

IN RICHMOND

Vlado's Charcoal Grill. 61 Bridge Rd. ☎ **03/9428 5833.** Reservations required, *well* in advance. Meal for two about A$100 (U.S. $80). AE, BC, DC, MC, V. Mon–Fri noon–3pm; Mon–Sat 6–11pm. BEEF.

This steakhouse is nirvana for meat-eaters, particularly visiting Japanese executives. Beef—sausages, liver, steak, and so forth—is grilled to perfection. Host Vlado Gregurek has a loyal following, so if you plan to dine here, make reservations up to two weeks ahead. Licensed and BYO.

IN ST. KILDA

The Pavilion. 40 Jacka Blvd. ☎ **03/9534 8221.** Reservations recommended. Dinner for two about A$90 (U.S. $72); less for lunch. AE, BC, DC, MC, V. Daily noon–10:30pm. Tram: 15 or 96 to Luna Park stop; then walk toward the sea. SEAFOOD.

The Pavilion is literally a stone's throw from the beach in Melbourne's favorite seaside community. Inside dining in slightly art deco surroundings is possible daily year-round. The informal contemporary eatery is in the former beach changing rooms, remodeled and refined by proprietors Kevin and Gail Donovan. The cuisine is mostly seafood. Pacific oysters are opened to order. You might also like to try the pan-fried filet of marinated ocean trout with a vinaigrette of dill and seed musturd; if seafood isn't your thing, perhaps try one of the vegetarian dishes. The wine list is very good.

A MOVABLE FEAST

The Colonial Tramcar Restaurant. ☎ **03/9696 4000.** Fax 03/9696 3787. Reservations required, *well* in advance; after 6:30pm, call mobile phone (☎ 007/33 2900). Early dinner three-course meal A$55 (U.S. $44); late dinner five-course meal A$75 (U.S. $60) Sun–Thurs, A$85 (U.S. $68) Fri–Sat. All drinks included. Early dinner daily at 5:45pm; late dinner daily at 8:30pm. Tram: Departs from and returns to stop 12 on South Bank Boulevard. INTERNATIONAL.

This is a way of combining good eating with an atmospheric ride around the city. The fully refurbished 1927 vehicles trundle along the tracks of Melbourne's scenic thoroughfares while you enjoy Pullman-style silver service and champagne. Seats covered in plush velvet, warm light glowing from brass lamps, and fresh flowers help to transport you to another era. Stabilizers ensure a smooth ride, and one-way windows have been installed so you can enjoy the passing scenery without the distraction of curious gazes.

The multicourse menu changes regularly and includes a choice of two entrees, main courses, and desserts. For example, following an appetizer of duck-liver bigarade, you select either seafood en cocotte Matthew Flinders or pepper-crusted kangaroo for an entree. The main offerings might be tenderloin of beef Sherwood or suprême of chicken colonial. A platter of Victorian cheeses is offered, followed by a choice of desserts like apple crêpe Port Arthur or coupe kallista. Coffee, mints, and liqueurs are served at the end of the meal.

5 Attractions

Visitors enjoy the conservative, almost old-world ambience of the city while they ride trams and wander through leafy parks and gardens. This is also a good spot for serious shoppers, those who enjoy fine dining, and theater buffs. In between sightseeing excursions and shopping trips, be sure to allow time for a traditional afternoon tea.

SIGHTSEEING SUGGESTIONS FOR THE FIRST-TIME VISITOR

If You Have 1 Day Start out at the National Gallery of Victoria, then, if you're a theater buff, visit the nearby Performing Arts Museum. After lunch do the walking tour I've included in this section and have afternoon tea at the Windsor Hotel. In the evening, travel to Phillip Island to see the fairy penguins.

If You Have 2 Days Spend Day 1 as suggested above. On Day 2 visit the Queen Victoria Market in the morning and the Melbourne Zoo in the afternoon. In the evening, dine on Melbourne's tramcar restaurant or eat in one of the city's myriad ethnic spots.

If You Have 3 Days Spend Days 1 and 2 as outlined above. On the third day, do a day trip to the Yarra Valley. Visit the Healesville Sanctuary, have lunch, and stop for tasting at some of the area wineries. This can be a self-drive excursion or you can join a coach tour.

If You Have 4 Days or More Use your first three days as suggested above. On the fourth day, make an excursion to Queenscliff with a stop at the National Wool Museum in Geelong. If there's time, stop at historic Werribee Park on the way back.

THE TOP ATTRACTIONS

✪ **National Gallery of Victoria.** 180 St. Kilda Rd. ☎ **03/9208 0203.** Admission A$6 (U.S. $4.80) adults, A$3 (U.S. $2.40) children, A$12 (U.S. $9.60) family. Daily 10am–5pm. Free tours Mon at 11am and 2pm; Tues–Fri at 11am, noon, and 1, 2, and 3pm; Sat–Sun at 2 and 3pm. Closed Good Friday and Christmas. Tram: Any southbound tram on Swanston Street to Stop 12.

The National Gallery contains an excellent collection of Aboriginal, colonial Australian, Asian, and European works. Be sure not to miss Tom Roberts's *Shearing the Rams,* one of the best-known paintings of its period. Also look for Frederick McCubbin's *The Pioneer.* Russell Drysdale, Sidney Nolan, and Arthur Streeton are also represented (as are Rembrandt and Picasso). For more information, the Gallery Shop sells a good selection of books about Australian art and artists. If you're fond of stained glass, note the ceiling in the Great Hall.

The Gallery Restaurant offers an à la carte menu. A kiosk sells snacks.

Rippon Lea. 192 Hotham St., Elsternwick. ☎ **03/9523 6095.** Admission A$7 (U.S. $5.60) adults, A$3.50 (U.S. $2.80) children; A$16.50 (U.S. $13.20) family. Daily 10am–5pm. Guided tours of house, daily 11am–3pm. Closed Good Friday and Christmas. Tram: 67 to Stop 40; then walk up Hotham Street. Bus: 216/219 from corner of Bourke and Queen streets, city to Stop 4. Train: Sandringham Line from Platform 11/12/13 at Flinders Street Station to Rippon Lea Station.

In the suburb of Elsternwick, 8km (5 miles) from the city center, Rippon Lea is a great Victorian house surrounded by 5.3 hectares (13 acres) of landscaped gardens. The first owner of the property was Sir Frederick Thomas Sargood, who started construction of the 15-room Romanesque-style house in 1868. By the time he died, in 1903, the mansion had grown to 33 rooms. In the 1930s the house underwent

Melbourne Attractions

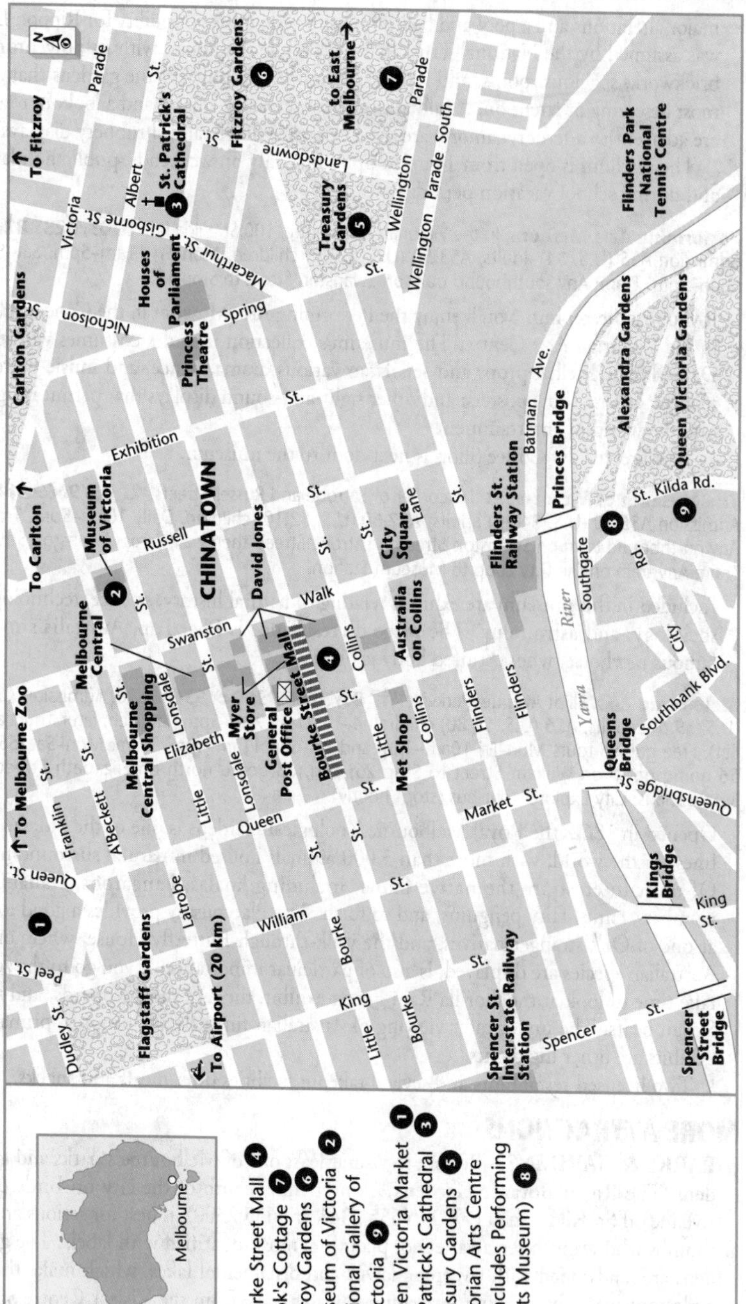

major alterations and a pool and ballroom were added. Responsibility for Rippon Lea was assumed by the National Trust in 1974. While the house, with its polychrome brickwork, spacious rooms, and stained glass, is interesting, it's the gardens that are most deserving of attention. A fully restored conservatory, a lake, and a lookout tower are adjacent to a fernery, an orchard, and extensive flower and shrubbery displays.

The tearoom is open from 11am to 4pm, but only on weekends, public holidays, and during school vacation periods.

Performing Arts Museum. In the Victorian Arts Centre, 100 St. Kilda Rd. ☎ **03/9281 8263.** Admission A$5 (U.S. $4) adults, A$3.50 (U.S. $2.80) children. Mon–Fri 11am–5pm, Sat–Sun noon–5pm. Tram: Any southbound tram on Swanston Street to Stop 12.

If you're a theater buff, you'll enjoy the Performing Arts Museum in the Concert Hall in the Victorian Arts Centre. The museum's collection includes costumes worn by Dame Nellie Melba; props and sets from various drama, dance, and music performances; artistic show posters; and other sight-and-sound displays that permit insight into the world of entertainment.

The Treble Clef Coffee Shop is next door to the museum.

The Museum of Victoria. At the corner of Latrobe and Russell streets. ☎ **03/9669 9888.** Admission A$5.30 (U.S. $4.20) adults, A$2.60 (U.S. $2.10) children. Daily 10am–5pm. Tram: Any northbound tram on Swanston Street to Latrobe Street; then walk across Swanston Street. Train: Any train on the City Loop to Museum Station.

Included in this museum are exhibits relating to natural history, science, technology, sociology, and astronomy. The pièce de résistance is Phar Lap, Australia's most famous racehorse, whose stuffed body is on view.

Melbourne Zoo. Elliot Avenue, Parkville. ☎ **03/9285 9300** or 9347 9530. Admission A$12 (U.S. $9.60) adults, A$6 (U.S. $4.80) children 4–15. Daily 9am–5pm (Jan–Feb, later Thurs and Sat). Free guided tours Mon–Fri 10am–3pm and Sat–Sun 11am–4pm. Tram: Mon–Sat, 55 or 56 going north on William Street to Stop 25; Sun, 68 going north on Elizabeth Street to Stop 23. Bus: City Explorer tour bus (stops hourly).

Opened in 1862, the Royal Melbourne Zoological Gardens is one of the oldest and finest in the world, with more than 3,000 animals housed in natural surroundings. Of most interest are the native fauna, including koalas, kangaroos, wallabies, wombats, emus, fairy penguins, and so forth. The Platypusary provides a good look at one of Oz's stranger natives, and the walk-through Butterfly House, where only Australian species are displayed, is also of particular importance. If you go to the zoo, take time to look at the Gorilla Rain Forest exhibit, the rare snow leopards, and the Syrian bears. The underwater viewing of Australian fur seals and arboreal primates exhibits are other highlights.

Two licensed restaurants and several takeout facilities offer meals and snacks.

MORE ATTRACTIONS

PARKS & GARDENS Be sure to visit at least one of Melbourne's parks and gardens. The **Royal Botanic Gardens,** 2km (1 mile) south of the city on Birdwood Avenue off St. Kilda Road (☎ 03/9655 2341 or 9655 2300), is best for serious green thumbs who want to see a variety of plant life, most identified with labels. The gardens are landscaped with sweeping lawns and ornamental lakes, which make them a pleasant place for strolling. Free guided walks leave from the Visitor Centre Sunday and Tuesday to Friday. The botanic garden's kiosk serves lunches and Devonshire teas. To get there, catch a tram on route 8 traveling south on St. Kilda Road and alight at Stop 21.

Nearby in **King's Domain,** you can visit **Latrobe's Cottage** (☎ 03/9654 5528), Victoria's first Government House. The cottage was built in England and brought out by ship in 1839. It's owned by the National Trust; admission is A$4 (U.S. $3.20) for adults and A$3 (U.S. $2.40) for children. The cottage is closed on Friday and open 11am to 4:30pm other days. Just across Birdwood Avenue, the **Shrine of Remembrance,** which honors Australia's fallen soldiers of World Wars I and II, Korea, and Vietnam, provides a good view of the city. From the top of the steps you can see right up Swanston Street to the landmark CUB (Carlton United Breweries) sign at the north edge of town. King's Domain is Stop 12 on a route 15 tram traveling south down St. Kilda Road.

The **Treasury Gardens,** with its lush lawns, lies to the east of the central business district. **A memorial to John F. Kennedy** is next to the lake. **Cook's Cottage,** built in 1755, is in **Fitzroy Gardens,** off Wellington Parade (☎ 03/9419 8742). The tiny bungalow was transported from the village of Great Ayton, England, in 1934 to mark Victoria's centenary, but today researchers have raised doubt about whether the English explorer ever actually lived in it. Admission is A$2.50 (U.S. $2) for adults and A$1.20 (U.S. $1) for children. It's open daily from 9am to 5pm. Treasury Gardens and Fitzroy Gardens can be reached by a route 75 tram traveling east along Flinders Street. Alight at Stop 14 for Treasury Gardens and at Stop 14A for Fitzroy Gardens.

ORGANIZED TOURS Local organized coach tours are offered by several companies, including **Melbourne Sightseeing** (☎ 03/9650 0088), **AAT King's** (☎ 03/9650 1244), **Gray Line** 03/9663 4455, and **Australian Pacific Tours** (☎ 03/9650 1511). In addition, **Moloney Aviation** (☎ 03/9379 2122; fax 03/374 2086) operates the *Penguin Express*—daily direct afternoon flights to Phillip Island to see the fairy penguins.

WALKING TOUR
Melbourne's Central Business District

Start: On Collins Street at Spring Street.
Finish: On Little Collins at Spring Street.
Time: Allow approximately one hour, not including shopping stops.
Best Times: Monday to Friday.
Worst Times: Weekends, when the CBD is less lively.

Don your Reeboks and see the city on foot, starting at the top of Collins Street, Melbourne's most interesting thoroughfare. Begin at the elegant:

1. **Old Treasury Building,** at the intersection of Spring and Collins Streets, dating from 1857. The impressive neoclassic structure built of brick and bluestone is faced with freestone. As you walk down Collins, the classy:
2. **Regent of Melbourne** (see "Accommodations" earlier in this chapter) is on your left and the:
3. **Melbourne Club,** a bastion of conservatism, is on your right. Continue downhill past the fashionable boutiques that give this area the name "the Paris end of Collins Street." On the corner of Russell and Collins, note the large:
4. **Uniting Church** and **the Scots Church,** across the street—both very pretty. The Scots Church, built in 1841, was originally quite plain; however, when gold-rush money poured into the city 10 years later, the church acquired Gothic trimmings.

Walking Tour—Melbourne's Central Business District

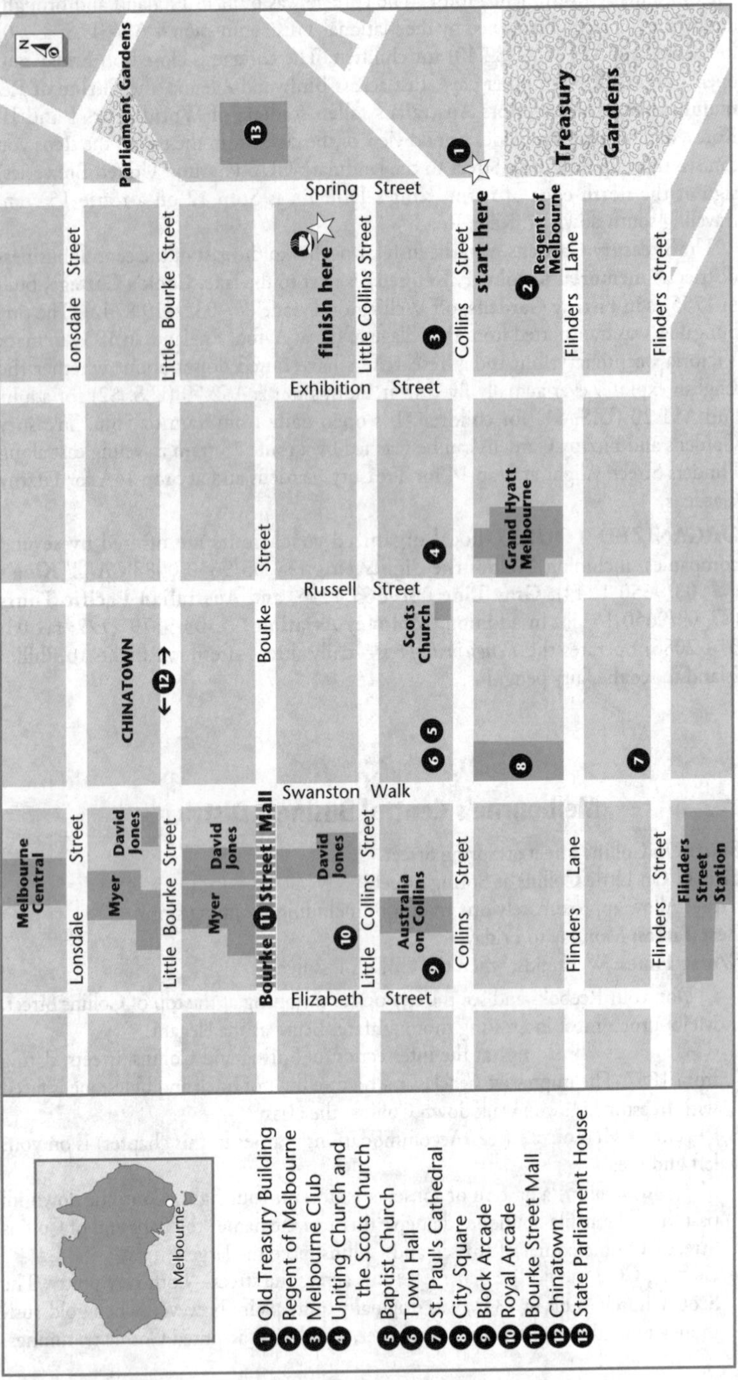

Continue down Collins Street. On your right you'll see the:

5. **Baptist Church,** which dates from 1845. The:
6. **Town Hall** (1867), at Collins and Swanston Streets, and:
7. **St. Paul's Cathedral** (1891), one block to the south, provide a sharp contrast to the modern:
8. **City Square** between them. Waterfalls, canopies, flowers, and periodic free concerts make this place popular for brown-bagging office workers. Continue down Collins Street past the Australia on Collins center and turn right into the:
9. **Block Arcade** (1892). Pause to admire its intricate mosaic floor and high domed ceiling before crossing Little Collins Street. Enter the:
10. **Royal Arcade** and wait just inside to see the mythical figures Gog and Magog (inside the dome) strike the hour. Walk north and you'll emerge on the:
11. **Bourke Street Mall** opposite the huge Myer department store. (David Jones has a nice women's lounge on the third floor.) Keep your wits about you in the *pedestrian* mall, because trams run down the middle of it. At the east end of the mall, turn left onto Swanston Walk and right onto Little Bourke Street. You'll find yourself in the midst of colorful:
12. **Chinatown.** Walk east to Spring Street and turn right. Pause to admire the handsome:
13. **State Parliament House,** dating from 1856. Guided tours are conducted Monday to Friday when the House is not sitting; call 03/9651 8362 for information.

WINDING DOWN If you're ready for a cup of tea or something stronger, take yourself to the wonderful **Windsor Hotel,** which faces Spring Street between Bourke and Little Collins. It has been pampering the city's weary visitors since 1883. (See "Dining" earlier in this chapter.)

6 Outdoor Activities & Spectator Sports

OUTDOOR ACTIVITIES

BICYCLING Extensive bike paths wind through the city and suburbs. Many bookstores sell "Melbourne Bike Tours," published by **Bicycle Victoria** (☎ 03/9328 3000), which describes 20 of the most popular routes. You can rent a bike from one of the **Hire a Bicycle** rental stores (☎ 018/534 383), open Monday to Friday from 11am to 5pm and Saturday and Sunday from 10am to 5pm. The charge is A$4 (U.S. $3.20) for half an hour, A$6 (U.S. $4.80) for an hour, A$10 (U.S. $8) for two hours, and A$22 (U.S. $17.60) for a full day.

GOLF The city's best-known course, the **Royal Melbourne** is in the bayside suburb of Black Rock, 24km (15 miles) from the center of town. This is a posh enclave, but if you're a member of an elite club at home you may get the privilege to play. The Royal Melbourne Golf Club is rated no. 6 in the world's top 100 by *Golf* magazine. Other notable links are the **Huntingdale, Kingston Heath, Commonwealth,** and **Yarra Bend** golf clubs. Yarra Bend, Yarra Bend Road, Fairfield (☎ 03/9481 3729), is one of the top public courses in Australia. Greens fees are about A$11 (U.S. $8.80); club rental is an additional A$10 (U.S. $8). If you need further information, contact the **Australian Golf Union,** 155 Cecil St., South Melbourne (☎ 03/9699 7944), or the **Victorian Golf Association,** 15 Bardolph St., Burwood (☎ 03/9889 6731).

Several companies specialize in personalized golf tours to local clubs. **Koala Golf,** 125 Beach Rd., Sandringham (☎ 03/9598 2574), can help you decide which course to play, assist you in renting equipment, obtain permission for you to play at private clubs, and provide transportation. Koala Golf also has offices in other Australian cities.

JOGGING & WALKING Melbourne's parks and gardens are ideal for stretching your legs. One of the most popular places is the 4km ($2^1/_2$-mile) track encircling **King's Domain.**

TENNIS **Flinders Park,** on Batman Avenue (☎ 03/9286 1244), is open to the public when it isn't hosting a tournament. The 15 outdoor and 5 indoor courts are available for rental Monday to Friday from 7am to 11pm and Saturday and Sunday from 9am to 6pm. Charges range from A$14 to A$30 (U.S. $11.20 to $24) per hour. Racquets are also available for rent.

You may also want to play at **Collingwood Indoor Tennis,** 100 Wellington St., Collingwood (☎ 03/9419 8911 or 9419 8185), where five synthetic-grass courts are available from 6am to 11pm. Court rental costs A$18 to A$32 (U.S. $14.40 to $25.60) per hour. Racquets, balls, and shoes are an extra A$4 (U.S. $3.20). Coaching is available daily from 7am to 6pm for A$36 to A$45 (U.S. $28.80 to $36) per hour. Use of the sauna and parking are free.

For further information, contact **Tennis Australia** at 03/9655 1177 or the **Tennis Association of Victoria** at 03/9510 3137.

SPECTATOR SPORTS

CAR RACING The Australian Formula One Grand Prix was held in Melbourne for the first time in March 1996. The annual event had previously always been held in Adelaide.

CRICKET November to March, everyone's attention turns to cricket and tennis. For on-the-spot insight into cricket, tour the **Melbourne Cricket Ground** and its large collection of memorabilia. The MCG's museum contains trophies, stamps, and postcards commemorating great batsmen, bats signed by victorious teams, pennants, famous players' old equipment, and so forth. The Australian Gallery of Sport and Olympic Museum, which includes portraits of well-known teams and players, is also at the Melbourne Cricket Ground. The gallery is open daily from 10am to 4pm (☎ 03/9654 8922). Admission costs A$5 (U.S. $4) for adults and A$2 (U.S. $1.60) for children. Guided tours of the MCG complex, Brunton Avenue, are available (☎ 03/9650 3001). To get there, take tram no. 48 or 65 to the Hilton Hotel and walk across the park to the members' entrance.

FOOTBALL Melburnians love their spectator sports, especially **Aussie Rules football,** which reigns supreme from late March to September. The **Australian Football League** season ends with the **Grand Final,** sort of a Super Bowl down under. For an estimated 65% of the 4 million people in the state of Victoria and thousands more from interstate, Grand Final day—the last Saturday in September—is not simply the climax of the Australian Football League's season, it's the high point of the year.

HORSE RACING Horse racing is a year-round passion. The **Melbourne Cup,** the country's richest race, is run on the first Tuesday in November. The **Victorian Racing Museum,** dedicated to the history of horse racing in Australia, is at the **Caulfield Racecourse.** It contains racing trophies, paintings, photographs, saddles, silks, and even scales together with a changing program of topical exhibitions and displays. The museum is open Tuesday and Thursday and race days from 10am to 4pm or by appointment (☎ 03/9563 4452). Admission is free.

TENNIS The **Ford Australian Open Tennis Tournament** is played at **Flinders Park,** on Batman Avenue (☎ 03/9236 1234), each January. The A$94-million (U.S. $75-million) complex has a retractable roof over center court for all-weather play. Guided tours, which cost A$4 (U.S. $3.20) for adults and A$2.50 (U.S. $2) for children, are offered Wednesday to Friday from April to September, subject to availability.

7 Shopping

THE SHOPPING SCENE

Throughout Australia, people talk about Melbourne as being *the* place to shop, for the number and variety of its stores are renowned. However, in terms of the items visitors usually seek, namely gifts and souvenirs, it probably isn't any better than Sydney. Melbourne's specialty is designer clothing. Perri Cutten, Trent Nathan, Prue Acton, Sally Browne, Adele Palmer, and Anthea Crawford—the stars of Australia's high-fashion scene—all operate boutiques in the Victorian capital, many of which are on Toorak Road in South Yarra and Toorak.

The city's main shopping area is in the central business district. **Melbourne Central** is a huge shopping complex between Latrobe and Lonsdale Streets, between Swanston Walk and Elizabeth Street. Here you'll find **Daimaru,** Australia's first international department store. **Australia on Collins,** between Collins and Little Collins Streets, is another bright new shopping complex. The other large department stores and many smaller shops are on **Bourke Street,** a pedestrian mall between Elizabeth and Swanston.

Arcades, chockablock with small specialty stores, also provide interest. Be sure to notice the **Block Arcade,** running from Collins Street to Little Collins, and the **Royal Arcade,** stretching from Little Collins Street to the Bourke Street Mall.

Like other cities in Oz, Melbourne has its share of markets. The **Queen Victoria Market** (☎ 03/9658 9600), covering several blocks between Peel, Victoria, Elizabeth, and Therry Streets on the northern edge of the city center, is a wonderful, slightly chaotic feast for the senses. Wares of every kind, plus fresh produce, are sold at more than 600 stalls. You can buy souvenirs, toys, clothes, furniture, bric-a-brac, leatherware, and all kinds of food—almost everything imaginable. It's open Tuesday and Thursday from 6am to 2pm, Friday from 6am to 6pm, Saturday from 6am to 3pm, and Sunday from 9am to 4pm. On Sunday, sales are limited to general goods and clothing—ranging from bargain-price designer fashions to secondhand gear. Get there on a route 55 tram traveling north along William Street and alight at Stop 13. Or take any northbound tram on Elizabeth Street; alight at the corner of Victoria Street.

You might also like to browse through the **Art and Craft Market,** held on the St. Kilda Esplanade, St. Kilda, on Sunday from 9am to 4pm.

SHOPPING A TO Z

ABORIGINAL CRAFTS

Aboriginal Handcrafts, at 125–133 Swanston St., on the ninth floor (☎ 03/9650 4717), is the place to go if you're looking for boomerangs, bark paintings, carvings, didgeridoos, and so forth. Open Monday to Thursday from 10am to 4:30pm and Friday from 10am to 5pm, this shop is largely run by volunteers, and profits are used to meet the needs of Aboriginal people.

Books

The **Hill of Content Bookshop,** a member of the Collins Booksellers Group, at 86 Bourke St. (☎ 03/9654 3144), has a good selection. Open Monday to Thursday from 9am to 5:30pm, Friday from 9am to 9pm, Saturday from 9am to 5pm, and Sunday from noon to 5pm; closed public holidays. Other **Collins Bookshops** are at 115 Elizabeth St. and 401 Swanston St.

Crafts

The ✪ **Meat Market Craft Centre,** 42 Courtney St., at the corner of Blackwood, North Melbourne (☎ 03/9329 9966), is a former meat market that's been converted into a center where craftspeople can work and sell their wares. This is an excellent place to buy high-quality Australian handcrafts, including ceramics, leather, glass, metal, textiles, and wood. Rotating exhibits focus on particular talents. Go Monday to Friday if you want to watch artisans at work. These include a bookbinder, milliner, jeweler, silk printer, and basket weaver. This special place is open Tuesday to Sunday from 10am to 5pm.

Department Stores

Daimaru, in the Melbourne Central complex (☎ 03/9660 6666), offers six floors of merchandise; open Monday to Thursday from 10am to 6pm, Friday from 9am to 9pm, Saturday from 10am to 6pm, and Sunday from 11am to 6pm. **Myer,** 314 Bourke St. Mall (☎ 03/9661 1111), has 12 floors of possible purchases and is the fifth-biggest department store in the world—it stretches over a two-block area; open Monday to Wednesday from 10am to 6pm, Thursday from 10am to 7pm, Friday from 10am to 9pm, and Saturday and Sunday from 10am to 6pm. **David Jones,** 310 Bourke St. Mall, also has an ample selection and also spans two blocks. Because of the number of exclusive boutiques, the eastern portion of Collins Street is known as "the Paris end."

Duty-Free Shops

Downtown Duty Free, 184 Swanston St. (☎ 03/9663 3144), sells the usual range of duty-free items—Cartier watches to Sony cameras and Kodak film to Wild Turkey bourbon. Downtown also has stores on Collins Street and Exhibition Street. Open Monday to Wednesday from 8:30am to 6pm, Thursday from 8:30am to 7pm, Friday from 9am to 9pm, Saturday from 9am to 5pm, and Sunday from 10am to 5pm.

Fashions

If you're in the market for a Driza-bone coat or an Akubra hat, try **Thomas Cook,** 58 Hoddle St., Abbotsford (☎ 03/9417 7555), and 246 Whitehorse Rd., Nunawading (☎ 03/9894 2316), or **Morrisons,** in the Como Centre, 299 Toorak Rd., South Yarra (☎ 03/9827 8255), or **R. M. Williams,** in the Melbourne Central complex (☎ 03/9670 7400).

Readers Recommend

"**Collins Place Art and Crafts,** on Collins Street between Spring and Exhibition streets (next to the Regent Melbourne Hotel), *operates every Sunday. There were 92 exhibits the day of our visit. The arts and crafts were, without exception, top quality with few duplications.*"

—Bruce Alloway, Edmonton, Alberta, Canada.

The following shops sell designer clothing: **JAG** (Adele Palmer), 459 Toorak Rd., Toorak (☎ 03/9827 2301); **New Dendy Centre,** 26 Church St., Brighton (☎ 03/9592 0396); **Anthea Crawford,** 1071 High St., Armadale (☎ 03/9824 7765); and **Perri Cutten,** 1083 High St., Armadale (☎ 03/9822 3984). There's also a Perri Cutten seconds store called **Overflow** at 193 Swan St., Richmond (☎ 03/9429 5435).

If you decide to wander down Toorak Road in Toorak, check out the **Liz Davenport** shop on the corner of Tintern Avenue. As you walk east there's **Crabtree & Evelyn, Sports Image, Benetton,** and **Henry Buck's** (men's clothes). Cross the street at Grange Road and take a look in **Sports Girl.**

The **Como Centre**, at the corner of Toorak Road and Chapel Street in South Yarra, has **Pierre Cardin, Morrisons,** and many others.

In addition to retail shops, **factory outlets** are dotted around the city, with a concentration of them on Bridge Road near Punt Road and Swan Street near Church Street in Richmond. Since these tend to change location and open and close faster than you can say "such a deal," I recommend that dedicated bargain hunters sign up with a pro. **Melbourne's Shopping Tours,** 21 Easey St., Collingwood (☎ 03/9416 3722, or 1800/134 181 in Australia), will get you where you want to go.

FOOD

Acland Street, St. Kilda, is renowned for its number of cake shops. Since many of these are owned by European Jewish immigrants, many foreign languages are heard throughout the neighborhood. Stroll down **Lygon Street** in Carlton if you like Italian sights and sounds. Several shops sell foodstuffs.

GIFTS & SOUVENIRS

The **Australiana General Store,** 1217 High St., Armadale (☎ 03/9822 2324), and at Shop 20, Collins Place, 45 Collins St. (☎ 03/9650 2075), and **Mainly Australian,** in the Royal Arcade (☎ 03/9654 5919), both have a good selection. In addition, you should look at **Yarrandoo Souvenirs and Native Art,** Shop 9, 131 Exhibition St. (☎ 03/9650 2461). Yarrandoo specializes in Aboriginal craft items but sells other souvenirs and gifts. The **National Trust Shop,** at Rippon Lea, 192 Hotham St., Elsternwick (☎ 03/9532 8298), also has nice things.

JEWELRY

Gemtec Australia, ground floor, 136 Exhibition St. (☎ 03/9654 5733), and **V. F. Trainor & Sons,** third floor, 289 Flinders Lane (☎ 03/9654 8361 and 9650 2129), both sell opals.

However, the most interesting place to shop for these stones is **Altmann & Cherny,** 120 Exhibition St., at the corner of Little Collins Street (☎ 03/9650 9685). It's open Monday to Friday from 9am to 5:30pm and Saturday and Sunday from 9am to 4pm and has a large selection of opal jewelry and unmounted stones. Mr. Cherny travels to Coober Pedy and Lightning Ridge, where he buys rough-cut opals to be cut and made into jewelry. Even if you don't want to shop, stop in and look at Olympic Australis—the largest precious-gem opal in the world. It was found in Coober Pedy, South Australia, in 1956 and is valued at over A$2 million (U.S. $1.6 million). It weighs 17,700 carats and is listed in the *Guinness Book of World Records.* Altmann & Cherny also cut and supplied the Andamooka opal presented to Elizabeth II in 1954.

Sheepskin Products

Victoria's Farm Shed is your best bet (see "Side Trips from Melbourne" at the end of this chapter).

8 Melbourne After Dark

Melbourne offers a variety of nightlife options, ranging from hot dance clubs to high-quality performing arts. The best source of current what's-on information is the "EG," the "Entertainment Guide" included in *The Age* each Friday.

THE PERFORMING ARTS

Half-price day-of-performance tickets can be purchased for live entertainment events, including dance, drama, and opera, at the **Half-Tix Kiosk** in the Bourke Street Mall (☎ 03/9650 9420 and 9649 8888). The booth is open Monday from 10am to 2pm, Tuesday to Thursday from 11am to 6pm, Friday from 11am to 6:30pm, and Saturday from 10am to 2pm. Tickets must be paid for in cash.

The Major Performance & Concert Hall

✪ **Victorian Arts Centre.** 100 St. Kilda Rd. ☎ **03/9281 8000** or 11 500 for ticket purchase. State Theatre tickets, A$40–A$73 (U.S. $32–$58.40); Playhouse, A$30–A$35 (U.S. $24–$28); Studio, A$15–A$20 (U.S. $12–$16); Concert Hall, A$35–A$40 (U.S. $28–$32).

The three theaters and the Concert Hall of the Victorian Arts Centre on the south bank of the Yarra River are the focal point of the city's cultural life. The **State Theatre** seats 2,079 on three levels. The motorized stage is large enough for elaborate productions of opera, ballet, musical comedy, or variety. The Australian Ballet Company, Australian Opera Company, Victoria State Opera, and many visiting companies perform here. The **Playhouse,** seating 888, is designed for drama productions and is used most of the year by the Melbourne Theatre Company. The **George Fairfax Studio,** seating 420, is a multipurpose auditorium with flexible seating. It's used for experimental theater and late-night cabaret.

A 115-meter (380 ft.) spire on top of the **Theatres Building** makes it the city's most identifiable landmark. Likewise, the round shape of the adjacent **Melbourne Concert Hall** makes it easy to spot. The excellent acoustics of this large hall, seating 2,677, are created by 30 Plexiglas shells suspended above the stage and 22 wool banners hanging along the walls on both sides. The Melbourne Symphony Orchestra and the State Orchestra of Victoria, as well as visiting orchestras, play in the Concert Hall. Luciano Pavarotti, Joan Sutherland, and Isaac Stern have also performed here.

Overseas visitors can make reservations for "An Evening at the Victorian Arts Centre" by contacting **ATS/Sprint** (☎ 800/423-2880 in the U.S. and Canada). The "Evening," offered Monday to Friday, includes a guided tour of the center, a pretheater dinner with wine in the Vic Restaurant, and the performance of your choice. (For details of the Vic Restaurant, see "Dining" earlier in this chapter.) The cost ranges from U.S. $71 to $126 per person, depending on what type of performance is selected. Other options, available Monday to Saturday, include dinner and a show, a show and supper, or champagne and chocolates during the intermission. The standard booking fee is U.S. $12. Reservations can be made up to 12 months in advance.

Tours: Guided one-hour tours of the theaters and Concert Hall and their adjacent foyers are offered Monday to Friday at noon and 2:30pm, costing A$9 (U.S. $7.20) for adults, A$6.50 (U.S. $5.30) for children, and A$20 (U.S. $16) for a family. Backstage tours, available on Sunday at 12:15 and 2:15pm, cost A$12 (U.S. $9.60). Children under 12 aren't allowed on the backstage tour. Call 03/9684 8151 or 9684 8152 between 9:30am and 5pm for further information.

THEATERS

Athenaeum Theatre. 188 Collins St. ☎ **03/9650 3504,** or 9650 1500 for tickets. Tickets, A$16–A$40 (U.S. $12.80–$32).

This building dates from the 1880s and is currently undergoing renovation to return it to its original appearance. The theater opened in 1924 and was, at one time, a cinema. The 960 seats are arranged on three levels. Performances vary from drama to musical theater and often include Shakespeare.

Comedy Theatre. 240 Exhibition St. ☎ **03/9662 2222,** or 9662 2644 for tickets. Tickets, A$30–A$44 (U.S. $24–$35.20).

The Comedy Theatre opened in 1928, but there has been a theater on this site since the founding of Melbourne. The theater, with 1,008 seats, has an intimate feel and a Spanish rococo–influenced architecture. The wooden-beam ceiling is original. Musicals and plays are the normal fare, though comedians and dance companies sometimes rent the theater for their performances.

Her Majesty's Theatre. 219 Exhibition St. ☎ **03/9663 3211.** Tickets vary, depending on show.

The original theater on this site, built in 1886, burned in 1928. Her Majesty's as it is today is a combination of the original Victorian front, saved from the fire, and the art deco interior from the 1934 rebuilding. This is a large venue—1,600 seats—usually used for short-run musicals. *Cats,* which ran for 12 months in 1988, was the last big success.

The C.U.B. Malthouse. 113 Sturt St., South Melbourne. ☎ **03/9685 5111.** Tickets, A$22–A$33 (U.S. $17.60–$26.40).

The Malthouse is a relatively new theater complex comprised of the Merlyn (445 seats) and the Beckett (196 seats) Theatres. It's the home of the Playbox Theatre Centre of Monash University, a theatrical production company whose primary artistic focus is on contemporary Australian theater. A gallery, a bar, and the Malthouse Cafe (open Monday to Saturday) are here.

Princess Theatre. 163 Spring St. ☎ **03/9639 0022,** or 9663 3300 to buy tickets. Tickets, A$20–A$60 (U.S. $16–$48).

This lovely Victorian theater hosted Andrew Lloyd Webber's *Phantom of the Opera* for over two years and is presently offering shorter runs of other big musicals. The 1,470-seat theater, designed by well-known colonial architect William Pitt, opened in 1886. It was first renovated in 1922, and was overhauled again in 1989 prior to the opening of *Les Misérables.* It has a dramatic marble staircase, beautiful murals on an ornate plaster ceiling, and a stained-glass window dating from 1901. The booking office is open daily from 9am to 6pm.

Sidney Myer Music Bowl. King's Domain, Alexandra Ave. ☎ **03/9684 8360.** Tickets vary, depending on performance.

This venue is a huge outdoor entertainment area used for opera, jazz, and ballet in warm months and ice skating in winter. It was presented to the people of Melbourne in 1959 by the Sidney Myer Charity Trust at the request of Mrs. Sidney Myer, widow of the founder of Australia's biggest department store. In 1980 it was handed over to the control of the Victorian Arts Centre Trust.

St. Martin's Youth Arts Centre. 44 St. Martin's Lane, South Yarra. ☎ **03/9867 2477.** Tickets vary, depending on performance.

Established in 1956, St. Martin's is a venue for live productions by and for young people. The Irene Mitchell Studio seats 80; the Randall Theatre has a capacity of 350.

THE CLUB & MUSIC SCENE

A COMEDY CLUB

✪ **The Last Laugh/Comedy Cafe.** 64 Smith St., Collingwood. ☎ **03/9419 8600.** Comedy Cafe, dinner and show, A$34–A$38 (U.S. $27.20–$30.40); show only, A$12–A$18 (U.S. $9.60–$14.40). The Last Laugh, dinner and show A$32–A$42 (U.S. $25.60–$33.60); show only, A$16–A$22 (U.S. $12.80–$17.60).

The Last Laugh is one of the original comedy clubs in Melbourne and features the best local and international comedy acts. It's open most nights throughout the year; dinner is served at 7:30pm and the show starts at 9pm. The Comedy Cafe, upstairs, is open only on Friday and Saturday nights; dinner is at 7pm and shows are at 8:30pm.

DANCE CLUBS

King Street is nightclub row in Melbourne.

Bobby McGee's Entertainment Lounge. In the Rydges Melbourne Hotel, 186 Exhibition St. ☎ **03/9639 0630.** Cover A$5 (U.S. $4) Wed–Sat after 8pm; free for hotel guests.

Upstairs from the popular Bobby McGee's Restaurant, the Entertainment Lounge is open daily from 5pm until late. The disco is popular with the 22-to-35 crowd after work and a younger set after 10pm. Complimentary hors d'oeuvres are served from 5 to 7pm Monday to Friday and drinks are sold two for the price of one during this time. The dance music starts at 9pm.

Lazar Melbourne. 240 King St. ☎ **03/9602 1822.** Cover A$10 (U.S. $8).

Open Friday to Sunday, this is one of Melbourne's most popular dance spots catering to a well-dressed over-25 crowd. A maximum of 2,000 merrymakers can be accommodated on three floors of what was once a warehouse. Live music is offered on Friday night. In addition to the dancing areas, there's also a piano bar.

Monsoon's Entertainment Studio. In the Grand Hyatt Melbourne, 123 Collins St. ☎ **03/9657 1234.** Cover A$8 (U.S. $6.40) Thurs, A$12 (U.S. $9.60) Fri, A$15 (U.S. $12) Sat; free for house guests.

Open Thursday to Saturday from 9pm to 3am, Monsoon's attracts a cross section of well-heeled patrons. These include visitors and locals who are members of this upmarket nightclub. The glittery Asian decor includes works of art commissioned in Tokyo. Live music is offered. Snacks and supper are available, as well as a full range of beverages.

JAZZ

Limerick Arms Hotel. 364 Clarendon St., South Melbourne. ☎ **03/9690 2626** or 9690 0995. Cover A$5–A$10 (U.S. $4–$8), depending on performer.

One of the best places in the city for jazz is the Limerick Arms. The pub dates from 1855 and is a cozy spot with a relaxed atmosphere. Live jazz bands—modern, improvised, contemporary, funk, blues, Latin—perform on Thursday and Sunday. Food is served, in addition to beer, wine, and a wide range of spirits (hard alcohol). The pub opens at noon and closes at 1am. The music starts about 10pm on Thursday and 6pm on Sunday.

THE BAR SCENE

COCKTAIL LOUNGES

Green Room. In the Regent of Melbourne, 25 Collins St. ☎ **03/9653 0000.**

The Green Room has comfortable lounge furnishings and is an ideal place for pre- and posttheater imbibing. On the lobby level, one floor above ground, the Green Room serves drinks and light suppers until midnight during the week and until 2am on Friday and Saturday. A pianist plays soothing music after 8pm during the week; a jazz band is featured on Friday and Saturday nights.

The hotel's **Black Swan Bar,** on the same level, is a sophisticated spot specializing in single-malt whiskies. It's open Monday to Saturday from 5pm to midnight. The **Atrium** and the adjacent **Piano Bar** on the 35th floor provide other options.

Rialto Bar. In Le Meridien at Rialto Melbourne, 495 Collins St. ☎ **03/9620 9111.**

The Rialto Bar is a picturesque courtyard with an atrium-style roof joining the historic Rialto and Winfield Buildings. Cocktails are served from noon to midnight or later.

PUBS

Cricketers Bar. In the Windsor Hotel, 103 Spring St. ☎ **03/9653 0653.**

This is one of several bars in Melbourne named and decorated in honor of the city's summer passion. Cricketers is an English-style pub popular with locals. Glass cases hold cricket memorabilia; plush green walls, green carpeting, and handsome mahogany woodwork create a traditional feel.

Mac's Hotel. 34 Franklin St. ☎ **03/9663 6855.**

Dating from 1853, Mac's is thought to be the city's oldest operating pub. It was originally a goldfield's coach terminus with stalls for over 100 horses and an ample yard for wagons. A special lockup was provided for the gold, along with accommodations for the gold escort. All that remains of this era is a watering trough at the front door. Mac's great claim to fame occurred on November 11, 1880, the day outlaw Ned Kelly was hanged. Emotions ran high, and one of the biggest fights ever seen in Melbourne broke out, nearly destroying the hotel.

Young & Jacksons. At the corner of Flinders and Swanston streets. ☎ **03/9650 3884.**

This is another landmark watering hole (also known as the Princes Bridge Hotel). Built in 1853 and opened for business in 1861, the hotel is known for its nude painting of Chloe, painted in Paris in 1875 and brought to Melbourne for the Great Exhibition in 1880. In 1908 the painting was purchased by Henry Young and Thomas Jackson and given a place in the bar. Chloe holds a special place in the hearts of customers, not the least of whom are the many servicemen who have paid tribute to her over the years. Some of them have painted replicas, and today Chloe look-alikes are dotted around the world.

A CASINO

Melbourne's **Crown Casino** opened at the corner of Flinders and Spencer Streets (☎ 03/9685 4200) in 1994. It offers 24-hour gambling, five restaurants, and entertainment on Tuesday and Wednesday evenings. As nice as it is, this is only a temporary facility, and the new casino in South Bank is expected to open at the end of 1996. It'll also be open 24 hours.

9 Side Trips from Melbourne

DANDENONG RANGES

Only 40km (25 miles) east of Melbourne lie the beautiful forest-clad hills of the Dandenong Ranges. Here is an opportunity to see native bush at its best and to tour several spectacular gardens. You can drive yourself or take a conducted excursion. The **Mount Dandenong Tourist Road** starts at **Upper Ferntree Gully** and winds its way through the villages of **Sassafras, Olinda, Mount Dandenong,** and **Kalorama** to **Montrose**. If you follow this route, plus make a detour through the **Sherbrooke Forest** to **Kallista,** you'll see a good sample of the local scenery. Craft shops and tearooms are dotted around the area.

SEEING THE AREA'S TOP ATTRACTIONS

Rhododendron Gardens, Olinda. Georgian Road, Olinda. ☎ 03/9751 1980. Admission A$6.50 (U.S. $5.20) adults; under 15 free. Daily 10am–4:30pm (5:30pm during daylight saving time). Closed Good Friday and Christmas. Train to Upper Ferntree Gully and then bus 698 along Mount Dandenong Tourist Road to Olinda.

This garden where thousands of "rhodies" and azaleas are planted in a 40-hectare (100-acre) setting of native and exotic trees deserves special attention. September to December is the best time to visit. A 3km (2-mile) planned walk leads you past incredibly colorful displays and to viewpoints from which you can see the Yarra Valley and beyond. A tearoom and small shop are on the property, and the staff are very helpful. On my first visit, the sky opened up just after we arrived and one of the gardeners, hearing my accent and noting my disappointment at not being able to tour the grounds, took me around in his service vehicle.

The William Ricketts Sanctuary. Mount Dandenong Tourist Road, Mount Dandenong. ☎ **03/9751 1300.** Admission A$5 (U.S. $4) adults, A$2 (U.S. $1.60) children 10–14; under 10 free. Daily 10am–4:30pm. Bus: 694 from Belgrave Railway Station to Olinda and then transfer to Croydon bus 688 to the sanctuary; or as directed for the Rhododendron Gardens above.

This garden features clay figures that are one man's vision of the Aboriginal Dreamtime. They were created by 95-year-old sculptor William Ricketts and are set among 6 hectares (15 acres) of fern gullies, rockeries, waterfalls, and stately mountain ash trees.

Bonsai Farm. Mount Dandenong Tourist Road, Mount Dandenong. ☎ **03/9751 1150.** Free admission. Wed–Sun 11am–5pm. Transportation: See William Ricketts Sanctuary above.

It's fun to see what's on display at the area's commercial garden nurseries. This place specializes in traditional and Aboriginal bonsai.

✪ **Tesselaar's Tulip Farm.** Monbulk Road, Silvan. ☎ **03/9737 9305.** Admission during Tulip Festival, A$7.50 (U.S. $6) adults; under 16 free, accompanied by an adult. During Tulip Festival (mid–Sept to mid–Oct), daily 10am–5pm; rest of the year, Mon–Fri 8am–4:30pm, Sat–Sun 1–5pm. Train to Lilydale and then bus 679.

From mid-September to mid-October, the show garden here is a photographer's delight. Hyacinths, ranunculi, daffodils, azaleas, rhododendrons, fuchsias, and cinerarias bloom in profusion, in addition to an amazing display of tulips. Four windmills and a coffee shop selling sweet Dutch treats complete the scene. Tulip bulbs are for sale year-round.

Puffing Billy Railway. Belgrave Station, Belgrave. ☎ **03/9754 6800** (Mon–Fri), or 03/9870-8411 for 24-hour recorded information. Admission A$15.50 (U.S. $12.40) adults, A$9 (U.S. $7.20) children 4–14. Operates daily, except Christmas. Trains from Flinders Street

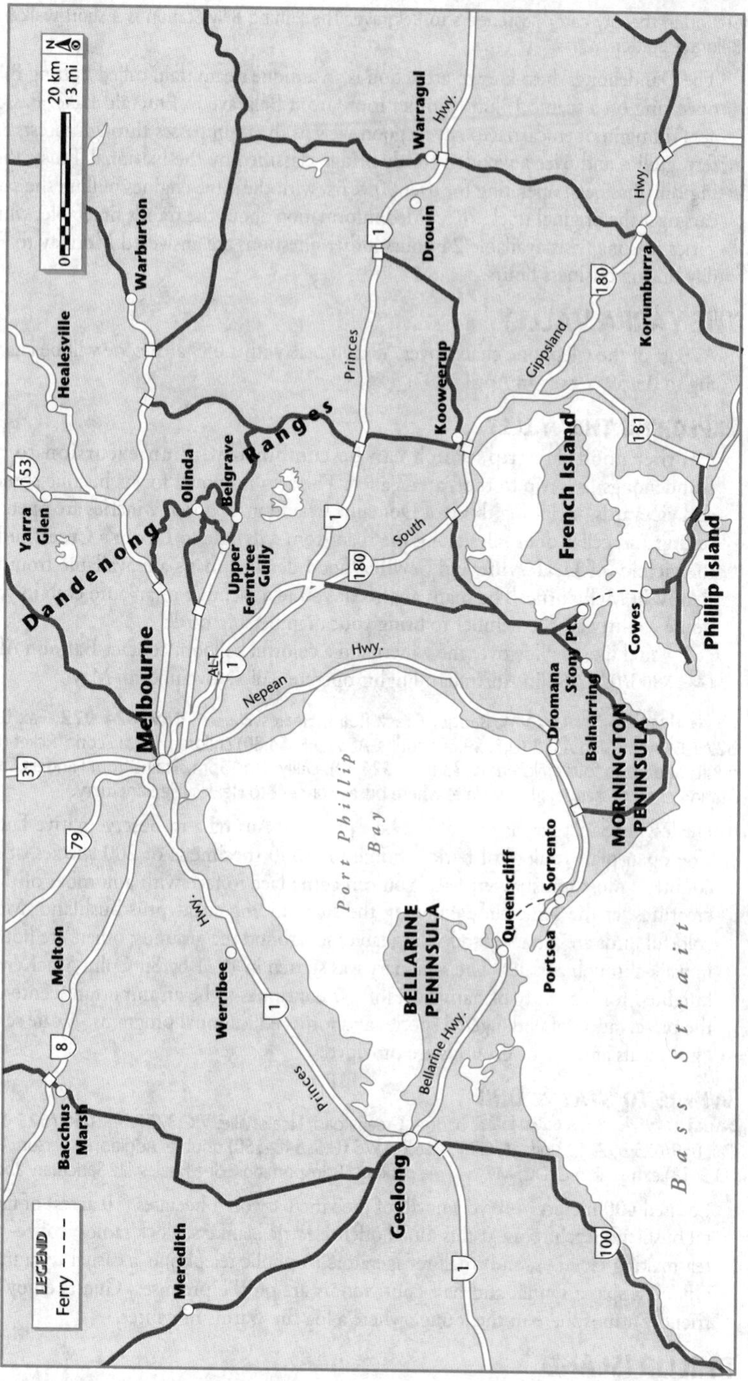
LEGEND
Ferry
0
20 km
13 mi
N
Melbourne
Dandenong Ranges
Healesville
Warburton
Yarra Glen
Olinda
Belgrave
Upper Ferntree Gully
Warragul
Drouin
Kooweerup
Princes
Hwy.
South
Gippsland
Korumburra
French Island
Phillip Island
Cowes
Stony Pt.
Dromana
Balnarring
MORNINGTON PENINSULA
Nepean
ALT
Port Phillip Bay
Sorrento
Portsea
Queenscliff
BELLARINE PENINSULA
Bellarine Hwy.
Bass Strait
Melton
Werribee
Bacchus Marsh
Geelong
Meredith
31
79
8
1
153
180
181
100
2354

Station in the city carry passengers to Belgrave. The Puffing Billy Station is a short walk from Belgrave Station.

The Dandenongs' best-known attraction is an antique steam train called Puffing Billy, operating on a scenic 13km (8-mile) route from Belgrave to Emerald Lake. Passengers riding in open carriages have a good view as the train passes through forests and fern gullies and over a wooden trestle bridge classified by the National Trust. Puffing Billy has been operating for over 90 years, with the same engines pulling the same cars over the original tracks. Recorded information about the train's timetable, which varies seasonally, is available 24 hours; other questions are answered Monday to Friday during business hours.

THE YARRA VALLEY

As part of the telephone changeover, all numbers with a 059 area code will be changing to 03/59xx xxxx in April 1997.

EXPLORING THE VALLEY

Another good day trip, which can be combined with an excursion to the Dandenongs, is a trip to the Yarra Valley. The area is known for its bucolic scenery and vineyards, including those of Domaine Chandon. A dozen wineries are open for tasting and cellar-door sales along the road from **Lilydale** to **Dixon's Creek** and in the vicinity of **Healesville** and **Seville.** Good detailed maps are available from the **RACV** in Melbourne. The maps are free if you're a member of an auto club in your home country and remember to bring your membership card.

If you'd like to glide over the wineries in a colorful balloon, contact **Balloon Aloft** (☎ 1800/028 568 in Australia). Flights operate daily November to May.

✪ **Healesville Sanctuary.** Badger Creek Road, Healesville. ☎ **059/624 022.** Fax 059/622 139. Admission A$12 (U.S. $9.60) adults, A$6 (U.S. $4.80) children 4–15; Econo Ticket (two adults and up to four children) A$33 (U.S. $26.40). Daily 9am–5pm. Trains from Flinders Street Station carry passengers to Lilydale, where buses connect to Healesville Sanctuary.

Healesville Sanctuary is one of the best places in Australia to observe native fauna. The open-plan zoological park is home to 1,800 specimens of 200 species of the country's most unusual animals. You can come face to face with a number of these creatures, at the same time enjoying the surrounding eucalyptus bushland. Many colorful birds are attracted to feeding tables set around the grounds; others are housed in walk-through aviaries. The sanctuary was started in 1921 by Sir Colin MacKenzie, knighted for his study of native wildlife. It continues to be an important center for the preservation of endangered species and for its educational programs. A café serves light meals and picnic grounds are provided.

WHERE TO STAY & DINE

Sanctuary House Healesville. Badger Creek Road, Healesville, VIC 3777. ☎ **059/625 148.** Fax 059/625 392. 12 units. A/C TV. A$65–A$75 (U.S. $48–$60) double. Additional person A$10 (U.S. $8) extra. AE, BC, DC, MC, V. Free parking. Transportation: See Healesville Sanctuary above.

Located 400 meters (440 yd.) north of the sanctuary on 4 hectares (10 acres) of natural bushland, each room at this motel offers electric blankets, clock radios, coffee- and tea-making facilities, and small refrigerators. A public telephone, a casual restaurant, a pool, a spa, a sauna, and half-court tennis are on the premises. Guests enjoy the friendly atmosphere in the lounge where a log fire warms in winter.

PHILLIP ISLAND

Besides the Penguin Reserve (below), there's a Koala Reserve on Phillip Island. The **Koala Conservation** (☎ 059/521 307) offers an opportunity to see these appealing marsupials in their natural surroundings. The **Phillip Island Information Centre** (☎ 059/567 447), open daily from 9am to 5pm, can supply you with information on Phillip Island.

Phillip Island Penguin Reserve. Summerland Beach, Phillip Island. ☎ **059/568 300.** Admission A$7 (U.S. $5.60) adults, A$3 (U.S. $2.40) children under 14, A$20 (U.S. $16) families. Visitor Centre opens 10am; penguins arrive at sunset. Phillip Island is 1½ hours by car from Melbourne. If you don't want to drive, several coach tour companies conduct daily excursions, and Maloney Aviation offers daily direct flights (see "Organized Tours" above).

The nightly parade of fairy penguins on Phillip Island is one of the best-known attractions in Australia. Every evening at dusk the little tuxedo-clad birds swim ashore and scamper across the beach to their sand-dune burrows. They're the smallest of the penguin species, measuring only about 33 centimeters (13 in.) high. A platform permits you to get a good view of the birds. Flash pictures aren't allowed because they frighten the penguins. Be sure to wear very warm clothes, as it can get mighty chilly down by the water while you're waiting for the penguins to appear. Walking shoes are also essential.

A kiosk selling takeout food opens an hour before the penguins arrive.

TYNONG

As part of the telephone changeover, all numbers with a 056 area code will be changing to 03/56xx xxxx in April 1997.

✪ **Victoria's Farm Shed.** Princes Highway, Tynong. ☎ **056/292 840.** Admission normally A$10 (U.S. $8) adults, A$3 (U.S. $2.40) children, but proprietors will deduct 20% if you tell them you're using this book. Daily 10am–4pm, with shows daily at 10:30am and 2pm year-round; sometimes an extra show at 3:30pm Nov–Mar. Drive (71km/44 miles east of Melbourne) or take a Melbourne Sightseeing coach tour (☎ 03/9670 9706).

On your way to Phillip Island or after visiting the Dandenongs, you might want to stop at Victoria's Farm Shed. In an informative one-hour show, various breeds of sheep and cattle are paraded in front of the audience, sheepshearing is demonstrated, and a cow is milked. Afterward, you move outside to see sheepdogs working. A shop on the premises sells sheepskins and wool products at very reasonable prices. A snack bar serves light meals, and a licensed restaurant offers a tasty barbecue lunch of prime beef steak, fish, or lamb with salads, damper, and dessert.

AROUND PORT PHILLIP BAY

As part of the telephone changeover, all numbers with a 052 area code will be changing to 03/52xx xxxx in March 1997.

Day-trippers from Melbourne have a choice of following the Princes Highway around the west side of Port Phillip Bay to Werribee and Geelong or taking the Nepean Highway, which goes along the east side of the bay and ends at Portsea. Those with the time to overnight along the way can combine the two options.

My suggestion for those with only one day: Start early, drive directly to Geelong, visit the wool museum, continue to Queenscliff on the Bellarine Peninsula, have lunch and explore a bit, and visit Werribee on the way back to Melbourne. If you have more time, stop at Werribee as you head south, have lunch and visit the wool museum in Geelong, and have dinner and overnight in Queenscliff. The next day, take the ferry from Queenscliff to Sorrento, explore the Mornington Peninsula, and either return to Melbourne, stay overnight at one of the two properties described below, or catch a ferry from Stony Point to Phillip Island.

The ***Peninsula Princess*** car-and-passenger ferry (☎ 052/582 3171 or 582 3244) makes about a dozen trips a day between the Bellarine and Mornington Peninsulas.

The crossing takes 35 to 40 minutes. The one-way fare for a car is A$30 (U.S. $24). Adult passengers pay A$3 (U.S. $2.40) and children are charged A$2 (U.S. $1.60); pedestrians pay A$6 (U.S. $4.80).

QUEENSCLIFF

In the 1880s the seaside town of Queenscliff at the head of Port Phillip Bay became a fashionable place for wealthy Melburnians to go for a holiday. Steamers made regular trips, carrying Victorian ladies and gentlemen, and a number of grand hotels were built to accommodate them. However, the community's heyday came to an end with the advent of motorcars early in this century. The vehicles opened up new destinations, and Queenscliff's popularity took a nosedive. The place remained of little interest to travelers until recently, when it was rediscovered as a pleasant weekend escape from the city. A few of the old hotels have been restored to their former glory and, with other mid-19th-century buildings, create a sedate old-world atmosphere. This is also a good excursion for those who enjoy the smell of salt air, beaches, water sports, and clifftop walkways with panoramic views of Bass Strait. A 110-year-old fort overlooks the narrow waterway through which all ships bound for Melbourne must pass.

Queenscliff (pop. 3,700) is 103km (64 miles) from Melbourne. You can drive there in about 1½ hours, taking the Princes Highway out of Melbourne and picking up the Bellarine Highway in Geelong.

WHERE TO STAY & DINE

✪ **Mietta's Queenscliff Hotel.** 16 Gellibrand St., Queenscliff, VIC 3225. ☎ **052/581 066.** Fax 052/581 899. 21 rms (none with bath). A$99 (U.S. $79.20) per person Mon–Thurs (including breakfast and dinner from simpler menu); from A$175 (U.S. $140) per person Fri-Sun (including breakfast and dinner in main dining room with wine). Ask about other packages. AE, BC, DC, MC, V. Train to Geelong; then bus from Geelong Station to Queenscliff.

Mietta's is run by Patricia O'Donnell, and the hotel, with a water view, was restored with great attention to detail. The public rooms are a joy—whether you dine, take tea, have a drink, or relax by the fire with a book. The "pink sitting room" has Chinese carpets and a pair of flowered wingback chairs in front of the fireplace. The "little sitting room" at the front of the house has a view of a park that slopes down to the seaside. In the "large sitting room" books, chess, and jigsaw puzzles are left out for guests.

The guest rooms have authentic period decors, including iron-and-brass headboards, hardwood floors, high ceilings, and Oriental carpets. Number 27, a spacious room with a working fireplace and a bay window, is my favorite. Since the hotel is a popular weekend escape for Melburnians, midweek rates are lower. Even if you don't stay overnight, stop by and have a drink or afternoon tea at the hotel. It's charming.

Dining/Entertainment: Superb gourmet cuisine is served in three areas: the formal main dining room, with crisp white tablecloths and an elaborate brass chandelier; the delightful courtyard dining room, with marble-topped tables from the Raffles Hotel in Singapore; and at umbrella-shaded tables in the garden.

Vue Grand Hotel. 46 Hesse St., Queenscliff, VIC 3225. ☎ **052/581 544.** Fax 052/583 471. 34 rms. TEL. A$295 (U.S. $236) double. Rates include dinner and breakfast. Ask about weekend and other packages. AE, BC, DC, MC, V. Transportation: See above.

The Vue Grand, dating from 1864, is a two-storied Victorian hostelry that has also been restored. The rooms have contemporary decors, but the public spaces are replete with period splendor. An indoor pool has taken the place of the original stables. There's also a gym and a spa.

Dining/Entertainment: French chef Stéphane Le Grand (a protégé of Paul Bocuse) offers a complete menu of delightful dishes. Meals are served in the dining room and in two courtyards.

GEELONG

✪ **National Wool Museum.** At the corner of Moorabool and Brougham streets. ☎ **052/264 660.** Admission A$7 (U.S. $5.60) adults, A$3.50 (U.S. $2.80) children under 16, A$18 (U.S. $14.40) family. Daily 10am–5pm. Closed Good Friday and Christmas. Geelong is a 45-minute drive from Melbourne. There's also regular train service, and the museum is a 10-minute walk from the station.

If you've heard someone say "Australia was founded on the sheep's back" and not understood what was meant—here's your chance to find out. Displays in this wonderful museum explain the importance of sheep farming in Australia—then and now—and provide historical background. Videos show sheepdogs working, you can feel several fleeces, and there's a chance to experience a shearing shed. It's especially interesting to follow the path of the fleece from the sheep's back to a finished wool garment. Working exhibits include a 1910 Axminster Jacquard carpet loom and a 1940s sock knitting machine.

The museum is in the former Dennys Lascelles 1872 woolstore, a building of great architectural and industrial significance to the wool industry. In addition to the museum there's a specialty wool store, Museum Gift Shop, and Lamby's Bistro—a licensed à la carte restaurant.

WERRIBEE

Werribee Park Mansion. K Rd. ☎ **03/9741 2444.** Park and picnic grounds, free; mansion, A$5 (U.S. $4) adults, A$2.50 (U.S. $2) children 5–14. Daily 10am–3:45pm (to 4:45pm weekends, public holidays, and during daylight saving time). Closed Christmas. Werribee is a 30-minute drive from Melbourne.

This 60-room Italianate mansion was built in 1877 for Scottish squatters Thomas and Andrew Chirnside. Known as "the palace in the paddock," this great house was, at that time, without rival in the colony. Today it stands on 130 hectares (325 acres) of bushland fronting the Werribee River. There is a free-range zoo adjacent.

MORNINGTON PENINSULA

As part of the telephone changeover, all numbers with a 059 area code will be changing to 03/59xx xxxx in April 1997.

Long a playground for Melburnians, the Mornington Peninsula offers safe beaches on Port Phillip Bay, rugged cliffs overlooking Bass Strait, coastal parks, and hinterland hills. A chair lift whisks passengers to the summit of 305-meter (1,006-ft.) Arthur's Seat, the highest point on the peninsula. If you prefer to drive, a good road winds to the top from Dromana. There are tourist information centers in Dromana on the Nepean Highway (☎ 059/873 078) and on Ocean Beach Road in Sorrento (☎ 059/050 099).

WHERE TO STAY & DINE

✪ **Delgany Country House Hotel.** Nepean Highway, Portsea, VIC 3944. ☎ **059/844 000,** or 1800/034 416 in Australia. Fax 059/844 022. 34 rms. A/C TV TEL. A$170 (U.S. $136) standard double midweek, A$240 (U.S. $192) standard double weekend; A$230–A$345 (U.S. $184–$276) executive, deluxe, or grand suite midweek, A$330–A$495 (U.S. $264–$396) suite weekend. Rates include continental breakfast. Ask about dollarwise packages. AE, BC, DC, MC, V. Free parking. Take a train from Melbourne to Frankston and bus 788 from there. Portsea is 100km (62 miles) southwest of Melbourne and 4km ($2^1/_2$ miles) from the ferry dock in Sorrento.

This grand mansion, built in 1927, was inspired by ancestral castles with Roman arches and Tudor battlements, and this character is still present. In addition to the years when it was a residence, Delgany has been a military hospital and, later, a school for the deaf. In 1989 it opened its doors as an elegant country-house hotel. Totally restored to its former splendor, the house is set in 4.8 hectares (12 acres) of private gardens abutting the Portsea golf course. Each guest room is tastefully furnished, some with fireplaces and spa baths. The drawing room has a grand piano, a huge open fire, and manor-house furnishings.

Dining/Entertainment: A meal at this country house is a memorable experience. French fare is prepared by chef Juliana Landrivon. Lunch is served daily from noon to 2:30pm and dinners are daily from 6:30pm.

Facilities: Outdoor heated pool, two tennis courts, and croquet lawn.

✪ **Warrawee Homestead.** 87 Warrawee Rd., Balnarring, VIC 3926. ☎ **059/831 729.** Fax 059/ 832 323. 4 rms. A$145 (U.S. $116) double. Rates include breakfast. Ask about midweek and weekend packages and discounts for extended stays. AE, BC, DC, MC, V. Free parking.

This is a great place to get a sense of what it might've been like to live in colonial Australia. One hour southeast of Melbourne, Warrawee Homestead was built in 1860 on a large farming property and later became a Cobb & Co. stopover. Today the house has a very pretty dining room with lace tablecloths, a big open fireplace, period furnishings, and the original Baltic pine floor. There's a sunny enclosed veranda where you can relax, and the whole place has a real sense of history. Proprietors Jane and Kieran Scott continue the process of restoring their 2 hectares (5 acres) of old-world gardens.

My favorite room is the honeymoon suite with a brass four-poster bed. Accommodations are offered nightly year-round and all meals are provided for guests. Nonguests can enjoy lunch, dinner, or afternoon tea on weekends year-round and Tuesday to Sunday during December and January. A two-course lunch costs about A$35 (U.S. $28); three-course dinners cost about A$45 (U.S. $36); afternoon teas are A$7.50 (U.S. $6). Fully licensed and BYO.

17 Victoria

Victoria occupies only 3% of the country, but there's a lot of variety within its borders. In addition to 1,300km (806 miles) of coastline, the state has desert in the west, a major river in the north, and mountains in the east. In between are forests, wine- and fruit-growing regions, and cities boasting rich gold-rush histories.

The mighty Murray River has its origins in the snow-capped high country of the northeast, and its course forms the border with neighboring New South Wales. The Murray's valleys produce prime vineyards and orchards. Mildura, Swan Hill, and Echuca are gracious riverfront towns where you can catch a ride on a paddle steamer.

The Grampians, in the western portion of the state, are scenic mountains popular with rock climbers, bushwalkers, and campers. The area has many rock shelters containing Aboriginal paintings, and the Brambuk Living Cultural Centre (☎ 053/56 4452) is a must for anyone interested in the Aboriginal culture. Good roads crisscross Grampians National Park, providing access to lookout points, lakes, waterfalls, and wide valleys. From June to November native flora puts on a colorful display, and all year long fauna, including kangaroos, koalas, and over 200 species of bird, is abundant. Hall's Gap, the gateway to the Grampians, is a three-hour drive from Melbourne.

The Great Ocean Road follows the coastline southwest of the state capital. Those who make this curvaceous trip are rewarded with outstanding ocean views. The shore on the eastern half of Victoria is less dramatic, but that doesn't prevent Wilsons Promontory National Park from being a favorite recreation area. The "Prom," as it's known, is 230km (143 miles) from Melbourne.

The center of the state was populated by hopeful gold miners in the 1850s. Relics of this era can be seen throughout places like Ballarat and Bendigo.

EXPLORING THE STATE

Intrastate train and coach service in Victoria is provided by **V/Line,** 67 Spencer St., Melbourne, VIC 3000 (☎ 03/9619 5000 or 13 22 32). This includes a wide network of interurban trains and an even more complete service of buses extending beyond the rail network. V/Line also offers day tours and overnight excursions (☎ 03/9619 8080) to places like Ballarat and the Great Ocean Road. **Kendell Airlines** (☎ 03/99670 2677) is the principal intrastate air

What's Special About Victoria

Top Attraction

- Ballarat's Sovereign Hill Goldmining Township, where Australia's history is re-created.

Activities

- Mildura, where you can ride down the mighty Murray River on a paddle wheeler.
- Snowy River National Park, in the eastern part of the state, a great place to go horseback riding.

Natural Spectacles

- The Twelve Apostles, highlight of the wonderful coastal scenery along the Great Ocean Road.

Beaches

- Lakes Entrance on the southeast coast—a seemingly endless stretch of ocean beach separated from an inland waterway by a row of sand dunes.

carrier. Southern Airlines flies to Mildura. Both V/Line and Kendell offer money-saving passes for those traveling extensively within Victoria. **Moloney Aviation** (☎ 03/9379 2122; fax 03/9374 2086) provides an air option to the Great Ocean Road, Phillip Island, and beyond.

While the vast majority of Victoria's four million residents live in Melbourne, some live on farms throughout the state and welcome visitors. If you fancy a farmer as a host, contact the **Victorian Host Farm Association,** 6th Floor, 230 Collins St., Melbourne, VIC 3000 (☎ 03/9650 2922; fax 03/9650 9434). In North America, bookings can be made through Intaussie (☎ 800/531-9222 in the U.S.). If you book directly with Victorian Host Farms Association, you'll pay A$120 to A$200 (U.S. $96 to $160) for two, including meals and lodging. The rate, which includes all meals, morning and afternoon tea, full-time hosting, accommodations, district tours, transfers from the nearest rail or bus station, and farm tours and activities, ranges from A$246 to A$286 (U.S. $196.80 to $228.80) for two people sharing.

Victoria Visitor Information Centre, Melborne Town Hall, at the corner of Little Collins Street and Swanston Walk, Melborne VIC 3000 (☎ 03/9650 1522; fax 03/9650 1212), is the best source of information. It's open Monday to Friday from 8:30am to 5:30pm, Saturday from 9am to 5pm, and Sunday from 10am to 5pm. Pick up maps and motoring details there or at the **RACV,** 422 Little Collins St., Melbourne, VIC 3000 (☎ 03/9607 2137).

1 Ballarat

113km (70 miles) W of Melbourne

The history of Victoria's largest inland city (pop. 90,000) is inextricably intertwined with the discovery of gold in 1851. The area had been used as sheep and cattle pasture since 1838, and by the mid-19th century a small township had developed. However, after blacksmith Thomas Hiscock found gold, hopeful miners from as far away as California flooded the region. Within two years, Ballarat had a population of nearly 40,000, including many Chinese who labored as cooks and at other auxiliary jobs in the goldfields. The difficulty of accessing the gold, some of which was under four layers of basalt, created a machinery- and equipment-manufacturing industry that has sustained the community since the last mine closed in 1918.

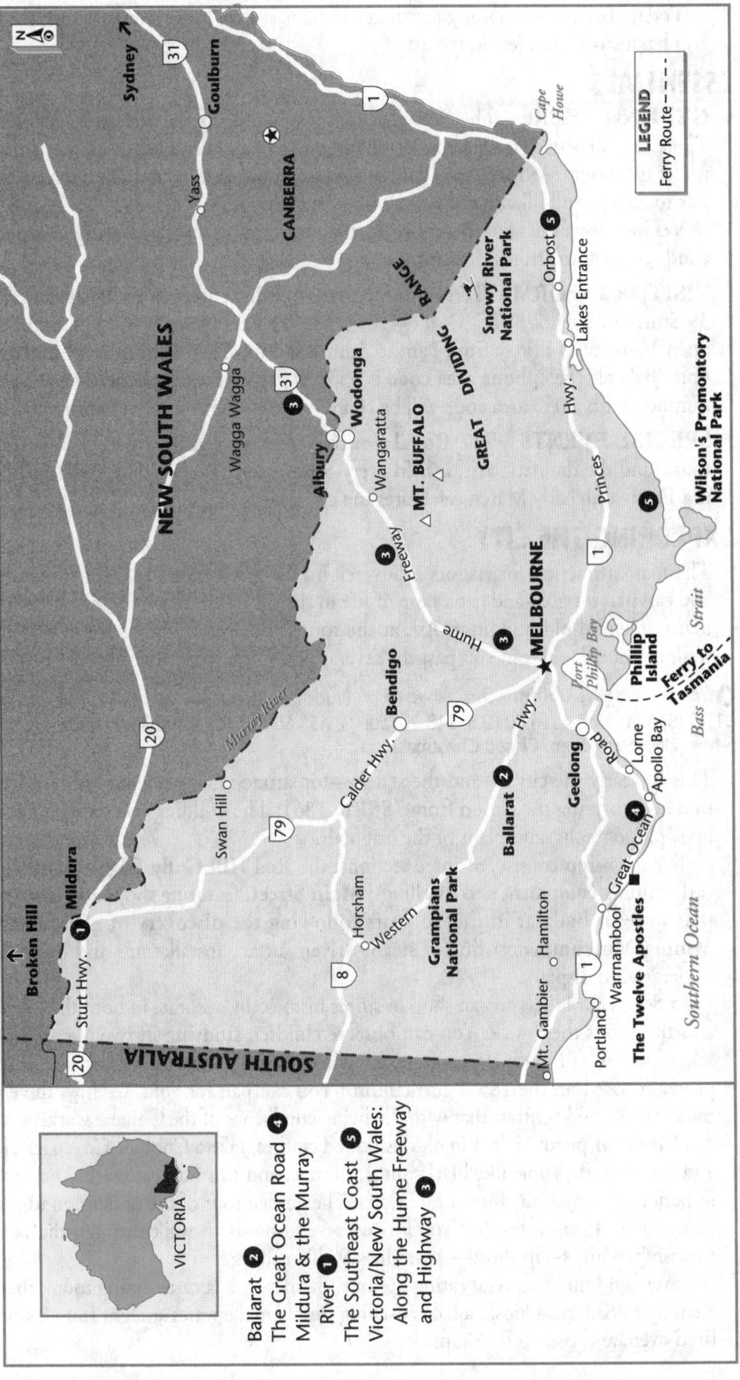
Ballarat 2
The Great Ocean Road 4
Mildura & the Murray River 1
The Southeast Coast 5
Victoria/New South Wales: Along the Hume Freeway and Highway 3
VICTORIA
LEGEND
Ferry Route
NEW SOUTH WALES
SOUTH AUSTRALIA
CANBERRA
Sydney
Goulburn
Yass
Wagga Wagga
Albury
Wodonga
Wangaratta
MT. BUFFALO
GREAT DIVIDING RANGE
Snowy River National Park
Orbost
Lakes Entrance
Cape Howe
Princes Hwy.
Wilson's Promontory National Park
MELBOURNE
Hume Freeway
Port Phillip Bay
Phillip Island
Ferry to Tasmania
Bass Strait
Bendigo
Calder Hwy.
Murray River
Swan Hill
Mildura
Broken Hill
Sturt Hwy.
Horsham
Western Hwy.
Grampians National Park
Ballarat
Geelong
Great Ocean Road
Lorne
Apollo Bay
The Twelve Apostles
Warrnambool
Hamilton
Portland
Mt. Gambier
Southern Ocean
2355

Today, Ballarat's economy continues to be based on heavy industry, but the city also has a strong interest in the arts.

ESSENTIALS

GETTING THERE The Western Highway connects Ballarat and Melbourne. There's no air service to Ballarat. V/Line trains can carry you from Melbourne in just under two hours (A$13/U.S. $10.40 one way). At the station, you can catch a shuttle bus to Sovereign Hill and the Gold Museum (below).

V/Line also offers coach service to Ballarat, and many sightseeing companies conduct day tours from Melbourne.

VISITOR INFORMATION Information is dispensed at **Ballarat Tourism,** 39 Sturt St., Ballarat, VIC 3350 (☎ 053/322 694; fax 053/327 977). This office is open Monday to Friday from 9am to 5pm and Saturday and Sunday from 9am to 4pm. Ballarat's **telephone area code** is 053. As part of the telephone changeover, all numbers with a 053 area code will be changing to 03/53xx xxxx in February 1997.

SPECIAL EVENTS The **Royal South Street Eisteddfod,** which focuses on music and the dramatic arts, is held every September/October. The **Ballarat Begonia Festival** in early March celebrates the city's floral emblem.

EXPLORING THE CITY

The main attraction for visitors is Sovereign Hill, a re-created colonial town where you can pan for gold and get a taste of life in the mid-19th century. Ballarat also has many splendid old buildings. Ask at the tourist office for a brochure describing a walking tour that'll lead you past the several significant local buildings.

✪ **Sovereign Hill Goldmining Township.** Bradshaw Street. ☎ **053/311 944.** Fax 053/311 528. Admission A$16.50 (U.S. $13.20) adults, A$8.50 (U.S. $6.80) children under 16; under 5 free. Daily 9am–5pm. Closed Christmas.

This is clearly the city's—and the state's—top attraction. Sovereign Hill is a living museum covering the period from 1851 to 1861: The buildings are based on drawings, photographs, and plans of the originals.

The township consists of three sections: the **Red Hill Gully Diggings,** showing early mining equipment and dwellings; **Main Street,** featuring shops and businesses that were in Ballarat in the 10 years following the discovery of gold; and the **Mining Museum,** consisting of steam-driven surface installations and impressive underground displays.

At Sovereign Hill, you can shop in stores historically accurate in both their design and the goods they stock. You can observe children studying in two Victorian-era schoolhouses. (Primary classes from anywhere in the state can book for a two-day program based on the 1850s curriculum.) You can pan for gold, see how the early miners lived, and contrast that with the living conditions of the Chinese workers. You can have your picture taken in old-fashioned clothes, take a Cobb & Co. coach ride, and watch craftspeople like blacksmiths, potters, and tinsmiths at work. Local folks in period costumes can answer questions. The guided tour of the underground mine takes about 45 minutes, but you'll need several hours to walk through the whole township. This is—in short—Australia's Williamsburg.

Sovereign Hill has several eating options. Besides an à la carte dining room, there's a family restaurant, a kiosk, a bakery selling freshly made wares straight from a wood-fired oven, and two coffee shops.

Gold Museum. Bradshaw Street. ☎ **053/311 944.** Admission A$4.50 (U.S. $3.60) adults, A$2.20 (U.S. $1.76) children. Sun–Fri 10am–5:20pm, Sat 12:30–5:20pm.

Across from Sovereign Hill is the Gold Museum, where samples of alluvial gold, gold nuggets, and gold coins are displayed. The exhibits depict life in the Ballarat area before the discovery of gold. There's also a major display on the Eureka Uprising (see below).

✪ **Blood on the Southern Cross.** At Sovereign Hill, Bradshaw Street. ☎ **053/311 944** or 053/335 777 for reservations. Admission: Show only, A$19.50 (U.S. $15.60) adults, A$9.50 (U.S. $7.60) children 5–15, A$52 (U.S. $41.60) family. Dinner and show, A$36 (U.S. $28.80) adults, A$22 (U.S. $17.60) children, A$106 (U.S. $84.80) family. Other packages combine daytime entry to Sovereign Hill with the show; entry, dinner, and show; or overnight accommodation, entry, dinner, and show. Mon–Sat two shows nightly (times vary seasonally).

This nighttime sound-and-light spectacular takes place across the 25 hectare (62-acre) panorama of Sovereign Hill. Imaginative sound and lighting techniques re-create one of the most important events in Australia's history. During the gold rush, miners had to buy a license from the government every month, whether or not they were finding gold. The miners resented the fee, especially because they didn't have the right to vote. The corrupt and abusive police conducted regular license hunts, further fueling dissension. When a publican guilty of murdering a miner was acquitted by the authorities, the miners rioted at his hotel.

On November 29, 1854, thousands of miners burned their licenses in a huge bonfire. The police countered with a ruthless license hunt. A few days later, the poorly armed miners gathered behind a stockade and were attacked by soldiers bearing firearms. The battle was over in 15 minutes, but 30 miners and 5 soldiers were killed. This incident forced the government to do something about the situation, and the hated licenses were replaced with "miner's rights," which cost only a fraction of the previous fee and included the privilege of voting. So the diggers lost the battle but won the war. The Eureka Uprising is significant since it's the only civil battle in the country's history.

Because this is an outdoor nighttime event, I suggest you wear warm, comfortable clothing and walking shoes.

City of Ballarat Fine Art Gallery. 40 Lydiard St. North. ☎ **053/315 622.** Admission A$2 (U.S. $1.60) adults; under 15 free. Tues–Fri 10:30am–4:30pm, Sat–Sun 12:30–4:30pm. Closed Good Friday and Christmas.

Established in 1884, this was the first provincial gallery in Australia. The foundation stone for the building was laid in 1887 to commemorate Queen Victoria's Golden Jubilee. Here you'll find a comprehensive collection of Australian art, especially from the colonial period and the Heidelberg School, plus the original Eureka flag.

WHERE TO STAY & DINE

Bell Tower Inn. 1845 Sturt St. (Western Highway), Ballarat, VIC 3350. ☎ **053/341 600** or 1800/032 978 in Australia. Fax 053/342 540. Reservations can be made through Flag Inns at 132400 in Australia. 75 rms. A/C MINIBAR TV TEL. A$85–A$140 (U.S. $68–$112) double. Additional person A$10 (U.S. $8) extra. AE, BC, DC, MC, V.

Located 6km (4 miles) west of central Ballarat, the Bell Tower offers five rooms that have tub/shower combinations and cooking facilities; 39 have spa baths in addition to showers; the rest have showers only. All offer coffee- and tea-making facilities, small refrigerators, electric blankets, queen-size beds, and radios. On the grounds are a heated pool, spa, sauna, playground, tennis court, trampoline, cocktail bar, and restaurant (closed Sunday).

✪ **Main Lead Motor Inn.** 312 Main Rd., Ballarat, VIC 3350. ☎ **053/317 533.** Fax 053/322 853. Reservations can be made through Flag Inns at 132400 in Australia. 25rms. A/C MINIBAR TV TEL. A$88 (U.S. $70.40) double. Additional person A$10 (U.S. $8) extra. AE, BC, DC, MC, V.

Ideally located within walking distance of Sovereign Hill, the Main Lead is an attractive two-story red-brick building. The rooms have exposed brick walls and beds with floral spreads; some have spa tubs and others offer large walk-in showers. I particularly like the upstairs rooms with cathedral ceilings and balconies. Lilians, a licensed restaurant, and an indoor pool and spa are on the premises. Lilians is open for lunch Monday to Friday and dinner Monday to Saturday.

2 The Great Ocean Road

Torquay: 94km (58 miles) SW of Melbourne

Port Campbell National Park: 285km (177 miles) SW of Melbourne

The rugged Southern Ocean crashes onto the coast of Victoria from one side of the state to the other, but only for a couple of hundred kilometers does a highway maintain close proximity with the sea. This portion following the shoreline is called the Great Ocean Road, beginning in Torquay, 94km (58 miles) southwest of Melbourne, and ending near Peterborough, some 200km (160 miles) later. The scenic route has been compared to California's coastal Highway 1 and the drive along the Italian Riviera.

Construction of the road was begun after World War I, as a memorial to those who'd lost their lives and to provide employment for returned soldiers. The going was rough. Equipment was sent overland by train to Dean's Marsh, and from there it was taken by wagons pulled by teams of 14 horses. It took two days to travel the 25km (15 miles) to Lorne. The workmen complained of low wages and rough conditions, but they did experience one pleasant windfall: A coastal steamer ran aground near the town of Kennet River in 1924 and had to jettison its cargo. Among the things that floated to shore were 50 barrels of beer and various cases of spirits; no work was done for the following two weeks. While building the road was a struggle, it was finally completed in 1932. In addition to providing coastal access to tourists, it has made viable the fishing industry in Lorne and Apollo Bay.

ESSENTIALS

GETTING THERE This scenic road is best enjoyed by car, which allows for stopping at the various viewpoints. It's completely paved, wide enough to be safe, and well signposted. There are no airports along the Great Ocean Road. However, Moloney Aviation (☎ 03/9379 2122; fax 03/9374 2086) offers a day trip that includes flying from Melbourne to Peterborough and then traveling by coach to the sights along the Great Ocean Road.

V/Line has regular train service to Geelong and Warrnambool with Friday-only connecting coaches along the Great Ocean Road.

VISITOR INFORMATION **Bell's Beach,** a few kilometers southwest of Torquay, is the site of the annual Surfing World Championships. It also boasts one of the longest right-hand waves on the continent. Nearby, Winkipop is another popular surf spot. The Park Information Centre, at **Port Campbell National Park** (☎ 055/986 382), has an interesting display and audiovisual show about the area. It's open daily from 10am to 5pm. The primary resort towns along the Great Ocean Road offering dining and lodging are Lorne (pop. 935) and Apollo Bay (pop. 1,162). Both also offer opportunities for surfing, fishing, golf, and bushwalking. The region's **telephone area codes** are 052 and 055. As part of the telephone changeover, all numbers with a 052 area code will change to 03/52xx xxxx in March 1997 and numbers with a 055 area code will change to 03/55xx xxxx in March 1997.

EXPLORING THE COASTAL ROAD

In some places the road skirts high cliffs well above the ocean; at others, it descends to sea level and curves along sightly sand beaches. One of the most spectacular areas is known as the ✪ **Twelve Apostles**—a row of great stone pillars emerging from the sea just a short way offshore. These sentinels are part of **Port Campbell National Park,** as are the other unusual features created by the sea from limestone cliffs: **Loch Ard Gorge** and **The Arch.** (Another landmark, London Bridge, collapsed into the sea in 1990.) This stormy coast has claimed 163 sailing ships. While they can't be seen from land, the wrecks can be explored with scuba gear. (Because they've been declared historical sites, you can remove nothing from them.)

WHERE TO STAY

IN LORNE

Cumberland Lorne Conference & Leisure Resort. 150–178 Mountjoy Parade, Lorne, VIC 3232. ☎ **052/892 400,** or 1800/037 010 in Australia. Fax 052/892 256. 51 one-bedroom, 35 two-bedroom, and 12 penthouse apts. TV TEL. A$185–A$200 (U.S. $148–$160) one-bedroom apt; A$230–A$245 (U.S. $184–$196) two-bedroom apt; A$285 (U.S. $228) penthouse. Ask about dollarwise midweek and weekend packages. No-smoking rooms available. AE, BC, DC, MC, V. Free parking.

On the main road in Lorne, 142km (88 miles) southwest of Melbourne, this resort is ideal for families who want to enjoy all the recreational opportunities available in Lorne. It's in the heart of the community, near all the activities. Each modern spacious apartment has a full kitchen, a washing machine and dryer, a spa bath, in-room movies, and a balcony with patio furniture. More than half have ocean views. Each apartment block is named for a shipwreck that occurred in the vicinity of the Great Ocean Road.

Dining/Entertainment: Chris' Restaurant, a casual bistro with indoor and outdoor seating, is open from 11am during the week and 9am on weekends. Horizons, the more elegant à la carte dining spot, is open Monday to Saturday during December and January.

Services: Baby-sitting.

Readers Recommend

Otway Ranges Deer and Wildlife Park, Great Ocean Road, Princetown (☎ 052/375 262). *"On the way to the Twelve Apostles, this place is well worth a visit. You can hand-feed wallabies and kangaroos. It's shortly before the Twelve Apostles and well signposted."*

—Wendy Gross and Bev Wybrow, Toronto, Canada

Facilities: Heated indoor pool, gym, sauna, two tennis courts, table tennis, billiards, two squash courts; bicycles, surf skis, and bodysurfing boards can be rented. The children's activity program includes beach games, movies, face painting, walks, and picnics. The resort's shopping plaza has 14 specialty shops, a beauty salon, a bank, and a post office.

Motel Kalimna. Mountjoy Parade (Great Ocean Road), Lorne, VIC 3232. ☎ **052/891 407.** Fax 052/892 318. 25 rms. TV TEL. A$74–A$165 (U.S. $59.20–$132) double. Additional person A$10 (U.S. $8) extra. Lower rates off-season. AE, BC, DC, MC, V. Free parking.

At the low-rise Kalimna, private balconies face the sea. A cocktail bar, a restaurant, a pool, laundry facilities, a tennis court, a barbecue area, and a games room are on the premises.

In Apollo Bay

Apollo International Motor Inn. 37 Great Ocean Rd., Apollo Bay, VIC 3233. ☎ **052/376 100.** Fax 052/376 066. Reservations can be made through Flag Inns. 24 rms. A/C TV TEL. A$90–A$119 (U.S. $72–$95.20) double. Additional adult A$15 (U.S. $12) extra; A$12 (U.S. $9.60) child under 12. Surcharge Sat night, Christmas, Easter, Melbourne Cup weekend, and public and school holidays. AE, BC, DC, MC, V. Free parking.

This may look like just another red-brick motel, but it's really much more. Six rooms have spa baths in very large bathrooms. There are also six two-story family units, and all quarters have small refrigerators, toasters, electric blankets, art deco interiors, hairdryers, and coffee- and tea-making facilities. The hostelry also offers a pool, spa, and guest laundry.

Near Woolsthorpe

Quamby Homestead. Caramut Road (R.M.B. 9130), Woolsthorpe, VIC 3276. ☎ or fax **055/692 395.** 5 cottages, 1 carriage house, 1 schoolhouse. A/C TV. A$135 (U.S. $108) per person in mews, A$160 (U.S. $128) per person in carriage house. Two-day package (including two dinners, two breakfasts, and picnic-hamper lunch), A$225 (U.S. $180) per person in mews, A$250 (U.S. $200) in carriage house. Rates include breakfast, afternoon tea, and dinner. Lower rates for extended stays. Children under 12 not accepted. BC, MC, V. Free parking.

Quamby is a wonderful historic homestead where you sleep in cottages and other buildings on a 26.4-hectare (66-acre) property surrounded by sheep and pretty gardens. The location is ideal: 32km (19 miles) north of Warrnambool and just a short distance from both the Great Ocean Road and the Grampians. Edna Goldman and Rodger Stebbing enjoy telling guests about William Lindsay, the immigrant from Scotland who cleared and drained 30,000 acres here in 1854. By the 1870s the property had grown to 70,000 acres and was the largest cattle station in Victoria. Unfortunately, the Lindsay grandchildren gambled and drank away their inheritance and died penniless, and Quamby was in ruins when it was sold in 1983. Today it has been beautifully restored and provides a good chance to experience rural life and understand an important aspect of Australia's history.

All the buildings are white with blue trim and surrounded by English-style gardens and lawns. You sleep in queen-size iron-and-brass beds with wonderful doonas and awaken to the sound of native birds, peacocks, and sheep. All accommodations have baths (some with showers only). Breakfast is served on the veranda of the main homestead. Roger is a very talented chef, and Edna's specialty is "looking after people." Tasty four-course dinners (included in the rates) are available to nonguests on Friday and Saturday night. Sunday lunch is also offered. You may bring your own wine or choose one from the Quamby list.

The hosts will happily make arrangements for you to watch shearing (September to December) or tour other local gardens and homesteads.

WHERE TO DINE

IN LORNE

The Arab Restaurant. 94 Mountjoy Parade. ☎ **055/891 435.** Reservations recommended. Main courses A$12.50–A$17.90 (U.S. $10–$14.30). No credit cards. Dec–Easter, daily 8am–midnight; Easter–Nov, daily 8am–9:30pm. INTERNATIONAL.

This popular bistro has been pleasing customers since it opened in 1956. Black-and-white photos on the wall show "bathing beauties" in the restaurant as it was then. Host Sammy Gazis writes the daily offerings—seafood, chicken, and steaks—on a chalkboard. The specialty of the house is chicken Kiev. Seated at a wooden table, you can watch your meal being prepared in the open kitchen. There's limited seating outdoors, and two levels inside. Save room for Sammy's apple crumble.

IN APOLLO BAY

$ **Bay Leaf Gourmet Deli.** 131 Great Ocean Rd. ☎ **052/376 470.** Reservations not accepted. Breakfast and lunch A$2–A$14.50 (U.S. $1.60–$11.60); dinner main courses A$5–A$16.50 (U.S. $4–$13.20). BC, MC, V. Breakfast served all day. May–Sept, daily 8am–2:30pm; Sept–April, daily 8am–2:30pm, Thurs–Sat and public holidays 6–10pm. CAFE.

The Bay Leaf serves the best breakfast for miles—maybe the best in Australia. Whether you choose an omelet, banana pancakes with rum butter and maple syrup, or a crumpet with honey, you won't be disappointed. The lunch menu changes daily and includes such items as tortellini with ham and mushrooms; smoked salmon, avocado, and cream cheese on rye; and hot roast beef and salad sandwich. Dinner possibilities include curry, smoked trout pasta, or risotto with pumpkin and sundried tomatoes. There are less than a dozen tables inside and a few more outside. Some locals just drop in for a cappuccino or a cup of Twinings tea and read the magazines provided. BYO. Highly recommended.

3 Mildura & the Murray River

544km (337 miles) NW of Melbourne, 400km (248 miles) NE of Adelaide, 297km (184 miles) S of Broken Hill

In the Aboriginal language, *mildura* means "dry red earth," which brings to mind much of Australia's landscape. Thousands of miles of inland terrain are rust-colored and barren. In the case of Mildura, however, this isn't true. When the natives named the area, it *was* indistinguishable from the land around it, but subsequently the largest irrigation scheme in the country has created 22,000 fertile hectares (54,340 acres) that produce wine and table grapes, olives, many types of citrus fruit, avocados, and melons. These horticultural achievements are possible because of the town's location on the banks of the Murray River and the know-how of California's Chaffey brothers—George and W.B. (William Benjamin).

The Chaffeys honed their skills in Etiwanda and Ontario, California, where they developed large-scale irrigation programs. George, the elder, was an engineer, and W.B. had a talent for business ventures. In 1887 they were invited by Alfred Deakin, a member of Victoria's Parliament, to transform the red earth along the Murray River into prime growing land. George Chaffey designed two triple-expansion pumping engines, and while they were being manufactured in England, newly arrived settlers set about clearing hundreds of hectares of scrub, erecting fences, and digging many kilometers of channels. By 1890 Mildura had 3,000 residents and 2,500 hectares (6,175 acres) of vines, citrus, and stone fruit. One pump continued operating until 1955; the other lasted until 1959. Today the oasislike community (pop. 19,360) is the heart of one of Australia's most important fruit-growing regions.

ESSENTIALS

GETTING THERE The drive from Melbourne takes seven hours. Kendell and Southern Airlines provide service to Mildura from Melbourne, Adelaide, and Broken Hill. The flight from Melbourne takes 1½ hours. There's no train service to Mildura.

V/Line operates daily coach service. The fare from Melbourne is A$51 (U.S. $40.80).

VISITOR INFORMATION Information is dispensed at the **Mildura Tourist Information Centre,** 101 Deakin Ave., Mildura, VIC 3500 (☎ 050/214 424), Monday to Friday from 9am to 5:30pm, Saturday from 9am to 4pm, and Sunday from 10am to 4pm. Mildura's **telephone area code** is 050. As part of the telephone changeover, all numbers with a 050 area code will be changing to 03/50xx xxxx in March 1997.

SEEING THE AREA

ATTRACTIONS

Mildura Arts Centre. 199 Cureton Ave. ☎ **050/233 733.** Admission A$2 (U.S. $1.60) adults; children free. Mon–Fri 9am–5pm, Sun 2–4:30pm. Closed Good Friday and Christmas.

The Mildura Arts Centre consists of **Rio Vista** (the former home of W.B. Chaffey), the **Regional Art Gallery,** and a 400-seat **theater.** The grand house, built in 1890, is interesting for itself and for the items of local history it contains. The dining room and smoking room are just as they were when the Californian was in residence. A variety of equipment used by the pioneers in this area is on display on the front lawn, including one of Chaffey's original pumping engines. This 6-meter-high (20-ft.), 750-horsepower engine transformed Mildura from a waterless wasteland into the most densely populated rural production center in Australia.

Mildura Workingman's Club. Deakin Avenue. ☎ **050/230 531.** Free admission. Mon–Sat 9am–noon.

Another point of interest in Mildura is the Workingman's Club, where the bar is nearly the length of a football field and has 27 beer taps. According to the *Guinness Book of World Records,* this is the Southern Hemisphere's longest.

✪ **Golden River Zoo.** Flora Avenue. ☎ **050/235 540.** Admission A$8.50 (U.S. $6.80) adults, A$4.25 (U.S. $3.40) children. Daily 9am–5pm. Closed Christmas.

Set on 14 hectares (35 acres) of lush Murray River frontage 4km (2½ miles) from the city center down 11th Street, this privately owned zoo is well worth a stop. You walk through large enclosures where native animals roam freely and can be petted and fed. A paddleboat cruise to the zoo departs Mildura Wharf at 9:50am and returns at 3pm. Snacks are sold from a kiosk on the grounds.

FRUIT & WINE PRODUCTION

The original settlers sun-dried their fruit because they couldn't get it to Melbourne markets before it spoiled. This changed when the railroad was put through to Mildura in 1903, but dried fruit remains an important product in this area. The packing companies here are among the world's largest. You can tour the **U.D.F.A. Shop** on the Calder Highway at Irymple (☎ 050/245 203). In town, the **Sunraysia Dried Fruits and Healthfood Centre,** 33 Deakin Ave. (☎ 050/231 760), shows a video on the industry and sells an amazing array of the product. The center is open Monday to Friday from 9am to 5:30pm and Saturday from 9am to noon. Light lunches and morning and afternoon teas using the local products are available.

The area's wineries also welcome visitors. **Mildura Blass Wines Limited,** Wentworth Road, Merbein (☎ 050/252 303), 11km (7 miles) northwest of Mildura, is open Monday to Friday from 9am to 5pm, Saturday from 11am to 4pm, and Sunday from 11am to 4pm (holiday periods only). Tours cost A$2 (U.S. $1.60). **Lindeman's Karadoc,** the largest winery in the Southern Hemisphere, is 29km (18 miles) southeast of Mildura in Karadoc (☎ 050/513 285); it's open daily from 10am to 4:30pm for tastings and sales.

THE MURRAY RIVER

The Murray River provides a number of activities. To begin with, you can watch the action as boats pass through the river's **Lock 11.** If you have a bit more time, why not take a two-hour cruise on the **PS Melbourne** (☎ 050/232 200)? This steam-powered paddlewheeler, built in 1912, leaves from the Mildura Wharf Sunday to Friday at 10:50am and 1:50pm and Saturday at 1:50pm. It's still driven by its original steam engine and boiler. The fare is A$15 (U.S. $12) for adults and A$6 (U.S. $4.80) for children 5 to 15; under 5 are free. A kiosk on board sells snacks and teas. Cruises don't operate on Christmas.

For an extended river experience you might like a two-, three-, or five-night cruise on the **M.V. Proud Mary.** You hear tales of the area and its heroes, bushrangers, and colorful characters as this paddlewheeler travels along the Murray. Daily shore excursions are included. The per person–double occupancy cost is A$398 (U.S. $318.40) for two nights; A$620 (U.S. $496) for three; and A$995 (U.S. $796) for five. For information, contact Proud Australia Holidays at 08/231 9472 (fax 08/212 1520). Another paddlewheel cruise option is the **Murray Princess**. The per person–double occupancy cost is A$235 to A$305 (U.S. $188 to $244) for two nights; A$380 to A$495 (U.S. $304 to $396) for three; and A$630 to A$830 (U.S. $504 to $664) for five. Shore excursions are extra. For more information, contact Captain Cook Cruises at 02/206 1144 (fax 02/251 4725).

The Murray is fed by the Darling River, which starts in Queensland, and the Murray-Darling system constitutes the longest river in Australia. Because the land is so flat, it's also one of the world's slowest rivers. When there's a flood in Queensland, it takes the water three months to reach Victoria and South Australia, so people have plenty of time to protect their riverfront property.

WHERE TO STAY

Chaffey International Motor Inn. 244 Deakin Ave., Mildura, VIC 3500. ☎ **050/235 833.** Fax 050/211 972. Reservations can be made through Flag Inns. 33 rms. A/C MINIBAR TV TEL. A$86–A$125 (U.S. $68.80–$100) double. Additional person A$10 (U.S. $8) extra. AE, BC, DC, MC, V. Free parking.

This is a modern two-story hostelry. In addition to its 33 rooms, the Chaffey has a cocktail lounge, restaurant, spa, pool, laundry, and playground. All rooms have coffee- and tea-making facilities, small refrigerators, in-room movies, and clock radios. Room service is offered and facilities for the handicapped are available.

$ **Mildura Grand Hotel.** Seventh Street, Mildura, VIC 3500. ☎ **050/230 511,** or 1800/034 228 in Australia. Fax 050/221 801. 105 rms, 7 suites. MINIBAR TV TEL. A$73 (U.S. $58.40) standard double, A$115 (U.S. $92) "Grand Room" double; A$110–A$320 (U.S. $88–$256) suite. Rates include breakfast. Ask about dinner, bed, and breakfast packages. AE, BC, DC, MC, V. Free parking.

The Grand Hotel, across from the train station, is a charming reminder of a more elegant era. Each room in the two-story 19th-century hostelry has a bath (20 have tubs), in-rooms movies, free daily newspaper, and coffee- and tea-making facilities;

suites have their own spa baths. A pool, spa, and sauna are in a charming garden setting. Meals are served in the dining room, and teas and drinks are available in a number of bars and lounges or around the pool. Large open fires warm these public areas in the winter. Room service is provided 24 hours.

4 Victoria/New South Wales: Along the Hume Freeway & Highway

If you're driving, the fastest route from Melbourne to Sydney is the Hume Freeway and Highway, a distance of 840km (520 miles). Most vacationers break this 12-hour journey with an overnight stay, but truck drivers and businesspeople in a hurry go nonstop. In Chapter 6 I described the northern end of the trip through the Southern Highlands outside of Sydney. Albury and Goulburn, both in New South Wales, are other logical places to pause. The turnoff to Canberra, the nation's capital, is at Yass if you're coming from the south and just past Goulburn if you're coming from the north.

WANGARATTA

AirWorld, on Greta Road in Wangaratta, Victoria (☎ 057/218 788; fax 057/222 388), 233km (144 miles) north of Melbourne, is worth a look if you're interested in antique aircraft. This aviation museum contains some 47 very old civil and military planes—most in flying condition. Some are the last of their type left in the world. Antique bicycles and cars are also on display. A 200-seat restaurant is on the premises. AirWorld is open daily from 9am to 5pm; admission is A$6 (U.S. $4.80) for adults, A$4 (U.S. $3.20) for children, and A$12.50 (U.S. $10) for families. There's no public transportation to this attraction.

As part of the telephone changeover, all numbers with a 057 area code will be changing to 03/57xx xxxx in February 1997.

WHERE TO STAY & DINE

Yaridni Homestead. Yarrawonga Road, Benalla (R.M.B. 1090, Goorambat, VIC 3725). ☎ **057/641 273.** Fax 057/641 352. 3 rms (1 with bath). With breakfast, A$95 (U.S. $76) double. With all meals and wine with dinner: A$95 (U.S. $76) per person. Dinner, bed, and breakfast rate also available. No credit cards. Free parking. Free transportation from train or bus station in Benalla.

About 40km (25 miles) south of Wangaratta and 10 minutes from the Old Hume Highway between Winton and Benalla, Yaridni is a 1,500-acre sheep property where handsome merinos roam over the parklike grounds and Rhyllis Siggers welcomes guests with open arms. It's about 8 hours from Sydney, 5 hours from Canberra, and 2½ hours from Melbourne.

The white ranch-style homestead sits on a rise at the end of a half-mile tree-lined drive. It offers three rooms—one with a bath, the others with shared facilities. It also has a large family room, a cozy lounge (living room) with fireplace, a sunny patio with wide views over the property, and a dining room where evening meals are served. You're invited to join farm activities, and Rhyllis's sons will shear a sheep and put Judy Dog through her paces, if so desired. Kangaroos graze in the paddocks at dusk. Children are welcome.

ALBURY-WODONGA

Straddling the border and the Murray River, 305km (189 miles) north of Melbourne, the twin towns of Albury, New South Wales, and Wodonga, Victoria, provide a convenient point at which to break the Melbourne-Sydney drive. Information on New South Wales and Victoria is available from the **Gateway Tourist Information Centre,** Lincoln Causeway, Wodonga, VIC 3690 (☎ 060/413 875), open daily from 9am to 5pm. It also provides a 24-hour phone service.

As part of the telephone changeover, all numbers with a 060 area code will be changing to 02/60xx xxxx in February 1998.

Seeing the Area

The **Albury Regional Art Centre,** 546 Dean St., on Queen Elizabeth II Square, contains the Drysdale Collection, European prints, and Australian photography. The **Albury Regional Museum,** Australia Park, Wodonga Place (☎ 060/214 550), is housed in the Old Turks Head Inn, dating from 1854. It's open daily from 10:30am to 4:30pm and admission is free. The **Botanical Gardens** would be an ideal place to stretch your legs.

Where to Stay & Dine

Albury Georgian Motor Inn. 599 Young St., Albury, NSW 2640. ☎ **060/218 744,** or 1800/028 273 in Australia. Fax 060/218 320. 19 rms, 5 suites. A/C MINIBAR TV TEL. A$76 (U.S. $60.80) double; A$85 (U.S. $68) suite. Additional person A$12 (U.S. $9.60) extra. AE, BC, DC, MC, V. Free parking.

Each room in this two-story motel has a tub/shower combination, a queen-size bed, a clock radio, a hairdryer, tea- and coffee-making facilities, and a small refrigerator. A restaurant is on the grounds and room service is available 15 hours a day. There's a pool and a spa; baby-sitting can be arranged. The motel is 1km (0.6 mile) from the rail station and 3km ($1^1/_2$ miles) from the airport on the Hume Highway.

Hume Country Golf Club Motor Inn. 736 Logan Rd., Albury, NSW 2640. ☎ **060/258 233.** Fax 060/404 999. 21 rms, 4 suites. A/C TV TEL. A$65–A$75 (U.S. $52–$60) double; A$95 (U.S. $76) suite. Additional person A$15 (U.S. $12) extra. Rates are 10% higher on public holidays. AE, BC, DC, MC, V. Free parking.

At this modern motel adjacent to a golf club, all rooms have toasters in addition to the standard facilities. The four VIP suites have two-person spas. Pool, laundry, and barbecue facilities are available. The golf-club complex includes a 27-hole course, modern locker rooms with showers, a pro shop, a day-and-night golf driving range, 100 poker (slot) machines, a bistro for quick meals, a cocktail lounge, and a restaurant. All rooms in the motel have golf-course views.

Hume Inn. 406 Wodonga Place, Albury, NSW 2640. ☎ **060/212 733.** Fax 060/412 239. 40 rms, 5 suites. A/C TV TEL. A$65–A$75 (U.S. $52–$60) double; A$74–A$86 (U.S. $59.20–$68.80) family unit; A$125 (U.S. $100) suite. A$5 (U.S. $4) surcharge on public holidays. AE, BC, DC, MC, V. Free parking.

At this two-story motel, the licensed à la carte restaurant is open daily and there's a pool and playground. Some rooms have queen-size beds and clock radios. All offer tea- and coffee-making facilities and small refrigerators. Baby-sitting can be arranged.

Gundagai

You might want to stop briefly in Gundagai, New South Wales, 491km (304 miles) north of Melbourne and 386km (239 miles) south of Sydney, to see the **"Dog on the Tuckerbox" memorial,** 8km (5 miles) north of town, which is celebrated in a popular Australian folk song, "The Road to Gundagai." **Rusconi's Marble Masterpiece,** a miniature cathedral made of 20,000 pieces of NSW marble, is worth a look, too. It's on display at the **Tourist Information Centre** on Sheridan Street.

GOULBURN

Even if I didn't tell you Goulburn is the center of a wealthy farming district, you might guess it when you see the high-rise horned ram towering over the **Big Merino Tourist Complex** on the Hume Highway (☎ 048/215 477). This all-inclusive pit stop is 681km (422 miles) north of Melbourne and 196km (121 miles) south of Sydney. It consists of a 24-hour gasoline station, a large gift/souvenir shop, a 400-seat Agrodome, the Billabong Restaurant, the 24-hour Viennaworld Restaurant, and an ice-cream parlor.

Several times a day Australia's top 20 ram breeds are presented in shows in the Agrodome. The one-hour entertainment also includes a shearing demonstration and information on the wool industry. Admission is A$6 (U.S. $4.80) for adults and A$3 (U.S. $2.40) for children. Many woolen items are sold in the complex's shop.

As part of the telephone changeover, all numbers with a 048 area code will be changing to 02/48xx xxxx in June 1998.

WHERE TO STAY

Lilac City Motor Inn. 126 Lagoon St. (Hume Highway), Goulburn, NSW 2580. ☎ **048/215 000.** Fax 048/218 074. 28 rms. A/C TV TEL. A$70 (U.S. $56) double. Additional person A$7 (U.S. $5.60) extra. Ask about lower rates through Aussie auto clubs. AE, BC, DC, MC, V. Free parking.

Should you decide to break your Melbourne-Sydney trip in Goulburn, the Lilac City Motor Inn is a nice two-story motel with a restaurant, room service, and the standard amenities. Facilities for the handicapped are available.

5 The Southeast Coast

The **Princes Highway** follows the perimeter of Victoria and New South Wales, connecting Melbourne and Sydney over a route of 1,080km (670 miles). Unlike the speedy Hume Highway trip, this journey is best done over two days. You may want to take longer, of course, especially if you stop to play golf, go boating, or enjoy the beaches. I described the coast from Sydney to the state border in Chapter 6. The highlights of the Victorian portion are Wilsons Promontory National Park, 230km (143 miles) southeast of Melbourne; Lakes Entrance, 319km (198 miles) east of Melbourne; and the Snowy River National Park, due north of Orbost.

WILSONS PROMONTORY NATIONAL PARK

Few Aussies who've been there can talk about the "Prom" without getting misty-eyed. The rugged wedge of granite projecting into Bass Strait is rich in wildlife and has been a national park since early this century. Nature lovers flock here to observe native animals, gaze at the magnificent scenery, hike through lush fern gullies, and stroll along deserted beaches. From late September to early December wildflowers bloom in profusion. Park entry is A$6.50 (U.S. $5.20).

The park is rich in bird life. Crimson rosellas are the most obvious, but honey eaters, cockatoos, kookaburras, and many others are here, too. It's also fairly easy to spot koalas, kangaroos, wallabies, wombats, and possums.

There are campsites and lodge-style accommodations at Tidal River. Sea kayaking is a popular activity. If you're interested, contact **Wilsons Promontory Seakayaking** at 056/881 233. The season for this sport is November to May.

As part of the telephone changeover, all numbers with a 056 area code will be changing to 03/56xx xxxx in March 1997.

WHERE TO STAY & DINE

$ Waratah Park Country House. Thomson Road, Waratah Bay, VIC 3959. ☎ **056/832 575.** Fax 056/832 275. 6 rms. A$100 (U.S. $80) per person Sun–Thurs (including four-course dinner and breakfast); A$245 (U.S. $196) per person for "Weekend Package" (including two nights' lodging, two breakfasts, and two four-course dinners); A$145 (U.S. $116) per person Sat night (including four-course dinner, lodging, and breakfast). AE, BC, MC, V. Free parking.

There are no hotels or motels in the national park, and even if there were I'd bet you'd still opt to stay at this lovely country house overlooking the western edge of the park and a dozen Bass Strait islands. No expense was spared in building Waratah Park: Each room features a different type of wood in its furnishings, a king-size bed with fluffy doona, a large spa bath, and a million-dollar view. However, what really makes this place special is the site: 30 hectares (75 acres) of elevated farmland where kangaroos, wallabies, and wombats graze at dusk.

Owners Bill and Paula Thomson relish pampering their guests and gourmet cuisine and fine wines are served in the Great Room, where a brick fireplace contributes to the welcoming atmosphere.

LAKES ENTRANCE

A series of interconnecting lakes and lagoons and a long expanse of beach make Lakes Entrance (pop. 4,100) a popular summer resort. The town is at the eastern end of the Gippsland Lakes: Lake King, Lake Victoria, Lake Wellington, Lake Reeve, and others provide a wonderful playground for boaters, waterskiers, windsurfers, and fishers. (Boats of all shapes and sizes can be rented in Lakes Entrance. Cruises and fishing excursions are also available.) The inland waterway is separated from the ocean by a thin sliver of sand dunes and a footbridge allows surfers, swimmers, and sun worshipers access to a seemingly endless stretch of beach.

Lakes Entrance is the base for Australia's largest commercial fishing fleet. Even if you don't choose to break your Melbourne-Sydney journey at this point, pause at **Jemmy Point,** 2km (1 mile) west of town on the Princes Highway, to admire the view.

As part of the telephone changeover, all numbers with a 051 area code will be changing to 03/51xx xxxx in March 1997.

WHERE TO STAY & DINE

Abel Tasman Motor Lodge. 643 Esplanade (Princes Highway), Lakes Entrance, VIC 3909. ☎ **051/551 655.** 12 rms. A/C TV TEL. A$50–A$81 (U.S. $40–$64.80) double. Rates are highest from Christmas to the end of Jan and Easter week. AE, BC, DC, MC, V. Free parking.

This two-story motel offers modern amenities and a pool. All rooms have lake views, radios, coffee- and tea-making facilities, small refrigerators, and toasters. First-floor rooms have private balconies.

Banjo Paterson Motor Inn. 131 Esplanade (Princes Highway), Lakes Entrance, VIC 3909. ☎ **051/552 933.** Fax 051/552 855. Reservations can be made through Best Western. 22 rms. A/C TV TEL. A$65–A$135 (U.S. $52–$118) double. Rates are highest from Christmas to the end of Jan and Easter week. Ask about lower rates through Aussie auto clubs. AE, BC, DC, JCB, MC, V. Free parking.

Six of the rooms at the Banjo Paterson have spa tubs and all are equipped with radios, hairdryers, videos, coffee- and tea-making facilities, and small refrigerators. A licensed restaurant and pool are on the premises, and room service is available.

SNOWY RIVER NATIONAL PARK

Adventurous travelers who don't mind driving on unpaved roads have the option of leaving the Princes Highway and wandering up through the foothills of Victoria's high country. The **Barry Way** follows the course of the Snowy River, passing through the rustic townships of **Buchan** and **Gelantipy.** The wilderness scenery in this area is breathtaking. One of my most vivid mental pictures of Australia was formed when I walked down to the river, at a point just south of the New South Wales border, and discovered the banks were covered with colorful California poppies. Besides being a beautiful drive, this route is a shortcut to **Jindabyne,** the gateway to Thredbo and the Snowy Mountains (see Chapter 6).

The **Buchan Caves** (☎ 051/559 264) are open to the public with several tours daily between 10am and 3:30pm. Both Fairy and Royal Caves are easily accessible and highly decorated with delicate calcite formations. Cave tours cost A$6.50 (U.S. $5.20) for adults, A$4 (U.S. $3.20) for kids 5 to 16, and A$17 (U.S. $13.60) for families in Royal Cave; and A$8 (U.S. $6.40) for adults, A$5 (U.S. $4) for kids, and A$20 (U.S. $16) for families in Fairy Cave. A kiosk sells snacks. The road to Buchan is paved all the way from the coast.

Horseback riding is popular in this area. If interested, contact **Snowy River Trail Rides,** Buchan Bruthen Road (R.M.B. 4030), Buchan, VIC 3885 (☎ 051/559 245). Rides cost A$15 (U.S. $12) per hour. Longer trail rides in the Snowy River country cost A$80 (U.S. $64) per day (all inclusive) for 2- to 10-day rides. These take place November to May.

Paul and Judi Sykes of **Snowy Mountain Rider Tours,** Karoonda Park, Gelantipy, VIC 3885 (☎ 051/550 220), host guests at their property and do day rides from there. These cost A$100 (U.S. $80) per day. They also organize longer, more adventurous trail rides, which involve camping for four or five nights. These cost A$400 to A$500 (U.S. $320 to $400) and take place November to March. Between the spectacular scenery, Judi's good cooking, and the pleasure of riding and sleeping out where, according to Banjo Paterson, "the night stars fairly blaze," this could be the thrill of a lifetime.

Tasmania

18

Australia's only island state looks more like New Zealand than mainland Oz. Tasmania is green and mountainous in some places, green and pastoral in others. It's sparsely populated, has cool wet winters, and is a great place for growing apples.

There are several good reasons you should spend the time and money to visit Tasmania. The first is wilderness scenery. Because it's so isolated, Tasmania's bush remains very much the way it was when Abel Tasman first sighted the island in 1642. (More than 20% of the island has been declared a World Heritage Area.) Dense rain forests, jagged mountains, alpine meadows, stands of Huon pines that predate European exploration, lush valleys, and wild rivers await adventurous souls. You can view some from the main roads, but the best are stashed away where only those willing to hike, climb, raft, or canoe will see them. South West National Park and the rugged West Coast are magnets for those who like roughing it.

This isn't to say the "holiday island" is only for athletes. In addition to beautiful wilderness scenery, Tasmania is well known for its colonial buildings. While other states have pulled down many of their Victorian and Edwardian structures, this kind of "progress" has eluded out-of-the-way Tassie. Lots of cozy bed-and-breakfast inns, quaint tearooms, and appealing eateries are housed in historic buildings. In this respect, Tasmania resembles England.

Were I packing for a trip to Hobart or Launceston, I'd leave room in my suitcase for all the handcrafts I know I'll buy. Many talented artisans are drawn to the island's slow way of life and appreciation of nature. While some of their products are sold on the mainland, the selection and prices offered in local craft shops are unmatched in other states. Pottery, wooden items created from Tasmanian trees, and hand-blown glass pieces are especially attractive.

In addition to wonderful wilderness, a plethora of colonial buildings, and crafts, the island state offers excellent trout fishing on more than 3,000 lakes. Arthur's Lake, Lake Sorell, and Great Lake, all in the central region, are anglers' favorites. If you like eating seafood but aren't interested in catching it, a large commercial fleet keeps local restaurants well supplied.

Seafood is only one aspect of Tasmanian cuisine. Visitors here can also look forward to cheese, cream, game, beef, fruit, vegetables, and wine that are some of the best Australia has to offer.

What's Special About Tasmania

Buildings
- Many colonial buildings, some functioning as B&Bs.

Top Attractions
- Port Arthur, the remains of a penal colony.
- Wilderness scenery, much of it on the World Heritage List.

Shopping
- For crafts—excellent selection and good prices.

Regional Food & Drink
- Tasmanian wine, both red and white.
- Fruits and vegetables, freshly picked in season.
- Seafood—including salmon, crayfish, trout, and oysters.

Activities
- Camping, hiking, and fishing in beautiful bushland settings.
- Sailing, a popular summer pastime.

Saturday Selections
- The Salamanca Market in Hobart, for arts and crafts.

Nothing in the state's appearance hints at its early violent and cruel history. First settled by Europeans in 1803, Tasmania was primarily a penal colony where convicts lived in terrible conditions and toiled hard until the last transportations in 1852. Unfortunately, this isn't the worst aspect of the island's story—the white settlers hunted the local Aborigines like animals.

EXPLORING THE ISLAND STATE

Tasmanians are very hospitable hosts who'll make you glad you took the time to visit. Try to go between mid-September and May, when the weather is best. The **Tasmanian Visitor Information Network** operates information centers in most Australian capitals and in 30 cities and towns throughout Tasmania. Be sure to pick up a copy of *Travelways,* Tourism Tasmania's free tourist tabloid, which is several cuts above the norm.

GETTING THERE Tasmania can be reached by many air services and by boat across Bass Strait. The ***Spirit of Tasmania*** ferry carries 1,300 passengers, with or without their cars, from Melbourne's Station Pier to Devonport on the island's north coast. The ship has all the modern conveniences, and unless the seas are rough the trip is comfortable and enjoyable. Facilities include a cafeteria, buffet bistro, fine-dining room, pool, sauna, and disco. The *Spirit of Tasmania* sails on alternate evenings at 6pm from Devonport and Station Pier, arriving the next morning at 8:30am. Reservations can be made with TT-Line at 03/9206 6233 in Melbourne, or 13 20 10 or 1800/030 344 in Australia. You can also make reservations for the *Spirit of Tasmania* by calling Intaussie at 800/531-9222 in the U.S. and Canada. Fares vary according to the time of year. The "holiday" period (mid-December to January and two weeks at Easter) is the most expensive. One-way adult fares range from A$99 to A$295 (U.S. $79.20 to $236), depending on the type of accommodation, which varies from hostel-type lodging to deluxe suites with private baths.

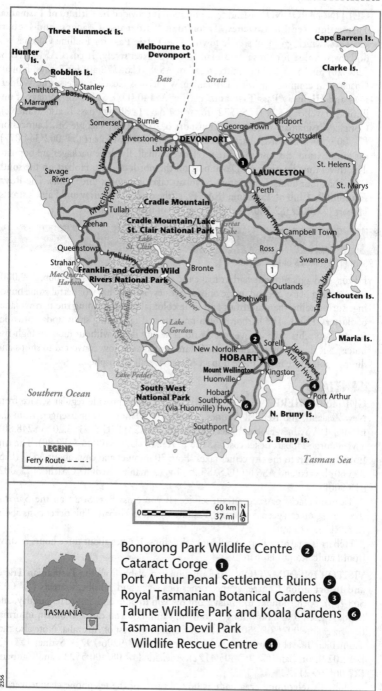

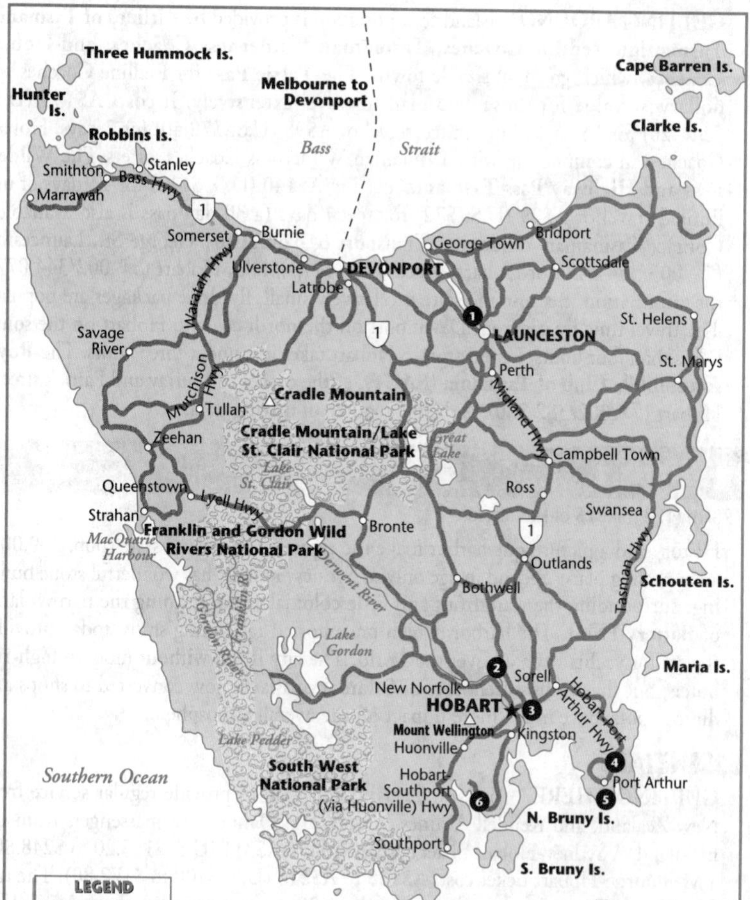

Three Hummock Is.
Hunter Is.
Robbins Is.
Melbourne to Devonport
Bass Strait
Cape Barren Is.
Clarke Is.
Smithton
Stanley
Bass Hwy
Marrawah
1
Somerset
Burnie
Ulverstone
DEVONPORT
Latrobe
Waratah Hwy
George Town
Bridport
Scottsdale
LAUNCESTON
St. Helens
Savage River
Perth
St. Marys
Murchison Hwy
Tullah
Cradle Mountain
Cradle Mountain/Lake St. Clair National Park
Great Lake
Midland Hwy
Zeehan
Campbell Town
Lake St. Clair
Queenstown
Lyell Hwy
Ross
Strahan
Swansea
Franklin and Gordon Wild Rivers National Park
Bronte
MacQuarie Harbour
Outlands
Derwent River
Tasman Hwy
Schouten Is.
Bothwell
Gordon River
Franklin R.
Lake Gordon
Maria Is.
Sorell
New Norfolk
HOBART
Hobart-Port Arthur Hwy
Mount Wellington
Kingston
Huonville
Lake Pedder
South West National Park
Southern Ocean
Hobart-Southport (via Huonville) Hwy
Port Arthur
N. Bruny Is.
Southport
S. Bruny Is.
LEGEND
Ferry Route
Tasman Sea
0
60 km
37 mi
N
TASMANIA
Bonorong Park Wildlife Centre 2
Cataract Gorge 1
Port Arthur Penal Settlement Ruins 5
Royal Tasmanian Botanical Gardens 3
Talune Wildlife Park and Koala Gardens 6
Tasmanian Devil Park Wildlife Rescue Centre 4
2356

GETTING AROUND Island transportation is provided by **Airlines of Tasmania, Tasmanian Redline Coaches, Tasmanian Wilderness Coaches**, and **Hobart Coaches,** which go to all sizable towns. The **Tassie Pass** for Redline Coaches is a dollarwise value for those who plan to travel extensively. It costs A$139 (U.S. $111.20) for 15 days of unlimited travel or A$98 (U.S. $78.40) for 7 days. Hobart Coaches, in conjunction with Tasmanian Wilderness Coaches, offers **The Wilderness and Highway Pass Tasmania,** costing A$140 (U.S. $112) for 14 days of unlimited travel or A$99 (U.S. $72) for seven days (a 30-day pass is also available). Contact Tasmanian Wilderness Transport & Tours, 101 George St., Launceston (☎ 003/344 442), or Hobart Coaches, 4 Liverpool St., Hobart (☎ 002/344 077), for information. Because the state is relatively small, fly/drive packages are popular. The travel time by car from Devonport on the north coast to Hobart on the south is less than four hours; Launceston to Hobart takes just under three hours. The **Royal Automobile Club of Tasmania (RACT),** at the corner of Murray and Patrick streets, Hobart (☎ 002/382 200), is the best source of driving data.

1 Hobart

198km (123 miles) S of Launceston

History and a picturesque harbor make the capital of the island state (pop. 200,000) an appealing place. Second in age only to Sydney, Hobart has wonderful stone buildings surrounding the waterfront and little colonial cottages lining the narrow lanes of **Battery Point.** The harbor, which once hosted tall sailing ships, today provides shelter for yachts from all over the world. The city is not without modern high-rise hotels, but the 1840s warehouses of **Salamanca Place,** now converted to shops and dining spots, have much more impact on the overall atmosphere.

ESSENTIALS

GETTING THERE Air New Zealand and Qantas provide regular service from New Zealand, and Kendell Airlines, Ansett, and Qantas carry passengers from the mainland. A Sydney-Hobart ticket costs A$194 to A$311 (U.S. $155.20 to $248.80); a Melbourne-Hobart ticket costs A$135 to A$216 (U.S. $108 to $172.80). The trip from the airport to the city center takes about 30 minutes and costs about A$17 (U.S. $13.60) by taxi and A$6.60 (U.S. $5.28) by Tasmanian Redline Coaches (☎ 002/313 900).

Tasmania lacks passenger train service. If you cross Bass Strait on the *Spirit of Tasmania,* you can get a connecting Redline Coach to Hobart. This ticket costs about A$32 (U.S. $25.60).

Hobart is a favorite port of call for cruise ships. It takes about three hours to drive from Launceston to Hobart.

VISITOR INFORMATION Information is available from the **Tasmanian Travel and Information Centre**, at the corner of Davey and Elizabeth streets (☎ 002/308 233), open Monday to Friday from 8:45am to 5pm and Saturday, Sunday, and holidays from 9 to 11am (longer hours in summer). You can also obtain information by calling 002/308 250 or 1800/806 846 in the rest of Australia. Note also that Tasmanian Travel Centres are in Melbourne (☎ 03/9206 7922), Sydney (☎ 02/202 2022), Brisbane (☎ 07/405 4122), Adelaide (☎ 08/400 5522), and Canberra (☎ 06/209 2122).

Hobart's **telephone area code** is 002. As part of the telephone changeover, all numbers with a 002 area code will be changing to 03/62xx xxxx in November 1996.

Hobart

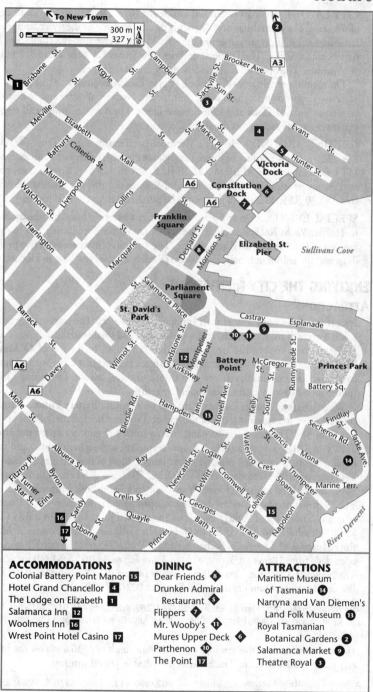

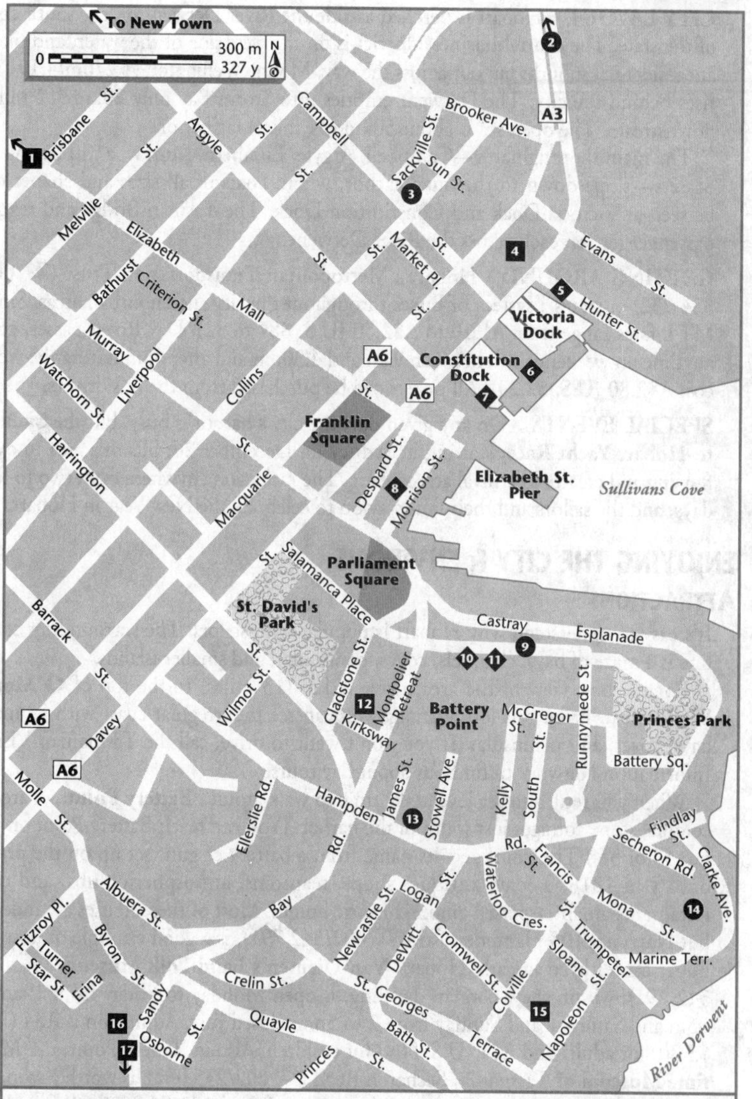

ACCOMMODATIONS
- Colonial Battery Point Manor 15
- Hotel Grand Chancellor 4
- The Lodge on Elizabeth 1
- Salamanca Inn 12
- Woolmers Inn 16
- Wrest Point Hotel Casino 17

DINING
- Dear Friends 8
- Drunken Admiral Restaurant 5
- Flippers 7
- Mr. Wooby's 11
- Mures Upper Deck 6
- Parthenon 10
- The Point 17

ATTRACTIONS
- Maritime Museum of Tasmania 14
- Narryna and Van Diemen's Land Folk Museum 13
- Royal Tasmanian Botanical Gardens 2
- Salamanca Market 9
- Theatre Royal 3

2357

CITY LAYOUT Hobart is perched astride the River Derwent on the south coast of the state. The central business district is on the west side of the water, and pleasant residential suburbs fan out across the way. Mount Wellington (1,270m/4,191 ft.) rises behind the city. The Derwent empties into Storm Bay only 20km (12 miles) downstream. The open sea is about 50km (31 miles) farther on.

The main thoroughfares—Campbell, Argyle, Elizabeth, Murray, and Harrington Streets—slope down to the busy harbor, where boats of all sizes and shapes can be seen at Victoria Dock and Constitution Dock. The Tasman Bridge and regular passenger ferries reach across the River Derwent.

GETTING AROUND Hobart's Metropolitan Transportation Trust (☎ 002/334 232) operates a system of **buses** throughout the city and suburban areas. Single MTT fares range from A1.10 to A$2.50 (U.S. 88¢ to $2); Day Rover passes, good anytime on weekends and between 9am and 4:30pm and after 6pm during the week, cost A$2.80 (U.S. $2.24). All tickets can be purchased from the bus drivers.

SPECIAL EVENTS On any given day, the city's harbor is busy, but the **Sydney-to-Hobart Yacht Race,** starting in Sydney on December 26, fills this area to overflowing and creates a carnival atmosphere. The race takes anywhere from two to four days, and the sailors and their fans stay on to celebrate the New Year in Hobart.

ENJOYING THE CITY & ENVIRONS

ATTRACTIONS

It's easy to understand why Hobart is popular with sailors. The surrounding coastline is a maze of bays, channels, coves, peninsulas, and smaller islands.

For the best view of the area, drive 22km (13 miles) to the top of ✪ **Mount Wellington.** From this lofty vantage you can see the irregular coast with its many bays, coves, and peninsulas. If you don't want to drive, call the Tasmanian Visitor Information Network to find out about day tours.

When you return to sea level, take time to walk around **Battery Point,** an area of colonial stone cottages just south of the harbor. (You can reach Battery Point on bus no. 53 or 55.) The point gets its name from a battery of guns set up on the promontory in 1818. Today, antiques shops, tearooms, atmospheric pubs, and cozy restaurants are interspersed among historic homes. Most of these houses are modest, but **Narryna,** 103 Hampden Rd. (☎ 002/342 791), is a good example of how the upper classes lived in early Hobart. **Van Diemen's Land Folk Museum** (☎ 002/342 791), within the Georgian dwelling, is open Monday to Friday from 10am to 5pm and Saturday and Sunday from 2 to 5pm; closed July. Admission is A$4 (U.S. $3.20) for adults and A$1 (U.S. 80¢) for children. Also in Battery Point, the **Maritime Museum of Tasmania,** Secheron Road (☎ 002/235 082), is worth a stop. It's open daily from 10am to 4:30pm, with an admission of A$2 (U.S. $1.60) for adults. The **National Trust** conducts walking tours of Battery Point on Saturday at 9:30am. For details, contact tour organizer Bill Foster at 002/237 570.

Runnymede. 61 Bay Rd., New Town. ☎ **002/781 269.** Admission A$5 (U.S. $4) adults, A$3 (U.S. $2.40) children. Daily 10am–4:30pm. Closed July, Good Friday, and Christmas. Bus: Lutana, route 20.

History buffs will love this gracious colonial home, built in 1836 and now the property of the National Trust. The house is furnished in period antiques.

Cadbury Chocolate Factory. Claremont. ☎ **002/490 111.** Tours, A$8 (U.S. $6.40) adults, A$4 (U.S. $3.20) children 6–15; younger children not admitted unless carried. Boat fare is A$20 (U.S. $16) adults, A$10 (U.S. $8) children 5–15; under 5 free. Tours, Mon–Thurs at 9, 9:30, and

10:30am, Fri at 9 and 9:30am. Closed Sept 1–11 and mid-Dec to Jan 18. Phone the Cruise Company at 002/349 294 for transport. Bus: 38 or 41.

For a change of pace, take a cruise on the *Derwent Explorer* and visit the Cadbury Chocolate Factory in suburban Claremont. Along the way you'll pass the **Naval Base, Government House,** and other landmarks. You must reserve ahead of time for factory tours.

Royal Tasmanian Botanical Gardens. On the Queen's Domain near Government House. ☎ **002/346 299.** Admission: Gardens, free; Conservatory, A$1 (U.S. 80¢). Daily 8am–4:45pm (until 6:30pm in summer).

If you like flowers, trees, and shrubs, visit the Royal Tasmanian Botanical Gardens, only 2km (1¼ miles) from the city center. Established in 1818, the gardens are known for their floral displays, conifers, and native plant collection. Colorful seasonal blooming plants are housed in the Conservatory. A restaurant provides lunch and teas.

Bonorong Park Wildlife Centre. Briggs Road, Brighton. ☎ **002/681 184.** Admission A$5 (U.S. $4) adults, A$2.50 (U.S. $2) children under 17. Daily 9am–5pm. Closed Christmas. Bus: 125 or 127. Drive north on Route 1 to Brighton; it's well signposted.

If you're interested in native fauna, visit the Bonorong Park Wildlife Centre, about 25 minutes' drive north of Hobart. The 6-hectare (15-acre) park houses native Tasmanian animals in a bush setting. The Bush Tucker Shed serves lunch, billy tea, and damper.

OUTDOOR ACTIVITIES

Tasmania is the ideal place for those who like a lot of action. At least four dozen operators will happily help you get organized for hiking, horsetrekking, sailing, caving, fishing, bushwalking, diving, cycling, rafting, climbing, kayaking, or canoeing. For a full listing, see the "Outdoor Adventures" section of *Travelways.*

Contact **Peregrine Adventures** (☎ 002/310 977, or 1800/331 124 in the rest of Australia; fax 002/348 219) if you'd like to raft the Picton or Huon River. This company also offers 5-, 7-, 11-, and 13-day raft trips on the Franklin River for those with more experience. Peregrine's East Coast Adventure is a six-day trip that involves mountain biking, walking, snorkeling, and rafting. Another good outfitter is **Rafting Tasmania** (☎ 002/278 293; tel/fax 002/279 516); it offers sea kayaking, rafting, and canoeing trips of 1 day to 11 days long.

Tas-Trek in Launceston (☎ 003/982 555 or 341 787), conducts four-wheel-drive excursions that last 1 day to 10 days. Some depart from and return to Hobart. The four-day Franklin River/World Heritage Area tour is especially popular. For information on Tasmania's wilderness regions, contact the **Department of Environment and Land Management,** 134 Macquarie St. (☎ 002/338 011).

Half-day downhill mountain bike, full-day, and longer cycling trips for a minimum of two people are organized by **Brake-Out Cycling Tours,** 27 Channel Court (P.O. Box 427), Kingston (☎ 002/291 999; fax 002/298 019). **Trout Fishing Safaris of Tasmania,** 2/45 Lansdowne Crescent, West Hobart (☎ 002/347 286), will happily take you to where the fish are biting. Daily all-inclusive charges are A$250 (U.S. $200) per person for two or more and A$350 (U.S. $280) solo. No trips during June or July.

For a view from the air, ✪ **Par Avion,** Cambridge Aerodrome (☎ 002/485 390; fax 002/485 117), operates scenic flights over wilderness areas in the southern part of the state. This is an ideal way to witness Tassie's mountains, rivers, plains, beaches, and dense bush. Those who want something a bit more experiential can join the trip that lands in South West National Park for a tour by boat and a barbecue lunch. The cost of A Day in the Wilderness is A$250 (U.S. $200). Trips depart at 9am and return at 5pm.

The **Royal Hobart Golf Club,** Seven Mile Beach (☎ 002/486 161), is an 18-hole championship course open to members of overseas clubs. "Ladies and gentlemen" pay A$30 (U.S. $24) to play here.

An extensive network of walking tracks (trails) is located on the slopes of Mount Wellington. These afford wonderful vistas of the surrounding area as well as pleasurable hiking. Pick up a copy of *Mt. Wellington Day Walk Map and Notes* from the **Department of Environment Tasmap Centre,** on the ground floor of the Lands Building, 134 Macquarie St. (☎ 002/303 382).

Shopping

The Hobart area is a great place to shop for Tasmanian crafts. I hope you'll be in town on Saturday because the ✪ **Salamanca Market,** from 8:30am to 2pm, is a treasure trove of items made from native woods, pottery, and glass. Many of the goods sold at the 200 colorful stalls are identical to those you could find in the adjacent Salamanca Place shops—the only difference is the price.

The **National Trust Shop,** 33 Salamanca Place (☎ 002/237 371) sells tasteful souvenirs and gifts on Monday to Friday from 9:30am to 5pm and Saturday from 9:30am to 1pm. Other places to browse or buy are **Handmark Gallery,** 77 Salamanca Place (☎ 002/237 895); the **Spinning Wheel,** 69 Salamanca Place (☎ 002/341 711); and the **Wilderness Society Shop,** 33 Salamanca Place (☎ 002/349 370). **Aspect Design,** 79 Salamanca Place (☎ 002/232 642), sells the work of jeweler Jon de Jonge and other Tasmanian artisans. Be sure to notice the Richard Clements glass bottles and the wooden boxes by Peter Gorring. Peter Rix does glass blowing on the premises.

The main shopping area of Hobart is centered around the **Elizabeth Street Mall,** between Collins and Liverpool streets. **The Cat and the Fiddle Arcade,** between the mall and Murray Street, houses interesting boutiques and shops. Store hours are Monday to Thursday from 9am to 6pm, Friday from 9am to 9pm, and Saturday from 9am to noon.

WHERE TO STAY

Besides modern hotels and motels, Hobart and the surrounding area offer a nice selection of homestays. If you'd like to overnight with a Tasmanian family either in town or on a farm, contact **Homehost & Heritage Tasmania Pty Ltd.,** P.O. Box 780, Sandy Bay, TAS 7005 (☎ 002/241 612; fax 002/240 472). Nightly bed-and-breakfast prices are A$86 (U.S. $68.80) double. In most cases private baths are provided. Some properties are totally self-contained (meaning entirely separate quarters with a kitchen).

Hosts belonging to the **Tasmanian Colonial Accommodation Association** (☎ 003/317 900) also welcome visitors to their self-catering country homes and host farms. Another option, **"colonial accommodation,"** refers to lodging in a building or cottage erected on its present site before 1901. The interiors are true to the period and contain either genuine antiques or reproduction furniture.

Very Expensive

Hotel Grand Chancellor. 1 Davey St., Hobart, TAS 7000. ☎ **002/354 535.** Fax 002/238 175. 222 rms, 12 suites. A/C MINIBAR TV TEL. A$230 (U.S. $184) double; A$370 (U.S. $296) executive suite. Additional person A$45 (U.S. $36) extra. Children under 18 free in parents' room. No-smoking rooms available. AE, BC, CB, DC, MC, V. Free parking.

The Sheraton is a posh property overlooking the picturesque harbor. More than half the rooms in the 12-story hotel have a view of the water and wharves. The attractive lobby boasts a polished granite floor, pale-gray walls, and a large curved window that frames the activity on Victoria and Constitution docks. Colorful sails are suspended from the top of a four-story atrium. All the quarters are spacious and have polished-granite baths. Ten executive suites have separate bedrooms with harbor views and large baths with separate showers and tubs, scales, hairdryers, and terry robes. An additional half bath is off the lounge. Eight rooms are equipped for the handicapped.

Dining/Entertainment: The Cove Restaurant and Atrium Cocktail Lounge enjoy a nice vista. Sullivans is an attractive grill. Drinks are served in the Spinnaker Bar.

Services: Concierge, 24-hour room service, laundry, valet, nightly turndown, baby-sitting, massage.

Facilities: Heated indoor saltwater pool, sauna, health club (with gym equipment and massage), unisex hair salon, business center, newsstand.

Moderate

✪ **Islington Elegant Private Hotel.** 321 Davey St., Hobart, TAS 7004. ☎ **002/233 900.** Fax 002/243 167. 8 rms. TEL. A$130 (U.S. $104) double; A$150 (U.S. $120) suite. Rates include continental breakfast. Children not accepted. No smoking permitted. BC, MC, V. Free parking. Islington is 2km (1.2 miles) from the city on the way to Mount Wellington. Take the A6 Highway from the airport to Davey Street; it's important to stay in the right lane and go straight ahead when road turns left. There are buses to/from the city.

The Islington is a delightful hostelry created from a gracious private home built in 1845 and owned by Sandra and David Dunkley. Throughout the Regency mansion, antiques, cedar woodwork, and elegant furnishings contribute to an air of gentility, calm, and tradition. French doors open onto a charming garden where breakfast is served. You sleep in queen-size beds, read free daily newspapers, and have the covers turned down for you at night. The Islington is on an avenue of stately old-world homes. The view of Mount Wellington is lovely, and a pool is on the grounds.

Wrest Point Hotel Casino. 410 Sandy Bay Rd., Hobart, TAS 7005. ☎ **002/250 112,** or 1800/030 611 in Australia. Fax 002/253 909. 264 rms, 14 suites. A/C MINIBAR TV TEL. A$100 (U.S. $80) Garden View room; A$110 (U.S. $88) River View room; A$198–A$220 (U.S. $158.40–$176) tower double; A$280 (U.S. $224) junior suite; A$380 (U.S. $304) executive suite. Additional adult A$30 (U.S. $24) extra. One child under 15 free in parents' room. Reservations can be made through Flag Inns. No-smoking rooms available. AE, BC, DC, MC, V. Free parking. The hotel is 3km (2 miles) south of city center. A taxi costs about A$5 (U.S. $4), and there's bus service.

The tower of the Wrest Point Hotel Casino is almost as much a landmark in Hobart as Mount Wellington. On the waterfront in the suburb of Sandy Bay, the 17-story hotel is easy to recognize on the skyline. It's popular with those who like to gamble, as the large casino is open daily. Most of the rooms are in the tower, which is round and creates pie-shaped quarters. A choice of bed sizes is offered. All have good views. Less expensive lodging is in the low-rise Motor Inn River View and Motor Inn Garden View sections. Ten rooms are designed for the handicapped.

Dining/Entertainment: The hotel offers a wide range of dining and drinking choices. These include a 24-hour coffee shop, the River View Lounge in the keno area of the casino, an Asian eatery, and a posh revolving restaurant on the top of the tower.

Services: Concierge, 24-hour room service, shoeshine, valet, baby-sitting, massage.

Facilities: Indoor pool, spa, gym, tennis court, sauna, mini-golf, Ping-Pong, beauty and hair salons, business center, casino.

Readers Recommend

The Lodge on Elizabeth, 249 Elizabeth St., Hobart, TAS 7000 (☎ 002/313 830; fax 002/342 566). *"This bed-and-breakfast is in a historically interesting house, and the hosts invite their guests to a complimentary predinner drink in front of the fireplace. When we returned from dinner, complimentary sherry was on the sideboard, and we enjoyed a very generous breakfast with the other guests."*

—Charlotte Bauer, Avon, Conn., U.S.A.

Colonial Battery Point Manor, 13 Cromwell St., Battery Point, TAS 7004 (☎ 002/240 888; fax 002/310 972). *"In Hobart we stayed in this elegant boutique hotel near Salmanca Place. The rooms were stunning; we had a great view of the harbor. Freddie the owner was very gracious, entertaining us with his life story, recommending his favorite local restaurants, and helping us plan our excursion to Port Arthur. There's an amazing garden in the back full of roses and several kids of lavender. They'll cook anything your heart desires at breakfast."*

—Lisa Renaud, New York, N.Y., U.S.A.

Serviced Apartments

✪ **Salamanca Inn.** 10 Gladstone St., Hobart, TAS 3000. ☎ **002/233 300,** or 1800/030 944 in Australia. Fax 002/237 167. 60 apts. MINIBAR TV TEL. A$164 (U.S. $131.20) one-bedroom apt for one or two; A$280 (U.S. $224) two-bedroom apt. Additional adult A$25 (U.S. $20) extra; A$15 (U.S. $12) each child 3–14. Ask about weekend and long-stay packages. AE, BC, DC, MC, V. Free parking. Bus: Sandy Bay Road.

It isn't surprising that the Salamanca Inn has won the Tasmanian Tourism Award. The property offers pleasant apartments around the corner from Salamanca Place and within walking distance of most attractions. All quarters have modern furnishings, full kitchens (with dishwashers), queen-size beds, in-room movies, and hairdryers. Facilities include a complimentary self-service laundry, an indoor pool, spa, and cheerful Gladstones restaurant. Baby-sitting can be arranged. Room service is offered during restaurant hours.

Woolmers Inn. 123 Sandy Bay Rd., Hobart, TAS 7005. ☎ **002/237 355,** or 1800/030 780 in Australia. Fax 002/231 981. 31 apts. TV TEL. A$90 (U.S. $72) apt for one or two. Additional adult A$14 (U.S. $11.20) extra; additional cild A$8 (U.S. $6.40) extra. Rates 10% higher Christmas–Jan. AE, BC, DC, MC, V. Free parking. Bus: Sandy Bay.

Woolmers Inn is 2km (1 mile) south of the city. The cozy units have one or two bedrooms and fully equipped kitchens. The baths contain tub/shower combinations and laundry facilities. The two-story complex has an attractive red-brick colonial-style exterior. One unit can accommodate the handicapped. Baby-sitting can be arranged. There's an eight-ball table in the house bar.

In Richmond

Prospect House. Main Road, Richmond, TAS 7025. ☎ **002/602 207.** Fax 002/602 551. 10 rms, 1 suite. MINIBAR TV. A$120 (U.S. $96) double; A$130 (U.S. $104) suite. Additional person A$25 (U.S. $20) extra. Rates include breakfast. AE, BC, DC, MC, V. Free parking. Drive or take a bus from Hobart.

Located 26km (16 miles) from Hobart, Prospect House is primarily known for its restaurant, but it also offers guest rooms, with antique furnishings and modern baths, in the original convict-built barn and haylofts. The property, winner of the 1992 Tasmanian Tourism Award, is set on 8 hectares (20 acres) of grounds, where there's a tennis court. Hosts Mike and Shauna Buscombe, direct descendants of the original owner, are sure to make you feel welcome. See "Where to Dine" below for details about Prospect House's award-winning fare.

Inexpensive

Wellington Lodge. 7 Scott St., Glebe, Hobart, TAS 7000. ☎ **002/310 614.** 5 rms (1 with bath). TV. A$70–A$85 (U.S. $56–$68) double. Additional person A$20 (U.S. $16) extra. Rates including breakfast. BC, V. No smoking permitted. Children under 12 not accepted. Free parking. Bus: 2.

Eric Littman hails from Glasgow, Scotland, and this late Victorian house (ca. 1900) he purchased, painted, and restored is a 10-minute walk from the center of Hobart. His friendly service is reason enough to stay here. One room has its own shower; the other four rooms share two baths. Throughout are hardwood floors. All quarters have wicker chairs, nice spreads with matching draperies, and coffee- and tea-making facilities; two have iron beds and three have wooden beds.

WHERE TO DINE

Tasmania is renowned for its fresh seafood, including king crab, oysters, crayfish, salmon, and other equally wonderful treats. If you choose from my recommendations, you'll also encounter some great game and wonderful wine lists. Prices are considerably lower than they would be for comparable cuisine on the mainland.

Expensive

Dear Friends. 8 Brooke St. ☎ **002/232 646** or 018/126 446. Reservations recommended. Main courses A$16.50–A$24 (U.S. $13.20–$19.20). Surcharge Sun and public holidays 10%. AE, BC, DC, MC, V. Wed–Fri noon–2pm (except Jan); Mon–Sat 6–10pm. TASMANIAN.

Centrally located Dear Friends has been awarded Best Restaurant in Tasmania every year except one since it opened in 1984. This no doubt pleases proprietor Chris Richards, who's actively involved in all aspects of this restaurant. It's one level above ground—what Aussies call the first floor—and, while there isn't a view, paintings done by Tasmanian artists make the walls interesting.

The specialty is Tasmanian produce, like game, seafood, and beef. You might start with carpaccio of King Island beef with virgin olive oil, slithers of fresh parmesan, and baby capers, dusted with black pepper. Another popular entree (appetizer) is boned charcoal-grilled quail on a Rösti potato with shredded vegetables and citrus-and-currant glaze. Main courses include deep-sea salmon with herb crust served on champagne sauce, filet of highland beef cooked pink and served with a reduction of peppercorns and red wine, and a duo of game—venison and hare with a red-currant reduction, two vegetable purées, and crisped leeks. Tasmanian cheeses and local stone fruit, poached and served in a liqueur of sauternes and lemon, are among the dessert offerings.

✪ **Mures Upper Deck.** Between Victoria and Constitution Docks, Hobart. ☎ **002/312 121.** Reservations suggested. Main courses A$19.50–A$25 (U.S. $15.60–$20). AE, BC, DC, JCB, MC, V. Daily noon–10pm. SEAFOOD.

Because this restaurant is on the waterfront, you're treated to a great view as well as outstanding seafood. In sunny weather you can sit on the deck and watch the fishing boats; at night the lights, boats, and wharf activity provide a wonderful backdrop. Owners George and Jill Mure—long involved in Australia's fishing industry—own three fishing boats and have been processors and even boat builders. They opened their first restaurant in 1974, moved to their present location in 1987, and have written a cookbook. With their background, they've built a reputation as being among Oz's foremost seafood restauranteurs. As you might have guessed, their own boats supply the restaurant with the freshest fish.

Your dining experience might start with oysters Mures style (eight natural oysters topped with diced smoked salmon, sour cream, and salmon caviar) or warm scallop salad tossed in garlic, ginger, coriander, chiles, and lemongrass and served with pea shoots. As a main course you could opt for seafood pasta (pan-fried prawns, scallops, fish, garlic, oregano, tomato, and feta cheese over homemade pasta and topped with parmesan) or salmon Abel Tasman (a salmon filet broiled and served on braised cabbage and apples with a mushroom-and-asparagus beurre blanc). There are vegetarian and beef dishes as well. The desserts can include baked bread-and-butter pudding and homemade ice cream. Mures is a delightful dining experience. Its complex also includes Lower Deck, a licensed family restaurant, and the Orizuru Sushi Bar.

The Point. In the Wrest Point Hotel Casino, 410 Sandy Bay Rd. ☎ **002/250 112.** Reservations recommended. Dinner for two about A$100 (U.S. $80); three-course City Lights dinner A$45 (U.S. $36); fixed-price three-course lunch A$25 (U.S. $20). AE, BC, DC, MC, V. Daily noon–2pm and 6:30–9:30pm. TASMANIAN/AUSTRALIAN.

The Point, a revolving restaurant on the 17th floor of the Wrest Point Hotel Casino, serves up spectacular harbor and mountain views as well as tasty lunches and dinners. The à la carte menu includes entrées like homemade venison sausages on lentils, duck liver in juniper-berry sauce, and Tasmanian smoked trout. Sample main courses are paupiette of sea-run trout, diced venison filet, and pan-fried John Dory filets. Prawns flambé are a specialty. If you can manage dessert, typical offerings are crêpes Suzette and apple beignets served with vanilla ice cream.

MODERATE

Drunken Admiral Restaurant. 17–19 Hunter St., Old Wharf. ☎ **002/341 903.** Reservations recommended. Main courses A$16.90–A$22.90 (U.S. $13.52–$18.35). Sun and public holiday surcharge 15%; Sat surcharge A$2 (U.S. $1.60) per person. AE, BC, DC, MC, V. Daily 6–11pm or later. SEAFOOD.

Opposite the Hotel Grand Chancellor on the waterfront, the Drunken Admiral is decorated with colorful sailing memorabilia from the colonial period. Tasmanian oysters are presented four ways: natural, grilled with garlic and butter, baked with chablis and cheese, and barbecued Aussie-style with bacon, homemade sauce, and a "dash o' grog." Drunken Admiral fish stew "ain't no ordinary stew. It's a little of everything the fishmonger had to sell at the docks this morning." Buccaneers' Revenge is squid, scallops, trevalla, and mussels that are pan-fried with tomatoes, onions, garlic, and olives. The salad bar is spread in a sailing dinghy. This is a popular spot, so book early.

$ **Moorilla Estate Vineyard Restaurant and Winery.** 655 Main Rd., Berriedale. ☎ **002/492 949.** Reservations recommended, essential Sun. Main-course lunch A$14–A$17 (U.S. $11.20–$13.60). AE, BC, DC, MC, V. Lunch and wine tasting daily 10am–5pm. Bus: 33, 35, 36, or 42. Ferry: Cruise boats depart Brooke St. Pier, Hobart, daily to Moorilla; the 40-minute journey costs A$10 (U.S. $8) one way. Head north on Brooker Highway and follow the signs. TASMANIAN.

The Moorilla Estate Vineyard Restaurant and Winery in Berriedale (about 10km/6 miles from Hobart) is a delightful place for a meal and some wine tasting. There's both inside and outside dining, all surrounded by extensive vineyards. The emphasis here is on Tasmanian food like local venison, spatchcock, or the catch of the day. The Moorilla Shop Cellar Door offers wine tastings, cellar door sales, morning and afternoon teas, ploughman's lunch, gifts, and souvenirs. The shop is open daily from 9am to 5pm. Special events are held at harvest time (March to May).

Mount Nelson Signal Station Restaurant and Gift Shop. 700 Nelson Rd., Mount Nelson. ☎ **002/233 407.** Fax 002/241 913. Reservations recommended at lunch, especially to get a window table on the veranda. Lunch main courses A$9–A$14 (U.S. $7.20–$11.20); afternoon tea A$7 (U.S. $5.60). Public holiday surcharge 10%. BC, MC, V. Daily 9am–5pm (morning tea/lunch/afternoon tea). Bus: 57, 58, or 59 from Franklin Square, or take a taxi (A$8/U.S. $6.40). TASMANIAN.

What a delightful spot, perched on the top of Mount Nelson with an uninterrupted view of water and islands as far as you can see. In 1811 Governor Macquarie ordered a flagstaff and guardhouse erected here. From 1830 to 1877 there was a semaphore station, from which messages were transmitted between Hobart and Port Arthur. The restaurant is housed in the cottage of the chief signalman. Today, there's indoor and outdoor seating and you're treated to delicious local produce. Lunch entrees (appetizers) include smoked salmon pâté and smoked trout. Sample main courses are fettuccini topped with scallops, prawns, and fish flavored with garlic and chiles as well as warm salad of marinated chicken grilled and served on mixed greens. For afternoon tea I suggest scones with Tasmanian cream and freshly made raspberry jam or Lady Nelson's Delight—a warm chocolate sponge sandwich filled with ice cream and topped with hot chocolate-fudge sauce. Proprietress Judith Cooper is a charming hostess.

✪ **Mr. Wooby's.** At the rear of 65 Salamanca Place. ☎ **002/343 466.** Main courses A$18–A$19 (U.S. $14.40–$15.20). AE, BC, MC, V. Mon–Fri 11:30am–2:30pm; Mon–Thurs 6–10pm, Fri–Sat 6–11:30pm, Sun 6–9pm. TASMANIAN.

This place is named after a man who owned a "goody stall" on the wharf in the 1870s. It was a ramshackle structure, but despite this he locked it each evening with a huge padlock obtained from the convict prison at Port Arthur. Needless to say, the sweets stall is long gone, but the name of the proprietor and a little of his eccentricity live on in Mr. Wooby's eatery. Once a jam factory, the building has thick stone walls with exposed girders; rafters show in the low ceiling. Proprietor John Addison retired after 40 years with Telecom (Australia's AT&T) and now enjoys being the host and chef. You can be served beer and wine only if you order a meal.

In Richmond

Prospect House. Main Road, Richmond. ☎ **002/602 207.** Reservations recommended, especially for Fri–Sat dinner and Sun lunch. Main courses A$17.50–A$22.50 (U.S. $14–$18). AE, BC, DC, MC, V. Daily noon–2pm and 7–9pm. Drive or take a bus. TASMANIAN.

Prospect House is in the village of Richmond, less than a half hour's drive from the center of Hobart. Built around 1830, the house exudes colonial country charm. The two dining rooms have marble fireplaces, high ceilings, and Oriental rugs. The restaurant is renowned for its gourmet cuisine and has won many awards. On a typical evening the entrées might include vegetable tart (a selection of fresh vegetables tossed in tomato-and-basil coulis and served in a light filo basket on steamed spinach leaves, with a light cheese sauce) and game pie (hare, wallaby, and venison with prunes, herbs, and a rich stock sauce served in a puff pastry pie accompanied by crème fraîche and homemade tomato relish). Sample main courses are lamb Wellington, aged venison marinated and lightly baked, and oven-baked spatchock. The wine list is extensive. Prospect House is owned and operated by the great-great-grandson of original owner Michael Kestell Buscombe and his wife, Shauna.

In Woodbridge

✪ **Woodbridge Hotel.** Channel Highway, Woodbridge. ☎ **002/674 604.** Reservations required. Main courses A$10–A$17.50 (U.S. $8–$14); Tasmanian platter of local specialties A$22.50 (U.S. $18); wine tasting A$1 (U.S. 80¢) each taste or A$5 (U.S. $4) for any six; kids' meals A$3–A$4 (U.S. $2.40–$3.20). AE, BC, DC, MC, V. Daily noon–2pm; Mon–Sat 6:30–8:30pm; wine tasting Mon–Sat 11am–10pm, Sun 11am–7pm. Drive, 30 minutes south of Hobart. TASMANIAN.

You don't normally look for great cuisine in a country pub, but this place is an exception. The Woodbridge Hotel is run by two generations of the Mason family. Brian and Elaine Mason and their daughter and son-in-law, Sandra and Murray Crowden. The meals are served in a casual room overlooking the D'Entrecasteaux Channel or on an outdoor covered patio. In addition to dining, you can enjoy wine tasting—the Woodbridge offers Tasmania's largest selection of Tasmanian wines—and bottle sales.

INEXPENSIVE

On Salamanca Place, there's a little Greek place called the **Parthenon. Flippers** is a floating fish-and-chips shop on Constitution Dock. Both of these are popular with budget diners.

HOBART AFTER DARK

THE PERFORMING ARTS

Theatre Royal. 29 Campbell St. ☎ **002/310 899** for information, or 002/346 266 for tickets. Tickets, A$7–A$39 (U.S. $5.60–$31.20), depending on performance.

The Theatre Royal was built in 1837 and is the oldest remaining live theater in Australia. Substantially restored after a 1984 fire, it has what Sir Laurence Olivier described as "perfect" acoustics and an elegant late Victorian decor. Tasmanian professional and amateur companies and professional companies from mainland Australia and overseas perform here regularly. The theater seats 747 on three levels—stalls, dress circle, and upper circle (what Americans call the orchestra, mezzanine, and balcony or upper mezzanine). Shows include dance, drama, comedy, revue, music theater, concerts, puppetry, and mime. Tours are given by arrangement for A$4 (U.S. $3.20).

THE CLUB & BAR SCENE

Atrium Lounge. In the Hotel Grand Chancellor, 1 Davey St. ☎ **002/354 535.**

The Atrium Lounge is a sophisticated watering hole and a good spot for a drink with a view of waterfront activity. Live music is offered.

✪ **Knopwood's Retreat.** 39 Salamanca Place. ☎ **002/235 808.**

Near the waterfront in the historic Battery Point area, this is a favorite local tavern/wine bar. The clientele is comprised of artists, poets, laborers, politicians, political activists, and other interesting folk. They enjoy the late Victorian atmosphere, alfresco seating, and live music, which varies from jazz and blues to rock and roll. Knopwood's opened in 1829 as a tavern and brothel for whalers. Personalities like Joseph Conrad and Roald Amundsen have called in for a drink. Some 145 beers and wines are offered.

Regine's Nightclub. In the Wrest Point Hotel Casino, 410 Sandy Bay Rd. ☎ **002/250 112.** A$5 (U.S. $4) cover charge Fri–Sun.

Regine's, open nightly from 9pm to 4am (sometimes 5am on Friday and Saturday), is popular with the "young and young at heart." The decor is reminiscent of the 1960s, with an open fire in winter. Karaoke is a big crowd-pleaser on Friday and Saturday and is the only live music offered. A wide range of beverages and snacks is served.

Spinnaker Lounge. In the Sheraton Hotel, 1 Davey St. ☎ **002/354 535.**

The Spinnaker is what I call an "upmarket public bar." It has the friendliness of a traditional pub and a clean and bright decor. This is a good place to chat with locals and an inexpensive spot for counter lunches. The entrance to the Spinnaker is on the side of the hotel.

A Casino

Wrest Point Casino. In the Wrest Point Hotel Casino, 410 Sandy Bay Rd. ☎ **002/250 112.** This casino was Australia's first legal gaming club. It continues to be a popular place with those who like blackjack, roulette, minidice, two-up, craps, baccarat, keno, and so forth. The table games in the main casino are open Monday to Thursday from 1pm to 3am, Friday and Saturday from 1pm to 4am, and Sunday from noon to 3am. Video gaming machines are available from noon every day in both the main casino and the Riverview Lounge.

Side Trips from Hobart

Port Arthur

I suggest you take a day to drive out to Port Arthur, where you can tour the remains of the penal colony. If you've got the time, stop in the historic village of **Richmond** and at the **Tasmanian Devil Park Wildlife Rescue Centre** on the way. The rural scenery is most enjoyable.

Richmond is only 26km (16 miles) northeast of Hobart and is the site of the country's oldest bridge (1823), a gaol (jail) that dates from 1825, and several old churches, including St. John's Roman Catholic (1837) and St. Luke's Church of England (1834–36). In addition to these colonial structures, Richmond offers a plethora of cozy tearooms, craft shops, galleries, and antiques stores. The riverbank is a nice spot for a picnic. If you're interested in overnight accommodations or gourmet fare, see my listings for Prospect House in "Where to Stay" and "Where to Dine" above.

The **Tasmanian Devil Park Wildlife Rescue Centre,** Port Arthur Highway, Taranna, 80km (50 miles) from Hobart (☎ 002/503 230), presents an opportunity to see some of the flora and fauna unique to the island state. Most of the park's animals, which include Tasmanian devils, quolls, eagles, and kangaroos, have been rescued after being injured or orphaned. All rescue work is funded by visitor entrance fees. The park is open daily from 9am to 5pm (longer hours September to April). The admission is A$8 (U.S. $6.40), with children paying half price.

The ruins of the penal settlement at **Port Arthur,** 100km (62 miles) southeast of Hobart, are Tasmania's number-one tourist attraction and one of Australia's most important historic sites. While the grounds are now peaceful—you could almost say picturesque—from 1830 to 1877 Port Arthur was the site of one of the country's harshest convict institutions. The infamous settlement was on the **Tasman Peninsula,** connected to the rest of Tasmania by a narrow strip of land called **Eaglehawk Neck.** To keep the prisoners from escaping, guards and savage dogs kept a constant vigil across this path, and the authorities circulated rumors that the surrounding waters were shark infested. As you pass Eaglehawk Neck, stop and look at the blowhole and other coastal formations, including **Tasman's Arch, Devil's Kitchen,** and the **Tesselated Pavement.**

At Port Arthur, you can tour the remains of the church, guard tower, hospital, model prison, and several other buildings. Because these structures have been damaged by fire and vandalism over the years, it's best to take a walking tour with a guide who describes what they originally looked like and what purposes they served. You can also rent a Walkman at the Information Office and tour at your own pace while listening to a prerecorded audio tour. Open daily from 9am to 5pm. Summer admission to the Port Arthur Historic Site (☎ 002/502 363) is A$13 (U.S. $10.40) for adults and A$6.50 (U.S. $5.20) for children 5 to 15, which includes a walking tour and cruise to the **Isle of the Dead,** off the coast of Port Arthur. Winter (July and August) admission is A$10.50 (U.S. $8.40) for adults and A$4.50 (U.S. $3.60) for children, without the boat tour. **Ghost Tours** of Port Arthur by lantern light leave nightly at 8:30pm (9:30pm during daylight savings), costing A$8 (U.S. $6.40) for adults and half price for children.

Where to Stay & Dine

Port Arthur Motor Inn. Port Arthur Historic Site, Port Arthur, TAS 7182. ☎ **002/502 101,** or 1800/030 747 in Australia. Fax 002/502 417. 35 rms. MINIBAR TV TEL. A$90 (U.S. $72) double. Additional person A$13 (U.S. $10.40) extra. Children under 12 free in parents' room. AE, BC, DC, MC, V. Free parking. Bus: Daily Hobart Coaches bus from Hobart.

Should you decide to overnight, this motor inn has comfortable rooms and a restaurant overlooking the historic site of the penal settlement. All quarters have clock radios, coffee- and tea-making facilities, and small refrigerators. You may use the self-service laundry and playground. Ghost Tour packages are available (see the Port Arthur listing above).

Port Arthur After Dark

For entertainment, you might want to view the original version of the 1926 silent movie *For the Term of His Natural Life,* screened nightly at 7:30pm from November to April at the **Broad Arrow Tea House and Coffee Shop,** on the historic site (☎ 002/502 242). The cost is A$5 (U.S. $4) for adults and half price for children 6 to 16. The film is also available on in-house video to guests at the Port Arthur Motor Inn all year. Much of the film was shot on location at Port Arthur.

The Huon Valley & the Channel Coast

Another delightful day-trip route leads southwest from Hobart and takes you past apple orchards to craft workshops, a wildlife park, and wonderful water views. Blooming cherry, pear, and apple trees are a bonus on this drive September to early November. The trees are laden with apples in March, and cherries are for sale in January.

Take Highway B64 from Hobart to the **Apple & Heritage Museum** (☎ 002/664 345), just past Grove. Located in a former apple-packing shed, the displays here provide insight into an era when people in the once-thriving apple industry worked by candlelight and earned about 50¢ a week. The museum is open daily from 9:30am to 5pm. Admission is A$3 (U.S. $2.40) for adults and A$1.50 (U.S. $1.20) for children under 16.

Continue down the east side of the Huon River on Highway B68, the Channel Highway. Just before the town of Cygnet, look for the **Cygnet Pottery,** 49 Cradoc Rd., Cygnet (☎ 002/951 957). It's open Tuesday to Sunday from 10am to 5pm and is a great place to learn about this craft and perhaps purchase a piece or two. Be sure to notice their original porcelain dolls and terra-cotta planters.

Continue south until you come to Highway C626. Turn left (east) and drive 7km (4 miles) to **The Deepings** (☎ 002/951 398), where you can watch woodturner Adrian Hunt at work. (Adrian and his wife, Roslyn, also offer country accommodations.) Be sure to notice the Deepings Dolls. Return to the Channel Highway and go south to Highway C627. Turn left and stop at the ✪ **Talune Wildlife Park and Koala Gardens,** RSD 1522, Cygnet (☎ 002/951 775), where former science teacher Mike Jagoe has assembled a large collection of native animals. Because this isn't a huge commercial operation (and because Mike is an extremely friendly "bloke"), you can hold, pet, and feed lots of creatures. Admission is A$6 (U.S. $4.80) for adults and A$2.50 (U.S. $2) for children. Open daily from 9:30am to 5pm. (The park also has three tourist cabins. Park entrance is included with lodging.)

Readers Recommend

Ross, The Midlands, Tasmania. *"Ross is the loveliest village we saw in Tasmania. It has a historic bridge, a lovely old church, and a beautiful elm-lined main street with colonial inns and cottages. The crafts shop was the most complete of any we saw in Tasmania. At the Village Tea Rooms on Church Street we thoroughly enjoyed rhubarb pie and delectable herb scones."*

—Katherine W. Ezell, Miami, Fla., U.S.A.

Farther along C627 you'll come to **Winterwood Winery** (☎ 002/951 864), where fruit wines, as well as grape wines, are made. Then enjoy the fantastic view while proceeding to the **Woodbridge Hill Handweaving Studio** (☎ 002/674 430), where you can watch Anna Maria Magnus at her loom using hand-spun wool and mohair to weave garments and rugs. Her large garden is open to the public for a small fee.

As you continue toward the coast, you'll see more really pretty ✪ **views of the D'Entrecasteaux Channel.** Just north of Woodbridge, you have the option of stopping at the **Woodbridge Hotel** for wine tasting, lunch, dinner, or overnight lodging (see "Where to Dine" above for more information). The return to Hobart from Woodbridge takes about 35 minutes.

2 Launceston

198km (123 miles) N of Hobart

Tasmania's second city is sited at the head of the Tamar River, 50km (31 miles) inland from the state's north coast. Surrounded by hills, Launceston is the center of a lush green farming region. Because of its easy access from the mainland, it's a handy place for you to start your exploration of the state. Often referred to as the Garden City, Launceston (pop. 92,000) has many fine parks and some excellent examples of colonial architecture.

ESSENTIALS

GETTING THERE The flight to Launceston from Melbourne takes 55 minutes and costs A$116 to A$187 (U.S. $92.80 to $149.60). Airlines of Tasmania will fly you up from Hobart for A$70 (U.S. $56). Coach transfer to the city from the airport costs about A$5 (U.S. $4). There are no passenger trains in Tasmania.

If you take the *Spirit of Tasmania* ferry across Bass Strait, the drive from Devonport takes about 1½ hours and the bus fare is about A$13 (U.S. $10.40). A Tasmanian Redline Coaches or Hobart Coaches ticket from Hobart costs about A$17 (U.S. $13.60).

Hobart is less than three hours away by car on Highway 1.

VISITOR INFORMATION The **Tasmanian Visitor Information Network** operates the **Tasmanian Travel and Information Centre** on the corner of St. John and Paterson streets (☎ 003/363 122). The **Royal Automobile Club of Tasmania** doles out maps and answers questions from its headquarters on the corner of York and George streets (☎ 003/313 166). Launceston's **telephone area code** is 003. As part of the telephone changeover, all numbers with a 003 area code will be changing to 03/63xx xxxx in January 1997.

CITY LAYOUT A pedestrian shopping mall is on Brisbane Street between St. John and Charles streets. The **Town Hall** is two blocks north on Civic Square. **City Park,** on the northeastern edge of the central business district, makes a pleasant spot for a picnic.

EXPLORING THE CITY & ENVIRONS

✪ **Cataract Gorge,** the result of violent earthquakes that ruptured Tasmania about 40 million years ago, is a scenic area with walking trails, picnic grounds, and splendid gardens located 10 minutes from central Launceston. The South Esk River flows through the gorge, which is traversed by a suspension bridge and a chair lift. Whether you go to hike or to photograph the view, you won't be disappointed. The hike to the Duck Reach Power Station takes about 45 minutes and should be attempted only by those with sturdy footwear; other walks are shorter and easier. The Gorge Restaurant serves meals and teas.

Mountain biking is a popular activity in this area. If you're interested, contact **Tasmanian Expeditions** (☎ 003/343 477). During summer this company offers four- to eight-day trips along the east coast.

National Automobile Museum of Tasmania. Waverley Road. ☎ **003/393 727.** Admission A$4 (U.S. $3.20) adults, A$2 (U.S. $1.60) children under 14. Daily 9am–5pm. Closed Christmas.

This museum shares the Waverley site and gives you a chance to see classic cars undergoing restoration, as well as completely restored vehicles. Children particularly enjoy the model car collection.

Old Umbrella Shop. 60 George St. ☎ **003/319 248.** Free admission. Mon–Fri 9am–5pm, Sat 9am–noon.

Of the local colonial buildings, the Old Umbrella Shop—now used as the National Trust Gift Shop and Information Centre—is one of the more interesting. The facade of the shop, dating from the 1860s, remains unchanged. Umbrellas used during the last 100 years are on display.

Waverley Woollen Mills. Waverley Rd. ☎ **003/391 106.** Tours, A$5 (U.S. $4) adults, A$3 (U.S. $2.40) children. Tours, daily 9am–4pm.

This business was established in 1874 and is still operating on the same site 5km (3 miles) northeast of town. On the tour, you see how animal fibers are turned into quality woolen garments. Hats, caps, ties, skirts, bush shirts, blankets, and jackets are sold on the premises. Teas and light lunches are available.

Entally House. Hadspen, 15km (9½ miles) from Launceston. ☎ **003/936 201.** Admission A$5 (U.S. $4) adults, A$3 (U.S. $2.40) children. Daily 10am–12:30pm and 1–5pm.

This is another historic property of note. Built around 1820, the lovely Georgian colonial, once the home of a Tasmanian premier, is furnished in period antiques. The surrounding grounds contain pretty gardens, a glasshouse (greenhouse), many mature trees, and a display of horse-drawn vehicles. Refreshments are sold on the premises.

Readers Recommend

Tascot Templeton Carpet Factory, 5 Best St., Devonport. *"This was one of the best tours we had. You need to make an appointment for the tour at the Information Office. There was no charge and it was better than the Waverley Woollen Mills in Launceston."*

—Bruce Alloway, Edmonton, Alberta, Canada.

Shopping

The **National Trust Shop,** in the Old Umbrella Shop (above), sells interesting gift items, and you won't want to miss the ✪ **Design Centre of Tasmania,** on the corner of Tamar and Brisbane streets (☎ 003/315 506; fax 003/315 662). Wonderful craft items from wood to glass—all made by Tasmanians—are sold in this attractive gallery on the edge of City Park. It's open Monday to Friday from 10am to 6pm, Saturday from 10am to 1pm, and Sunday from 2 to 5pm.

If you're in Launceston on a Sunday, you might want to go to the **Yorktown Square Market,** at the rear of the Launceston International Hotel. This is an ideal place for buying local craft items. The market is open from 9am to 2pm.

Where to Stay

Expensive

✪ **Alice's Place.** 17 York St. (mail address: 129 Balfour St., Launceston, TAS 7250). ☎ **003/342 231.** Fax 003/342 696. 1 cottage. TV. A$145 (U.S. $116) cottage for one or two. Additional person A$50 (U.S. $40) extra. Rates include breakfast ingredients. No credit cards. Free parking.

Like Ivy Cottage next door (see below), Alice's Place is owned by Helen Poynder. However, this attractive spot, which sleeps four, isn't actually old. An expert in restoring colonial buildings, Helen created Alice's Place from bits and pieces of historic places that were being razed, doing much of the work herself. The result is charming quarters that are a bit roomier than those of Ivy Cottage and share the same wonderful garden. Alice's Place has its own washing machine and dryer.

Novotel Launceston. 29 Cameron St., Launceston, TAS 7250. ☎ **003/343 434,** or 1800/642 244 in Australia. Fax 003/317 347. 165 rms and suites. MINIBAR TV TEL. A$160 (U.S. $128) double; A$200–A$400 (U.S. $160–$320) suite. Additional person A$20 (U.S. $16) extra. Children under 16 free in parents' room. Ask about packages. Weekend rates about 50% lower. No-smoking floor available. AE, BC, DC, MC, V. Free parking.

This city center hostelry is Launceston's most elegant. All rooms have clock radios, hairdryers, tea- and coffee-making facilities, small refrigerators, in-room movies, and free daily newspapers. Standard rooms have two double beds or a king-size bed. Jackson's Tavern is a popular watering hole, and the Avenue Restaurant is an upmarket coffee shop. Services here include a concierge, 24-hour room service, laundry, valet, and baby-sitting. There are also a self-service laundry, business center, beauty salon, and gift shop.

Moderate

Innkeepers Colonial Motor Inn. 31 Elizabeth St., Launceston, TAS 7250. ☎ **003/316 588,** or 1800/030 111 in Australia. Fax 003/342 765. 61 rms, 2 suites. A/C MINIBAR TV TEL. A$110 (U.S. $88) double; A$140 (U.S. $112) suite. Additional person A$18 (U.S. $14.40) extra. Lower weekend rates. Children under 3 free in parents' room. No-smoking rooms available. AE, BC, DC, MC, V. Free parking.

The Colonial combines old-world ambience with traditional comfort and facilities. The Old Grammar School has been incorporated into the complex, but those who desire tried-and-true standard motel lodging will feel right at home here. The rooms have attractive furnishings and modern amenities like clock radios, hairdryers, tea- and coffee-making facilities, small refrigerators, in-room movies, and free daily newspapers. The Quill and Cane Restaurant was once a big schoolroom; Rosie's Tavern, central Launceston's liveliest nightspot, was formerly the boys' gymnasium.

✪ **Ivy Cottage.** 17 York St. (mail address: 129 Balfour St., Launceston, TAS 7250). ☎ **003/342 231.** Fax 003/342 696. 1 cottage. TV. A$125 (U.S. $100) cottage for one or two.

Additional person A$30 (U.S. $24) extra. Rates include breakfast ingredients. No credit cards. Free parking.

This is one of the most interesting places at which I've ever stayed. Proprietor Helen Poynder has restored the Georgian cottage (ca. 1840) with loving attention to detail. The two bedrooms not only are furnished with antiques but are replete with accessories and fascinating bric-a-brac—for example, period clothing and a wonderful doll collection. You stay here on your own, cook for yourself, and come and go as you please. Helen lives nearby and is happy to answer questions and chat, but she also respects your privacy. The slate-floored kitchen is equipped with absolutely everything you might need for preparing a meal, and the hostess urges you to take fresh herbs from the garden as required. The bath has a wonderful claw-foot tub with a metal shower surround. Two working fireplaces, games and books, and a cheerful old-world flower garden are other plusses.

Helen also offers nine other cottages: one at **Alice's Place** (above), three theme cottages known as **Alice's Hideaways**, and five cottages collectively known as the **Shambles.**

Inexpensive

Lloyd's Hotel. 23 George St., Launceston, TAS 7250. ☎ **003/314 966.** Fax 003/315 589. 18 rms. A$55 (U.S. $44) double. Rates include breakfast. BC, MC, V. Free parking.

Lloyd's is an older-style property offering comfortable accommodation. Hosts Berkley and June Cox have traveled overseas and extend warm hospitality to guests. Each room has a private bath, a refrigerator, and coffee- and tea-making facilities. Some have a TV. The central location and secure parking are a bonus.

WHERE TO DINE

Expensive

✪ **Fee & Me.** 190 Charles St. (at the corner of Frederick Street). ☎ **003/313 195.** Reservations recommended. Main courses A$21 (U.S. $16.80). AE, BC, MC, V. Mon–Sat from 7pm. MODERN AUSTRALIAN.

Built in 1835, the grand mansion that houses Fee & Me was one of Launceston's most gracious homes. It later was converted into a hospital, even later into corporate headquarters. Today it's the place where lucky diners enjoy the meals prepared by the Fee & Me team. Sample entrees are charcoal-grilled quail, chili oysters, and scallops with goat cheese and pesto. Sample main courses are trevalla with leeks and mushrooms, roast duckling, and a mixed grill. The wine list is extensive. Fee & Me won the Best Restaurant Award in Tasmania in 1992.

Moderate

The Owl's Nest Restaurant. In the Penny Royal Watermill Motel, 145–160 Paterson St. ☎ **003/316 699.** Reservations recommended. Main courses A$11–A$14.50 (U.S. $8.80–$11.60). AE, BC, DC, MC, V. Daily 6–8:30pm. TASMANIAN.

The Owl's Nest offers an interesting menu based on fresh local products. All dishes are available in either entree or main-course portions. These include salad of smoked salmon and cucumbers, sweetbreads in seeded-mustard sauce, barbecued quail with peppercorns, tomato-and-basil fettuccine, and honey duckling with orange sauce. The Owl's Nest, with a colonial decor, is adjacent to a historic 19th-century water mill that has been reconstructed on the grounds. It's a 10-minute walk to the city center.

Shrimps. 72 George St. (at the corner of Paterson Street). ☎ **003/340 584.** Reservations recommended. Main courses A$15–A$22 (U.S. $12–$17.60). AE, BC, DC, MC, V. Mon–Sat noon–2pm and from 6:30pm. SEAFOOD.

It's impossible not to notice Shrimps, whose exterior is pumpkin with a red metal roof and forest-green trim. Its style is classic Georgian and it was, in fact, built in 1824 and restored in 1980. A sign near the door says it's "a fine example of one of the few classical Georgian corner buildings in Launceston." If you dine here, you'll choose between fresh Tasmanian mussels, oysters Tzarina served with crème fraîche, abalone tempura, and more unusual dishes like a Spanish seafood omelet. Save room for dessert.

Victoria's on City Park. In City Park, at the corner of Tamar and Cimitiere streets. ☎ **003/317 433.** Reservations recommended. Main courses A$12.50–A$17.50 (U.S. $10–$14). AE, BC, MC, V. Daily noon–2:30pm; Wed–Sat 6pm–closing. TASMANIAN.

This is a charming coffee shop with oversize windows looking out on the park. Drop in for a sinfully delicious dessert, such as chocolate mousse, apple Danish, or chocolate, rum, and mint cream puffs. For lunch you could have quiche and salad, one of several kinds of pasta, or one of the creative sandwiches.

INEXPENSIVE

$ **Janet's Lunchbar.** 2 Paterson St. (near the corner of Paterson and George streets). ☎ **003/341 095.** Reservations not required. Light lunch for one A$5 (U.S. $4). No credit cards. Mon–Fri 8am–5pm, Sat 8:30am–2:30pm. LIGHT LUNCHES.

Janet's is a little deli in the city center. This is a great stop to pick up sandwiches for a picnic. Hot roast rolls—either beef or lamb—are the specialty. You might also like to try the home-cooked egg-and-bacon pie or the vegetarian lasagne. Janet also offers a selection of savory pasties—the feta and spinach is my favorite.

3 Cradle Mountain & Lake St. Clair National Park

Tasmania has many beautiful wilderness areas, but it's generally agreed that the national park, encompassing both Cradle Mountain and Lake St. Clair, is one of the most spectacular regions. The 1,545-meter (5,100-ft.) mountain dominates the north end, and the long, deep lake is in the most southerly section. Between them lie steep mountains, flat plains, dozens of lakes, several rivers, majestic forests, and scenic valleys. **Mount Ossa** (1,617m/5336 ft.), the state's highest point, is in the center of the park. The World Heritage Committee added Cradle Mountain/Lake St. Clair National Park to their list of the world's most precious places in 1982.

ESSENTIALS

Cradle Mountain & Lake St. Clair National Park is in the northwest quadrant of the state. Queenstown is on approximately the same level as the park's southern border. Devonport is 85km (53 miles) north of the park. Lake St. Clair is 173km (107 miles) northwest of Hobart.

GETTING THERE An airstrip is near Cradle Mountain Lodge at the north end of the park. **Par Avion** (☎ 002/485 390) will fly you there from Hobart. **Devonport Aviation** (☎ 004/279 777) provides transfers from Devonport. If you're coming from Launceston, the **Launceston Flying School and Charter Service** (☎ 003/918 477) will fly you to Cradle Mountain. There are no passenger trains in Tasmania.

Tasmanian Wilderness Transport (☎ 003/344 442) operates coach service from Devonport (2 hr.) and Launceston (3 hr.). From either place the one-way fare is A$35 (U.S. $28) and the round-trip costs A$65 (U.S. $52). It also provides transfers from Hobart to Lake St. Clair (3 hr.; A$35/U.S. $28 one-way, A$65/U.S. $52 round-trip). Hobart to Cradle Mountain via Strahan costs A$70 (U.S. $56) one-way (an overnight stop in Strahan is required). All Tasmanian Wilderness services have commentary on board.

Motorists can enter the park on only two roads: From the north you can drive to Dove Lake and Waldheim Chalet; from the south you can drive to Derwent Bridge and Lake St. Clair. The drive from Devonport to Cradle Mountain takes 1 1/2 hours; from Launceston about 2 1/2 hours.

VISITOR INFORMATION The **Visitor Information Centre** (☎ 004/921 133; fax 004/921 120) near Cradle Mountain Lodge is just within the park boundary. It has displays and brochures that tell about the region's World Heritage Area, geography, flora, and fauna, as well as a number of items available for purchase. It's open from 8am to 5pm daily. The **telephone area code** is 004. As part of the telephone changeover, all numbers with a 004 area code will be changing to 03/64xx xxxx in March 1997.

The entry fee to the national park is A$8 (U.S. $6.40) per vehicle for one day or A$2.50 (U.S. $2) per person per day for pedestrians, cyclists, and coach passengers. There's also a "holiday" pass, good for up to two months and costing A$25 (U.S. $20) per vehicle, and a "backpacker" pass, good for two months and costing A$10 (U.S. $8) per person. Annual passes are also available.

SEEING THE AREA

Don't leave the area until you've driven the 8km (5 miles) from Cradle Mountain Lodge down to ✪ **Dove Lake.** The view of this beautiful body of water and Cradle Mountain is picture-postcard material. The lake, encircled by rugged mountains, was formed by a glacier.

I also recommend that even the least athletic folks take the less-than-10-minute walk from the lodge to Pencil Pine Falls.

A daily program of walks and outdoor activities is planned by the staff at **Cradle Mountain Lodge** (below). These range from short excursions to longer, more arduous hikes. The guided walks, abseiling (mountaineering), rock-climbing excursions, and trout-fishing trips are open to registered guests, including campers. A nominal charge is levied for activities requiring equipment. Many people, of course, prefer to go off on their own, and this is perfectly all right as long as they're properly equipped and aware of safety essentials. There are lots of trails for all fitness levels; these are well marked and maintained without disrupting the natural setting.

The most popular hiking trail in the park is the **Overland Track,** an 80km (50-mile) route that links Cradle Mountain and Lake St. Clair. The trek takes 5 to 10 days. The trail passes through almost every type of country—from highland moors to dense valley rain forests. Every summer hundreds of people of various ages and countries make this hike. Lodging is in huts spaced out along the way. Even in summer, hikers must be prepared to deal with sudden inclement weather. **Cradle Mountain Huts,** P.O. Box 1879, Launceston, TAS 7250 (☎ 003/312 006; fax 003/315 525), organizes guided versions of the Overland Track. The fee of about A$1,250 (U.S. $1,000) per person includes transfers to/from Launceston, meals, guiding, and accommodations in huts along the track. Trips last six days.

Between June and October it's possible to cross-country ski in the park. Swimming is a popular pastime in summer.

At the southern end of the park near Derwent Bridge, there's a ranger station and campgrounds. Day hikes can be done from here, and **Lakeside St. Clair Wilderness Holidays** (☎ 002/891 137) offers cruises on Lake St. Clair (A$16/U.S. $12.80).

WHERE TO STAY & DINE

✪ **Cradle Mountain Lodge.** P.O. Box 153, Sheffield, TAS 7306. ☎ **004/921 303,** or 1800/030 377 in Australia. Fax 004/921 309. 4 lodge rms (none with bath), 96 self-contained cabins. Lodge rooms, A$104 (U.S. $83.20) double; Pencil Pine cabins, A$153 (U.S. $122.40) per cabin. Spa cabins A$198 (U.S. $158.40) per cabin. Additional person A$26 (U.S. $20.80) extra. Children under 3 free in parents' room. Cradle Campground, A$8 (U.S. $6.40) per adult, A$6 (U.S. $4.80) per child; A$22 (U.S. $17.60) bunkhouse bed for adult, A$12 (U.S. $9.60) bunkhouse bed for child. BC, MC, V. Free parking. Transportation: See above.

If you love the outdoors but have no desire to sleep in a tent; enjoy hiking, kayaking, and canoeing but want a hot shower and a clean bed at the end of the day; like eating next to a roaring fire but don't want to wash dishes—this is the place for you. This remote mountain lodge has comfortable rooms, good food, friendly staff, and big open fireplaces—all surrounded by magnificent scenery. The two-story timber building, with a peaked roof and verandas where hikers remove muddy boots before going inside, looks like an inn you'd find in the Alps.

Pleasant rooms with shared facilities are in the lodge and cozy cabins are spread across the grounds. Each modern wood cabin has a pot-bellied stove, bath (with hot shower), small kitchen, and comfortable bed. Spa cabins are carpeted and have spa tubs as well as showers.

Hearty meals are served in the big dining room in the lodge, which is just rustic enough to be invigorating. Rather than choosing from a published wine list, you're free to make your selection from the well-stocked wine cellar. Drinks are served in a country-style tavern, where a welcoming fire blazes in a stone fireplace. At night, wild animals from the nearby forests come right up on the verandas to claim the edible goodies left out for them. This is a great opportunity to see opossums, wallabies, and Tasmanian devils up close.

Nonstaying guests are welcome and can enjoy meals and teas in the lodge. Hot breakfast costs about A$10 (U.S. $8) and continental is about A$6 (U.S. $4.80). Lunches, ordered from a chalkboard menu, range from A$7 to A$12 (U.S. $5.60 to $9.60). Five-course family-style dinners are A$30 (U.S. $24). Morning and afternoon teas cost about A$3 (U.S. $2.40).

In the United States you can make reservations *only* for Pencil Pine and Spa cabins at Cradle Mountain Lodge through **P&O Resorts** (☎ 408/685-8902 or 800/225-9849; fax 408/685-8903). Book less expensive options directly with the lodge.

Ⓢ **Lemonthyme Lodge.** Off Cradle Mountain Road, Moina via Sheffield, TAS 7306. ☎ **004/921 112.** Fax 004/921 113. 8 rms (none with bath), 4 self-contained two-bedroom cabins, 14 luxury cabins (7 with spa). A$80 (U.S. $64) double room; A$150 (U.S. $120) cabin. Children under 14 charged A$15 (U.S. $12). Three-course dinner A$25 (U.S. $20) extra; breakfast from A$9.50 (U.S. $7.60). AE, BC, MC, V. Free parking. Lemonthyme Lodge is 70km (43 miles) southwest of Devonport. The management can provide transfers, or you can take the Tasmanian Wilderness Transport coach (A$35/U.S. $28), which will drop you 8km (5 miles) from the lodge and the management will pick you up. If you're driving, call for directions.

This remote lodge offers comfortable accommodations for those who really want to get away from it all. The lodge rooms are sparsely furnished and share baths down the hall, but the new "wilderness suites" are lovely and come with down comforters and private balconies with table and chairs. All cabins have Huon pine furniture, nicely appointed baths, minibars, and log fireplaces. Lemonthyme Lodge is the largest log cabin in the Southern Hemisphere, constructed of ponderosa pine and set on 109 acres. All meals are served in a rustic dining room, where there's a big open fire. You can help yourself to complimentary coffee and tea throughout the day.

If you stay here, you can take walks in the surrounding bush, go fishing, go on four-wheel-drive trips, or drive over to Cradle Mountain.

4 The West Coast

Strahan: 296km (184 miles) NW of Hobart, 245km (152 miles) SW of Devonport

Tasmania's west coast boasts steep mountain ranges, deep gorges, swift rivers, rain forest, and wilderness. It's a region of sharp contrasts—the "moonscape" at Queenstown is the result of intensive mining and industrial activity; the pristine Franklin and Gordon Rivers are included in a World Heritage Area. Strahan, at the head of Macquarie Harbour, is a historic port and the starting point for cruises through the harbor to the Gordon River.

ESSENTIALS

GETTING THERE **Tasmanian Wilderness Transport** (☎ 003/344 442) provides service to Strahan from Hobart on Saturday. The trip departs at 8:30am, stops at Lake St. Clair for two hours, and arrives in Strahan at 4:45pm. The cost is A$40 (U.S. $32) one-way, A$75 (U.S. $60) round-trip. TWT also provides service from Devonport and Launceston on Saturday. It takes about 5¹/₂ hours, with a 2¹/₂-hour stop at Cradle Mountain, and costs A$40 (U.S. $32) one-way and A$75 (U.S. $60) round-trip. The low-season (Easter to November) schedule is slightly different.

Tasmanian Redline Coaches provide service from Hobart to Strahan Monday to Saturday, departing at 8:30am and arriving at 4:15pm. The fare is A$34 (U.S. $27.20) one-way.

The drive from Hobart to Strahan takes about 4¹/₂ hours without stops. From Devonport, allow about 3¹/₂ hours. While the roads are paved and well marked, I don't recommend you do either trip after dark.

VISITOR INFORMATION Information about the World Heritage Area is available at the **Ranger Station,** Customs House, Strahan (☎ 004/717 122). It's open Monday to Friday from 8am to 5pm. The **telephone area code** is 004. As part of the telephone changeover, all numbers with a 004 area code will be changing to 03/64xx xxxx in March 1997.

EXPLORING THE AREA

Gordon River cruises depart Strahan Wharf daily at 9am. The half-day trip returns at 2pm after traveling across Macquarie Harbour and down the Gordon River. A stop is made at Heritage Landing, where you get a taste of rain forest. During January, there's also a half-day cruise at 1:45pm.

The full-day trip returns at 3:30pm and follows the itinerary of the half-day trip, with an additional stop at Sarah Island, where there are ruins of a penal settlement that was abandoned in 1833. The fare for the half-day trip (including morning or afternoon tea) is A$44 (U.S. $35.20) for adults and A$24 (U.S. $19.20) for children 4 to 14. The full-day fare (including tea) is A$62 (U.S. $49.60) for adults and A$30 (U.S. $24) for children. Lunch can be purchased on board the vessel.

Bookings can be made with **Gordon River Cruises,** P.O. Box 40, Strahan, TAS 7468 (☎ 004/717 187; fax 004/717 317).

While the cruises are the main attraction in the area, you can also enjoy jetboat rides, flightseeing in a seaplane that lands on the Franklin River, four-wheel-drive tours, and fishing. In Zeehan, 42km (26 miles) to the north, the **West Coast Pioneers Memorial Museum** is worth a stop. It's open daily and admission is free.

WHERE TO STAY & DINE

✪ **Franklin Manor.** The Esplanade, Strahan, TAS 7468. ☎ **004 717 311.** Fax 004/717 267. 14 rms, 4 cottages. TV TEL. A$145 (U.S. $116) standard double, A$165 (U.S. $132) double with spa bath or cottage. Rates include breakfast. BC, MC, V. Free parking. Transportation: See above.

This is easily one of Australia's nicest B&Bs. Built in 1890—Strahan's heyday—for the harbormaster, the house was restored in 1988. Today it's owned by gracious hostess Bernadette Woods, who immigrated from Ireland in 1983 and was once the manager at Cradle Mountain Lodge. All rooms have tub/shower combinations, tea- and coffee-making facilities, beautiful comforters and coordinated draperies, heaters, electric blankets, iron or brass queen-size beds, clock radios with cassette players, and small refrigerators. They're spacious and have old-world decors, handcrafted timber cabinets, and large windows that make them sunny. Five also offer large spa baths.

Gourmet meals, prepared by chef Rodney Charles, are served in two atmospheric dining rooms. Three-course dinners cost about A$38 (U.S. $30.40). The handsome Huon pine bar in the foyer and the wine cellar operate on the honesty system. You choose what you want and note your selection in a notebook. An adjacent lounge is where coffee is served after dinner and you can relax throughout the day. Taped classical music, an open fire, and large arrangements of dried flowers contribute to the charm of this room.

Bernadette fixes picnic lunches for those going on day trips and is a good source of information on things to do in the area.

Gordon Gateway Chalets. Grining Street, Strahan, TAS 7468. ☎ **004/717 165.** 10 one-bedroom units, 2 two-bedroom units. TV. Off-season (May-Dec), A$80 (U.S. $64) double. In season, A$100 (U.S. $80) double. BC, MC, V. Free parking.

These modern units are on a hill and have excellent views of the harbor and Strahan township. Each has cooking facilities, a bath with shower, contemporary furnishings, and local Huon pine and blackwood timbers. Electric blankets and cozy comforters are standard. Breakfast is provided on request at an additional charge. You have the use of a self-service laundry and a barbecue area, and there's a playground for children. One unit is designed for the disabled.

19 Canberra

Canberra is unique in Australia. Other cities were founded near the mouth of a river whose natural harbor could be made into port facilities. Canberra isn't even on the coast. Other cities survived because minerals, particularly gold, were discovered nearby. Canberra has no mineral wealth. Other cities were founded in the 19th century and grew gradually and naturally. Canberra, begun in 1913, was carefully planned before the first brick was laid.

Why is the nation's capital unique? The story begins with federation in 1901. As soon as Queen Victoria agreed to the establishment of the Commonwealth of Australia, the need for a site for the national government became an issue. Archrivals Sydney and Melbourne each wanted to become the federal capital. To appease them, Australian leaders chose to follow the U.S. example of a federal district, and in 1908 a place between the two cities was chosen. The Australian Capital Territory (ACT) was at that time nothing more than a sheep-grazing region. The work of creating a capital out of the bush began in 1911 with an international competition for a city plan. Walter Burley Griffin, a Chicago landscape architect and contemporary of Frank Lloyd Wright, won the contest. In 1913 the federal capital was named Canberra—an Aboriginal term for "meeting place."

1 Orientation

ARRIVING

BY PLANE Canberra is well served by the daily flights of Ansett and Qantas. The fare from Sydney is A$141 to A$177 (U.S. $112.80 to $141.60) for the 40-minute flight. The same discounted fare from Melbourne is A$198 to A$247 (U.S. $158.40 to $197.60) for a 55-minute flight.

The **Canberra Airport,** about 10 minutes from the city center, has car-rental desks, a gift shop, a newsagent (a kiosk where magazines and newspapers are sold), and a currency exchange, but it lacks lockers, showers, and a post office. Stamps are sold at the newsagent's and a mailbox is provided for cards and letters. A bar and bistro are available. A taxi to the city center costs approximately A$12 (U.S. $9.60).

What's Special About Canberra

Museums

- The National Gallery of Australia, a treasure trove of the nation's art.
- The National Science and Technology Centre, a hands-on science center.

Monument

- The Australian War Memorial, a tribute to those who gave their lives.

Activities

- Cycling on Canberra's many miles of bike paths.

Parks & Gardens

- The city's extensive greenbelts and parklands.
- The Australian National Botanic Gardens, the best collection of native flora.

Top Attraction

- Parliament House on Capital Hill.

Buildings

- The High Court of Australia, an impressive concrete-and-glass structure.
- The Telecom Tower, providing a lofty viewpoint.

Man-Made Spectacle

- Lake Burley Griffin, contributing significantly to the city's overall beauty.

Events

- Floriade, Canberra's annual floral festival—from mid-September to mid-October.

BY TRAIN You might want to consider taking the train to Canberra. Countrylink's *Canberra Xplorer* makes the journey from Sydney in four hours; the fare is A$51.80 (U.S. $41.45) in first class and A$37.85 (U.S. $30.28) in economy. Children are half price. Countrylink also offers dollarwise day-trip and overnight packages to Canberra from Sydney. For more information, call Countrylink at 02/379 3077 (or 13 22 32 in Australia). V/Line provides service from Melbourne. The Canberra Link is a combination of train and coach travel taking a total of about eight hours. The fare is A$59.60 (U.S.$47.68) in first class and A$45 (U.S. $36) in economy. Children pay a little more than half fare. For further details, call V/Line at 13 22 32 in Australia. Canberra's Railway Station is about 3km (2 miles) southeast of Capital Hill.

BY BUS A Greyhound-Pioneer (☎ 06/257 5091, or 13 20 30 in Australia) ticket from Sydney costs A$30 (U.S. $24) for adults and A$15 (U.S. $12) for children; the trip takes 4 to 4½ hours. A Greyhound-Pioneer ticket from Melbourne to Canberra costs A$55 (U.S. $44) for adults, A$44 (U.S. $35.20) for children. Several sightseeing bus companies in Sydney, including AAT King's and Australian Pacific Tours, offer day trips to Canberra. Intercity buses arrive at the **Jolimont Tourist Centre,** at the corner of Northbourne Avenue and Alinga Street, in Civic.

BY CAR The ACT is within the state of New South Wales. Sydney is 306km (190 miles) northeast and Melbourne 651km (404 miles) southwest. If you drive from Sydney via the **Hume and Federal Highways,** the trip will take 3½ to 4 hours.

VISITOR INFORMATION

Canberra Tourism (☎ 06/205 0044, or 1800/02 6166 in Australia; fax 06/ 205 0776) dispenses information and books accommodations from an information center on Northbourne Avenue, Dickson (just south of Morphett Street). The office is open daily from 9am to 5pm. A fast-food eatery/souvenir shop is next door.

A host of free events—from concerts to competitions—is part of the annual **Canberra Festival** held in March. The 10 days of frivolity end on Canberra Day (a local public holiday), always the third Monday in March.

Floriade, Canberra's annual floral festival, is held between mid-September and mid-October and includes spectacular floral displays, complemented by music, dance, and theater events. Admission is free. For more information, call the Floriade hotline at 06/257 5092 (or 1800/026 166 in Australia). Floriade will take place from September 14 to October 13, 1996.

CITY LAYOUT

Walter Burley Griffin's plan for Australia's capital has stood the test of time. Canberra is an attractive, carefully designed city that functions well as the seat of the federal government and as a desirable place to live. The Chicago architect didn't envisage that 300,000 people would one day inhabit his city, but because parks, gardens, and open space were important to him, the many residents of this model metropolis consider themselves lucky. In addition to the planned greenbelts, those who live in Canberra enjoy excursions into the surrounding Australian Capital Territory, which remains a sparsely populated rural region.

Griffin hadn't seen the site for the capital when he created his prize-winning design, but it's hard to imagine him having done any better even if he had. **Capital Hill**, where the **Parliament House** opened in 1988, is the center of a hub from which more than half a dozen avenues radiate. Each of these broad tree-lined streets leads to a traffic circle from which more roads emanate, like spokes in a wheel. Around each hub, the streets form a pattern of concentric circles. This unusual traffic plan is one of the hallmarks of Griffin's design. The other notable feature is the man-made lake he stipulated, created by damming the Molonglo River. Today, **Lake Burley Griffin** contributes to the city's overall beauty and provides a welcome recreation area.

Not everyone admires Canberra. Some say the city is so well planned it's boring and sterile. Others complain the circular street system is hard for newcomers to navigate. I appreciate the capital's treasure trove of museums and galleries and find the fresh modern architecture a pleasant change from that of other Aussie cities. Admittedly, I've gotten lost in the spokes going from one hub to the other, and you might be wise to use public transport or take taxis. Because this is a horizontal, rather than a vertical, city, the distance between points of interest precludes walking. However, if you're fit you can tour the area of greatest national importance on foot: The major sights are in the **Parliamentary Triangle,** a pie-shaped wedge whose boundaries are **Kings Avenue, Parkes Way,** and **Commonwealth Avenue.**

While extensive walking isn't practical, cyclists can rent a bike and move around Canberra on its 120km (74 miles) of bicycle paths. Commonwealth Avenue leads across the lake to City Hill, the commercial heart of the capital. **Northbourne Avenue** is the main thoroughfare in this central business district, known officially as **Canberra City** and locally as **"Civic."** Separate centers for national and municipal functions were part of Walter Burley Griffin's plan. The **Telecom Tower** on **Black Mountain** and the viewpoint on **Mount Ainslie** provide spectacular wide-angle vistas of the entire region. The best time to visit Canberra is in spring (September to November) or autumn (March to May).

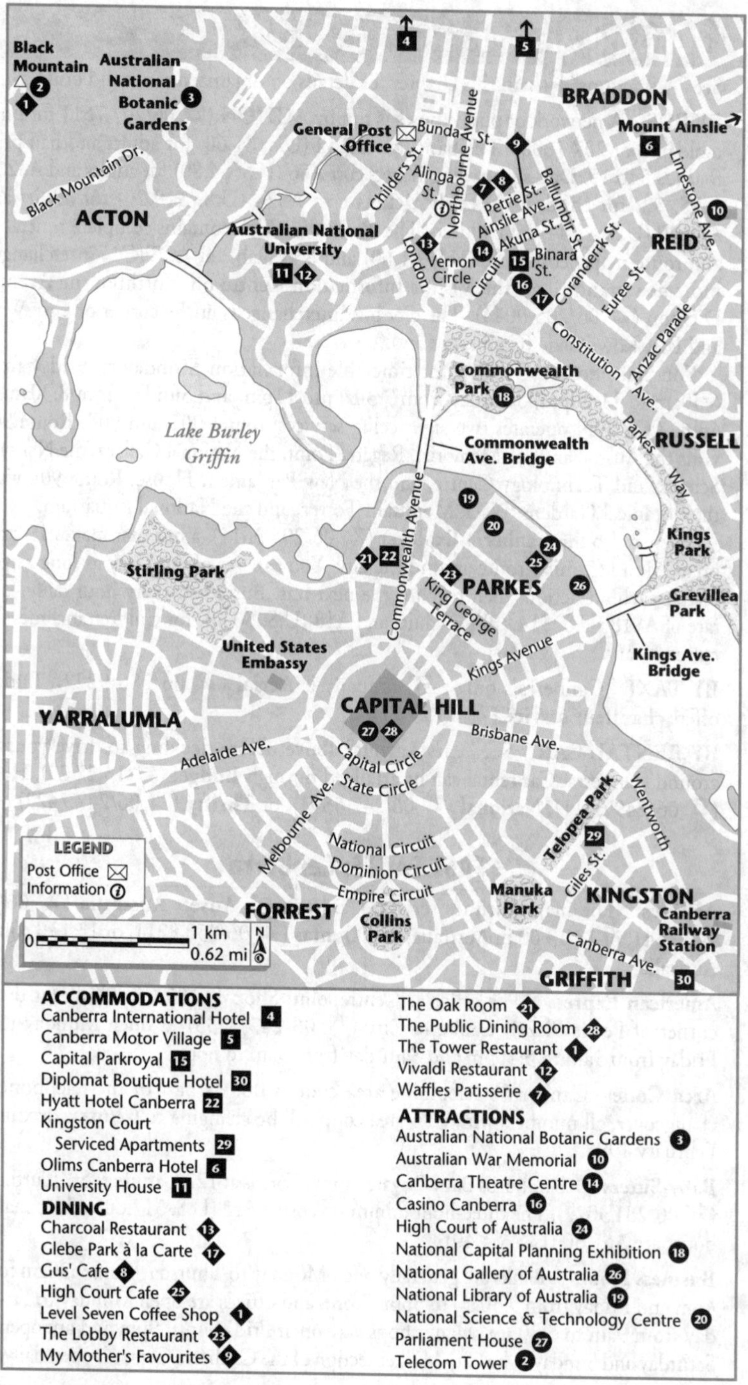

ACCOMMODATIONS

- Canberra International Hotel 4
- Canberra Motor Village 5
- Capital Parkroyal 15
- Diplomat Boutique Hotel 30
- Hyatt Hotel Canberra 22
- Kingston Court Serviced Apartments 29
- Olims Canberra Hotel 6
- University House 11

DINING

- Charcoal Restaurant 13
- Glebe Park à la Carte 17
- Gus' Cafe 8
- High Court Cafe 25
- Level Seven Coffee Shop 1
- The Lobby Restaurant 23
- My Mother's Favourites 9
- The Oak Room 21
- The Public Dining Room 28
- The Tower Restaurant 1
- Vivaldi Restaurant 12
- Waffles Patisserie 7

ATTRACTIONS

- Australian National Botanic Gardens 3
- Australian War Memorial 10
- Canberra Theatre Centre 14
- Casino Canberra 16
- High Court of Australia 24
- National Capital Planning Exhibition 18
- National Gallery of Australia 26
- National Library of Australia 19
- National Science & Technology Centre 20
- Parliament House 27
- Telecom Tower 2

2 Getting Around

See "Attractions" later in this chapter for details on organized tours and cruises.

BY BUS A network of public buses is run by **ACTION** (☎ 06/207 7611 for timetable info or 207 7600). The basic fare is A$2 (U.S. $1.60) for adults and half price for kids 5 to 15. **Day-sightseeing** tickets cost A$6 (U.S. $4.80) for adults and A$2.50 (U.S. $2) for children. **Weekly tickets** cost A$24 (U.S. $19.20) for adults and A$9.30 (U.S. $7.44) for children. The *Bus Book,* which contains complete timetables and route maps, costs A$2 (U.S. $1.60) and is available at ACTION interchanges, most newsstands, and the Visitor Information Centre on Northbourne Avenue, Dickson (☎ 06/205 0044). The city bus interchange is at the corner of City Walk and East Row, Civic (Canberra City).

You can phone ACTION for timetable information Monday to Friday from 6:30am to 11:30pm, Saturday from 7:30am to 11pm, and Sunday from 8:30am to 6pm. ACTION operates two sightseeing services: routes 901 and 904. Route 901 visits the Australian War Memorial, Regatta Point, the National Gallery, the National Science and Technology Centre, and the New Parliament House. Route 904 visits the Botanical Gardens, Black Mountain Tower, and the National Aquarium.

There's also the **Canberra Explorer** (☎ 06/295 3611), a bus that makes 19 stops on a 25km (15-mile) route around the city. You can get off and stay as long as you like at each attraction, then reboard the next bus. Buses run every hour daily. The fare of A$18 (U.S. $14.40) for adults and A$8 (U.S. $6.40) for children includes full commentary.

BY TAXI Canberra's only taxi company is **Aerial** (☎ 06/285 9222). Budget offers **chauffeur service** (☎ 13 27 27).

BY RENTAL CAR See "City Layout" above before deciding to drive yourself around Canberra. Car rental can be arranged through **Budget** (☎ 13 27 27), **Hertz** (☎ 06/249 6211), **National** (☎ 06/247 5591), or **Thrifty** (☎ 06/247 7422).

FAST FACTS: Canberra

Airlines The major airlines serving Canberra are **Ansett Australia** (☎ 06/249 7641, or 13 13 00 in Australia) and **Qantas** (☎ 06/250 8211, or 13 13 13 in Australia).

American Express The office at Centrepoint, Shop 1, 185 City Walk (at the corner of Petrie Plaza), Canberra City (☎ 06/247 2333), is open Monday to Friday from 9am to 5:15pm and Saturday from 9am to noon.

Area Code Canberra's telephone area code is 06. As part of the telephone changeover, all numbers with a 06 area code will be changing to 02/6xxx xxxx in February 1998.

Baby-Sitters All Suburbs Baby Private Home Care is at 122 Caruthers St., Curtin (☎ 06/281 3027). The three-hour minimum costs A$22 (U.S. $17.60); additional hours are A$5.50 (U.S. $4.40).

Business Hours Banks are generally open Monday to Thursday from 9:30am to 4pm and Friday from 9:30am to 5pm. Stores and offices are open Monday to Friday from 9am to 5:30pm. Many shops stay open Friday until 9pm and are open Saturday and Sunday. The City Market section of the Canberra Centre is open daily.

Car Rentals See "Getting Around," above.

Currency See "Information, Entry Requirements & Money" in Chapter 3.

Currency Exchange Cash traveler's checks at banks, at American Express (above), or at Thomas Cook, at the Petrie Plaza entrance of the Canberra Centre, open Monday to Friday from 8:45am to 5:15pm and Saturday from 9am to noon.

Dentist Canberra lacks a dental emergency referral service. Two dentists with conveniently located offices are Dr. A.W. Bubear (☎ 06/247 8400) and Dr. D.R. Robertson (☎ 06/248 0161), both in the City Walk Arcade, Canberra City.

Doctor The Capital Medical Centre, 2 Mort St., Canberra City (☎ 06/257 3766), is open Monday to Friday from 8:30am to 5pm.

Drugstores The Canberra City Pharmacy, at the corner of East Row and Alinga Street, Canberra City (☎ 06/248 5469 or 248 6491), is open daily.

Embassies/Consulates The representatives of the major English-speaking countries are in Yarralumla: the **British High Commission,** Commonwealth Avenue (☎ 06/270 6666); the **Canadian High Commission,** Commonwealth Avenue (☎ 06/273 3844); and the **U.S. Embassy,** Moonah Place (☎ 06/270 5000).

Emergencies In an emergency, dial **000** to call for an ambulance, the fire department, or the police.

Eyeglasses For eyeglass repairs, go to OPSM Express, 4 Bailey Arcade, East Row (☎ 06/247 8980).

Hospitals For medical attention, go to the Woden Valley Hospital, Yamba Drive, Garran (☎ 06/244 2222); or call the Accident & Emergency Department at 06/244 2611 (24 hours).

Hotlines Lifeline, 06/257 1111; Rape Crisis Centre, 06/247 2525; Drug/Alcohol Crisis Line, 06/205 4545 (24 hours); Suicide Prevention, 02/331 2000; Poison Information Centre, 06/285 2852.

Libraries The National Library, Parkes Place (☎ 06/262 1111), is open Monday to Thursday from 9am to 9pm, Friday and Saturday from 9am to 5pm, and Sunday from 1:30 to 5pm.

Lost Property Inquire at the local police station.

Luggage Storage/Lockers There's a luggage-storage room in the train station in Kingston. Each item left costs A$1.50 (U.S. $1.20).

Newspapers/Magazines Canberra's daily newspaper is the *Canberra Times.*

Photographic Needs City Market Fast Photo, Shop 4a City Market, Bunda Street, Civic (☎ 06/248 5545). sells a large range of cameras, film, and batteries and offers one-hour processing. Located opposite the Canberra Centre, this shop is open daily.

Police See "Emergencies" above or call 06/256 7777 for general inquiries.

Post Office The Canberra Post Office (GPO), Alinga Street, Canberra City (☎ 06/201 7070 or 209 1370), is open Monday to Friday from 9am to 5pm. Smaller branches are located throughout the area.

Radio You'll hear classic hits on 2CC (1206 AM) or 2CA (1053 AM), classical music on ABC (102.3 FM), rock on 104.7 FM or 106 FM, and national news and information on ABC Radio National (846 AM).

Restrooms You'll find them near the city bus exchange, City Hill, London Circuit.

Safety Canberra is generally quite safe. However, it's always a good idea to stay out of parks and dimly lit places at night.

Taxes There's no GST, no hotel tax, and no sales tax added to purchases in Canberra.

Taxis See "Getting Around" earlier in this chapter.

Telegrams/Telex Send these from the post office (above).

Television Channel 9 (Australian Broadcasting Company) offers news, current affairs, educational programs, and entertainment. Channels WIN, PRIME, SBS, and TEN CAPITAL broadcast sports, entertainment, news, and so forth.

Transit Information Call ACTION timetable information at 06/207 7611.

Useful Telephone Numbers Citizen's Advice Bureau, 06/248-7988; Australian National University, 06/249 5111; Lesbian Line, 06/247 8882; Gay Contact, 06/247 2726; Women's Information and Referral Centre, 06/205 1075.

3 Accommodations

Australia's national capital offers a good range of lodging at prices lower than those of many other big cities. Since many people come to Canberra for business during the week, weekend rates are often lower.

IN THE CITY CENTER

Capital Parkroyal. 1 Binara St., Canberra, ACT 2601. ☎ **06/247 8999,** or 1800/020 055 in Australia. Fax 06/257 4905. 287 rms, 6 suites. A/C MINIBAR TV TEL. From A$210 (U.S. $168) standard double; from A$225 (U.S. $180) parkview double; A$460–A$660 (U.S. $368–$528) suite. Additional person A$20 (U.S. $16) extra. Lower weekend rates. Children under 15 free in parents' room. No-smoking rooms available. AE, BC, DC, MC, V. Free parking.

The centrally located Capital Parkroyal is part of the National Convention Centre complex overlooking Glebe Park. The impressive garden setting includes pools, watercourses, and fountains. All rooms have clock radios, terry robes, hairdryers, tea- and coffee-making facilities, small refrigerators, and in-room movies. The majority have one queen-size bed or two doubles. Deluxe quarters have king-size beds. Five rooms were designed for the handicapped.

Dining/Entertainment: The hotel has two restaurants, Blundell's and the Glebe Cafe, and two bars offer drinks.

Services: Concierge, 24-hour room service, nightly turndown, free daily newspaper, laundry, valet, baby-sitting.

Facilities: Pool, health club, gym, sauna, business center.

IN YARRALUMLA

✪ **Hyatt Hotel Canberra.** Commonwealth Avenue, Yarralumla, ACT 2600. ☎ **06/270 1234,** or 1800/222 188 in Australia. Fax 06/281 5998. 249 rms and suites. A/C MINIBAR TV TEL. A$295 (U.S. $236) standard double; A$320 (U.S. $256) deluxe double; A$350 (U.S. $280) Pavilion Terrace (Regency Club) quarters; A$650 (U.S. $520) executive suite; A$1,200–A$1,600 (U.S. $960–$1,280) Diplomatic Suite. Additional person A$40 (U.S. $32) extra. Children under 18 free in parents' room. Ask about weekend packages. No-smoking rooms available. AE, BC, DC, MC, V. Free parking.

This is the capital's poshest hotel, ideally sited in the shadow of the new Parliament House and between Lake Burley Griffin and the Parliamentary Triangle. The Hyatt is a renovation of the Hotel Canberra, a historic landmark built in 1924. The gracious ambience of the National Trust building was preserved while luxurious lodging and dining facilities were installed. All staff members wear 1920s-style outfits, and the hotel has the low-key atmosphere usually associated with a country club.

Some 39 rooms are in the original two-story section; these have small windows and tend to be a little dark. The majority of lodging is in the new four-story section, and these rooms are spacious, have pleasant beige/cocoa decors, and marble baths with separate tub and shower stall. Each offers a radio, a terry robe, a hairdryer, tea- and coffee-making facilities, a small refrigerator, in-room movies, and king-size or twin beds. Deluxe rooms on the fourth floor of the north wing have the best lake views.

Dining/Entertainment: Meals and drinks are served in the Promenade Cafe, the Tea Lounge, the Oak Room (winner of the 1990 Australian Tourist Commission Award for fine dining), the Speaker's Corner, and Griffin's.

Services: Concierge, 24-hour room service, free daily newspaper, laundry, valet, nightly turndown, shoeshine, massage.

Facilities: Indoor pool, extensive fitness center with daily aerobics classes, gym, sauna, spa, tennis court, business center, bike rental.

IN DICKSON

Canberra International Hotel. 242 Northbourne Ave., Dickson, ACT 2602 ☎ **06/247 6966,** or 1800/026 305 in Australia. Fax 06/248 7823. 152 rms and suites. A/C MINIBAR TV TEL. A$120–A$160 (U.S. $96–$128) double; A$140–A$160 (U.S. $112–$128) suite. Additional person A$15 (U.S. $12) extra. Children under 12 free in parents' room. Lower weekend rates. AE, BC, DC, MC, V. Free parking. Bus: 382 or 431.

Before the Capital Parkroyal and the Hyatt were built, the Canberra International was the city's most prestigious address. The three-story hotel offers standard rooms and one- and two-room suites, 10 with kitchens. All quarters have hairdryers, irons and ironing boards, in-room movies, clock radios, tea- and coffee-making facilities, and small refrigerators. Two are equipped for the handicapped.

Dining/Entertainment: Meals and drinks are served in the Garden Terrace Restaurant, the Gazebo Cocktail Bar, and the Lemon Tree Brasserie.

Services: 24-hour room service, free daily newspaper, laundry, valet, baby-sitting.

Facilities: Outdoor pool, gift shop.

IN GRIFFITH

Diplomat Boutique Hotel. Canberra Avenue and Hely Street, Griffith, ACT 2603. ☎ **06/295 2277,** or 1800/026 367 in Australia. Fax 06/239 6432. 68 rms and suites. A/C MINIBAR TV TEL. A$120 (U.S. $96) double; A$140–A$160 (U.S. $112–$128) executive room. Additional person A$10 (U.S. $8) extra. Lower weekend rates. Children under 18 free in parents' room. AE, BC, MC, V. Free parking. Bus: 371.

The white contemporary Mediterranean-style hotel is about 3km (2 miles) from the Parliamentary Triangle and about 6km (4 miles) from Civic. Most rooms face onto a multilevel atrium and are spacious and modern. Two-thirds have tub/shower combinations; all have hairdryers, irons and ironing boards, clock radios, tea- and coffee-making facilities, fresh fruit, and small refrigerators. Some deluxe suites have spas.

Dining/Entertainment: Meals are served in the Diplomat Bar & Grill, an informal eatery at the base of the atrium.

Services: Room service during limited hours, baby-sitting.

Facilities: Outdoor pool, sauna, gym, video movies.

IN KINGSTON

$ **Kingston Court Serviced Apartments.** 4 Tench St., Kingston, ACT 2604. ☎ **06/295 2244.** Fax 06/239 9499. 36 apts. A/C TV TEL. A$100 (U.S. $80) apt for two. Additional adult A$10 (U.S. $8) extra; additional child A$5 (U.S. $4) extra. AE, BC, DC, MC, V. Free parking. Bus: 352.

Kingston Court is a good choice for those who want the comforts of home. Each 100-square-meter (1,000-sq.-ft.) unit has its own washing machine, dryer, kitchen with dishwasher, and balcony or courtyard. The quarters are cleaned five days a week; the towels are changed daily. Kingston Court is 1km (0.6 mile) from the Parliamentary Triangle and about 6km (3½ miles) from Civic. Telopea Park is across the street. The only drawback is that this three-story building has no elevator. A pool, a gas barbecue, and half-court tennis are provided on the premises.

IN BRADDON

✪ **Olims Canberra Hotel.** At the corner of Limestone and Ainslie avenues, Braddon, ACT 2601. ☎ **06/248 5511,** or 1800/020 016 in Australia. Fax 06/247 0864. Reservations can be made through Flag Inns. 126 rms and suites. MINIBAR TV TEL. A$95 (U.S. $76) standard double; A$125 (U.S. $100) deluxe double; A$140 (U.S. $112) suite. Additional person A$15 (U.S. $12) extra. Children under 12 free in parents' room. AE, BC, DC, MC, V. Free parking. Bus: 385.

The Olims Canberra was remodeled not long ago and thankfully the original section was retained. The Ainslie Hotel, which opened in 1927, was known for its high pitched gables and attic windows, a style called "English deco." The building was classified by the National Trust in 1981 and more than A$5 million (U.S. $4 million) has subsequently been spent in upgrading and extension efforts.

Today 37 standard rooms remain in the original part and the rest are in a tasteful addition. (Only standard rooms lack air conditioning.) All quarters are spacious and nicely furnished. The 33 suites are on two levels, with kitchen and lounge (living room) downstairs and bedroom and bath upstairs. Standard rooms offer a choice of twin or double beds; in the new section, king-size, queen-size, and twins are available. Some rooms overlook the attractive central courtyard. The hotel's bistro/carvery is open daily for moderately priced lunches and dinners. The restaurant serves breakfast and dinner Monday to Saturday. There's also a beergarden and a bottle shop. Civic is just over a kilometer away. Room service is available 24 hours a day.

IN ACTON

University House. On the campus of the Australian National University, Balmain Crescent, Acton (G.P.O. Box 1535, Canberra, ACT 2601). ☎ **06/249 5211.** Fax 06/249 5252. 145 rms, suites, and apts. TEL. A$99 (U.S. $79.20) twin with bath; A$105 (U.S. $84) suite; A$110 (U.S. $88) one-bedroom apt; A$155 (U.S. $124) two-bedroom apt with bath and kitchen. AE, BC, DC, MC, V. Free security parking. Bus: 434.

Whether or not you have business at ANU, University House is a pleasant and out-of-the-ordinary place to stay, conveniently within 2km (1¼ miles) of the city center. All rooms offer a small refrigerator, a toaster, and coffee- and tea-making facilities. The apartments have kitchenettes. Meals are served in Boffins Restaurant and The Cellar Bar. University House has tennis courts and easy access to walking and jogging tracks.

IN O'CONNOR

$ **Canberra Motor Village.** Kunzea Street, O'Connor, ACT 2601. ☎ **06/247 5466,** or 1800/026 199 in Australia. Fax 06/249 6138. 38 motel units, 44 powered sites. A$89–A$99 (U.S. $71.20–$79.20) double. On-site vans A$39 (U.S. $31.20). Powered sites A$22 (U.S. $17.60). Ask about lower rates through Aussie auto clubs. AE, BC, DC, MC, V. Free parking. Bus: 381.

The Canberra Motor Village offers motel lodging, on-site vans, and camping sites about 5km (3 miles) northwest of Civic. The 38 motel units have private baths, TVs, and phones; some have cooking facilities and some air conditioning.

4 Dining

IN THE CITY CENTER

MODERATE

Charcoal Restaurant. 61 London Circuit. ☎ **06/248 8015.** Reservations required well in advance. Main courses A$15–A$27 (U.S. $12–$21.60). AE, BC, DC, MC, V. Mon–Fri noon–2:30pm; Mon–Sat 6–10pm. INTERNATIONAL.

This well-established Canberra favorite has been serving thick, juicy steaks to bureaucrats and their buddies for 30 years. You can choose either King Island sirloin or rump, T-bone, filet mignon, carpetbag steak (eye filet with a pocket of oysters), pepper steak, or steak Dianne. Other dishes include chicken Kiev, Creole blackened fish, Snowy River trout, and curry pot. The central location no doubt adds to the Charcoal's popularity. Things can get really busy for lunch, when every red leatherette chair is occupied. Good wine list.

Waffles Patisserie. 50 Northbourne Ave. ☎ **06/247 2913.** Reservations recommended. Main courses A$8–A$13.50 (U.S. $6.40–$10.80). AE, BC, DC, MC, V. Daily 8am–well past midnight. CAFÉ.

At Waffles, tasty dishes are served by a friendly staff in a pleasant atmosphere. The peach-and-gray decor and large windows create a light, airy feel. Technically, this is a "licensed pâtisserie," which means it specializes in pastry—in this case, waffles—and is licensed to serve alcoholic beverages, but that's only half the story. Waffles are the specialty at breakfast, but a selection of eggs and cereals is also available. Pasta, burgers, and open sandwiches are served for lunch, as are many kinds of dessert waffles. Waffles also does takeout.

INEXPENSIVE

Gus' Cafe. Next to the Centre Cinema in the Garema Arcade, Bunda Street. ☎ **06/248 8118.** Reservations not required. Homemade soup with bread A$4–A$5 (U.S. $3.20–$4); main courses A$4–A$7.50 (U.S. $3.20–$6); desserts A$1.60–A$4 (U.S. $1.30–$3.20). Sun and public holiday surcharge A50¢ (U.S. 40¢) per person. DC. Daily 7am–midnight. LIGHT CONTINENTAL.

Gus' is a popular local hangout. Canberrans congregate here to read the newspaper, meet friends, and munch on things like focaccia, Black Forest cake, and carrot cake. The cheesecake, made fresh daily by proprietor Goronwy Price, is excellent. If you're ready for a meal, I recommend homemade Hungarian goulash with noodles or knodel (dumplings). Seating is both indoors and out, and magazines and board games are provided for use while you sip your cappuccino. BYO.

IN YARRALUMLA

The Oak Room. In the Hyatt Hotel Canberra, Commonwealth Avenue. ☎ **06/270 1234.** Reservations recommended. Main courses A$22–A$34 (U.S. $17.60–$27.20); fixed-price three-course lunch A$34.50 (U.S. $27.60). AE, BC, DC, MC, V. Tues–Fri noon–2pm; Tues–Sat 7–10pm. MODERN AUSTRALIAN.

This elegant restaurant won the Australian Tourist Commission's 1990 award for "Best Fine Dining Restaurant," and it isn't hard to understand why. Chef Gary Hague creates interesting dishes that are neither too simple nor too belabored. His entrees (appetizers) include a medley of marinated raw seafood, enhanced by fresh basil around a crisp autumn salad and green wasabi; tender South Australian lobster tail lightly pan-fried in herb butter and surrounded by champagne/wild mushroom beurre blanc; or Oriental-flavored beef tartare accompanied by red currant/ginger

Quick Bites

Glebe Park à la Carte, adjacent to the Casino Canberra at 15 Coranderrk St., Civic (☎ 06/257 6512), is a light, airy food court with eight outlets serving various kinds of food. You can eat lunch or dinner for A$4 to A$10 (U.S. $3.20 to $8). One entrance faces the plaza of the National Convention Centre. **Pasta Palace, Flaming Wok, Ali Baba,** and the others are open daily from 11am to 8:30pm. The brewery/tavern stays open until 11pm.

At Shop 5A, City Market, Bunda Street, Civic, ✪ **My Mother's Favourites** (☎ 06/247 8840) proprietor David Cox sells wonderful muffins that could be the basis of a picnic breakfast in your hotel room. Open daily from 9am to 5pm.

sauce and served with warm oven-baked buckwheat blinis. The main courses are equally creative. The menu changes monthly.

When entering the dining room you walk past extensive wine cellars—white to the left, red to the right—into the oak-paneled room, divided into intimate spaces. One room with 10 tables has been designated no-smoking; the other has eight tables. Both areas have fireplaces and art deco decors. Three private dining rooms are ideal for politicians and others needing privacy.

IN ACTON

✪ **Vivaldi Restaurant.** In the Arts Centre on the campus of the Australian National University. ☎ **06/257 2718.** Reservations recommended on weekends. Main courses A$15.50–A$19.50 (U.S. $12.40–$15.60). AE, BC, DC, MC, V. Mon–Fri noon–2pm; Mon–Sat 6–10pm. Bus: 434. CONTEMPORARY AUSTRALIAN.

This restaurant has an appealing casual ambience created by lots of green plants, cane springback chairs, exposed brick walls, and faux-marble tables. It's licensed and BYO, and most diners arrive toting their bottles. The clientele includes politicians, university staff, and local residents. The printed menu is the same for lunch and dinner, but at lunch there's also a chalkboard menu announcing dishes like boned rainbow trout filled with seafood mousse and spinach fettuccine tossed with prosciutto, black olives, and roasted red capsicum. If you order from the printed menu you could start with angel-hair pasta with duckling, asparagus, snow peas, and emerald capsicum butter, then follow with turkey breast and smoked salmon wrapped in spinach puff pastry with smoked-salmon hollandaise. Vivaldi boasts a large no-smoking section, which the management is hoping to expand.

WITHIN THE PARLIAMENTARY TRIANGLE

MODERATE

The Lobby Restaurant. King George Terrace. ☎ **06/273 1563.** Reservations recommended. Main courses A$16.50–A$19.50 (U.S. $13.20–$15.60). AE, BC, DC, MC, V. Mon–Fri noon–2:30pm; Tues–Sat 6:30–10pm. Bus: 352, 357, 358, or 359. INTERNATIONAL.

The Lobby, close to Capital Hill, is a popular haunt for politicians and others with government business on their minds. Entrees include a selection of terrines and pâtés served with homemade chutney as well as spiralli and tortellini pasta cooked with Italian sausage, chiles, olives, and basil. The main courses are eclectic: whole boned Snowy Mountains trout, a selection of satays on a bed of salad, and escalopes of fallow deer in a red wine, leek, and bacon sauce. The desserts include forest-berry pudding with crème anglaise and strawberries Romanoff (in season, of course).

INEXPENSIVE

High Court Cafe. In the High Court Building. ☎ **06/270 6828.** Reservations not required. Main courses A$3.85–A$10.50 (U.S. $3.10–$8.40). Children's portions half price. No credit cards. Daily 9:45am–4:15pm. Bus: 234, 350, 352, or 358. INTERNATIONAL.

This café, overlooking a wide grassy area and Lake Burley Griffin, is a good spot for a morning or afternoon tea break or a light lunch while you're sightseeing. For lunch you could have pasta, a ploughman's platter, pan-fried sea perch, or something classically Aussie like a meat pie and chips. For tea, be sure to try their fluffy scones with your cuppa.

Public Dining Room. In Parliament House. ☎ **06/277 3990.** Reservations not accepted. Carvery lunch A$8 (U.S. $6.40); other lunch items A$4–A$8 (U.S. $3.20–$6.40). BC, MC, V (with A$10 minimum purchase). Daily 9am–4:45pm; carvery 11:30am–2:30pm. Bus: 231, 234, 235, or 777. AUSTRALIAN.

This cafeteria is a handy and inexpensive place to eat lunch or just enjoy a beer after you've toured Parliament House. There's indoor and outdoor seating and it's all very light and bright. The menu reads like a list of archetypical Australian dishes: fish and chips, sausage rolls, meat pies, roast meat with "veg," and lamingtons for dessert.

ON BLACK MOUNTAIN

EXPENSIVE

The Tower Restaurant. In the Telecom Tower. ☎ **06/248 6162.** Reservations required. Main courses A$19.50–A$35.50 (U.S. $15.60–$28.40); buffet lunch A$24.50 (U.S. $19.60); fixed-price lunch A$25.50 (U.S. $20.40) for two courses, A$32.50 (U.S. $26) for three courses; fixed price dinner A$45.50 (U.S. $36.40) for three courses. Weekend and public holiday surcharge 10%. AE, BC, DC, MC, V. Daily noon–3pm and 6–9pm. INTERNATIONAL.

For dining with a view, the top spot in town is the revolving restaurant in the Telecom Tower on Black Mountain. The Tower Restaurant occupies a lofty site 54 meters (178 ft.) above the top of the mountain. Sunset is my favorite time here, but whether you dine during the day or at night the view is spectacular. And the food is also good. There's a fixed-price menu at lunch, but you can also choose à la carte. For dinner, you might start with broccoli-and-vegetable terrine, seafood tartlets, or warm quail salad. Main courses include boned loin of lamb, Atlantic salmon cutlet on leek purée topped with lemon-and-dill butter, and kangaroo filets flamed in brandy and served with pepper cherries. The wine list, which features maps of Australia's wine-producing regions, is both interesting and educational.

INEXPENSIVE

Level Seven Coffee Shop. In the Telecom Tower. ☎ **06/248 6162.** Reservations not required. Quick lunch A$8–A$10 (U.S. $6.40–$8). AE, BC, MC, V. Daily 9am–9pm. FAST FOOD.

This inexpensive eatery is a good spot for a quick bite while you savor the view from the lofty lookout. No fancy fare—just sandwiches, burgers, soft drinks, and so forth. Snacks in the Tower Kiosk cost even less.

5 Attractions

As the national capital, Canberra has a wealth of impressive government buildings and is, in many ways, a repository of the country's treasures.

IN THE PARLIAMENTARY TRIANGLE

✪ **Parliament House.** On Capital Hill. ☎ **06/277 7111.** Free admission. Daily 9am–5pm (later when Parliament is in session). Guided tours 9am–4pm when Parliament isn't sitting. Bus: 231, 234, 235, or 777.

Since it opened in 1988, Parliament House has become Canberra's top attraction. The building was designed by the New York firm of Mitchell, Giurgola, and Thorp (Thorp is an Australian) and is the culmination of the city plan conceived in 1912 by American Walter Burley Griffin. Like Griffin, the New York architects entered their design for the building in an international competition and won. The new Parliament House would've pleased Griffin, for he urged that when it was eventually constructed it should be functionally as well as symbolically "the people's house." In keeping with this idea, the architects created a structure with extensive public access. The design is very distinctive, merging into the top of Capital Hill; only a national flag the size of a double-decker bus rises above the natural curve of the hill. The grass lawns that cover the roof can be used for picnicking and play 24 hours a day. The view from the roof can only be described as spectacular. No doubt it gives egalitarian Aussies some satisfaction knowing they can walk over the heads of their representatives.

Free 50-minute guided tours are offered throughout the day. You can also wander through on your own or rent a 40-minute Acousti guide (A$3/U.S. $2.40). You must make reservations for gallery tickets if you want to observe Parliament in session. Write to the Sargeant of Arms, Joint House Department, Parliament House, Canberra, ACT 2600, or call 06/277 4889. There's a bookstore off the foyer and a post office on the first floor. The Public Dining Room is an inexpensive self-serve eatery (see "Dining" earlier in this chapter).

High Court of Australia. Overlooking Lake Burley Griffin, Parkes Place. ☎ **06/270 6811.** Free admission. Daily 10am–4pm. Bus: 234, 350, 352, or 358.

The High Court building was opened by Elizabeth II in 1980. The impressive 40-meter-tall (132-ft.) concrete-and-glass structure overlooks Lake Burley Griffin. Several interior features are of note: These include the large tapestry in Courtroom One in which symbols of each state are incorporated, and the various native timbers, donated by the states, which lend elegance to the courtrooms. You must stay at least 10 minutes if the court is in session. It's most likely to be in session on the Tuesday, Wednesday, and Thursday of the first two weeks of the month.

✪ **National Gallery of Australia.** Parkes Place. ☎ **06/271 2502,** or 06/271 2501 for recorded information. Admission A$3 (U.S. $2.40) excluding major exhibitions; under 15 free. Free guided tours daily. Daily 10am–5pm. Closed Good Friday and Christmas. Bus: 234, 350, 352, or 358.

This attraction is next door to the High Court and linked by a pedestrian bridge. It features permanent and special exhibitions of Australian and international art. These are displayed in 11 galleries over three floors, with sculptures in the garden. You might want to look for Jackson Pollock's *Blue Poles,* Monet's *Haystacks at Noon* and *Waterlilies,* and de Paolo's *Crucifixion.* Among the most interesting Australian works is Sidney Nolan's Ned Kelly collection.

National Library of Australia. Parkes Place. ☎ **06/262 1111.** Free admission. Reading rooms and Exhibition Galle7ry, Mon–Thurs 9am–9pm, Fri–Sat 9am–5pm, Sun 1:30–5pm; guided tours, Tues–Thur at 2pm. Closed Good Friday and Christmas. Bus: 350, 352, or 358.

The National Library is the information resource for the nation. It houses over five million books, as well as huge collections of paintings, maps, manuscripts, films, music, newspapers, and oral histories. In addition to reading rooms, the library offers a bookshop specializing in Australian literature, history, and biography, and souvenirs. Dining facilities include a self-service bistro and a restaurant, both licensed.

National Science and Technology Centre. Between the High Court and the National Library, King Edward Terrace. ☎ **06/270 2800.** Admission A$8 (U.S. $6.40) adults, A$4 (U.S. $3.20) children 4–16; under 4 free. Daily 10am–5pm. Closed Christmas. Bus: 350, 352, 358, or 777.

This is a hands-on science center enjoyed by kids and adults alike. Some 180 interactive exhibits deal with the mysteries of science and demonstrate their day-to-day use. Topics include waves, robotic dinosaurs, force, sound, light, earthquakes, communications technology, and mathematics. The NSTC makes science exciting, interesting, and fun by encouraging you to interact with the exhibits. Meals and snacks are served in a cafeteria.

National Capital Planning Exhibition. Regatta Point, Commonwealth Park. ☎ **06/257 1068.** Free admission. Daily 9am–5pm (to 6pm in summer). Closed Christmas. Bus: 901.

Even though it's across the lake from the other attractions, the National Capital Planning Exhibition is still within the Parliamentary Triangle. Here are excellent displays and a film that explain Canberra's origin and design. This is a must for anyone who wants to understand the full scope of the city. The Planning Exhibition also provides a good point from which to view Lake Burley Griffin, the Captain Cook Memorial Water Jet, and the Carillon. A neighboring kiosk and licensed restaurant serve meals and snacks.

OUTSIDE THE PARLIAMENTARY TRIANGLE

Because Canberra is the nation's capital, 70 countries maintain embassies here. While you can't go inside most of them, it's fun to drive past and note the ethnic architecture. Many of the embassies are in the suburb of Yarralumla. The **Embassy of the United States,** on Moonah Place (☎ 06/270 5000), is built in the style of colonial Williamsburg. The architecture of the **India High Commission,** Moonah Place (☎ 06/273 3999), was inspired by the Moghuls. The **Greek Embassy,** on the corner of Empire Circuit and Turrana Street (☎ 06/273 3011), is a modern derivative of classic Greek style. The **Embassy of Thailand,** on the corner of Empire Circuit and Adelaide Avenue (☎ 06/273 1149), has a sloping roofline that rises to points on either end, which is characteristic of sacred Siamese Buddhist buildings. You may also be interested in the High Commissions of **Britain** (☎ 06/270 6666), **Canada** (☎ 06/273 3844), and **New Zealand** (☎ 06/270 4211), all on Commonwealth Avenue.

✪ **Australian War Memorial.** At the head of Anzac Parade on Limestone Avenue. ☎ **06/243 4211.** Admission (including guided tours) free. Daily 10am–5pm; guided tours on request. Closed Christmas. Bus: 302 or 303.

The War Memorial is one of Canberra's top attractions, drawing more than a million visitors annually. I hope you'll take time to tour this impressive collection of historical artifacts and displays that tell about the wars in which Australia has been involved. I can think of few other experiences that offer as much insight into the country. It's a sobering but not depressing experience. The Aussies have served alongside Americans in many conflicts, including Europe and the Pacific during World War II, and seeing these experiences from their viewpoint is fascinating. Don't miss the displays relating to Gallipoli, the World War I bloodbath in which so many Anzac (Australia and New Zealand Army Corps) troops lost their lives.

Telecom Tower. Black Mountain Drive. ☎ **06/248 1911.** Admission A$3 (U.S. $2.40) adults, A$1 (U.S. 80¢) children under 17. Daily 9am–10pm. Bus: 904 (Mon–Fri).

The Telecom Tower, rising 195 meters (644 ft.) above the summit of Black Mountain, is the loftiest spot in town for getting a bird's-eye view of the landscape. For the admission fee, you're whisked up to an enclosed viewing gallery, 58.5 meters (193 ft.) above ground, and to two open viewing galleries, 62 and 66 meters (205 and 218 ft.) in the air. Those who dine in the revolving Tower Restaurant (see "Dining" earlier in this chapter) are entitled to a refund of their admission charge. There's also a coffee shop on Level 7 and a kiosk.

Australian National Botanic Gardens. On the slopes of Black Mountain. ☎ **06/250 9450.** Free admission. Daily 9am–5pm. Closed Christmas. Bus: 434 or 904.

These gardens contain the world's best collection of Australian native flora. More than 6,000 species are under cultivation, and excellent printed guides (available at the Information Centre) help you find your way around. In addition, walks of various lengths are marked and plants along the way are labeled. Guided tours are offered free of charge.

ORGANIZED TOURS

Several bus companies offer escorted sightseeing tours of Canberra. These include **ACTION** (☎ 06/207 7611 or 207 7600) and **Murrays** (☎ 06/295 3611 or 295 3677).

Or you can board the **Canberra Explorer** bus (☎ 06/295 3611 or 295 3677) and stay on for the complete one-hour, 25km (15-mile) circuit—and then go back later on your own to the places that interest you. This costs A$18 (U.S. $14.40) for adults and A$8 (U.S. $6.40) for children.

Canberra Cruises (☎ 06/295 3544) offers 1½-hour cruises on Lake Burley Griffin. These cost A$12 (U.S. $10) for adults, half price for children.

6 Outdoor Activities & Spectator Sports

OUTDOOR ACTIVITIES

BALLOONING **Balloon Aloft** (☎ 06/285 1540) will take you up, up, and away on an unforgettable sunrise trip over the city. Forty-five-minute flights cost A$185 (U.S. $148) per adult and A$120 (U.S. $96) per child, including a champagne picnic. Half-hour weekday flights cost A$130 (U.S. $104) for adults and A$80 (U.S. $64) for kids, including champagne or orange juice and a flight certificate.

BICYCLING Rent a Bike from **Mr. Spokes,** at the ferry terminal, Acton Park (☎ 06/257 1188), and take advantage of Canberra's 120km (74 miles) of cycleways. Some picturesque paths follow the shore of Lake Burley Griffin; others head out through the suburbs. It costs A$8 (U.S. $6.40) per hour for adults and A$7 (U.S. $5.60) per hour for children. Helmets are compulsory and included in the rental price. Mr. Spokes is open daily.

BOATING Contact **Dobel Boat Hire Pty. Ltd.,** on the north side of Lake Burley Griffin and just east of Commonwealth Avenue, Acton Jetty, Acton (☎ 06/249 6861), if you want to rent catamarans, paddleboats, sailboards, rowboats, or other vessels. Rates are A$8 (U.S. $6.40) per half an hour and A$14 (U.S. $11.20) per hour. **Lake Burley Griffin Boat Hire** (☎ 06/249 6861) has canoes for hire.

GOLF The 18-hole course closest to the city center is the **Yowani Country Club,** on the Federal Highway in the suburb of Lyneham (☎ 06/241 2303 or 241 3377). Greens fees are A$35 (U.S. $28) for 18 holes and A$23 (U.S. $18.40) for 9 holes. Club rental costs an additional A$13 to A$20 (U.S. $10.40 to $16). You *must* reserve in advance.

SWIMMING The 50-meter (162-ft.) indoor heated pool at the **Australian Institute of Sport,** Leverrier Street, Bruce (☎ 06/252 1111), is open to the public at certain times of day. This facility is about 8km (5 miles) northwest of Civic. Adults pay A$3.50 (U.S. $2.80) to swim or A$6 (U.S. $4.80) to swim, spa, and sauna.

TENNIS The **National Tennis and Squash Centre** is on the Federal Highway in Lyneham (☎ 06/247 0929). Squash courts cost A$10 to A$14 (U.S. $8 to $11.20) per hour, depending on when you want to play. Tennis courts rent for A$12 to A$16 (U.S. $9.60 to $12.80). There are also courts at the **Australian Institute of Sport** (see "Swimming" above). Court rental is A$10 to A$20 (U.S. $8 to $16) an hour inside and A$8 to A$10 (U.S. $6.40 to $8) per hour outside.

SPECTATOR SPORTS

Canberra's teams includes **rugby league, basketball, waterpolo, baseball, hockey,** and **soccer.** Many of these matches are held at the Australian Institute of Sport, Bruce Stadium, Battye Street, Bruce (☎ 06/253 2111).

7 Shopping

The **Canberra Centre,** which fills four square blocks between City Walk and Ballumbir Street between Petrie Street and Akuna Street in Civic, is the city's best place to shop. Some 150 specialty stores of all types fill the three-story atrium, which, because of the amount of glass used, feels like a conservatory. **David Jones** and **Grace Bros.** are the major department stores. You'll also find **Target, Venture,** and **Supa Barn** here. The **City Market** section, which includes a butcher shop, a bakery, fruit and vegetables sellers, a deli, and several fast-food outlets, is open Monday to Thursday from 9am to 6pm, Friday from 9am to 9pm, and Saturday and Sunday from 9am to 5pm. The rest of the stores are generally open Monday to Thursday from 9am to 5:30pm, Friday from 9am to 9pm, Saturday from 9am to 4pm, and Sunday from 10am to 4pm.

My favorite shop is the ☎ **Craftsman's Collection,** on the center's first floor (☎ 06/257 4733). The crafts sold here are made of Australian materials, by Australians, in Australia. These include pottery, jewelry, glass pieces, and wood items. Be sure to notice the Dingo Pottery and Mathew Larwood's glass work.

Travellers Maps and Guides in the Jolimont Centre, 67 Northbourne Ave., Civic (☎ 06/249 6006), stocks a wide range of helpful maps and travel accessories. Open daily.

8 Canberra After Dark

THE PERFORMING ARTS

Canberra Theatre Centre. London Circuit, Civic Square, Civic. ☎ **06/257 1077,** or 06/257 1077 for tickets, or 1800/802 025 in Australia. Tickets A$30–A$55 (U.S. $24–$44).

This is the best-known venue for the performing arts. A wide range of productions—from rock to Shakespeare—takes place here. The Canberra Theatre Trust presents the National Festival of Australian Theatre every October. This event features the best of contemporary Australian theater and artists. The theater, built in 1965, has 1,189 seats. Check the Saturday *Canberra Times* for what's-on information.

THE CLUB & MUSIC SCENE

Canberra Tradesmen's Union Club. 2 Badham St., Dickson. ☎ **06/248 0999.** No cover.

There's something for nearly everyone in this large club, 4km (2 1/2 miles) north of Civic. The Canberra Bicycle Museum is here, with about 60 unusual bicycles on display. You can also have dinner in one of 10 restored trams, and there are rooms full of poker and card machines—over 280 in all. Housie (bingo) is played about 20 times a week, and there are five snooker tables. Naturally, a wide range of drinks is available at several bars. A "tinnie" (can) of Fosters will set you back A$2 (U.S. $1.60). The club is open 24 hours.

✪ **Dorette's Bistro.** 17 Garema Place, Civic. ☎ **06/247 4946.** Cover A$2–A$4 (U.S. $1.60–$3.20) Fri–Sat.

There's no doubt about why Dorette's is popular. There's live music here every night, the modern Australian food is good (if you choose to eat), and the ambience is that of a small European bistro. Jazz is king five nights a week, but Wednesday is for classical music and Sunday is just for folk and blues. The music starts at 8pm during the week and at 9pm on Friday and Saturday.

Dorette's is on the first floor (one level up from ground) overlooking the fountain in Garema Place, which is a pedestrian plaza. The decor includes ceiling fans, large modern oil paintings, and wooden tables and chairs. Dinner is served daily from 6 to 10pm; light suppers, daily from 10pm to midnight or later. You don't have to eat, but there's a A$15 (U.S. $12) per-person minimum charge for those occupying dining tables on Friday and Saturday nights. No minimum applies to the cocktail tables. Happy hour is 5:30 to 6:30pm daily. Reader M. Cecilia Wendler of Blaine, Minn., writes about Dorette's: "We enjoyed our meal (and service and music) so much that we chose to return there for our last night in town."

Tilly's (Divine Court Cafe). At the corner of Wattle and Brigalow streets, Lyneham. ☎ **06/249 1543.**

This popular place offers a high caliber of live entertainment. The music is most frequently, but not always, jazz. Phone to see what's on.

A CASINO

Casino Canberra. In Glebe Park, 21 Binara St., Civic. ☎ **06/257 7074,** or 1800/806 833 in Australia. Free admission.

This casino offers a range of games, like baccarat, roulette, and blackjack. It's open from noon until 6am on weekdays and 24 hours on weekends. Two restaurants and three bars are on the premises. Dress regulations prohibit leisure wear, running shoes, and denim. Men are required to wear a jacket or tie after 7pm.

Appendix

A Metric Measures

Length

1 inch (in.)			=	2.54cm				
1 foot (ft.)	=	12 in.	=	30.48cm	=	.305m		
1 yard (yd.)	=	3 ft.			=	.915m		
1 mile	=	5,280 ft.					=	1.609km

To convert miles to kilometers, multiply the number of miles by 1.61 (for example, 50 mi. × 1.61 = 80.5km). Note that this conversion can be used to convert speeds from miles per hour (m.p.h.) to kilometers per hour (kmph).

To convert kilometers to miles, multiply the number of kilometers by .62 (example, 25 km × .62 = 15.5 mi.). Note that this same conversion can be used to convert speeds from kilometers per hour to miles per hour.

Capacity

1 fluid ounce (fl. oz.)			=	.03 liter		
1 pint (pt.)	=	16 fl. oz.	=	.47 liter		
1 quart (qt.)	=	2 pints	=	.94 liter		
1 gallon (gal.)	=	4 quarts	=	3.79 liters	=	.83 Imperial gal.

To convert U.S. gallons to liters, multiply the number of gallons by 3.79 (example, 12 gal. × 3.79 = 45.48 liters).

To convert liters to U.S. gallons, multiply the number of liters by .26 (example, 50 liters × .26 = 13 U.S. gal.).

To convert U.S. gallons to Imperial gallons, multiply the number of U.S. gallons by .83 (example, 12 U.S. gal. × .83 = 9.96 Imperial gal.).

To convert Imperial gallons to U.S. gallons, multiply the number of Imperial gallons by 1.2 (example, 8 Imperial gal. × 1.2 = 9.6 U.S. gal.).

Weight

1 ounce (oz.)			=	28.35g				
1 pound (lb.)	=	16 oz.	=	453.6g	=	.45 kg		
1 ton	=	2,000 lb.	=			907kg	=	.91 metric ton

To convert pounds to kilograms, multiply the number of pounds by .45 (example, 90 lb. × .45 = 40.5kg).
To convert kilograms to pounds, multiply the number of kilos by 2.2 (example, 75kg × 2.2 = 165 lb.).

Area

1 acre			=	.41 ha		
1 square mile	=	640 acres	=	2.59 ha	=2.6 sq. km	

To convert acres to hectares, multiply the number of acres by .41 (example, 40 acres × .41 = 16.4ha).
To convert hectares to acres, multiply the number of hectares by 2.47 (example, 20ha × 2.47 = 49.4 acres).
To convert square miles to square kilometers, multiply the number of square miles by 2.6 (example, 80 sq. mi × 2.6 = 208 sq. km).
To convert square kilometers to square miles, multiply the number of square kilometers by .39 (example, 150 sq.km × .39 = 58.5 sq. mi.).

Temperature

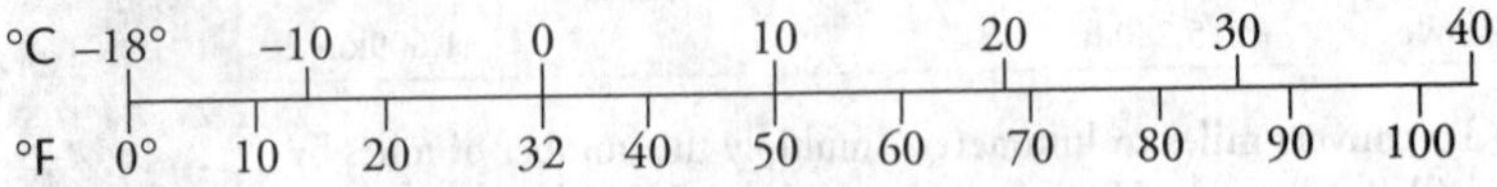

To convert degrees Fahrenheit to degrees Celsius, subtract 32 from °F, multiply by 5, then divide by 9 (example, 85°F−32 × $^5/_9$ = 29.4°C).
To convert degrees Celsius to degrees Fahrenheit, multiply °C by 9, divide by 5, and add 32 (example, 20°C × $^9/_5$ + 32 = 68°F).

B An Aussie/Yankee Lexicon

According to the encyclopedia, Britain, Canada, South Africa, New Zealand, Australia, and the United States—as well as a few other places—are all English-speaking countries. While this is true in theory, those of us who've traveled in these lands know that communication difficulties arise because of the use of idioms, colloquial expressions, and the difference in accents. I've never experienced a serious language problem down under; rather, I've found our choice of words to be a built-in ice breaker, an excuse to start a conversation.

This is not to say I've never embarrassed myself or caused a few giggles. I remember the time I was at the home of a new Aussie acquaintance and asked to use the *bathroom.* I was shown the way down the hall, but once inside I realized the one piece of plumbing I needed was nowhere in sight. I obviously didn't know that in Australia the bathroom is a room in which there's a bathtub and I should've asked for the *toilet.* And then there was the time I verbally blasted the chap who asked me if I'd go to a *hotel* with him. I'd have responded differently if I'd realized that in Oz, *hotel* is synonomous with *pub* and he was just inviting me to have a drink.

New Zealanders share many expressions with their cousins across the Tasman, but they aren't immune from oral errors. A Kiwi who requests to be *knocked up* will get the same quizzical response in Sydney that he'd receive in San Francisco or New York. He will only be asking to be awakened, but Aussies and Yanks will think of a much more physical act.

However, these down-under relatives share bemusement when they hear Americans talk about *rooting* for the home team. They'd *barrack* for their favorite squad and do their *rooting* in the bedroom.

The following list of Aussie words and expressions is intended to save you a few red-faced moments, help you order what you want to eat, and get you where you're going. If you're particularly interested in the language used in the sparsely inhabited back country, you might want to order *The Ringer's Book of Outback Terms and Phrases.* The 22-page volume is available for A$6 (U.S. $4.80), including airmail postage, from the Australian Stockman's Hall of Fame and Outback Heritage Centre, G.P.O. Box 171, Longreach, QLD 4370 (☎ 076/58 2166; fax 076/58 2495).

The Dinkum Dictionary: A Ripper Guide to Aussie English by Lenie (Midge) Johansen, is another collection of Aussie-isms. Look for it in bookshops down under.

Air conditioning Refers to both heating and cooling the air
Aussie An Australian
Barby Barbecue
Bathroom Where one bathes
Beetroot Beets
Bickie barrel Cookie jar
Billabong Water hole in a usually dry river
Billy Tin container used for boiling water over an open fire
Billy tea Tea boiled over an open fire
Biscuits/bickies Cookies
Bloke Guy, man
Bon bons Cylindrical party favors containing a prize similar to that found in a box of Cracker Jack (U.S.); called Christmas crackers in New Zealand
Bonnet Hood of a car
Boot Trunk of a car
Boxing Day The day after Christmas
Brasserie A casual restaurant
Brekkie Breakfast
Bum Backside (if you mean a guy who's down on his luck, say *tramp*)
Bushranger Outlaw, bandit
Bushwalking Hiking (U.S.), tramping (N.Z.)
Chemist shop Drugstore
Chips French-fried potatoes
Chook Chicken
Cobber Friend
Cozzie, bathing costume, swimmers, togs Swimsuit
Crook Sick
Cuppa Cup of tea
Doona Quilted eiderdown comforter
Drover Cowboy
Dunny Slang for toilet, but really an outhouse
Esky Styrofoam cooler (U.S.), chillybin (N.Z.). A large esky is often called a *car fridge.*
Entree Smallish first course; appetizer
Fair dinkum True, real, genuine
Fancy-dress party Costume party
Fête A function to raise money for a charity, church, school, or similar
Flog Sell
Footpath Sidewalk
Footy Football
Frankfurt or saveloy Hot dog
Galah A noisy pink-and-gray native parrot; anyone who talks a lot, especially foolishly
Gaol Jail
German sausage Bologna
Gidday or g'day Hello (good day)
Greenies Ecology-minded activists
Grog Booze
Gumboots Waterproof rubber boots (U.S.), Wellingtons (Britain)
Gum tree Eucalyptus tree
Hotel Public licensed hotel, a pub, a bar
Ice block Popsicle
Jackeroo Male apprentice ranch hand
Jilleroo Female apprentice ranch hand
Joey Baby kangaroo in the pouch
Jumbuck Sheep

Jumper Pullover sweater (U.S.), jersey (N.Z.)
Kerb Curb
Knickers Underwear, undies
Lift Elevator
Lollies Candy (U.S.), sweets (Britain)
Loo Toilet
Mackintosh A rubberized raincoat
Mate Friend (not spouse)
Matilda Slang for swag (see *swag,* below)
Napkin or nappy Diaper (in a restaurant, ask for a *serviette,* see below)
Newsagent A kiosk where magazines and newspapers are sold
Ocker A stereotypically uncultured Australian male
One off One of a kind
Oz Australia (the Lucky Country)
Poker machine Slot machine
Pom or Pommie Person from England
Postie Letter carrier
Pozzie Position, location
Prawn Shrimp
Queue Line, waiting in line
Return ticket Round-trip ticket
Rocket Arugula
Rubber Pencil eraser (the one used for birth control is a *condom*)
Sandshoes Sneakers
Serviette Napkin
Sheila Female (slang)
Shout Treat someone to a drink, buy a round
Silverbeet Swiss chard
Silverside Corned beef
Singlet Sleeveless undershirt
Sister Nurse
Snags Sausages (U.S.), bangers (N.Z. and Britain)
Station Ranch
Sticky beak A nosy person; the act of being snoopy
Strides Trousers
Stubby Short brown bottle of beer
Swag A bundle or roll carried across the shoulders
Swagman A man who travels about the country on foot, living on his earnings from occasional jobs; such a person often carries his possessions in a swag.
Ta Thank you
Telly Television
Thongs Jandals (N.Z.), flip-flops (Britain)
Tinny Can, as in "a tinny of beer"
To call To visit
To ring To phone
Troppo, bonkers Mentally disturbed
Tucker Food
Ute Pickup truck
Wireless Radio (also known to younger Aussies as a *trannie*)
Wowser Prude, killjoy
Yabby An Australian freshwater crayfish
Yank American
Yarn Conversation

C Menu Terms

ANZAC Biscuits Cookies made with rolled oats and golden syrup; so named because they were often mailed to the ANZAC fighting forces.
Balmain bug An edible crustacean first discovered in Sydney Harbour and named after a Sydney suburb. Similar delicacies found around Brisbane are called Moreton Bay bugs. Also known as a slipper lobster.
Barramundi Large freshwater fish found in the northern part of Australia; giant perch
Beetroot Beets (often found sliced on Aussie sandwiches)
Billy tea Tea boiled over an open fire
Biscuit/bickie Cookie

Capsicum Bell pepper
Carpetbag steak A thick cut of beef stuffed with oysters
Chips French-fried potatoes
Coral trout A popular eating fish found in the vicinity of the Great Barrier Reef
Crayfish A freshwater crustacean; crawfish
Damper A type of bread made from a simple flour-and-water dough with or without a leavening agent and cooked in the coals of an open fire or in a camp oven
Donner kebab Gyros in pita bread
Entree A smallish first course; appetizer
Frankfurt, saveloy Hot dog
German sausage Bologna
Jewfish A popular saltwater eating fish
John Dory A thin deep-bodied popular food fish found in Australian waters
Lamingtons Pieces of sponge cake covered with chocolate icing and shredded coconut
Lemonade 7-Up
Meat pie A two-crust pie filled with stewed cubed or ground meat (usually beef) and gravy
Mud crab A large edible crab found in the mangrove regions of New South Wales and Queensland
Pavlova A large soft-centered meringue filled with whipped cream and garnished with fruit (for a great pavlova recipe, see p. 406).
Pawpaw Papaya
Porridge Oatmeal
Prawn Shrimp
Roast dinner Roast beef or leg of lamb served with potatoes and other vegetables that've been cooked with the meat
Rocket Arugula
Rockmelon Cantaloupe
Salad bar A buffet of prepared salads like potato, three-bean, and coleslaw
Scone A biscuit, often served with jam and clotted cream
Shandy A drink in which beer and lemonade are combined (see *lemonade* above).
Silverbeet Swiss chard
Silverside Corned beef
Snags Sausages (U.S.), bangers (N.Z. and Britain)
Sweets Dessert
Tomato sauce Catsup
Vegemite A yeast-based vegetable extract used as a spread on bread
Witchetty grubs Large white edible larvae of certain Australian moths and beetles
Yabby An Australian freshwater crayfish

D Distance Chart

	Adelaide	Albany	Alice Springs	Ayers Rock	Brisbane	Broken Hill	Cairns	Canberra	Darwin	Hobart*	Kununurra	Mackay	Melbourne	Mount Isa	Perth	Port Hedland	Surfers Paradise	Sydney
Adelaide		2675	1555	1597	1992	513	2858	1230	3261	999	3248	2100	747	2734	2720	3847	2028	1475
Albany	2675		3594	3636	4269	2790	5135	3905	3735	3674	3735	4377	3422	4773	409	2105	4305	3791
Alice Springs	1555	3594		446	3026	1670	2307	2785	1706	2554	1693	2391	2302	1179	3639	3289	3106	2831
Ayers Rock	1597	3636	446		3472	1712	2753	2827	2152	2596	2139	2837	2344	1625	3681	3737	3552	2873
Brisbane	1992	4269	3026	3472		1479	1710	1315	3672	1970	3659	1010	1718	1847	4314	5289	80	1031
Broken Hill	513	2790	1670	1712	1479		2345	1100	3376	1113	3363	1783	861	2105	2835	4531	1559	1161
Cairns	2858	5135	2307	2753	1710	2345		2938	2953	3291	2940	700	3039	1128	5180	4570	1790	2636
Canberra	1230	3905	2785	2827	1315	1100	2938		4233	903	4400	2325	651	2724	3950	5646	1235	302
Darwin	3261	3735	1706	2152	3672	3376	2953	4233		4260	880	3037	4008	1825	4206	2510	3752	4095
Hobart*	999	3674	2554	2596	1970	1113	3291	903	4260		4247	2971	252	3070	3719	5338	2074	1141
Kununurra	3248	3735	1693	2139	3659	3363	2940	4400	880	4247		3024	3995	1812	3326	1630	3739	4096
Mackay	2100	4377	2391	2837	1010	1783	700	2325	3037	2971	3024		2719	1212	4422	3654	1090	2061
Melbourne	747	3422	2302	2344	1718	861	3039	651	4008	252	3995	2719		2818	3467	5286	1822	889
Mount Isa	2734	4773	1179	1625	1847	2105	1128	2724	1825	3070	1812	1212	2818		4973	3442	1927	2396
Perth	2720	409	3639	3681	4314	2835	5180	3950	4206	3719	3326	4422	3467	4973		1696	4393	3996
Port Hedland	3847	2105	3289	3737	5289	4531	4570	5646	2510	5338	1630	3654	5286	3442	1696		5369	5692
Surfers Paradise (Gold Coast)	2028	4305	3106	3552	80	1559	1790	1235	3752	2074	3739	1090	1822	1927	4393	5369		933
Sydney	1475	3791	2831	2873	1031	1161	2636	302	4095	1141	4096	2061	889	2396	3996	5692	933	

Source: Australian Tourist Commission. Distances are in kilometers; to convert to miles, multiply kilometers by .62 (or by 5/8).

*Road distance to Hobart excludes the Melbourne–Devonport ferry journey.

Index

Chicago '96
Denver/Boulder/Colorado Springs, 2nd Ed.
Disney World/Orlando '96
Dublin, 2nd Ed.
Hong Kong, 4th Ed.
Las Vegas '96
London '96
Los Angeles '96
Madrid/Costa del Sol, 2nd Ed.
Mexico City, 1st Ed.
Miami '95-'96
Minneapolis/St. Paul, 4th Ed.
Montreal/Quebec City, 8th Ed.
Nashville/Memphis, 2nd Ed.
New Orleans '96
New York City '96
Paris '96
Philadelphia, 8th Ed.
Rome, 10th Ed.
St. Louis/Kansas City, 2nd Ed.
San Antonio/Austin, 1st Ed.
San Diego, 4th Ed.
San Francisco '96
Santa Fe/Taos/Albuquerque '96
Seattle/Portland, 4th Ed.
Sydney, 4th Ed.
Tampa/St. Petersburg, 3rd Ed.
Tokyo, 4th Ed.
Toronto, 3rd Ed.
Vancouver/Victoria, 3rd Ed.
Washington, D.C. '96

FROMMER'S FAMILY GUIDES

(Guides to family-friendly hotels, restaurants, activities, and attractions)

California with Kids
Los Angeles with Kids
New York City with Kids
San Francisco with Kids
Washington, D.C. with Kids

FROMMER'S WALKING TOURS

(Memorable strolls through colorful and historic neighborhoods, accompanied by detailed directions and maps)

Berlin
Chicago
England's Favorite Cities
London, 2nd Ed.
Montreal/Quebec City
New York, 2nd Ed.
Paris, 2nd Ed.
San Francisco, 2nd Ed.
Spain's Favorite Cities
Tokyo
Venice
Washington, D.C., 2nd Ed.

FROMMER'S AMERICA ON WHEELS

(Guides for travelers who are exploring the USA by car, featuring a brand-new rating system for accommodations and full-color road maps)

Arizona and New Mexico
California and Nevada
Florida
Mid-Atlantic

FROMMER'S SPECIAL-INTEREST TITLES

Arthur Frommer's Branson!
Arthur Frommer's New World of Travel, 5th Ed.
Frommer's America's 100 Best-Loved State Parks
Frommer's Caribbean Hideaways, 7th Ed.
Frommer's Complete Hostel Vacation Guide to England, Scotland & Wales
Frommer's National Park Guide, 29th Ed.
USA Sports Traveler's and TV Viewer's Golf Tournament Guide
USA Sports Minor League Baseball Book
USA Today Golf Atlas

Frommer's Best Beach Vacations

(The top places to sun, stroll, shop, stay, play, party, and swim, with each beach rated for beauty, swimming, sand, and amenities)

California
Carolinas/Georgia
Florida
Hawaii
Mid-Atlantic from New York to Washington, D.C.
New England

Frommer's Bed & Breakfast Guides

(Selective guides with four-color photos and full description of the best inns in each region)

California
Caribbean
Great American Cities
Hawaii
Mid-Atlantic
New England
Pacific Northwest
Rockies
Southeast States
Southwest

Frommer's Irreverent Guides

(Wickedly honest guides for sophisticated travelers and those who want to be)

Amsterdam
Chicago
London
Manhattan
New Orleans
San Francisco

Frommer's Driving Tours

(Four-color photos and detailed maps outlining spectacular scenic driving routes)

Australia
Austria
Britain
Florida
France
Germany
Ireland
Italy
Scandinavia
Scotland
Spain
Switzerland
U.S.A.

Frommer's Born to Shop

(The ultimate travel guides for discriminating shoppers from cut-rate to couture)

Great Britain
Hong Kong
London
New York

Frommer's Food Lover's Companions

(Lavishly illustrated guides to regional specialties, restaurants, gourmet shops, markets, local wines, and more)

France
Italy